THE WAR
ILLUSTRATED

GENERAL DWIGHT DAVID EISENHOWER, G.C.B.

Supreme Commander Allied Expeditionary Force in Western Europe from December 1943, U.S. General Eisenhower was C.-in-C. for the Invasion of Europe, June 6, 1944.

THE WAR
Illustrated

Complete Record of the Conflict
by Land and Sea and in the Air

Edited by

SIR JOHN HAMMERTON

Volume Eight

The EIGHTH VOLUME of THE WAR ILLUSTRATED contains the issues numbered 181 to 205, covering the period May 1944 to April 1945. As foreshadowed in the preceding volume, the present absorbing chronicle is of triumphant combined operations, of swift series of far-reaching Allied successes on a scale unparalleled in world history.

France, Belgium, Luxembourg, Poland, Greece, almost all Italy, and parts of Holland and Yugoslavia were freed, the Siegfried defences crunched to dust, the Saar and Ruhr pounded to impotence by Allied bombers. Triumph piled on triumph : from mighty D-Day landings in Normandy to the crossing of the Rhine in force nine months later ; from final liberation of Soviet soil to the close siege of Berlin and Vienna by Marshal Stalin's valiant and incomparable Armies.

In Burma the 14th Army, pushing south in circumstances of well-nigh overwhelming difficulty, achieving immortal fame, recaptured Mandalay and drove the Japanese invaders headlong. On the many-islanded Pacific front General MacArthur returned as conqueror to the Philippines. The enemy, blasted from hide-outs in these islands, saw their vaunted navy shattered and scattered, Allied warships steaming into their home waters, Allied troops landing on Japanese territory, and Tokyo, capital of the Nippon empire, set furiously ablaze by aerial armadas.

Politically, the highlight of the period was the momentous Crimea Conference in February 1945 : when, in a spirit of complete unanimity, Mr. Churchill, President Roosevelt and Marshal Stalin formulated plans for Victory and Peace in the West and announced the summoning, for the month of April, of a United Nations' Conference at San Francisco.

Speaking on German soil to British troops, in March, our Prime Minister declared, " Anyone can see that one good strong heave all together will end the war in Europe, beat down tyranny, and open the path to Peace and the return to the Homeland." We close the volume with Armies of the Western Allies across the Rhine, driving on for the heart of Hitler's shrinking Reich.

Published 2000
Cover Design © 2000
TRIDENT PRESS INTERNATIONAL
ISBN 1-58279-107-4 Single Edition
Printed in Croatia

General Index to Volume Eight

THIS *Index is designed to give ready reference to the whole of the literary and pictorial contents of* THE WAR ILLUSTRATED. *Individual subjects and persons of importance are indexed under their own headings, while references are included to general subjects such as* Burma; Tunisia; Pacific; U.S.A., etc. *Page numbers in italics indicate illustrations.*

7

List of Maps and Plans

Index of Special Drawings and Diagrams

Errata and Addenda

P. 90, illustration showing H.M.S. Inconstant is of the cruiser (built 1914-18 and now broken up) not the modern destroyer of the same name now in service.

P. 93. The metal track shown in the picture is not Sommerfeld track, as stated in the caption, but pressed steel planking.

P. 274, bottom line of caption. For R.E.s read R.A.O.C.

P. 357, third line of caption. For bomb-wrecked read wrecked Allied.

P. 357, fourth line of caption. For Allied bombing read enemy bombing and shelling.

P. 614, col. 3, line 20 from bottom. For Commander read Commodore.

Vol 8 — The War Illustrated — N° 181

Edited by Sir John Hammerton

SIXPENCE

MAY 26, 1944

IN HONOUR OF THE RUSSIAN FALLEN in Stalingrad this temporary memorial has been erected to unknown Red Army soldiers who died in the fierce fighting for the city; a permanent monument will later take its place. In a recent statement, the Vice-President of the Academy of Architecture of the U.S.S.R. said that plans were being made to lay out the centre of the reconstructed city in broad squares, adorned with mighty monuments to the heroes of Stalingrad.

Photo. Pictorial Press

NO. 182 WILL BE PUBLISHED FRIDAY, JUNE 9

Our Roving Camera Looks at the Housing Problem

CARAVANS serve at least as a temporary measure to overcome the housing problem near Elstree, on land which prior to the war was a holiday camp site. Some 20 families live in the caravans, which are either rented or self-owned; the inhabitants are Service people, munitions workers and evacuees, whose children attend the village school. The community is self-contained and well-ordered. Left, the caravan "town" at Elstree; and (below), inside a caravan, where space is limited and domestic arrangements are simple; cooking is done individually on stoves with cylinder-contained gas or coal fires.

Photos, Daily Mirror, Topical Press, Planet News

PAGE 2

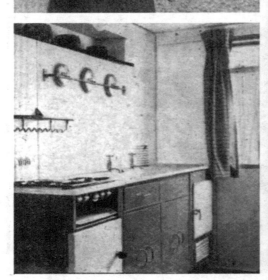

EMERGENCY HOUSES to help immediate needs in post-war Britain were mentioned by Mr. Churchill in his broadcast on March 26, 1944. One of the pre-fabricated steel houses, of which it is hoped to build 500,000, has been erected in London (bottom left). The house has a living-room, two bedrooms, kitchen (above left), and bathroom, lavatory and shed. Another type of two-storey, pre-fabricated house produced by a Hull firm (bottom right) was recently erected in just under nine hours. Workmen are seen laying the floors (centre right).

THE BATTLE FRONTS

by Maj.-Gen. Sir Charles Gwynn, K.C.B., D.S.O.

WITH the approach of the long awaited Second Front the atmosphere became almost unbearably tense by the beginning of May. Rumours and speculations from a multitude of sources provided a variety of forecasts of its date, points of attack and methods that gave ample scope for choice. The odds were long, however, against any of them proving more than partially correct, but they served to indicate the difficulty the Germans would have in adjusting their dispositions to meet the threat without unduly dispersing their resources in an attempt to be strong everywhere. Personally, with so many possible permutations and combinations, including a number of unknown factors, I was content to wait and see what the Allied Command would produce.

The lull in major operations—other than the air offensive—which set in towards the end of April served only to increase the tensity of the situation and to give additional subjects for speculation. How long would it last and where would it be broken—on the Russian front, in Italy or in the Balkans?

RUSSIA

On the Russian front it seemed at any rate pretty certain that the lull would not last as long as in 1943. Then, although mud brought operations to a standstill for a considerable time, the main reason for the prolongation of the lull was the exhaustion of both sides after the winter campaign and the necessity of carrying out extensive reorganization before embarking on major operations again. This year the Russians show no sign of exhaustion and they have demonstrated their ability to maintain their offensive under most adverse ground conditions. North of the Pripet Marshes the lull is probably due to ground conditions which in the north are worse and persist longer than in the south, but south of the Marshes it may be no more than an unusually long pause made desirable by the coincidence of several reasons. The main reason I judge is that the offensive, having split the enemy's forces into two groups, has now two distinct objectives, which call for considerable regrouping of the armies before launching major operations in divergent directions.

Secondly, the distance the offensive has already covered has immensely increased the length of lines of communication which almost certainly must require to be improved before they can stand the strain of maintaining a major offensive. A third reason is that the offensive between the objective in Poland and the objective in the lower Danube area has reached the Carpathians, which encroach on both lines of renewed operations, limiting their scope of manoeuvre. With the passes still blocked by snow, operations across the Carpathians on a major scale are presumably out of the question. But, perhaps more important, the melting of the snows has brought the Dniester, Pruth and Sereth temporarily down in flood which improves the German defensive position; and, where the foothills of the mountains encroach on the area of operations, tributaries in spate are a particularly serious obstacle. Comparatively small swift flowing torrents may often prove a greater obstacle to military operations than large rivers whose levels are less liable to sudden and extreme fluctuation. On the whole, however, on the southern front seasonal conditions tend to limit the scope of operations rather than to bring them entirely to a standstill as mud can do in the north.

The unexpectedly rapid fall of Sevastopol on May 9 was a fitting climax to what I think was one of the most brilliant achieve-ments of the Soviet military forces. The initial break-through into the Crimea was a masterpiece of planning and execution, but the Sevastopol defences were so strong that it seemed probable that a prolonged siege might be necessary. That the Russians were able in three weeks to complete preparations for the final assault and to overwhelm the defence in three days' fighting was an amazing proof of their organizational and tactical ability.

BURMA

While the lull continued in Europe more interest could be taken in Far Eastern operations. In Burma the situation was certainly obscure and not a little disturbing. The Japanese offensive which had isolated a considerable body of

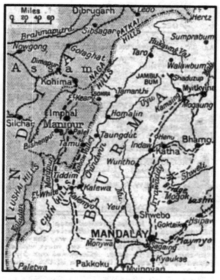

FAILING TO TAKE KOHIMA, Allied base in Assam, Japanese troops were, on May 15, 1944, concentrating in the area of Imphal in the Manipur State, where strong Allied forces barred the way. In Northern Burma the Allies were advancing in the Mogaung valley.
By courtesy of The Times

our troops in the Imphal area and was attacking the small garrison at Kohima on its main line of communications would, in ordinary European warfare, have undoubtedly produced an alarming situation.

IT was difficult to realize that in Burma, although operations were conducted by fairly large forces of well-equipped troops, they had largely the character of guerilla warfare, and only in the open Imphal plain could battles of a normal type develop. There the isolated force had the advantage of superior armament owing to the inability of the Japanese to bring up large numbers of the more powerful weapons because of their indifferent communications, and once they emerged from the surrounding jungle their attacks were therefore practically bound to fail. Nor was the isolated force likely to suffer from lack of supplies, for its large reserves could be frequently supplemented by air transport.

The situation at Kohima was more serious, for there not only was the garrison very much smaller, but the Japanese were able to close in on it from the surrounding jungle. Only the very gallant defence of the garrison prevented a regrettable incident, damaging to our prestige, and one which might have enabled the Japanese to infiltrate up to and interrupt the railway which provides the line

of communication with General Stilwell's force in the north. It was only after a period of some anxiety that a relieving force broke through the blocks on the road between Kohima and the railway and was able to replace the original garrison by fresh troops. A general counter-offensive against the Japanese detachments, dispersed and dug in over a wide area at inaccessible points in the jungle difficult to locate, was impracticable and counter-measures were perforce of a guerilla character. Carried out on an extensive scale by troops based on the railway and by the Imphal force they may have met with considerable success, dislodging and inflicting heavy casualties on Japanese detachments. The Japanese are having difficulty in maintaining supplies; these difficulties will probably greatly increase in the monsoon season which has begun and they may compel the Japanese to withdraw.

Meanwhile, General Stilwell's Chinese troops, covering the construction of the new road, which may one day link up with the old Burma road to China, are making steady progress, and the main communications of the Japanese opposing them have been cut by the Chindit airborne force which has established itself on the railway leading north from Mandalay. That force has been reinforced, but little information about its operations, evidently also of a guerilla character, has been given. Air communications with it during the monsoons obviously present difficulties, but apparently there is confidence that a technique has been developed which will overcome them. Japanese attacks on its central stronghold at Henu have all been driven off.

FAR EAST

The progress of the air-sea offensive in the southwest Pacific (see map, p. 4), now far ahead of schedule, is very encouraging. It is very clear that under the umbrella of carrier-borne aircraft amphibious operations can be carried out at a constantly increasing range. In an attempt to be strong everywhere the Japanese shore-based aircraft have to be distributed over many points, with the result that detachments are liable to be overwhelmed by the surprise attacks of carrier-borne aircraft and long-range shore-based bombers, leaving detachments of ground troops such as that at Wewak without air support to be isolated or dealt with by landing parties in due course. Meanwhile the magnificent purely land operations carried out by Australian troops under appalling difficulties of terrain and climate which ended in the capture of Madang should not be forgotten or underrated.

Pattern of Allied Attack in the Pacific War

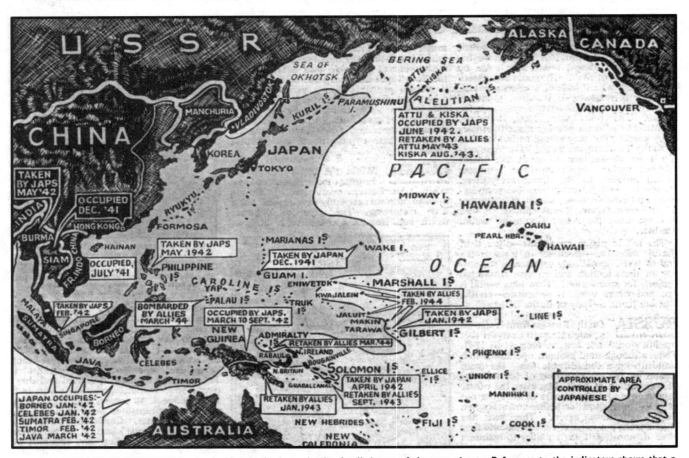

GENERAL STRATEGIC POSITION in the Pacific war is shown in the detailed map of the area above. Reference to the indicators shows that a considerable number of vital places captured by the Japanese in their initial offensive of 1941-42 have been recaptured or are in the process of being recaptured by the Allied forces, slowly but steadily pushing the enemy back the way they came. On Mar. 29, 1944, the U.S. Pacific Fleet prepared the way for further strategic progress by attacking Palau Islands; these are the most westerly of the Carolines, and the attack was by far the deepest penetration made into Japanese territory in the Pacific to date. Heavy sea and air blows were struck at Truk, Japanese naval base, on April 29 and 30. Wake Island had also been subjected to air attacks, indication of the manner in which the Allied arm ever lengthens its reach.

SURPRISE ASSAULT LANDINGS on the New Guinea coast in the rear of the Japanese, which entailed the greatest assembly of Allied air, sea and land forces ever seen in the south-west Pacific, resulted in the capture of Hollandia and Aitape in Northern New Guinea by April 28, 1944, and in the trapping of an enemy force estimated at 60,000 men between these places and Wewak and Madang. Madang itself fell to Australian forces on April 24. With the exception of a small area in the north-east of New Britain, covering Rabaul, in which region another big force of Japanese has been trapped, this island is in Allied hands. Up to May 11 all Japanese efforts to supply, reinforce or evacuate the doomed garrisons in New Guinea, New Britain, New Ireland and the Solomons had been smashed.

Courtesy of The Daily Telegraph

In New Guinea Another Japanese Base Falls

THREE-DAY AIR POUNDING of Japanese positions paved the way for the great Allied landings at Hollandia (Dutch New Guinea), Aitape and Tanahmerah Bay on April 22, 1944 (see map in facing page). Hollandia looks peaceful (1), but it is now the centre of Allied military activity. Dutch civil authorities arrived there with the troops, to handle the affairs of the first Dutch territory recaptured from the enemy. In typical New Guinea terrain, U.S. infantrymen wade across a jungle stream, while a heavy calibre machine-gun posted on the bank covers their advance (2). Parachute bombs drop towards a grounded Japanese plane, which a second later was blown to pieces (3). At the enemy airfield at Hollandia (4), wrecked installations and aircraft burn after the devastating air attacks which preceded the landings.

Photos, U.S. Official, E.N.A., New York Times Photos, Keystone

PAGE 5

THE WAR AT SEA

by Francis E. McMurtrie

PRIMARILY the invasion of Europe is a naval undertaking, based on Allied superiority in sea power. No landing in hostile territory could be undertaken with much prospect of success in the absence of such superiority, since it would be liable to interception on passage, or to subsequent isolation from reinforcement in the event of naval support proving insufficient. It was sea power which enabled the successful landings in North Africa and Sicily, and at Salerno and Anzio, to be accomplished without serious loss or subsequent interruption. A landing effected, the Navy has still to keep open the sea routes by which supplies and reinforcements of all kinds must be kept constantly flowing to sustain the invading armies.

An essential feature of a really successful invasion is some element of surprise. Hence the secrecy with which preparations for the great expedition are surrounded. Travel to Ireland and elsewhere has been forbidden, and even the dispatch of diplomatic mails by neutral embassies and legations has been suspended to guard against the danger of warning being conveyed to the enemy.

For a considerable time past the Germans have been endeavouring by every possible device to discover not only the date when the invasion will begin, but also the points selected for the first landings. Though conditions of weather and tide must govern the former contingency, there is still a considerable period during which prospects should be favourable, and to narrow down the date to a definite few days would assist our foes immensely. Still more valuable would it be for them to make certain where the blow will fall, so that they might concentrate all their defensive measures at the right spot. Actually there are so many possibilities that they are in danger of dissipating their resources in a vain endeavour to be strong everywhere.

NORWAY and Denmark Offer Attractions to Invader

Thus there has recently been a tendency to forecast an Allied stroke in Norway, where harbours abound and German communications are extended across a stretch of sea where interruption should not be difficult. In an endeavour to extract information concerning this possibility, neutral papers have been furnished with paragraphs, inspired from Berlin, to the effect that there have been troop concentrations in Iceland, from which the blow may therefore be expected to come.

Again, the flat peninsula of Denmark, whose people have recently followed the example of the Norwegians in organizing a stubborn passive resistance to the Nazi domination of their country, offers certain attractive features to an invader. German occupation forces have therefore been strengthened and some of the more likely landing places barred by fortifications.

IN the Netherlands, coastal areas have been flooded, and threats to destroy the dykes and inundate the greater part of the fertile fields of Holland with salt water on a large scale have been uttered. Farther south, along the French coast, what has been variously termed the Atlantic Wall or Western Wall has been constructed. It consists of a series of fortifications, reminiscent to some extent of the Siegfried Line, paralleled by minefields both in coastal waters and along the shore. To baffle the mine-detecting devices which have been used successfully in the past by Allied armies, German land mines are now reported to be made of non-magnetic material. It may be assumed, however, that the ingenuity of our experts will be equal to overcoming this artful precaution.

There is, of course, no reason why the invasion should be confined to the Atlantic coasts held by the enemy. For this reason the inhabitants of certain parts of the Riviera have been compelled to evacuate their dwellings at short notice, in case a descent should be made from Corsica and their assistance be invoked by the invaders.

All this shows how perplexed and worried the Germans must be, and how necessary it is that they should be prevented from ascertaining with any approach to certainty the plans which are now maturing for their discomfiture. It is always within the power of the Allies, owing to their superior sea power, to change the direction of the attack at the last moment; or several landings can be started, some of which may prove ultimately to be mere feints, designed to draw enemy strength in the wrong direction.

LANDING craft have been assembled in such numbers that it is probable there are few harbours around the British coasts facing the Continent without their quota of these specially designed vessels. American shipbuilding resources now undertake the construction of such craft as a first priority, having as their target the provision

IN THE WAR AGAINST JAPAN Britain's submarines, ever-increasing in number, will be a powerful factor in the intensified actions to come. Already, operating in the Indian Ocean, they have struck many vital blows at Japanese supply lines. (See p. 616, Vol. 7.) Preparing for further missions in the Far East is this submarine, into which stores are being loaded (right), while one of its deadly torpedoes is taken aboard (left), ready to send yet another enemy vessel to the bottom. Average number of torpedoes carried is six. *Photos, Fox*

of 80,000 of them. Already more than a fourth of this total is officially stated to have been delivered.

All these vessels will be under naval control, manned and commanded by personnel of the Royal or Allied Navies or of the Royal Marines. Fortunately, the exceptional qualifications of the latter corps for the conduct of amphibious operations are at last being adequately recognized.

There has been more activity in the Channel of late, as the lengthening days leave the enemy fewer hours of darkness within which to transfer supplies along the French coast by sea. A smart action on April 26 resulted in a German destroyer of 1,100 tons being sunk by four British destroyers of the "Tribal" type, supported by a new cruiser named Black Prince, whose commanding officer (Captain D. M. Lees, D.S.O., R.N.) was in charge of the whole operation.

Three of the destroyers in question were the Athabaskan, Haida and Huron, new vessels of close on 2,000 tons belonging to the Royal Canadian Navy. The fourth was

the older destroyer Ashanti, of 1,870 tons, a unit of the Royal Navy. Nothing has been said officially to indicate the class to which H.M.S. Black Prince belongs, but according to the Swedish Navy League Annual, "Marinkalender," she is of an improved Dido type. The official photograph reproduced in page 614, Vol. 7, showed just such a ship engaged in supporting the Anzio landing.

IN a second encounter three days later the Germans would seem to have laid a trap for the Canadians (see story in page 25). In pursuing enemy light forces towards the French coast, the Athabaskan was torpedoed by one of the small craft which are incorrectly referred to as E-boats, though the German name for them is S-boats (*Schnellboote*). They are actually equivalent to our own motor-torpedo boats. About 130 of her officers and men appear to have been rescued, though many of these are prisoners. The enemy did not escape scatheless, for one of their destroyers was driven on to a shoal, where her destruction was completed on May 7 by our motor-torpedo boats under Lt.-Cmdr. T. N. Cartwright, D.S.C., R.N.V.R.

H.M.S. Grenville Rams E-Boat in Midnight Battle

AFTER A FAST SEA CHASE off the Anzio beach-head at midnight on Mar. 24, 1944, the British destroyer, H.M.S. Grenville, rammed and sank a German E-boat which she had previously crippled by gunfire. Back in port gunners, who helped to stop the E-boat before it was rammed, busy themselves fusing shells for the Grenville's guns, in readiness, perhaps, for another victory of the same kind. H.M.S. Grenville replaces a destroyer of the same name which was sunk in the North Sea on Jan. 20, 1940.

Photo, British Official

How Glider Troops Went to Burma 'Broadway'

DARING PENETRATION behind the Japanese lines in Burma, 200 miles east of Imphal, by airborne troops commanded by the late Maj.-Gen. O. C. Wingate, was achieved by an air commando force under Col. P. J. Cochran, U.S.A.A.F., on March 5, 1944. Two sites were selected for the landing, called "Broadway" and "Piccadilly." But as later reconnaissance showed Piccadilly to be obstructed, the entire glider force went to Broadway, most arriving safely. To relieve congestion another airfield was constructed, and up to March 11 thousands of men, more than 500,000 lb. of stores, 1,183 mules and 175 ponies were landed by air.

Maj.-Gen. O. C. Wingate, D.S.O. (wearing topee) and Col. P. J. Cochran give British and U.S. flyers a final briefing (1). A mule is coaxed aboard a transport plane (2). The glider force lined up, tow ropes ready (3). A tow plane and glider pass over the Chin Hills en route to Broadway (4). Allied fighting men sit round their glider, crashed on landing (5).

Precipitous Heights of the Imphal Road

ALONG STEEP TWISTING WAYS, such as this mountain road from Ukhrul to Imphal (capital of Manipur State in Assam on the borders of Burma) over which an Allied tank is seen advancing, British forces move also against the Japanese at Kohima, 87 miles from Imphal. Through some of the most difficult country in the world, overcoming immense physical obstacles, our 14th Army is pushing on. On May 8, 1944 the enemy was counter-attacking on the Ukhrul-Imphal road. See also map in p. 771, and illus. p. 773, Vol. 7. PAGE 9 *Photo, Indian Official*

Mighty is Canada's Help to the United Nations

Apart altogether from the epic story of her armed forces, the great Dominion of Canada's records of industrial and engineering triumphs, in furtherance of Allied war aims, verge on the miraculous. Facts substantiating that statement are here presented by HAROLD A. ALBERT, who has worked in close touch with the Wartime Information Board in Ottawa.

CANADA at war has expanded a 15-ship navy into a sea force of over 600 vessels and has become a naval power third in strength among the United Nations. Her anti-submarine craft have taken over half the burden of convoying merchant ships across the North Atlantic ; and her shipyards, almost non-existent in 1939, have repaired more than 5,000 damaged merchant ships and serviced more than 3,000 naval vessels.

Her air force had a pre-war strength of only 4,000 men. Now the R.C.A.F. has 38 fighter and bomber squadrons overseas, and for every Canadian in these squadrons there are 11 other R.C.A.F. air crew members with the R.A.F. In addition, Canada has organized, trained and equipped from her own factories a fighting army of over 500,000 and has handled contracts for over 10,000 million dollars' worth of munitions. While this has been going on, she has keyed her farm production to the highest point on record and has become a world trading nation second only to Britain and the U.S.A.

These facts are amazing. They serve to illuminate the striking energy and singleness of purpose of the Canadian people. They are so impressive that one discovers almost with shock and disbelief that there are only 11,500,000 people in the entire Dominion—two or three million fewer than in Yugoslavia ! Yet this is the Canadian miracle. Her people have the largest gun plant in the Empire, and its assembly lines have been turning out 25-pounders and other guns faster than the rival records established by Krupps in Germany or by the Soviets at Magnitogorsk. Her small-arms ammunition factories alone produce a million rounds a day. Her slipways are disgorging cargo ships at the rate of 20,000 tons a week. These statistical highlights are outshone in turn by the quiet feats that have been going on in Canada month by month since the outbreak of war. Among them are epics of engineering skill and ingenuity rivalling the greatest achievements in the history of man.

EARLY in 1941, for instance, the big aluminium smelting plants at Arvida, 130 miles north of Quebec, reached the peak of their power. New dams, barricading the flood waters of the Lake St. John area and yielding a hydro-electric output of 840,000 h.p., had already made Canada the world's third largest producer of aluminium. These fully tapped the only available natural energy, but nearly double their power output was needed if Arvida was to meet the demands of Allied aircraft and armaments. The Canadian engineers were unperturbed. By the spring of 1942, 10,600 men drawn from all the eleven Provinces were working night and day in ten-hour shifts, lifting the Saguenay River, one of the deepest rivers in the world, from its valley bed and creating an artificial waterfall. Toiling in secrecy they have created within two years a mightier power development than Boulder Dam in the U.S.A. A few miles upstream from Arvida, the new Shipshaw Dam and power-station totals a 1,500,000 h.p. capacity, and Canada's aluminium output is now thought to surpass that of the entire pre-war world.

At Goose Bay, in the Newfoundland territory of Labrador, the building of the

FROM THE NORMAN OILFIELD near the Great Bear Lake to the Whitehorse refinery goes the pipeline, on its way surmounting the 8,000-ft. high Mackenzie Range. The map shows its situation and course to the distribution point, whence the oil travels westerly to the Aleutian Islands and southwards to other centres. Output of Norman Wells exceeds 3,000 barrels a day.   *By courtesy of The Sphere*

greatest airport began at scratch when twenty Canadian lumberjacks waded ashore from an icebreaker three years ago. It was a spot lost in a savage and impenetrable hinterland. Its only approaches were from the sea. Within three days the lumbermen had built a log jetty. Within three weeks sea supplies were being landed at a permanent dock. The first five tractors to be landed became enmeshed in the mud of a spruce swamp. The Canadians laid logs as a road, and manhauled the tractors to firmer terrain.

The first blizzards buried the equipment in snowdrifts thirty feet deep. The men slept in tents, with the temperature at 50 degrees below zero. For all that, they finished a gravel runway for the first supply planes, and in another 30 days they cleared and levelled a 21-mile road to a gravel pit. Before the spring they had rolled out three runways. In March 1942 the base officially became an R.C.A.F. station—and Goose Bay is

geometrically patterned with shining concrete runways, 6,000 footers, designed to take the largest aircraft now in blueprint form. All around rise the warehouses, machine shops, oil reservoirs and buildings of a modern town, one of many to have shot up in the past five years in the northern wilderness. (See illus. p. 88, Vol. 7.)

More recently, the R.C.A.F. construction men laid out an airport on a remote island beach off northern British Columbia. It fills a great need for land-based aircraft operating out of the Northern Pacific area; and the main steel mat runway, 4,700 feet long, was laid and the entire operation completed in 13 days, three days ahead of schedule.

THEN there is the Canol Project—from the telescoped words, Canadian Oil—an immense engineering operation which opens up a vast oil-field within 75 miles of the Arctic Circle. The contract was signed less than two years ago. The U.S. War Department visualized the difficulties of fuelling the Alaskan war bases from the States and, in effect, arranged with Canada for oil supplies from Norman Wells on the Mackenzie River. It was no obstacle that Norman Wells was divided from the Alaska Highway by some 550 miles of unmapped territory, including the mountain range of the Yukon Divide. It was no obstacle that the Norman Field lay 1,500 miles north of a railhead and hemmed from the sea by the ice barriers of the Arctic Ocean. The U.S. Corps of Engineers, the Royal Canadian Corps of Signals and 3,000 Canuck civilians joined hands in organizing a 1,500-mile road-and-river transport system up through Canada's northern interior, sailing tractors, jeeps, and fuel tanks across the lakes, hauling tugs ashore and dragging them from lake to lake over 16-mile land barriers.

Seven crews were sent into the field to find a route across the ice and tundra of the Yukon hump. The seventh succeeded, and soon an oilpipe began to wriggle its way from Norman Wells to Whitehorse. Today it has been extended for 1,600 miles to the Alaska ports, and the output of the Norman Field, its limits still uncharted, is believed to exceed 3,000 barrels a day.

Starting with petroleum as the raw material, the manufacture of synthetic rubber in Canada was put in hand in 1942, when plans were made for a plant with a production capacity of over 30,000 tons a year.

These are only a few of the miracles of Canada at war, miracles achieved by a pioneer nation in backing the words of their Minister of Finance : " We aim to make a reputation for Canadian achievement in this war that will be the talk of the world for generations, that will be the pride of ourselves, our children and our children's children."

Dominion Enterprise Keeps War Industries Busy

THOUSANDS OF LOGS float outside this Ottawa sawmill (1) waiting to be converted to war purposes. At Shipshaw, in North Quebec, workmen are rushing to finish one of the world's greatest water-power projects ; huge generators such as these (2) will put an extra 1,500,000 h.p. behind aluminium and aeroplane production. Millions of eggs are powdered for dispatch to Britain (3). Storage tanks (4) of the £30,000,000 Norman Wells oil scheme (see facing page). PAGE 11 *Photos, Canadian Official, Pictorial Press, Paul Popper, Canadian Film Board*

Our Colonies in the War: No. 8—Sierra Leone

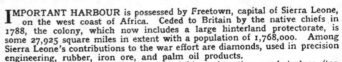

I MPORTANT HARBOUR is possessed by Freetown, capital of Sierra Leone, on the west coast of Africa. Ceded to Britain by the native chiefs in 1788, the colony, which now includes a large hinterland protectorate, is some 27,925 square miles in extent with a population of 1,768,000. Among Sierra Leone's contributions to the war effort are diamonds, used in precision engineering, rubber, iron ore, and palm oil products.

Scenes in Freetown's harbour (top left), and native market-place (top right). Atlantic anti-submarine patrol and convoy work are carried out by aircraft of this naval air station in the bush (below) ; in charge is Commander C. Oliver Foley, O.B.E., R.N. (centre left), formerly responsible for all survey work and aircraft moorings on Imperial Airways routes from Southampton to Singapore. *Photos, British Official and Pictorial Press*

Empire Premiers Tackle War and Peace Plans

Next stages in the war, and organization of the peace to follow, were points of discussion before the Empire Prime Ministers who came to Britain for the Conference which opened at 10, Downing Street, London, on May 1, 1944. From Canada, Australia, New Zealand, South Africa and Southern Rhodesia these stout-hearted leaders came, each cognizant of his own tremendous responsibility, soberly aware that on their united decisions largely rested the prospects of mankind. The last conference of Empire Premiers was held after the Coronation in 1937.

Mr. Churchill, who presided at the first meeting of this first wartime conference of Prime Ministers of the Commonwealth, is seen (left) with Mr. Curtin, Australia. Above Sir Godfrey Huggins, Southern Rhodesia. Below, at a dinner given by the King and Queen to the Premiers at Buckingham Palace, are, left to right : Mr. Fraser (New Zealand), Mr. Curtin (Australia), Mr. Churchill, H.M. the King, Mr. Mackenzie King (Canada), General Smuts (South Africa). PAGE 13

Blockade-Running Now a Desperate Axis Gamble

Increasingly urgent need of the enemy for certain war commodities is aggravated by Allied patrols taking mounting toll of Axis blockade-runners on the seas. The unenviable lot of officers and crews engaged in that losing gamble is presented here by CAPT. FRANK H. SHAW, from first-hand knowledge of its hazards—for he also has "run" contraband of war.

ROYAL NAVY submarines ran the air-blockade of Malta and saved that island from total destruction and starvation. The petrol, ammunition and food carried there kept the R.A.F. in the air to beat off Axis bombers, the ammunition helped to shoot down such of the raiders as our Spitfires, Gladiators and Hurricanes missed, and the food maintained the stamina of the people of the George Cross Island.

Blockade-running is desperate work. Myself, I have run contraband of war to various bellicose states, mostly in a condition of revolution, for the Latin American countries used to be regularly "agin the Government"; in such circumstances, avoiding the guardships and look-out craft is a hair-raising job. But it requires a war of this present magnitude to reveal the blockade-runner at its best—and worst.

The Axis powers are extremely anxious to interchange war-essentials: raw products for finished fighting-tools. But for German machine-tools to reach Japan entails a very lengthy voyage which bristles with hazards, and whose ultimate goal is usually that Port of Missing Ships whence no vessel returns. Probably seventy-five per cent of Axis contrabandists have been self-scuttled; most of the remainder have been sunk by Allied action.

Their existence has not been enviable. With increasing air and sea-power the Allied watch on such sly merchants has been practically unbroken. The widest detours are necessary to steam from the Western Pacific to the Eastern Atlantic, when it is remembered that the Panama Canal, the Magellan Straits, and all other short cuts from Orient to Occident are under the closest surveillance. Ports of refuge and refuelling are few and scattered, and every such port is well known to the Allied sea and air sentinels. If a ship fills up with fuel and stores for her crew's consumption to the extent necessary for what might easily prove to be a twelve months' voyage, valuable cargo-space is sacrificed. That means that only ships of considerable size are serviceable in the blockade-running game; and the bigger the ship, the more easy her detection.

THERE is also need for speed in times of crisis, which means very powerful engines and boilers, occupying much space. Since Axis blockade-runners are all more or less heavily armed large crews are needed, not only to perform the usual ship work but also to handle the guns in event of emergency, as there is a ninety per cent chance of such occurring. During a year of solitary voyaging, of long periods of hiding in lonely bays, remote from the normal sea-routes, of incredibly wide detours, a lot of food and water are consumed. But certain commodities, such as rubber, aluminium and wolfram are vitally necessary to the production of munitions: and as even comparatively small quantities have their value the Axis considers such risks and privations justified.

Normally, a runner steaming from Japan to Germany would go down the Pacific almost to the fringe of the Antarctic ice, the thick, stormy weather serving as a shroud to her movements. She could then steer either east around Cape Horn or west around Good Hope. The latter route would be the more dangerous, because of the regular sea-watch maintained by the South African Air Force, which runs systematic patrols over a wide area of ocean, and the South Atlantic squadrons of the Allied navies. The coasts of Tierra del Fuego and the south Argentine, however, afford many opportunities for hiding; and the Argentine has shown itself friendly disposed towards the Axis.

STILL, the great oceans are wide; and if we owned ten times the ships and aircraft at present in Allied possession we could not

AFTER SCUTTLING THEIR VESSEL, the crew of the 4,793-ton German armed ship Silvaplana pull towards the British cruiser H.M.S. Adventure; the entire company, including 100 German navy personnel, were rescued. Trying to run the blockade from the Far East with a cargo of rubber and tin, the Silvaplana was intercepted 200 miles off Cape Finisterre. *Photo, Central Press*

maintain a full patrol all the time. One need only survey the seas from the air at a height of, say, 1,000 feet, to realize what an infinitesmally small speck a big steamer can appear. But a blockade-runner in open sea is of no real use to anybody: it is only when she reaches an Axis port with her cargo that she acquires value. And it stands to reason that the Allies tighten their watchfulness at the chief focal points of a journey. The Straits of Gibraltar are now definitely denied to Axis surface ships. There remain the Biscayan ports, the Norwegian fjords, and the Baltic as possible havens. Except to an occasional submarine the whole Mediterranean, east and west, is barred completely to Axis sea-forces.

But every route to the Norwegian hide-outs, the Baltic harbours and the Biscayan ports is today patrolled as closely as human ingenuity can patrol it. Only by night, and preferably in thick weather, can a useful landfall be attempted. This calls for consummately accurate navigation, at which the Germans do not excel, being prone to grow hysterical when faced with difficulty. This fact accounts for most of the Axis blockade-runner sinkings taking place either in the Bay of Biscay itself or in its approaches. Between the Canary Islands, in Spanish possession and conceivably somewhat friendly to the Axis, and Biscay, there is not one inch of cover, especially now, when French West Africa has come into Allied occupation. Dakar at one time afforded an excellent

halting-place for the runner to rest and refit in readiness for the hazardous skelter to Biscay. Now there is no shelter to be found at Dakar—only long-range air-patrols, with light, fast naval surface ships to carry out unbroken policing.

The acquisition of bases in the Azores has helped the Allies to fine-comb every degree of this area of the Atlantic, through which the runners must pass if they are to reach port. And this stretch of sea is almost phenomenally clear of cloud and fog. The atmosphere is the most transparent in the whole world, and the water is aglow by night with glittering phosphorescence, so that the wake and bow-wave of a ship can instantly be detected from the air. Also, our night-patrolling aircraft carry the revealing Leigh-Light, designed originally as an anti-U-boat device, but equally valuable against surface craft. Once a runner is spotted from the air it is hardly necessary for the aircraft to attack, although this has been frequently done with excellent results. The patrol above can call up naval vessels to complete the victory, well knowing that their superior speed in a sea where no hiding-place is available will enable the Navy to intercept or overtake the fugitive and compel either its surrender or its scuttling.

Life for the crews of such ships is appallingly monotonous, the only constant thing being fear of detection and destruction. In the narrow limits of such a lonely ship, with nothing whatever to relieve the boredom, men grow mentally unstable. Food is usually scarce and badly cooked. The wireless picks up Allied news-bulletins, with their serial tales of increasing victory—if the Gestapo agents aboard each blockade-runner permit such news to be received and passed on to the crew. The discipline aboard such blockade-runners must necessarily be tyrannically severe, for the slightest laxity is apt to precipitate trouble of a mutinous nature.

HUMAN nature can stand just so much. How many cases have occurred of crews overpowering their officers and surrendering the vessel to Allied patrols will not be made public until the need for secrecy ends. But the end is more usually the sighting of an Allied patrol, the headlong chase, and then the challenging fire that tells the actors in the grim drama that the game is up. Escape is hopeless. There are few, if any, big Axis surface ships in the open now to provide a formidable escort. Whether it be a long-range Sunderland dropping bombs and depth-charges, or a warship bracketing with heavy shell, Nemesis overtakes the worn-out enemy crew.

A U-boat, a complicated mass of internal machinery, has little spare space for cargo. Aircraft cannot carry sufficient freight to justify their use against Allied air-power. Blockade is a formidable weapon, as exercised by the Allied powers it is practically a fatal weapon. Yet, despite Hitler's so-called U-boat blockade, 99 per cent of our surface ships now get through, as compared with the one per cent success of the Axis.

Maj.-Gen. IVAN PANFILOV

Vasili Yakolev

A GUERILLA   V. Neshinsky

Along the Battlelines with Russia's War Artists

WIDE encouragement is given to artists in the Republics of the Soviet Union. The Red Army has its own studio and employs artists specifically to paint battle scenes. Others dispose of their pictures in the socialist market or through a co-operative. The same economic laws apply as to other workers, many artists working in their own studios, while others join large studios run by the State. The cream of artistic production during the first 18 months of war was recently displayed at the Great Patriotic War Exhibition held at the Moscow Tretyakov Gallery, the collection later going on tour. Representative examples, notable for imaginative conception and vigorous execution, are given in these pages.

EXPLOIT OF TWENTY-EIGHT GUARDSMEN OF THE PANFILOV DIVISION   D. Mochalsky

SPRING ON THE DONETS — Aléxander Gorpenko

A MEETING IN LIBERATED STALINGRAD

THIS WE WON'T FORGIVE THEM — Kukryniksi

URALS ARTILLERY PLANT — Peter Vasiliev

PRISONERS OF WAR : SOUTH-WESTERN FRONT — Alexei Laptev

Constantine Finogenov

INHABITANTS OF LIBERATED VILLAGE

Pavel Malkov

BOMBARDING PAULUS' MEN : STALINGRAD

Constantine Finogenov

A CAVALRY CHARGE

Alexander Deineka

TANKS ON THE UNIVERSITY EMBANKMENT: LENINGRAD

Mikhail Platunov

VIEWS & REVIEWS
Of Vital War Books

by Hamilton Fyfe

I READ in a Times leading article not long ago that "we are in the midst of a revolution." I dare say a good many people who read that wondered what it meant and didn't altogether like the sound of it. But it is profoundly true, and I have just been looking through a book which shows how the change is working.

Revolution is change, a change in the State—the State meaning those who wield the supreme power in a nation. Once the barons had this power in England. Then the kings secured it, having beaten the barons in the Wars of the Roses. Then the kings lost it, through the folly of the Stuarts, and the landed aristocracy held it. They kept it for a century and a half, until they were compelled by the Reform Act of 1832 to share it with the commercial, manufacturing and financial interests. Gradually these latter gathered it into their hands and squeezed out the landed interest. Now, during the past few years, the power has been passing to the mass of the nation. That is what The Times meant.

What the mass of the nation will do with it no one can say. Some look forward to better government than we ever had before—better, that is, for the people as a whole. Some think it will be the ruin of the country. Probably it will be much the same as, more or less, it always has been. "The mixture as before !"

But in many directions certain alterations have been made in our ways of thinking, in public opinion, in the relations between different sections of the community. Wellington described his soldiers as "the scum of the earth." When he said "the battle of Waterloo was won on the playing-fields of Eton" (if he ever did say it) he was praising his officers at the expense of the Other Ranks. That view of the private soldier prevailed up to the end of the 19th century. A young man who enlisted was thought to have disgraced his family. Officers treated their men as if they were criminals or children.

The Old-Style Bullying Tone

Even during the last war I was re-volted by this. I was staying in the trenches with a Fusilier battalion. The C.O. was a friend of mine, a very good chap with many up-to-date ideas. But he spoke to his N.C.O.s and privates in a harsh, almost bullying tone—just because this was customary, because he had always done it. The men didn't seem to mind. They were used to it. But it gave me a shock.

Now that couldn't, I think, happen today. I say "I think." I may be wrong. Some officers may think the best method of ensuring good discipline is to "put the fear of God" into the private soldier. If there are any such, I hope they will read the book, Psychology and the Soldier, by the Rev. Norman Copeland (Allen and Unwin, 5s.). It may change their ideas. It will show them, at all events, how the attitude towards the man in the ranks has shifted since they were young (I assume they must be getting on in years or they would have noticed this shift already).

Mr. Copeland is an Army chaplain. He has been in the Service fifteen years, a comrade as well as a padre, a student as well as a teacher. He gives his book as its secondary title, "The Art of Leadership." His aim is to show that "putting the fear of God" into men (he uses the phrase himself) is the worst way to turn them into good soldiers. To get the best out of them their officers must first understand them, then they must like them ; they must regard them as fellow-men, must study them individually, make allowances for their defects, try to develop whatever ability there is in them. "In order to lead a man must be in advance of his group. He cannot lead from behind or even from the ranks. He can shout or shove, but shouting and shoving are always exhausting and rarely effective. An appointed leader must be accepted by the led as the most able man in the group before he is followed blindly. It is not sufficient that he should have ability. The effect of his personality must be such as to inspire confidence in his ability."

Psychology and the Soldier

MR. COPELAND says he is interested in psychology. Of course he is, or he wouldn't have written this book. What he means is that he enjoys studying human nature. As a psychologist in the technical sense he is not very acute. He says, for instance, that there must be a standard of behaviour in every group of men, either that of "the clean, alert, cheerful, honest, virtuous and clever, or that of the dirty, lazy, dishonest, vicious and stupid." There speaks the parson rather than the scientific investigator. He ought to have noticed that often the dishonest people are the cleanest and sometimes the most

MAJOR TOM BRIDGES, D.S.O., of the 4th Royal Irish Dragoon Guards (later General Sir Tom Bridges, K.C.B., K.C.M.G., who died on Nov. 26, 1939), was the hero of the drum-and-whistle episode related in this page. The scene was St. Quentin, the date August 27, 1914.

cheerful, that the clever ones may be lazy or the dirty ones virtuous in a conventional way.

However, for practical purposes this active-minded, kindly padre knows quite enough about the behaviour of men and the reasons for it to make him a safe guide. He knows that discipline need not be compulsion. Discipline is aimed at keeping people in order. But "a good disciplinarian can influence a group of people to keep themselves in order." He knows too that, while discipline is more necessary to the soldier (a fighting man generally) than to anyone else in the world, "there is a vast difference between the discipline which restricts and irritates and the discipline which exists as a useful incentive."

Importance of the Personal Touch

Here is a less obvious piece of advice. "Always call men by their names. When we call a man by his name we give him an identity. He is no longer a man in the crowd, but an individual. We have given him a sense of importance and a feeling of confidence and respect." The story is told of Lord Roberts riding beside a column of tired troops on the march and asking, "Who is that man—and that—and that ?" and then speaking to them, using their names, encouraging them with little personal touches. He made them feel he knew them personally. "They were good for another ten miles."

Another story is quoted to prove how a glint of fun will sometimes do what no exhortation or entreaty can effect. A Dragoon Guards major was sent to bring in some stragglers who were exhausted. He found them listless, apparently too weary to move. They sat and lay in the square of a small French town. He was puzzled. He had to get them going. What could be done ? His eye lit on a toyshop. He went in, he bought a tin whistle and a child's drum. He had a trumpeter with him. "Can you play The British Grenadiers ?" he asked. "Right. Then take this whistle and play it. I'll play the drum."

They went round the square, playing for all they were worth. The tired men looked up, light came into their eyes, their lips opened in smiles, they stirred, they looked round to see what the row was about. Then they broke into a roar of laughter and scrambled up and followed. Not a man was left behind.

Mr. Copeland mention Napoleon's saying, " Moral force in war is worth three times as much as physical force," and he thinks Napoleon might have said more than three times. But he might have made it clear that moral force in this connexion does not mean that the army with a good cause which it believes in is sure to win. That would be a very dangerous doctrine, as harmful as that which Mr. Copeland preaches when he suggests that if we constantly repeat, "Thou art the Lord our God and we are Thy people," the British Empire is bound to triumph.

Many armies have fought in good causes, many which have believed they were the Lord's people have been utterly defeated and destroyed. The Boers in South Africa believed it ; what higher principle had we to fight for ? But we beat them. The Finns thought they had a sacred principle, and were enthusiastic about it, but the Russians won because they were better equipped and led and had larger forces.

Leadership is of special interest just now. It may turn the scale in theatres of war where forces seem equally matched. In Montgomery we have a leader of the classic type ; he would endorse all this book says about establishing close relations between officers and men. That is how he won the trust and devotion of the 8th Army.

A New Stalingrad Rises from the Ashes of War

CITY OF HEROES, Stalingrad stoutly met the Nazi onslaught of September 1942, and in the subsequent prolonged and bitter fighting was all but razed to the ground. The enemy succeeded in occupying the greater part of the city ; then came the Russian counter-blow which trapped the German 6th Army and culminated in the city's relief on Feb. 2, 1943. Today the resurrected town begins to assume a foremost place in the resurgent life of freed Russia.
The once-dead Volga waterfront grows busy again (1) ; the archway marks the limit of Gen. Chuykov's front line. In the famous tractor plant, where the last remaining German invader was exterminated, a wall plaque commemorates the Red Army's deeds ; alongside it a poster announces a football match in the plant's stadium (2). A girl plasterer (3), who has quickly learned to handle the trowel, helps to rebuild the city ; other citizens work with a will in a once-shattered street (4). See story in p. 25. *Photos Exclusive to*
THE WAR ILLUSTRATED

Red Marine Commandos Raid the Crimea Coast

STRIKING SWIFTLY and often during the battle for the Crimea —which on May 9, 1944, came to an end with the storming and capture of Sevastopol, last German hold on the Peninsula—marines of the Soviet Black Sea Fleet have made many commando raids to wipe out Nazi coastal garrisons, their successes greatly aiding the triumphal progress of the main Russian forces (see map in p. 778, Vol. 7).

Fast motor boats of the Soviet Black Sea Fleet with a landing party of marines start off on a coastal raid (1). Undetected, they reach the beach ; armed with automatic weapons and grenades, and hauling behind them a heavy wheeled machine-gun (2), they move quickly inland, pausing to observe when danger threatens (3). Their objective reached—an inhabited place held by the Germans—the marines take up fighting positions and turn their full fire-power on the surprised enemy.

Photos, Pictorial Press

Hounds of War Now Go to Training School

Loaned for the purpose by patriotic owners, dogs are being trained in England for a number of important war duties, including the guarding of Service installations and property at home and overseas, on lines described here by LEIGH M. SCULLY. The Nazis also have their war-dogs —and our Commandos have learned by practical experience how to deal with these.

"WAKE up, you ! One of the dogs has gone sick, and you've got to take his place ! " is the caption to a new Army cartoon unofficially issued at an important Air Service Command post where dogs are used as guards, each dog releasing three men for more important duties.

The U.S. Eighth Air Force headquarters started the scheme some months ago in England when they opened a dog-guard training school. Men from all parts of the country were sent there to learn to handle the animals and train them for their war duties. Men and dogs are trained as a team, so that when they complete their term at the school they virtually "talk the same language." Some of these massive dogs are killers, and it is fascinating to see how implicitly they obey their masters.

It is a stiff course for the dogs. They are taught discipline, how to manage a stranger, how to keep him in captivity, and how to trail and pick up scents at prescribed distances. Dogs are assigned to a post just as an ordinary soldier would be, and incidentally they don't grouse about their guard duties, but take a pride in their work ! An e pert at the training school tells me that the u e of dogs for guard duties was first started as an experiment, but they have proved so efficient that they are now used extensively. In the last war dogs were used chiefly as messengers by Royal Engineers signals detachments. Their use as guards for Army property is a new development.

" IT is necessary for us to keep them in constant training," one of the school trainers told me. " We follow a daily routine for teaching them obedience. In the exercises we have to wear a leather sleeve to protect us against their teeth. This helps the dogs to learn the proper way of attacking an intruder." Two dogs which never leave the heels of the two school instructors are Wolf and Danny, pedigree Alsatians lent by their British owners for the duration of the war. Not all these dogs are killers, but their method of attack is not a happy experience, and their watchfulness is such that no sniping Nazi would be able to get a shot in before the dog's teeth penetrated his uniform.

There is evidence that genuine "killer" dogs, including Alsatians and other large breeds, are being trained by the Reichswehr as part of their anti-invasion defences. There is reason to believe that large numbers of them are stationed at frequent intervals along certain stretches of the coasts of France, Belgium and Holland, to give the alarm when anyone approaches from the sea at night.

Each of these sentry dogs is in charge of a German N.C.O. detailed for its training. It is drilled to run to its master, who would be on sentry-go near by, to give warning of suspicious noises out at sea. The Germans believe that their "Alsatian Guard," with their acute sense of hearing, can pick up sounds that would fail to register on the most sensitive sound-detection apparatus. They claim that their most skilfully trained killer-dogs can detect even a carefully-propelled rowing boat when still a considerable distance off shore.

It is no myth that these dogs exist. They have been encountered by British Commando units on their spasmodic raids, and from some of these forays have come back stories of savage attacks by German-trained dogs.

IT is even reported that as a result of encounters with dogs, many Commandos now carry their knives on the left hip instead of on the right. The reason is that Commando soldiers, instinctively raising their right arms to keep the dogs at bay, lost a split-second in getting the knives in the right-hand position.

One difficulty of training dogs of the Alsatian type for this work is, although they have good natural "guard" properties they do not willingly obey more than one master.

Thus each dog has to be under the command of one sentry with whom it has been trained possibly for several weeks. In Australia the experiment is being tried of dogs with radio control, and the first tests have shown that the scheme may be of use in jungle warfare where dogs are used to follow a scent. A midget short-wave radio set is strapped on a harness worn by the dog, or carried on a stout collar ; it works from dry batteries, and will receive for about 60 hours before new batteries are fitted. The sets are flatly tuned and give good quality—so that a dog, hearing the midget loudspeaker behind his ear, at once recognizes his master's voice.

WITH this radio control, a man can call on or call off several dogs at once. As all the receivers will be tuned to one frequency the radio control does not upset any other form of radio transmission used. In training, gramophone records of the "master's" voice are used, while he stands near the dogs and alternately shouts real words of command. After about a week the dogs accept the loudspeaker as a real "voice," and the radio control works quite well even though the master at the microphone may be several miles away.

FOUR-FOOTED FORCES are in training at special schools for war dogs in Britain. Thousands have already completed their course and will carry out patrol work, guard munition dumps and Army headquarters and do other duties. Above, A.T.S. kennel maids groom Alsatians ; below, a war dog receives first aid. See facing page.

Photos, Sport & General

Man's Best Friend Helps Him Fight the Enemy

RADIO GUIDES THE ACTIONS of this white Alsatian (1), which has been trained to obey words of command (from its concealed master) transmitted through the small wireless receiving set strapped to its body; the set (5) is sufficiently powerful for the voice to be heard clearly. U.S. Marines use scouting dogs to track down Japanese snipers in Pacific island jungles (2). This war-dog acts as sentry on a R.A.F. airfield (3), while another has a message for delivery placed in its collar (4).

Photos, Keystone, Planet News, Pictorial Press

How They Fight the Malaria Menace at Anzio

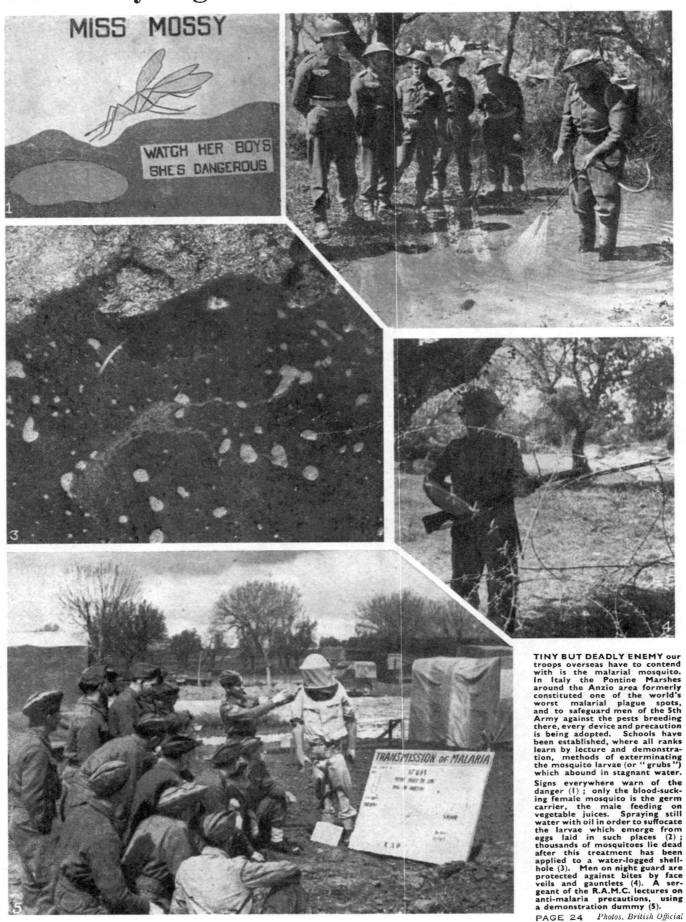

TINY BUT DEADLY ENEMY our troops overseas have to contend with is the malarial mosquito. In Italy the Pontine Marshes around the Anzio area formerly constituted one of the world's worst malarial plague spots, and to safeguard men of the 5th Army against the pests breeding there, every device and precaution is being adopted. Schools have been established, where all ranks learn by lecture and demonstration, methods of exterminating the mosquito larvae (or " grubs ") which abound in stagnant water.

Signs everywhere warn of the danger (1) ; only the blood-sucking female mosquito is the germ carrier, the male feeding on vegetable juices. Spraying still water with oil in order to suffocate the larvae which emerge from eggs laid in such places (2) ; thousands of mosquitoes lie dead after this treatment has been applied to a water-logged shell-hole (3). Men on night guard are protected against bites by face veils and gauntlets (4). A sergeant of the R.A.M.C. lectures on anti-malaria precautions, using a demonstration dummy (5).

Photos, British Official

I WAS THERE! Eye Witness Stories of the War

We Knew Our Sister Ship Would Sail No More

Two recent actions off the Ushant shore were notable as being the first naval actions which ships of the Royal Canadian Navy have ever fought against enemy surface fighting ships. This account of the passing of the gallant Athabaskan, set afire and torpedoed on April 29, 1944, is by a Naval correspondent who was aboard H.M.C.S. Haida.

WE heard the cry, "Athabaskan has been hit!" and as we turned to look at her we saw flames enveloping her superstructure. The action had hardly commenced. Two Canadian Tribal destroyers had discovered two enemy destroyers of the Elbing class close in on the French coast, and suspected others near by, and immediately closed to engage. Athabaskan (Lieut.-Cdr. J. H. Stubbs, D.S.O., R.C.N.) fired the first starshell. She was directly astern of Haida (Commander H. G. DeWolf, R.C.N.) and only a few cables distant.

Our guns opened immediately after, and under the spread of starshell we sighted the enemy ships, two of them, racing along the coast. They attempted to repeat the tactics of two nights previously, when we had sunk one and damaged three of their destroyers. They were making smoke and hoping to get away under cover of it. The action blazed furiously, and it was just after the first few salvos had been fired that Athabaskan was hit. It was a hazy, starlit night, about an hour and three-quarters before dawn.

We saw the flames spreading over Athabaskan but she steamed on, her guns thundering. Enemy starshell was all about us at the time, and shells were splashing around and between the two ships. Another shell seemed to strike Athabaskan aft, and she slowed down. H.M.C.S. Haida, her gunners repeating their fine performance of two nights previously, hammered the enemy ships, while Cdr. DeWolf ordered a smoke screen to shield Athabaskan, meanwhile maintaining the engagement. Hits were observed and a small fire broke out in the leading enemy destroyer and then, as we concentrated on the nearest one, we saw our salvos strike home and flames appear through the smoke screen.

It was about this time that a sudden explosion made us realize that Athabaskan had reached the end. We saw a burst of flames and knew our sister ship would sail no more. The odds were now more than two to one against Haida, but Cdr. DeWolf continued directing the engagement. Another salvo and another struck the enemy ship, and the flames mounted higher. It was obvious that both enemy ships were confused. The burning one opened a vicious fire in the direction of the other, mistaking her apparently for us as she fled. As our target appeared stopped, we closed, pounding her as we came in, only to realize, as we saw the rocks, that she had been driven ashore out of control.

Haida then turned back to where we had last seen Athabaskan. Bobbing lights appeared on the surface as we closed the area, lights from the new type R.C.N. lifejacket. Nosing gently in to where the lights were thickest, Cdr. DeWolf stopped Haida and ordered all life rafts over and all boats

H.M.C.S. ATHABASKAN, which was sunk on April 29, 1944, during the Channel engagement described in this page. Of her complement of about 200 men, 40 were rescued by H.M.C.S. Haida, 6 by her motor-boat which reached home safely, while 83 were reported prisoners of war.

Photo, British Official

PAGE 25

lowered. The sea was covered with thick heavy fuel oil from Athabaskan's tanks. Those of Haida's crew who could be spared from the guns lined the rails, shouting encouragement to those in the water. "Come on, boys, this is Haida!" they cried, and the survivors shouted back and blew whistles. They were covered with oil, and they slipped in our hands as we helped them over the side. Several of Haida's crew, including Mr. L. Jones, the Gunner (T), and Lieut. John Coates, R.C.N.V.R., went down the nets, accompanied by several Haida ratings, to help the survivors on board.

Up on the bridge the Captain, Cdr. DeWolf, leaned over and encouraged the swimmers steadily. "Come on, chaps, swim in to the ship's side!" he told them, and the survivors did so. One survivor coming in looked up and grinned. "Good old Haida," he said, "you beat us to it again," referring to the Elbing destroyer which Haida had intercepted and sunk in the previous fight two nights before. "We got the one that got you!" the Haida boys told him cheerfully.

The whaler was lowered and let go, and then the motor launch went down. Three of Haida's crew, knowing there was little hope that the ship could wait for them, did an amazingly brave thing very coolly. They got the motor-boat clear in record time, started up the engine and calmly proceeded to round up survivors who were too far away from the ship to reach it. It was less than half an hour to dawn. A lighthouse abeam of us on the French coast kept flashing steadily, and the shore was plainly visible less than three miles away. Reluctantly, Cdr. DeWolf gave the order to depart, and we went, leaving the gallant crew in the motor-boat to pick up as many as they could and utilize the whaler also. The motor-boat had fuel for six hours at a speed of ten knots. It had all necessary gear, including a compass and a Verey pistol. As we pulled clear, two of Haida's men who were down on the scramble nets were unable to get up, and they jumped clear. They were wearing the new lifejackets.

From a raft close alongside a voice, believed to be that of Lt.-Cdr. Stubbs, hero of North Atlantic actions against U-boats, was heard to shout, "Get away, Haida, get clear!" It was the kind of thing that this very brave and gallant gentleman who captained H.M.C.S. Athabaskan would say in such circumstances, though it left him, covered with oil on a drifting raft, to meet a cold, unfriendly dawn off the enemy coast.

Bulldozing With the 5th Army at Anzio

Despite the fact that it lacks the glamour attached to many other military activities, Royal Engineers who drive bulldozers are proud of their task—which is, mainly, to construct tracks and roads, often under fire. Cpl. L. P. Dymock, R.A.F., sent us this story from the Italian beach-head.

THE giant diesel-driven bulldozers are a product of America's great engineering firms. They have proved themselves indispensable in our battles. First ashore in an initial landing they prepare the way for tanks, which are in the forefront of the waiting trucks which, with men, guns and stores, are ready to pour from the landing craft.

Great advances have been made in the waterproofing of these machines, so that they are capable of operating under water.

Sapper Griffiths, of Doncaster, commonly known as "Diablo" to the Italians, has been in the many landings in this theatre of war. He has had some interesting adventures, including being snapped on his mighty "steed" by President Roosevelt's personal photographer. In Griffiths' view, mines are the greatest danger to the bulldozer; but the drivers are comparatively safe from the splinters, having a few tons of steel between them and the explosion. During the Anzio landing his machine was hit a number of times by small-arms fire, but this did not

affect the mechanical efficiency of the great caterpillar.

While advancing in Sicily he worked beyond the infantry. He told me: "I had been making a diversion through a large village, clearing away the rubble and generally making a road. When returning along the road to my bivvy an infantry officer told me to get out of the way as his company intended to capture the village I had just left!"

Many instances have occurred where, during the demolition of buildings, search has revealed a cellar to be full of liquor. The most notable occasion was when enough lager was found for a regiment; the point about this incident was that they almost did not bother to see if there was a cellar into which the bulldozer might go tumbling! Celebrating with the same golden liquor, the boys were suddenly told to shut up and blow out the lights as in the vicinity of the garden a German patrol was loitering—evidently in search of the liquid that was cooling-off our Tommies' parched throats.

BULLDOZERS HAVE PROVED INVALUABLE to the allies in the speedy preparation of roads and airfields and in the multifarious other construction jobs which mobile warfare entails. Here one of these highly efficient mechanical monsters is seen clearing a debris-blocked street in the Italian port of Anzio. The useful work performed by bulldozers in this beach-head area is described in this and the preceding pages.
Photo, British Official

radio message ordered us to land at a forward airfield, to fly six urgent casualty cases back to base. We set course south, escorted by Hurricanes, two flying close in to ward off any possible hit-and-run attack, while the four others criss-crossed in and out of the clouds, searching for enemy fighters which might have looked on "P for Peter" as easy meat.

Below, we saw the landing strip, deserted save for its small windsock hanging from a bamboo pole. We touched down to pick up our cargo, and left the Hurricanes patrolling the sky. Eight stretcher cases came aboard, mostly Gurkhas, but there was one British soldier among them, a private from Tutshill, Monmouthshire.

I asked him what had happened. He pointed south, where smoke from mortar fire and shells showed as they burst in the sky. "We ran into a machine-gun burst," he said. "We were accompanied by Gurkhas, and trying to edge round a Japanese pimple (a small concentration, heavily armed with machine-guns). Johnny Jap must have seen us as we were coming through the trees, and they outnumbered us four to one. The scrap didn't last long, and when it was over the stretcher-bearers came out to help get back the wounded. We were sneaking back when the Japanese opened fire and many of

Parking the bulldozer one evening behind a house partly requisitioned for billets, the Italian women who had been wailing that the Germans had stolen all their goods rushed in front of Griffiths frantically waving him back. Thinking it was a mine, he got out to have a look and there they were, clawing up the ground, digging out wine, grain and food.

Sapper Terrent, of Horsham, whose nickname is "Digger" (he earned that by

previously serving with the Aussies), came up from El Alamein with an Australian Division in the last push. His invasions include Sicily, Reggio, and Anzio, where he helped to clear the beaches and roads. Terrent works with Griffiths, sharing dugout and adventures. These two, like others who operate bulldozers, are not envied. They are fully aware of the magnificent job they are doing, and are proud of the praise given them by many high-ranking officers.

We Dropped Supplies to the Troops in Burma

During a recent operation from a Bengal airfield a plane of R.A.F. Transport Command flew to a front line outpost a load including 47,000 cigarettes, 6,000 boxes of matches, tinned milk and an assortment of other supplies, then returned with wounded, as told below.

SEEN from "P for Peter" the other fast transports made a grand sight on our port and starboard sides, their combined slipstream shooting a violent duststorm towards the hangars. We took our place at 8,000 feet. We were well above the clouds, and the fierce sun made the interior of the aircraft too hot for comfort. After flying for two hours we were met by a squadron of Hurricanes which escorted us to our dropping point. We were over rugged, desolate country. As far as the eye could see, hills up to 3,000 feet zig-zagged awkwardly over the horizon. We were well within range of enemy fighters. The jungle beneath, a densely-vegetated maze of green sprawling between the valleys, was no place for a forced landing.

We broke formation and descended, to fly in line astern, playing follow-my-leader through valleys and skimming hilltops and rivers until our formation leader circled a hill, eight miles farther on. Parachutes from the first two aircraft had already landed right where the troops waited for them. Our turn came, and we made our run.

I sat in the co-pilot's seat, and watched the crew in the fuselage, stripped and sweating, as they piled the heavy packages at the exit, ready for the next run. Five packs were poised ready, with another five directly behind. They weighed from 80 to 140 pounds each. The contents were packed in tins with a small parachute on top, enclosed in a cover with 12 feet of rope fastened to an attachment inside the aircraft. The crew

were secured by safety belts tied to a longeron. "Red light on !" shouted the Flight Sergeant near the tail, and the crew got their hands under the packages. The bell rang insistently and everybody heaved like mad to get 13 packages overboard before the bell rang again, three seconds later.

The process was repeated until the last package had been dropped, and we circled to make sure that the load had landed safely before setting course for base. But "P for Peter" had not finished the mission. A

WHEN THE SIGNAL BELL RINGS these men of a supply-carrying aircraft in Burma will push overboard the bulky packages of vital stores, as is told in the accompanying eye-witness account.
Photo, British Official

the stretcher cases already wounded were killed, along with the orderlies." He swore vehemently.

When all our patients had been made comfortable, we took off and rejoined the waiting fighter escort, to set course for base, where ambulances were ready to rush the wounded to hospital.

For Stalingrad's Citizens a New Era Dawns

Wonderful plans are in operation to put the city of "steel-hearted" citizens on its feet again. How the dreadful scars left by the Nazis are being obliterated is here described by the famous Russian writer, Z. Mokhov, by courtesy of Soviet War News Weekly. See also illus. p. 29.

I WENT to see the gift sword sent by King George VI to Stalingrad's defenders. The King's gift is displayed in a special room, where there is always a Guard of Honour. Scores of people come to see it every day—not only Stalingrad people, but visitors who have arrived from all parts of the U.S.S.R. to pay homage to the city of world renown.

Pigalev, chairman of the City Soviet, showed me the King's gift. I read over and over again the inscription to the "steel-hearted citizens," engraved in English and Russian on the blade. Pigalev remarked,

"We treasure this sword as a symbol of the fighting friendship between the peoples of the Soviet Union and Great Britain." Pigalev is an engineer by profession. He invited me to his study, where a number of engineers and architects from Moscow were waiting to confer with him about a big new medical institute and hospital, to be equipped according to the very last word in medical science. Dozens of plans and sketches were pinned to the walls and spread over Pigalev's desk. The sites are already being cleared.

That same evening I attended a review of plans for the restoration of schools, children's homes and nurseries. This year 18 million

MORE AND MORE MATERIALS for the reconstruction of the hero city of Stalingrad pour in daily, to be handled without delay by men and women labourers eager to push the great task ahead. 85 per cent of all buildings in the city were destroyed in the winter battles of 1942-43. But by the end of 1943 over 1,000 houses as well as over 10,000 cottages had been built, and more than 100,000 people have moved from the tents, cellars and dugouts where they had been forced to live to these new homes. (See also illus. in p. 20.)
Photo, Pictorial Press

roubles have been allocated for this purpose. Forty-five schools were opened last year, but the population is growing by leaps and bounds. The number of children has nearly doubled.

The City Soviet plans to spend over 37 million roubles on dwelling - houses during 1944. The Dramatic Theatre and the Summer Theatre are being restored. Five cinemas were opened last year. Several more are almost ready. There is a fair prospect that many clubs and other cultural institutions will be reopened shortly. Over

67 million roubles are being spent on the restoration and extension of the tramways, the water supply, drainage system, shopping centres, public baths and other municipal services. Stalingrad expects to break the back of this part of the job before 1945.

The "Red October" plant is in production again, turning out rolled steel. The Tractor Plant has sent tanks to help the latest offensives. The workers at these great enterprises also find energy to help in the reconstruction of their city. The Tractor Plant

is supplying labour, transport and building materials for a new polyclinic, a maternity hospital, four kindergartens, two schools with places for 1,600 children, and bath-houses.

During the winter Stalingrad railway junction had its work cut out to handle the immense volume of freight, as gift trains sped to the city from all over the Soviet Union with building materials, food, household goods, machinery. But now the ice has cleared from the Volga, and the transport problem will be easier.

OUR DIARY OF THE WAR

APRIL 26, Wednesday *1,698th day*
Australasia.—Alexishafen, W. of Madang in New Guinea, occupied by Australians.
Sea.—In naval action off Brest, German destroyer sunk by new cruiser H.M.S. Black Prince.
Air.—U.S. aircraft bombed Brunswick without loss. At night Bomber Command sent over 1,000 aircraft to Essen and Schweinfurt.

APRIL 27, Thursday *1,699th day*
Russian Front.—Soviet bombers made heavy night raid on Lvov.
Australasia.—Main Hollandia airfield in New Guinea occupied by U.S. troops.
Air.—Two daylight attacks by U.S. bombers on aerodromes and marshalling yards in France. R.A.F. heavily bombed Friedrichshafen, Lake Constance, at night.

APRIL 28, Friday *1,700th day*
Mediterranean.—Genoa and other Italian ports attacked by Allied bombers.
China.—Announced that Chengchow, Honan, fell to Japanese on April 22.
Air.—Airfields and military installations in France bombed by U.S. aircraft. Air-frame factory at Oslo attacked by R.A.F.

APRIL 29, Saturday *1,701st day*
Mediterranean.—Day and night raids on Toulon, Genoa, Spezia and Leghorn.
Pacific.—U.S. carrier-based aircraft bombed islands at Truk ; 120 Jap aircraft destroyed on the ground and in the air.
Sea.—In action in English Channel Canadian destroyers Haida and Athabaskan crippled enemy destroyer ; Athabaskan was torpedoed and sunk. Submarine H.M.S. Syrtis reported lost.
Air.—Mass daylight raid on Berlin by U.S. bombers and fighters. By night Lancasters bombed aircraft factory at Clermont Ferrand and explosive works near Bordeaux.

APRIL 30, Sunday *1,702nd day*
Mediterranean.—Day raid by U.S. bombers on factories and rly. yards near Milan. R.A.F. bombers again attacked Genoa, Spezia and Leghorn at night.
Russian Front.—Long-range Soviet aircraft bombed rly. junction of Brest-Litovsk.
Pacific.—Japanese islands near Truk again attacked from sea and air ; Liberators bombed Wake Island.

Air.—U.S. bombers attacked aerodromes and railway yards in France by day ; R.A.F. bombed ammunition dump at Maintenon and rly. yards at Acheres and Somain.

MAY 1, Monday *1,703rd day*
Russian Front.—Soviet bombers made mass raid on Lvov.
Mediterranean.—Announced that German Gen. Kreipe had been captured in British raid on Crete.
Air.—U.S. aircraft attacked Pas de Calais and rly. yards in Belgium and N. France. R.A.F. dropped 2,500 tons of bombs by night on factories and rly. yards in France and Belgium.
General.—First wartime conference of Dominions Prime Ministers opened in London.

MAY 2, Tuesday *1,704th day*
Russian Front.—Soviet aircraft made day and night attacks on aerodromes and rly. stations in Lvov, Stanislavov, Roman and Sambor.
Mediterranean.—Allied bombers attacked harbour at Spezia, rly. yards at Florence and rly. bridge at Spoleto.
Air.—U.S. bombers attacked Pas de Calais and railway centres in France and Belgium. Leverkusen, near Cologne, and railway yards at Acheres bombed by Mosquitoes at night.

General.—Mr. Eden announced Anglo-American agreement with Spain, restricting supply of wolfram to Germany.

MAY 3, Wednesday *1,705th day*
Burma.—14th Army in Arakan captured heights overlooking Maungdaw-Buthidaung road.
Mediterranean.—R.A.F. bombers made first night attack on Bucharest.
Air.—R.A.F. bombers made heavy attacks on military depot at Mailly, aircraft stores at Montdidier and ammunition dump at Chateaudun in face of fierce fighter opposition. Low-level precision attack by Mosquitoes on a house in The Hague was announced.
General.—Announced that Military Mission from Marshal Tito had arrived in London.

MAY 4, Thursday *1,706th day*
Mediterranean.—Budapest railway yards bombed at night by R.A.F.
Sea.—Submarine H.M.S. Stonehenge announced overdue and presumed lost.

MAY 5, Friday *1,707th day*
Italy.—R.A.F. dive-bombers smashed Pescara Dam in Adriatic sector of front.
Mediterranean.—Day and night attacks by Allied bombers on Rumanian targets, including Ploesti, Campina and Turnu-Severin.

Burma.—Our troops attacked at all points on the Kohima front.

MAY 6, Saturday *1,708th day*
Mediterranean.—Allied aircraft again attacked Rumanian targets, including Brasov, Pitesti, Campina and Turnu-Severin.
Pacific.—Guam, in the Marianas, bombed by U.S. aircraft.
Air.—Liberators bombed Pas de Calais area. At night R.A.F. made heavy attack on rly. yards at Mantes, N.W. of Paris and ammunition dumps near Tours and Le Mans.

MAY 7, Sunday *1,709th day*
Burma.—Announced that after defeating enemy counter-attacks in Mayu Range our troops withdrew from Buthidaung.
Russian Front.—Soviet troops broke through main lines of Sebastopol defence area.
Mediterranean.—Day and night raids on railway yards at Bucharest ; railway bridge near Belgrade also bombed.
Air.—Over 1,500 U.S. bombers and fighters made daylight attack on Berlin. R.A.F. sent out six forces at night to bomb airfields and ammunition dumps in France.
Sea.—German destroyer crippled on April 29 was destroyed by our light coastal forces.

MAY 8, Monday *1,710th day*
Air.—Berlin and Brunswick attacked by over 1,500 U.S. bombers and fighters : 119 enemy fighters claimed as destroyed. At night R.A.F. bombers attacked railway yards near Mons and airfield near Brest.

MAY 9, Tuesday *1,711th day*
Russian Front.—Sebastopol taken by storm after three days' fighting by troops of 4th Ukrainian front.
Italy.—Eighth Army troops advanced in Adriatic sector following enemy withdrawal.
Sea.—Announced that during April number of enemy submarines sunk exceeded number of Allied merchant ships sunk.
Air.—Heavy attacks by U.S. bombers on eight aerodromes and three railway yards in France, Belgium and Luxembourg. Night raids by R.A.F. on factories at Annecy and near Paris. Mosquitoes dropped 4,000 lb. bombs on Berlin.

★ ======== *Flash-backs* ======== ★

1940
May 3. *Landing of Polish troops in Norway announced.*
May 5. *Norwegian Ministers arrived in London.*

1941
April 26. *German parachutists captured Corinth. South African troops occupied Dessie in Abyssinia.*
April 28. *Germans under Rommel captured Sollum.*
May 6. *Stalin became Premier in place of Molotov.*

1942
April 29. *Japanese took Lashio (Burma) by mass assault.*
May 3. *Second "Baedeker" raid by the Luftwaffe on Exeter.*
May 8. *Japanese aircraft bombed Chittagong in Bengal.*

1943
May 2. *Japanese raided Darwin in Northern Australia.*
May 7. *Ports of Tunis and Bizerta captured by Allies.*

" S " FOR SUGAR, veteran Lancaster of Bomber Command, recently completed her 100th operation from her British base. R.A.F. maintenance staff were preparing her for a sortie when this photograph was taken ; in the foreground is some of the bomb load she took with her on the trip, including a 4,000-pounder and 500-pounders. Now with an Australian squadron, "S" for Sugar took part in 60 sorties with the original Pathfinder force and has been crossing enemy territory for two years, during which time she has dropped 1,000,000 lb. of bombs and used 150,000 gallons of petrol doing it. Grim mockery of the boast made by Field Marshal Goering are the bomb tally markings of her many trips ; also painted there are the D.S.O. and two D.S.C.s won by previous captains.

Photo, G.P.U.

THE WAR IN THE AIR

by Capt. Norman Macmillan, M.C., A.F.C.

EUROPE is the focal centre of the United Nations' air strength. In the United Kingdom is a great array of air power —Bomber Command, Air Defence of Great Britain, No. 2 Tactical Air Force, and Coastal Command U.K., together with the U.S. Army 8th and 9th Air Forces. In the Mediterranean there are the Mediterranean Command of the R.A.F. and the U.S. Army 12th and 15th Air Forces, called the Mediterranean Allied Air Force. In Eastern Europe is the Red Air Force. And at sea there is the British Fleet Air Arm which can operate on the northern side of the European square right up to the Barents Sea. Now these air forces that surround Hitler's Europe are able to send into the air some 10,000 aircraft every twenty-four hours, not counting the Coastal Command which operates mainly over the sea.

COMPARE this with the capacity of the Luftwaffe in its palmiest days, the days of the Battle of Britain when the people and Air Force of the United Kingdom stood alone, and Hitler had no other combatant Power to face. Then the Luftwaffe would put into the air perhaps a thousand aircraft by day and about half that number by night, a total of around 1,500 during the twenty-four-hour period.

Today seven times that number of aircraft are engaged in the strangulation of German military power in Europe. Some are engaged in direct assaults upon targets of immediate military value, others are employed against longer-range factory output, some against communications by land, inland waterways, and sea lanes. But generally speaking we are witnessing during the pre-invasion period an Anglo-American version of the Battle of Britain in reverse. It is more than the Battle of Germany, although that is what it is leading up to. It is the Battle of Europe.

BATTLE for a Continent Waged by Air Alone

This leads one to the thought that air battles must be designated by territorial agglomerations much vaster in area than the designations accorded to either sea or land battles. For example, we have had during this war such sea battles as those of the River Plate, and Cape Matapan, Midway Island, and the Coral Sea. We have witnessed land battles such as the Battle of Egypt, of Stalingrad, of Sicily, the Solomons, and so on, in all of which the air has played a prominent part. But during this pre-invasion period, when the armies mass for the triple-Service assault upon the German Western Armies, we see a battle for a continent waged by air, and by air alone.

It is convenient, but incorrect, to speak of a Battle of Berlin. This air assault, carried out by successive attacks by night and day at varying time intervals, against one of

the largest of the world's capital cities, is no more than an incident in a far larger battle. It is, as it were, what happens in the case of one ship in a great naval battle—to liken the air action to a sea action. It is not more than that.

And there are so many features in the great air attack upon Fortress Europe—the striking down of the heavy industries whose products go to the manufacture of large guns, tanks, ships, submarines, armoured trains, shells, bridges, and a thousand-and-one important items of military necessity in war ; the systematic crushing of the enemy aircraft industry in widely dispersed parts of the continent ; the damaging and destruction of enemy aircraft in the air and on the ground to add to the difficulty he must find in replacing aircraft torn out of the production line by the bombers ; the pin-point attacks upon specialized targets where isolated factories or even individual houses in cities are demolished.

PIN-POINT Bombing Has Reached a High Degree of Accuracy

The recent attack by Mosquitoes upon a house in The Hague is a specimen case. Here was a house containing matter useful to the enemy, the destruction of which would be of corresponding usefulness to the Allied High Command. Presumably from a humanitarian point of view it was decided that it was necessary to destroy that one house, and to leave its neighbouring houses on either side safe. A surprise day attack from a low altitude did the strategists' work. It was not the first time that such attacks have been made. It is many months since the similar attack upon the Gestapo headquarters in Oslo hit that special building standing in a comparatively crowded part of the Norwegian capital (see illus. p. 264, Vol. 6). Such accurate bombing brings to the aeroplane a new use in war, and places in the hands of directing generals the power to destroy a pin-point target at a distance of hundreds of miles with as much accuracy as gunfire over one-hundredth part of the range. Such attacks require a different standard of intelligence work behind the enemy front. If it were possible to gain knowledge of the exact situation of a number of vitally important buildings containing key matter, it

TWENTY-EIGHT NAZI PLANES stood to the credit of Wing Commander J. E. Johnson, D.S.O., D.F.C. by May 5, 1944 when, leading a Canadian Spitfire wing over France, he shot down one more German. Some time before, on March 25, he destroyed his 26th and 27th enemy aircraft during a three-minute battle.
Photos, British Official : Crown Copyright

should become possible to use aircraft to dislocate the organization of the enemy staff to such an extent as to throw his machinery of offence and defence out of gear. This would be bringing the artillery of the air into action against the enemy staff with a vengeance.

IT is noteworthy that during General Auchinleck's offensive in Libya a bomb landed on a table around which enemy staff officers were gathered, a perhaps lucky shot which caused disorganization in the Afrika Korps next day. But low-level high-speed bombing has reached such a degree of accuracy when carried out by skilled pilots that it is possible to direct bombs into openings no larger than railway tunnels.

The great air battles are now battles of huge areas, covering so much territory and doing so so quickly as to counter the feint and parry of the defence. Our limiting factor may even now be the area available for bases from which to launch our aircraft, for the territory in possession of the United Nations is comparatively restricted for the operation of such great air forces.

THE question is then to determine, as far as possible, how long it will take with the aircraft which can be deployed from existing bases to pull the enemy down. It may even be that the 7,000 sorties a day which can be directed against German-held Europe by the United Nations' air forces based in Britain and the Mediterranean are not enough, and yet represent something approaching the maximum in operational possibilities.

Should this prove to be so it leads at once to the argument that territorial restrictions handicap the full employment of the Allies' air power. And, just as General MacArthur found it imperative to employ surface forces to capture airfields in the South-West Pacific from which he could strangulate Japanese naval and military power in that area, it may be that it is necessary for General Eisenhower to seize airfields in Western Europe from which to expand the air offensive against Germany. Every airfield captured by the invasion forces will add power to the Allies in the air, and curtail still more the defence efficiency of the Wehrmacht in air, on land, and at sea. More airfields may be the master key to the shortening of the war.

FIRST SPITFIRES OVER THE REICH, one of which is seen here about to take off, flew 700 to 800 miles on a sortie on April 26, 1944 across territory between Aachen and Cologne ; they attacked grounded enemy aircraft and a goods train, returning without loss. PAGE 29

Allied Awards for British Services Rendered

Ldg. Aircraftwoman I. G. LEASK was presented by Gen. Spaatz, Commanding General of the U.S.A.A.F. in Europe, with the Legion of Merit Medal for "extraordinary fidelity to duty and exceptionally meritorious service rendered." On July 2, 1942, she located and identified a U.S. air formation which had become lost at sea.

L./Bombardier W. REGAN, R.A., received the U.S. Soldier's Medal, presented by Lt.-Gen. Mark Clark, 5th Army commander, on Dec. 25, 1943, for gallantry in saving a U.S. pilot from a burning plane at Pantellaria.

W/Cmdr. W. DRAKE, D.S.O., D.F.C., of the R.A.F. Shark Kittyhawk Squadron, won the United States D.F.C. while operating with the U.S. 9th Air Force.

Capt. M. RICHMOND, R.N. (centre), and Capt. R. G. ONSLOW, R.N., on April 20, 1943, received the Order of the Red Banner from M. Maisky, then Soviet Ambassador in London. Russian decorations were awarded to a number of other officers and men of the Royal Navy and Merchant Navy for "valour and courage" in the delivery of armaments in Arctic convoys.

Sgt. J. DEARDEN, R.A.F., won the American Air Medal for "meritorious achievements" in photographic reconnaissance for the U.S.A.A.F. The medal was presented at a joint British and U.S. decoration ceremony held at a U.S. Army Air Station in England in October 1943.

C.S.M. REGINALD ALLEN, of the Parachute troops, received the American D.S.C. from Gen. Eisenhower, Supreme Allied Commander, for bravery in stopping a German advance.

PAGE 30   *Photos, British Official; G.P.U., Associated Press, Planet News*

I DARE say you have sometimes felt a shade impatient as you have listened night after night, week in week out, to the statement that our aircraft have been engaged on "mine-laying in enemy waters." I know people who have said, "Why worry about that so often ?" Those people did not know the great value of the work that the mine-layers do, or the effect it is having on the course of the war at sea. The mines they lay are magnetic ; in the four years since the use of these began more than 500 enemy ships have been sunk by them, a loss to the Germans of about a million tons of shipping. It was the enemy who first brought the magnetic mine into play ; we soon found the answer to it. He must be sorry he ever started the game, for it has hurt him far more than it did us. He has had to send out very large numbers of minesweepers, but these cannot clear all the dangers out of the way. Warships as well as cargo and troop-carrying vessels have been destroyed. We mined the Kiel Canal long ago. Now we have mined the Danube. All the coasts of countries under the Nazi yoke have been made unsafe for their ships. So when you hear the familiar phrase now, don't be under any misapprehension. It is telling you something important, something you should be glad to hear.

HISTORY is going to be rewritten. A committee of historians drawn from many nations will compile the annals of Europe for boys and girls between sixteen and eighteen years old. A handbook for teachers of history is also in preparation. But how are the new histories going to deal with characters like Napoleon and Hitler ? Unless children are taught from their earliest school-days that many of the men known as "Great" were enemies of the human race and ought to be remembered with loathing rather than admiration, the world is certain to go on as it has done since the earliest recorded times, with war as its most constant and most absorbing industry. Alexander the Great was a madman, Frederick the Great was a scoundrel, Napoleon the Great (so-called to distinguish him from his nephew, Emperor Louis, whom Victor Hugo derided as "the Little") was a man of immense ability crazed by foolish ambition. Hitler and Mussolini appear to be merely successful gangsters, comparable with Al Capone and Legs Diamond. Their methods are identical with those of the Chicago underworld. Yet, if historical precedent is followed, they will be presented as great men a hundred years hence. If we want that new world, about which politicians chatter so much, we must tell the truth about the old world. History has never yet done that.

WHAT baffling divergences of opinion there are among the "experts" about food and the way to use it so as to enjoy the best health ! When I saw that one of the chief medical authorities attached to the Ministry of Food had been inveighing against starting a meal with soup, I wondered how many hundreds of times I had heard or seen that view expressed by doctors—and how many speak just as often in the exactly opposite sense. The safest guidance in such a matter is given, it seems to me, by those who are really "experts," that is, in the original meaning of the word, people who have tried, experimented, experienced. The French know more about feeding than any other nation. They have better digestions than any other civilized race. You don't see in France the masses of indigestion remedies that are so widely sold elsewhere. Well, the French always start their principal meal with soup. It doesn't seem to do them any harm. There is a good deal to be said for making a meal off soup, and soup alone—with plenty of

bread put into it or eaten dry. For those who have to work again directly after they have done eating, this is as good a lunch as they could have—palatable, satisfying and nourishing—if it is well made, of course. Weak soup is nasty, as well as bad for one.

J. M. BARRIE used to make fun of the Athenaeum Club after he had been elected to it under the rule which admits men distinguished in literature, science or art, without making them go through the ordinary process—the rule which has enabled the Committee to invite General Eisenhower and other American commanders of high rank to become members. Barrie told of washing his hands next to a man who looked nervously at him, but did not say anything. Barrie said "Good evening." The man instantly asked him : "Will you dine with me ?" And when he saw that Barrie looked surprised, he added: "You are the first person in this club who has ever spoken to me and I have been a member for twenty-five years." That was in the days, now a good long way back, when the Club was supposed to be "infested with bishops." It was then a much more solemn place than it is now—or was in earlier days. Thackeray gave an account of a talk he had there with Macaulay, of a very lively description. Now that there is far less of the standoffishness that Barrie satirized, the flow of cheerful talk in the dining-room and the smoking-room after lunch is like that of any other West End club. The Americans will not find it different in this respect from the older clubs in New York, which are none of them very gay.

THIS month Assize Courts have begun hearing divorce cases. The change will be scarcely noticed, yet it marks a social revolution. A hundred years ago, and for long after 1844, it was very hard indeed for an ill-matched couple to dissolve their union. This could be done only by carrying a private Bill through the House of Lords, an expensive process which none but wealthy people could afford. Every attempt to give any other Court power to grant divorce was bitterly resisted, not only by the Churches one and all, but by the mass of the nation. It was said that any such step would break up the social fabric, do away with family life, destroy the sanctity of marriage. When the Bill to establish a Divorce Court as part of the King's Bench Division was introduced in 1857, it passed through only because Lord Palmerston, as Prime Minister, said he would

keep Parliament sitting until it did. And none of the dreadful results predicted came to pass. Now under the stress of war we have gone a step farther and nobody seems at all perturbed about it.

DANGER to life has always been the parent of superstition. Wars make most of us more credulous, readier to believe gossip, more anxious to invoke the protection of unseen powers. Just now jewelers are cashing-in on this and making a lot of money. They can sell twopenny-halfpenny "charms" or "amulets" for about ten times what they used to cost. A little button with the figure of Saint Christopher on it could be bought for sixpence before the war. Now it cannot be obtained for less than 5s. 6d. Some men wear this in their buttonholes (at the risk, I take it, of being " crimed " on the charge " improperly dressed ") ; others conceal it under their clothes. Another saint much in demand is Saint Anthony. If you can pay in pounds instead of shillings, you will find no difficulty in purchasing a medallion in enamel and platinum or gold. Seems a lamentable waste of money to me.

WE hear a great deal about profiteering, which means taking advantage of the war to overcharge for goods or services ; but I know of many cases in which the convenience and benefit of the community are put before personal gain. I looked at a sheaf of notices in a suburban shop-window the other day and saw one offering to repair watches and clocks. I took a clock to be mended, received it back in good going order, and was charged what seemed to me a very reasonable sum. The repairer told me about himself. He is in the building trade, and "making the wheels go round" is a sideline with him. He does it largely to oblige poor folk who rely on a clock to tell them when to get up from their beds, and he makes them pay as little as possible. He could get work of the kind at far higher rates, but he will not take it. He was asked to call at a house where there were nine clocks, not one of which would go. He took the likeliest, put it right in three days, and charged 7s. 6d. The owner said he had been told in the shops that it would cost 15s. and take ten weeks. He offered the man the job of repairing all the clocks and promised good money. The offer was declined, because this would have meant turning away the people who brought their alarm clocks and old silver " turnip " watches, which they could not do without. That man is, I consider, a true philanthropist, a friend of his fellow-men. All honour to him !

More Forts to Pound the Heart of Germany

BOMBING MISSIONS LIE AHEAD for these U.S. Flying Fortresses carrying out tactical training at a centre in Florida. At this large school crews of Fortress and Liberator aircraft are coached in high-level precision bombing. Apart from the various combat theatres, America has at home four complete air forces, plus many commands for personnel training and experimental work. Total strength of the Army Air Forces is estimated at 2,385,000 officers and men.

Photo, Keystone

Printed in England and published every alternate Friday by the Proprietors, THE AMALGAMATED PRESS, LTD., The Fleetway House, Farringdon Street, London, E.C.4. Registered for transmission by Canadian Magazine Post. Sole Agents for Australia and New Zealand: Messrs. Gordon & Gotch, Ltd.; and for South Africa: Central News Agency, Ltd.—May 26, 1944. S.S. *Editorial Address:* JOHN CARPENTER HOUSE, WHITEFRIARS, LONDON, E.C.4.

Vol 8 **The War Illustrated** N° 182

SIXPENCE

Edited by Sir John Hammerton

JUNE 9, 1944

DELIVERED BY DONKEY POST are the letters and parcels sent to men of a heavy bombardment group of the 15th U.S.A.A.F. in Italy.   Commanded by Lt.-Gen. Nathan Twining, who is responsible for strategic bombing operations, the 15th U.S.A.A.F. is one of the units of the Mediterranean Allied Air Force, whose formation, replacing the Mediterranean Air Command and the N.W. African Air Forces, was announced on Jan. 27, 1944, by Gen. Sir H. Maitland Wilson, Supreme Commander in the Mediterranean. *Photo, U.S. Official*

NO. 183 WILL BE PUBLISHED FRIDAY, JUNE 23

New War-Angles Seen by Our Roving Camera

N.F.S. MOTOR CYCLE SECTION (above) is part of one of the Overseas Columns which will support the Army Fire Services when the Western assault commences ; all the men are volunteers, and must be over 19 and not 41 by the end of 1944.   The stark realities of a prisoner-of-war's life are brought home by this replica of a German prison watch-tower (left), part of an exhibition held in the heart of London by The Daily Telegraph, with the help of the Red Cross and St. John War Organization.   Thousands learned from it how Allied prisoners really live whilst behind the enemy's barbed wire.

PRE-FABRICATED CONCRETE BARGES to help the transport of our vital war supplies are being mass-produced at a British shipyard, as shown above. The barges are 84 ft. long, with a deck-width of 22 ft. 6 ins. and their dead-weight capacity is 200 tons.   There are 174 free-cast concrete units to each barge assembly, and construction is quite simple.

DRILLING FOR COAL in the Welsh mountains is this native from the Philippines (above), whose home islands the Japanese at present occupy.   He is one of many experts who have been engaged in mining tasks of this kind in various parts of the world ; working for the Government on behalf of a Canadian drilling company, they are making a grand contribution to the war effort.

FLY-SWATTING the mechanical way is now the method of dealing with insect pests which rob our country of fruit supplies, which are more valuable than ever in these war-days. A tractor (left) equipped with a multi-spray jet apparatus, throwing a liquid which is certain death to the pests, is driven through an orchard, doing the work of many men using the old bucket and syringe, and in half the time.

Photos, Topical Press, Fox, Keystone, Daily Mirror

THE BATTLE FRONTS

by Maj.-Gen. Sir Charles Gwynn, K.C.B., D.S.O.

THE offensive which opened in Italy on the night of May 11-12 had obviously a different object from that of previous operations there. It was generally believed that the landing at Salerno was undertaken with a view to a rapid advance up the peninsula in order to secure air bases from which Central and Eastern Germany could be attacked. The German forces in Italy were at the time not strong and it was probably assumed that they would be used to defend the Po plain and the Alpine passes, leaving it mainly to the troops that had evacuated Sicily to delay our advance.

If that was the original German intention, the success they achieved in preventing a rapid exploitation of the Salerno landing and the difficulties we encountered in winter weather, clearly induced them to reinforce their Southern force. Yet they still remained on the defensive and kept a large part of their army in the north—possibly owing to a fear that we might undertake a landing in rear of their Southern group. By that time it had become evident that our advance up the peninsula would prove more difficult than was expected, and the Anzio landing appears to have been undertaken with the more limited objective of manoeuvring the Germans out of their positions opposite the 5th and 8th Armies and opening the way for an advance on Rome, which became the immediate objective.

I doubt if it was expected that the Germans would move practically the whole of their army in Italy to the South to counter the Anzio landing, and only an early counter-attack on the Anzio beach-head by the comparatively small reserve force in the Rome area appears to have been anticipated. When, however, the Germans decided to use their whole army in the Southern area not only to reinforce their front opposite the 5th and 8th Armies, but also to mount a formidable deliberate counter-attack against the Anzio beach-head, the whole aspect of the situation again changed. The Anzio beach-head after some anxious days held firm, but it had lost much of its original meaning. It had failed to manoeuvre the Germans out of their main defences, and with the Anzio force deprived temporarily of offensive power, the project for capturing Rome had little chance of quick success.

ONE must admit that the original plans of the Allies had been successfuly countered, but it may be questioned whether in doing so the Germans have not been drawn into an unsound strategical position. They are apparently not strong enough to take the offensive, but are committed to fighting defensively with long lines of communications, vulnerable to air attack, in their rear, and with indifferent lateral communications between them. An army on the defensive has always to consider the possibility of having to withdraw, and plenty of room for retreat is normally an advantage ; but space offers few advantages if movement within it is restricted. It may be a disadvantage, increasing the difficulty of reinforcing and supplying the defence if it stands and making a rapid withdrawal difficult and costly.

Should a withdrawal become necessary it would probably have to be conducted as a slow retreat involving frequent and heavy rearguard actions. This would seem to be the position the Germans are in now, and the Allied offensive makes it difficult for them to extricate themselves from it. They have elected to stand and fight, and General Alexander's object is evidently to destroy them where they stand or force them into a difficult fighting retreat. The capture of Rome has, for the time being at least, ceased to be a military objective.

The Germans have on many occasions

ONE WEEK AFTER OUR NEW PUSH in Italy, on May 18, 1944, the directions of thrusts south and north of Cassino are indicated by arrows in the map above. By May 23 Cassino had fallen ; beyond Itri, near the Appian Way, Terracina was captured on May 24, and in the central sector the Hitler defence zone (shaded arc) had been cut in half near Pontecorvo. *By courtesy of The Daily Express*

shown great skill in extricating themselves from dangerous positions into which faulty strategy has led them, but their tendency has been to hold on too long when well-timed retreat might have saved them. Sometimes this has involved them in complete disaster, in others unnecessary losses of men and material, and I cannot recall a single instance where such obstinacy has improved their general strategical situation. Tactically a detachment may justifiably be ordered to hold a point to the last man and last round, and it may have great effect on the result of the battle. Of course, an army or any large body of troops whose retreat is cut off should similarly refuse to surrender as long as it can exercise any influence on the general situation, but it can never strategically be justified to place it in a position which involves complete destruction.

The German attempt to drive us into the sea at Salerno was, of course, correct and it may even be questioned whether they should not then, as they did later at Anzio, have reinforced their Southern army from

their reserves in the north for a resumption of the counter offensive in greater force. Possibly uncertainty as to the attitude of the Italians in the north and because at the time they had fewer troops in Italy were the reasons why they fell back on the defensive. In the circumstances a defensive may have been justified, since it could be successfully carried out by a comparatively small force.

The Anzio landing, however, forced Von Kesselring's hand. He had either to retire or to employ practically the whole of his army. One certainly cannot quarrel with his decision to take the latter course so long as he used it offensively in his attempt to destroy the Anzio force. When that attempt failed, and when the developments of the war elsewhere made it clear that he could expect no reinforcements which would enable him to renew his offensive in greater strength, it became more than questionable whether he was right in committing practically the whole of his army to the defensive so far south. It must have been obvious that with the approach of summer the potential offensive power of the Allies both on land and in the air would increase, and that they would not suffer from lack of reserves. Moreover, the developments of the general war situation suggested that the drain on German resources in men and material should be reduced to a minimum in Italy ; and that, it would seem, could best be achieved by delaying action rather than by accepting decisive battle, which, even if it succeeded in retaining ground of no great strategic importance, in the widest sense would certainly involve heavy expenditure of men and material at a time when they could ill be spared.

IT seems probable that the best Von Kesselring can now hope for is that he should be able at some stage to carry out a belated and difficult retreat. A rapid disengagement and retreat such as Rommel carried out in Libya must be out of the question in view of Italian topography, the size of his army and the extended range of fighter aircraft. A slow fighting retreat on the Sicilian model might be more practicable, but the size of his army would be a serious handicap in retreat and it would tax his ability to disengage without serious disaster.

Kesselring has shown that he—like the majority of German commanders — possesses great executive qualities ; but, as on many other occasions, German higher strategical direction, perhaps influenced by Hitler himself, seems likely to prove faulty. Again and again it has over-reached itself and has been drawn by initial success into weak strategical situations and belated decisions which have either led to complete disaster or have imposed desperately difficult tasks on subordinate commanders. The Crimea provides the most recent example, but we have good reason to hope that Italy will give another—disappointing as our campaign there has for so long been. If we can achieve a success there it will obviously have a much more important strategical effect than had any of our previous failures or partial failures.

Although our offensive in Italy may be considered as the forerunner of the great impending offensives in the West and East it probably has no exact chronological connexion with their opening dates. The timing, however, ensured that Kesselring was neither likely to receive reinforcements nor be able to spare any of his reserves for transfer to more decisive theatres.

5th and 8th Armies Break the Gustav Line—

IN THE OPENING STAGES of the great new offensive in Italy by the 5th and 8th Armies, which began on May 11, 1944, anti-tank gunners wait to move up into battle (above). The preliminary artillery barrage of great violence lights the night sky (circle). Medium tanks of a combined French and U.S. force approach the shell-blasted village of Cosma E'Damiano (below). The Gustav Line was the first Allied objective; it was breached by French troops on May 14, and three days later it was officially announced as having ceased to exist.

Photos. British and U.S. Official

—in Terrific New Push to Smash Kesselring

DOUGHTY WARRIORS FROM INDIA man roadside slit-trenches during the advance (above), while a camouflaged Sherman tank (circle) moves up to the Liri River, and the crew of a Bren-carrier pause for observation in the same sector (below). Note shellbursts in the distance. All were engaged in piercing the Gustav Line, which is reported to have derived its name from an aged pre-Hitler Berlin driver of a horse-cab who, to show how strong he still was, drove to Paris and back and became known as " Iron Gustav." PAGE 37 *Photos, British Official*

THE WAR AT SEA

by Francis E. McMurtrie

As the day draws nearer the Germans are evincing increasing anxiety concerning the coming invasion of Europe by the Allies. In an effort to conceal their nervousness they have lately adopted a more boastful tone, asserting that they will meet the attack on the beaches and there repel it ; whereas previously they had suggested that they were prepared to suffer an Allied penetration of sixty miles or more.

In neutral countries these symptoms of enemy apprehensions are becoming more and more prominent. For the third time a consignment of military maps of Sweden has been discovered in German postal bags in transit through that country to Norway. Naturally this has caused indignation and disquiet in Stockholm, feelings which were scarcely allayed by the curious explanation offered by the German Minister. He declared that it was necessary for the German troops in Norway to be provided with maps of the frontier between the two countries "in view of what might happen in the event of an Allied invasion of Norway."

British naval operations on the Norwegian coast during May have certainly shaken Nazi nerves. Early on May 6, Barracuda aircraft of the Fleet Air Arm, protected by fighters, carried out a successful attack on enemy shipping off Kristiansund. This port is about 80 miles from Trondheim, and should not be confused with Kristiansand, on the Skagerrak, much farther to the southward. Ships carrying Swedish iron ore from Narvik must pass Kristiansund on their passage to Germany. The aircraft were flown off from carriers forming part of a force detached from the Home Fleet, under the command of Captain N. V. Grace, R.N., in H.M.S. Berwick, a 10,000-ton cruiser. (See map above.)

In the course of the attack two supply ships were sunk, a large tanker was torpedoed and bombed, and an escort vessel and another ship were damaged. Two enemy planes were shot down ; we also lost a couple of aircraft. This exploit followed ten days after a similar attack by our carrier-borne aircraft on a German convoy off Bodo, in the north of Norway. Hits were scored on four supply

ships and an escort vessel, three of the former being set on fire and the largest one grounding. In addition, a large supply ship in Bodo harbour was left blazing. Five of our aircraft were lost. Our submarines in northern waters have also been busy of late ; during April one or two tankers and a supply ship were sunk by them and six other vessels more or less severely damaged by torpedoes. The catapult ship Schwabenland was so injured she had to be beached to prevent her sinking.

ELABORATE Precautions Against Sudden Descent by the Allies

With all these blows falling one after the other it can well be understood that the enemy are kept in a constant state of alarm. Nor is it only in Norway that such uneasiness is prevalent. A little farther south, in the Jutland peninsula of Denmark, elaborate precautions are being taken to guard against a sudden descent by the Allied forces. It is believed that the Germans have been studying the plans propounded by Admiral of the Fleet Lord Fisher in 1914. These aimed at utilizing British preponderance at sea to strike a blow at the heart of Germany.

Lord Fisher advocated the landing of British troops on the North Frisian Islands and the coast of Schleswig-Holstein (the southern part of Denmark, which the Prussians filched in 1864; they still contrived to retain the greater part of it after 1918, thanks to a cleverly manipulated plebiscite). This sudden invasion under the protection of the British Fleet was to be merely a diversion, intended to withdraw attention from the real attack, which was to be made in the Baltic. By transporting several Russian divisions from Riga to the Pomeranian coast, at a point less than 100 miles from Berlin, the enemy would, it was argued, have been thrown into complete confusion. When Frederick the Great was confronted with a similar peril from Russia at a critical period of the Seven Years' War, he was so upset that he contemplated taking poison. Had not the Russian Empress died at this juncture, it is possible that he might have done so, and the history of Prussia would have been changed. (See map above.)

PLAN FOR INVASION of Germany by way of the Baltic as advocated by Lord Fisher in 1914, and outlined in the accompanying article, is illustrated in this map.

New ships which Lord Fisher had ordered for use in the project were ultimately expended elsewhere, and the whole scheme was pigeonholed ; but the subsequent knowledge that it had been under discussion undoubtedly impressed the Germans deeply. When their withdrawal from the shores of the Gulf of Finland starts, the dread of a landing in the rear of the retreating armies will be accentuated by the recollection of the Fisher proposals.

Marshal Tito is recently reported to have appealed for the transfer to his control of the ships of the Yugoslav Navy which he declares are at present playing a more or less inactive part in the Mediterranean. With their aid he has hopes of gradually expelling the Germans from the many islands that fringe the Dalmatian coast on the eastern side of the Adriatic. As originally constituted, the Royal Yugoslav Navy comprised four modern destroyers, four submarines, six small minelayers, ten motor-torpedo-boats, an aircraft tender, four ex-Austrian torpedo-boats built during the last war, and an ancient cruiser used as a training ship, besides some auxiliaries.

When the country was invaded many of these ships fell into Italian hands, though one destroyer, the Zagreb, was blown up by her officers and men to avoid that fate. A submarine, the British-built Nebojsa, and a motor-torpedo-boat, the Velebit, escaped and joined the Allies, but the latter vessel was afterwards lost. Of the Italian prizes, the destroyers Dubrovnik and Ljubljana were renamed Premuda and Sebenico, respectively. Both are believed to have been recovered by the Allies as the result of the Italian collapse. There is also the corvette Nada, formerly H.M.S. Mallow.

A ship which is reported to have hoisted Tito's flag is the Split. This destroyer was laid down at the Yugoslav port after which she is named in 1939. Presumably she was completed and put into commission by the Italian Navy in 1941-42, and has now been manned by the Yugoslavs again.

In the case of the old cruiser used as a training ship, previously mentioned, there was a curious sequel. Originally this vessel was the German Niobe, launched as far back as 1899. In 1926 she was bought by the Yugoslavs from the German Government and refitted for training duties. Manned by Germans, she was sighted by Allied aircraft aground on one of the islands already mentioned. An attack was made upon her by British motor-torpedo-boats on the night of Dec. 21-22, 1943, and she was thus destroyed.

RICHELIEU, 35,000-TON FRENCH BATTLESHIP, exercising with the British Home Fleet, opens fire with her short-range weapons at an aerial target. Disabled at Dakar, North Africa, on July 8, 1940, when Lt.-Cmdr. Bristowe, R.N., crippled her steering gear and propellers by exploding depth charges against her stern, she has been refitted in America and now operates with the Allies. See also illus. p. 504. Vol. 7.
Photo, British Official

Royal Indian Navy Backs the Burma Battles

STRIKING POWER OF THE INDIAN NAVY is indicated in this photograph of an alert and watchful, well-armed escort vessel bringing up the rear of a flotilla of landing-craft heading for another surprise attack on the Mayu Peninsula in the Arakan region. The Royal Indian Navy is composed of large forces of sloops, minesweepers, trawlers and coastal craft; its size has increased enormously since war began and recruits from all over India are constantly swelling its personnel strength.

Photo, Indian Official

Seaborne Raiders Strike at Arakan Japanese

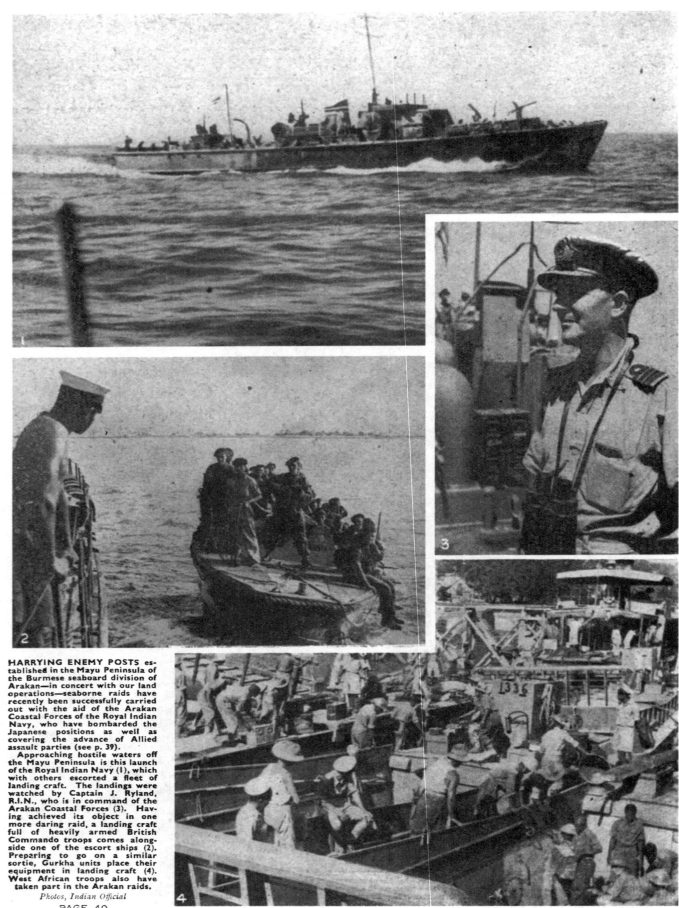

HARRYING ENEMY POSTS established in the Mayu Peninsula of the Burmese seaboard division of Arakan—in concert with our land operations—seaborne raids have recently been successfully carried out with the aid of the Arakan Coastal Forces of the Royal Indian Navy, who have bombarded the Japanese positions as well as covering the advance of Allied assault parties (see p. 39).

Approaching hostile waters off the Mayu Peninsula is this launch of the Royal Indian Navy (1), which with others escorted a fleet of landing craft. The landings were watched by Captain J. Ryland, R.I.N., who is in command of the Arakan Coastal Forces (3). Having achieved its object in one more daring raid, a landing craft full of heavily armed British Commando troops comes alongside one of the escort ships (2). Preparing to go on a similar sortie, Gurkha units place their equipment in landing craft (4). West African troops also have taken part in the Arakan raids.

Photos, Indian Official

Our Colonies in the War: No. 9—The Bahamas

CONSISTING OF 700 ISLANDS, with a total area of 4,375 square miles, the Bahamas have as their capital Nassau (4), key port on sea routes between Florida, New York, Cuba, Haiti and Jamaica, besides vital inter-island communications (see map). The Bahamas are almost self-supporting and, industrially, the islands are striving to aid the United Nations with the production of a new and superior fibre called sanseveira—a project of great value in view of the loss of Manila hemp. Another revolutionary war effort lies in the agreement between Britain and the U.S., instituted in the spring of 1943, by which native labourers of the Bahamas work on Florida bean and sugar plantations (2). Thousands have been engaged and the results have been invaluable. Facilities for the establishment of naval and air bases in the Bahamas were granted to America by Britain in 1940.

H.R.H. The Duke of Windsor, the Governor, takes the salute at an R.A.F. parade at Nassau (1). A meeting of the Legislative Council of the Bahamas (3) which, under the Governor, administers the islands.

Photos, British Official; West Indian Committee, Pictorial Press, Stanley Toogood

Ships and Men of the Convoy Rescue Service

Manned by Merchant Navy and Royal Navy personnel, steamers that once plied a quiet trade around the coasts of Britain now patrol the broad Atlantic on life-saving duties, as outlined here by KEITH COOPER. Much rescue work, carried out valorously and in perilous circumstances, lies to their credit. Thousands of survivors plucked from death's jaws call them blessed.

WHEN the U-boat offensive was at its height in 1941, and losses among crews of the Merchant Navy were high, the Admiralty, in conjunction with the Ministry of War Transport, decided upon a scheme to aid those seamen unfortunate enough to be thrown into the Atlantic as the result of enemy action. At first the rear ship in convoy took upon itself the task of picking up survivors from merchantmen that had suffered attack; eventually, as the result of much thought, the Convoy Rescue Service was formed.

Duty of ships belonging to this Service was to take up position at the rear of the convoy, and at all times go to the assistance of seamen struggling in the water. In the course of such work the vessels would be exposed to danger, it was realized, so small ships, quick on the helm, and offering only a restricted target for U-boats, had to be found.

FOUND they were—among the coastal steamers that used to carry on important trade around the coasts of Britain. It was feared at first that these craft would never stand the dangerous and treacherous Atlantic. But they have; and in just over two years of work the Convoy Rescue Service has been responsible for saving 3,563 officers and men of the Allied Merchant Services.

Heavily armed, possessing a good turn of speed, the rescue ships are formidable, and they perform escort duties until called upon to snatch from the sea men in distress. Life aboard these rescue ships is hard indeed, with quarters often swamped with water, yet the crews, proud of their calling, continually sign for duty. In normal times, about thirty men would form the crew of a rescue ship; today, because of the important work, the vessel has seventy men aboard her.

During the years that this branch of the convoy system has been at work, much has

MEN OF A CONVOY RESCUE SERVICE VESSEL make final preparations in the lifeboat (above), which will soon be on its way to pick up survivors of a wrecked ship. The survivors are found, and aided by the lifeboat crew they go aboard the rescue vessel by means of the scramble net (bottom left). See also facing page. *Photos, Associated Press*

been learnt from hard experience. At first survivors picked up from the sea were offered little beyond shelter. Today, first-class hospitals and operating theatres, wards, and comfortable bunks for at least a hundred men, are standard. As soon as survivors are taken aboard, their clothing is removed and they are given a rub-down by experts. They are then put to bed with hot-water bottles and the medical men give them an overhaul. If a man is suffering from any hurt or illness, these doctors give prompt treatment.

One of the most difficult tasks, at the best of times, is to get survivors aboard the rescue ships. At first the men on the vessel engaged upon life-saving duties had to introduce novel methods, and rely upon their strength; but science has been called on to play a part. Now, rescue ships are equipped with boom nets; with these they drift towards the men in the water and "trawl them up." A large wicker basket is suspended over the sea, with a member of the crew standing in it. He assists men from the sea into the basket, and so aboard the rescue ship. In addition, the sides are hung with scramble nets and Jacob's ladders so that the crew can haul aboard men who reach the rescue ship's sides. Navigating officers and men of this Service are drawn from the Merchant Navy, but the medical officers, sick bay attendants, gunners, and signallers are from the Royal Navy.

There isn't a risk that the rescue ships will not take. A Canadian tanker was blasted to pieces when a U-boat's torpedo crashed into her. The forepart, with no one aboard, drifted away in the blizzard that was raging. Fifty men, who had clung to remnants of the ship, thought they were doomed. But a rescue ship got quickly to work. In spite of the weather, U-boats and torpedoes, she rescued every man who had been aboard the tanker, though it took her over forty hours to complete the task.

ON another occasion, when a tanker was sunk in the Atlantic, the rescue ship Perth picked up the crew. One man had a smashed skull, and an immediate operation was necessary. While this was being performed a U-boat surfaced a few hundred yards away, and every gun aboard the Perth opened fire. And still the operation went on, to a successful conclusion. The man with the smashed skull is now serving aboard a rescue ship!

Crews of these little-known but very important ships get many a thrill. To chase tiny lights in a storm—lights aboard rafts or lifeboats—is no child's play. But hardships are counterbalanced by the satisfaction of hauling aboard grateful and often badly wounded men. As they all say: "There is no greater work than saving the life of another man." This motto of the rescue ships is one reason why our Merchant Navy puts to sea with so much confidence; they know, if fortune is against them, that a Convoy Rescue ship will be not far away.

Pre-War Cargo Boats Perform a Mercy Task Now

SAVED FROM THE SEA, a mariner receives artificial respiration on the rescue vessel's deck from a medical orderly ; meantime his companion, snatched from the same fate, is brought aboard in a sling (1). The rescue ship's doctor attends to a stretcher case, while other survivors look on (2) ; in the operating theatre of the ship's hospital an injured seaman receives prompt and highly skilled attention (3). Nothing is overlooked ; a resuscitated seaman is fitted out with a new set of clothing (4). See also facing page.

PAGE 43   *Photos, Associated Press*

Allied Flyers Cross the 'Roof of the World'—

ONLY DIRECT SUPPLY ROUTE BETWEEN CHINA AND HER ALLIES is the airway over the Himalaya mountains, between N. India and Yunnan in China, a distance of some 750 to 1,000 miles, here (1) being followed by an aircraft of the India-China wing of U.S. Air Transport Command. The Buddhist Monastery which stands 16,500 ft. above Lake Tali in the Himalayas is seen (2) from a supply plane flying at 18,000 ft.; at 21,500 ft. The "Hump," as the mighty mountain chain is called. looks like this (3).

Photos 2 and 3 exclusive to THE WAR ILLUSTRATED

—Carrying Supplies for China's Fighting Men

AT THE EASTERN END OF THE CHINA AIR ROUTE a transport plane comes in over a village to its airfield (1). Vast stocks of oil for the aircraft are stored near the terminal point in India in tanks such as this (2) being constructed by Indian engineers. Besides supplies, the planes carry over the hazardous airway military officials, technicians and diplomats, who must wear oxygen masks at such altitudes (3). Our capture of Myitkyina airfield in Burma (announced May 18, 1944) may eventually relieve pressure on the airway by reopening of land routes.

This Will be a Task as Big as the War Itself

The last shot fired and the last bomb dropped, we shall be forced to tackle the awesome problems of repair, renewal and rehabilitation. Half the world will lie in physical, political and economic ruin. How the United Nations Relief and Rehabilitation Administration is preparing to go to work to clear up the mess mankind has made of things is explained here by JOHN ENGLAND.

BEFORE this war we knew that patriotism is not enough. We now know that charity also is not enough. The rebuilding of the world—and our immediate problem is Europe—calls for more than charity. It involves the recruitment of the finest organizing brains, plus the mobilization of every kind of necessity from iron ore and coal to medical stores and seed.

U.N.R.R.A. (United Nations Relief and Rehabilitation Administration) is, therefore, primarily a job for thinkers and not for sentimentalists. The root principle which it has been decided to apply to this mammoth problem may be simply stated as putting first things first. In other words: Who has first claim on relief, and what material things are most needed for immediate post-war service ?

Already U.N.R.R.A. has made up its mind about these points, and a vast skeleton plan has been articulated for the application of relief throughout freed Europe. To get some notion of the magnitude of this undertaking it is necessary to bear in mind the central truth— that U.N.R.R.A.'s job is precisely as big as the war itself.

HERBERT H. LEHMAN, U.S. Administrator of U.N.R.R.A. Born in 1878, last-war colonel, he was Governor of New York State, 1933-42. *Photo, Topical Press*

Surely that is an impressive thought. Everything the war has destroyed is to be rebuilt, remade, set going, rendered fruitful again. Already the United States has voted £350,000,000 as an initial instalment, and Britain has contributed £80,000,000.

A newly-formed branch of the Army, known as the Civil Affairs Division, will deal with the host of administrative problems that will arise when the Allied troops first land in Europe. A new staff—G.5—is attached to General Eisenhower's headquarters for the direction of this Division, which is commanded by Lieut.-General A. E. Grasett. On the heels of the invading troops Civil Affairs detachments, equally composed of British and Americans, will come into action. Their most immediate concerns will be with such things as feeding and finding shelter for civilians and restoring damaged public services. In general, their task is to see that civilian problems do not interfere with military operations. The long-term policy of restoring life to the liberated territories will be taken over by U.N.R.R.A. in collaboration with the governments concerned, as soon as conditions permit.

U.N.R.R.A.'s first consideration after the war, then, will be to help the liberated countries to help themselves. As soon as an area is liberated, U.N.R.R.A. will supply the peasantry with all that is necessary to get agriculture going—that means new temporary housing, agricultural machinery, seeds. For Europe, once so fecund, has been mainly a battlefield, and its restoration to maximum crop yield is the surest and sanest way to end the semi-starvation which has been for millions the common lot through these dark years.

But individual enterprise, whether urban, such as manufacture, or rural, such as wheat growing, can function only under law and order and proper public administration. U.N.R.R.A. here will have to assist in reshaping the civic governments of these lands, and this it will do by assisting the proper people of each nation to get their public life going again. How ? By the loan of technicians, by money grants, by the supply of materials.

CONSIDER some of the items. The war has destroyed electric lighting town plants, hydro-electric enterprises, sewage and drainage systems. All these, for rehabilitation, call for machinery, engines, dynamos, thousands of miles of wires and cables, to mention but a few items. In this great work there will be no such thing as a colour bar or racial discrimination, and need will be the yardstick alone. We in England have been so fortunate in the matter of food that we are apt to forget, or not to realize, that under the Nazi heel Europe starves. The supply of food is Number One on the U.N.R.R.A. list. It is proposed to mobilize shipping for this purpose and to set up communal feeding arrangements at once.

Some notion of the tragic state of Europe's enslaved people may be inferred from a recent statement by the Belgian Prime Minister. He said that the dietary of Belgium was now so low that very few women were having children. Which brings into view yet another aspect of U.N.R.R.A.'s task— the prevention of epidemics and diseases which may result from the long years of privation, decline in hygiene, and destruction of public works. Thus medical help, both by way of personnel and supplies, is to be on a lavish scale. And this not alone for the benefit of the

CLOTHING THE NAZIS' VICTIMS will be the task of Mr. L. R. Allan, D.S.O., O.B.E., (centre) of the Hosiery and Knitwear Export Group, which in London, in June 1943 showed for the approval of representatives from nine Allied Nations garments designed for the liberated European peoples. *Photo, Keystone*

stricken peoples of Europe, but for the protection of our armies. For U.N.R.R.A. envisages United Nations troops in control until such time as Europe can defend herself against all subversive elements.

There is another aspect of this work—the repatriation of displaced people, 20,000,000 in Europe alone, and in Asia even more. Many of these people are weakened by hunger and disease, many are sick in mind and body—both. Whenever possible U.N.R.R.A. will return people to the homes from which they were ejected by the invading Germans. The Red Cross has prepared lists of such people, with details concerning their former homes. It has a card index that contains 15,000,000 names.

In the view of those directing the work of U.N.R.R.A., this handling of the dispossessed millions constitutes one of the most terrible and dreadful of the aftermaths of war problems. "The world," said Mr. F. B. Sayre, Assistant to the U.S. Secretary of State, "has never faced any problem of human woe comparable to it." What master brain, it may be asked, can orchestrate this vast, world-wide scheme for creative effort ? The man who recently accepted this burden is Mr. Herbert Lehman, former Governor of New York State.

LEHMAN is a rich banker, and the son of a rich banker. Relief work comes as no novelty to him. In the last war he directed the raising of £15,000,000 for the relief of war suffering, and distributed it on equal lines that revealed those qualities which have resulted in the present appointment. Stout, silver-haired, with fine dark eyes, Mr. Lehman is quiet-voiced and imperturbable. His strength lies in his capacity to achieve a synthesis, and no man ever needed more that faculty than he who has the co-ordination of this terrific task.

"We must feed these people !" is the cry. Yes, but where is the food ? And if it exists, say in the Argentine, where are the ships to bring it across the ocean ? Where are the railway engines and the rolling stock to transport it throughout Europe ?

That is how it is. But the central hard core of hope-producing fact is this : this time we are not leaving post-war social and economic and political problems to stew into another broth of hate and ultimate war.

G.5 HEADQUARTERS TEAMS such as this are training at centres in America and Britain for work in Europe with the Allied armies. These field units are equipped for all possible emergencies. G.5, as explained in this page, is the military liaison with U.N.R.R.A. *Photo, Keystone*

Photo, Royal Canadian Navy

Canada Helps to Win Battle of Atlantic

Allied crushing of the Atlantic U-boat menace, now all but total, has been in large measure due to the vigorous part played by the Royal Canadian Navy. Consisting of 16 ships and 1,700 men in 1939, it now numbers 700 ships and over 80,000 men, ranking third in naval might among the United Nations. Here H.M.C.S. "Prince Robert," Canada's first anti-aircraft cruiser, is depth-charging a U-boat.

47

Attack is the Royal Navy's Watchword—

Steadily mounting strength of the Allied Navies bodes ill for Japanese shipping, already heavily hammered in the Pacific. British submarines in increasing numbers are refitting for action in Far Eastern waters; alongside the depot-ship there is activity in the conning-tower (1), while other vessels arrive (2). New aircraft and carriers rapidly augment the power of the Fleet Air Arm; in the escort carrier H.M.S. "Searcher" (3), a Wildcat fighter is brought to the flight deck by lift.

—From Cruiser to Sloop It's the Same

Among the Royal Navy's host of warships, youth and age team up together to confound the enemy. H.M.S. "Jamaica" —8,000-ton Mauritius class cruiser—is but two years old; her torpedoes helped to sink the "Scharnhorst" in 1943. Here is one of her 6-in. gun crews at work (4). In contrast is H.M.S. "Folkestone," one of our older sloops, whose battle-hardened crew (5) proudly boasts of having "the finest set of beards that have gone to sea in this war."

49

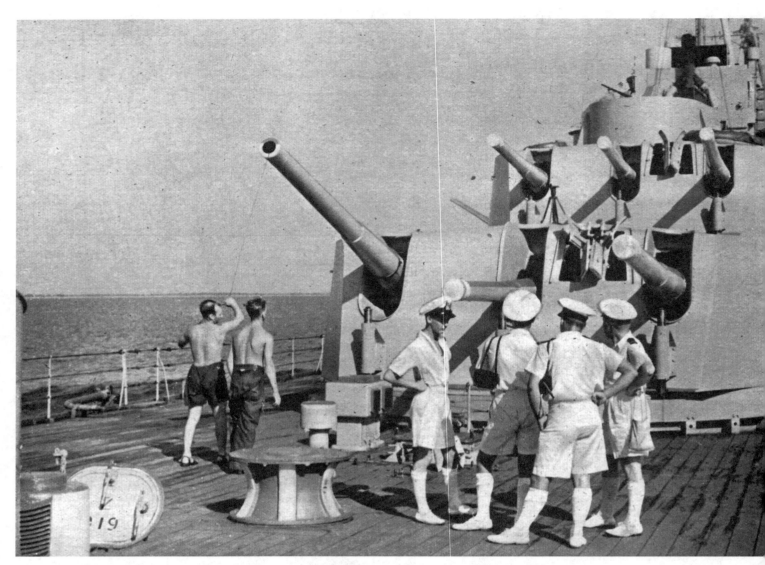

Eastern Fleet Guns Prepare

Since 1942, units of the Allied Navies operating under Admiral Sir James Somerville in the Indian Ocean have constituted our Eastern Fleet, whose sudden sally against enemy-held Sumatra on April 19th, 1944, fore-shadowed the trouble to come for the Japanese. Ships of the Eastern Fleet are constantly preparing for a trial of strength with the enemy, and here a cruiser's 6-in. guns are being calibrated, or tested for accuracy. An Ordnance Artificer lowers the weight down the barrel (top) prior to sponging out before the shoot, and later (left) a gunner's mate sets the "rakes"—used to measure the spread of shots—according to the angles given him by the Staff Gunnery Officer.

Photo, British Official

VIEWS & REVIEWS Of Vital
Of Vital
War Books

by Hamilton Fyfe

MAN is an unaccountable creature. Every now and then there appear among human beings what we call imaginative geniuses. They peer into the future. They suggest what it may bring forth. They sketch for us the shape of things to come. They point out possibilities of all kinds—pleasant, dangerous, attractive, terrifying.

One might suppose that such men—they are always men : women for some reason have never taken much interest in the future—would be encouraged to elaborate their suggestions. One might fancy that experiments would be made along the lines of their ideas. What happens ? Exactly the opposite to this. Their sketches are derided as fantastic, their warnings go unheeded ; we even pay for large and powerful organizations which make every possible effort to persuade us that the developments outlined are quite impossible and that, even if they could be realized, we should be better without them.

One such organization is the War Office. I can remember some forty years ago reading a romance in which H. G. Wells predicted the coming of "land ironclads," monsters of steel which could roam on land as battleships and cruisers did at sea, which would be unpierceable by any shells at that time known, and would make any army possessing them easily victorious. Here was a hint which might have seemed to the War Office at any rate worth considering.

But the War Office, regarding itself as a bulwark against innovations—being paid, as it supposed, to keep warfare static—took no notice whatever. This was all the more stupid for the reason that in the South African War at that time going on effective use had been made of armoured trains. Probably that put the idea of "land ironclads " into Wells's receptive imagination. If these things were useful on rails, how much more valuable their deadly work could be if they ran around without rails ! But no one at the War Office—no one in authority, that is—had any imagination at all. The hint passed unheeded.

ANOTHER prophecy of Wells's was war in the air. When he made it no flying machine existed. In a few years private inventors had picked up the notion and, although they obtained no help from any official source, had brought the aeroplane to a stage at which it could at any rate rise up a few hundred feet and remain in the air for as much as an hour at a time. Not even then, not even when the submarine—foreseen by Jules Verne long before Wells was writing—had been developed and adopted by the world's navies, did the War Office learn the lesson that " these writin' fellers" sometimes hit on an idea worth following up. As late as 1912 a plan for land ships to be used in war was sent into the War Office and turned down.

You might have thought that with our small regular army such a weapon as this would have appealed strongly to the military chiefs. It was then the practice of Continental armies to give battle in solid formation. "Shoulder to shoulder" was still their motto. What a chance for these ironclads on land to plunge through their ranks, not only mowing down vast numbers, but spreading such terror and dismay among the rest as the soldiers of the ancient world felt when they first saw elephants brought into the fighting line. But no, the generals and the bureaucrats shook their sapient heads and let the opportunity go by.

It was not even to the credit of the War Office that the Tank (as it came to be called in order to hide what we were making from the enemy) was adopted in the First Great War. It was due to the Admiralty's ex-

The Triumph of The Tank

periments, undertaken by order of Winston Churchill, then First Lord. Kitchener called them "toys." Scarcely any of the generals taking active part in the war had any use for them—until they proved at Cambrai in 1917 that Wells had been right after all.

BETWEEN the wars we had another chance to get ahead of other States in the manufacture and handling of Tanks. A number of modern-minded officers, realizing that we lived now in a mechanized world and that warfare could not stay out of it, devoted their energies to laying foundations for a mechanized army. The War Office frowned on them, took them away from this most necessary work, told them they were victims of an obsession. Nevertheless we had, when the Second Great War opened, a certain number of Tanks, though nothing like as many as the Germans, and nothing like as good, if we can trust Mr. David Masters, who tells us in With Pennants Flying (Eyre & Spottiswoode, 9s.) that they did not get to France in sufficient force, or in time, or with strong enough fire-power, to keep back the torrent of German invasion when it poured over the Low Countries and France.

Of the First Armoured Division, which did not land on the Continent until May 22, 1940, by which time it was too late to hold up the German advance, "only an odd Tank or two" were left by May 30. The light Tanks were already obsolete. The heavier ones were more or less capable of standing up to the enemy Tanks, but there were no more than twelve of them ! That First Armoured Division "was doomed before it started." It "contained the cream of British manhood, trained to the highest degree of technical efficiency," and they "drove cheerfully into battle," but they had not "the remotest chance of success."

After that the construction of Tanks was taken out of the hands of the War Office, though the organization of them had to be left in its hands. The spirit in which it carried this out is shown by their being organized in "squadrons" and troops, the men in them being known as "troopers," and by their being called Dragoons and Hussars, and having "pennants flying." You can tell at once that cavalry officers made that arrangement. Pretend they are cavalry ! If we must change our beautiful prancing chargers for these horrible stinking engines with their hideous din, let us keep the same old names to remind us of the " good old days " !

WELL, it isn't what they are called, but what they do that matters, and the Royal Armoured Corps have done a magnificent job in many war areas. Mr. Masters tells of numberless acts of the most daring courage and the most ingenious initiative performed by the crews of our Tanks. They have a worse time even than the crews of submarines. There is only just enough room inside for the men and machinery, the turret gun, the shells and the wireless set. The men must be cramped at all times, and when the Tank gets very hot during an engagement and they cannot open anything they suffer badly for want of air. But they keep cheerful and settle down marvellously soon to a life of the utmost discomfort and frequent danger.

Of course, Tank tactics have altered a great deal since it was supposed that they might be able to win battles by themselves. They are useful only when they work with infantry and with aircraft, and whereas it was thought not long ago that the Tank must clear the way for the infantry, now the infantry more often clears the way for the Tank. They have been of most value when they had only scattered resistance to meet, as in France and Belgium. Against fixed defences and stubborn opposition they have so far not been able to make much headway.

THEY were immensely useful in the wide spaces of the desert, but it was due to heavy losses among them that Wavell had to retreat before the Germans, after he had pushed the Italians out of Cyrenaica in his amazing lightning campaign of 1941. His armour was so crippled that "his advanced units were forced to cast aside their worn-out Tanks " and learn to use the ones they captured from the Italians. We did not lose the Tanks which might, later, have stopped Rommel in a sudden blow, as Mr. Churchill told the House of Commons, relying on incorrect information. " They were whittled away day after day by Rommel's guns." Montgomery's greater success in Africa was due to his understanding of Tank warfare and the care he took not to let his " armour " be " whittled away."

What will be the future of the Tank no one can say. About its past, one can only declare that the scientists who improved it, the factory workers who made it and the men who took it into the field are deserving of the highest praise, while the army chiefs, both military and civil, who stood in its way so long deserve—well, I can't think of any punishment bad enough for them.

SHERMAN TANK races for a bridge thrown across the River Liri in the Cassino area during the new Allied push in Italy. Significance of the tank in modern warfare and the immortal deeds of the Royal Armoured Corps are dealt with in the book reviewed in this page. See also illus. pp. 36 and 37. PAGE 51 *Photo, British Official*

Britain's Battle Padres are Front Line Men

IN THE SPIRIT OF CRUSADERS, Britain's Royal Army Chaplains are preparing to face field dangers when the Allied assault from the West commences by going through a " toughening " course at a country headquarters in the Midlands (known locally as the " Padre's Battle School ") where they learn the arts of self-preservation. The padre knows how to use camouflage (1). With his companions he learns how to infiltrate through a village, to dodge the fire which may threaten him (2). Captain the Rev. L. Davies (3) has served in India, Iraq, Persia, Syria, Egypt and Sicily ; now he is at Anzio in Italy, where he is seen (4) leaving his dugout " rectory." This padre (5) trains to go with our airborne forces.   PAGE 52   *Photos, British Official ; Topical Press*

These Whip the Cream of the German Armies

WAITING FOR THE COVER OF DARKNESS before pushing on in the great new drive in Italy (see pp. 36 and 37), men of the 8th Army rest by the side of a wrecked railway track. After months of fluctuating battles in restricted areas they and our American, French, and Polish Allies, together with New Zealand and Indian troops, are at last engaged in a full-scale offensive against the enemy in more open country and are proving once more that the German best is not their super o.

Photo. British Official: Crown Copyright

Indomitable Spirit of the Red Air Force

Alexei Khlobystov is typical of the pilots of valiant Russia skilled in aerial warfare : gambling almost light-heartedly with the Angel of Death in the Valley of the Shadow, enjoying to the full the exhilaration of brilliant triumph as yet another enemy flyer spins to his doom. This vigorous sketch is by KONSTANTIN SIMONOV, playwright and official Red Army war correspondent.

SITTING in the cabin of his fighter plane, prepared to go up at a moment's notice, Alexei Khlobystov looked around him. Glancing at a near-by machine he suddenly recalled the first plane he had ever seen close at hand. It was near Moscow. A U-2 had unexpectedly landed in the courtyard of the plant where he then worked. It was an old, battered machine and yet he, a boy at the time, had felt a strange thrill pass through him and a desire to climb into the cockpit, take hold of something (he did not exactly know what) and go up into the air. He liked to make his wishes come true quickly, and half a year later he was flying an aviation club plane.

On July 1, 1941, he brought down his first Junkers—and became so excited that his temperature shot up, and from the cabin he was taken straight to hospital. In the autumn, after destroying his fourth plane, he plummeted to earth, shearing off tree-tops as he fell. Later, as he lay in hospital with several ribs broken, it sometimes seemed to him that breathing was difficult, not on account of his injuries but because of the hospital air—because he could not climb into a plane, go up and take a deep breath high in the sky. And when he was asked, "Khlobystov, do you want to fly a new type of plane ?" he only nodded, and closed his eyes, because he was afraid to answer out loud. He was afraid that a fit of coughing would seize him and he would be ordered to remain in bed. Finally, with an effort, he said, "I do !"

HE had found himself in the hospital bandaged all over, without helmet and flying suit. Now, as he was going out, his flying suit was brought to him and a thrill passed through him just as it did when he saw the old U-2. A month later he was flying this new machine, with short, sturdy wings and a sharp, shark-like nose. His period of duty came to an end, and he walked towards a dugout with his comrades. In the dug-out talk turned to the day when his picture was printed in all the papers.

The day was a restless one and he was very tired. Of course he was tired. First he flew on reconnaissance patrol with Captain Posdnyakov, then went up to attack ground objectives, then had his plane refuelled. He stood by while the ground crew worked, and thought how fine it would be to get an hour's sleep. But he had been ordered to take off again in half an hour. He heard petrol bubbling as it flowed into the tank. By the sound he could judge just how much had been poured in. Another five minutes and he would be ready to take off. And they did take off—Posdnyakov, and he and four other lads, still young and with hardly any combat experience.

He remembers well his first feeling when 28 enemy planes were sighted. The feeling was that Murmansk was in danger. The fact that there were 28 of them he realized later. It was not frightening, but serious, very serious. "Take a look—how many we have against us !" he said to Posdnyakov over the wireless, and in the earphones heard the Captain's reply :

"Look after the youngsters. I am going to attack !" A minute later they were fighting. One Messerschmitt fell. A thought flashed through Khlobystov's mind that now there were only 27. His greatest fear was for the youngsters, and he turned and veered to cover their tails. A Messerschmitt 110 passed below. Making use of the advantage

in height, Khlobystov went after it. Clearly he could see the gunner's head and the burst of tracer bullets that whizzed by. The distance between the two planes decreased steadily. The gunner dropped his head and fired no more.

Now they were flying low over a wood, and a hill loomed up ahead. At that moment,

Snr.-Lt. ALEXEI KHLOBYSTOV, Soviet air ace (top), first Russian pilot to ram two German planes in one action, whose epic story is related in this page. Back safely, he examines his damaged aircraft (below).
Photos, Pictorial Press

when the natural action was to pull on the steering column and zoom up, he decided to ram the Messerschmitt. To climb meant to let the enemy escape. He glanced back and saw three more enemy planes coming up from behind. Because the German was so near, and he could distinctly see the tail

with the black cross on it, Khlobystov thought clearly and calmly that in a moment he would find himself slightly to the left and behind the Messerschmitt, would raise his right wing and strike it against the enemy's tail . . . The blow was short and hard. The Messerschmitt hit the hill, and Khlobystov zoomed up. It seemed strange that his right wing was shorter than the left, that its tip had been sliced off. At that moment he heard Posdnyakov's voice, for the last time : "I have shot down one !" the captain announced triumphantly.

KHLOBYSTOV's plane was no longer as manageable as it used to be. It no longer seemed to be a part of his own body. The Soviet planes formed a circle while the Germans, who had regained their self-possession after the ramming, resumed frontal attacks. Posdnyakov was seen to drive straight at a German ace.

Later, when he was back on the ground, Khlobystov realized that the captain had made up his mind to bring down the enemy leader at the cost of his own life, if need be, in order to force the Germans to break formation. The two fighters collided at tremendous speed ; the German had refused to swerve and they fell down together. A second later Khlobystov realized that now he was the commander ; Posdnyakov was no more, and on him rested full responsibility for the combat.

"I am assuming command," he said over the radio. "I am going to attack. Protect my tail !" He saw two German fighters coming straight at him. His fuel tanks were practically empty, the enemy was still numerous, and behind his back were four young pilots for whom he had now become the only commander. When he made up his mind to ram the enemy he no longer believed that he would escape alive. His only thought was that if he did ram, the Germans would scatter and his comrades would break out of the ring. He calculated for a fraction of a second. As the German on the right turned away, Khlobystov hit the one on the left with his damaged wing. The blow was heavy. He lost control, and felt himself being drawn down after the spinning German. But he believed, somehow, that his machine would stand the strain.

WHEN he rose from the ground and realized that he was alive, through his mind flashed the words which he later said at Posdnyakov's funeral : "A score of vengeance !" And now people came running up, the commander was embracing him—everything began to whirl around, and he was overcome with fatigue . . .

. . . One Polar night we were leaving the north. "Is Khlobystov on duty tonight ?" we asked. "No, he is not," replied the commanding officer. "He is in the hospital. Yesterday he rammed his third German plane and baled out. He was rather unlucky. He had been wounded in the arm and leg at the outset of the combat, and realizing that he would not be able to fight for long he rammed the enemy. It's just like him : he can't bear to see a German escape alive."

I recalled Khlobystov's face with the light, audacious, boyish smile and the shock of unruly hair. And I realized that he was one of those people who, while they may sometimes make mistakes and take needless risks, have the gay and indomitable heart that never admits defeat or considers a venture to be too great.

Soviet Might Wins Back the 'City of Glory'

FALL OF SEBASTOPOL— whose name means " City of Glory "—was another great Soviet triumph in which all arms shared. Last German stronghold in the Crimea, it was retaken after three days of intensive fighting in which General Tolbukhin's 4th Ukrainian Army and Soviet air and sea forces co-operated in the greatest combined operation yet undertaken by Russian forces. Sebastopol had been in German hands since July 3, 1942.

Great damage has been done to the city by the enemy occupiers; Lenin Street, the main thoroughfare, lies in ruins (1). Soviet sailors, who played such a gallant part in the defence of Sebastopol in 1942, return again as conquerors, entering the city through a shattered archway (2). The Soviet naval colours are hoisted over Lenin Square (3). German soldiers, hands raised in surrender, emerge from hiding-places (4)

Photos, Pictorial Press, Planet News

'The Faithful Durhams' Toughen-up for Battle

TRAINING for further triumphs, men of a Durham Light Infantry battalion (regimental badge at left) manhandle a five-pounder gun across a treacherous sand waste (1); two leap to the top of a barbed-wire surmounted wall (2) during an assault course practice. Learning to be a dispatch rider is this private (3); his grandfather, father and two brothers have all served in this same regiment. Vehicle maintenance is of supreme importance to any army, and this traditionally tough North Country regiment makes certain that theirs are always in trim (5). Great importance also attaches to mail from home, here being distributed by the post corporal (centre, 4) to his colonel (right), major (left) and regimental sergeant-major (second from left). The Durham Light Infantry, formed in 1756, have a regimental nickname which they have proved on many fields—"The Faithful Durhams." In this war they have fought with great distinction in France, and in the North African, Sicilian and Italian campaigns. *Photos, British Official*

I WAS THERE!
Eye Witness
Stories of the War

In the Jungles of Assam Where Wild Battles Sway

Dispatched on April 11, 1944—thirteen days before the British garrison of
Kohima had been relieved by troops of the 14th Army—this story had to
be taken 500 miles by Graham Stanford of The Daily Mail before he could
cable it to London. See also illus. page 9.

For the past four days I have been chasing the Japanese attack over 50,000 square miles of the wildest country in the world—a battlefield which broadens every day as the enemy plunge deeper into the jungle and climb higher into the mountains in daring attempts to cut the lines of communication which the Allies have carved out of this fantastic country in the past two years.

From out of the besieged garrison at Imphal, main British base, where the Maharajah stays with his people, I climbed by plane to 10,000 ft. to clear cloud-shrouded mountains and trace the winding, precipitous Manipur road down to the hillside township of Kohima. There, a few days ago, a small party of British convalescent soldiers played a brave part in repulsing suicidal Japanese attacks.

Then I went down to an airfield hidden in the heart of the jungle, and on by truck, jeep, and on foot to follow trails of war through the once-peaceful, still green,

They are flying hundreds of sorties in support of our ground troops.

When I last flew over the Manipur road you could follow the trail of dust churned up by columns of our motor-transport climbing the road from Dimapur to Imphal and then onwards to the Burma border and the River Chindwin. Now the road was just a ribbon of red, and there was no movement. The Japanese have cut the highway

SHELLBURSTS envelop a Japanese position on the Tamu Road (above) during the Imphal battles in Manipur State. On May 22, 1944, British forces, having practically eliminated the enemy in the Kohima area, were pressing the Japanese back on the defensive. A U.S. soldier unwraps ammunition sent down by parachute to units fighting in North Burma (left). See story in this page.
Photos, Indian Official, Keystone.

road. They cling to the jungle-flanked tracks that lead down to the road; set up their ambushes and establish blocks so that the road may be denied to us.

There were no signs of war until we neared Kohima and then you could see great pillars of smoke rising more than a thousand feet into the air. Kohima—reputed to be the healthiest spot in Assam, and site of a convalescent hospital—is divided into two distinct parts. There is a native village, and one mile northwards the so-called residential quarter, where the convalescent home is situated. It was the village that was blazing, fired by our artillery shelling Japanese who had established a foothold in the native bazaar. For days and nights a mad battle raged in Kohima. Defending the resort were a handful of garrison troops and 35 British troops convalescing from typhus.

After the first Japanese charges had been held, the little band were shelled over open

sights at 800 yards range. An order to withdraw was given—and never received. At last strong reinforcements arrived and the garrison had a well-deserved rest. After Kohima we flew on over miles of more mountainous country until we had passed over the last razor-edged range and had touched down at an airfield in the heart of the tea-growing country.

We found a canteen in an old village hall and were served by the middle-aged wife of the local district commissioner who apparently played fairy godmother to all British troops. From here we began to trek by truck, jeep, and on foot until we reached the railhead of Dimapur, where there was no excitement but only confidence on all sides in the ability of British and Indian troops to drive the Japanese from Assam. Troops, armoured vehicles and guns were already trundling up the road to meet the enemy.

Dhansiri valley, where many a tea planter's luxurious bungalow is now a dormitory for the troops.

When I took off from Imphal in a plane loaded with supplies there was a strange, almost uncanny quiet in this plain, which is the granary of Assam. From dawn to dusk every day these transport pilots drive their planes over this scattered battlefield, carrying thousands of pounds of supplies. Yet week after week goes by with no losses, and pilots continue oblivious to flying strain. Technique of air supply is being revolutionized in this theatre of war. Pilots from other theatres say they would never have believed air supply could be carried out on such a scale as it has reached, and with so few casualties.

As we made our way over 8,000-ft. mountains and down the Manipur road we passed a squadron of Vengeance dive-bombers which had just returned from an attack near Kohima, scene of the present bitter fighting.

twice between Imphal and Kohima and they have a road block 39 miles from Dimapur. But—fearful of our continual air attacks—they are apparently making little use of the

I Walked in Odessa's Guerilla Army Catacombs

Impregnable stronghold of 10,000 Russian guerillas who by night dominated
the city for the last fortnight of the German occupation, the vast system of
winding and complicated passages beneath the streets and buildings of the
famous Black Sea port was recently visited by Paul Winterton, The News
Chronicle special correspondent. See also illus. pp. 778-779, Vol. 7.

The city of Odessa is built on a yellowish limestone so soft that it can be cut with a saw or shaped with an axe. Ever since 1794, when Odessa was built, the inhabitants have been quarrying this stone for their houses. That is why there is now a complicated labyrinth of shafts and tunnels twisting haphazardly below the city.

The depth of the passages, the recent home

of a real "underground movement," varies from about four yards to forty yards below the surface. In some you have to crawl on your belly or crouch down. In others you can walk erect for tens of miles along passages six feet wide and ten feet high. Naturally, in the old days, the catacombs were used by smugglers since they link with the port. Criminal elements used to make them their headquarters.

THE RED FLAG FLIES AGAIN IN ODESSA, Soviet city which was recaptured from the enemy on April 10, 1944. Red Army officers are here displaying it from the balcony of the Lunacharsky Theatre while happy citizens watch from below. The theatre was saved from destruction by the underground guerilla army, whose story is given here. *Photo, Pictorial Press*

During the enemy occupation of Odessa the catacombs served three purposes. When the Rumanians were attacking in 1941 and Luftwaffe bombs were raining down on the city, many thousands of women and children took shelter in the caves. In the last few weeks of the occupation they provided a safe hiding-place for innumerable thousands of men who would otherwise have been driven away to serve the enemy. Finally they were an impregnable base for the partisans.

I met the commander-in-chief of the guerillas yesterday in a small upper room in the workers' quarter of Odessa. His name, which deserves to become famous, is Anatol Loschenko. During the occupation he used the name of "Volgin" and was addressed by the guerillas as "Comrade Major," though, in fact, he had no military rank. Loschenko, a chemical engineer, was the ideal type to lead a movement which, in addition to waging a desperate, stealthy warfare with the enemy, also had thousands of civilians on its hands below ground.

H E is thirtyish, with a calm, kindly face, bright, determined blue eyes, very strong, white teeth and black hair brushed straight back. He possesses—and has exercised—the qualities of a natural leader. Largely through his efforts and personality an organization was built up in Odessa strong enough to break the enemy's nerves. Loschenko told me:

It was in January 1943, when the great German retreat began, that we started our preparations. We collected a little capital, bought provisions, set up a small flour mill and sausage factory, and stored food in the catacombs. Because there are no natural springs, we sank deep artesian wells and sometimes collected water from walls and roofs. We had a radio station and a printing press, and we set up an underground hospital with cots and sheets and all medical equipment.

We went out on night sorties. One night we had pitched battles with the Rumanian police and brought 67 prisoners back into the catacombs, where we kept them with many others until we could hand them over to the Red Army. When the Germans began to blow up the city before leaving we did everything possible to hamper them. We caught groups of soldiers in the act of setting buildings on fire and rushed them down into the caves. We saved the theatre by cutting wires leading to a charge of dynamite which the Germans had laid.

We continually cleared mines from areas in the port and succeeded in saving part of it. Night after night German preparations for demolition were rendered useless. We prevented part of the Telephone Exchange from being destroyed. The Germans and Rumanians began to get panic-stricken. At night the streets were ours. Their worst trouble was that they could never find out how many of us there were underground—one thousand or ten thousand!

On April 8 they issued an order that no one must appear in the streets after 3 p.m., and that all windows must be closed and all doors left open. Arms were brought to us by our women, as men dare not appear on the streets at all in the last fortnight. Tommy-guns, rifles and revolvers could be bought from Rumanian and German soldiers for cash. A rifle cost from 50 to 100 occupation marks, a tommy-gun 250, a revolver 150 to 200—with ammunition, of course. We exchanged bread for hand grenades. We also raided enemy dumps.

Our biggest windfall was when several hundred Slovaks deserted from the German Army and joined us, with arms and food. They brought trench mortars and automatic rifles. In the end 5,000 of us were armed—50 per cent. If the other half had been armed, too, we could have seized the city. As it was, we came out into the open when the Red Army drew near and fought the Germans in the streets in daylight, killing many hundreds of them. We guarded the entrances to the catacombs very well. The Germans knew where some of them were, but not all, for there are so many all over the city. Anyone coming into the catacombs was disarmed. We always let everybody in, but not everybody out. We had passwords which were changed every day. It was a constant battle of vigilance and wits.

One day a girl came and said she was a parachutist dropped with instructions from the Red Army for us to suspend operations for a time. But when we had given her wine she confessed that she had been sent by the Gestapo under a threat of death for her family. We kept a list of traitors. Sometimes men whom we regarded as traitors were persuaded to come over to our side with valuable secrets. We maintained direct contact with the approaching Red Army by means of scouts and radio.

That was Loschenko's story. Then he led us down into the catacombs to see for ourselves just how the guerillas had lived and worked. The entrance was half hidden among the rubble of a demolished building. By the light of flaming wicks stuck into bottles of petrol we squeezed through a two-foot wide hole and half slid, half scrambled, down a narrow funnel until we were thirty yards below the surface.

T HERE were traces of German attempts to blow up the opening with grenades, but it soon became obvious why they had made no attempt to break into the catacombs and drive the guerillas out. In these winding and complicated passages one man could hold up a battalion. No German ever dared to go in—no German was ever sent in. It was the guerillas' impregnable stronghold.

We walked about 400 yards in an eerie semi-darkness. It was very hot and stuffy, and Loschenko said that when the atmosphere got too bad the civilian residents were moved to different sectors of the caves, which were all divided up into districts. Here and there water trickled down the yellow walls. The guerilla headquarters was a large chamber divided into a number of "rooms" by low stone walls. Each room had its own special function—one of them was labelled "Command Point for Forming Guerilla Bands." There was another smaller chamber for making anti-tank petrol bottles.

When we left the workers' district hundreds of people gathered round us near the entrance to the caves and waved good-bye. They had all lived down below—they all knew and loved and trusted the guerilla leader Loschenko and his assistants. They were certainly proud of their catacombs.

I Saw the Tricolour Flying Over Mount Majo

In the Allied offensive in Italy which opened on May 11, French troops under General Alphonse Juin made a spectacular advance through country beautiful to the tourist, but incredibly difficult to the tactician. This story by L. Marsland Gander, who drove up the Garigliano Valley in their wake, is reprinted by courtesy of The Daily Telegraph.

T O reach the village of S. Andrea from a former front-line position I motored in a jeep for two and a half hours and found the lovely Garigliano Valley now free from the German invader.

Across the river lay the heights the French had captured, piled one behind the other, rugged, scrub-covered, and sometimes thickly wooded.

To climb on foot to the 2,600-ft. summit of Mt. Faito, unhampered by wire and mines, takes the ordinary hiker three and a half hours. French Spahis, Chasseurs, Senegalese and Moroccans overran this and a score of other heights in three days against stiff opposition and under shell- and mortar- fire.

In the gently shelving fields bordering the river, red with poppies which gleamed among the rank grass, there was grim evidence of battle. We passed two hastily dug graves, an American medium tank damaged and overturned, two lorries upside down off the road.

The going now became difficult as we overtook supply columns of the advancing army, and the jeep bounced and rattled over shellholes. Frequently we were shot off our seats by the violent jolting, but always

made safe landings in the vehicle again. Drivers cursed at one another and at the smothering dust which changed all our pigmentation, but in reality everybody was

GENERAL ALPHONSE JUIN, commander of the French troops who in the magnificent mountain drive, described in the accompanying story, broke the vaunted Gustav Line on May 14, 1944. General Juin also fought in France and North Africa. *Photo, U.S. Official*

in the best of humour. When we had halted in one of the numerous traffic blocks a passing poilu grinned delightedly at us and said: "Eighth Army bon."

French sailor gunners of a battery which I had visited previously came clattering past over the very road which they had shelled so often with 6-in. guns. I remembered as they hailed us the painstaking way in which they had been improving their camp and emplacements as if they were there for the rest of the war.

Passing lorries and jeeps were all named according to their owners' fancy. I noticed "Pantagruel," "Port Lyautey," and "Lulu" among many others. One lorry carried an oil painting of General de Gaulle on the windscreen.

At last we were climbing by a tortuous road in a slow procession of jeeps into S. Andrea, which snuggles among the hills, every house a medieval fortress in itself.

As usual the solid stone houses of this little village had stood the bombardment well. A pathetic group of about a dozen women, children and old men stood outside a house they had converted into a shelter by piling loose stones outside the walls and windows.

As much in relief at the end of their torment as in joy at the sight of their liberators, these people of a sorrow-ploughed country were in astonishingly good spirits. Wreathed in smiles, they cordially welcomed me into their temporary communal dwelling, where a French sergeant was nursing a baby on his lap.

French 105-mm. guns firing in the valley roused shattering echoes which turned every shot into a cannonade. But here there was no enemy retaliation.

The village was still beset with mines and booby traps. Two gallant French officers had that morning, in the moment of victory, been killed by a mine.

ONE OF MANY SHATTERED NAZI TANKS which lay on the outskirts of the Italian village of Castelforte, at the southern end of the Gustav Line—which it was announced on May 15, 1944, was taken by French forces, two of whom are seen passing through the village. For months Castelforte had been one of the main bastions of the enemy line. French troops engaged include Moroccan, Algerian and Senegalese units.
Photo, British Official

A Piper Cub flying overhead to pick up French wounded was a demonstration of how far and fast the advance had gone through this difficult country, where the Germans, like ourselves, had been forced to depend on congested mountain trails.

In the steep central square, sitting among the rubble at a trestle table, was a placid and corpulent town major. He told me S. Andrea was taken by Senegalese, who stormed the surrounding heights, forcing the garrison to capitulate.

Just what was involved in this feat was apparent when one looked at the mountains. Through glasses I could see the Tricolour flying on Mt. Majo.

OUR DIARY OF THE WAR

MAY 10, Wednesday *1,712th day*
Air.—Railway centres and airfields in France and Belgium bombed by U.S.A.A.F. by day and R.A.F. at night.
Mediterranean.—U.S. aircraft bombed Wiener Neustadt aircraft factory ; railway yards at Budapest attacked by night.
China.—Offensive in West Yunnan launched by Chinese troops across Salween river.

MAY 11, Thursday *1,713th day*
Italy.—Fifth and Eighth Armies launched offensive against the Gustav Line.
Air.—U.S. heavy bombers attacked marshalling yards in France, Belgium, Luxembourg and W. Germany ; at night R.A.F. bombed railway yards at Boulogne and Louvain.
Russian Front.—Soviet aircraft bombed Lublin railway junction.
Sea.—Admiralty announced sinking of two U-boats in Atlantic by frigate H.M.S. Spey.
General.—Announced that Major-Gen. R. G. Sturges, Royal Marines, had been appointed head of Special Service Group (Commandos).

MAY 12, Friday *1,714th day*
Air.—Over 750 U.S. bombers attacked four synthetic oil-plants near Leipzig and one in Czechoslovakia. Railway yards in Belgium bombed by R.A.F.
Italy.—5th Army French and U.S. troops made progress against Gustav Line, supported by Allied naval forces. Heavy bombers attacked ports and railway centres in Northern Italy.
Russian Front.—Soviet aircraft bombed railway junctions of Dvinsk (Latvia) and Tartu (Estonia).

MAY 13, Saturday *1,715th day*
Air.—Large force of U.S. bombers attacked oil refinery near Stettin, Focke Wulf plant at Tutow on Baltic, and marshalling yards at Osnabruck ; Thunderbolts dive-bombed airfield near Bremen.
Italy.—5th Army troops captured Castelforte. Allied bombers attacked railway communications on Brenner Pass line.
Russian Front.—Soviet bombers attacked Brest-Litovsk, Polotsk and Narva.

MAY 14, Sunday *1,716th day*
Italy.—French troops of 5th Army captured Mt. Majo and made breach in Gustav Line. Allied bombers attacked railway yards in Po Valley. U.S. naval forces bombarded enemy positions round Formia and Itri.
Russian Front.—Soviet bombers attacked railway junctions near Lvov.
Air.—Mosquitoes bombed Cologne at night.
Home Front.—15 German aircraft destroyed in raids on S. and S.W. England.

MAY 15, Monday *1,717th day*
Air.—U.S. heavy bombers attacked Pas de Calais area ; at night Mosquitoes bombed Ludwigshafen.
China.—In Western Yunnan, Chinese troops continued to make progress towards Burma.

MAY 16, Tuesday *1,718th day*
Italy.—Pignataro captured by Indian troops of 8th Army.
Air.—Mosquitoes bombed Berlin at night.
Russian Front.—Soviet aircraft bombed railway junctions at Minsk, Baranovichi and Kholm.

MAY 17, Wednesday *1,719th day*
Burma.—Main airfield at Myitkyina captured by Chinese-American troops under Brig.-Gen. Frank Merrill.

East Indies.—Aircraft from Anglo American carrier force attacked Surabaya, Java ; ten ships sunk and heavy damage done to floating docks, oil installations and airfields.
Australasia.—American forces landed on Wakde Island, off New Guinea.
Sea.—Announced that H.M. frigates had sunk two U-boats in N. Atlantic.
General.—Announced that V.C. had been awarded posthumously to Major C. F. Hoey for gallantry in Burma.

MAY 18, Thursday *1,720th day*
Italy.—Cassino captured by British troops, and Monastery Hill by Poles.
Mediterranean.—Allied heavy bombers attacked Ploesti (Rumania) and Belgrade and Nish (Yugoslavia).
General.—Announced that V.C. had been awarded to Major H. R. B. Foote for outstanding gallantry in Libya in 1942.

MAY 19, Friday *1,721st day*
Italy.—Spezia, Genoa and Leghorn attacked by Allied heavy bombers.
Air.—U.S. bombers and fighters attacked Berlin and Brunswick ; R.A.F. bombed railway yards at Orleans, Le Mans, Boulogne and Tours.
Sea.—Admiralty announced destruc-tion of at least two U-boats during passage of convoy to Russia.
Australasia.—U.S. troops completely occupied Wakde Island.
General.—Announced that 47 British and Allied air force officers had been shot by Germans after mass escape from prison-camp.

MAY 20, Saturday *1,722nd day*
Air.—New record in offensive from Britain set up ; almost 5,000 bombers and fighters attacked 12 railway centres and nine airfields in France and Belgium.
Italy.—Battle for Adolf Hitler line began ; Americans captured Gaeta on west coast.

MAY 21, Sunday *1,723rd day*
Italy.—5th Army troops captured Fondi on Appian way.
Air.—Allied fighters and fighter-bombers attacked transport facilities from Brest to east of Berlin, shooting up more than 300 locomotives. At night R.A.F. bombers made heavy attack on Rhineland port of Duisburg.
Burma.—Chinese-American troops occupied one-third of Myitkyina.

MAY 22, Monday *1,724th day*
Air.—Kiel was main target of U.S. escorted heavy bombers. By night more than 1,000 R.A.F. bombers attacked Dortmund and Brunswick as well as Orleans and Le Mans.
Italy.—Hard fighting for the Adolf Hitler line continued.
China.—Chefang, on Burma Road W. of Salween, captured by Chinese troops.
General.—First official announcement of work of Italian patriots in enemy-occupied Italy.

MAY 23, Tuesday *1,725th day*
Italy.—British and U.S. troops of 5th Army in Anzio beach-head launched offensive against perimeter defences, synchronized with attack by Canadian Corps of 8th Army to break Adolf Hitler Line in the Liri valley.
Air.—U.S. heavy bombers, escorted by more than 1,000 fighters, attacked airfields, marshalling yards and other targets in France and Western Germany. At night Mosquitoes bombed Berlin and Dortmund.
China.—Chinese forces began a general counter-offensive in Honan.

★ ═══════════ *Flash-backs* ═══════════ ★

1940
May 11. Formation of new British War Cabinet announced.
May 22. U.K. Emergency Powers Act passed, giving Government control over persons and property.

1941
May 14. Large reinforcements from Britain arrived at Singapore.
May 15. R.A.F. bombed Syrian airfields used by German aircraft.

1942
May 10. Mr. Churchill warned Germans that if gas used against Russia, British would retaliate.
May 15. First British forces retreating from Burma reached Indian frontier.

1943
May 11. U.S. troops landed on Attu Island in the Aleutians.
May 12. All organized Axis resistance in Tunisia ended.
May 16-17. R.A.F. mine-laying Lancasters breached Mohne and Eder Dams in Ruhr basin.
May 22. Dissolution of Comintern announced from Moscow.

THE WAR IN THE AIR

by Capt. Norman Macmillan, M.C., A.F.C.

IF this war has been the forcing-house of aeronautical development for military purposes that the First Great War also was, it has at the same time, like the earlier conflict, left its mark on the transport side of aviation. Most of the projected transport aircraft of 1939 were necessarily shelved in Great Britain because scarcity of military aircraft was so great that neither factory space nor tools, and hands to operate them, could be spared to carry on an aircraft-building programme that did not seem to lead to a definite military end.

Indeed, it is extraordinary, now in 1944, to look back at the British military air outlook in 1939, and realize that no preparations had here been made for parachute troops, or glider-borne soldiery, or dive- or fighter-bombers; the largest force we could put forth when Norway was invaded numbered 92 aircraft. But for the efficiency of our fighter-aircraft and of the pilots who flew them in the Battle of Britain—and for the somewhat late-in-the-day decision to give priority to fighter aircraft construction because we could not build enough aircraft to satisfy all our requirements—we might never have had the opportunity to gain time to catch up on the wily enemy we faced alone and (as we have done before) outmatch him technically and numerically.

THE position that existed then in the military sphere of aviation may even now exist in the transport sphere of aviation. This does not mean that we are not capable technically of producing the finest transport aircraft in the world. Undoubtedly, we can produce the equal of the world's best, and may even say without seeming to be immodest that some such aircraft of ours might excel those produced elsewhere in some particular class or characteristic.

It is now generally known that a number of British aircraft firms are engaged on the research and construction of special aircraft for post-war transport. But the fact still remains that the needs of the military situation dominate the aircraft industry, and for that reason they dominate the minds of men.

We did not suddenly produce a perfect Lancaster bomber or Barracuda torpedo-bomber. The Spitfire has not reached its present stage of super-performance without the passage of time necessary for the accumulation of experience which can be gained only by practical methods. And so, in the same way, it is scarcely to be expected that transport aircraft can reach their full development until they have been put into service and passed through the mill of usage. And most of the air transports of today are employed for military purposes. Thus it is impossible not to give a mental bent, and a practical one, to the somewhat specialized requirements of the war in regard to the design, construction, and employment of these aircraft.

AIRCRAFT Design Dictated by Special Circumstances

Take a few of the factors which condition the design of aircraft. First, there are the types of engine available. Engines today are designed for military purposes first and foremost. Does it follow that they are equally suitable for transport use? Air-frame constructional methods, and wing construction also, are related to the carriage and employment of warlike armament and stores. Shape and size of aircraft are dictated by the same consideration.

No doubt it is for these good and sufficient reasons that experienced military designers like Mr. Chadwick, of A. V. Roe & Co., and Mr. Frise, of the Bristol Aeroplane Co., have stated that they do not look for any great departure from accepted aeronautical practice in the construction of transport aircraft for some ten years after the war.

Now it is generally accepted that the current types of military aircraft were sired mainly by civil types of aircraft. The low-wing, retractable undercarriage, single-engined fighter sprang from such types of aircraft as the Supermarine Schneider Trophy racers of 1927–31, and the Lockheed Orion six-passenger transport of 1931. The original medium bombers which we possessed at the beginning of this war were the offspring of aircraft like the Northrop Delta and the Britain First; aircraft such as these were like civil prototypes of the Battle and the Blenheim. The four-motored bomber class was preceded by aircraft like the Ensign and Albatross, and the Sunderland flying boat was a direct conversion from the Empire-class commercial flying boat.

WHEN the war began the commercial air routes and the aircraft and personnel that operated them passed directly under Government control, and became for all practical purposes servants of the State in much the same manner as the Merchant Navy. Then Ferry Command was instituted to bring aircraft from outside Britain to the United Kingdom and to fly aircraft needed abroad to their destinations, while Air Transport Auxiliary was already engaged in the ferrying of aircraft internally in Great Britain. Air Transport Command of the R.A.F. followed in due course as a natural development of the expanding air situation; and, later still, the Air Transport Command of the United States absorbed the overseas transport company of Pan-American Airways within its rapidly growing organization.

British Overseas Airways and a few internally operated airlines in the United Kingdom represent almost the sole remaining civil transport aircraft operating concerns plying in a quasi-civil transport manner in and without the United Kingdom. Meanwhile, air transport as such has grown to dimensions never visualized by the pre-war military mind, and is employed almost exclusively for war transport purposes, as indeed it must be while the war continues.

NEW Departures Relegated to Uncertain Future Date

It seems, therefore, that the past and present situation is one wherein the orthodox views of Mr. Chadwick and Mr. Frise are justified, because military necessity cannot afford to risk the unorthodox design with its too-frequent attendant delays. So we stick to the accepted types of aircraft for immediate production, while planning new departures for the future when there will be more time to devote to the development of such special kinds of aircraft as the flying-wing—which dispenses with tail and body and presents the perfection of streamlining to reduce resistance to the minimum. And we stick to the reciprocating engine for transport aircraft because it is today the most efficient for the purpose, relegating jet propulsion and gas turbine to an uncertain future date.

BUT the great contribution which the war in the air is making towards the future of transport flying is the ground organization —the air routes, aerodromes, transport methods of operating through the world's most difficult sections of the atmosphere. Here the forcing house of war is producing great growth, and who knows but that the air invasion fleets that may descend upon Europe will change the whole character and art of war. Certain it is that war in the air and war on the ground will be influenced out of all present measure by the developments of transport aircraft, and that we are only at the beginning of the demonstrations of the use of air transport in war strategy.

In connexion with air transport developments, reference should be made to illustration in pages 44–45; and to articles and illustrations in pages 316, 362–363 and 716–717 in Volume 7.

U.S. MITCHELL B.25 BOMBERS and an invasion convoy pass each other on the way to deal the Japanese in the South-West Pacific yet more powerful blows. The bombers are heading for the enemy base at much-raided Rabaul in New Britain; the invasion convoy vessels, seen leaving their wakes in the water far below the planes, are steering a course for New Ireland. See map in page 4.

Photo, New York Times Photos

8th U.S.A.A.F. is Germany's Daylight Scourge

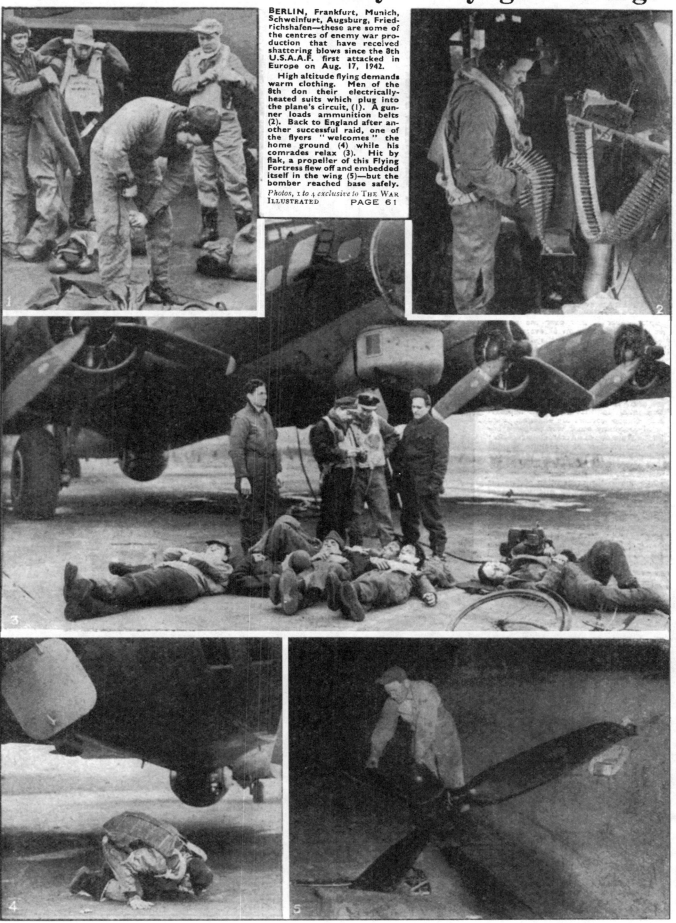

BERLIN, Frankfurt, Munich, Schweinfurt, Augsburg, Friedrichshafen—these are some of the centres of enemy war production that have received shattering blows since the 8th U.S.A.A.F. first attacked in Europe on Aug. 17, 1942.

High altitude flying demands warm clothing. Men of the 8th don their electrically-heated suits which plug into the plane's circuit, (1). A gunner loads ammunition belts (2). Back to England after another successful raid, one of the flyers "welcomes" the home ground (4) while his comrades relax (3). Hit by flak, a propeller of this Flying Fortress flew off and embedded itself in the wing (5)—but the bomber reached base safely.

Photos, 1 to 4 exclusive to THE WAR ILLUSTRATED   PAGE 61

Ulster Makes Dress-Lengths for Our Planes

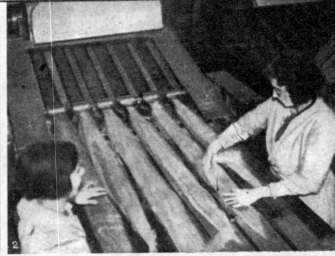

VITAL MUNITION OF WAR is the linen made in Northern Ireland from home-grown flax, and which in peacetime brought beauty to everyday life in the form of fine damask ; now it helps R.A.F. wings to spread ever farther over the enemy. Used in the construction of every operational aircraft made for the R.A.F. in Britain, linen is found in many "key" points in the framework of a plane, including wings, fuselage, joins and seams generally. Flax production in Ulster has increased five-fold since the war began (see pp. 650 and 651, Vol. 7), and today there are some 105,000 acres under cultivation in an industry in which approximately 60,000 workers are engaged. Flax is used for many other war purposes besides the main one of aircraft construction ; in the manufacture of parachute harness webbing alone, at the end of 1943 some 35,000 yards were being supplied weekly to the R.A.F.

Stage one in the preparation of flax for spinning is the roughing and piecing of the fibre (1), which is then machine-hackled, emerging from the front of the machine in a continuous ribbon (2). After four or five stages it arrives at the roving frame (3), then goes to the loom for weaving (4). It took more than 1,000 yards of linen to "clothe" this civil version of the Vickers Warwick plane (5).

Photos, Topical Press, Charles E. Brown

IN the earlier days of the War, when my space was more abundant, I often gave excerpts from letters that came from readers of THE WAR ILLUSTRATED overseas, to illustrate the remarkable way in which the sea communications of the Empire were being maintained even during the most violent phases of the U-boat attacks. Eventually the pressure on my space prevented my sharing with my readers glimpses of these interesting epistles, and there is no probability of my resuming a practice which I was sorry to discontinue, but it happens that among my correspondence this week is a letter from Mr. Kenneth G. McDonald, of Kingston, Jamaica, in which occurs a paragraph that I must find a corner for, as it is a timely reminder in an intimate way of how thankful we should be to the Royal Navy for enabling our merchantmen to maintain those overseas communications that are the lifeblood of our Empire. Here is the paragraph:

"I immediately decided that I should like to subscribe to your Magazine, with a view to keeping a permanent record of the war. I therefore had a local dealer, the Educational Supply, Ltd., import for me the copies weekly, and here, I think, is the best reflection on the wonderful way in which the Royal Navy has been keeping the sea-lanes open, to even such a far distant place as little Jamaica, for I am proud to say that I now have six complete bound volumes and I am well on the way to completing the seventh. Even through the darkest days my copies arrived with almost clock-like regularity. Of course, there were a few from time to time which were lost, but even those I was able to replace. These volumes have not only been a source of great information to me, but have succeeded in putting right many arguments which we have had on various happenings of the war."

UPTON SINCLAIR has put many ideas before his multitudinous readers since he wrote the book which brought him into fame at a bound. The idea behind The Jungle was that the peasants from Lithuania and other countries of north-eastern Europe ought to be better treated when they reached the United States. They expected to find liberty after fleeing from the German Kaiser or the Russian Tsar, and what they found was only another form of slavery. Sinclair drew a picture of their sufferings in the Slaughtering Yards of Chicago which sent a shudder though this country as well as his own. But the Americans saw in the book a warning against the dirty, disgusting manner in which their canned foods were prepared. The sale of these fell off so rapidly and heavily that the canners reformed their methods at once. I went through one of their factories a year or so after The Jungle appeared and saw the women who packed the meat into tins having their nails manicured to ensure perfect cleanliness! Since then Sinclair has contributed numerous suggestions for human progress, some good, some not so good. His latest is that Hitler, when he has been beaten and taken prisoner, shall be sent to a charming island off the coast of California with an almost perfect climate and exquisite scenery. I doubt if that will meet with much approval. It seems to me just silly.

THAT an old person should take on a war job at 83 astonishes many people who have not been noticing the signs of the times. The job is not a very heavy one. The great-grandmother whom I have been hearing about sorts the clean clothes in a laundry. But it still seems almost a miracle to some of us that a woman of her age should be able to do any work at all. So it would have been fifty years ago. But today the people who were formerly thought to have finished their working days when they reached sixty are still energetic long after that. It looks as if Nature were adapting herself to the change that is predicted by population experts. They say that everywhere the numbers of the human race will decrease. They expect Britain to have not more than five to ten million inhabitants in a hundred years' time. The proportion of young folks to old folks will become much smaller. It will be necessary for the old to keep on working as long as they can. Already there has been a marked change in this direction, and it must continue unless something should happen to send population figures bounding up again, which does not seem likely.

IF the Ministry of Information must drop into poetry it might, I think, aspire to produce verses composed on accepted standards. I read in a fishmonger's shop these lines printed on a card which the Ministry distributes:

When my shop is cold and empty
Don't look at me in woe;
Fishing-boats have gone a-sweeping
For the mines laid by the foe.

Then my eye wandered round and I saw another card with this quatrain on it:

The fishermen are saving lives
By sweeping seas for mines.
So you'll not grumble, "What, no fish?"
When you have read these lines.

Doggerel such as that would disgrace a class of ten-year-olds. A State Department ought to keep up to a decent standard if it insists on circulating verses, for which I myself can see no need. But almost all advertisers now regard the public as a large child whom they must amuse. This would-be comic element is vastly overdone and very seldom amusing.

THE decision of the Town Council in a big seaside resort not to have prayers before they begin their meetings has caused a good deal of comment. As war is believed to make us more religious, the proposal that this should be done at Brighton was expected to win the support of a large number of councillors. Those who wanted a chaplain to be appointed quoted, of course, the example of the House of Commons. The opposition members might have replied by pointing out that very few M.P.s attend the prayers which precede every sitting of the House of Commons. They might also have mentioned that the Lords do not pray. But they kept to local objections, which were strong enough to defeat the proposal. Nobody said anything about having prayers at the end of meetings. These would seem to be far more necessary. Often the things Town Councils do are such that they ought to ask pardon for doing them, and some councillors are so persistent in provoking scenes that their colleagues might be glad to put up earnest petitions for their removal to some other place of activity.

IN a tea-shop the other day an American soldier gave a tip of half-a-crown for a meal costing about as much. It was generous —but thoughtless. All those sitting near who saw what he had done looked at one another and lifted their eyebrows. They knew it was pardonable ignorance of what custom should suggest as a limit for tipping. He did not want to swank or make others who gave the usual tip look uncomfortable. He just didn't understand that in such a matter as this we observe certain social conventions of our own. If the incident stood alone, there would be no need to say anything about it, but there are many like it occurring every day. Half-a-crown was no doubt exceptional, but the tips American soldiers give are generally on the high scale as a rule. This is the kind of thing that is likely to add to the resentment British soldiers are inclined to feel about the difference in the pay of the two armies. It would have been wise to tell the Americans when they arrived about this and other social habits of which they should be made aware.

THERE is very little objection among our troops to officers being saluted and regarded generally as professional superiors. But there is in certain units (I know of one in Dorset, for instance) some resentment about officers being treated as superior human beings when off duty. This unit has a cinema, and the other day a crowd of privates was waiting to go in as soon as any seats were empty. As they waited, they saw officers stroll up and walk in, knowing that seats would be found for them. The reply to this is, "It has always been like that, and the officers most insistent on such privileges are those who have risen from the ranks. Should any of the grumblers receive commissions, they will regard the social barrier between officers and Other Ranks as highly desirable, indeed necessary."

Whilst Death Rains Down from China's Sky

SHELTERING FROM JAPANESE BOMBS, war-experienced refugee Chinese women crouch with their children in a slit-trench while enemy planes are overhead. On April 8, 1944, Japanese forces launched big attacks in the Honan Province—which is known as the granary of China—but their hold on the key Peking-Hankow railway was broken by the Chinese capture of Suiping on May 13.

Photo, Keystone

Printed in England and published every alternate Friday by the Proprietors, THE AMALGAMATED PRESS, LTD., The Fleetway House, Farringdon Street, London, E.C.4. Registered for transmission by Canadian Magazine Post. Sole Agents for Australia and New Zealand: Messrs. Gordon & Gotch, Ltd.; and for South Africa: Central News Agency, Ltd.—June 9, 1944. S.S. *Editorial Address:* JOHN CARPENTER HOUSE, WHITEFRIARS, LONDON, E.C.4.

Vol 8   *The War Illustrated*   N° 183

Edited by Sir John Hammerton

SIXPENCE   JUNE 23, 1944

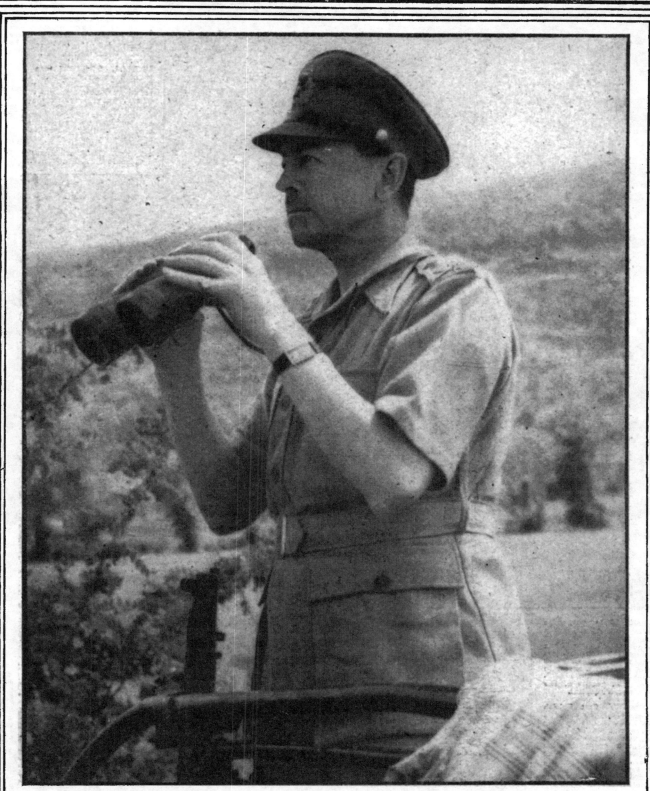

GENERAL SIR HAROLD ALEXANDER, G.C.B., C.S.I., D.S.O., M.C., Commander-in-Chief of the Allied Armies in Italy, watched keenly the successful progress of our troops as they engage the enemy at the commencement of the great new offensive on May 11, 1944. General Alexander was appointed Commander-in-Chief on December 24, 1943. On May 12, 1944, in an order of the day addressed to his forces in English, French, Italian, and Polish he declared, "We are going to destroy the German armies in Italy."

Photo, British Official

NO. 184 WILL BE PUBLISHED FRIDAY. JULY 7

Our Roving Camera Sees War Prisoners Return

FREE MEN AGAIN after more than four years behind German barbed wire, some of over 600 repatriated British prisoners smile happily from the decks of the Swedish mercy ship Gripsholm (left) which landed them at a British port recently. The Gripsholm sails under a " safe conduct " on such humanitarian voyages and carries on board representatives of the Protecting Power (Swiss) and International Red Cross Committee.

W.R.N.S. SORTERS are busy (below) at an Admiralty depot in Britain classifying snapshots taken by holiday-makers abroad in travel-easy peace days. In response to a Government appeal, millions of topographical photographs taken by people who had travelled in Europe, also in Japan and in what are now Japanese occupied territories, have been collected. They will provide invaluable tactical information.

MENACING, but now quite harmless, is this big German gun (above) captured at Tripoli, which has been brought to London. Soldiers are cleaning the war scars from the 25-ton monster in preparation for its exhibition to the people of the Empire's capital.

COVENTRY, first British provincial city to suffer a concentrated enemy air attack—on Nov. 14, 1940— was also among the first to produce a comprehensive post-war redevelopment scheme. The Cathedral Church of St. Michael, with its 300-ft. spire, is now only a shell (right). The steeple beyond is that of Holy Trinity, also devastated. This recent photograph shows the clearance effected in the cathedral vicinity

Photos, New York Times Photos, Planet News, Fox, J. Dixon Scott

THE BATTLE FRONTS

by Maj.-Gen. Sir Charles Gwynn, K.C.B., D.S.O.

SINCE I last wrote it has become increasingly clear that General Alexander's offensive was conceived with the idea of bringing about one great battle in which the enemy might not only be driven from his defensive positions, but be defeated beyond hope of recovery. The Anzio attack was delivered not in order to induce Von Kesselring to retreat and open the way to Rome, but if possible to prevent the escape of his 10th Army. So much one can conclude from the timing and direction of the blow.

How far Alexander will completely succeed in his object remains uncertain while I write, for Kesselring is a skilful commander and modern weapons have great delaying power, although the fallacy of the one-time fashionable belief that they gave the defence mastery over attack has never been more clearly proved than by the collapse of the Gustav and Hitler positions.

It has been an extraordinarily interesting battle in many ways, apart from the great issues involved. Never has one been fought over such an amazing variety of terrain, or over terrain which seemed to offer such immense advantages to the defence on both high and low ground. The Gustav and Hitler positions might have served as a text book example of the ideal defensive position, with no obvious points of weakness, and with secure flanks resting on the sea on one side and on a great mountain range on the other.

The composition of the attacking army was even more varied, and in a single battle seldom can four distinct national armies have been each given its separate role. When one comes to the composition of the national groups in detail never surely since Babel can there have been such an assemblage of races united for a single purpose. The Polish Army was, I suppose, the most homogeneous, and with it were working American tanks and artillery. The American Army was, of course, exclusively American, but I imagine it would have been difficult to find in it a unit composed of men sprung from a single ethnological stock. The French Army, largely colonial, was recruited from many different African tribes and races, but it was the British Empire contingent that could produce the greatest diversity of language, colour, race and geographical origin in its several units and formations.

BRITISH, Indian, Canadian and New Zealand formations provided its major sub-divisions, but other units, especially the ancillary units which did splendid work, showed an amazing variety of origin. That this astonishing mixture successfully worked to one plan and defeated an army which claimed to be drawn from the most homogeneous and most martial stock in the world was indeed a triumph, tending to upset the belief that certain races inherently possesss greater martial virtues than others. No one could fail to recognise the necessity for tact in the commander of such an army or the unerring judgement displayed by General Alexander in assigning to each of his national groups the tasks which best suited its characteristics.

Yet it is impossible to say which of the tasks was the most difficult, since they differed so greatly in character. The mountains north of Cassino formed the greatest physical obstacle, and it was on that front that infantry possessing very special qualities of individual endurance and activity was needed. It was assigned to the Poles, who had already proved their aptitude for mountain warfare and were essentially an infantry army. In the Liri valley the British had a greater variety of physical obstacles to deal with, though of a less formidable character, water being perhaps the greatest. It was on this front that the enemy were thickest on the ground and had prepared the strongest artificial defences. It was a front which required the assistance of armour and tremendous weight of artillery support to reduce the volume of fire the enemy could develop from front and flanks.

ON the French front, mountains, though less precipitous than those the Poles had to deal with, were again the main physical obstacle. Infantry of great dash and activity were required, but probably a greater weight of artillery support could be given them than on the Polish front. Although the ground lent itself to defence it seems probable that difficulties of supply and deficiencies of lateral communication limited the size of the defence force to a greater extent here than in the Liri valley. It was, however, far from being a weak sector of the enemy's front. The American task included both the forcing of

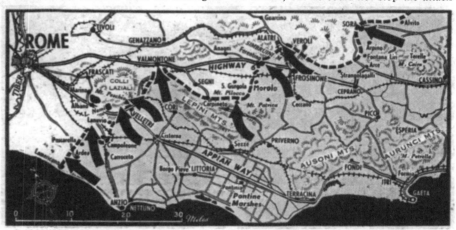

SMASHING BREACH AFTER BREACH in Kesselring's right flank, south of Rome, pivot of his entire retreat, the Allies by June 1, 1944, were advancing in five thrusts in that area, as indicated above. U.S. forces established on the Alban Hills north of Velletri were overlooking the city ; in the coastal area British forces were driving up the Ardea Road. At Frosinone, near Highway 6, the 8th Army was pushing on. On the night of June 4 troops of the 5th Army entered Rome, the Germans withdrawing north of the capital. *By courtesy of The Daily Mail*

the defile between the mountains and the sea and the capture of the mountains which overlooked it. Here again the enemy were in strength and had good artificial cover, so that to reduce the volume of the defenders' fire the attack required the support of armour and massed artillery on a scale that only the British and American Armies could produce.

Whatever were the respective difficulties of the various sectors of the front it is clear that each of the groups fought with the greatest determination and had each made definite progress before they obtained the benefit of the progress of the groups alongside. Only the Poles coming up against the pick of the German troops in appalling ground were definitely held up, though they held on firmly to what they had gained. But, well as all did, it is frankly agreed that it was the French who in the first days of the battle made the breach which led to decisive results. Beginning with the magnificent feat of capturing the key strong points of Monte Majo they "followed through" with amazing rapidity over rugged terrain in which the speed of foot of the African natives and their cavalry were prominent factors. In difficult country with bad lateral communication the Germans do not seem to have been able to exploit their usual counter-attacking defence tactics.

Their "follow through" carried the French at Ausonia across the main lateral communication of this part of the Gustav position, thus interfering with the movements of German reserves. Maintaining the momentum of the attack northwards they not only penetrated right through the Gustav position but well into the forward defences of the Adolf Hitler line. The breach thus made must undoubtedly have helped the 8th Army to advance from the bridge-head they had established across the Rapido, forcing the Germans to withdraw from Cassino, which had been by-passed. British and Polish troops mopped up the rearguard detachments. No one grudged the Poles the honour of seizing Monastery Hill, and everyone rejoiced that the French had given such proof of revival of their famous fighting qualities.

The Gustav line was captured in under a week and the momentum of the offensive was so admirably maintained that the Germans were unable to rally on the Hitler position except in its very strong northern sector covering Highway 6. This Kesselring attempted to use as the pivot of a new defensive position, until the break-through from the Anzio beach-head convinced him that he must retreat if he was to have any hope of escaping complete disaster. He still fought desperately in the Liri valley to check the advance of the 8th Army while he regrouped his armies, but he could not stop the attack by the Canadians, nor could he prevent the Anzio thrust penetrating to Valmontone, where it brought Highway 6 under artillery fire.

THE only way of escape for Kesselring's 10th Army then lay by the circuitous mountain roads from the Liri valley to the Rome-Pescara trans-Apennine highway. He could no longer hope to defend Rome, but in order to cover his lines of retreat which converged on Rome he used his 14th Army, reinforced by three divisions from north Italy, to hold the Alban hills. While that position held, the 10th Army, covering its retreat by desperate rearguard actions, by mines and demolitions, could still escape through Rome and avoid being separated completely from the 14th Army. It must have heavy losses during its retreat and will be exposed to air attack on mountain roads.

The unopposed capture of Rome was a great political success brought about by military victory, and it resulted primarily from Alexander's concentration on the defeat of the enemy's armies. Left with no alternative but rapid retreat, Kesselring refused to entangle himself in the streets of Rome. That being so, he would not only have exposed himself to the execration of civilized peoples, but would have further reduced his chance of saving the remnants of his armies. He has paid a heavy penalty for the strategic mistake of committing himself to a decisive battle south of Rome.

After Four Long Years D-Day Dawns at Last

ON THE EVE OF INVASION hundreds of England's by-roads became busy assembly points for the gathering hosts of liberation (above). Stretching along a tree-lined country lane is further evidence of Allied determination in this vast arsenal of shells (below), piled under cover, ready for the guns. General Eisenhower, Supreme Allied Commander of the British and U.S. Expeditionary Forces, talks to Canadian soldiers before operations begin (left). *Photos, Canadian Official, Planet News*

"AN IMMENSE ARMADA of more than 4,000 ships and several thousand smaller craft have crossed the Channel . . ." These were the words of Mr. Churchill announcing the commencement of the long-awaited invasion in the West on June 6, 1944. The great assault took place between the hours of 6 a.m. and 8.15 a.m. on that morning, and at 9.30 a.m. Communiqué No. 1 from General Eisenhower's Supreme Headquarters announced that landings had been made on the north coast of France, and that General Montgomery was in command of the 21st Army Group (which included British, Canadian and U.S. forces) carrying out the attack.

Mr. Churchill said the landings were the first of a series in force on the European continent, and that 11,000 first-line aircraft were backing operations. He revealed that our forces had penetrated enemy defences inland to a distance of several miles, and that successful landings of airborne troops "on a scale far larger than anything that had been seen so far in the world" took place with little loss and great accuracy. Fighting was in progress around Caen in Normandy, which is nine miles inland and has an airfield : situated on the River Orne, it is the most important road junction in the south-eastern part of the Cherbourg Peninsula and is 130 miles from Paris.

Allied Invaders Storm Germany's 'Atlantic Wall'

FOUR YEARS TO THE MONTH after the B.E.F.'s fighting withdrawal from France, the forces of liberation have returned to that country, magnificently equipped for whatever battles lie ahead, firm in the resolve to lift the Nazi yoke and to crush the aggressors for all time. Confronted now with the immediate prospect of war on four fronts, in Italy, in the Balkans, in Western Europe, and in Russia, the Germans may well hear the knell of doom.

On June 6, 1944, Supreme Headquarters, Allied Expeditionary Forces, stated that opposition from the enemy coastal defences was not so serious as had been expected, a fact which gives the lie to the German boast of the impregnability of their "Atlantic Wall," which at one time they claimed would hold back any assault, no matter how massive. Air preparation before the landings was described as "a magnificent job." On the night before the invasion force went in, between midnight and dawn more than 5,000 tons of bombs were rained down on ten enemy coastal batteries in the greatest single bombing attack yet recorded. This terrific bombing was supported by 640 naval guns, ranging from 4-in. to 16-in. The bulk of the naval forces engaged were British and American, but ships of the Royal Canadian Navy, and the French, Norwegian, Dutch, Polish and Greek Navies also co-operated.

ENSURING FOOD SUPPLIES for our fighting men about to embark on the liberation of Europe, one of many field-kitchens goes aboard a landing ship (top). The landing craft set out on the great assault guarded by the Royal Navy, the guns of one of whose ships are seen in the foreground (centre). Allied Naval C.-in-C., Admiral Sir Bertram Ramsay, watches the armada sail (centre right). Part of the greatest sea force the world has ever seen waits for the signal to go (bottom). At least 100 invasion vessels can be counted in this photographed section alone. *Photos, British and U.S. Official; Keystone*

THE WAR AT SEA

by Francis E. McMurtrie

THERE is no doubt the complete success of the Allied landings in Normandy on June 6, 1944, was due to thorough preparation and the use of overwhelming force. Lack of these two essentials had much to do with the very different results which attended the Gallipoli landings in 1915.

Our foes, on the other hand, tried to be strong everywhere, and thus failed miserably at the point where the attack was delivered. Their only hope of repelling the Allies was either to interrupt the expedition by sea, which they were not strong enough to do, or to beat back the troops as they attempted to land. It may now be asked, is there anything they can do by naval means to interfere with the steady progress of the invasion ?

It is indeed beyond doubt that the German fleet must be acutely feeling the man-power shortage. U-boat casualties in the past eighteen months must have been appalling. For the whole of this time, drafts have had to be made on the complements of surface warships to make up fresh crews for new submarines. Nor have other naval losses been light. Two thousand officers and men went with the Bismarck, and some 1,500 more in the Scharnhorst. Destroyers, minesweepers, motor-torpedo-boats and other small craft are being sunk with increasing frequency, adding considerably to the toll. It is improbable that there is any considerable reserve of skilled naval ratings remaining.

It may be assumed that any enemy action at

tion mines, which are controlled from the shore and exploded electrically when a ship is seen to be in the field, may either be avoided or set off prematurely by counter-mining. All these dangers and difficulties were foreseen and provided for in the plans made for the Allied attack, no fewer than 200 minesweepers being included in the invasion fleet. Other ships that have been mentioned officially include the British battleships Nelson, Rodney, Warspite and Ramillies, and the U.S. battleships Nevada, Texas and Arkansas, and smaller vessels.

One of the biggest difficulties under which our foes are labouring in Europe today is that of maintaining supplies, especially in the more distant countries which they still occupy. This has been well illustrated of late by the series of raids which the Fleet Air Arm has been carrying out on convoys proceeding up and down the Norwegian coast. Most of this traffic goes through the "leads," the channels between the mainland and the fringe of islands which extends for the greater part of the distance from the North Cape to Stavanger. For a long time past these convoys had been suffering from intermittent attack by our submarines, as well as from bombing by Coastal Command and Bomber Command aircraft in the south.

Now that aircraft carriers are available in greater numbers, with longer-range fighters to protect the bombers, the Fleet Air Arm is coming more and more into the picture. In the past two months there have been six such attacks, including the one on the Tirpitz on April 3, 1944. These have taken a steady toll of merchant vessels, besides damaging escort vessels, so that there is a shortage of both. Escort vessels in Norwegian waters consist mostly of trawlers, minesweepers and miscellaneous auxiliaries. Not only are the losses in ships and cargoes hard to replace, but the enforcement of longer intervals between convoys in itself leads to shortage of supplies.

U.S. BATTLESHIP, ALABAMA, 35,000 tons, is seen here at anchor somewhere off an Allied base of operations. She is armed with nine 16-in. guns (in turrets of three), twenty 5-in. dual purpose, and sixteen 1·1-in. guns, as well as fifty 40-mm. and machine-guns. She is also equipped to carry and launch fighter aircraft by catapult. Her normal complement is 2,000 men. Belonging to the Washington class, she has five sister ships.
Photo, Keystone

Before the landing hints were thrown out that the heavier ships of the German Navy were being kept in reserve for such an emergency ; but this could hardly have applied to a landing in France, though it might just possibly refer to one in Denmark, about which the enemy, as described in my last article (see No. 182, page 38), were extremely apprehensive. This becomes clear if the question is asked, where are the principal surface ships of the German Navy ? Of its four battleships, the Bismarck and Scharnhorst are at the bottom of the sea, and the Tirpitz and Gneisenau are crippled, and could hardly have been made seaworthy in time to play any useful part in such operations. This leaves only ten ships of any importance, apart from the incomplete aircraft carriers Graf Zeppelin and Peter Strasser, the construction of which has evidently been abandoned. These ten are the pocket battleships Admiral Scheer and Lützow ; the heavy cruisers Prinz Eugen and Admiral Hipper ; the light cruisers Nürnberg, Leipzig, Köln and Emden ; and the ancient coast defence ships Schlesien and Schleswig-Holstein. All are believed to be in Baltic ports, and their inactivity for many months past leads one to suspect that some, if not all, of them have been laid up, probably for lack of trained crews.

sea against the Allied invasion will now come from submarines. This was the experience in North Africa, but it did not in any way affect the issue. Since Allied naval forces are ready for such attacks, the slaughter of submarines is likely to be great.

A WEAPON capable of being used at night is the motor-torpedo-boat, or *schnellboot*, as the Germans call it. Commonly but incorrectly referred to in this country as the E-boat, this type of vessel depends for any success it may achieve on speed and stealth. In daylight it has no chance, being at the mercy of aircraft or destroyers ; but at night it is impossible always to guard against it. Several of these enemy craft have been destroyed near the landing beaches.

Much the most dangerous obstacle which our invading forces encountered was the minefield. This may consist of either magnetic, acoustic, contact or observation mines. Various methods of defence against the magnetic and acoustic types, or combinations of these, have been perfected, of which the best-known is the de-gaussing girdle encircling a ship. Contact mines can be dealt with by sweeping, or deflected by the paravane, special mine defence gear which is streamed from the bow of a ship. Observa-

Conditions which the British naval personnel engaged in these raids have to face are severe. To carry out attacks through blinding snowstorms, with the prospect of dying of cold very quickly if shot down in icy water, calls for skill and courage of a high order. Flying off and landing on the decks of aircraft carriers, from which two feet of snow may first have to be cleared, is no job for a novice. Men who work on the slippery decks in the teeth of icy wind and snow deserve equal credit for the success of these expeditions.

TYPES of aircraft used in the Norwegian operations include the Barracuda, Corsair, Hellcat and Wildcat. The first-named can either dive-bomb or release torpedoes, as circumstances may dictate. The other three types (all American designs) can be used as fighter-bombers when necessary, and the effectiveness with which they meet any attempt by the Luftwaffe to interfere is most notable. On various occasions they have shot down Focke-Wulf and Messerschmitt machines. Ships from which these raids have been launched include the modern fleet aircraft carrier Victorious and her more antiquated consort, the Furious, together with the smaller American-built escort carriers Emperor, Fencer, Pursuer, Searcher and Striker.

Royal Navy Drops Shells on the Appian Way

AID FROM THE SEA to our land offensive in Italy was given by the 5,450-ton cruiser H.M.S. Dido, which, escorted by U.S. destroyers, on May 13, 1944, shelled the Appian Way (Highway 7, leading to Rome) in the Terracina area and also heavy enemy artillery opposing the 5th Army in the Gaeta sector. One of the destroyers (above) lays a smoke screen to cover the movements of the Dido, from whose bridge (below) the bombardment is directed by the Gunnery Officer (seated centre). Rear Adm. J. M. Mansfield is seen on right, in white tunic and steel helmet. PAGE 71 *Photos, British Official*

MOVING UP INTO BATTLE over the Cassino plain, massive Sherman tanks roll on to help smash the Germans at San Angelo, important village south of Cassino in the Gustav Line area. This photograph was taken during the early stages of the concerted Allied attack on the Gustav Line which commenced on May 11, 1944. Initially, in the Cassino plain push tanks took a primary part, advancing by day while the infantry moved up at night to consolidate. Against fanatical enemy resistance the Allied tanks and British and Indian infantry of the 8th Army stormed their way through barbed wire entanglements and minefields under a rain of fire directed against them from fortified enemy positions on the mountainside above. The key point of San Angelo fell on May 13.

Photo, British Official

They Plucked a German General Out of Crete

In truly audacious manner one of the most successful enterprises of Combined Operations was carried out on the night of April 26, 1944, when Maj.-Gen. Kreipe, commander of the 22nd Panzer Division in Crete, was spirited away by a small British patrol from the Nazi-occupied Greek island and transported to Egypt, and later to Britain, as a very chagrined prisoner of war.

IT now may be in the mind of Karl Heinrich Georg Ferdinand Kreipe that he was born under an unlucky star. For the superstitiously minded, that suspicion would seem to have foundation in the fact that he was a thirteenth child—in a family of fifteen. Born at Niederspier, in Thuringia, in 1895, he commenced his career in the German army in 1914. And now, on this April night of 1944, he was about to have that military career terminated for him in as dramatic a fashion as could well be devised.

His last-war record in France had been not undistinguished; and for services rendered to the Fuehrer as a regimental commander at Leningrad he had received the Knight's Cross. He had fought also in the Kuban bridgehead, and at Mariupol. His crowning triumph was but five weeks old. For that length of time he had been commander of the 22nd Panzer Grenadier Division (known as the Sebastopol Division) in Crete, and now he was being driven home from his headquarters to his villa (stolen from the Cretans in May 1941) in a luxurious car. Just a few miles south of Heraklion that villa lay, and he was accustomed to do the journey without escort; for what manner of harm could befall him from these islanders ground firmly beneath the German heel?

Nevertheless, befall him it did. The first intimation came in the sudden twinkling through the dusk of a red light swinging slowly in the centre of the lonely road. Unsuspected by Major-General Heinrich Kreipe, behind that waving light stood British officers operating under the command of General Sir Bernard Paget, C.-in-C., Middle East. They had been landed by the Royal Navy on a lonely part of the coast and had painstakingly reconnoitred the scene of their present exploit so that it was as familiar to them as their own home towns. The commander of the small raiding force was a major, with a captain of the Coldstream Guards as his assistant; names, for the time being, must be suppressed.

At the behest of the red traffic light the car-driver pulled up, the door of the car was wrenched open, and the officer who had been holding the lamp made a brief but staggering statement to the effect that the general must consider himself a prisoner. The sight of automatic weapons convinced Kreipe that this was no joke.

SWIFTLY the driver was bundled out of his seat to the back of the car, a British officer took the wheel, turned the car, and—the two prisoners carefully "covered" by their captors—drove off back through Heraklion, passing through 22 control posts without challenge from the sentries, the two pennants of a divisional commander flying from the bonnet ensuring safe passage.

They had no time to waste. They had another rendezvous to keep with the Royal Navy, at a spot 30 miles beyond Heraklion. At that point on the coast, where a vessel was waiting for them, the car was abandoned and the party embarked: the British joyously, the two Germans numbed with bewilderment. The last act of the small raiding force before leaving the island was to deposit in the car a sealed letter addressed to the German authorities:

"Gentlemen,—Your divisional commander, Kreipe, was captured a short time ago by a British raiding force under our command. By the time you read this he and we will be on our way to Cairo. We would like to point out most emphatically that this operation has been carried out without the help of Cretans or Cretan Partisans, and the only guides used were serving soldiers of His Hellenic Majesty's forces in the Middle East.

"Your general is an honourable prisoner of war, and will be treated with all the consideration due to his rank. Any reprisals against the local population will be wholly unwarranted and unjust. Auf Baldiges Wiedersehen (I see you soon).—Signed, Major, Commanding Raiding Forces, and Capt., Coldstream Guards. P.S.—We are very sorry to leave this motor-car behind."

TOUGH GREEK GUERILLA FIGHTERS in Crete wage ceaseless war against the despoilers of their country, swooping down from mountain hide-outs in fierce sorties which keep the enemy constantly on the jump. The German authorities strongly suspected them of complicity in the kidnapping of the commander of the island's military garrison, as related here. *Photo, Greek Official*

And the general's reactions? When he had recovered somewhat from his astonishment he ventured, "This puts me in a very difficult position. I have lost my job and have no responsibilities left. This is going to be a great strain for me. I don't know how I'll employ my time."

Meanwhile, discovery of the abandoned car had set the Germans a first-class problem. The letter did nothing to enlighten them as to the tactics employed to bring about this almost incredible coup. It did not seem possible that the kidnapping could have been conducted without local help or that the general could have been taken far—in spite of the assertion in the letter.

THE Cretan guerillas were strongly suspect. After the seizure of the island by the Nazis in the spring of 1941 the invaders found themselves continually harassed by these intrepid fighters. From end to end of the island the guerillas ranged, taking nightly toll of the enemy's posts and destroying communications. Harsh repressive measures were adopted against them, by strong forces sent for that purpose in 1942; but the spirit of the guerilla bands remained unbroken.

Was this present "outrage" to be credited to them? The afternoon after the abduction leaflets showered down upon Crete's hillsides and coast, informing all whom it might concern that bandits had captured the general, that his whereabouts must be known to the population, and that unless he were handed back to the authorities within three days all the local villages of Heraklion province would be razed to the ground. So far as is at present known, the threat has not been carried out. And still the Germans are wondering as to the precise purpose behind this abduction of one of their generals.

GENERAL HEINRICH KREIPE, until recently Nazi Commander in Crete (right), photographed on his arrival in Cairo as a prisoner of war. The astonishing story of his surprise capture on the island by a small British raiding force is given in this page. It was announced on May 25 that the captive general had arrived in Britain by air. PAGE 73 *Photo, British Official*

Workers Step-up Production on Soviet Farms

BACKING RUSSIA in her mighty war effort, Soviet collective farmers are striving valiantly to increase production. Notable contributors are the Soviet Central Asian republics, principal of which is Uzbekistan; it supplies more than 50 per cent of the Soviet Union's raw cotton and is the main source of rice supply. Women, old men and children work on the Uzbekistan collective farms. A nurse of a workers' crêche takes care of baby for mother (1). Sturdy schoolgirls help to remove soil from newly dug irrigation ditches (2). Local ancients have patriotically formed themselves into a special Old Ploughmen's Brigade (3). Expert milkmaid evacuated from the Ukraine, Martha Ivanova (4) is instructor in an Uzbek village. At the dinner-time break, women field workers listen to the latest war news read by their leader (5).

Exclusive to THE WAR ILLUSTRATED

Britain's Colonies in the War: No. 10---Cyprus

STRATEGIC STRONG-POINT in the Eastern Mediterranean, Cyprus, which proved a deterrent bastion against further German progress in the area during the critical days of the African campaign, has been a British colony since 1925. The island, 3,572 square miles in extent, is chiefly an agricultural producer, sending fruit and vegetables to help feed our Middle East armies and also to Britain. Among other war materials produced are quantities of asbestos and chrome.

Contribution of a high order in the active war theatres has been made by the Cyprus Regiment (comprising transport and pioneer companies) which has served in Greece, Crete, Egypt, Libya and Abyssinia ; it was the first colonial regiment to contact the enemy in France.

Unloading stores on the quayside at Famagusta, the island's chief port (3). British gunners of the A.A. defences receive instruction in the use of field radio transmission sets designed to increase their already high efficiency as marksmen (1), while another " class " of men handle a light Bofors gun, watched by General Sir Bernard C. T. Paget, K.C.B., D.S.O., M.C., C.-in-C. Middle East Forces (2, carrying cane), during a tour of inspection. On the ancient ramparts of Famagusta, men of a naval signals post keep watch (4). *Photos, British Official*

New Guinea Shipyard Speeds Pacific Offensive

IN A CLEARING IN DENSE JUNGLE on the New Guinea coast, U.S. Army engineers have set up a miniature shipyard for the quick assembly of newly-arrived L.C.M.s (Landing Craft, Motors) which are delivered there in crated sections. These are moved into position at the yard (1), a motor is unpacked (2), and a bow section is swung into place (3). The completed L.C.M.s will play their part in Allied operations aimed at driving the last Japanese out of the last acre of captured territory in the Pacific.

PAGE 76

Photos, Planet News

Here the Allies Prepare for a Last Round-up

FURTHER SPECTACULAR BLOW TO THE JAPANESE in the Pacific was achieved by the great Allied landing at Hollandia, Dutch New Guinea, on April 22, 1944, which has since proved a lever for the splitting-up and reduction to scattered groups of enemy strength in that area and in British New Guinea, at Madang, where an Australian force is advancing along the coast.

Since the Hollandia fighting further progressive steps have been made in the landing on Wakde Island and the mainland coast opposite, 125 miles west of Hollandia, on May 19 ; and on Biak Island in the Schoutens group, 200 miles west of Wakde, on May 27. Control of Biak Island with its three airstrips commanding the western tip of New Guinea may give the final impetus needed for the successful conclusion of the Solomons, Bismarck Archipelago and New Guinea campaign.

BY DUG-OUT CANOE Australians cross a jungle river (1). Taking advantage of a pause in the pursuit of the enemy, a group of Allied soldiers (including Australians, Dutch and Americans) have a yarn and a smoke (2). " Corduroy " roads made from coconut tree logs provide the only possible path for transport over swamp land (3). An Australian examines Dutch New Guinea paper money, part of his Army pay (4). Natives receive treatment from an R.A.A.F. doctor (5).

Photos, Australian Government   PAGE 77

Background of the Fleet Air Arm's Success

Acting extremely important roles behind the scenes in dramatic performances of our naval aircraft are indefatigable research workers, tireless experimenters, daring test pilots, skilled mechanics who repair damaged planes. Varied activities of these "silent men" who help to keep the Fleet Air Arm flying and always up to scratch are dealt with here by JOHN ALLEN GRAYDON.

SINCE they received new types of aircraft the Fleet Air Arm have daily become more prominent, their daring exploits paving the way for more than one Royal Navy victory. It is generally recognized that aircrews of the Fleet Air Arm are among the best trained and most efficient in the world, yet behind these flying-sailors is a band of silent men with one main task: to keep the F.A.A. flying, and make sure that their "wings" are kept in tip-top condition.

One of the best known of these "silent men" is Vice-Admiral Bell Davies, V.C., who commands the Royal Navy's test aircraft carrier, H.M.S. Pretoria Castle. This vessel, used for a short time as a luxury liner before the war, on the South African route, operated as an armed merchant-cruiser in the South Pacific late in 1939 and early in 1940. Then it was decided to make her a test aircraft carrier. Her superstructure was removed, the builders commenced work, and the Pretoria Castle took her present shape.

ABOARD this special vessel Vice-Admiral Bell Davies, in the course of a single day, must watch some of the most amazing landings in the world. Great experiments have taken place aboard her; experiments that have played a part in the advance of the Fleet Air Arm, and added hitting power to the machines they fly into battle.

Before any new type of plane takes its place in the Fleet Air Arm's armoury it is tested aboard the Pretoria Castle, whose Commander of Flying is that distinguished young officer, Commander Peter Bramwell, D.S.O., D.S.C., considered by many to be one of the greatest naval aviators in the world. The Commander, who has over 2,000 flying hours to his credit, has tested everything from Mae West lifebelts to aircraft due to be sent into action. He has also operated from the Ark Royal, fought in the skies over the beaches of Dunkirk, and was the first to land a Spitfire on the deck of an aircraft carrier.

When it was realized that the Fleet Air Arm would have to have an improved fighter to defend convoys, experts thought it im-

VICE-ADMIRAL R. B. DAVIES, V.C., C.B., D.S.O., A.F.C., R.N., one of the most senior pilots in the Fleet Air Arm. Formerly Rear-Admiral Commanding Naval Air Stations, he retired in 1941, went to sea again as a Convoy Commodore, and now commands H.M.S. Pretoria Castle. *Photo, British Official*

possible because of landing speed. But Commander Peter Bramwell had other ideas. For two weeks he practised landing on the tarmac of a Fleet Air Arm service station. Then he landed on the dummy deck laid out on the station. Then, his great moment, he brought the "Spit" down safely aboard the test carrier.

THERE are many other men upon the Pretoria Castle who have a love for naval aviation, and are willing to risk their lives so

that our high standards can always be improved upon. H.M.S. Pretoria Castle, test carrier, may not have the glamour of the late Ark Royal, but because of the skill of those who work aboard her Britain's floating aerodromes are now among the finest in the world.

Another strange ship that plays an important part in the activities of the Fleet Air Arm is H.M.S. Merlin. A rating aboard this craft once said to me: "I'd rather serve on her than most ships, for it'd take a big torpedo to reach you up there." You see, the Merlin is a large Fleet Air Arm airfield in the north, where they have some of the finest workshops of their kind in the world. About 1,500 civilian workers are employed there, 400 of them women.

CAPTAIN R. D. Nicholson, in command of the Merlin, has under him a staff which can deal with every type of aircraft used by the Fleet. Planes that have been damaged in action, crashed, or are due for overhaul come in regularly. Rare is it that the workers aboard have a minute to spare, owing to the increased tempo of the war at

COMMANDER P. BRAMWELL, D.S.O., D.S.C., R.N., under whom the experienced teams of Fleet Air Arm pilots and observers of H.M.S. Pretoria Castle carry out tasks on which much of our air striking power at sea depends. He was the first man to land a Spitfire on an aircraft carrier's deck. *Photo, British Official*

sea. The aim of all these workers, who are made to feel that they are part of the Royal Navy, is to put into the air the perfect aeroplane. And they do!

NEARLY every Fleet Air Arm machine, whether or not it is damaged, goes to H.M.S. Merlin after it has flown 240 hours to undergo a major inspection. This means, for the most part, that the plane is taken to pieces, each bit is carefully examined, and then the aircraft is rebuilt. Before the planes are sent back for active service they are handed over to a band of first-class test pilots —now serving as officers in the Fleet Air Arm —who put them through their paces and make sure they are perfect. In fact, efficiency and perfection are the two words that stand out for everyone to see in H.M.S. Merlin.

ONCE A LUXURY LINER, H.M.S. Pretoria Castle now has a big war job to do as an experimental aircraft carrier from whose decks aircraft and all the many adjuncts to flying at sea are given exacting tests. On board the Pretoria Castle representatives of British and American aircraft industries can watch their products under test; manufacturers and aircrews can then pool improvement suggestions on the spot. PAGE 78 *Photo, British Official*

San Giorgio's Bell May Yet Ring for Victory

In a battered street of San Giorgio in the Liri Valley, south of Cassino, where despite the ruin of the church the bell still hangs in the tower, American and French tanks and armoured cars assemble prior to attacking the next objective. San Giorgio had been successfully stormed by French troops of the 5th Army on May 15, 1944. By May 26 the entire original German defence line across Italy was shattered and the enemy was withdrawing to the north and west.

From Strong Defences German Hordes are Hurled—

Photos,
Co.

Scrap-iron for battlefield salvage collectors is this knocked-out German tank (1) in the Ausente Valley, north of Cassino ;
2½ miles south of that shattered town, in San Angelo, the crew of a 6-pounder anti-tank gun (2) hold themselves in readiness.
Beyond San Angelo, taken by Indian troops of the 8th Army on May 13, 1944, after bitter fighting in caves and cellars,
men of a Priest self-propelled gun snatch brief rest after a heavy night barrage (3).

—As 8th Army Smashes Through the Gustav Line

Waiting for glimpse of enemy movement is this British sniper (4) in the ruins of San Angelo. Beyond lies Pignaturo, on a steep rocky crag honeycombed with caves, hammered for months by our long-range artillery, and stormed by Indian troops on May 16, 1944 ; this (5) was the town's main thoroughfare. Entrenched in a lane-side (6) during fighting which led to the capture of San Angelo and Pignaturo. The Hitler Line, beyond, was pierced on May 23.

Our French Allies Score Notable Victories

In the early stages of the breaking of the Gustav Line, French troops of the 5th Army, operating in a mountainous sector south of the Liri Valley, seized the dominating height of Mt. Majo, then captured San Ambrogio and Ausonia. French gunners armed with shovels (top) pass a crippled German Mark III tank as they move on to choose and prepare a new gun site. Their guns and stores pass through the village of Castelforte, which was occupied by U.S. tanks of the 5th Army on May 13.

VIEWS & REVIEWS

Of Vital War Books

···

by Hamilton Fyfe

DAVID GARRICK was watching Kitty Clive on the stage. He followed her movements with admiring eye. He listened to her voice, entranced by its variety and charm. At last he turned round to someone who sat with him in the stage box. "Dammit," he burst out, "she could act a gridiron!"

I feel much the same kind of envious delight in Captain Liddell Hart's new book. It is about war. It is called Thoughts on War (Faber, 15/-). Most people's thoughts on that topic would be jejune and depressing. This book is alive on every page, tingling with vigour, suggesting trains of reflection which lead one far from the battlefield; offering comments on life, as well as instruction for dealing out death most effectively, which make it, open where you will, a philosophical, historical, topical volume of value to every intelligent man, woman, and I had almost added "child."

For its simplicity is one of its chief virtues. There is no attempt at fine writing. No wrapping-up of ordinary statements in technical language in order to make them appear profound. Liddell Hart is an artist in words. His Yea is Yea and his Nay, Nay. He never leaves you in doubt as to his meaning. He never fears, for example, to show up the weakness of the military imagination, the dullness of the military mind.

As to Tanks, he is painfully frank. He quotes without comment (none is required!) the War Office docket on a design sent in before 1914: "The man's mad." He notes Kitchener's opinion of the Tank when he first saw one: "A pretty mechanical toy, but such machines would never win a war." The head of the Royal Engineers, who are supposed to be brainier than other branches of the Army, said, when shown the early designs, that they were in "the realms of imagination, not of solid fact."

Similar blindness marked the attitude of even the more thoughtful among leading soldiers to the possibilities of the air. When Foch watched the 1910 Circuit of the East in France, which proved the reliability of the new invention, he exclaimed: "That is good sport, but for the Army the aeroplane is no use."

Liddell Hart liked soldiering. He was sorry to be invalided out of the Army. But he has come to see more and more that officers "seal up parts of their mind."

The Army for all its good points is a cramping place for a thinking man. As I have seen too often, such a man chafes and goes—or else decays. And the root of the trouble is the Army's rooted fear of the truth. Romantic fiction is the soldierly taste. The heads of the Army talk much of developing character yet deaden it—frowning on the younger men who show promise of the personality necessary for command, and the originality necessary for surprise . . . There are few commanders in our higher command.

Most of them are "desperately conventional" and in war "recklessly cautious." I knew many staff officers and made acquaintance with a good few of our generals during the 1914 war. I know how right Liddell Hart is. With a few exceptions such as "Tim" Harrington and Thomson, who became Air Minister for a short while, they were none of them "educated truly for a higher role than that of brigade or divisional commanders, where the need for scientific calculation and imagination is preponderant over that for fighting qualities." How Montgomery, who is unconventional in so many ways, attained the front rank I cannot guess. Both in our Army and the American there is a strong preference for "regular guys"—that is, men who live by rule, do what they are told and ask no questions, respect tradition, worship the God of Things as They Are.

So far as I can judge this is not so in the Red Army. It is nearly ten years since I was in Russia, and it is hard to know what to believe if you aren't on the spot to check

---

Can We Get Rid of War?

---

statements made in books and papers by personal observation. But there does seem in the Russian Army to be a preference for "irregular guys." It is often asked, "Why have the Russians done so much better against the Germans this time than they did last time?" The reason appears to me to be simple. The Tsar's officers were a social caste, like ours used to be—and in some degree still are. If you doubt this, look at a number of soldiers in any train or bus or on any railway station, and see if you have any difficulty in separating officers from privates. You probably won't have!

In the new Russian army there is almost no difference. I have seen generals sitting in theatres next to privates. I remember noticing on a Kiev railway platform the last time I was in that fascinating city a colonel with a fine bushy beard seeing somebody off. In the carriage with the somebody were some soldiers. He chatted to them in a friendly way. He would have been horrified by the admission which a Guardee officer made to Liddell Hart that "Guards discipline is frankly based on fear." That can be justified only by regarding the "other ranks" as lower animals. "Not a pleasant attitude, and historically unsound."

Now that all our officers must pass through the ranks before being given commissions the notion "gentlemen must lead" will be forgotten. We shall be able to draw on a vastly larger pool for our military leaders —not limit ourselves to a small number drawn from the upper and middle classes, but pick out brains and initiative from pretty well the entire youth of the country.

I say "we shall be able to do this." I cannot assert that we shall do it. The Civil Service has not perceptibly altered since it was thrown open to competition, in which boys who started from elementary schools gained many of the top places. Sir James Grigg was one; he has not made any changes in War Office methods, either as permanent secretary or as Parliamentary chief.

Liddell Hart is not sanguine about this being the last war. Indeed, he assumes all through that there will be other wars. He does not throw his *Thoughts* into the form of a treatise or an argument or even a survey. He just selects them from his writings between 1919 and 1939, groups them under certain headings, and prints them piecemeal. This makes the book unusually interesting as a browsing ground for minds in search of nutrition, and also makes it easy to read.

It has this advantage too. He can return again and again to a subject at intervals, without any danger of wearying the reader by a long-drawn-out disquisition. Thus he hovers frequently round the query, Can we get rid of war? Yet he does not sum up all the pros and cons so as to strike a balance. He leaves us to do that for ourselves.

ON the dispute whether war can be made to pay, he is inclined to take the side of Sir Norman Angell, who wrote The Great Illusion 35 years ago, to show that it could not. But he "still has a doubt whether war could not be made to pay—by a new Bismarck who had both the power and the calculating intelligence to control and to stop it at the point where extra expenditure promised no adequate return." Hitler fancied he could play this part. He offered to end the war after he had overrun Poland in the autumn of 1939. Bismarck would not have been so silly as to think he could do that. "No acquisitive State is likely," the book says, "to embark on war unless it has reason to believe that it will gain an adequate result for its efforts." Bismarck had good reason to believe in 1870 that he could defeat the French and, as one result, create the German Empire. Hitler believed he could by a succession of rapid blows knock out both France and Britain. He was right about France, but ludicrously wrong about Britain. His most astounding miscalculation was his notion that he could annihilate the Russian armies in a few weeks. "A man who is partly blind is not likely to see clearly in any direction," says Liddell Hart. He is speaking of dictators, blinded by ambition and conceit. Some who call themselves democrats have their eyes weakened also.

OFFICERS AND MEN OF THE RED ARMY AND NAVY know how to relax as well as fight : during a lull a navy man entertains comrades of all ranks with a traditional dance. Soviet Forces discipline is strong, but the genuine comradeship referred to in this page prevails above all else.   **PAGE 83**   *Photo, Planet News*

How 5th Army Linked up with Anzio Beach-head

DRAMATIC MEETING of troops from the main 5th Army in Italy with patrols from the Anzio beach-head took place at 7.30 a.m. on May 25, 1944—an outstanding event in the campaign's history. General Mark Clark, Commander of the 5th Army (centre), is seen at the meeting place surrounded by cheering British and U.S. soldiers (1). A British beach-head sergeant greets his U.S. opposite number from the main 5th Army forces (2). First British armoured car to arrive at the spot was "overwhelmed" by our triumphant troops (3). On the road near the meeting-place soldiers exchange stories and cigarettes after the link-up (4).

Photos, British Official and British Newsreels

Allied Units Blast Japanese on the Burma Fronts

MONSOON WEATHER, prevailing between June and September, precludes until the end of the latter month possibility of startling developments in the Burma campaign, which has see-sawed backwards and forwards for many weeks over a large area, with the Allies making, on the whole, slow but sure gains against the Japanese invaders. Having secured a foothold on Indian territory in the Manipur State, near Imphal (the main Allied base), the enemy dug in against pressure from General Slim's 14th Army. Other Allied units operating inside Burma had made good progress. It was announced on June 6, 1944, that in North Burma Americans, Chinese and Chindits and levies commanded by General Stilwell were closing their grip on the three main Japanese bases—at Myitkyina, at Mogaung and at Kamaing, a triangle in which the enemy is fighting a losing battle.

While no great Allied advance is to be expected until the monsoon months are ended, it is believed that by then the South-East Asia Command will be fully prepared to strike directly and heavily at the centres of Japanese occupation in Burma.

DURING SEVERE FIGHTING in the Imphal area, men of a West Country regiment swept the Japanese from " Nippon Peak," a hill of strategic importance overlooking the Tamu supply road used by our forces. After the battle, enemy dead were cremated on the slopes of the hill (1). With the Japanese only a few hundred yards away in the jungle, Gurkhas cut bamboo stakes with their kukris to form a protective barrier for their newly won position (2). Camouflaged from air observation is this British gun emplacement from which Japanese positions in the Imphal plain were blasted (3). Men of the 13th Frontier Force Rifles, some concealed in fox-holes from which they had ejected their opponents, cover infantrymen engaged in the unpleasant but necessary task of collecting enemy dead who fell during the Nippon Peak action (4).

Photos, Indian Official

This Is how We Mobilized for Total War

Those who toil in "civvies" or dungarees have seldom been exposed to the searchlight of publicity. Not that they do not deserve it. That is made abundantly clear in Manpower: The Story of Britain's Mobilization for War (prepared for the Ministry of Labour by the Ministry of Information and published by H.M.S.O. at 9d.), reviewed below by E. ROYSTON PIKE.

As a people we are not given to the revolutions of barricades and bloodshed. The only revolution that is mentioned in most English history-books was a very quiet and gentlemanly affair, William taking the place of James with hardly a ruffle on the surface of contemporary life. There have been other revolutions—not political, but social and economic, as when the medieval system of husbandry was converted into one in which sheep-farming was predominant, and that other and much more important, when the agricultural England of the 18th century became the urbanized and industrialized England that we have inherited. There is yet another revolution, the one we are living through at present. It may be said to have begun on May 22, 1940, when the Emergency Powers (Defence) Act passed through all its stages in both Houses of Parliament and received the Royal Assent.

It was quick work, such as must have surprised and confounded those who used to argue that parliament is old and creaking and cannot do its job. That it can move quickly, as speedily as any vauntedly - efficient dictatorship, was proved on that May afternoon. The circumstances admittedly were conducive to instant action. The French were already showing signs of collapse, Mr. Churchill had flown to Paris to stiffen their faltering resistance, the German hordes were pouring over the French plains and rivers, the grim spectre of invasion was already threatening us from across the Channel. The hour called for rapid decisions, for determined measures. The call was answered. "It is necessary," said Mr. Attlee, the Leader of the House, "that the Government should be given complete control over persons and property, not just some persons of some particular class of the community, but all persons, rich and poor, employer and workman, man or woman, and all property." With no opposition the Government's proposals were accepted : on the very same afternoon a regulation was issued under the Act empowering the Minister of Labour and National Service "to direct any person in the United Kingdom to perform such services in the United Kingdom as might be specified in the direction."

Such vast powers over life (and property) had never before been entrusted to any British Government, to any Minister of the Crown. One unacquainted with our thoughts and ways might be forgiven for assuming that on May 22, 1940 we became a totalitarian country, since in law everybody and anybody were henceforth liable to be "directed" to any job that Mr. Bevin or his officers might think fit. But Hitler bludgeoned his way to power ; in Britain, power over our lives and property was freely given for the time being to the Government so that victory might be won, and that most speedily and surely.

Our liberties are not lost, but merely in abeyance ; and even though there have been complaints of individual cases of hardship and misdirection, the Minister's most bitter critic could not in truth accuse him of flouting the wishes of organized labour, of neglecting to secure the co-operation of the employers, of acting undemocratically in the interest of a class or faction, or of showing a lack of understanding and sympathy for the human factor. A great and possibly thankless task was thrust upon Mr. Bevin's broad shoulders ; and perhaps the greatest tribute that can be paid to him is that it is difficult to suggest any other figure in the world of industry, whether on the masters' side or on the men's, who would or could have made of the business a better job.

Immediately the powers were granted the mobilization of Britain's labour-power began. The result may be expressed in figures, though figures are bare and unrevealing things when taken by themselves. Out of

Mr. ERNEST BEVIN, Britain's Minister of Labour (centre), watches a group of girl trainees and their instructor at a work-bench in an L.C.C. Technical Institute where the girls are being taught war jobs. Similar institutes and technical training centres all over the country have turned out thousands of skilled workers. *Photo, Fox*

Britain's 33,100,000 persons between the ages of 14 and 64, nearly 23 millions are "gainfully employed," whether in the armed forces at home and abroad, in civil defence, in industries directly devoted to the satisfaction of war needs or in those industries and services which are deemed to be necessary for the carrying on of civilian existence. Of the 17,200,000 women included in the group nearly ten million are occupied in essential household duties, and many of these are in paid employment, full or part-time, while another million are rendering voluntary service.

Some seven million women are in industry or the Forces. There are nine million children to be looked after, usually by women. Furthermore, about a million men and women of 65 and over are engaged in paid employment. By the middle of 1943 there were 1,200,000 more men employed on making munitions than at the end of the last war ; and the proportion of women aged 14 to 59 in the Forces, munitions, and essential industries is about double the proportion of 1918. More than twice as many married women and widows are employed today as before the war. Indeed, 90 per cent of the single women of 18 to 40, and 80 per cent of the married women and widows without dependent children are in the Forces or industry. No other country, it may be said, has mobilized its womanhood on such a scale as Britain.

This mobilization of women was a new and particularly tricky business. Women who not long ago were shop assistants or domestic servants, waitresses or chorus girls, manicurists or hairdressers, housewives in cottage or mansion, are now working to produce aircraft and tanks, guns, bombs, and shells. They have stepped into the shoes of men who have gone to the war. They are doing jobs such as have never fallen to woman's lot in all the many hundred years of our history. Millions of women have been placed in war jobs that were not of their own choosing. A new distinction has been introduced, one between "mobile" and "immobile" women, the latter being those who because of their domestic responsibilities cannot be given jobs away from their own area. A very large proportion of women are in this category, most of them married women engaged in household duties, often with children under 14 ; and women whose husbands are at home, even when their domestic duties are not such as to prevent their taking a war job, are not asked to go to work beyond daily travelling distance.

But also included among the "immobiles" are the wives of men serving in the Forces and the Mercantile Marine. Some of these may have no children, domestic duties, or indeed little to keep them busy ; but they have not been sent to work in districts away from their homes because of their husbands' fear that their homes would be broken up in their absence. All the same, as everyone knows, the great majority of Servicemen's wives are at work. Many of them (let it be added) are at work when they would be better employed looking after their young children at home—but they have to go out to work to supplement their allowances.

If the mobilization of women has been the most remarkable, the most startling, of the changes brought about by the industrial mobilization, there are many others that will not escape the attention of the social and economic historian. Trade Unionism is now most definitely "on the map" : the trade union official has a recognized part to play in the nation's economic life. Casual labour at the docks and in such industries as building has been practically abolished.

Wage rates have increased pretty generally, and actual wages earned show a great advance over pre-war. Working conditions have been vastly improved (though much remains to be bettered). Millions of meals are served every day in works' canteens; and "music while you work" has become a recognized institution. The welfare officer is now to be found in every large works, and many local authorities have established wartime nurseries for the reception of children of women engaged in full- or part-time work. Hostels have been opened in all parts of the country, in which thousands of "mobile" women and girls have made a home from home.

These are just some aspects of the change that has come over Britain since that afternoon a little more than four years ago. Some of them we may regret, but taken all in all, the story of how Britain mobilized her men and women in the Second Great War is one of which we may well be proud.

Welfare of Our Wartime Working Millions

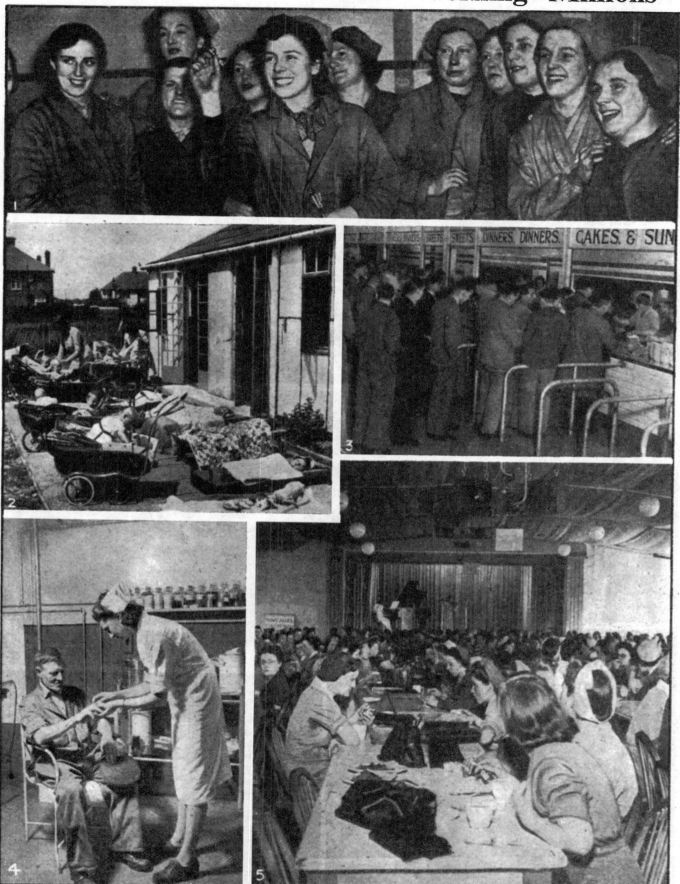

IN BRITAIN'S WAR-GEARED FACTORIES everything possible is done to ensure for the workers conditions as nearly ideal as can be contrived. Relaxation is of first importance, and here munitions girls in free moments enjoy a game of darts.] (1). Nurseries care for working mothers' babies (2). Modern kitchens provide good, cheap food (3) and concerts are arranged for workers at meal-times (5). Well-equipped medical clinics are always ready to deal swiftly and expertly with minor injuries (4). See also facing page.

Photos, British Official, Fox, Illustrated

At the End of the Great Battle for Cassino Hill

BARRIER TO OUR PROGRESS in Italy for long months, Cassino town and the monastery-fortress on the hill above it fell to the 8th Army on May 18, 1944. British troops captured the town, Poles took the hill and all that remained of the monastery (1). Its chapel altar had been piled high by the Germans with tinned food and boxes of ammunition (2); an Allied soldier examines a basket of shells in a mortar position in the courtyard (3), from which the enemy had fired on our troops; and on shelves more mortar shells were found (5), further proof of the manner in which the Nazis had turned a sacred edifice into a fortress and made its reduction by the Allies a necessity. Some Polish infantry, recovering from the last bitter fight, rest in the catacombs (4); a mine detector —one which helped to clear the path to victory—leans against the wall behind them. See story in facing page.

Photos, British Official: Crown Copyright

I WAS THERE!

Eye Witness Stories of the War

Things I Saw in Battle-Smashed Cassino Abbey

Dating his dispatch from Cassino, Italy, on May 19, 1944, John Redfern sent to the Daily Express this account of his visit to the remains of that historic building in the Gustav Line around and about which bitter battle for so long raged. See also facing page.

THE Abbey was sealed off today while Polish soldiers groped in the masses of fallen stone for delayed-action explosives, ammunition dumps, or paratroopers in hiding. The searchers have already discovered that the Germans put some prepared charges under the ruins, but they did not blow them when they left to surrender. Although the British and Polish flags flutter on the top of the highest remaining fragment of wall of the buildings, it is conceivable that there are still odd Germans in hiding under the tortured masonry.

This was shown last night when 40 paratroopers sneaked out of the cellars under the main part of the Abbey or the pill-boxes near it. They were fully armed. But the sentries were waiting for this kind of thing. They challenged the moving shadows. As soon as the Germans realized the Poles had seen them, they threw down their arms and surrendered. Odd Germans may still be hid away living on tinned food in the hope of a chance of getting out during the night.

They know that on the surface sentries cannot use lights because of enemy observers on Monte Cairo, which is three times higher than Abbey Hill. It is believed that underground ammunition stores may yet be discovered. One of the prisoners volunteered that at the surrender the Abbey garrison had enough ammunition for a month and supplies for 1,000 men. All this explains why from today onwards strict control is being applied to all "arrivals" at the Abbey. Officers who want to drop in for the purpose of telling a traveller's tale afterwards in their mess will not be allowed to go up.

A colleague and I were the last of the visitors today. We had to leave the jeep and clamber for one hour and a half over loose stones. It was essential to follow the broad white ribbon, blood-splashed in many places, to keep on the track free of mines or booby traps. This white tape follows on to a part the Poles now call "The Lane of the Dead Men." Here today the bodies of the Polish soldiers who fell near the monastery were being collected, labelled and covered with blankets, before burial in the hillside soldiers' cemetery. Each Polish grave there has a bottle rammed neck-down into the soil in front of a wooden cross. Inside the whisky bottle or beer bottle, or anything obtainable, is a piece of paper with the details of how the soldier fell.

ON up the white tape line, with hesitant moments occasionally where the tape disappeared, we climbed into the Abbey building after several attempts. On the last lap the rubble was pounded into powder, and I slipped back several times. War has ravaged the Abbey. The Germans have turned it into a gigantic ash-can. At the foot of one fine stairway are thousands of empty tins. The great and graceful font in the baptistry is filled with used plates, greasy and dust-covered. In what was the forecourt the scene is a mixture of Salvador Dali and a nightmare.

A few feet from the great headless statue of Saint Michael is the abbot's motor-car buried in rubble so that only the back of the saloon is visible. Upside down near the car is a wooden pushcart for a child. A pace or two on there is a gold and white chasuble, a vestment used by the priest celebrating mass, which has been slashed and then flung across broken columns. These Germans did not let the religious significance of many things in here worry them. One fellow had the altar cloth as coverlet for his bed. Near the bed of another was a chalice, which seemed to have served as a shaving vessel.

Candlesticks, fractured and battered, lie among the stones. But they were damaged probably by bombs. Other ecclesiastical vestments—amices, albs and stoles—are scattered about. Someone flung a purple stole out of the window so that it dangled from a corner. Not all the removals had been wanton. The Germans had taken a silver Christ and fastened the figure to a rough wooden cross above a mound of soldiers' graves amid the ruins. I met another soldier who was taking away a cross. He was a Pole, a good Catholic. "We borrow this for our soldiers' chapel," he said, "we have so little there."

The monastery is too wrecked to make it possible to pick out parts of it without a plan. But in what appeared to be the monks' rooms, or perhaps the sacristies, I found an Italian copy of the Forsyte Saga, a 1,000-page encyclopedia through which a bullet had passed, and, scattered around, packets of ultramarine blue and other colours for illuminating missals and the like. They must have been badly served for light, but that was well for them in this gaping skeleton of a building. Down here there is plenty of space between the low iron-framed beds which they had evidently collected from the monks' quarters.

On a table are six opened tins of rations and three mess plates with sardines and potato untouched. Littered over the floor are packets of Esbit, a brand of fuel tablet with which they heated their mugs of coffee. The chief civil affairs officer of Amgot walked into Cassino at noon yesterday. Tonight Amgot issued a communiqué saying: "No civil affairs officer will be posted in Cassino because there is nothing left to administer." But, though much of the bombed and shelled Abbey is a heap of dust, it can be rebuilt entirely is the view of Major Norman Newton, an American who is Amgot's monuments officer.

We Wrestled at Sea with a 100-m.p.h. Gale

The destroyer H.M.S. Inconstant recently survived a terrific storm, the worst in her commander's long experience. For three-and-a-half days she had to heave-to before reaching harbour with structural damage and many depth charges lost overboard. The story of her struggle with the gale is told here by Sub.-Lieut. A. C. List, R.N.V.R.

WE were escorting a northbound convoy when we ran into the gale, which eventually reached 100 miles an hour. The convoy was scattered. We battened down all hatches, and it was impossible to get from one end of the ship to the other. I was on the bridge with the commanding officer, Lieut.-Cmdr. J. H. Eaden, D.S.O., R.N., of London, and the navigating officer, Lieut. R. S. S. Ingham, D.S.C., R.N.V.R., of Wigtownshire. The waves were coming right over the bridge, and we were up there for about 10 hours before we could safely get away.

Suddenly, the depth charges amidships started to break loose. The Gunner, Mr. R. P. Burgess, R.N., of Carshalton, Surrey, was below when he heard the depth

UNION JACK AND POLISH FLAG fly side by side over the shattered remains of Cassino Monastery, finally stormed and taken by the Poles on May 18, 1944. The Monastery fell at 10.20 a.m., and at 5.30 p.m. the two flags were hoisted, the Poles who had fought so grimly for this moment mounting a guard of honour. See story in this page.

PAGE 89   *Photo. British Official*

charges rolling round the deck over his head. He went on deck and tied a life-line round his waist. Leading Seaman T. A. Pryce, of Plymouth, paid out the line while Mr. Burgess scrambled to the depth charges.

All this time the waves were crashing down on the ship and Pryce tied the line to a stanchion. It was a good job he did, as one wave washed Mr. Burgess through the guard rails, and but for the life-line he would have gone overboard. Mr. Burgess called for volunteers, and Able Seaman C. Pemberton, of Blackpool, Able Seaman B. D. Wilde, of Mansfield and Able Seaman J. Ambrose, of Liverpool, went up to help. They hadn't been working long before the ammunition locker broke away under another wave and trapped them all underneath it.

The First Lieutenant, Lieut. M. Hayward-Butt, R.N., of Bude, went to their assistance, but another wave tore away the iron ladder leading up to one of the gun platforms. As it swung round, it hit the First Lieutenant on the forehead and knocked him unconscious. When the men under the locker were released, they were all suffering from severe injuries to their legs. Eventually we got all the injured below. Meanwhile, the ammunition locker had been washed over the side as though it had been matchwood.

We were pretty badly knocked about when we reached harbour, both the whaler and motor-boat being smashed as well. We collected the remainder of the convoy and carried on to our destination. We were in harbour just about long enough to refuel when we went out to help another convoy

H.M.S. INCONSTANT, the story of whose epic battle with raging seas is related in this and the preceding page. A destroyer of the Intrepid class, H.M.S. Inconstant has a displacement of 1,370 tons and a complement of 145 ; her armament includes four 4·7-in. guns, five 21-in. torpedo tubes, and she is also specially fitted for mine-laying. A destroyer of this type costs about £320,000 to build.

Photo, Topical Press

which had been coming up behind us. There was a pack of U-boats waiting to attack, but we got there first.

I Flew Over Hitler's Front Line in the West

To within 30 miles of Paris, H. M. Moynihan, News Chronicle special correspondent, flew over France on May 20, 1944. His account of the country thus seen reveals it as desolation—marshalling yards empty of freight ; and roads, railways and rivers deserted. It was, he says, a "dead land."

IN the co-pilot's seat of a Mitchell medium bomber I flew last evening to within 30 miles of the centre of Paris. Our route took us nearly 200 miles over Hitler's front line—areas on which a world's attention is being focused. This is what I saw: deserted roads, railways, stations and marshalling yards like forgotten toys ; rivers unrippled by craft. It was the "dead land" of which I had heard from pilots who for months have been operating day after day unchallenged in the skies of Northern France.

"Targets in Northern France" has become the refrain of nearly every Air Ministry communiqué. To the crew of R for Roger yesterday afternoon's briefing prepared them for another routine job—their 29th since last November. Yesterday evening their 500-pounders were required for fuel dumps and hangars at Creil airfield, 30 miles from the centre of Paris.

For myself, it was in more ways than one a novel experience. My maiden flight was to be an operational one. Of this, Flying Officer Desmond Martin, New Zealand pilot of R for Roger, was kept in ignorance until our safe return. Flying above cloud over the Channel the three squadrons of Mitchells crossed the French coast, its white cliffs, outer wall of enslaved Europe, gleaming below. Now the fields of France stretched to the horizon, a flat patchwork of grass, ploughland and woods interlaced with roads.

We flew too high to distinguish details in the pattern below—details that might convert a tranquil countryside into a region bristling with the weapons of defence. At several points a cluster of bomb craters indicated locations of the "military targets" that are being pounded with systematic regularity by our fighter-bombers and medium bombers. Smaller clusters of craters were visible at frequent intervals, looking like rubbed ink stains on a green and brown carpet.

From a forest criss-crossed by a regular pattern of paths much could be guessed, nothing observed. The Germans, masters of the art of concealment and surreptitious movement, had left no clue here for the daylight observer.

The roads and railways, along which the convoys and freight trains, moving under cover of darkness, are carrying the materials and equipment for the defence of the West Wall, were deserted. In an hour's close scrutiny I saw two heavy vehicles, one car and one motor-cyclist, moving specks in seemingly depopulated countryside. Marshalling yards, pitted with old bomb wounds, were empty of freight—no puff of smoke indicated activity on the miles of rail below.

Pilots with whom I have talked in the past weeks have told the same story. Some have not seen a train in months. On the evening's operation the three squadrons of escorting Spitfires returned again without a fight. Over the target as our bombs went down two puffs of black smoke drifted by. The half-hearted effort by ground defences was our only proof that the country below was enemy-occupied. Only 30 miles from the target, visible on a clearer day, lay Paris. The return trip was equally uneventful. We left behind a target well covered, sprouting smoke. On another airfield north of Paris Marauders were carrying out a similar attack. Forced to reserve its main strength for the invasion, the Luftwaffe has no place at present in the skies over France.

I Watched an Unbeatable Army Come Home

Sent to Dover in May 1940 as a war reporter, Ronald Camp of the News Chronicle has now recalled in that newspaper (on May 31, 1944) some of the things he did and saw in the front-line town during that bleak period in our military history. His flash-back to Dunkirk days will stir solemn memories in the minds of many readers of " The War Illustrated."

THE Dover bookseller who sold me the Ordnance Survey map of South-East England gave me a careful scrutiny and I left his shop wondering if he too believed all the rumours of the landing of German parachute-spies.

An hour later I knew the answer. By that time I had been "detained" by security police and was being interrogated by a polite but grim officer who was disposed to believe my credentials, but was taking no chances.

"The map ? Yes, I bought it. Why ? Just to plan possible escape routes out of Dover, in case—well, for an emergency, to get stories back to London." The officer asked, looking at the pencilled routes : "If the German Army lands here. Is that what you mean ?" I meant exactly that.

This was Dover, four years ago. I had been the first reporter sent there to cover—anything. You could hear the German guns across the Straits. There was very little

official news ; what there was, was bad and no one had any doubts that the Germans were coming. At the Grand Hotel—a ruin now—the first survivors of the disaster in France had already arrived, a trickle of dazed people which was to grow in a few days into a wave of hundreds of thousands flooding into the little towns all along the South-East Coast.

Overriding the dread we all experienced was the strangest exhilaration. Children in Dover were still playing in the streets and on the waterfront as close as they could go to the barbed wire and the anti-aircraft guns dotting the promenade. In the shops food was plentiful ; so was bright talk. In the pubs people were drinking harder. Four years ago, and the pictures remain vivid.

There was a bomber pilot in the hotel at X near by. His flying field was only a short distance away. "Well, chaps, I've got to go," he said, jerking his thumb towards France. "Pour me a Guinness

STRETCHING FROM SHORE TO SHORE were the armadas of the "little ships" at the time of the Dunkirk evacuation, between May 29 and June 3, 1940; the one seen in the foreground is packed to the rails with British and French troops. A flash-back to those sombre Dunkirk days is provided in the accompanying story by a war correspondent who saw the home-coming from his post at Dover four years ago.
Photo, British Official

the bombs fell and the music and the roller skaters went round and around.

Then the thing happened. There were ships sinking in sight of shore, machine-gun bullets flattening themselves in the streets. We saw the first destroyer back from Dunkirk, its bow wave a foaming arc making everything but funnels and bridge invisible. The destroyer slowed, turned for harbour; we saw them then, hundreds of British soldiers clinging to her decks. We couldn't even shout. Even the roller skates were silent.

After that the desperate, incredible medley. Horror, grief, humour, policemen weeping as the troops came ashore; the wonderful women of Folkestone, Dover, Ramsgate and the other places ransacking their homes for sheets for emergency bandages—did they ever get new bed linen?—pushing wooden hand carts around the towns, collecting food, crockery, tea; boats and ships, big and little, laden until they were unseaworthy, forging into dock, turning and going back, the crews working until they dropped or died.

The Channel at night glowed; flickering, blood-red, great pillars of fire belched into the smoke-blackened night sky over the French coast. And by day the writhing smoke clouds marked the funeral pyres of an army's equipment. Everything seemed chaotic, yet everything had a strange orderliness, and by day and night the hospital trains moved out and the empty trains came in for all the thousands who waited.

We did not know then or for some time after of the men who stood by along the cliffs and beaches. Fifty rounds apiece was wealth of ammunition then. They stood ready to fight while the defeated army came home. And the men who had lost? I was asked time and time again, "What did they look like?" They looked awful. But they looked, I said, unbeatable, because their spirit was unbroken even then. And that was four years ago today.

when you hear my car leave; I'll be back to drink it before the froth has gone." We did that. We heard him go, saw his plane, one of only three, flying out over the evening-sunlit water. There was a lace of froth still on the drink when he returned, oil on his face, flying helmet in his hand.

Two naval officers, thick black oil from head to bare feet, came into the hotel. There was no room, but room was made for them. Was it bad? they were asked. Worse, the

lieutenant assured us. "Six brand new pipes I had, all on appro', too. Lost the lot. But I saved these." He carefully wiped oil from his binoculars.

There was a raid on the harbour area. We were in the area. Standing at the hotel door we saw the flashes and were shaken by the noise. What was the curious persistent moaning, rattling sound—a new weapon? No. The skating rink was still in session, an ack-ack gun firing almost on its doorstep;

OUR DIARY OF THE WAR

MAY 24, Wednesday *1,726th day*
Italy.—Canadian armoured units went through breach in Adolf Hitler line; Terracina and Pontecorvo captured.
Mediterranean.—U.S. heavy bombers attacked factories and airfields near Vienna and military installations at Graz and Zagreb.
Air.—Forts and Liberators attacked Berlin; medium bombers attacked airfields and railways in France. At night R.A.F. bombed Aachen and Antwerp.

MAY 25, Thursday *1,727th day*
Italy.—Patrols from 5th Army main front made contact with patrols from Anzio beach-head; U.S. troops captured Cisterna.
Balkans.—German parachutists attacked Marshal Tito's headquarters, but did not succeed in capturing him.
Mediterranean. — Allied heavy bombers attacked Lyons and Toulon railway yards.
Air.—Nine marshalling yards and four airfields in France and Belgium bombed by heavy force of U.S. bombers.
Pacific.—U.S. Pacific Fleet announced attacks on Marcus Island on May 19 and 20, and on Wake Island on May 23, by carrier-borne aircraft.

MAY 26, Friday *1,728th day*
Italy.—Places captured by 5th and 8th armies included Cori, San Giovanni, Piedimonte and Monte Cairo.
Mediterranean.—Railway centres at Lyons, St. Etienne, Grenoble and Nice bombed by Forts and Liberators.
Air.—Airfields and bridges in N. France attacked by U.S. 9th Air Force.

MAY 27, Saturday *1,729th day*
Air.—U.S. heavy bombers attacked railway yards at Ludwigshafen, Mannheim, Karlsruhe, Saarbrucken and Strasbourg. By night over 1,000 R.A.F. planes attacked military depot at Bourg-Leopold, near Antwerp, and railway yards at Aachen and Nantes.
Mediterranean.—Escorted heavy bombers in great strength attacked railway yards at Marseilles, Avignon and Nimes.
Pacific.—Allied troops landed on Biak Island, off Dutch New Guinea.
China.—Japanese launched new offensive against Changsha, capital of Hunan.

MAY 28, Sunday *1,730th day*
Air.—U.S. bombers and over 1,200 fighters attacked synthetic oil-plants near Leipzig; rocket-projectile Typhoons destroyed a German military headquarters in N. France. Railway centre of Angers bombed by R.A.F. at night.
Mediterranean.—Allied heavy bombers attacked harbour installations at Genoa.
Italy.—Ceprano and Belmonte captured by 8th Army.

MAY 29, Monday *1,731st day*
Air.—Two thousand U.S. aircraft attacked two fighter factories in Poland and five in N. Germany.
Mediterranean.—Italian-based heavy bombers attacked aircraft factories and airfields at Wiener Neustadt; German troop concentrations in Jugoslavia bombed.
Russian Front.—Soviet bombers attacked airfields near Roman and Husi, Rumania.

MAY 30, Tuesday *1,732nd day*
Air.—Two thousand U.S. planes attacked aircraft factories and airfields in Germany and railway yards in Belgium and France; French road and railway bridges bombed by medium bombers.
Italy.—8th Army troops entered Arce.

Mediterranean.—Allied bombers attacked factories near Wiener Neustadt and railway yards at Zagreb (Yugoslavia).
Russian Front.—Germans attacking N. of Jassy, Rumania, drove small wedge into Soviet defences.

MAY 31, Wednesday *1,733rd day*
Air.—U.S. bombers found new targets in railway yards at Hamm, Osnabruck, Schwerte and Soest; at night R.A.F. bombed French railway centres at Trappes, Tergnier and Saumur.
Italy.—Velletri virtually surrounded by U.S. troops' occupation of Monte Artemisio.
Mediterranean.—Allied bombers attacked Ploesti and Turnu-Severin (Rumania); at night R.A.F. attacked Iron Gate railway on the Danube.
Russian Front.—Further German attacks N. of Jassy repelled by Soviet forces.

JUNE 1, Thursday *1,734th day*
Italy.—8th Army troops entered Sora and Frosinone.
Air.—R.A.F. bombers attacked railway yard at Saumur.
Sea.—Carrier-borne aircraft of Fleet Air Arm bombed enemy convoy off Norway.

JUNE 2, Friday *1,735th day*
Italy.—Valmontone and Velletri captured by 5th Army troops; Ferentino occupied by 8th Army.
Air.—Nearly 1,000 U.S. heavy bombers attacked Pas de Calais without loss; road and rail bridges in France bombed. R.A.F. bombed Trappes at night.
Russian Front.—U.S. Flying Fortresses landed on airfields in Russia after bombing Rumanian targets.

JUNE 3, Saturday *1,736th day*
Air.—Forts and Liberators bombed military installations in Pas de Calais and Boulogne areas; road and rail communications in France also attacked. R.A.F. bombed objectives on French coast.
Italy.—Lanuvio and Nemi in German line S. of Rome, captured by 5th Army.
Russian Front.—Violent German attacks N. and N.W. of Jassy again repelled.

JUNE 4, Sunday *1,737th day*
Italy.—Rome occupied by 5th Army troops during night of June 4-5.
Air.—U.S. heavy bombers attacked targets near Boulogne and railway centres and airfields in N. France; radio installations in N. France also bombed.
Russian Front.—Soviet bombers made mass raid on Kishinev.

JUNE 5, Monday *1,738th day*
Air.—Military installations near Boulogne and Calais attacked by U.S. heavy bombers; radio installations in N. France and Channel Is., and road and rail communications in France also bombed. In a record night of bombing, more than 1,300 R.A.F. planes attacked ten German coastal batteries.
Russian Front.—At night Soviet bombers made mass attack on Jassy.
General.—King Victor Emmanuel signed decree transferring royal powers to his son, the Prince of Piedmont.

JUNE 6, Tuesday *1,739th day*
Western Front.—Allied air-borne and sea-borne troops began landing on the coast of Normandy, supported by very heavy naval and air bombardments.
Russian Front.—U.S. Russian-based bombers attacked airfields at Galatz, Rumania, and returned to Soviet bases.
General.—Gen. de Gaulle broadcast from London to the French people.

★ ══ *Flash-backs* ══ ★

1940
May 27. *Royal Navy sank concrete-filled blockships at Zeebrugge.*
May 28. *Allied forces captured Narvik, destroyed harbour works.*
June 2. *Mr. Eden broadcast that four-fifths of the B.E.F. were safely back from Dunkirk.*

1941
May 25. *King George of Hellenes escaped from Crete to Egypt.*
June 1. *British troops entered Baghdad after the collapse of the Rashid Ali revolt in Iraq.*

1942
May 24. *General Stilwell arrived in Delhi after twenty days' trek through the Burmese jungle.*
June 3. *Japanese bombed Dutch Harbour, United States naval base in the Aleutian Islands.*

1943
May 30. *Organized Japanese resistance ended on Attu Is., Aleutians.*
May 31. *Announced that French Fleet at Alexandria joined Allies.*
June 1. *Heavy naval and air bombardment of Pantelleria began.*

THE WAR IN THE AIR

by Capt. Norman Macmillan, M.C., A.F.C.

THE institution of an Eastern Command of the United States Strategic Air Forces in Europe is an event of outstanding military and political importance, marking the beginning of new developments in the employment of air power. The first mission devolving from the setting up of this new Command was the bombing of targets in Hungary and Transylvania on June 2, 1944. It is not, however, in the selection of targets, but in the organization of the surface servicing of the Force that the real innovation lies.

The formation of Fortress bombers left airfields in Italy escorted by long-range Mustang fighters. They alighted on Soviet territory with an additional escort of Red Air Force Yak fighters. This was the first demonstration of the principle of a shuttle air operation between east and west Europe, instead of the more familiar out-and-home method of working. Incidentally, it is a method of bombing operation which I suggested when Russia first came into the war. But for that I claim no particular prescience, for its advantages were so apparent that many must have been aware of them even if few wrote about them.

The military advantages are both strategical and tactical. The tactical advantage lies in the use of favourable geographic siting of Allied airfields: (1) to reduce the distance to be flown when attacking distant targets, so that a greater weight of bombs can be carried in lieu of petrol ; (2) to enable fighter escorts to accompany the bombers throughout their mission due to the mileage falling within the range of the fighters ; (3) to reduce the strain on the aircrews, airframes, and engines by cutting down not only the time of flight, but more particularly the time spent over enemy territory, thus maintaining the efficiency of the aircrews and aircraft of the force over a longer period of operation ; (4) to add difficulty to the opposing air force's interception of the bombers, thereby offering the pilots and bombardiers the best conditions for accurate bomb-aiming.

THE strategical advantages are not less important. The choice and situation of targets to be attacked is greatly increased and widened. The Air Staffs of both Allies are brought together to work towards a common military policy. The maximum use is made of all available airfields. Part of the man-power resources of both Allies is pooled. And for the first time foreign aircraft are accorded in war the same airfield facilities as warships had long been accustomed to enjoy in harbourage. Thus a step has been taken in the direction of the international strategical employment of military aircraft.

This was not the first time that shuttle bombing services had operated. Bomber Command of the R.A.F. on July 15, 1943, sent a force of Lancasters to night-bomb transformer stations in Italy ; this force flew on to land in North Africa, and when returning to England bombed the port of Leghorn in the night of July 24. Other targets in South Germany and Italy were attacked to a similar formula. But in these attacks the aircraft were dispatched from and arrived at airfields under the control of the same military authorities. No political concessions were involved.

With the U.S. and Russian shuttle-bombing the political issues were the primary problem, and it is said that these were the subject of discussion at the Moscow Conference in

OUR FIRST TACTICAL AIR FORCE dealt shattering blows to German supply routes while the Allies closed in on Rome, as this photograph of bomb craters and abandoned vehicles shows. Main role of the First Tactical Air Force (under Maj.-Gen. John K. Cannon), composed of fighters, fighter-bombers, and light and medium bombers, is to secure air superiority over battle areas and to disrupt local road and rail communications. *Photo, British Official*

October 1943. No doubt the England-North Africa shuttle-bombing by Bomber Command was a useful factor in the discussion, as must have been also the photographic evidence of the destruction wrought in Western Germany by the strategic-economic bombing of Bomber Command and the U.S. Army 8th Air Force.

The man-power problems involved in air warfare on its present scale are vividly illustrated by the bomb tonnage figures for May 1944. A year ago the tonnage dropped by American bombers in Europe was comparatively small compared with the figures for Bomber Command. In May 1944 the total tonnage dropped by the Strategic Air Forces of Britain and the U.S. (not including the

bomb weight dropped by the Tactical Air Forces over the battlefronts) exceeded 100,000 tons. Of this total the U.S. Strategic Forces in Britain and Italy dropped about 60,000 tons by day and 7,600 tons by night. Bomber Command from the United Kingdom dropped 37,000 tons. These figures show clearly that industrial man-power is the factor that controls the air-power potential of a nation, and suggest the necessity for a Treaty to regulate the size of post-war air forces in a manner similar to the Washington Treaty of 1922 for the regulation of the size of navies, unless some other international formula can be found to control post-war air policy.

Aircraft have been used to attack German military headquarters in Western Europe by pin-point bombing, and the accuracy of this method of attack is now so high that special measures for security and for the protection of headquarters of military importance will have to be devised. Whether it is better to bomb and follow the attack by dropping parachutists, as was done in the attempt to capture Marshal Tito in Yugoslavia at the end of May, must depend on the prevailing circumstances, but it is probable that this form of parachutist infiltration behind the enemy "front" will be developed as never before with the major invasion operation in Europe.

MEANWHILE, on the Italian front Allied aircraft have found important communication targets in the road transport which Kesselring was compelled to use during daylight when the Fifth and Eighth Armies forced the German retreat from the Anzio perimeter and the defensive lines to the south. Allied aircraft sorties there rose to over 3,000 a day, and on May 26 no fewer than 610 vehicles were destroyed behind the German front. This daily road-strafing began on May 24 and continued daily. Strategic aircraft attacked rail communications throughout south-eastern France, there interfering with German troop movements towards Italy, the Brenner Pass rail route having been previously attended to by bombers and blocked.

In Western Europe the main targets have been railway communications. Heavy attacks have been made by day and night against railway key centres with the object of reducing the transport facilities between industrial Europe and the "West Wall." In May Bomber Command dropped 28,500 tons on comparatively small targets, a diversion from its urban area attacks.

British aircraft have been using rocket projectiles—officially called unrotating projectiles—since June 1943. They are essentially weapons for low and close attack. Targets attacked with them have been mainly the smaller vessels, but German army headquarters buildings, radio stations, and railways have also been singled out for rocket attack. Small ship draught is too shallow for torpedo attack, and the rocket has proved superior to the skip-bombing and cannon-gun form of attack against them. Four rockets are carried under each wing. Their discharge shock is taken by the air. They can be fired in pairs or in one salvo of eight. Their cordite propellant is electrically ignited by a small platinum fuse wire when the pilot presses a firing button. (See illus. p. 94).

Metal 'Carpets' for Our Front Line Airfields

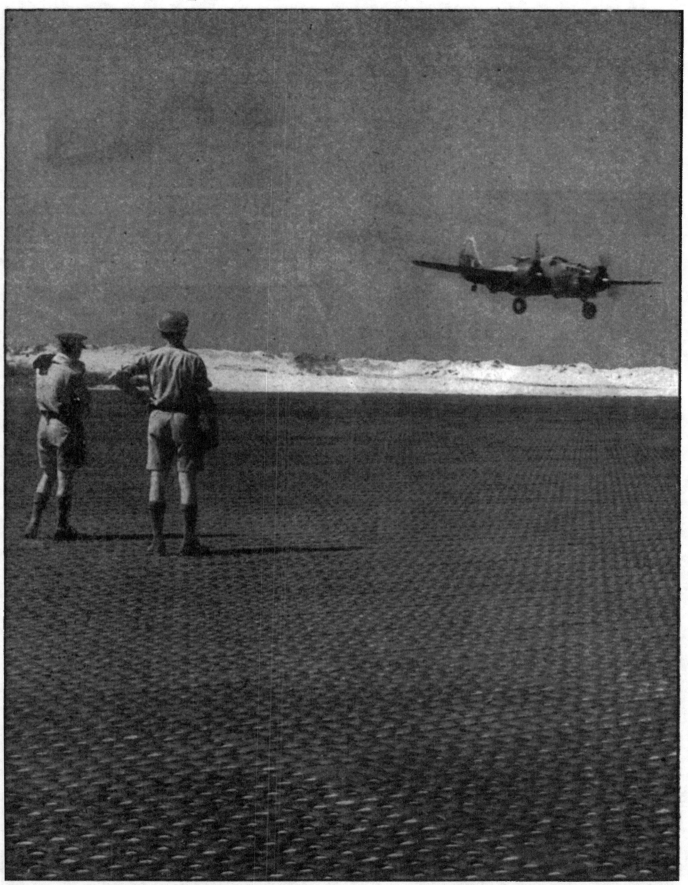

SWIFT MAKER OF LANDING GROUNDS is the Sommerfeld track—a strip of metal "netting" tautly stretched between stiff edges and firmly picketed at the sides. Transported in 25-yd. rolls, it can be speedily laid down on any flat ground and is strong enough to carry the heaviest vehicle up a sandy beach. Strips laid side by side form an admirable surface for aircraft runways and emergency landing-grounds. A Baltimore medium bomber of the Desert Air Force is about to land on one of these meshed airfields in Italy.

Photo, British Official

R.A.F. Rockets Equal a Warship's Broadside!

NEW WEAPON OF THE R.A.F., the rocket-projectile is being used with increasing success against enemy targets on land and at sea. Six feet long, the rocket consists (apart from its explosive head) of a tube filled with cordite; when fired, a fuse ignites the cordite and the resultant gas-flow propels it at terrific speed. Eight rockets are carried by a plane, four under each wing, and they can be fired in pairs or all eight together, the effect of such a salvo being comparable to that of a light cruiser's broadside. A Beaufighter of R.A.F. Coastal Command uses its rockets (1). H. M. the King recently inspected the latest rocket-equipped Typhoon aircraft (2).

FOUR FIGHTERS OF COASTAL COMMAND—Hurricanes, Beaufighters, Typhoons and Swordfish—have all been adapted for rocket firing. One instance of their striking power is evident in the result of a special mission to eliminate a German military headquarters in Northern France, undertaken by rocket-projectile Typhoons of the Second Tactical Air Force on May 28, 1944; only battered walls of the building remained standing after that visit. R.A.F. ground crews load rockets into the guide rails of a Beaufighter (3). An enemy armed trawler under rocket fire (4); one of the projectiles can be seen on the right. *Photos, British Official*

OF all our Allies to which do we feel most akin? I should say the Norwegians. This is natural, for we are closely related to them. Since the Normans, or North-men, began coming to England, long before the Norman Conquest, we have been mixing our blood with theirs. We inherit from them our aptitude for seamanship. I don't say our love for the sea, because sailors, I notice, are always looking forward to the day when they will be able to live permanently on land, and most Britons are seasick if the waves are more than inch high! But we do produce good seamen. We did in the time of masts and sails, and we do still. This we owe to our ancestors from "Norroway o'er the faem," as the old ballad called it. Now we have another tie of friendship with the Norwegians. We have fought together for the same great cause—to keep alive the flame of freedom. How much the Allied cause owes to Norwegian seafaring men, soldiers and airmen few people yet realize. If they will spend 6/- on a book just published by Hutchinson, with the authority of the Royal Norwegian Government Information Office, they will learn a great deal. That book, Fighting Norsemen, by R. B. Nyquist, does not tell all that these "bonny fighters" have done. That must wait. But it tells a great deal in a very attractive style.

MOSTLY they acted in co-operation with British forces. But sometimes they struck entirely on their own, a blow at the Germans whom they hate with a concentration that is surprising in so placid and kindly a people. For example, at a place on the coast of northern Norway fishmeal and herring-oil factories were being used greatly to the enemy's advantage. A raid was planned in which only native sailors and soldiers were to take part. In a destroyer, one of those sent to Britain by the Americans, they started across the North Sea, slid into a fjord, expecting to be met with enemy fire; were not molested; landed without meeting any opposition. For nearly three hours they stayed on shore, distributing food to the inhabitants, whom the Germans kept on short rations, and completely destroying the factories and other buildings useful to the enemy. Then they re-embarked and steamed quietly away. Few of their exploits were so easily accomplished. But nothing daunts them.

MRS. CHURCHILL in her charmingly spoken talk on the wireless about her Red Cross Fund, which deserves all the support we can give, described the Nazi system as "the worst tyranny the world had ever known." That is her husband's way of looking at it, and a dutiful wife always agrees with her husband—in public, at any rate. But whenever I hear or read this description I enter an inward protest. Hateful as it is, abominable as its crimes are, we give it too much importance when we pretend that nothing like Nazism has ever been seen before. I should say the Spartans were far more uncomfortable than the Germans were during the six years of peace after Hitler grabbed power. Of the notorious Duke of Alva, governor of the Netherlands in the 16th century, it was said that his executioners shed more blood than his soldiers. The Pharaohs of Egypt enslaved whole populations and made them build the Pyramids. The Israelites under Joshua went through Palestine with fire and sword, extermin-

ating, burning, destroying. For 30 years in the 17th century the wars of religion made Germany a hell. Humanity has always known the rule of oppressors and that rule has varied little throughout the ages. Sometimes it has been a little worse in one direction, sometimes rather more humane in another. But always coldly cruel and at the same time senseless, for always in the end the tyranny has collapsed. But it has always begun again either in the same place or somewhere else.

HOW it is with folks who live out of sight and sound of aircraft passing overhead in vast numbers to bomb the enemy, I don't know; but I feel sure those who do see and

WING COMMANDER R. H. McCONNELL, D.F.C., was the first pilot of the Royal Air Force Coastal Command to use rocket projectiles in an action against the enemy. Commissioned in the R.A.F. in 1935, Wing Commander McConnell gained his decoration in 1940. See also facing page. *Photo, British Official.*

hear this daily are more affected by the thought of casualties to a small number of the crews than by that of tens of thousands who might be killed in battle. It is because one knows that in each of those machines roaring over there are a few young men who may not come back—that there are bound to be some who will not—and it is this that makes reflection so poignant. It is brought close home to us. Battles happen a long way off. No one who has not been in or near one has any exact idea of what they are like. When we hear that very large numbers have been killed, we have no clear picture in our minds of how they met their death. But we can imagine in the most painful detail how these boys in the bombers and fighters may meet their fate. When we see them come back our hearts are thankful. This time, at any rate, they have escaped to fight again.

BREWERS are doing very well, making large profits, paying big dividends; their shares increase in value. But will this continue? I notice a significant change near where I live. A baker's shop, where even now there is always a tempting array of cakes

and bread in the window, is frequented at all hours of the day by soldiers, and by workers in overalls, for cups of tea and buns. They make it a sort of teashop, filling it so full at times that customers for loaves or tea dainties have to edge their way through to the counter, smiling good-naturedly at the men sitting there with cups in their hands. Will the taste for beer give way to a liking for tea? In a good many men it may. Australians prefer tea—not here, perhaps, but they do in their own country, and they drink an enormous lot of it, as I can testify.

WHAT makes men endurable is that they are so much like boys. However solemn they try to be, whatever airs of wisdom they give themselves, one touch of schoolboy fun breaks down their pretences, and they become delightfully natural. I was in the House of Commons the other day. Some discussion was going on about fish which involved a complaint about bad smells. Mr. Boothby got up and said: "I was in Aberdeen recently"—he sits for one of its divisions—"and the stench was intolerable." There was an immediate and joyful roar of laughter. It was exactly what would have happened in one of the lower classes if a master had given such an opening. I felt more kindly then to M.P.s than I have for a long time. The House really does need renewing with some fresh and younger material. It has been there nine years and looks it. It is a tired House. Everyone knows what everyone else will say (if they get a chance). There is an air of weariness and strain about the place; it was refreshing to see this dispersed for a moment by that burst of schoolboy hilarity.

HOLLYWOOD is the place to make money. The largest income in the United States is earned by Mr. Louis Mayer of the well-known film company. He makes £756 a day. And Leslie Howard, who went there with nothing, left £62,000 when he died, though he was still quite a young man. I remember hearing a story of a visit to the bank manager by a boyish actor and his father who went to see if they could arrange for an overdraft so that the son might try his luck in California. That was Leslie Howard, who rose to the front solely by merit and force of character. He well deserved all the monetary reward he earned.

HAD anyone foretold fifty years ago that the Salvation Army would some day plan to build headquarters for itself in London at an expense of half-a-million pounds, the prophet would have been thought crazy. The Army was then looked on as a passing nuisance. It was small and noisy, sneered at by intellectuals, disliked by the conventional for its intimate street-corner discussions about the ways of the Almighty and the sinful human race. Its finance depended on the pennies of its members for the most part, though it had some few supporters who gave General Booth large sums to be spent exactly as he thought fit without accounting to anybody. He had a good idea of business himself and he gathered together men who were first-class accountants. The S.A. headquarters were destroyed in an air-raid three years ago and to the compensation that will (they hope) be received from War Damage Insurance there will be added large sums raised all over the world for a spacious and striking block on the old site in Queen Victoria Street, London.

Avenger Takes Off on its Mission of Death

LAUNCHING TORPEDOES FROM THE AIR is the special task of this Avenger aircraft, here seen taking off from the flight deck of a U.S. aircraft carrier operating against the Japanese in the Pacific. Powered by a 1,700 h.p. Wright Cyclone engine, and armed with ·50 and ·30 calibre machine-guns and one 22-in. torpedo, the Avenger has a speed of 270 miles an hour. In May 1944 it was announced that the U.S. Navy alone will soon have a force of 37,700 planes.

Photo, Keystone

Printed in England and published every alternate Friday by the Proprietors, THE AMALGAMATED PRESS, LTD., The Fleetway House, Farringdon Street, London, E.C.4. Registered for transmission by Canadian Magazine Post. Sole Agents for Australia and New Zealand: Messrs. Gordon & Gotch, Ltd.; and for South Africa: Central News Agency, Ltd.—June 23, 1944. S.S. *Editorial Address*: JOHN CARPENTER HOUSE, WHITEFRIARS, LONDON E.C.4.

Vol 8 · The War Illustrated · Nº 184

Edited by Sir John Hammerton

SIXPENCE

JULY 7, 1944

VICTORY FOR OUR ARMOUR NEAR BAYEUX was the outcome of the first heavy clash with enemy tanks in Normandy on June 9, 1944 ; above, a British tank crew, wrapped in blankets, is seen taking a brief rest between spells of violent action. Brought across miles of water by ship, or landed from the air, our armoured monsters pushed on inland. Trying to stem the flow, especially in the Caen area, the Germans threw into battle increasing numbers of tanks, including the big Mark VI Tigers. *Photo, British Official*

NO. 185 WILL BE PUBLISHED FRIDAY, JULY 21

Our Roving Camera Speeds Airborne Troops

ON A SCALE never before attempted, the use of airborne troops in the Allied invasion of France met with such quick and outstanding success as to remove any last doubt as to the value of this form of modern warfare. Air landings at specially selected points in many cases caught the enemy completely by surprise, and all tasks allotted to the airborne forces were carried out. In the early stages of the assault, approximately 24,000 parachute troops, equivalent to two airborne divisions, were flown over in 1,000 Army transport planes; thousands more went by glider. See stories in pp. 120 and 121.

Stirling aircraft line a runway in Britain, preparatory to taking off with their loads (1). Parachute troops fill the inside of one aircraft (2); others read with anticipatory pleasure the pointed remarks chalked on the side of their glider (3). Crossing the Channel troop-carrying planes tow gliders (4); below them, leaving a broad wake on the water, are Allied naval units, also headed for France.

Photos, British and U.S. Official

THE BATTLE FRONTS

by Maj.-Gen. Sir Charles Gwynn, K.C.B., D.S.O.

IT is high time to stop using the term Second Front. It has long ceased to be accurate, though it conveniently defined our strategic aims. Now that those aims have taken concrete shape we should, I think, talk of the Western Front until such time as the general term is superseded by the names of its sub-divisions.

The landings in Sicily and at Salerno gave some indication of the immense preparations that have to be made for a large-scale amphibious operation—sufficient at least to silence those who had clamoured for the immediate opening of a second front as if it were only necessary to give the order. Yet few can have realized the complexity of the task until D-Day was passed and General Montgomery's armies were safely established on the coast of Normandy.

Fewer still, I think, realized the risks of failure or the consequences of failure which might disastrously have affected the whole strategic situation and have prolonged the war indefinitely, even if it had not affected its ultimate issue. The mere fact that Rommel—who, if no great strategist, is at least an excellent tactician—was confident that the beach defences were impregnable should make us realize the greatness of our achievement and the risks of failure involved.

BEFORE the war it was generally and justifiably held that it had become more than ever impracticable to land a large modern army with all its essential equipment on the coasts of a fully armed and prepared enemy. All the tactical advantages that modern weapons had conferred on the defence over the attack could be exploited even more effectively than in a purely land battle. While, strategically, the mobility conferred by mechanization and improvements in road and railway communication to a large extent reduced the advantage held by a seaborne force of being able to mask its intention till the last moment.

Even if a surprise landing could be effected (which was improbable in view of the potentialities of air reconnaissance and the strictly limited stretches of coast which at all favoured attack) the defenders' reserves could be moved to the danger point more rapidly than the attacking force could disembark in strength. Uncertainty of weather conditions and the necessity to capture a port which would ensure the uninterrupted landing of heavy material added considerably to the manifold difficulties of the invader.

ENEMY'S Labour and Ingenuity Finally Brought to Nought

What has brought this seemingly impossible enterprise into the category of practical operations and successful achievement in spite of the immense labour and ingenuity the enemy had expended in making security doubly sure ? Primarily, it was the refusal of one man, or perhaps a small group of men, to admit impossibilities, and their courage and foresight in embarking on preparations extending over a period of years and on an unprecedented scale with one object in view—a triumph of Faith.

Obviously, the first essential was to establish such naval and air supremacy as would ensure a high degree of protection to the armada in its passage across the sea and during the actual landing. Yet preparations were set in motion long before it could be guaranteed that the requisite degree of supremacy would ever be attained. Actually it was recognized that the danger of underwater and air attack, especially at night, although it might be minimized, could never

be completely eliminated and the risks were courageously accepted. Some idea has been given by the Press of the immense organization that had to be built up ; of the numbers of ships that had to be constructed and assembled, of the great variety of landing craft that had to be designed and built, and of the amount of specialized training that had to be given to all concerned in the operation. Yet I doubt if any single brain can grasp the full complexities of the preparations. They were the achievements of a great team working together to a single end, but with highly specialized functions ; and the results were amazing. (See article in p. 110.)

WHAT impresses me most is that this immense undertaking was launched in the full knowledge that the possibility of bringing it into fruition might never arise, and that, even if the opportunity materialized, vagaries

GENERAL EISENHOWER'S CALL TO THE INVASION TROOPS

SOLDIERS, sailors and airmen of the Allied Expeditionary Force ! You are about to embark upon the great crusade toward which we have striven these many months. The eyes of the world are upon you. The hopes and prayers of liberty-loving people everywhere march with you.

In company with our brave Allies and brothers-in-arms on other fronts, you will bring about the destruction of the German war machine, the elimination of Nazi tyranny over the oppressed peoples of Europe, and security for yourselves in a free world.

YOUR task will not be an easy one. Your enemy is well trained, well equipped and battle-hardened. He will fight savagely.

But this is the year 1944 ! Much has happened since the Nazi triumphs of 1940-41. The United Nations have inflicted upon the Germans great defeats, in open battle, man-to-man. Our air offensive has seriously reduced their strength in the air and their capacity to wage war on the ground. Our Home Fronts have given us an overwhelming superiority in weapons and munitions of war, and placed at our disposal great reserves of trained fighting men.

THE tide has turned. The free men of the world are marching together to victory. I have full confidence in your courage, devotion to duty and skill in battle. We will accept nothing less than full victory. Good luck ! And let us all beseech the blessing of Almighty God upon this great and noble undertaking.

Order of the Day issued to each individual of the Allied Expeditionary Force, June 6, 1944.

of the weather or other unforeseeable circumstances might lead to disastrous failure in the course of a few hours. That so great a measure of success has been achieved is due mainly to the courage and efficiency of the human element—sailors, soldiers and airmen—and the perfection of the equipment which they operated. Perhaps especial credit should be given to the efficiency of the Navy, including the Merchant Service, which was fundamental to the success of the operation. When one considers the number of amateurs recruited into these Services, and called on to carry out unfamiliar tasks often requiring a great display of initiative, it may well be questioned whether any but a nation with natural maritime instincts could have adapted itself to an undertaking so far outside the range of normal experience of war.

The success of the initial landing, apart from these considerations, turned, I think, on three bold decisions, all of which contributed an element of surprise. First and most courageous was the decision to start the operation in what the enemy deemed were prohibitive weather conditions. General Eisenhower presumably must have been ultimately responsible for the decision, though he could hardly have made it without the concurrence of his Naval advisers whose professional responsibility must have been even greater.

I cannot believe that the decision would have been made if it had not previously been decided, breaking away from all precedent, to start landing at low tide. For in a rough sea the enemy's elaborate underwater defences would surely have proved an impassable obstacle. Now that it has been tried out, the landing at low tide may seem to have been an easy solution of the problem of dealing with the underwater obstacles on which the enemy so greatly relied—yet it was not a solution that would seem to have occurred to Rommel or to the designers of the defence system, strangely enough.

COURAGEOUS Decisions Helped to Win Battle of the Beaches

Of course, it involved the exposure of the assaulting troops to fire for a longer time. In the past it would also have meant man-handling heavy weapons over long distances. The possibility of landing tanks and other mechanical vehicles from the leading landing craft and the effective covering fire which could be directed by Naval guns and aircraft on the enemy's weapons sited to bear on the beaches, greatly reduced these former disadvantages ; and obviously the importance of being able to clear passage through the obstacles while they were exposed at low tide outweighed them. Rommel, confident in the impregnability of underwater obstacles covered by fire, had apparently committed an unduly high proportion of his available troops to his forward defences and trusted to his armoured reserves being sufficient to counter-attack at any points where his front might possibly be penetrated.

Also, there was the decision to land a large force of airborne troops in advance of the sea landing. It was a courageous decision, for if the seaborne force had failed to get ashore or had been seriously delayed, the airborne force must have been sacrificed to a man. In the event, the airborne force not only accounted for some of the enemy's weapons which bore on the beaches but, what was probably more important, engaged enemy reserves which might have been used in early counter-attacks on the beach-head.

ESTABLISHMENT of Bridge-head Primarily for Offense

These decisions all contributed to the winning of a protective beach-head. Thenceforward, disembarkation could proceed with little interference by the enemy. There remained to be accomplished, however, the establishment of a bridge-head covering a sufficient area to admit of the deployment of forces adequate to undertake major offensive operations. The establishment of a beach-head is essentially a defensive step—but a bridge-head, though partially intended to provide a defensive position in depth in which an enemy counter offensive in force can be met, has primarily an offensive object.

AT the time of writing, the battle of the bridge-head is still in progress. Much has been accomplished owing to the consistently offensive action of our troops, which from the first has compelled Rommel to use his reserves piecemeal in fierce costly counter-attacks, and to the delays imposed on the movements of his strategic reserves caused by air attacks on his road and railway communications. The battle of the bridge-head cannot, however, be considered to have been conclusively won until all enemy attempts to forestall our major offensive operations have been defeated, and until we are in possession of the port of Cherbourg as a guarantee that an uninterrupted volume of supplies and heavy equipment can be maintained. For instance, without an adequate port at which rolling stock and other railway material can be landed, our armies would have to operate without railway communications.

Readers are referred to map in page 106

After the D-Day Storm that Smote the Hun

THE ALLIES cracked it, then a bulldozer (one of many) pushed pieces of it into the sea, aided by a crane ; the section of " West Wall " being dealt with (1) is at Port en Bessin, stormed by Royal Marine Commandos during the initial landings in Normandy. Two members of an Allied tank crew stretch out for forty winks ; others lean against it, making the most of the opportunity to write home (2). Letters and parcels from home reached the beach-head soon after fighting began ; a batch is being sorted (3) for delivery. General de Gaulle, instigator of the resistance movement after France collapsed in June 1940, returned to his native land again on June 14, 1944, on a short visit ; he toured liberated areas, and at Bayeux received a tremendous welcome (4). Thousands of men, women and children sang the Marseillaise.

Photos, British Official, Keystone

Britain and Canada Fight as One in Normandy

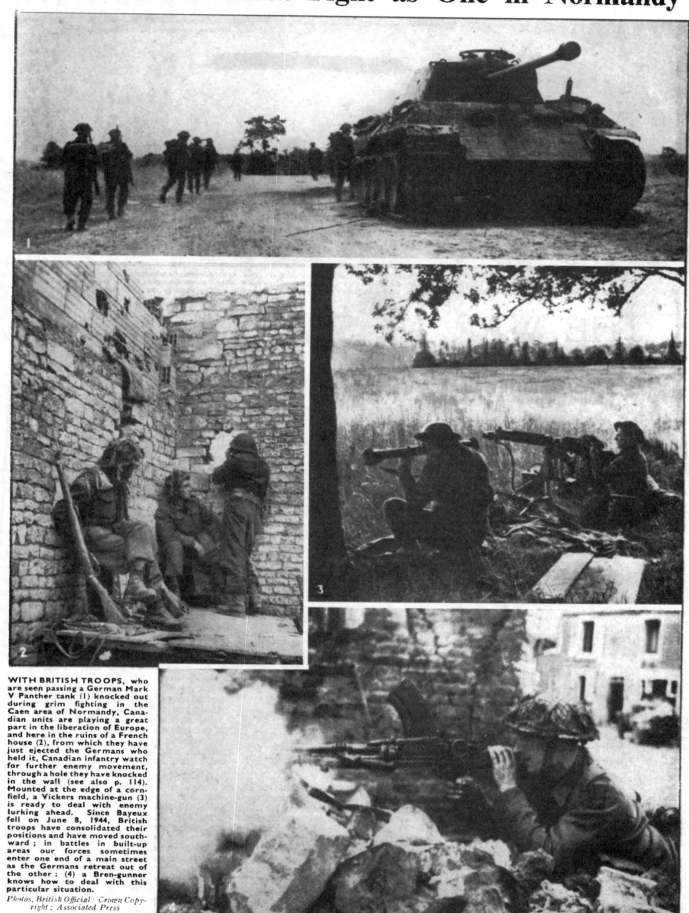

WITH BRITISH TROOPS, who are seen passing a German Mark V Panther tank (1) knocked out during grim fighting in the Caen area of Normandy, Canadian units are playing a great part in the liberation of Europe, and here in the ruins of a French house (2), from which they have just ejected the Germans who held it, Canadian infantry watch for further enemy movement, through a hole they have knocked in the wall (see also p. 114). Mounted at the edge of a cornfield, a Vickers machine-gun (3) is ready to deal with enemy lurking ahead. Since Bayeux fell on June 8, 1944, British troops have consolidated their positions and have moved southward; in battles in built-up areas our forces sometimes enter one end of a main street as the Germans retreat out of the other: (4) a Bren-gunner knows how to deal with this particular situation.

Photos, British Official: Crown Copyright; Associated Press

THIS RHINO FERRY (centre background), laden with trucks and ambulances for delivery on the Normandy invasion coast, is seen leaving its mother vessel—a big tank landing craft. The Rhino Ferry, of U.S. design, and made of pre-fabricated hollow boxes of light steel, can be used for pontoon-bridging the short distance between landing ships and beach, or employed as a wharf, or dry-dock or, as this photograph shows, as a self-propelled barge.

Photo, British Official

THE WAR AT SEA

by Francis E. McMurtrie

THOUGH certain of the details have still to be filled in, enough is now known of the Allied invasion of Normandy to make it plain that it is the greatest as well as the most successful combined operation that has ever been undertaken. After all their efforts to ascertain where the blow was most likely to fall, the Germans were in the end taken by surprise. Over 4,000 ships of every kind, together with immense numbers of landing craft, were able to proceed across the Channel, breach the enemy coast defences and land large armies where desired, all without appreciable interference by the enemy sea or air forces.

This vast armada must have been collected from ports all over the United Kingdom, though the greater proportion was concentrated beforehand in southern harbours. To ensure surprise, it may be assumed that the use of wireless was restricted to a minimum ; thus communications needed to be severely limited. Everybody concerned seems to have known exactly what had to be done, so that the operation of crossing the Channel and landing the troops was carried through without a hitch.

SUPERIOR sea power was the foundation on which this success was based. Not only was ample tonnage available, in the shape of merchant vessels and landing craft, to transport the troops to the beaches, but very strong naval forces were provided for duty as escorts, for the bombardment of German gun emplacements, and to clear the minefields which presented the most dangerous obstacle of all. After the landings had been completed, these naval forces continued to support the invasion by shelling enemy concentrations of tanks and artillery, and protecting the sea supply routes against attack by enemy light craft. In fact, sea power played just as important a part as it did in the North African and Sicilian landings.

In Washington it has been revealed that the contribution of the United States Navy to the operation numbered 1,500 ships, comprising the battleships Nevada, Texas and Arkansas, the heavy cruisers Augusta, Quincy and Tuscaloosa, over 30 destroyers, and large numbers of destroyer escorts, transports and landing craft. It should be explained that

"destroyer escort" is the official rating of an American type of escort vessel, corresponding to British frigates of the "Captains" class.

British warships numbered about twice as many as American, and are known from Press reports to have included the battleships Nelson, Rodney, Warspite and Ramillies ; cruisers Ajax, Apollo, Arethusa, Argonaut, Belfast, Bellona, Black Prince, Ceres, Danae, Diadem, Enterprise, Frobisher, Glasgow, Hawkins, Mauritius, Orion, Scylla, and Sirius.; destroyers Algonquin, Ashanti, Beagle, Brissenden, Eskimo. Haida, Huron, Javelin, Kelvin, Melbreak, Scourge, Sioux, Tartar, Urania, Versatile, Vidette, Wanderer and Wrestler ; the monitor Roberts ; frigates Duff, Stayner, Tyler and Torrington ; and the auxiliaries Glenearn, Glenroy, Hilary, Prince David and Prince Robert. Of these ships, the Algonquin, Haida, Huron, Sioux, Prince David and Prince Robert belong to the Royal Canadian Navy, the growth of which since 1939 has been absolutely phenomenal.

More than 200 minesweepers of various types formed an important element of this fleet, together with a number of warships belonging to our European Allies. There were the French cruisers Georges Leygues and Montcalm, with the destroyer La Combattante, in which General de Gaulle took passage for his visit to Normandy ; the Polish cruiser Dragon and destroyers Blyskawica, Krakowiak and Piorun ; the Norwegian destroyers Glaisdale, Stord, and Svenner ; and the Dutch gunboats Flores and Soemba. Two Italian destroyers are also believed to have been present.

ONE of the surprises of this operation has been the rapidity with which naval guns have knocked out shore ones. While there is no doubt that fire control methods have improved out of all knowledge since the Belgian coast bombardments of the 1914-18 war, it is still true that a gun mounted in a battery on shore has definite advantages over one in a ship. There is a limit to the amount of armour that a warship can carry, but a fort can be protected to any extent desired. A ship can be sunk, but a silenced battery can be re-established, repaired or re-manned.

Yet in the last few weeks the naval gun has triumphed every time. One reason for this has been the thoroughness of air reconnaissance, enabling the exact position of every gun emplacement to be ascertained, so that it can be wiped out by an overwhelming concentration of fire. Spotting of the fall of shot from the air has been developed till it is almost an exact science, depending largely upon very carefully co-ordinated communication by signal between ship and observer. Previous experience in Italy and elsewhere has also borne good fruit. Having said all this, it still remains a fact that the gunnery of the Allied warships has been exceedingly good, testimony to the keenness and trained efficiency of naval officers and men. That these statements are in no degree exaggerated may be judged from the chorus of praise for the achievements of the naval guns from the Allied armies and from independent Press observers afloat and ashore.

UP to the time of writing, no news has come of Allied naval losses, beyond the statement that two U.S. destroyers were sunk, and reports of landing craft wrecked. Though German claims in this connexion may generally be disregarded as exaggerated out of all proportion to the truth, it is significant that on this occasion they have been unusually modest. Their own losses, on the other hand, have been severe, having regard to the few ships at their disposal. On June 7 three enemy destroyers were attacked by Coastal Command aircraft in the Bay of Biscay. One of these was set on fire, a second slowed down perceptibly, and a third had stopped when last seen. Attacks were also made on the same date upon coastal craft of the type which the Germans call S-boats, but which for no logical reason are commonly referred to as E-boats. Two of these were sunk and a third may have shared their fate.

A day later another enemy m.t.b. was attacked with rockets by fighter aircraft and was almost certainly destroyed. Off Ushant a force of German destroyers was brought to action by six British destroyers ; one of the enemy ships was torpedoed and sunk and a second was driven ashore. In other encounters more than a dozen German m.t.b.s and motor minesweepers and several armed trawlers were lost, while air attacks on the harbours of Havre and Boulogne are believed to have accounted for a good many more. Some of these losses have been admitted by the enemy. We lost a motor torpedo boat in one engagement.

Great Sea Guns Blast Hitler's French Coast

NAVAL MIGHT OF THE ALLIES helped to ensure success of the initial invasion landings in France on June 6, 1944, with intense bombardment of the beach-head areas, and later supported our troops advancing inland. H.M.S. Warspite, veteran British battleship, pounds the coast with her 15-in. guns (1). Closer inshore destroyers add to the softening-up process (2), and the U.S. battleship Texas joins in (3). Valuable part in the invasion operations was taken by the Royal Canadian Navy; a landing craft (4, in foreground) from H.M.C.S. Prince David, laden with Canadian troops, heads for a Normandy beach. See stories in pp. 122, 123.

Photos, British Official; Royal Canadian Navy, Associated Press

These Men Lead the Mighty Liberation Forces

OFF A BEACH-HEAD in Northern France, and close to the battles there raging, one of the most significant conferences of this war took place on the afternoon of June 7, 1944. For four and a half hours, General Eisenhower, Supreme Commander of the Allied Expeditionary Forces, with Admiral Sir Bertram Ramsay, Allied Naval Commander, cruised there on board a British warship. General Montgomery joined them to discuss the situation.

The Allied commanders on deck after their cabin conference (1)—Gen. Eisenhower (centre), Adm. Ramsay (left), Gen. Montgomery (right). On a beach U.S. invasion commanders "talked things over." (2—left to right)—Rear-Adm. A. G. Kirk, Commander of the Western Naval Task Force ; Lt.-Gen. Omar Bradley, Commander of the U.S. ground invasion forces ; Rear-Adm. J. L. Hall, Jnr., commander of an assault task force under Rear-Adm. Kirk. Air Chief Marshal Sir Trafford Leigh-Mallory, K.C.B., D.S.O., Commander-in-Chief Allied Expeditionary Air Force (3). Air Chief Marshal Sir Arthur Tedder, G.C.B., Deputy Supreme Commander (4). German prisoners turn to stare as Gen. Montgomery drives past in a jeep (5).

Photos, British Official ; Associated Press, Planet News

On Normandy Beaches Won Back from the Nazis

POWER OF OUR LIBERATING FORCES is indicated in this photograph (1) taken by a combat cameraman of the 9th U.S.A.A.F. It shows just a few of our big and little ships lying off a beach-head of Northern France, protective barrage balloons overhead. Digging in at a strong-point near the coast, British troops make themselves at home (2). Carrying bicycles, infantrymen wade the few remaining yards ashore to help consolidate our hold on territory regained from the Nazis (3).

Photos, British and U.S. Official. P.N.A.

MOUNTING TREMENDOUSLY FROM DAY TO DAY is the build-up of the Allied front in Northern France. Above, sea lines indicate four landing-points at Luc, Langrune, St. Aubin and Bernières, where British and Canadian forces went in. On June 13, 1944, reports showed that Allied divisions along the Normandy front, starting from the eastern flank, included the British Sixth Airborne, the Third, the Fiftieth (Northumbrian), and the U.S. First divisions. Keypoints taken in the first fortnight's fighting spread out on our line of advance (roughly from Troarn to the port of Quinéville, whose capture was announced on June 15) include Bayeux, Isigny, Carentan and Ste. Mère-Eglise. By June 18 the Allies had swept due west from Carentan across the Cherbourg peninsula to Barneville-sur-Mer on its west coast, turning thence to its tip to break into Cherbourg on June 25.

Specially drawn for THE WAR ILLUSTRATED *by Félix Gordon*

With the 'Suicide Squads' Who Cleared the Way

An 80-mile breach in the vaunted West Wall on the Normandy coast lies at the back of our Armies in France. It can now be revealed how, in fantastic circumstances, British scientists stole the beach-head secrets, and how the first cracks of that breach were made by Royal Navy men and Marines and Royal Engineers shortly before zero hour on June 6, 1944.

WRIGGLING inland on their stomachs, blackened faces within an inch of the ground, a number of men who had been secretly landed in darkness at a point on the French coast went calmly about their work—probing here and there with special instruments, making notes and generally behaving as do fantastic visions in an uneasy dream. Noiselessly they continued their crawl, and no crack of a shot to indicate

ANTI-LANDING CRAFT OBSTACLES such as this being examined by a Naval officer and a Royal Engineer officer were intended to be invisible to oncoming craft at high tide. Their purpose was to rip a gaping hole in any vessel approaching the Normandy beaches.
Photo, British Official : Crown Copyright

that their movements had been spotted by a German sentry.

Half a mile or more in different directions, members of this silent party went: scouring the beaches until they were satisfied their mission was well and truly completed. Assembled at last at the appointed rendezvous back at the sea-edge they packed up their instruments and the soil-samples which these had secured, put away their notes and departed for Britain, as mysteriously as they had arrived.

These "bright lads" (as one of them described his adventurous party) were civilian scientists, and the information and specimens they brought back with them proved of inestimable value to the authorities in whose hands lay the final planning which should put the assaulting troops ashore dead on time on D-Day—which yet lay months ahead.

A GREAT deal had been learned of the nature of the ground and of the defences where our landings might eventually take place, through innumerable photographs secured by low-flying planes of the R.A.F.; and, appertaining to the topography and terrain characteristics, old French books— some published before the 18th century— had yielded much that was of use. This midnight crawl of the scientists over Hitler's weapon-bristling beaches added the final footlines and marginal notes. Summed up, all this diversely gleaned information resulted in invasion-rehearsals in Britain which went far towards ensuring the assault troops' brilliant success.

From the crawling scientists' painstaking charting was discovered where treacherously soft patches of beach would be encountered, where boggy ground and slippery clay and firm or shifting sand would have to be negotiated. The beach obstacles they had sketched were reproduced on British beaches and assaulted by way of rehearsal. Landings were practised on British coastline stretches

identical in nature with the Normandy beach-heads. Vehicle types to be used in the actual landing were decided upon as the outcome of these practices, and where necessary they were specially adapted. Angle of slope of the beaches made it desirable that some should be waterproofed (see article in page 110) and others considerably lightened.

At dawn of the day appointed for attack, suicide squads—they call themselves, officially Landing Craft Obstacle Clearance Units— went in to clear the way for the troops who were speeding in their wake across the Channel. These Naval parties and Royal Marines and Engineers had the task of clearing all the beaches of the sudden death so plentifully besprinkled there. Up to their necks in water they mostly worked at this touch-and-go job.

THERE were stout steel pickets with thick supporting rods driven into sand or turf or concrete, each 7 feet high and 8 feet wide and weighing a ton and a half, placed there to rip the bottoms out of landing craft and tanks. Other steel obstacles blocked beach exits. There were continuous rows of angle-iron hedgehogs, and rows of steel rails set upright or at a sharp angle. Timber tripod obstacles were concealed at high tide, to impale landing vessels. There were anti-boat cables, and numerous types of mines— some hanging from stake-ends and capable of being detonated at a touch.

Weary indeed, and bloodshot and nerve-frayed were these suicide men when at last they rested. They had been sniped at from pillboxes, and whilst they laboured some of the beach areas had been under bombardment by our own naval forces. They didn't talk much of their comrades who fell, but one swift picture of their ordeal has been given by a correspondent to whom one spoke :

It was the toughest job we've ever had. Some of our plans went just as scheduled and others all went screwy. For instance, we were a little late getting in and the water was higher than we expected. We had to work with water up to our necks, sometimes higher. Then there were the snipers. They were nipping us off as I was working with two blokes on a tough bit of element, when suddenly I found myself working alone. My two pals just gurgled and disappeared under water.

Naturally they could not deal in the short time at their disposal with all the thousands of deadly obstacles and booby traps that,

hidden or exposed, littered the landing areas, and one officer observer has recorded how his craft was among the few that met with dire misfortune :

Her bottom had been ripped by one of the thousands of obstacles. With the water rising well over her engine-room plates, and her engines out of action, the Commanding Officer decided to beach her. At low tide it would be possible to patch her up and make the passage back to her home-port and carry on with the "shuttle-service." The tide receded a long way, to reveal an amazing sight on the beaches. Thousands of rusted iron girders, bolted together in threes like stacked rifles, had been driven into the clay and sand. Their jagged edges at high-tide either barely protruded above the water or, more often, were just submerged. Between them wooden stakes were driven into the beach to which shells, mines, and other under-water traps had been attached. How so few craft had sustained really serious damage was a miracle. That there was not a single landing-craft bigger than the smallest assault craft—and of these there were very few— actually sunk, throughout our sector, was a tribute to those who designed and built them, as well as to the seamanship of the crews.

Bulldozers smashed down, and mobile cranes tore away, iron girders and stakes with utmost speed to enable successive waves of assault craft to come in. There were great lines of barbed wire, and where this had not had gaps blown in it by the naval bombardment it had to be cut for the infantry to pass through and get at what ever chanced to lay immediately beyond—enemy trench systems, pill boxes and gun emplacements.

EACH man of the demolition parties carried T.N.T., and as their work took them farther up the beaches some were detailed to blast passages through concrete or masonry sea-walls which in some places were about 20 feet high and many feet thick—though nothing like a continuous "wall" was anywhere encountered. The solid "wall" as popularly visualized was a phantom of Nazi bluff; but what there was of it rocked and splintered throughout invasion day and intermittently throughout the night and next morning, and mines of every description continued to detonate.

"Occasionally" (said another war reporter) "the men dealing with them miss one, but not often. Then a man or vehicle sets it off, and the man goes to a hospital or a grave, and the vehicle to a repair crew or junk heap." . . . Salute to the Brave !

ENORMOUS EXPLOSIONS occurred on the French foreshore as enemy mines were touched off by such men as these of the Royal Navy. As members of Landing Craft Obstacle Clearance Units their task, in co-operation with Royal Marines and Engineers, was to deal with deadly obstructions in the path of our assault troops. How these "suicide squads" shaped on D-Day—and subsequently—is told in this page. **PAGE 107** *Photo, British Official : Crown Copyright*

'Blimey, it's Churchill!' the Soldiers Said

TO SEE FOR HIMSELF, Mr. Churchill crossed the Channel in the destroyer H.M.S. Kelvin and spent seven hours ashore on the Normandy beach-head on June 14, 1944. With him went General Smuts, Prime Minister of South Africa, and Field Marshal Sir Alan Brooke, G.C.B., D.S.O., Chief of the Imperial General Staff. On the way across H.M.S. Kelvin bombarded a German position.

On the destroyer's bridge Mr. Churchill chats to Field Marshal Sir Alan Brooke (1). From the duck which brings him ashore the Premier sets foot on French soil, to be warmly greeted by General Montgomery (2) and "mobbed" by working parties of Army and Navy men as he tours a captured town (3). German planes came over, but were engaged and driven off; the Premier, General Smuts, General Montgomery and Field Marshal Sir Alan Brooke watch the air battle (4). General Montgomery obtains information from fishermen (5) at a captured port.

Photos, British and U.S. Official

Reinforcements Move Up to the Western Front

IT MIGHT BE A COUNTRY LANE IN ENGLAND with care-free soldiers on a route march. But the scene is Normandy, and these infantrymen of ours are moving up to a front-line position. British Divisions now engaged in France include the 6th Airborne, and the 3rd and 50th (Northumbrian). The latter was in the spearhead of the British assault on D-Day, earning high praise for " a first-class performance in the face of very adverse conditions and stout enemy opposition." The 7th British Armoured Division also is busy out there. *Photo. British Official*

Miracles of Planning Behind the Great Invasion

No less renowned a warrior than Marshal Stalin has paid tribute to the brilliant success of our assault on Western Europe. "In the whole history of war," he said, "there has not been any such undertaking, so broad in conception, so grandiose in scale and so masterly in execution." The military organization that helped to make this triumph possible is briefly outlined below:

TRAINS cancelled and trains late : these were annoyances suffered in varying mood by the civilian on the eve of D-Day—and promptly forgotten when, on the morning of June 6, 1944, the world thrilled to the announcement that a gigantic armada had crossed the Channel and the siege of North-Western Europe had commenced.

In vast camps and remote villages all over Britain extreme activity, surpassing anything that had gone before, had reigned whilst we finally gathered our assault forces and

MILITARY SIGN on a road leading to a British port of embarkation warns those who can't help not to hinder. The steady flow of invasion troops across Britain was assisted by the widening of roads and the strengthening of bridges. *Photo, British Official*

gave them the strength to do that which they are now accomplishing so magnificently. Roads echoed to the thunder of almost endless convoys as the appointed day approached ; and on the railways fell an especially heavy burden—the transportation in two months of 230,000 soldiers criss-cross over the face of Britain to the several invasion marshalling centres, together with 12,000 tons of baggage.

In those eight weeks close on 2,000 special trains ran non-stop to ports whence the invasion was to be launched. Tanks and other war vehicles to the number of 7,000 went by rail. For heavy tanks special flat-bottomed wagons had had to be constructed, to the order of the War Office. To all this was added other stupendous traffic which cannot be specified here—yet complete order reigned where might have been expected chaos. The result was that every ship that in due course sailed across the Channel was loaded up with just that cargo for which it had been earmarked. Thus brilliantly shone just one of the many and almost bewilderingly varied facets of the scheme involving naval, land and air forces in a combined operation on the smooth running of which the whole fate of the gigantic venture hung as on a thread.

THE fact that Allied forces also were involved added to complications which, long before D-Day, had of sheer necessity to be smoothed into an indivisible and unconquerable power to shatter as speedily as possible the resistance of the enemy.

As far back as the closing days of 1941, when we were slowly recovering from the disastrous Dunkirk period of the previous year, this problem of landing an army in full strength on the mainland of Europe was engaging the keenest brains. But operations in the Mediterranean area had then to be given priority.

During that period the pattern of our ultimate plans was emerging. From Combined operations at St. Nazaire in March 1942, and in August at Dieppe, much was learned. The lay-out of the supposedly formidable West Wall was revealing its secrets to the British Intelligence Staffs. Invasion maps, covering all parts of Western Europe where operations might eventually take place, were prepared by the million ; in this work practically every firm in Britain whose plant was capable of, or could be adapted to, the printing of maps was employed by the Survey Department of the War Office, the greatest precautions meanwhile being taken against leakage of any scrap of information likely to be of use to the enemy.

Operations against Sicily and the Italian mainland followed the Casablanca Conference of early 1943. At the end of March of that year the 1944 "Second Front" preparations entered on a new and vigorous phase. An Anglo-American staff representing all three Services (Army, Navy and Air) made an accounting of all resources that would be available early in 1944, and compiled plans for the invasion.

A GENERAL scheme was submitted to British and U.S. Chiefs of Staff, and finally approved by the Prime Minister and Mr. Roosevelt at the Quebec Conference in August 1943. Administrative preparations then went forward apace, special training of the forces was speeded up, and complete co-ordination by air and naval forces was arranged to the satisfaction of General Eisenhower, who assumed the appointment of Supreme Commander in January 1944. Upon him devolved responsibility for decision as to the actual date of the assault.

Supply, provisioning and transport all had to be fitted into the master plan. Here entered administrative problems of the very first magnitude—the concentration of large troop formations in areas near to points of embarkation, with the minimum dislocation of the civilian population, to be followed by

WATERPROOFING our assault vehicles for the dash to the Normandy coast was a high-speed pre-invasion task, as mentioned in this page. Here jeeps are being prepared for the waterproofing process.

Photo, U.S. Official

the movement of the concentrated troops to marshalling areas, where they would be divided into assault troops, first reinforcements and follow-ups and then split into unit parties and craft loads for embarkation. Coastal shipping for the cross-Channel transport of troops had to be arranged for, without "robbing" the country unduly of the wherewithal to obtain essential supplies for home and factory use. Loading berths had to be decided upon, and special "hards" constructed to add to berthing facilities. The movement of requisitioned coastal ships to selected ports and points of loading provided many a headache.

EVERY planned movement and route, by land and sea, had to be according to exact time-table. For each beach-head secured, ships were to be loaded with a mixed cargo : food, ammunition, signals equipment, engineering and ordnance stores, water and medical supplies, each in carefully calculated quantity per ship. Furthermore, responsibility for transporting R.A.F. materials needed at airfields captured or constructed devolved upon the Army.

Among major considerations which had to be settled well in advance was that concerning types of invasion vehicles. The D.U.K.W.s (amphibious lorries), which had served so well in the invasions of Sicily and of the Italian mainland, required for their manning—for this greater occasion—large numbers of water-trained R.A.S.C. personnel; and for the operating of fast launches in connexion with beach and port unloading, special motor-boat companies had to be organized. For all lorry drivers instruction in manoeuvring through deep water from the assault craft was necessary.

ONE simple type of craft from which troops can wade ashore suffices to transport an infantry battalion. But their vehicles, and tanks, and artillery, necessitate the employment of manifold types of craft. These must all be at the right spot at the right moment, and in sufficient numbers. One problem in connexion with the landing of vehicles on the French beaches worried the Directorate of Mechanical Engineering, until a system of waterproofing was evolved. This not only protects vehicles against the corrosive effects of sea water, but enables the engines to function in a depth of water to which the craft may be not ordinarily adapted. That our tanks drove on to the Normandy shore through six feet of water is due to one of the greatest "rush" jobs of this war.

Chiefly, this task of waterproofing the invasion vehicles fell to the Royal Electrical and Mechanical Engineers. Enough steel plate was used in the process to lay an armoured road from London to Berlin, and it was produced by the round-the-clock efforts of our combined steel sheet-rolling industries. Army and civilian lorries to the number of 250 were engaged for eight weeks in transporting the material from the 280 factories handling it, to R.A.O.C. depots ; 500,000 components the R.A.O.C. received and assembled and then issued to some 5,000 different depots for fitting.

Hand-in-glove with all this went medical preparations, and far-seeing arrangements for the transport of the sick and the wounded from the beach-heads to Britain, either by sea or by air. Pay day on the beaches passed without a hitch, thanks to the Paymaster-General's forethought ; and within a day or two of the landing letters were being collected for delivery home—and letters from home being received by "the boys" sharing the brilliant triumphs of those early June days.

Allied Tanks and Equipment Pour into Normandy

Shepherded across the English Channel by the Allied Navies under Admiral Sir Bertram Ramsay, tanks and equipment in ever-increasing quantities land on wide stretches of the Invasion Coast in broad daylight. With barrage balloon protection, calmly and methodically the work of unloading goes on. Many vehicles, such as the tanks in the top photograph, have been specially waterproofed to keep their mechanism unaffected by immersion in deep water as they drive ashore.

Foothold Gained on the Northern Coast of France—

Under cover of naval and air bombardment, American assault troops plunge through the surf from a landing craft (1) on June 6, 1944, to the shore, where they are here seen from the air (2). Confronted by withering enemy fire they take cover behind beach obstacles (3). At the end of a day of very heavy conflict in one beach sector, they gained a hundred yards of ground, " hanging on by their eyelids " declared General Montgomery ; but a few days later they were 10 miles inland.

—Our Men are All Set for the Liberation of Europe

British infantry and Red Cross personnel (4) wade in from the sea in the wake of comrades who are battling their way inland through the Normandy countryside. Tow-planes and gliders swarm overhead (5) carrying more reinforcements, while landing craft lie close inshore. In the first 24 hours the Battle of the Beaches was won; in a week the Allied front extended 60 miles, with maximum depth of 18 miles, crowning with triumph the greatest combined operation in history.

Canadians Contribute to the Haul of Prisoners

Photos, Canadian Official

In six days from the landing prisoners numbered 10,000. This wayside station in Normandy (top) was a German strong-point. It is now in Canadian hands, and the lined-up prisoners await marching orders. They were still preparing an "impenetrable defence" when the blow fell. Another morose half-dozen (bottom) are seen with their guards; in the background, casualties receive attention. The Western Canadian Infantry Brigade formed part of the British 3rd Division.

VIEWS & REVIEWS Of Vital War Books

by Hamilton Fyfe

A SWEDISH statesman some centuries ago was sending his son out into the world and giving him advice. Better advice than Polonius gave Laertes, though that was not bad. Oxenstierna said, "Don't believe what you are told, my boy. Investigate for yourself. Make up your own mind. Then you will be astonished to find with how little wisdom the world is governed." I suppose few ages have had more glaring examples of this than the one we live in.

I have been reading a book which shows how the muddles and intrigues of politicians made possible the attempt Japan is making to become all-powerful in the Pacific. That attempt could not have been made, says Willard Price in his Japan's Islands of Mystery (Heinemann, 10s. 6d.), if the mandate for protecting these territories which stretch across the ocean for thousands of miles had not been given by the 1919 Peace Conference to Japan. The risk of doing this was not absent from some American minds. President Wilson felt they might be a threat to the United States. But secret treaties between Britain, France and Japan prevented him from standing out against this gift of enormous value to a possible, indeed a probable, enemy.

It was laid down in the mandate that the islands should not be fortified or used as naval bases. Mr. Price, who is American, blames the "easy-going" officials of the League of Nations, "comfortably leather-chaired in Geneva," for not keeping a closer watch and discovering that Japan treated this proviso with contempt. He does not complain of the secret diplomacy that promised the islands to Japan. That happened before the United States entered the war in 1917, and he says that "if America had been moved to fight for democracy when Germany first flung down the challenge in 1914, instead of after three years delay, it might have prevented the rising of many ghosts which haunted President Wilson at the peace table." He blames "American vacillation and lack of clear-cut policy" for the failure to safeguard American interests in the Pacific, by letting territories vital to the security of those interests fall into the hands first of the Germans and then of the Japanese.

WHEN the U.S.A. fought and beat Spain, the islands were part of the spoils of victory. All that the U.S.A. kept were the Philippines and Guam. The rest was returned to Spain. Spain sold it to Germany for £700,000. The Germans were more energetic than the Spaniards had been.

The Spanish period had been largely a regime of priests who forced their religion upon the islanders with the bloody assistance of soldiers. Rebellions were frequent.

The Germans worked up the trade in dried coconut (copra) and were making a profit when the 1914 war came. Then Japan rushed in and seized Micronesia (which means The Little Islands) before British ships on the same errand could get there. The Japanese made it quite clear they meant to hold them, if necessary to fight for them. So the easy way out seemed to be to give them the mandate to take care of them. Japan did this thoroughly, not in the interest of the inhabitants but of its own ambitions.

Not only did they make the islands strong for use in war; they also introduced new methods in cultivation and new crops which have brought about an economic revolution. Production of copra has been improved and quickened. Some of the finest sugar-cane in the world is grown. Tapioca, used by cake and confectionery makers everywhere in powdered form, has been planted on what seemed barren land. Pineapples and pigs are raised in vast numbers. That is an example of wisdom in government, but the Japanese spoil it by their criminal folly of believing they can make profit out of war.

Willard Price and his wife managed to see a good deal of Micronesia in spite of the obstacles thrown in the way of anyone who wanted to visit there. A German who got in some ten years ago complained that he had been followed about wherever he went. The explanation offered was that he had been discovered to be tubercular, and it was neces-

---

An Island Whereon to Spend Eternity?

sary to take great care of him. He mistook hospitality for shadowing! Another traveller, a U.S. colonel of Marines, disappeared and was stated to have drunk himself to death, but the general belief was that the Japanese had poisoned him.

AMONG some of the islanders head-hunting still goes on. I have often wondered what its origin could have been. It is now practised as a kind of sport. How it started was explained by one of the "kings." At a time when there was not enough to eat—"too many people, too little food"—each group of tribesmen tried to thin out the population by killing as many of other tribes as they could. Warriors were sent out to trap unwary men, women or children, and fall on them unawares. "If we could stop a young mouth from a lifetime of eating, it was even better than stopping an old one." So what Karl Marx called economic warfare was waged in its simplest form in Palau.

The South Seas have been described so often as earthly paradises that it will surprise and shock most people to learn that the natives are an unhealthy lot. Everywhere the population is decreasing. "Long time ago," lamented a chief, "only old men died; now young men die." They die from diseases of the stomach and lungs. They die from leprosy, dysentery, venereal complaints. These last have been brought to them, as tuberculosis was, by white people. But they have only themselves to blame for weakening their constitutions by living in thatched-roof huts, which are shut up tightly in bad weather and at all times are damp, frousty and dark.

Their ancestors taught them to plunge fever sufferers in the sea to cool them, and to lay anyone with a chill on them as close as possible to a fire. They still do it. Some of them wash their dead chiefs' bodies after death and drink the water, hoping to acquire his strength. So much was their working capacity diminished by illness that the Japanese in self-defence established up-to-date hospitals and efficient health centres.

IT is impossible to avoid thinking that the islanders would be better off if white men had never found them. One of the most intelligent whom Mr. Price talked to deplored the "benefits" supposed to have been brought to them. He said they got on very well without them. They were contented and quiet. Now they were being made restless, anxious to be doing something, even if it was quite useless. "On the athletic field near the school a track has been made where boys may run round in a circle. That is what civilization is—running round in a circle."

But if the people are in many ways disappointing, the beauty of the scenery cannot be exaggerated. While we picture Truk, the Japanese naval base, as a fortress bristling with guns, grim and horrid, it is in truth more lovely even than Tahiti. It is "a cluster of 245 islands in a vast iridescent lagoon surrounded by a coral reef." Once there was a huge volcano here. Its summit was divided up into many summits. The land gradually subsided; only the tops of the mountains were left above water. These are now Truk. There are also pink coral islands which are flat, while the volcanic remnants are like towers and minarets "clothed from sea to summit with bread-fruit and banana trees, coconut palms, scarlet bougainvillea and crimson hibiscus, brilliant against the deep blue South Sea sky." Mr. Price says if he could choose a spot in which to spend eternity, he would think twice about Truk.

It would have to be de-Japped, of course. Well, it will be. And then we must hope white people will be careful not to make such glaring mistakes in government as they made in the past—with the result that we are tangled up in this world war.

SET AFIRE BY CARRIER-BASED AIRCRAFT of the U.S. Navy, bombed Japanese vessels are seen lying off the thickly jungled Palau Islands in the Pacific after the heavy attack there on March 29, 1944; other enemy ships fled before the attack. This vital Japanese base, which lies some 480 miles from the Philippines, was severely damaged. The story of these enemy-held islands is dealt with in the book reviewed in this page. *Photo, Planet News*

Freedom Returns to Stricken Towns of France

ONE AFTER ANOTHER towns and villages of Normandy have had the Nazi yoke lifted by the advancing Allied armies. Isigny, a small commercial town some three miles inland (1), was captured on June 10, 1944. Cheering crowds greeted our forces in Bayeux, and two little girls presented bouquets to the officers who addressed them (2). Capture of Bayeux on June 8 deprived the enemy of the most direct line of communication from the Cherbourg peninsula to the valley of the Seine and to Paris. The Germans flooded the area round Carentan, key transport and communication centre (3), which the Allies first entered on June 12. The town of Ste. Mère Eglise (4) was taken on June 6. See map in p. 106.

Photos, British and U.S. Official, and Associated Press

We Have Won Battle of the Beaches—*Montgomery*

THE situation today is that these landings that we have made on the coast of Normandy have all been joined up into a solid line—a continuous lodgment area from right to left.

The violence and the power and the speed of our initial assault carried us right over the beaches and some miles inland very quickly, except in one special case. On these beaches there were concrete defences and in a great many cases they were passed with enemy garrisons remaining in them.

I said beforehand that every man must be imbued with one idea and that was to penetrate quickly and deeply into enemy country and peg out claims inland. The conception that you land on the beaches and get a little bridgehead, then dig in—that is no good. You must penetrate quickly and deeply. Those defended localities which still held out when we were three miles inland had to be dealt with and reduced later. In that process we had losses because they were held by stout-hearted Germans who fought very well indeed in their concrete-built boxes.

On the beach where the landing of American troops took place east of the Carentan estuary, they found a German field division which had been brought up from behind to thicken the coastal crust and was in process of carrying out an exercise. Very heavy fighting went on on the American beach on D-Day, swaying back and forwards, and by the evening the leading troops were not more than 100 yards inland, hanging on by their eyelids . . . Today those troops are miles inland.

The situation was retrieved by three things—(1) the gallantry of the American soldiers; (2) by the very fine supporting fire given from the sea by the Allied Navy; and (3) by the very good fighter-bombers, who came down low to shoot up the Germans at close range. I should think that the retrieving of that situation from a very difficult and unpleasant situation to a very good one is probably one of the finest things that has been done in this operation.

The Western Canadian Infantry Brigade, which is part of the British Third Division, has been in the thick of the fighting since the first day. The brigade landed on the beaches, went right away to its objective inland and still stands there.

The support given to our armies by the Navy and Air Force has been superb—without it we could not have done it. The heavy bombing of the Fortresses and the other bombers was one of the big factors which made our getting on shore so quickly really possible. Our soldiers—American and British—have already got the measure of the enemy.—*From a talk by Gen. Montgomery to War Correspondents in Normandy, June 12, 1944.*

FIRST FOOTHOLDS SECURED on the coast of Northern France in the early morning of June 6, 1944, our forces lost no time in pushing inland. Behind a massive tank-destroyer British infantry shelter from German snipers while preparing to return their fire (1). Battery of well-camouflaged heavy 105-mm. self-propelled gun-howitzers smashes enemy attempts to hold up one of our advancing groups (2). Allied troops and transport move on through a captured village from which the Germans had only recently been ejected (3). PAGE 117 *Photos, British Official*

Heart of a Fallen Empire Beats Freely Again—

TWELVE DAYS AFTER OUR NEW OFFENSIVE in Italy, which was launched on May 23, 1944, the Allies entered Rome. Mussolini's balcony, from which the ex-dictator was wont to harangue his crowds, provides our troops with a grandstand (1). General Mark Clark, Commander of the 5th Army (in jeep, left), talks to a priest outside St Peter's (2). Transport in front of the monument to King Victor Emmanuel II (3); it also marks the Italian Unknown Soldier's grave. Romans greet our troops (4).

Photos. British and Canadian Official

—As Allies Reach the End of the Road to Rome

ARMOUR OF THE 5th ARMY rolls past the ancient Colosseum in Rome, which our triumphant troops occupied on the night of June 4, 1944, while cheering Italians line the pavement. Before the liberators, Kesselring's forces were retreating miles to the north, pursued by our advance mobile columns and battered by our air forces. The Colosseum, erected by the Roman emperor Vespasian in A.D. 72, was inaugurated in A.D. 80, by Titus, whose armies at that time were occupying part of Germany.

Photo, U.S. Official

I WAS THERE!

How We Smashed Into Western Europe

How went the first hours of D-Day? In these personal stories glimpses are given of some of the actions and incidents that made June 6, 1944, memorable as the actual commencement of the greatest combined operation known to mankind—the mighty assault on Hitler's fabled fortress in the West to free the enslaved peoples of Europe.

I PARACHUTED into Europe at two minutes past one a.m. this morning, six-and-a half hours before our seaborne forces began the full-blown invasion of Festung Europa; and I have seen, done and experienced a lot since then. I was near the shore, hiding from Nazi patrols as I watched our first forces go ashore from the sea at 7.15. I have seen a few thousand paratroops and glider-borne troops, whom I nominate now as the bravest, most tenacious men I have ever known, hold the bridgehead against Hitler's Armies for over sixteen hours despite overwhelming odds.

Our job as an airborne force was to silence a vital coastal battery, which if still in operation might have blown our ships to bits as they came to the shore. We silenced it. And our other just as vital job was to secure two important bridges over the canal and river north of Caen, to prevent them from being blown up, and to hold them against all-comers until the main Armies arrived. We are still holding them. They are still intact.

I emplaned in "C for Charlie," a great black bomber, at 11.20 p.m., and we took our place in the taxi-ing line of planes that stretched from one end to the other of one of the biggest airfields in Britain. There were Lancashire men, Yorkshiremen and North-umbrians mostly in our "stick" of para-troopers, the beefiest bunch of armed men I have ever seen. Preceding them by half an hour were the gliders and planes of para-troopers who were going to make a do-or-die attempt to take vital bridges before they could be blown up. Those gliders were going to crash themselves on the buttresses of the bridges themselves, and then, aided by paratroopers, were to capture the bridges and all surrounding land. It was our job to

bring them aid within thirty minutes of their surprise attack, and to "infest" the whole area for a hundred square miles around to prevent the Nazis from counter-attacking.

It was five minutes to one when the light snapped off and a hole in the plane was opened. Under it we could see the coast of France below—and a garish sight it was, for flak from the coast defences was spouting flame everywhere. In great globes of red and purple it burst all round our plane as it coasted in and down to the dropping zone. And we were scared by it—until the red light flashed before our eyes and then swiftly changed to green, and we were all madly shuffling down the hole and jumping into space. I looked, as I twisted down, for the church I had been told to spy for a landmark, and for the wood where we were later going to rendezvous as a fighting force. But the wind had caught me, and was whisking me east. Faster and faster I twisted, and I had to wrestle with my straps to get me straight. By that time I had come down in an orchard outside a farmhouse. And as I stood up

with my harness off and wiped the sweat off my brown-painted face, I knew I was hopelessly lost. Dare I go to the farmhouse and ask for directions? Suddenly there was a rip and tear in my flapping jumping-smock, and I flung myself to the ground as machine-guns rattled.

There was silence, then two more smashing explosions. Hand-grenades, this time. I could now see figures manoeuvring in the moonlight. I dived into the next field, and began to run at the crouch. And then, suddenly, at the farther edge there were two more figures. They were coming towards me, and they were carrying guns. What might have happened is one of those "ifs" of my private history—only there was a crash of Sten gun fire instead, and both men crumpled up not fifteen yards from me. Into the field stealthily came five men to challenge me—and I was with our own paratroopers again.

For two long, weary hours we wandered the country. We hid from German patrols in French barns. We shot-up a Nazi car speeding down a lane. When we were lying in a ditch on the outskirts of a village, a youth appeared with a German flask full of Normandy wine and, after we had drunk it, he led us, by a roundabout route, away from the enemy. And just after 3 a.m. we made our rendezvous—the bridges. Over both the river and the canal, spans were in our hands and firmly held by paratroop machine-gunners. Only beyond, in the west country, could tracer be seen and the noise of battle heard as we beat back a Nazi counter-attack. And then, at 3.20 every Allied

paratrooper behind the so-called Atlantic Wall breathed a sigh of relief as he heard the roar of bombers coming in slow, bombers towing gliders towards the dropping ground.

We watched them in the pale moonlight and glare of flak, unhooking, and then diving steeply for earth. We saw one, caught by ack-ack, catch fire and fly around for three or four minutes, a ball of flame. We heard the crunch of breaking matchwood as gliders bounced on rocks and careered into still-undestroyed poles. Out of every glider men were pouring, and jeeps, and anti-tank guns and field guns—and we knew that if Nazi tanks did come now we could hold them.

And now, as a faint glow began to appear in the eastern sky, our eyes turned upwards and westwards. For there was a roaring that rapidly grew to a thunderous roll that never stopped. We knew the climax of phase one of the invasion was approaching now. Here were bombers, swarming in like bees to give the Nazi coastal defences their last softening-up before our seaborne forces landed. And what a sight it was to see. We were about two miles away, but the shudder of explosions lifted us off the ground. Soon the sky was lit with a green and purple glow from burning Nazi dumps, and still more bombers swarmed in.

As dawn came I moved across country

BRITISH AIRBORNE TROOPS, down to earth in Normandy, promptly dig in (above). The British 6th Airborne Division has won high praise in the invasion battles; stories are given in this page and in page 121. Giant Hamilcar gliders, towed by Halifaxes, are about to touch-down in a French field (top); the fast and light tanks they carry will emerge ready for immediate action.

Photos, British Official

BATTLE-DUSTY BRITISH COMMANDOS are here seen moving up, with Allied transport, through a shell-smashed Normandy town near hotly-contested Caen. They have been in the thick of the fighting since our assault on Western Europe began on June 6, 1944, and have well been called " the fine cutting edge of the British Army." *Photo, British Official*

through Nazi patrols to get nearer to the coast. Wherever we moved there were traces of our airborne invasion. Emptied containers, still burning their signal lights, were scattered in fields and orchards.

Wrecked gliders littered the ground, some of them splintered to matchwood. There were parachutes lying everywhere. Eventually we reached high ground overlooking the coast

and waited until our watches showed 7.15. A few minutes before it there was an earth-shaking holocaust of noise. Approaching the coast under cover of naval ships, the invasion barges were coming in, and coming in firing. It was a terrific barrage that must have paralysed the defences. Then ships began nudging towards the beaches. The invasion at long last had begun !—*Leonard Mosley, for Combined Press*

It was 4.15 a.m. Mortars and machine-guns chattered. I was in a panic. My one desire was to get back home. Suddenly : " Push ahead, and for God's sake keep flat ! " came a voice, that of a captain who had come over in my glider. Chin-deep in filth I slid along, feeling very weak. I drew myself forward with my hands, which were cut and pierced and stung by nettles. I parted some reeds, and the rustle brought bursts of machine-gun fire and bullets from a sniper across the field. I continued to inch along the ditch, getting wetter, colder and more hungry.

At 4 p.m. the ditch was still my shelter. I was still face down, flatter than a worn rug. In my crawling I met Lieutenant-Colonel Charles Schellhammer, of New York. He had been in my glider and I felt a little better. We were able to get out of the ditch and start new tactics of hedge crawling. There were still plenty of snipers around and they began to practise on us, following us all along the hedge. At one place there was a 7 ft. gap which had to be cleared in a leap. Lieutenant-Colonel Schellhammer made it and beckoned to me. Weak and dispirited, I started across like an Olympic champion, but slipped right in the middle. All records for picking oneself up and proceeding were broken then and there.

I had lost my tin hat. Lieutenant-Colonel Schellhammer ordered me to go back for it. I suddenly hated him with a black venom— but I dived back and got it. The tactics baffled the sniper so much that he didn't shoot ! However, things improved, and by 5.30 that afternoon the area was cleared of snipers and we reached a little town which had just been captured by Americans. An old French woman came with a bottle of cognac which I gulped. " The Boche has gone. The war is over," she said. Ten minutes later the Germans counter-attacked and the war started all over again. Eager to keep out of trouble I hiked for the woods and spent a miserable night with an American colonel and a very dolorous cow in a clump of super-sharp raspberry bushes.

I wandered all next day and reached a temporary Command Post. That was Wednesday, and in the evening a platoon of Germans raided us as we were digging in.

I was getting shock-proof. I flopped into my hole and slept. Then I proceeded to the H.Q. establishment. A sergeant who watched me from a distance introduced me to his friends as the " best in the hedge-crawling business." It is an honour I am proud to accept. I calculate the Germans used about 5,000 rounds of ammunition on me that first day.—*Marshall Jarrow, Reuters*

I Went With the First Glider-borne Troops

I LANDED with the first glider forces in the invasion. It was dark, it was deadly, and we landed in a country of stinking swamps and hidden snipers. Almost the whole time I was there I had to take evasive action from the enemy. I crawled as I have never crawled before. When I left the fighting area I left behind me my face-print in the mud of Normandy's ditches.

I went over with the first glider group from Britain before dawn on D-Day. Never before had I been in a glider, and my own experience has shown me that the men who fly in gliders are among the world's toughest. They risk a crash landing, to start with, and are usually given a hot reception because the enemy has been put on the alert by the prior arrival of paratroops. We took off in the dark with scores of large transport planes hauling the heavily loaded gliders off the aerodrome at intervals of about 20 seconds.

We headed into heavy weather towards France. The glider heaved and pitched. Soldiers on either side of me were sick. I chewed gum vigorously, according to directions, swallowed some seasick pills and tried to think of something funny. I couldn't. The aerial procession was a sight I shall never forget. The sky looked like a giant Christmas tree, aglow with heaving clusters of red and green lights. In a little over two hours we reached the French coast, which was ablaze with light. We approached by an indirect route. Then it began. Flak started ripping through the fabric sides of our glider, but no one was hit despite our slow pace and low altitude.

Suddenly we went into a sickening dive as we dropped our tow-line. " Hold tight. We're going

down ! " yelled the pilot. Great balls of fire started to stream through our glider as we circled to land. I loosened my safety-belt to remove my Mae West and could not get it fastened in the excitement. I was thrown to the floor as our glider smashed and jarred on the earth, slid across a field and crashed into a ditch. For a moment I lay half-stunned, but the red-hot zip of machine-gun bullets an inch or two above my head revived me in a hurry. I took a wild dive out of the emergency door and fell into a ditch, waist-deep in stinking water overlaid with scum.

Storming Ashore with the 50th Division

WE landed soon after seven a.m. on June 6, from an assault craft. As our line of craft approached the shore the Navy's guns were blazing and smashing shells into fortifications guarding the strip of the beach we had to take. Just ahead of us, tank landing-craft were already inshore and tanks were racing up the shingle. German 88-millimetre guns got on to them and there were several direct hits which knocked out the tanks. Others came on.

We had no time to see how they got on, as our craft were by this time bumping on to the beach. Three hundred yards ahead of us was a concrete wall about 20 feet high. It was really a road embankment with a road running along the top. It was embrasured and the Jerries were lining the top and potting away at us, sweeping with their machine-guns and hurling down hand-grenades as we swept forward.

Several of our lads fell, but we dashed forward and got under the base of the wall where the Jerries couldn't get at us. More

of our landing-craft were coming inshore. I took a glimpse backward and saw one go up in flames. It had hit one of their under-water obstructions. I had seen these poking up out of the water as we came in, but we missed them. They were long ramps sticking up from the sea-bottom like inclined planes, and intended to rip the bottoms out of our craft. In addition they had bottles of explosive attached to the protruding end, which went up on contact. It was one of these that apparently upset the craft I saw go up.

Jerry was fighting hard to stop us landing, but soon the beach was swarming with our chaps. My party worked along the base of the wall and then charged over the open beach. There was sloping ground away on our left which led up to the top of a road where the wall petered out. We fought our way up this slope and got into the wooded ground above. This was full of Jerries. The wood was criss-crossed with low stone walls, just like Sicily. There were snipers behind these walls and they let us

H.M.S. RODNEY hurled 16-in. shells at the Normandy coast while landing-craft sped to the beaches under cover of the terrific bombardment from her guns and those of other Allied warships (see story below)
Photo, Keystone

have it. The chap next to me fell, shot through the neck. He was dead. Among the woods there were also trenches which the enemy was defending strongly. We drove them out with Tommy-guns and rifle fire as we advanced, but the men behind the walls were causing us a lot of trouble and casualties. The first of our chaps had got through the wood and were working round the Jerries manning the top of the wall when

a grenade lobbed over and exploded at my feet. I got this smack in the head and was out of the battle. Jerries were by this time popping off with their mortars.

The beach and wood became very hot places, and there was a certain amount of barbed wire among the trees, but it was low and we had got through it without much difficulty. When Jerry went back a bit, still fighting pretty hard, I made my way back to the beach and, with other wounded, was loaded on a ship—and here I am. It was a lively party, but we shifted Jerry from his strong points and everything was going well when I left.—*Sgt. G. Maynard of the 50th Division, as told in hospital to R. Monson.*

It was too close to be healthy, and from the splashes we judged the guns to be 5·9-in. or 6·1-in., big pieces to have got into position so quickly unless they were mobile. The Germans had taken the bait wholly, and flash after flash revealed them as they tried to pin down the weaving cruisers.

I took my eyes from the binoculars for a second to peep through my armoured slit at the blistered and blackened barrels of the old "Spite's" guns. They were already trained on the "new tenants," cocked so aggressively so that where I sat 20 feet above the captain's bridge I could almost look down their grizzled muzzles. They were only waiting the order of Captain Kelsey to spit out the inferno of flame and brown smoke speeding their ton-weight of high explosive to its billet. "Open fire!" came the order from the bridge. The Director Layer—an experienced warrant officer—pressed a foot-pedal which can fire all the main armament in one mighty broadside.

We of the Warspite Shelled the French Coast

FOUR men with their eyes glued to their powerful binoculars mounted in the control tower from which the fire of this battleship is directed shouted together "there he goes again!" as a winking light on the shoulder of the skyline this afternoon betrayed a powerful German gun in action. It had obviously been dragged into position overnight to take the place of the battery which we had knocked clean out with our 15-inch salvos yesterday. The new arrivals had dug themselves in near the old position probably because no other so completely commanded our beaches.

They had no intention of interfering with us. Seeing the devastation of yesterday so near them, they probably had a healthy respect for our gunnery, but they betrayed their activity by a few unostentatious ranging shots which they put out to sea. What they wanted to do was to take advantage of the hazy distance between us and them to get on with their real job of harassing the beach without being spotted by guns like ours which could answer back. It was part

of the schedule of the cruisers Frobisher and Scylla to investigate certain targets reported to them by aircraft, and so they were instructed as they passed nearby to let the new occupants have a few salvos. It was hoped that the Germans would return the fire and so give us an opportunity of marking them down accurately for the attention of our heavier guns. I was in the director control tower when one of the gunnery officers' team reported "Frobisher has opened fire, sir."

"Now we will see if Jerry accepts the bait," said the gunnery officer ("Guns"). It was a few seconds later that the cry went up from the watchers, of whom I happened to be one. The new, and very temporary, tenants bit all right, and the tell-tale gun flashes from the all but invisible skyline were quickly translated into a target for our "B" turret. Distance, angle of sight and a dozen other readings were transmitted to the G.T. "table" in the bowels of the ship from which all the guns get their instructions.

In the meantime, another of our team had noted the fall of shot about the two cruisers.

Two ranging shells went screaming away through the volcano of smoke and flame which blotted everything from our view temporarily. "Guns" imperturbably noted the passage of the seconds. It was amazing how all the crew could tell you exactly when the projectiles were going to burst. "Splash!" sang out "Guns," using the technical slang to indicate that the shot had fallen; and peering through my binoculars I saw two fountains of grey smoke spring up from the side of the hill. We were "right for line" as they say, but a little short. "Up 200" and "right one" were the instructions that sent the next two ranging shots screaming on their path. Then whoops of delight rang through the D.C.T. as the next salvo spouted high above the horizon, exactly where we had seen the gun flashes of the "new tenants."

"That will make them think again, but let them have another for luck!" said "Guns." Away screamed another salvo and as the "projjies" hurtled on their way still echoing faintly back at us the German battery flashed again. "Wait until this one reaches you!" Again we seemed dead on the target, and behind the dun-coloured bursts of our shells a great cauliflower of angry smoke spread and drifted to leeward in a heavy pall.

DURING MOPPING-UP OPERATIONS in a Normandy area east of Caen, important communications centre, British airborne troops move a captured German anti-tank gun into firing position (centre) behind the village, which they had first subjected to a heavy mortar barrage, taking great toll of the enemy defenders. The magnificent work of the airborne troops went far towards helping "Monty" win the first round of the final bout with Rommel. See also illus. p. 98, and stories in pp. 120 and 121.

Photo, British Official: Crown Copyright

In the absence of a spotting aircraft to give us a bird's-eye report, we could only gauge our success by whether or not the "new tenants" manned their guns again. There was no sign of life and no further reply to Frobisher's fire, nothing from that direction harrying the beach, and we came to the conclusion that the gun site was again "to let."

Though we had fired until dusk on Tuesday we were ready again by 6.30 this morning. The first target reported to us came at 7.40 when spotting aircraft recommended for our attention a group of transport attached to a Panzer column two miles north of Caen. It was moving south-westerly along a road. Three two-gun salvos landed smack in the middle of them, and then, shifting range a thousand yards, we put three more salvos into some more transport concentrated near a village. The aircraft reported so many of the vehicles destroyed that they did not consider it worth our while continuing.

Then we had indicated to us some strongly held earthworks in a wooded area south of a village. Including our ranging shots we only needed to put 20 rounds into this strongpoint before we received the report that it appeared to be totally destroyed. Next came news of a troublesome German A.A. battery of five guns lying on high ground and, ranging on it, we quickly knocked out four of them.—*W. F. Hartin, Combined Press*

We Carried Canadian Troops to the Beaches

They look like beer bottles, these mines, and they are coloured black. They hang on tripods stuck in shallow approaches to the beaches, and you see them if you approach at low tide. They do not hurt fair-sized ships, but if you are in small assault landing craft you have a tough go of it; but if it is at all possible you carry out your assignment—to deliver troops. That was the assignment of Canadian seamen, who were charged with bringing Canadian assault troops on to the beaches when Western Europe was invaded this morning.

I was aboard H.M.C.S. Prince David when she weighed anchor off the coast of France and giant davits dropped her landing craft on to the water. Forty-foot craft churned away in a perfect line, and the Canadians in them tightened their grips on their weapons—members of the crew, youngsters from every part of Canada and veterans of Combined Operations landings at Dieppe, North Africa and Sicily.

They ran into no opposition until a hundred yards from the beaches, then choppy waters dashed them against these "beer-bottle" mines. Some craft were blown up, but there were few casualties among the troops and they waded through three feet of water on to sandy shores. By afternoon seamen had hitch-hiked their way back to the Prince David on other landing craft while soldiers were advancing through the town in wake of scores of tanks. Mines had failed to stop them, and except for sporadic mortar and machine-gun fire there was no large-scale resistance in that sector.

Day broke under clouded skies after we had spent days aboard ship waiting. At first, life aboard the Prince David was as free from concern as a jaunt in a St. Lawrence River pleasure liner. That was appropriate enough, because at one time the Prince David had been on the luxury run between Boston and Halifax. Then she was taken over by the Royal Canadian Navy and converted to an armed merchant cruiser. After service in the Pacific she was sent across the Atlantic as a mother ship. Technically she is called a Landing Ship Infantry, but if you want to be informal you call her a mother ship—the same name that was given to hundreds of large craft that made part of the fleet of four thousand ships converging on Western Europe. Let Able Seaman James Morgan tell his story:

Our only trouble came from mines. There was hardly any mortar or machine-gun fire. When we left the David and joined with the rest of the flotilla the sea was a little rough, but that was all. We saw only about six German planes and they didn't come near us. As we approached we could see what our bombing had done to the village. Not a house stood undamaged. A machine-gun nest in a church steeple about a hundred yards away rattled away, but one of our bombers swooped down on it. All along the beaches other craft were landing and we would just walk in.

The water was about three feet deep. A bullet skimmed my ear and struck the soldier next to me. I don't think he was badly hurt. All troops got on land all right and they no sooner did than we hit a mine and the craft blew up. The crew were okay, though, and we waded ashore to regroup ourselves and get a lift out with the heavier tank-landing craft that were not affected when the mines exploded under them. Tanks gathered in dozens, and the troops we had carried gathered behind them to advance into the village itself. I saw a couple of civilians run out to greet them. I also saw a couple of French Canadians standing guard over eight German prisoners. By this time there was very little stuff dropping near us . . .

When the David's assault crew rejoined the ship they were cheered lustily by their mates, who had begun worrying about them. The cheers died down as another large landing craft drew alongside. It contained casualties—the first they had seen. They were Royal Marine Commandos. Wounded men were taken to the sick bay and the hastily converted wardroom, and landings from the Prince David continued.—*Gerald Clark, aboard H.M. Canadian ship Prince David*

OUR DIARY OF THE WAR

JUNE 7, Wednesday *1,740th day*
Western Front.—Allied troops cleared all landing beaches of the enemy.
Air.—Allied heavy bombers attacked airfields and railway communications from Bay of Biscay to the Seine.
Mediterranean.—Heavy bombers attacked Ploesti oil refineries, railway yards at Brasov and Pitesti, and Iron Gate canal at Turnu Severin.

JUNE 8, Thursday *1,741st day*
Western Front.—Capture of Bayeux announced by Allied Headquarters.
Italy.—Civita Castellana occupied by 5th Army, and Subiaco by 8th Army.

JUNE 9, Friday *1,742nd day*
Air.—R.A.F. attacked airfields in N.W. France, and Etampes railway junction; Mosquitoes bombed Berlin.
Italy.—Fifth Army captured Viterbo, Vetralla and Tarquinia.
Mediterranean.—Targets in Munich area, railway yards at Nish, and harbour at Porto Marghera (near Venice), attacked by Allied heavy bombers.

JUNE 10, Saturday *1,743rd day*
Western Front.—Isigny and Trévières captured by U.S. troops. Gen. Montgomery established H.Q. in France.
Air.—Heavy attacks by Allied planes on airfields in Normandy and Brittany. At night, rail centres at Orleans, Dreux, Achères and Versailles bombed by R.A.F.
Mediterranean.—Lightnings bombed oil refinery at Ploesti. Munich, Avignon and Arles attacked by heavy bombers.
Russian Front.—Soviet troops launched offensive against Finns in Karelia, capturing Terijoki.
Pacific.—U.S. carrier-borne aircraft attacked Guam, Saipan and Tinian Is. in the Marianas.

JUNE 11, Sunday *1,744th day*
Western Front.—U.S. troops occupied Lison; British reached Tilly-sur-Seulles, S.E. of Bayeux.
Air.—Heavy bombers struck at rail centres of Nantes, Evreux and Tours.
Mediterranean.—Allied bombers attacked Constanza and Giurgiu and oil installations at Smererovo (Yugo-slavia).
Russian Front.—U.S. Russian-based bombers attacked Rumanian airfields and landed in Italy.
Italy.—8th Army occupied Pescara and Avezzano.
Pacific.—Liberators made daylight attack on Truk.
China.—Japanese troops occupied Changsha, capital of Hunan.

JUNE 12, Monday *1,745th day*
Western Front.—U.S. troops captured Carentan. Fighting between British and German armoured units between Caen and Tilly-sur-Seulles.
Air.—Over 1,400 U.S. heavy bombers struck at airfields and bridges in France. At night over 1,000 R.A.F. planes bombed Gelsenkirchen, Cologne, Arras, Cambrai and Amiens.
Pacific.—U.S. Pacific Fleet again attacked bases in the Marianas.
General.—Mr. Churchill, Gen. Smuts, Gen. Eisenhower and U.S. chiefs of staff toured Normandy beach-heads.

JUNE 13, Tuesday *1,746th day*
Western Front.—Allied troops entered Pont l'Abbé, Montebourg and Troarn.
Air.—U.S. heavy bombers attacked airfields and bridges in France. At night, Mosquitoes bombed railways and bridges behind the battle fronts.
Mediterranean.—Italian-based bombers attacked aircraft factories near Munich.
Russian Front.—Soviet long-range aircraft bombed airfields at Brest-Litovsk, Bielostok, Pinsk, Minsk, Bobruisk and Orshi.
Pacific.—Liberators bombed airfields and seaplane base at Truk.
Home Front.—First German pilotless aircraft appeared over England.

JUNE 14, Wednesday *1,747th day*
Western Front.—Enemy counter-thrust at Carentan repelled. Allies gave ground at Montebourg.
Air.—More than 1,500 U.S. heavy bombers struck another record blow at airfields in France, Belgium and Holland. R.A.F. bombers in first daylight attack since 1942 dropped 12,000-lb. bombs on Havre E-boat pens.
Pacific.—U.S. carrier-based aircraft attacked islands in Bonin group, 700 miles from Tokyo.
General.—Gen. de Gaulle visited Bayeux and other towns in Normandy.

JUNE 15, Thursday *1,748th day*
Western Front.—Allied troops captured Quineville, on east of Cherbourg Peninsula.
Air.—Strong force of heavy bombers attacked railway yards and airfields near Bordeaux, Paris, Angouleme and Tours. At night, R.A.F. bombed E-boat pens at Boulogne, and railway centres of Lens and Valenciennes.
Italy.—8th Army troops captured Orvieto.
Japan.—New U.S. Super-Fortresses bombed steel works at Yawatta, on Kyushu Island.
Pacific.—American troops landed on Saipan Island, Marianas.
Home Front.—Continuous attacks on Southern England by pilotless planes began

JUNE 16, Friday *1,749th day*
Western Front.—St. Sauveur, in Cherbourg Peninsula, captured by Americans.
Air.—R.A.F. attacked synthetic oil centre of Sterkrade, Ruhr, and bombed pilotless plane ramps in Pas de Calais.
Italy.—5th Army troops occupied Grosseto with extensive airfields.
Mediterranean. — Allied bombers raided oil refineries near Vienna and Bratislava.
General.—King George VI visited Normandy beach-heads.

JUNE 17, Saturday *1,750th day*
Western Front.—Strong-point of Douvres, north of Caen, captured by Royal Marine Commandos.
Burma.—Chinese troops captured Kamaing in Mogaung valley.
Mediterranean.—French troops landed on Elba with Allied air and naval support.

JUNE 18, Sunday *1,751st day*
Western Front.—Cherbourg Peninsula cut off by U.S. troops reaching Barneville on west coast.
Air.—Britain-based Fortresses and Liberators bombed oil plants in Hamburg, and pilotless plane ramps in Pas de Calais.
Russian Front.—Soviet troops broke through Mannerheim line towards Viborg.
Pacific.—In attack on U.S. fleet off Saipan, 353 Jap aircraft shot down.

JUNE 19, Monday *1,752nd day*
Western Front.—Tilly-sur-Seulles finally fell to British, and Montebourg to Americans.
Air.—Allied heavy bombers bombed pilotless plane emplacements in Pas de Calais.
Mediterranean.—All German resistance ceased in Elba.
Pacific.—U.S. carrier-aircraft sank or damaged 14 Jap warships between Marianas and Philippines.

JUNE 20, Tuesday *1,753rd day*
Western Front.—Allied troops attacked outer defences of Cherbourg.
Air.—Heavy Allied attacks on Pas de Calais launching platforms. Twelve synthetic oil plants in Germany bombed by Fortresses and Liberators.
Russian Front.—Viipuri (Viborg) captured by Soviet troops of Leningrad front.
Italy.—8th Army entered Perugia.

Flash-backs

1940

June 12. *Allied force including 51st Division cut off at St. Valery.*
June 13. *Paris declared open city.*
June 15. *Germans occupied Verdun and outflanked Maginot Line.*
June 20. *French Government asked Italy for an armistice.*

1941

June 7. *Mass Japanese raids on Chungking, capital of Free China.*
June 16. *President Roosevelt ordered closing of German consulates in the United States.*

1942

June 10. *Germans opened new offensive on the Kharkov front.*
June 13. *Japanese landed on Attu in the Aleutian Islands.*
June 17. *British withdrew to Egyptian frontier, leaving strong garrison in Tobruk.*

1943

June 7. *French Committee of National Liberation formed in Algiers under Giraud and De Gaulle.*
June 11. *Island of Pantellaria occupied by Allied forces.*

THE WAR IN THE AIR

by Capt. Norman Macmillan, M.C., A.F.C.

Throughout the twelve days' interval, between the break-out from the Anzio beach-head and the capture of Rome, aircraft of the No. 1 Tactical Air Force of the Mediterranean Allied Air Command scoured the roads leading to the battle area from enemy-occupied Italy to destroy enemy road communications. During the Allied attack against the German Army, Kesselring's supply problem became so acute that he was forced to use road transport by day, whereas formerly he had kept his road convoys hidden by day and moved them only at night. The fighter-bombers and medium-bombers sought their targets with pitiless efficiency. By night the roads were lit by parachute flares. Allied aircraft were flying over 3,000 sorties daily ;

verse weather reports caused a postponement for 24 hours. The delay was not for flying weather, but for sea weather for the landing craft. This gave the air bombardment forces a further 24 hours for preparing the "softening" of the enemy-held zone. On June 5, up to 750 Fortresses and Liberators with about 500 escorting fighters attacked bridges, rail communications and radio towers. Mustangs bombed German army lorries. Thunderbolts bombed bridges, railway intersections and locomotives at Conflans, Gisors, Mézières, Beauvais, and Mons ; factories at Conflans and Juziers ; and a radio station at Louviers.

By June 6, 25 railway and 9 road bridges had been destroyed, and only one railway and 5 road bridges were standing across the

IT TRIED TO INTERFERE with our advance in Normandy, so this Messerschmitt 109 G.6—one of the Germans' principal single-engined fighters—was shot down near our lines in the Tilly-sur-Seulles sector to the south-east of Bayeux, in which neighbourhood some of the most violent armoured battles in this present fighting in France have taken place.
Photo, British Official

610 vehicles were destroyed and 561 damaged on May 26 ; on June 4 at least 1,200 German road vehicles were destroyed.

Close cover for the armies was given over the fighting zone. Before the break-out from the Anzio beach-head a Spitfire squadron moved in to operate from a landing strip one mile from the enemy advanced positions. Dumps and stores were guarded by the R.A.F. Regiment. The cover was continuous. On June 3, M.A.A.F. flew 2,100 sorties and saw only one enemy aircraft in daylight. The German armies, almost isolated, were unable to withstand the drive of the Allied Armies. Rome was entered on June 4, 1944, and as the soldiers were entering the city about 750 bombers of the M.A.A.F. were attacking railway targets on both sides of the French-Italian frontier. Kesselring's retreat was rapid, with aircraft pounding away at his flying columns pulling north into Tuscany.

June 4 was the seventeenth successive day of air attack on military targets in northern France. June 5 was to have been the day of assault against the Normandy coast, but ad-

Seine between Paris and the sea ; 16,000 sorties had been flown against 85 railway centres, and radio installations had been heavily attacked. Heavy bombers had attacked coastal targets by day and night.

From 11.30 p.m. on June 5 to sunrise on June 6, Bomber Command made ten attacks each with a hundred or more heavy bombers against German naval guns and land howitzers along the French coast bombing through ten-tenths cloud by pathfinder marker methods—the greatest single night attack on record, with over 5,000 tons of bombs dropped.

At 6 a.m. on the 6th day of the 6th month landings were made by surface forces on the Normandy beaches of the Cherbourg peninsula. Before dawn the biggest-ever airborne forces had already landed by parachute and glider, and jeeps, artillery, bombs, petrol, ammunition, rations followed by air ; light tanks were flown in by Hamilcar gliders towed by Halifaxes. At dawn more than 1,000 U.S. heavy bombers supported by hundreds of medium and fighter bombers

hammered the coast defences, roads, rail bridges, and troop concentrations. More than 10,000 tons of bombs were dropped in 7,500 sorties in weather which compelled low flying. Never were there fewer than 200 fighters over the beaches.

Mr. Churchill stated that the Allied air force operating against the German army in this operation was over 11,000 aircraft, a world record force. R.E. Pioneers and R.A.F. Servicing Commandos landed with the first troops, and in three days Spitfires were flying from landing strips in Normandy. The bombing forces grew speadily larger day by day, even bombing areas where German snipers were secreted. Wounded began to be evacuated by air ambulances.

Strategic air power has been applied in recent weeks to reduce the enemy oil reserves. This strategy worked well against Rommel before the final victory in North Africa. Attacks have ranged far and wide over Europe, from Ploesti oilfields to synthetic oil plants in Germany, and storage tanks in Austria and Hungary. Berlin was bombed three nights running—June 9, 10, and 11—by Mosquitoes with 4,000-lb. bombs, and on June 16 by Bomber Command's heavies, More than 1,000 Fortresses and Liberators screened by up to 1,000 Mustangs, Lightnings and Thunderbolts, bombed Berlin by day on June 21.

On June 13, Germany began bombing Southern England with pilotless bombers, p-planes for short. These weapons, constructed mainly in steel, are not radio-controlled, but directed by an automatic pilot, set before take-off. Here they differ from the radio-controlled glider bomb. P-planes are launched from concrete platforms heavily protected against bombing. Their take-off is assisted, probably by rocket accelerator. More will be known about launching methods following the inspection of platforms overrun by Allied forces in the Cherbourg peninsula, an area wherein were more than a quarter of the robot-planes' launching sites.

The present p-plane fuselage is 21-ft. 10-in. long, with a maximum width of $32\frac{1}{2}$ inches. Wing span is 16 ft. They are petrol driven and jet propelled by a reaction unit mounted above the aft end of the fuselage, and fly at between 300 and 350 m.p.h. Range is about 150 miles. A thrumming noise accompanies their flight. The exhaust shows as a glow and flash behind the tail; when this "light" goes out (i.e. when the engine stops) the p-plane dives and the synchronized explosion follows from five to fifteen seconds later.

The explosive, carried in a warhead rather like the marine torpedo charge—indeed, the p-plane is a real air torpedo, a hitherto much misused term—is contained in a thin casing in front of the fuselage, bringing the overall length up to 25-ft. $4\frac{1}{2}$-in. The explosive power is equal to a German 1,000 kilogramme (one ton) bomb. Since their introduction these missiles have been used by day, but more by night. Targets claimed by the Germans to have been attacked include Greater London, Southampton and Portsmouth.

Since the p-plane attack began, in addition to continued counter-bombing of launching sites, Britain's anti-aircraft defences—guns and day and night fighters, including the new Tempest fighter—have been organized to meet the new weapon, and many p-planes have been shot down into the sea or on open country.

Allied Wings that Rule the Skies in Normandy

SUPPORTING OUR ASSAULT TROOPS, Marauder bombers smashed early German attempts at reinforcements of stormed beach positions in Normandy by blasting road and rail junctions, such as this one smothered by high explosives (1), and covered our landing-craft as these beached (2). Air Vice-Marshal H. Broadhurst, D.S.O., D.F.C., A.F.C. (3) is Air Officer Commanding an R.A.F. Group operating from the first R.A.F. airstrip to be built in France since 1940, from which these Spitfires are about to take off (4).   PAGE 125   *Photos, British and U.S. Official*

How the Wounded Come Home from the Beaches

FIRST CASUALTIES IN FRANCE were back in Britain on the day that the invasion commenced. A wounded man is carefully hoisted from a beach landing craft aboard a troopship lying in the Channel (1). Comfortable on bunks inside a returning tank landing craft, casualties are homeward bound (2), and eventually are helped ashore (3). An ambulance receives a stretcher case for transit to hospital (4), where a blast-deafened soldier gains relief at the sure and gentle hands of a woman doctor (5).

PAGE 126   *Photos, Planet News, Associated Press, Fox, Daily Mirror*

LIKE all celebrated military geni- uses, Napoleon made some colossal mistakes. But he had so much practice in war and thought about it so constantly that he arrived very often at sound con- clusions, even if he did not always act upon them. One remark of his is specially appro- priate to the present war situation. "You may," he said, " win a battle with an army smaller than that of your enemy, but to win a war you must have superiority in numbers." That is what gives us certainty that the United Nations will win this war. We may have set-backs. We almost certainly shall have them. The Nazis are not nearly beaten yet, so far as all the signs go. But in time they will find that we are everywhere superior to them in numbers. Not only in numbers of men. Already we have far more aircraft. Already we have probably more artillery. We have always had more ships. We shall have before very long more of everything. Then the German generals will see that it is useless for them to keep up the fight and, as professional soldiers, they will refuse to sacrifice their men uselessly. They will bump off Hitler as readily as they forced the Kaiser to depart in 1918, and will 'then throw up the sponge. Napoleon's maxim will have been proved true once more.

CURIOUS things one reads in the newspapers! Here is an item that I had to look at two or three times—"Noel Coward is to fly up and down the Burma border sing- ing in the monsoon rain to British troops." What a picture this brought into my mind's eye—the author-composer fitted with wings, sailing under grey wet skies and piping away hard as he flew! Well, I dare say he would take on even that job. He has had many different ones during the war, and I under- stand he did them all competently. Certainly his film efforts—In Which We Serve, and This Happy Breed— have been valuable contributions to the war effort. I cannot say as much for his Blithe Spirit, which is now nearing its fourth year, I believe ; but it must have added very con- siderably to his fortune. Its success is due to its knockabout incidents and to skilful acting, but it has amused many thousands and that also is War service. I have seen it twice with great enjoyment.

WAR makes "the common man," as President Wilson called him, feel that he has become—for the time, at any rate— more important. The "common woman" too. Dwellings for the mass of us used to be put up according to the ideas of the small builder. Very poor ideas they were. Houses were built in long rows all alike, and as ugly outside as they were incon- venient within. Now housewives are con- sulted as to what they want their kitchens and their parlours and their bedrooms to be like. And in Norfolk men are being asked to say what size the gardens attached to council houses ought to be. Some want an acre, others say one-sixth of an acre would be as much as they could manage to cultivate. The latter is about the size of the average allotment. Some people, not men only, but women, too, occasionally, are able to cope with two allotment patches, but it means hard work. If the worker has only spare time to put in, after a day's work, say, or in between the manifold labours of keeping a house going, such a piece of land, 60 ft. by 180, is too large. An acre would mean

a whole-time job, I should think. Few people have any notion how large an acre looks. It will be instructive to see what the general opinion in Norfolk turns out to be.

HARROGATE air, known to be of a peculiarly bracing, energizing character, has had a most satisfactory effect on Post Office workers who have been there since they had to leave London because of the bombing. I had occasion to write to the P.O. Savings Bank Department for a relative, who had lost a warrant posted to her. I expected to get a printed acknowledgement in a week or so, and possibly a reply in the course of a month. But within five days after I had posted

BRIGADIER-GENERAL H. S. VANDENBERG of the U.S.A.A.F. was appointed Deputy Supreme Commander-in-Chief of the Allied Expeditionary Air Force on April 19, 1944. Aged 45, he was previously Chief of the Allied North West African Strategic Air Force. His decorations include the D.S.M., D.F.C., Legion of Merit and Air Medal.
Photo, U.S. Official

my letter came a full answer, courteous and helpful, telling my friend what she must do. Mr. Leon Simon, head of the branch to which I wrote, must be a new kind of official— a much better kind than those to whom we have been too long accustomed. To deal so promptly with a query in wartime and with so much extra work to be done is really marvellous.

ALL Americans who have come to this country of late express surprise at the quiet way in which we accept the tidings of great events in the war. All Britons who have been in the United States recently comment on the excitability of the population, their readiness to fly off the handle either at good news or bad, and to swallow absurd stories when there is no news at all. For instance, the story printed in a Washington journal that the talk of a Second Front was merely intended to scare the enemy seems to have been widely credited and talked about. A well-known American newspaperman, H. R. Knickerbocker, who discovered where the

Nazi leaders had stowed away their illgotten fortunes and how large these were, says that in New York they chattered about the invasion all the time for weeks before it started. He found this tiresome. When he reached here, however, he felt frozen by the cold looks he received when he said any- thing about it. How is it, by the way, that the original inhabitants of America, the Indians, were the most reserved, silent, inscrutable of beings, while the present Americans seem to possess exactly opposite characteristics?

WHAT is there about the name George that prompts so many people to use it humorously ? "Let George do it" has long been a familiar phrase. Why should George be selected as the goat to bear all sorts of burdens ? And why do airmen call the mechanical pilot which, in certain circumstances, can be left to direct a war plane for long distances while the live pilot sits back and reads or twiddles his thumbs—why is that called "George"? Is it because there are so many front- rank funmakers with this Christian name ? George Formby, George Robey, Wee Georgie Wood, George Gee—I could go on reeling them out for a long time. I should guess that George is not a name many parents choose for their baby sons at present. It may join Marmaduke and Augustus and Cuthbert, which used once to be fairly common and now are turned into jokes.

WILL baseball become as popular in Britain as it is in the United States as the result of its being played here by Americans and Canadians and being taken up by British soldiers too ? The last- named, I hear, are in the Middle East being provided with bats and balls and masks and gloves so that they can play the game properly. It is far better to watch than cricket. Something is going on all the time, and going on quickly. There are no long "overs" without a run being scored. You do not have to sit and wait while a batsman walks from the pitch to the far-away pavilion and another walks out. The excitement at ball games in America and Canada surpasses even that of our football matches. As a game to play, baseball is also better than cricket, for there is not all the long waiting about while your side is batting.

POSTERS in London are telling the world that "the British Empire is founded on God's word and on God's Sunday." If any of the millions of Moslems, Hindus, Sikhs, Jains, Buddhists or Jews in the British Empire read that, it cannot make them feel very much at home in it. For none of them believes the Bible to be God's Word, nor do they regard Sunday as it is regarded by a certain type of Christian. This kind of thing is ill calculated to draw the bonds of Empire more tightly among all its peoples. As to Sunday, that is misleading too. For the millions of Roman Catholics and Anglo- Catholics in the Empire do not hold at all the view as to "keeping it holy" which is held by a small number of Protestant sects. They make it a holiday, not a holy day. And if it is still taught that it was ordained by the Almighty after He had created the world in six days and decided to rest on the seventh, how can we justify resting not on the last but on the first day of the week ? This kind of street hoarding theology does more harm than good, I fear.

Pacific Signpost is Victory Indicator

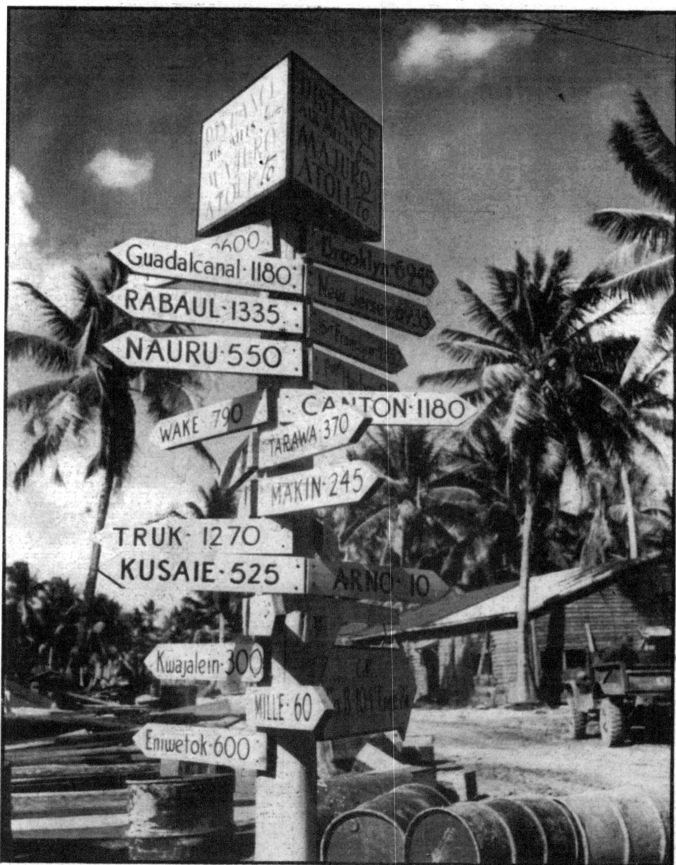

Guadalcanal · 1180
RABAUL · 1335
NAURU · 550
WAKE · 790
CANTON · 1180
TARAWA · 370
MAKIN · 245
TRUK · 1270
KUSAIE · 525
ARNO · 10
Kwajalein · 300
MILLE · 60
Eniwetok · 600

Photo, Keystone

POINTING THE WAY TO VICTORY—and to home after victory is won—is this American-made signpost in Majuro Island in the Marshalls group, in the Pacific, first Japanese territory to be invaded by the Allies, February 1944. Other pointers are directed towards Guadalcanal, cleared of the enemy by Feb. 10, 1943 ; Kwajalein (Marshall Islands), taken by U.S. forces on Feb. 5, 1944 ; and Eniwetok, west of the Marshalls, captured on Feb. 18, 1944. Rabaul, Nauru, Wake, Truk, all important Japanese bases in the Pacific, have been "softened up" preliminary to final seizure.

Printed in England and published every alternate Friday by the Proprietors, THE AMALGAMATED PRESS, LTD., The Fleetway House, Farringdon Street, London, E.C.4 Registered for transmission by Canadian Magazine Post. Sole Agents for Australia and New Zealand : Messrs. Gordon & Gotch, Ltd. ; and for South Africa : Central News Agency, Ltd.—July 7, 1944. S.S. *Editorial Address :* JOHN CARPENTER HOUSE, WHITEFRIARS, LONDON, E.C.4.

Vol 8 # The War Illustrated N° 185

Edited by Sir John Hammerton

SIXPENCE

JULY 21, 1944

OPENING THE GATES OF FRANCE REDEEMED—symbolic of the complete liberation of all enemy-occupied territories—General de Gaulle (right), accompanied by high-ranking French officers, enters Bayeux, cleared of the Germans by our Forces on June 8, 1944. First French town to be freed, Bayeux has twice before been occupied by English soldiers—in 1346, at the start of the Hundred Years War, and again in 1417, in the reign of King Henry V.

Photo, Planet News

NO. 186 WILL BE PUBLISHED FRIDAY, AUGUST 4

Behind-the-War Scenes With Our Roving Camera

A.T.S. POLICEWOMEN training for service with the troops in Normandy are given a lesson in French during a lecture on French Local Administration by Warrant-Officer J. Christie, of the Army Education Corps.

MAIL FOR MERCHANT NAVY officers and men in ships supplying the Allied forces in France is handled by Combined Office Merchant Navy Operations (COMNO). These girls are sorting a day's accumulation of letters.

STEEL HELMETS FOR LAND ARMY GIRLS is the order of the day in Kent, coastal county which since the early months of the war has been continually exposed to front-line perils. With the advent of the flying bomb this headgear is still more desirable.

ST. PAUL'S CATHEDRAL provides fire-watchers with plenty of exercise. Above, a midnight alert has sounded. Swiftly, working by torch-light, team members run out a length of hose—with the towering reredos as background. The reredos is undamaged, though the altar in front of it was smashed when the cathedral was hit during one of the early air raids. The height of the building is such that upper parts are beyond the "throw" of any fire-pump; special pumping machinery carries water to the lofty dome.

R.A.S.C. TRANSPORT CORPS animals are in readiness to replace lorries and cars in "difficult" terrain. Animals, officers and men go through strenuous courses. Right, limber teams riding rough country: a test of endurance which only the fittest in man, animal and machine survives.

Photos, Associated Press, Topical Press, Keystone, Fox

THE BATTLE FRONTS

by Maj.-Gen. Sir Charles Gwynn, K.C.B., D.S.O.

THE end of June found the Germans in by far the most serious strategical situation they had yet to face. The fall of Cherbourg meant the definite establishment of a western front, and the rapid collapse of their defensive position in White Russia was a disaster which knocked out the king pin of their eastern front. Both were strategic disasters of the first order and both revealed the immense offensive power the Allies had developed. The situation in Italy had also deteriorated so greatly that it had been necessary to send reserves to the German general Kesselring which could ill be spared from France and yet were insufficient to give him much hope of stabilizing his front. If Cherbourg had stood a prolonged siege, even if it had held out for a month or six weeks, it would have gone far to reduce the value of the footing the Allies had gained in Normandy. The footing could undoubtedly have been firmly held and possibly have been considerably extended, but no far-reaching offensive operations could have been undertaken from it until an adequate port was secured.

It is in fact astonishing that it was practicable, in spite of desperately unfavourable weather, to disembark reinforcements and supplies on the beaches sufficient to maintain the offensive operations which led to the capture of the fortress and pinned down Rommel's reserves. It must be realized, however, that a general offensive and an advance to more distant objectives would have entailed immense and constantly increasing demands which a beach organization could not have met. Only the most perfect organization could have met requirements during the first three weeks, and we have yet to learn what the effort cost in loss of stores and landing craft from weather alone, though we know it must have been high.

The final assault on Cherbourg was delivered with immense dash and determination ; coupled with the tactical skill shown in outflanking and by-passing the enemy's strong points, it is evidence of the very high standard of training that has been reached by American troops. The success of the operation, however, depended largely on whether Rommel could be prevented from intervening with his armoured reserves. That he was unable to make any counter-attack from outside the ring of encirclement was entirely due to the vigorous offensive attitude of the British and Canadian troops in the Caen-Tilly area which pinned all his available reserves to that sector of his front. That offensive action must, however, have made heavy demands on the reserves of munitions and material which Montgomery had been able to accumulate—demands which might rapidly have increased if Rommel had been able to launch an attack on a large scale.

CHERBOURG was Intended to Withstand a Long Siege

I think it will therefore be recognized that under the conditions of weather which made the replenishment of munitions, supplies and full air co-operation uncertain, Generals Eisenhower and Montgomery made a notably bold decision when they refused to be deterred from pursuing their offensive policy. Less determined leaders might well have been tempted to adopt a defensive attitude until conditions were more favourable, and thus have lost the opportunity of exploiting the initial success of the landing. That the Germans fully realized the strategic importance of denying Cherbourg to the Allies and that they had taken every precaution to enable it to stand a long siege cannot be questioned. The mere fact that they entrusted its defence to somewhat inferior troops is proof of their reliance on its impregnability.

The collapse of the front in White Russia may have more immediately disastrous results. The consequences of the loss of Cherbourg may not be fully felt for some time, but in Russia the whole structure of the front is crumbling. I admit that I had thought, after the Russian successes of the winter which enabled them to threaten the positions at Vitebsk and on the upper Dnieper from both flanks, that the Germans were only clinging to that line in order to hold the Red

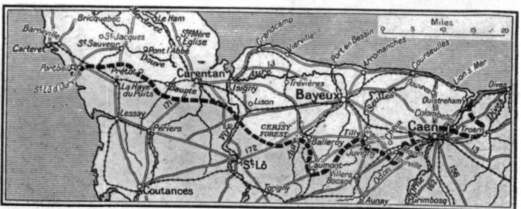

BATTLE FOR CAEN flared up afresh on June 25, 1944, when British infantry of the 2nd Army broke out of the Normandy beach-head perimeter, which had been static for two weeks, and drove a salient into enemy positions S.W. of that town. Our armour and infantry crossed the River Odon on a front of two miles on June 28 and established a bridgehead towards the River Orne which withstood several sharp counter-attacks. The approximate position on June 30 is indicated above.

By courtesy of The Times

Army at a distance and to blunt the edge of any offensive delivered against it. The position was obviously strong and very large forces would be needed to capture it, which seemed to make it probable that the Russians would select weaker sections of the front for their initial offensive. If, however, a major offensive developed here I believed that the Germans would resort to elastic delaying defence, and carry out a well-planned co-ordinated withdrawal to a shorter front.

IN the light of events it would seem that the Germans were over-confident in the strength of the position, and, believing that the main Russian offensive would come on Marshal Zhukov's front towards Lvov, were surprised by the weight of the offensive north of the Pripet and the time of its delivery. Possibly they considered that the preparations for the offensive, which they must have observed, only indicated a threat designed to draw their reserves northwards. This would explain why they seem to have left the bulk of their Panzer Divisions with Von Manstein and to have been weak in the air when the blow fell. Here again they may have used too high a proportion of inferior divisions in what they assumed to be impregnable defences ; otherwise it is difficult to understand the rapidity with which the Russian victory was achieved.

When the danger was fully realized the lack of good and direct lateral communications must have been felt, making it impos-

sible to rush up reserves from other sectors in time to attempt to retrieve the situation. Nor can it have been possible to dispute seriously the air superiority the Russians had established, for many of the German airfields in the combat zone had been overrun or put out of action at an early stage. Once air superiority, or anything approaching equality, is lost it is difficult to recover ; and almost impossible when the army which relies on it is in retreat.

KEY-POINT Encirclement Plan Gains Soviet Victories

Although the Germans must have envisaged the possibility of being compelled to withdraw from Vitebsk and the upper Dnieper at some stage, it is quite clear that they have not voluntarily withdrawn on a preconceived plan and that they have suffered an unexpected and crushing disaster. The Russian plan of encircling each of the key-points of the front while combining it with a wider pincer attack towards Minsk, which might have provided a rallying pivot in rear, was well designed to break up attempts to carry out a well co-ordinated last minute withdrawal.

The amazing capture of Minsk a few hours after the Germans had broadcast that it must and would be held at all costs came as a surprise even to those who realized the state of demoralization of Busch's troops, of which the capture and killing of so many senior generals is convincing proof. The city was apparently taken without severe fighting, in spite of the arrival of fresh reinforcements, and its abandonment was evidently due to a panic decision—for although it was bound to fall in due course, the Russians' outflanking thrust could hardly have been strong enough to effect immediate encirclement.

We can only conclude that the Russians have again shown an amazing ability to break through the strongest defences, and what is even more surprising, the Germans have again signally failed in defence of much stronger positions than the Russians have successfully held on other occasions. Comparing the defence of Leningrad, Moscow and Stalingrad with the rapid failure of the German defence on the Don, at Orel, in the Crimea and now at Cherbourg and Vitebsk, one wonders if there is something radically wrong with German tactical theories. I suspect that when it comes to the attack or defence of really strongly fortified positions the Germans pay the penalty for over-reliance on armour to the neglect of developing the full power of artillery, to which both in attack and defence the Russians have owed their successes. Armour is, of course, of immense value in mobile operations and as a co-operative weapon, but infantry and artillery are still the dominant arms where armies are locked in close combat.

British 2nd Army in the Normandy Campaign

GERMAN SNIPER whose last battle has been fought and lost lies prone beside a knocked-out enemy tank (1) in the Tilly-Caen sector of the Normandy front; just ahead of the tank a British soldier, wearing the new type steel helmet, snipes from the cover of a thicket. Captured in heavy fighting during the last week of June 1944 two German officers tramp back to a prisoners' compound under the watchful eye of a cheery, diminutive Tommy (2). Enemy snipers had the exact range of an exposed spot on a road used by our infantry; speedy but cautious movement was called for (3). Across open country a British assault wave, of which these two are members (4), eager to get to work with the bayonet, went into the attack in the Tilly area on June 26. As a result of brilliant operations extending over 30 days, the key-town of Caen was captured by British and Canadian troops on July 9, and Rommel was in slow retreat.

Photos, British Official

Swiftly Advancing Red Army Regains Vitebsk

IN THE BIG SOVIET OFFENSIVE hourly gaining momentum, forces of the 1st Baltic Front, commanded by General Bagramyan, and of the 3rd White Russian Front, under General Chernyakhovosky, in Central Russia on June 25, 1944, captured Vitebsk, covering the approaches to East Prussia, a fortress in German hands since July 1941. Red Army men wave tommy-guns in captured Vitebsk and their cheers re-echo across the River Dvina (top). Citizens crowd round the victors (bottom) after three years of savage German occupation of their town. Rolling on in three thrusts (see arrowed map), by July 3 the Russians had taken Minsk, last great fortress held by the Germans in White Russia.

Photos, Pictorial Press. Map by courtesy of News Chronicle

BRITISH CRUISER H.M.S. GLASGOW (foreground) and **U.S.S.** Quincy, units of a bombardment task force, at 15,000 yards range fired broadside after broadside into German shore batteries at key-points on the fringe of Cherbourg Harbour, enemy long-range and shore batteries returning the fire vigorously until silenced. This bombardment, in support of our ground forces, started shortly after midday on June 25, 1944, and lasted more than three hours.

Photo British Official : Crown Copyright

THE WAR AT SEA

by Francis E. McMurtrie

Finnish insistence on fighting to the last ditch for the benefit of Germany must inevitably affect the naval situation in the Baltic. Already the enemy, in accordance with the pact made by Ribbentrop with the Finnish Government, has been obliged to send some of his scanty reserve of troops to the aid of the Finns. These forces were landed at Helsinki (the Finnish capital) and at Turku. The former port is situated on the Gulf of Finland near its narrowest point. Approach to the harbour is guarded by the fortress of Sveaborg, which was bombarded by the British fleet during the war of 1854-56 ; in those days, of course, Finland was an appanage of Russia, as it looks like becoming again before long.

Turku, formerly known as Abo, is about 100 miles farther west, outside the gulf. At a shipbuilding yard there submarines were built to German designs during 1929-33, when U-boat construction was still prohibited in Germany by the Treaty of Versailles. In this way our enemies carried out useful experimental work, which enabled them to resume submarine construction in good time for the present war without infringing the letter of the Treaty. At the same time, the Finnish Navy was enabled to acquire a number of submarines for next to nothing.

Transports bringing the German troops to these two places were escorted by the heavy cruisers Admiral Hipper and Prinz Eugen, a " pocket battleship " (either the Lützow or Admiral Scheer), and three destroyers. These constitute the backbone of the German Navy, for its only two genuine battleships, the 45,000-ton Tirpitz and 26,000-ton Gneisenau, are completely disabled, and incapable of proceeding to sea. In addition to the duties just accomplished, these ships will have to undertake the task of convoying to Ulu (formerly known as Uleaborg), the Finnish port near the head of the Gulf of Bothnia, reinforcements and supplies for the German army which occupies Northern Finland. Until his death in a flying accident recently, this army was under the command of General Dietl.

It may be assumed that the Soviet armies will continue their advance along both the northern and southern shores of the Gulf of Finland, supported by the ships of the Baltic Fleet. These comprise two old battleships of over 23,000 tons, three or four cruisers, and a number of destroyers and smaller craft. Sooner or later these movements will have the effect of exposing German sea lines of communication with Northern Finland to attack by Soviet submarines, motor-torpedo-boats and aircraft, which have already done serious damage to German coastal traffic along the Estonian coast.

Russian and German Naval Strengths in the Baltic

To strengthen their position the Germans are believed to contemplate the occupation of the Aaland Islands. From their position at the entrance to the Gulf of Bothnia, flanking the approaches to the Gulf of Finland to the south-eastward, and to Stockholm south-westward, these islands have always been a key-point in Baltic warfare. In past centuries they have belonged sometimes to Russia and sometimes to Sweden, but since 1919 they have been Finnish. A naval action was fought there between Russian and Swedish squadrons in 1790 ; and in 1854 the island stronghold of Bomarsund was reduced by a British squadron under Captain W. H. Hall, as a preliminary operation of the Baltic campaign.

Since the strength of the Russian Navy in the Baltic is no more than equal to that of the German, it has been suggested in the Soviet press that reinforcements may be sent through the Stalin Ship Canal by the Allies. This canal connects Soroka, on the White Sea, with Leningrad, and its whole course has now been freed by the defeat of the Finnish forces in that region. These do not appear to have done any important damage to the locks. Much of the course of the canal follows natural features, making use of the river Svir and Lakes Ladoga, Onega and Vyg as part of the route. Depth of water is sufficient to take the largest destroyers, or even light cruisers.

In the English Channel naval interference by the enemy with the sea communications of the Allies grows steadily weaker, while the occupation of Cherbourg affords the Allies the inestimable advantage of a fine protected harbour through which men and materials can be poured into Normandy at a much more rapid rate. In almost every encounter the Germans have lost a unit or two, either destroyers, motor-torpedo-boats or minesweepers, so that their forces must now be seriously depleted. Air raids on Havre and Boulogne have inflicted further losses.

There has been little mention of U-boats in this connexion, though before the invasion the German public were told that these were being reserved for this especial purpose. Now it is argued by the enemy that submarines are at too great a disadvantage in the narrow and shallow waters of the Channel.

According to later reports from Admiral Nimitz, Commander-in-Chief of the U.S. Pacific Fleet, the defeat inflicted on the Japanese off the Mariana Islands was more severe than at first believed, although the ships of the opposing fleets never sighted each other. It is evident that the Japanese attached considerable importance to the retention of the island of Saipan, in the Marianas, which is capable of being used as a base for attacks on Japan. With the exception of Guam, captured from the Americans in December 1941, it is the most populous and highly cultivated island of the group. That the Japanese garrison was a strong one may be judged from the fact that United States Marines and Army formations struggling for its possession lost, between June 15 and 28, no fewer than 9,752 officers and men in killed, wounded and missing. What this means will be realized when it is added that the total U.S. casualties in Normandy from June 6 to June 20, including hard fighting with a German division which was carrying out an anti-invasion exercise at the point where American troops landed, were not more than 24,162.

In addition to a fleet aircraft carrier, two oil tankers and probably a destroyer, the Japanese fleet attacked by U.S. naval aircraft between the Marianas and the Philippines is now known to have lost a second aircraft carrier of smaller size. A large aircraft carrier is also believed to have been sunk by an American submarine. The fleet carrier of the Syokaku type already known to have been damaged is now stated to have been hit by three 1,000-lb. bombs, and a light carrier by seven of 500 lb. Therefore, not less than five enemy aircraft carriers have been either sunk or put out of action for some time to come. Enemy aircraft destroyed over Saipan totalled 402. Conquest of Saipan was completed on July 8.

British Troops March Through Freed Bayeux

STALWARTS OF OUR 2nd ARMY marching triumphantly through the cobbled streets of ancient Bayeux on June 8, 1944, were warmly welcomed. The German occupiers had been killed or ejected or taken prisoner—though the crack of a sniper's rifle still rang out occasionally. At that early date of the Normandy campaign Bayeux had the distinction of being the first French town to be set free. Also it had the good fortune to escape bombardment ; the 13th-century cathedral (in background) showed no sign of damage. PAGE 135 *Photo, British Official*

Great Climax of Allied Assault on Cherbourg—

ONE OF THE FINEST DEEP-WATER HARBOURS in Europe was secured to the Allies when strongly fortified Cherbourg in Normandy fell to our forces by June 27, 1944. Large-calibre coastal defence guns in reinforced forts (1) were shattered by air, and sea bombardments. Strongpoints were overcome; this fort (2) is being entered by U.S. advanced troops. On the hill overlooking the port these infantrymen (3) were seeking the tunnel entrance to Fort du Roule whilst its batteries still fired.

PAGE 136   *Photos, U.S. Official, Planet News, Associated Press*

—Nazi Naval and Military Commanders Surrender

CAPTURED WITH 800 GERMAN TROOPS in a subterranean passage under Fort du Roule on June 26, Lieut.-General Carl Wilhelm von Schlieben, commander of the Cherbourg garrison (centre, facing camera), and Rear-Admiral Hennecke, Sea Defence Commander of Normandy (left), formally surrendered to Major-General W. Lawton Collins (right), commander of the U.S. 7th Corps, at his headquarters after the taking of the town and whilst numbers of Germans were still fighting. These Nazi wounded (top) were making their way through the streets under the protection of a Red Cross flag.

Photos, Associated Press, Planet News

Nurses Were Soon Tending Our Men in France

Photos, British Official : Crown
Copyright ; Planet News

WITHIN A WEEK of the Allied landings on the Normandy coast, nurses of Queen Alexandra's Imperial Military Nursing Service, wearing regulation Army battle-dress had crossed over from England to the beach-head and, with the assistance of R.A.M.C. personnel and the Pioneer Corps, had erected marquees and established a fully-equipped general hospital to house 600 patients. Most of these nursing Sisters had seen service before in this war—in France and the Middle East.

Nurses and R.A.M.C. orderlies remove a soldier-patient from the mobile operating theatre (I) back to his bed. Off duty, the nurses live under canvas ; they are well versed in the art of adjusting tent-pegs and guy ropes (2). When night bombing is in progress they sleep in slit trenches ; here (3) they prepare their beds. A newly-erected American Field Hospital in the Cherbourg peninsula seen from the air (4).

How Crab Tanks Clear the Nazi Minefields

EXPLODING A WIDE PATH for our infantry waiting to advance (1), and for guns, tanks and other vehicles about to go forward (4) through minefields in Normandy, the Crab flail-tank goes ahead and beats the ground with chain-ends, thus setting off buried anti-personnel and anti-tank mines. Close-up of chains (2). The Crab in action (3). Incorporating the best points of three previous types, it helped to clear the invasion beaches before commencing operations inland. The Sherman is the tank chiefly adapted to this purpose. PAGE 139 *Photos, British Official*

For Lack of a Drink a Battle May Be Lost

Shells, cartridges and food may be in ample supply, and courage and leadership of the highest order, but if thirst afflicts an army all its elaborate equipment may stand for nought. In this page HARRIMAN DICKSON explains how our fighting men on the various fronts are safeguarded against horrors and perils that may arise through lack of water.

An elaborate system of water supply for Second Front troops had been worked out so that when they landed on the coast of Normandy they were able to take their own drinking water with them. Mobile reservoirs, each holding thousands of gallons—taken from reservoirs in this country—had been standing ready. Each is mounted on a railway truck and, the landing effected, they were stationed at supply bases and other strategic points on the invasion coast for immediate dispatch to any of our advancing troops who might encounter water shortage.

New Zealand troops stationed on Nissan Island in the Solomons have their own water diviner, Sergeant L. R. Varnham, who roams the island with his hazel twig searching for supplies. In the hands of an expert, the V-shaped twig jerks spasmodically when the searcher is in the immediate vicinity of an underground spring; and Sergeant Varnham's twig betrays hidden supplies in various parts of that island where fresh water is otherwise difficult to come by.

REMARKABLE stories can be told of the part played by thirst in this war. In the Libyan campaign the 8th Army needed 5,000 tons of water every day, and to secure it considerable resource and initiative on the part of the Royal Engineers in that arid country were called for. They tapped a variety of sources. From lakes in the highlands of Kenya, Uganda and Abyssinia, water travelled over two thousand miles through the Sudan and Upper Egypt to Cairo and Alexandria. Thence the R.E.s had constructed a pipe-line to Tobruk capable of dealing with 2,500 tons of water daily. Fifteen hundred tons a day were shipped to Benghazi and another 300 tons were landed from lighters at the main beaches. There still remained 700 tons a day to be found somewhere. Again the water diviners played their part, tracking down a number of new sources of supply by means of their hazel twigs. Thus, plus

water distilled from the Mediterranean, was the remaining 700 tons provided.

Later in this campaign an astonishing incident occurred. It happened in those fateful days of early July 1942 when it looked as though Rommel would smash his way through to Alexandria. In fact, on July 3 he did penetrate our lines at El Alamein, with three very reduced panzer divisions. A number of his men then came upon a pipe-line stretching as far as the eye could see, and to them it was a wonderful sight. For nearly a whole day they had been without water. Immediately they shot holes in the pipe-line, dropped down and drank their fill. Then they pushed on towards Alexandria, and the following morning were within sight of it, when up came a weary section of the British Army to deal with them. It was a peak moment of the campaign. One battle-worn section of the German Army faced an equally exhausted section of the British Army. For some time the battle swayed to and fro, then the Nazis began to withdraw.

Shortly afterwards, over a thousand men of the 90th Light Panzer Division moved towards our lines with their hands above their heads, obviously surrendering. They seemed to move very uncertainly, and then the British soldiers noticed the twisted expression on their faces, the swollen lips. On the very day the Germans had broken through, our engineers had been testing that particular pipe-line. To test a pipe-line in the desert you use sea water: fresh water is far too precious. The men of the 90th Panzer Division had swallowed gallons of salt water; and, in the end, it was thirst that drove them to surrender.

EVEN in 1933 the War Office was sufficiently interested in the work of water diviners to send Captain A. J. Edney of the Royal Engineers, an expert "dowser," to a congress of diviners. Today, a very elaborate water organization has been devised to keep soldiers, sailors and airmen adequately

PRIMITIVE BUT EFFECTIVE is this well in Dutch New Guinea, from which an Australian and a Netherlands East Indies soldier are drawing water. Difficulty in getting adequate supplies is often very great in this theatre of war; in some islands diviners have successfully used their powers. *Photo, Australian Official*

supplied even in the most difficult circumstances. The Royal Engineers have a compact pumping equipment of which use was made in the Anzio beach-head in Italy. In the first place they set up water points, tapping all suitable streams, then pump water into sandbagged tanks, from which water trucks can be filled at high speed. Water for washing purposes is run by pipes to the bathhouse, a structure built by a company of R.E.s in a few days; it can provide baths for as many as four hundred men a day.

Water for drinking purposes receives elaborate treatment. The Army now has its mobile laboratories which can travel close to the front line, with all necessary equipment to test the purity of food or water. When the enemy is in the habit of polluting all the water supplies before he retreats, it is vital to have the water analysed before it is used in any way. The mobile laboratories can carry out these tests at speed. The water may need filtering, or it may need treatment with chlorine. Whatever the trouble there is always an answer. One particular water point in the Anzio beach-head supplied 40,000 gallons a day; special water trucks distributed it. In mountainous country the Army uses specially trained mules with water panniers. And in emergency water can be dropped by planes to encircled troops or marooned seamen.

At sea the problem of fresh water may become as vital as in the desert or the jungles of Burma, particularly to shipwrecked men adrift in boats. The Ministry of War Transport, in collaboration with a group of experts, has devised a compact distiller which converts sea into fresh water at the rate of five pints an hour. The distiller was the result of many months' experiment, and it was finally chosen from several other distillers (see illus. p. 11, Vol. 7). The choice was made by a handful of seamen selected at random from merchant ships. What I will call Mr. K.'s seemed the best from their point of view. Today a large proportion of lifeboats on merchant ships are fitted with this apparatus.

WATER SUPPLIER FOR THE BRITISH ARMY is this pipe point north-east of the town of Bayeux, which was taken by the Allies on June 8, 1944; it is one of many set up in various parts of the Normandy front. Attached to the truck is a trailer-tank into which water is flowing from one of the pumps fixed to the lines laid along the ground. PAGE 140 *Photo, British Official*

5th and 8th Armies Advance on 150-Mile Front

NORTHWARD FROM ROME the armies of the Allies in Italy swept the Germans before them in a retreat which assumed more and more the nature of a flight. On the west, the 5th Army went forward on a broad front to extend their mastery over the plain of Tuscany; by July 6, 1944, U.S. advance units were within fifteen miles of the great port of Leghorn. Inland, the French were driving on north of Siena, which they captured on July 3. In the more difficult country to the east, British 8th Army troops were engaged in a fierce struggle round Lake Trasimeno, where the Germans put up a considerable fight for the road to Florence.

At the east end of the front on the Adriatic coast (where Ancona port was threatened) a useful part in the capture of Ascoli Piceno was played by Alpini units of the Corps of Italian Liberation, while behind the enemy lines in Northern Italy partisans were encouraged to become more audacious in sabotage. Kesselring attempted to delay General Alexander's advance by extensive demolitions while his troops fell back to the so-called "Gothic Line" between Pisa (north of Leghorn) and Rimini.

CITIES OF UMBRIA province fell into Allied hands one after the other as General Alexander's armies pressed on through Italy. Two days after the fall of Assisi, on June 18, came the capture of Perugia; Sgt. C. Read of the Royal Corps of Signals is standing before the city's war memorial (2). Indian troops sharing in the triumphal progress of the Allies marched into Terni (1); this much-bombed centre of railway and road communications, lying midway between the east and west coasts, was the principal objective of the first drive north from Rome, and was occupied on June 15. Parallel with our advance on the mainland, French troops landed on June 17 on the island of Elba (3) with Allied naval and air support, and by the 19th had overcome all German resistance there. Black arrows on map indicate Allied thrusts on June 28.

Photos, British and U.S. Official; map by courtesy of The Daily Mail

Streets as Battlefields and Towns as Forts

Towns defended with determination can most effectively hold up a modern army—a lesson slowly and painfully learnt by ourselves and the enemy during the course of this war. New methods of attack are being evolved and, as suggested in this article by DONALD COWIE, are now being applied to problems of this nature facing our liberating forces in Western Europe.

"YOU found little Cassino a tough nut to crack. Well, I hope you have considered, when estimating the duration of the war, how many Cassinos there will be on the way to Berlin!" That remark was made to the writer by a neutral military expert, who had carefully studied the methods of the Germans in this war. And it was, if only for the moment, like the shock of cold water.

Had it not been firmly established by Cassino, in confirmation of the lesson taught at Stalingrad and so many other battles in built-up areas, that towns held with determination could halt the progress of a modern mechanized army more effectively than any other means?

Thus the writer remembered another conversation he had had with a tank commander who had fought in many campaigns. This man had been asked why tanks were so "timid" in towns. And he had replied: "You just try driving a number of tanks into an urban area defended by troops in the houses and office-blocks and cellars. Not only are you partly blind, with your gunlayers' and aimers' visions restricted to lamp-posts and walls, with occasional downstairs windows and doors, but you are terribly vulnerable. Anti-tank artillery can snipe at you from devastatingly close quarters, having the clear vision that you lack. Even the crudest methods, such as the dropping of petrol bombs from rooftops and upper windows, the toppling over of coping stones, can destroy you before you have an opportunity to hit back.

"MEANWHILE, your greatest asset, mobility, is countered by the rubble in the streets, or the actual narrowness of them. Why, I once saw a Sherman hopelessly jammed in one of those little Sicilian towns. It had become wedged between buildings in a narrow street, and could go neither backwards nor forwards. Ugh! No built-up areas for me!"

Is the tendency of this article clear? Perhaps it may be put briefly in this way, that if towns have been proved by the experience of the present war to be more defensible than any other kind of position against modern attack, then we can expect that north-western Europe, studded with towns, will present some very ticklish problems to our invasion forces. And that is just exactly what is now happening in Normandy.

There is little doubt about the fact of towns being easily defensible. First revealed in the Spanish Civil War by the prolonged resistance of Madrid and other cities, it should have been recognized by ourselves as a most useful discovery. Then we and the French might have stood longer in the blitzkrieg storm of 1940; certain Malayan towns, and finally Singapore and Rangoon, might have delayed the Japanese for months if defended street by street.

BUT the Russians watched and understood. "No city should be otherwise than in complete ruins when an enemy takes possession," was their virtual commandment to military subordinates, and so the German flood was eventually halted and turned back, not in great pitched battles, not on the open plains or on the river banks, but amid the remorseless rubble of cities, towns and their suburbs—Leningrad, Smolensk, Rostov, Voronezh and, what will remain the classic text-book instance, Stalingrad!

What was the reason? An answer has been partly given in that tank commander's remarks. Since modern strategy and tactics depend almost entirely upon mobility, anything which "grounds" tanks, lorries and other vehicles is fatal to the success of their missions. But there is more to it than that. Second in importance to mobility is firepower, the terrible capacity of modern artillery and automatic small-arms for destroying anything soft in the open. The Germans had to retreat in Italy till they reached Cassino, or our superior fire-power would have broken their line. Upon reaching the town, however, they could defy our fire-power for many months.

They could also defy our bombs, sometimes rained down in the heaviest concentrations of history. This was because they always had *some* protection in this as in other towns, and it is remarkable what man will endure provided that he does not feel altogether naked. In every town there are strong buildings. When they are blasted to shells the defenders descend to cellars, tunnels, and catacombs. Meanwhile, they

CONCEALED IN THIS WRECKED HOUSE in Cherbourg the sniper's position was a precarious one—with Allied soldiers watching for the betraying movement that would give them their target. *Photo, Planet News.*

excavate still deeper refuges, and the rubble above provides them with fortifications from behind the midnight shelter of which they can sally forth in raids and counter-attacks.

That the Germans have appreciated the military significance of these facts has been revealed not only by their defence of Cassino but also by the system employed by them in Russia to hold certain localities. This "hedgehog" system, as it was called, used towns as nuclei of defence, surrounded by artificial strongpoints, all connected by trenches or tunnels so that the garrison could be switched quickly from one sector to another.

Therefore it is but realistic to assume that the enemy will try to halt our progress in north-western Europe and elsewhere by a series of stubborn stands in certain key towns—such as, for example, the Channel ports, then Rouen, Amiens, Arras, and Lille. The desperate German defence of Caen in Normandy suggests that this is, indeed, his intention. Above all, he will almost certainly hope to defend his own towns of the Rhineland and Ruhr Valley, where he will not suffer from the handicap of a hostile local population. And it is feasible that if we played his game, and sat down as besiegers before each of these strongpoints in turn, then our journey to Berlin would indeed be protracted.

FORTUNATELY we will not do so; or we will not if we observe what Cassino and Russia taught us. Undoubtedly that Italian town and those Russian "hedgehogs" protected the enemy for a long time, so long as we and the Russians took them seriously and attacked them frontally. But once we left Cassino temporarily alone and attacked elsewhere, and once the Russians learnt to by-pass the "hedgehogs," the enemy was checkmated. He could continue to hold out for a while in an island of resistance, but with the knowledge that he could obtain no more supplies and must ultimately surrender if he did not retreat. Usually he retreated, and the town was no longer a fortress.

The moral has been for us, accordingly, that the road to Berlin may be a surprisingly swift and direct one, provided that the forces of retribution, like the Pilgrim on his progress, keep straight on. That is the answer to the neutral military expert; while our tankmen, always steering as clear of the rubble as possible, should not be prevented from fulfilling their true functions of smashing the enemy's armour and isolating his impotent "hedgehogs" one by one.

BRISTLING WITH OBSTACLES such as the logs, iron stakes and heaps of rubble seen here, the streets of some of Normandy's towns and villages are proving tough going for the advancing Allied forces. Resistance in these desperately defended localities has been bitter; Tilly-sur-Seulles changed hands more than once, in house-to-house fighting, before it finally fell on June 19, 1944. PAGE 142 *Photo, British Official: Crown Copyright*

D-Day Morning in Fields of Northern France

Across the English Channel on June 6, 1944, stretched an airbridge formed of great numbers of towplanes and gliders, protected by thousands of Allied fighters. Here, through clear June skies, soar planes that towed some of the troop-packed gliders to Normandy in advance of our ground forces; their mission completed, they head for their bases in England. Empty gliders bestrew the fields, whilst men that occupied them have rallied to strike mighty blows for the liberation of Europe.

143

When the Allies Swept Across Cherbourg Peninsula

Through St. Sauveur outskirts (1) Allied troops advanced on June 17. By June 27 Cherbourg had fallen. "The striking advances which gave the Americans the entire neck of the peninsula," said Mr. Henry A. Stimson, U.S. Secretary of War, "were due in large part to British and Canadian operations at the south-eastern end of the front." After the battle of Isigny inhabitants returned (2). The crew of this camouflaged gun (3) received the enemy range by phone from a spotting plane.

Photos, Br
Asso

The King Visits His Victorious Armies in France

H.M. the King crossed in the cruiser Arethusa to a Normandy beach-head on June 16, drove inland to General Montgomery's headquarters and inspected Allied officers and troops (4) after a special investiture. Seen from the air after its capture, the smashed town of St. Sauveur (5) stands at an important road junction. Down a lane in the Lingèvres area (6) pointed a 6-pounder gun, ready at point-blank range to open fire if the wish of its crew—a glimpse of the enemy—were fulfilled.

Eastward Lies the Road to Paris

When Cherbourg had fallen, the road to Paris was the part of this bullet-pierced sign (1) that held interest for Allied troops in Carentan, occupied on June 12. Enemy snipers lurked in Christot village near Tilly-sur-Seulles : these watchful British troops smoked them out (2). In the main street of Tilly, centre of communications west of Caen, Royal Engineers searched for mines (3), which were left in abundance by the Germans when they were driven out on June 19.

by Hamilton Fyfe

THERE are many surprising things in Mr. A. D. Divine's new book, Navies in Exile (Murray, 12s. 6d.), but the one that astonished and delighted me most is the lovely picture of a sailing minesweeper in the Mediterranean. It is yacht-rigged, but the vessel itself is like one of those sturdy, safe-looking Dogger Bank fishing-boats which bring us the cod that tastes so different here from what it does when eaten fresh in Newfoundland. The idea of a sailing boat doing the hazardous work of clearing mines was so unexpected, the contrast between its beauty and the grim ugliness of war so pathetic, that I have turned to the photograph again and again.

It is the Greek Navy which sends out these peaceful-looking craft for most useful service to the war effort. Not much else has it been able to do with the force it had five years ago. Nearly all of that was lost in the struggle with Italy. But the ashes of it produced a phoenix, a new force, with 350 officers and about 6,000 men. Britain has provided them with six new destroyers of the Hunt class ; they have three submarines, and, says Mr. Divine, "week by week, year by year, since the disastrous days of 1941, they have played magnificently their part." A similar tribute is paid to the Norwegian Navy. Its spirit may be illustrated by the action of a whaling skipper whose ship had been turned into a naval patrol-boat. She had one gun, and was guarding the entrance to the Oslo Fjord. In the darkness of an April evening the skipper sighted a force of heavy ships entering the waters of that " firth," as we should call it, which goes up to the capital of Norway. He challenged, but received no answer. Then he signalled to the big ships to heave-to. This was ignored also. So, with his one gun, he opened fire. The patrol boat took on the whole of the German naval force sent to play its part in the brutally mean, unprovoked attack on the Norwegian people.

"INSTANTLY from the German line came the flash and thunder of an overwhelming reply." The patrol boat was a wreck within a few seconds. The skipper had both legs severed, but he was still conscious ; he told his crew to scramble into their one boat and, as they were doing this, and finding it too small for everybody, he muttered, "I'm no good, anyhow," and rolled over the side into the sea. I wish there were a poet living who could celebrate that as Tennyson celebrated the fight which the little Revenge put up against the naval might of Spain.

There are many stories of gallantry in this book, but none to match that. Here, however, is one of a different kind, which did immense credit to the cleverness as well as the courage of a Yugoslav naval officer, commanding a motor torpedo-boat in the Adriatic. Its speed was 29 knots at best. Eleven Italian destroyers were looking for it on a dark night ; they could do between 35 and 40 knots. They sighted the torpedo-boat and challenged. " The Yugoslavs could not fight. They could not run. There was no shadow of hope," Mr. Divine writes. But he is wrong. There came into the captain's mind an idea which had the germ of hope in it. What the Italians were demanding was the password. They had to know whether he was a friend or foe. "Quick," said the captain to the man with the flickering signal lamp, "ask the second ship of their line for the password !" It was asked for—and given !

Instantly the signaller passed it on to the first ship, which was satisfied. The torpedo-boat went ahead and sailed straight through the Italian line.

Numerous have been the exploits of Polish naval commanders and seamen. Here is one of the most thrilling. A Polish motor gun-boat was taking part in shepherding a British convoy through the English Channel. A strong force of E-boats came out to attack the convoy. As it was too strong for the M.G.B., this was ordered to retire. But the

Exiled Navies and the Nelson Touch

Polish lieutenant in command had something wrong with his eyesight, the same complaint that on a famous occasion attacked Nelson. He did not see the signal—or did not appear to see it. He went on towards the E-boats.

There were six of them. Each was about the size of his own, and had much the same armament. "Full speed ahead ! " he ordered and shot in amongst them. All his guns were firing almost before the Huns realized they were being attacked. They made some attempt to reply, but they didn't like the look of it. They drew off and fled as fast as their engines would carry them. The threatened attack had been nipped in the bud. One against six had been victorious. The convoy steamed on without interference. It was a case of " the blind eye " all right, but the lieutenant's commanding officer said that " results fully justified this following of precedent." The Nelson Touch had succeeded again.

Better known, but well worth re-telling, is the saga of the Polish submarine Orzel, which was in the Gulf of Danzig at the start of the war, and was told to set out and attack German ships in the Baltic. As soon as she started, E-boats attacked and the submarine had to submerge for two hours. During that time ten depth charges were heard to explode near the vessel. When after dark she carefully nosed her way out

into the open sea, she was scraped by wire cables of moored mines or sweeps.

In the Baltic the Orzel found no enemy ships to attack, and when she had searched in vain for a week repairs were needed and she had to put into Tallinn in Estonia. Here the authorities, either in fear of or in league with the Nazis, decided to disarm and intern the submarine, although it had a perfectly good legal claim to shelter for as long as it took to finish the repairs. At once the suggestion, " Let's make a run for it ! " was put forward and accepted unanimously.

THE crew had burned their documents and charts ; their guns had been removed. Some of their torpedoes had been taken, but six remained. On a Sunday morning the commander cut the cable of the lift which raised the torpedoes and then went on deck, slating the Estonians for carelessness in letting it break. They looked at one another. It was Sunday. Mending the cable would be a long job. Why not put it off till Monday ? This they did. Only a small guard was left on board. Departure was fixed for midnight. But between eleven and twelve an officer arrived to inspect the guard. There was a delay of two hours. At last the signal was given. The guards were seized, gagged, carried below. All cables were cut. The engines were started. The Orzel edged away towards the port entrance, but not knowing the way to it exactly, she ran on a shoal. By this time the alarm had been given. Guns began booming. Rifle and machine-gun fire became furious. Fortunately, the smoke of the exhaust screened the submarine from sight and not a hit was made. She escaped to sea, but had to crash-dive immediately, for she was caught by searchlights, and batteries sent over six-inch shells. Surface craft also hurried out to drop depth charges. Though the Orzel made off, she had to stay under water all next day because it was felt that planes would be looking for her.

When the crew felt fairly secure from pursuit they put the Estonian guards in a boat near land with plenty of food and whisky and started to comb the Baltic for any German ships they could put their six torpedoes into. They found none. At the end of a fortnight they had scarcely any water, very little fuel. They could have put into a Swedish port and been interned, but that did not appeal to them. They determined to make for Britain. When they reached here, having come through many other perils, they were told " You can't be the Orzel. The Orzel has been lost ! " The story of the Orzel never will be.

IN the course of his accounts of these and other exiled navies—the French and the Dutch, with glances at Belgium and Denmark—Mr. Divine indulges in some interesting speculations. He thinks it may be said some day that the invasion of Norway lost Hitler the war. In that operation the German Navy was crippled. It lost something like one-third of its cruisers and destroyers. This prevented it from " playing havoc with the evacuation of Dunkirk " and making possible a landing on the British coast under cover of the Luftwaffe.

Again the Germans missed their chance, Mr. Divine thinks, with the magnetic mine. "Had it been manufactured in vast quantities and utilized in a single tremendous laying in every stretch of shoal water about the United Kingdom, in every channel and harbour entrance, it might have dealt us a crippling blow." As they did not do this, as they began with a small number, we had time to discover its secrets and the answer to it.

MINESWEEPING IS THE TASK of this Greek sailing ship, an example of one of the activities of the lesser vessels of the gallant Royal Hellenic Navy—to which tribute is paid in the book reviewed in this page. PAGE 147 *Photo, British Official*

Readers are referred to THE WAR ILLUSTRATED *p. 124, Vol. 7, for the story of our mastery of the magnetic mine.*

Battle-Torn Tarawa Atoll Now an Allied Base

FIRST MAJOR BLOW was struck by the Allies against the Japanese in the Central Pacific on November 20, 1943, when landings were made on Tarawa and Makin atolls in the enemy-occupied Gilbert Islands, 1,000 miles north of the Solomons; three days later Allied occupation was complete. In this desperate fighting Tarawa, chief Japanese air base in the Gilberts, became a shambles; but it was speedily transformed to an efficient Allied base.

One of the first steps in producing order out of battle chaos was to import a small saw mill with which to make planks for building purposes (1). Lt.-Col. E. J. C. Finny (2-left) and Capt. R. B. Marfack, British administration authorities, were with the U.S. forces who drove out the Japanese. Tarawa airfield, reconditioned for Allied warplanes (3). Street scene (4) shows huts and tents so placed as to make the most of cooling breezes and shade from the few remaining trees. See also pp. 503, 591 and 594, Vol. 7.

Photos, Associated Press

PAGE 148

Vital Burma Supply Road Freed by 14th Army

WEST YORKSHIRE

CRUSHING BLOW to Japanese aspirations in Burma was the final clearance of the vital Imphal-Kohima supply road, announced on June 25, 1944. For many weeks the Japanese had clung to this key area until cracked by continual Allied pressure. Tanks and men of the West Yorks Regiment (whose badge is shown above) push on against the Japanese on the Imphal-Kohima road (1), while one of the many road-blocks with which the enemy had hoped to stem the advance is torn down (2). All that remains of a battle-wrecked village taken by our troops (3). Allied supply mules toil up steep paths to forward positions (4).

Photos, Indian Official

Men of the Maquis are Striking for France!

A special communiqué issued on June 17, 1944, by Supreme Headquarters of the Allied Expeditionary Force detailed the considerable part that has been—and now more than ever is being—played by the Maquis, the secret Army of the French Forces of the Interior, towards the liberation of their country. Just who these valiant patriots are is explained by JOHN ENGLAND.

"GUERILLA operations against the enemy are in full swing," announced a communiqué from S.H.A.E.F., "and in some areas the army of the French Forces of the Interior are in full control. At the end of the first week of operations on the shores of France the army of the French Forces of the Interior has, with its British and American comrades, played its assigned role in the battle of liberation."

Let us turn back the clock to 1943, when Germany made forced labour absolute for young Frenchmen. Resistance at once stiffened and "ne va pas en Allemagne" (don't go to Germany) became the watchword. That followed the census of all men born between 1912 and 1921, about 130,000 being affected, according to Vichy, of the total of nearly a million registered for forced labour. Before then men could only be persuaded to go to work for the enemy; the Compulsory Labour Service instituted a two-year period: The Maquis (a Corsican word for the dense undergrowth of that island) was the reply of French youth to that.

No less than 200,000 young men dodged registration. In the Limoges region only forty per cent registered. Chambery did not

of persuading these patriots to submit to the foreign yoke. Promises were made of amnesty. When this failed force was brought to bear, in particular against the numerous bands who had retired to the Haute Savoie, there to wage a guerilla war against the invader, without organized arms, without proper commissariat, without camps, often without food or shelter.

IT was to the Haute Savoie that the ruthless Darnand sent his armed police, but without much success, and soon there were bands of these spirited young men in every "inaccessible" part of France. These youths suffered many losses on the snow-covered mountains of the Mediterranean, and Darnand claimed that he had cleaned up the menace. It was an empty brag, for the men of the Maquis are more active than ever—in the Savoy, the Limousin, the Dijonnais and the Ardennes. They are in Brittany and in the Jura, they have strongholds even in Toulon and Bordeaux regions and in the Pyrenees.

The Maquis bar no foreigner who cares to join their ranks, and many have, including Fascist-hating Italians and Republican Spaniards. It includes radicals, socialists,

communists, and royalists too. Right, Left, Reds, Pinks and Blues, it is all the same. In the matter of leaders the Maquis have been fortunate, for many officers rallied to them, most notable of all General de Lattré de Tassigny, who later escaped from France and was in command of the French army which captured Elba in June 1944. Every man who makes his way to the hills or to the forests and is ushered into the hut or tent of the local captain must take an oath of fidelity, expecting no rewards, uniform or medals: only hardship, danger, outlawry, hunger and thirst.

The Maquis had in the early days only one source of firearms—setting aside secret stores which date back to the defeat of 1940; they had to carry out raids, and some of these have been spectacular in their daring. And it is a capital offence to lose one's arms, a severity dictated by the extremes of necessity. A man instructed to secure food or clothing sets forth from the secret camp for the nearest town or police or military store; often food and goods are pressed upon him without demand for payment. The peasants, too, have been a source of strength to the movement, hiding men and secreting food for them.

THE Maquis waged war by means of sabotage, and as the months passed became more and more daring. Referring to them in a speech some time ago, General de Gaulle said; "We can guarantee that inside France combatants, many of whom are now taking part in small-scale actions, will participate in the great military effort of the French and the Allied armies by attacking the enemy in the rear on orders from the French command in accordance with the operational plans of the inter-allied High Command."

And now? Since D-Day (June 6, 1944) the ranks of the Maquis have continued to swell, absorbing police and gendarme and Vichy army deserters complete with their arms. On that day the French Provisional Government in Algiers announced that members of this underground movement were helping Allied airborne troops and attacking communications leading to the battle zone. It was further stated, on June 14, that the organization was recognized by the French Provisional Government and that all troops served under the orders of responsible leaders. Their official status as the French Army of the Interior was further marked on June 25 by the announcement that General Koenig, of Bir Hakeim fame, had been appointed to direct the operations of all resistance forces in France under and by authority of the Allied C.-in-C.

ON D-Day an appeal was made by Supreme Command H.Q. to the Maquis asking them to try to delay enemy reinforcements being brought up to the Normandy coast during the first twelve hours of the Allied invasion. The reinforcements were delayed three and a half days! With almost fiendish energy the partisans are paralysing rail and road traffic, destroying bridges, damaging canals and locks, and interrupting telegraph and telephone communications.

Subterranean cables, in spite of being well defended, have been attacked and destroyed, and transformer stations have been the objective of well-directed and executed sabotage. German garrisons have been harried, street fighting has occurred, villages occupied, enemy detachments wiped out, and prisoners taken. And still it is rising—this enemy-dreaded might of the Maquis: a grim shadow of doom behind the German lines.

DRILLING IN SECRET, these young men of the Army of the Maquis prepared themselves for warfare against the Nazi occupiers of France. Despite German patrols and Vichy police, defiant townsfolk of Bourg-en-Bresse—north-east of Lyons, in the Department of Ain—erected this bust (right) on the pedestal of a former statue removed for use as scrap metal, and filed past it on Armistice morning 1943. *Photos, Free French Official*

supply one man. In Savoy 800 registered, but of those called up seventy-five per cent escaped. They became refugees, outlaws, "hill men." They were the first men of the Maquis. In their heroic and seemingly hopeless resistance to the all-powerful and all-pervading Nazis, there was something sublime—and futile, or so it seemed then. It is not possible to state with certainty the total number of young Frenchmen in the Maquis today; estimates range up to 500,000.

Faced with this dramatic recoil from the Nazi tyranny, Vichy tried many methods

Armour Speeds to Combat on the Western Front

SWEEPING ON PAST INFANTRY-HELD POSITIONS, a Sherman tank, followed by a dispatch rider, rumbles along a dusty Normandy road to further action in the Tilly-Caen area. In this crucial sector, where Rommel massed most of his armour, British and Canadian forces kept German tank formations from moving towards Cherbourg. By June 28, 1944, when the troops emerged from difficult country around Tilly into an open plain more suited to the deployment of armour, many clashes occurred with the enemy's Panthers and Tigers; climax came to our furious assaults when on July 9 Caen fell. See map in p. 131.

Photo, British Official

Our Colonies in the War: No. 11—The Cameroons

REMEMBERING the days of Teuton misrule, that part of the Cameroons which became British after the Germans were defeated there in February 1916 is helping to ensure another defeat for the enemy. Lying between our colony of Nigeria (see pp. 586 and 587, Vol. 7), by whose government it is administered under a mandate, and French Equatorial Africa, the British Cameroons is a strip of land running the whole length of the Nigerian border with a total extent of some 34,000 square miles. Pulling its weight with Nigeria, the British Cameroons is producing bananas, rubber, tea, palm oil, castor seeds and cocoa for the war effort; bananas particularly being of great value, as tons of them, dried and made into banana "dates," go to feed our troops in West Africa.

Tons of shelled castor seeds are spread out in the sun to dry (1). Green tea leaves are poured into a rolling machine (2). Tapping a rubber tree; an incision is made in the outer bark which frees the sap (latex rubber) and allows it to flow into the collecting cups (3). Great bunches of bananas fill the ripening sheds (4), which are served by railed trucks. *Photos, Nora Haydon*

I WAS THERE! Eye Witness Stories of the War

I Saw a City Below the Germans' 'West Wall'

Parts of Hitler's Normandy coast defences, boosted in loud propaganda as the impregnable "West Wall," really were amazingly well prepared. Alan Moorehead, for Combined Press, has recorded a day he spent in going through one such area—abandoned in panic at short notice.

I WENT into about twenty dugouts all concealed under the trees. Here was a complete underground city, the work of two years or more. Wooden steps made of saplings lead you beneath the surface and then you are surrounded by concrete and masonry. Everything was abandoned apparently at five minutes' notice. The mess-room is about eighty feet long by twenty feet. It has a piano, four radio sets, a bar stocked with German Pilsner beer, German gin and whisky and cigars (or the relics thereof). There are several chests full of sports gear—footballs, jerseys and shorts.

Another dugout is a central office with a telephone exchange, table lamps and many cupboards filled with books, papers, forms and all the impedimenta of a lavish pre-war city office. A third dugout contained sides of beef. A fourth had about thirty bicycles and a workshop. A fifth contained officers' sleeping quarters, rigged up with dressing-table, curtains and comfortable beds with sheets.

I went into half a dozen store-houses containing tinned pork, fruit and vegetables, thousands of rounds of all kinds of ammunition, signalling sets, flags, clothing, boots, rifles and machine-guns, with all their spare parts. Then there was the kitchen, a sort of dream kitchen with electric boilers and cookers all fitted with elaborate gauges. I came on underground piggeries and stables, fitted with the most modern equipment, underground hangars for tanks and lorries. In the sculleries there was a great butter churn.

At the moment when our assault was launched the Germans were in the act of bundling up parcels to send home to their families. Each parcel contained three pounds of fresh Normandy butter. Above ground there were many more curious and pathetic things. The German officers' dogs were chained at a series of neat wooden kennels. Those that had not died when the battle swept over, lay in a coma of hunger and thirst at their chains. Everywhere roamed German horses, their eyes white with fear at the shelling. Some were still harnessed to their long wooden coffin-like wagons. Others were being ridden by the Tommies. Others, which had broken legs, were being shot by our officers. The very birds in this green and unreal wilderness were lying dead on the ground ; others had been winged or crippled by the flying shrapnel.

I watched a group of Tommies kill and cut up a German pig. A little farther on a Sten gunner had bagged two geese. A third group was frying the liver the men had cut from some animal during the battle. This then was a German Regimental Headquarters.

From it a network of trenches fans out. One trench, about eight feet deep, zig-zags down to the sea three miles away. I imagine you could walk for five miles through trenches and pillboxes almost without coming to the surface at all. I leave you to imagine the vast labour and expense sunk in this empty undertaking—years of work and everything lost in a day. The crust was simply not strong enough to hold. We paid for it, of course.

Today I have been by many fresh graves which the French have piled high with Normandy roses in pink and red and white. And yet the officer who commands the Medical Corps on this sector told me in his new tented hospital today that he had catered for very many more casualties than we have had. As for the wounded, they are probably

WRECKED GUN EMPLACEMENT which formed part of the "West Wall" (see story in this page), now a piled mass of shattered concrete, being inspected by U.S. troops.
Photo, Associated Press

getting better and quicker treatment than they have had before. Penicillin has been issued right down to first-aid posts.

General Montgomery has been here and has given praise in a way I have never known him do before. It must have been pleasant for him to see among our booty a number of British vehicles of the Morris make which the Germans apparently captured at Dunkirk in 1940 and were still using.

A Gale Nearly Wrecked Our Invasion Fleet

How the build-up of our great attack in Normandy was nearly brought to a halt in its third week is told by W. F. Hartin (by arrangement with the Daily Mail). Only superb seamanship by hundreds of young sailors handling their cumbersome invasion craft in the teeth of a howling Channel gale saved the Army from a serious setback.

FOR two nights, as vessels dragged their anchors, plunged into one another with a sickening grinding sound and were swept by 8-ft. waves, the situation to us who were in the midst of this fury seemed touch and go. We were in mid-Channel when the full force of the north-east wind, meeting the tide, piled up a mountainous beam sea. I was in one of the Navy's motor-launches, a sturdy patrol vessel used to most hazards of these treacherous waters.

Suddenly, three times in succession, we were nearly capsized. As every man clung to the nearest hand-hold, the water hissed along the deck, burying the starboard half in boiling foam. We looked at each other without attempting to speak, because the same thought was in all our minds—"This is the end. She is not going to right herself." Each time the vessel swung back crazily to port it was as if she were bracing herself for the final plunge, when she would roll over completely to starboard.

Then the captain, Lieut. G. S. Parsons, R.N.V.R., saw his chance, snapped out an order to put the helm hard over, and the little ship bravely dug into the sea head-on. She shivered as she hit one wave after another, but we were comparatively safe. The story of the next 12 hours is one of relentless fight, zig-zagging across these seas, when each turn might have been fatal.

Hour after hour we tried to edge nearer our part of the French coast, and after 12 hours' passage we managed to get an anchorage in the lee of some big ships miles from where we were scheduled to arrive. We soon realized our troubles had barely begun. In the eerie twilight of this, the shortest night of the year, we could hear above the hiss of the waves and the shrieking wind the yet

MASSIVELY CONSTRUCTED GERMAN STRONGPOINTS such as this overlooked the Normandy beach-head. From this fort guns swept the beach, until Royal Navy shells silenced it. It was then used as an Allied command post. Immensely strong and well-equipped defence works, theoretically impregnable but hurriedly abandoned during our assault, are described in the story above. *Photo, Associated Press*

more ominous sound of ships grinding together.

Landing craft out of control pounded against us. Our anchors dragged, and we lost one. We, too, were drifting, and before we could tackle the situation the ship was flung heavily on a sandy bottom and pounded by a terrifying surf. In another second we would have been rolled over, a plaything of the storm, but just in time we managed to get our engines going and headed for deeper water. The appalling sight of the beach in the dreary grey of the morning told its own tale of craft that had piled together and been ground to matchwood. Feverish salvage work was going on all round, and most remarkable of all, when we reached our appointed anchorage next afternoon, the laborious process of keeping the Army supplied had not been brought to a standstill.

Still, angry seas were flinging the small craft up and down the sides of the big ships from which they were taking cargoes in slings. It was a feat of seamanship to get these small fellows alongside without getting them smashed. It was another to get them loaded, and yet another to get the cargoes ashore. But despite the combined heroism of thousands of men, the supplies came ashore all too slowly. The tonnage landed that day was small.

It was decided that the next day—whether the weather abated or not—our giant landing ships would go in "taking all risks," and land direct on to the storm-swept and wreck-cluttered beaches. It was realized that this would probably mean a dead loss of these ships, for it was doubtful if they could ever be refloated in a seaworthy condition after the pounding they would receive.

Fortunately, the wind died down after 3½ days, and on Thursday morning our whole invasion coast lay lapped in a glassy sea. Unloading went on apace, though not all the damage could be put right at once. The serious aspect was the 3½ days' delay in passing cargoes to France. It took several days of intense activity to make good the depleted dumps ashore. A north-easterly gale of such ferocity—it blew in 70 m.p.h. gusts—is not recalled within the memory of the most experienced Channel pilots, and blowing, as it did, straight into the Baie de la Seine, it piled up such a sea that all calculations of tides were confounded.

UNLOADING AMMUNITION INTO A LANDING CRAFT, one of the first to reach the Normandy shore on D-Day. The gigantic flow of supplies continued despite almost insuperable difficulties, including one of the worst Channel gales in living memory; how this brought us to near-disaster in the third week of the campaign, when the beaches were crying out for ammunition, is told in the story commencing in the previous page.	*Photo, P.N.A.*

We Broke Through the Hills Around Cherbourg

Twenty days after the initial assault, Cherbourg fell to the Allies. It was at 3.30 on the afternoon of June 24, 1944, that American troops saw for the first time the city spread out below, and here a war correspondent gives his impressions of the momentous occasion. Alan Moorehead's story is published here by arrangement with the Daily Express.

IT was an uplifting moment. We could see the buildings fringing the water's edge, the warehouses along the docks, and beyond this, in the calm sea, the outer

DEEP UNDERGROUND TUNNELS in the German defence system of Cherbourg had entrances such as seen here. In the background an Allied soldier examines a captured mortar.	*Photo, Planet News*

concrete breakwaters of the harbour. All the green land between us and the sea—about a mile—was swarming with Germans. They brought us to a sudden halt on the road by firing almost point-blank out of a stone farmhouse. On the right they kept up a running fight through the undergrowth with machine-guns.

And on the left, just as I was watching with my glasses, a thicket of trees suddenly opened up with great trailing balls of fire coming towards us. These were the German rockets. As their phosphorus burned away the air was filled with a breath-taking noise, a sort of whirling and tearing, and a second later the farmyard below us disappeared in walls of dust and smoke. About the same time half an acre of ground half a mile away appeared to rear itself slowly and lazily in the air until it formed an immense mushroom of smoke and the noise of the explosion came rushing across the fields at us.

We were pinned down on a sunken road under almost continuous rifle and machine-gun fire. It kept hitting with vicious little whacks against the piled-up earth beneath the hedge. So long as we did not bob up

above the level of the embankment we were perfectly safe there in the strong June sunlight. The embankment was four feet thick and those shots that missed simply whizzed by harmlessly overhead.

Some of the infantry slept oblivious of the noise and the presence of the enemy in the next field. Some brewed coffee. Some edged up the hedge nearer and nearer to the Germans. The American general, who looks like a successful business man, was striding about, highly delighted with it all. "Come on," he called to us, "if you want a good view, go up that hill." All around us was the recent wreckage of battle: a group of dummy German guns made out of saplings, the still warm German dead lying at their foxholes, a burning cowshed, the dead beasts in the fields among the torn telephone lines, and the litter of mess-tins and empty meat cans scattered up the road.

A haze began to drift over Cherbourg towards the evening when the Americans advanced for their last run down to the sea. It had been as balanced and as decisive a break-through as any I have seen in this war—the power of the offensive machine against fixed positions. Coming up to the Regimental Command post one could feel the sense of expectancy and eagerness among the staff officers. The colonel said, "I think we are going to have better luck today."

He selected a good observation point for us on his map, and added: "Right now there is a German ack-ack gun on it firing at our forward troops, but we will have it within an hour for you. Just wait till I get the artillery to dump something on it." He picked up his telephone, and presently the dumping began. While we were waiting the colonel explained that little knots of Germans had been by-passed in our rear and had been holding out for three days. "But, hell," he said, "you don't go any place unless you by-pass." All this took place under the low branches of an apple orchard in full leaf, and there were with us a couple of British Guards officers who had come up to see the fight.

Midday was zero hour, and as it struck, the colonel picked up his telephone and told his general : "We are all ready to go !"

Then it started. There was no great barrage, no cloud of aircraft, no great noise. The infantry simply vanished into the forest with the sound of the light, quick coughing of their machine-guns. Yet the next six hours were packed with more incident than I can put down here. At the start a French irregular came up to my jeep with a Russian in civilian clothes. He wanted the Russian shot as a spy. But we managed to dissuade him and pushed on.

Within an hour we had gone clean through the main German perimeter. On either side of the lane there were deep concrete dugouts with many abandoned enemy guns—places with running hot and cold water and electric lights. The hedges and trees were badly damaged by blast and the German dead lay spaced along the roadside ditches. About 4,000 yards from the city limits we came on the main German encampment, with some 20 or 30 camouflaged barracks sunk beneath the surface and linked with underground concrete passageways.

Some 400 Germans were holding on here, but they fled in panic as the Americans burst

SOME OF THE THOUSANDS OF GERMANS who surrendered in the arsenal of Cherbourg march through the captured town to a prisoners-of-war cage, as " guests " of the Allies for the duration of the war. A statue of Napoleon in the background stares stonily at the procession. Fall of the arsenal was announced on June 27, 1944.
Photo, Planet News

through the trees. A dozen shuddering and frightened horses stampeded about the sloping parade ground. In the officers' quarters and the storehouses we found cases of brandy and tubs of butter, many radio sets, big stacks of office equipment, bottles of eau-de-Cologne and such an array of

toilet things that you might think the German effeminate if you did not know him. And so we came through the outer defences of Cherbourg to the hills above the city—the infantry feeling their way along the hedges, the jeeps and the guns slowly trundling up the roads.

OUR DIARY OF THE WAR

JUNE 21, Wednesday   *1,754th day*
Western Front.—Allies occupied Valognes in Cherbourg Peninsula.
Air.—Over 1,000 British-based bombers attacked Berlin area and with Mustang fighter escort flew on to Russian base.
Pacific.—Aircraft of Eastern Fleet struck at Port Blair, capital of Andamans.

JUNE 22, Thursday   *1,755th day*
Western Front. — Encirclement of Cherbourg almost complete ; heavy fighting continued in Tilly area.
Air.—Heavy bombers again attacked flying-bomb sites in Pas de Calais ; at night R.A.F. bombed railway yards at Rheims and Laon.
Burma.—Whole of Kohima-Imphal road cleared of Japanese.

JUNE 23, Friday   *1,756th day*
Western Front.—Pressure on Cherbourg defences increased.
Air.—Flying-bomb sites again attacked by heavy bombers ; road and rail communications in France also bombed.
Mediterranean.—Allied bombers attacked Ploesti and Giurgiu, Rumania.
Russian Front.—New Soviet offensive launched round Vitebsk on central front.
Pacific.—U.S. carrier-borne aircraft attacked Iwo in Volcano Islands.

JUNE 24, Saturday   *1,757th day*
Air.—Road and rail communications over wide area of France hit by Allied bombers ; flying-bomb sites in Pas de Calais again attacked.
Pacific.—Guam and Rota Islands bombed by U.S. aircraft.

JUNE 25, Sunday   *1,758th day*
Western Front.—British 2nd Army opened attack S.W. of Caen towards River Odon.
Air.—Allied heavy bombers attacked airfields and oil dumps in France.
Italy.—5th Army troops entered Piombino on west coast.
Mediterranean.—R.A.F. made night attack on Shell Koolaz oil refinery near Budapest.
Russian Front. — Soviet troops breached defences covering Orsha and Bobruisk on central front.

JUNE 26, Monday   *1,759th day*
Western Front.—Cherbourg fell to Allied troops ; Gen. Schlieben and Adm. Henneke captured.
Russian Front.—Vitebsk and Zhlobin captured by Soviet troops.

Mediterranean.—U.S. Russian-based bombers and fighters attacked oil plant at Drohobycz, Poland, and landed in Italy. Mediterranean-based bombers attacked oil refineries in Vienna area.
Italy.—Chiusi captured after bitter fighting.
Pacific.—U.S. warships bombarded Jap positions in Kuriles, and carrier-based aircraft attacked Marianas.
Burma.—Chindit and Chinese forces captured Mogaung, near Myitkyina.
China.—American air base at Hengyang, near Canton-Hankow railway, captured by Japanese.

JUNE 27, Tuesday   *1,760th day*
Western Front.—Allied troops in Tilly-Caen area crossed Caen-Villers Bocage road.
Air.—Halifaxes bombed military installations in N. France ; railway centres of Vitry-le-Francois and Vaires, east of Paris, also attacked. Rocket-carrying Typhoons demolished German Army Corps H.Q. south of Cherbourg Peninsula.
Mediterranean.—Military targets near Budapest, and railway yards at Brod, Yugoslavia, attacked by Allied bombers.
Russian Front.—Soviet troops occupied Orsha, south of Vitebsk.
General.—Following Ribbentrop's visit, Finnish Govt. declared for closer pact with Germany.

JUNE 28, Wednesday   *1,761st day*
Western Front.—Allied armour and infantry crossed the river Odon.
Air.—Airfields near Laon and railway yards at Saarbrucken attacked by U.S. bombers ; night attacks by R.A.F. on Metz and Blainville.
Mediterranean.—Italian-based bombers attacked oil refineries near Bucharest.
Russian Front.—Soviet troops forced the Dnieper and stormed Mogilev, east of Minsk.
General.—Philippe Henriot, Vichy Propaganda Minister, killed by French patriots.

JUNE 29, Thursday   *1,762nd day*
Western Front.—Enemy resistance ceased at Maupertus airfield, Cherbourg.
Air.—U.S. bombers attacked many aircraft factories and oil plants in Germany ; R.A.F. bombed flying-bomb sites.
Russian Front.—Soviet troops captured Bobruisk, S.E. of Minsk.

JUNE 30, Friday   *1,763rd day*
Air.—Airfields and road and rail communications in France attacked by R.A.F. and U.S. bombers ; at night Mosquitoes bombed oil plant near Homberg, on the Rhine.
Russian Front.—In Minsk direction Soviet troops forced River Beresina on wide front.

General.—U.S. Govt. severed diplomatic relations with Finland.

JULY 1, Saturday   *1,764th day*
Western Front.—Last enemy resistance ended in Cap de la Hague area of Cherbourg.
Air.—Liberators bombed flying-bomb sites in Pas de Calais ; R.A.F. made night attacks on Western Germany.
Italy.—5th Army captured Cecina, S. of Leghorn.
Russian Front.—Borisov, strongpoint on approach to Minsk, stormed by Red Army.
Pacific.—Noemfoor Island, off Dutch New Guinea, bombed by U.S. aircraft and shelled by Allied warships.
General.—State of siege proclaimed in Copenhagen following Danish strikes.

JULY 2, Sunday   *1,765th day*
Western Front.—Allied bridgehead across the Odon stood firm despite continuous enemy assault.
Air.—U.S. and R.A.F. bombers attacked flying-bomb sites in N. France.
Russian Front. — Minsk-Vilna and Minsk-Brest Litovsk railways cut by Soviet troops.
Mediterranean.—U.S. bombers attacked oil refineries and airfields near Budapest and railway yards in Yugoslavia.
Pacific.—U.S. troops landed on Noemfoor Island.

JULY 3, Monday   *1,766th day*
Russian Front.—Minsk, capital of White Russia, captured by Soviet forces ; street fighting in Polotsk to the north.
Italy.—French troops occupied Siena.
Air.—Allied medium bombers attacked enemy transport and munition dumps in Normandy.
Burma.—Ukhrul, Japanese base on Indo-Burmese frontier, captured by British 14th Army.

JULY 4, Tuesday   *1,767th day*
Western Front.—Allied forces made two major attacks : in Caen area, Carpiquet captured by Canadians ; in base of Cherbourg Peninsula U.S. forces advanced on La Haye du Puits.
Air.—U.S. heavy bombers attacked airfields in Paris area.
Russian Front.—Soviet troops captured Polotsk and advanced to within 55 miles of Vilna.
General.—Copenhagen strike ended following concessions by Germans.

★ ~~~~~~~~~~ *Flash-backs* ~~~~~~~~~~ ★

1940
June 23. Gen. de Gaulle announced provisional French Government to continue the war.
July 1. German battleship Scharnhorst bombed at Kiel.
July 3. S.S. Arandora Star, taking German and Italian internees to Canada, sunk by U-boat.

1941
July 1. Germans captured Riga and reached the river Beresina.
July 3. Broadcast by Stalin calling for guerilla warfare and scorched earth policy in Russia.

1942
June 21. Japanese landed on Kiska in the Aleutian Islands.
June 25. Gen. Eisenhower made leader of U.S. forces in Europe.
July 1. Germans reached Alamein.

1943
June 20-21. Friedrichshafen attacked by R.A.F. Lancasters which flew on to North African bases.
June 23-24. R.A.F. shuttle-bombers raided Spezia from North Africa and returned to British bases.
July 4. General Sikorski, Polish C.-in-C., killed in air crash.

THE WAR IN THE AIR

by Capt. Norman Macmillan, M.C., A.F.C.

SINCE the beginning of the P-plane bombardment of Southern England, the Germans have maintained as great a continuity of attack as possible by night and day. Anti-aircraft defences and fighters have taken an increasing toll of the crewless raiders, and the Prime Minister remarked on June 30, when visiting A.A. batteries with General Sir Frederick Pile (G.O.C.-in-C. A.A. Command), " It's a pity there were no Huns in them ! "

So far official policy is still to maintain complete silence on the percentage of P-planes brought down by the defences. There must always be a balance between the harm done by careless gossip and the advantage gained in refusing the enemy accurate information, but in this case, when there are no aircrews to return to state where the bombs exploded, it must be more than usually difficult for the enemy to check up their results by photographic reconnaissance.

Whole areas would have to be photographed to discover where damage had occurred in built-up zones. But even this immense task of photography and subsequent assessment would not disclose the number of P-planes destroyed by the defences, for those that explode on open country at the end of a normal flight do not excavate the huge craters which so easily betray the explosions of ordinary bombs, and thus cannot be readily assessed even by expert photography.

THE most that photographic reconnaissance results can show is the percentage of hits in built-up areas. There seems to be no way for the enemy to discriminate between misses and P-planes destroyed. Obviously, the most efficient way to employ a battery of P-planes would be to have spotter aircraft over the target area, able to report results by radio as is done for gunnery shoots. Otherwise, the shooting of the P-plane battery must be blind. No doubt the fighter squadrons of Air Defence of Great Britain would welcome the chance of having a crack at German spotter planes over Southern England. And the policy of withholding information which might be useful to the P-plane batteries is certainly justifiable.

The Germans have given this weapon the term Vergeltungswaffe (reprisal weapon) with the abbreviation V1. It has now appeared in several varieties, with wing spans of 16 ft., 18 ft., 23 ft., and even up to about 30 ft. The first has a speed of nearly 400 m.p.h. and the second about 350. The 2,200 lb. of high-blast explosive contained in the warhead makes this weapon more powerful than a one-ton bomb whose total weight includes all the metal. Height of flight above the English coast has been about 2,500 ft. by day and rather lower by night.

APART from the fighter, gun and balloon defences against the P-plane, the bomber attacks against the launching platforms (now totalling 50,000 tons) have continued and sometimes significant periods of quiet followed these attacks. Moreover, while the bombers make the attacks the enemy cease launching P-planes. On the other hand, it is clear that this diversion of bombing effort from German cities to military targets behind the French coast must provide relief to hard-hit German industries and cities. But the growth of Allied shuttle-bombing must make it increasingly difficult for Germany to find safe sites for the manufacture of weapons. On June 21, U.S. Army 8th Air Force Fortress bombers from Britain attacked oil plants in Ruhrland, 50 miles south-east of Berlin, and other targets, and flew on to airfields behind the Central Russian front. They were escorted throughout by Mustang P-51B long-range fighters.

Previously (July 1943) British bombers from Britain attacked targets in Italy and landed in North Africa, repeating their attack on the return journey. In June 1944 U.S. bombers shuttle-bombed Rumania from airfields in Italy and Russia.

The strategic use of air power includes withholding attacks in addition to making them. This strategy was used at Beda Fomm by General Wavell's Army of the Nile. It was used again by General Eisenhower in connexion with the invasion of Normandy. The plans to bomb the Loire bridges before the invasion were not put into use because, taken in conjunction with the bombing of the Seine bridges, they might have disclosed the probable zone of invasion. By D-Day all the Seine railway bridges were down, the Loire

FLIGHT-SGT. M. ROSE, of Glasgow, who shot down the first flying bomb (P-plane) in daylight draws a sketch for the benefit of an Intelligence Officer and fellow fighter-pilots. See also illus. p. 158. *Photo, British Official*

bridges were then made the first object of attack, and all were quickly brought down, disrupting all rail traffic from the south of France to Normandy. These actions greatly hampered the movements of German troops and made it necessary for German tanks to be brought up to the fighting zone on their own tracks, to the detriment of the mechanism through wear and tear.

GERMAN Tanks Blasted by Lancasters in Normandy

The strategic bombers of Bomber Command have also been thrown into the fighting in Normandy. After the fall of Cherbourg the troops of the British 2nd Army that crossed the river Odon were fiercely counterattacked by enemy forces, including many tanks. In the afternoon of June 30 Bomber Command sent a force of 250 Lancaster night bombers, heavily escorted by fighters, to the aid of the 2nd Army. In the space of a few minutes they dropped more than 1,000 tons of bombs on Villers Bocage and a restricted wooded area where enemy tanks were concealed—part of June's 56,000 tons.

In Normandy, too, tactics similar to those used successfully in the Pacific against Japanese ships were used against the German army. A Typhoon squadron skittle-bombed a German Corps H.Q. in a château at St. Sauveur Endelin. The bombs were released at zero feet and disappeared into the house, which thereupon disappeared too.

Towards the end of June the Luftwaffe began to offer more opposition on the Normandy front. Allied pilots reported increasing numbers of aircraft in the Chartres airfields area. But bombing, and attacks with rockets, cannon and machine-guns have pushed German air-bases far back from the fighting zone. As a result the Luftwaffe have been forced to construct new, small satellite fields from south of the Loire to Belgium and Holland to enable their aircraft to operate. Twenty-five German aircraft were destroyed over Normandy on June 29, a larger number than in the earlier days of the fighting.

THE raising of his score of victories to 33 brought Wing Commander J. E. Johnson, D.S.O., D.F.C. (see illus. p. 29), one ahead of the R.A.F.'s previous highest scorer Group Capt. A. G. Malan, D.S.O., D.F.C. Although the present war has outlasted the duration of the last war, fighter-pilots' scores are notably lower. Nine pilots' scores equalled or bettered the current R.A.F. best. These were : Bishop 77, Mannock 73, McCudden 50, McElroy 41, Little 40, Fullard 39, Ball 38, Collishaw 38, Barker 33; five of these pilots won the V.C. and five survived the war. The only fighter-pilot who has won the V.C. in this war is Nicolson, who gained the decoration for bravery in an action in which he shot down his first opponent. In this war the majority of V.C. awards in the R.A.F. have gone to Bomber Command. Why ?

SUPPLIES FOR TROOPS IN NORMANDY are dropped by parachute from Stirling bombers in response to a radio request from an airborne division. The vastness of the scope of operations of the R.A.F., the closeness of its co-operation with our ground forces, and the lack of enemy interference in this enterprise are suggested here by the great number of parachute supplies being sent down over an extensive area. PAGE 156 *Photo, British Official*

Casualties Carried by R.A.F. Transport Command

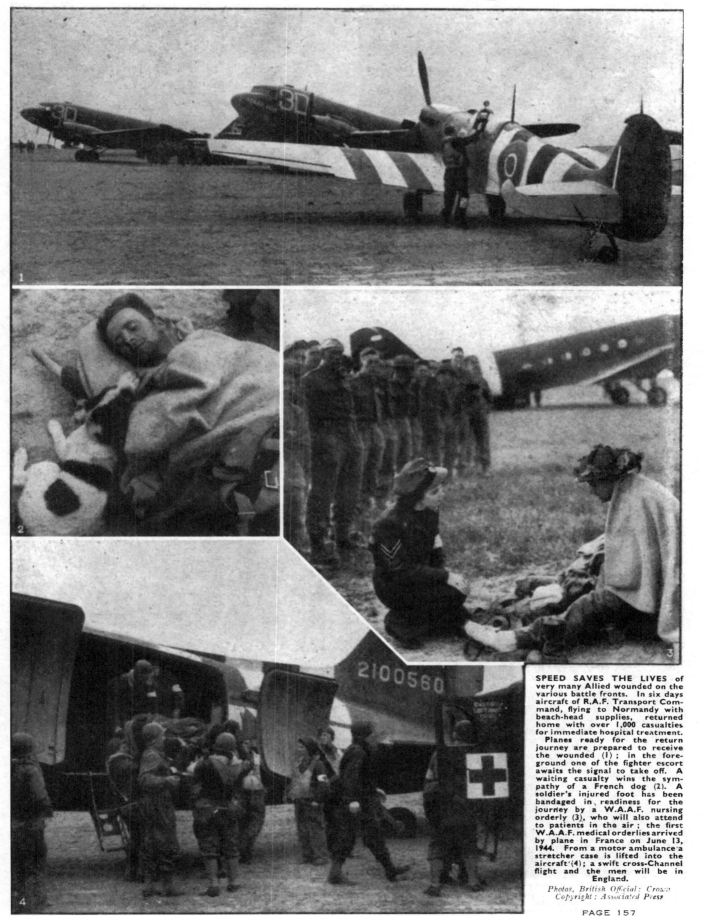

SPEED SAVES THE LIVES of very many Allied wounded on the various battle fronts. In six days aircraft of R.A.F. Transport Command, flying to Normandy with beach-head supplies, returned home with over 1,000 casualties for immediate hospital treatment. Planes ready for the return journey are prepared to receive the wounded (1); in the foreground one of the fighter escort awaits the signal to take off. A waiting casualty wins the sympathy of a French dog (2). A soldier's injured foot has been bandaged in readiness for the journey by a W.A.A.F. nursing orderly (3), who will also attend to patients in the air; the first W.A.A.F. medical orderlies arrived by plane in France on June 13, 1944. From a motor ambulance a stretcher case is lifted into the aircraft (4); a swift cross-Channel flight and the men will be in England.

Photos, British Official: Crown Copyright: Associated Press

Southern England Attacked with Flying Bombs

LAUNCHED MAINLY AGAINST LONDON from bases in France, flying bombs or pilotless planes (sectional drawing, top right) totalled 2,754 up to 6 a.m. on July 6, 1944. Many were intercepted and shot down by R.A.F. fighters. This one (1) started its 350 m.p.h. journey (2) from a camouflaged launching base in the Pas de Calais, similar to several captured near Cherbourg by the Allies (3). Caught in a network of tracer shells, bullets, searchlights and flak, another flashes to extinction—blown up by gunfire (4). See also p. 156.

Not so many people are coming forward this year to promise help in bringing in the harvest. Partly this may be due to the cold weather of May and June. Most folks are liable to think conditions will go on being whatever they happen to be at the moment. If it rains, they say " We are in for a rainy summer.'' If the wind blows from the north with a razor-edge to it, when it ought to be soughing warmly from the south-west, they anticipate months of it. There is just as much chance that August will be very hot as that the inclemency of spring and early summer will continue. But there is another reason lessening the response to the appeal for workers in the field. This is that many of the younger men and girls who harvested last year supposed that they would get a holiday with lots of time to themselves and nothing very strenuous to do when they were on duty. They found out their mistake and were disappointed when they could not "make whoopee'' as they had expected. That is what one of the field-workers has been telling me. She adds that for those who take it in the right spirit no holiday could be healthier or more enjoyable, as well as valuable to the country and our great Cause.

I AM told that a good many Dutch army officers and business men in Holland were believers in Nazism as a system of government, but I cannot think that they are of the same opinion still. The same used to be said, with more truth I fancy, of Swedish military and commercial men, for, according to people who have lately been in Sweden, this pro-Nazi feeling has by no means disappeared. They certainly were on the side of the Germans in the First Great War. The Swedish aristocracy and upper middle class are inclined to domination. There is a story in one of Robert Louis Stevenson's Vailima Letters about trouble in a South Sea Island. Some native chiefs had been imprisoned for stirring it up and it was feared that a rescue might be attempted. A young Swedish officer, who was in command of the small international force stationed there to keep order, proposed to store dynamite in the gaol and blow it up if any attempt were made to get the prisoners out. He actually secured enough explosive to do this. Stevenson was highly indignant. Public feeling was aroused, the risk to the whole community was realized, and the plan was ruled out. But it was a pointer to the sort of way that young Swedes had been taught to think.

"THE more things change, the more do they remain,'' says the paradoxical French proverb, with characteristic French love of literary epigram. It is a proverb frequently proved to be true. Mankind is like the pointer to a weighing machine, which swings away to the left as you weigh yourself and, as soon as you get off, swings back again to its abiding-place. See what is happening in Russia. First a tremendous upheaval. Everything in the melting-pot. " Never be the same again," said the wiseacres. But watch what happens. A little while ago religion was brought out and dusted and set up again to be practised without hindrance or even discouragement. Now horse-racing has been restored to its place among popular entertainments. It would not be surprising to see Stalin become sovereign. Oliver Cromwell nearly became king, not because he wanted a crown and sceptre—far from it— but because monarchy was the only form of government the mass of the English people at that date could understand. For all practical purposes Stalin is Tsar already, and a far more competent one than Russia ever had before, as well as far more anxious for the welfare of his nation as a whole. If it seemed desirable—at present it does not—that the title should be added, I fancy no objection would be raised—though the title would probably not be that of Tsar.

MUCH surprise has been expressed about the quantities of food found by our troops in Normandy. But if the Highlands of Scotland were to be invaded, the invaders

LIEUT.-GENERAL SIR MILES DEMPSEY, K.C.B., D.S.O., M.C., commander of the British 2nd Army, comprising all the British troops in France, led the famous 13th Corps of the 8th Army in N. Africa, Sicily, and Italy. *Photo, British Official : Crown Copyright*

would be equally astonished to find people there eating so much better than they do in our cities and towns and even in most villages. I have had a letter from someone enjoying a holiday in the foothills of the Cairngorm Mountains. "We get any amount of cream," he says, "and really more eggs than can be good for us. Yesterday, counting the puddings and sauces made with them, we reckoned we consumed half-a-dozen each." You may say, "Ah, yes, the Black Market !" Not at all. The explanation is simply that in the village there are so many cows and so many chickens, and the spot is so remote from a railway, that the local produce must be consumed on the spot. That is also the reply to ill-natured people who say the Normans must have been food hoarding. They used to supply other parts of France, especially Paris, with the produce of their fruitful soil. As it can't be taken away by rail or road, it stays there. And the troops get the benefit of it, I am glad to say.

HERE is an illustration of the way in which languages grow. I first heard the word "maquis" when I was sailing in the Mediter-ranean many years ago and noticed a very agreeable scent in the air. I was told we were near Corsica and that all over the island grow flowering perfumed shrubs. They were what I could smell out at sea. Later when I landed and walked about the place I came to love the maquis as much as one loves the South African veld with its scent of mimosa so heavy in the hot air. It must be a local word, for I cannot find it in French dictionaries ; but it cropped up a year or so back in the news about the French partisans in the mountains of their homeland. They were then termed "the men of the maquis." They have become maquis themselves (see article and illustrations in p. 150), and no doubt the word will remain with us, meaning "guerilla troops who fight in wooded districts." Only purists who would like languages to be cut-and-dried products of pedantry will raise any complaint. Lots of words in every language have originally meant something other than what they now mean. Any language that becomes stiff and stereotyped is already half dead.

A SYMPATHIZER with my lament over the doggerel issued by a Government Office about fish and exhibited in fishmongers' shops, sends me these wretched lines which he saw in an omnibus :

Sprightly Stephen thinks awhile,
Then climbs to Top Deck with a smile,
Leaving the Lower Deck for fares
Of folk who cannot tackle stairs.

For seventy years we have been trying to educate the masses—that is, to give them some sense of literary form, to supply them with a standard for judging between decent English and illiterate drivel. We have failed so completely that it seems to be time we tried some other method of mind-cultivation. For, mark you, it is not merely that the products of elementary schools tolerate rhymes of this character. These are produced and put up in public places by those who manage omnibus companies and by those who are in charge of Government Offices. These people have in all probability been at secondary and perhaps at " public " schools, yet they have no feeling for literary values whatever. Why not drop education on literary lines and teach boys and girls to use their hands, make them study machines, train them by engineering courses ? It might give better results.

LIFE is a series of surprises. Most people are surprised when they find themselves married. Children, when they come, cause unexpected wonderment by all they do and say. Discovering that we have grown old is a surprise. Dying may be—we don't know— the greatest surprise of all. Certainly every war that has been fought since long-range weapons and fast-moving vehicles were invented has upset all the plans made by military commanders. It was supposed that this war would be like the last one; it has turned out completely different. The sort of fighting that goes on now in France and Italy suits young men of spirit far better than sitting in trenches and occasionally labouring across no man's land to take part in a big attack. It gives opportunity for individual exploits, for initiative and ingenuity. It gives the private soldier more exciting work to do, and it is more dangerous to generals than war used to be. Half a dozen have been killed on the enemy side in Normandy.

North Italy: a Wave in the Permanent Way

Photo, British Official: Crown Copyright

BEARING WITNESS TO THE ACCURACY of Allied bombing of enemy rail communications in Northern Italy is this twisted section of a main line which received a direct hit; on the left can be seen a derailed tanker wagon. Speeding up the rate of our drive far beyond Rome were special mixed task forces composed of tanks and mechanized infantry; by July 5, 1944, they were heading north-west of Perugia (captured on June 20 by the 8th Army) towards the city of Florence.

Printed in England and published every alternate Friday by the Proprietors, THE AMALGAMATED PRESS, LTD., The Fleetway House, Farringdon Street, London, E.C.4. Registered for transmission by Canadian Magazine Post.   Sole Agents for Australia and New Zealand: Messrs. Gordon & Gotch, Ltd.; and for South Africa: Central News Agency, Ltd.—July 21, 1944.   S.S.   *Editorial Address:* JOHN CARPENTER HOUSE, WHITEFRIARS. LONDON, E.C.4.

Vol 8　The War Illustrated　Nº 186

SIXPENCE

Edited by Sir John Hammerton

AUGUST 4, 1944

HOW ARE THE MIGHTY FALLEN! This German 60-ton Tiger tank, shorn for ever of its deadly power and now hurled on its side and with one track missing, yet retains one degree of usefulness—it provides shelter from the rain for a resting British soldier on the Italian front. Enormous losses of armour and equipment have been suffered by the enemy in our latest offensives ; as much as possible is salvaged for prompt repair and re-use by the Allies, or for shipment as scrap for conversion into new weapons. *Photo, Keystone*

NO. 187 WILL BE PUBLISHED FRIDAY, AUGUST 18

Our Roving Camera Visits Allied Air Forces

INDIAN AIRFIELDS find elephants useful for hauling grounded aircraft, which they do with the same unconcern as they handle timber. At a Fleet Air Arm station in the Indian Ocean area one pulls its weight at the end of ropes in order to get a plane into position (left).

RUSSIAN MECHANIC gets to know something about a Fortress engine from a U.S. aircraftman at a field somewhere in the Soviet Union (below). Occasion was on June 2, 1944 after the first "shuttle" raid carried out by bombers of U.S. Strategic Air Forces in Europe, which attacked targets in Rumania before proceeding to bases prepared for them in Russia; on June 6 they bombed oilfields at Galatz from these bases.

U.S. 'BLACK WIDOW' NIGHT-FIGHTER is named after a deadly spider found in America. It is reputed to be one of the largest and most powerful pursuit aircraft yet built. Otherwise known as the Northrop P-61, the Black Widow has two Pratt and Whitney engines, a tricycle undercarriage and, as this rear view shows, unusual twin fuselages.

IN NORMANDY the famous Spitfire was known only by repute until the Allies landed in France. These French children (above) crowd round ground staff men of an R.A.A.F. squadron operating in the bridge-head to admire one of their planes, and even have the thrill of standing on its wings. The R.A.A.F. is playing a big part in covering operations with our ground forces on the Western Front.

CAEN CATTLE could not resist approaching to investigate this strange object which suddenly fell from the skies into their field (left). The wings and engine were all that remained of a German fighter, which a few minutes before had been circling and twisting overhead in vain endeavour to escape the bullets of the R.A.F. plane that eventually brought it down.

Photos, British and Australian Official, Planet News, Keystone

THE BATTLE FRONTS

by Maj.-Gen, Sir Charles Gwynn, K.C.B., D.S.O.

SINCE I last wrote, Germany's situation has continued to deteriorate rapidly. For many months the threat of the opening of a western front and the air offensive based on Britain had exercised a very great influence on the eastern front, immobilizing Germany's reserves and steadily undermining her war industries. But the German General Staff and people were confident that their western wall had been made practically impregnable by the precautions taken; and if, contrary to all expectations, the Allies did succeed in effecting a landing it was believed that they could be crushed decisively before they could become really dangerous, without diverting troops from the east to an extent which would endanger the situation there. Since it was held that a successful counter-stroke or failure to effect a landing would convince the Allies that a negotiated peace was all they could hope for, the western was looked on as the front where the decisive battle would be fought. Now that the Germans have seen a great army successfully landed and so firmly established that hopes of crushing it by a counter-offensive have practically disappeared, the shock to their morale can be well understood.

BUT what may have an even greater effect on their morale is the concrete proof that the opening of the western front had already had disastrous effects on the eastern front. Their own military authorities have been forced to excuse the catastrophe which has overwhelmed Von Busch's Army and opened the gateway to East Prussia, by claiming that it had been necessary to withdraw reserves from the east in order to reinforce Rommel. The two Panzer Corps that were withdrawn might well have averted the most disastrous consequences of the Russian break-through, and it is evident that they arrived too late in the west to enable Rommel to crush Montgomery's armies before they were firmly established, or materially to improve his situation. It would seem that the German High Command have repeated the blunder which in 1914 sent two army corps racing across Europe to repel the Russian invasion of East Prussia only to arrive too late to affect the situation there; while their presence in France might well have tipped the scales on the Marne.

FRANCE

In Normandy there has been much heavy fighting, but it is clear that up to the time of writing Montgomery has made no attempt to launch a far-reaching general offensive, and he may not be ready to do so for some time yet. His objects so far have evidently been, while building up his resources, to gain room for the effective deployment of his armies in depth and thus avoid the danger of congestion at his base of operations when his whole force is set in motion. By strong local attacks to gain ground at a number of points he also maintained heavy pressure on Rommel, compelling him to dissipate his reserves and subjecting him to processes of attrition which must always be more severely felt by the numerically weaker army. Under this pressure Rommel, in attempts to recover lost ground, was induced to deliver a series of costly counter-attacks in which his strong panzer force, with which he hoped to regain the initiative and possibly deliver a decisive counter-blow, has suffered heavily. Montgomery, on the other hand, has retained the initiative continuously in spite of the handicap of weather, which on occasions greatly restricted air co-operation to which he attaches so great importance.

THE Germans now admit that their hopes of staging a counter-offensive before Montgomery was firmly established were shattered by the air offensive against the road and railway communications by which they had confidently relied on being able to bring up rapidly their strategic reserves. Once again German High Commanders failed to appreciate the offensive potentialities of their opponents, and it is somewhat surprising that their reserves were held so far back, considering how thoroughly our air supremacy had been established and how clearly the Cherbourg peninsula was indicated as the most probable scene of an initial landing attempt.

The interruption by bad weather on several days of our air offensive enabled the movements of German reserves to be accelerated, but Montgomery's persistent attacks drew them into battle as they arrived. Rommel is now very definitely on the defensive and his object must be to keep Montgomery's armies within a restricted area. He cannot afford to carry out an elastic defence, for it would entail a constant increase in the length of his front, already overlong for the troops he has available. The loss of Caen and La Haye du Puits, the bastion positions covering his flanks and the roads and railways which will probably dictate the direction of Montgomery's major offensive thrusts, must have been a heavy blow to him—Caen in particular, when finally cleared, will greatly facilitate further Allied operations.

Should Rommel be forced to abandon his hold on the base of the Cherbourg peninsula, operations would be bound to become much more mobile and fluid. At present it is, of course, absurd to compare the rate of progress in Normandy with that of the great Russian offensive. In Normandy no decisive break-through has yet been attempted, and in Russia, though it has now been so magnificently accomplished, it was not attempted until after many months of preparatory attacks and a building up of communications and resources very similar to that now in progress in Normandy. Once a break-through is achieved operations take on a new tempo, especially when the enemy is deficient of reserves available to cover retreat by rearguard actions. In that case such centres of resistance as are encountered can be by-passed with impunity

SOVIET FORCES continued to press against the German armies on the Latvian border and in the Lithuanian regions, as here shown. On July 16, 1944, Grodno, covering the approaches to East Prussia, was taken, while by July 19 the Red Army was closing in on Brest-Litovsk. *By courtesy of News Chronicle*

by advanced guards and left to be mopped up by the main body, but the rate of the advance depends mainly on the supply services of the pursuing army keeping pace, and the efficient working and organization of the base of operations.

RUSSIA

The Russian break-through, so astonishingly complete and overwhelming, was in itself evidence of perfect preparation and planning as well as of the quality of the troops; but the maintenance of the amazing speed of the follow-through can to an even greater extent be attributed to the completeness of the preparations for the offensive. Critical as Rommel's position is in Normandy, the crisis there is far from having reached the stage it is in on the eastern front. The invasion of East Prussia may have even a greater effect on German morale than the penetration of the west wall; but it would have a less direct effect on the strictly strategical situation than if Lindemann's forty divisions in the Baltic States become isolated and incapable of taking any effective part in the defence of the homeland. It is not yet known what orders Lindemann has received, but his apparent inaction suggests that again the German High Command has hesitated to reach a decision until too late—possibly owing to Hitler's obstinacy or the divergent advice given to him. The offensive by Yeremenko's 2nd Baltic Army on the Sokolniki front should be well calculated not only to add to the difficulties of Lindemann's position but to give effective protection to the flank of Bagramyan's 1st Baltic Army against any counter-offensive Lindemann might attempt to deliver.

YEREMENKO'S offensive, and Koniev's offensive on the Lvov front, were also evidence that the Russians have no intention of depending on one concentrated drive, but are fully prepared to open new fronts of attack when previous blows have compelled the Germans to alter the dispositions of their reserves, or when it has become difficult to maintain the impetus of the initial attacks. Such strategy is particularly well calculated to maintain relentless pressure on a weakening adversary deficient of reserve power, and was, of course, that adopted by Foch in 1918.

Koniev's offensive may prove to be the most devastating yet launched, for although the Germans expected it and had concentrated most of their armoured divisions to meet it, they may have been forced to send some of their reserves to the north. Moreover, since Koniev started 200 miles farther west than the northern offensive, the momentum of his drive to Lvov and the Carpathian passes should be further maintained.

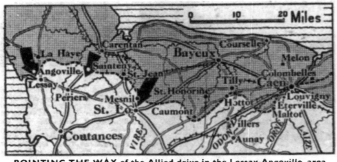

POINTING THE WAY of the Allied drive in the Lessay-Angoville area and district of St. Lo, arrows on the map above show the position as it was on July 14, 1944. St. Lo fell on July 18, on which date, in the Caen area east of the Orne river, a new British break-through gained more ground. PAGE 163 *By courtesy of News Chronicle*

Vital Key-city Captured on Normandy Front

MOPPING UP in the streets of Caen, British infantry turn against the enemy a Hotchkiss machine-gun which they had captured (right). Originally a German invention, an adapted type of Hotchkiss has been used by our Forces; it is a light machine-gun, firing .303 ammunition, the same calibre as our infantry rifle.

ABANDONED ENGINE in the Caen area, whose tank had been punctured by a shell, provides good cover for advancing British troops engaging German units on the other side of the railway line (below). The soldier on the left uses his rifle, while his comrade is armed with a Piat Projector, an anti-tank weapon which fires a 2¾-lb. bomb and is effective against tanks and pill-boxes up to 115 yards.

ALLIED CONVOY, carrying vital supplies and more men, passes down the main street of war-battered Isigny (above), captured by our Forces on June 10, 1944, losing no time in exploiting every yard of territory we have gained on the western front.

BATTLE AFTERMATH in Caen found this key-city (left), freed by British and Canadian troops on July 9, 1944, badly damaged; but the citizens were joyful at their release from hated German rule. Capture of Caen was an important strategic step, prelude to a breakthrough into open country and use of the full weight of our armour.

Photos, British Official

Victories Garnered in Red Army's Drive West

WITH EVER-INCREASING PRESSURE, Red Army troops of the 1st Baltic Front, on July 4, 1944, took one of their major objectives since their armies emerged in the Vitebsk region last winter—the important town and railway junction of Polotsk, main gateway for the drive on Latvia and most advanced strongpoint, in the south, of the powerful German forces there. (Left) General Ivan Bagramyan, Commander of the 1st Baltic Front. (Right) Soviet infantry engaged in hard street fighting before the final capture of Polotsk.

MOGILEV, fortress in the German "Fatherland Line" defence system in eastern White Russia, was captured on June 28, 1944. Tanks of General Zakharov's 2nd White Russian Front are here seen entering the town, their crews waving encouragement to its inhabitants.

KARELIAN ISTHMUS OFFENSIVE against the Finns was launched on June 10, 1944. Eight days later the Russians had broken the Mannerheim Line (which they had smashed before, in 1940), and on June 16 they took Viipuri. Here Red Army men penetrate a captured trench system.

MINSK, CAPITAL OF WHITE RUSSIA, round which remnants of the German divisions driven back from the "Fatherland" and Beresina lines had formed along with the city's powerful garrison, fell to Soviet forces of the 3rd White Russian Front, under General Ivan Chernyakhovsky (right), in co-operation with those of the 1st White Russian Front, under Marshal Rokossovsky, on July 3, 1944. In the capital, Red Army officers talked with liberated women citizens (left).

Photos, U.S.S.R. Official, Pictorial Press, Planet News

THE WAR AT SEA

by Francis E. McMurtrie

FROM their present rate of advance it appears likely that the Soviet armies will have entered Riga by the time these lines appear. Riga is not only a valuable port, with a secure harbour at the southern end of the Gulf of Riga, but its possession should effectually cut the communications of the German armies in Estonia, unless these can be evacuated by sea. Neither side can claim control of the Baltic, but the Germans may be expected to cling as long as possible to the three large islands which partially block the mouth of the Gulf of Riga, to facilitate the safe passage of transports from Tallinn (Reval) to Danzig or ports farther west.

The three principal islands in question are Dago, Oesel and Moon, or to give them their Estonian names, Hiiumaa, Saaremaa and Muhu. All are low-lying, with considerable areas of marsh and woods. In the channels separating them from the mainland of Estonia it would be possible for motor-torpedo-boats, submarines and other small craft

to lie in wait for transports passing outside the islands. These islands formed an important feature of the Russian plan for resisting the German advance in 1916-17. In October of the latter year there was a naval action here, in which the Russians lost a battleship and several smaller craft, being obliged to withdraw their forces from the islands in consequence. In the German invasion of 1941 it was not possible to make so considerable a stand at this point.

According to rumour, German forces have occupied the Aaland Islands in the entrance to the Gulf of Bothnia, farther to the northwestward. Evidently the enemy hope, by controlling these two groups on opposite sides of the Gulf of Finland, to keep clear the approaches to Tallinn, and so leave open to their troops in Estonia a way of retreat by sea.

On the other hand, occupation of Riga would enable the Soviet forces to land on the Dago group and use these islands as a base for the motor-torpedo-boats and submarines which are likely to be the transports' most dangerous foes at sea.

AMERICAN occupation of the island of Saipan, in the Marianas, is now complete, all organized resistance having ceased. From the strength of its garrison, which certainly exceeded 20,000, it is evident that the enemy regarded it as their principal fortress guarding the approaches to Japan from that direction, as well as a major supply base for their conquests in the South-West Pacific. Up to the date of the last report, nearly 16,000 enemy dead had been buried by the U.S. forces, and many more bodies were awaiting burial. Over 1,600 Japanese soldiers and some 14,000 civilians had been made prisoners.

In the course of the fighting, Vice-Admiral Chuichi Nagumo, Commander-in-Chief of the Japanese fleet in the Central Pacific, and Read-Admiral Yano were both killed. Nagumo was in command of the Japanese forces which delivered the surprise attack on Pearl Harbour on December 7, 1941. He

was also in command at the Battle of Midway, which marked the turning point in the struggle in the Pacific, and was subsequently appointed port admiral at Sasebo, a naval base comparable to Chatham.

WITH its two airfields and deep-water harbours, Saipan should provide a capital base for combined operations against other islands nearer Japan. In the meantime, aircraft carriers fuelled and stored at Saipan should find no difficulty in carrying out attacks on Japanese ports, regardless of the abominable announcement by the enemy that captured airmen will be killed. Yokosuka, the port of Tokyo, is only about 1,350 miles distant; and the principal intervening groups, the Bonin and Volcano Islands, have already been heavily raided. (See facing page.)

It does not of course follow that Japan itself will be the next target. An attractive alternative would be the Philippines, which lie some 1,500 miles to the westward of Saipan. With a native population which in the past two years has learned to fear and detest the Japanese interlopers, and would be ready to aid American forces in the event of an invasion of Mindanao or Luzon, the enemy must feel considerable uneasiness in the Philippines.

From the fact that Guam and Rota, two other islands in the Mariana group slightly to the south-westward, have been assailed by gunfire, bombs and rockets, it was conjectured that these may be the next objects of attack; and as I write, news comes that a landing has been made in Guam, which was an American possession from 1898 to 1941, falling to Japanese assault shortly after the Pearl Harbour raid. Owing to the refusal of Congress to vote funds for its fortification in pre-war years, it was incapable of offering prolonged resistance.

It is the superior sea power of the Allies which here, as in Europe, enables them to threaten attack at various points without the enemy being able to do anything about it.

Owing to the late date at which they were announced, more than five weeks after D-Day, details of Allied naval losses during the great landing in Normandy have attracted comparatively little attention. Yet the very small number of ships sunk is really remarkable, in view of the magnitude of the operation and the elaborate arrangements made by the Germans to cope with it in the way of mines, obstructions and fortifications. Actually these losses comprised six destroyers, four frigates (or in American naval parlance, destroyer escorts), one fleet minesweeper, one trawler and three auxiliaries. Landing craft lost have still to be announced.

WITH the exception of H.M.S. Boadicea, launched in 1930, all the destroyers were new vessels built during the war, i.e. H.M.S. Swift and a sister ship, the Norwegian Svenner (formerly H.M.S. Shark), and the U.S.S. Corry, Glennon and Meredith. This is the second Meredith the United States Navy has had sunk since war began, the earlier one having been lost in action with the Japanese in the South-West Pacific in 1942, and replaced by the present ship.

One of the frigates was of the "River" type, H.M.S. Mourne; the other three, H.M.S. Blackwood and Lawford and the U.S.S. Rich, were units of the "Captains" type. The fleet minesweeper was the U.S.S. Tide, a two-year-old vessel of 700 tons, and the trawler was the Lord Austin, taken up in the early days of the war for minesweeping duties. The three auxiliaries were the U.S. transport Susan B. Anthony and fleet tug Partridge, and the British vessel Minster, a small cargo vessel built in 1924 for the Southern Railway's cross-Channel service.

No particulars of the sinkings have so far been published, except in the case of the Svenner, which has been torpedoed.

H.M.S. BLACK PRINCE, acting with U.S. naval units and backing American land forces, contributed a stirring chapter to the invasion of Normandy. One of Britain's newest cruisers, she steamed close inshore for ten days, pin-pointing targets which ranged from beach pill-boxes to gun emplacements and enemy infantry concentrations inland. Out of 35 specially indicated targets she destroyed 20 for certain. Lower photograph shows the Black Prince, which suffered no casualties and no damage, returning to port, her mission ended; above, a Wren tests her telephone equipment on docking.

Photos, British Official

Saipan's Capture is a Bombing Threat to Tokyo

FURIOUS BATTLE FOR SAIPAN ISLAND, Japanese stronghold in the Marianas, in the Pacific, which began with the landing of U.S. troops on June 15, ended 25 days later with complete victory for the Allies. Length and ferocity of the struggle surpassed any other battle previously fought in the Central and S.W. Pacific areas.

On this island, little more than 70 square miles in extent, the Japanese had a garrison of over 20,000 men, the strongest force the Americans have yet encountered on any one occasion since the opening of the Allied counter-offensive against the Japanese in August 1942. Of that garrison 95 per cent perished. American casualties were 2,359 killed, 11,481 wounded, and 1,213 missing.

Prize of the victory at Saipan was the airfield which, less than 1,500 miles from Tokyo (see map), brings the mainland of Japan within bombing range ; hence Saipan's new nickname—" Bomb Tokyo " island. The island's harbours also provide an excellent base for future Allied attacks throughout the Central Pacific. On June 15 and on July 5, 1944, U.S. Super-Fortresses attacked Japan (see p. 189) from bases in the India-China-Burma theatre.

AMMUNITION CASES LINE THE WAYSIDE, part of the great mass of Allied war materials poured into Saipan Island, as troops and vehicles move up (1). Prisoners, taken as the enemy were squeezed from position after position, were marched back to quickly erected stockades (2). Much use was made of " Alligators " or amphibious tractors in bringing U.S. reinforcements from the warships lying off the island ; here one is seen reaching the beach (3), while another lies stranded off shore, its occupants wading the last few yards. PAGE 167 *Photos, Planet News, Associated Press*

In Praise of the Heroes of the Stokehole

What sort of men are these who, down below the waterline, see nothing of the battle when the destroyer they man is hotly engaged : who labour on though engine-room and stokehold become a scalding inferno and shell splinters hurtle through the confined space like shrapnel ? Capt. FRANK H. SHAW puts these highly-trained specialists of the Royal Navy "on the map."

I⊤ is no longer a matter of thunderously whirling cranks ; semi-magical turbines supply the enormous power needed to drive a modern destroyer through the water at a speed approximating to fifty miles an hour. Nor is it a grimy business of hurling tons of Welsh steam coal into the incandescent and ever-hungry furnaces, for the stoker of to-day turns a tap or two and so adjusts the mixture of steam, oil and air that makes a warship's fuel.

"The sort of job," as a stoker, first-class, told the writer, "you can do in white kid gloves and a boiled shirt !" When the compliments are paid to the Royal Navy a full share should be tendered to the Black Squad, from the resolute and infinitely resourceful chief engineer to the lowliest stoker. The engines and boilers are the real vitals of a ship of war, and on their exact functioning —under all conditions—depends the turn of the scale between victory and defeat.

The men responsible for developing phenomenal power of speed at short notice

motions of a small ship swinging at speed through Atlantic combers are exaggerated below the waterline, and men keep their footing only with difficulty and a sense of awareness. To lose footing might well mean to crash up against hot steel. And, come what might, the engines must keep moving if the bridge so directs.

ON prompt, intelligent obedience to commands might depend the life of the ship and the members of her crew, for a touch on the telegraph may mean an added, lightning-quick burst of speed that will enable the destroyer to escape a busy torpedo, or a quick stop that baffles the aim of a battleship's gunners ready to send a crushing salvo at the hurrying target. Destroyer captains can time the shell flights to a nicety, after seeing the sharp flash of the discharge ; and if the Black Squad are reciprocative— as they invariably are—the captain can fling his ship out of the danger-zone before the big shells arrive at their assumed target.

If hit below, the engine-room and stoke-

tive lighting in the event of damage occurring to the main supply. Shell-hoists and a host of complicated gear come under his most exacting surveillance.

And Black Squad ratings are quick to assist the "chippy-chap"—the carpenter or shipwright—if the plugging of splinter-holes becomes a vital need. At such times they display an aptitude of improvisation that can not sufficiently be admired. Furthermore, each stokehold rating is a fully-qualified fighting man, adept in the use of rifle, bayonet, hand-grenade and machine-gun—so that if the destroyer has to dispatch landing-parties ashore, the "below-the-waterline" ratings take part with their shipmates of the deck.

The chief of the Black Squad is the warrant engineer, one of the marvels of the Navy of to-day, as highly-qualified a mechanic as can be found in this mechanical age. Starting in all probability as a stoker, he has graduated up through the various degrees : leading-stoker, stoker petty officer, and mechanician, to his present commissioned warrant rank. Ranking as an officer, he enjoys wardroom privileges. Usually "The Chief" is one of the most warmly welcomed of all the wardroom mess.

On his own engine-room plates he is lord paramount of his steamy domain, conversant with all his engines' tricks and whimsicalities — as engines that are liable to be savagely overworked are wont to have. Destroyer-engines are unlike the more sober machinery of, say, a freighter—they must be ready at an instant's notice to jump from a crawl to lightning-like haste, and stop dead. The Chief has to assure himself that enough steam is always in hand—since you never really know when the emergency will arise to demand a furious burst of speed. A destroyer acting as escort to a convoy might receive a rapid command from a higher authority to proceed "all out" to an indicated destination, perhaps to salve the crew of a castaway lifeboat spotted from the air, or a shot-down airman. That means subjecting the machinery to a severe test ; and if it failed the fault would be laid at the Chief's door.

THE STOKER'S JOB in the Royal Navy has been "cleaned up" very considerably, as told in this page, but there is still dirty work to be done. This member of the Black Squad (left) is probing the tubes of a ship's furnace with a ribbon brush; soot is collected and emptied into special containers (right). *Photos, British Official*

are highly-trained specialists : trained the Navy way, which makes allowances for practically every contingency. When first recruited into the Service they may be men without the faintest idea of mechanics. The Navy spruces them with a bit of drill, fits them out in natty uniforms to give them self-respect, consigns them to the most arduous, dangerous job existing aboard a ship of war.

DANGEROUS indeed the work is. For in ninety-nine cases out of a hundred, when an enemy attacks or defends itself it concentrates its fire on the machinery of a hostile ship, in the hope of crippling its opponent's furious speed and leaving it a hulk on the surface, to be pounded to scrap at leisure. Similarly, U-boats send their torpedoes as near the destroyer's engine-room as they can aim them, thus hoping to arrest the power that hurls the lean hull towards their destruction. A stopped ship is more or less a useless ship, since gun-fire alone has small power against a submerged foe.

It is hot in the vibrating shell that is a destroyer's engine-room. Men work stripped to the waist, even though ice clings everywhere on deck. There is a constant deafening noise, for only by applying the blowers can the draught necessary to achieve speed be obtained, and blowers are noisy. The

hold are liable to turn into scalding infernos. A burst main steam-pipe is enough to scald the entire complement to death. Fast-moving machinery—there are dynamos and pumps constantly at work in addition to the turbines—when hit by shell-fragments is apt to throw off clusters of splinters which rage through the confined space like shrapnel. The plating of a small ship is almost paper-thin, and though chilled steel of the highest quality is used, such metal is not adequate protection against high velocity projectiles.

Then, too, the fact that in all probability the hatches are closely battened down, to prevent big water from penetrating below, is prone to create a sort of claustrophobia in the minds of men whose nerves are not of the steadiest. Nothing can be seen of whatever fight is in progress : the engine-room must simply obey orders and put its imagination to sleep until the emergency is past—one way or another !

Damage must be made good if mechanical ingenuity permits. For running repairs it would be difficult to find the superiors of a destroyer's engine-room staff. They can perform miracles. The electrician is responsible for all electric circuits, from those illuminating the gun-sights to the main supplies, and is required to provide alterna-

I⊤ is the Chief who makes steam and keeps the engines moving when the ship has received a savage wound. Imperturbable, amid scalding steam, wounded men and flying debris, knowing the destroyer is likely to go to the bottom with a sudden plunge, he keeps the wheels in motion ; and when the order to abandon ship is given, he stands by —last man below—to cut off the fires and blow down the steam, so that the boilers shall not burst and destroy men struggling in an oily sea amongst the wreckage.

Acts of stark heroism among the Black Squad are uncountable—coolness under fire and in dire emergency seems to be a commonplace. When a deck-man is blown up, he usually falls into the sea ; when a stokehold rating is blown up he is usually mangled in an almost hermetically sealed death-trap. Imagine the horror of seeing the walls of your steel prison suddenly cave in to the impact of a torpedo, followed by a Niagara-like inrush of water, and knowing that the engines must turn until the bridge gives the signal to go ! The courage of Casabianca was trifling as compared with that of the average member of the crew below the waterline.

The Bailey Bridge that Triumphs over Demolitions

Mr. D. C. BAILEY, O.B.E. (2), who has designed every bridge but one in current Army use.

OVER THE ENORMOUS GAP which German demolition squads had blown in this bridge in Italy, our men and heavy armour were soon speeding in pursuit of the enemy—across a Bailey Bridge, the nose of which is here seen (1) about to be launched.

FROM A ROUGH SKETCH on the back of an envelope was evolved a piece of equipment which has revolutionized bridge-building for our armies in the field, speeding their advance in North Africa, Sicily, Italy and Normandy. This Bailey Bridge—praised by General Montgomery as "Quite the best thing in that line we have ever had. It does everything we want. It will be needed everywhere we operate in Europe"—was invented by Mr. D. C. Bailey, of the Ministry of Supply.

Designed to cross gaps up to 240 ft. without the help of pontoons, in conjunction with these the span is lengthened considerably. In its lightest form the Bailey can carry 20 tons; construction can be doubled or trebled to take our heaviest tanks. Fitting together like a jig-saw puzzle, each section is ten ft. long and has seventeen parts. Nine other parts are used for the bridge foundation.

TRIPLE TIER specimen (3) In the first stage in bridging a gap the Bailey is built on rollers on the bank, each span as completed being pushed out and over. Only one steel pin is required for each join.

UNDER FIRE from enemy guns our Royal Engineers finished the approaches to this Bailey Bridge (4) which they had thrown across the Caen Canal in record time. The heaviest part can be handled with ease by six men. The American Army have adopted the idea, using it as standard equipment under the name of the Panel bridge, and components of British and American-made bridging can be interchanged. When the bridge went into mass-production in England all kinds of firms co-operated including makers of bedsteads, window-frames, paper, canoe-paddles, and a greenhouse manufacturer.

Photos, British Official ; Daily Express

2nd Army Infantry Stormed this Nazi Bastion

FIERCE BOMBARDMENTS by artillery, aircraft and naval vessels preceded the capture of Caen in Normandy on July 9, 1944. The Germans themselves did their utmost to ravage wantonly before they were driven out. Besides normal military demolition, they ruthlessly destroyed the contents of many historic buildings. Above is a view over the rooftops of Caen after the battle.

TREADING WARILY because of the possibility of stepping on undiscovered mines which the Germans sewed thickly in the streets, more British troops (left) enter Caen to consolidate the hold they had won.

MAIN STREET in the captured city (below), showing rows of buildings still standing after our terrific bombardments. It was estimated that, in spite of the danger to themselves, 30,000 inhabitants remained, awaiting their hour of deliverance.

Photos. British Official

Hunting Out the Lurking Hun in Shell-Torn Caen

HUB OF TWELVE MAJOR ROADS of great military value is the key-town of Caen, capital of the Calvados department of Normandy. Defended fiercely by the Germans since our first landings, it finally fell to British and Canadian units. In the course of the battle the town suffered extensive damage and the retreating enemy left its streets heavily mined; here a British patrol is searching a debris-strewn thoroughfare for lurking snipers. In the background is the tower of the 14th-century cathedral of St. Pierre.

Photo, Associated Press

New Zealand's Premier Sees His Troops in Italy

THE Right Hon. Peter Fraser, Prime Minister of New Zealand, it was announced on May 20, 1944, travelled to Italy specially to meet and congratulate the men of the renowned New Zealand Division which had served in Libya, Egypt, Greece and Tunisia, as well as distinguishing itself in Italy. Mingling with his troops, who greeted him with cries of, "It's Peter Fraser—good-day, Pete!" the Prime Minister thanked and shook hands with hundreds of them.

In an extensive tour he saw for himself the impressive quality under field conditions of this famous Division from his home country. Later, on June 10, he visited Rome, first member of any United Nations Government to enter the freed city, and had audience with the Pope, who sent his blessing to the people of New Zealand. Returning home, he paid high tribute to the people of Southern England for the way they were standing up to the flying bomb ordeal.

GATHERING THEM IN GROUPS ABOUT HIM, Mr. Fraser thanked the men wherever he went (1), and during his tour saw some of New Zealand's fierce-fighting Maoris (2). The Premier sat on the beds in Army hospitals chatting to the patients (3). In an armoured car with Major-General Sir Bernard Freyberg, V.C., K.C.B., D.S.O., G.O.C. of the New Zealand Division (4, left), Mr. Fraser (right) went to the fighting line; he also visited the ruins of Cassino Monastery (5). The Dominion's armed forces have already won 7 V.C.s in this war. *Photos by courtesy of the New Zealand Government*

Town After Town Falls on the Road to Florence

SIENA—IMPORTANT BASTION in German defences before Florence, and a medieval Italian town of great historical interest—fell to French troops of the 5th Army on the morning of July 3, 1944. French native troops, leading a mule train, wind along a road just before the final assault (1). Leverage for the Allied successes at this stage was effected by the 8th Army who, it was announced on June 19, occupied Assisi, 60 miles south-east of Siena. In that town a British soldier passes under an arch, behind which is the church dedicated to St. Francis of Assisi in 1253 (2). Another 8th Army step was the capture of Castiglione in the same area, on June 26, where our infantry are here seen (3) mopping-up on a street stairway. Ancona, on the Adriatic coast, fell to Polish units on July 18.

Photos, British Official

Bulldozing to Victory on All Fighting Fronts

The driver of this astonishing mechanical navvy, which carries no armament, is open to be shot whilst he gets on with his task of levelling an airstrip, cutting a road, smashing a track through a forest, filling bomb and shell craters, pulling a store-laden sledge, hauling equipment up a cliff or assaulting enemy pillboxes. ROBERT DE WITT here tells something of the story of the diesel engined 400 h.p., 22-ton bulldozer and its smaller versions.

THE ingenious foreman of a road gang got the idea, a few years ago, that the powerful tractor he was working would be more useful if it had fixed in front of it a flat metal shield which would enable its full power to be applied to pushing loose earth to one side. He asked his firm's blacksmith to fix it for a trial, and thus the bulldozer was born.

Today there are thousands of bulldozers on every Allied front. The machine has shown that although it carries neither armour nor guns it is a weapon as indispensable to a modern army as tanks and artillery. At the beginning of this war it was considered a "behind the lines" vehicle, a machine for preparing fortifications quickly and for

part in the landings on Attu in the Aleutians can be quoted. The work of these bulldozers was to push a road across a valley to get urgent supplies to the troops. The bulldozers were on top of an almost precipitous mountain. They were wanted in the valley below, immediately. Engineers decided there was only one way to get them down in time —topple them over and let them roll. Six of them were sent driverless over the edge. They turned over and over all the way down. Not one was put out of action! Those that landed right way up were driven off at once. Those that landed upside down were righted and, although somewhat battered in appearance, were perfectly fit for the task they had to do.

In one of the Pacific landings some Japanese snipers were giving a lot of trouble from their concealment in foxholes. The driver of a bulldozer saw his chance. With covering fire to keep the Japanese down he approached, the roar of his engine unnoticed in the noise of battle. At just the right moment the metal shield dropped down, pushed out the right amount of earth and killed and buried the snipers in one motion.

PERHAPS the most fantastic assault on a pillbox ever made was carried out by Royal Engineers using a bulldozer on the Normandy beaches. A deeply dug-in pillbox manned by resolute Germans was holding up our troops, its machine-guns sweeping the beach. The bulldozer was taken round to the "blind spot" of the pillbox. Then it picked up earth and began to angle it into the loopholes. One after another the loopholes were completely blocked by feet of earth. That pillbox was finished, and the bulldozer returned to more prosaic but not less useful work in clearing the beaches for vehicles and stores to come ashore.

There are few parts of the world now in which bulldozers are not working for the Allies, and it would be difficult to overestimate the value of the enormous manufacturing capacity for these machines which exists in the United States. It was bulldozers, pulling out trees by their roots, pushing earth and rock into embankments and out of cuttings, that enabled the Alaskan Highway to be built in record time. The original Burma Road was built by some ten million labourers working with baskets and the most primitive tools. The new road-link with China will be built faster with the aid of bulldozers that stand up to the Tropics as well as they do to the Arctic.

CLEARING TONS OF RUBBLE from the streets of war-blasted Valognes, in France, a bulldozer works with speed and power undreamed of in the old pick-and-shovel days. Immediately an enemy position is taken, bulldozers commence to clear roads through the debris of artillery and aircraft bombardment to facilitate our swift advance. Other mighty tasks they perform are described in this page. *Photo, U.S. Official*

clearing up the rubble when the army had gone through.

Now it is a front-line weapon, not following the tanks and guns but in many cases clearing the way for them. In the fighting in Italy the bulldozers have again and again been right in the front, pushing aside rubble from houses dynamited by the retreating Germans to make roadblocks. For the landings in Normandy bulldozers were loaded so that they could get ashore first and clear a way up the beaches for tanks, trucks and men and supplies.

BULLDOZERS have developed considerably from the crude pushing affair devised by Roy Choate. They have become more and more powerful, and fitted with controls that enable the pushing shield to be lifted and its angle adjusted according to the task in hand. The biggest bulldozers now have diesel engines developing more than 400 horsepower. They are very strongly made, able to take a tremendous amount of punishment from rough work without being any the worse for it. The largest weigh over 22 tons and are able to push around several tons of earth or rubble, doing the work of a hundred or more men quickly and neatly.

To show the punishment these vehicles will stand the case of half-a-dozen that took

The tremendous power of bulldozers explains to a considerable degree the speed with which recent landings in the Pacific have been consolidated and exploited. Their work is not limited to levelling-out airstrips, filling bomb and shell craters, cutting roads. They are used as powerful tractors, capable of pulling enormous quantities of stores on special or improvised skids. They can bulldoze landing ramps and push out earth and rock at a bridge-head to give a firm foundation. They can pull equipment up cliffs by means of cables and winches. They have even been used for tearing up roads covered with anti-personnel mines, simply churning up the earth and pushing it aside. They are amongst the most adaptable machines ever invented, and in the hands of a skilled driver there seems to be nothing that man or horses could do that a bulldozer cannot do in one-hundredth the time.

As it carries no armament you would not think of the bulldozer as a weapon of offence. Generally the drivers have to sit in rather an exposed position and just be shot at while they get on with the job. Scores have been killed and injured while working their bulldozers within view of the enemy. It is no surprising that when they get their chance they like to get their own back.

Correspondents report that the sensational advance of the Russians in Finland was largely due to the bulldozers which, accompanied by tommygunners, laid broad tracks through forests along which more men and machines could be brought up at unexpected speed. The Germans have no machines, either in quality or number, to compare with those going into action for the Allies. These machines are part of the explanation of the speed with which German demolitions and roadblocks have been negatived in Italy and France. The powerful throb of bulldozers at work was heard immediately Cherbourg surrendered.

IN Britain we see these machines levelling aerodromes and making new railway sidings at almost incredible speed. Some have put in "overtime" clearing sites for post-war building estates. The machines are familiarly known as "dozers" or "cats." The latter name comes from the caterpillar tracks which are an essential feature. The "bulldozer" is rather less obvious. The business of catching and throwing cattle for branding on ranches in America has long been called "bulldozing." It is hard, sweating work, and apparently the similarity between it and pushing tons of earth around struck the first users of these mechanical navvies. They christened their machines "bulldozers" and the name has stuck.

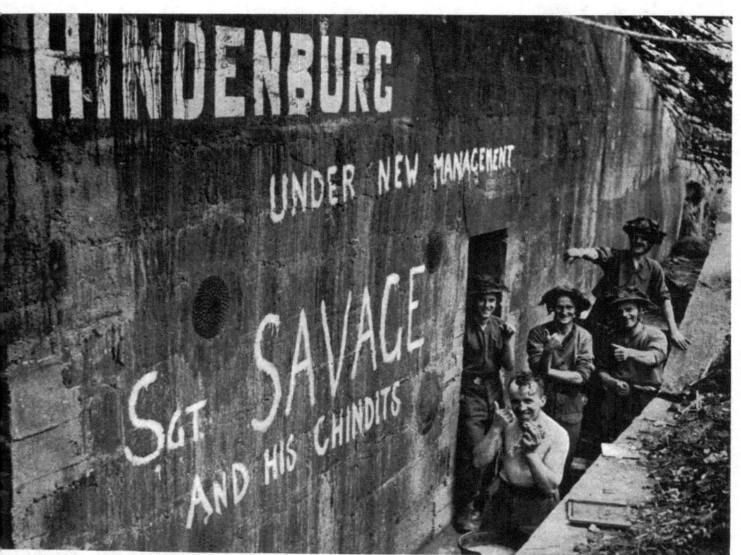

HINDENBURG
UNDER NEW MANAGEMENT
Sgt. SAVAGE
AND HIS CHINDITS

Conquests of Second Army in Normandy

Organized by Field-Marshal von Rundstedt, German "West Wall" defences were burst asunder in the first rush of the Allies against the Normandy beaches. Formidable strongpoint was the Hindenburg Bastion, enormous concrete emplacement with elaborate system of trench communications. But this was put under new management, as emphasized by chalked comments of the British Bofors gun crew who made themselves at home therein (above). Within days of the landings, 1,313 square miles of France had been liberated. Specially fierce was the fighting in the Tilly neighbourhood when, on June 26, possession of villages was contested house-by-house: a British patrol pause for observation in St. Mauvieu (right).

Photos, British Official

British Infantry and Armour Pressed on to Caen

Churchill tanks co-operated magnificently with British and Canadian infantry of the 2nd Army in the great break-through towards Caen—hinge of Rommel's right flank (until captured on July 9) and strategic gateway to Paris: waist-deep in undergrowth troops follow in the wake of a Churchill crashing through a hedge (1). Our armour passes a knocked-out enemy Tiger tank near Rauray (2). Churchills leading, infantry advance to the attack through a cornfield (3).

Ph

In the Wake of Battle Refugees Return Home

British guns in action (4) during the heavy artillery preparation for our attack in the Tilly-Caen area. The tide of battle has barely receded when refugees return to their homes—or what is left of these. Troops in occupation add to their sympathy ready aid: a cartload of family possessions is helped along the churned-up road of Cheux village (5), between Tilly and Caen, shortly after the British-Canadian fighting line had passed beyond on June 27.

8th Army Leaves Rome Far Behind

Within 24 hours of the Allied entry into Rome, columns of the 6th South African Armoured Division swept through the city to become the spearhead of the advance towards Florence : their Recce carriers passed through the gateway of Orvieto (2), 70 miles beyond Rome, on June 14. British 25-pounders hastened in pursuit of the enemy through Allerona (4), 90 miles north of Rome, captured on June 19. A day later, 8th Army troops entered Perugia (1), 100 miles to the north; the 16/5th Lancers led the column, and attacking infantry included men of the Rifle Brigade. Churchill tanks (3) were used for the first time in Italy on May 17 : so excellent was their work in support of the Canadian Corps when the latter broke through the Adolf Hitler line that the Canadians, as a privilege, requested the brigade concerned to " bear the Maple Leaf on their tanks."

Photos, British Official

VIEWS & REVIEWS
Of Vital War Books

by Hamilton Fyfe

I BELIEVE that most people, when they hear on the wireless about what "the Chindits" are doing in Burma, imagine them to be native levies. The sound of the name seems inevitably to suggest that. The late General Wingate, who coined it for the force of irregulars he trained and led, took it from the mythological beast, half-lion, half-griffin, of which images stand outside Burmese pagodas to keep off devils. This is called "Chinthey." He meant it to symbolize the co-operation between ground and air forces. How effective that co-operation is, how the force is able to do without lines of communication, which would be next door to impossible in jungle country, and how skilful the R.A.F. pilots are in landing supplies of every kind on very small target grounds, I understand far better now than I did before I read Mr. Charles J. Rolo's book, Wingate's Raiders (Harrap, 8s. 6d.). It gives a fascinating, fully detailed account, based on the stories of Major J. B. Jefferies and Squadron-Leader R. Thompson, who took part in them, of the "raids" which caused the Japanese so much trouble and so much anxious uncertainty last year, and which have now developed into a regular and most valuable feature of our military operations in the Far East.

Wingate's methods were the same in Burma as they had been in Abyssinia, where he organized the force which went with the Negus when he re-entered the country. He attacked only when and where it suited him. In pitched battles that might go on for a long time his Chindits would have been overwhelmed by numbers, would have had no chance of success. So what he did was to "bedevil the Japs with murderous nocturnal forays and lightning daytime raids." His men surprised the enemy over and over again; struck hard and, before they had recovered from the shock, were off again, nowhere to be found. "Times of darkness, mist and storm" were what he wanted.

His men trusted him absolutely. He never set them impossible tasks. He made them do things that were intensely difficult, but his imagination showed him that they were things which could be done. He insisted on the necessity for imagination in a military leader. "Every military operation," Wingate held, "must be seen as a whole, as a problem in time and space, pictorially. There must be scrupulously accurate realism in its details. Most commanders' minds present them with a series of pictures showing their troops moving victoriously from point to point. These pictures are completely bogus." How many of the catastrophic retreats in which I participated between 1914 and 1918 could have been avoided if British and French, Russian and Rumanian generals had possessed this gift of "an anxious, meticulously accurate and ever active imagination."

BUT Wingate thought, too, there is always an element of luck in a leader's success or failure, and that an unlucky general must be sacked, "however good a general he may be." On that principle Mr. Churchill has acted more than once. It is perfectly sound, hard though it may be on individual commanders. Troops will not fight their best for men they do not believe in. Every one of the Chindits put every ounce of himself

into whatever he was told to do because he felt certain that Wingate knew it was the right thing, the only thing to be done in the circumstances.

The hardships they went through were colossal. Often they were very short of food. They had to swim rivers or cross them in dug-outs with enemy bullets flicking all about them. They sometimes struggled through tall, tough, prickly elephant grass at the rate of a hundred yards an hour. Diseases weakened and killed them, though they were kept fairly free of malaria by

Wingate of the Chindits

sweating hard—one of Wingate's hunches; "he made us sweat all right!" they said. Ticks and lice, and red ants up to three-quarters of an inch long and "with a needle-sharp bite" made sleep uneasy, if not impossible. A king cobra might suddenly rear up from the ground to one-third of his fifteen-foot length, swaying from side to side, poised to strike. Scorpions hiding under stones which men moved to clear sleeping-places inflicted nasty bites. They always had to be on the alert for herds of wild elephants.

WHEN they got out after their expedition had taken them within a hundred miles of the Burma Road, which was so badly needed

The late Maj.-Gen. ORDE CHARLES WINGATE, D.S.O., creator and leader of the Chindits, is here seen (facing camera) with some of his Chindits at an outpost on the Assam-Burma frontier. Exploits of this almost legendary figure are described in the book reviewed in this page. (See also pp. 46-49, Vol. 7.)
Photo, Keystone

as a highway for supplies to China, and after exploits more exciting and more perilous than any that were ever invented by boys' story-book writers, they were a pitiable sight. They had set out strong, hearty, well-muscled. Now muscles had become stringy tendons, arms and legs were emaciated, stomachs caved inwards, ribs stuck out. Some were partly deaf, others scarcely able to speak—effects of starvation. They had eaten roots, which tasted good but had no staying power. They had cut up and grilled snakes of the python variety, which "tasted rather like fish." They were "bare-footed, bearded, wearing foul-smelling rags," when five of them staggered into a group of spruce-looking British officers having tea. They had got out, an operation far more difficult than getting in; and they had done it only just in time.

WHAT had they accomplished? Most important of all, they had staved off the invasion of India. They had shown that in jungle fighting we could do better than the Japanese. That had given the enemy something to think about; it had also helped to bring many Burmese round to a belief in Allied victory, which made them more ready to assist us. On the whole, the Burmese were friendly. I know there are those who feel that if when their Premier, now the chief Japanese quisling, came to London in 1940, to ask that his people might have self-government—if we had then met him in a more accommodating spirit, and if at the same time we had decided to take no chances with the French in Indo-China, the Japanese might never have entered Burma at all—and we might not have lost Singapore. On the other hand, that quisling U. Saw is known to have left a very bad impression on all who had contact with him during his London visit, and these may be no more than the "ifs" of History which make it so interesting a study.

With a man like Wingate, however, directing our strategy, such possibilities cannot be ruled out. That is why his accidental death was such a heavy loss to us. He was everything the usual kind of British officer in the past has not been. He had very wide interests. He would talk on almost any subject. He was, like a good many men who have excelled in war, firmly religious, though not sectarian. He quoted the Bible a lot, because he had been brought up on it, and because it, like Shakespeare, contains something suitable for every occasion. But he thought there was good in all forms of faith in the unseen—and would, no doubt, have admitted something bad as well. He was very strong physically, tough in constitution as well as muscular and hard. He had no respect for big-wigs of any kind. He had endless rows, of course, but he could throw off their effect with a grin and a cheery "I'm not really as crazy as people think." He did not smoke, because once he gave it up for a year in order to save money for a trip to the Libyan Desert and found himself fitter without cigarettes; but he liked good food and good wine, though he believed one could not really enjoy them unless they had been earned by periods of hardship.

He made an immediate impression on Mr. Churchill and on Field-Marshal Wavell, whereas the reaction of Haig to him would have been "Impossible bounder!" and that of Mr. Neville Chamberlain "Very odd uncomfortable man!" Not a great leader, for the reason that he did not have the opportunity to cope with a great task; but one who would pretty certainly have shown greatness given the chance.

How Our Dogs Detect Land-Mines in France

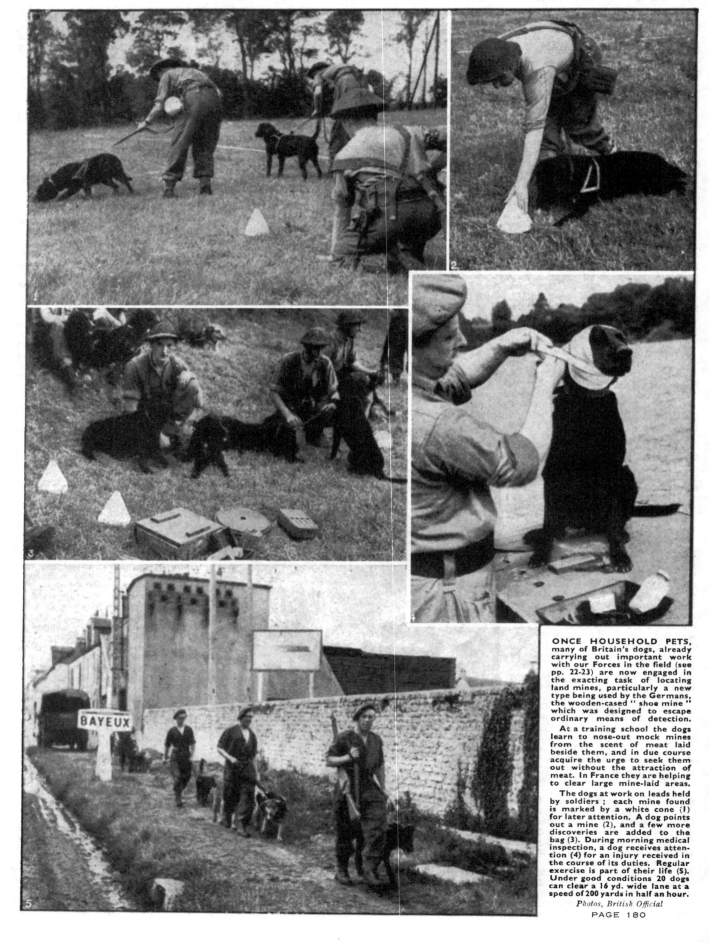

ONCE HOUSEHOLD PETS, many of Britain's dogs, already carrying out important work with our Forces in the field (see pp. 22-23) are now engaged in the exacting task of locating land mines, particularly a new type being used by the Germans, the wooden-cased "shoe mine" which was designed to escape ordinary means of detection.

At a training school the dogs learn to nose-out mock mines from the scent of meat laid beside them, and in due course acquire the urge to seek them out without the attraction of meat. In France they are helping to clear large mine-laid areas.

The dogs at work on leads held by soldiers ; each mine found is marked by a white cone (1) for later attention. A dog points out a mine (2), and a few more discoveries are added to the bag (3). During morning medical inspection, a dog receives attention (4) for an injury received in the course of its duties. Regular exercise is part of their life (5). Under good conditions 20 dogs can clear a 16 yd. wide lane at a speed of 200 yards in half an hour.

Photos, British Official

Here Our Armour Outfought Rommel's Panzers

AFTER THE GRIM TANK CLASHES which preceded the capture of Caen on July 9, 1944, British tanks are here seen halted in a street, while an anti-tank gun unit sets up at a corner. Engaged in the Normandy fighting was a new British type, the Cromwell tank, which has a 75-mm. gun and a special high-capacity engine ; further hitting power was given to Allied armour by American-built Sherman tanks recently fitted with the famous British long-barreled 17-pounder gun.

Photo, British Official

Anti-Aircraft Command's Detectives at Work

Behind the announcement that our A.A. guns have shot down enemy planes or flying bombs
lies a story of keen detective work by Intelligence Officers who investigate success claims sent
in by batteries and apportion credit between friendly rivals. The following account of this by
no means easy task was given to "The War Illustrated" by A.A. Command Headquarters.

GUNS can shoot at planes seven miles away. If they score a hit the plane may limp on, or glide into the next county. Or, as often happens, it may come down in the sea. How are the gunners and A.T.S. to know whether they have scored a "Cat One" (plane definitely destroyed), a "Cat Two" (plane damaged so seriously that it probably failed to return to base), or a "Cat Three" (plane damaged)? How are they to know that the wreckage which a farmer finds in his field is the plane they engaged, or one shot down by guns 20 miles away? Or perhaps one shot down by a night fighter?

The Intelligence Officer must find out. He must link up shooting with wreckage. If all planes fell close to the gun sites which fired at them it would be easy. If targets could be followed by camera from the first order of "Fire," the evidence would be conclusive. But there are a hundred and one snags.

The first place the I.O. makes for is, naturally, the site claiming a kill. He takes statements from eye-witnesses. For a Cat One where the raider or its wreckage cannot be found, he must find two independent witnesses who will say they definitely saw the plane falling in flames. Then he may call on police, Royal Observer Corps posts, A.R.P. wardens, fire watchers, coastguards, naval officers, and any others who may possibly have seen the engagement.

Interrogation of witnesses must never be left to inexperienced questioners, or the claim may become confused, or left till it is too late to get the missing pieces needed to complete the evidence picture. If he does not trace the witnesses quickly they may have gone home to bed, or they may be shift workers who cannot be found for hours. Here are some typical instances of an I.O.'s search for the story to back up the guns' claims.

Six Focke Wulf 190s swept in over a certain S.E. coast town, and thanks to our guns and fighters only one went back to France, damaged. Light gunners saw their shells blow the tail off one over Deal, and down it went into the sea. Everybody, including coastguards and police, saw it, and there was no mistaking a certain kill.

The gunners claimed another, but the A.A. Intelligence Officer couldn't immediately find anyone who would state they saw it hit by shells and come down. An hotel keeper said he saw both planes hit, and men on searchlight sites said they were certain the guns got it. The I.O. went from one witness to another. His search took him to a range where firing was in progress, and rather than delay his search for evidence he risked a dash across the fields during salvos, and collected statements from gunners. Eventually he obtained the full report. It was a week before two swastikas went up on the guns' scoreboard, with three to the R.A.F.

At Hastings, one Sunday, twenty raiders came over during lunch-time. A policeman on point duty vouched for one being hit by A.A. shells, and his statement brought a Cat One when added to others. It took twenty-four hours to track down another claim, based on one plane being seen to break away from its formation and lose height going out to sea. The I.O. questioned passers-by every 200 yards along the streets. Eventually a Cat Three was awarded.

An I.O. watching an action over Dover saw a red glow in the clouds, then a splash in the harbour. Everyone said it was an oil bomb. Next morning the I.O. went down to the quay and said to the skipper of a mine-sweeper: "Will you look out for plane wreckage and let me know if you see anything?" At four in the afternoon the boat returned with a flying suit, a pilot's log in German, and nine oxygen bottles. It was enough. Another Cat One for the guns.

Who shot the plane down is sometimes a tricky question. Several sites may fire during the same few seconds, and shell-bursts are seen enveloping the target. Whose shells did the trick? Every battery is keen to chalk up one more Nazi on its scoreboard, and there is keen rivalry. Sometimes it is possible to decide this on action reports by sites. They all keep a log of the exact time their shells leave their gun barrels, and the instrument operators can say exactly in which direction, and when, the target starts

GENERAL SIR FREDERICK A. PILE, K.C.B., D.S.O., M.C., G.O.C.-in-C. Anti-Aircraft Command since 1939. Aged 59, he entered the Royal Artillery in 1904 and served in the 1914-18 war. From 1937 to 1939 he commanded the 1st A.A. Division of the Territorial Army. *Photo, Topical Press*

to lose height. But the enemy pilot may lose height purposely to fox the gunners, to make them think he has been hit, so they will leave him alone. As he loses height a badly placed round luckily gets him. So many things are possible!

IT is not enough for a captured Luftwaffe pilot merely to state that his plane was brought down by A.A. fire. This information would seem to the layman to be all that was necessary to give an award to the guns making success claims at the time, but some German flyers are so proud of their skill in the air that they won't admit having been shot down by an R.A.F. night-fighter. Their attitude is that a hit by A.A. fire is just a matter of bad luck, to be dismissed as such. This verbal evidence from prisoners is never accepted by the I.O. He seeks out the wreckage and makes up his report only from what he sees and can find out from the shell splinter holes or bullet strikes.

In a raid early this year the official score sheets of enemy bombers destroyed over Britain showed that Anti-Aircraft Command and the R.A.F. were each credited with half of one particular raider. The pilot baled out, not far from London, from a bomber which had been engaged with 40 rounds of A.A. fire at 11,000 feet. When captured, he claimed that he had been shot down by flak, and showed a splinter wound in his heel to prove it. But when his aircraft was examined, the strikes of a Mosquito's cannon shells were also found. So there was nothing for it but to share the kill—half a bomber each way.

Frequently the factors to be taken into account in assessing A.A. claims after a raid are so involved that definite awards to gunners on the ground cannot be granted to an individual gun site. On February 20, for example, during a two-phase raid on London, a Ju. 88 crashed in a suburban area. A very large number of heavy A.A. sites and Home Guard rocket batteries had been engaging the raiders and there were no R.A.F. claims. The award was granted to the London A.A. defences as a whole.

A SINGLE Ju. 88 over the south coast in the middle of April this year caused a lot of work when the I.O.s investigated its crash. The raider dropped no bombs and committed no "hostile act" at all, but in the early morning light it circled around in the mist on a sortie which no one could define. It was the only daytime raider that day. It was destroyed, but not until six days later was the award finally granted. The following A.A. troops were then credited with half a "Category One": An all-male heavy A.A. battery, a mixed heavy A.A. battery, a light A.A. battery (Bofors guns), a searchlight battery (machine-guns). The other share went to R.A.F. fighters.

This matter of delay in settling claims wheri verification is difficult had an amusing sequel shortly after the first American A.A. batteries were deployed in Britain's air defence system. They had been fighting extremely well on several nights without securing a longed-for "Category One" success. However, on April 19, just after midnight, when three enemy planes were accounted for by A.A. fire, a U.S. battery at Dover claimed to have hit one of the raiders. Together with the British regulars at Dover they were awarded a half share in a "Category One," thus making history in American records as the first official successful engagement with a German plane over Britain.

The difficulty came when, two days later, a claim from a U.S. battery in London was verified, resulting also in a share, for another plane shot down on the same night. There was nineteen minutes difference in the two engagements—and the Americans in London had actually scored before the Yanks at Dover, but the former took more investigating than the latter. Strangely enough, a third U.S. battery, at Folkestone, got a Cat Three that same night.

Up to the time of writing, since the beginning of the war Anti-Aircraft Command has accounted for 831 enemy planes shot down, 236 probably destroyed, and 420 damaged. Of these 70 have been definitely destroyed by the guns alone since January 1, 1944. Proof of all these successes has been established by A.A. Command's Intelligence Officers. But to assess the value of anti-aircraft guns in a defended area only in terms of planes shot down or damaged is an underestimation of their power, for it is also part of the role of anti-aircraft defences to prevent bombers from being able, accurately, to approach their targets in bombing runs. Many a German raider has been forced to turn back without ever reaching even the fringe of the capital. Anti-Aircraft Command's success in this role of defence could never be gauged by its Intelligence Officers; only the Germans would know! But the Germans are left guessing as to how many of their flying bombs are shot down over Southern England by the gunners of A.A. Command!

Our Plan of Campaign against the Flying Bomb

HITTING BACK at the flying bomb, with which, on June 15, 1944, the Germans began to attack London and Southern England generally, Air Defence of Great Britain lost no time in coping with the menace. As early as August 17-18, 1943, the important German research and experimental station at Peenemunde, on the Baltic, had been attacked. R.A.F. fighters soon perfected their attack technique which destroyed flying bombs, while A.A. fire added its quota, and new methods of deploying barrage balloons were adopted. After a flying bomb patrol, an Intelligence Officer (right) takes notes (1). A.A. men drag in a " kill " (2). Evacuation of London's children began again on July 3, 1944 (3). Air Marshal Sir Roderic Hill, A.O.C. Air Defence of Great Britain (4), who himself took part in the fighters' operations against the flying bomb. London's first new deep shelter opened on July 9, 1944 (5).

Photos, British Official: Crown Copyright; G.P.U., Keystone, Planet News

China Enters 8th Year of Her Fight for Freedom

JAPAN STRUCK at unprepared China on July 7, 1937—and for seven long years, regardless of all sacrifices, China has fought valiantly against a better equipped foe.

Training in the use of firearms is given to Chinese recruits by U.S. instructors (1). Part of the Ledo Road (2), which Allied engineers have driven from Assam across the Patkai Range into the Hukong Valley in Burma, eventually to link up with the old supply route to China, the famous Burma Road. Early in 1944 Madame Chiang Kai-shek (3—centre), wife of the Generalissimo, opened a War Orphans Home near Chungking. Chinese troops, seeking out the enemy, ford the Tanai River in Burma (4).

I WAS THERE! Eye Witness Stories of the War

Over Caen I Saw the Flag of Freedom Raised

British troops fresh from battle formed a guard of honour in the square outside the grammar school of Caen, in Normandy (captured by the 2nd Army on July 9, 1944), and presented arms as the flag of De Gaulle was hoisted. The historic event was witnessed by George McCarthy of the Daily Mirror.

I THINK that hastily improvised ceremony was the most impressive I have ever seen. Outside there were gathered a crowd of French civilians—soldiers of the resistance. The guard of honour was provided by half a company of British troops; not tall Guardsmen chosen for the pomp of ceremonial, but tough little fighting men with the dirt of battle still on their boots and their battle dress. The resistance leader blew a whistle. We all fell silent. He gave an order and his little troop came to attention. A British command rang out. The troops presented arms.

The tricolour emblazoned with the cross of Lorraine was hoisted. It stuck half-way. And perhaps that was a symbol, too, for 3,000 French civilians have died in this battle to set a people free. The resistance leader spoke again. He beat time and we all sang the Marseillaise. There was no music and we were a little flat and off the tune, but never can even Frenchmen have sung it with more relief or more tired joy.

The song ended and the Frenchmen broke into shouts of "Vive De Gaulle," and "Vive les Alliés." Just down the street the battle was raging. During the singing and the cheering the guns near by were roaring. The Germans across the river were firing anti-personnel shells, which burst overhead.

A formation of Messerschmitts, the largest I have ever seen in France, roared through the low clouds, pursued by our bursting flak. But the French just went on cheering for De Gaulle and the Allies. Then they broke up into groups and came forward to greet the British. "This is a great day, monsieur!" they exclaimed, as they shook our hands.

The Underground Battle Was Won

I went inside the grammar school. It was crowded with people who had found shelter there from the bombs and the guns. Mothers and children clasping each other as they perched on stacked bags of flour and other food, nuns tending a great room full of wounded, pails of soup passing through, nurses carrying in water and bandages; that was the grammar school of Caen. Men came round to tell me of this chief of resistance who had led the singing in the square. "He is a great man," his lieutenant told me. "He has organized all the fighting and all the underground. When this battle began the Gestapo were on his tail. He eluded them. Two days ago he was surrounded in a house. He crawled through a garden, climbed a wall and escaped."

The chief came in. He is probably thirty-six, but looked older today. He told me how he and his little army carried on the fight. "It was dangerous, deadly work and our forces were very small. But the battle was won."

A young Frenchman came forward. He said three weeks ago a party of five Rover Scouts cycled in here from Paris. They had heard that the English had landed in Normandy, and hastened here to be in the fight. For three weeks they had played a big role in the underground movement. Then, when the battle began, they had taken arms and joined the fighting men. Last night they left again. They explained that their mission was to fight Germans. Their place was always in the rear of the enemy.

There is great damage in the town. Fires are still smouldering. Men and women are picking what they can from the debris that had been their homes, just as the people of London have gathered up the remnants of their possessions after a heavy raid. It is not a pleasant sight, a big town after a battle. It is a procession of death and destruction and burning. There is a trail of broken tramway wires and telephone lines. Unburied dead litter the gutters. There are dead dogs and heaps of discarded equipment.

And amid the ruin and desolation the people are cheering us and the children are running up to clasp our hands. Before the landing there were 60,000 people in this town. The Germans ordered an evacuation, and 20,000 left. Many more old people got out when fighting approached, but others refused to leave. They knew that if they stayed they would be free. So they stayed and saw the battle through—not too high a price, they think, to pay for liberation.

One father and mother came up to speak to me. She was in tears, and he held a photograph in his hand. It was a picture of their son. He is Paul Collette, a French sailor aged 21, who went out to shoot the traitor Laval in the streets of Versailles. He wounded him and was caught. The Germans took him away. His fate is still unknown.

As I drove out, skirting the shell-holes in the main road and evading the debris, the German guns opened up again. Shells were falling near the road, and they were bursting behind me as we drove past the shell-torn village of Carpiquet and the hangars where the Germans had fought so hard.

SIGN OF RELEASE from the tyrant's yoke is the Free French flag of Lorraine here being hoisted with simple ceremony in the Place du Lycée beside the abbey church of St. Etienne in Caen. The part played by men of the French resistance movement in the liberation of this Norman city is related in this page. See also pp. 164, 170-171. *Photo, British Newspaper Pool*

Tornado-like a Flying Bomb Roared Down at Me

Readers who have not been exposed to the peril of flying bombs will specially appreciate this vivid little pen-picture of the coming of the bomb, the impact and explosion and the dread aftermath, as experienced by W. A. E. Jones. His story is given here by arrangement with the Daily Herald.

SPLINTERED bark whipped clean from the beech trees by the blast sears past my head. A cold, swishing wind like a miniature tornado carries my hat away. The ground quakes. Great spouts of mud spatter down. Through the choking, oily smoke, I can see the tall trees bowing, cracking, falling. Then the leaves fall. They fall languidly.

My car is buried under a mantle of green until it looks like a curved mound of camouflage. A woman lies near me. She is dead. One of her shoes has been ripped from her foot. Her stocking is torn open. Her little brown dog is there too. His country walk ended in death for him. Now the leaves are mercifully covering him. An old man—his tweeds are plastered with soil—peers from a bush, says shakily, "Where did it go?" So I point to a tangle of green metal that has dug itself into the grass a few yards from us. It is all that is left of the flying bomb that roared down on us a minute ago.

I had a ringside seat for this robot. I had a close-up of Hitler's indiscriminate warfare on Southern England—and I am able to

CATCHING UP WITH A FLYING BOMB, an R.A.F. fighter (1, left) closes in to destroy this indiscriminate German weapon directed against our civilian life. A reconnaissance plane, getting on the tail of another flying bomb, took this remarkable photograph (2). Plume of black smoke rising above the trees (3) marks the end of yet another, this time shot down by our gunners. (See also illus. p. 183.)
Photos, G.P.U., U.S. Official

write about it because a tree saved my life. It took the blast. There's no symmetry about that tree now. It has been stripped of its branches. It looks now like a decrepit, bare old skeleton creaking dolefully as it droops over the scene.

Down one side of the tree the bark has been sheered off. The sharpest knife couldn't have done a cleaner job. The robot bomb raced towards us in a downward glide. We dived for cover. We huddled in the grass, waiting. Then the explosion. When I could hear again I listened to a woman's voice crying shakily, "Look, look. I'm alive !" The woman was leaning from a wrecked window. Her home was a ruin. But she was still alive and she wanted us to know all about it. Then there were more voices. On all sides there were voices of people who had survived their nearest brush with death.

We began to realize at that moment that we had all escaped—save the old woman and her brown dog. A butcher's boy cycling by jumped from his machine. He tore his apron from him, offered it "for bandages for the wounded." Nurses from a hospital in their impeccable white uniforms dashed into the debris as it still creaked and heaved. They brought comfort with them. They brought soothing words with them and cool fingers to tend the injured. A barmaid—she was a big woman—loomed up. She had a tray of drinks with her. She was mighty popular.

Soon, very soon, this "incident" was under control. And all its untidiness was receding and life was going on again. "It doesn't take long to put things right, does it ?" said my chauffeur as he picked the splintered boughs from the running board. As we came home we drove down a street where another flying bomb had dropped an hour or two before.

You could hear a piano tinkling in a house that was patched up with tarpaulin and boarding.

It was the house of the local music master. He was there with a pupil. The lesson was going on. Away in another street a man was turning the handle of his barrel-organ. Two little girls hopped around him. "Say, Mister," they chanted, "has your monkey been bombed ?" They had been bombed. For all that was left of their home was being heaped on a handcart that would soon be on its way to another house ready for them at two hours' notice.

I Travelled the Red Army Road to Vitebsk

Enemy-occupied for three years, Vitebsk was retaken by Soviet forces on June 26. Capt. Eugene Krieger, Izvestia war correspondent, watched the Russian advance, and in this story (reprinted by arrangement with The Star) tells what he saw in this devastated Central Russia town.

I WAS driving along the roads of Belorussia to Vitebsk when I learned that Chausy, 70 miles to the south, had been taken. At once my memory went back to those grim days in the summer of 1941, when thousands of refugees were fleeing from burning Minsk. Children were crying for their mothers ; Soviet artillerymen were setting up heavy howitzers with which to counter by point-blank fire the avalanche of panzers which a year or so before had flattened out the fields and vineyards of France.

On a road running parallel to ours I saw a column of tanks dashing towards Chausy. German aircraft flew overhead. Our only chance of escape was to outstrip the panzers and slip across the river, which divided the town in two. We just managed it. That was on July 15, 1941.

Now, in June 1944 I have travelled that road again. Long before we got to Vitebsk we were caught in a flood of iron and steel. Soviet motors were roaring on the ground and in the air. Endless columns of vehicles were dashing ahead at a steady 40 to 50 kilometres an hour.

We were deafened by the roar which arose from every kind of fighting machine—from motor-cycles with their protruding machine-guns, weaving through the narrow gaps in the iron flood, to heavy tanks, armoured cars, troop carriers, tractors towing long-range guns, lorries loaded with pontoons, trucks piled with mines and shells, wireless cars and staff cars.

The metal of the Urals workers is flowing like scorching lava across Belorussia. In it German divisions are perishing, German steel is melting and hope is withering in Germans' hearts. The Red Army had forced the Western Dvina, skirted Vitebsk from the north and south, and, closing the ring far beyond the city, swept into one vast pocket the picked German troops and the makeshift battalions which had been rushed to the front from deep in the rear.

German prisoners were being questioned at our staff headquarters. They declared they had been ordered to hold the left bank of the Western Dvina at all costs until June 26, on which day they were promised " big reinforcements " for the relief of Vitebsk. But these " big reinforcements " found themselves caught in the same pocket, and on the morning of June 26 the Red Flag was waving over the city. On the southern side of the pocket the Germans attempted to break through across a bridge.

They were allowed to mass and then mown down by a sudden and devastating squall of artillery fire. It was a holocaust. Today the road is jammed with scorched and battered German trucks, and wagons loaded with ammunition and supplies. The actual assault of Vitebsk began at five a.m. The Germans had taken up positions on a line strengthened by an intricate system of trenches, wire entanglements and minefields.

This was pounded to pieces by the Soviet artillery, and within a few hours our troops had broken into the outskirts. The Germans launched four counter-attacks, but the Soviet artillerymen rushed their guns into the thick of the fight in the city's streets, and by evening our troops had reached the river, which divides the town in two.

All the bridges had been destroyed by the Germans, except one. This, too, was mined, and the Germans were preparing to blow it up, but Soviet sappers dashed forward and the Nazis were driven back.

We met a group of 150 captured Germans on that bridge. The officers marched in front. All had iron crosses on their breasts, and most of the soldiers wore decorations. The cathedral in the centre of Vitebsk had been blown up by the Germans, and Cathedral Square was pitted with shell-holes.

Everywhere we came across similar scenes of destruction. The Germans had dynamited the railway station, the post office, hospitals

and clubs, children's homes—in fact, every large building. Every house in Station Avenue, Vitebsk's favourite promenade, was wrecked. But the surviving inhabitants crept from their cellars and hiding-places, weary and wan, but weeping with joy at being free again.

Today the wrecked and mutilated city is still filled with smoke from the fires. Troops are still marching through the streets, heavy guns rumble over the cobble-stones. The last Germans are being ferreted out of cellars in the distant outskirts. But peace is again wrapping its soothing veil around the smoking ruins.

IN WRECKED BUT FREED VITEBSK life begins to assume some normality again, as a woman member of the Red Army, whose job is that of traffic regulator, takes her stand beside the signpost at a street crossing (left). Returning to their homes with their few possessions are these inhabitants of the city who had hidden from the enemy in the country outside (right). How the Red Army finally stormed Vitebsk is described in the story commencing in the page opposite.

Photos, Pictorial Press

OUR DIARY OF THE WAR

JULY 5, Wednesday *1,768th day*
Western Front.—Canadian troops held firm at Carpiquet against counter-attacks.
Air.—Allied bombers attacked airfields in Low Countries and flying-bomb sites in Pas de Calais.
Russian Front.—In White Russia, Soviet troops captured Smorgon, on Minsk-Vilna railway; in Karelia, Salmi, N. of Lake Ladoga, was occupied.
Mediterranean.—U.S. bombers on final lap of shuttle-mission attacked railway yards in S. France on way from Italy to Britain. Liberators bombed submarine pens at Toulon.
Pacific.—Allied bombers attacked Yap and Woleai in Carolines.

JULY 6, Thursday *1,769th day*
Air.—Allied aircraft attacked targets in N.W. Germany, airfields in France and military installations in Pas de Calais.
Russian Front.—Soviet troops occupied Kovel, S.E. of Brest Litovsk.
Home Front.—Mr. Churchill announced that, between June 15 and July 6, flying-bombs launched against London and S. England numbered 2,754, causing 2,752 fatal and about 8,000 other casualties.
General.—Germans announced that Field-Marshal von Rundstedt, supreme commander in West, was displaced by Von Kluge.

JULY 7, Friday *1,770th day*
Western Front.—Allied troops crossed river Vire and launched attack S.E. of Carentan; heavy air bombardment of Caen.
Air.—More than 1,000 U.S. bombers attacked oil plants and aircraft works near Leipzig; at night R.A.F. bombed flying-bomb depot in caves N.W. of Paris.
Mediterranean.—Italian-based bombers attacked oil plants at Odertal, Silesia.
Italy.—Allied troops captured Rosignani, 12 m. from Leghorn.
Japan.—U.S. Super-Fortresses again bombed Yawata steel works and Sasebu naval base on Kyushu Island.

JULY 8, Saturday *1,771st day*
Western Front.—British and Canadians launched three-pronged attack on Caen.
Air.—Railway communications from Loire to Channel and from Paris to Nantes attacked by Allied aircraft.
Russian Front.—Baranovichi, S.W.

of Minsk, captured by Russians; Soviet troops broke into Vilna.
Pacific.—Organized Japanese resistance ceased on Saipan Island. U.S. warships shelled Guam in Marianas.

JULY 9, Sunday *1,772nd day*
Western Front.—Main part of Caen captured by 2nd Army; Germans held suburb of Vaucelles across the Orne.
Russian Front.—Lida, railway junction E. of Grodno, captured by Red Army.
Italy.—Volterra, S.E. of Leghorn, captured by 5th Army troops.
Pacific.—U.S. carrier-borne aircraft attacked Guam and Rota, in Marianas.
Home Front.—First of new deep shelters opened in London.

JULY 10, Monday *1,773rd day*
Western Front.—2nd Army attacked from Odon bridge-head towards Orne.
Air.—Transport and communications in N. France attacked by Allied aircraft.
Russian Front.—Vilna encircled and by-passed; Dvinsk-Kaunas road cut.
Burma.—All organized Japanese resistance ended in Ukhrul.

JULY 11, Tuesday *1,774th day*
Western Front.—Gen. Montgomery announced total to date of 54,000 prisoners in Normandy.
Air.—About 1,000 U.S. bombers attacked Munich area.

JULY 12, Wednesday *1,775th day*
Air.—More than 1,000 U.S. bombers again attacked communications and other targets in Munich area; Lancasters bombed flying-bomb sites in France.
Russian Front.—Troops of 2nd Baltic Front opened new offensive, capturing Idritsa on Moscow-Riga railway.
Mediterranean.—Railway centres in S. France attacked by Allied heavy bombers.

JULY 13, Thursday *1,776th day*
Air.—Third consecutive attack on Munich area by U.S. bombers; night attacks by R.A.F. on railway centres in N. France.
Russian Front.—Vilna liberated by 3rd White Russian army after five days' fighting.
Mediterranean.—U.S. heavy bombers attacked railway yards on Milan-Venice line and oil storage tanks at Porto Marghera and Trieste.

JULY 14, Friday *1,777th day*
Air.—Lancasters attacked flying-bomb installations; rail and road communications in France also bombed.

Mediterranean.—Naval installations at Toulon attacked by U.S. heavy bombers.
General. — U.S. Govt. recognized French Committee of National Liberation as de facto authority for civil administration of France.

JULY 15, Saturday *1,778th day*
Western Front.—2nd Army launched night attack between Odon and Orne.
Air.—Night attack by R.A.F. on flying-bomb depot in caves at Nucourt.
Russian Front.—Red Army forced river Niemen, E. of East Prussia.
Mediterranean.—About 750 U.S. bombers attacked oil refineries at Ploesti.
Pacific.—U.S. carrier-borne aircraft made twelfth consecutive attack on Guam, Marianas.

JULY 16, Sunday *1,779th day*
Air.—Heavy force of U.S. bombers attacked Munich and Saarbruecken areas.
Russian Front.—Grodno, 45 miles from E. Prussian border, captured by Russians; new Red Army offensive launched E. of Lvov.
Italy.—Arezzo fell to troops of 8th Army.

JULY 17, Monday *1,780th day*
Air.—Railways and bridges on German supply routes in France heavily attacked by U.S. bombers; Lancasters attacked rocket-site in N. France with 12,000-lb. bombs.
Russian Front.—Soviet troops captured Sebezh, near Latvian border.
Italy.—8th Army troops advancing N. of Arezzo crossed river Arno.

JULY 18, Tuesday *1,781st day*
Western Front.—British and Canadians of 2nd Army broke through E. of the Orne and S.E. of Caen, preceded by very heavy air bombardment. St. Lo fell to U.S. troops.
Air.—Heavy force of U.S. bombers attacked German air research stations at Peenemunde and Zinnowitz on Baltic.
Russian Front.—Announced that in three days' fighting round Lvov more than 600 places, including Krasnoye and Brody, had been liberated by Russians.
Italy.—Ancona, Adriatic port, captured by 8th Army Polish troops.
Pacific.—U.S. warships shelled Guam from close range.

Russian Front.—Pinsk, E. of Brest Litovsk, and Volkovysk; E. of Bialystok, captured by Soviet troops.
Mediterranean.—Oil refineries and railway yards in Hungary attacked by Allied bombers.
Italy.—French troops of 5th Army captured Poggibonsi, N. of Siena.

★ ══ *Flash-backs* ══ ★

1940
July 9. French warships at Alexandria agreed to demilitarization.
July 11. German air attacks on Channel convoys began.
July 18. Aaland Islands to be demilitarized at request of U.S.S.R.

1941
July 8. Soviet Military Mission arrived in London.
July 12. Anglo-Soviet agreement signed in Moscow for mutual assistance against Germany.

1942
July 12. Germans began drive towards Stalingrad following failure to capture Voronezh.

1943
July 5. Germans launched abortive offensive in Kursk and Orel sectors of Russia.
July 9-10. Allied airborne and seaborne forces landed in Sicily.
July 15. Russians launched offensive in direction of Orel.

THE WAR IN THE AIR

by Capt. Norman Macmillan, M.C., A.F.C.

Air war news is good from all fronts but China. I will deal with the Chinese situation later. For a moment let us glance at the other zones.

It is now agreed that the pre-invasion work of the British and American air forces operating from the United Kingdom (and to a lesser extent from Italy) played a great part in making the Normandy landings the unexpectedly swift and light-casualty successes they were. The cost of this advance contribution was not a light one to the air forces concerned.

In the first five months of 1944 the R.A.F. lost 1,483 bombers and 276 fighters; the U.S.A. 8th A.F. lost 1,407 bombers and 673 fighters; the U.S.A. 9th A.F. lost more than 100 medium and light bombers. Flying in these lost aircraft were 24,260 men (equal to two divisions) who died or were taken prisoner, and these figures do not include those who were flown back dead or wounded in planes that returned. But the sacrifice of the army of the air was not in vain. The communication system operated by the Wehrmacht was so dislocated that reinforcements could not be rushed to Normandy when the Allied army landed, and the consolidation of the bridge-head was thus made sure with relatively small casualties. In addition it must be credited to the continued bomber and fighter attacks, and sweeps by the Allied air forces, that the Germans have been unable to maintain adequate air forces over the three fronts—in Normandy, Italy and Russia.

The total tonnages of bombs dropped have reached figures which are still soaring to new records. U.S. bombers dropped 58,750 tons of H.E. and incendiary bombs on Europe in June. Bomber Command, too, broke all records by dropping 56,000 tons in that month.

In Russia air power has played an important part in the successes of the Red Army in White Russia. Over this vast battlefield, where the warfare has been of the kind commonly called "fluid," Red Air Force Stormovik battle-planes, escorted by fighters, have ranged with penetrating effect over the German forces. In waves of from 30 to 50 the Stormoviks have made deadly attacks on troop concentrations and supply lines, and have been counted as one of the major factors in the great Russian victory leading, so far, to the capture of Vilna.

The shuttle-bombing of the U.S. air forces has continued to affect the war adversely for the enemy on all fronts. The heavy bombers have used all Europe as though it were a baseball ground. Leaving Britain on June 21, led by Col. J. M. Blakeslee Don, of Ohio, they bombed oil-plants at Ruhland, 50 miles S.E. of Berlin, and landed in Russia; en route from Russia to Italy they bombed the oil refinery at Drohobycz in Galicia; flying from Italy to Britain (where they

landed on July 5) they attacked the rail centre of Beziers, near Montpelier in southern France. They were escorted throughout the whole journey of 7,000 miles by long-range Mustang fighters which shot down 7 German fighters on the first leg and 12 on the second.

New applications of bombing power were witnessed. Two daylight attacks were made on June 14 by Lancasters and Halifaxes of Bomber Command against Le Havre harbour. These bombers dropped 12,000-lb. bombs in the water to raise tidal-waves inside E-boat pens, and among a concentration of R-boats and other vessels. A similar attack was made on the following day against Boulogne by Lancasters and Halifaxes. At least 80 vessels were sunk or damaged in the two harbours.

Bomber Command played a part in the air and artillery bombardment that preceded the fall of Caen to the infantry and tanks. At dusk on July 7 a force of 450 Lancasters and Halifaxes concentrated 2,300 tons of bombs on German troops, tanks, guns, defence posts and strongpoints in the north part of this important inland port. The British troops, waiting their turn to attack, were awed by the spectacle, in which they saw for the first time an air attack on the scale

applied to industrial targets in Germany. As in the latter raids the bomb-aimers were aided by the Pathfinder Force's markers.

The Pathfinders were the first aircraft to be equipped with the British Mark XIV bomb-sight which permits accurate bomb-aiming even when the aircraft is banking. With earlier British bomb-sights it was necessary to fly the aircraft both straight and level to enable the aiming to be made with accuracy so that the bombs would hit the target. Amid the growing artillery barrages, and with the intensifying air fighting by day and night, it was often impossible to fly the aircraft in conditions suitable to the scientific requirements of the fastidious bomb-sight. Moreover, with the development of the tremendously swift mass raids there was no opportunity for the recurrent runs over the target which were such a feature of almost all the earliest bombing attacks by British aircraft. The first run had to be the unloading run in most cases. Scientists began work to meet the new requirements, and the Mark XIV sight was issued to the Pathfinders first in August 1942. All Bomber Command aircraft now have it. It was used in the battles of the Ruhr, Hamburg and Berlin. U.S. medium bombers use the same sight under the designation T.1 sight.

In the night of July 6 Super-Fortresses of the 20th Bomber Command of the U.S.A.A.F. attacked naval installations at Sasebo and the steel works at Yawata, on Kyushu Island. This was their third attack against Metropolitan Japan. They are at present employed as the equivalent of a naval task force in connexion with Pacific strategy. But in China the war situation is not satisfactory. The present Japanese advance in the Changsha area threatens to form an armoured Japanese line across all China, endangering future raids against Japan proper. The repulse of this Japanese move is considered essential to the success of future operations in the whole of the South-East Asia zone. Meanwhile, two difficulties in China are the reported famine conditions which are said to be affecting the Chinese army, and the delivery of much Allied war material into the hands of independent war-lords, who apply it to their own personal ends. Clearly the pressure of Admiral Nimitz's Pacific sea and air power towards China's mainland may have to be further increased to speed the actual " Normandy " assault on the Chinese mainland.

In the Pacific zone the battle for airfields continues with growing success. The seizure of Saipan in the Marianas is an event of note (see pp. 166, 167), as are the attacks against Guam and Iwojima and Chichijima islands (Bonin Group). But will the air ring perimeter contract swiftly enough for Chiang Kai-shek?

Air-minelaying closed the Kiel and Königsberg canals in the early summer. Mosquitoes were used for this work. Recently the Danube has been similarly closed. And ranging far across Europe the oil-war bombers have been busy burning up many of Hitler's sources of the essential war spirit, in refineries, storage plants and synthetic producing units. Railways and bridges were hit, too

FROM THIS LONG-RANGE ROCKET SITE near Watten, in the Pas de Calais district of France (top), the Germans hoped to send death-dealing explosives against this country to add to the anti-civilian missions of their flying bombs. But Allied aircraft spotted it and smashed it, leaving the site closely pockmarked with accurately placed bombs (bottom). PAGE 188 *Photos, British Official*

Japan Bombed Again by America's New 'Heavies'

BOEING-29 SUPER-FORTRESSES, U.S. Army's new high-altitude long-distance bombers, have attacked the Japanese in their own islands. On June 15, 1944, they hit Yawata at the northern extremity of Kyushu, and the enemy's biggest iron and steel works ; on July 7 the attack was repeated. Super-Fortresses (1) have a wing-span of over 141 ft., and four engines each of 2,200 horse-power. The tail fin, 27 ft. in height, dwarfs a normal plane (2). Super-Fortress (3, nearer camera) and Flying Fortress compared.

Photos, U.S. Official, Keystone

Wonder-drug Penicillin Saves Limbs and Lives

ONE OF THE MOST POWERFUL WEAPONS in mankind's armoury against disease might have remained undiscovered but for the fact that Professor Alexander Fleming, Professor of Bacteriology at the University of London and St. Mary's Hospital Medical School, was interested in what, by sheer accident, had happened to a deadly microbe culture he had under observation : this had been spoilt by a green mould caused by the chance arrival of a minute airborne fungus spore. Noticing that the deadly microbe colonies in the vicinity of the green mould began to disappear, he realized that here might lie the way for another great step in the endless fight against disease, and he began to experiment with the mould. Later it was identified as Penicillium notatum, and the antibiotic (anti-disease microbe substance) it produced was named penicillin.

Between the original discovery by Professor Fleming and the finding of a successful means of producing penicillin in purer and more concentrated form, years had to pass. In 1938 Professor Sir Howard Florey, Professor of Pathology, Oxford University, took up the search which finally led to success and proved penicillin capable of killing many deadly disease germs. By 1943 much progress had been made in producing penicillin in laboratories in Britain, Canada, Australia and America.

Today the wonder-drug is saving the limbs and lives of our wounded in battlefields everywhere, while an indication that penicillin, hitherto restricted to military use, will be released for civilian treatment was given by Mr. Churchill; on July 6, 1944, referring to the flying bomb attacks on this country, he said that penicillin would be available for all casualties caused.

AT WORK ON HIS GREAT DISCOVERY, Professor Alexander Fleming has before him mould specimens from which penicillin is extracted (1). Professor Sir Howard Florey, who took up the research and helped it to final success (2). A woman laboratory assistant (3) inoculates sterile culture with spores which will later produce penicillin. A steam container ensures that the culture flasks themselves are absolutely sterile before the mould goes in (4). The vital mould growing in a culture flask (5). *Photos, British Official, Topical Press, Keystone*

A FRIEND who has fought both in Italy and in Normandy tells me of the difference between the people in those two theatres of war. When the British troops arrived in Calabria and made their way slowly up the peninsula, the Italians all said with relief, "Now the war for us is over!" The Norman peasants said the opposite. "Now we can begin the war!" they exclaimed. The Italians are reported by all I have talked to from that country to be sick of all public matters. They want to interest themselves only in their daily occupations, their homes and families. They have no faith in any leaders. The House of Savoy, which has held them together for some three-quarters of a century, no longer commands their respect and will probably be dismissed. Where are the statesmen who can lead the nation back to order and prosperity? Those are questions which thoughtful British soldiers who have been among them are asking.

THERE is another contrast between Italians and Frenchmen of the North which strikes all who have been on both fronts. The Italians welcomed our troops with excited exuberance. They threw flowers to them, gave them wine if they had it, shouted *Viva Inghilterra* as they ran alongside the columns on the march. But our men could not get rid of the fancy that they might have given the Germans the same sort of reception. The Normans throw no flowers, do not cheer, though they do hand out what they have in the way of food and drink. But they show that they are honest-to-God haters of the Germans and that they are genuinely happy to see the men who are going to drive the oppressors off French soil. They are not demonstrative folk, these farmers and smallholders of the country between the Channel and Rouen. Maupassant described them with exactitude in his short stories, showing them as hard-working, thrifty to the point of miserliness, secretive where property is concerned, cheerful, and fond of a joke if it is a fairly obvious one. Pleasant people I have always found them as acquaintances. It would be difficult to form real friendships among them, I fancy.

GEGEN *Dummheit kampfen Götter selbst vergebens*, says the well-known line of Goethe—"against stupidity even the Gods fight in vain." But it is not true in the long run. Stupidity defeats itself. Napoleon was vastly more intelligent than most of the adventurers who have aimed at world-domination. But Napoleon did stupid things. The most stupid thing he did was to march his armies into Russia. That broke him. On this point the teaching of history is so plain that it seems impossible anyone could fail to profit by it. Well, Hitler failed, and his stupidity has broken him. For two years he had everything in his favour. If he had insisted on Goering continuing the Battle of Britain a bit longer, he would in all probability have weakened us so much in the air that he might have been able to invade Britain, relying on his bombers to deal with our naval forces. That was a colossal blunder, but not his worst. If in the middle of 1941 he had concentrated on the effort to crush the forces of the British Empire, there was a chance that he would, for a time at any rate, have succeeded. Instead, he repeated the mistake Napoleon had made: he marched into Russia. And now—well, now he knows!

IT is one of the oldest of jokes that farmers always complain of the weather. No one who has farmed, or had an allotment, or even cultivated a small garden, will make fun of farmers for that. If you are trying to grow things, you are bound to find our climate annoying. You are almost certain to grumble. Unless you have a phlegmatic temperament which enables you to take everything calmly as it comes, you are pretty sure to take gloomy views about the chances of your crops, whatever they may be. A long drought makes you think all your vegetables will be dried up. Frosts and high winds seem certain to ruin your fruit. Sunless weather suggests that nothing will ripen properly. But fortunately these fears almost

Maj.-Gen. SIR FRANCIS WILFRED DE GUINGAND, K.B.E., D.S.O., Chief of Staff to the 21st Army Group commanded by General Montgomery. Aged 44, a brilliant administrator, he was behind successes gained by the 8th Army in North Africa, Sicily and Italy. He was created a K.B.E. (Knight Commander of the British Empire) for his part in planning operations in Normandy.
Photo, Associated Press

always turn out to be unfounded. Nothing is so bad as it looks. This year there were at one time the most melancholy predictions as to what the wheat harvest would be. Now we are reassured. Spring-sown wheat will not be quite as good as last year, but the autumn-sown may be better. Sugar beet prospects are excellent. Fruit is nothing like so bad as growers feared a month or two ago. We shall not have to tighten our belts after all.

ONE surprise of the wartime theatre was the long run of Oscar Wilde's romantic comedy, An Ideal Husband. It was beautifully acted, and at a small playhouse, but even that would not seem to account fully for its popularity. One explanation is that it deals with "high life." When it was written, duchesses were social leaders (Dame Irene Vanbrugh acted one gloriously); young men of fashion thought a lot about their clothes and their buttonholes; the whirl of gaiety in the London Season from May to July made its votaries really glad when it came to an end and they could go to Cowes for yachting,

or to the Highlands for shooting, or to some Continental Spa for their stomach's sake, so that they need not stay up till three or four in the morning and perpetually be lunching and dining out. The interest taken now in this sort of existence and those who led it resembles that with which other audiences look at Love for Love, depicting a social scene still farther away from our own time. And possibly the number of titled persons in the cast may please spectators rather tired of the middle-class comedies that have been holding the stage so long. Fifty years ago, when Oscar Wilde was writing, almost all plays were about the aristocracy. Since Freddie Lonsdale produced On Approval, which has recently been made into a film, I can hardly remember one that has dealt with dukes, marchionesses, and the like.

DUE doubtless to the pace at which the war compels us all to live I find that events which at the time were of immense importance retain but fuzzy outlines in most minds. How many could state offhand, for instance, the objects of our surprise landings in North-West Africa 21 months ago? Realization of this fading of memory was brought home to me with something of a shock, when in exchange for a shilling I recently acquired a copy of The Army at War: Tunisia—an extravagantly generous and admirably illustrated publication prepared for the War Office by the Ministry of Information.

The coldly official narrative—a compressed mass of dates, figures and places—reminds me that the objects to which I allude were "to effect a landing in Morocco and Algeria; to rally the local French to the Allied cause and ultimately to occupy Tunisia so as to menace from the rear the enemy forces opposing the 8th Army; to re-open communications through the Mediterranean, and to secure a base for subsequent operations against the underbelly of the Axis in southern Europe." This shillingsworth gives the data of the part played so magnificently by our land forces, up to the complete collapse of the Axis armies engaged, and the capture by the Royal Sussex Regiment of Von Arnim on May 12, 1943. Results of those victories are evident now in our Continental successes.

I OFTEN hear comments on the change that the war years have made in the opinions of many Conservatives, especially the younger ones, in the House of Commons. Among Socialists there has been a noticeable shift of view-point as well. Mr. Herbert Morrison, for example, who not many years ago was for nationalizing all big industries wholesale, now says in a Fabian Society pamphlet that anything of that kind is ruled out as a matter of immediate practical politics. He does not think the nation would agree to it and, even if they did, it would be impossible. He speaks "as one with some experience of administration." Just so! Then there is Mr. A. L. Rowse, one of the Socialist intellectuals, who believes that, while we shall reach out to greater equality, we must "see that individual quality and enterprise, private and personal freedom, are not ironed-out, but preserved and even enriched." If the Socialists put the brake on, and Conservatives step on the gas, they will be able to work together and we may move forward as a whole towards a New Society which will develop naturally and peaceably from the old.

R.A.F. Chaplain as Newsboy in Normandy

ADOPTING A HIGHLY APPRECIATED ROLE, an R.A.F. squadron-leader chaplain in one of the Normandy bridge-head sectors delivers eagerly awaited newspapers, which were flown from England on the same day, to ground staff engaged in servicing a Mustang aircraft. Vicars and curates, who normally receive the rank of squadron-leader on entering the R.A.F., are promoted in the same way as other officers—consideration being given to suitability in their office, and length of service.

Photo, British Official: Crown Copyright

Printed in England and published every alternate Friday by the Proprietors, THE AMALGAMATED PRESS, LTD., The Fleetway House, Farringdon Street, London, E.C.4. Registered for transmission by Canadian Magazine Post. Sole Agents for Australia and New Zealand : Messrs. Gordon & Gotch, Ltd. ; and for South Africa : Central News Agency, Ltd.—August 4, 1944.   S.S.   *Editorial Address* : JOHN CARPENTER HOUSE, WHITEFRIARS, LONDON, E.C.4.

Vol 8   *The War Illustrated*   Nº 187

SIXPENCE

Edited by Sir John Hammerton

AUGUST 18, 1944

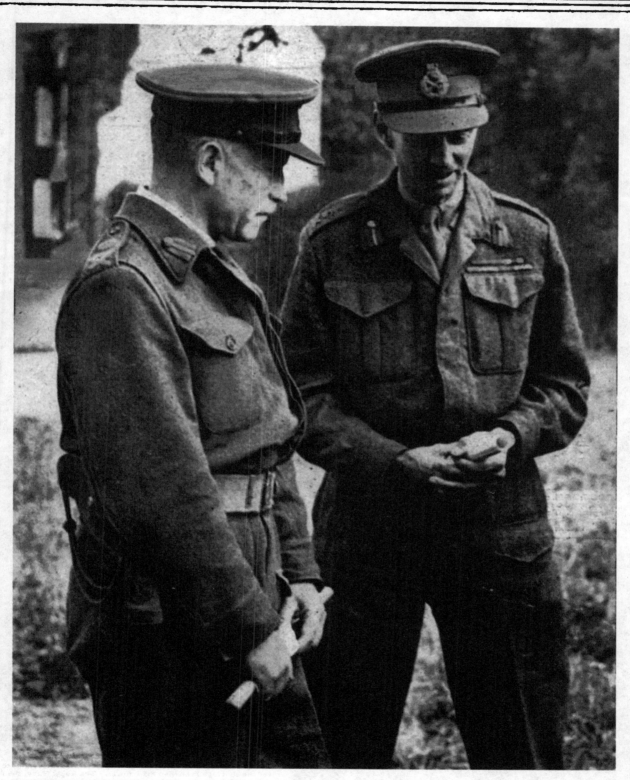

TWO OF BRITAIN'S INVASION CHIEFS are Lieut.-Gen. Sir Miles Dempsey, K.C.B., D.S.O., M.C. (right), Commander of the British 2nd Army in Normandy, and Lieut.-Gen. Sir Richard Nugent O'Connor, K.C.B., D.S.O., M.C. (left), Commander of British armoured forces in the Caen area; aged 55, General O'Connor won the D.S.O. and bar and the M.C. in the 1914-18 war. Both Generals served in North Africa, and both were at the Staff College, Camberley, with General Sir Bernard Montgomery.   *Photo, British Official*

NO. 188 WILL BE PUBLISHED FRIDAY, SEPTEMBER 1

Our Roving Camera Sees War's Impact at Home

HARVESTING IN FULL SWING on the Buckinghamshire hills : the crop is oats, and girls in the foreground are stooking sheaves to allow them to dry out before they are collected. People from all walks of life are holiday volunteers and spare-time workers this year, as they were last, when 500,000 became amateur "farmers' boys."

CONTROL ROOM of one of London's new deep tunnel shelters, first of which was opened on July 9, 1944, is the nerve-centre of a refuge designed to hold 8,000 people. Amenities include bunks, cloakroom facilities, canteens, and well-equipped medical aid posts staffed by St. John Ambulance and British Red Cross nurses under a resident doctor.

SERVICE MEN LEND A HAND in vital war tasks in Britain, to help meet the shortage in civilian man-power. The Royal Navy, the Army and the R.A.F. have each loaned some of their personnel ; as volunteers for this " change-over " they continue to wear Service clothes and receive their normal rates of pay. Some gain proficiency as railway firemen and cleaners : Sgt.-Pilot Forster, very much " grounded," emerges from beneath a locomotive after emptying the ashbox (above). Royal Naval Commandos, who have been on several operations, help after flying bomb visitations ; their main job is re-tiling roofs of damaged buildings (left). *Photos, Sport & General, Planet News, New York Times Photos, Associated Press*

THE BATTLE FRONTS

by Maj.-Gen. Sir Charles Gwynn, K.C.B., D.S.O.

WHETHER Hitler and Himmler really succeeded in crushing the revolt of the generals did not, I think, matter much to us. The mischief was already done, for though the Reichswehr may continue to fight a losing battle it is impossible to believe that any army can maintain its morale when it knows that numbers of its most esteemed leaders have openly shown that they consider the war has been lost—and that through the incompetence of the High Command. The amazing success of the Russian offensive, skilfully as it has been conducted and despite its overpowering weight, could not have been achieved if the German Army as a whole retained anything of its former spirit.

One cannot help suspecting that some at least of the astonishing number of German generals who have been taken prisoner knew that an internal clash was imminent, and preferred captivity to being forced to take sides in a struggle whose outcome was still doubtful. They can claim that they remained with their troops, but it is hard to believe that they tried to take opportunities to escape with some part of their forces before the net closed. Granted that the action of partisans and the Russian cavalry probably added to the difficulty of escape, and that orders from Hitler not to retreat may have obscured their better judgement. Such an order might often involve Divisional H.Q. in the battle, but even they and still more Corps H.Q. should normally aim at being in a position to take a broad view of the situation and to retain power of exercising control.

RUSSIA

Koniev's offensive on the Lvov front has had a more rapid and complete success than might have been expected, for here if anywhere the Germans were fully prepared. Yet it is on this front that the break-through has made the most astonishing progress, and there have been most evident signs of the enemy's demoralization. Hitler's orders that Lvov should be held at all costs invited a new catastrophe, and the same applies to Brest-Litovsk, Bialystok and Dvinsk—the capture of all these fortress towns with their large garrisons, announced on July 27 and 28, of course representing an immensely more important success than their abandonment by the retreating army.

By the end of the first month of the offensive it was evident that Koniev and Rokossovsky were driving with all speed to gain the crossings of the Vistula, while Zakharov was well placed to cover Rokossovsky's right flank and to turn the line of the Narew River. It was clear that the Germans would be hard put to it to hold the line of the Vistula and Warsaw. It was obvious too that the three Baltic armies were aiming at isolating and destroying Lindemann's northern armies.

It was not so clear whether Cherniakovsky and Zakharov's armies would simultaneously attempt the invasion of East Prussia from the east. They had forced a crossing over the Niemen and established bridge-heads on its left bank, and by doing so had apparently drawn most of the available German reserves. But whether stiffening opposition had checked further progress, making a pause necessary to close up and consolidate communications, or whether it suited Russian plans better to wait till East Prussia has become a dangerous salient, was a matter for speculation.

There had been an absence of information from this section of the front lately, but as far as could be gathered Cherniakovsky was making no vigorous attempt to close in on Kaunas. It seemed possible that he might be playing on German anxiety to save East Prussia and would not press his attack until Rokossovsky and Zakharov threatened to isolate the forces defending it. Whatever the future held in store, the achievements of the Red Army in the first month of the offensive had established a new speed record and had once again exposed the amazing incompetence of the German High Command.

FRANCE

In Normandy, perhaps owing to a somewhat loose use of the word "break-through," expectations were disappointed when the massive attack which cleared the Caen bottle-neck turned out to have only limited objectives. Personally, I never imagined that a break-through with unlimited objectives was attempted. The mere facts that no attacks were made simultaneously on other sectors and that the attack was delivered on a very narrow front seemed to indicate clearly that the object was to remove the cork from the bottle-neck and to gain a bridge-head in the open country beyond.

Admittedly, all objectives were not gained in the initial attack, but it should be recognised that although the cork had been removed the bottle-neck remained, cramping immediate exploitation of success. The existence of the bottle-neck was in fact sufficient evidence that no offensive on a great scale could be staged until a substantial bridge-head was secured beyond it and new routes opened. Presumably but for the interruption caused by weather the initial success would have been followed up promptly in order to gain a bridge-head of the size required.

FAILURE to reach all the objectives aimed at led to criticism of the tactical methods adopted, particularly the use of tanks to lead the assault. I would not, however, attempt to form any opinion on the point without

RUSSIAN PRESSURE on the 1,000-mile battle front extending from Pskov in the north to Stanislavov in the south is indicated by the arrows above. By August 1, 1944, the Red Army was closing on Warsaw, moving towards Riga, capital of Latvia, and approaching East Prussia. *By courtesy of The Daily Telegraph*

much more detailed knowledge of the terrain conditions and of the information available when plans were drawn up. It is clear that Rommel reacted with great speed, and it is possible that too much reliance was placed on his movements being hampered by the cratering of roads. No doubt alternative routes had been reconnoitred with a view to the rapid switch of his anti-tank weapons.

THE preliminary air bombardment of the factory area has also been criticized, but it seems to have accomplished its object and to have been skilfully planned to minimize the disadvantages revealed at Cassino. I should imagine, however, that tanks were used to lead the assault on the grounds that they could traverse the devastated area at greater speed than infantry and might therefore have a better chance of anticipating the enemy's reaction. Critics, in any case, might allow for the fact that if everything always went as planned a general's job would be an easy one, and, in particular, that our troops in Normandy are opposed by the pick of the German Army commanded by a general who certainly has great executive capacity.

Although the clearance of the Caen bottle-neck has been a step forward, preparatory to launching a full-scale offensive, the bridge-head across the Orne will probably require enlargement before anything decisive can be attempted. The time has come, however, when preparatory operations will be on a greater scale and on wider fronts.

ITALY

Meanwhile, in Italy, General Alexander's armies continue to make steady progress, and Kesselring is back in the forward zone of the Gothic Line: the time must be approaching when the German High Command will have to decide whether he is to attempt to hold that position at all costs or to withdraw to the Alpine passes. In view of the lessening importance of the Italian air bases owing to the Russian advance, and the pressing need of the Germans for reserves, it would not be surprising if the latter alternative were adopted. Possibly, however, hopes of gathering the harvest of the Po valley might affect the decision.

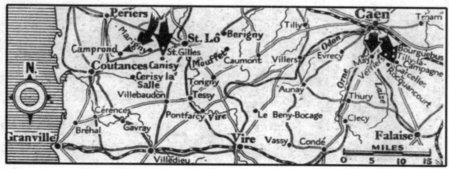

IN THE NORMANDY BATTLES the Allies, thrusting on from St. Lo area, took the towns of St. Gilles and Marigny on July 27, 1944, continuing past Coutances, Villebaudon and Cerences, to capture, on July 31, Avranches, south-east of Granville. Around Caen progress was limited, but new British attacks in the Caumont area had progressed well, a deep salient having been made in the German line towards Vire in the south. PAGE 195 *By courtesy of the News Chronicle.*

Russians Crack More Bastions in Berlin Drive

PSKOV, strongpoint covering roads to southern Estonia, was captured by troops of the 3rd Baltic Front, under General Ivan Maslennikov (above), on July 23, 1944. The town was set ablaze by the retreating enemy (right).

LVOV'S TREE-LINED MAIN STREET, the spacious and imposing Academic Boulevard (left), as it was in pre-war days. Economic, political and regional centre of the Ukraine, big railway junction and bastion covering strategic roads to southern Poland, Lvov was captured by Red Army troops of the 1st Ukrainian Front on July 27, 1944. Soviet tanks (right) manoeuvre into position during the final encirclement of the enemy that garrisoned the city. For two days street battles raged, tanks, cavalry and infantry taking part in the action which cleared it at last of the invaders. See also map in p. 195, and illus. p. 201.

Photos, U.S.S.R. Official, Planet News, Pictorial Press

Great Gaps Torn in Nazi Line across France

WEST OF ST. LO, captured by U.S. Forces on July 18, 1944, the Americans launched a new attack on July 25 to break the German hold on the south of the Cotentin peninsula. By August 3 their armoured columns had driven beyond Avranches and reached Rennes and Dinan in Brittany. Encountering enemy fire, U.S. troops dashed across a road to cover (left). An American tank shepherds in German prisoners waving white flags (above), hatless and dishevelled, representatives of thousands more.

ON THE CAEN FRONT the British 2nd Army, taking up the running of the American offensive, attacked around Caumont on July 30. Faced by six of the nine German armoured divisions in Normandy, they made good progress, reaching Vire by Aug. 3. In a rain-flooded street a British military policeman directs troops (above). Mr. Churchill visited Normandy again on July 21 and was photographed with British soldiers (right). *Photos, British and U.S. Official, British Newspaper Pool, Keystone*

THE WAR AT SEA

by Francis E. McMurtrie

Admiral C. W. NIMITZ (right), C.-in-C. U.S. Pacific Fleet. Recent outstandingly successful U.S. Navy actions were the bombardments preceding landings on Guam Island and Tinian, in the Marianas group, on July 20 and 23, 1944, respectively. *Photo, Keystone*

FROM the very start of this war, Germany put her entire trust in the U-boat as the principal weapon with which to defeat British sea power. In this respect the enemy plan of campaign differed materially from that of thirty years ago. In 1914 scarcely any German seems to have realised the potency of the submarine as a means of destroying shipping; and during 1915 and the early part of 1916 its use was limited by a reluctant consideration for the feelings of neutrals. Not until Jutland had made it plain that there was no hope of gaining victory at sea by surface battle was all restraint abandoned.

As a result the United States was drawn into the war following persistent attacks on American vessels engaged in peaceful trade. Thus in the ultimate issue the U-boat campaign proved Germany's undoing, though not until its prosecution had inflicted well-nigh fatal damage, as figures attest. During four black weeks of 1917 nearly 900,000 tons gross of shipping were sent to the bottom. Had this rate of destruction continued, it was a mathematical certainty that by the end of the year there would have been just enough tonnage left to Britain to bring food, leaving nothing over for the transport of troops, munitions, fuel and other vital necessities.

fare meant nothing to the Germans; it was just another scrap of paper.

During the past four and a half years the enemy again came near to success in their nefarious undertaking. In 1941-42 shipping losses were so severe that the submarines seemed to the German naval authorities to have victory within their grasp. During those two years the Battle of the Atlantic was for the Allies a desperate struggle for survival, but in 1943 came the turn of the tide. Now more U-boats are being sunk every month than merchant ships, and the German submarine service has come to be regarded as a suicide club.

NOT until the struggle is over and access has been had to enemy records shall we know exactly how many German, Italian and Japanese submarines have paid the penalty for their depredations. It has been stated that Italian losses total 84, which is probably pretty close to the truth. It would leave the Italian Navy with a residue of between 60 and 70, excluding vessels of the midget type. Some of these, of course, are in German hands and may have been destroyed since. Japanese figures are more uncertain, but it is probable that more than 20 have been accounted for in various ways. This

Unquestionably the knowledge that under present conditions there is only a faint chance of survival must be disheartening for the personnel. At the present time the rate of slaughter of U-boats almost certainly is higher than one in two, which has been assumed to be the average for the whole war. Moreover, the majority of the more skilful and daring of the enemy submarine captains has been killed or taken prisoner, leaving only the less efficient and enterprising to carry on the conflict. In such circumstances it may be assumed that there is no strong desire on their part—still less on that of their crews—to make contact with convoys, as even if a successful attack can be made, escape afterwards is highly unlikely. This alone goes far to explain the rarity of U-boat attacks on shipping in recent months.

OWING to the high proportion of surface blockade runners intercepted en route from Japan to Germany during 1943, an effort is believed to have been made to carry on the traffic by submarines. The vessels chosen for this purpose were probably the large supply U-boats already mentioned, together with a few big Italian submarines fitted out specially. Even in this service submarines are believed to have proved a failure, so that Germany's desperate need of rubber, gum, tin, oil and other Eastern products has not been relieved; nor is Japan's shortage of machine tools, ball bearings, and so on, likely to be assuaged by anything the Germans can send in return.

Slowly but surely the war is drawing nearer to Japan. Tinian Island, like its neighbour Saipan, has now passed into American occupation with its fine airfield. Reconquest of Guam is making steady progress, and the bombardment of the Palau group is another warning to the enemy that retribution approaches closer daily. In the Indian Ocean the port of Sabang, at the north-western extremity of Sumatra, has again been attacked by Allied ships and aircraft of the Eastern Fleet, and its equipment and storage facilities have suffered damage. The appointment of Admiral Sir Bruce Fraser to be Commander-in-Chief of the Eastern Fleet may be taken as an indication that the time is not far distant when fresh attacks will be made on Japan from this quarter.

Shortage of shipping is perhaps the greatest trouble from which Japan is suffering at the present time. Not only have a great many transports and supply vessels been destroyed by air attack in the Solomons, New Guinea and the Dutch Indies, but United States submarines are waging an unending campaign against enemy shipping in Far Eastern waters, sinking a larger tonnage every month

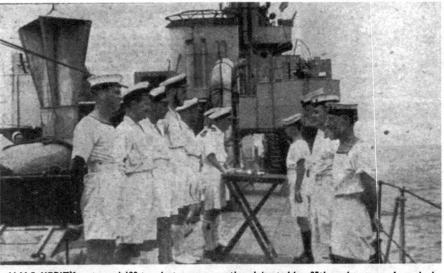

H.M.S. VERITY, veteran 1,120-ton destroyer, recently celebrated her 25th anniversary. Launched in 1919, she has served all over the world. Engaged in convoy work on the outbreak of war, in 1940 she took General McNaughton, the then G.O.C. Canadian Forces, to France, later bringing Queen Wilhelmina from the Hook of Holland. During Dunkirk she rescued some 20,000 soldiers. Here her Commanding Officer is receiving requests—which may vary from leave, promotion or welfare to "permission to grow a full set of whiskers." *Photo, British Official: Crown Copyright*

Recalling these facts, it seemed to Hitler and his naval advisers that if submarine warfare were waged without limit from the start, its success might be regarded as a certainty. With this in mind, the German Government in 1935 concluded an agreement with Britain by which, while the ratio of German naval strength was fixed as 35 per cent of that of the Royal Navy, the *Reichsmarine* was permitted to build submarines (a right denied by the Treaty of Versailles) up to a percentage of 45 in the same relation.

U-BOAT construction had already been resumed before this agreement was actually signed; and it was no doubt calculated that in another four years enough submarines would be available to furnish the means for prosecuting a fresh war against the world's sea transport. Of course, the fact that Germany had also subscribed to a pact renouncing unrestricted submarine war-

would leave over 100 still in service, without allowing for losses of which nothing is known outside Japan.

Germany possessed 70 submarines at the outbreak of war, as compared with 28 in 1914. They have been added to at a far faster rate than in 1914-18, when 344 were actually completed, 226 more begun but not finished, and 212 projected but never built. By mass production methods the Germans are believed to have turned out over 1,000 U-boats since September, 1939, including some of a special supply type, which for a time were used to refuel and revictual submarines out on patrol. It is probably no exaggeration to assess the losses of the U-boat flotillas in this war at 50 per cent —or not less than 500 submarines to date. In other words, out of every two U-boats that have sailed to prey upon shipping one has failed to return.

8th Army Riflemen Patrol the Arno Valley

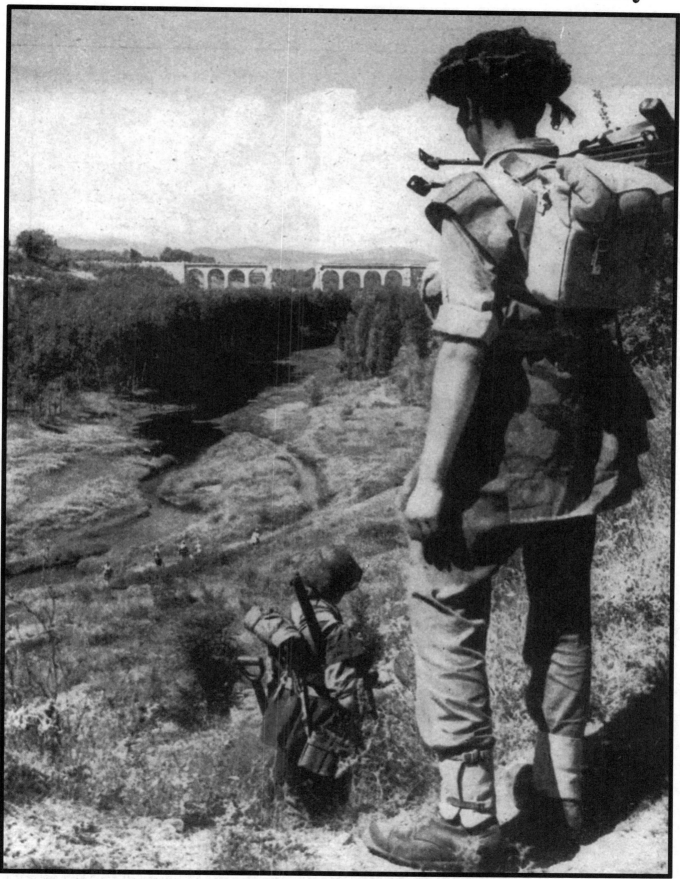

THE RIFLE BRIGADE reconnoitred the difficult country ahead for concealed German positions in the valley of the Arno, north of the captured Italian town of Arezzo (see page 200). Defending the approaches to Florence five German divisions were massed by August 2, 1944, in a 30-mile arc—including their best formations in Italy: the 4th Parachute Division and the 3rd and 29th Panzer Grenadiers, supported by Tiger tanks. The Rifle Brigade has been serving in Italy as part of an armoured division since March.

Photo. British Official: Crown Copyright

Advance to Arezzo Heralds Fall of Florence

TRIUMPH FOR BRITISH TANKS, guardsmen, riflemen and Indian troops of the 8th Army was the capture, on July 16, 1944, of Arezzo, in the centre of the coast-to-coast battle line in Italy and the keypoint of the German defences guarding Florence and the Gothic Line. It was taken after a three-weeks' struggle, the final days of which cost the Germans dearly in men and material. Our aircraft had gone into action in the preliminary stages of this advance, and here (1) Fleet Air Arm and R.A.F. personnel get a Seafire into fighting trim at a forward airfield. A Sherman tank passes a de-tracked and knocked out German Panther (2). British troops dug in to give covering fire to patrols clearing a village near Arezzo (3). Infantry on the march, one of them wearing a "non-regulation" sun-hat (4).   PAGE 200   *Photos, British Official*

Irresistible Red Armies Swept On Into Poland

OVER A RIVER AND ONWARDS surged tanks, guns and men of the 1st Ukrainian Front, under Marshal Koniev, towards Lvov, key to Southern Poland (see illus. p. 196) ; for days completely encircled, the city was captured on July 27, 1944. Lvov is an important junction of railways to Warsaw, Cracow, Breslau and Budapest ; it was the third biggest city of pre-war Poland.

SIXTY THOUSAND GERMANS, including generals, marched through Moscow on July 17, 1944—but not as the conquerors they had hoped to be. Captured in White Russia, they were on their way to prison camps in Siberia, watched by grimly silent crowds of Muscovites. German forces had advanced to within 12 miles of Moscow in 1941 ; their repulse was due in part to Marshal of Tanks Pavel A. Rotmistrov (in circle), Russia's greatest exponent in the theory and practice of tank warfare.

Photos, U.S.S.R. Official, Pictorial Press

IN THE FRONT LINE NEAR CAGNY, south-east of Caen, men of the 2nd Army await the order to attack. Each carries a pick or shovel ready for instant digging-in on reaching new positions, and a D.R. stands by to take back word of the assault to headquarters. This incident was a preliminary to operations which resulted, at the end of July, in the establishment south-east of Caen of a new line extending from Caumont, east of the Orne river, through Bourguebus and Frénouville to the neighbourhood of Troarn, a distance of about 20 miles, with a varying depth, in the whole area won, of from 2 to 10 miles.   *Photo. British Official.*

They Tend the Front Line Sick and Wounded

Ministering angels of the battlefields go to their tasks from Britain with no illusions as to the hardships and perils they themselves must face in the execution of their duties. Theirs is no glamorous holiday from the humdrum round of home duties but a stern facing-up to tragic realities of the fighting front, as shown here by GEORGE GODWIN. See also page 138.

QUEEN Alexandra's Imperial Military Nursing Service has made known its need for a thousand nurses for the front line, to staff such medical and surgical units as mobile casualty clearing stations for succouring Allied wounded in the battlefields of Western Europe and Italy. In no previous war have nurses been called upon to work in such conditions of extreme danger, hardship and endurance.

Mrs. L. J. WILKINSON, O.B.E., R.R.C., Matron-in-Chief of Queen Alexandra's Imperial Military Nursing Service. Serving in the 1914-18 war, when she was awarded the Royal Red Cross (First Class), she was in France again in 1940. She gained the O.B.E. in 1943.
Photo, British Official: Crown Copyright

Let us glance for a moment at how the whole problem of nursing was brought within the pattern of the national "man-power" at the start. In 1939 the Ministries of Health and National Service required all State Registered Nurses and Certified Midwives to register. That was the first occasion when a census of nurses had been made on national lines. It revealed the fact that the country had a reservoir of some 80,000 qualified nurses and midwives, and it made possible their appropriate distribution. In April 1943 the Ministry of Labour required all nurses and midwives to register at their local offices, for by that time we had need of 11,000 nurses.

NURSES were then classified into groups —those immediately available, those unemployed, in industry or married, and those who had nursing experience but were not engaged in nursing. Between 1939 and 1943 many nurses and women with nursing experience had entered the women's Services. They were henceforth free to quit the Services for their own job of nursing. And those who had gone on to war work were taken off and returned to this great central pool. So much for the general way in which this vital public service has been directed during the war. What of the Q.A.I.M.N.S.?

This Service, whose grey and scarlet uniform is everywhere familiar, is divided into three sections. First, the regular section, then the reserve, then the T.A.N.S. (Territorial Auxiliary Nursing Service). It is for this Service that the gallant thousand are required. What sort of conditions will they have? Their work, it is true, will be done under the hardest conditions; but they will have the compensation of possessing a higher status than ever before. For these women will rank as officers and wear the appropriate rank badges—lieutenant, captain, major, and so on. In place of the familiar scarlet and grey they will wear khaki, for there is a shortage of the standard cloth. For the rest of the war period these nurses will wear a uniform like the A.T.S., which is a great break with tradition. Their pay starts at £105 a year, all found.

IT is not generally known that the V.C. is a decoration which may be won by a woman, for the regulations governing that award state that the act of gallantry must be one performed in the face of the enemy in the field. It is therefore possible that this war will see the award of the V.C. to the first woman recipient. In the past most army and other service nursing has been done at base hospitals. Today these nurses share the full ardours of war and already there is a casualty list which tells more eloquently than words of the reality of these perils. It was nurses of the Q.A.I.M.N.S. who stuck it out on the beaches at Dunkirk in 1940; these staffed the long processions of ambulance trains in France. They have served in hospital ships, and in many countries, and now again in France. They have worked under perpetual bombings and under intense shell-fire.

Yet, despite a magnificent record of courage, devotion and endurance, few stories have been told of these self-sacrificing and uncomplaining women. Incidentally, it is the hall-mark of the "pukka" nurse that she does not dramatize her work, but takes it in a matter-of-fact way, doing her job quietly and efficiently in every manner of circumstance. There was one such nurse who was torpedoed and shot into the sea. For

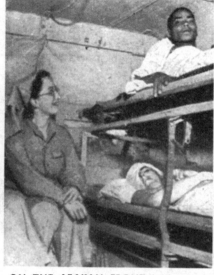

ON THE ARAKAN FRONT in Burma, a Q.A.I.M.N.S. nurse sits in an ambulance ready to tend wounded soldiers waiting to be taken by air to a hospital in the rear. Air ambulances are saving many lives on this front.
Photo, Indian Official

twelve days she was one of a party in a life-boat. She held a daily "sick parade," she comforted men when hysteria broke down their courage, she operated on boils with an iodine-dipped safety-pin, she instituted a daily salt-water bucket bath to allay thirst. In short, she handled the whole human boatload with the competence and quiet assurance of a Ward Sister in a civilian hospital in peace time.

Nurses on active service handling casualties in the forward area often have to put up with conditions which would appal a tough man. Consider the delicate operation of giving a blood transfusion. This operation is now performed under canvas or in any sort of available cover behind the front line—in leaky tents with floors slippery with wet mud, often with nurses in attendance who have not had their clothes off for a week, by nurses whose hours run to anything up to eighteen per day.

Such, very briefly, are circumstances in which our Service nurses are succouring our men to-day. How do they "take it"? Maybe the best answer is found in the casual remark of a nurse serving in Arakan, at a casualty clearing station close to the front line. She said, laughing: "We are the most forward women in Arakan!"

IF you enquire who these women are, the answer is they come from London, from Ireland and Scotland, from provincial cities and towns—that they are, in short, a cross section of the British nursing service and the inheritors of a tradition which goes back in direct line of descent to those crude, rough hospitals of the Crimea where Florence Nightingale laid the foundation of modern Service nursing.

At the head of Q.A.I.M.N.S. is Matron-in-Chief Mrs. L. J. Wilkinson, who had been Chief Principal Matron in India since 1942; she succeeded Dame Katherine Jones, as Matron-in-Chief, in July 1944.

Many who responded to the appeal for front line nurses are girls who had only just completed their hospital training and attained to the dignity of State Registration.

ARRIVING IN NORMANDY a few days after the Allies battered their way ashore, these members of the Q.A.I.M.N.S., clad in battle-dress, are being detailed for duty by their Senior Commandant Matron (extreme right). Their purpose was to set up at once on the beach-head a general hospital to house 600 patients; aided by R.A.M.C. and Pioneers, the task was accomplished in record time. PAGE 203 *Photo, British Official: Crown Copyright*

Hard-hitting Spearheads of Our 2nd Army Front

GREAT WEIGHT OF BRITISH ARMOUR, sweeping ahead of a combined British and Canadian advance east of the River Orne in Normandy, included American-built Sherman tanks (I) here seen moving up through standing crops. Improved Shermans, fitted with the British 17-pounder gun (2), joined in the thrust. A Cromwell followed by another Sherman crosses a bridge (3) ; one of the latest types of British cruiser tank, the Cromwell, incorporates a 75-mm. gun. Eastward across the Orne via " London Bridge " speeds yet another armoured column (4).

Roar of British Guns Rolls over Norman Plains

OBSERVATION TOWERS, skilfully located between tall trees and with their tops camouflaged to blend with the foliage, are used by our forces on the Western Front. This tower (1) was built for a flash-spotting unit of a Royal Artillery survey regiment ; the men who watch from the summit platforms note flashes from enemy gun positions and pass the information back, by field telephone, to our own batteries for accurate retaliatory action.

At dawn a gun of a 5.5 in. medium battery joins in a massed barrage ; shells are stacked ready for the non-stop pounding (2). So fierce was the firing that the barrels of this 25-pdr. battery had to be cooled at regular intervals with water (3). Each time this heavy 155 mm. gun was fired the shock raised clouds of choking dust (4) ; it is fitted with recoil absorbers, seen above the control part of the barrel

Photos, British Official, British Newspaper Pool

'Red Duster' Flies Again in Swedish Ports

Five small British Merchant Navy blockade-runners, audaciously defying Hitler's navy and the Luftwaffe, succeeded in establishing a regular service between Britain and neutral Sweden —after a break of 3½ years—returning with, among other war cargoes, vital ball-bearings. Facts about this daring enterprise are told here by Capt. FRANK H. SHAW. See also page 217.

TECHNICALLY, the Merchant Navy is a civilian, non-combatant force ; since the day hostilities opened it has been in the front line of activity, braving the seas and every fiendishness that Hitler's ingenuity could devise. Its losses, in men and ships, have been colossal ; but there is no record of any single ship failing to sail on schedule. Out of such unfaltering record it stands to reason that any occurrence deserving outstanding praise must be a remarkably fine feat indeed. Consider now the almost fantastic story of the little Red Ensign blockade-runners . which have defied the worst Hitler's navy and air force could do, to maintain a regular service between Britain and Sweden.

The picture of Francis Drake was hung in the cabin of each of the five gallant midget ships concerned. The names of this defiant quintet deserve to be honoured equally with the Golden Hind and the stoutest hearts-of-oak that ever took the sea with Good Queen Bess's august blessing. The Ellerman-Wilson Line, noteworthy through many years for trading in the harsh, hostile Baltic, were given the responsibility of operating the Gay Corsair, commanded by Capt. R. Tanton, O.B.E. ; the Gay Viking, Capt. H. Whitfield, O.B.E. ; the Hopewell, Capt. D. Stokes, O.B.E.; the Master Standfast, Capt. C. R. Holdsworth ; and the Nonsuch, Capt. H. W. Jackson, O.B.E.

This 20th-century task of singeing Hitler's moustache contained many factors that would have shaken even the stout soul of Drake, who never had to contend with mines, moored and magnetic, or with U-boats or hostile aircraft, E-boats, powerful destroyers, land-based torpedoes, and the multifarious ingenuities of the modern, war-minded scientists. This in no wise detracts from Sir Francis's gallantry ; it only enhances that shown by the captains and crews of the Red Duster's little ships, which made a regular habit of defying the myriad dangers of the Skager-rak—a poisonous stretch of water at the best of times ; which plied to and fro almost with the regularity of a peacetime mail-line, and conveyed to this country materials of which she stood sorely in need.

THE ships concerned were specially designed for this unique service of running the gauntlet through seas bristling with potential death. They had to be small, to allow of quick manoeuvring through minefields that were refreshed on every possible occasion by German mine-layers—surface, sub-surface and aerial. They had to be fast, because when liable to be chased they needed ability to dodge salvos of shell and straddles of bombs. But speed without volume promised to be of little value : express

M.T.B.s could have run the gauntlet any day ; but these sea-wasps are totally incapable of carrying considerable freights ; consequently, the Drake Flotilla, as these ships might well be honoured in future references, had to be roomy and capacious, where every possible inch of space could be devoted to the snug stowage of cargoes. The fact of their unqualified success speaks volumes for the ingenuity of their designers and builders, as it glorifies the sterling, audacious courage of their youthful crews.

"Give us the tools," said the Prime Minister on a memorable occasion, "and we will finish the job." The little craft got

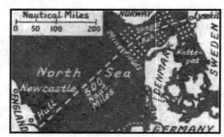

MOUTH OF THE SKAGER-RAK (see above) is heavily mined, yet gallant little vessels of the Merchant Navy—including the Gay Viking (below)—ran the German blockade to exchange war essentials with Sweden, as told in this page.   Photo, British Official

their working tools, and the personnel performed such a job of work as deserves to live in history until the Red Ensign—otherwise the Red Duster—disappears for ever from the world's vast oceans. It was not that one solitary, breathless blockade-busting run was performed. Week by week, through the period of long nights, the shuttle service of unequalled value persisted. It was in the early part of last year—1943—that the operation was first conceived. The specially designed ships were built. Diesel engines were installed, as being capable of giving a high rate of speed without the sacrifice of too much engine-room and bunker-space. Since anything but defensively-armed merchant ships were liable to internment in the Swedish neutral ports to which the modern "mosquitoes" plied, only strictly defensive armament could be carried—deck-guns aft, Oerlikons and high-angle A.A. guns for defence—quite legitimate—against hostile assaults from the air. Thus the small flotilla did warships' work whilst lacking warships' aggressive armaments, and deserve all the more credit on that account.

The crews—each ship carried about 20 men—packed close, in order that valuable space might not be unduly encroached upon. The living conditions of these men approxi-

mated those of the crews of our submarines and light coastal craft : hot cooked food was a rarity, exercise a practical impossibility. And when the service was started, in the autumn of 1943, the North Sea and Skagerrak waters were about at their worst. As an old navigator of these waters, in fair weather and foul, I can only stand amazed at the consistent temerity with which the hundred-odd men concerned faced the fearful odds of their voluntary trade. They had to dare thick fogs, ever-altering minefields. The North Sea gales were continuous and tumultuous. Leading lights and landmarks were practically non-existent ; the nights of that first bitter winter were long and dark—very, very dark.

IT was impossible to display so much as a glimmer of light even to guard them from collision with friendly or neutral craft. Each eastward voyage was so dexterously timed that the ships reached the Skager-rak, the area of greatest danger, as the darkness intensified. This called for expert navigation —navigation of hair's-breadth precision. The sun was valueless, and the main aids were compass and sounding-lead. The masters and crews were specially trained to feel a way across the North Sea's hidden bottom. But Hull men—who predominated in the crews—are notoriously skilful at such work ; it is an inherited tradition with the stolid Yorkshiremen that the bitter sea washing their coast exists only to be beaten in fair fight—though the North Sea generally fights foully : getting its challengers down for the count and then hammering home its most savage blows.

And so, thrusting through noisy seas, blasted by screaming winds of almost incessant ferocity, liable to immediate sinking by enemy attacks from all dimensions, the persistent armada carried to Sweden commercial commodities required by that neutral country, and exchanged them for ball-bearings by wholesale—and ball-bearings mean as much to the machinery of modern war as does oil—and a multitude of other material without which our successful conduct of the war could not be guaranteed. Invaluable passengers were conveyed, too—that entailed even closer stowage of the human element aboard. Details of the cargoes borne both ways must necessarily be kept secret ; but it is no exaggeration to say that but for the fidelity and toughness of these men and ships, the present invasion of Europe might well have been impossible.

SWEDEN welcomed the adventurers, rejoicing to see a resumption of trade with her old commercial friend. Although Germany did all in her power to interrupt the comings and goings of the little armada, Sweden sturdily held that she was entitled to conduct such trade. Our British die-hards were welcomed in Lysekil—the Swedish port selected for harbourage—with open arms. They were fêted, much to the disgust of the Germans ; and the crews moved jauntily ashore among the very nationals whom they were defying day by day.

Not all the little ships escaped. The Master Standfast fell a prey to enemy activity. She was taken as good prize by the Germans ; that she fought gallantly is proved by the fact that her captain died in the performance of his duty ; Captain Holdsworth deserves a place in British sea-history comparable with any non-combatant merchant-adventurer whose deeds have helped to shed lustre on the British flag.

Naval Aid for Our Armies of Invasion

Through death-strewn, narrow waters and under shore-battery fire two great invasion armies were successfully carried to the Normandy coast and landed on open beaches with the combined protection of Allied sea and air forces and the help of the Merchant Navies of Britain and America.

Since those June days, food and water, petrol and oil, ammunition, vehicles and spare parts, and great reinforcements have been transported without intermission—" Making it possible," in the words of General Sir Bernard Montgomery, C.-in-C. 21st Army Group, in a message of thanks to Admiral Sir Bertram Ramsay, Allied Naval C.-in-C. Expeditionary Force, " for us to fight when you had put us ashore."

Above, on the deck of a British warship anchored off a beach-head, the crew of a Bofors A.A. gun covers shipping unloading supplies. Right, troop transports and landing craft approach the coast.

Photos, British Official; Pictorial Press

Beaufighters

Supplementing the brilliant wo
Allied navies, supporting our
the Continental field, one of th
"strike" forces R.A.F. Coast
mand has ever put in the air
down through cloud to mast-t
on July 15, 1944, and surprised,
and smashed an entire German
off the south coast of Norway
the Beaufighters departed, u
every one of the nine ships—
urgently needed war carg
written off the Nazi roll. One

Enemy Convoy

last seen going down, the re-
were either on fire or crippled.
d trawler (1, foreground) bursts
e ; in the background another is
y ringed with near-misses. At
t of the attack (2), four of the
ters are seen in devastating
Enemy gunners abandon their
(3) as this trawler begins to
water-level. R.A.F., Canadian,
n and New Zealand squadrons
l Command participated in this
emely successful operation.

Guns of Navy Take Part in Land Battles

As they bombard enemy strong-points ashore gun crews of the Royal Navy rely for correct ranges on men of Forward Observation Bombardment units, among whom are many naval telegraphists from H.M. ships; here spotting for the Navy's guns are (1) an infantry officer and a sergeant and, in the trench, a naval rating in battle-dress. From the bridge of a U.S. escorting destroyer (2, left) the British cruiser H.M.S. Dido is seen bombarding shore targets to the west of Gaeta, in Italy. Changing guns on the upper forward turret of H.M.S. Ramillies (3), which helped considerably to break up concentrations of enemy armour around Caen in Normandy; in the first ten days of the invasion operations Ramillies hurled nearly 1,000 tons of shells on German defence positions.

Photos, British Official

VIEWS & REVIEWS Of Vital War Books

by Hamilton Fyfe

I HAVE been reading what its author calls "an angry book." He offers no apology for it. He makes the same answer that the prophet in the Bible made to Jehovah when he was asked "Doest thou well to be angry?" His answer was "I do well."

Mr. George Soloveytchik claims that he has every right to feel anger against "successive British governments which have refused to govern," and as a result of that refusal "have sent hundreds of thousands of heroic young men to slaughter or enemy prison camps." He extends his indignation to "the Allies who declared war on Germany without bothering to wage it" and were so "blind, cowardly and inefficient" that they inflicted "on millions of men and women all over the world the horrors of invasion, terrorism and slow death."

He expands this indictment as follows: The Allies, "having exhausted their efforts to evade war at almost any price, having surrendered one vital bastion in Europe after another, and refused to fight for Czechoslovakia," declared war, but did not wage it.

They each proceeded to attend to their own affairs, while carefully refraining from attacking Germany in the west—the only effective help they could have given the Poles.

Britain, it is suggested, was even more to blame than the French for the "phoney war."

After eight months there were still many hundreds of unemployed as well as many hundreds of thousands of young men duly registered for military service still waiting to be given anything to do.

The war did not begin for us, Mr. Soloveytchik says, until Hitler invaded Scandinavia (April, 1940).

It took the tragedies of a defeat in Norway, the invasion of the Low Countries and a ghastly break-through to the Channel ports before a change of government became possible, and with it a much speedier adaptation of the nation to the life-and-death struggle in which it had become engaged.

This did not save us, however, from the consequences of allowing the British Empire to become "the greatest collection of unprotected loot in the world."

This is the heavy indictment Mr. Soloveytchik brings against the rulers of his adopted country during the past twenty-five years or so. He does not bring it for the sake of raking up old muddles and blunders and crimes. His book, *Peace or Chaos?* (Macdonald, 10/6) is designed to show how Britain shook herself free of Baldwinism and Chamberlainism, stood alone against fearful odds for a year, and has since redeemed the reputation of our race for obstinate, unbeatable opposition to tyranny. It is a plea for British leadership of the most vigorous and enlightened kind after the war.

Mr. Soloveytchik was born in Russia. He came to this country 25 years ago and took up British citizenship. He can therefore speak of himself as "one of us," yet at the same time he can look at our history with detachment and our problems with the perspicacity of a looker-on who has seen more of the game than the players who were engaged in it. At times he shows that he has not quite assimilated the British point of view. For example, he says on page 212:

Our case is the greatest case there ever was. A cynic might say that in being forced to take up arms we had greatness thrust upon us, while the idealist would argue that we are fighting to protect freedom and democracy. There is a modicum of truth in both these views.

On Page 215 he accuses those who claim that Britain is fighting "solely for the common good" of "cant, sanctimoniousness and defeatism," and states roundly that "every single one of the United Nations is at war because it has been constrained by direct or indirect attack to fight for survival."

I do not remember hearing anyone claim that we were altogether disinterested when we decided to intervene in the affairs of Europe and to defend Poland and Rumania against the Nazi menace. That isn't the sort of thing Britons are in the habit of saying. Nor do I think it could be successfully argued that we intervened because we

War's Aftermath: Peace or Chaos?

were directly threatened. Hitler, in fact, wanted to come to an agreement with us and it is on record that Mr. Chamberlain's "dearest wish" was to reach such agreement. In the hope of doing so he abandoned the Czechs. Only when it appeared that other nations one after the other would have to be abandoned did he bow before the rush of public feeling and warn Hitler that he must reckon with us if he tried to treat others as he had treated the Czechs. It was, therefore, for the sake of weaker peoples that we declared our readiness to take up arms, and in writing that I cannot feel guilty of defeatism, sanctimoniousness or cant.

NOR does it seem fair to blame "our paranoiacs" for wanting to group together various small nations for purposes of defence, or "our Press" for saying that the small States were really responsible for the war, that their squabbles and economic nationalism were at the root of the crisis, that they remained neutral far too long, and could not defend themselves when invaded. Such a line has not been taken by any section of the British Press that carries much weight. That Holland and Belgium did make things more difficult for us at the beginning of the war is undeniable. The insensate belief of their

HITLER PLASTERED, as to the back of his left hand, after the bomb attempt on his life reported on July 20, 1944. He is seen here at his Berlin headquarters with Goering, who arrived shortly after the incident, which was generally regarded as the first real crack in the German structure. On the left is Admiral Doenitz. PAGE 211 · *Photo, News Chronicle*

rulers in the possibility of remaining outside the struggle was a positive hindrance to us. But we have not reproached them, we have on the contrary treated them as if from the first they had been at one with us.

However, it is the future more than the past that matters most. Let us see what Mr. Soloveytchik proposes British leadership should aim at. Chiefly, of course, the prevention of a Third World War, for which Germany's military leaders are believed to be making plans already. But here he creates for himself a difficulty. He believes that "in every State there exists an inherent tendency to expansion."

Indeed, I believe that it would be quite as legitimate to talk of the State's "instinct of expansion" as it is to talk of the individual's instinct of reproduction.

If that is so, then how can we hope to check the German tendency to expand? In the face of so imperious an instinct, what is the use of setting up obstacles that nationalism will sweep away?

The truth seems to me to lie in another direction. What Mr. Soloveytchik calls an instinct I should call a delusion, created and fostered by politicians, journalists, philosophers, and other people who have nothing better to do than increase their importance by appearing as "national leaders" and making their nations believe they can make themselves happier and richer by dominating and oppressing other nations. The Swiss have never suffered from this delusion. The Scandinavians have not shown any symptoms of possessing such an "instinct" since the time of Charles the Twelfth. And those are nations which Mr. Soloveytchik singles out for special commendation.

In his plans for keeping the Germans in order he drops his theory and gets down to facts. Instinct or no instinct, they have got to be shown that the rest of the world does not mean to let them disturb its peace any longer. They have been disturbing it since 1859, when Bismarck was the arch-deluder, noisily supported by politicians, professors and pen-men. Hitler is merely a caricature of Bismarck. The policy, the ambitions, have been the same ever since then. The rest of the world could have stopped that policy, could have snuffed out that ambition, if it had enjoyed clear vision instead of seeing through a glass darkly. Now the job has to be done thoroughly, and it is more difficult now than it would have been thirty years ago, when Page, American Ambassador in London, was astonished that it had not been tackled already.

ONE of Mr. Soloveytchik's ideas clashes with what Mr. Churchill has said more than once with emphasis. This is the idea that Germany should be forcibly divided up into small States. It must be dismissed, therefore, as outside the range of possibility. With the suggestion that we should do what the Germans have long and falsely accused us of doing—encircle the Reich—there will be widespread sympathy. The author wisely pours scorn on the notion that it should be "invaded by an army of no doubt well-meaning English-speaking schoolmarms, tutors, padres, quakers, Y.M.C.A. workers, missionaries, and other vegetarians," who would "re-educate" the Germans.

But there ought to be, he says, strict frontier supervision, so that the immense imports of iron, copper, bauxite, fats, oil, petrol, and a whole series of other raw materials essential to rearmament, which were allowed to flow in between 1933 when Hitler secured power and 1939 when he made war, shall be made impossible. That will be generally approved also. But not everybody will agree with the writer and Dr. Goebbels, from whom he quotes the sentiment, that in making peace it is power and not morality that counts. Is not that the very sentiment we are fighting against?

The Japanese are being Driven out of Manipur

AFTER CLEARING THE ENEMY from the 45 miles long Imphal-Kohima road on the Burma-Manipur front, which they achieved by June 25, 1944, British and Indian troops despite monsoon weather pressed on against the Japanese in that region.

Behind tanks, British and Gurkhas move up (1); tumbled hills in the background indicate the difficult terrain with which they have to cope. The monsoon wind, sweeping over a flooded R.A.F. airfield, picked up this plane and turned it over; ground staff and a mobile crane undertook to set it right again (2). In dense elephant grass Japanese snipers lie hidden; covered by a Bren gun British troops stalk them (3). Awaiting their turn to go into action are these Gurkhas (4); behind are transport planes which will take them and supplies to the fighting line.

Photos, British Official: Crown Copyright; Indian Official.

How Freed France Kept Bastille Day in 1944

ANNIVERSARY of the Fall of the Bastille which, 155 years ago, heralded the death of a former tyranny and birth of a new France, was celebrated in appropriate manner on July 14, 1944, in French towns and villages liberated by the Allies. In Bayeux, cleared of the Germans on June 6, Allied troops and civilians paraded before the 1914-18 war memorial (1). At Courseulles, one of the first villages to be freed, a French child placed a wreath on the grave of a British soldier who fell in the early hours of D-Day (2). A military band grouped before the flag-draped war memorial at St. Ouen de Rots (3). U.S. soldiers danced with the French in Cherbourg (4). With simple ceremony the great anniversary was marked amidst the ruins of La Haye du Puits (5).

Catapults give R.A.F. Pilots a Flying Start

Ships that carry an aeroplane as part of their normal equipment haven't the deck space to provide a runway for the plane to take off under its own power. The answer to that conundrum is the catapult device which launches plane and pilot into the air at 55 miles an hour from the stationary position. HARRIMAN DICKSON has visited a training school for these pilots.

THE day I crossed the ferry to visit the R.A.F. station where they train catapult pilots, there was a choppy sea and a sharp wind blowing. Ships of all kinds lay at anchor, slatternly tugs, broad merchant ships and a sprinkling of warships. One at least among them had a strange-looking apparatus fitted across her decks. I was destined to see a larger version of this device in operation.

I approached it via a tunnel, part of an old fort which, centuries ago, had protected this part of Britain from invasion. I came out of the tunnel, and there was the giant trellis-work of steel lying across its concrete base like the huge skeleton of some prehistoric monster. This is the device which three years ago put a spoke in the U-boat's wheel and made the attacks of German long-range bombers a very hazardous business. In those days the battle of the seas was the most vital battle of all, and ships far out in the Atlantic had no protection against prowling German bombers capable of flying long distances without refuelling. Then catapults were fitted to hundreds of ships. R.A.F. pilots became part of the crew, and high-speed fighters were punched into the air from a small deck space whenever an attack threatened. Many of the pilots who volunteered for this dangerous work were trained at the catapult centre I visited. I watched the whole process while I was there.

Despite its weight and proportions, the catapult was so perfectly balanced on its spindle that it could be swung into the wind by one or two men without any great effort. The whole thing was not unlike an enlarged and carefully corrected version of the schoolboy's catapult. I watched a plane trundle towards the giant crane standing beside the catapult. The pilot remained in the plane while the grapples of the crane were fitted into position and plane and pilot were hoisted into the air, swung gently across, and dropped down on to the superstructure of the catapult, a framework of steel legs designed to carry the weight of the plane and distribute it evenly. Below the framework of legs, and within the main steel trellis, were three massive rams, which gave the plane its drive, each ram taking up the impulse from the last and finally conveying it to the plane. The latest catapults used on our merchant ships work upon a similar principle.

THE Direction Officer of the training school waited until the plane was in position, then walked over to examine the catapulting charge, something like a seven-pounder shell, but filled with cordite instead of high explosive. A nod from him and the armourer inserted the charge into the breech just as though he were loading a gun.

Above their heads, the pilot glanced over his controls and then waved his arm to the Direction Officer. Already various flags had conveyed a variety of signals to and from the catapult crew, and all was ready for the firing of the shell. It is a tense moment for a pilot about to make his first trial catapult take-off. He doesn't quite know what to expect.

The arm of the D.O. fell, the armourer

"FLYING FLOSSIE" is the name given to this boat-shaped, water-filled steel tank on wheels used in testing plane catapults as explained in this page. Here it is "in flight," doing 70 miles per hour.
Photos, British Official: Crown Copyright

pulled a wire lanyard. But there was no deafening explosion. Instead, the metal rams suddenly leapt to life, the whole framework of legs shot forward and at a certain point automatically collapsed, leaving the plane in the air. It had been whisked from a standstill to 55 miles an hour, and another first-time flight from the catapult apparatus was successfully completed.

THE trial process does not end at this school. To make the catapults foolproof, the Fleet Air Arm uses an interesting device nicknamed "Flying Flossie." It consists of a boat-shaped steel tank on wheels, without motor, wings or propeller. The tank is filled with water until it equals the weight of the type of plane about to be flown, and then it is fitted to the catapult and flung into the air. It travels at a speed of about seventy miles an hour, and after a short flight crashes into the sea, where it is later recovered by a tug.

With the pilots trained and the "operations" catapult proven, serious work begins. On board a variety of ships the catapult pilots have already played a vital part in defeating attacks on our convoys, spotting for battleships, and reconnoitring enemy positions. The life of the catapult pilot is distinctly more hazardous than that of the normal Fleet Air Arm pilot, because he has no aircraft carrier's deck waiting his return. In the case of merchant ships, the pilot, once he has taken off and dealt with any attacker, has the choice of these alternatives: he can make for the nearest land, or he can risk a landing in the sea and there wait for his ship to pick him up.

ON one occasion, miles off Iceland, a pilot was catapulted from the deck of his ship to tackle an approaching bomber. Cloud and poor visibility made his job difficult, but once the bomber sighted him it beat a hasty retreat. Then the pilot turned to find his own ship again, and there was just a grey waste of water with no sign of mast or rigging, and not even a puff of smoke. He knew his position in relation to Iceland, and from his petrol gauge estimated that he might just make it. He set his course accordingly, and finally crash-landed with an empty petrol tank. From there he returned to England by flying boat, and within a very short time was on the high seas again, had warning of an approaching bomber, and was catapulted away once more. This time he shot the bomber into the sea.

GOING ABOARD THE PARENT SHIP and being replaced on the launching catapult by means of a dock crane is this Hurricane fighter, after alighting on the sea. The idea of catapulting aircraft from merchant ships was suggested by Mr. Churchill in 1941, although the Navy had used the method in warships long before. Cata-fighters belong to the M.S.F.U. (Merchant Ship Fighter Unit); vessels are known as C.A.M. ships—Catapult Aircraft Merchantmen. 　　　PAGE 214

Spitfire Cameras in Action High Over Normandy

PHOTOGRAPHIC RECONNAISSANCE is the speciality of one of the newest members of the famous fighting Spitfire family—the long-range Mark XI; there are three versions, powered respectively by the Rolls-Royce Merlin 61, 63, and 63a engine, which gives a maximum output of more than 1,650 h.p. Providing for great range, extra fuel tanks, additional to the two main tanks in the fuselage, are fitted in the leading edges of the wings—in the space usually occupied by guns. The plane has a span of 36 ft. 10 ins. and is just over 36 ft. long.

Men who fly these Spitfires belong to the R.A.F. Photographic Reconnaissance Unit, which had its origin in a special flight formed in October 1939 from remnants of a peacetime survey unit. First Spitfire was used for reconnaissance in April 1940, when Kiel was photographed.

A Spitfire Mark XI above the clouds, about to dive down to take its pictures (1). Into its dive (2), its terrific speed (to date undisclosed) carries it through "enemy action." A fitter mounts the camera (3) which, electrically operated, can take 500 pictures, photographed horizontally or obliquely. After a flight, pilots are interrogated (4). Leaning on the wing of a plane P.R.U. men examine their pictures (5).

Photo "recce" pilots helped the planners of our invasion of Europe by producing minute-detail photographs of the territory over which the Allies would fight. Not an inch of a 3,000-mile coastline was neglected, and from nearly half a million photographs experts pieced together the mosaic.

Photos, British Official, Chas. E. Brown, Fox

New Awards Raise this War's V.C. Roll to 93

Temp. Lt.-Col. H. R. B. FOOTE, D.S.O.
Of the Royal Tank Regiment, Royal Armoured Corps, Lt.-Col. Foote (left) gained the Victoria Cross in Libya during the period May 27 to June 15, 1942. In one action, his own tank knocked out, he changed to another and, although wounded, continued to lead his battalion. The second tank disabled, he continued on foot under intense fire. By his brilliant leadership he defeated a German attempt to encircle two British divisions.

Major C. F. HOEY, M.C.
On Feb. 16, 1944, in the Ngakyedauk Pass in Arakan, Burma, Major Hoey (right) of the Lincolnshire Regt., badly wounded, rushed an enemy strong post, killing the occupants before he himself fell. He was awarded the V.C.

Actg. Naik NAND SINGH
Of the 11th Sikh Regt., Indian Army, Naik Singh (below) won the V.C. in Burma on March 12, 1944. Crawling up a steep, knife-edged ridge under heavy fire, with the bayonet alone, and wounded, he took three Japanese trenches single-handed, killing seven of the enemy.

Pilot Officer C. J. BARTON, R.A.F.V.R.
Posthumously awarded the V.C. for conspicuous bravery in a raid on Nuremberg on March 30, 1944, Pilot Officer Barton (above) took his crippled Halifax to the appointed target. On the return journey, with only one engine working, he crashed in attempting to avoid houses in England.

Temp. Captain R. WAKEFORD
In the Cassino fighting in Italy, on May 13, 1944, Capt. Wakeford (above) of the Hampshire Regt., accompanied only by his orderly, killed a number of the enemy and took 20 prisoners. Later, seriously wounded, he consolidated another position. For selfless devotion to duty he won the V.C.

Major J. K. MAHONY
Of the Westminster Regt. (Motor), Canadian Army, Major Mahony (above) during the establishment of a vital bridge-head across a river in Italy, and in the face of determined enemy attack, on May 24, 1944, showed great courage, exposing himself wherever danger threatened until all enemy attempts to destroy the bridge-head had failed. This action gained him the V.C.

Fusilier F. A. JEFFERSON
In an attack on the Gustav Line in Italy on May 16, 1944, Fusilier Jefferson of the Lancashire Fusiliers (above) destroyed with a Piat Projector a German tank threatening an important position. His action, for which he won the V.C., saved his company and broke the enemy counter-attack.

Photos, British Official, "Daily Mirror," G.P.U., Planet News

I WAS THERE! Eye Witness Stories of the War

How We Ran the Blockade in the Gay Corsair

Captain Robert Tanton, O.B.E., Merchant Navy skipper, has told to a News Chronicle reporter the part his little ship the Gay Corsair has played in bringing to Britain tons of invaluable war materials available only in Sweden —sailing defiantly from an East Coast port, past German planes and E-boats and over minefields into a blockaded Swedish harbour. See also p. 206.

MORE exciting than the Malta convoy run, in a way, this blockade running. I was a first officer then with Ellerman's Wilson Line. I was sent for and asked if I would like to volunteer for a special job. I volunteered. Next morning I had been promoted to captain, and five of us met in a private room in the owners' office. There we were briefed. They told us we had to get through to Sweden. Our route ran straight across the thickest minefields.

We slipped out of the Humber in convoy. A few hours later we had engine trouble, and when the trip really began we were all alone in the North Sea. The Gay Corsair was only 125 ft. long. There was no comfort aboard, and we all knew that we should be on constant alert all the way across.

We flew our Red Ensign all the time and the pictures of Drake and Mr. Churchill we had aboard gave us a feeling of adventure. The boys were ready for the whole German shooting match. It was daylight when we left England, and nearing dusk when we reached the Skager-rak. Then we crowded on all our speed—and it was plenty. We just shot through the sea.

There were plenty of floating mines in front of us, but the look-outs gave up watching them after a bit. Our bow wave was pushing ahead of us, and we simply drove at full speed right through the mines. The wash we threw up carried them past our bows.

The Skager-rak was the worst part of the voyage. A German patrol plane spotted us and our gunners went into action with their Oerlikons. The German turned away and disappeared. It was very cold and very wet, and we were weary. Our look-outs spotted German patrol ships and the Germans saw us, but the engineers poured on everything, and we slipped by the E-boats without action.

We were pleased with ourselves, of course. As we entered the little Swedish harbour there was the German consul standing on the pier. He was glaring at us, but my boys weren't worried. I must say that they were not very polite. They greeted the consul with—well, like British sailors greeting a German consul —you can imagine !

Captain ROBERT TANTON, O.B.E., commander of the Gay Corsair (story on the left). Scorning the difficulties of the enterprise he declared, " If one can get through, two can ! " —a neat " play " on the ship's badge, a toucan (bottom). *Photos, News Chronicle*

I Dodged the Germans for Five Weeks in Caen

A Lancaster bomber pilot from London, Squadron Leader E. Sprawson, D.F.C., wearing patched blue overalls and a dirty scarf, told a Reuter correspondent of his adventurous introduction to the old Norman city and of his five weeks' sojourn there with friendly French civilians before British troops arrived and threw the Germans out.

I WAS shot down by a fighter over Caen on D-Day. Five of us baled out— I don't know if the two gunners made it or not. French civilians who had just got out of the centre of Caen to avoid bombing happened to be in the field where I landed. They had me out of uniform into these clothes within 20 minutes of my landing. They are very brave people with plenty of guts and determination. They had realised what would happen if I was caught —I would be taken prisoner and they would be shot for hiding me. We went back into their house in the town and they treated me as a member of the family.

I had no rations, so they insisted on sharing theirs with me. We were lucky and lived on the produce from a little allotment, the milk from a couple of cows and the very limited rations distributed daily to the townspeople. I got two square meals a day. My chief worry was to know what to do. Allied broadcasts advised us to evacuate the town, but I could see myself trickling into Switzerland by about 1946 and decided to stay where I was in the hope that our troops would arrive before long.

Another idea was to move into open country out of the way of concentrated bombing and shelling. But being British and individual, I thought I would have much more trouble concealing my identity. There was only one really bad bombing. I was right in the middle of it. I walked through Caen twice when it was full of Germans.

Though I speak French and could make myself understood I could never have passed myself as a Frenchman. Last night when we were in the cellar of the house in Rue de Moulin, jutting on to the main thoroughfare of Boulevard Des Allies, a great deal of scuttling about by the Germans took place. They had lots of armed patrols slinking along the streets while the crowd jostled south.

For the last fortnight civilians in Caen have been living for this day. We heard you were two miles away, and then one mile But there was still no sign until this morning. A 12-year-old boy rushed in to me and said very excitedly, " Here are the Allies ! " I went out and saw a British sergeant. I told him I was British, but it was difficult for him to believe me. I showed him my identification papers and told him to put me under arrest if he had any doubts. He put me in the charge of an officer who took me to the colonel of the regiment.

My friends in Caen had spread the tale that I was a Frenchman who had lost everything and was so shocked that I was unable to speak. Until this morning other French civilians with whom I had come in contact daily did not know I was English. There were collaborationists about who would have reported me at once if they had heard me talk.

Most of the French in Caen were definitely for us. They realised that the bombing was necessary, and were determined to accept it as worthwhile, although after some of the heaviest raids it is understandable they would occasionally let slip a few nasty things. And now I am longing to be in uniform again and have another smack at Jerry.

JAMES CONWAY (right), burly motor mechanic of the Gay Corsair, with other members of the crew. The little ship is only about 125 feet in length but is highly powered. See story above. *Photo, Keystone*

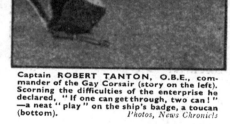

Squadron-Leader E. SPRAWSON, D.F.C., aged 33, was commissioned in the R.A.F. in 1934. He was awarded the D.F.C. on June 16, 1944, " for achievements worthy of the greatest praise " during many sorties over Germany. His latest adventure is related by himself in this page. *Photo, Evening Standard*

We Shelled German Targets at 11 Miles Range

There is at least one German who can vouch for the accuracy of the guns of the cruiser H.M.S. Arethusa during the bombardment of Normandy. This unfortunate Hun was perched on the top of a chimney stack in a factory area acting as spotter for the shore batteries. The story is told by the Arethusa's gunnery officer, Lieut.-Commander H. T. Burchell, D.S.C.

H.M.S. ARETHUSA, 5,220-ton cruiser, the story of whose bombardment of the Normandy coast is told here by her gunnery officer. Here seen at Malta before the war, she is armed with six 6-in., eight 4-in A.A., two 3-pounder guns, and six 21-in. torpedo tubes. *Photo, Fox*

I WOULDN'T have had his job for all the tea in China. We were nearly ten miles out, but we managed to get within about 25 yards of the chimney although we didn't actually hit it. We started a couple of large fires and we heard later that the chimney had been destroyed by our aircraft.

We were at the head of the column of bombarding battleships and cruisers, and our position was on the eastern flank. Our original target was a shore battery, but hardly had we commenced firing when a number of enemy destroyers came out of Le Havre and opened up on us. We switched our fire on them and they scuttled back to harbour without causing any trouble. We then returned to our original target and put it out of action.

Forward observers ashore sent back positions of targets which varied from the gentleman on the chimney to tanks, lorries, infantry and gun batteries. We also had a crack at a chateau which was being used as enemy headquarters. We were eleven miles out, but got at least three direct hits. The chaps ashore were very pleased with our shooting and one Brigadier signalled that we had broken up three counter-attacks on his troops. In all we got rid of 2,282 rounds of ammunition.

We were attacked many times by enemy aircraft at night, but were not hit. You would have thought that with all those thousands of ships lying offshore they couldn't have missed, but they did. We had two near misses, and that was all.

In a Burning Plane I Crashed in Yugoslavia

In some thousands of sorties to Yugoslavia there has been only one accident. It happened on the night of July 16, 1944, when a transport plane carrying personnel stalled above its goal and crashed from 400 feet. Among the survivors were Major Randolph Churchill, attached to the staff of the Maclean Mission to the National Liberation Movement, and Philip Jordan, war correspondent for Combined Press, who here relates the adventure.

WE are all being looked after with the greatest kindness and enthusiasm in various partisan hospitals and billets here, but the fact that in the fifteen hours we have so far been here it has been impossible for our generous hosts to attend and provide dressings for any but the seriously burned or fractured is some testimony to the grave shortage of medical supplies from which the army still suffers.

Our own medical supplies, along with everything we possessed, except the clothes which remain with us, were consumed in the fire. Our perished crew was drawn from Australia, Canada, South Africa and Britain. Our failure was a double tragedy, for there was no return journey for the wounded partisans who were waiting so patiently for us in the fields.

Nothing that I know is more forlorn than this corrugated country when you fly over it in the dark night. Once the last faint shimmer of Adriatic waters has gone it is as though the world has gone also, and you were in a void with neither purpose nor direction. The stars went out; the new moon had not risen. Even our wings were not visible except when summer lightning gave them substance. The only lights were sparks from exhausts which flew past like tracers. Once we flew over a road convoy,

a row of moving lights that went out as we approached.

When the end came it came slowly. Far below us like an inverted constellation seen in an amber mirror, our own strip came suddenly to view. We saw the safety flare exchange recognition signals and then we went down in steep and steady spirals. Until we were within 400 feet all was well. It was dark when we hit the ground, but when those of us who were lucky enough to regain consciousness two minutes later opened our eyes the aircraft was illuminated by what seemed thousands of little candles, for the flames were burning from one end to the other, flicking in through every split joint.

There had been darkness and cold, but now there was infinite light. It was no more reality than the transformation scene in a pantomime. It was enchanting until I realised that my own hair was one of the candles and that the fallen jack was across my body making movement difficult. When we "put ourselves out" and went to the door it would not open, but they say we squeezed out between it and the aircraft's body.

Later when we had forced the door others walked or were carried out, but they could not get them all. A young British signaller from the North Country and a partisan were noted to have been searching for bodies in the flaming plane. Then all the Verey lights in the plane went off, and it collapsed.

I don't believe we quite knew what had happened. Maybe we don't know yet, for none of us has any sense of tragedy or destruction even though men we knew and liked and respected and one partisan girl were incinerated beside us. Maybe we haven't yet had time to feel anything but physical things, and they have hardly begun yet except for those who are badly hurt.

GERMAN PARACHUTE TROOPS drop during their abortive attempt to capture the Bosnian headquarters of Marshal Tito on May 25, 1944. Marshal Tito and Allied officers attached to his staff, including Major Randolph Churchill, the Prime Minister's son, had escaped into the mountains an hour before. A later adventure is related in this page. *Photo, Keystone*

Our Unwanted Cargo was an Unexploded Mine

After Landing Craft Tank 513 had touched down on the Normandy coast and her cargo of troops and vehicles had gone ashore her Commanding Officer, Lieut. D. S. Hawkey, R.N.V.R., discovered that there was every possibility of the craft being blown sky-high during the return trip.

I THOUGHT we had cleared the beach obstacles, but when we left I found one of the mines attached to the obstacles had become caught in our landing ramp. It was firmly lodged, and although it hadn't exploded it was liable to do so as soon as anything touched the detonator. My First Lieutenant, Sub-Lieutenant B. D. Davis, R.N.V.R., of Norbury, wanted to go for'ard and cut it loose, but I didn't think it advisable.

We came all the way back across the Channel with this mine stuck in our bows, and we couldn't lose it. I decided I couldn't enter harbour with it still there, so we tried to get rid of it. We rigged a wire from the ramp to the capstan with the idea of shaking the mine loose as we ran the ramp into the swell. I cleared the upper deck, and the party needed for working the capstan got under cover. I was standing on the bridge keeping well down, and giving orders to the capstan crew through the loud-hailer.

Unfortunately, we heaved in a bit too hard, and instead of shaking the mine loose we pulled it inboard. By a stroke of luck it fell sideways and the detonator was knocked off without exploding it. No time was wasted in throwing the mine over the side.

On our next trip we were left behind by the remainder of the flotilla when we developed engine trouble, and we lost sight of them before the engines were repaired. As soon as the engines were running I tried to catch up with the remainder of the flotilla, but I didn't see them even when we reached the beaches. I discovered later that they had had a spot of bother with some E-boats and I had passed out of sight of them.

After we had unloaded we towed back another landing craft that had been damaged. The weather was very bad—the worst known in the Channel for years—and as we had to tow the other craft alongside us, we sustained some minor damage. We reached port safely and underwent repairs. When we rejoined the flotilla I found we had been reported as missing, as the flotilla had lost touch with us after the engine trouble.

SALVAGE FEAT EXTRAORDINARY was performed by one of our L.C.T.s (Landing Craft Tanks) which, broken completely in two, returned to a southern port in Britain in the manner shown above. The stern half of the vessel, containing the engine, took the bow half in tow and thus brought herself home!
Photo, British Newspaper Pool

OUR DIARY OF THE WAR

JULY 19, Wednesday　　1,782nd day
Western Front.—Faubourg de Vaucelles, Caen, captured by British 2nd Army.
Air.—U.S bombers attacked aircraft and chemical works in S. and S.W. Germany. R.A.F. bombed flying-bomb storage depot at Thiverny, near Paris.
Mediterranean.—Allied heavy bombers attacked factories in Munich area.
Italy.—U.S. troops entered the port of Leghorn.
Japan.—New Japanese cabinet formed under Gen. Koiso and Adm. Yonai, following resignation of Tojo and entire cabinet.

JULY 20, Thursday　　1,783rd day
Western Front.—2nd Army widened corridor in German front east of the Orne.
Air.—U.S. bombers from Britain and Mediterranean attacked German aircraft factories and oil plants. R.A.F. bombed rocket-site in northern France.
Russian Front.—In new offensive from Kovel, Russians made 90-mile breach in German defences.
Pacific.—U.S. forces landed on Guam in the Marianas.
Germany.—Announced that attempt on Hitler's life had been made by group of Army officers ; Himmler appointed C.-in-C. of Home Army.

JULY 21, Friday　　1,784th day
Air.—U.S. bombers from Britain and Italy again attacked aircraft and ball-bearing factories in S. Germany.
Russian Front.—Ostrov, near Latvian border, captured by Red Army.
General.—Gen. Stuelpnagel, German commander in occupied France, injured in attack by French patriots.

JULY 22, Saturday　　1,785th day
Western Front.—Allies resumed attack on the Orne front.
Air.—R.A.F. attacked flying-bomb sites in N. France.
Russian Front.—Kholm, inside 1939 Polish frontier, stormed by Red Army. Ponevezh on Dvinsk-Kaunas railway also captured.

JULY 23, Sunday　　1,786th day
Mediterranean.—Ploesti oil installations bombed by Allied aircraft.
Germany.—Hitler issued Order of the Day to Army stating that " traitor clique " had been wiped out.

JULY 24, Monday　　1,787th day
Western Front.—Announced that Mr.

Churchill had made three-day tour of Normandy.
Air.—R.A.F. made very heavy night attack on Kiel.
Russian Front.—Pskov, near Lake Peipus, captured by Russians ; street fighting in Lublin.
Italy.—U.S. troops reached outskirts of Pisa.
Pacific.—U.S. troops established beachhead on Tinian Island, Marianas.
General.—Moscow announced formation at Kholm of Polish Committee of National Liberation. H.M. King George VI arrived in Italy to visit the forces.

JULY 25, Tuesday　　1,788th day
Air.—R.A.F. made very heavy night attack on Stuttgart.
Russian Front.—Lublin, railway junction S.E. of Warsaw, captured by Soviet troops.
Germany.—Nazi salute to replace military salute in all ranks of German army.
Western Front.—British 2nd Army began attack astride Falaise road S. of Caen ; U.S. troops attacked W. of St. Lo.
Air.—R.A.F. dropped 12,000-lb. bombs on rocket site at Watten, Pas de Calais. Another heavy night attack on Stuttgart.
Russian Front.—Soviet troops completed encirclement of Lvov. U.S. fighter

aircraft attacked airfields in Poland from Russian bases.
Mediterranean.—Allied bombers attacked tank works at Linz, Austria.
Pacific.—Allied warships and aircraft of Eastern Fleet bombarded harbour of Sabang, Sumatra.
Germany.—Goering and Goebbels appointed to organize total mobilization in Germany.

JULY 26, Wednesday　　1,789th day
Western Front.—U.S. armoured columns reached St. Giles and Marigny, W. of St. Lo.
Air.—R.A.F. bombers attacked railway junction at Givors, S. of Lyons. Mosquitoes bombed Hamburg.
Russian Front.—Narva, Estonian border town, and Deblin on the Vistula, captured by Soviet troops ; Tilsit, East Prussia, bombed by Russian aircraft.
Mediterranean.—Allied heavy bombers attacked military installations in Vienna area. U.S fighters returned to Italy from Russia, bombing Rumanian bases on the way.

JULY 27, Thursday　　1,790th day
Western Front.—Strong counter-attacks against Allied advance S. of Caen.
Russian Front.—Dvinsk and Rezeknes (Latvia), Siauliai (Lithuania), Lvov, Bialy-

stok and Stanislavov captured by Soviet troops.
Air.—Radio and electrical factories in Belgium attacked by U.S. bombers. R.A.F. bombed flying-bomb sites.
General.—Soviet Government signed agreement with Polish Committee of National Liberation.

JULY 28, Friday　　1,791st day
Western Front.—Coutances cleared of the enemy by Allied armoured columns.
Russian Front.—Brest Litovsk, Yaroslav and Przemysl captured by Red Army.
Air.—U.S. bombers attacked Leuna oil plant at Merseburg. R.A.F. bombed supply depots for flying bombs and made night attacks on Stuttgart and Hamburg.
Mediterranean.—Allied heavy bombers attacked Ploesti oil installations.

JULY 29, Saturday　　1,792nd day
Air.—U.S. bombers again attacked Leuna oil plant. R.A.F. bombed rocket supply depot near Watten. Mosquitoes bombed Frankfurt by night.
Russian Front.—Soviet troops reached Jelgava (Mitua), 22 miles from Riga.
Far East.—U.S. Super - Fortresses bombed steel centre of Anshan, Mukden and Tangku, port of Tientsin.
Balkans.—Allied land, sea and air forces raided Himara, on coast of Albania.

JULY 30, Sunday　　1,793rd day
Western Front.—British 2nd Army launched attack pivoting on Caumont.
Russian Front.—Soviet troops broke through towards E. Prussia from bridgeheads west of the Niemen.
Italy.—Eighth Army closed in on Florence.
Mediterranean.—Allied bombers attacked airfield and aircraft works near Budapest.

JULY 31, Monday　　1,794th day
Western Front.—Avranches occupied by U.S. armoured columns.
Air.—Munich and Ludwigshaven areas attacked by more than 1,200 U.S. bombers. R.A.F. bombed flying-bomb supply depot and railway junction at La Roche.
Russian Front.—Soviet forces captured Jelgava (Mitau), Latvia. Street-fighting in Kaunas, Lithuania. Siedice, east of Warsaw, captured by Red Army.
Mediterranean.—Allied bombers attacked oil plants at Ploesti and Bucharest.
Pacific.—New Allied landings at Sansapor, in Dutch New Guinea.
General.—Adm. Sir Bruce Fraser appointed C.-in-C. Eastern Fleet in succession to Adm. Sir James Somerville.

★ ════════ *Flash-backs* ════════ ★

1940
July 23. *Provisional Czechoslovak Government formed in London, recognized by Britain.*
July 30. *Demobilization of French North African and Syrian armies announced.*

1941
July 20. *Stalin became People's Commissar for Defence of the Soviet Union.*
July 30. *U.S.S.R.-Polish agreement signed in London ; Polish army to be formed in Russia.*

August 1. *Diplomatic relations between Britain and Finland were broken off.*

1942
July 20. *Russians captured bridgeheads at Voronezh on Don.*

1943
July 19. *Marshalling yards at Rome bombed by U.S. aircraft.*
July 21. *National Committee of Free Germany formed in Russia.*
July 22. *Palermo, Sicily, captured by Allied forces.*
July 25. *Mussolini resigned ; Badoglio became Prime Minister.*

THUNDERBOLT FIGHTER-BOMBER, undercarriage wheels about to fold flush with the wings, roars into the cloud-flecked sky above Normandy and on to attack a target. A U.S. aircraft, it is carrying two 250 lb. bombs slung beneath each wing and an auxiliary petrol tank under the fuselage. Armed with eight 0.5 in. machine-guns, the Thunderbolt has a wing-span of 41 ft., length of 32 ft. 8 in., speed of 400 m.p.h. *Photo, Associated Press*

THE WAR IN THE AIR

by Capt. Norman Macmillan, M.C., A.F.C.

FIFTEEN hundred miles south-west of Wake Island and 1,600 miles east of Manila in the Philippine Islands lies Guam, the southernmost island of the Marianas group, and one of the stepping stones across the great Pacific Ocean. Before the war Guam was one of the stopping places for the China Clippers of Pan-American Airways on the San Francisco–Philippines–Hong-Kong route. Indeed, it was the last stop before reaching the Philippines. That was its importance then, as now. It became an American possession in 1898, during the war between the United States and Spain. For America it became a naval station. This island, 32 miles long and ten wide at the widest part, had a pre-war population of about 21,000, mostly Chamorro, one of the Malayan families. Fewer than 1,000 non-natives lived there normally. Its interior is jungle, with savanna, sword grass, and liana-hung trails. Its highest hill is 1,334 feet high. (*See* map p. 167.)

This island of 206 square miles received a 17 days' naval and air bombardment from an American task force prior to the landing made on July 20, 1944—with the support of carrier aircraft and surface combat units of the Fifth Fleet—by U.S. Marines and Army assault troops. The landing operations were directed by the naval officer who commanded the amphibious operations against Sicily. The landings were made on both sides of the five-miles peninsula of Orote which juts out from the west coast of the island. Wave after wave of dive-bombers added their power to the blast of shells that swept the Japanese positions. The Japanese cannot withstand this deadly dual form of bombardment.

SEA-AIR power has shown its effectiveness already in the Pacific. As the war against Japan proceeds to its inevitable end in the defeat for the first time of that predatory people, the employment of marine-air power will rise continually to ever-increasing fury. The configuration of Japan proper lends itself to attack by sea-borne aircraft—a long series of narrow islands running in a gentle crescent. But air power directed against Japan will not all be sea-borne, as the Boeing B-29's have already demonstrated. With the capture of Saipan and Tinian islands, and the imminent capture of Guam and Rota islands, the American forces will

hold the four southernmost islands of a chain which runs almost due north to Tokyo itself. The science of the construction of take-off points for aircraft has developed enormously during this war, and one of the most important features of military engineering is now the ability to construct air strips where before this war it would have been thought impossible to do so.

MOREOVER the increasing power of aircraft engines—which has risen since the war began from between 1,000 and 1,500 h.p. to a range that now reaches 3,000 h.p.— has made it possible to take off under conditions that would have been dangerous before. Even on rocky islands, or on tropical coral atolls, it is possible to make strip runways, and so get aircraft up and down. The innumerable islands of the Pacific Ocean in the area where the war against Japan is now raging provide a great number of fixed aircraft "carriers" whose value is to that huge war zone as was the value of Malta to the Mediterranean. The war in the Pacific is therefore still at the stage of a fight for the possession of fixed air bases, each new victory pushing forward the advanced landing fields towards the great combat areas where Japanese power will have to be defeated to overthrow Hirohito and his robber barons.

The Japanese have demonstrated how clever they are at maintaining communications, by running ships along the coast of China. Before their communications with Malaya and the Netherlands East Indies and the Philippines can be seriously cut, it will be necessary to move the air bases forward island by island and so provide air cover on a scale that will make even the air cover provided against the German submarine menace seem puny by comparison. Moreover, the rear areas will then still need air cover, and this is where the value of the islands now being captured will excel in strategical value to the Allies their previous use to Japan, for the Allied carrier task forces will penetrate into the inner hostile waters with a protective land-based air force in their rear.

As I see it, the sea-air war against Japan divides into two strategic zones—one contained within the area bounded by the Aleutians, Midway, the Gilberts, the Solo-

mons, New Guinea and the Philippines; and the other bounded by India, Australia, New Guinea and the Philippines. In each area the possession of the Philippines is the key. Every move made by the American naval and air forces under Admiral Nimitz points to the Philippines as the first great strategic objective, and the underlying strategy of General MacArthur is corroborative pressure towards a common goal. It is within the southern half of the first-named great area that air pressure has been most applied, and wherever its power has been used to aid the occupational forces the Japanese have been squeezed to destruction and defeat. The Japanese pre-war air development of the Palau islands provides a useful stepping stone on the way to Mindanao.

Meanwhile over Europe great air blows have been maintained against the German dominated Continent, both in the fighting fields and in the strategic zones lying within them where industry strives to produce the weapons for the enemy. Here I regret to have to mention that Warburton, the greatest of our photographic pilots, is posted missing.

THE work of the aircrews who undertake these tasks is arduous, dangerous, less spectacular, perhaps, than the fighting and bombing; but it is the basis of our air-war intelligence. Often these men have flown unarmed aircraft far into enemy territory to secure photographs, relying on the speed of their aircraft and the height at which they flew for safety. Not always did they return. One pilot I knew flew an unarmed Mosquito on a mission to the Salzburg area, and did not get back; he had made many flights before, passing over Europe almost as the airline pilots did before the war began; on that run over the Austrian Alps he was unlucky. (*See* illus. page 215.)

It is remarkable how front-line troops can withstand the terrible bombardments rained upon them from the air. Thousands of tons of bombs fall upon their defences. Yet our advance does not move swiftly forward afterwards. Why? I believe it is due to over-concentration of bombardment. We now bomb heavily only 2,000 yards from our own troops and in a concentrated enemy-held zone. Just outside that zone the enemy are as secure as our own troops. The science of bombing forward troops has advanced little from the last war except in weight of attack. In the interval the science of defence in depth has been developed. It seems that concentrated blast attack from the air must give place to an aerial adaptation of the creeping barrage of artillery.

Tedder's Carpet Laid Down on Western Front

ONCE GERMAN FORTIFIED POSITIONS near Sannerville, south of Caen, this carpet of craters was laid by R.A.F. Lancasters and Halifaxes preceding a British offensive in Normandy. Highly concentrated and astonishingly accurate bombing completely obliterated the defensive works. Bombs with slightly delayed action were used, so that the ground should be cratered so deeply as to be impassable by enemy armour—development of the famous technique associated with Air Chief Marshal Sir Arthur Tedder, G.C.B. (see p. 516, vol. 7). PAGE 221 *Photo, British Official*

Britain's Colonies in the War: No. 12—Gambia

LINKED WITH BRITAIN FOR OVER 350 YEARS, since 1588 when Queen Elizabeth granted a patent to English merchants to trade with the country, is Gambia in West Africa, which became a Colony in 1888. After this war had broken out—especially when from June 1940 to May 1943 the Mediterranean was closed to Allied shipping—Bathurst, capital of Gambia, gained importance as one of the stopping-places on the West African air transport routes.

Gambia, with an area of some 4,132 square miles and a population of 199,520 has several organizations to help the Allied effort, including the Gambian Women Workers, composed of Europeans and non-Europeans; during the early days of the Battle of the Atlantic these voluntarily assisted and cared for shipwrecked seamen; they also helped to equip Gambians serving in the Army. Volunteers for the Army, Navy and Merchant Navy have been many. Products useful to the war effort include vast quantities of ground nuts or monkey nuts (oil from which is used in the manufacture of margarine and soap) and rice, hides, rubber and wax.

Millet and rice are the staple food of the people, and the home-growing of these crops helps greatly towards easing difficulties arising from war-time reductions of other supplies; it also releases tons of valuable shipping space for other vital service in the cause of the United Nations.

TRANSPORT DIFFICULTIES ARE SURMOUNTED by employment of ox-drawn carts (1), and paired containers carried shoulder-wise (2); the latter are here filled with millet, one of the staple foods of the natives. A Gambian who qualified as radio operator in the Merchant Navy (3). From a gigantic mound of harvested ground nuts (5), bags weighing 90 lb. are carried up a precarious gangway to an ocean-going vessel moored at the very edge of Kuntaur, 150 miles up the Gambia River (4).

Photos, L. H. Saunders, G. McCormack, Sport & General

"WHEN will the War end?" was the pointblank question put to me by a friend one sultry afternoon recently when we sat down to tea at his country cottage after enjoying the excitement of watching a Tempest shoot down a flying bomb nearby on the Sussex weald. Although my main preoccupation since September 1939 has been the study of the War News, I should not venture an answer to such a question with the slightest belief that my opinion was more likely to be accurate than that of my barber, who had given me some astonishing information about pilotless planes which I knew to be amusingly wrong. But I could at least tell my friend with absolute confidence that the prophecies of the astrologers made in solemn conference at Harrogate towards the end of 1941 that the War would end in a victory for the Allies by January 31, 1942, did not fit in with the facts as I knew them! Indeed, one of the minor victories of the War has been its devastating exposure of these persons who used to make a profitable business of interpreting the secrets of the stars for the amazement of the credulous.

ONE of the most high-spirited women of my acquaintance is a lady of seventy-nine : the mother of five stalwart sons and four tall and elegant daughters! Her husband, a dear friend of mine, died in 1916, while all her sons nobly discharged their duties in the last War and came through it scatheless. She has been living in recent years in a flat in a North London suburb where, in the second week of the flying-bomb blitz, the building containing her flat was so badly blasted that she lay for nine hours amongst the ruins of her home before she could be released. Knowing her extraordinary vitality and remembering her light-hearted nature, I am not surprised that after she had recovered from the shock, in an emergency hospital to which she had been rushed clad only in her nightdress and with a blanket around her, she seemed little the worse for her exciting experience. She was kept under observation for a week before being removed to the home of her eldest son in a southern suburb, where flying-bombs have been even more numerous than in the north. When it was necessary to bring her travelling clothes from her bomb-blasted home to fit her up for removal, not one item of her clothing could be found at her wrecked flat : she had nothing beyond the nightdress in which she had been rescued from the wreckage ! Looters had removed her entire wardrobe. In Berlin these looters would have been found and shot out of hand. It might be a good thing to invent some sort of punishment just a little short of shooting for our own looters : for looters, especially in circumstances such as these, are vermin, be they English or German.

THE Finnish ruling class offers us another illustration of the truth that people who have struggled hard for freedom themselves often struggle quite as hard to prevent others being free. While Finland was under the harsh domination of the Tsars, it had the sympathy of the civilized world. When it was freed it began at once to impose, as far as it could, an even more brutal domination on the Karelian people. In 1918-19 the atrocities committed by Finns filled those who knew about them with horror. The object was to prevent the Karelians from throwing in their lot with Russia and force upon them subjugation to Finland. Once more we have proof of the correctness of what Lord Palmerston, with his wide experience as Foreign Minister, said about "a passion in the human heart stronger than

the desire to be free from injustice and wrong—that is the desire to inflict injustice and wrong upon others." Clemenceau's opinion was the same : "I have worked for liberty for forty years," he observed in 1914, "but the Frenchman's idea of liberty is suppressing somebody else." Lord Salisbury, when he was Prime Minister, saw concealed behind most religious movements and "great moral efforts" what he called "the steady enemy of human liberty—the desire of men to grasp power, to force others to conform to their ideas." Oliver Cromwell put the same thought into other words when he remarked bitterly : "Everyone loves liberty but none will give it."

WHERE Clemenceau and Lord Salisbury went wrong, it seems to me, was in attributing to Frenchmen as a race and to men in general this stupid craving for power. The mass of mankind do not feel anything of the kind. They want to be left alone and they are quite ready to leave others alone—if their minds are not perverted and their imaginations luridly fired by the incitements of cunning or crazy agitators. Palmerston was himself such an agitator when he stirred up the British nation to the point of making war (the Crimean War) on Russia in 1854. He was a cunning one. Hitler is a crazy one, as were the Finnish rulers who succeeded men of ability and good sense and filled the minds of the Finns with foolish visions of spreading Finnish rule as far as the Ural Mountains ! Some of those who, during the time when they struggled towards freedom, passed for able, sensible men, have revealed themselves in their true

Captain F. J. WALKER, C.B., D.S.O., R.N., whose death was announced on July 10, 1944. Ships under his command sank 20 U-boats, 15 of which were destroyed by the famous 2nd Escort Group of which he was senior officer (see pp. 710-711, Vol. 7).

Photo, Sport and General

characters since they became rulers. One of them, named Tanner, was a Co-operative Society leader, well-known to co-operators in Britain. He has been one of the most obstinate believers in a Nazi victory over the United Nations. I wonder which side some of our Co-operative leaders would come down on if they had to choose, like Tanner, between supporting National Socialism, which is Fascism, or real Socialism of the Russian type ?

A PRIVATE in a French Canadian regiment lately in Britain, now in France, told me how he escaped from France two years ago because he was disgusted with Petain, Laval, and all the Vichy gang. He got into Spain across the Pyrenees. He was a Frenchman of France ; many others like him escaped. Also there were German deserters from the army of occupation. Reaching the Spanish frontier, they had to explain themselves to the authorities. This they managed to do fairly well and arrangements were made to send them to their respective "fatherlands." They had to go through a lot of examinations, and any who did not answer up quickly were turned over to the Spanish police, who passed them on to agents of Hitler's Gestapo, and they were sent back to France. But a good many made their escape, and some of them are back in Europe now, like the "French Canadian" whom I met.

AN American soldier who watched a cricket match at Lord's could not understand why four members of one team did not go to the wicket at all. He was told that their side had "declared"—that is, decided not to send any more of its men in to bat and put the other side in. He shook his head bewildered. He was equally puzzled by the slowness of the run-getting. One batsman was in for nearly an hour and got fewer than fifty runs. In America, this soldier said, such dead-alive performers would have had lemonade bottles thrown at them. He contrasted the solemnity and leisureliness of it with the brisk excitement of baseball—as I have previously done in this page—and said he could not discover what the English found so attractive in watching cricket. There were thousands of people at Lord's that day. They had all paid for admission. What was more, they all seemed to be enjoying themselves. He gave it up ! As, of course, others of us would be baffled in contemplation of the "sportsmanship" of those who throw lemonade bottles !

SOMEONE remarked the other day that the Americans, who are with us in such large numbers, winning, like Macbeth, "golden opinions from all sorts of people," seldom seem to use the expressions with which the talkies have made us so familiar and which most cinema-goers suppose to be integral parts of the language spoken in the United States. They do not, for instance, speak of undertakers as "morticians" or say "they funeralized" instead of buried somebody. We too have expressions that appear in advertisements and sometimes on shop fronts which we do not use in conversation. I have seen lately a rat-catcher described as a "rodent operator," and over a shop selling powder and make-up the word "cosmetician." I remember the late Sir Henry Lunn being immensely amused by "mortician," and he also quoted with glee from a price-list issued by a Methodist church in America :

For smoothing the features of deceased—one dollar.

For imparting to the features a look of contentment —two dollars.

For giving to the late departed the appearance of Christian peace and resignation—five dollars.

How much would be charged for making it appear that the deceased was really glad to be dead was not stated.

British 17-pounders Pursuing the 'Tigers'

IMPROVED IN BRITISH FACTORIES by the fitting of a longer-range and more powerful gun—the 17-pounder—American-built Sherman tanks, which can out-manoeuvre the enemy 60-ton Tiger, claimed to be the biggest tank in the world, on any type of ground can now out-fight it. At over 1,000 yards the Sherman's hitting power is terrific. Above, they are seen rumbling to action through a Normandy village near Caen. In its original form the British 17-pounder was a wheeled anti-tank gun and is still used as such.

Photo, British Official

Printed in England and published every alternate Friday by the Proprietors, THE AMALGAMATED PRESS, LTD., The Fleetway House, Farringdon Street, London, E.C.4. Registered for transmission by Canadian Magazine Post. Sole Agents for Australia and New Zealand: Messrs. Gordon & Gotch, Ltd.; and for South Africa: Central News Agency, Ltd.—August 18, 1944. S.S. *Editorial Address:* JOHN CARPENTER HOUSE, WHITEFRIARS, LONDON, E.C.4.

Vol 8 *The War Illustrated* Nº 188

SIXPENCE

Edited by Sir John Hammerton

SEPTEMBER 1, 1944

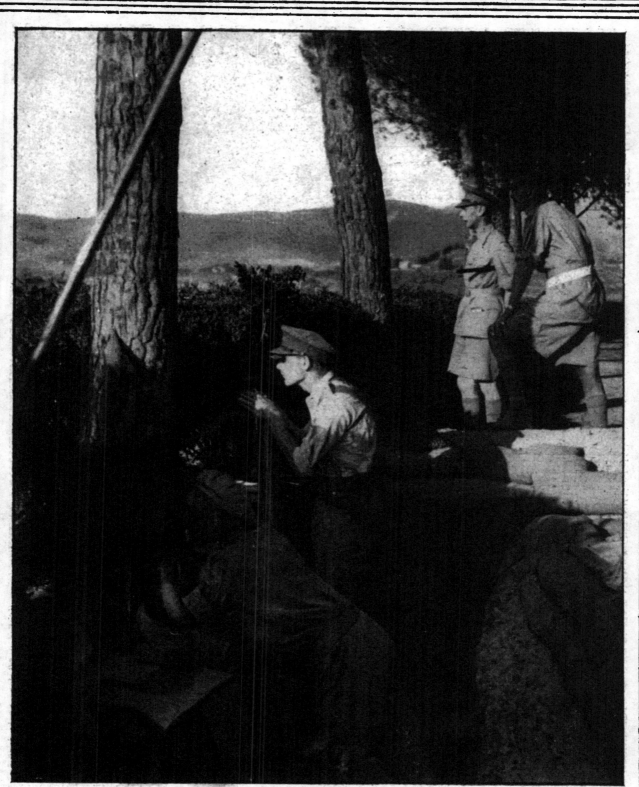

OUR KING IN ITALY (background) watched with keen interest, from a forward observation post, shells bursting during an artillery duel in a target area some four miles beyond the 8th Army front line, north of Arezzo, which was captured on July 16, 1944. His Majesty went to Italy on July 23, and spent twelve days visiting units of the Navy, Army and R.A.F. as well as the Dominions and Allied forces. He returned to Britain on August 3.

Photo, British Official

NO. 189 WILL BE PUBLISHED FRIDAY. SEPTEMBER 15

Our Roving Camera sees Women at War Overseas

WEATHER CLERK W.A.A.F. (above) is attached to a Middle East Meteorological Unit. With a theodolite she checks the speed of the wind which, together with other conditions, must be known, with the nearest approach to certainty, before a plane may take off. During his visit to Italy, from July 23 to Aug. 3, 1944, H.M. the King inspected W.R.N.S. officers of a shore base in the Naples area (right).

CANADIAN NURSING SISTERS (above) make themselves comfortable under canvas in a field in Normandy. Inside their tent is a ground-sheet-lined slit trench as protection against any shrapnel which might come their way. Personal belongings give a touch of home to rough-and-ready military surroundings.

BEACH-HEAD W.A.A.F.s (above) make friends with a little French girl and villagers living near their station in Normandy. Background to the meeting is a burnt-out German vehicle —one of hundreds destroyed during the early stages of our advance. Like other Service women overseas, W.A.A.F.s are engaged in tasks which are speeding the day of final victory

FIRST A.T.S. to arrive in Normandy leave their landing craft at one of the beaches (left) en route to take up duties with General Montgomery's 21st Army Group. Many of the clerk grade went on the special request of the Army officers and branches they had worked with in England, and a specially prepared "luxury camp" awaited their arrival. A.T.S. of 19 or over may volunteer for service abroad.

Photos, British and Canadian Official

THE BATTLE FRONTS

by Maj.-Gen. Sir Charles Gwynn, K.C.B., D.S.O.

THE great Western offensive has at last begun, and up to the time of writing has made amazing progress. We are told that the whole operation has so far followed broadly the course planned many months ago, but in detail its development must have depended on the skilful leadership of Generals Eisenhower and Montgomery and on the high qualities of their subordinate commanders and troops. The campaign is evidently now entering on a new and highly mobile phase in which it is impossible yet to predict developments, particularly the course the enemy will attempt to take.

It seems certain that if Hitler remains in supreme control he will at all costs attempt to retain possession of the bases from which his flying bombs and rockets are discharged. His military advisers, on the other hand, now that the outer perimeter defences have been broken, would probably advocate a withdrawal to the inner defences of the Fatherland, concentrating all available forces in the desperate attempt to win a compromise peace and to save the *Reichswehr* from defeat in detail. With the Russians surging forward from the east and the Luftwaffe completely outmatched, it would, however, be a forlorn hope.

Rommel, though his troops have fought with immense determination and skill, has been out-manoeuvred and has time and again been caught on the wrong foot, especially when, induced to believe that Montgomery's main blow would be struck in the east, he was unable to shift his weight in time to check the break-through in the west. The British thrust in the centre from Caumont contributed still further to throw him off his balance. The desperate attempts he, or his deputy after Rommel was wounded, made in numerous fierce counter-attacks to restore equilibrium only served to accelerate the weakening of his strength. The Canadian attack on the Caen front deprived him of his last secure foothold at a time when the gambling counter-attack at Mortain, made by Gen. Hausser, commanding the Seventh Army—possibly a belated and forlorn attempt to cut the communications of the Americans at Avranches—left him with his main armoured reserve desperately weakened and fully committed.

IT should now, I think, be appreciated that the weeks of preparation and stubborn fighting that followed D-Day were amply justified and were not the result of exasperating delay or indecision. When the opportunity to strike home occurred, or I should prefer to say was created, everything was in readiness to exploit it and the blow was delivered in no uncertain manner. It is not yet clear whether the great offensive opened at a pre-arranged moment or whether, as I am inclined to believe, it was started with a brilliant exploitation by commanders on the spot—of an opportunity that was worked for. Its development seems to show less signs of a set piece programme than of admirable control exercised according to circumstances. No doubt, however, the objectives of the offensive—such as the occupation of Brittany and the capture of its ports—were laid down in the original plan and may have a still unrevealed meaning.

Before the great achievements of D-Day and the two months that followed are obscured by perhaps greater events to come, it may be well to recall what was accomplished in that period. Criticism of what seemed to some to be unnecessary delays may be remembered longer than what had to be done before the offensive could be launched. Moreover, it must not be forgotten that during the period we were opposed by picked troops of the German Army commanded by a general of undoubtedly great capacity, who had had ample time to make his plans and to carry out the defence works he considered essential in a terrain that lent itself to defence. The great feat of carrying the Army across the seas and the landing of the first parties in face of opposition was so obviously a triumph of organization and skilful planning that it must always appeal to the imagination and cannot be forgotten.

I DOUBT, however, if it is fully realized how critical was the four days' battle for the Normandy beaches, during which the enemy's strong points had to be captured and counter-attacks defeated. It was a soldiers' battle which only highly trained troops possessing initiative and the offensive spirit could have won, and it is astonishing that at no point did the landing fail or counter-attacks achieve any considerable success. Rommel had then already suffered a double

IN FLORENCE, five of the six bridges across the River Arno were destroyed by the Germans in an attempt to delay the Allied advance in Italy. Only the Ponte Vecchio (in the background, above) remained intact; this bridge was rebuilt in 1362 and became famous for the goldsmiths' shops flanking its sides. In the foreground is the smashed S. Trinita bridge. The demolition failed to achieve its purpose. On August 11, 1944, the enemy withdrew from Florence. *Photo, British Official*

defeat. He had counted on making the landing practically impossible, and had calculated on annihilating any troops that might reach the shore before they could establish a firm foothold.

Up to that stage, if Rommel had won, our great undertaking would have been a costly failure, but probably not of such a disastrous nature as would have prevented our Supreme Command making another attempt. The danger of the undertaking ending in a really crushing disaster, however, increased as more and more men and equipment were landed, thereby adding to our stake. Rommel's plans had failed, but his army had not been defeated; it might still be used, when its strategic reserves arrived, in an overwhelming counter-offensive. What was the most dangerous phase of the undertaking had yet to be passed. That it was passed successfully was due partly to the air offensive which delayed the arrival of Rommel's reserves and upset the carefully prepared plans for their rapid concentration.

Partly it was due to the speed with which the Navy, in spite of the most adverse weather, continued to pour troops and material on to the beaches. But I think chiefly it was due to the continuous offensive operations conducted by the Army which not only secured more room for defence should Rommel's counter-offensive materialize, but also forced him to employ his powerful armoured force, of great offensive potentialities, in a defensive role, dissipating it in local defensive counter-attacks. During that stage our offensive operations, except those that led to the capture of Cherbourg, were not of a sensational character, but they were directed with admirable generalship and conducted with amazing energy by the troops.

Individually, the attacks could not achieve outstanding victory, but cumulatively they inflicted the third, and strategically perhaps the most decisive defeat on Rommel by preventing the materialization of his counter-offensive. Gradually he was forced into attempting, by purely defensive action, to seal up the Allied Armies in the peninsula. For that course he possessed great facilities. His defensive front was not over-long for the troops he had available to hold it. Its flanks rested securely on the sea, and the terrain lent itself to defence. He had a powerful, highly mobile reserve. His great weakness lay in the inferiority of his air arm.

But however strong a defensive position is, defensive action carries with it the inherent disadvantage of loss of the initiative, and the commander of the attacking force can always win a measure of success by concentrating superior power at his selected points. Sooner or later Rommel's seal was bound to crack and to break away from its flank anchorages. But it meant desperately hard and skilfully directed fighting. Now that the seal has been broken and the campaign has entered on a new and more sensational phase, let us not forget the prolonged series of operations that led up to the breaking nor under-estimate their importance.

IT must now be apparent that a premature attempt to break through would probably have led to costly failure, and even if it had created a breach the opening would have had little value if everything had not been in readiness to exploit it. The volume of the flood which poured through the gap and the strength of the attacks delivered against what remained of Rommel's seal surely give ample evidence that the weeks of preparatory fighting and work were not wasted.

The capture of the Brittany ports and the transfer of General Eisenhower's H.Q. to Normandy suggest that the risk of another opposed landing in Western Europe need not be accepted. Moreover, the capture of stretches of the French railways intact with rolling stock is a great asset secured by the far-reaching nature of the break-through.

Troop Carriers Astride the Caen-Falaise Road

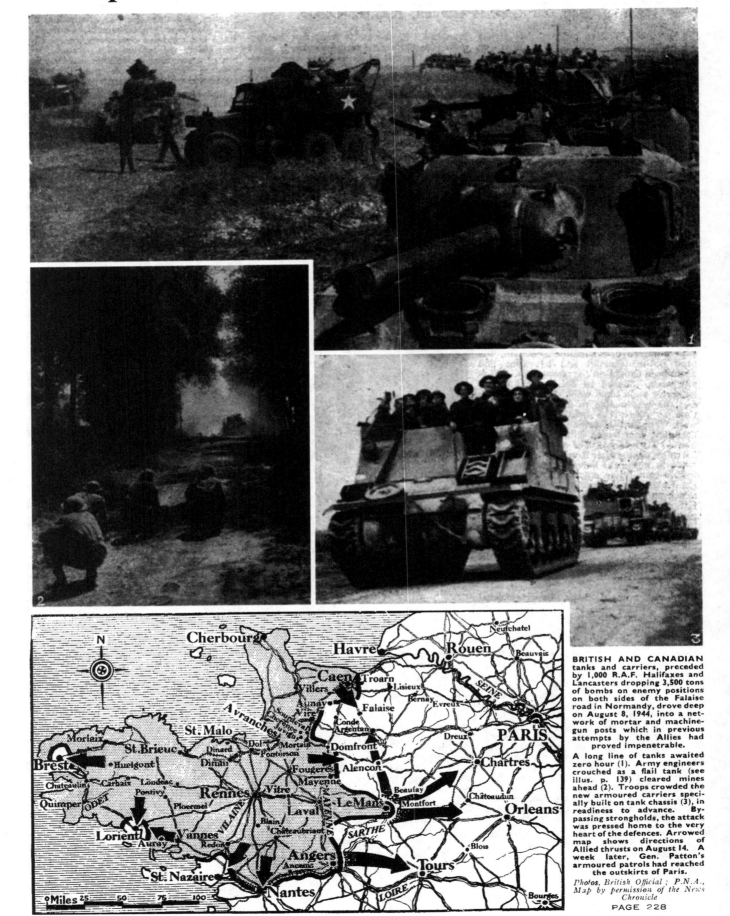

BRITISH AND CANADIAN tanks and carriers, preceded by 1,000 R.A.F. Halifaxes and Lancasters dropping 3,500 tons of bombs on enemy positions on both sides of the Falaise road in Normandy, drove deep on August 8, 1944, into a network of mortar and machine-gun posts which, in previous attempts by the Allies had proved impenetrable.

A long line of tanks awaited zero hour (1). Army engineers crouched as a flail tank (see illus. p. 139) cleared mines ahead (2). Troops crowded the new armoured carriers specially built on tank chassis (3), in readiness to advance. By-passing strongholds, the attack was pressed home to the very heart of the defences. Arrowed map shows directions of Allied thrusts on August 14. A week later, Gen. Patton's armoured patrols had reached the outskirts of Paris.

Photos, British Official ; P.N.A., Map by permission of the News Chronicle

Anti-Tank Defences Broken by 1st Canadian Army

FOR THE FIRST TIME IN HISTORY operating as a complete Army, Canadians (until July 31, 1944, included in the British 2nd Army) under the command of Lieut.-General H. D. G. Crerar thrust forward east of the River Orne in Normandy, and by August 8 captured May-sur-Orne, part of a powerful German anti-tank defence line. In carriers (above) they moved to the assault ; victory gained, troops relaxed (below) and there was time at last to read a letter from Home.

Photos, British Newspaper Pool, New York Times Photos

THE WAR AT SEA

by Francis E. McMurtrie

At the time of writing, certain aspects of the war at sea bear a distinct resemblance to the situation in the autumn of 1918, so far as Germany is concerned. Then as now she was deserted by her principal Allies in Europe. Her heavy ships (though she possessed far more in those days) were in no position to put to sea except as a suicidal measure ; and the submarine campaign against shipping had definitely failed. Whether a spirit of revolt is stirring in the *Reichsmarine*, as it was in 1918, still remains to be discovered ; but in view of the unrest in the *Wehrmacht* it would not be surprising if, in the larger surface ships at all events, there were no longer any desire to continue the struggle.

Reports that the 45,000-ton battleship *Tirpitz* has been undergoing steam trials

the end of the *Tirpitz* will be similar to that of the *Admiral Graf Spee*, which scuttled herself in preference to continuing the fight. If the *Graf Spee's* men lost heart so easily in the early months of the war, no better spirit is to be expected from the crew of the *Tirpitz*, which, even if it is at full strength, must be thoroughly disheartened after its ship has been disabled first by torpedoes from midget submarines (see illus. p. 649, Vol. 7) and then by bombs from naval aircraft (see pp. 776, 777, Vol. 7). Moreover, in the interim their sole remaining consort, the *Scharnhorst*, risked a sortie against an Allied convoy, only to be caught in a trap and destroyed. The moral of this event is unlikely to have been missed by the ship's company of the *Tirpitz*.

Early in November 1918 the U-boat

thrown into the Battle of the Atlantic just at the time when the numbers of our escort vessels were drastically reduced by three factors. One of these was the defection of the French Navy ; a second, the necessity of reinforcing our Mediterranean Fleet to meet the "stab in the back" from Italy ; and the third, the loss of a number of destroyers and the disabling of 70 more in the evacuation of Dunkirk.

It may be assumed that, with the advance of the Allied armies in France, German submarines at sea will have been instructed by wireless not to return to French Atlantic ports but to seek other havens of refuge, such as Trondheim or Bergen. There is no certainty therefore that any large number of U-boats will be found in Brest, Lorient or St. Nazaire, unless under refit and incapable of proceeding to sea. Those suffering from minor defects may be expected to proceed coastwise to La Pallice or the Gironde, or intern themselves in Spanish ports. Any that take the risk of putting straight to sea are likely to encounter Allied patrols, which it may be assumed are keeping the Brittany and Biscay coasts under strict surveillance. Departure at night is no longer a safeguard, for official accounts of U-boat hunts have made it plain that the Royal Navy is equipped with anti-submarine devices which enable touch to be kept with the movements of U-boats during darkness.

Prior to the Allied invasion, there are believed to have been about 100 U-boats based on French Atlantic ports. Perhaps as many have been operating recently in the Mediterranean ; those based on Toulon have no doubt fled since the Allies landed in the Riviera. Only a few are thought to be in the Black Sea, to which area they must have proceeded by way of the Danube. Some are in Norwegian waters, and the main reserve is to be found in the Baltic, including older submarines used for training and new ones awaiting crews or undergoing trials.

DISAFFECTION in Higher Ranks Has Been Checked by Himmler

In 1918 the U-boat personnel were the last people to be touched by the disaffection that was rife in the rest of the German fleet. Towards the end of October it was proposed to send the battleships to sea in an effort to restore the morale of their crews by action ; but it was too late. A general refusal of duty was impending when one of the larger submarines, U 135, was ordered to proceed to the Schillig Roads, at the mouth of the Elbe, and attack the battleships Ostfriesland and Thüringen, which were in a state of open mutiny. The captain of the submarine discreetly requested orders in writing, and as these were not forthcoming there was no further development beyond the entire collapse of German resistance everywhere. It may not be long before the armed forces of the Third Reich reach a similar frame of mind, though for the moment Himmler seems to have checked the movement in the higher ranks of the services.

ROCKET-FIRING BEAUFIGHTERS of R.A.F. Coastal Command never lose an opportunity of crippling or sending to the bottom German shipping they encounter. This photograph was taken during a recent attack ; on each side three rockets are seen hurtling towards an enemy escort vessel off the French Biscay coast. She sank shortly afterwards. *Photo, British Official*

with a view to proceeding from her remote anchorage in the Altenfjord to the Baltic should be received with caution. It is true that with Finland showing signs of dropping out of the war the position of the German forces in the north of Norway is becoming increasingly precarious ; but it has to be remembered that the distance from the Altenfjord to the Kattegat is over 1,200 miles. Though it might be hoped to make the passage through the "Inner Leads," or channels between the Norwegian mainland and the islands fringing it, this would not necessarily preclude interception. Recent British attacks by sea and air on shipping around Kristiansund illustrate the very keen watch which is being kept on these waters.

Any attempt to regain the shelter of the Baltic would be for the Tirpitz a counsel of desperation. It may be hoped to retain her more or less intact as a bargaining counter when the time for surrender arrives ; but if so, it is only another proof of German misconception of Allied intentions, which are to accept nothing but unconditional submission. In all probability, therefore,

flotillas in the Atlantic and Mediterranean were recalled to Germany in view of the hopeless position. It is possible that before long we may hear of a similar order being given by Grossadmiral Dönitz. Though nearly three times as many U-boats have been built in this war as in 1914-18, already their losses approximate to a similar percentage. Up to the end of July the number destroyed totalled over 500, and today submarine sinkings are more frequent than those of merchantmen—a complete inversion of the state of affairs which formerly obtained.

LOSS of French Atlantic Coast U-Boat Bases Foreshadowed

American occupation or investment of the ports of Cherbourg, Brest, Lorient and St. Nazaire must have been a heavy blow to Dönitz, especially as it foreshadows the loss in the near future of La Pallice, Rochefort and Bordeaux, the other principal U-boat bases on the French Atlantic coast. It was the facilities afforded by these ports, seized by Germany in June 1940 that enabled heavier concentrations of U-boats to be

Reinstatement on the active list of Admiral Sir J. Somerville is a measure which has something of the flavour of an afterthought. Placed on the retired list less than three months before the outbreak of war, on the recommendation of a medical board, Admiral Somerville took a leading part in the evacuation of British forces from Dunkirk and Boulogne ; was in command of Force "H" which held the Western Mediterranean and took convoys through to Malta in 1940-41 ; and became Commander-in-Chief of the Eastern Fleet after the disaster in which H.M.S. Prince of Wales and Repulse, with Admiral Sir Tom Phillips, were lost. In that capacity he directed recent bombardments of Japanese bases in the Netherlands East Indies.

One-way Traffic to Victory in Normandy

ROADS WERE PACKED with men, tanks and supplies as British forces from the Caen area swept towards the strategic village of St. Martin des Besaces, in an effort to keep up with the retreating Germans. About five miles south of Caumont, St. Martin fell at the start of the 2nd Army's drive, on July 30, 1944. German resistance was fierce, but weight of metal—and the insuperable courage of our men—prevailed, and strong points in this locality were speedily neutralized.

Photo, P.N.A.

AFTER BITING INTO BRITTANY, on August 2, 1944, Gen. Patton's armour sped through Pontorson, 6 miles south of the Gulf of St. Michel, in which lies the historic island of the same name, with its 13th-century town and famous Benedictine abbey, well known to British peacetime tourists. In striking contrast to this picturesque place is the jeep approaching it across the half-mile causeway. The Germans left St. Michel untouched, and it was first entered by three Allied war correspondents. The abbey was founded in 709 by St. Aubert, Bishop of Avranches, obeying the commands of the Archangel Michael, who, appeared in a vision : in his honour it was called " the Abbey of St. Michel, Archangel, of the Peril of the Sea",—apparently referring to fear of inundation.

Photo, Planet News

Our Hospital Ships on the Cross-Channel Run

Mostly ex-passenger liners of normal build, lacking defence and frequently without escort, rendered vividly conspicuous by giant Red Cross emblems, distinctive colour of hull, and brilliant night illumination, hospital ships are supposed—by international agreement—to be immune from attack. But every voyage may be perilous, as explained here by Capt. FRANK H. SHAW.

WHILST many of the Allied casualties are being carried at speed from the battlefields of Western France to hospitals in Britain by means of air-transport, our hospital ships are in full employment. Their value is inestimable ; for though the distance between war and the comparative peace of the base hospital is short—less than an hour by transport aircraft—the seaborne craft afford facilities for expert treatment that are not forthcoming under other circumstances.

Our hospital ships may have an easier time today than they had in the past—the Luftwaffe being half-impotent—but with a desperate enemy struggling to stave off defeat by all means in his power, dastardly attacks on these ships are only too likely to continue. The narrow waters of the English Channel are proving to be one of the world's bitterest battlefields. By all the recognized war-codes, hospital ships are considered immune from enemy attack—the Red Cross they conspicuously display is supposed to render them sacrosanct to belligerent eyes. A hospital ship is simply a floating stretcher, highly magnified ; it carries wounded men, and women to minister to them. Such a vessel does not carry even defensive armament, but trusts to her recognition marks for immunity. Even bloodthirsty barbarians have recognized such sanctity.

But the savage, desperate enemy of today has dissociated himself from all the recognized humanities. He has attacked hospital ships regularly—almost systematically, exactly as he has frequently opened fire from the shelter of the raised white flag. The irony of such attacks is that, as often as not, some part of the hospital ship's human cargo is of the same nationality as the attackers ; for when the wounded are considered, race, creed and colour no longer enter into the argument. A stricken man is simply an object of sympathy, deserving of ready aid and comfort.

THAT is, to all but Huns or Japanese. Sight of the safeguarding sign—Red Crosses lavishly exhibited, distinctive colouring of hull, night illumination, and so on—appears to breed a Berserk lust in their souls, which can only be satisfied by wanton destruction. Aboard a normal freighting ship conveying reinforcements and supplies across to the Normandy coast, night brings some cessation of anxiety. In the night a darkened-down ship is not easily visible from above, though the throb of her propellers is audible to U-boats' listening devices. Seen from high up there is little likely to betray such a freighter's presence other than the white wake and bow-wave, and the spray thrown by the wind tends to obscure all clear-cut outlines. Only by dropping flares can an aircraft discover its target ; and to drop flares is to invite an A.A. barrage.

But in a hospital ship sunset means "Lighten ship !" and she at once becomes vividly conspicuous, observable for miles, both from sea-level and from the stratosphere. The giant Red Cross emblems painted on decks and bridge-awnings, and the high topside at bow and stern are floodlit. This makes her visible from every angle ; she is also as audible as the ordinary freighter to the hostile sound-locators. Electrically lit crosses stud her upperworks. Since all Allied vessels darken down at nightfall, it stands to reason that such a radiance of light can indicate only a hospital ship, which, if not full of wounded and sick, is at least hurrying to their succour. Notwithstanding this, a large number of Allied hospital ships

have been wantonly destroyed by bomb or torpedo—with all hands.

Axis claims that such vessels are using their safeguarding symbols to camouflage military activities, and that warlike stores are conveyed to the fighting areas in their holds, are, of course, gross lies. A nation that is a past-master in falsehood has excelled itself in making such statements.

BECAUSE the enemy use their own ostensibly sacred vessels for such purposes does not mean that the Allies do. Germans judge us by their own lawless, treacherous standards. So they sink our Red Cross ships without mercy, as a mad dog bites everything within reach, without regard to consequences. The odds against the hospital ship are long. The vessels are highly conspicuous by day and by night. White topsides with the easily recognizable green bands —at a period when practically all seagoing tonnage is either camouflaged or painted battleship grey—and the vivid Cross symbols sufficiently identify her. She is, therefore, easy to attack ; and, lacking defence, is as easily destroyed.

H.M. Hospital Ship NEWFOUNDLAND, displacement 6,791 tons, deliberately bombed by the Germans on Sept. 13, 1943, off Salerno, on the coast of Italy. All the doctors, every ship's officer, and five nurses were killed ; about 100 U.S. nurses who were aboard escaped.
Photo, British Official

She frequently sails without escort, though the nature of her employment often brings her nearer to the actual firing-line than usually happens with defensively armed merchantmen, for the sooner the wounded can be handed over for the highly skilled attention available aboard, the better their chance of recovery. Many hospital ships close-in almost to the beaches across the Channel, exactly as they did at Salerno and Anzio ; and although deliberate sinkings have not thus far been reported from Normandy, off the Italian coast one such ship at least was dive-bombed deliberately—whilst her lights were blazing—and sunk ; several others were severely damaged, with loss of life and added pain and suffering to the injured passengers. Other Red Cross ships have been wantonly torpedoed in open water.

The inhumanity of sinking a hospital ship is worse even than assault on a hospital ashore. The helpless patients are deep down in the hull, and their hope of rescue is prejudiced. Many, by reason of their wounds and shell-shock, are not in full possession of their faculties ; they suffer cruelly in such attacks, even if by a miracle their lives are

preserved. With a ship steaming alone, the hope of rescue is lessened. It is not only the wounded and sick who suffer from these dastardly outrages, but the surgeons, nurses, and hospital orderlies. The actual crews run an equal risk. It may be said, without fear of contradiction, that hospital ships' crews are the bravest of the brave—even in the Merchant Navy. They go into the firing-line weaponless, knowing themselves to be special targets for bestial inhumanity. They do so unflinchingly, because they are merchant seamen, and it is their plain duty.

When attack—almost inevitable as the enemy grows more and more desperate— develops, the prime consideration of each ship's crew is to safeguard as many as possible of the helpless passengers. There are many recorded instances of almost incredible self-denial. A bombed ship, below decks, quickly becomes an inferno of fire and wreckage, but the unvoiced creed of every crew is : " Women and wounded first ! " Far too often such sacrifices are, alas ! in vain. Hospital ships are not specially constructed to withstand attack, they are mostly ex-passenger liners of normal build ; and a hit from a bomb or torpedo is as likely to shatter them or break their backs as if they were normal tonnage. The ordinary freighter can hit back, her crew can secure some satisfaction by blazing away at a treacherous enemy, and can—nowadays —practically be confident of help arriving from escort or rescue ships.

THERE is, accordingly, every justification for arming hospital ships against an enemy who refuses to abide by the laws of the Geneva Convention. There is also every justification for requiring them to sail in complete darkness, since the preservative symbols are disregarded. Innocence is no safeguard against packs of ravening wild beasts. Indeed, it has been shown repeatedly that the advertisement of innocence incites the aggressor to more cold-blooded attacks. Naturally, retribution will be demanded against the perverted criminals responsible for such outrageous excesses. Massacring wounded who should be protected by the Red Cross is a penal offence. The Axis should be warned that not only past but future offences will be punished by death.

There is one way by which hospital ships could be given a fair chance. Ambulance aircraft, conveying wounded from battlefield to base in the present operations, do not carry distinguishing marks, because they are used to ferry war stores from base to battlefield ; and if they were so distinguished, the enemy would be able to lay a true accusation against them of masquerading as innocent. Why, therefore, should not hospital ships be similarly utilized ? Why not have the characteristic markings painted out altogether, so that they are not required to stand out boldly against the general mass of shipping ; and why not arm them defensively, exactly as general freighters are defended against air and submarine attack ? If this were done, if the ships were allowed to take a chance equal with their fellow Merchant Navy ships, their hold space could be usefully employed on outward runs for supplying our troops without infringement of the Convention.

When the time comes for punishment of the criminals, the time for adequate reward for hospital ships' crews, from commander to lowest rating, should also arrive, if not before. For a sailor, soldier or airman to rescue wounded under fire more often than not means the award of the Victoria Cross. On this showing, every member of a hospital ship's personnel is a potential V.C.

Purged of the Scourge French Life Begins Anew

IN THE WAKE of our advancing armies there is liberation and renewed hope—antithesis of the oppression and despair spread by the Germans.

At Montebourg, in Normandy, freed on June 19, 1944, a French family await transport to take them back to their homes (1), and calm returns to this refugee (2) as she thinks of better days ahead. Watched by a friendly U.S. soldier, fishermen again peacefully mend their nets in the harbour of Barfleur (3). In their drive south from Caen, British forces captured Le Beny Bocage on August 1 : a gendarme officer warmly welcomes the first troops to enter, and citizens add their greetings (4). During the fighting in the Caen area, some 20,000 citizens sheltered in deep-hewn quarries along the bank of the River Orne ; in the quarries French nuns ran a hospital (5) with 500 beds.

Photos, British Official ; Planet News, Keystone, Associated Press, P.N.A.

Bradley's Blitzkrieg Freed Brittany's Capital

TEARING THROUGH GERMAN POSITIONS in Brittany, on August 4, 1944, General Bradley's armoured forces swept into and took the town of Rennes, capital of the province, 60 miles from St. Nazaire. Jeeps poured through one of the streets, U.S. soldiers mingling with the happy citizens (1) ; some of their comrades display a captured battle trophy (2). In the main square of sunlit Rennes a vast and jubilant crowd gathered to welcome the bringers of freedom (3).

Photos, Keystone, Planet News

'Legion of the Lost' Fought on in New Guinea

When Timor Island fell to the Japanese in February 1942 the Australian "Sparrow Force" won resounding fame by continuing to fight in the jungles for many months (see p. 714, Vol. 6). Escaping to Australia, they were reorganized as a commando unit and then proceeded to New Guinea. Some of the remarkable exploits of these indomitable warriors are narrated in this article.

LATE one afternoon, natives ferried across the Ramu River, in New Guinea, seventeen green-clad, sun-burned men. Leaving their forward unit in the Ramu Valley, a patrol pushed forward behind the Japanese lines for information. They went as far as the Finisterre Range, far up the Valley, but found no sign of the enemy.

Passing through a native village on their way out they left three of their party, one on guard and two men sick. Some days later the main party returned to this small native village, having given the neighbourhood a thorough searching.

In the half light of morning, before the men were due to stand-to, the enemy struck. A whistle sounded—the Japanese signal for attack—and the fight was on. Men jumped from bed, half-dressed, to hurl grenades and meet the enemy in the pre-dawn light. For a few hectic minutes the fight was fierce, then numbers told and the patrol was forced to retire. They had lost all their gear, and at roll-call six men had failed to rally.

That is what fighting in New Guinea is like. You may be the best scout or jungle fighter in the world, but you can never be sure if the enemy is twenty feet or twenty miles away from you. To prove this, one officer of the party lay in a hole for five hours within ear-shot of the Japanese, waiting his chance to regain his unit. Harried by the enemy following up their success, the party travelled through heavy jungle and spent that night shivering in a tropical rainstorm; they were without food for nearly two days. One man,

who had to get out without his boots, covered fifteen miles of thorn-studded scrub track before reaching headquarters.

To get to the Ramu Valley they covered many weary miles of country, unrivalled for roughness anywhere in the world. They climbed tooth-sharp hills, like Mount Otto and the Wesia Mountains. They scaled the Bismarcks—a range of over 10,000 feet, with the 14,000 feet Mount Wilhelm towering above them. They paddled their gear across swift-rushing rivers on machine-made and home-made rafts that often tumbled men and gear into the torrent. When rivers could not be forded by normal means the Air Force dropped them life-belts and ropes; and men, loaded to the neck, swam across, clinging to those ropes.

THEY took the risk as part of the day's work. Acts of high courage were everyday matters. One man walked along the Ramu Valley as a decoy, and as a result the Japanese were successfully ambushed, losing forty-five killed and fifteen wounded out of a total of a hundred. The enemy attacked often and with fierce determination, in one village making no less than six attempts in one day, only to be repulsed each time with great loss.

In one such attack a man was wounded. For sixty hours he staggered along bush tracks before coming up with the rest of his patrol. He had eight bullet wounds in his body and five sword slashes round his head. It took three weeks to get him to a bush hospital—yet he lives. Another, an officer,

SCENE OF THE EXPLOITS of the "Lost Legion" in New Guinea. On April 24, 1944, Australian forces advancing along the Ramu Valley, took the key-point of Madang. By August 1 they were west of the Sepik River.

was wounded five times in an attack, and became lost; it was six days before he regained his unit, stoutly maintaining that he could still kill Japs.

These men of Timor patrolled far to the Japanese coastal points and brought back information which proved invaluable in laying the foundations of the subsequent Allied victories in New Guinea. One party went "into the blue" for twenty-nine days, and owing to wireless failure nothing was heard from them after the second day. But they pushed on and returned with the information their Commander required.

This Australian "Legion of the Lost" was a complete self-contained fighting unit, with its own medical officer and a hospital, together with a cunningly-hidden headquarters in a pocket of the jungle. Its supplies and mails were dropped by a watchful Air Force, whose admiration of these resourceful men is of the very highest. The headquarters was in the usual mosquito-ridden place, studded with a few native huts and paved with logs to give a footing through the mud.

DESPITE the rigours of their task they found time to adopt and rear five kittens, named after the Dionne quins. Although some of the best scouts in the world were members of this force, they were never able to account for the father of the kittens. He was never seen or even heard in the district.

This mystery provoked a great deal of discussion! It was a strange sight to see a tough jungle fighter, just back from a patrol where death stood at his shoulder, sitting in front of "headquarters," playing with a tiny kitten.

But this was a lonely life, far from the amenities of civilization, and playing with a kitten was a heaven-sent outlet. Off duty they found time to laugh and this laughter —and that wonderful sense of comradeship cemented on the jungle paths of New Guinea by the common peril of duty—made for something that even civil life never offered.

They ask no banners, they wave no flags, and expect no blare; but now and again they appreciate a thought. A man comes off patrol, to be greeted with a firm handshake and a "Glad to meet you, Jack!" that means more to him than he could express.

Although the story of their achievements, first in Timor and then in New Guinea, cannot yet be told in full, enough is known to prove that the Australian soldier is still equal to the toughest task set him, even when confronted with the most difficult country in the world—that he can fight and win as well as his brothers fighting on other fronts. In the final story of the Australian fighting forces of this war the "Lost Legion" will have a high place.

'GREEN SNIPER'S PIMPLE' Australians called this 4,500-ft. height in the Ramu Valley (see map above) held by the Japanese for months, and barring our advance towards the important coastal town of Madang. The hill fell to the Australians, here seen climbing its precipitous side, after a heavy air attack. On December 27, 1943, they clawed their way up to complete victory. See also illus. p. 715 Vol. 7:

Photo, Australian Official

Stronghold of Saipan Torn from Japanese Hands

ANOTHER STEP NEARER the Philippines and Japan was the American capture of the island of Saipan in the Marianas group in the Pacific, which was entirely in U.S. hands by July 10, 1944, after a 25-days' campaign. Heavy bombardment from the air, sea and land paved the way for the entry into Garapan, the capital, on July 4, where few houses remained standing (1). U.S. Marines, pushing the enemy across Saipan, had to face continual fire; a combat photographer secured this dramatic picture of a marine hit by a bursting mortar shell and holding his head as he was about to fall (2). An American soldier tosses a smoke bomb into a Japanese foxhole (3). Tanks played a part in the conquest, and here (4) one rumbles victoriously down the shattered main street of the capital. See also p. 167.

Photos, Keystone, Planet News, Associated Press

Under the Japanese Heel in Shanghai Today

Cut off from the rest of the world for two-and-a-half years in Japanese-occupied Shanghai are communities of British, Americans, Dutch and European stateless refugees. This account of their fate and how they have contrived for themselves tolerable conditions of life in internment was given to Dr. ERNEST WERTH and is exclusive to " The War Illustrated."

THE telephone rings. The voice from the other end sounds familiar. For years I had not heard my old friend ; and now, half-frightened, half-delighted, I burst out : "Good heavens ! Where are you speaking from ?" "Silly question !" comes the answer. "From our City office !" "But you are supposed to be interned by the Japs in Shanghai !" I exclaim. "That's right, but I am back."

When, that same evening, we met for the first time in years a full account of Japanese-occupied Shanghai was given to me. What my friend reports about life and conditions there may interest many readers of THE WAR ILLUS-TRATED. Not without good reason was Shanghai named the "New York of the Far East." As in the U.S. metropolis, in this Chinese city of more than four million inhabitants skyscrapers and huge modern departmental stores tower up ; enormous wealth and abundance were found side by side with direst poverty. Today, however, we are particularly interested to hear about the European colony and its fate since the outbreak of the War with Japan.

Many Refugees from Russia

At that time there were living in Shanghai approximately 30,000 Europeans, amongst them 3,000 to 4,000 British, 1,000 Dutchmen, 5,000 French, as well as nearly 5,000 Americans. By far the greatest European community was that of between 15,000 and 20,000 Russians who had fled from Russia after 1918. Britons, Americans, Dutchmen and others dwelt in the so-called International Settlement, an extra-territorial concession under its own government, the Municipal Council, in which, together with Chinese, all European nations were represented.

After the outbreak of war, on the night of December 9-10, 1941, the occupation of the International Settlement by the Japanese started in true Pearl Harbour style. At 4 a.m. Japanese aeroplanes appeared over the harbour and bombed a British gunboat, which sank, firing to the last. Next morning, against all international law and treaties, Japanese troops marched into the extra-territorial district. From that very moment these Prussians of the East started a terror regime over the whole area. Chinese patriots put up as much resistance as they could, and surprise attacks and bomb explosions were of almost daily occurrence.

ALL Allied nationals—British, American, Dutch, but not French—were compelled to close their offices, which were occupied by the Japanese military authorities. The famous Sassoon Hotels, Cathay and Metropole, became Japanese Headquarters and all the abundant stocks and provisions were, of course, seized at once. All Allied men, women and even children had to wear red armlets with an "A" for American, a "B" for British, "N" (Netherlands) for Dutch. Restrictions of all kinds followed, the frequenting of theatres, cinemas and other places of entertainment was forbidden and a curfew varying according to the season was imposed. Notwithstanding initial promises that international treaties, guarantees and laws would be strictly adhered to, the Japanese military authorities soon started to arrest prominent persons under all kinds of pretences, and later on turned to general internment. A special camp for political suspects was established in Haifong Road. There tortures were applied by Japanese "gendarmes" in order to elicit political secrets.

Today about 3,000 British, 1,000 Americans and 1,000 Dutch are living in internment camps, the largest of which is Chapai. Families are dwelling in hutments which they have fitted up themselves, and they have organized, as well as circumstances permit, schools, hospitals and other institutions. The Swiss Red Cross cares for these camps as far as possible and has repeatedly been asked to intervene in order to improve the worst sanitary conditions. None of the inmates of the camps is allowed outside the barbed wire, which is strongly guarded by Japanese soldiers.

A special class is formed by about 18,000 European stateless refugees, for the greater part Jews, who from 1937, thanks to the liberal attitude of the Chinese government,

AGGRESSIVE SUPPORTERS of expansionist Japan are Adm. Yonai (left), former C.-in-C. Japanese combined fleet, and Gen. Koiso, Governor-General of Korea, who, it was announced on July 22, 1944, were chosen to form a new cabinet, replacing that led by Gen. Tojo.
Photos, Associated Press

found an asylum in Shanghai from concentration camps in Germany and other European countries. They had already managed to begin building up a fresh existence, and soon one could observe the European influence of these refugees in the main streets of the city. Elegant window dressing, fashionable dresses, handbags, cosmetics and so on appeared, and new industries sprang up which were already of some importance in the economic life of China. The Germans, however, seeing in these refugees enemies of Nazism, intervened and on May 18, 1943, the Japanese Navy and Army High Command issued an order according to which all European fugitives who had arrived in Shanghai after 1937 had to live within a designated area.

Primitive Reservation Conditions

THE refugees were forced to give up their living within three months—people who had travelled 10,000 miles, often under appalling and adventurous conditions, to find some shelter and peace in Shanghai. The old Japanese quarter Honkew, separated from Shanghai proper by the famous Garden Bridge and completely destroyed during the Chinese-Japanese war in 1937, became the reservation. Since then, 18,000 of these Europeans have been living in Honkew. They have rebuilt the district to some extent and established themselves to the best of their ability, often under most primitive

conditions. Although the quarter is not fenced in with barbed wire, it is closely guarded by Japanese gendarmes and latterly by a police corps which the refugees organized and recruited amongst themselves. To leave the district the inhabitants need a permit.

AFTER a time workshops and factories were started, partly by transferring machinery from other parts of Shanghai, and the production began of textiles, chemicals, pharmaceutical and other products previously imported from Europe. All kinds of crafts are represented, from tailoring to cobbling and watchmaking. The people have, of course, themselves produced all their household furniture, beds and kitchen utensils. In the community, which organized co-operative administration, there live today approximately 10,000 men, 5,000 women and 3,000 children. Diseases which the wretched sanitary conditions might have produced were prevented by scrupulous cleanliness and stringent precautions. Consequently, mortality is much less than amongst the Chinese population under the Japanese yoke. Many well-known doctors, technicians and scientists have put their services at the disposal of the community, and their work may become an important factor in the rebuilding of China after the war.

Self-Help at Honkew

About 5,000 persons who cannot support themselves are housed in an institution, maintained for the greater part by earlier immigrants not affected by the Japanese order previously mentioned, and by Red Cross Organizations as far as is possible under war conditions. The whole Honkew Community has voluntarily submitted to a tax system, and out of its revenues the poor are assisted and hospitals installed. One of these already has some hundred beds, an operating-theatre, X-ray and other modern equipment handled by refugee doctors. Every possible care is taken of youth ; schools are at work, sports grounds have been laid out and are being steadily improved by the boys and girls themselves. Thus these refugees have created tolerable conditions of life.

ASSEMBLIES or meetings in camps or houses are forbidden for all Shanghai Europeans. So is distant radio reception. Installation for short waves had to be removed from sets, and nobody was allowed to listen-in to foreign news. Only one official Russian local transmitter using various languages can be heard, and it reports only from the European theatre of war ; the Pacific may not even be mentioned. All public utilities, gas, water and electricity, previously in British and American hands, have been taken over by the Japanese and are managed by them. All the important British, American and Dutch banks, shipping firms and insurance companies are closed.

The Chinese are putting up against the Japanese a very successful passive resistance. Shanghai used to be the only harbour in the Far East which had huge stocks of provisions. It was the centre of importing and trans-shipment for the immense Chinese hinterland. These stocks have been removed by the Chinese patriots in many mysterious ways and remain unobtainable by the greedy Japanese. The Chinese underground movement is well organized. Hundreds of thousands of patriots are waiting for the signal from their great leader Chiang Kai-Shek to rise and destroy the Japanese oppressor when the hour strikes.

Photos, Sport & General,
Keystone

Shadow of German Doom Cast over Normandy

" On every battlefield all over the world the Armies of Germany and Japan are recoiling," declared Mr. Churchill on August 2, 1944. On the Western Front, advancing south of Caumont, a column of British infantry and anti-tank guns (top) headed for the hotly contested Bois de l'Homme on August 1. Through the remains of Periers (bottom), important communications centre north of Coutances, U.S. armour passed after the town's capture by the American 1st Army on July 27.

239

Rokossovsky Leads the 1st White Russian Front

Flying aces of the Red Army have earned the admiration of even the R.A.F. Among them is Fighter-Pilot, Hero of the Soviet Union, Capt. Mayorov (1) in a plane presented by workers of the Mongolian People's Republic. Capture of Lublin, covering the approaches to Warsaw, on July 24, 1944, was effected by forces under Marshal Rokossovsky : Soviet snipers (2) helped to clear out the defenders. Rokossovsky, C.-in-C. of the 1st White Russian Front (3), plans fresh conquests.

Photo

All-Conquering Red Forces at Germany's 'Gates'

"It is the Russian Armies," said Mr. Churchill, "who have done the main work in tearing the guts out of the German Army." That operation was in full blast when, on July 27, 1944, Marshal Rokossovsky's warriors captured Lvov; over the freed town the Soviet Flag was hoisted (4) as artillery passed through (5). Amphibious tanks crossed the River Bug (6) by July 22, in the drive to Lublin and Warsaw. By August 5, Soviet forces had smashed through to the frontiers of East Prussia.

Last Stages in the Fight for Florence

Overcoming fierce resistance in the central sector of the Italian front, General Alexander's forces reached the outskirts of the city of Florence by August 4, 1944 ; tankmen of the Canadian Armoured Force moved up in Shermans (top left). East of Arezzo the enemy began to withdraw on July 22, and our artillery in the valley between Mts. Cedrone and Arnato hastened the retreat : a Bofors crew in action (top right). An Indian patrol cautiously approaches a hide-out of snipers (bottom).

by Hamilton Fyfe

IF an individual is a danger to his neighbours, if he makes unprovoked brutal attacks on them, his neighbours do not say, when the police take him into custody, that he really was not responsible and ought not to be punished. They recognize that for the sake of social peace and order he must be punished—if possible in some way that will prevent his committing the same sort of crimes again.

But when we have to deal with nations that behave towards others with deliberate savagery, that defy justice and decency, that proclaim themselves "master-people" who have the right to oppress and rob everyone else, we find that the case is altered.

I have read a number of books on the problem "How to Ward off a Third World War." All the writers apply to the Germans every kind of abusive epithet, say they are collectively to blame, denounce them as enemies of the human race. Yet when it comes to the question of dealing with these criminals the writers soften. They say we must discriminate, we must not be too hard on them, we must not forget that the Germans are necessary to a prosperous European economic system.

This last plea is the strongest, and it is purely selfish. It is not the result of pity: it comes from the desire to keep customers. It is being put forward in the United States as well as in Europe. Mr. Dewey, candidate for the Presidency, voiced the opinion of business men when he said lately "peace terms must not be too rigid." Now an American lawyer, Mr. Louis Nizer, in a book called What To Do With Germany (Hamish Hamilton, 7s. 6d.) proposes that these terms should be "economically generous" and looks forward to the German people "benefiting from an improved world economy." Mr. Nizer is far from arguing that the Germans as a nation are not to blame:

> Never again must we be deluded into misplacing responsibility for German aggression. It is not the leader of the day, whether he be Charlemagne, Barbarossa, Frederick Wilhelm, the Great Elector, Frederick the Great, Bismarck, the Kaiser, or Hitler, who wages war against mankind. It is the German people.

The German people, Mr. Nizer declares, "have ever been arch-conspirators against civilization. They have deliberately plotted to destroy it and subdue all mankind to serfdom. They have given their brains, their energies, and their very lives through the centuries in fanatical devotion to this task. This is the greatest indictment of a people in all history."

YET the Germans are not to suffer for their misdeeds. The Allies should draw up peace terms "chiefly designed to serve the economic health and growth of Germany." That is to say, Germans are to "share in the immediate food relief which will be extended to Europe during the emergency period following the armistice," and they are then to be given every assistance towards regaining their prosperity.

What would be the certain consequence of their becoming prosperous again with the help of the nations now fighting against them? They would say, "Well, we haven't lost much after all. We are back where we were before we 'forced war upon the world for the second time with determined criminality'" (Mr. Nizer's words). They would listen eagerly to crazy agitators, ambitious politicians, and generals anxious to try again.

I consider both Mr. Nizer's attitude towards the German people and his suggested method of dealing with them foolish and dangerous. It seems to me to be nonsense to talk about the Germans in general—the pleasant, kindly farmers and innkeepers, the authors and newspaper men, the workers, skilled and unskilled, whom I have known—"conspiring against civilization, making barbarism an ideal, distorting nationalism into a ritual of international murder." As Hedda Gabler's husband says in Ibsen's play, "people don't do such things."

Punishment to Fit the Nazi Crimes?

But don't suppose that I acquit the German people of guilt. If Mr. Nizer said they have allowed their rulers to do "such things," and have applauded their rulers when victories were won (as in 1859 over Austria, and in 1864 over Denmark, and in 1870 over France), and have made no effort to become good Europeans, he would be quite right. If the Germans in general have not harboured criminal designs themselves, they have been accessories both "before and after the fact," as the law puts it, to the crimes that have been committed, and are still being committed, in their name.

THEREFORE, in my view, they should be treated in such a way as to fix for ever in their minds, and in the minds of any nation that might feel inclined to behave as they have behaved, the conviction that such conduct does not pay. To put them on the same level as the peoples whom they have savaged and tortured and massacred, and to help them by every means in our power to regain their prosperity, would simply encourage them to prepare for revenge and a third attempt at world domination.

BLACKENED REMAINS of the church of Oradour-sur-Glane, near Limoges, inside which, on June 10, 1944, German S.S. troops after an orgy of street killings incarcerated men, women and children before setting fire to the church, in which they had also placed explosives. Punishment of such war criminals is one of the subjects of the book reviewed in this page. *Photo, Keystone*

I see another objection besides this to Mr. Nizer's plan, which is obviously drawn up to please Big Business (do not forget that just the same view was taken last time, when Sir Arthur Balfour, created Lord Riverdale, said we must rearm Germany). This other objection is that it will not be left to the United States or to Britain to decide what shall be done with Germany. Can we imagine the Russians, whose country has been devastated, or any of the nations that have suffered terribly at the hands of German tyrants, agreeing to measures intended to put German business on its feet again and based on the idea that "every consideration shall be extended to improve the standard of living in Germany"?

EVEN if the other measures recommended in the book were to be carried out—the execution of 150,000 Nazis as well as a very large number of others who aided and abetted them; the sentencing of hundreds of thousands to terms of imprisonment; the close control of every branch of German industry; the abolition of "the entire educational system" and the substitution for it of a new one designed by the Allies and carried out by an International University staffed mainly by non-Germans—even if these could be put into operation, which I do not believe possible, the restoration of German prosperity by Allied help would still make a large number of half-lunatic Germans feel it would be worth while to have another shot at world supremacy and induce the mass of the people to allow the trigger to be pulled.

I believe the only way to teach Germans that they have acted like wild beasts—much worse than wild beasts—and that they are loathed by the rest of the human race, except perhaps the Japanese; and that conduct such as theirs is not going to be allowed to pay or to go unpunished (as it did last time), is to put a ring round them and keep them within it, cut off from the rest of the world, until they show that they have every intention of living in peace and contentment with the rest.

Seeing that Germany is surrounded by peoples whom Germans have tried to turn into slaves, and on whom they have practised the most appalling cruelty, it would not be difficult to create that ring of isolation. They have in the past complained without justification that they were being encircled. Let them really suffer encirclement.

LET them live on what they can produce themselves. They would have enough food to keep them alive. Permit no imports of any kind. Then they could not manufacture weapons of war. Do not send our troops, who have already been through such hard fighting experience and so long away from their homes and normal lives, to pass years in occupying Germany. Shutting the Germans up would have a far better effect and would avoid risk of Allied soldiers having to intervene in civil war and probably being attacked by both sides.

Mr. Nizer sees that something must be done to counteract the "poisoning of generation after generation of German minds." He sees that what he calls "de-mentalization" is more necessary than disarmament for the future peace of Europe.

> Against such mania, self-decorated with patriotism and "world-mission," it is futile to hurl moral preachments. German education has established another level of morality, which scorns our own and is impervious to its nobility. Nor can appeals to reason be indulged in, for reason has coagulated into cruel concepts which regard decency as weakness.

Surely it follows from this that the only thing to do with Germany is to make her understand that the rest of the world will not tolerate such mania any longer. I submit this cannot be done by giving her back her trade.

R.A.F. Smash Flying Bomb and Rocket Sites—

FLYING BOMBS DON'T ALWAYS FLY, as the top photograph of a Pas de Calais launching site shows : B, C, D, and E mark where four of the missiles crashed and slid along the ground ; the launching ramp itself (A) was straddled by our bombs.   Below is a large structure, also in the Pas de Calais, believed to be connected with the use of long-range rockets, on which R.A.F. 12,000-lb. or " earthquake " bombs landed : a thick concrete dome covers underground workings (1), near which a 100-ft. crane was being used (2).

Photos, British Official

IN CONSTANT ACTION against the flying bombs, some of which scatter incendiaries, our heavy and light anti-aircraft batteries, recently re-deployed specially to cope with this form of air attack, add very satisfactorily to their tally of kills. Each shell fired is aimed directly at the flying bomb: in this particular circumstance a more effective method than the "box" barrage used so successfully against aircraft.

The A.T.S., who played such a fine part in our anti-bomber defences, soon proved themselves vital in this battle too. In the operations room (1), nerve centre of the A.A. batteries, they plot the course of flying bombs from information received from the R.A.F. and Royal Observer Corps, while others operate a rangefinder out of doors (2). Flashes leap from a gun muzzle during a night action (3); rate of fire is so rapid that the gun appears to be firing in more than one direction at the same time. Gunners bring in remains of a "doodle bug" (4). Shell bursts thicken in the sky as a flying bomb approaches (5).

Photos, British Official, Planet News, Fox, G.P.U.

Will The Nazi War Machine Run Dry and Crash?

A yearly average of 12,000,000 tons of liquid fuel has been needed by Germany to support her mechanized forces alone. The supply now is running dangerously short; for the Nazi home front, too, the fount of essential fuel is almost dry. Dr. EDGAR STERN-RUBARTH explains whence supplies have been forthcoming—and how the red light of danger now glows for the Reich.

GERMANY is extremely poor in natural oil. There are but a few small wells near Wietze, in Hanover, which were hardly worth exploiting before the war. Before squeezing her into his political serfdom, Hitler found Rumania willing enough to sell to him the better part, and finally all, of her production, then the largest in Europe. With the conquest of Poland he found a second reservoir north of the Carpathians, the oilfields of Borislav, Drohobycz, Stanislovo, and Jaslo.

Technical progress accounts for the now rich yields of his own Hanoverian wells, of an originally neglected field at Zistersdorf, in Austria, and of the previously unimportant and only field in France, at Pechelbronn in Alsace. But all that together would not have given him more than half the desired quantity of the precious fuel; and that is why, on the one hand, he ordered his armies' mad drive into the Caucasus and, on the other hand, had hastened the development of plants for the hydrogenation of coal and lignite.

There are no official figures; but a total requirement of between 13 and 15 million tons a year, between 10 and 12 of them for purely military purposes, is a guess based on sound foundations. Theoretically, Hitler was just able to get these quantities during the first three or four years of "his" war, and even to accumulate some emergency stocks by looting the huge fuel dumps of Norway, Denmark, Holland, Belgium and France. But always it was a rather precarious balance, as the table of approximate production figures (tons) in this page shows.

OIL-SHALE, potato spirit and other substitutes had to make up for the missing quantities, while generator gas came to the rescue, with an ever more restricted allocation of liquid fuel for civilian transport and other requirements, up to the end of the fourth year of war. The scores of oil refineries, originally mostly in Rumania, were multiplied by new or enlarged plants all along the river Danube, in Hungary, Austria, Czechoslovakia and Germany; new hydro-genation plants were commissioned wherever coal and lignite deposits permitted, in the Ruhr valley, in central Germany, in Moravia, so as to make up for the natural depletion of the Rumanian wells, hastened by war conditions and the lack of necessary machinery. And without the Allies' systematic bombing campaign even the demands of a three-front war might have been met, to some extent.

	1940	1942	1943
Rumania, raw oil	6,500,000	6,000,000	5,000,000
Poland, raw oil	700,000	650,000	600,000
Hanover, raw oil	75,000	150,000	300,000
Pechelbronn, raw oil	60,000	100,000	150,000
Zistersdorf, raw oils ..	0	200,000	300,000
Germany, synthetic fuel	4,800,000	5,300,000	5,500,000
	12,135,000	12,400,000	11,850,000

MONTHS of Allied bombing have altered all that. Systematically, one after the other, refineries and hydrogenation plants have been flattened out all over Germany and occupied countries; the oil wells themselves, at Ploesti and near Pitesti in Rumania, became one of the foremost targets of British and American bomber fleets operating from Italy and, of late, from Russia; and, together with their huge distillation plants at Giurgiu, Constantza, Campina and elsewhere they should be pretty well devastated by now. The main plants—there are about 24 altogether—for synthetic fuel: the Leuna-Werke the I.G.Farben Trust's and probably all Europe's biggest industrial works, between Halle and Merseburg, the same combine's plant at Ludwigshafen, the Scholven plant at Buer in the Ruhr valley, and many minor ones, shared that fate. Nor did the smaller refineries along the Danube escape; and as careful watch was kept over all repairs done by specialists running around like rats in a cage, Allied air attacks were renewed as soon as improvement seemed imminent.

The results became, eventually, disastrous for Hitler's war machine. The total output of fuel, natural as well as synthetic, fell in June 1944 to only 30 per cent of the requirements of the German forces alone, at a time when their stocks had dwindled to a bare two months minimum quota for the army and three months for the air force. During that month of crisis the Nazis managed to increase the output to nearly 50 per cent, only to see it affected again by new and heavier attacks, while their meagre stocks had been further depleted. First priority over all war material and ammunition was granted to machinery and repair material for oil plants of any kind; all technicians, engineers and workers who had ever held a job in an oil or hydrogenation plant were at once released from the armed forces and the most drastic orders for economizing petrol and lubricants were issued.

Thus the German railways, already ramshackle and overburdened, were deprived of 25 per cent of their quota of lubricant oils and fats; the tank training units, and even the Luftwaffe in all its training camps, base airfields and transport wings, suffered a cut of no less than 50 per cent; the subsidiary army units such as engineers, pioneers, signallers and so on were wholly or partly deprived of their motorized transport and, like the ambulances in all towns and cities not under permanent threat of air attacks, were provided with makeshift equipment for going back to horse-drawn locomotion.

CLUMSY, heavy, generator-gas driven vehicles put in an appearance, even in front of our own jeeps and motor-lorries of the latest design; and the 10th Panzer Division in Normandy, except for its tanks, runs entirely on wood-gas. Apart from the official and decreed economies—disastrous as their consequences may be with whole units plodding along at a speed of two or three miles an hour while others move with ten times that speed—the lack of sufficient stocks everywhere, and of fuel for transport engaged in carrying petrol to forward units, has brought about local shortages which seriously endanger military operations. Hundreds of planes and thousands of vehicles, tanks, and guns had to be abandoned to the Russians simply because there was no fuel—not even enough to destroy them.

This state of affairs is bound to become still worse with the loss of the Polish oilfields (Borislav and Drohobycz fell to the Russians in August 1944). A Russian penetration into the Wallachian plains would accomplish that which our air assaults systematically prepared: Hitler's loss of well-nigh all his supplies in natural oil. He may fight against these looming shadows of utter defeat by cutting out all motorized transport at home, and by depriving industries and craftsmen of the small ration so far left to them.

But all that will only accelerate his breakdown. For the workers, engaged in 10, 12 or 14 hours of daily uninterrupted toil, will be unable to reach their benches; and thousands of small but useful factories all over Germany and in occupied countries will have to close down for lack of petrol or paraffin oil for driving their engines. Thus the collapse of Hitler's war machine within a very few months is inevitable, because he will be unable to feed its motor.

ANOTHER GERMAN OIL REFINERY RAN DRY after the R.A.F. visited these storage depots at Donges, near St. Nazaire, France, where great destruction was caused in two heavy attacks on July 23 and 24, 1944. The giant storage tanks were blown open, buildings were flattened, and an oil tanker lying off the quay was tossed on its side. *Photo, British Official*

From China Our Allies Press On to Burma

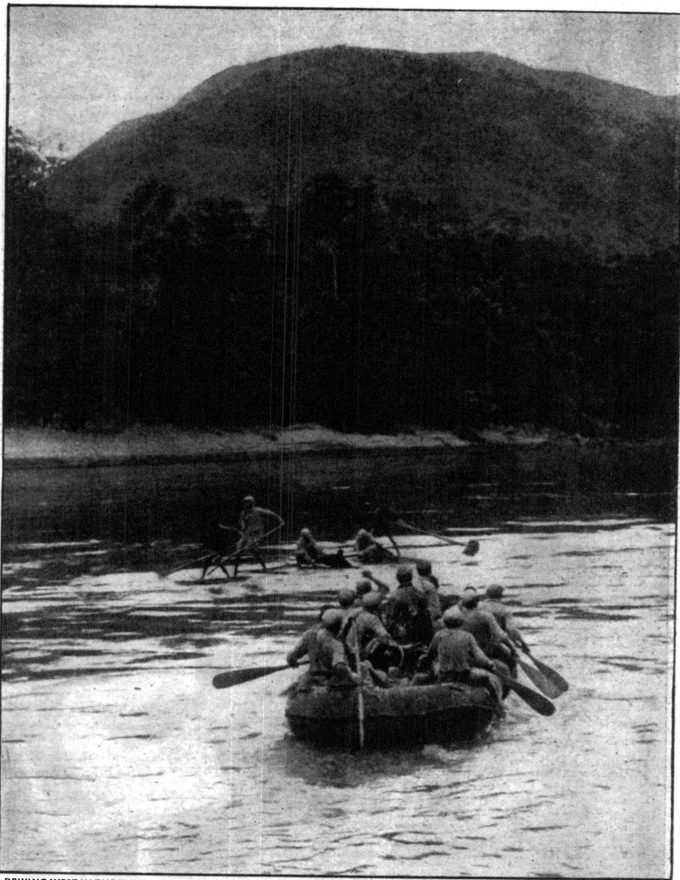

DRIVING WEST IN THE YUNNAN PROVINCE of China towards a junction with the Allied forces in Burma, our Far Eastern comrades-in-arms cross the Salween River in rubber boats and makeshift bamboo rafts in their determined forward push. By August 5, 1944, they had reached a point some 50 miles south-east of the North Burma town of Myitkyina, Japanese base held by them for two years and captured by the Allies on August 4 after months of bitter fighting.

Photo, U.S. Official

How Russia Cares for Her Wounded Warriors

IN THE QUIET of a Red Army hospital, after the furious clangour of the field, Soviet fighting men receive all the kindness and highly skilled care known to Russian medical science that is their due. Given doctor's permission, a patient can order any delicacy he fancies; this Ukrainian airman (1, right) chose a tureenful of borshch, a soup made from cabbage and other ingredients. Gift parcels are distributed regularly (2). Patients are informally entertained by outstanding performers with plays, concerts and recitations: an actress (3) recites to her audience. A woman surgeon performs a delicate lung operation (4). In the rest room recuperating men relax (5).

Photos exclusive to
THE WAR ILLUSTRATED

I WAS THERE!

Eye Witness Stories of the War

We Pounded the Japanese Stronghold of Sabang

The crippling 35-minute surprise attack by Admiral Somerville's Eastern Fleet on July 25, 1944, against the dockyard, harbour installations, wireless equipment and workshops at Sabang, the Japanese-held naval base in Sumatra at the entrance to the Straits of Malacca, is described here by Reuters correspondent Alan Humphreys, who was on board the flagship.

AT the rate of ten tons a minute, 350 tons of steel and high explosive struck Sabang in the 35 minutes the bombardment lasted. Battleships, cruisers and destroyers poured shells varying from 4-in. to 15-in. into the base at close range. When the flagship turned away after completing her firing she was only two miles from the green, jungle-covered hills which rise steeply from the sea around Sabang. It was the first time that any Allied naval surface force had been in sight of Sumatra since the dark days of the Japanese onrush in 1942.

The fleet reached its objective unobserved and the first thing the Japanese knew was intensive strafing by carrier-based Corsair fighters. Among the Corsairs' targets were three airfields, including one at Kota Raja on the Sumatra mainland. Confirming suspicions that Japan's air strength was weak, only four aircraft were found and all destroyed. Disturbing as was the air raid to serene Japanese slumbers, the first reaction of the defenders when they saw the powerful battle fleet closing in must have been one of extreme dismay.

The fleet was divided into five forces for the operation. The carriers with their escort stayed a considerable way out at sea. The aircraft went strafing, were ready to deal with any Japanese aircraft coming up, provided an umbrella over the warships and acted as spotters for the guns. Battleships made up another force. A third force which included Dutch warships penetrated the harbour and dealt with installations at Sabang. Two other forces were devoted to attacks on coastal targets east and west of Sabang.

Just before 6.55 a.m.—zero hour—the loudspeakers announced: "Two minutes to go!" An unusual silence developed, so that sounds normally unnoticed became insistent—the remote slap of spray, the faint hiss from the funnel, the bubbling whistle of wind in the wires just overhead. Then

with a great belch of flame, a greater belch of orange-brown smoke, a blast of hot air and a jolt back on to the heels, the first salvo was fired from the big guns at a range of 17,000 yards.

A rating fired his own shot. "Share that lot amongst you!" he said, as the guns roared. One by one resonant booms told that the other battleships had joined in the bombardment. Then began the process described beforehand by a gunnery officer, of "inflicting the maximum damage in the minimum time." The particular target of the flagship was the military barracks area, and in the words of the same gunnery officer, the Japanese garrison there was given "a new type of reveille in the form of a 15-in. 'brick'."

For the next quarter of an hour it was a rapid succession of jarring explosions. The force going into the harbour was firing

furiously, one destroyer depressing a multiple pom-pom and spraying the defences with that also. Three Japanese batteries inside the harbour engaged these warships, a number of bursts throwing up grey gouts of water all round and close to them. On the run in, one battery was silenced the workshops and wharves were attacked, and a large crane was seen to topple over. Two batteries were silenced on the run back. The report on the operations concluded with the words "quite a skylark!"

The remainder of the fleet carried out the bombardment unmolested. It appeared there were no coastal batteries. All the time a great cloud of smoke was steadily thickening over Sabang, a testimony to the weight and accuracy of the bombardment. The Japanese defenders, who made only the slightest reaction to the air attack, apparently nettled at last, whistled up their aircraft, possibly from Sumatra, possibly from Malaya.

Two hours after the fleet withdrew, a Japanese two-engined bomber was reported approaching. It was shot down by Corsairs. Shortly afterwards a Zero fighter found the fleet. He came in as close as ten miles—then started to run home. He reported from 14 miles away, then 25, then 28. At this point the fighters cried "Tallyho!" and a moment later the Zero went into the sea 30 miles away.

I Visited a Bombed-Out Flying-Bomb Site

Pointed at Bristol, bombed by Allied Air Forces into abandonment, a flying bomb installation at Martinvast, Normandy, has been inspected by war correspondent Peter Duffield. His story, and interview with the former owners of that site, appear here by arrangement with the Evening Standard.

FIVE years ago, in the uneasy but peaceful summer of 1939, Count and Countess Hubert Pourtales lived in one of Normandy's truly idyllic chateaux. They lived as they had always lived, smoothly and gently. Their world—their castle and their village. The Count, then 76, was serving his forty-eighth year as mayor of the tiny hamlet of Martinvast, six kilometres south of Cherbourg. A herd of fine Normandy cattle grazed over his rich green 250-acre dairy farm. His foals were numbered among the finest French thoroughbreds. His castle, filled with treasured furnishings and unsurpassed tapestries, was one of Normandy's show pieces. You will find his racehorses in the Stud Book. The years passed . . .

Last November they began to build the great steel and concrete flying-bomb site on the count's green, wooded acres. They came in hordes, German workers, foreign workers, enlisted French workers. Tented camps sprang up under the hedges and the trees. A new German regiment moved into the château—an A.A. command which elbowed the count, countess and their 53-year-old daughter, Countess d'Hauteville, still closer into their three remaining rooms. The fields were porcupined with Hun emplacements. Everything was camouflaged. The work went on in November and December. The year 1943 turned.

"The first time you raided us," said the Countess d'Hauteville, "was on January 14 at 9 p.m. How could I forget? It was apparent that they knew the location of the bomb site, guarded, hidden and secret as it was. And you must have known the château was the German H.Q."

The first raid burned half the château almost beyond recognition, blew great gashes in the sturdy old masonry, crushed one tower, obliterated the tennis court, smashed every window—and blew the German H.Q. clean out of the castle. "They left first thing next morning," said the countess, "taking nearly all our furniture, looting and drinking their way from Martinvast."

For a time the count and his family were left alone both by the Germans and the Allied Air Force. Furnitureless, they moved out to the little lodge at the end of their avenue drive, but the Germans came back, and so did the bombing.

"The next big raid," said the countess, "was on May 8, when the bomb-site and the castle were again attacked. That time you set the farm on fire. There were some Germans hiding there, but only one of them was killed. During the May 13 raid we hid in the old eleventh-century tower, which is the oldest part of the château. By then we were alone at nights except for the surrounding A.A. gunners. The workers no longer remained in the camps during the night. They had been driven by your bombing to Barneville, about 15 kilometres away. They

JAPANESE-HELD NAVAL BASE at Sabang in Northern Sumatra was on July 25, 1944, subjected to a fierce bombardment by Allied warships and carrier-based aircraft, as told above. The photograph shows a Barracuda plane which took part in a previous attack on Sabang by the Eastern Fleet on April 19, leaving behind it columns of smoke rising from fires started there. See map in p. 774, Vol. 7.

Photo, British Official

used to come to work every morning by bus. Yes, the raids did some good.''

As the tall, white-haired Countess d'Hauteville made that selfless remark to me today she was standing among the ruins of her once beautiful home. Through the empty crusts of arched windows we looked out on the acres where a torrent of high explosives had fallen. There, in the bomb-pitted pasture land, the last foal of a long lineage of thoroughbred horses had toppled dead in the bombing.

Behind us, as we stood gingerly on some remaining floorboards, the rooms were bare of all save dirt and debris. Pieces of finely carved ceiling, shreds of tapestry, sections of carved stone mantelshelves, alone bore witness to bygone beauty.

"Yes," she repeated, "the raids did some good. I have never seen our bomb site. Always we were told to keep away. It was secret, very secret, they told us. Even the French workers were unable to get information."

We took the Countess on her first visit to the bomb site. She looked silently at the long, twin concrete ramps, the curving bombproof storage tunnels, the concrete assembly hangar, the narrow gauge rails that were to transport the bomb to the ramp, the sunken, apparently non-magnetic, pillar box where the gyro was to be adjusted and controls set.

We inspected one element of the emplacement after another. It was scattered over perhaps 30 acres of her ground, each section

DRAGGED ON A WOODEN TROLLEY, this flying bomb is being moved to a launching ramp in France for discharge against Southern England. This is the first German official photograph to reach this country of " Revenge Weapon Number One " at its starting-point. See the accompanying story, and illus. pages 244-245.
Photo, Daily Express

small and remote from the others. It was superbly camouflaged, surely invisible from the air. We saw no direct hits on concrete buildings themselves, but craters pitted the linking roadways and the warm, rich acres of earth between sections. There was no doubt of the delaying effectiveness of the Allied bombings !

enough for Lvov. It must be Przemysl." The salutes which bring everyone into the streets or to the windows are those which celebrate the liberation of the capital of a Republic, like Kiev, Minsk and Vilna. They get 24 salvos from 324 guns and on those occasions windows rattle and buildings seem to shake.

Nowadays it gets around beforehand that a big salute is expected. Little boys, who see everything, notice exceptionally large numbers of guns being brought in from the outskirts to take up their positions on appointed sites along the Moscow river. And the news goes around. A.A. battery crews which fire the salutes are men, but on the roofs Red Army girls fire off the rockets. It is a responsible job, for they have to get them all into the air together, but it is a job they like. Incidentally, it is reliably reported that the rockets are part of the vast booty captured from the Germans. I hope it is true.

When those Victory Salvos Roar in Moscow

Since the guns of Moscow fired their first thunderous salvos in August 1943 in celebration of the liberation of Orel, there have been many scores of these salutes to enliven and encourage the Muscovites and the Allies in general. Paul Winterton, News Chronicle special correspondent, sent the following descriptive report from Moscow on July 31, 1944.

THE salute now follows a well-defined ritual. About fifteen minutes before it is due to take place the Moscow loudspeaker network announces : " In a few minutes there will be an important communication. Listen to our broadcast." This is repeated several times. Then at the appointed time a male announcer reads in ringing tones the Order of the High Command naming the town taken. About ten minutes later the guns start.

The salute itself has not changed in style — the only change was found after the Kharkov salute, when it was found that, while tracer bullets helped to give a spectacular pyrotechnical display, they tended to fall on the

heads of people afterwards. So now we have just guns and rockets. First you see the red flash of the guns in the sky, then hear the roll of explosions, and, last of all, the crack of hundreds of red, green and white rockets soaring skywards from dozens of rooftops. All over Moscow when the rockets are at the top of their flight the streets become as light as day.

After a time you can learn to judge the importance of the event being celebrated without hearing the announcement. For small places there is a salute of 12 salvos from 124 guns. For big towns 224 guns fire 20 salvos. The expert will cock his ear to the window and say : "Hum, that's not big

Street crowds which watch the salutes are just as large and just as eager as they were when the first salvos were fired. Round caps are still thrown into the air as the rockets go up and there is eager discussion of the latest victory. There was never a time when the movements of the Red Army were more closely followed than now, and that is natural enough because there was never a time when their activities were so exciting.

I was in a theatre the other night when a salute was announced on the radio. In the interval between acts the director of the theatre came on the stage and told us Bialystok had fallen. There was loud clapping and then all stood for the national anthem. In the middle of the anthem the director called for cheers for the Red Army and for Stalin. There is no doubt that spirits are very high. Forty-one salutes in just over a month—forty-one towns recaptured—would make anyone cheerful.

These summer nights, of course, the rockets lose some of their effect. Fireworks ought to be a winter sport. Generally speaking an effort is made to keep the salute until it is beginning to get dark—ten or eleven o'clock is the favourite time—but when you have a day like last Thursday (July 27), with five salutes to work off in an evening, you have to make an early start. What with the national anthem played five times and 100 salvos from 224 guns and then cheerful music from loudspeakers going on until one in the morning, I think that was about the noisiest night I have ever known in Moscow. Well, nobody minds noise in a good cause !

MOSCOW'S VICTORY GUNS announce yet another Red Army triumph, their flashes and the rockets above illuminating the Kremlin. First time the Russians heard there was on August 5, 1943, when, to celebrate the double victory of Orel and Byelgorod, Marshal Stalin ordered a salute of 12 salvos of 120 guns. See story above. PAGE 250 *Photo, Pictorial Press*

They Bake 1,000 Loaves a Day for Invasion Craft

Admiral Sir Bertram Ramsay, Allied Naval C.-in-C., has sent a message of congratulation to the men in the landing ships engaged in the vitally important work of building up supplies in Normandy. Here is the story of one of these little ships—a Landing Barge Kitchen—by a Naval reporter.

WE found her amid a huddle of ships on a Normandy beach when the tide was out—a queer, top-heavy-looking craft surmounted by a battery of galley chimneys. At some time in her career she had been a Thames lighter. But now, equipped with twin rudders, twin screws and engines which will drive her through the water at twelve knots, she is the Sailors' Joy. Officially this strange craft is one of ten L.B.K.s—Landing Barge Kitchens—which are providing hot meals for the men in hundreds of small craft which are helping to ferry supplies from the ships to the Normandy beaches.

The mud exposed hereabouts at low tide does not always smell pleasantly, but this afternoon the L.B.K. is baking bread for six hundred men. Mud or no mud, this spot smells good to one who knows hard compo biscuits. The C.O., wearing a white pullover and flannel trousers, was walking around his craft. He was critically examining the work of the crew, who were giving the hull a new coat of white paint. The C.O. is Midshipman J. S. McIntyre, R.N.V.R., of Berwick-on-Tweed. He is nineteen and very proud of his first command.

"This is definitely an occasion for painting ship," he said. "We have a reputation to maintain : already we have been recommended for our accounts, for the cleanliness of the ship and the high standard of the food we serve. Our complement is 25 men, including thirteen cooks, nine seamen and three stokers. Until recently we supplied, every day and in all weathers, hot meals for 500 to 700 men. Now we are baking 1,000 lb. of bread a day. Our last dinner was served to 600 men. On the menu were roast pork, cabbage and baked potatoes, followed by fruit and custard. Among the craft we supply are L.C.M.s, L.C.V.(P.)s and supply and repair barges.'' That is a considerable achievement for thirteen cooks, among them men who until recently were a miner, a bricklayer, and a factory hand. The Commanding Officer invited us on board.

We found a ship spotlessly clean, a floating kitchen in which was installed the most up-to-date equipment, including oil-fired

HUNGRY LINE UP for a hot meal at the serving hatch of a L.B.K.—landing barge kitchen—whose achievements in feeding the crews of small craft busy about the Normandy beaches are recounted here.
Photo, British Official

ranges, automatic potato peelers and refrigerators. Pots and pans were polished until they shone. In a rack on the starboard side were scores of golden loaves, still warm from the ovens. The Chief Cook, Petty Officer R. F. White, of Shepperton, Surrey, has had immense experience in field bakeries and kitchens. He took part in the Africa landing and was later in the Sicily operations. He appreciates the splendid work of his present shipmates.

"Except for two leading cooks I do not believe any of them had been afloat before D-Day," he said. "The weather then was so bad that we lost both rudders and had to turn back. All but five of the crew were seasick, for we were rolling until the decks were awash." The Landing Barge Kitchen is one of the most popular ships in the armada off the Normandy coast.

On a calm night, when ships come alongside, more than one hundred and twenty craft have called for the insulated canister of steaming meat and vegetables, and safari jars of soup, coffee or tea. In rough weather the squadron leaders organize the distribution of the food to their own craft. The Kitchen is always busy, for it must be prepared to supply hot meals at any time.

"During the gale, when we were dragging our anchor nearly to the beach, and we were constantly being shelled by enemy batteries, the cooking still went on," said Petty Officer White. "We had many near misses. One shell dropped five yards away and peppered the meat safe with shrapnel. We are a lucky ship. There were no casualties. During all that time we victualled the Army or anyone who came on board. These ships are fitted out to carry about a week's supply of food for 800 men." Petty Officer White is particularly proud of one fact. During the whole of one month—June—corned beef was issued for only one supper, and then it was disguised as cottage pie.

OUR DIARY OF THE WAR

AUGUST 1, Tuesday *1,795th day*
Western Front.—Granville cleared of the enemy. Le Beny Bocage captured by Allied troops.
Russian Front.—Kaunas, Lithuania, captured by Red Army. Polish Underground Army in Warsaw began open fighting against Germans.
General.—Marshal Mannerheim became Finnish President in place of Ryti.

AUGUST 2, Wednesday *1,796th day*
Western Front.—Allied formations reached Vire, south of Caumont.
Air.—Flying-bomb depots and road and rail bridges in N. France attacked by Allied bombers.
Balkans.—Allied land, sea and air forces raided two islands off Dalmatian coast.
General.—Turkish Govt. broke off diplomatic and economic relations with Germany.

AUGUST 3, Thursday *1,797th day*
Western Front.—American armour reached Dinan and Rennes in Brittany.
Air.—Allied aircraft attacked flying-bomb depots in N. France, and railways at Saarbruecken and Strasbourg.
Russian Front.—Soviet troops forced the Vistula S.W. of Sandomierz.

AUGUST 4, Friday *1,798th day*
Western Front.—Second Army tanks reached Villers Bocage.
Air.—U.S. heavy bombers attacked experimental station at Peenemunde and German oil refineries.
Italy.—S. African troops of Eighth Army reached outskirts of Florence.
Burma.—All organized Japanese resistance ceased in Myitkyina.
General.—Purge of German Army announced.

AUGUST 5, Saturday *1,799th day*
Western Front.—Allied armour reached Redon in Brittany. Villers Bocage and Aunay-sur-Odon, Normandy, captured.
Air.—U.S. bombers attacked oil plants and armament works in Germany. R.A.F. dropped 12,000-lb. bombs on U-boat pens at Brest.
Russian Front.—Soviet troops captured Stryj, in Carpathian foothills.

AUGUST 6, Sunday *1,800th day*
Western Front.—German armoured attack at Mortain smashed by rocket-firing planes.

Air.—R.A.F. bombed flying-bomb bases and U-boat pens at Lorient. U.S. bombers again attacked German oil plants and armament works.
Russian Front.—Drohobycz, Polish oil centre, captured by Red Army. U.S. bombers from Britain landed in Russia after bombing aircraft works near Gdynia.
Mediterranean.—Allied bombers attacked railways and oil storage areas in Rhone Valley and U-boat pens at Toulon.
Pacific.—First of three attacks by Allied aircraft on Davao airfield, Philippines.

AUGUST 7, Monday *1,801st day*
Western Front.—1st Canadian Army launched offensive south of Caen.
Air.—More than 1,000 R.A.F. bombers attacked German line south of Caen.
Russian Front.—Borislav, chief Polish oil centre, captured by Soviet troops. U.S. bombers attacked oil refinery in Poland from Russian bases.

AUGUST 8, Tuesday *1,802nd day*
Western Front.—Canadians made progress towards Falaise.
Air.—More than 600 U.S. bombers operated in support of Allied troops in Caen area.
Russian Front.—U.S. bombers left Russian bases, bombed Rumanian airfields, and landed in Italy.
Germany.—Field Marshal Witzleben

and seven other high officers condemned and hanged for plot against Hitler.
China.—Hengyang, on Hankow-Canton railway, fell to Japanese after two months' siege.
General.—Announced that Polish armoured division was in action with Canadians in Normandy.

AUGUST 9, Wednesday *1,803rd day*
Western Front.—Le Mans occupied by Allied forces.
Mediterranean. — Allied aircraft bombed lock-gates of important canal near Venice, and oil plants and airfields in Hungary.
Sea.—Announced that number of U-boats sunk during the war exceeded 500, greater than number of merchant ships sunk.
General.—Gen. Eisenhower's H.Q. moved from Britain to France.

AUGUST 10, Thursday *1,804th day*
Air.—Allied aircraft attacked railway targets east, north-east and south-east of Paris and bombed fuel depots.
Far East.—Super-Fortresses bombed Nagasaki, Japan, and Palembang oil refinery, Sumatra.
Pacific.—All organized Japanese resistance ceased in Guam.
General.—Formation of joint Anglo-American airborne force announced. Removal of Gen. Maitland Wilson's H.Q. from N. Africa to Italy announced.

AUGUST 11, Friday *1,805th day*
Western Front.—Allied troops entered Angers and Nantes.
Italy.—Announced that German troops had withdrawn north of Florence.
General.—Announced that Mr. Churchill had arrived in Italy.

AUGUST 12, Saturday *1,806th day*
Western Front.—German 7th Army began to withdraw from Mortain-Vire sector.
Air.—R.A.F. made heavy night attacks on Brunswick and Opel works at Russelsheim.
Mediterranean.—U.S. bombers on shuttle-trip bombed airfield near Toulouse from Italian base and returned to Britain.
General.—Mr. Churchill met Marshal Tito and Yugoslav Premier in Italy.

AUGUST 13, Sunday *1,807th day*
Western Front.—Announced that American troops from Le Mans had reached Argentan, south of Falaise.
Air.—Allied aircraft harried German withdrawal in France ; over 1,000 heavy bombers attacked roads on the Seine, from the sea to Paris.
Mediterranean.—Allied bombers attacked railway bridges in Southern France.

AUGUST 14, Monday *1,808th day*
Western Front.—Canadians resumed offensive towards Falaise in conjunction with U.S. troops from Argentan.
Air.—R.A.F. bombers attacked German positions before Canadian advance. Transport facilities in France and Germany heavily bombed by Allies.
Russian Front.—Osowiec, stronghold 18 miles from E. Prussia, captured by Soviet troops.
Mediterranean.—Allied heavy bombers continued to attack military installations in S. France and N.W. Italy.
General.—Announced that French armoured division under Gen. Leclerc was operating in France.

AUGUST 15, Tuesday *1,809th day*
Mediterranean.—British, U.S. and French troops landed on southern coast of France between Nice and Marseilles ; airborne landings also carried out.
General.—Announced that American Third Army was in action in Northern France, under Gen. Patton.

★ ========== *Flash-backs* ========== ★

1940
August 7. British made military agreement with Gen. de Gaulle.
August 15. Croydon airport bombed in German daylight raid.

1941
August 15. Soviet-Polish military agreement signed in Moscow.

1942
August 5. Germans captured Voroshilovsk and crossed River Kuban.

1943
August 4. Russians captured Orel.
August 5. British troops entered Catania, Sicily.
August 12. U.S. aircraft bombed Japanese bases in Kurile Is.
August 14. Italian Government declared Rome an open city.
August 15. U.S. and Canadian forces landed on Kiska Island, in the Aleutians.

THE WAR IN THE AIR

by Capt. Norman Macmillan, M.C., A.F.C.

THE part played by air power in the invasion of Normandy was referred to by Air Chief Marshal Sir Trafford Leigh-Mallory, C.-in-C. Allied Expeditionary Air Force. He made these important points:

Before the invasion constant watch was maintained over the Channel by Allied aircraft. The moment German reconnaissance planes appeared they were chased back. In the six weeks prior to the invasion the Luftwaffe made but 129 reconnaissance flights, of which only 11 penetrated to the English coast.

Because our air power had smashed all enemy radiolocation stations, the movement of the colossal fleet steaming from the English coast since six o'clock on the morning of the previous day was not known to the enemy until one o'clock on the morning of D-Day. He lost many valuable hours for troop movement.

Here is the reverse side of the picture. If air forces on both sides had been completely wiped out the invasion would not have been attempted. The Germans, with the magnificent communications of Northern Europe, would have been able to build up their forces in the lodgement area at a speed which would have made it impossible for us to embark on the operation with any hope of success.

Turning again to the obverse side, in the three months before D-Day Allied air forces from the United Kingdom destroyed over 2,600 German aircraft in combat. In 2 months since D-Day 1,800 were destroyed in the battle area. In July Allied aircraft destroyed 400 tanks. When the Americans broke through at Coutances, Allied fighter-bombers destroyed 147 enemy tanks in one day. In July fighter-bombers destroyed over 3,000 German motor transport vehicles.

THIS is nothing short of a turning of the tables. In the first Battle of France in 1940 the Luftwaffe enjoyed air supremacy and their armoured forces were as powerful on the ground. They swept across France with astonishing speed. Today the Germans are reaping where they sowed. In the same area from which the last British troops were evacuated from France during the night of June 19-20, 1940—from the same ports of Cherbourg, St. Malo, Brest, and St. Nazaire —the present Allied counter-assault is proceeding under conditions as favourable to Allied arms as those that favoured German arms in France in 1940. Indeed the conditions are more favourable, for the Germans cannot evacuate Europe and retire, as we did, into a base where we could prepare for the return stroke.

It is now increasingly clear that the turning-point of the whole war was the August-October Battle of Britain in 1940, when about 1,000 first-line aircraft of Fighter Command and the Anti-Aircraft Command between them inflicted the first defeat upon the Wehrmacht. Note that that was before Hitler took over the supreme command of the German forces. The Battle of Britain was won against the professional German general staff. Now, after four years of continuous air warfare against the Luftwaffe, the Allied air forces have gained complete supremacy of the air, and obtained for the Allied Expeditionary Force the conditions which the Luftwaffe failed to provide for the German expeditionary force of 1940.

DURING the four years which have elapsed, technical advances in aircraft have been marked—in range of flight, load carried, operational height, and speed. The Mosquito can carry to Berlin twice the bomb-load at double the speed of some of the bombers we possessed when the war began, and it does this more safely with a crew of two than the former aircraft did with crews of four and five. We did not have a fighter-bomber when the war began; now we have a whole stable of them. Of this type Mallory said: "The fighter-bomber is a splendid weapon for exploiting a victory, and when the enemy begins to fall back all along the line it is a weapon we intend to use to the utmost."

Production of the Hurricane ceased during the first half of August 1944. The latest Hawker fighter is the Tempest. It has been used against the flying bombs (some carrying about 20 incendiaries), powered

Group Capt. J. D'ARCY BAKER-CARR, A.F.C., was chiefly responsible for the development of the rocket projectile used by our Typhoons, with which he had experimented since August 1942. Aged 38, with 15½ years service in the R.A.F., he was previously a fighter pilot.
Photo, British Official.

with the 2,200 h.p. Napier Sabre engine; a 24-cylinder, liquid-cooled, sleeve-valve H-type engine hitherto used in the Typhoon.

The jet-propelled Messerschmitt-163 fighter has been reported in action, first on July 30 and again on August 9, 1944. This aircraft has a single jet-propulsion unit. So far it has shown no advantage over Allied fighter aircraft. The jet-propelled fighter is essentially a high-altitude machine, and would not shine at the lower levels. It is therefore unlikely in its present form to make a good fighter-bomber, or to be a practical instrument in the Normandy fighting.

MEANWHILE, all over Europe the air war against German oil supplies continues as the major strategic employment of air power. Attacks against communications form the principal strategico-tactical task. Tactical engagement includes attacks against the launching sites and storage depots of the flying bombs, and concentrated operations within the fighting zones in France and Italy. In Normandy, Bomber Command applied its area bombing methods with success around Caen, with the Army units ready for immediate follow up. The precision of these attacks is their most remarkable feature, despite the fact that in one such bombardment the Command can drop as great a weight of high-explosive in 20 minutes as the artillery could fire in a week!

Fighting ceased on Guam by August 10. The use of the air bases captured in the Marianas Islands has brought the air ring tighter around Japanese-occupied territory. From the Marianas air attacks have been made against the Volcano Islands 690 miles from Japan, and against targets in Mindanao in the Philippines. The oil centre of Palembang in Sumatra has been bombed from West New Guinea.

The ejection of the Japanese from Myitkyina (Burma), has enabled greater supplies to be flown to China, for the aircraft have been re-routed over a lower section of the mountains. Even petrol for U.S. aircraft operating from within China must be flown in in this way, and the bombing of Japan proper by Super-Fortresses depends on this. Latest raid was against Nagasaki. Hengyang, one of the bases from which Japan proper is bombed, was captured by the enemy on August 8.

Allied airborne combat troops, transport aircraft and gliders that carry them, in Western Europe have been combined into one command approximating to the size of an Army of the Allied Expeditionary Force in France. Its commander is 45-years-old U.S. Lt.-Gen. L. H. Brereton, with British Lt.-Gen. F. A. M. Browning as Deputy Commander.

R.A.F SERVICING COMMANDOS prepare a fighter for action at a forward dispersal point in a Normandy cornfield. While Commandos lift a bomb from the ground before loading it onto the plane, an armourer, perched on a wing, attends to its machine-guns and cannon. The sheaves of corn in the foreground had been carefully " stooked " to prevent damage by the planes to this valuable food.
Photo, British Official

Typhoon Rockets Smashed Great Panzer Thrust

ANSWERING A CALL for maximum air support received from the Americans on Aug. 8, 1944, during a massive panzer counterattack directed towards the sea near Avranches, south of Cherbourg, rocket-firing Typhoons of our Tactical Air Force lost no time going into action—and won the greatest aircraft-versus-tank victory of the war to that date. In all, some 135 German tanks and 200 vehicles were accounted for.

Rows of rockets lie ready to replenish the Typhoons (1). German communications were also attacked; smoke trails mark the rockets' downward course (2). French peasants examine wonderingly an enemy tank blown on its back by a Typhoon (3). Wing Cmdr. C. Green, D.S.O., D.F.C. (4), led a Typhoon wing; it destroyed 38, probably destroyed 14 others, and damaged 12 German tanks, firing more than 800 rockets and 24,000 rounds of ammunition. Devastation wrought by the Typhoons (5). Rocket projectiles were first designed as anti-aircraft missiles and for attacks on enemy shipping.

Photos, British Official

Britain's Colonies in the War: No. 13—Mauritius

STOUT SUPPORT from another small but strong British Empire island, Mauritius, which became a British colony in 1814, aids the United Nations towards victory. Lying in the Indian Ocean, in Port Louis it has vital links with Colombo, Durban and Madagascar (see map). Cyclones which frequently sweep the island would destroy crops such as corn, so the cultivation of sugar cane, which usually stands up to such conditions, is the main industry, although some tea and fibre hemp are also produced. Recent Government grants voted Mauritius and Jamaica £35,000 for the development of the sugar industry and, perhaps more important, installation of food yeast factories. Food yeast, which looks like a cereal, is rich in protein and will play a big part in future world dietary. Mauritius has its own regiment fully trained for modern warfare. Salvage forms another useful contribution ; while wartime restrictions of food supplies are eased by special Nutrition Demonstration Units.

Mauritians are eager to learn how to make best use of their food from the demonstration experts (1). Sugar cane is brought in high-wheeled carts to factories for processing (2). Barges unload scrap metal at a quayside (3). Under jungle conditions the Mauritius Regiment trains (4). *Photos, British Official*

I HAVE just had a letter from a Welsh M.P. who has been appealed to by some of his constituents to redress a wrong committed by one of my assistants. But "committed" is hardly the word, as it concerns an omission. By a process of guessing and sleuthing I suspect my correspondent may be Mr. James Griffiths, Labour M.P. for Llanelly, for the signature offers only a dim clue to his identity. I might state the gravamen of the charge thus : that I did knowingly cause to be drawn and reproduced in No. 176 of THE WAR ILLUSTRATED a certain illustration, to wit a map, chart, or diagram purporting to show the strategic importance of Ulster in this War, and did omit therefrom the name of a certain region of the island of Great Britain, to wit the Principality of Wales. Indeed, my correspondent could have strengthened the indictment by pointing out (as I have just blushed to notice) that the word ENGLAND in the said diagram (for it is *not* a map) impinges upon Welsh territory to the extent of EN. Now, I used to keep a form-letter of reply to those perfervid Scots who rush to their inkpots whenever they see England or English used where the word should more correctly be Britain or British ; but this is the first time that I have come up against the racial and territorial pride of the Welsh ! I would not tolerate the slightest affront to gallant little Wales, but the fact is that the diagram had no occasion to mention Wales, and hardly any need to indicate Scotland and England, as the outline of the British Isles is surely familiar to every reader, and the place names that mattered were given. The essential lines of Ulster's strategic importance towards America and Europe were very clearly shown, and *that* was the sole purpose of the diagram —a very instructive one, let me add. Thus, oddly enough, I find myself apologizing for an error of my own discovery which was not in the original charge : the draughtsman had no right to start the word England well over the border of Wales. In a map properly so-called that would be inexcusable, in a sketchy diagram I hope the offence may be forgiven.

WHAT sort of a propagandist Goebbels would be if he were left alone it is impossible to say. With Hitler always butting in, the Doctor's efforts to humbug the German people and mislead foreigners are ludicrously ineffective. What could be more confusing to Germans, and disheartening as well, than the absurd stories concocted about the plot against the Fuehrer ? The wisest thing would have been to say nothing about it, just to round up the ringleaders quietly and liquidate them. When Hitler yelled "The generals want to kill me ! " millions of his dupes must have asked themselves, "Why do they want to kill him ?" For the first time their silly minds began to entertain doubts as to his being the man they thought him to be. No one could have struck so telling a blow against him as he struck himself. I should think, too, Goebbels must, being a clever journalist, see how stupid it is to shout threats of what secret weapons are going to do. Raising hopes that are not to be fulfilled has the worst results on morale. The Americans were prudent enough not to say a word about their new explosive until it had actually been used against Japanese forces with devastating consequences.

EINSTEIN is said to have had a hand in preparing that compound, which appears to be more appallingly destructive than anything previously devised. He is known to have been working for the U.S. Navy's Ordnance Bureau. That shows how far the atrocities committed by Germans against Jews and others have moved the world-famous professor from his former pacifist attitude.

He is an American citizen now and lives at Princeton, the pleasant university town, where he carries on his researches into gravity and electro-magnetism in a bare study which has little in it but a deal table and deal shelves filled with books. He does not spend much time in reading though. He says over-indulgence in books weakens the capacity for thought, which I am sure is true. He does not over-indulge in tobacco, either ; he smokes only three pipes a day. He does not drink at all—alcoholically, I mean. He can often be met in a Woolworth store, beaming on his fellow-customers and picking out five or ten cent articles that may come in useful some day, he says.

WE used to hear often enough during the interval between the wars that another world-wide conflict would "destroy civilization." Hardly anyone took any notice. Almost everybody fancies that the conditions in which they happen to live are unalterable, eternal ; their imaginations are not equal to picturing any other conditions. But in how many ways has that prediction been fulfilled during the past five years ! Civilization has not been destroyed, perhaps, but it has been suspended in numerous directions. We have cars, but we cannot use them. We have brought aircraft to a high pitch of efficiency, but they are not for any but the armed forces and a very few persons who travel on war errands. It used to take little more than six hours to get to Edinburgh by a fast train. Now it takes between ten and eleven. Then consider the shortage of books. Books are a necessary element of civilization. Yet it is hard, if not impossible, in Britain today to

Lt.-Gen. F. E. MORGAN, C.B., whom Mr. Churchill, in his speech on August 3, 1944, named as the head of the British and American staff behind the Normandy invasion planning. Aged 50, he served with distinction with the Royal Artillery in the 1914-18 war.

PAGE 255   *Photo, British Official*

buy those which are most worth reading, because they are not being re-issued as they used to be. Cheap editions of famous works are for the time being a thing of the past. An enormous quantity of paper is still wasted—on foreign political pamphlets, for example ; but publishers are kept very short.

HOW hard it is to arrive at the truth about anything has been amusingly illustrated by a dispute in newspapers as to how Leghorn should be pronounced. Some persons who have lived there contend that Leghorn is right with the accent on the "orn." Others, also claiming to know their Italy well, say the Italians put the accent on the "Leg" as most of us do. In modern Italian the name is not Leghorn at all, but Livorno, which appears to be a lazy corruption of the other. Some Italians, however, appear to say Legorn or Leg-orn still. I have never been more struck by the conflicting statements about what ought to be easily ascertainable facts than when controversy arose as to the expression Herr Bethmann-Hollweg used at the beginning of the 1914-18 war about the Treaty which guaranteed the independence of Belgium. When he was told by the British Ambassador in Berlin that Britain considered herself bound by that instrument, the German Chancellor said something about "a scrap of paper." Sir Edward Goschen, our Ambassador, told Mr. Valentine Williams, then a correspondent in Berlin, that his words were *ein Stück Papier*. Later, Goschen said the conversation was conducted in English ! The Chancellor himself stated that his expression was *ein Fetzen papier*. So what can one believe ?

THE French countess whose château in Normandy was used as headquarters by a German staff and almost entirely ruined by our bombs, and who said when our troops arrived, "Your bombing did some good ! " (see story in p. 249), had her counterpart in one of the Devon farmers turned out for a time so that American troops might practice warfare over his ground. Now this bit of country near Kingsbridge is being restored to those who lived there. This particular farmer went back a week or two ago and looked at the shattered buildings and devastated fields. But he had in his pocket a newspaper telling of the splendid way the Americans had driven the Germans before them in Normandy and Brittany, and all he said was, "Well, it was worth while. They made good use of our land if they learned to fight like that on it ! "

NOT many people seem to know much about the City Companies, the livery guilds which have survived from the centuries when all members of a trade had to belong to one, and when they played a very useful part in the organization of industry—an indispensable part, indeed. The City means the City of London, the square mile over which the Corporation rules with the Lord Mayor at its head, and which is said to represent more money than any other square mile in the world. Each of the Companies had a Hall of its own. Most of them were fine old buildings. They numbered thirty-five. Now only five stand unscathed by bombing. Others can be repaired. Twenty-three have been completely destroyed, and the question is, Shall they be rebuilt when rebuilding is possible ? Mostly they were used for purely social purposes. I used to dine with the Clothworkers, the Saddlers, the Carpenters, the Skinners, the Vintners in the years when the City Corporation and its Companies were attacked by Radicals for uselessness and extravagance. Very elaborate dinners they gave, and some of them presented each guest with a box of most expensive chocolates in a velvet or red leather case. It was extravagant, but they had plenty of money much of which was devoted to charities. Now, though they are less wealthy, they have many other uses for their funds.

The 'Factory Removers' Went to Colombelles

POUNDED TO RUBBLE by the R.A.F. was this huge cement works at Colombelles, an industrial district north-east of Caen in Normandy. The Germans had made good use of its high points as observation posts from which to watch British movements. Together with German guns and snipers concealed there, it was obliterated by the new and terrifically powerful bombs known as " factory removers " during a concentrated attack on this area on July 18, 1944.

Photo, British Official

Printed in England and published every alternate Friday by the Proprietors, THE AMALGAMATED PRESS, LTD., The Fleetway House, Farringdon Street, London, E.C.4. Registered for transmission by Canadian Magazine Post. Sole Agents for Australia and New Zealand: Messrs. Gordon & Gotch, Ltd.; and for South Africa: Central News Agency, Ltd.—September 1, 1944.   S.S.   *Editorial Address:* JOHN CARPENTER HOUSE, WHITEFRIARS, LONDON, E.C.4.

Vol 8   *The War Illustrated*   N° 189

Edited by Sir John Hammerton

SIXPENCE   SEPTEMBER 15, 1944

BRITISH AND CANADIANS JOINED UP IN NORMANDY when armoured cars of a Canadian reconnaissance unit, driving hard from south to south-east of Caen, contacted advanced British troops after the successful crossing of the River Orne during the night of August 7, 1944. The offensive, preceded by a terrific air bombardment, was part of a vast sweeping movement which trapped the bulk of the German 7th Army in the Falaise " pocket." See also illus. pp. 271-273.
Photo, British Newspaper Pool

NO. 190 WILL BE PUBLISHED FRIDAY, SEPTEMBER 29

Victory Sidelights seen by Our Roving Camera

MAGNETS were used to salvage thousands of screws (above) scattered in the wreckage of a factory hit by a flying bomb. Grounded for overhaul, a flying bomb "killer" records in swastikas painted on its side (top right) the number it has intercepted and caused to crash harmlessly.

TWO-WAY TRAFFIC is a familiar sight at South Coast ports. While R.A.M.C. personnel wait to embark for France, newly-landed prisoners queue up for trains to internment camps : at the port where this photograph (below) was taken 10,000 had been landed up to August 17, 1944.
Photos, British Official, Daily Herald

LAST HURRICANE to be produced (manufacture of this particular type ceased in August 1944), this fighter (left), named "The Last of the Many," is piloted by Group Capt. Bulman, who tested the first Hurricane to take the air in 1935. These famous aircraft, together with Spitfires, made history in the Battle of Britain in 1940.

U.S. LOCOMOTIVES, which for a time hauled British goods trains, were hoisted (below) in full working order, on to cross-Channel boats for shipment to France ; a few hours after landing they were in service in the Cherbourg peninsula. (See also p. 239, Vol. 7).
Photos, New York Times Photos, Daily Mirror, British Newspaper Pool

ALLIED COMMANDERS, in a hayfield in France on August 21, 1944, discussed next moves against the stricken enemy. Back view, left to right, Generals Crerar, Dempsey, Montgomery, Bradley and Hodges.
Photos, British Official

THE BATTLE FRONTS

by Maj.-Gen. Sir Charles Gwynn, K.C.B., D.S.O.

SINCE I last wrote, great events have followed each other at a bewildering pace. The liberation of Paris politically and sentimentally if not strategically is certainly the greatest, and the fact that it was liberated by the French themselves is an additional reason for rejoicing. The possession of such a great road and rail centre will send to accelerate the development of General Eisenhower's plans.

Some time ago I suggested that once Rommel was forced from his anchorage at the base of the Cherbourg peninsula the war would enter on a new and mobile phase. I admit, however, that I never expected that it would develop with such rapid and devastating results. I had not allowed for the complete mechanization of the American Third Army, nor even been certain that it would appear on the Normandy battlefields. Much less did I expect the Germans to make the enormous blunder of allowing themselves to be caught in a pocket when their gambling counter-attack towards Avranches had obviously failed. That blunder may not have altered the results of the war, but it has certainly greatly hastened the complete disruption of the German western front.

The inner Falaise pocket has now been liquidated, and such troops that escaped from it are, as I write, being exterminated in the outer pocket formed on the south bank of the Seine. A fair number may have escaped across the river; but disorganized, and having lost the greater part of their transport and heavy equipment, they can be in no state to meet General Patton's armoured columns which have already crossed the Seine west of Paris. The disaster which befell what was Rommel's Army involved the best and most mobile troops of the other German armies in France which von Kluge sent to its assistance. In actual losses of men and material the disaster is on the Stalingrad scale, and it is the more catastrophic since the army destroyed represents a much higher proportion of the troops on the western front than Von Paulus' Army did on the eastern front.

RESULTS achieved by the armies under Gen. Montgomery's command have been of themselves sufficient to disrupt the whole German outer defences in the west, and the landing of General Patch's armies in the south and the great achievements of the French Forces of the Interior make it doubtful whether the Germans will save enough from the wreck to enable them to rally on their original west wall. The Maginot Line, even if its works have been reversed to face westward, and the Siegfried Line, will not prove impregnable unless adequate numbers of good troops are available to hold them.

There can be no doubt that the Normandy battle was responsible for the disorganization of German defensive plans that enabled General Patch's armies to land with comparatively light opposition. The landing was, however, so admirably planned and executed that no delay occurred in getting material ashore and in building up the bridge-head. The conditions were, of course, vastly different from those in Normandy, where not only was stiff resistance encountered but where it was necessary to secure a defensive position on which a major counter-stroke could be met, and within which preparation for far-reaching offensive action could be made. Weather conditions were also obviously very different in the Channel from those of the Mediterranean in summer. All the conditions when the new landing took place called for rapid and bold offensive action, and General Patch seized his opportunity without hesitation.

THE capture of Marseilles, isolation of Toulon and advance to Grenoble within a week give proof of the energy he displayed. There is every reason to believe that the landing of stores and heavy equipment will be able to keep pace with his advance, especially as the Port of Marseilles and railways leading from it have probably not been extensively damaged. If he can maintain the pace of his original thrusts—and, with the action of the French Forces of the Interior greatly reducing the power of the Germans to delay him, that is not improbable—there is every hope that he will be able to join hands with Montgomery's right wing before any large numbers of the Germans in Southern France escape encirclement.

If the situation of the Germans in France is desperate the situation on their eastern front is equally serious, despite the temporary relief their counter-attacks have given them. Their armies isolated in the Baltic States have little chance of escape, and with the defection of Rumania and the resumption of the Russian offensive towards the Danube, their troops in the islands of the Levant and throughout the Balkan countries are in an even worse predicament: Kesselring's armies in Italy have lost one escape and supply route and will find it difficult to disengage if they attempt to retreat.

Even before the attempt on Hitler's life I was convinced that the majority of the generals of the regular Reichswehr realized the war was lost and were looking for a way to bring it to a speedy end. To prolong the struggle until, and after, Germany itself had been invaded (as Hitler declares he will do) would mean exposing the country not only to the devastation caused by an ever intensifying air attack but to the even greater devastation resulting from resistance on land.

I do not believe that many generals were actually involved in the plot against Hitler, and in any case, with the Reichswehr engaged in the fighting on the outer defensive perimeter, it would have been difficult to ensure sufficient force to crush Hitler's supporters by a military coup d'etat. The warning Hitler has received probably makes it all the more difficult to stage a military revolt without a civil war on a great scale, and one in which the issue would be uncertain owing to the quality of the S.S. troops and their fanatical loyalty to Hitler.

On the other hand I cannot believe that, so long as they commanded troops still capable of fighting, German generals would ever take the responsibility of seeking an armistice without the authority of a central Government. That would be contrary to their conception of discipline and be held to tarnish the honour of the Reichswehr, which must be protected at all costs. Is there any escape from this obvious dilemma? I suggest that the generals may have found one which would satisfy their idea of honour, hasten the end and save Germany from the worst consequences of invasion. We have seen them flinging their last reserves into violent and costly counter-attacks on the frontiers of East Prussia, on the Vistula and in France; counter-attacks which cannot achieve more than temporary results.

THE expenditure of reserves they entail fits in badly with Hitler's determination to maintain the struggle, buying time with space till the innermost ring of resistance is reached. It would, however, fit in with the conception that the inevitable surrender should take place outside the limits of the Fatherland, and thus involve only invasion by armies of occupation. I should, therefore, not be surprised if the generals refuse to retire across the German frontiers but will fight it out beyond them, till their troops, as at Stalingrad, are incapable of fighting any longer and survivors surrender piecemeal. Such a policy would, of course, entail the destruction of the Army: but it might be claimed on the one hand that it would save its honour, and on the other that it would save the Fatherland from the devastating effects of continued resistance within its borders. It would certainly shorten the final death struggle.

Over the broad Seine Allied Tanks Thundered

WEST OF PARIS, U.S. Army engineers rapidly constructed a pontoon bridge (top). Jubilant crowds assembled outside Chartres cathedral as Allied flags were hoisted on the spire (left); the city, 55 miles south-west of Paris, was freed on August 17. The map (right) shows the changing scene in France up to August 25; arrows indicate Allied thrusts. *Photos, Keystone. Map, Daily Express* PAGE 260

Here are Nazi Prisoners Coming in at the Double

"THE END OF THE WAR is in sight," declared Gen. Montgomery on Aug. 21, 1944. Prisoners came in thick and fast and "at the double" (top). Citizens of Deauville, seaside resort on the Channel coast, freed on August 22, gave thanks to their liberators (left). A helping hand was appreciated by this old lady of Falaise (above). *Photos, British Newspaper Pool*

THE WAR AT SEA

by Francis E. McMurtrie

COMMAND of the sea enabled the Allies to land in the south of France on August 15, 1944, and so cut off the escape of the majority of the enemy forces to the west of the Rhone. Knowledge of this and similar facts must inevitably weaken the morale of more distant German garrisons, such as those in the islands of the Aegean (see illus. p. 269). Now that Rumania and Bulgaria have changed sides, their line of communication with Germany through Greece, Albania and Yugoslavia is wearing extremely thin, and a landing in force on the Dalmatian coast would soon cause it to snap. It does not necessarily follow that such a landing will be effected just yet, for it may be found simpler to fasten upon the enemy's communications by sea with Greece. In any case, attacks by Allied surface warships, submarines and aircraft are likely to be intensified in the present situation.

In Norway the German position is equally unhappy. Patriots there are taking advantage of the situation by organizing sabotage on a large scale. One recent achievement of this kind was the destruction of a large depot in Oslo containing 50 aircraft, twice as many aeroplane engines, large stocks of spare parts and quantities of irreplaceable tools. Considerable supplies of explosives must be in the hands of the Norwegians for such a coup to have been possible.

ANOTHER proof of growth of the resistance movement is that many students threatened with conscription for forced labour in Germany have taken to the mountains, whence they wage guerilla warfare against the hated enemy. This must make things very uncomfortable for the second-rate German troops who now garrison Norway, composed chiefly of old men, boys, and men who have been rejected for general service on account of various ailments and disabilities. A proportion of these are said to be suffering from melancholia. All the sound troops have been withdrawn to bolster up the crumbling fronts elsewhere.

IN the Baltic, German efforts to effect a "Dunkirk" withdrawal from Estonia do not appear to be prospering. A considerable number of enemy vessels have been sunk by the Soviet Navy's light forces and aircraft in the Gulf of Finland, including an entire division of destroyers of the so-called "Elbing" type. These are ships of 1,100 tons, with a main armament of four 4·1-in. guns each. Further fighting may be expected in this quarter.

For German vessels in the Black Sea, escape appears now to be impossible. They include a few small submarines, some motor-torpedo-boats and motor-launches, and a number of local craft which have been armed and fitted out as patrol vessels. Though a few contrived to pass through the Bosphorus and Dardanelles disguised as merchantmen, directly Turkey's attention was drawn to the matter egress was barred for the rest.

Some of the German craft in French ports on the Bay of Biscay have already given up hope of escaping and have been interned at the Spanish port of Pasajes. Vessels at Havre and Dieppe have tried to get away to the northward under cover of darkness, only to be intercepted by Allied naval forces and aircraft. Those that were not sunk had to seek such shelter as could be found, some running into small fishing harbours and others beaching themselves. Probably valuable material and personnel were being carried in some of these vessels, few of which are likely to find their way back to Germany.

IN this connexion curiosity was aroused by the mention in an official communiqué of a British destroyer named Retalick. No destroyer of this name had before been reported to exist ; and it would seem on the face of it to be a name more appropriate to one of the American-built frigates of the "Captains" class, to which it is possible she may in fact belong. How many of these frigates are actually in service is not known, but the names of more than 30 have now been released officially on this side of the Atlantic ; and from references in the American Press their total number is believed to be not less than 100. Some are propelled by steam turbine engines, others by Diesels. Armed with 4-in., 40-mm. and 20-mm. guns, together with a plentiful supply of depth charges, they have accomplished much useful work as convoy escorts in the North Atlantic.

With the fall of Toulon the French Navy has regained control of its most important naval base. The dockyard is an extensive one, with dry docks capable of accommodating the largest warships in the French Fleet. How many of the numerous ships in the yard will be found in serviceable condition is uncertain at the time of writing, as the majority were scuttled, set on fire or otherwise badly damaged by their own officers and men to prevent their being made use of by the Germans in November 1942. The sister battleships Dunkerque and Strasbourg, of 26,500 tons, each mounting eight 13-in. guns, are the most valuable units. One if not both have since received further damage in action with Allied bombers, so it is uncertain whether they can be made seaworthy in a reasonable time. Probably both will need to be extensively reconstructed.

TOULON a Great Asset to the French Navy

There are seven cruisers, few of which are likely to be useful at present. Four are ships of 10,000 tons armed with 8-in. guns ; these are the Algérie, Dupleix, Foch and Colbert. The remaining three are the 7,600-ton Jean de Vienne, La Galissonière and Marseillaise, all armed with 6-in. guns. How many destroyers are in the port is uncertain, but the number is estimated to be between 20 and 30. Some of these are known to have been repaired and put into service by the Germans. They vary in size from 2,569 tons to 1,319 tons, and in speed from 37 to 33 knots. There are believed to be over 20 submarines, of from 1,379 to 548 tons. Some of these again have probably been appropriated by the enemy, and may have been lost or taken elsewhere.

Fleet auxiliaries include the seaplane carrier Commandant Teste, of 10,000 tons, and the netlayer Le Gladiateur, of 2,293 tons. There are also three old battleships dating from before the last war, the Provence, L'Ocean and Condorcet. The two latter were removed from the effective list some time ago and adapted for use as harbour training ships. How much further injury the Germans may have inflicted on these ships before surrendering is another problem. No doubt they have done their best to render the dry docks useless by blowing up the pontoons and wrecking the pumping plant.

After taking all this into account, the regaining of a naval port such as Toulon gives the French Navy an asset of much value. Up to now the only useful bases under its own flag in the Mediterranean were Bizerta, Oran and Algiers.

STATIONS MANNED, this M.T.B., with recognition sign white-painted on its deck, leaves for another spell of Channel patrol—shepherding Allied ships to and from the French coast. Motor-torpedo-boats of the Light Coastal Forces of the Royal Navy contribute in no small measure to the success of our landings on enemy-occupied shores. See also p. 501, Vol. 7.

PAGE 262

A New Chapter Opens in the Story of Florence

FREED ENTIRELY FROM GERMAN OPPRESSION by August 22, 1944, the people of Florence thrilled to the sight of men of the 8th Army passing through the city. In the background is Il Duomo, fourth largest church in the world, dating from 1298. On August 11 officials of AMGOT (Allied Military Government of Occupied Territory) had crossed from the south bank of the river Arno, which divides the city, to the north bank, with food for the civilians. Except for five of its famous bridges, this famous Italian city escaped serious destruction, but in streets and buildings German snipers remained active for several days.

Photo, British Official

Craft that Land our Men on Enemy Beaches

" We will fight on the beaches . . ." said Mr. Churchill when in those dark hours of 1940 invasion threatened England. Fate decreed that they should be not of this country but of enemy territory. Inseparable from Allied landings on the coasts of France and Italy and elsewhere is an astonishing variety of vessels, described by ALEXANDER DILKE. See also illus. pp. 656-657, Vol. 7.

THE first experimental models of our landing craft were tried out in the Clyde in pre-war days, Britain being the pioneer of these adjuncts to large-scale invasion. In the years that have passed since those first squat little vessels chugged in Scottish waters, hundreds of shipyards in Britain, Canada, the United States and other countries have been building more and more landing craft, of different types.

Today the United Nations have great armadas of these vessels. Figures are secret, but Mr. Donald Nelson has mentioned the production of 20,000 vessels of fifteen special types already built, with 80,000 landing craft as the total of the programme, these figures being for the U.S.A. alone. Britain has built thousands of landing craft also, using small yards on estuaries and "forgotten" ports and prefabrication on a great scale.

Learning to Put a Ship Ashore

Britain also has trained the sailors to man the landing craft, most of them " hostilities only " men, whose work before the war was quite unrelated to the sea—bus drivers, factory hands, farmers, and so on. Perhaps when they expressed a preference for the Royal Navy, many of them expected to serve on a battleship or in a submarine. But the insatiable demand for experienced sailors for destroyers, and other ships on convoy duty, meant that the "amphibious navy" had to be built up from men who were newcomers. They have been trained at a hundred little places round our coasts and have learned to handle their craft in all kinds of weather. Their chief task is to do what seamen ordinarily spend their lives trying to avoid—put their ship ashore.

LANDING craft are flat-bottomed, square-bowed and of shallow draught. They have to be most things which the ordinary deep-water sailor would consider bad. Some of the types of landing craft and many of their details are secret. But it is possible to give interesting information that shows we have developed what is virtually a new form of warfare, as revolutionary in its way as the tank warfare developed in the 1914-18 war.

There are the amphibious craft, equally at home on land and water ; the small landing boats, not capable of a long sea voyage and carried close to the scene of action on larger vessels ; landing craft tanks and landing craft men which can be grounded to pour out their loads of men, tanks and vehicles through their bows which let down to form ramps ; and there are the big transports. An invasion fleet implies an immense variety of vessels. Standing off the beaches are warships of all kinds laying down covering fire.

EXPERIENCE has shown the need for landing craft to protect themselves, and there are a number of specialized ones. They have their own smoke apparatus, and can call upon the fast motor-gunboats if necessary. Some barges are crammed with A.A. weapons which can be continuously in action. Others, used in Pacific landings, carry rocket guns. Where an ordinary gun's recoil would necessitate a large ship and heavy mountings, the non-recoiling rocket missile can be fired from a small vessel. The craft can thus give cover to the men they are landing.

Most novel of the amphibious vehicles is the Duck, or to be correct DUKW. The popular name is a " happy accident " ; coincidence made the factory serial letters for a boat, a lorry-body and a lorry-chassis into DUKW. The Duck has at the rear a double set of wheels between which is fitted a propeller which can be engaged by the driver, some of its motive power when in the water also being derived from the treads of the wheels, which are kept turning. With this heavy load the engine must remain in low gear while the Duck is in the water, but it gets up a speed of several knots and is perfectly controllable. The Ducks proved themselves in the Sicily landings, and since.

The enormous advantage of the Duck is that it goes straight ashore with its load. Men, ammunition and stores do not have to be transferred at the beaches ; the Duck can drive straight on with its load to the battle lines. It cannot, of course, make a long sea voyage, but must be dropped from a large ship near the beaches. The Ducks go aboard under their own power, fully loaded, are carried close to the scene of action and then launched by methods that remain secret. Basically they are U.S. six-wheel trucks modified to make them float. They

PREFABRICATED SECTION of an L.C.I. (Landing Craft Infantry) on the railway from an American factory to the shipyard for final assembly. *Photo, Associated Press*

are now being built by the thousand, and are manned by the R.A.S.C. In the early days of Ducks, the leader of a V-shaped formation saw a destroyer signalling him frantically. Anxious to know what he was doing wrong, he spelled out the signal. It was a derisive " Quack ! Quack ! " (See p. 301, Vol. 7.)

" Invasion barges " seems a ridiculous term to apply to the L.C.T. and L.C.M., the largest of which are more than 350 tons, can take 250 men and have a range of 1,500 miles with a maximum speed of, perhaps, 18 knots. The crew required for the largest craft may be up to 35 men, and their quarters being cramped they have to " rough it." The craft is strictly functional and old ideas of shipbuilding and design went by the board to make it fit its special task. The majority are of steel, with considerable armour protection against small arms and cannon fire. One of the special difficulties encountered was mounting the compass in the all-steel structure, but this was overcome by demagnetizing.

"Alligators" in the Pacific

All our invasion craft so far described have been driven by propellers. Other methods of propulsion have been tried. At the time of the Japanese onslaught on Pearl Harbour the U.S. were experimenting with an amphibious craft whose caterpillar treads became paddles in the water, and considerable numbers were ordered. Known as " Alligators," they were subsequently used in numerous Pacific island landings. (See illus. p. 167.) One of the difficult tasks that designers have to face is the best size for invasion craft. The bigger the ship, the greater its efficiency. But big craft are more difficult to control, and they entail the risk of "many eggs in one basket." The Japanese have never used large craft and have always mixed their cargoes, carrying tanks, lorries, artillery, machine-guns and men all in one unit.

THOSE who have had to decide on the United Nations invasion craft building programme have constructed " made to measure " craft, in the right numbers and of the right type for each landing place. Admiral Luetzow, the German naval spokesman, devoting one of his latest broadcasts to the Allies' invasion navy paid high tribute to its efficiency, and he said the craft varied from 2½-ton amphibians through 18-ton landing craft and 250-ton landing barges to 5,000-ton transports carrying as many as 20 tanks. In attendance on our invasion craft are clumsy-looking but efficient landing barge kitchens (L.B.K.s) ; these did specially good work off the Normandy coast, as told in p. 251.

IN SOUTHERN FRANCE the first German prisoners were taken as the Allied troops landed on Aug. 15, 1944. By midnight 700 Nazis had been captured ; next day they numbered over 2,000. Above, some of the startled, hatless Germans march to the beach-head. In background is a L.C.I.(L)—Landing Craft Infantry, Large—which carried some of our troops over and returned with the prisoners.

Mightily We Smote the Hun in Southern France

ANOTHER TERRIFIC BLOW TO GERMAN HOPES was dealt by the Allies on August 15, 1944, when British, U.S. and French troops made a landing in force in Southern France, on beaches between Nice and Marseilles. Before the landings were carried out, in the early morning, a formidable air force, which entailed the use of 14,000 airmen, poured down on to the German defences a cascade of bombs. At dawn hundreds of parachute troops were dropped to seize vital positions.

Lieut.-Gen. A. Patch (left), Commander of the Allied 7th Army. As the Allies moved triumphantly on, a U.S. soldier found time to hand sweets to children at a wayside house (right). An Allied patrol passes a sunken tank turret mounted with a 20-mm. gun and a machine-gun, part of the enemy defences at the coastal town of St. Raphael, which was in our hands on Aug. 17 (centre left). Parachute troops descend in mass on strategic key-points (bottom).

Photos, U.S. Official, Keystone, Associated Press

GERMANY'S ARMOURED VEHICLES, employed without success to stop the Allied advances in France, include a wide range of types. On almost every occasion the British and American forces, meeting the most formidable weapons the enemy could produce—vanquished the war machines on which the Nazis pinned their hopes.

Apart from one or two freak weapons, which lasted little longer than their initial try-out in the field, all types of German armour used in France and elsewhere are shown in the sketches in this page.

Bulwark of German tank strength consists of the semi-obsolete Mark IV; the very manoeuvrable Mark V Panther, with a 75-mm. gun; and the 60-ton Mark VI (2) Tiger, which has a powerful 88-mm. gun (originally an anti-aircraft gun) with an extreme range of 16,000 yards, although its accurate knock-out range is much less—some 4,000 to 5,000 yards. The 88-mm. gun is matched by the famous British fast-firing and hard-hitting 17-pounder, now mounted on a high proportion of Sherman tanks. Another German 88-mm. type of armoured vehicle is the Ferdinand mobile gun,

and there is the 88-mm. Hornet; also the 7.5-cm. assault gun on a Mark III tank hull, the 10-cm. howitzer Wasp, and the Bumble Bee, with its 15-cm. gun-howitzer on a Mark IV chassis.

Perhaps the most interesting pieces of German armour—apart from the Beetle explosive tank, which is electrically controlled towards its target by means of a long cable, and its larger version, the B-4, which is man-driven as close as possible and then radio-controlled—are the mobile pill-box, which is towed upside down on detachable wheels and then, turned right way

up, is sunk into the ground wherever required, and the Panzer-Nebelwerfer multi-barrelled rocket gun, which has also an ordinary mortar version. (See illus. p. 724, Vol. 7.)

Many German tanks have been found abandoned because of lack of fuel. Destruction by the Allies of railways forces the enemy to bring up their armour by road, with consequent wastage of fuel and a shortening of the combat life of the vehicle; a heavy tank consumes about one gallon of fuel per mile, and engine replacement or complete overhaul is essential after 600 miles.

Drawn by G. H. Davis, and reproduced by courtesy of The Illustrated London News

Labels on illustration:

- MOBILE LIGHT ANTI-AIRCRAFT GUNS.
- "HORNET" MOBILE 88 mm GUN ON MARK IV TANK CHASSIS.
- PILL-BOX IN POSITION.
- ARMOURED AMBULANCE ON SEMI-TRACKED CHASSIS.
- MOBILE ARMOURED ANTI-AIRCRAFT GUN.
- "BUMBLE BEE" 15-cm MOBILE GUN ON MARK IV CHASSIS.
- ARMOURED TRACTOR.
- MOBILE STEEL PILL-BOX IN TOW.
- "WASP" 10cm ASSAULT GUN MOUNTED ON K.VII CHASSIS.
- "B-4" EXPLOSIVE TANK. THE DRIVER STEERS THE MACHINE TO WITHIN A FEW YARDS OF ENEMY LINES, AFTERWARDS IT IS RADIO CONTROLLED.
- "BEETLE" CONTROL CABLE.
- PANZER-NEBELWERFER MULTI-BARRELED ROCKET GUN.
- 88 mm "FERDINAND" (OR "ELEPHANT") MOBILE GUN.
- 88ML MOBILE PART-ARMOURED DUAL PURPOSE GUN.
- 7.5-cm ASSAULT GUN ON MARK III TANK CHASSIS.
- "TIGER" MARK VI(2) TANK WITH ENLARGED TURRET. WEIGHT 60 TONS. MAX SPEED 8 M.P.H.
- ELECTRICALLY PROPELLED AND CONTROLLED "BEETLE" EXPLOSIVE TANK.
- MARK V "PANTHER" TANK. MAX SPEED 30 M.P.H. WEIGHT 45 TONS.

'Magic Carpets' Help to Keep our Forces Moving

Bogged vehicles and grounded aircraft are millstones around the neck of an army ; if its transport
ceases to flow, offensive action becomes impossible and defence a matter of uncertainty. How
perplexing ground-problems have been ingeniously solved for our forces in France and elsewhere,
by the provision of portable roads and airstrips, is explained by Lieut.-Col. R. M. LESTER.

As our armies advance towards Hitler's inner lines of defence, portable roads and aircraft runways are being laid in forward positions, thus enabling our tanks and other vehicles to move over the worst kind of ground, and our aircraft to land on and take off from advanced bases. Tremendous use was made in North Africa, Sicily and Italy of these "magic carpets," and on them we were operating Allied aircraft from the Normandy beach-head shortly after D-Day. Before the end of the first day of our landing in France our armoured vehicles and lorries were moving along these portable roads.

THIS was made possible by the development of what is known as Sommerfeld Track, the principle of which is that of a spider's web, as already roughly copied by man in the tennis racket. It is a light metal carpet made of wire netting strips, reinforced with steel bars. The engineers lay it in rolls of 25 yards, about 10½ feet wide, with loops at the edges. For aircraft runways widths are linked together by threading the steel bars through the marginal loops ; then a bull-dozer or caterpillar tractor stretches the whole thing taut, the runway then being fastened to the ground by steel spikes driven at the outer edges. Although the landing strip has not the usual hard surface it is perfectly adequate for heavy aircraft.

The material is so light and portable that a runway can be carried in eighteen 12-ton lorries ; the material for a concrete runway of the same dimensions would need 2,500 such lorries. Thus considerable economy in transport is effected. The first of these runways was tried out on an English downland during an Army exercise without any preparation other than levelling the site. Just before this war experiments had been carried out in Palestine, and these were continued, after the outbreak of war, in a small country garden in England. Early in 1940 the Army authorities carried out tests, and this material of light weight, in easily portable loads, was found to be admirably suited to the purpose. So production was started, at first in a small workshop, later on a rapidly expanding scale in the factories.

Extricating Bogged Bombers

In 1941 the first operational track was laid at a fighter station, and it is still in use and giving every satisfaction. Attention was turned meanwhile to the production of special tools that would help to reduce the time taken in laying the track. It was early in 1942 that selected units of the Royal Air Force succeeded in laying a track in 11¾ hours. The next development was that of wooden flexboards, on the principle of continuous duckboarding ; these are laid as wheel tracks, transversely arranged, and held closely together with steel bands which are secured through the timber, the ends of these bands being formed into loops and welded.

The boards are flexible, to suit uneven ground, and can bridge small gaps and holes. Heavy lorry loads can be transported over grass runways on airfield construction jobs by making use of these boards, and no wheel ruts are left in the grass. The R.A.F. uses them for extricating bogged bombers, and for aircraft standings. A great advantage is that they can be removed from site to site as required, for use over and over again.

ON D-Day, as transports reached the Normandy beaches Royal Engineers were ready to perform their particular task without further orders. Sappers and pioneers leapt overboard with their pickets and sledge-hammers and started unrolling the first twenty-five-yard strip of Sommerfeld Track. With our fighters and anti-aircraft batteries giving cover protection, lorries were slowly moving along the tracks as they were laid out. These were linked up with the nearest permanent roads, and soon tanks and other vehicles were proceeding in great convoys. Ducks — our amphibious carriers — ran straight out of the sea up these newly laid tracks, sometimes negotiating steep inclines. They were each carrying over two tons of bombs, for the use of our aircraft in their task of blocking the enemy's lines of communication.

Four Canadians, flying Spitfires, were the first pilots to land there. A captain of the Royal Engineers was in charge of a unit at work on the airfield, which they had set up in about 36 hours. They had been training, of course, for this work for many months, becoming as proficient in track drill as an infantryman in platoon drill. Every hour found the airfield nearer completion, and when the pilots landed there again the following morning it was fully equipped for servicing aircraft and for carrying out minor repairs.

Swamp Converted to Airfield

It is possible to overcome the problem of marshy ground by laying a matting under the track. As an example of how the greatest difficulties in this direction can be speedily overcome, there is the case of a piece of ground near the Volturno River, in Italy, which our Engineers found to be little more than a swamp. Yet in a matter of hours they had levelled the ground, laid out the rolls of steel matting, and converted it into a fully serviceable airfield.

PRESIDENT ROOSEVELT, in a message to Congress, stated that—among other material—44,500,000 yards of Sommerfeld Track had been received by the United States from Britain under Reverse Lend-Lease. There is no doubt that this is one of the outstanding inventions which has made possible our invasion of Europe. What would we not have given to have had such facilities in the last war, when we recollect the endless bogging of vehicles in the appalling mud of the Somme ! In Viscount Allenby's campaign, too, the problem of transporting vehicles over the desert sand was a very serious one, and sheep hurdles were put down to form as firm a surface as possible. The Germans in the last war requisitioned all the curtains they could get hold of in East Prussia, nailed them to wooden frames and placed them on the ground in the region of the Masurian lakes, thus providing very temporary roads for their vehicles.

The "battle of the building-up" in all theatres of war owes much to these portable roads. And there is a post-war aspect of this invention : it will prove invaluable in the making of temporary roads wherever new territories are exploited, or where building takes place on unpromising sites.

THE BAYEUX BY-PASS IN NORMANDY, along which Allied transport is seen passing, was swiftly laid with the Sommerfeld Track which is described in the accompanying article. Without that ingeniously devised track, construction of the road would not have been possible in such a short time as was necessary for our advance. PAGE 267 *Photo, British Official*

Nazis were Snatched from Albanian Stronghold

SURPRISE BLOW was struck in the early hours of July 29, 1944, when British forces, including seasoned Commandos, raided the Albanian mainland, two miles south of the village of Spilje (see map below). Land, sea and air forces co-operated in this successful venture which resulted in the overwhelming of the German garrison and contact with partisan forces in this area. It was the biggest combined operation carried out by the Allies in the Balkans, and lasted for 10 hours after the landings had been made under cover of darkness.

British sharpshooters, merged in the dense shade of a tree (1), covered the advance of comrades pushing on to the objective. With rifles strapped to his sides as emergency splints, a casualty was carried back for first-aid attention (2). Through a wood, under enemy fire, Commandos cautiously made their way forward (3). German prisoners (4) helped to carry boxes of medical supplies back to our landing-craft off the shore.

Photos, British Official

British and Greek Commandos in Aegean Raid

SHOCK TROOPS of Britain and Greece, harassing the enemy in the Aegean, hold down thousands of German soldiers and guns. On the night of July 13-14, 1944, these Commandos assaulted the Dodecanese island of Symi (see map), a few miles north of Rhodes. Landing secretly, the raiders took up positions overlooking the castle of the Knights Hospitallers and attacked at 7 a.m. By the afternoon the enemy had been overwhelmed; the entire garrison, which included Italian Fascists, was liquidated and large quantities of ammunition were destroyed.

In an emplacement overlooking Symi harbour a sergeant prepares the demolition charge for an enemy gun (1). Sappers about to go ashore to blow up German installations (2); two of their comrades, already established on the island, concealed themselves among rocks (3), covering the approach of other raiders assailing an enemy billet. One of the landing craft leaves its base ship, those left behind giving a hearty send-off (4).

Photos, British Official. Map by courtesy of The Times

The Story Behind Britain's Vast Radio Blitz

Every hour of the 24 the air over Europe is charged with the War-Voice of Britain sent out by the B.B.C. In frantic endeavour to quell the unceasing Voice from London the Nazis are devoting more time, money, personnel and material than they are expending on their own broadcasting, as explained here by Capt. MARTIN THORNHILL, M.C.

It is doubtful if the threat of death ever deterred Europeans under the Nazi heel from listening-in to London. At any rate, Goebbels has frankly admitted the failure of the extreme penalty by setting up a Broadcasting Defence Department with dictatorial powers and summary orders to smash Britain's big radio blitz. Staffed by the best experts Germany can produce, this Department at once decided on a policy of jamming on a scale never before considered practicable.

On the orders of Berlin's "Jam Chief," regional controllers now charge the ether over Europe with a barrage of miscellaneous din which would make the uproar of the world's biggest menagerie sound like a monastery by comparison. First, programmes to be attacked are selected, then instructions are sent to hundreds of widespread jamming stations, most of which function in local Gestapo headquarters.

When the programmes start, a medley of Morse, gongs, bird screeches, loud cross-

every radio station on the Continent. Full well did the Nazis realize the value of quick seizure of local wireless centres. The first "soldiers" to ride into a city were radio engineers; in a matter of hours, sometimes minutes, the transmitters were mouthing mealy quisling welcomes to the "saviours" who had come to deliver the people from oppression."

By the middle of 1942 the Nazis were boasting that their powerful controlled European network was exerting more radio influence on world opinion than that of any other country. Yet the British stood firmly by the conviction that victory could be brought nearer by months, perhaps years, by supremacy on the air. And at the end of that year our Controller of Overseas Services claimed that "Britain was nearing parity with the Axis powers," that "the United Nations as a whole could now compete with the Axis in the short-wave field." Out of a beginning with four people, broadcasting for 10 hours a day on a programme allowance

Working over 16 hours a day, Radio Bari has been relaying daily six B.B.C. broadcasts in Italian, and five American programmes, and pumping into German-held territory a daily commentary on the war, along with detailed information of German troop dispositions and instructions for sabotage.

That our control of this first-class station seriously worries the enemy is patent from his repeated but ineffectual attempts to block the transmissions, much as he jams those going out to the rest of Europe direct from the B.B.C. For the entire radio offensive is supported by intelligence work which enables us to keep strictly abreast of requirements. Trained radio scouts all over Europe counter every move of the Gestapo, and keep the B.B.C posted on day-to-day reception and listener-reaction.

It is known exactly what types of wireless sets are being used in respective areas. Easy instructions are broadcast as to how the range of the less powerful instruments can be increased so as to hear London more distinctly, and hints on how to reduce jamming. If the Germans augment their jammers, the B.B.C replies by transmitting the same programme on several separate wave-lengths.

A vital factor in building up an audience was the security of listeners. A favourite Nazi dodge was to introduce, without warning, a distinctive jamming note so that radio sleuths listening near houses can detect sets tuned in to London. Radio intelligence enables the B.B.C. to warn listeners when this expedient is imminent. In fact, this aspect of the radio offensive has reached such perfection that not only the inception of the underground movement by the V-campaign, but its rapid increase and expansion throughout Europe, has been due almost exclusively to sustained support from the B.B.C. Thousands who might never see the underground news sheets learn their contents via London radio.

Of the immense influence wielded by the Voice of Britain the B.B.C. have ready evidence, much of it from official action taken by the Nazis themselves. A certain U-boat commander returned home and reported that his and two other submarines had been attacked by British aircraft. The other U-boats, he declared, had declined to open fire, attempting to escape by submerging. But before they could do so the aircraft had swooped and sunk them both, making off when confronted by the guns of the third. The lucky captain was congratulated on his escape. But his satisfaction was short-lived. When the version put out by the B.B.C. reached German official quarters the ungallant commander was promptly court-martialled. It was his ship, not the others, that had stopped firing and had plunged to safety.

It may seem odd that Germany should have accepted London's word rather than that of one of her own nationals. But it is further proof of the faith that German as well as other listeners place in the news and propaganda coming to them from the B.B.C. If official German quarters will discredit their own news sources, preferring to rely on statements from London, how much more will the mass of the people incline to belief in British propaganda?

When the war was going well for Germany the truth provided Nazi propagandists with first-class material. Now the boot is on the other foot!

ADDING ITS VOICE to the 24-hour-a-day B.B.C. broadcasts, the new radio station, A.B.S.I.E. (American Broadcasting Station in Europe), the control room of which is seen above, helps to carry the word of the Allies to those oppressed peoples not yet relieved by our military might. Broadcasting in many languages, including German, A.B.S.I.E.'s first transmission, which consisted of news bulletins and music, was on April 30, 1944. *Photo, Planet News*

talk, musical discords, machine saws, hammers on anvils, and factory whistles fills the air. If the noise seems ineffective, the listening controllers call up still more jammers in the frantic endeavour to quell the unceasing voice from London.

The voice? There are scores, hundreds of voices. Yet not long ago, in face of increasing Nazi victories, the best our aerial propagandists could do was to fight a stiff rearguard action. Inevitably the worsening military situation had a tragic effect on the propaganda position. There seemed little to say that would help the cause of freedom, and far too many hours a day in which to say it. We were losing everything; more important, from the publicity point of view, we were being progressively deprived of the only bases from which it might be possible to meet the enemy "on the air" on anything like equal terms.

For only on the air would it be practicable to exert any pressure on Germany or German-Europe at all. But the difficulty was, how to do it, with the Nazis in control of almost

of £10 a week, the service had now grown to three separate programmes broadcasting 24 hours a day in 15 languages, and employing nearly 500 people.

Today, under the very nose of the Gestapo, many thousands of the slaves of Europe listen hourly to the heralds of coming liberation in the voices of kings and queens, prime ministers, diplomats and patriots. In 24 languages on 26 wave-lengths over 600 persons wage—non-stop—the B.B.C.'s radio war on Hitler's Europe. And Hitler, himself a keen believer in radio splutter, who planned to protect his subjects against propaganda *with* propaganda, is now confronted with the memory that it was Britain's skilful use of this weapon that ruined German morale in the last war.

The first really effective use in the present conflict of this, the primary weapon in our psychological armoury, was when the excellent radio station at Bari was put into reverse against the enemy in northern Italy and throughout the Balkan peninsula.

Photos, British Official,
British Newspaper Pool

Von Kluge's 7th Army Trapped in France

British and Canadians drove a great wedge on August 8, 1944, into the enemy lines south of Caen towards Falaise—at the mouth of the " trap " wherein by August 20 part of the German 7th Army was being annihilated. Our transport and men on the Caen-Falaise road (above), with distant fires caused by 1,000 R.A.F. bombers which attacked on the previous night ; below, bombs burst on German positions during the following daylight raid by 600 Fortresses.

Closing in for the 'Kill' in Normandy

Advancing on Falaise to help close the " trap," British troops liberated Aunay-sur-Odon on August 5, 1944 ; ten days later their armoured patrols had entered Vassy, through which our men are seen (1) moving on. British and Canadian transport on the Caen-Falaise road (2) ; Rocquancourt village (right) was captured on August 8. Relieving Churchills moved up to battle positions as Shermans which had been in heavy and continuous action made their way back (3) to the Vassy main road.

P
B
T

Here is Peace for the Vanquished Hun

Demolitions in the wake of the retreating enemy are countered by the speedily-erected Bailey bridge, across which a flail tank for exploding mines is being shepherded (4). On the Falaise outskirts a village was entered by Polish troops, one riding a white horse (5) captured from a German transport column trying to escape from the Normandy " trap." Before retreating the Huns buried some of their dead in elaborate graves, past which a British 5·5-in. gun rumbles (6).

Respite from Battle for Man and Beast

Photos, British Official

Indifferent to British guns and vehicles, cows amble leisurely to the milking-shed of this Normandy farm (top) around which for three weeks fighting had raged; to the watching gunners they are symbols of Home. A chance to remove the dust of conflict is jumped at by the troops; the bathe completed they line up at the mobile laundry for clean underwear (bottom)— grateful to the R.E.s who make this refreshing behind-the-lines service possible.

VIEWS & REVIEWS Of Vital War Books

by Hamilton Fyfe

I SUPPOSE that everyone who takes any interest in the war (a surprising number of people don't) knows something about the San Demetrio, a tanker torpedoed and set on fire, abandoned by her crew, then re-manned and, after the most tremendous exertions and hardships, brought into the Clyde with five-sixths of the oil saved. Most of us read about it at the time ; some of us have seen the film. (See p. 597, Vol. 3.) It is a great story, which makes one feel immensely proud to belong to the same race as the men who figured in it. But that is only one of many stories which produce the same effect and which are to be found in Capt. Frank H. Shaw's new book, The Merchant Navy at War (Stanley Paul, 12s. 6d.).

Another exploit of the same kind received next to no publicity, but was not less worthy of it. Here again a ship had to be abandoned. She seemed to be sinking ; her bows were under water, her propeller revolving in the air. However, she did not sink, so next day the crew went back and made up their minds to save her. This time it was not fire but water which they had to fight. There was a huge hole in the bow, where the torpedo had struck. The stern was still sticking up. The first thing to be done was to get her on an even keel. They "worked like maniacs" for twenty-four hours, and did it. Then they had to shore up the water-tight bulkheads which kept the sea from flooding the whole ship. That too was accomplished, and then they limped home, steering with difficulty, making very few knots, an easy prey for a U-boat if there had been one about. Luckily there wasn't. For some reason the name of the vessel still has to be kept secret.

I CAN introduce you by name, however, to the British freighter Ajax, of 7,000 tons, speed ten knots. Meet also her captain, name of Adams—Capt. Elias Adams. Not a popular captain. Didn't want to be popular. Saved money wherever he could. Crew called it "cheese-paring." Adams didn't mind. When the Admiralty put a gun on board he groused, because sailors would be needed to work it, and they would have to be paid. But two of his mates qualified "Very Good Indeed" in a gunnery course, so they were given charge of the gun and the captain was pleased.

But he didn't remain pleased long. He grudged the time occupied in training a gun crew, and he did not like them being on the poop, which he had always kept to himself. He had no use for deck guns. Also he resented being told how to handle his ship when it was sailing in convoy. Altogether, Captain Adams was not having a good war.

Then one day a U-boat hit the Ajax with a shell. The gun on the poop went into action. Captain Adams became another man. They were shelling his ship. They had torn a hole in her side, they had shot away her funnel. The quartermaster at the wheel was hit. Cool in spite of his fury, the captain took the wheel and

steered as well as he could steer a motionless ship, to turn her stern towards the enemy, thus presenting a minimum target. There was a considerable swell. Several rounds were fired by Sloane, the mate, all of them failing to hit. Enemy shells fell perilously close, one fetched away the mainmast. Another set the ready-for-use ammunition near the gun on fire. There was imminent risk of a major explosion, which would have put the gun out of action and rendered the Ajax helpless. Other members of the crew dashed in and at great risk threw the threatened ammunition

overboard. The fire-and-wreckage party ranged hoses and put out the flames. Sloane went on serving the gun.

At last he registered a hit on the U-boat, but it was not enough to put her out of action. She went on firing with her two guns and manoeuvred at top speed, twenty knots, to avoid being hit again. After an Ajax lifeboat had been "blown to match-wood" the mate, thinking of their chances of escape, asked if the captain was going to abandon ship. "Abandon be damned !" was the answer. "We've not started fighting yet. If I come aft to show you——!"

Limelight on Our Merchant Navy

He did not go aft. He led a party to extinguish a fire caused by a shell. While he was engaged in this, another shell found its mark and he was wounded. He knotted a bandage round the wound, and carried on. At this point the mate made another hit on the U-boat, which lessened her speed ; he followed this up by another that silenced one of her guns. The U-boat fired now only "in a desultory fashion" ; but she began loosing-off torpedoes. Fortunately, the range was too great for them to take effect.

> The Ajax was by now a good deal of a wreck. Without her funnel, her upper paint practically burnt off, she seemed derelict. The port wing of her bridge had gone and she was leaking in several places ; but the gun remained undamaged, though the U-boat had tried to burst shrapnel over its position in the hope of putting the crew hors de combat.

As for the U-boat, only her conning-tower now showed above water. She seemed to have little fight left in her. Now was the moment to get away, for the chief engineer announced that he could give steam in spite of heavy damage to the

engine-room. But the captain had no thought of escape in his mind. "Carry on shooting !" he ordered, and in a short while the Germans were seen to be abandoning ship. When eighteen were in the water there was an explosion. The U-boat blew up—nobody knew why.

The eighteen were rescued. "No one would believe we'd licked a Hun," said the captain, "unless we took back souvenirs." It was a magnificent "licking," with odds of more than two to one against the Ajax, two guns to one and twenty knots to ten.

Captain Shaw is severe, and justly so, on the neglect of precautions for the security of merchant ships between the wars. The Admiralty, "with its sublime, obsolete faith in gunnery," persisted in believing that cannon could "hit targets well under water." They gave merchant ships deck-guns as defence against submarines submerged. Had they provided depth-charge throwers and charges to be thrown, there would have been far fewer losses, Captain Shaw says.

THEN freighters were too slow for the increased speed of U-boats. They had no detector devices. They were sent often at first without escort. During the First Great War "the idea of convoys was received with considerable antagonism" by the Navy, and by merchant seamen as well. And the Admiralty put up the First Lord not long ago to tell the House of Commons that "about as many fast merchantmen had been sunk by the enemy as slow ones." Why, Captain Shaw says, did not some M.P. inquire, "How many fast ships were sailing in slow convoys ?" Convoys must move at the pace of the slowest ships in them, and we have far too many slow ships.

How shamefully we neglected the Merchant Navy during those twenty years of "peace which was no peace" the book shows, with pardonable indignation. I remember seeing in the River Fal rows of ships, just rotting. The men who had been their crews and officers were rotting, too. Many ships were sold to Germany, many to Japan. "The most vital national service was ignored and neglected. There was no vision." Have we learned our lesson or shall we do the same again ? The Merchant Navy ought to be recognized as part of the Royal Navy. It is absurd to keep up the barrier between the two services.

MERCHANT NAVY OFFICERS arrive at a South Coast port after completion of special duties across the Channel—each carrying his own gear, in Army packs. They have no batmen as have officers of the Royal Navy, and in the book reviewed in this page Capt. Frank H. Shaw makes a number of wise suggestions for raising the status of, and improving conditions of service in, our incomparable M.N.

PAGE 275

Photo, British Newspaper Pool

French Army Fights Again in its Native Land

REGULAR FRENCH TROOPS were reported in action in France on August 14, 1944, fighting by the side of the Americans. They were the 2nd French Armoured Division which had been formed in North Africa in May 1943, and finally trained in England.

As proudly they drove through the streets of St. Mère Eglise (liberated on June 6, 1944), during our thrust for Cherbourg) the townspeople flocked to give them warm welcome (1). French women ambulance drivers waiting to embark for France (2).

General Jacques Phillipe Leclerc, Commander of the 2nd French Armoured Division (3); he is famed for daring desert raids he led during the North African campaign. A portrait of General de Gaulle decorates a half-track vehicle (4). Flowers were thrown by this girl as tanks rolled through her village (5). On August 25 it was announced that elements of the 2nd French Armoured Division had entered the streets of Paris.

Photos, U.S. Official, Planet News

Through Shattered Falaise Avenging Armour Sped

BIRTHPLACE OF WILLIAM THE CONQUEROR, the ancient town of Falaise, 20 miles from Caen in Normandy, from which 4,000 citizens had fled, was set ablaze by the Germans before British and Canadians occupied it on August 17, 1944. Falaise was the keypoint of the great trap which engulfed Von Kluge's army; and by the light of the fires that raged there our troops hounded down the last of the outfought garrison. British armoured cars are here seen hastening through the ruins in pursuit.

Photo, British Newspaper Pool

Before the Red Armies a Name Immortal Ran

No glamour of the front-line warrior surrounded the sapper major. Yet his name liveth for evermore in the annals of the Soviet brave; to the death he proved how nobly they also serve who only pave the way. This vivid record, written exclusively for "The War Illustrated," is by KONSTANTIN SIMONOV, playwright and official Red Army war correspondent.

WHILE the battles on the Desna were still going on, in September 1943, we were stranded because of a breakdown at a most awkward spot—a temporary bridge which the sappers were hastily throwing across the river. It so happened that in the half-hour that we were delayed, three or four German aeroplanes attacked the crossing and began to drop bombs all around it. The working-party fell flat on the ground, but the little swarthy major in command would not permit a moment's delay; the advance depended on them. He got the working-party to its feet again and, enemy planes still circling overhead, the building of the bridge went on.

I might have forgotten the episode had it not been for the fact that certain circumstances reminded me of it again in the days of the great advance in the spring of 1944. It was during the fighting around the Dnieper. We had to overtake the army, which had gone far ahead. Every now and again we would come upon a name that seemed fated to be our travelling companion. It was written on bits of plywood nailed to telegraph poles, on the walls of houses, or chalked on the armour of a half-wrecked enemy tank. "No mines—Saveliev," or "Road examined for mines—Saveliev," or "Skirt this area on the left —Saveliev," or "Bridge built—Saveliev." Sometimes there was just "Saveliev," and an arrow pointing ahead.

It was obviously the name of the officer in command of sappers who marched with advance units and cleared the road for the army. The notices were frequent and detailed and, what was most important, thoroughly reliable. After driving 200 kilometres and seeing 20 or 30 of these notices, I suddenly remembered the swarthy little major who had commanded the bridge-building over the Desna, and it occurred to me that he might be the mysterious Saveliev, marching ahead of the troops in the role of guardian angel. When we reached the river Bug, we spent the night in a village where there was a field hospital. In the evening we gathered around the lamp and had tea with the doctors. I don't remember how it came about that I spoke of Saveliev's notices.

"Yes, we have travelled nearly 500 kilometres by those notices," the chief surgeon said. "It's a famous name in these parts. In fact, it's famous enough to send some women crazy! Don't be annoyed with me, Vera Nikolayevna, I'm only joking." He turned to a young woman doctor, who made a gesture of protest.

"It's no joke as far as I can see," she retorted. Then, turning to me, she said: "You're going on ahead, aren't you?" I told her that that was my intention.

"You know they make fun of what they call my superstitious feeling," she went on, "but my name is Savelieva, and I sometimes fancy that it is my brother who leaves these notices on the roads. I haven't heard anything of him since the beginning of the war. We parted in Minsk. He used to be a road-building engineer in peacetime. I keep fancying that he might be this Saveliev; indeed I really believe he is!"

"Yes, she believes it," the chief surgeon said, "and she gets really angry because this Saveliev doesn't put his initials on the notices."

"It's very irritating," she exclaimed. "If only it said A. N.—for Alexander Nikolayevich—I'd feel quite certain about him."

"And do you know what she did once?" the chief surgeon turned to me. "She wrote on a notice-board: 'Which Saveliev is this? Alexander Nikolayevich? His sister, Vera Savelieva, field mail box 1390, is looking for him.'"

"Did you write all that on the notice-board?" I asked.

"Yes, I did. They laughed at me, and told me that the sappers come back this way. If you're going on ahead, you might ask at Divisional Headquarters. I'll write down my address for you. If you do hear any news, please drop me a line."

I promised, and she tore off a scrap of newspaper, wrote down her mail box number and held it out to me. As I put it away in my pocket she watched my movements closely, as though to make sure the note was in a safe spot.

THE offensive continued. I came across the name Saveliev often, on and beyond the Dniester. "Road examined for mines—Saveliev." "No mines—Saveliev." And sometimes again the name alone and an arrow pointing ahead. When we were in Bessarabia in April of this year, I happened to be with a rifle division, and mentioned Saveliev's name.

"Why, of course we know him. It's my sapper battalion commander Major Saveliev. A splendid sapper. You must have seen the name very often?"

"Very often," I agreed.

"I should think so. He's the man who clears the roads for the whole army, and not only for our division. His name is known throughout the army, though very few have ever seen him. He's gone over 500 kilometres of road. Yes, his is a famous name, an immortal name I should even call it." The crossing at the Desna came back to me again, and I told the General I'd like to see this Saveliev.

"Oh, you'll have to wait. If we have a temporary halt then you'll see him. But now

you can't; he's somewhere ahead with the reconnaissance units."

"What's his first name?" I asked.

"Alexander Nikolayevich. Why?"

Then I told the General about my encounter at the hospital. "I believe he's from the reserve," he said, "although he's such a fighter now you'd think he'd been in the army a hundred years. Yes, this must be the man you're looking for."

THAT night I searched my pockets for the paper on which Dr. Savelieva had written her address, and I sent her a few lines saying that her feeling about the signature on the notices had proved correct, and that soon she'd have travelled a thousand kilometres on her own brother's trail. I remember being very pleased with myself at the moment for not having lost the address and having kept my promise, despite my dislike of letter-writing. But before the week was out I regretted it.

The bridge over the Pruth had not yet been built, but two perfectly sound ferries were plying with monotonous regularity between one bank and another. We were driving up to the left bank when I noticed on the shield of a wrecked German self-propelling gun a familiar notice: "Crossing in order —Saveliev." I crossed the Pruth on a leisurely ferry, and when I reached the opposite bank I looked around for the usual notice. Twenty paces away, at the edge of a precipitous bank, I noticed a freshly-made mound with a wooden pyramid on which someone had evidently expended great pains. Under a five-pointed tin star at the top of the tablet was the inscription: "Here lies Major A. N. Saveliev, who died a sapper's glorious death during the crossing of the Pruth."

Beneath this someone had inscribed in red paint (obtained heaven knows where!) the words that have acquired the lustre of splendid tradition since our first winter campaign in 1941: "Forward to the west!" Lower down, a square piece of glass protected a small photograph. I looked closer and saw that it was an old snapshot, worn at the edges. It had evidently been carried in a tunic pocket for a long time, but it was still possible to recognize that same little major whom I had seen at the crossing over the Desna.

I lingered for a long time before the memorial. The emotions that stirred me were complex, and I was sorry for the sister who had lost her brother—perhaps before she had received the letter. And then a forlorn feeling came over me. It would not be the same on the roads now without that familiar signature. We waited while the ferry unloaded our cars, then pushed on. Fifteen kilometres distant, at a point where deep banks sloped down on either side of the road, we saw piles of anti-tank mines, resembling huge pancakes. And on a telegraph pole there was a little piece of plywood with the words: "Road examined for mines —Saveliev."

THERE was nothing supernatural about this, astonishing as it seemed at first. It was simply that here, as in many units which have had the same commander for a long time, the sapper battalion was accustomed to calling itself "Saveliev's." His men honoured their commander's memory by carrying on the task of clearing the road for the army and leaving his name in every section they passed through. There was something of lofty symbolism in this simple action of the men who went ahead.

SOVIET SAPPERS day and night risk their lives to clear away land mines laid by the retreating enemy in the path of advancing Red Army forces. With their curiously-shaped detectors this group had discovered nearly 2,000 cunningly concealed explosives. The inspiring record of a sapper major is given in this page. *Photo, Pictorial Press*

Soviet Guns Reach the Soil of the Reich

ON THE EAST PRUSSIAN FRONTIER German troops were urged by Hitler to stand firm : retreat before the oncoming Soviet Forces would be regarded as " the gravest of crimes." But the exhortation bore no fruit. On August 17, 1944, Red Army troops led by Gen. Ivan Chernyakhovsky crossed the River Sesupe and reached the frontier north-west of Mariampole, prepared to carry the fight to German soil : their mobile guns are seen (1) passing horse-drawn transport. On the central front the Russians closed in for the assault on Warsaw : tanks carrying infantrymen (2) pass on their way towards the Polish capital. Russian-trained and equipped Polish troops commanded by Gen. Rola Zymierski haul a gun into position (3). Map shows limits of the Russian advance up to August 6. *Photos, U.S.S.R. Official, News Chronicle, Pictorial Press. Map, New York Times.*

Over Guam Island 'Old Glory' Flies Again

FIRST U.S. PACIFIC ISLAND taken by the Japanese, in December 1941, Guam, in the Mariana group, was regained on August 10, 1944.

The sea before Guam was churned to foam as hundreds of U.S. landing craft drove in during the first landing (1). Maj.-Gen. R. S. Geiger, U.S. Marine Corps (2), veteran of Guadalcanal, led the expeditionary troops. Burning Japanese out of a hidden pillbox, a marine crawled ahead with a flame-thrower with comrades behind him ready to shoot (3). " Old Glory "—the U.S. flag—tied to a boat-hook was flaunted in the face of the enemy (4).

Photos Associated Press, New York Times Photos, Planet News

I WAS THERE! Eye Witness Stories of the War

We Opened the Fourth Front in Southern France

British, U.S. and French troops landed on the Riviera on August 15, 1944 —and within a week 2,000 square miles of territory in the South of France had been liberated. Maurice Fagence of The Daily Herald, who was aboard the flagship, tells the story of the preliminary bombardment.

I HAVE just seen the fourth front open in the chilly, misty hours of dawn. We were due to land our first men at 8 a.m. At 8.51 I can write that they are pouring on to the beaches. At this early hour there seems astonishingly little response from the enemy. He may well be lying doggo, but I prefer to believe his coastal defences are either stunned or obliterated by the air-sea bombardment that is still shaking our flagship like a tin toy in a bath.

More than 1,000 Allied ships lurked in the offshore mists when over the loudspeakers came the warning : "Now, here it is," followed by a command that pinned the gunners to the guns and infantry to their stand-by points. American ears paid no undue attention to the first warning. It is the traditional preface to an American naval order, but to us British it sounded a well-chosen piece of Americanism to describe—what everybody engaged in this vast operation believes it to be—the last challenge to Hitler to find reserves to resist the grand assault that is going to finish the war.

Well, here it certainly is. Afloat in a sea aflame with orange fire and acrid with cordite fumes, and semi-stupefied by the roar of it all, I try to sort out my impressions. These ships around me assembled at a dozen different points in the Mediterranean to fox the enemy. For days and nights they steamed. Yesterday, when we were well knit into a monster fleet, Admiral Cunningham and General Maitland Wilson skidded around us in the fastest, slickest British destroyer afloat with the message that what we were going to do is destined to make history, and might prove the final blow to the enemy.

I talked on the bridge with the admiral commanding this particular naval force, which is concerned with the central part of a ten-mile front. "They've promised me bombardment by 1,300 bombers just before the attack, and they've even promised me bombs that make no dust," he said. The first sign of battle came from the enemy-held coast when a signal light hissed into the sky. We were still watching the spot when an American destroyer nearby spat smoke and a shell towards the coast.

British destroyers opened up just as vehemently, then more Americans joined in. Finally the great shadowy shapes of battleships, almost hidden in the mist farther out to sea, began to roar out broadsides. Destroyers sailed up saucily towards the shore and poured in close-range stuff. And those 1,300 bombers weighed in, giving us a close-up picture of what a Berlin bombing must look like. The bombers left, and it was the turn of the rocket ships. They threw sheets of fire that made even the oldest warhorses jump until the noise died down just in time to give our ear-drums a reprieve as the first wave of infantry went ashore.

It is now 9.15, and I hear the voices of beachmasters, calm, confident voices, telling what size boats can now get in with little difficulty. At 9.30 we ourselves ease towards that strangely quiet beach. An American tank lies wrecked on the beach, victim of a coastal mine which our rocket ships failed to detonate. A cloud of dust rises from where a small squat beach-house had stood. Some minutes before, the Germans opened fire from this house on a tiny British flak ship standing offshore.

So a destroyer butted in like a big brother. Just one blow and the column of dust shot up. From a hotel high on the coast that rises to some hundred feet inland a group emerges with a white flag. The weak response of the enemy is astonishing, inexplicable and welcome. As I hand over my message for transmission a hundred prisoners are coming down to our beaches and the seventh wave of our infantry leap from their barges.

I Saw the Mad Colonel of St. Malo Surrender

Having sworn to defend St. Malo, in Normandy, to the last drop of blood, Colonel von Auloch headed an ignoble procession of 605 Germans to surrender—the day after Hitler had presented him with the Oak Leaves to the Iron Cross, which he wore when he gave in. Montague Lacey, Daily Express correspondent, sent this story from the Citadel on August 17, 1944.

A FEW minutes before four o'clock this afternoon, the German commander of the Citadel, Colonel von Auloch, the mad colonel with a monocle and a swaggering walk, led 605 men from the depths of his fortress and broke his promise to Hitler that he would never give in to the Americans. The colonel goose-stepped up to surrender, with a batman carrying his large black suitcase, and another in attendance round him flicking the dust from his uniform, and as they went by an American soldier called out : "What a corney show ! "

Colonel von Auloch is the man who wrote to the American commander attacking the Citadel to say that a German officer never surrenders, and for 15 days he sat tight 60 feet below ground in the safety of his underground shelter. By tonight the Americans would have been sitting on top of his fortress, which would have become a mass grave for all the men in it. By holding out, Colonel von Auloch has not affected the course of the war one jot. What he has done is to cause the almost complete destruction of the old town of St. Malo, and sow further seeds of hatred in the hearts of the French.

Even as I write, the townspeople gathered in the Place above are shouting and shaking their fists at the Germans from the Citadel. As the Germans pile into trucks to be taken away, the older men somehow look ashamed and stupid, but the young Germans are still

ASSEMBLED FOR INVASION OF SOUTHERN FRANCE, some 70 vessels of a great armada of ships are here seen at anchor in a port of southern Italy waiting for the order from Vice-Admiral Kent Hewitt, U.S.N., to proceed. Ranging from battleships downward, the invasion fleet included units of British, U.S., French and Canadian Navies, and vessels flying Dutch, Greek and Belgian ensigns. The landings took place on August 15, 1944. See story above, and illus. p. 265.

Photo, U.S. Official

COLONEL VON AULOCH, monocled and swaggering, wearing the Oak Leaves to the Iron Cross —presented to him by Hitler the previous day—leaves the Citadel of St. Malo to surrender, after he had sworn to defend the position to the last drop of blood. The dramatic story of the capitulation commences on page 281. *Photo, Keystone*

grinning and arrogant. The Citadel fell dramatically just an hour before American infantrymen were ready to assault the fortress for the third time, and just as a squadron of Lightning bombers swept in to shower incendiary bombs on the place.

All last night and throughout this morning heavy guns had pounded the Citadel, a main blockhouse surrounded by about a dozen entrances from the mine-like caverns below. The Americans ate their lunch in the wrecked streets before they formed for the attack. At 2.30 p.m. a big white flag appeared on one of the pillboxes. No one took much notice, for at 3 o'clock a fighter-bomber attack was to be laid on. Soon after 3 o'clock the first Lightning swept in. It came down to 50 feet and planted a couple of incendiaries square on top of the Citadel. More white flags were then run up—there were now five flying in the breeze.

The pilot of the second bomber saw them and dived without dropping his bombs. But he opened up his guns as a sort of warning as he flew round followed by the rest of the squadron. The airmen waited long enough to see a batch of Germans come from the Citadel and a bunch of Americans walk up the hill to the fort carrying a coloured identification flag.

Now there was a mad scramble to the Citadel. Word soon went round that the Germans had surrendered. Everyone raced down the hillside to see the sight. First out was Colonel von Auloch still barking orders to his officers and men who were almost tumbling over themselves to obey. Two senior officers were with him, one of them a naval commander. They were all trying to make an impressive display in front of the Americans.

THEN a curious thing happened. An elderly German, a naval cook, broke ranks and ran up and embraced a young American soldier. The German was lucky not to be shot and the guards lowered their guns just in time. But no one interfered when the U.S. soldier put his arms round the German. They were father and son. The German spoke good American slang and was allowed to stay out of the ranks and act as interpreter. He had been 14 years in America, he said, and went back to Germany just before the outbreak of war.

Colonel von Auloch counted all his men as they filed out carrying their belongings. There were Poles among the party, some Russians and about a dozen Italians. Still shouting orders, Von Auloch was put in a jeep and driven away to Division Head-

quarters. He refused to talk about his surrender and so did his soldiers.

Down in the labyrinth of tunnels of the Citadel there was the usual destruction and signs of panic. Clothing and equipment were strewn all over the place. There was still plenty of food, water and ammunition

—and the usual heaps of empty bottles.

Colonel von Auloch's room was in the lowest and safest part of the fort. It was about eight feet by ten feet, and furnished only with two leather armchairs and a bed. It seemed to be the only room with a wash basin and running water.

On the desk stood an electric lamp and a telephone; nearby was a tray containing coffee, and two postcards which the colonel was about to write. I have one of these cards now. It shows a picture of Goering and Hitler smiling as they ride through cheering crowds. On the back is the stamp which the colonel had just stuck on—a beautiful pictorial stamp of a fortress castle.

The big guns of the fort were wrecked, and all the Germans had left were machine-guns and other small arms. With the prisoners who came out of the Citadel was a little party of American soldiers who had been captured last Friday. They had crept up to the fortress at night with explosives in an attempt to wreck the ventilation system.

When all the surrendered garrison had been driven away or marched away, several hundred French people gathered round shaking each other by the hand, cheering and singing their national anthem. And one day, soon perhaps, the Citadel where the mad colonel surrendered will be one of the sights the people of St. Malo will point out to visitors coming here again from England for their holidays.

How Our Buttoned-Down Tanks Charged Through

Described here by News Chronicle war correspondent Norman Clark as "the most motorized army in the world," the U.S. 3rd Army under General Patton was on August 22, 1944, smashing on towards Paris. He tells how the tanks made mad dashes through village and hamlet to force a passage through small pockets of the enemy who might be there.

FOR the most part each large town commanding a road junction is enfolded in the grip of columns that by-pass it to encircle it; when they see this threat developing the German forces defending the town pull out, often to find their escape cut off by our tanks already across the road behind them.

Where the road is long and straight the tanks "button down" their turrets to make mad dashes through some village or hamlet where small pockets of the enemy might be established. This is the quicker way of forcing passages through the enemy.

To bring up infantry and mount an attack on the village as the military manuals say it should be done would take time and give the enemy an opportunity to mine an area ahead and reinforce a strong-point. So the tanks go through like some mad cavalry gallop. Not often are they ambushed. More than once they have charged an enemy anti-tank gun and its crew, coming upon them while they were still camouflaging and sand-bagging the position.

In whichever direction you choose to go today the roads of France are hidden under an endless and increasing flood of transport. The cottages and houses which bank the rivers of vehicles shake and quake as heavy tanks, transporters and lorries, piled high with supplies, roll on.

You come to villages where they have not yet raised the Tricolour; others where it is flying for the first hour in four years. You are just a jeep in this procession of moving vehicles. For hour after hour the wheels turn; you are caught, perhaps, between a tank and an armoured car, smothered in the dust and fumes of back-firing exhausts, and must keep your place in the convoy. At night the noise and the spluttering fang-like dynamo sparks from the tank in front of you (you cannot move

out of range of the hot blast of its motor) and of returning supply lorries ache your head and your eyes. The nightmare continues through the night.

On the piled lorries men fall asleep while the driver keeps position, his eyes straining to catch the tail-light of the vehicle in front, and alert to brake when the convoy halts. Voices shout at you in the dark, "Is this the road for ——?" "Where is —— headquarters?" But the most motorized army in the world—the U.S. Third Army—moves

GENERAL PATTON, exploits of whose armour are narrated above, was named as commander of the American Third Army on August 15, 1944. In recognition of his spectacular leadership the U.S. Senate confirmed his rank of Lieut.-General, previously withheld on account of a face-slapping incident in Sicily (see p. 287). *Photo, Associated Press*

ever onward, one column swirling off down a side road to make more of the highway mileage of France ours. Like streams of quicksilver it darts over the countryside to seize another cross-road junction before the Germans can get there.

In daytime the traffic is four-banked where the road widens. When the convoys are stopped the men fall out of the lorries to fall asleep in the shade of a hedge or tree. The air of this part of France is heavy and oppressive. Along the roads you come upon strange happenings. When we were outside Le Mans we were stopped by a French couple. They were on bicycles, and on pillows strapped to the luggage-carriers were their two children.

The man asked : "Is this the road to Paris ?" Yes, we said, but did he know that this part of France was a battlefield in which it was better not to travel ? "Oh, that's all right," he replied. "My wife and I cycled from Paris two days ago to fetch our children back from their grandfather's farm near Argentan. They have been staying with him for the summer, and now we're taking them back to Paris because the war is as good as over. We had no trouble getting here."

You find, however, that the next cyclist who hails you will tell of seeing 500 German tanks and many guns on the way from the capital. Which to believe ? Farther east as we returned the V-salutes of the villagers we passed 200 buxom women, their hair tied with handkerchief bands, giving us the clenched fist of the Soviet. They stood on rows of benches with the hammer-and-sickle flag behind them, and cheered the onward march of the tanks and big guns rumbling past, the dust-black faces of the drivers and commanders grinning back under their helmets.

We turned into the "Red Hat" restaurant

IN ORLEANS' PLACE DU MARTOI American troops in jeeps paused to gaze at the statue of Joan of Arc, the "Maid of Orleans." The pedestal is battered but the statue is undamaged, and for the first time in four years there were displayed the Tricolor and flags of the Allies. The town was liberated in General Patton's lightning advance on August 17, 1944. *Photo, U.S. Signal Corps*

outside which these 200 Russian women stood absorbing the sight of weapons of war moving to secure the destruction of Germany. In the dance hall of what had been a road-house 215 women had their sleeping quarters. Through a Russian-born French interpreter, M. Constantin Politoff, we heard their story as they surrounded us. Four months ago 1,500 Russian women had been seized in their homes around Leningrad, snatched from their husbands and children, and brought to France in cattle-trucks to labour for the Germans.

They had been put to work unloading mines and other war materials from trains shunted into the Le Mans sidings. They had been made to work during bombing raids. We left them dancing in a shack which had been their overflow dormitory, one of the women playing a guitar. Their laughter was free and unsuppressed, and they flung themselves about and chased each other like children. Their German captors had gone—they were watching a column pursuing them back to Germany, and their new-found happiness was unbounded.

OUR DIARY OF THE WAR

AUGUST 16, Wednesday *1,810th day*
Air.—U.S. bombers attacked oil plants and aircraft works in Central Germany. At night R.A.F. bombed Kiel and Stettin and laid mines in Stettin Canal.
Western Front.—In S. France advancing land troops made contact with airborne forces. French Forces of Interior rose in strength over southern and central France.

AUGUST 17, Thursday *1,811th day*
Western Front.—Falaise and Troarn captured by British and Canadians. U.S. 3rd Army occupied Dreux, Chartres, Chateaudun and Orleans.
Russian Front.—Red Army reached frontier of E. Prussia N.W. of Mariample.
Mediterranean.—Allied bombers attacked Ploesti oilfields.

AUGUST 18, Friday *1,812th day*
Western Front.—German retreat from Argentan pocket towards the Seine heavily attacked by Allied aircraft.
Air.—Allied bombers attacked airfields in N. France and bridges on the Meuse in Holland and Belgium. R.A.F. made heavy night attack on Bremen.
Russian Front.—Sandomierz on the Vistula captured by Soviet troops.
Mediterranean.—Allied heavy bombers again attacked oil installations at Ploesti.

AUGUST 19, Saturday *1,813th day*
Western Front.—French Forces of the Interior rose in Paris.
Air.—Allied heavy bombers attacked oil storage depot at La Pallice.
General.—Heavy fighting continued in Warsaw between Germans and Poles.

AUGUST 20, Sunday *1,814th day*
Western Front.—British troops entered Argentan. Falaise gap sealed off. Toulouse liberated by F.F.I.
Air.—Road and river crossings in France bombed by Mosquitoes by light of flares.
Russian Front.—Soviet troops made progress in S. Estonia, but gave ground south of Riga.
Mediterranean.—Allied bombers attacked oil refineries in Silesia and Slovakia.
Pacific.—Super-Fortresses again bombed district of Yawatta, Kyushu.
General.—Gen. de Gaulle arrived in Cherbourg.

AUGUST 21, Monday *1,815th day*
Western Front.—Allied forces crossed the Seine on both sides of Paris. French troops entered suburbs of Toulon.
General.—Gen. Koenig appointed Military Governor of Paris.

AUGUST 22, Tuesday *1,816th day*
Western Front.—Sens, S.E. of Paris, captured by Gen. Patton's Third Army.
Russian Front.—In double drive on Rumania, Russians captured Jassy and advanced towards the Danube and Galatz.
Italy.—Announced that whole of Florence was in Allied hands.
Mediterranean.—Allied bombers attacked oil plants in Silesia and Austria.
General.—In Paris patriots occupied all public buildings, but fighting continued.

AUGUST 23, Wednesday *1,817th day*
Western Front.—S.E. of Paris Allied forces reached Corbeil and Melun. In Normandy Evreux was captured. In the south French troops occupied Marseilles and U.S. troops reached Grenoble.
Russian Front.—Tilsit, East Prussia, bombed at night by Red Air Force. Akkerman on Black Sea captured by Russians.
Mediterranean.—Allied bombers attacked military installations near Vienna.

General.—Announced that new Rumanian Government accepted Russian peace terms and Rumania would fight on Allied side.

AUGUST 24, Thursday *1,818th day*
Western Front.—Units of French 2nd Armoured Division entered Paris. Allies occupied Cannes, Antibes and Grasse.
Air.—More than 1,900 U.S. bombers from Britain and Italy attacked oil refineries and aircraft works in Germany and Czechoslovakia.
Sea.—Coastal Command aircraft bombed enemy shipping evacuating from Le Havre.
Russian Front.—Kishinev, Rumania, captured by Red Army.
Pacific.—Allied carrier-borne aircraft attacked Padang in Sumatra.

AUGUST 25, Friday *1,819th day*
Western Front.—Gen. de Gaulle entered Paris. Elbeuf, south of Rouen, and Honfleur on Seine estuary, liberated.
Air.—Allied bombers attacked Peenemunde research station and oil and aircraft plants in Germany. At night R.A.F. bombed Opel works at Russelsheim and chemical works at Darmstadt.
Russian Front.—Tartu, Estonia, captured by Red Army.

Pacific.—Heaviest yet Allied air attack on Palau Is. in the Carolines.
General.—Agreements signed between Great Britain and France and U.S.A. and France regarding civil administration in liberated territories.

AUGUST 26, Saturday *1,820th day*
Western Front.—Allied troops across the Seine at four points between Paris and the sea. Paris bombed by Luftwaffe.
Air.—R.A.F. made heavy night attacks on Koenigsberg and Kiel.
Pacific.—Allied air attacks on seven Japanese isles including Yap and Iwo.
General.—Bulgarian Government decided to withdraw from the war. Announced that German troops were being disarmed.

AUGUST 27, Sunday *1,821st day*
Western Front.—Allied forces reached the Marne at Lagny. Toulon cleared of the enemy.
Air.—R.A.F. and U.S. bombers attacked oil plants and railways in Germany.
Russian Front.—Soviet troops captured Rumanian Danube port of Galatz.
General.—Announced that German resistance has ceased in Bucharest.

AUGUST 28, Monday *1,822nd day*
Western Front.—U.S. troops reached Chateau Thierry on the Marne. British secured another bridge-head on the lower Seine.
Air.—R.A.F. bombers attacked flying-bomb sites in N. France. U.S. fighters bombed rail, road and river transport.
Mediterranean.—Allied bombers attacked oil refineries and railways in Austria and Hungary.
Russian Front.—Danubian port of Braila and Black Sea port of Sulina captured by Soviet forces.

AUGUST 29, Tuesday *1,823rd day*
Western Front.—U.S. forces under Gen. Patton captured Soissons, 55 miles north-east of Paris. In the south, French troops advanced through Nimes towards Montpellier.
Italy.—In their advance towards the Gothic line, 8th Army crossed the river Arzillo.
Russian Front.—Troops of the 3rd Ukrainian Army captured Black Sea port of Constanza.
General.—Mr. Churchill returned home from his extensive tour of the Mediterranean theatre of war.

★━━━━━ *Flash-backs* ━━━━━★

1939
August 23. *German-Soviet Pact of Non-Aggression signed.*

1940
August 19. *British evacuated Somaliland, N.E. Africa.*
August 24. *First bombs fell in Central London ; 52 raiders brought down.*
August 25. *First British bombs dropped on Berlin.*

1941
August 25. *British and Russian forces entered Persia.*

August 28. *Russians announced that Dnepropetrovsk had been evacuated by Red Army.*

1942
August 19. *Combined Operations raid on Dieppe area, lasting nine hours.*
August 26. *Japanese landed at Milne Bay, New Guinea.*

1943
August 17. *All enemy resistance ended in Sicily after 38-day campaign. Allies entered Messina.*
August 23. *Kharkov recaptured by Red Army.*

THE WAR IN THE AIR

by Capt. Norman Macmillan, M.C., A.F.C.

A FORTNIGHT'S air bombardment preceded the assault on the Riviera coast of France by the forces under General Maitland Wilson. At seven o'clock (first light) on August 15, 1944, heavy bombers and medium and light tactical aircraft bombed gun positions, troop concentrations, strong points, supply dumps, beach obstacles, inland airfields and communication lines. The actual invasion began with the descent of paratroops (see illus. p. 265), who landed in waves of up to 1,000, followed by airtugs towing gliders carrying troops, jeeps, and 75-mm. howitzers. Then came the main force in beach assault craft, their approach to shore covered by aircraft and a naval bombardment of coastal guns (see story in p. 281). More than 14,000 airmen were in the air during the landings.

Allied aircraft quickly secured absolute mastery of the sky above an area stretching from the beach-head inland to 30 and 50 miles. Great forces of bombers smashed rail and road bridges in the hinterland, far up the Rhone valley. The quick success of the air operations in the chosen battle area showed how we have gained in battle experience, through the knowledge acquired from the Commando assaults against Norway, the bitter trial of Dieppe, the attack on Sicily, and the first great Continental invasion in Normandy.

Superimposed upon the organizational excellence of the assault were the newest methods of placing troops just where they were most needed, and covering them with the latest fire-power weapons. During the final five minutes of the pre-assault barrage 14,000 rocket projectiles were fired from ships and aircraft into the Riviera beaches selected for the first beach landing parties.

THE eclipse of the Luftwaffe enables air forces of the United Nations to concentrate ever more strongly against the surface forces of the Wehrmacht. Bombers can carry heavier loads of bombs, and both the Hurricane and Thunderbolt were stepped up to take one 1,000-lb. bomb under each wing. Now the American light bomber Havoc has been stepped up to take one 500-lb. bomb under each wing, thus increasing its bomb-load to a total of 3,000-lb. Without the mastery of the air which had been gained by the constant aggressive action of the fighters and bombers of the United Nations it would have been impossible to restrict the speed and manoeuvrability of the fighter-bombers and light bombers by the addition of bomb load under their wings—where the exposed bombs create additional resistance and add to the outboard weight.

On page 220 I wrote of the probable adoption of an aerial adaptation of the creeping barrage of artillery. It was just such an employment of air power that blasted the way through the defences of the German Seventh Army in Normandy and enabled the Allied Expeditionary Force to break through to victory. The method of application was different from the artillery method only in its timing. The bomb barrage was employed to cover a selected area, into which a high density of bombs was poured—anything up to 5,000 tons. Then the ground forces moved forward. When they were again held up the process was repeated, and by a succession of such blows the German defences in depth were broken faster than it was possible for new defences to be prepared in the rear.

HERE is the outstanding feature of this war. The former idea of defence has vanished. Air attack is now stronger than defence when it has received sufficient preparation in material and in organization. By the employment of air power in the battle area, it is possible to make all the preparations for demolition attack at a distance in safety, and then carry out the destruction in extremely brief time.

So far as is now known, the only security of an army against this form of overhead attack lies in the possession of superior air power. Thus the battle of Normandy is the culmination of four years of air war, during which the Luftwaffe has been beaten from its position of superiority over the battlefield to one of great inferiority. This prelude was not the prerogative of the British and American and Allied air forces alone. The 60,000 German aircraft that have been destroyed on the Russian front during the past three years were a great contribution to Allied air superiority over France. It should be real-

ized that Germany has been fighting in the air on three fronts for three years, and it was the triple effort against foes with increasing air strength that decimated the Luftwaffe.

From the beginning of the war until the beginning of June 1944, Germany produced about 110,000 aircraft, reaching peak production in 1942. British aircraft production in the same period was about 90,000. Without Russia and America, British air power would not have equalled German. Russian aircraft output has probably been about 60,000 in the same period ; Russian aircraft losses have been stated as about 31,000. Combined American and British Empire aircraft production from 1940 to 1943 inclusive was 255,000. Combined German, Italian and Japanese production was about 190,000.

In the spring of 1944 German aircraft production was down to an annual rate of about 20,000 (excluding flying bombs, of which 7,250 were fired from the middle of June to August 21, 1944). Moreover, aircraft production in Germany then gave a bias in favour of fighters, unlike the position during the peak year of 1942 when bombers had priority.

FOR 1944 the combined British Empire-American output is estimated at about 140,000. Thus the air superiority of the Allies is a growing one industrially. Meanwhile, the German aircraft factories are being bombed, while Allied aircraft factories are immune from attack. The flood of Allied air power is rapidly growing to proportions which will utterly swamp the German air defences everywhere as the ring contracts about the Reich.

Bearing these figures in mind, it is well to recall the words of General Montgomery in his special message addressed to the armies under his command on August 21, 1944 : " I doubt if ever in the history of war air forces have had such opportunities or have taken such good advantage of them. The brave and brilliant work of the pilots has aroused our greatest admiration. Without their support, we soldiers could have achieved no success."

From the South East Asia Command comes the same heartening tale. The defeat of the Japanese in their drive against the Manipur State of India, designed to cut the lifeline to China, was in great measure due to the supply of the Imperial, American and Chinese forces by air. Throughout the Pacific the Allied air might is playing a great part in sweeping the Japanese back whence they came.

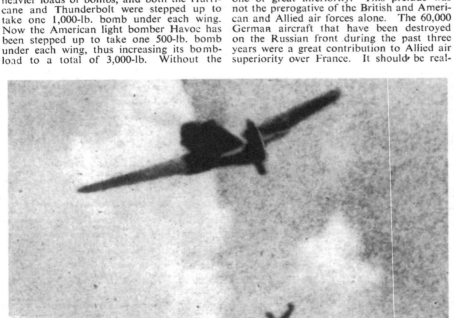

THE NAZI PILOT BALED OUT, leaving his ME 109 to be finished off by the Allied fighter-pilot responsible for his hurried exit after brief combat over French territory. The parachute has yet to open, hence the undignified position of the unnerved Luftwaffe warrior who has " had enough."

Photo, U.S. Official

How R.A.F. helped the Maquis to Set Paris Free

ARMS AND SUPPLIES for the Maquis—secretly raised Army of the French Forces of the Interior—fighting for the liberation of Paris were dropped in large quantities by R.A.F. Bomber Command. American bombers also played a big part in the operations : a Flying Fortress, skimming the tree-tops, sends down by parachute vital packages over the countryside (1) : the contents later to be collected by Maquis (2) at a house on the Chateaudun outskirts. Maquis enter the town of Argentan (3), and patrol in F.F.I. trucks (4).   PAGE 285   *Photos, British and U.S. Official*

Wild Beauty Now Covers Our London War-Scars

SUMMER has come to London, and an army of wilderness commandos has invaded City street and suburban avenue. Staunch and sturdy, these wild soldiers are already firmly entrenched. They are at their own particular action stations on the blitzed sites of the Metropolis . . . Dandelion and dock, thistle and daisy, coltsfoot, bindweed, nettle and clover—they have stealthily reclaimed the capital of Britain.

On the cleared London sites that remain as memorials of the Great Blitz is now spread a bright carpet of green, patterned with gold and white and mauve. The pattern changes as one crosses London. In Clapham Park, for instance, there is one damaged site in a residential road that is covered by an almost solid mass of big-headed dandelions. The round yellow tops stand bravely among the bright flush of unmown rank grass. The note they strike in that road of trim front lawns and close-clipped privet hedges is bizarre and garish, yet somehow free and joyous.

A bus ride east, in Chaucer's Southwark, bindweed crawls and clambers over a scattered flooring of loose stones. Across earth now covered by the lowly vine the Canterbury Pilgrims may have passed. Over the cobbles of neighbouring roads the life of the City continues to flow with noisy rhythm, while seedlings thrive in their rich dust.

TO the north, in the bombed side-streets of Islington, couchgrass, as hardy and enduring as the English oak, raises its bayonet-shaped leaf while its long, vivid root burrows deeply into grey earth that trembles when the train shuttles into or out of King's Cross and St. Pancras. Thistles, in purple bloom, have won foothold on the barren spaces that were Kensington houses.

Indeed, there is an unending variety to the evidence of this invasion by Nature. In the drab purlieus of Tottenham Court Road (which somehow succeeds in being never quite English), birds have made their nests behind the bars of exposed fire-grates. Grass shoots are springing along Holborn, once described as the world's busiest mile. No grass had seeded and sprouted there for 500 years. Seedlings have fought for life and won on the torn and scarred slope of Ludgate Hill, which has probably been grassless for seven centuries. It may well be that plant-life has returned to nooks and crannies of London that have not known green shoots since a Roman legion built its camp on the north bank of the Thames.

THE three years that have passed since the heavy raids on London have returned some of the City streets to the state they were in after the Great Fire; the Cockney grasses and weeds have established themselves. Their roots could now successfully defy a hoe. Nor are they to be found only in a few widely-separated districts. Every London borough now has its patches of built-up streets reclaimed by the long-defeated wilderness.

There is more genuine countryside today in many of Central London's back streets than in some village streets in the heart of Britain. It is as though Nature has covered the City's scars with a cooling green salve. There seems an aptness about the whole process, a significance attaching to this casual yet full-scale invasion. The sprouting of seasonal grasses and weeds, embodying, as they seem to, the resilience and pert vigour of the Londoner, has brought colour and hope to the battered streets.

LEONARD R. GRIBBLE

These photographs, specially taken for THE WAR ILLUSTRATED *by J. Dixon-Scott in August 1944, show St. Paul's from Warwick Square, and St. Mary-le-Bow from Watling Street.*

Editor's Postscript

WHEN it was complained to Abraham Lincoln that Grant, the only successful general on the Northern side in the American Civil War, drank too much whisky, Lincoln said, "I wish I knew the brand he drinks. I'd send my other commanders a barrel apiece!" Is President Roosevelt thinking the same about General Patton, who, for all I know, may be a life-long teetotaller? This officer was reprimanded for striking a private soldier in a temper, and the rank of Lieut.-General, to which he would have been entitled, was withheld from him. Then he was given a command in Europe, and gained a place in history by his handling of the American army that carried on such a blitzkrieg as not even the Germans equalled in their conquest of the Continent. Evidently General Patton's ire can be turned against the enemy with the most satisfactory results. Those who advocated his dismissal from the Service must be wondering whether the ordinary rules of conduct ought to apply to commanders of armies. Anyhow, the amazing energy and fierceness of his leadership in France were promptly recognized by the confirmation of his rank of Lieut.-General.

NOTHING will impress future ages more forcibly, when the histories of this war come to be read, than the exactitude with which the date of the United Nations' readiness to strike was predicted. Perhaps "predicted" is not the right word. It was not a guess or a prophesy: it was a calculation. When Mr. Churchill said early in 1942 that by 1944 we should be in a position to begin driving the enemy out of occupied Europe, sighs of dismay went up. Few people believed the war could last that long (because they did not want it to!). But those of us who were admitted behind the scenes of the great show that was being prepared knew the Prime Minister had given that date after long and close collaboration with those who were directing the preparation. Full time had been apportioned for turning out the material and the munitions required, for training the troops, for weakening Germany's output of war machinery. Plans were drawn up two years in advance for the strategy that was to be followed. And since the invasion of Normandy, at the beginning of June of this year, the carrying-out of those plans has been steadily proceeded with.

TO whom the credit for this long and patient build-up of a force that should be irresistible will be chiefly given by historians we cannot tell. Much of it to Mr. Churchill, much to General Eisenhower, a good deal to General Montgomery, though he came into it only after his brilliant Desert and Tunisian campaigns had been completed. What a contrast with the absence of planning that had such an unhappy effect on our war effort last time! Haig was no planner. Pershing came in too late to do much in that line. We had no one at home like Mr. Churchill to keep up an unceasing demand for plans and the means to operate them. Until Foch took over the supreme command there was really no strategy on our side at all so far as the Western Front was concerned. Outside his soldiering Foch was not an intelligent man. He said in 1919, "Germany is finished. There is no longer a Germany." But he had a first-class military mind, and his hammer-blows made Ludendorff quail and give in.

HOW well the British and American Governments have been kept informed about what was happening in France I realized better than I had done before, when I had a talk a few days ago with a Frenchman who had been back and forth between this country and his own some dozen times. A braver soldier of freedom than this peacetime professor does not exist. Wartime professor, too, actually, for he kept his chair at a French university while he was doing his valuable work for the cause. For a long time no suspicion fell on him. Then he was caught. Arrested in his home, he looked on while Gestapo agents searched for incriminating documents. He knew they would find plenty. 'In an hour," he told himself, "I shall be dead." But then he thought he might as well die kicking, so with a sudden rush he upset a heavy desk on to the policemen, ran into another room, jumped out of a window, and hid in a garden not far off till pursuit died down. He knew what to do then. In a marvellously short time a British plane landed in a field, picked him up, took off again, and brought him to England. Sounds incredible, but it is true!

ANOTHER interesting talk I have had was with an expert in psychology who replies to questions sent in to a woman's weekly paper. It seems that nearly all these questions are now concerned with sex problems. Innumerable wives ask for advice because they have ceased to love their husbands or because they think their husbands have ceased to love them. Large numbers have had babies while their husbands were far away on active service. Unmarried girls piteously tell how they have been promised marriage by soldiers of one or other of the Allied armies and have somehow discovered that these men have wives in their own countries. There is nothing new or surprising in all this, the psychologist assured me. Such happen-

Lt.-Gen. L. H. BRERETON, former commander 9th U.S.A.A.F., was appointed, on August 10, 1944, commander of the First Allied Airborne Army. This consolidates airborne troops—including British, United States and Polish—of the Supreme Headquarters, Allied Expeditionary Force.
Photo, U.S. Official PAGE 287

ings are a concomitant of all wars. Between 1914 and 1918 the same cries for help went up. Unfortunately, in very few cases can any real help be given. Still, if those who seek it feel that the answers they receive show understanding and sympathy, their minds are to some extent relieved and they are given more courage to face their difficulties.

WE often hear that there is too much centralization of government and that local authorities are not given enough scope. But lately I have been noticing a number of cases in which local authorities have been getting into trouble with the law. For instance, the Corporation of Battersea in London were fined £20 for heating a greenhouse at a cemetery, where people buy flowers to place on graves. Then the Brighton J.P.s nearly broke the Motor Fuel Regulation which forbids unnecessary use of petrol. A woman summoned for some trifling offence failed to appear before them, and the magistrates on the Bench said "Send a car to fetch her." She lived six miles away! The magistrates' clerk stopped that. In Hampshire the police authorities have come into conflict with the legal profession. They have recently been themselves instructing barristers to conduct police prosecutions. Barristers with the support of the Bar Council, their trade union executive, say this should be done by the legal officers of the Crown. It is good to know that watch is kept on this kind of activity by persons "dressed in a little brief authority."

ON the other hand, there is a growing tendency to resent what are perfectly reasonable, and in fact necessary, inquiries by officials. A question was asked in Parliament the other day about a Board of Trade query as to why an applicant for an alarm clock wanted it. Was such investigation permitted, the questioner wanted to know. He ought to have known without asking that anyone really requiring an alarm clock would readily give particulars as to why it was required. Anyone objecting to do so would naturally be suspect. I cannot myself see any great objection to asking railway passengers "Is your journey really necessary?"; but the very idea seems to arouse most people's worst passions. Another instance of interrogation which is more naturally resented has been the subject of a parliamentary question. Inspectors on London Tube railways have been in the habit of asking anyone whom they suspected of trying to defraud the Passenger Transport Board where they worked and what they earned. They have now been told to stop this. Mere suspicion does not justify such queries, the Home Secretary says.

NEWSPAPER readers frequently comment on the number of misprints in wartime journals. This is due partly to the more than usually hurried conditions in which newspapers have to be produced, and partly to the additional strain put upon the meticulously careful "reader" in the newspaper offices. The duty of the "reader" is to go through all the proofs, having the "copy," which is the original, read out to him and correcting mistakes that compositors may have made in "setting it up." These Correctors of the Press, as they call themselves, are thoroughly competent and it is rare for misprints to get past them. The story of the "battle-scarred veteran" who was turned into a "bottle-scarred veteran" came from America, where less care was taken. One of the funniest errors I have noticed lately was in a news item about a question to be asked in the Commons by Sir Ernest Graham-Little. It ended with the statement, "Sir Ernest Further asks whether Mr. Willink" will do so-and-so. Compositor and reader must both have thought there was an M.P. named Further!

How We Crossed the Orne at Thury Harcourt

ROYAL ENGINEERS in working "undress" paved the way for British and Canadian troops advancing on the village of Thury Harcourt on the River Orne, south of Caen in Normandy. They are here preparing the foundations of a ford across a narrow neck of the water by laying fascines, or bundles of tree-branches. These will support the wooden track already being laid on the far bank. The village was finally cleared of Germans by August 15, 1944.

Photo, British Newspaper Pool

Printed in England and published every alternate Friday by the Proprietors, THE AMALGAMATED PRESS, LTD., The Fleetway House, Farringdon Street, London, E.C.4. Registered for transmission by Canadian Magazine Post. Sole Agents for Australia and New Zealand : Messrs. Gordon & Gotch, Ltd. ; and for South Africa : Central News Agency, Ltd.—September 15, 1944. S.S. *Editorial Address:* JOHN CARPENTER HOUSE, WHITEFRIARS, LONDON, E.C.4.

Vol 8

SIXPENCE

The War Illustrated

Nº 190

Edited by Sir John Hammerton

SEPTEMBER 29, 1944

IN LIBERATED PARIS tanks of the 2nd French Armoured Division presented an impressive spectacle as they passed the Arc de Triomphe. On August 25, 1944, the German General von Choltitz had surrendered the capital to General Leclerc after 50,000 members of the French Forces of the Interior and unarmed patriots had risen against the enemy garrison and some 10,000 Germans had been made prisoners in the city. See also illus. pages 303-306.

Photo, Planet News

NO. 191 WILL BE PUBLISHED FRIDAY, OCTOBER 13

Afloat and Ashore with Our Roving Camera

MOTOR-TORPEDO-BOATS are the fighting midgets of the Royal Navy; officially, they are part of our Light Coastal Forces. Of these little ships which dash and scurry over the wild waters of the Channel searching for enemy targets, the Fairmile (above) is typical. It is 115 feet in length, with a complement of 30 ratings and 3 officers. Armament includes two 21-in. torpedoes, and pom-pom and Oerlikon guns.

MOBILE X-RAY VANS (left) call at British factories to look into the health of war-workers. X-ray photographs, which have been taken by the thousand, reveal the internal condition of those who sit for their "portraits," and according to the findings of the experts so is the medical treatment. Each unit consists of radiologist, three radiographers, doctor, marshal, three clerks and the van driver.

AERIAL LIGHTHOUSE KEEPER is one of the wartime positions so capably filled by W.A.A.F.s. After intensive training, the girls "man" and maintain these lighthouses which are so valuable a part of the night-flying equipment of R.A.F. bomber stations. Attending to her specialized job, the 20-year-old W.A.A.F. on the right was in peacetime a clerk in a draughtsman's office.

RUSSIAN OFFICERS IN NORMANDY, on a recent visit to an R.A.F. airfield under the guidance of a British officer (pointing), included Vice-Adml. Kharlamov (head of the Soviet Military Mission in England), Maj.-Gens. Skliarov and Vasiliev, and Col. Gorbatov. Above, they are watching Typhoons.

STAPLE INN, historic 16th-century building in London's Holborn, was one of the Capital's show places badly damaged during the flying-bomb attacks. Rescue workers are seen (above) removing from the wreckage ancient relics and such other items as were worth the risk and trouble of salvaging.

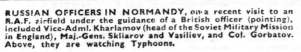

PAGE 290   *Photos, British Official; Keystone, Planet News, Central Press*

THE BATTLE FRONTS

by Maj.-Gen. Sir Charles Gwynn, K.C.B., D.S.O.

So much has happened in the fortnight since I last wrote that if we were dealing with an enemy of normal mentality it would be safe to predict that the inevitable end would be reached in a few days. Rumania, Bulgaria and Finland have all accepted the situation and have followed the example of Italy—Rumania and Bulgaria to the full extent of changing sides. Hungary alone of the satellite countries remains in the enemy's camp, and even she would probably get out of it if she could, and if she were not so hostile to Rumania.

German mentality, and in particular Nazi mentality, being what it is, it would be rash to assume, however, that no further great exertion will be needed. I feel certain that the Reichswehr will not go down as in 1918 without a final battle when confronted with terms of unconditional surrender. Weak as the defences of the German western frontier now are through lack of adequate numbers of good troops to hold them, they nevertheless present a formidable obstacle which we cannot expect to break through without a bitter fight.

The momentum of the great pursuit through northern France can hardly be expected to carry us through such an obstacle without a pause to close up and re-group for a very different type of operations, and of course a pause gives the enemy time to reorganize and to some degree recover his morale. I have not the least doubt that the Siegfried Line will break under a fully organized attack, but there should be no disappointment if the attack takes longer to develop and to be carried through than the speed of the pursuit phase might lead us to expect.

There is always, however, the possibility that when the full extent of the disasters in France and Rumania and the strategic implications of the defection of the satellite nations are better known in Germany, there may be a complete breakdown of morale. There are indications that the Russians are now ready to renew on a major scale their offensive on the Vistula and against East Prussia. A break-through there would be even more decisive than in the west where the Rhine affords a second line of defence which has no counterpart in the eastern front.

FRANCE

The amazing speed with which Montgomery's 21st Army Group took up the pursuit when it had dealt with the Falaise pocket and with the remnants of the 7th Army south of the Seine will, I hope, convince everyone of the absurdity of drawing critical comparisons between the rates of progress of armies operating in what is almost a military void and those encountering stiff resistance. In the one case, progress is in the main limited by the difficulty of maintaining supplies—that in itself alleviated by low expenditure of munitions—and in the other, progress is checked by projectiles and mines.

Conversely it may be noted how the most rapid pursuit when it has covered long distances can be checked, even by disorganized and largely demoralized armies who find a line on which they can stand and fight. We have seen this happen in Russia, in Italy and now again in France. What, I think, deserves our special admiration is the speed and energy with which the British 2nd Army and the Canadians took up the pursuit when they had crossed the Seine after fighting which must have caused a considerable amount of disorganization, exhaustion and great expenditure of munition supplies.

In their pursuit they had to cross river lines in their widest reaches and encounter enemy groups that, although in retreat, had not yet been engaged in battle. Furthermore, the Canadians especially had to deal, either by by-passing or by capture, with enemy garrisons left to deny us the use of the Channel ports. As a single feat the 2nd Army's final dash from Brussels which took the garrison of Antwerp by surprise and secured that great port practically intact perhaps deserves the greatest credit and achieved results of the highest importance.

The capture of Antwerp and the closing of the 15th German Army's line of retreat to the north is proof that the speed of the

Lieut.-Gen. SIR OLIVER LEESE, commander of the 8th Army in Italy (left), explained the battle situation to Mr. Churchill—Gen. Alexander looking on—previous to watching an attack on a German-held ridge, after the Maturo had been crossed, on August 26, 1944.
Photo, British Official

pursuit had a great strategic object and was not inspired merely by competitive ambitions.

ITALY

The great and exciting events in the west should not distract our attention from the other battle fronts. In particular we should not under-estimate the part played by General Alexander's Army Group in Italy. It has had a long and difficult campaign, and by its unceasing pressure has forced the enemy to expend reserves he badly needed elsewhere. In particular we may well believe that General Patch's landing and rapid advance, including the capture of Toulon and Marseilles, could not have had such immediate success if German divisions had not been sent from France to reinforce Kesselring.

Now Kesselring himself is in a precarious position. His immensely strong Gothic Line has been broken and he will almost certainly be forced to undertake a long and difficult retreat. Alexander has again exploited the inherent advantages of the offensive—surprise and the concentration of force at the selected point—which when skilfully used will overcome the strongest defensive position. The general similarity between Alex-

ander's methods against the Cassino Line and now against the Gothic Line, and Montgomery's methods in the Cherbourg peninsula is easily detected. Kesselring has proved himself to be a good and determined general, particularly by the way he rallied and reorganized his defeated armies, but his stand to cover the Lombardy Plain has weakened rather than strengthened the present German situation ; for his army has become nearly as useless and wasteful a detachment as was the force left in the Crimea and as are the German armies in the Baltic States and northern Finland.

For that, the German Higher Command's strategy is responsible. German military historians will not be able this time to ascribe their defeat to the breakdown of the Home front, and they will have little cause to complain of the fighting qualities of their troops or the technical efficiency of the General Staff. It seems certain, therefore, that much will be written about the baleful influence Hitler has exercised on the higher direction of the war in order to protect the reputation for infallibility of the great General Staff. Hitler may be treated as a transient phenomenon, but the General Staff may emerge again.

If Hitler has been mainly responsible for German disasters, there can be little doubt that Russian recovery from disaster has been due to Marshal Stalin. But he also is mortal, and the interesting matter for speculation is whether he has created a machine that will long survive him. It would seem that he probably has, judging from the number of brilliant generals his regime has produced, and from the amazing efficiency with which the administrative part of the machine has worked. It is hard to believe that an organization built on such wide foundations could collapse rapidly.

RUSSIA

Meanwhile, the question of the moment is when will the decisive encounter on the Russian front begin. Malinovsky and Tolbukhin have brilliantly carried out their part in the Rumanian campaign, but both in Rumania and in Finland the successful issue was due more to patient and far-seeing diplomacy than to the purely military operations. It is on the Polish and East Russian fronts, where the main armies of both sides face each other, that the decisive military struggle must take place. Hard as the Germans have been fighting, the constant counter-attacks they have delivered can only have tended to exhaust their strength, and the issue when the final test comes cannot be in doubt.

FAR EAST

With the German war approaching its end, it is perhaps insufficiently realized how much progress has been made in the war with Japan. Air and sea operations conducted against her have become almost as great a menace to her sea communications as the U-boat ever was to ours in the Atlantic.

Her main Fleet can no longer operate outside the range of shore-based fighter aircraft, and cannot prevent the steady advance of American naval and air bases towards Japan's home bases and towards her lines of sea communication. In Burma the Japanese attempt to invade India and to interrupt the construction of land communications with China have been decisively defeated, though at heavy cost to our own troops, whose operations under the most trying conditions have hardly been followed with the attention they deserve.

The Empire certainly has taken its full share in the land counter-offensive against Japan, including of course Australian operations in New Guinea. Moreover, that share is likely to increase when weather conditions permit of more extensive operations in Burma and as more shipping becomes available for amphibious enterprises,

When Allied Armies Reached the Siegfried Line

THE ALBERT CANAL, which runs from Antwerp to the Meuse, in Belgium, was crossed by British and Dutch troops against strong enemy resistance on September 7, 1944, when the first bridge-head was established at Beeringen. Blown up by the retreating Germans, the bridge (above, background) over the canal was restored by Royal Engineers: a British tank has just crossed it, whilst a Dutch soldier of the Princess Irene Regiment (right) and a British sergeant share guard duties at the approach of the bridge.

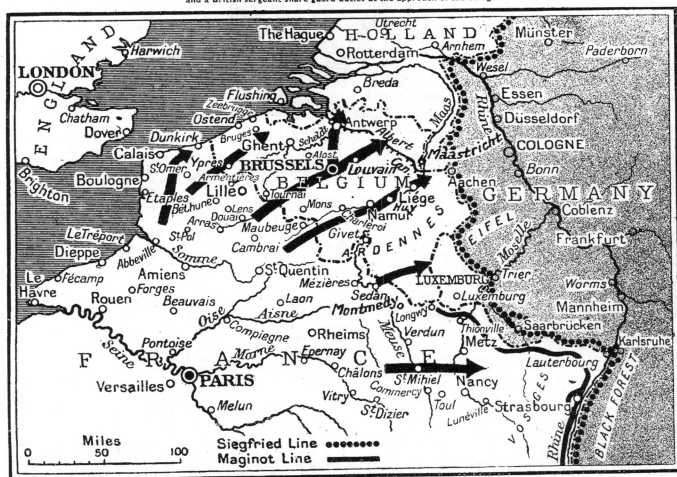

A MIGHTY ARC, 225 miles long, of Allied forces in France and Belgium threatened the German frontier defences : by September 15, 1944, the U.S. 1st Army had crossed the frontier and broken into the outposts of the Siegfried Line near Aachen ; farther north, the British 2nd Army on the Escaut Canal was within ten miles of the border ; the U.S. 3rd Army driving on from Nancy had joined up with the 7th Army near Belfort. Arrows on map show directions of Allied thrusts on September 11.

Photo, British Official. Map by courtesy of The Times

The Gothic Line Breached on a 20-Mile Front

IN ITALY THE 8th ARMY opened an attack on the Gothic Line on August 26, 1944. By September 3 the defences had been breached from Pesaro in the Adriatic sector to a point 20 miles inland. British, Canadian, Indian, Italian and Polish troops took part; the Polish Corps was opposed by the same German forces—the 1st Parachute Division—against whom it had fought at Cassino. Poles handle a 3-in mortar in a farmyard (1). During the onslaught civilians sought safety in a tunnel (2). A British signaller operates his portable radio set on the road (3). British infantry and Shermans on a captured hill position (4).

Photos, British Official

THE WAR AT SEA

by Francis E. McMurtrie

In announcing the formation of the Royal Naval Scientific Service, inaugurated on September 7, 1944, the Admiralty released some information concerning technical developments during the war. There was no scientific organization in the Navy before 1914-18, but during those years a large number of scientists were brought into the service from the universities and from industry. By 1939 these numbered about 600, a figure which has since been expanded by some 3,000 temporary entries. Hitherto they have been divided into scientific, technical and chemical pools, but have now been embodied in a single organization under the Director of Scientific Research.

Members of the R.N.S.S. will be on a similar footing to those of the Royal Corps

revolution in the equipment of warships. Working as it does in darkness and fog, radar has been of inestimable value to the Royal Navy. The uncanny way in which touch was maintained with the Scharnhorst off the North Cape in the darkness of an Arctic night is now explained.

Wartime improvements in radio—now adopted as the official term for wireless, though its similarity to radar seems likely to lead to occasional confusion—have been almost as far-reaching. Communication can be maintained over greater distances, with less liability to interruption. Moreover, as proved during the Normandy campaign, it is now possible to keep open a great many lines of wireless communication at once.

THE FRENCH CRUISER EMILE BERTIN, 5,886 tons, complement 567, took part in the Allied invasion of Southern France on August 15, 1944. From her decks, during a lull in the bombardment, eager eyes of the sailors are directed at the coastline of their native land so soon to be liberated completely from the dominance of the Hun.
Photo, British Official

of Naval Constructors, and will be given training and experience at sea, for which purpose they will wear the uniform of the equivalent naval rank, just as naval constructors do. Otherwise it is, of course, a purely civilian service.

RADAR Works for the Navy in Darkness and in Fog

Of the various fields of operation to which scientists have contributed improvements during the war, the most important is radar, the official term covering what was previously known as radiolocation. Its development has absorbed the majority of the temporary scientists and engineers, whose work is carried on in close collaboration with Army and Air Force experts.

Before the present war the movements and fighting activities of our warships were largely dependent on the human eye, as used by look-outs, sight-setters and range-finders. Radar has been perfected to an extent which altogether supersedes these arrangements, and has indeed entirely altered the face of sea warfare. It has involved a complete

There has also been a big advance in anti-submarine detection methods, though these proved adequate in coping with the initial U-boat attack at the start of the war. Equipment today is altogether different and can do much more. Fire control has been similarly improved, the factor of rolling motion in a ship having been given especial consideration in the present system.

In 1939 magnetic mines laid by enemy aircraft gave serious trouble, until the dismantling of an unexploded specimen by Lieut.-Commander J. G. D. Ouvry led the way to the antidote (see p. 124, Vol. 7). As a result of examination it was found that the German magnetic mine was almost identical with the type we had ourselves begun to lay in 1918. This knowledge was of the utmost value, more especially as we had been faced with the task of sweeping up these mines after the Armistice in that year and therefore had a pretty good idea of how to deal with them.

Later the Germans produced an acoustic mine, as well as variants combining the two

principles in different ways; but our scientists were always ready to meet enemy ingenuity with an effective counter-measure. In fact, we have contrived to keep ahead of the Germans in every department whenever a novel sea weapon has been brought into use. In torpedoes we were superior to the enemy from the outset, the only enemy device which has given us any trouble being the German acoustic homing torpedo. In normal laboratory work the progress made in this war has been so great that it is now possible for two girls to carry out analyses of steel samples at the rate of a thousand a day, work which would have occupied about 500 people in the last war.

Hopes that a large number of trawlers would be returned to their owners by the Admiralty, which took them over in 1939, were encouraged by the news that a couple were actually handed back recently. It is true, of course, that trawlers are unlikely to be wanted in large numbers for operations against the Japanese in the Far East. But it must not be forgotten that in European waters the Germans have laid immense numbers of mines which will require to be swept up as soon as hostilities cease. This work will fall largely upon the trawlers, since the majority of fleet minesweepers may be expected to go to the East next year. Thus the prospects of immediate release of trawlers for fishing can hardly be expected just yet.

GREATER Naval Activity Expected in North Sea

The two that are reported to have been returned, the Aquamarine and Onyx, are understood to be vessels over 30 years old, no longer so suitable as they were for naval purposes. It is possible, however, that most of the wooden drifters which were taken over by the Admiralty at the outbreak of war may become available to resume their work on the herring fisheries. There must be in existence considerably over a hundred of these useful vessels, which are of smaller size and lower engine power than the average trawler.

Now that the German Navy has been driven out of the Channel with heavy loss, it may be expected that there will be greater naval activity in the North Sea. For two or three years past there have been regular encounters there between our coastal craft (motor-torpedo-boats and motor-gunboats) and those of the enemy, in which the advantage has invariably lain with us. Of late, night engagements off the Hook of Holland and the Frisian Islands have been increasingly frequent.

Before long the Germans will have to abandon Dutch harbours as they already have those of France and Belgium. No effort will be spared to harry enemy submarines and surface vessels as they retreat towards their own coast and ultimately to the Baltic. Not only our light coastal craft, but also cruisers and destroyers may be expected to take part in this work, as they already have done in the Channel. To oppose this weight of attack the Germans can have little left. Since D-Day they are believed to have lost eight destroyers or large torpedo boats in the Channel, some in action with our own destroyers and others as the result of attacks by Coastal Command. They may try to bring back from Norway the destroyers which were stationed there with a view to intercepting Allied convoys to and from the northern Russian ports. Some of these destroyers were hit and badly damaged during the concentrated attacks made by the Fleet Air Arm on the Tirpitz and other ships in Altenfjord in August 1944. It is not known to what extent the Tirpitz herself suffered on this occasion, as the ship was hidden by smoke screens which hindered effective reconnaissance from the air.

In Belgium's Capital Hitler Went Up in Smoke

BRITISH TANKS rumbling through Brussels were mobbed by delighted crowds who clambered up for a ride wherever foothold could be found (top). It was one of the most amazing manifestations of joy in the world's history. Early on September 3, 1944, Allied troops entered Belgium, freed Tournai, swept on north and east, and in the evening entered the capital. Outside the Bourse de Commerce the people cheered themselves hoarse as Hitler's portrait was ceremoniously burned (bottom).

Photos, British Official, British Newspaper Pool

DRAMATIC RETURN OF THE CANADIANS TO DIEPPE, on the Channel coast of Northern France, on September 1, 1944—when they captured the town without having to fire a shot—must have brought back to many of them terrible memories of the fiercely-contested Reconnaissance in Force of August 19, 1942. Men of these same units of the 2nd Canadian Division—the Essex Scottish, the Royal Hamilton Light Infantry, and the Royal Regiment of Canada—had then been mown down on the beaches and in the streets. Now, as roars from the French greeted this historic return, other Dieppe units were approaching—the South Saskatchewan Regiment, the Black Watch and the Toronto Scottish. At the great liberation parade on September 3, in the Rue Claude Grouland (above) General Crerar took the salute.

Photo, Associated Press

Young Surgeons in Action With the Royal Navy

Dealing calmly and competently with casualties while his ship is reeling in battle and himself in danger, restoring life to survivors of a wreck, giving succour to crashed airmen, operating for appendicitis during a raging Atlantic gale, decoding secret signals in his spare time : these are among the responsibilities of the Naval Surgeon, as described by Capt. FRANK H. SHAW.

"SURGEON, R.N." is his title. In small ships, however, he is usually "Surgeon, R.N.V.R.," for wartime expansion of the Navy does not permit the regular red-ringed men to go round. And usually he is young—until he has played a part in his first action ; that ages even the most care-free ex-medical-student in a very short time.

Captains and deck-officers see most of the game ; the surgeon, stowed away in the stripped wardroom, sees most of the after-effects. In Nelson's Navy the value of a naval engagement was assessed by the size of the "butcher's bill"—men got promotion according to the number of casualties—and the work of Nelson's surgeons inevitably savoured more of the abattoir than the hygienic clinic.

Cruisers, aircraft-carriers and battleships are equipped with a sufficient medical staff and these are furnished with up-to-the-minute operating theatres, sick-berth stewards, even nurses : the last word in blood-transfusion machinery is at instant call ; all the messy work entailed by action can be conducted below the waterline in armoured security (if even the biggest battleship can be deemed secure) but the small-ship "Doc" must make shift with improvisations nine times out of ten, even though his little ship is in the firing line ten times for its big brother's once.

THERE is, in a destroyer, no recognized cockpit : usually the officers' wardroom is converted into a hospital, with surgical instruments laid out where normally eating utensils would be arranged. One sick-berth steward is at hand to administer an anaesthetic, pass an artery forceps or otherwise make himself as useful as a whole, highly-trained staff. There is no warranty, as a destroyer races into close action, that an enemy shell will not make its first hit in the wardroom, thus wreaking havoc amongst the best-laid plans. No wonder Navy surgeons claim executive rank ! They haven't even the protection of sand-bagged bridges or armour-plated gun positions.

A big responsibility attaches to these youngsters, many of them fresh from the training hospitals, who have never previously been required to accept responsibility of the major sort. There is no court of appeal to which to turn when the dilemmas come. But experience teaches them the art of "making-do"—and their record throughout the war has been a proud one. When no action is pending, they are usually asked to serve as "code-and-cipher" officers, disentangling the innumerable secret signals brought down below by the wireless telegraphists ; and there is always enough purely local practice to keep their minds occupied, for hurrying small ships are hotbeds of minor casualties : scalds, burns and contusions, even more serious harm, often need immediate attention.

In the Thick of Grim Activity

A destroyer, the Navy's maid of all work, seems to attract to herself all the flotsam of salt water. A protecting aircraft, for instance, might crash into the sea ; or a Catafighter pilot might bale out in near proximity. Naturally, the small ship hurries to the rescue, to salve survivors ; and as the exigencies of war sometimes compel a crashed airman or aircraft crew to be immersed for lengthy spells, the ailments thus arising demand attention, to say nothing of serious gunshot wounds, or the scorching horror of petrol burns. Or a ship's lifeboat, adrift for days—even weeks—might be sighted,

manned by an emaciated, despairing crew ; then it is up to the ship's M.O. to provide comfort and easement for the sufferers, to work over them assiduously, encouraging every flickering spark of hesitant life ; to improvise remedies for immersion-foot, starvation, exposure and the countless evils that afflict those cast away in open boats, especially in a North Atlantic winter.

It is seldom that skilled assistance is available to the Doctor, for in small ships every member of the limited crew is a specialist, with his own appointed niche to fill in the general scheme. There are, of course, volunteers : an off-watch officer, a rare passenger ; but few of these have any knowledge of the trade of medicine, and are apt to perpetrate blunders ; the Doc must supervise everything they do with the closest care.

Surgeon-Lieut. **MAURICE J. HOOD, D.S.C.,** of the R.N.V.R., lost his life after saving a young American seaman suffering with acute appendicitis. Rather than risk seamen's lives in transferring him to the British destroyer from which he had been summoned, he remained aboard the merchant vessel. Three days later it was torpedoed and sank in seven minutes. Lieut. Hood had previously won the D.S.C. for jumping, in a gale, from the icy deck of his destroyer to another vessel to attend to 81 wounded men. *Photo, G.P.U.*

It is, however, when the small ship joins action that the surgeon finds himself in the thick of grim activity. Modern war-wounds are horrible ; bursting H.E. shears through human flesh and bone impartially ; amputations are frequently urgent ; abdominal wounds demand far better care than the hasty cockpit of action can offer. The surgeon has to do his best, as the mangled bodies are borne down the awkward companionway by the stretcher-parties. A whole gun-crew might be borne below in quick succession, every man savagely wounded. Opiates must be administered in sharp order to ease the agonized suffering bred of lacerated wounds : a whiff of ether here, a morphia tablet or injection there. With the whole crowded sick-bay a veritable shambles, a young, untried man might be excused for losing his head ; but the small-ship doctor seldom does this : he tackles the different problems with the stoic resolu-

tion taught in the surgical wards of the hospital of his training. No matter if the wardroom is ablaze from end to end, that enemy shells are screaming imminently near, that the ship is shaking and staggering at heavy hits, that she is jolted half-way out of the water by shell-bursts close alongside, or near-misses by 1,000-lb. bombs ; he must continue his merciful labours without a tremor. And, since the wounded take their courage from him, he must affect a coolness and unconcern that he probably does not feel ; for any next moment might find the surgeon blown up through the decks overhead, and swimming for dear life outboard.

Hurled into Littered Scuppers

With choking wafts of cordite smoke causing horrible inconvenience ; with the oily smoke of the protective screen that belches like something solid from the gushing funnels, to be drawn down below through the ventilating fans, until the wardroom is as murky as a London street in its worst fog ; with the ship rolling and pitching to an extent that hurls the suffering patients from operating table into littered scuppers, unless miracles of prompt assistance are given, being a destroyer surgeon in action is anything but child's play, indeed.

The only thing to do is to keep one's nerve, to do as much as—and a little more than—one pair of hands is capable of performing. It might mean a consecutive stretch of uncounted hours on duty ; it might mean that as the cockpit is filled to suffocation-point with his own shipmates—men he has learnt to know, admire, even to love—a fresh batch of salved enemy wounded is hauled aboard, each man suffering even more grievous hurt than his own associates. And humanity dictates the same careful attention to all ; for a wounded man ceases to be an enemy the moment he is laid on the bloodied deck of the rescuing-ship.

No wonder the London Gazette publishes so many instances of "devotion to duty under enemy fire," on the part of naval surgeons. They have earned many proud decorations, and they have earned them well. Not for them the comparative ease and security of a peaceful country general practice, or a hospital interne's busy, ordered existence. They'll tell you that most of the seagoing surgeon's work consists in killing time, in acting as mess president, in deciphering complicated signals ; but they know what they know. It occasionally happens, even in the best regulated ships, that emergency operations are required for appendix trouble and the like ; and the youngster who has practically never attempted even a minor operation is confronted with a set of circumstances that demands instant action.

A destroyer was boring an uneasy way through a North Atlantic gale that threw her about like a chip in a maelstrom, when a rating chose that inopportune moment to develop acute appendicitis symptoms. There was need for instant operation. Everything was made ready ; the agonized patient was anaesthetised, laid out on the hastily-cleared wardroom table. The young surgeon made the initial incision with a trembling hand ; it was his first abdominal case. Hardly had he done this when the lively destroyer did everything but turn turtle. Doctor, aides, patient, all slithered in a tangled heap to leeward. "But that roll did the trick," said the surgeon. "When we picked up the patient his appendix stuck up through the incision like a flag-pole ; all I had to do was suture it and cut—a first-class recovery !"

Over the Seine in Hot Pursuit to Brussels

CONFIDENT and cheerful, British troops (above) hauled a flat-bottomed boat through the streets of the ancient town of Vernon, 14 miles north-west of Mantes, on the left bank of the Seine, in preparation for the crossing which was effected by British and Canadians on August 26, 1944.

"A little classic" was how this crossing was described by Lieut.-General B. G. Horrocks, commanding the British 2nd Army corps, whose armour made the spectacular dash from the Seine to Brussels—206 miles in 6 days against steady opposition. This corps was moved across American lines of communication and, complete with bridging material, formed up at Vernon (which the Americans had captured) on August 24, for the crossing two days later.

ROYAL ENGINEERS laid a pontoon bridge across the river (right) as soon as the infantry had overcome enemy resistance. Skilfully and swiftly the way was thus paved for the transport to the far bank of light guns and Bren carriers to support the troops pursuing the Huns.

AFTER enemy guns laying down a barrage had been silenced by Allied artillery, our men, without cover, embarked in their flat bottomed boats (above) and crossed under rifle and machine-gun fire.

This thrust had commenced in the area of Dreux; the Seine crossed, our armour sped on through Beauvais, Amiens, Arras, Douai and over the Belgian frontier, to reach Brussels on September 3. Men of the Maquis and the Belgian "White Army" were given the tasks of preventing bridges being destroyed, locating and reporting enemy mines, and mopping up by-passed groups of Germans.

WRECKAGE of a beaten army in headlong retreat, hoping to escape across the Seine, was strewn along part of the river bank. Transport vehicles, mostly horse-drawn, and immense quantities of stores and material, had been shattered by Allied bombing (below).

Photos, British Official, British Newspaper Pool

Memories were Stirred on Battlefields Regained

FROM THE PAS DE CALAIS to the Argonne the Allies swept forward, aided in the great drive by French Forces of the Interior. Near Fouilley, at the beginning of Sept. 1944, British armour passed 1914-18 war graves overlooking the Somme Valley (1) in 1940 the Battle of the Somme had opened on June 5.

Our troops approaching the railway station at Arras (2) on Sept. 1, 1944, trod ground that in May 1940, was the scene of a magnificent stand by a British force against overwhelming German onslaught.

Canadians gained the wrecked town of Rouen on August 30, 1944 ; from the cathedral the Tricolour flutters (3). On June 9, 1940, Rouen had fallen.

In Amiens (4), regained on August 31, 1944, bare-headed German prisoners halted as members of the F.F.I. carried the bodies of fallen comrades to their last resting-place. German motorized columns had reached Amiens on May 21, 1940.

Photos, British Official; British Newspaper Pool, New York Times Photos

How We Blasted the Huns with Flame in France

When Britain's fortunes were at lowest ebb in 1940—when the Army had returned almost weaponless from Dunkirk and the full fury of Hitler's hordes threatened this country—Ramsgate beach saw the first active steps taken towards the development of amazing new weapons which are now searing great paths through the enemy's most formidable defences.

At dusk on July 14, 1944, a Scottish regiment launched an attack on a German position north of Esquay in Normandy. Strongly entrenched in the edges of woods and along the hedgerows, the enemy could not easily be overcome by any ordinary plan of engagement. But this assault was to hold surprises for the Germans against which they could not hope to stand.

Astride a roadway the attack went in—one troop of tanks on each side of the road, each troop followed by a platoon of the infantry, one section keeping close up to the armour. Suddenly through the half-light enormous flames roared out and licked fiercely at the hedgerows and forward undergrowth of the woods. Bushes and saplings were wrapped in fire. In that fiery, crackling inferno no man could live.

From this awesome threat of being consumed the Germans turned and ran, presenting their backs as targets for the bullets of the Scottish infantry. Some stayed, and were burned. And the position was taken without loss to the attackers. Subsequent interrogation of prisoners left no shred of doubt in the minds of the questioners as to the devastating and utterly demoralizing effect of this flood of liquid fire from our Crocodile flame-throwers.

For this section of the enemy it was the first (and for many the last) experience of Britain's new device for blasting a way into Normandy and so through France. Others had already made its fearsome acquaintance. Thirty-five minutes after our landing on D-Day (June 6) our Crocodiles went into action, and they led the British 2nd Army in the advance to Crépon (9 miles N.E. of Bayeux). Our flame-throwing Crocodiles, Wasps and Lifebuoys took part in almost every operation, fighting with every British and Canadian formation in the Normandy bridge-head.

"The Churchill Crocodile is the most powerful flame-thrower in the world today," declared Mr. Geoffrey Lloyd who, as Minister of Petroleum, formed in 1940 the organization known as the Petroleum Warfare Department. "With its special fuel it shoots a flame that is truly terrifying and deadly. We designed this weapon to burn out the strongpoints of the Atlantic Wall and Hitler's 'Fortress-Europe' and to save the lives of our infantry carrying out the assault. All this has developed from our first crude experiments to improvise burning oil defences on the beach at Ramsgate on a June afternoon in 1940. All of us who were there became keen believers in the effectiveness of flame warfare. That band grew and included people with the most varied, and indeed unorthodox, qualifications."

From those first hasty experiments, undertaken in every circumstance of personal danger, our three flame-throwers have developed. The Germans, who had used flame-weapons in the last war, were well provided for this war with new equipment on improved lines. We started from scratch, but fortunately we were possessed of ample stocks of oil. Not until the Dieppe raid did our troops go into action with anything of the sort : then the Commandos used flame-throwers of an early type to such effect that a German coastal battery was put out of action.

Our Ramsgate beach experimenters suffered painful burns and injuries, but the research went on—with all possible haste, for there was every likelihood of an attempted landing on our shores by the enemy, and our immediate objective, in the event of that happening, was to fling a protective curtain of flame over Britain from the beaches, the harbours, the lanes and the highways.

A satisfying measure of success was achieved in these preparations, and it became possible to switch from thoughts of defence to assault. In due course there rolled from the factories (the Ministry of Supply being responsible for production) these mighty weapons whose use has been attended with such tremendous success.

Immense efforts were called for on the part of the firms concerned, varying from foundrymen to footwear manufacturers and from racing car builders to laundry engineers ! The workers, pledged to secrecy, were given a glimpse of the result of their labours by films and demonstrations. Discouragements, inevitable in the evolution of any novel weapon, were many ; types were changed, modifications were introduced, older attempts outmoded. There came the final call for a last lap sprint for D-Day. The Crocodiles were needed 35 minutes after the Normandy landing. Nobly the workers responded. They even collaborated in the special and urgent training of the troopers who were to man the flame-throwers.

That early work of the Petroleum Warfare Department had indeed borne striking fruit. Speaking of the later work on the mobile flame-throwers in Bren Carriers, Mr. Geoffrey Lloyd said, "We owe a great debt of gratitude to General Macnaughton and the Canadian Army, particularly the Engineering Corps. Their enthusiasm matched our own. The Canadian Army carried out the first practical trials with the new weapon and the Canadian Government placed the first large order."

Fitted to the heavily armoured Churchill tank, the most powerful and effective of these flame-throwers is the Crocodile. The armoured trailer which carries the fuel is towed by the tank, and the fuel is led forward through an armoured pipe. Should need arise, the trailer—universally articulated so that it can move in any direction—can be jettisoned by means of an ingenious device.

The trailer itself is controlled from inside the tank, and its movements are indicated by pilot lights mounted on a panel in front of the tank commander. This makes it unnecessary for the commander to expose himself to enemy fire in order to see just what is happening at any given moment. One specially useful and interesting point about the new type of fuel that is used—it can be projected to distances of over 150 yards—is that it can be fired around corners, so that it will ricochet and produce persistent flame in every cranny of pillbox and trench.

The Lifebuoy flame-thrower, deriving its name from its appearance, has a ring-shaped tube as container for the fuel, with a spherical container for compressed gas, the device being carried on the operator's back. The flame is projected from a " gun " which incorporates an igniting mechanism. The range is about 50 yards, and the Lifebuoy has been used with outstanding success by our parachute-troops, and Commandos, and Canadian infantry. For dislodging the enemy from otherwise "awkward" positions and exposing them to the small-arms fire of the infantry it is in all ways admirable.

Where more devastating and "frightening" action is required, the Wasp—intermediary between the Lifebuoy and the Crocodile—is available. Its larger fuel supply and greater mobility render it more suitable than the Lifebuoy for big operations. This thrower is fitted to a Universal Carrier. Tanks containing the liquid fuel and compressed gas are mounted on the carrier, the flame-gun projecting through the front armour.

A MIGHTY FLAME REACHING TO 150 YARDS originates in the fuel-trailer (left) of the Churchill Crocodile flame-thrower and is emitted from the projector nozzle (right) in the nose of the tank, which is seen in action in the facing page. The armoured trailer is towed by the Churchill, the connexion being so devised that it can move in any direction and be disconnected if necessary. The special fuel passes from the tanks in the trailer to the nozzle via an armoured pipe.

Photos, British Official

Terrifying British Weapons throw Liquid Fire

THE LIFEBUOY FLAME-THROWER in the aiming position (above), and in action (right). The ring-shaped tube, or "lifebuoy," carries the special fuel; the spherical container in the centre is charged with compressed gas. Igniting mechanism is incorporated in the "gun."

THE CROCODILE flame-thrower is fitted to the heavily armoured Churchill tank, and the devastating and demoralizing flame is thrown forward 150 yards or more (above). What is perhaps even more terrifying to the enemy, the flame will bend and search him out in trench and pillbox corners. See facing page.

THE WASP is fitted to a Universal Carrier, the flame gun (above) having a range equal to that of the Churchill Crocodile. Pipes lead from the projector to fuel and compressed gas tanks which are easily removable; in the field they can be taken out quickly if it is desirable that the carrier should resume its normal role, and can be replaced at once if flame-throwing operations against the enemy are to be resumed.

Wasps in action (left) can go forward in the face of heavy gunfire, the body of the carrier being bullet-proof. Their larger fuel supply and greater mobility make the Wasps more suitable for large-scale operations than the man-carried Lifebuoy.

The story of the development and use of these new weapons is told in the facing page.

Photos, British Official : Crown Copyright; New York Times Photos, G.P.U.

An End to this World-Curse of German Minorities!

A complicated problem which the post-war world will have to unravel is that of German minorities
in foreign lands. In the past a continual source of trouble, they have been ever ready to turn
Fifth Columnists in the service of the Reich. Here HENRY BAERLEIN points out future dangers
and how, with foresight and determined action, they might be avoided.

WHEN the German armies in Russia were advancing towards Stalingrad and the River Volga, a most necessary step was taken by Marshal Stalin—which, according to the German radio, was "shamelessly barbaric." If the 80,000 Germans, most of them Swabians, who dwelt on the banks of the great Volga had not been evacuated to the Urals, by Stalin's orders, there can be no doubt that some of them would have continued to function as very active Fifth Columnists.

There are other European countries which, after the war, will have to face a similar problem ; if they leave it unsolved it will be to their peril. Such is the nature of the German abroad that he scarcely requires any propaganda from Berlin. For instance, when after the last war the two small districts of Eupen and Malmedy were incorporated in Belgium and given tolerant Belgian government, the German minority was most unhappy without the severe discipline to which their compatriots in Aachen and Cologne were being subjected, feeling like lost sheep. This yearning for the jack-boot will have to be taken into account chiefly by Czechoslovakia and Poland.

THE three or four million German-speaking inhabitants of the Sudeten districts of Czechoslovakia will be reduced to perhaps 1½ millions after the war, for many have fallen in the East, others have secured positions in Germany, and at least 20 per cent are painfully aware that their names are on the lists of war criminals. It is thought that those who remain will not automatically be granted Czech citizenship, but will have to ask for it ; and that perhaps two-thirds will receive the provisional grant of it, that is to say, "first papers," dependent on their behaviour, as in the United States.

There should be no self-determination for villages, but for the nation. In other words, the policy of allowing a village with 20 per cent of Germans to have a German school at State expense is likely to be abandoned ; a citizen enjoying full rights will have to know the State language. Others may remain as aliens without vote, and in the event of unemployment preferential treatment would be given to full citizens. By bitter experience the Czechs have learned that their legislation between the two wars was far too liberal for the mentality of those who were persuaded that the republic would never endure. Of course, the old and strong mountain frontier of Bohemia should be restored to what Mr. Chamberlain called "an unknown country." It should be reinforced by Slovak and Ruthenian peasants from the more arid parts of the Republic, and by inviting the Lusatian Serbs to come in from Saxony, where even Hitlerian methods have not succeeded in obliterating the Slav spirit of these sturdy folk.

Land-Grabbing Policy in Poland

In the 1886-1918 period, during the activity of the Colonizing Commission, the Reich spent over 500 million gold marks on subsidies designed to increase the number of Germans in the Polish provinces. After years of expropriation of Poles in favour of Germans, and of subsidizing German landowners, 26 per cent of the arable land in the province of Poznan (western Poland) was in German hands, although the Germans formed only 9·1 per cent of the population.

THE colonization of East Prussia, much earlier, had a hostile and Germanizing character. And when Poland was restored, after the last war, the Germans everywhere in the country were egged on, if that was needed, by their Press in Poland to prevent normal and peaceful relations between Poles and Germans. Any German who refused to obey the leaders of the *Deutsche Vereinigung* (the principal German minority organization) was boycotted by all the members in social and business life.

The German minority in Poland in 1939 —when Hitler was hysterically screaming that their life had been rendered unendurable —had no less than 394 elementary schools, 15 high schools and 13 for girls, using the German language, maintained at the expense of the Polish Government. When the western parts of Poland were parts of the Reich, the Poles, although admitted by official German statistics to be in the majority, were treated as second-class citizens, with no schools in their own language. After this war the Poles will have to see to it that this Trojan horse is well muzzled !

In 1939 when the population of Rumania reached the 20 million mark, the number of German settlers there amounted to some 800,000, many of them descended from the men brought in by the old Austrian Empire in the eighteenth century as "Frontier Regiments" against the Turks. They enjoyed special rights, which have been preserved, so that in February 1942 Iuliu Maniu, the revered Liberal leader, wrote to Marshal Antonescu pointing out that the Germans were becoming a State within the State, viewing with equanimity the disappearance of Rumania and working for the "Danube State" which was to be the guardian of that most important European traffic-artery, the Danube, and of the shortest way to India.

Curious Position of Hungarians

In the last Yugoslav census of 1931 it was seen that about 500,000 Germans (i.e. 3·59 of the population) lived there, enjoying the fullest freedom. In Slovenia the heavy industry was in their hands, while their banking position became ever more potent. It is interesting to note that the German minority sent no complaints to the League of Nations, and even Hitler, in 1938, said bluntly that "the German minority is nowhere better off than in Yugoslavia." Nevertheless, their leader in Parliament, a certain Herr Hamm, made a speech demanding not only "cultural" but also political autonomy. One of the measures Yugoslavia will have to take after the war is to investigate what happened after the agrarian crisis from 1930 onwards, when Germans, using assumed names or openly, began to acquire landed property on the northern borders of the country and by the side of railways and canals. Once bitten . . . !

The Hungarians find themselves in rather a curious position, for the German doctrine of the Herrenvolk is the same as that which the Hungarians have themselves carried on for centuries against the Slavs and Rumanians in their country. Now Basch, the leader of the half-million Germans, has obtained for them such conditions that Hungary has become economically completely dependent on the Reich. This was to the advantage of Hungary's feudal class, but the only hope for the future prosperity of that country lies with a people whose democratic instincts have never been allowed to develop.

WHEN Transylvania was arbitrarily divided by the Axis between Hungary and Rumania, most German settlers found themselves in the former country. With Rumania now very prudently throwing in her lot with the Allied Nations, who, of course, did not recognize the Axis award, the wiser of these Germans will return to their economic activities, not participating in the conflict of words—possibly of deeds—between the two countries.

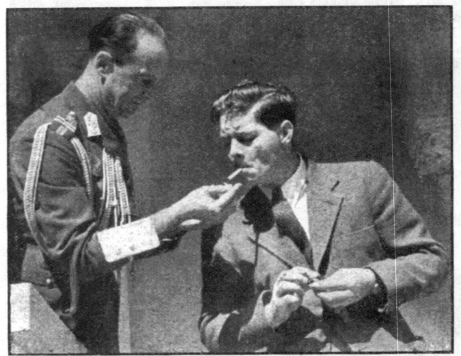

KING MICHAEL (right), 22-year-old ruler of Rumania, gave a lead to other satellite States when he quitted the Hitler alliance. In a dramatic proclamation on August 23, 1944, he announced that his country had ceased fighting the United Nations and would forthwith support them in the prosecution of the war.

Photo, Associated Press

Cheers and Homage in Paris Freed

Entering Paris with French and U.S. troops on Aug. 26, 1944, British soldiers received a specially tumultuous welcome (above) as soon as their battle-dress was recognized by the wildly delighted Parisians—free to live their own lives again after four years of German oppression.

At the tomb of the Unknown Soldier beneath the Arc de Triomphe (right) three of our warriors paid solemn tribute to the past glories of France and greater glories yet to come. General de Gaulle, who reached Paris on the evening of August 25, placed on the tomb a wreath in honour of France's sons who fought and fell by the side of the British in the war of 1914-18.

Photos, British Official, British Newspaper Pool

De Gaulle Symbolizes France's Liberation—

From the Arc de Triomphe down the Champs Elysées, across the Place de la Concorde and so along the Rue de Rivoli (1) General Charles de Gaulle passed between cheering multitudes. Not yet, however, had the last acts of Nazi terrorists been recorded in the annals of the capital; as units of the 2nd French Armoured Division passed in procession through the world-famous archway (3) shots rang out to mar one of the greatest celebrations ever held in Paris.

—Whilst Snipers' Bullets Whine Overhead

From cheers to threat of death by snipers' shots aimed from a building in the Place de la Concorde : the startling interruption turned celebrations into a scurry for cover. Lamp-posts and even barbed wire "knife-rests" gave to crouching figures some fancied sanctuary from the hail of lead (2). But the jubilation of a city freed at last could not be stifled, as this sea of happy faces photographed in the Place de l'Opéra (4) vividly testifies.

The Last Round-up of Frenzied Huns

Patrols of General Leclerc's 2nd French Armoured Division reached Paris on the evening of August 24, 1944, and made contact with the F.F.I. Twenty-four hours later organized German resistance had ceased; but fanatical snipers had yet to be silenced. French troops proceeded with the mopping-up (top), whilst a lone comrade in another street did execution with a light machine-gun. In the battle for liberation 1,496 French people were killed, 552 wounded.

VIEWS & REVIEWS Of Vital War Books

by Hamilton Fyfe

WE at home felt badly when we heard day after day two years ago of things going badly in Burma. What do you suppose were the feelings of the men on the spot as they had to retreat before the hordes of oncoming Japanese ? The airmen especially, who were outnumbered so heavily by the enemy, but who believed they might hold on if only the Army could stay put. They were doing magnificent work. To be pulled back made them both sad and furious.

How they took it, Kenneth Hemingway lets us see in Wings Over Burma (Quality Press, 15s.) without indulging in any complaints or laments, but allowing their thoughts and feelings to appear through the slangy talk of himself and his fellow-airmen as they sit in their mess, hurry to their airfield when the telephone calls them, go up on bombing raids or escort flights, get back and talk their day's or night's work over.

They seem to have been, even for airmen, an unusually cheerful lot. The author himself is a man with an infinite capacity for enjoyment. He could find delight in being out before dawn on a February morning when " a battledress top " was needed to keep in the warmth of a body going out into cold air, with the task of raiding a Jap airfield awaiting him.

> I find one never wearies of being first out on an aerodrome, whatever the circumstances, whether it be an operational or quiet station. It is a satisfaction constantly pleasing, as fishing is to an angler or country walks to a townsman.
> Whatever the clime, at dawn comes an expectancy, the optimism with which one makes New Year resolutions. The hangars, the surrounding country, and the aircraft all glisten as if they had been cleaned with a bucket of dewdrops. Though it is a modern scene brushed with machinery, oils, steels and glycols, its essence is the maturing of the spirits of Drake's galleons, Nelson's ships of the Line.

Mr. Hemingway, you can see, is something of a poet.

It is not cold in Burma in the daytime. The heat is described as almost unbearable. The clothing worn is of the lightest after the sun has gained power, which it does very quickly. Yet at a great height in the air the temperature is low again, so warm clothes must be worn, whatever the thermometer on the ground says. It was a harassing life the airmen led. How harassing they fortunately scarcely realized until they had a holiday. Only a couple of days, but that, in the midst of a campaign, was enough. Two weeks would have been too much. After a fortnight

> ease permeates a man's being ; his resolves and reactions, like a jigsaw of many pieces, cannot be reformed into the mien of a compleat fighter in a day . . . Twelve days of refined food, baths, clean clothes, and you like civilization, subconsciously maybe, too much !

But for two days they were thoroughly contented

> with no telephone by our side all day and every day to ring suddenly and raise our hackles, with none of the tension of that sitting around in the dust and heat, and then patrolling, patrolling again, and more sitting ; and among it the sudden skirmishing dog-fight and the scrambling from sweaty heat to too cool a comfort above.

They spent their holiday at a military hill station, Maymo. On the road to it they passed through Mandalay. They had expected picturesqueness, and from a distance its pagodas, hundreds of them, supplied it ; but inside . . . . .

there was garbage strewn on the pavements ; its inhabitants looked as if they wanted a wash, and the stucco of the buildings in the main streets was more often than not peeling in a porriginous dinginess.

The cantonment, when they came to it, surprised them by its fine buildings, trees and gardens, golf and sports grounds, spacious houses, brick and half-timbered as in a London suburb, with well-kept drives up to them and a setting of smooth lawns. In a large, luxurious residential club they found quarters of the most comfortable

---

Battle by Air: the Burma Background

---

order, with excellent food and hosts of servants. It was like an English hotel, and the likeness was intensified by the way the people in the dining-room " avoided each other's glance," and took no notice of anyone not in their own party.

ONE cannot help wondering whether all the care and thought that went to the perfecting of places like that in the Far East, and in India too, might not have prevented some of the set-backs that befell us, if they had been devoted to the business instead of the pleasures of life. And whether, perhaps, it would not have been better if, instead of separating themselves so ostentatiously from the life of the Burmese, the British had entered more into that life and won liking and respect, which would have made the people our friends in time of trouble. As it was, Mr. Hemingway says, " like most onlookers, they tended to favour the winner."

An Anglo-Burmese girl (which means British father, native mother) told him what she thought, quite frankly. She was intelligent, quick to laugh, composed in manner. " One great fault," she said, " has been that you British have kept to yourselves. Our families are educated, and our people are happy, they like entertaining . . . that

attitude of yours naturally creates resentment." So it came about that men of the British forces had to be always " on the *qui vive* for some hostile Burman popping up knife in hand." It is only fair to add that in other parts with which this author was evidently not acquainted the Burmese gave us a good deal of help. We should have received more from them if we had taken more trouble to make them like us.

WE suffered in the Far East from shortcomings in the past and from muddling at the moment of danger. We ought not to have lost Burma. Mr. Hemingway does not deal with the reasons for our losing it, though he lets us see they caused a good deal of heart-searching at the Front. We need not have lost it if quick decisions had been taken. In the House of Lords some two years back Lord Addison read out a letter written by the colonel commanding a Scottish regiment, who was posted as " missing, believed killed." This told how a plan was framed to forestall the Japanese landing in Siam. Put into operation at once, it would have stopped them seizing a base for their attack on Burma. But it was held up because our Intelligence Service reported Siam as a friendly nation, whose neutrality we must not infringe. When the Japanese landed it became clear at once that the Siamese were on their side, and had been all the time.

Many of us must have wondered how, when airmen reassemble at a meal after some big flight in which many have gone down, and see the unoccupied places, they feel about their comrades who have left them, and whether it makes them gloomily reflect, " It may be my turn to-morrow." Mr. Hemingway deals with this.

> One soon forgets. Our faces quieten at such news, we mutter indistinguishably sometimes when it is someone in our own squadron, yet to imagine that pilots moon about afterwards with grim faces and, when they next go into action, snarlingly press the gun-button with " And that's for George " is plain tripe. We are at war ; our instinct is to push such incidents away in the subconscious and get on with the job. It affects us only when we are growing " operationally tired " or when the man killed has been such a key personality in the squadron that his extinction is comparable to losing an elder brother or young sister. Besides, the pinch of salt to every stew of grief is the selfish thought it might be yourself next. Naturally we refuse to brood over that.

Passages like this give the book a value beyond that of its topical interest and the light it throws on the conditions of the Burma campaign in the air.

SPITFIRES IN BURMA established clear superiority over the Japanese Zero. Here in a forward airfield " Spits " are lined up for the fray ; in the foreground, surrounded by boxes of ammunition, the pilots are waiting. The manner of life our airmen led previous to the evacuation of Rangoon is described in the book reviewed in this page. *Photo, Indian Official*

Russians at Bucharest and East Prussian Border

SOVIET ARTILLERY EIRED ON GERMAN TERRITORY in East Prussia when, on August 17, 1944, Red Army forces reached the enemy frontier north-west of Mariampole: for the first time in this war the Germans were given a dose of their own land-war medicine. The shelling of German soil was a milestone in the great summer offensive, staged all along the front from Finland to the Carpathians, which carried the Russian forces 350 miles forward, and brought about the defection from the Axis of Rumania, Finland and Bulgaria.

STALIN'S TANKS ROLLED INTO BUCHAREST on August 31, 1944, after troops of the 2nd Ukrainian Army had advanced 35 miles from Ploesti in a day. This victory, in which the tanks figured largely, followed the rout of the Germans who had made a last-minute stand north of the city. As the Russian armour passed through Rumania's capital people thronged the streets to make plain their welcome of these representatives of the onsweeping Red Army. See illus. p. 302.

Photos, Pictorial Press; U.S.S.R. Official

Armed Might that Gladdened the Heart of France

THOUSANDS OF U.S. TROOPS, with tanks and other armoured vehicles passed through the streets of Paris on August 29, 1944, on their way to the front. In a two-hour procession massed infantrymen marched down the Avenue des Champs Elysées to the Place de la Concorde, where Lieut.-General Omar Bradley, commander of the 12th Army Group, and General Charles de Gaulle took the salute. In the background is the Arc de Triomphe, draped with the Tricolour.

Photo, Associated Press

Royal Air Force Regiment in Action Overseas

On the Burma front, in desert battles from Alamein to Tripoli, in Sicily and Italy and France, the youngest branch of the youngest British service—the R.A.F. Regiment—has won undying fame. This article, specially written for "The War Illustrated" by Sgt. A. J. WILSON, tells of the origin and splendid achievements of this now mighty corps.

"JUST a minute, chum!" The leading aircraftman with the flash of the R.A.F. Regiment on his shoulder looked around as the call came from a hospital train which stood at the up-line platform of a station in Southern England. At an open carriage window was a wounded soldier of a famous North Country regiment just back from the Normandy battlefield. The soldier thrust his arm through the window and shook the airman's hand.

"I've been wanting to do that ever since I first saw your lot in action!" the soldier said. "They're doing a grand job over there—good luck to all of you!" Like many other British troops who carried out the landings in Northern France on D-Day, the soldier and his comrades had been surprised to see men of the R.A.F. Regiment in the first landing craft which nosed their way through the minefields and other obstacles off the Normandy coast.

BUT for the Regiment, this was by no means their first major action. They had gained their battle experience in the Western Desert and in Tunisia ; they had taken part in the landings in Sicily and Italy, and had won undying fame on the island of Cos in the Dodecanese. The Regiment had, in fact, seen as much of the enemy at close quarters as many of the Army units with whom they shared the hazards on the beaches of Normandy.

The R.A.F. Regiment's chief task, at home and overseas, is the defence of airfields from attack, both from the air and from the land. In France, every British aircraft which operates from the captured airfields or landing strips laid down by construction units does so under the protection of anti-aircraft guns of the Regiment. Night and day, the airfields are guarded and vital points picketed by the men in khaki and blue. Aircraft, pilots, ground crews and stores are all dependent for their safety on the watchfulness of the airmen-soldiers.

It is now four years since the R.A.F. began to provide their own airfield protection. In 1940, when the German Army was roaring westwards across Europe, smashing everything in its path, ground defence units were formed within the R.A.F. to guard our airfields from the invasion which seemed so imminent. Army officers, many of them last war brigadiers and colonels, were specially selected to command the units and sent hurriedly off to vital bases, the single thin ring of a pilot officer on the sleeves of their new blue uniforms contrasting strangely with the rows of ribbons on their chests.

Ready for the Nazi Onslaught

The chief equipment of these first units were Vickers and Lewis guns—and pikes ! The unit commanders themselves had to make their own arrangements for the manufacture of pikes. Nearly everything had to be improvised. At some stations the men managed to get hold of some small cars which they armoured, while one unit was presented with a couple of five-ton lorries, with concrete gun turrets, which proved almost too heavy to move. Through the anxious days of the Battle of Britain the men stood ready at their action stations, waiting for the invasion that never came.

The rapid expansion of the R.A.F. in the following year made it clear that if the airmen were to continue to look after their own airfields many more men would be required and the individual units put under central control. Eventually, after many Air Ministry

and War Office conferences, it was agreed to form a special corps ; and on February 1, 1942, the R.A.F. Regiment officially came into being, with Major-General C. F. Liardet, C.B., D.S.O. (now Sir Claude Liardet), taking charge as Commandant of the Regiment and Director General of Ground Defence.

EACH R.A.F. Home Command was given a Chief Defence Officer, who was responsible for the administration of all Regiment squadrons in that Command, and a comprehensive training programme was arranged. All men did the basic training of an infantry soldier in the regular Army, a battle school was started and there was specialized training for the anti-aircraft gun crews. They took part in combined exercises and very soon reached a high pitch of efficiency. At first the scheme applied only to home service, but within a few months squadrons were on their way to all parts of the world where there were R.A.F. aircraft operating.

Out in the Middle East, where Rommel's dash across the Desert had brought him to within a few miles of Alexandria and Cairo,

Major-General SIR CLAUDE LIARDET, C.B., D.S.O., Commandant of the R.A.F. Regiment and Director General of Ground Defence since February 1942. In this page some of his Regiment's exploits in France and other theatres of war are related. *Photo, British Official*

the Regiment was built up to considerable strength ; and shortly before the British attack at El Alamein, Air Vice-Marshal Coningham, commanding the R.A.F. forces, sent for his Defence Officer and outlined the plan for the great offensive. Together they studied the maps, the Air Vice-Marshal pointing out the enemy airfields he hoped to occupy during the advance.

The battles in the Desert from Alamein to Tripoli gave the men of the Regiment their first taste of working in co-operation with the Army in the field and their first chance to get to close grips with the enemy. On the move forward, their anti-aircraft guns helped to give constant protection to convoys, while picked flights went ahead with the infantry (and sometimes without them) to ensure the immediate occupation of enemy airfields. Many times they cleared up pockets of resistance and worked under shell fire and bombing attacks, getting their guns into position.

They cleared mines and unexploded bombs, searched for booby traps and dealt with enemy snipers ; in fact, they did everything to get the captured airfields ready for immediate use by their flying comrades. It was their work which enabled the leap-frogging R.A.F. to give the enemy no rest from air

attack as he went tearing back towards Tripoli with the 8th Army close on his heels

Meanwhile, other squadrons of the R.A.F. Regiment had embarked in the great invasion fleet for North Africa, and, with their comrades from the Western Desert, they played a vital part in the final stages of the Tunisian campaign. For a time some squadrons were attached to Army units in the line for battle experience and later the airmen were among the first British troops to enter Bizerta and to pass through Tunis, following the armoured forces into the city. In a few days they took more than 3,000 Axis prisoners and captured a vast quantity of valuable equipment, as well as mounting their guns on the captured airfields.

Gunning the Germans at Cos

In Sicily, and in Italy, men of the R.A.F. Regiment were again in the first landing barges, and at Cassino this year they held part of the Allied line in the mountains north of the town. But perhaps the most glorious chapter in the history of the Regiment in its first two years of war was at Cos, where its men were continually in action from the day of the British landing in September 1943 until the island was retaken by the Germans three weeks later. Even after resistance to strong enemy tank and infantry attacks seemed hopeless, they continued to fight on in the hills against overwhelming odds.

Through many ground-strafing raids the guns of the Regiment were the island's only defence against air attack. It was impossible to dig in the guns or protect them in any way, and in almost every raid the unprotected crews suffered casualties from the cannon and machine-gun fire of German fighters or from the tail gunners of the bombers

A Royal Artillery officer who escaped from the island paid this tribute to the men : "All of us who saw the R.A.F. Regiment gunners in action were impressed by the grand spirit of the gun teams, who were determined to fight their guns no matter how easy a target they presented. There was a cheery and defiant courage about them and a pride in their Regiment which impressed us all. We will always remember them for their unfailing cheerfulness, their determination to fight their guns to the end and their great courage. We were all proud to know them."

IT was with the same determination and courage that squadrons of the Regiment embarked for Normandy on the night of June 5, 1944. They knew their job and they were determined to see it through. On the beaches they went about their task of unloading and dispatching their equipment calmly and efficiently, and by the time the construction work on the first air landing strip had begun their anti-aircraft guns were in position to ward off enemy air attack. One squadron landed in eight feet of water, and the lorries carrying their anti-aircraft guns were submerged. Although their guns were 12 hours in the water they were all in action against enemy aircraft by nightfall.

For many hours during those first few vital days the men of the Regiment worked under constant shell fire, but they had their reward when their guns shot down the first German aircraft to be destroyed from the ground in Normandy. They have added many more to their "bag" since then. Today the R.A.F. Regiment in France are moving forward with the great Allied Armies and are looking forward to the time when they will take their guns across the Rhine to mount guard on the airfields of the Reich.

Airmen-Soldiers Deeply Versed in Craft of War

IN EGYPT the R.A.F. Regiment went into action for the first time when it helped to capture Rommel's advanced air bases at Daba and Fuka, on November 4, 1942, and rounded up 200 prisoners ; Bren gunners (left) covering advancing riflemen await the order to move up. In the Imphal Valley, Burma, aircraftmen in a trench (right) point out a Japanese position to Sqdn.-Ldr. Ryalls (2nd from right), commanding officer of all R.A.F. regiments in the Valley. The Regiment ordinarily works in very close co-operation with the Army in the field.

CONCEALMENT PLAYS A BIG PART in attack as well as defence, and here the art of camouflage is strikingly demonstrated during an airfield exercise in Normandy by ten men of the R.A.F. Regiment. Invisible in the lower photograph—prone in the herbage, still as death itself—on the word of command the ten men spring to their feet (centre) revealing how very effectively they were hidden, with no aid other than that provided by Nature. See also facing page.

Photos, British Official : Crown Copyright

They Helped to Drive the Japanese from India

FIGHTING THROUGH DENSE JUNGLE, swamps and swollen rivers and up rocky mountains, troops of the British 14th Army ousted the last remnants of organized Japanese resistance from India by August 17, 1944, five months after the invasion of the Manipur State. After covering 130 miles of some of the world's roughest routes, our men had succeeded in their immediate objective.

Under the command of Brigadier L. E. C. M. Perowne (1)—leader of "Newcomb's Rifles" during the fighting in France in June 1940—tough fighters of the 23rd Brigade queued up to receive sorely needed clothing (3). Much of the work of driving the enemy out of Northern India was accomplished by men of the Devon Regiment, some of whom, wounded, are seen about to enter a jeep (2) to be taken to a base hospital. Other wounded cross a temporary wire bridge constructed by Indian engineers (4). The Imphal-Tiddim Road, scene of savage fighting, stretches like a giant snake through the jungle (5); it is now cleared of the enemy.

I WAS THERE!

Eye Witness
Stories of the War

•••

This Was the End of Our Serfdom in Brussels

After one of the most terrific forward drives of the war—our armoured columns covered 206 miles in six days—the Belgian capital was captured by the British 2nd Army on Sunday, September 3, 1944. A famous Belgian journalist, Louis Quievreux, here describes this dramatic chapter in the city's history. His story is reprinted from the News Chronicle.

FOR the past three days I have been watching, with eager interest and with a satisfied sense of revenge for four years of humiliation and persecution, the ceaseless stream of battered and exhausted German troops through the main thoroughfares of Brussels. The crumbling of the Nazi administration of Brussels began on August 29, when the news spread like lightning that the Gestapo was leaving the beautiful modern building they had occupied since 1940.

I went there and saw them at work, piling up stolen furniture in all kinds of vans and burning heaps of documents. On that same day German girls of the civil and military services—the "mice" we called them because of their grey uniforms—were ordered to leave within 24 hours. You should have seen them dejectedly waiting for machine-gun riddled, wood-gas operated lorries. They were no longer the laughing, haughty girls whose bottle and necking parties had for long months shocked the people of a hungry capital.

This is where the Brussels White Brigade struck. About 100 "mice" were ordered to heap their luggage at an hotel where it would be picked up by a special van. The van came, but it was a White Brigade one, and into it the "mice," smiling with relief, piled their belongings. Fifteen minutes later the real van arrived.

At the Barriere de St. Gilles, 100 yards from the grim-looking prison where thousands of Belgian patriots have been imprisoned and tortured, I saw, on Saturday, this heart-rending scene. A Black Maria was taking away several civilian prisoners. It was followed by a crowd of women shouting out the names of their relatives in the hope that they would hear. Through holes torn in the cloth unknown hands were waving adieu. A youth thrust his head between two warders armed with tommy-guns, but he was thrown back.

The main square before the Gare du Nord was the place where tens of thousands of Bruxellois for three days watched the retreat from their city. Dust-covered, exhausted Germans, passing on tireless bicycles, in lorries showing traces of the recent fighting, in carts drawn by lank horses, could see the people of Brussels seated outside cafés sipping beer and lemonade. "Now," said one beaming citizen to me, "we have a genuine news-reel, not a faked one such as we have had for four years."

The St. Jean Barracks, near the Gare du Nord, were so crammed that tents had been erected in the front yards. Among the weary soldiers the crowd passed smiling ironically. So strong is the feeling of anger for all the atrocities committed here that not a glass of water, not a cigarette was offered to the routed Germans. Then a long column of brand new amphibious tanks came along and stopped. The crews huddled themselves on the pavements or on the mudguards and fell into a heavy sleep. Not even an air-raid alarm moved them.

During the night of Sunday the White Brigade went into action at several places. At Molembeek several garages filled with lorries were blown up. The noise of explosions and of gunfire, and the news that our Allies had entered Tournai, kept everybody awake. Everywhere could be seen groups of Germans selling what they could—lorry tires, bottles of rum, margarine, bicycles. All the Germans were anxious to get civilian clothes.

Some days ago Belgian journalists who had not been working for the German Press and barristers and officers of the Belgian Army received a threatening letter from the Rexist Party in which they were told that they would be shot should a Rexist member in their street be shot. I disappeared for some nights !

Rexists were executed, but there were few reprisals ; the Rexist Party had already disbanded, forsaken by its former protectors. At the Gare du Nord Rexist families and legionaires waited for three days in the hope of getting a train for Germany. Their hopes were in vain. The Germans dropped them. A German officer, who was also a teacher of English, said to me : "We do not like traitors. We just use them."

On Saturday, Sept. 2, the Brussels newspapers of the German Press appeared for the last time. In an editorial entitled "God save Belgium," the "Nouveau Journal" said that the newspapers would not be published on Monday. It announced an era of revolution and of trouble. A crowd mad with joy welcomed the first British cars on the southern outskirts of Brussels at 7 p.m. on Sunday. Flags of all the United Nations were hung from

GESTAPO' RECORDS were consumed in the blaze when the retreating enemy fired the magnificent Palais de Justice in Brussels (above). Situated on a height in the centre of the city, the huge building commanded much of Belgium's capital, and it was here that the Gestapo kept its archives. British armoured forces advanced 206 miles in six days, and by this lightning-like drive prevented the Germans from removing their documents. See story above, and illus. pp. 295, 298.

Photo British Newspaper Pool

balconies and windows. Near the Avenue Louise, the Rue de Livourne and the Rue de Florence, German soldiers were shooting at passers-by. Two German cars stood in the deserted Avenue Louise.

I cycled towards the Place Ste Croix, where stands the huge building of Brussels Radio. The quisling announcers and the staff had gone. The Belgian flag was flying mast-high above the building, now occupied by gendarmes. The gendarmes had been ordered to defend the premises against all attacks. It was dark when I went back, and I ran into violent firing at the Porte de Namur, which armoured cars had reached about 9 p.m. Shots were exchanged with isolated snipers.

The scene all along the Chaussee de Charleroi to Uccle was splendid. People danced and sang in the light of fireworks ; members of the Independence Front, armed with rifles, pistols and grenades, were wildy cheered. In the Avenue Brugman two

American tanks were surrounded by a crowd of hysterical people. A Brussels fire brigade engine swung past and the firemen announced that German cars were coming in this direction. The crews of the tanks took up battle position, but a dozen people who were sitting on top of the tanks refused to jump down. An American soldier fired a pistol in the air to make them do so. But it was a false alarm.

Before leaving Brussels the Germans destroyed the great copper dome of the Law Courts and set fire to a wing which had been occupied by the military court. The Burgomaster of Brussels, Mr. Van de Meubbroek, was back at the Hotel de Ville on Monday morning, where he received British officers. This morning Brussels is full of British and American armoured cars and tanks. The first London soldier with whom I shook hands was Driver J. Heatley, of Pownell Road, Hackney.

They either huddled beneath them or ran blindly for the futile cover of the hedges. They ran in the direction of the fire, shouting that they had surrendered. They gave up in hundreds upon hundreds. There was no fight left in them any more, and now here you can see what is left by the battle in the warm midday sunlight. It is exactly like one of those crowded battle paintings of Waterloo or Borodino—except, of course, the kind of wreckage is different.

EVERY staff car—and I suppose I have seen a hundred—is packed with French loot and German equipment. There is a profusion of everything—field-glasses and typewriters, pistols and small arms by the hundred, cases of wine, truckloads of food and medical stores, a vast mass of leather harness. Every car is full of clothing, and every officer seems to have possessed a pair of corsets to take home. If you want a car you walk up and take your pick—anything from a baby tourer or a volkswagen to a ten-ton half-track. The Tommies start them up and go off through the orchards. Two Russians in German uniform stand stupidly on the river bank, and they timidly hold out cigarettes to anyone who comes by. They stand in the middle of piled-up riches they never dreamed of before —purses crammed with notes that have fallen from dead men's bodies, radio sets and dumps of clothing looted from the French.

At St. Lambert I Saw the End of German Might

The obliteration of the German 7th Army in France was a grim and ghastly feat. Writing from the village of St. Lambert, on August 22, 1944, Alan Moorehead, of The Daily Express, describes what happened to the panzers when at last they met our troops head-on.

THE best of Von Kluge's Army came here en masse forty-eight hours ago. They converged upon the village to fight their way out ; long caravans of horses and gun-carts, tanks and half-tracks, hospitals and workshops, artillery and infantry. It was the sort of panzer battle array that the Germans have used to terrorize Europe for four years. We knew no combination to stand against it. And now here in the apple orchards and in the village streets one turns sick to see what has happened to the panzers. They met the British and the Allied troops head-on, and they were just obliterated.

UNTIL now I had no conception of what trained artillerymen and infantry can do, and certainly this is the most awful sight that has come my way since the war began. It begins in the back streets of St. Lambert, where the German columns first came in range of the British fire. The horses stampeded. Not half a dozen, but perhaps 300 or more. They lashed down the fences and the hedges with their hoofs and dragged their carriages through the farmyards. Many galloped to the bank of the River Dives and plunged headlong with all their trappings down the 12-foot bank into the stream below, which at once turned red with blood.

Those animals that did not drown under the dragging weight of their harness or die in falling kept plunging about among the broken gun-carriages and trampled to death the Germans hiding under the bank. The drivers of the lorries panicked in the same way. As more and more shells kept ripping through the apple trees they collided their vehicles one against the other and with such force that some of the lighter cars were telescoped with their occupants inside. At some places for stretches of 50 yards, vehicles, horses and men became jammed together in one struggling, shrieking mass. Engines and broken petrol tanks took fire and the wounded pinned in the wreckage were suffocated, burned and lost. Those who were lucky enough to get out of the first collisions scrambled into the ditches and ran for cover across the open fields. They were picked off as they ran. One belt of shellfire fell on the Dives River bridge at the moment when two packed columns were converging upon it.

Those vehicles and beasts and men on the centre of the bridge were all pitchforked into space at once. But so many fell that soon the wreckage piled up level with the bridge itself and made a dam across the river. At the far entrance to the bridge, where a number of heavy guns were attempting a crossing, a blockage was caused and took fire. Those in front apparently tried to struggle back. Those behind, being utterly bewildered, tried

to push on. And so the whole column was wedged immovably until it was in flames.

I suppose there were about 1,000 German vehicles of every sort lying out in the fields behind. All these came under fire. The Germans made no attempt to man their guns.

TOKENS OF DEFEAT, German helmets by the hundred marked the scene of large-scale surrenders on the Falaise road, as observed by this British soldier and told in the accompanying story of the rout of a German army on one of this war's grimmest battlefields.

Photo, New York Times Photos

Too Weak to Cry any More

I have just picked my way across the wreckage to the house on the far side of the orchard. It is full of Germans—Germans beaten and numbed into senselessness. Like animals, they seem to have no will of their own. They are all armed with machine-pistols and rifles, but no one takes the slightest notice of them. It would be absurd to think that they would fire, and nobody has any time to take their arms from them and lead them into captivity.

Over at the hospital it is far worse. The dead and the wounded lie together. Living or dead, there is not much difference in the appearance of the men. Many hours ago life ceased to count for anything at all. The wounded keep dying, but quietly so that one is not aware at any given moment of just how many are surviving. They are all jumbled on top of one another and the stench makes it difficult for one to refrain from being sick.

Outside, a Canadian soldier is mercifully going round shooting wounded horses with a Luger pistol. It would be equally merciful if he did the same for some of these enemy patients who are beyond hope and too weak to cry any more. At any rate I have just directed this mercy killer down to the river where there are about 30 horses wounded and unable to get up the steep banks. Long ago they stopped trying and they stand patiently in the water waiting unconsciously to die.

Germans Flung Helmets Away

I do not know the limits of this battlefield, since I have been here only four hours. It stretches, I know, for about a mile up the Falaise road, because for a good part of that distance you see the line of many hundreds of German helmets flung away by the enemy at the moment of their surrender. I have just selected a volkswagen to get me back to my billet. The back seat is piled up with the belongings of the man who now lies dead by the front wheels. He had taken the precaution, I note, of procuring a civilian suit, which is always a good thing for you if you are going to desert.

WELL, there could be no reason in this ghastly scene. I think I see the end of Germany here. This was their best in weapons and men, their strongest barrier before the Rhine. It has been brushed aside and shattered into bits. The beaten Wehrmacht is a pitiful thing.

Our Kill-or-Capture Raid on Thira Island

The enemy-occupied Greek island of Thira was the recent objective of a raiding party, as described here by Sgt. Instructor D. B. Henderson of Perthshire. He tells how the German radio station was destroyed, the barracks shot up and severe casualties inflicted on the surprised garrison.

Sgt. Instructor D. B. HENDERSON, who took part in the Thira operation which he describes in this page, is here seen with his tommy-gun. The map shows the location of Thira, one of the Grecian Cyclades islands.
Photo, British Official

WE landed on the coast of the island during the night, and after marching inland for a short distance got under cover before dawn broke. There were two patrols, each under an officer, and a lieutenant of the Greek Army as interpreter.

The main party was to attack the barracks, in which we had been told there were 38 Italians and 10 Germans, while a smaller party was to blot out the radio station and clean up an outpost at the village of Meri-Vigli. It was a pitch black night, with the faintest crescent of a new moon showing in the sky as we left our hideout for the attack. My instructions were to get a good position covering the small house in which the German officer and his corporal lived, and kill or capture them when they came out to see what the main attack was all about.

Owing to the high walls around the house and the fact that I was single-handed, I found that I could not get a site where I could cover both the back and the front. I got in position behind the wall where I could cover the front door—because that was the nearest to where the main party would attack.

When it came to within a few minutes of zero hour, I began to feel a bit tense and hoped that I could make a clean job of it quickly ; but when the attack did start the German officer stubbornly refused to do a thing, although he must have heard the racket. There was quite a wind blowing, but no one could have slept through the sound of the grenades exploding and the bursts of sub-machine-gun fire.

It was at this point that I decided to lob a grenade through the front window and liven them up. After the second one I heard people moving inside, but they went towards the rear. I dashed round to the back, but could only hear footsteps hurriedly retreating down the narrow lane. Since it was too dark to shoot, I threw another grenade and then followed down the lane, but saw nothing. Next morning we learned that one of my grenades had probably killed the corporal, but unfortunately the commandant seemed to have got away unhurt.

Meanwhile, the small patrol had everything go perfectly for them. They surprised a German in bed in the first house they entered, and made him show them where the corporal, also caught in bed, was sleeping. After this they bagged six more sleeping Germans and then went to the radio station, which was unguarded, and blew it up, returning in safety to the main body . . .

Meanwhile, the main party had a brisk engagement with the enemy in their billet in the Bank of Athens building, some few minutes of confused hand-to-hand fighting in the pitch dark, and the Greek interpreter was killed and a sergeant mortally wounded. At least three Germans were killed and two wounded, while nine of the Italian Fascists were killed and the same number wounded. As original reports had over-estimated the number of the garrison it was thought that practically all had been killed, wounded or made prisoners.

We withdrew to our hideout in the hills, then went farther back as we were being hunted from the air. Four Junkers 88s, two seaplanes and a fighter circled over us at a height of under 300 feet, but fortunately they did not locate our hiding-place and we left the island in safety that night.

OUR DIARY OF THE WAR

AUGUST 30, Wednesday *1,824th day*
Western Front.—Beauvais reached by British troops and Rheims by Americans. Canadians entered Rouen.
Air.—U.S. bombers attacked targets in Bremen and Kiel areas, following night attack on Stettin and Koenigsberg by R.A.F.
Russian Front.—Rumanian oil centre of Ploesti captured by Red Army.
Pacific.—Allied naval and air forces began four-day attack on Bonin and Volcano Is.

AUGUST 31, Thursday *1,825th day*
Western Front. — British forces reached Amiens and established bridgehead over Somme. Gen. Eberbach, commander of German 7th Army, captured. U.S. troops crossed the Meuse near Sedan.
Russian Front.—Soviet troops entered Bucharest, Rumanian capital.

SEPTEMBER 1, Friday *1,826th day*
Western Front.—Canadians entered Dieppe without fighting. British reached Arras. Americans occupied Verdun.
Russian Front.—Danubian port of Giurgiu captured by Soviet troops.
Balkans.—Attack on German communications in Yugoslavia launched by Yugoslav Liberation Army in conjunction with Allied air forces.
Pacific.—Liberators made heavy attack on airfields at Davao, Philippines.
General.—General Montgomery promoted Field-Marshal.

SEPTEMBER 2, Saturday *1,827th day*
Western Front.—51st Division captured St. Valery ; Lens, Mons and Douai also captured.
Italy.—Announced that 8th Army had broken through Gothic Line. 5th Army captured Pisa.
Russian Front.—Red Army reached Bulgarian frontier between Danube and Black Sea.
Pacific.—Heaviest yet Allied air attack on Davao, Philippines. Halmahera in the Celebes also bombed.
General.—Announced that Finnish Govt. was prepared to negotiate peace with Russia.

SEPTEMBER 3, Sunday *1,828th day*
Western Front.—Allied troops entered Belgium and liberated Brussels. Abbeville captured. In southern France, U.S. and French troops entered Lyons.
Air.—R.A.F. heavily attacked airfields in Holland. U.S. bombers attacked Ludwigshafen area of W. Germany.
Pacific.—Allied naval and air forces attacked Wake Island.

SEPTEMBER 4, Monday *1,829th day*
Western Front.—Antwerp, Louvain and Lille occupied by Allied troops.
Russian Front.—Soviet troops, in co-operation with Rumanians, captured Brasov and Sinaia.
General.—" Cease fire " sounded on Russo-Finnish front.

SEPTEMBER 5, Tuesday *1,830th day*
Western Front.—Allied troops captured Namur and Charleroi.
Air.—U.S. bombers attacked Karlsruhe, Stuttgart and Ludwigshafen. R.A.F. bombed Havre and Brest.
Russian Front.—Soviet troops occupied Pitesti (Rumania) and Wyszkow, 30 miles N.E. of Warsaw.
Sea.—Announced that carrier-borne aircraft had made repeated attacks on German battleship Tirpitz in Alten Fjord, Norway.
General.—Russian Govt. declared war on Bulgaria.

SEPTEMBER 6, Wednesday *1,831st day*
Western Front.—Courtrai and Armentieres cleared of the enemy.
Air.—R.A.F. bombers heavily attacked Emden ; Brest again bombed.
Russian Front.—Soviet troops captured Turnu-Severin, reaching Rumanian-Yugoslav frontier. Ostrolenka, on Narew approaches to E. Prussia, also taken.
General.—Bulgarian Govt. asked Russia for an armistice.

SEPTEMBER 7, Thursday *1,832nd day*
Western Front. — British forces crossed Albert Canal and reached Bourg-Leopold. Ypres captured. U.S. 3rd Army made two crossings of the Moselle.
Home Front.—Announced that of 8,000 flying bombs launched in 80-day attack, some 2,300 reached London area.

SEPTEMBER 8, Friday *1,833rd day*
Western Front.—Canadians occupied Ostend unopposed. U.S. troops captured Liege. In southern France Allies captured Le Creusot and Besancon.

Air.—Over 1,000 U.S. bombers attacked oil plants and factories in Germany.
Russian Front.—Soviet troops entered Bulgaria and captured Sumla, Rustchuk, Varna and Burgas.
Pacific.—U.S. carrier-borne aircraft attacked Mindanao in Philippines and destroyed Japanese convoy of 52 ships.
Far East.—Announced that Super-Forts had again attacked Anshan steel works, near Mukden, Manchuria.
General.—Bulgarian Government declared war on Germany.

SEPTEMBER 9, Saturday *1,834th day*
Air.—More than 1,000 U.S. bombers attacked targets at Mannheim, Ludwigshafen, Mainz and Duesseldorf. At night, R.A.F. bombed Muenchen-Gladbach.
General.—Soviet troops ceased war operations in Bulgaria.

SEPTEMBER 10, Sunday *1,835th day*
Western Front.—Full-scale attack opened against Le Havre. U.S. troops entered city of Luxembourg. Ghent finally cleared of the enemy. Canadians entered Zeebrugge.
Air.—Over 1,000 U.S. bombers attacked tank and aircraft factories in southern Germany.
Pacific.—Carrier-aircraft attacked Palau Is. Truk also bombed.
General.—Mr. Churchill arrived in Canada for conference with Roosevelt.

SEPTEMBER 11, Monday. *1,836th day*
Western Front.—U.S. 1st Army crossed Luxembourg-German frontier north of Trier. French captured Dijon.
Air.—More than 1,000 U.S. bombers attacked oil plants from Leipzig to Hanover ; 175 German fighters destroyed. R.A.F. bombed oil plants in the Ruhr in daylight and at night attacked Darmstadt.
Pacific.—Units of U.S. Pacific Fleet bombarded Palau Islands. Carrier-aircraft attacked central Philippine islands.

SEPTEMBER 12, Tuesday *1,837th day*
Western Front.—U.S. 1st Army made second crossing of German frontier east of Eupen. German garrison at Le Havre surrendered. Fort Eben Emael, Bruges and Bourg-Leopold occupied by Allies.
Air.—U.S. and R.A.F. bombers again attacked oil plants and aircraft works in many parts of Germany.

★ ===== *Flash-backs* ===== ★

1939
September 1. *Germans invaded Poland. Start of this war.*
September 3. *Britain and France declared war on Germany. Liner Athenia sunk by U-boat.*

1940
September 3. *Agreement whereby Britain leased to U.S.A. bases along Atlantic seaboard.*
September 7. *Heaviest air attacks yet made on London ; 103 German aircraft destroyed.*

1941
September 8. *Announced that British, Canadian and Norwegian force had raided Spitzbergen.*

1943
September 3. *8th Army troops landed on toe of Italy.*
September 8. *Gen. Eisenhower announced surrender of Italy.*
September 9. *Allied forces landed at Salerno, near Naples.*
September 12. *Hitler's H.Q. announced release of Mussolini.*

SEAFIRE III WITH FOLDED WINGS (left) for compact stowage in aircraft-carrier hangars ; folding reduces the wing-span of 36 ft. 8 ins. to nearly one-third. In service with the Fleet Air Arm—it made its first operational appearance on D-Day—it is a naval version of the Spitfire. Latest and fastest Spitfire is the 5-bladed 2,000 h.p. Mark XIV (right); it has operated against flying bombs. Armament consists of three alternative arrangements of 20-mm. cannon and ·5 and ·303 machine-guns.
Photos, British Official ; Charles E. Brown

THE WAR IN THE AIR

by Capt. Norman Macmillan, M.C., A.F.C.

BY September 8, 1944, the 2nd Tactical Air Force was operating from airfields in Belgium, and rocket-firing Typhoons that day attacked barges on the Rhine. The chimes and strokes of Big Ben came direct from Westminster over the radio that evening at nine o'clock, after an indirect transmission beginning on June 16, 1944. The direct emission of this world-famous time signal marked the close of the flying bomb Battle of London, which began on June 13, seven days after the first Allied troops had stormed the Normandy beaches.

It came to an end when the Allied Armies driving through the disorganized German Armies in Northern France had thrust their armour so far forward as to draw a cordon round the Channel coast from which the flying bombs had been launched, thus cutting off the supplies, which, owing to bombing attacks, had been on an expenditure basis, with small stocks kept in the launching area—the crescent-shaped coastal zone from Le Havre to Ostend.

Up to September 4 a total of 8,070 flying bombs was estimated to have been launched against England, and there was a further attack during a short period before daybreak on September 5. It does not necessarily follow that this must be the last attack, for some of the bombs which have entered the area singled out for attack, mainly Greater London, have come from a due easterly direction, launched from aircraft.

DURING the night of September 1/2, two component aircraft laden with explosive landed in England. They did little damage and caused no casualties when they blew up. They were presumed to be the lower components of the composite Messerschmitt 109 and Junkers 88, in which a single pilot seated in the cockpit of the 109 controls both aircraft, and releases the Junkers to fly on towards its intended target. One such German version of our Mayo composite aircraft was shot down into the sea off Normandy.

Just as the tank came into the last war too late for full development, so the flying bomb has come into this European war. It is still in a comparatively crude stage and is capable of much development. Should the world be unable to abolish war, the means has been devised to make air warfare still more terrible

in the future. The nature of this weapon, employed as a long-range bombardment missile, demands a new regard for geographical considerations when considering the configuration of post-war Europe. German exposure of this weapon is opportune, for its use by the enemy will no doubt cause Allied expert advisers to take into consideration its range of action in relation to important European cities when fixing the future German frontier in the west ; and it will probably be necessary to create a deep neutral zone inside Germany's frontiers to ensure that no launching sites are secretly erected in later years against the outbreak of another planned war.

FASTEST Fighters to Catch and Kill the Flying Bombs

The forces that had to be mustered to provide defence against the flying bomb indicate the power of this type of weapon. Eventually there were 800 heavy and 2,000 light guns with 20 American batteries (one-eighth of the heavy guns) concentrated along the south-east coast under Anti-Aircraft Command. Balloon Command had 2,000 balloons, flying two and three cables instead of the normal single cable, thanks to the lift obtainable through the lower height at which the balloons had to fly.

The flying bombs came over from below 1,000 feet up to 2,500 feet at a speed of from 350 to 400 miles an hour. Fighters maintained standing patrols of between 30 and 40 aircraft during periods of sharp attack. The aircraft used by A.D.G.B. were the Tempest, Mustang and the Griffon Spitfire, for only the fastest fighters were fast enough to catch the prey. The Spitfire XII is a low-level Griffon-engined aircraft. The latest Spitfire is the Mark XIV, fitted with the Rolls-Royce Griffon 65, developing over 2,000 h.p. for an even weight in lbs. This engine has a two-speed supercharger and a five-blade Rotol constant speed airscrew. Power is maintained up to 40,000 feet.

These three types of fighters destroyed 1,900 flying bombs. The Tempests got 578 ; one of them, flown by Sqdn. Ldr. Berry, shot down over 60. Spitfire XIVs brought down over 300. Guns destroyed 1,560 and the last line of defence, barrage balloons,

279. Of the bombs launched, 29 per cent got through to the London area, 25 per cent were erratic or inaccurate (some diving into the sea), and 46 per cent were brought down by the triple defences. Successful defence was due to timely warning by intelligence agents, followed up by air photographic reconnaissance which disclosed the nature of the threat and many of its testing, manufacturing and launching sites and depots, and bombing by British and American aircraft to the vast tune of 100,000 tons of bombs, which destroyed all the original launching sites and delayed the plan for five months.

The value of the information and action taken before the flying bomb attack is shown by the fact that 23,000 houses were destroyed or damaged beyond repair, while 870,000 houses (some seriously damaged) need repair. That was done in less than three months by a depleted force of flying bombs whose maximum assault rate was 200 in one day, and whose average rate was about 100 a day. Had the enemy's intention not been discovered the assault might well have been four times as heavy and lasted many months longer. To prevent that, 2,900 pilots and other members of aircrews gave their lives during the great bombardment of the flying bomb bases, many of which were outside the action limits of the fastest fighters. These men deserve to be remembered with the 375 fighter pilots killed and 358 wounded in the first Battle of Britain in 1940.

DEFENCE improved from the beginning of the attack to the end. In the beginning 33 per cent of the bombs were brought down and a greater number got through to the London area. In the end 70 per cent were brought down and 9 per cent reached London. On August 28 only four got to London and 97 were brought down.

But aviation has demonstrated its merciful side simultaneously with the other. Thousands of wounded have been evacuated from France by air, mostly in Dakotas carrying 18 stretcher or 24 walking cases. Death rate has dropped from 16 per 1,000 by sea to one per 1,000 by air. This has been due mainly to speed and smoothness of travel to skilled hospitals ; the deaths have mostly occurred after some time in the United Kingdom.

Meanwhile, Hitler Europe is getting more heavily bombed—the Opel works at Russelsheim on August 12 and 25, Konigsberg on August 26 and 29, the Ruhr on August 27, Stettin port and canal on August 16 and 29 ; the port of Kiel was attacked by British and U.S. bombers on July 18, 23, August 4, 6 and 16, and Emden on September 6.

Quick Bases for Spitfires in Southern France

EMERGENCY LANDING STRIPS speedily established by the R.A.F. in Southern France enabled overwhelming air cover to be given to Allied forces pushing on into the interior. From such sites as this (3) roots, rocks, stones, and other obstacles were grubbed up to secure a level base ; on the completed strip (1) Spitfires are at their dispersal points. R.A.F. men, making short work of airborne supplies, unload a long-range fuel tank from a Dakota transport plane (2). See also p. 310.

Photos, British Official

How Paris was Relieved from Peril of Famine

MR. CHURCHILL'S PROMISE OF FOOD for the French capital, as soon as it should be liberated, was promptly kept. British and Canadian Army lorries delivered first consignments of the thousands of tons of sorely needed provisions on August 28, 1944. Vehicles (above, and below) displayed heartening words.

IN SOUTHERN FRANCE distribution centres for supplies captured by the advancing Allies from the Germans were set up. Above, citizens of Besne gather around to draw their free rations. Men of the Maquis are seen standing by.

SHOPS HAD BEEN PLUNDERED by the Germans and shelves of the Paris stores laid bare. But against such emergency as this vast food stocks had been piled in the United Kingdom; from those stocks supplies had been arriving in Normandy since D-Day, to be held in the Civil Affairs depots until required. Unloading sacks of flour from a lorry in a Paris square (above), our men laboured and joked amidst an extremely appreciative assembly of onlookers.

Photos, Canadian and U.S. Official, British Newspaper Pool

Editor's Postscript

WIDELY spread I find the delusion that "if we get rid of Hitler, the German people will be all right." This is the veriest nonsense. To attribute the conceit and brutality of Germans to Nazi teaching shows complete ignorance of what they were before Hitler was born. They have been taught for the best part of a century that they were destined by Providence (" their old German god," as the late Kaiser called him) to be a "master-race" and rule the world. They were especially encouraged to look forward to a day when they would establish themselves in Britain, which they believed to be decadent, anaemic, and too frivolous to defend itself successfully. No English writer knew the Germans better than the author of Elizabeth and Her German Garden and so many more books of delicious humour and sentiment and close observation. In most of these she shrewdly criticized them, and in The Caravaners, written thirty-five years ago, she drew an unforgettable portrait of a Prussian officer, one of the Pomeranian "vons," who let himself go on the subject of his country's future. The Germans, he firmly believed, had "a right to regard themselves as specially raised by Almighty God to occupy the first place among the nations."

JOURNEYING through the south of England, he noted with satisfaction that it looked rich, "as if there were money in it." His thought when he caught sight of the village churches and snug parsonages was that "some day perhaps—and who knows how soon?—we shall have a decent Lutheran pastor in his black gown preaching in every one of those churches." He decided that everything English was unmethodical, happy-go-lucky, effeminate, and non-military. The food was "uneatable" (though, being a greedy person with a huge appetite, he ate plenty of it). The inhabitants were "asses." When he went to church, he disliked the frequent change of positions, standing, sitting, kneeling ; and he considered this " one of the keys to the manifest decadence of the British character." It was highly irreverent ; and, though he deplored irreverence, he could not altogether regret it, since it would undoubtedly land the British nation all the sooner " in the jaws of Germany." And "How good it will taste !" he reflected longingly. That was not exaggerated. I knew many Germans who held similar views and did not conceal them. In the north they were almost all of that kidney. I am sure that nothing could be more misguided than to suppose that Hitler and his fellow-criminals are responsible for the idiotic pride which has led the Germans so disastrously astray.

HOW are they to be cured of it? How are the children who are taught all the nonsense about the glory of the Third Reich and their own superiority to other nations to be given back sanity and induced to prefer decent behaviour ? That problem is forced on the notice of theatre-goers by the play from the United States which has started a run in London with every prospect of long success. The play is called Tomorrow the World. The words are a quotation from the German song which ends with the boast that tomorrow the Germans will conquer the whole world. The principal character is a boy of twelve. He is the son of a German who won a Nobel Peace Prize and was murdered by the Nazis. He has been told that his father was a traitor and a coward who committed suicide. He speaks of Jews in foul terms. He recites what he has learned of Nazi doctrine with ludicrous enthusiasm. His mother was American and

his uncle, a young college professor, manages to get the boy out of Germany and into the United States. He causes dismay, of course, insists on wearing his Nazi uniform and heiling Hitler ; begins spying on his uncle, who is engaged on important war work ; and makes a murderous attack on a little girl who has discovered what he is doing and will not promise to keep quiet about it.

The uncle is at his wits' end. In a fit of ungovernable rage he almost throttles his nephew, who is saved by the girl he is going to marry, a Jewess, who has been called filthy names by the young devil. She feels pity for him instead of anger, and it is she who persuades the professor not to hand him over to the police. She thinks that he can be reformed because tears come into his eyes when he hears that the little girl had, just before she was attacked, bought a present for him. Through all his punishments he had never cried. Now, the fiancée fancies, he can be approached by means of his desire for affection. So he stays in the professor's house.

IT is an interesting play, very good "theatre," acted brilliantly. But I cannot pretend it offers convincing proof, or even hope that this little Nazi reptile would ever be turned by kindness into a decent human being. The Jesuits say " Let us have a child up to the age of seven, and he will never break away from what we have taught him." I do not think that is of universal application. I know of some cases in which there has been

General JACQUES PHILIPPE LECLERC, commander of the 2nd French Armoured Division which entered Paris on August 24, 1944. The division consisted of Frenchmen who had fought in Africa and later were equipped and trained in England. *Photo, Planet News*

a breakaway. But generally speaking it holds good. How are German boys and girls into whose heads and natures Nazi lies and bestialities have been driven from their earliest years to be converted into civilized beings ?

THE more we learn about previous civilizations the more we find they resembled our own. The Cretans had domestic plumbing arrangements like ours (though we do not know whether they made jokes about plumbers as we do). The Romans had central heating, and so on. Now it is suggested by a learned Mexican who has studied the ancient Mayan civilization, which flourished in his country, that the Mayas knew all about penicillin many hundreds of years ago ! They cured infection with mould growing on damp wood or food made from certain plants, and penicillin, it appears, is just that. (See p. 190 for facts and figures concerning penicillin—"one of the most powerful weapons in mankind's armoury against disease.") They also had herb remedies for many other diseases, including tuberculosis and leprosy. When the Spanish invaders of South and Central America brutally destroyed the systems of civilized life that they found there, the secrets of these cures were lost. Now one has been rediscovered (this is the theory put forward), and it is possible others might be. Let us hope so, anyway.

MORE of us eat sweets now than ever before, I suppose. The scarcity of alcohol—you can hardly call beer alcoholic these days, though it may taste quite good and prove an agreeable thirst-quencher—creates among those who were accustomed to sherries or cocktails before lunch, and port after dinner, and whiskies-and-sodas before going to bed, a craving for something to take its place. That craving can be supplied, in part at any rate, by sweets. Even persons who are not affected in that way regularly purchase their ration of chocolate or boiled sweets, for the reason that they feel they would be missing something if they did not. At a bridge evening I went to last week there were dishes of candies, as the Americans call them, on a side-table, as well as boxes of cigarettes, and I noticed that nearly all the guests ate some. For children they are really a necessity, most doctors will tell you ; but that must depend on the kind of food the little ones have. However, unless candies are eaten in large quantities, which is scarcely possible just now, they don't do any harm to anyone . . . except to the diabetics !

BICYCLING was never more in favour than it is today, in spite of the difficulty in buying machines. I have never seen larger flocks of cyclists than those which now sweep over many of our roads when work ends for the day—and I suppose also when it begins, though I don't see that ; not even in The Hague or Copenhagen, where there always seemed to me to be more people on wheels than on foot. When first the low bicycle, the Safety, came into use it was ridden for the most part by people who took up cycling simply as an amusement. We used to ride in Battersea Park and sometimes have breakfast in the refreshment kiosk which stood in that very delightful "lung" of south-west London. It was quite the fashionable thing to do. That paved the way for the taking-up of the bicycle by the million as a means of getting to and from work and out into the country at week-ends. This gradually went out of favour until a few years ago. Now if you want a really good machine you have to pay a high price. I heard of one going for as much as £30 the other day. But there are, of course, much cheaper articles to be had, and sometimes a deal can be made by way of barter. An advertisement in a London paper offered three bottles of gin in exchange for one, which would be the equivalent of about £4.

Our Tanks Chased the Nazis out of Lisieux

BRITISH ARMOUR CLIMBED THE HILL past the famous basilica of St. Therese (above) after the enemy had been routed out of Lisieux in Northern France. The Germans had strong positions dominating the eastern end of the town, but by August 24, 1944, they had been overwhelmed. Then, by-passing Le Havre and Dieppe and outflanking the flying-bomb sites between those towns, the Allied thrust across the Seine and the Somme developed on a spectacular scale.

Photo, British Newspaper Pool

Printed in England and published every alternate Friday by the Proprietors, THE AMALGAMATED PRESS, LTD., The Fleetway House Farringdon Street, London, E.C.4. Registered for transmission by Canadian Magazine Post. Sole Agents for Australia and New Zealand : Messrs. Gordon & Gotch, Ltd. ; and for South Africa : Central News Agency, Ltd.—September 29, 1944.   S.S.   *Editorial Address :* JOHN CARPENTER HOUSE, WHITEFRIARS, LONDON, E.C.4.

Vol 8

The War Illustrated

Nº 191

SIXPENCE

Edited by Sir John Hammerton

OCTOBER 13, 1944

YUGOSLAV WALKING ARMOURY, this smilingly confident partisan of Marshal Tito's National Army of Liberation sets out to harass a German retreat line. So successful was their offensive launched against the Germans—with the co-operation of the Royal Navy, units of Land Forces Adriatic and aircraft of the Balkan Air Force—on Sept. 8, 1944, that by Sept. 17 the Dalmatian islands of Korcula, Hvar and Brac had been freed. Four days later Tito's forces were drawing their net around Belgrade.
Photo, British Official

NO. 192 WILL BE PUBLISHED FRIDAY, OCTOBER 27

At Home and Far Away with Our Roving Camera

BRITAIN'S DIM-OUT succeeded the black-out on Sept. 17, 1944, when a modified form of lighting appeared in many thoroughfares. A street scene in Rochdale, Lancs, the first English town to have the new "side street standard" lighting in operation. Other towns will follow suit as labour permits.

REPATRIATED PRISONERS of war from Germany, numbering 1,025, received a tumultuous welcome on Sept. 15, 1944, when they arrived aboard the British liner Arundel Castle, at Liverpool.

EMERGENCY HUTS totalling 10,000 to provide temporary homes for 50,000 bombed-out people in the London area during the winter formed part of the recent plan for rehousing the homeless. Below, one of the prefabricated huts.

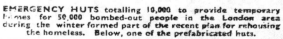

RUMANIAN-SOVIET ARMISTICE was signed in Moscow on Sept. 13, 1944, by Mr. L. Patrascanu, head of the Rumanian delegation. Soviet Foreign Commissar Mr. Molotov is seen on the extreme left ; Marshal Malinovsky, commanding the 2nd Ukrainian Front, signed for the Soviet Union.

"HELLO, THERE, FRANK, OLD BOY!" was Mr. Churchill's greeting to President Roosevelt when these two great leaders met for discussions on the future conduct of the war, at the second Quebec Conference, on Sept. 11, 1944. They ended their talks on Sept. 17.

Photos, British Official; Planet News, Keystone, Pictorial Press, New York Times Photos

THE BATTLE FRONTS

by Maj.-Gen. Sir Charles Gwynn, K.C.B., D.S.O.

EVERYONE admits that airborne troops have done most valuable work in Burma, in Algeria, in Sicily and in the Normandy landing, but I think some may have doubted whether the achievements of the comparatively small forces used on those occasions warranted the formation of a large airborne army. It may be argued that as airborne troops must always be comparatively lightly armed and have little mobility after landing, their offensive potentialities are limited, and though they may seize by surprise and be able to defend important localities there is always a considerable risk of their being overwhelmed by the enemy's reserves before they can be supported by more heavily armed forces.

The decision to form a large airborne army has, however, amply justified itself. They may greatly accelerate the advance of the main armies ; and the enemy's shortage of reserves minimizes the risks run by their bold use well ahead of supporting forces. There is no reason to suppose that the airborne army was constituted especially in anticipation of the situation that developed in Holland, but it is hardly possible to conceive a situation which would give better opportunities for its effective use.

Not only was the enemy short of reserves, greatly disorganized and deeply committed to his encounter with the British 2nd Army, but he still had fears of a seaborne invasion.

which smaller detachments could be usefully employed. The knowledge that large airborne forces exist adds to the problems which confront the German commanders. The necessity of retaining reserves available to deal with possible airborne landings will tend to cause dispersion of forces somewhat similar to that caused by fear of seaborne landings—a fear which was the primary cause of the destruction of the 15th and 19th German Armies in France.

A TOKEN Battle to Save Hun Commander's Honour

It will be noted that so far there have been no signs of a co-ordinated German withdrawal to a shorter front either in the east or the west. Practically everywhere German armies are fighting bitterly where they stand, even where, as at Brest, resistance was continued after it had ceased to serve a useful purpose ; or as in Italy, where refusal to retreat seems to invite disaster. It is perhaps premature to claim that this tends to confirm my theory that the Reichswehr generals, apart from those willing to obey Hitler's instructions, are in the main fighting to maintain the honour and traditions of the Reichswehr and are determined that the final battles of the war should as far as possible be fought outside German territory or on its frontiers.

That the generals have different views on what will satisfy their conceptions of honour

the 3rd and 7th Armies in front of it, in the Lorraine and Belfort gaps respectively. The 1st Army has penetrated far into, if not completely through, the Siegfried defences and has clearly proved that these defences were not as formidable as was expected.

IT has been found that they were inadequately armed and held by second-class troops, but the main weakness was that the Germans did not have the reserves or artillery support required for effective counter-attacks. On the Lorraine front and in the Belfort gap the Germans appear to have concentrated the best of their reserves, and there resistance has been more effective than on the 1st Army front, although the troops have depended more on cover provided by natural features and on counter-attacks than on artificial defence works. The exceptionally strong works of the

457,346 HUNS 'IN THE BAG'

German prisoners taken by five armies of the Allied Expeditionary Force on the Western Front since D-Day (June 6, 1944) amounted to 457,346, it was announced on September 21, 1944, the total being made up as follows :

British 2nd Army —	— —	73,000
Canadian 1st Army	— —	52,971
U.S. 1st Army	— — —	173,375
U.S. 3rd Army	— — —	76,000
U.S. 7th Army	— — —	82,000

fortress of Metz have resisted attack, but like all fortresses it absorbs large forces for its defence, which must ultimately be sacrificed if the place is surrounded.

If a fortress cannot be used as a pivot for a major counter-stroke, as is the case now with Metz, its main function is to block railway lines or roads that the attacker would need as he advances ; but a large fortress is generally a wasteful means of achieving that object. General Patton's Army has been reinforced and is now making steady if slow progress east of the Moselle. It will be interesting to see whether the Germans opposing him will, as they are driven back, attempt to make a decisive stand on the Siegfried Line or merely use it as a delaying position. There would seem to be a considerable likelihood that they may be too exhausted and disorganized when they reach it to make use of its full potentialities and in any case by that time it may have been turned by General Hodges' Army advancing through Luxembourg.

MALINOVSKY'S Westward Drive Reaches Hungarian Plain

On the eastern front the main Russian offensive against East Prussia and in Poland has not yet been launched, although Rokossovsky's capture of Praga, and Zakharov's of Lomza and the line of the Narew, are preparatory steps of great importance. Meanwhile, however, the Russians appear to have decided to deal once for all with the German armies in Estonia and Latvia which might at last make an effort to escape, now that the surrender of Finland has removed the chief strategic object they may have had. Already the Estonian group has lost the ports by which it in part has been evacuated, and its main communications with the Latvian group have been cut. The Latvian group is in hardly a better position now that Bagramyan's renewed offensive has almost reached Riga. In the south, Hungary is almost equally threatened ; for Malinovsky's westward drive has reached the eastern side of the Hungarian plain, and Petrov's 4th Ukrainian Army is striking from Poland into the northern Carpathian passes. Still farther south, Tolbukhin's advance through Sofia towards Nish in the Morava valley, and Tito's increasing strength, make the withdrawal of any considerable part of the German forces in the Aegean Islands, Greece and Yugoslavia almost impossible. As these groups are liquidated full Allied power will be released for the final encounter.

FALL OF PRAGA, Warsaw suburb east of the Vistula, announced by Marshal Stalin on Sept. 14, 1944, marked the end of the first phase in the battle for the Polish capital. Praga witnessed fierce house-to-house fighting before the Russians and Poles finally beat down German resistance. The victorious forces included Russian troops of the 1st White Russian Front and soldiers of the 1st Polish Army. Soviet infantry are seen (above) entering the suburb. *Photo, Pictorial Press*

That was one side of the picture ; on the other it could be seen what immense assistance would be given to the 2nd Army if stepping stones were secured over the three great rivers, the Maas, the Waal and the Lek, which seemed likely to delay greatly, if not to stop, its advance. These rivers formed a deep triple obstacle, and given time they might be strongly defended. On the other hand, their passage meant that the line of the Rhine, which elsewhere provided a second defence position behind the Siegfried Line, would be turned.

FURTHERMORE, the operation gave a good prospect of cutting the lines of retreat of the large German forces still in western Holland, since the main railways leading to Germany run parallel with and close to the rivers. Whether such an opportunity for employing airborne troops in great force will ever recur is doubtful, but in any case there are certainly likely to be occasions in

we may conclude by comparing the attitude of the German commander at Brest with that of the conduct of the commander of the strong group that surrendered near Orleans. The proposal of the latter that there should be a token battle to save his honour savoured of the Middle Ages, if not of comic opera. There no doubt have been many humorous episodes during the war, but surely none on such a large scale.

The situation in Holland is, at time of writing, much the most interesting ; partly because novel features have been introduced and partly because it would seem to give greatest scope for generalship. But the situation on the front of the American Armies has also special points of interest. All three armies are now meeting stiff resistance, and the great speed of their progress has been checked : that of the 1st Army on the Siegfried position, and that of

Thrusting Through Holland Towards the Ruhr—

BRITISH 2nd ARMY VEHICLES formed this great convoy moving up in Holland. It was reported that one column stretched for 60 miles as it made its way from Belgium towards the Dutch frontier.

EINDHOVEN, liberated on Sept. 19, 1944, was the first large town in Holland to fall to Allied forces. Citizens waved and cheered in the beflagged streets as British armour passed through in the direction of Nijmegen.

DUTCH RESISTANCE MOVEMENT members rounded-up many stray Germans as our men pushed onward, clearing towns and villages of the enemy. These patriots (left) made their first capture at Valkenswaard, a town close to the Dutch-Belgian border (see also illus. p. 341). The fury of the present and the peace and calm of the past were strikingly contrasted as British tanks rolled on towards the front through characteristic Dutch scenery (right).

Photos. British Official

—Bitter Was the Fighting for Nijmegen Bridge

ONE OF THE GLIDERS which carried troops of the 1st Allied Airborne Army to Holland crashed in a turnip field without injury to the crew. Dutch civilians hastened to offer assistance.

NIJMEGEN ROAD BRIDGE, spanning the Waal, or Dutch Rhine (top right), captured intact by Sept. 21, 1944, was taken in the face of German anti-tank and 88-mm. guns holding the southern approach. U.S. airborne infantry forced a crossing of the river 3 miles downstream and captured the northern end of the bridge. After 2½ hours of fierce fighting British tanks penetrated the southern defences : above, they are seen carrying U.S. airborne troops on the way to Nijmegen.

Photos, British Newspaper Pool, U.S. Official, E.N.A

THE WAR AT SEA

by Francis E. McMurtrie

FOR some little time past, naval operations against Germany have been gradually assuming a different complexion. No longer does one hear of determined attacks on convoys in mid-Atlantic by "wolf packs" of a dozen or more U-boats. That submarine attacks have ceased is by no means true; but they have fallen off so much in vigour, frequency and extent that it may be fairly said that they no longer constitute a serious menace to our communications. Of course, this is no reason for the slightest relaxation in vigilance, for given the opportunity the danger would soon reassert itself.

As it is, with no port in Western Europe at their disposal south of the Scheldt, the U-boats must find themselves severely restricted in their approaches to the trade routes. Our anti-submarine forces, on the other hand, have fewer exits to watch, enabling them to concentrate all the greater force at any particular point when the occasion arises.

Still more remote is the date when a raid on commerce by German surface warships was to be feared. The Bismarck and Scharnhorst lie at the bottom of the sea; the Gneisenau is reported to be a dismantled hulk in a Baltic port; and the Tirpitz, having sustained damage in four Allied attacks, seems less likely than ever to leave her remote anchorage in the innermost recess of the Altenfjord.

GERMAN coastal forces have suffered heavily in evacuating French ports, and are likely to incur further losses before they leave those of the Netherlands. It would seem from a recent utterance of Grossadmiral Dönitz that the Reichsmarine has been given the thankless task of sacrificing itself in the hope of saving some remnants of the German Army threatened with capture as one port after another on the French, Belgian or Italian coast is invested. Small naval craft are given the desperate task of running the blockade of these ports in the hope of bringing away high military officers or technical specialists. Larger vessels with no chance of escape are sunk in harbour entrances as blockships. Some of the garrisons of French ports are reported to have

been stiffened by a reinforcement of picked naval officers and men.

With the fall of Brest was revealed the extent and massiveness of the construction of the celebrated U-boat pens. It has been reported that these are roofed with concrete 15 feet thick, and that preparations had been made to add another eight feet to it. No wonder there were few penetrations as the result of Allied bombing! As most of these cave-like shelters appear to have been left intact, they will presumably be taken over by the French Navy as part of the facilities of the naval base, which have otherwise been considerably reduced by enemy demolitions.

PORTS Threatened by Latest Allied Advances in Italy

In Northern Italy several ports of importance are about to fall into Allied hands. First of them is likely to be Spezia, headquarters of an Italian maritime department in peacetime. A town of over 100,000 inhabitants, it possesses both constructional and repair facilities. The disabled cruisers Bolzano and Gorizia are believed to be there; these are ships of 10,000 tons with main armaments of 8-in. guns. Also there is the new fast cruiser Claudio Tiberio, of 3,362 tons, which is probably still incomplete, and two obsolete cruisers of negligible value, the Bari and Taranto. The last-named, which was originally the German Strassburg, was taken over by the Italian Navy under the conditions of the Peace Treaty of 1919. In 1935-37 she was refitted, and according to the latest reports was wrecked by Allied bombers last August as the Germans were endeavouring to utilize her as a blockship.

Somewhat farther north is Genoa, with a normal population of close on 650,000. Though bigger than Spezia, it is of less consequence as a naval base, but has more important shipbuilding resources. These may by now have completed four fast cruisers of the 3,362-ton type, the Cornelio Silla, Paolo Emilia, Claudio Druso and Vipsanio Agrippa, but in view of the shortage of materials this is very doubtful. The Germans are able, however, to dispose of a certain number of smaller vessels.

On the other side of the Italian peninsula the three principal ports threatened by the

Allied penetration of the Gothic Line are Venice (headquarters of a maritime district), Trieste and Pola. Such warships as exist are believed to be concentrated at Trieste, where the torpedoed battleship Conte di Cavour was taken for refit after her long stay on the mud in Taranto harbour; damage is believed to be so extensive that it is questionable if she will ever be fit for service again. At Trieste also is the 35,000-ton battleship Impero, built at Genoa, and brought from there in semi-complete condition in 1943. Neither of these ships is likely to offer serious opposition to our advance, except possibly as floating batteries for the defence of the port.

They may have suffered from the attentions of Allied aircraft, which recently succeeded in reducing to a wreck the Trans-Atlantic liner Rex, at Capodistria, not far from Trieste (see illus. on this page). Two cruisers of 4,200 tons were laid down at Trieste in 1939 for the Siamese Navy. Though they were in due course appropriated by the Italians and later by the Germans, it is improbable that they have been finished. Though shipbuilding facilities exist at Venice, that dockyard is primarily for maintenance.

IN the Netherlands, now in process of liberation, there are important shipbuilding centres where incomplete fighting ships may be found. Farthest south is the Schelde yard at Flushing, where torpedo craft and submarines used to be built for the Royal Netherlands Navy. An incomplete destroyer, in tow, was the target for an air attack there last month. The Wilton-Fijenoord combine at Schiedam is also an important yard, building destroyers and submarines.

Another extensive undertaking is the Rotterdam Dry Dock Company, which used to divide orders for destroyers and submarines with the Wilton-Fijenoord Company. At Amsterdam is the Nederlandsche Scheepsbouw Maatschappij, which built the Dutch cruisers Sumatra, Heemskerck and Tromp. It may be assumed that the Germans have not failed to make the utmost use of all these resources to supplement their own, which have suffered heavily from bombing.

A little-known section of the Royal Navy which is concerned with the clearance and rehabilitation of wrecked ports taken from the enemy is the Salvage Division. Though little publicity has been given to its work, its skilled personnel have rendered invaluable service in this direction.

ITALIAN LINER REX, intended by the Germans to be used as a blockship in Trieste harbour, was bombed by rocket-firing Beaufighters on Sept. 8, 1944. The attack was carried out in two waves, and the Rex sustained 123 hits. Above, rockets falling near the ship. Right, two-thirds submerged, smoke rising from stem to stern.

Photos, British Official

Those U-Boat Pens Were Not So Bomb-Proof!

THE 40-FOOT HOLE IN THE STEEL-AND-CONCRETE ROOF of this U-boat shelter at Brest is marked up to the credit of the R.A.F. Others of these notorious submarine pens, claimed as absolutely bomb-proof by the Germans, and from which they had so frequently launched attacks against Allied shipping in the Atlantic, were found in similar condition—cracked wide open by block-busters—when U.S. forces under General Middleton took possession of the port. The garrison, commanded by General Ramcke, ran up the white flag on Sept. 19, 1944.   PAGE 327   *Photo, British Official*

Fiercely Contested Channel Ports Regained

ISOLATED ENEMY RESISTANCE POINTS on the French coast fell one by one to the Allies in September 1944. Brest capitulated by Sept. 20 : Germans are rounded up (1), and a tank destroyer fires its 75-mm. gun to clear a street (2). Flame throwers went into action in the final attack on Havre (3) ; Bren carriers entered the town (4), which surrendered on Sept. 12. Near Boulogne, in Canadian hands by Sept. 21, R.A.M.C. men, assisted by French civilians, evacuated British wounded under fire (5). PAGE 328   *Photos, British and U.S. Official; British Newspaper Pool, Keystone*

Blasting at Last Through the Siegfried Line

THRUSTING INTO THE REICH, men of Lieut.-General Hodges' U.S. 1st Army crossed the Luxembourg-German frontier north of Trier on September 11, 1944. Within 24 hours a second powerful American wedge had been driven into Germany, infantry and tanks penetrating 10 miles south of Aachen into the Aachen State Forest (4) on their way to attack the Siegfried Line defences.

On September 15 the Line was breached: infantry and engineers clearing away series of steel road obstructions (1). A jeep with trailer follows a path blasted by American engineers through concrete "dragons'-teeth" (2). The problem set by a 15 ft. tank trap was surmounted by this jeep (3). U.S. infantrymen march towards Aachen (5); by September 16 the city was virtually surrounded.

Photos, Associated Press, Planet News

British Second Army's Epic Dash to Brussels

Lieut.-Gen. B. G. Horrocks, C.B., D.S.O., who commanded the British corps which, at the end of August 1944, covered the 206 miles from Vernon on the Seine to Brussels in only 6 days, here tells how the Belgian capital was captured by brilliant desert tactics. This astoundingly swift advance is outstanding even among the whirlwind achievements of modern mobile warfare.

THE advance began with the capture, on August 6, of Mont Pincon in Normandy, a vital feature which dominated the whole countryside and without which the forward movement would have been impossible. It was captured in twenty-four hours' heavy fighting by tanks and infantry. Six tanks fought their way to the top and stayed there among the enemy for three hours, until the infantry arrived.

The Germans showed all the familiar signs of cracking, the same as in the desert, during the push from Mont Pincon to Condé. It was necessary to keep up constant pressure, attacking daily in spite of the weakened state of some divisions, which suffered considerable casualties, especially among the junior officers. We literally blasted our way to Condé, using concentrations of guns wherever we were held up. Every operation we did was simple. We didn't try anything complicated.

The crossing of the Seine at Vernon was "a little classic." American troops had

Boche going, and it wasn't the time for tidiness ! The leading armoured units, which cleared the way for the main force, had covered 18 miles against steady opposition by August 29. By August 30 the main armour was up, and the fast push to the east began.

It wasn't a push round the flanks ; we had villages with enemy in ahead all the time. We found as many as eight 88-mm. guns in some villages. The key-point of the advance came when the armoured columns, which had already advanced 25 miles against steady opposition to the Beauvais area, were ordered to push on all night for Amiens.

THE tanks covered the additional 43 miles in the night and captured the Amiens bridges intact by the first light. August 31, 1944, was spent in crossing the Somme, and on September 1 the armour was ordered to push on to Arras and Douai, using the same tactics as in their advances in the desert, and covering the 40 miles in the day, leaving the flanks open. Our flanks were exposed, but

you've got to take chances ! The shortest distance covered in one day was 15 miles of difficult country towards Douai. The next day the tanks raced 75 miles to Brussels, and Antwerp was entered on September 4.

The men were magnificent. When we bumped into opposition the tanks got behind it and the infantry followed up. One infantry division held 65 miles of road during the advance, with the Germans trapped between the British and the coast, trying to break out. The Germans so trapped were variously estimated at between 120,000 and 200,000. They consisted of men from many units, including the "Duodenal Division" of elderly men. Some of these were in the fighting at Antwerp, where the commander of the German division was captured. Prisoners from 182 different units were taken in this area.

Germans Were Left Guessing

The speed of our advance was largely due to the help of the French Maquis and the Belgian "White Army." They were given the tasks of preventing bridges from being blown up, reporting mines and mopping up by-passed pockets of the enemy. They carried them out everywhere unless the enemy was too strong, when troops were sent to help them. They are very brave chaps.

Co-operation between the British and the Americans also speeded up the advance. The Americans, at the request of the British, cleared Tournai for the tanks. There was no organized front in this area, and the Germans did not know exactly what troops they had ahead of us. The S.S. troops were still fighting, and unless we finish the S.S. it is sure that our children will be doing it in 20 years' time.

From an interview given by Lieut.-Gen. B. G. Horrocks to British United Press war correspondent William Wilson, in Brussels.

pushed up along the river banks from the south and captured the town. Then the entire British corps was moved across their lines of communication at the same time as they were pulling back. This was carried out without one serious hitch. On August 24 the British began concentrating a force of infantry and bridging material at Vernon. It was done with great secrecy, and British troops were not allowed to go near the river banks, where they might be seen by the Germans, who believed there were only Americans there.

To Dominate the Crossing

The entire force formed up at Vernon without the enemy's knowledge. Then, at 6.30 p.m. on August 26, all available artillery and mortars suddenly laid down a barrage, and the infantry began crossing the river (see illus. page 298.) They crossed under cover of a smoke screen in ducks and assault boats, some of which got caught on submerged islands because the level of the river had changed. The bridge-head was consolidated next day, and the troops who had crossed were ordered to go on in every direction and dominate the crossing for at least ten miles. All the armour for the push to Brussels moved eastwards across the Seine into the wide bridge-head and was ordered to start the push from a situation which can only be described as "untidy."

We had got across and had to get the

Lieut.-Gen. B. G. HORROCKS, C.B., D.S.O. (left of centre group in top photo) watched British 2nd Army men pass through Amiens, which was entered on August 31, 1944, on their way to Brussels. The town was reached after an all-night drive through rain and mud ; the speed and surprise of our entry prevented the destruction of three bridges over the Somme, although demolition charges had been prepared under them. Above, a 17-pounder anti-tank gun in a street of Antwerp, which was freed on September 4. PAGE 330 *Photos, British Official*

Line-Up of Our Forces Against Western Germany

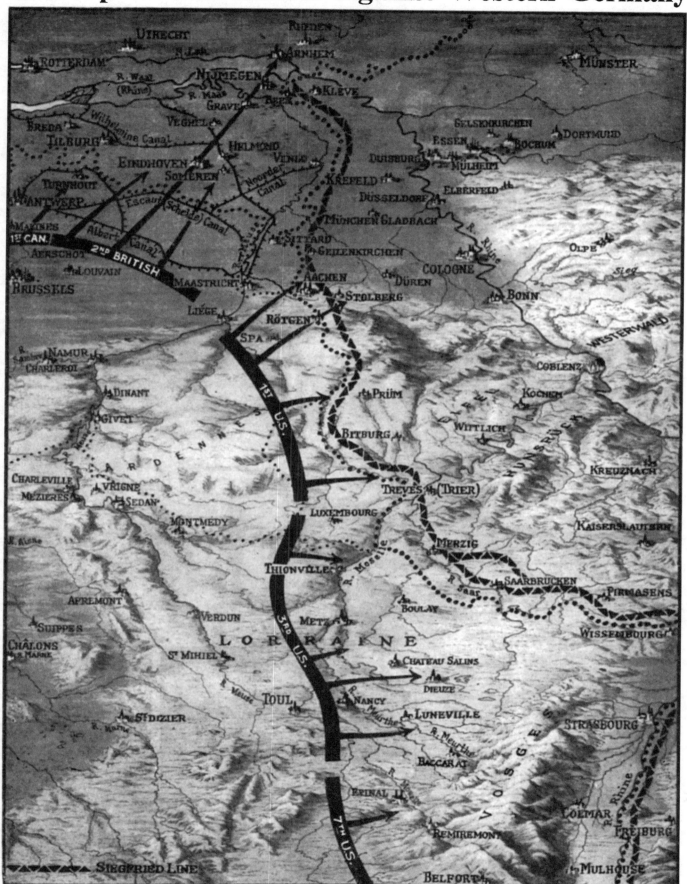

DISPOSITIONS IN LATE SEPTEMBER 1944 of the five Allied armies under Gen. Eisenhower; arrows show directions of thrusts at Germany.   From Brussels to Belfort direct is 255 miles.   Lieut.-Gen H. D. G. Crerar's 1st Canadian Army and Lieut.-Gen. Sir Miles Dempsey's British 2nd Army form the 21st Army Group commanded by Field-Marshal Sir Bernard Montgomery.   Lieut.-Gen. C. Hodges' 1st and Lieut.-Gen. G. S. Patton's 3rd U.S. Army constitute the 12th Army Group commanded by Major-Gen. O. Bradley.   The 7th U.S. Army is led by Lieut.-Gen. A. M. Patch.   PAGE 331

How the Wehrmacht Scrambled out of Belgium---

CLEARING OUT of Brussels and Malines as victorious Allied armies advanced, in September 1944, retreating Germans took all they could lay hands on. Belgian civilians who had looked forward to these days of liberation, through four tormenting years of enemy occupation, watched their former conquerors depart: German troops left the Belgian capital by the northern exit and took with them quantities of flour in horse-drawn carts (1). Other Huns made haste to board the last tram from Brussels (2) at 2 p.m. on Sunday, September 3, as British advanced tanks approached from the south.

Citizens of Malines were entertained by the comic spectacle of a reluctant pig which escaped into the road from a German truck (3) as numerous lorries piled with loot, including boxes of food and cases of wine, wended their way out of the town. (4). Cyclists escaped on machines stolen from civilians. The photographs on this page were taken secretly by two Belgians at the risk of their lives.

Photos, Planet News, New York Times Photos

—With British Troops and Armour at its Heels

OUR ADVANCE towards the Belgian-Dutch and German frontiers was further speeded on September 17, 1944, by a great airborne landing in Holland itself (see p. 349). Hard fighting had occurred along the Albert Canal in Belgium, but by Sept. 12 the enemy defences before Holland had been smashed.

British infantry rode on Sherman tanks to clear pockets of resistance near the Dutch frontier (1). Heading for Holland, our armoured units drove past the world famous Town Hall in Louvain (2). Under covering fire from a Bren gun, infantrymen dashed across a bridge in the Antwerp docks area to take up new positions (3). Self-propelled U.S. 155-mm. guns mounted on Sherman tank chassis were the first heavies to fire into the Reich; the target was S.W. of Aachen on the Aachen-Liége road. The guns opened their barrage with 21 rounds of 100-lb. H.E. shells (4). By Sept. 19 American troops had advanced 11 miles through the Siegfried Line in the Trier sector.

Photos, British Official ; New York Times Photos, Planet News

The Rise and Fall of Hitler's Flying Bombs

"Except possibly for a few last shots, the Battle of London is over," declared Mr. Duncan Sandys, M.P., Chairman of the War Cabinet Committee on operational counter-measures against the flying bomb, on September 7, 1944. How Germany's attempt to destroy London with her vaunted V1 weapon was foiled makes one of the most memorable war stories. See also pages 335-338.

"DIVER, diver, diver!" The words drummed into the ears of a telephone operator at Air Headquarters, Air Defence of Great Britain, a few minutes after 4 o'clock in the morning of June 13, 1944. The code message came from the Royal Observer Corps station at Dymchurch, Kent; it marked the moment for which the authorities had long been prepared.

Two members of the Corps had seen the first flying bomb, approaching over the sea, and in less than 40 seconds their warning in code had been received at headquarters: the whole intricate machinery of defence was at once set in motion, to what effect has been recorded by Capt. Norman Macmillan, M.C., A.F.C., in page 316. The "human side" of this great story contains material for many an epic narrative.

Difficulties of our airmen in getting to grips with this devastating weapon, especially in the early stages of the battle, can be summed up in the following statements :

"We found that by getting in to 200 yards' range we could hit the target. If we were farther away we missed. If we were nearer our aircraft were liable to be damaged by flying debris. In fact, quite a number were brought down. After the first fortnight or month we had so improved our tactics that we were knocking down at least 80 per cent of our sightings. The three squadrons in my wing destroyed 600." This by a Wing-Commander who led the first Tempest wing into action against the flying bomb and himself shot down 23.

Squadron-Leader J. Berry, of Carlton, Nottingham (his photograph appears below), said: "Our chief difficulty was that, though we could see the bombs much farther away at night, we could not easily judge how far away they were.

All we could do at first was to fly alongside the fairly slow bombs and remember what they looked like at lethal range. In this way a very good interception system was worked out before the new shilling range-finder was issued."

That shilling rangefinder, which provided "the complete answer" to pilots' difficulties, was the invention of Sir Thomas Merton, unpaid scientific adviser to the Ministry of Production. He told a Daily Mail reporter that 24 hours after he was first struck by the idea he had manufactured a prototype. In less than a week the manufacture of hundreds was in full swing. "The rangefinder must remain secret," he said, "as its possibilities in this war may not yet be exhausted. But I can say that it is very small and no heavier than a box of matches. It was one of those ideas that look so obvious afterwards."

NEW and resourceful tactics were evolved by our fighter pilots. One, who ran out of ammunition after destroying two doodle-bugs and wanted to tackle a third, brought his fighter alongside of it and slid his starboard wing-tip beneath the port wing of the bomb. A flick of the control column and the "diver," its delicate gyro mechanism thrown out of balance, spun to earth. The pilot reported this novel method of attack when he arrived back at base, the news spread, and soon other pilots were repeating the trick. It was not always easy; they were compelled sometimes to make two, three and even four attempts before the flame-erupting target crashed.

Another pilot discovered that the best position for an attack was slightly behind and to one side of the flying bomb, when it

became possible to shoot off the jet or a wing. At times fighters would co-operate with ground defences to bring the missiles to destruction; several flying bombs were destroyed by heavy and even light A.A. fire after having been "flipped down" to a convenient height by an obliging fighter.

HEAVY A.A. guns, moved to suitable sites, were supported not on the usual 15 ft. of concrete but on improvised "mattresses" of railway lines and sleepers. For this purpose 35 miles of lines and 22,500 sleepers were collected from 20 different railway depots.

There were instances of pilots who deliberately "steered" flying bombs into balloon barrage concentrations. The greatest balloon barrage in the history of the R.A.F. was massed to support the defences; at the height of the menace nearly 2,000 balloons were brought from every part of Britain and concentrated into an area to the south-east of London. Altogether they destroyed 278 flying bombs out of those which escaped the outer defence rings of A.A. guns and fighters.

To step-up the production of balloons the Ministry of Aircraft Production demanded of one factory an all-out effort. "We were offered," said the managing director of the firm concerned, "the use of another factory and urged to discontinue making our dinghies and lifebelts, but we knew these things were also of vital importance, so decided to appeal to our workers. They put in such a spurt that we increased the production of balloons by a very considerable proportion without affecting our output of dinghies and other things. Young girls and women toiled to the limit of their endurance, inspired by the fact that they were helping to defeat the flying bomb." The youngest of those girls and women was 14 and the oldest 68 !

BALLOON sites were completed swiftly, and to link these with headquarters thousands of miles of telephone cable—much of it borrowed from Army formations on the spot to save time—was laid by G.P.O. engineers, assisted by men of the R.A.F. Signal Units and Royal Signals and manned by W.A.A.F. telephonists. The vigil of the crews who manned the sites was continuous.

Thousands of W.A.A.F. personnel played their part in the flying bomb battle, as photographers, photographic interpretation officers, plotters, balloon fabric workers, cooks, and so on. A.T.S. girls also were well to the fore. And non-Service girls at London's telephone switchboards did a magnificent job in helping to keep the phones going during the attacks. Gas and water services were frequently interrupted—and as frequently put into operation again. The work of the various transport staffs was of the very highest order : 78 bus workers of the London Passenger Transport Board were killed and 1,410 injured.

Worst hit district of London was Croydon, with 75 per cent of its houses damaged. In a single day 8 bombs dropped there, and 15 in one week-end : 211 of its citizens were killed. Engaged in repairing London's damage, in August, were 1,500 naval ratings, each vigorously upholding the Royal Navy's tradition of "Jack of All Trades." These Servicemen were called in to ease the heavy burden suddenly thrust upon the heroic and ever-willing Civil Defence organization, every branch of which toiled unceasingly to save life and mitigate the hardships suffered by the "man-in-the-street." A first-hand description of such rescue work is given in page 347

Sqdn.-Ldr. J. BERRY, D.F.C. and bar (below), top-scoring pilot in the battle against the flying bombs, of which he destroyed 60, all but three of them between sunset and dawn. His Tempest was damaged on several occasions by the explosions of his robot targets. *Photo, Central Press*

THE FAMOUS GUARDS CHAPEL, attached to Wellington Barracks, London, was hit by a flying bomb during a Sunday morning service in June 1944, and casualties were caused. Men (above) at work in the Chapel's shell. PAGE 334 *Photo, Planet News*

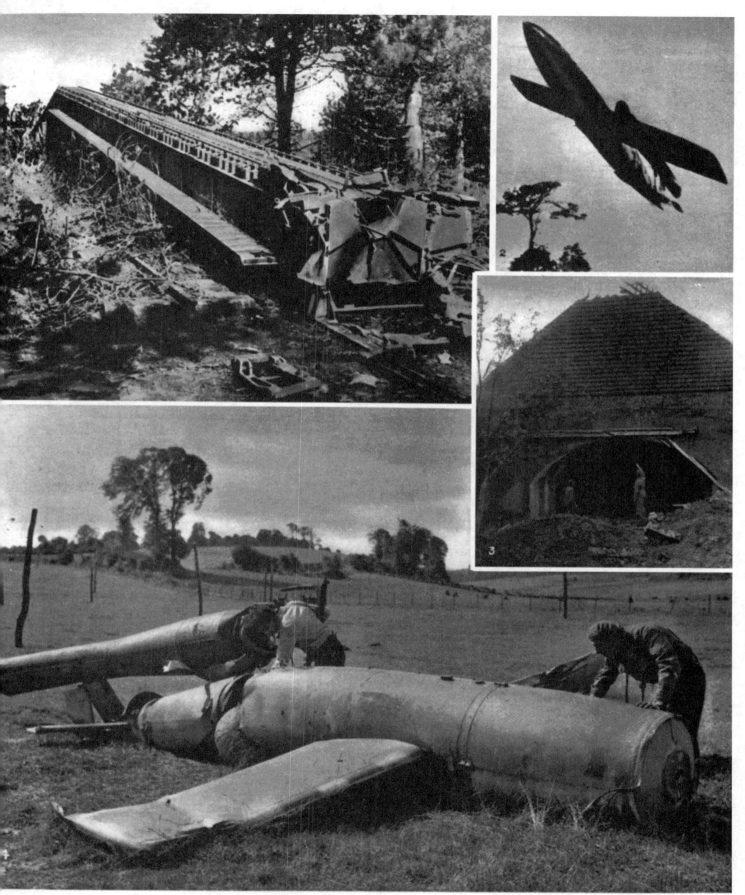

When Hitler's V1 Left its Lair for England

Many flying-bomb launching sites were put out of action by the Germans themselves before they were captured : a disabled runway (1) found at Belloy-sur-Somme, near Amiens. "This indiscriminate weapon," as Mr. Churchill called it, was an unpleasant sight as it took the air (2). Sometimes it failed to function (4) and crashed near its launching site. Camouflage was employed to conceal flying-bomb depots from the R.A.F., some assembly houses having roofs resembling farm buildings (3).

335

Guns and Fighters Battled in Doodle-bug Alley —

In one day 97 out of 101 flying bombs were shot out of the sky. Sharing in the hard-won victory of this Second Battle of London, hundreds of coastal guns and fighter-planes were continually in action. Shell-bursts from an A.A. battery clustered thickly (1) as a flame-spouting bomb droned towards the capital. At a range of only 40 yards this R.A.F. pilot (2) destroyed his diving target ; punctures in his Spitfire were caused by the bomb's mid-air disintegration.

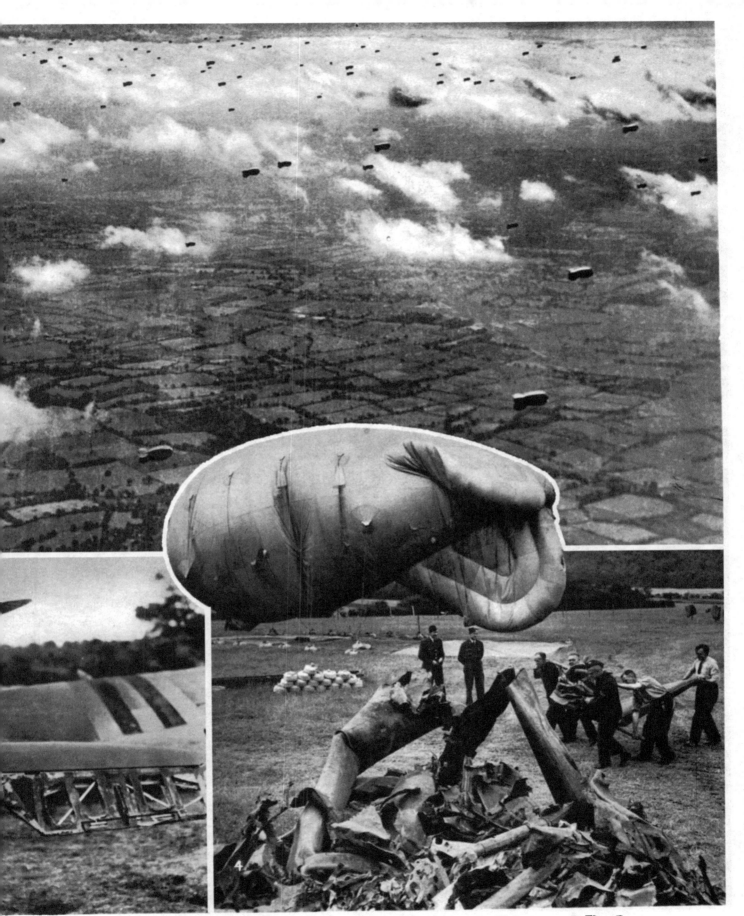

— Cabled Balloons Formed Last Line of Defence

Of bombs which slipped through the first two lines of our triple defence and entered the balloon barrage area—the greatest concentration ever put into the air—nearly 15 per cent were brought down through collision with the cables ; 278 were thus destroyed up to September 10, 1944.   Here is a small section of the sky-barrage guarding towns of Southern England (3). From open fields surrounding the many sites the litter was daily collected and added to numerous scrap-heaps (4).

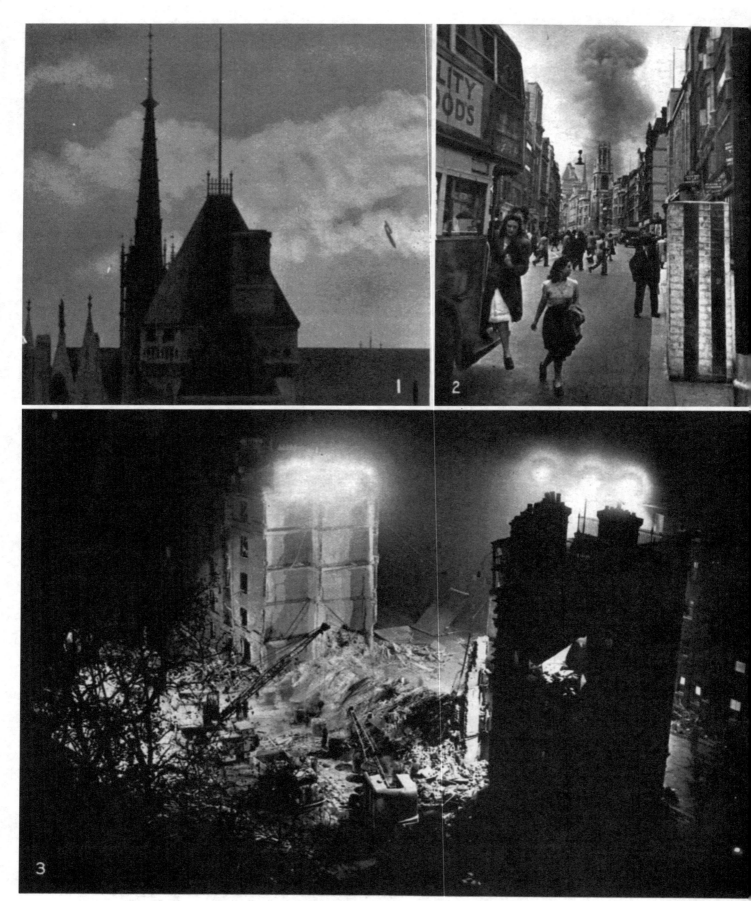

London's Head was Bloody but Unbowed

Photos, Associated Press, Daily Mirror, Daily Express

Almost at the end of its final glide—motor cut out, impact and shattering explosion a matter of seconds only—a flying bomb (1) just missed the Law Courts in London. Frequenters of Fleet Street passed on almost unheeding as a pillar of smoke (background, 2) marked the crashing of a bomb in the Aldwych, almost the proverbial stone's-throw from them. Ripped apart in the dead of night, a block of flats sets heroic C.D. rescuers toiling with the aid of searchlights and cranes (3).

VIEWS & REVIEWS Of Vital War Books

by Hamilton Fyfe

"Join the Navy and See the World" urged a pre-war poster. But during the past five years the men of the Army and Air Force have been quite as far afield as the sailors and marines. Never before has there been such an uprooting of men from their homelands on so vast a scale, never before such a planting of them down among far-off races, in lands that had hitherto been to them nothing more than unfamiliar names.

The soldiers of the ancient Roman Empire travelled as far to the west as Britain, as far south as the Sahara, as far east as the Black Sea. Those were short distances compared with what Allied troops have accomplished in this war. Soldiers and airmen from Britain have been almost all over the world. Canadians have fought in Sicily, Australians in the Western Desert and Egypt, South Africans in Somaliland, New Zealanders in Greece and Crete.

Those were only two of the countries where New Zealand forces have been sent, and it is very doubtful whether they ought to have been sent there. Mr. Walter Nash in his book, New Zealand, a Working Democracy (Dent, 8s. 6d.), defends the decisions of Mr. Churchill and the N.Z. Cabinet to send them and other troops for the sole purpose of "honouring the promise of assistance which the Greeks had been given." Mr. Nash admits "there was little expectation that the Germans could be held," but he argues that "a pledge had to be honoured, however costly it might be."

That seems to me altogether wrong. In war a promise of help is given in certain circumstances. If those circumstances alter so as to make it plain that assistance cannot be of any value, then it is mere Quixotism to keep the promise. It means throwing away many lives and much material without in any way benefiting those to whom the promise was made. That "the successful evacuation of Allied forces from Greece and subsequently from Crete was a magnificent achievement which will most assuredly find an honoured place in the annals of British naval history" is true; but the question whether the Navy ought to have been called on to achieve it will be debated as long as military history is written.

What is certain is that the New Zealanders fought bravely and skilfully in the Near East, as they have done wherever they went. They are usually self-reliant and at the same time unusually good at working together and with other units.

Long hard years of pioneering in a virgin country brought home very forcibly to New Zealanders the necessity of self-help. They learned this lesson well and have not forgotten it. In the desert sands of Libya, in the skies over German cities, and on cruisers and carriers in the southern seas these traits of individual initiative and responsibility are a characteristic of thousands upon thousands of young New Zealand men.

They learned, too, that the individual can only thrive if all join in helping one another. Thus there emerged side by side with a deep faith in the value of individual freedom an equally firm belief in the value of collective organization for the individual as well as for the nation.

A large part of Mr. Nash's book is filled with the description of the system which he calls "a working democracy." That is undeniably correct, and Mr. Nash is the right person to tell us about it, for he was one of the Ministers chiefly concerned in its creation. Behind that effort, which gave such excellent results, was "the recognition

that the community as a whole through its organized government must be collectively responsible for the welfare of its members." But along with this went "emphasis on individual rights and freedom"; there was no attempt to force people to alter their ways and their outlook. Thus the capable and honest men who laid the foundations of the new system were able to make "necessary political and economic adjustments smoothly," teaching the rest of the nations, ourselves included, a most useful lesson and "offering a practicable example of the kind of social organization—the kind of laws and institutions—that may well become typical of most democracies tomorrow."

"Practical" — that is the key-word. Changes were made "as the need for them arose." No doctrine, no theory, no so-called philosophy was allowed to dominate action. Reforms were carried out, not "according to plan"; that is, not as part of any preconceived transformation of society, but "as the need arose." If New Zealanders have any philosophy, which most of them would emphatically deny, regarding philosophers as a bunch of "long-hairs" with cranky notions, their philosophy is a conviction that "the best and fullest possibilities in life for themselves and their children" can be attained by the use of "common sense, combined with a realistic approach towards most problems and a strong humanitarian instinct."

Pattern of Life in New Zealand

For seven years what is known as a Labour Government has been in power. It is in fact representative not merely of one side in politics but of the nation in bulk. Its basic principles are (1) the care of the old "because they have worked to make it possible for us to enjoy the standards we enjoy today" (that would not be true in all countries, would it ?); (2) that those who render useful services are entitled to the full fruits of their labour ; (3) that "resources must be so organized as to ensure the maximum production of useful goods and services, and that these shall be available to those who render useful service, if they are able, so that all may enjoy good standards of life, with security and leisure"; (4) that collective planning is necessary "both to make the best of our resources and to ensure that human needs are satisfied to the utmost."

Already, says Mr. Nash, the New Zealand worker can be fully employed at standard rates of wages. "He is guaranteed security against the hazards of ill-health, old age and invalidity. All children have equal educational opportunities from the kindergarten to the university. Every family can have a home and a home life with all that those terms imply." From this we can understand why the New Zealander, whether in the forces or working at home, feels a special personal interest in winning the war. If Japan had succeeded in her criminal endeavour to rule and enslave all the Pacific nations, the New Zealand system would have been turned into one of forced labour without liberty of any kind, for the advantage of a degenerate ruling race.

MR. WALTER NASH, whose book is reviewed in this page, was born in England in 1882. New Zealand's Minister of Social Security from 1938-41, he was appointed Minister to America in 1942. *Photo, Topical Press*

The Japanese plot has failed—so far, but Mr. Nash warns us against supposing that it will be a simple matter to dispose of Enemy Number Two when once Hitler, Enemy Number One, has been crushed in Europe. He believes Japan will fight to the bitter end and be "an even more determined foe when her cause is an utterly hopeless one than she has proved to be when everything was going in her favour." That does not accord with my reading of the character of the men who direct Japanese policy. Judging by what has happened in the past, I should say they will try to get out as soon as they see their defeat is certain. That Japan can continue to exist as an independent power much longer seems to me most unlikely. The four hundred millions of Chinese are bound to overwhelm the one hundred million Japs, and the two countries will then be amalgamated under Republican government. It is not improbable that this government might join the Federation of Socialist Soviet Republics, of which Russia is at present the largest unit.

Whether this would make for peace or for other wars no one can say. Certainly both Russia and China will be members of whatever international body is formed to take the place of the League of Nations, and will have great influence on its activity. Mr. Nash is of the same opinion as Mr. Churchill about the old League. It could have prevented war "if its machinery had been applied in its full vigour." Because Baldwin was too King Log-ish and Neville Chamberlain too King Stork-ish in the interest of Big Business and High Finance, the League languished. Nobody believed in it. If the warnings in a memorandum drawn up by the New Zealand Government and sent to the League in 1936 had been attended to, war could have been avoided.

For the immense quantities of food we have received from New Zealand, for the reverse Lease-Lend aid which the Dominion has given to the United States, for the instant response its people made to the Call to Arms, we owe debts of gratitude that must not be forgotten. We may also in the near future be indebted to them for the pattern of a State that can be described with accuracy as "a working democracy," not less efficient in peace than it is in war.

Desert Battle to Save World's Food Supplies

A special British military force, numbering 1,000 officers and men, is fighting on a vast front to free the world of countless appallingly destructive pests now threatening millions of pounds' worth of vital crops. How this strange war, directed from the London headquarters of the Anti-Locust Research Centre, is being waged is told by Captain MARTIN THORNHILL, M.C., F.R.G.S.

EVERY twelve years invasion by huge hordes of locusts, which have on occasion threatened the economic security of nearly half the world, reaches its most dangerous peak. The year 1944 is one such critical period, and it is feared that it may be the worst on record. "Hoppers," estimated to be mobilizing in unprecedented strength, are accordingly being systematically attacked in their Arabian breeding grounds. The most determined onslaught ever made against the world's worst menace to food supplies, its object is to prevent the giant grasshoppers from sweeping across the desert and stripping the Middle East of the crops now vital to stricken Europe.

The British expedition in Arabia is part of an international campaign, stretching from Russia, through Syria, Palestine, 'Iraq, Persia, Egypt, the Sudan and Ethiopia, to beyond Uganda and Kenya. So interested is the world in the enterprise that the United

dug pits, and then slaughtered, in Cyprus alone : there, 300 tons of locust eggs have been destroyed in a single season.

Egypt, annually ravaged since Biblical days, had its worst invasion of all time in 1915. Here, too, there were defence measures—of a kind. Enormous trenches trapped 7,866 million of the pests, weighing 13,500 tons. This catch was not for the whole season, but during a single phase of it. Individual farmers have original methods of frustrating the common enemy. I have seen Arab smallholders spread the smooth pages of large illustrated magazines before their plots in the path of creeping hordes of hoppers grounded for feeding ; unable to climb the glossy sheets, the marauders bypassed the plots while their owners genuflected in thanks to Allah.

As the years pass, more up to date and efficacious methods have been used against the invaders. Shortly before the Eighth

Officer Beer, of Birmingham, who has flown with the Russians on several anti-locust spray swoops, pays high tribute to the efficiency of the Red Air Force pilots. "For their job," he says, "they often come down to within 15 feet of the ground—a task needing considerable skill and nerve."

UNTIL recently it was thought there were two types of locust, the individual and the swarming. It has now been found that there is one only, and that swarming is caused by local conditions. This migratory species closely resembles, but is much larger than, the English grasshopper. It deposits its eggs in the sand, and the young hoppers hatch out in 4-6 weeks. Far from being dangerous only at the flying stage the locust is destructive at every turn of its career—larva, flightless "hopper" stage and adult. During the second stage of their evolution, lasting another 4-6 weeks, the hoppers move along in vast swarms several miles wide, laying waste all the ground they traverse. It is during this period that the treated bran is laid in their path. They eat it for the water that is mixed with it.

Thus it is essential to wipe out locusts during breeding, and first reports of the success of modern methods come from East Africa. There, one anti-locust unit alone laid down 8,045 bags of bait, 10 tons of molasses saturated with the new poison compound D.N.O.C., destroying 526 separate hopper and flying swarms.

Starting from the Turkana district in N.W. Kenya, the swarms threatened to destroy thousands of tons of food crops in the East African territories. "The infestation can only be described as terrific," stated an East Africa Command communiqué, "but vast areas of hoppers were completely wiped out." More than 7,000 square miles of territory, largely desert country with no water or road communications, was quartered by 200 motor vehicles, including ambulances, mobile workshops and water tankers. The personnel which made up this desert army included 60 British officers and N.C.O.s, 2,000 African troops, 2,000 Turkana tribesmen, and seven civilian experts.

COMBATING THE LOCUST MENACE in India, Russian airmen consult with Indian locust specialists. They are here seen plotting on a map the positions of swarms from reports sent in by British and Indian troops who act as observers on the pests' flying routes. As told in this page, Russia has often helped to overcome the threat to India's crops. *Photo, Indian Official*

States, Russia and India are helping substantially with funds and equipment. Supreme scientific direction comes from the Anti-Locust Research Centre in London, under Dr. Uvarov, the world's greatest living locust expert. Conferences on locust-control held in Cairo and Nairobi in 1943 were attended by experts from many States.

IMAGINE your home county swept clear of vegetation in a few hours and you have some idea of the problem confronting this new great organized 12-months' offensive against an almost incredibly destructive foe. When this war put a stop to it, science had all but won a fight which has been going on for centuries and from which the enemy has always emerged victorious—and small wonder, for a single flight of locusts over the Red Sea is estimated to spread over an area of at least 2,000 square miles. Settling, they strip vast territories, in very short time, of every vestige of vegetation. Taking flight again, they settle in pastures new. When the season's ravage is over enormous tracts lie devastated, barren for twelve months.

One memorable swarm, providentially blown into the sea during a storm, was cast up on the South African coast, the massed bodies of the monster insects forming a 4-ft. high bank five miles long. In one year 56,000 million were captured in specially

Army knew the Qattara Depression, a 50 by 125-mile swarm which threatened that and the surrounding area was diverted into the desert by an army of 2,000 men with flame-throwers, while aircraft sprayed the swarming sands with poison dust. It was shortly afterwards—in the spring of 1942—that the first large-scale offensive was launched against locusts in an effort to save Allied shipping by preserving from ravage the summer's food crops grown in the African colonies to supply the North African and Middle East armies. Entomologists had reported new remote trans-Arabian breeding grounds, and huge consignments of poisoned bran were shipped to those areas, and the "nurseries" extensively treated during the locusts' wingless stage.

That campaign was financed by the British Government, Russia, India, Africa and Middle Eastern Powers co-operating. In the present offensive the Soviet are one of the most ardent collaborators. The subject of Russian alliance with the Middle East Anti-Locust Union may well have been on the agenda of the Teheran Conference. India and Persia are close neighbours of the Soviet Union, and well-equipped Russian aircraft, with their own mechanics and ground staff, are now helping materially to overcome the locust threat to India's foodstuffs. Flying

THE Force that has now been swallowed up by the Arabian Desert is still more exceptional. The men belong to the R.A.S.C., Signals, R.A.M.C., and Army Catering Corps, and all have served at least two years in the Western Desert. There are two distinct parties. Both, with their technical experts, started from Egypt. One, a 250-vehicle convoy, under Major Pickavance of Liverpool, travelled through Palestine, Syria and 'Iraq to the head of the Persian Gulf and then down the tracks of Saudi Arabia. The second, commanded by Major William Horsfall of Wetherby, Yorks, crossed the Sinai desert to 'Aqaba, and then down the west coast of Arabia. At the head are special navigation cars to pilot the columns of locust hunters through the roadless wilderness of 3,000 miles.

From the Army Welfare Department the expedition received half a million cigarettes, footballs, boxing gloves, darts, indoor games, books, gramophones and records. The only link between the locust hunters in a land seldom penetrated by white men, and the outside world, is by radio reception from the B.B.C. To make local purchases the officer in charge of catering carries bags of gold sovereigns, every one bearing a king's head, since Arabs, regarding women as the inferior sex, part with less goods for queen's-head coins !

First Dutch Town Entered by British Ground Troops

VALKENSWAARD, the first town in Holland to be entered by British ground troops on their way to Eindhoven, was liberated by the British Second Army on September 17, 1944. This photograph shows British armour in the centre of the town, where tanks and other vehicles were temporarily stationed in the cobbled streets. Situated close to the Dutch-Belgian frontier, Valkenswaard represented an important capture for General Sir Miles Dempsey's forces which subsequently drove on through Eindhoven to Nijmegen. PAGE 341 *Photo, British Newspaper Pool*

'Seven-League Boots' are Winning Pacific War

Air and sea power, combined in a new strategical pattern and backed by modern mechanical devices on land, have given the fabled "seven-league boots" to Allied forces in the Pacific. The once-derided technique of "island hopping" has indeed produced most spectacular results in this theatre of war, as explained by DONALD COWIE.

ROOSEVELT once said that if MacArthur conquered an island a month it would take him 100 years to reach Tokyo. The President was expressing, back in the gloomiest days of the Pacific war, the popular revulsion against what the Americans derisively called the "island-hopping" strategy of MacArthur. Why the somersault since? Why, that is, do we now consider the end of the Japanese fight to be not so distant after all, and acknowledge that "island-hopping" has indeed done the trick?

The answer to these questions contains one of the most remarkable strategic discoveries of modern warfare. It is that seven-league boots have been given to the island-hoppers by the development of carrier-borne aircraft so that they can by-pass hundreds of miles of occupied islands at will and, landing far in their rear, remove those garrisons from the war without firing a shot against them.

Consider what happened in the Marianas, those islands within bombing range of Japan which an American task force ripped from a vicious enemy in less than two months, between June 15 and August 10, 1944. To begin with, they should never have been attacked, by all the text-book rules, till the Americans had first conquered and absolutely reduced (1) all the Caroline Islands to the far south, (2) the island of Guam to the near south, and (3) Wake Island to the east. You don't besiege Paris before you have taken Caen, or Genoa before you have taken Naples. It is not done.

But that is precisely what the Americans did. Ignoring the "strongest Japanese base in the south-west Pacific," at mighty Truk in the Carolines, taking no more notice of heavily-fortified Guam and Wake Islands than if they had been held by impotent children, our Allies steamed stolidly ahead through the blue, hundreds of miles across open sea, and struck. By so striking, and taking the Japanese utterly by surprise, and securing suddenly a great base for themselves

hundreds of miles in the rear of the defensive screen which their enemy had so carefully erected, the Americans accomplished in a month or so what might otherwise have taken them several years to win.

Even in the tactics of the assault on the Marianas they were gloriously unorthodox. Reading from south to north, first comes Guam, then Rota, then Tinian, and finally, nearest Japan, the strongest island of Saipan. Our Allies calmly sailed past Guam, Rota and Tinian, to attack Saipan alone. They could mop up the others afterwards, as they did.

Again by-passing the enemy stronghold at Truk, the next moves were made on September 15, 1944, when simultaneous landings took place on the Palau Islands, west of the Carolines, and on Morotai Island, 300 miles south-east of the Philippines. The Palau Islands were stormed by American Army and Marine forces; other Allied forces which landed on Morotai were under the command of General MacArthur, who himself took part. Thus two spearheads, 650 miles apart, pointed straight at Mindanao in the Philippines, and threatened to isolate the Japanese garrison of 200,000 in the East Indies.

So it has been almost from the beginning in the south-west Pacific, if the successive steps of General MacArthur's and Admiral Nimitz's forces are carefully analysed.

MacArthur jumped up the Solomons in a series of leaps, often leaving strong Japanese fortresses behind. To this day an enemy garrison still bristles, and starves, in the fetid jungles of Bougainville Island in the Solomons. After struggling forward in New Guinea for some months, MacArthur seemed to say "Oh, to hell with this!" and leapt right over the heads of the Japanese to attack northern bases, to land in New Britain. And then, having isolated strong Rabaul, he sped with those seven-league boots right across to the western or Dutch part of New Guinea, hundreds of miles away.

So we come to the crux of the matter. What *are* those interesting seven-league boots which similarly enabled Admiral Nimitz's naval forces to jump from the remote Gilbert Islands to Saipan near Japan in less than a year, losing only 6,000 men to the Japanese 55,000 in the same time? The "boots" are aircraft, used by men—and this is important—with a remarkable faculty for digging themselves in quickly.

FIRST our Allies produced planes adapted for the purpose, long-range bombers and fighters, troop-carriers, naval aircraft of many new types, and had them ready in record time. Then they built the ships, thousands of landing-craft, at least 22 big new aircraft-carriers. The bombers went out first, to smash Japanese air and naval ports, to sink enemy shipping. Next the big expeditions set sail or took to the air—and were protected throughout by such a hornet swarm of long-range and carrier-borne aircraft that the enemy was unable to interfere with them.

The enemy could not bomb them, because the American air umbrella was too strong; he could not attack them with his fleet, because American aircraft and submarines threatened to sink his precious ships wherever they so much as showed smoke on the horizon. He had only the one fleet, irreplaceable, and that must be kept for the final inshore defence of Japan.

So aircraft have enabled our Allies to disregard orthodoxy and, by continual by-passing, to advance in months over a Pacific distance which would otherwise have taken years. (No need to worry about the Japanese bases thus by-passed; isolated from home, they must rot.) Undoubtedly it has also been a very great naval occasion. Without the aircraft, however, those armadas of merchantmen, and landing-craft, and supply ships such as tankers, could never have thrust so far and so invulnerably. Their protecting warships would have had to fight great sea battles against the Japanese navy on equal conditions, or probably on unequal conditions. As it is, the aircraft alone have kept Japanese naval and air opposition completely at bay.

But there is one other factor in addition to the air weapon which has made this remarkable strategy possible—and it was referred to above when it was said that the men using the seven-league boots have a rare faculty for digging themselves in quickly.

ONCE it was necessary to capture enemy-held bases in order to have bases yourself. Bulldozer, roller and tractor in efficient American hands have altered all that. Why attack a heavily fortified base like Wewak in order to obtain landing facilities when troops can leap to Hollandia, over two hundred miles to the west, and create an equally good base there? An excellent alternative to taking Truk is to build a bigger and better Truk elsewhere, which is just what a clever army with new methods can do, almost overnight. One more text-book rule is out-dated!

Since the Japanese obviously based their Pacific defence on that ancient text-book, and since our American Allies have won their success up till now with sideshow forces, reserving the strongest for the European theatre, we can safely predict some startling Pacific developments tomorrow, when all is concentrated against the Far Eastern enemy. We ourselves may start some by-passing, possibly via Singapore up the Indo-China coast. The final big American hop might land them in the centre of Tokyo while we are still wondering how long it will all take

BY-PASSING JAPANESE ISLAND STRONGHOLDS in the S.W. and Central Pacific, Allied forces in this vast theatre of war isolated enemy garrisons and wrenched from the Japanese vital bases hundreds of miles apart. Enemy defensive plans were violently disrupted as a result of the Americans' "island hopping" in the areas shown in this map.

Burma Border Outpost Cleared by 14th Army

TAMU VILLAGE, adjoining Kabaw Valley in Manipur State, was wrested from the Japanese in early August 1944 by the British 14th Army when the latter crossed the Burma border to clear the last of the enemy out of India. Buddhist temples were found damaged (1). American ambulance returns to Tamu with casualties (2). A knocked-out Japanese tank is taken in tow by British troops (3). Moth plane waits in a clearing to take-off with wounded (4). Corner of a Japanese graveyard near the captured village (5). PAGE 343 *Photos, British and Indian Official*

How Belgium's White Army Aided Allied Advance

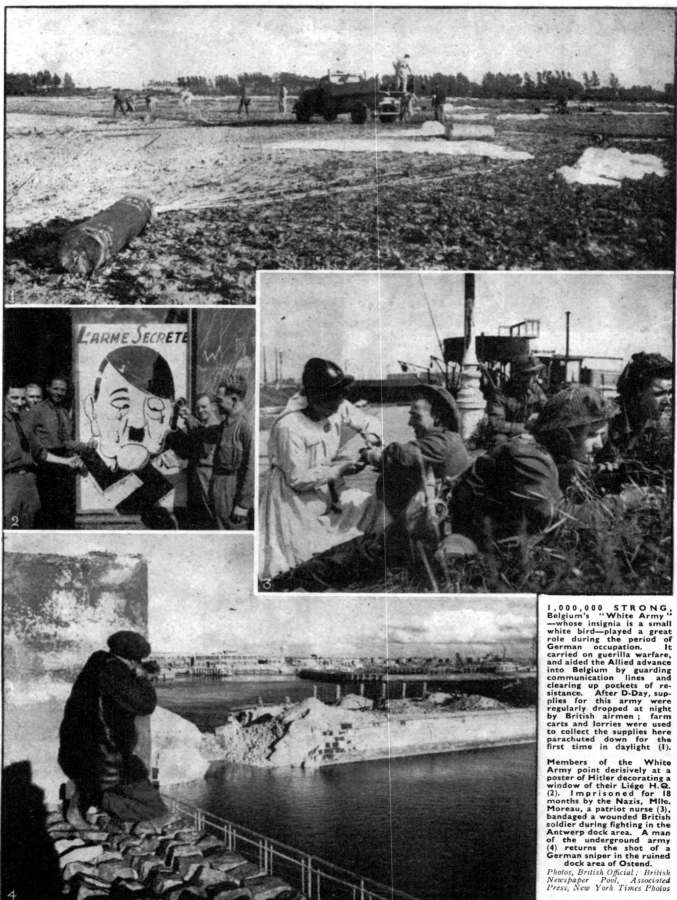

1,000,000 STRONG, Belgium's "White Army" —whose insignia is a small white bird—played a great role during the period of German occupation. It carried on guerilla warfare, and aided the Allied advance into Belgium by guarding communication lines and clearing up pockets of resistance. After D-Day, supplies for this army were regularly dropped at night by British airmen; farm carts and lorries were used to collect the supplies here parachuted down for the first time in daylight (I).

Members of the White Army point derisively at a poster of Hitler decorating a window of their Liége H.Q. (2). Imprisoned for 18 months by the Nazis, Mlle. Moreau, a patriot nurse (3), bandaged a wounded British soldier during fighting in the Antwerp dock area. A man of the underground army (4) returns the shot of a German sniper in the ruined dock area of Ostend.

Photos, British Official; British Newspaper Pool, Associated Press, New York Times Photos

I WAS THERE!

Eye Witness
Stories of the War

Dutch Fields were Bright with our Parachutes

The sensational descent of the First Allied Airborne Army behind the German lines in the Netherlands on September 17, 1944, was yet another remarkable demonstration of our air supremacy. Michael Moynihan, News Chronicle war correspondent, flew in a Halifax glider-tower with the great armada and kept this diary of the momentous occasion.

THIS was an army in flight. Flight, not in the German sense, for we were headed towards Holland. From horizon to horizon the sky was alive with Allied aircraft; Dakotas carrying paratroops, Halifaxes, Stirlings, great gliders weighted with men and material. One of the greatest airborne operations in history was under way. The Dutch coast appeared through the haze of the warm afternoon. To the men of the First Airborne Army it was the promised land. Within 45 minutes they would be in action on enemy-held soil. The full story of this great and historic operation cannot yet be told. My story is confined to one airfield among the many from which the airborne armada took off; and on that airfield the one plane.

M for Mike is the Halifax from which I witnessed this stupendous undertaking. Our job was to tow a Hamilcar, the world's biggest glider, right into Holland. Our freight consisted of two Bren-gun carriers, our " passengers " five North-Country men of the Airborne Army.

It was over a week ago that I came to this airfield in the West Country, but not until yesterday did " operations market " become a reality. At 11 in the morning the camp was sealed. Sentries guarded its boundaries. The bus service to the local town was cancelled. In all parts of the camp final preparations were made; troops assembled their equipment. Halifax crews went over their charts and maps for the last time with a thoroughness that could leave no room for mistakes.

They Joked Before Action

At six o'clock this morning the sleeping camp was roused for its great day. Ground crews had been working all night on Halifaxes. The two long rows of Horsas and Hamilcars waited, the latter already filled with their equipment—carriers and guns. Beside the assembled force, glider and tug pilots were briefed. The Group Captain read a message from the A.O.C., wishing pilots and crews all luck in the great mission.

In the warm autumn morning of this fourth anniversary of the Battle of Britain, troops and crews stood beside the giant machines that were soon to take them into action. They joked over cups of tea flavoured with rum; chalked the names of girl friends on the sides of their gliders. At the end of the long column of aircraft, M for Mike waited beside a Hamilcar that bore the macabre inscription, " The undertaker and his stiffs."

WE were the 13th and last of the Hamilcar towers. Staff-Sgt. Hill and Sgt. Openshaw were pilot and co-pilot of the Hamilcar. At 10.50 we taxied to the long runway. At 10.53 we were airborne. This is the diary I kept of an historic flight.

11.45.—We are flying in a blue sky, cloudless except for aircraft, and what an exception ! On our starboard side, front and behind, the armada stretches. M for Mike is not standing up well to the strain of the 15 tons dead weight behind. The other 12 Hamilcars have outdistanced us. The pilot and navigator decide to cut off a loop in our course to make up time. We are off now on our own. 2,000 ft. below people are coming out of country churches and staring up at us in wonder.

12.15.—Approaching the coast. Navigator says : " I have cut off as much as I can, but we are going to be hellishly late."

12.30.—Stirlings towing Horsas to port. Farther ahead aircraft are as thick as flights of swallows as far as the haze of the horizon.

1.0.—We have no chance now of catching the Hamilcars. Must risk a " lone wolf " approach perhaps 30 minutes late over our objective. To port a Horsa has broken adrift and goes down to the sea, a Stirling circling with obvious concern.

1.15.—We are over Holland. From the bomb-aimer's turret in the nose I see a flooded countryside, the water is still and looks like green slime from which rooftops, trees and telegraph poles protrude. First of the great fighter escort sighted—Mosquitoes hedge-hopping below us, Spitfires above.

1.20.—First signs of life below—groups of civilians staring up from country roads and village greens.

1.30.—Scores of Dakotas are passing to our starboard—on the way home. This is the Continent, but it seems to be "traffic on the left." None of the flak has been active.

1.35.—Three Horsas have made a forced landing. Dutch people are streaming across the fields from a village towards them.

1.50.—Dakotas coming up to port—reassuring to have their company. Flak has just come up from near our objective, like hammer blows on the floor of the plane. Flak bursts 50 yards to port.

1.55.—This is it. "O.K., boys. I'm casting off now," says the glider pilot. "Thanks for lift." They're away. Below, the fields north of the Rhine are cluttered with gliders. To port there is a wonderful spectacle as the Dakotas disgorge their troops. The sunlit area is bright with parachutes. In a village houses are on fire. The fighting seems to have moved west. Smoke rises from the woods and a large area of gorse is on fire. I see "the undertaker" touching down among the litter of gliders, a perfect landing. I can just see the nose swing back to let out the carriers. The parachutists are now down—their chutes scattered through the field like bright crushed apples.

2.0.—Headed for home. We have climbed above clouds and seem to be all alone in this remote mutable upper-world. For fighters or flak we have been all along and still are a sitting target. But the enemy appears to have been thoroughly stunned.

2.10.—Coffee is being passed round.

2.25.—By the flooded coast a ship shot up by Rocket Typhoon is blazing and sending up a huge cloud of black smoke.

2.30.—Over the coast. "O.K., boys. Back to Merrie England," says the navigator.

2.50.—A motor-boat is speeding below to the rescue of a detached Horsa.

3.30.—3,000 ft. over the Sunday quiet of England. On the Thames yachts and rowing-boats are gliding. " Oh, to be in Civvy Street ! " sighs one of the crew.

4.20.—We are coming down. We are home !

CROSSING A LOWER REACH OF THE RHINE, with the peaceful-looking Dutch countryside spread out below, these R.A.F. Halifaxes towing British Horsa gliders are nearing their destination. They formed a small part of the vast armada that carried the First Allied Airborne Army to Holland, as related in the story above. See also illus. p. 349. PAGE 345 *Photo, British Official*

BOUND FOR HOLLAND in a C.46 transport aircraft, these British parachute troops shared in the great adventure embarked upon by the First Allied Airborne Army on September 17, 1944 (see story in p. 345). By September 21, more troops had been landed in the area of Nijmegen—scene of fierce German resistance.
Photo, British Official

I Saw the Maginot Line Come to Life Again

With hardly a shot having been fired, a stretch of the Maginot Line fell to U.S. 3rd Army troops on September 11, 1944. Cornelius Ryan, of The Daily Telegraph, found that the Germans had not demolished or mined any part of it ; even the guns were still oiled and in working condition.

I STOOD beside a French boy of 18 this morning in murky, damp darkness, 100 ft. below the level of the earth in the electrical power house, and watched him as by the light of a torch he pressed the starter button of the huge Diesel engine. With a low hissing a flywheel began to spin, and one by one red lights flickered on the control panels flanking each wall, lights flashed on in the damp ceiling and a deep whirring note resounded throughout the miles of tunnels.

Very much as the French had left it in 1940,

the Maginot Line had come to life again. It had been "switched on" for our benefit. The whole of that vast power-house was as clean as a new pin, with everything in working order. There were shining Diesel engines, huge transformers, complete air-conditioning plant, lifts capable of hoisting 250 tons, and an electric railway. This particular fort, only one of a hundred which dot the countryside, had for its occupying force during the four years of occupation only one German. All its complicated machinery has been cared for by three Frenchmen and this boy, and

the Germans had paid them 5f. 40c., or about 6d. an hour to do it.

For nearly three hours I was shown over the whole fort by this youth. The main entrance is concealed in a dense forest near the little village of Crusnes. Driving through this forest we came to a squat, black, concrete fort which contained the main entrance. It was about 30 ft. high and about 80 ft. wide. In its centre stood two iron gates wide open. Anybody could have entered.

Just inside the entrance was a pit right across a tunnel, about 14 ft. wide and 12 ft. in depth. To cross, one had to walk over the iron rungs of a ladder. The walls on each side of the tunnel were lined with a heavy electrical cable, and down the centre ran twin railway lines. On one set stood a small electric engine, which received its power from overhead cables.

We reached the lift and began the long walk downstairs, which followed it spiral fashion down to the very depths of the earth. Reaching the bottom we walked perhaps a mile to the power-house, where the young Frenchman busied himself with the giant Diesel engine and then threw the starter which brought it to life. We continued the tour aboard an electric train, which nosed along tunnels, past the men's quarters, magazines, storehouses and gun emplacements commanding each tunnel.

At the end of one such tunnel we stopped at a solid one-foot thick steel door weighing 10 tons, which divided the fortifications and could be used as a means of defence or as a fire-door. Then the little train began the long climb to one of the main overground forts. We left the train and walked the remaining distance, passing hand-operated shell hoists, to the interior of a cupola.

In the centre, rising high into the darkness, ran a mass of machinery, which was the main base of the guns on the top, pointing outwards from the overhead fort. On each side of this machinery were two automatic shell lifts, much the same as on battle-cruisers. Here also was mechanism to turn the whole turret. Once again we boarded the electric train and journeyed along another tunnel to one of the observation points. This was another cupola, but instead of guns it had four wind slits about a quarter of an inch in depth.

IN THE MAGINOT LINE, in the Thionville sector, units of the French Forces of the Interior man a light machine-gun. A visit to the Line is described above. *Photo, Keystone*

We Salute the Men Who Tunnel Through Death !

Civil Defence Rescue men have earned the admiration of the whole civilized world. Preston Benson of The Star tells the inside story of their activities in the debris of a London building shattered by one of the 8,070 flying bombs launched by the Germans against Southern England up to September 4, 1944.

I WAS allowed to worm my way through the choking brick and mortar dust and the smell of gas, to scramble over masses of girders and jagged masonry, past the stout lorries and the three 7-ton mobile cranes which lifted great baskets of debris into the lorries to get it away.

Around me in the shadow of a vast gash in a block of flats that had collapsed on itself on being struck by a flying bomb were the Rescue men, stripped to the waist, the sweat wriggling down through the thick coating of dust on their sun-browned bodies. They were the Civil Defence Rescue units. Alongside them were specially-trained Rescue men from the Army, who had been called in. They were working tremendously, these men. I never saw men work so hard or intensely, except, perhaps, once in 1940, when I went to a Midlands iron foundry and half-naked men there laboured at the furnaces as if the entire war turned on them. Here men were saving life. Five people were still believed to be trapped.

The "incident"—a quaint word to describe a big bomb disaster on the edge of inner

London—had occurred shortly after daybreak. Seven had been taken out alive, one dead. It was now late afternoon. "Five more," said a man with a notebook in his hand. "We shall want the lights tonight, by the look of it." An officer took that up to be sure that the batteries of 300-watt flood lamps would be there. "Can't leave anything to chance," he remarked, "though there was a time when the public threatened us when we had dimmed headlights on a job like this."

It was living debris, an immense pile of it, dangerous stuff that would move if a wrong bit was extracted. Walls weighing scores of tons overhung the job. One looked tottery to me. "A tie-rod's keeping that up," I was told by a man with four-year stripes. "We'll have to risk it. We'd like to shore it up. Can't do it. Not time. We're cutting through here."

"How d'you know there's somebody in there ?" I asked.

"Information. You start these jobs by asking a lot of questions. It saves time. Ask wardens, anybody . . . But just a minute, old man. Shut up a bit."

Everything went dead silent. Shovellers, lorry men, everyone. Motors shut off. Men held their hands up at their shoulders, spreading out their fingers and shaking them for silence. Everyone held their breath, listening hard. One man bent down, putting his ear at the end of a pipe sticking out of the debris. A sweating labourer wagged a forefinger at a distant point of the debris. Was it a groan? I could not tell. Some slight movement of wood? "Tunneller, perhaps," my guide whispered. But nothing sure.

Then at it again . . . Round the other side at the entrance of the tunnel, scarcely enough to take a man, I thought, an armoured tube ran in. "He's in there with a mask on. Remote respiration control. Sounds as if he's sawing. That bloke'll get through anything."

I'd soon seen enough. You cannot watch this kind of thing for long, as you would gaze at a peacetime fire. "If I stop here I'll be wanting to help," I said, excusing myself. "Okay, mate," said my guide. "The public always feel like that. But except for clearing bits away you'd be in the way. I remember soldiers from a barracks who came to help. They worked like mad at loose roof timbers, attacked brickwork with crowbars, and piled the stuff on our chaps tunnelling into the basement. Skilled job this. Not for amateurs."

As we walked aside he told me. "You have to have expert knowledge of buildings and be trained," he said. "Tunnelling's almost an art. You might get in there and find yourself in a wardrobe. Knock the ends out and move it along with you, bit by bit, as a shield. Or go through a wall. I've known that. You've to know what you dare take out, what you must leave. All the time looking for a void.

"That's where they often are. Down comes a beam or the joists, leaving a trapped person in a triangular space. A void. You're trained for it in great dumps of debris, with live persons deliberately imprisoned underneath. They volunteer for it and get into the dump through a back door. Or are pinioned down and the stuff piled on. It's just like the real thing. You go in,

FLYING BOMB VICTIM, dug out from the wreckage of his home by heroic Civil Defence rescuers, receives first-aid attention. Scenes such as this became commonplace in London and Southern England in the summer of 1944.
Photo, Fox

tunnelling. Making frames as you go along. Why, we've even had competitions at it."

They are trained, too, to get people down from high floors; to convey casualties by human chain along tunnels; to make the essential preliminary reconnaissances by which a few minutes' delay saves hours. "Once knew a chap," said my guide, "who worked a kitchen table along as a frame and got people out. Last thing you do is to

start taking stuff from the top. Start at the lowest possible level and work into it. Or run a cutting through and then tunnel sideways. Tunnel upwards, too."

"What would you do if you met a gas-stove?" I asked.

"Go round it. Or through it! Metal bedstead's one of the worst things. Generally got to be cut. You can sometimes use a short-handled miner's pick in a tunnel or a New Zealand lumber jack. We have all the tools precisely arranged in a van, so that we can pick them out in the dark. We're really specialists, of course. Carpenters, plumbers, fitters, riggers, steel erectors, timber men, mattock men—from the building trades. Got a lot of teams in London from the country. They're keen, I tell you."

"What was your worst job?"

"Oh, I dunno. We once reached a woman sitting on a chair. She was pinned down at her head and we had to get the chair down to get her out. Cut its legs off to lower her. Then four fellows made a human chain to carry her out. One of my mates once reached a kid. Right in. 'Hello!' said the kid. 'Hello!' he said, 'You all right?' 'Yes,' said the kid, 'but I'm frightened.' Been in there two hours. Crawled out and got up and limped to the ambulance. Didn't want carrying. Only about ten, too. One of our fellows got a tunnel under a three-storey job and found a casualty pinned down. He had to amputate an arm under the direction of a doctor administering anaesthetic."

Two things he impressed upon me. "Tell people," he said, "that if they see some of our fellows walking up and down smoking fags and taking it easy, they're probably gassed and are being walked about to recover. And tell 'em to let their wardens know where their Morrisons are in the house and when they go away—even for a week-end. That'll save us risking our lives! Scores of us on this job in London have been killed. Hundreds seriously injured too." Somehow, I thought, there ought to be a Salute for Rescue. But my man was already back on his job. "Think we might get the N.F.S. floods here tonight, sir?" he was asking his officer.

OUR DIARY OF THE WAR

SEPTEMBER 13, Wednesday 1,838th day
Western Front.—Neufchateau, S.W. of Nancy, captured by 3rd Army. French troops of 3rd and 7th Armies linked up at Chatillon-sur-Seine.
Air.—Heavy attack by U.S. bombers on oil plants and aircraft factories in Germany, following night attacks by R.A.F. on Frankfort and Stuttgart. R.A.F. bombed Osnabruck by daylight.
Mediterranean.—Allied bombers attacked Oderthal and other oil plants in Poland and Silesia.
Russian Front.—Soviet troops captured Lomza, on R. Narew, near E. Prussia. Russian bombers attacked Budapest.
General.—Terms of armistice between Rumania and United Nations announced.

SEPTEMBER 14, Thursday 1,839th day
Western Front.—Allied troops in Belgium reached Leopold Canal. Dutch and U.S. forces freed Maastricht in Holland.
Russian Front.—Praga, suburb of Warsaw east of Vistula, captured by Soviet and Polish troops.
Baltic.—Germans attempting to land on island of Hogland repulsed by Finns.
Pacific.—Announced that 501 Japanese aircraft and 173 ships were destroyed in three days' air attacks on Philippines.
Home Front.—Continuous shelling of south-east coast area by German cross-Channel guns.

SEPTEMBER 15, Friday 1,840th day
Western Front.—U.S. troops broke through main Siegfried Line east of Aachen. Nancy liberated by F.F.I. and U.S. troops.
Air.—Kiel again attacked in force by R.A.F. at night. Lubeck and Berlin also bombed. Lancasters attacked German battleship Tirpitz off Norway with 12,000-lb. bombs.
Mediterranean.—Allied bombers attacked Athens airfields.
Pacific.—Allied forces landed on Peleliu, Palau Is., and on Morotai, N. of Halmahera.

SEPTEMBER 16, Saturday 1,841st day
Western Front.—Allies fighting in outskirts of Aachen. Modane, at western end of Mont Cenis tunnel, captured.

Air.—R.A.F. heavily bombed airfields in Holland and Germany at night.
Russian Front.—Soviet troops entered Sofia, capital of Bulgaria.

SEPTEMBER 17, Sunday 1,842nd day
Western Front.—1st Allied Airborne Army landed in Holland at Eindhoven, Nijmegen and Arnhem.
Russian Front.—Soviet Latvian offensive opened south-east of Riga.
Pacific.—Allied troops again landed in Palau group, on Angaur island.
Balkans.—Announced that Yugoslav Army of Liberation had freed central Dalmatian Islands.

SEPTEMBER 18, Monday 1,843rd day
Western Front.—Advanced armour of British 2nd Army made contact with airborne units in Holland.
Air.—Allied aircraft again bombed gun positions in Holland. At night R.A.F. made heavy attack on Bremerhaven.
Russian Front.—Soviet armies launched double offensive in Estonia.
Poland.—Large force of Allied bombers flew supplies to Warsaw and landed at Russian bases.
Pacific.—Allied Eastern Fleet and carrier-aircraft attacked rail centre at Sigli, Sumatra.

SEPTEMBER 19, Tuesday 1,844th day
Western Front.—Eindhoven in Allied hands. Resistance ceased at Brest.
Air.—U.S. bombers attacked railway and supply targets east of the Rhine. At night R.A.F. bombed Rheydt and Munchen-Gladbach.
General.—Armistice between Finland and United Nations signed in Moscow.

SEPTEMBER 20, Wednesday 1,845th day
Western Front.—Allied land and air forces linked up in Nijmegen area. Poles reached Scheldt on six-mile front.
Russian Front.—Soviet aircraft bombed Debrecen (Hungary) and Csop (Ruthenia).
Pacific.—First attacks by Allied carrier-aircraft on shipping and airfields in Manila area of Philippines.

SEPTEMBER 21, Thursday 1,846th day
Western Front.—Nijmegen cleared of the enemy. British 2nd Army infantry advanced towards Arnhem.
Air.—U.S. bombers attacked oil plant at Ludwigshafen, and rail yards at Mainz and Coblenz.
Italy.—Greek and Canadian troops of 8th Army captured Rimini.
Pacific.—Another heavy attack by U.S. carrier-aircraft on Manila shipping and

airfields; 40 ships sunk and 357 aircraft destroyed in two days.
SEPTEMBER 22, Friday 1,847th day
Western Front.—British 2nd Army continued to advance towards Arnhem despite enemy flank attacks. All organized resistance ceased in Boulogne. Allied troops captured Stolberg, E. of Aachen.
Russian Front.—Soviet troops stormed Tallinn, capital of Estonia.
Poland.—Units of Polish Home Army in Warsaw established contact with advanced Soviet units on west bank of Vistula.

SEPTEMBER 23, Saturday 1,848th day
Western Front.—Allied supply-corridor north of Eindhoven cut by enemy; some reinforcements crossed Rhine at Arnhem.
Air.—Gun emplacements on island of Walcheren bombed by Allied aircraft. At night R.A.F. made heavy attacks on Neuss, N.E. of Aachen, Munster and Bochum.
Russian Front.—Soviet troops occupied Estonian port of Pernau.
General.—Announced that all Swedish Baltic ports to be closed to foreign shipping from September 27.

SEPTEMBER 24, Sunday 1,849th day
Western Front.—Further attempts to reinforce Allied airborne troops on north bank of Rhine at Arnhem.
Russian Front.—Units of Soviet Baltic Fleet captured port of Baltiski, Estonia.

SEPTEMBER 25, Monday 1,850th day
Western Front.—British airborne troops at Arnhem withdrawn south across the Rhine at night.
Air.—More than 1,200 U.S. bombers attacked rail yards and oil plants behind Siegfried Line.
Russian Front.—In Estonia Soviet troops captured port of Haapsalu.
Balkans.—Cetinje, capital of Montenegro, captured by Yugoslav Army.
General.—Allied Command called on 12,000,000 foreign workers in Germany for active resistance.

SEPTEMBER 26, Tuesday 1,851st day
Western Front.—Allied salient from Eindhoven extended east to the Maas.
Air.—R.A.F. dropped 3,500 tons of bombs on Calais and Gris Nez.
Italy.—Allied troops crossed the Uso (Rubicon) north of Rimini.

★ *Flash-backs* ★

1939
September 17. Soviet troops entered Poland. Courageous sunk.

1940
September 15. Battle of Britain at climax; 185 German aircraft shot down.
September 17. City of Benares, taking children to Canada, sunk by U-boat.

1941
September 16. Germans claimed to be in Leningrad suburbs.

September 21. Russians evacuated Kiev after 45 days' fight.

1942
September 16. Germans fighting in outskirts of Stalingrad.
September 23. Antananarivo, Madagascar, captured by British.

1943
September 14. French Commandos landed on island of Corsica.
September 16. Australians captured Lae, in New Guinea.
September 25. Smolensk captured by Red Army.

THE WAR IN THE AIR

by Capt. Norman Macmillan, M.C., A.F.C.

THE strategic purpose of the 1st Allied Airborne Army has been well demonstrated in its employment in Holland. The first landings were made from noon on Sunday, September 17, 1944, at Nijmegen, Eindhoven and Arnhem, to secure the vital crossings of the water-belt of the Meuse and the Rhine delta, to assist the advance of Field-Marshal Montgomery's army group over this difficult country. The day's operations involved almost 1,500 transport aircraft and several hundred gliders. (See story in p. 345, and illus. p. 349.)

Time and again during this war—in the German invasion of France, in the jumps of the Eighth Army across the North African desert, in the German and Russian drives across the Steppes—it was evident that the maximum forward surge of an armoured and mechanized army is today in the neighbourhood of 400 miles. When this distance has been covered it is necessary to halt, to obtain supplies in the forward areas, and to regroup those units which have become separated into an ordered, integrated army that is once more able to break down the resistance which time has given the enemy opportunity to organize. This was the position which Field-Marshal Montgomery's army group appeared to have reached when the Allied Airborne Army of British, American and Polish troops literally leapt into the battle zone ahead of the ground army.

It seems to have been taken for granted by the general public (so accustomed has it become to miracles of organization) that the Airborne Army should have left England, to be fighting in Holland two hours later. Yet this was no less than a third invasion of Europe from the west. The air column of troop transports, tugs and gliders took two hours to pass over the English coast, stretching for 300 miles across the sky, so that the invasion was accomplished at a speed of 150 m.p.h.

THIS is about the same speed as that of the Junkers 52 air-transports used by the Germans which have fallen easily in large numbers to British, American and Russian fighter pilots. The German attempt to reinforce Tunisia in the later stages of that campaign brought disaster to convoy after convoy of these aircraft. Their greatest success was in Crete in 1941, when there was almost no fighter opposition. How different is the position in reverse today. We have larger airborne forces than the Germans possessed. We fly them to battle in greater numbers in a single convoy. But the Luftwaffe is powerless to interfere.

The Airborne Army convoy flying to Holland was protected by a huge escort of fighters, which formed a protective arch above the columns of flying fighting men, and the Luftwaffe was unable to put any aircraft into the air to attack the Allied aircraft during the landings. In advance of the operation, Allied fighters and bombers flying by day and night crushed ground opposition by destroying more than 100 enemy flak positions within the operational area.

ON the next day, almost as many aircraft and gliders flew reinforcements and supplies to the fighting units of the 1st Airborne Army. Allied losses in the two days were only two per cent. The weather was ideal for the landing of this greatest air invasion in history, with little wind to make the drops hazardous for the parachutists, and with clear vision for the glider pilots. On the second day Eindhoven was taken, the first large Dutch town to be freed from the Germans. By Thursday 11,500 sorties had been flown and operations were continuing.

ARMOUR Co-operated with the Airborne Troops

The airborne landings and the tank thrust of the ground army were co-ordinated. While the airborne troops held key-points in a corridor running north-north-eastwards, the armour swept towards them, crossing undamaged bridges at St. Oedenrode, Vechel and Grave. On Thursday, September 21, British tanks crossed the Rhine at Nijmegen (see illus. p. 325) and thrust on towards Arnhem, nodal point of the last river barrier whose possession was being bitterly contested between the German defenders and the airborne invaders. The crossing of the River Lek (arm of the Rhine) there would have taken the most northerly army of the Western invasion forces to the plains that run eastward to Berlin and south-eastward to the heart of the Ruhr at Essen ; but this crossing failed, and the remainder, some 2,000 men, of the British 1st Airborne Division were withdrawn south across the Lek on the night following Monday, September 25.

Everywhere the air activity of the Allies rises to fresh endeavours. Polish parachute commandos were dropped on Warsaw on September 19 by bombers. Fortresses dropped supplies to the Polish defenders of Warsaw in daylight and flew on to alight in Russia. While the Canadians were battling into Boulogne the R.A.F. dropped 3,500 tons of bombs on the German defences in the city. Cities ahead of the American

AIR CHIEF MARSHAL SIR A. TEDDER, Deputy Supreme Cmdr. Allied Expeditionary Force (right), discussed plans with Lieut.-Gen. F. A. M. Browning, C.B., D.S.O., Deputy Cmdr. 1st Allied Airborne Army, before the start of the invasion of Holland. *Photo, British Official*

armies were heavily bombed. The hopeless plight of the Luftwaffe is made clear by the official statement that only 200 German aircraft were put into the air against 5,000 Allied planes on D-Day. The Red Air Force has raided Budapest and other targets in Hungary. The growing effect of the Balkan debacle is followed by reports of German withdrawals from Crete and Greece.

The lost reverse side of the picture was found by U.S. troops, advancing through Brittany, in German guides printed for German parachute troops who were to have invaded South-West England. Marked " For Service Use Only," the guides contained photographs taken by spies before the war, including the Truro, St. Austell, Newquay, Ponsanooth viaducts and the Brunel Saltash-bridge across the Tamar. Many of these photographs, taken for an invasion that never came off, were probably filmed by cadets of the German training battleship Schleswig-Holstein which visited south-west England in 1938 and who freely roamed the countryside with cameras. Ribbentrop, when Ambassador, made a close study of Cornwall.

For the U.S. Navy is reported the mightiest Sea-Air Force, with 100 aircraft carriers by the end of this year. It looks as though Americans will possess the most powerful surface and air-cover Navy in the world.

ON September 15 Allied forces landed in Palau and Halmahera islands, both spearheads for the Philippines, fewer than 500 miles distant. In Peleliu airfield in the Palaus, U.S. Marines captured the finest airfield in the Western Carolines, but fierce fighting continued on the island where the Japanese garrison resisted strongly. On September 17, U.S. troops landed on Anguar, most southerly island of the Palaus. The rocket weapon is coming more and more into use ; 10,000 were used against the Japanese in the Carolines. This British invention was freely handed to the Americans for their war use.

The Philippines have come in for heavier bombings, especially Davao, in Mindanao, almost due west of Peleliu and due north of Halmahera in the Moluccas. Manila, capital of the Philippines, was attacked by a carrier-borne force which destroyed 250 Japanese aircraft and several ships. On September 18 British carrier-borne forces heavily damaged Sigli railway repair and maintenance centre in Sumatra ; Barracudas dropped heavy bombs under the protection of Corsair fighters ; one aircraft was lost in this operation, which formed part of a softening-up programme in Sumatra and the East Indies from the west.

DROPPING SUPPLIES BY PARACHUTE, B.24 Liberators of the U.S. 8th Army Air Force swooped over the Dutch countryside, as troops of the 1st Allied Airborne Army waited below for vital supplies and equipment. The landscape was strewn with the gliders and discarded parachutes of our men who had landed in the rear of the enemy. PAGE 348 *Photo, U.S. Official*

1st Allied Airborne Army Descends on Holland

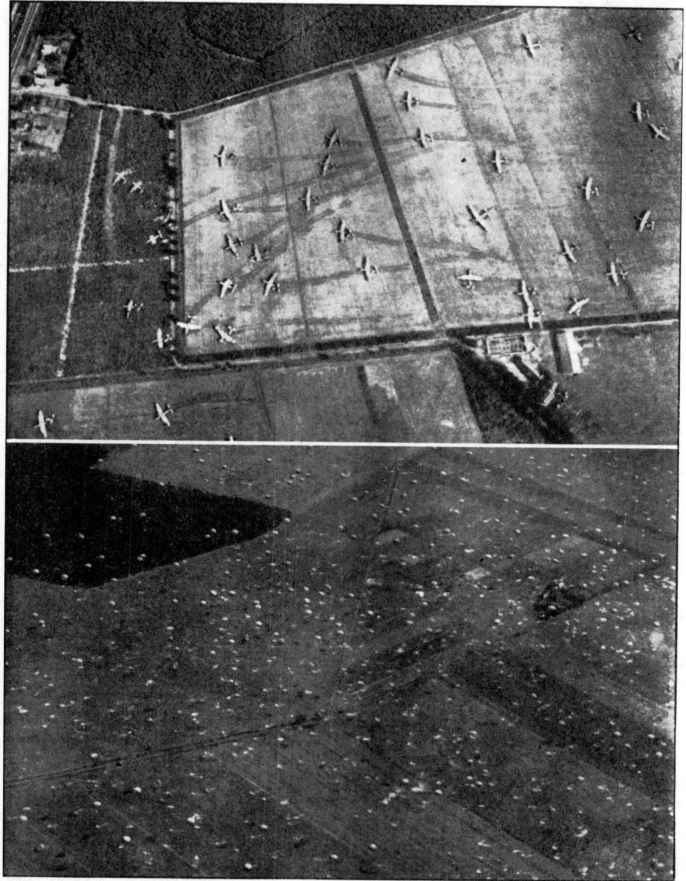

ENGULFING THE DUTCH LANDSCAPE, hundreds of Allied parachute troops floated to earth on September 17, 1944 (bottom). Following these came the gliders : each is seen at the end of a skid-track made in landing (top). This mighty armada of troop transports, glider-tugs and gliders swept out from England, over the North Sea and the water-barriers of Holland to land in the enemy rear. Later, land forces of the British 2nd Army linked up with the airborne troops at Eindhoven and Nijmegen. See story in p. 345.

Photos. British Official

Exploits of Our Special Air Service

Col. D. STIRLING wearing the regimental badge of the S.A.S., of which he was co-founder and first commanding officer.

DRAMATIC secret of the war, the existence of a unit of British parachutists who penetrate enemy territory, raid airfields, destroy planes on the ground, upset communications and ambush transport columns, was revealed when the story of the Special Air Service (S.A.S.) was officially released after the liberation of Paris. It was the S.A.S., which had been in action first in Africa and later in Italy, that was largely responsible for the swift Allied advance in France that thrilled and astonished the world. These small groups of specialists caused chaos and panic deep behind the enemy lines and disorganized resistance long before the break-through of the main Allied armies.

The S.A.S. was created by two young officers, Lt. (later Col.) David Stirling of the Scots Guards and Commandos, and Lt. Jock Lewis of the Welsh Guards and Commandos. Their theory was that small groups of hand-picked specialists could operate with great effect behind enemy lines, specially to deal with the menace of the Me.109s which were able to harass unchecked convoys and troops in the darkest days of the African campaign.

Those two officers were given permission to start a school in the desert, called "Stirling's Rest Camp," where the first 73 volunteers from the 8th and 11th Commandos were put through a training devised by Lt. Lewis which applied to officers and men alike. Each recruit had to be a parachutist; he had to be an expert in the use of small arms and in close combat, and he had to be tough enough to endure a 100-mile march with a heavy pack.

The Long Range Desert Group

The first operation of the S.A.S. in Africa was carried out on November 18, 1941, in a 30 m.p.h. wind against a German aerodrome; it ended in disaster and the S.A.S. lost about half of their numbers. The second attempt was in December 1941, when men of the S.A.S. flew to Galio, 90 miles south of Benghazi, surrounded the aerodromes and attacked aircraft and Luftwaffe personnel with success beyond their most ambitious dreams. They were taken close to their objectives by the Long Range Desert Group with whom henceforth they were to collaborate closely. The success of those marauding parties increased with experience. In 1942 they tried the experiment of travelling in jeeps, each mounted with two twin-sets of Vickers aerial M.G.s and one single Vickers. As a result the jeep was officially adopted as ideal for S.A.S. work. Fed and equipped by secret Long Range Desert Group patrols, S.A.S. would stay behind the German lines, sometimes for two months at a time, causing havoc among enemy military concentrations.

By September 1942 the unit, still shrouded in secrecy, had grown to 300 strong. Except for 30 Frenchmen it was entirely British, with a ratio of officers to men of about 1 to 10. During the famous 8th Army push, the S.A.S. were operating behind the German lines all the way; they were the first

S.A.S. PATROL set off cheerfully on a hundred-miles' desert trek to rejoin their lines. Men of this special unit, attached to the 8th Army, were the first to establish contact with the 1st Army in Tunisia.

to effect the link-up of the 1st and 8th Armies in the last stages of the Tunisian campaign. It was during this operation that Col. Stirling was captured. As Lieut. Lewis had been killed in an earlier raid, Lieut.-Col. R. B. Mayne now took command of the unit.

His task was to start the invasion of Sicily and to eliminate the coastal batteries; S.A.S. destroyed four of them and took over 500 prisoners. Four days later they were landed farther up the coast to storm Fort Augusta, and after another re-embarkation made a new landing at Bagnara, where they took the first German prisoners of the campaign.

The effectiveness of these operations called for expansion, and early in 1943 further units of the S.A.S. were formed from the nucleus of a small force which had been used to raid the coast of France. Operations were undertaken in North Africa and Sicily, but the real chance came when Italy was invaded. Now Col. Stirling's ideas came into full effect in the mountainous country.

The first task of the detachment was to act as reconnaissance for the Airborne Division which landed at Taranto, and at Termoli they helped a Special Reserve Brigade to fend off the first serious German counter-attack. During the advance, the emphasis on initiative and independence which marked the training of the S.A.S. paid high dividends. Led by a young cavalry officer who had escaped from Greece, they harried the enemy ceaselessly. A member of the expedition described their progress as a stalking match which was won by the quickest man on the draw.

They Commandeered a Train

S.A.S. parties had special success in a kind of Robin Hood system of operations against the German and Italian Fascists. They captured a Carabinieri barracks, and commandeered one of the King of Italy's cars and 3,000 gallons of petrol. On another occasion they surprised a German unit preparing an ambush for them. It so happened that the ambush was ambushed! A French Squadron commandeered an Italian train and drove it through enemy country to a concentration camp where they captured the guards, released the prisoners and brought the whole party, including the Italian colonel commandant, back by train.

Another exploit was the destruction of an important railway bridge. After being landed by the Royal Navy, a small S.A.S. party mined the bridge and then lured the carabinieri, who should have been guarding it, on to it just in time for the bridge to be blown up—together with the guards. During many of these operations the S.A.S. received valuable help from the Italian Navy.

Recently a SHAEF communiqué referred for the first time to the S.A.S. by name and to the manner of work they were doing behind enemy lines in France. But not until the war is over will it be possible to do full justice to their exploits; these stories will add honour to their regimental badge, a winged dagger bearing the words, "Who Dares Wins."

IN THE ENEMY'S REAR during the 8th Army's push through Libya, S.A.S. men continually harassed the coastal road from Tripoli to Sart. Riding in jeeps, they sometimes adopted the head-dress worn by Arabs (above). A French parachutist is seen handing cigarettes to Arab soldiers of the Tunisian Army (centre).

Photos, British Official

I HARDLY pick up a paper or review without finding suggestions as to what should be done with Germany when fighting stops in Europe. But there may be no formal ending of the War. No body of Germans with whom we could negotiate is yet in sight. The Nazis might attempt to carry on sporadic guerilla warfare, and it would take some time to exterminate them. But that's the idea of a pessimistic friend of mine, it's not my idea. But in that case Germans would no doubt be fighting against one another in civil conflict. What should we be doing in the meantime? Presumably trying to establish some sort of stable government in Germany. It will be necessary, Mr. Pethick-Lawrence has been saying, to "find a substitute for the whole Nazi structure, which extended from the judges to the teachers, the typists and the messengers." For this we shall have to rely on Germans "whose record would justify their employment." How difficult this will be is shown by the eagerness of people in the towns of the Reich already occupied by Allied troops to explain that they never had any use for Hitler or Nazism and will be very glad to see the last of them. Would you trust such assurances? Would you believe what those people said? I see that Montgomery still stands by his forecast that the War will end this year, but puts the date nearer Christmas than Patton, who is for October 31. Montgomery, most inspiring of all our great soldiers, has never let us down in achievement or in judgement of events, but after Arnhem, even he sounds optimistic to me now!

NEVER has there been a war which devastated so many places familiar to very large numbers of the people who follow its course on the map. As soon as the invasion of Europe had started names began to be mentioned which many of us knew as those of pleasant little seaside places on the Normandy coast, simple and cheap and much frequented by Parisians because they were only a short distance away, and inland towns that tourists know well, such as Caen and Avranches. Then came Mont St. Michel and Brittany. Next, the Riviera came into the picture—St. Raphael, Cannes, Nice, Mentone. Then Belgium, which for long has been a favourite holiday ground for British travellers who do not want to travel far. Bruges, Antwerp, Brussels, Ostend, the Ardennes awakened memories of delightful trips like that which Thackeray described in one of his Roundabout Papers. And then Aix-en-Chapelle, Germanized into the ugly name Aachen, and Cologne, where so many of us have gazed at the Cathedral and the Rhine and bought the original Eau de Cologne at the shop *gegenüber dem Julichsplatz*. Is it still there, I wonder?

HOW important it may be in coming years to attract visitors to our country is fortunately being realized. Mr. Ernest Bevin dwelt on it in his speeches as the Catering Act, as this went through the House of Commons. The Government is now being asked to appoint "an official national tourist organization." At Glasgow a school for future hotel managers has been opened, and another is to follow in London. But, of course, the best way to learn hotel-management is to go in at the bottom and pass through all branches of it. Swiss and German hoteliers used to send their sons round to learn the trade in this way. They knew every aspect of the job and all its most intimate details, from dish-washing to managing a large staff and planning meals. British hotels are, as a rule, badly-managed because so many of them are under the rule of men or women without any training at all. Unless we alter this—"reform it altogether,"

as Hamlet says—we shall not succeed in persuading tourist agencies to send us the visitors we shall need.

WHY shall we need them more than we have done in the past? Because we must have something fresh to exchange for all the foods and other commodities we want from other lands. Our exports which paid for these used to be mainly cotton and woollen goods, coal, iron, steel and motors. But now so many nations that took these things from us are producing them within their own borders. Our largest export in the years just before this war was machinery, which enabled the purchasers to make at home all sorts of articles they once bought from us. Another help to us in paying for our imports used to be the interest on our very large foreign investments. This interest, paid in the currency of the countries which owed it, was turned into fruit or wheat or maize or timber (to take a few examples), and these cargoes were sent here in exchange for our coal or cotton pieces or motors or iron and steel. Now those investments have been heavily reduced, and also the shipping and banking services we rendered to the rest of the world have shrunk. So we must look elsewhere— and tourist traffic would be a great help.

"AS drunk as goats." Thus an American officer described some Germans who were captured in a state of inebriety. Why goats? I am sure goats do not get drunk. They are, like all animals, abstemious, not eating more than they require, not needing stimulants to buck them up. I have often thought we are unfair to many animals when

ADMIRAL SIR W. H. COWAN, K.C.B., M.V.O., 73 years of age, was awarded a Bar to his D.S.O., it was announced on Sept. 4, 1944. As Commando Liaison Officer, he took part in a reconnaissance raid on Mt. Ornito, Italy, and rescued a wounded colonel under fire. PAGE 351 *Photo, News Chronicle*

we compare human beings with them. Why "sick as a cat"? Why "dirty dog!" as a term of abuse? Why call anyone who is greedy or unclean in person a pig? Pigs prefer to live in clean sties, and, if fed regularly, show no indecent rapture over their food. "Brave as a lion" is complimentary, but untrue. Lions are not courageous by nature. "Timid as a mouse" suggests quite wrongly that mice are more nervy than other very small beasts. "Stupid as a hen" may seem justified, if you have had occasion, as I have, to study the habits of hens. But, after all, they do lay fresh eggs. Isn't the stupidity rather on the part of the officials who prevent our getting them fresh? I live near a farm which has to send its eggs away somewhere —nobody knows their destination, but they are sure to be stale when they get there— and I have to put up with stale ones from some other part of the country.

"THOSE Germans certainly didn't get drunk on British beer!" a soldier friend of mine said bitterly when he heard about them. Complaints of the weakness of our national brew reach me from all sides. Dilution is admitted. It is unavoidable if the vastly increased demand for beer is to be met. The brewers get the same quantities of materials as they did before, but owing to (1) the scarcity of whisky and wines and (2) the fact that people have more money to spend and little else to spend it on, the increase this year in the number of barrels consumed is round about a million. That tells its own story. The best beer is made by local firms which do not send it out of their own area. They can keep up a fairly high standard and supply all who want it. What goes to the troops and the Navy and Air Force is specially brewed in order that it may keep. It is possibly stronger than your "local" can offer.

I FIND it strange that anyone should think of suggesting that horses should once more be used on a large scale in war. Some seem to want cavalry regiments to be mounted again instead of being packed into tanks and armoured cars. They have evidently never seen a battlefield in days when horses were ridden by cavalrymen and harnessed to guns and artillery supply carts. Never have the horrors of war been so burned into my imagination as they were by the sight of the poor creatures rolling in agony or lying exhausted while life drained slowly from them, or galloping up and down in a frenzy of fear and pain. It is one of the advantages of mechanized warfare that we do not now force these beautiful and highly-strung animals to undergo torture and misery for our benefit. Return to that system would be barbarous. It is no more than a wishful dream in the heads of people who would like to bring back cavalry because of its appearance and romantic associations.

I HEARD some indignant comments on the result of a quiz among soldiers as to the most eminent women in Britain. It appears the only eminent woman most of the soldiers could think of was Jane of the Daily Mirror. The indignant commentators had never heard of this lady. I was able to inform them that she appears daily in a strip cartoon in various stages of undress. I confess it never occurred to me that she could be of interest to grown men. However, it is now quite evident that she is, and I really do not see why any fuss should be made about it. Some of us prefer looking at the Venus of Milo or Botticelli's Primavera, but "everyone to his taste," and there is nothing new in the discovery that the great majority of men and women are blind to beauty and easily caught by the merely showy or the commonplace. I ventured to inquire of the indignant ones if they had ever done anything calculated to improve the taste of the masses. They looked down their noses and one muttered, "Can't be improved." To which I answered, "Then why worry?"

Monty the Conqueror at Historic Vimy Ridge

THE CANADIAN WAR MEMORIAL on Vimy Ridge, unveiled by King Edward VIII on July 26, 1936, was visited in early September 1944 by Field-Marshal Montgomery shortly after our men had swept beyond in the great dash to Belgium. The leader of the victorious 21st Army Group (British 2nd Army and Canadian 1st) is in reflective mood as he pauses on the steps of this impressive Memorial, north-east of Arras, which commemorates the heroic spirit of our kinsmen who fought and fell at the historic battlefield in the 1914-18 war.

Photo, British Official

Printed in England and published every alternate Friday by the Proprietors THE AMALGAMATED PRESS, LTD., The Fleetway House, Farringdon Street, London, E.C.4. Registered for transmission by Canadian Magazine Post. Sole Agents for Australia and New Zealand : Messrs. Gordon & Gotch, Ltd. ; and for South Africa : Central News Agency, Ltd.—October 13, 1944. S.S. *Editorial Address*: JOHN CARPENTER HOUSE, WHITEFRIARS, LONDON, E.C.4.

Vol 8 # The War Illustrated N° 192

SIXPENCE

Edited by Sir John Hammerton

OCTOBER 27, 1944

CANADIANS AT THE MENIN GATE, following the liberation of Ypres on September 7, 1944, paid their tribute to the memory of 55,000 officers and men whose names are inscribed upon the Memorial. Unveiled on July 24, 1927, the Menin Gate Memorial was erected in honour of " the Armies of the British Empire who stood here from 1914-18 and to those of their dead who have no known graves." Through the arch is seen the tower of the rebuilt Ypres Cloth Hall.

Photo, Associated Press

NO. 193 WILL BE PUBLISHED FRIDAY, NOVEMBER 10

Home Front-Line Tour With Our Roving Camera

SEA FORTS OF CONCRETE AND STEEL built to guard the Thames Estuary from enemy mine-laying aircraft consist of circular towers each mounted on four concrete legs rising from the river bed, and connected by bridges. Six of these grouped towers carry A.A. guns ; the seventh is a control tower. They are linked to the land by telephone, and manned by R.A. and other specialists.

DOVER'S ORDEAL ENDED with the surrender of Calais on October 1, 1944. In the area of Britain's " front-line town " 2,226 shells fell during four years' bombardment which began on August 12, 1940. Townsfolk emerged from their cave shelters to join in the celebrations of " liberation day." See also page 382.

LONDON'S mainline stations recently reverted to a pre-war lighting standard. Paddington (above) led the way on October 2, 1944, when platforms and staircases were brilliantly illuminated for the first time since the beginning of the war. The majority of the capital's termini subsequently adopted the new lighting system—estimated at five times the war-lamp strength.

BRITISH JET PLANES were used with great success against the flying bombs. Constructed by the Gloster Aircraft Co., this aircraft (left) was the first of its type to be propelled by a turbine engine jet, and was first flown in 1941. See also page 380.

Photos, British Official; Fox, Planet News, Topical Press

THE BATTLE FRONTS

by Maj.-Gen. Sir Charles Gwynn, K.C.B., D.S.O.

THE airborne landing in Holland admittedly failed to achieve its object completely, but it accomplished enough to have made the heavy sacrifices entailed more than worth while, although inevitably the losses had in the main to be borne by one gallant division. We now know how nearly we came to complete success, and but for the weather it probably would have been achieved. Weather delayed and circumscribed the movement of the British 2nd Army's supporting force ; it limited the amount of air support which could be given both to the force landed and to the 2nd Army's thrust ; it was one of the reasons why the landing of the second wave of the Arnhem Division was delayed for nearly twelve hours ; and it greatly interfered with the delivery of food and munitions by air (see pages 366-370).

Those were all great handicaps which could not have been foreseen, though they tend to show that even in its present state of development air power is so sensitive to weather that plans must take into consideration what course should be pursued if air co-operation relied on fails to materialize. In this case, of course, there was no alternative but to carry through plans with what co-operation could be given ; but in other cases postponement or modification of plans, requiring quick decisions, may be advisable, and the decision is easier to make if the situation which has arisen has been envisaged as a possibility beforehand.

ALLIED Pressure Maintained with Utmost Intensity

The whole enterprise afforded a complete illustration of the potentialities and limitations of airborne forces which should be generally recognized. The failure at Arnhem illustrated their limitations ; but equally the capture of the great Nijmegen bridge, the importance of which is immense, proved their potentialities. By no other means is it conceivable that the bridge could have been captured intact, and had it been destroyed the enemy would have been left in possession of one of the strongest defence positions on his whole front.

Since the failure at Arnhem there has been hard fighting of a localized character, induced partly by the enemy's desperate attempts to retrieve a dangerous situation and by the Allied operations to improve their position both defensively and offensively. It would, I think, be incorrect to believe that the enemy has succeeded in stabilizing the situation because no large scale offensive has been launched since the enemy began to make a determined stand. There has been only a pause, such as must always be expected when stiff opposition is at last encountered after a long advance.

It has, in fact, been surprising, considering the length of communications, the damage caused to railways by air attacks and the enemy's demolitions of port facilities, that pressure has been maintained with such intensity, and that such considerable operations as the capture of Brest, Le Havre, Boulogne and Calais have been carried through concurrently. The pause may be of considerable duration before the offensive is renewed on a maximum scale, but there is no reason to suppose it will be so prolonged as to cause its postponement till after the winter. It is obviously desirable to give the enemy no respite and there is every indication that General Eisenhower is preparing for a major effort, though at what points he may strike is, of course, his secret.

The 1st U.S. Army's attack on the Siegfried line north of Aachen, though it has

considerable weight, is evidently not the big thing but rather a preliminary attack which may increase the enemy's uncertainty as to how best to dispose his reserves. I think we may be certain that when he is ready General Eisenhower will aim at achieving a complete disruption of the German front, and will be prepared to exploit success to the utmost and with little regard to seasonal conditions.

THERE is perhaps a tendency to exaggerate the necessity of suspending operations in the late autumn or winter based very largely on Passchendaele experience. The Russians have shown how much can be accomplished even in a particularly wet, unfavourable winter. Furthermore, it must be remembered that the ground surface and roads have not been cut up, as they were in the last war, by prolonged fighting and heavy military traffic, and so long as the front does not become stablized 1917 conditions will not

recur. Troops undoubtedly may suffer great hardships, but they are for the most part fresh and in good physical condition to withstand them. Armour could in most places operate and, with immensely better roads, maintenance of supplies should not present the difficulties encountered during the final advance in 1918, especially as mechanized transport is now immeasurably more efficient and available in vastly increased numbers.

COULD a Counter-Offensive Be Staged in the West ?

On the assumption that the Germans may be able to stabilize the front and thus secure a respite, I have seen it suggested that they may still hope to stage a counter-offensive in the west when spring comes. Those who read the article in question, and did not attach sufficient weight to the writer's final conclusion that any such attempt was bound to fail, may have found the premises of his discussion somewhat alarming. To stage a counter-offensive of any weight it would obviously be necessary to build up a substantial reserve during the winter, fully organized and equipped. To support the suggestion it was therefore assumed that the Germans may succeed in withdrawing their troops from Finland, thus setting free those

in Norway to join the reserve, that they may also be able to withdraw their armies from the Baltic States, from the Balkans, from Italy and from Hungary and possibly also some elements from the main eastern front.

No doubt, if all that were successfully accomplished, though it is a very wide assumption, a numerically large force might be formed. But it would certainly have to be very extensively re-equipped and reorganized, a process which would take a considerable time after the troops had reached home territory. Moreover, obviously such withdrawals would release very large Allied forces to increase the pressure on Germany's defensive fronts, now none too strongly held. It is therefore probable that a considerable part of such troops as became available would be required to reinforce them.

Apart from such considerations I do not think that the Germans, after their disastrous experience in the Kursk salient in July 1943 are at all likely to embark on another gambling counter-offensive, especially as they have acquired a healthy respect for the quality of British and American troops and their commanders. I cannot help feeling

THREE MAIN ALLIED THRUSTS were in progress on the Western Front at the beginning of October 1944. North of the Antwerp-Turnhout Canal the 1st Canadian Army linked with the British 2nd Army, while General Dempsey's troops advanced to within two miles of Arnhem. U.S. 1st Army tanks broke through the Siegfried Line north of Aachen and reached the Cologne Plain. This map shows the positions of the Allied lines on October 5. *By courtesy of The Times*

that the author of the suggestion was amusing himself by constructing a bogy.

I am much more impressed by the difficulties which will be encountered, should Himmler succeed in organizing ruthless partisan warfare, when the Allies, as I am convinced they will, penetrate deep into Germany. Although I do not believe that the majority of the Reichswehr, in particular its officers, would take much part in such activities yet no doubt the young fanatical elements in the S.S. formations provide particularly good material for Himmler's purpose. The success of any form of guerilla warfare, however, depends on the sympathy, and at times the active co-operation, of the ordinary population. It is possible, or even probable, that no large section of the German people would willingly give such assistance, but they would certainly be subject to terrorization if they did not. Should the situation arise it will undoubtedly have to be dealt with firmly by the occupying troops and, if possible, before the partisans are well organized and have learnt how to operate most effectively. The British Army has had considerable experience of resistance in this form, and one of the chief lessons it has learnt is the danger of not taking it seriously enough, and of not being permitted to act promptly when it is first encountered.

Sherwood Rangers Our First Troops in Germany

FIRST BRITISH TROOPS TO ENTER THE REICH were the Sherwood Rangers (Notts Yeomanry), a mechanized cavalry unit. On Sept. 24, 1944, they crossed the German border at the village of Beek, 4 miles S.E. of Nijmegen. Against a background of wrecked German houses a conference was held on a Sherman (1), during the arrival of Honey Recce tanks, the first of which crosses the border (4). At the frontier post (2), a Ranger is ready to cover his comrades. Dutch women greeted our men (3) at a cafe displaying the white flag.

Photos, British Official

Dempsey's Men in the Corridor Through Holland

WIDENING THE EINDHOVEN-NIJMEGEN CORRIDOR, General Dempsey's forces crossed the Bar-le-Duc canal at Someren, south-east of Eindhoven, on September 22, 1944, and three days later reached Deurne, in the direction of the German frontier. During the advance the village of Asten was captured : a 2nd Army infantryman watches one of our tanks passing down a burning street (1). Bomb-wrecked vehicles at Eindhoven (2), and on the road to Arnhem (3), testified to the effectiveness of Allied bombing.

PAGE 357
Photos, British Official : British Newspaper Pool

ONE OF BRITAIN'S 'SECRET WEAPONS,' whose devastating fire-power has now been revealed to the enemy in full, is the Landing Craft Tank (Rocket), seen in action above. A large number of rockets can be fired in 30 seconds, and at considerable range. The effect of these rockets falling in a small area is such that the fire from one craft is roughly equivalent to the fire of 30 regiments of artillery or 30 cruisers each mounting twelve 6-in. guns, when related to the time over which the bombardment takes place.
Photo, Canadian Official

THE WAR AT SEA

by Francis E. McMurtrie

IN a recent speech Mr. Churchill referred to " a further measure of modernization and tropicalization " which our battleships have undergone in readiness for service in the Far East. This process of modernization is believed to have included : (a) the fitting of the latest type of radar (radio-location gear) ; (b) the mounting of much additional armament.

Similar extensions of armament and other equipment have been effected in H.M. ships of almost every category. Apart from such major improvements, concerned mainly with the fighting efficiency of our warships, various minor alterations have been made which affect living conditions in cabins and on the mess decks. This war has driven home the lesson that the well-being of Service personnel must be looked after if the best results are to be secured ; and in a broadcast at the end of last month Admiral Sir James Somerville referred feelingly to the discomforts which are, unfortunately, inseparable from tropical warfare.

IN addition to its responsibility for radar, radio and other " gadgets," the Royal Naval Scientific Service (the establishment of which was described in page 294) is closely concerned in the improvement of living conditions afloat. Control of humidity and additional ventilation are two of the chief aims. In " darkening ship "—the naval equivalent of the black-out—difficulties are aggravated. A man who feels a draught on turning into his hammock is very apt to put his sock into the ventilator. Indirect control of ventilation is the solution for this sort of difficulty.

For the benefit of men working under tropical conditions in a closed compartment, such as a wireless cabinet, it is covered in special material which does not absorb the sun's rays. In the Arctic the object instead is to keep people warm. Certain ships have been specially designed for service in high latitudes, but in others it has been necessary to insulate living accommodation to maintain a habitable temperature.

Not only habitability, but the problem of making it easier for men to perform mechanical operations of every kind is engaging the attention of the R.N.S.S. All points in the design of mechanism are watched carefully, and the positions of starting handles, switches, etc., arranged so that they can be got at easily. Power aid is brought in wherever necessary to enable a man to do things without the exertion of undue force. This, of course, is not a novel idea; it is embodied in the steering engine, and is encountered ashore in the use of electricity to assist the operation of levers in railway signal boxes and of points at a rail crossing. In the Royal Navy a wide field for such improvements has been found. Results have been gratifying, proving that to enable a man to do his job in greater comfort is to add to his efficiency.

SOVIET Submarine Successes Against German Transports

What has become of the German fleet in the Baltic ? According to Swedish reports little has been seen of it for some considerable time, beyond fleeting glimpses of a couple of ships, believed to be the 10,000-ton cruisers Prinz Eugen and Admiral Hipper. Yet, excluding the dismantled battleship Gneisenau, the aircraft carrier Graf Zeppelin and the cruiser Seydlitz, both incomplete, there are believed to be eight other warships of importance in German Baltic ports. These are the " pocket battleships " Lützow and Admiral Scheer, the coast defence ships Schlesien and Schleswig-Holstein, and the cruisers Nürnberg, Leipzig, Köln and Emden.

It is extraordinary that more use has not been made of these ships in resisting the Russian advance through Estonia and Latvia. Quite a number of enemy transports—certainly not less than six, and probably over a dozen—seem to have been sunk or obliged to beach themselves as the result of persistent attacks by Soviet submarines, motor-torpedo-boats and aircraft. No attempt appears to have been made to provide escorts of sufficient strength to withstand these attacks.

Nor does the German Navy seem to have figured in the struggle to retain the important islands at the mouth of the Gulf of Riga— Oesel, Dagö, etc. With these islands in their possession, the Russians have not only isolated Riga but have obtained complete control of the approaches to the Gulf of Finland, from which their fleet is now free to emerge. Its exact composition is doubtful, but Swedish sources consider that the old battleship Oktiabrskaya Revolutia and two heavy cruisers (one of them the ex-German Petropavlovsk) are certainly in seaworthy condition. Materials may not have been available for completion of repairs to the old battleship Marat.

EVIDENTLY the Russians felt sufficiently confident of German impotence at sea, to ignore the risk involved in landing troops in the Aland Islands, the strategic value of which had given rise to earlier reports of a German garrison having been installed there. There are at least three possible explanations of the absence of the German fleet from the scene of such important operations. One is that it has been resolved to husband all remaining naval resources for the defence of purely German territories such as East Prussia and Pomerania, now in imminent danger. Another is that reserves of naval personnel have been depleted by drafts made to man the defences of the Eastern and Western fronts, threatened by the advancing Allied armies. A third is that the vast number of mines laid in enemy waters in the Baltic by the Royal Air Force has caused the disablement of the majority of German heavy warships just when their services are most urgently needed. It may be that the truth will be found to include elements of all three explanations.

GREEK Islands Reoccupied by R.N. Landing Parties

In the Aegean the Royal Navy has recently been busy cutting the last lines of communication between the German-held islands and the mainland of Greece. Samos, Levitha and Cythera were amongst the first islands to be reoccupied, generally by landing parties from H.M. ships, who were later replaced by military detachments. Of late every vessel attempting to run the blockade with German evacuees has been intercepted and sunk, so that the enemy have had to fall back on their scanty supply of troop-carrying aircraft as a means of escape. Crete and Rhodes are the principal islands still in German hands, but their surrender has now become inevitable. The Navy has also been busy covering landings in the Peloponnesus, in Albania and on the Yugoslav islands that fringe the Dalmatian coast.

2nd Escort Group Raise U-Boat Toll to 500

FORMIDABLE U-BOAT HUNTERS, the 2nd Escort Group—composed of frigates and sloops (see pages 710-11, Vol. 7), and already holding a remarkable record for enemy submarine sinkings—recently returned home from another hazardous patrol. They had added three more to their total of kills. Ships of this famous Group included H.M.S. Loch Fada, Wren, Dominica and Loch Killin, seen during patrol (2) from the sloop Starling. The Wren (1) photographed from the Starling, stands by to rescue German survivors struggling in the water after their U-boat had been destroyed. Looking down at the Starling's impressive array of depth charges, ready for possible action (3). On August 9, 1944, it was announced that the total number of U-boats sunk during the war to that date exceeded 500. *Photos, British Official*

Dodging Destruction With Cargoes of Death

That on the many far-flung battle fronts our fighting men have not gone short of ammunition is due in large measure to the "powder ships." HOWARD JOHNS writes here of hair's-breadth escapes of indomitable men who serve aboard these vessels and by their labours and skill help to keep well fed the ever hungry Allied guns.

FOR security reasons the world is rarely told of the great work performed by the men who serve aboard the ammunition ships. These vessels, among the most coveted targets for enemy U-boats, have scores of times run the gauntlet of torpedoes, mines, and dive-bombers to sustain our armies and far-flung naval forces, yet the men who make up their crews take all this danger for granted. "I wanted to serve aboard an ammunition ship because my father, and grandfather, did in the last war," one young seaman said to me. "And, anyway, I do feel I'm doing something worth while."

The German Navy, and possibly the Luftwaffe, have in the past offered a bonus to anyone sinking an ammunition ship, so every time they leave port for the high seas these vessels know they are number one priority so far as enemy U-boats, or long-range bombers, are concerned.

IN the main, Britain's fleet of powder ships has developed over the war years, although in 1939 there were several craft that had been specially constructed for this ever-dangerous task. They had blast-proof steel bulkheads, thousands of automatic sprinklers which could flood any part of the vessel in case of fire, steel curtains to isolate the flames, and special arrangements aboard for jettisoning burning cargo.

As our war effort grew it was realized that the time taken to build such craft could not be spared, so merchantmen were re-built and transformed into "powder ships."

Our armies, and navies, as well as the R.A.F., have never gone short of ammunition, thanks in no small measure to the dare-devils who serve aboard the ammunition ships.

Would Explode With One Hit

When Malta was blockaded one ammunition ship, at great risk, ran through the Sicilian Narrows with a cargo of T.N.T. destined for the defenders of the Island. When she was half-way to Malta a German aircraft swooped low—and every man aboard the ammunition ship prepared to defend the vessel. It is a wise old saying among men of the powder ships: "Fight if you have to. Run if you can." After all, there is no sense fighting aboard a vessel that would explode with one hit! If you can get your cargo through, do so. These crews, however, love a fight, and when this particular plane began to shadow them, more than one gunner longed to send a shell into the blue heavens—but the skipper decided to wait.

For several hours the machine remained overhead; then, when its petrol must have been running low, another enemy machine appeared and took over the duty of shadowing the powder ship. Then, straight ahead, an enemy convoy appeared, obviously running across supplies to Rommel. Everyone aboard expected trouble, but kept cool, and the lone vessel steamed clean through the middle of the Axis convoy!

Shortly afterwards a British fighter appeared in the sky, engaged the German, and shot him into the sea. Then, in a menacing manner, the Spitfire turned towards the ammunition ship. A hurriedly flashed signal made the pilot aware that a British ship was below, and he escorted her to the nearest Allied port.

There the strange story of the "protection" given by the enemy aircraft was told, and the reason revealed. Apparently the Luftwaffe had been told to escort an Italian vessel to a North African port. Before they could link up with it, however, the Navy had captured the Italian ship, and the Germans had mistaken the British powder ship for the Italian! Anyway, by keeping cool the Britishers ran through an Axis convoy, avoided German fighter cannon shells, and managed to get through to Malta with a most valuable cargo.

SOMETIMES these vessels have not been so fortunate. On one occasion—again in the Mediterranean—a powder ship, that had been developed from a captured Italian schooner, was attacked by a Heinkel. The gunners, in great form, shot down the plane, but before he made his death-dive the pilot signalled the ammunition vessel's position to an Italian patrol ship. Soon she was attacking the British craft, who replied with her small 12-mm. gun. But it was a hopeless fight, and when the powder ship, destined for Tobruk, was fired amidships, the captain ordered his crew to climb into the lifeboat. They did not want to do this —but orders are orders! Then, when the Italian patrol ship drew close to the schooner the British captain turned towards her, and drove his flaming vessel at the enemy craft. There were shouts of alarm from the Italians as the schooner bore down upon them. Then, when it had reached the Axis craft, the flames reached the T.N.T. There was a terrific explosion. The Mediterranean, over a vast area, appeared to "jump." When the smoke cleared, shattered wood and twisted metal were all that remained of the powder ship and her gallant skipper.

Aflame With a Cargo of T.N.T.

On the Russian convoys the German U-boats and planes appeared to mark the ammunition ships out for special attention. During one hectic trip a large ammunition ship was bombed so often that the crew began to take it as a matter of course and thought it strange when the whistling of bombs was not to be heard! Twice torpedoes, aimed at her by U-boats, missed by inches and struck other vessels. But the ship with its precious cargo reached a Russian port, every member of the crew shaken but triumphant.

They had just settled down for the night when German bombers resumed the attack, and fire-bombs, hitting the deck, went through to the T.N.T. Although they knew the chances of coming out alive were slight, every member of the crew rushed to the threatened area and fought the flames, while German bombers, winging their way overhead, concentrated on the flaming target. And those seamen again defeated the enemy. Although many were badly burnt, they beat out the flames, then, in the darkness, took as much as possible of the T.N.T. from the vessel.

Ammunition ships, as I said earlier, are the vessels the Army and Navy rely upon to feed the guns, and it takes time to train men to handle such a delicate cargo. The enemy knows this; that is why the order was issued "Always go for ammunition ships." But it takes more than orders by the enemy to defeat men of this breed.

FIRE-BOMBS RAINED DOWN and set this ammunition ship ablaze. Dodging the flames, and well-nigh smoke-choked, the trained and war-hardened crew have no immediate thought for themselves. Their first duty is to prevent the conflagration reaching the munitions in the holds; at all costs a cargo of this nature must be delivered.

Photo, Keystone

Canada Mounts Guard at Calais Headquarters

CALAIS FELL TO THE 1st CANADIAN ARMY after a combined air and artillery attack on October 1, 1944. Over 7,000 prisoners were taken as the German garrison left their blazing strong-points ; among them was their commander, Colonel Schoerner. Before the final assault was made that brought enemy resistance to an end, a 24-hour truce enabled some 20,000 French civilians to leave. In the town itself the entrance to the former headquarters of the once-triumphant Wehrmacht was guarded by this Canadian rifleman.

Photo, Associated Press

Dutch Fight Their Way Home With the Allies

ADVANCING INTO HOLLAND with the Allied forces in September 1944, men of the Princess Irene Brigade (the Royal Netherlands Army) returned to their country as liberators after four years of exile. Maastricht, one of the first Dutch towns to be freed, welcomed the homecomers on September 14. A Boy Scout was among the crowd to greet Prince Bernhard as the latter drove in a jeep to the Town Hall (1).

Named after the second daughter of Princess Juliana and Prince Bernhard, the Princess Irene Brigade, composed of Dutch troops trained in Canada and Britain, achieved a fine record in Normandy; Cromwell tanks belonging to this brigade pause in a Belgian village en route for the Dutch frontier (2). Children waved to the lorries as a convoy set off (3). A corporal of the Dutch Marines (4), and a 6-pounder anti-tank gun with a Bren-gunner in position in a wood (5).

Photos, British Official ; Pictorial Press

Battle-Trained Postmen Handle Front Line Mail

Under the leadership of Brigadier Lane, Director of Army Postal Services, the Army Post Office functions magnificently, striving through enemy fire, rain, wind and tides to get letters from home to our fighting men. Postmen parachuted into Normandy on D-Day ; and in other campaigns they have performed difficult duties in praiseworthy fashion, as told by KEITH COOPER.

THE men of the Army Post Office belong to the Royal Engineers, and for the most part were employed in the General Post Office before the war. They perform highly-skilled duties, but before engaging in that work they have to undergo the battle courses and specialized training of a fighting man.

The day following our landing in France people in Britain received letters from Normandy. The majority wondered how such a service was possible ; the answer is the smooth working of long-term plans drawn up by the Army Postal Services. The Army Council, realizing the great morale-booster they have in a well-organized communications system with hearth and home in Britain, went to infinite trouble to make sure that the Army's postmen were given the best possible facilities ; and the postmen were determined to give of their best.

When the initial airborne landings were made in France men of the Army Postal Services were among the first to parachute to earth. Their sorting frames, and other essentials for their work, were also parachuted, in specially-constructed containers. Aboard the gliders men of the Army's own post office, together with their gear, touched down deep in France on D-Day, while others of the same unit were among the first to set foot on the beaches. In shell-craters, often with the battle close at hand, these men went about their work. And rare was it that even enemy action prevented them from continuing their difficult task of sorting the mail.

THEY have to take advantage of the shipping available, every load being taken to its destination by a courier detailed by the Army Postal Services. In this connexion it helps considerably if people keep down the weight of their letters, writing on both sides of the paper—and correctly address them. An average of 9,000 letters a day are incorrectly addressed, resulting in confusion and delay.

Over a thousand A.T.S. are today performing valuable sorting work at the home postal centres through which mail for overseas passes, and it speaks well of their skill that men who in civilian life were experienced postal workers have given them high credit for a job well done. These women greatly aid the ever-expanding postal service of the British Army, and play an important role in making sure that mail is on time.

ON the Western front the Army Postal Services are developing a routine service and it is hoped before long to establish one similar to that organized when the B.E.F. was in France. After the A.P.S. left France in 1940, and there was little work for them to do as the British Army overseas was small, most of these postmen were among the few well-armed soldiers who defended our coasts against the possibility of a German invasion—a fact not generally known outside Army circles.

In Crete and in North Africa they took part in some of the fiercest fighting of the war. Their battle training stood them in good stead every time, for although their chief function is, of course, tending the mail, like other units of the Royal Engineers they can be relied upon to perform any duty with satisfaction and relish.

On one occasion, in North Africa, a battery of the Royal Artillery desired to take over a spot used by the Army Postal Services. The latter's C.O. explained that it was quite impossible for them to remove their gear immediately, but said they had no objection

to the gunners sharing the site. This was agreed upon. But the first blast from the guns blew all the letters from the sorting racks ; so the postmen battened down the letters with weights, and then helped to bring up ammunition ! For two days they assisted the battery, resuming their own duties when the gunners moved forward.

THE letters for men in forward areas go up to the line with orderlies sent down to collect the rations. The Germans appear to take a great delight in trying to snatch these mail bags from our men, and on at least one occasion a bag, in no man's land, has been under fire for eight hours, after it had been dropped by an orderly running for cover. Eventually a daring sergeant dashed out and recovered it.

In the Field the Army Postal Services, night and day, are performing feats of hard work that rarely appear in the news. Getting a good flow of mail through to the men at the front means not only fighting the enemy, but tides, wind, rain and bad fortune. The success of these endeavours is reflected in the satisfied state of mind of the fighting men who regularly get their letters from home.

TWO-AND-A-HALF MILLION LETTERS every week were handled by an Army Postal Depot in the Midlands. Members of the A.T.S. (above) sort parcels and other postal matter. A kerbstone "sorting office" (top) was organized as a temporary measure by a regimental sergeant-major after the British 8th Army entered Florence on August 12, 1944 ; sorting racks—and a roof—and other refinements came later. PAGE 363 *Photos, British Official; Keystone*

Red Army Triumphant in Estonia and Bulgaria

TALLINN, CAPITAL OF ESTONIA, fell to the Russians on Sept. 22, 1944, after a spectacular 50-mile dash along the shores of the Gulf of Finland by Marshal Govorov's tanks and assault infantry. The capture of this important naval base deprived the Germans of a valuable escape port. By October 10 the whole of the Estonian mainland had been liberated and the Russians had landed on Oesel, last outlying island, and were mopping-up remnants of German resistance there. Citizens of Tallinn are seen greeting the Red Army in one of the city's squares.

VARNA, BULGARIAN PORT ON THE BLACK SEA, was occupied by Soviet forces on September 8, 1944, after they had driven south into Bulgaria from the Rumanian border. Taken without opposition, Varna played an important part after 1941 as a base from which the German-Bulgarian attacks were launched against the Red Army. Troops of the 3rd Ukrainian Front collaborated with the Soviet Black Sea Fleet in capturing the port. Russian motor patrol boats are seen entering the harbour.

PAGE 364

Photos, Pictorial Press

The Tragic End of Polish Resistance in Warsaw

BATTLE OF WARSAW which began on August 1, 1944, when the Red Army's summer offensive had advanced almost to the outskirts of the Polish capital, ended in tragic capitulation by the besieged Poles on October 2. Lieut.-Gen. Komorowski (Gen. " Bor "), C.-in-C. Polish Home Army, stated in his final message to the Polish Government in London that " Warsaw has fallen, exhausted and without means to carry on the fight."

The capital suffered great devastation, as shown in the photograph of the wrecked street along which a heavy German tank plunges (4). Enemy troops easily penetrated barbed wire defences— according to this German photograph (1) taken on August 31. Bitter fighting raged in Warsaw's main thoroughfares : the German H.Q. in Pilsudski Square (5). Two R.A.F. men were honoured for the part they played in dropping supplies to the Polish Patriots : F o J. D. Johnston (2) received the D.F.C., and W o A. Toft (3) the D.F.M.

Photos, British Official ; Keystone, Planet News PAGE 365

Immortal Story of the Airborne Men of Arnhem

For nine days in September 1944 men of Britain's airborne forces battled against huge odds to hold ground they had gained at Arnhem in Holland: an exploit intended to open a gateway to North-West Germany. Something of "this glorious and fruitful operation," as Mr. Churchill described it, is told below. See also pages 348 and 367-370.

"OUR task," said Major-General Urquhart, C.B., D.S.O. and bar, Commander of the 1st Airborne Division of the British Army, "was to secure the Arnhem Bridge if we could, and anyhow secure a bridge-head north of the River Lek. We hoped that the 2nd Army would be with us within 24 hours. That was the most optimistic estimate. We ourselves thought we might possibly have to hold 3 or 4 days" . . . They were there for nine bitter days. "Eventually we held a perimeter 900 yards broad and 1,200 yards in depth."

Had it been possible to get a complete airborne division down in one lift the outcome might have been very different; but it was not possible. And because of flak the R.A.F. was unable to land the airborne forces nearer than 8 miles of Arnhem town. Moreover, stronger and earlier opposition than was expected was encountered. But at the end of the first day one battalion of the division was on the bridge and the rest of the division was on the town's outskirts. The battalion removed the explosive charges and the Arnhem Bridge was ready to be crossed by the 2nd Army advancing north.

densed, makes solemn yet thrilling reading:

About five kilometres to the west of Arnhem on that last day (September 25) I saw the dead and the living—those who fought a good fight and kept the faith with you at home, and those who still fought magnificently on. They were the last of the few. I last saw them yesterday morning as they dribbled into Nijmegen. They had staggered and walked and waded all night from Arnhem about ten miles north, and we were busy asking each other if this or that one had been seen. I walked up to one young lieutenant to ask him about his sergeant—a stout lad if there ever was one—and he started to explain what had happened and then turned away. Remember, all of those men have been practically ten days and nights under the most murderous concentrated fire I have seen in two wars. Then he turned again and said: "It's hell to be pulled out when you haven't finished your job isn't it?"

THAT'S the way they all felt. It doesn't occur to them that if they hadn't held that horde of enemy at Arnhem, that force would have been down at Nijmegen upsetting the whole applecart. That was yesterday morning. Late on the afternoon before, we were told that the remnants of the 1st Airborne Division were going to pull out that night. The enemy was making it impossible for the elements of the 2nd Army to relieve us. We were told to destroy all our equipment with the exception of what would go into one haversack. We were told to muffle our boots with bits of blanket and be ready to move off at a certain time. When the various officers were told to transmit this news to that thin straggle of hard-pressed men around the pitifully small perimeter, a great silence seemed to come upon them even in the

middle of the shelling. The ones I saw just drew a deep breath and said: "Very good, sir." Then they faded away to crawl out on their stomachs and tell their men.

Perhaps I should remind you here that these were men of no ordinary calibre. They had been in that little space mortared and shelled, machine-gunned and sniped from all around. When a tank or a self-propelled 88 gun broke through, two or three of them detached themselves and somehow or another put it out of business. For the last three days they had had no water, very little small arms ammunition, and rations cut to one-sixth. Luckily, or unluckily, it rained, and they caught the water in their capes and drank that. These last items were never mentioned—they were airborne, weren't they? They were tough and knew it.

Well, at two minutes past ten we clambered out of our slit trenches in an absolute din of bombardment, a great deal of it our own, and formed up in a single line. We held the tail of the coat of the man in front, and set off like a file of nebulous ghosts from our pock-marked and tree-strewn piece of ground. Obviously, since the enemy was all round us, we had to go through him to get to the River Rhine. After about two hundred yards of silent trekking we knew we were among the enemy. It was difficult not to throw yourself flat when machine-gun tracers skimmed your head or the scream of a shell or mortar-bomb sounded very close. But the orders were to keep going.

THE back of my neck was prickling for all that interminable march. I couldn't see the man ahead of me—all I knew was that I had hold of a coat-tail, and for the first time in my life was grateful for the downpour of rain that made a patter on the leaves of the trees and covered up any little noises we were making. At every turn of the way there was posted a sergeant glider-pilot, who stepped out like a shadow and then stepped back into a deeper shadow again.

As we came out of the trees I felt as naked as if I were in Piccadilly Circus in my pyjamas, because of the glow from fires across the river. The machine-gun and general bombardment had never let-up. Verey lights were going up over us. We lay down flat in the mud and rain and stayed that way for two hours till the sentry beyond the hedge on the bank of the river told us to move up over the dyke and be taken across. After what seemed a nightmare of an age we got our turn and slithered up and over on to some mud flats. There was the shadow of a little assault craft with an outboard motor on it. Several of these had been rushed up by a field company of engineers. One or two of them were out of action already. I waded out into the Rhine up to my hips; it didn't matter, for I was soaked through long ago—had been for days. A voice that was sheer music spoke from the stern of the boat saying: "Ye'll have to step lively, boys, it ain't healthy here." It was a Canadian voice, and the engineers were Canadian engineers.

We helped push the boat off into the swift Rhine current and with our heads down between our knees waited for the bump on the far side—or for what might come before. It didn't come. We clambered out and followed what had been a white tape up over a dyke. We slid down the other side on our backsides, we sloshed through mud for four miles and a half, me thinking, "Gosh! I'm alive! How did it happen?" In a barn there was a blessed hot mug of tea with rum in it, and a blanket over our shoulders, and then we walked again all night. After daylight we got to a dressing station near Nijmegen. Then we were put in trucks, and that's how we reached Nijmegen. That's how the last of the few got out to go and fight in some future battle. No matter what battle that is, I know they won't let you down.

MAJOR-GEN. R. E. URQUHART, C.B., D.S.O. and bar (extreme right), commander of the British 1st Airborne Division that fought at Arnhem, returned to England on Sept. 29, 1944. He landed at an airfield in the Midlands in a U.S. troop-carrying plane and is here seen talking to glider pilots who accompanied him on his homeward journey. He was invested with the insignia of Commander of the Bath by H.M. the King at Buckingham Palace on October 9. *Photo, G.P.U.*

But though they could not "make it," the 2nd Army was able to complete the capture of the vital Nijmegen Bridge, to the south: the airborne men's gallant stand at Arnhem locking up German forces which otherwise would have been thrown into the Nijmegen battle. Approximately 8,000 men were dropped in the Arnhem area, those engaged in the great battle including gliderborne troops of the South Staffordshire Regt., the King's Own Scottish Borderers, and the Border Regt.; and men of the Dorsetshire Regt. and Polish parachute troops reinforced the Division.

"We decided on evacuation," said Maj.-Gen. Urquhart, "when it was clear we could not last another 24 hours. Our exit by two roads to the river came off better than I dared to hope." When the withdrawal of some 2,000 survivors from this bridge-head, which had become a trap when bad weather prevented adequate airborne reinforcements being dropped, had been successfully completed, Maj.-Gen. Urquhart received from Field-Marshal Montgomery this message:

"I want to express to you personally, and to every officer and man in your Division, my appreciation of what you all did at Arnhem for the Allied cause . . . In years to come it will be a great thing for a man to be able to say, 'I fought at Arnhem.'"

The story of the evacuation, by Stanley Maxted, from which the following is con-

Reinforcements for our Sky-Troops in Holland

" The largest airborne operation ever conceived or executed," in the words of Mr. Churchill, " achieved a further all-important forward bound in the north " when on September 17, 1944, the 1st Allied Airborne Army commenced landings at Nijmegen, Eindhoven and Arnhem, to seize important bridges and extend the great corridor the British 2nd Army was driving through Holland.   Aircraft towing gliders with reinforcements soared over a windmill (above) at Valkenswaard, south of Eindhoven.

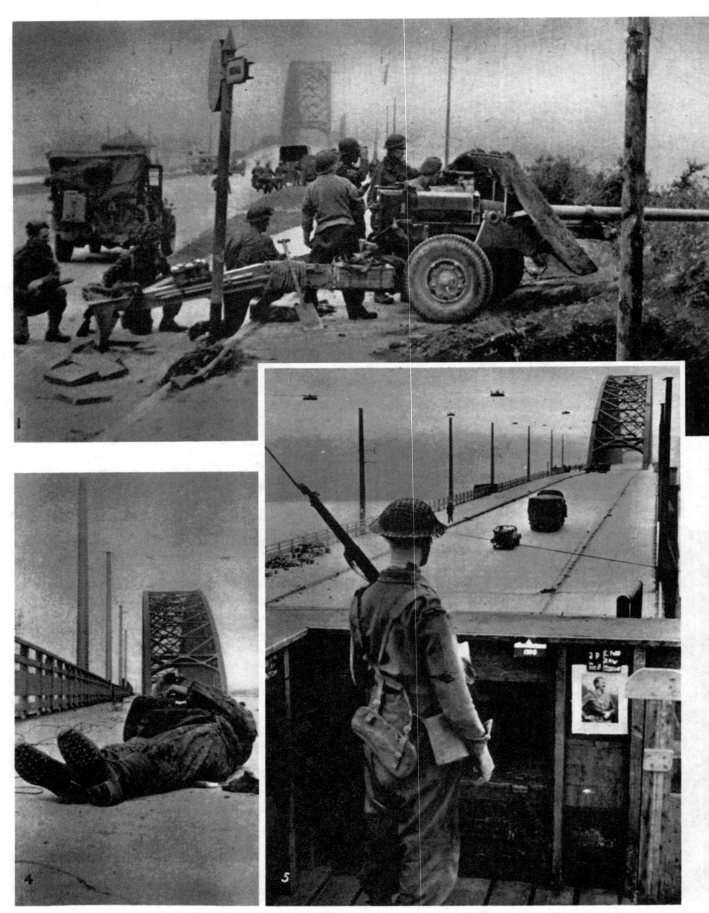

The Vital Bridge at Nijmegen was Captured Intact—

Stormed from the south by tanks of the Grenadier Guards after U.S. airborne infantry had landed and prevented its demolition, the bridge over the Waal (Dutch Rhine) was taken intact by September 21, 1944. A 17-pounder kept watch across the river (1) whilst 10,000 lb. of explosive placed in the bridge piers by the enemy were removed. A British corporal and a sapper assisted in the removal (2); British and U.S. airborne troops helped to stack the 200-lb. dynamite charges (3).

Ph

—To Speed the Great Thrust to Northern Germany

Wreckage of the fierce fight to be cleared from the bridge included the last of the enemy defenders (4). Guarding the approach, a British sentry occupied the former German command post (5), which still displayed a framed portrait of Hitler. Past smashed vehicles our transport was soon speeding (6) towards the next river ahead—the Lek, an arm of the Rhine—beyond which, at Arnhem, the British 1st Airborne Division had been dropped to battle against overwhelming odds.

British Valour in the Hell that was Arnhem

Photos, British and
U.S. Official

In hundreds the parachute troops of the 1st Airborne Army were dropped in landing areas from transport planes (1). Some, hard-pressed in their foxholes at Arnhem, bombarded German positions with three-inch mortars (2). Glider-borne troops of the Border Regiment, in a hastily-dug slit-trench, others lining the hedge beyond the road (3), waited tensely to repel attack by the enemy 100 yards away. Glider Pilot Regiment men searched for snipers in a shell-riddled school (4).

VIEWS & REVIEWS
Of Vital War Books

by Hamilton Fyfe

Facing me as I sit at my typewriter is a wall on which hang a number of Japanese colour prints. I have collected them gradually. Their beauty has given me pleasure for many years. Today I have noticed something about them that I never realized before. All the figures in them have cruel, sinister or cunning expressions on their faces. They are figures of actors, they are expressing the emotions proper to their parts; it had not struck me until today, when I glanced up at them from Mr. Joseph C. Grew's book, Ten Years in Japan (Hammond, 15s.) which I was reading, that all those emotions are of a harsh, threatening, belligerent character. And, according to Mr. Grew, who was United States Ambassador in Tokyo, that character is very quickly assumed by Japs when anything occurs to put them out, or when they are stirred to offensive demonstration by propaganda. In this they are very much like the ordinary run of North Germans.

When the Japanese attacked Pearl Harbour in December 1941 (Mr. Grew had warned Washington they might as far back as January of that year), little animosity was shown against foreigners in the capital for some days. The Japanese employees at the Embassy behaved very well indeed: they had always been treated by Americans with kindness and courtesy; they repaid this by loyalty in the dark hour. But when a few days had passed, other Japs who did not know any Americans and who were told to regard them as enemies began to behave badly and in a short time the feeling against both Americans and British in Tokyo was bitterly hostile. Even before war came Mr. Grew had seen many instances of overbearing, insolent conduct when there was no provocation whatever and, though he puts it on record that "there are no finer people in the world than the best type of Japanese," he comes to the reluctant conclusion that there are not many of them and that at present they have next to no influence in public affairs.

For a long time army officers, not of highest rank, have decided how the country shall be governed and what its foreign policy shall be. The Navy seemed to be a stabilizing factor. Its officers were not bellicose, they kept aloof from politics. But by 1938 there had come a change. The naval chiefs now felt they had too long allowed the army to "get all the glory" and had acted "merely as a beast of burden" for it. They resolved to make a bid for naval supremacy in East Asia as soon as the chance offered. By this time the army was in a position to create that chance. By assassination the more violent officers had removed some of the wisest of the Emperor's counsellors and had terrorized others. They obtained control over the Government. The only hope left to Japanese men of knowledge and understanding was that the Emperor's well-advertised desire for peace would prevent any disastrous outbreak. Count Makino, a leading member of the Cabinet, said in 1935, "There will never be any danger from military Fascism or Communism or any other kind of 'ism,' simply because the Emperor is supreme and will always have the last word." That must have been deliberate deception. Makino must have known that the Emperor was as weak and stupid as Oriental hereditary rulers generally have been. He did nothing to ward off the coming catastrophe. He may have been deceived by the declarations of his Ministers which so completely humbugged so many of the world's governing men.

One thing Mr. Grew learned and emphasizes: very few Japanese tell the truth if it be to their interest to lie. Yet they may not know they are lying. One of the most dishonest of their politicians told Mr. Grew: "We are too honest to be good poker players." Mr. Grew thinks he believed that. He says their mental processes and methods of reaching conclusions are radically different from those of Europeans and Americans.

The Westerner believes that because the Japanese has adopted Western dress, language and customs he must think like a Westerner. No greater error can be made.

The Japanese Art of 'Let's Pretend'

When a Jap makes an agreement about anything, he intends to keep it—as long as it suits him to do so.

It isn't that he necessarily has his tongue in his cheek when he signs the obligation. It merely means that when the obligation runs counter to his own interests, as he conceives them, he will interpret the obligation to suit himself and, according to his own lights and mentality, he will very likely be perfectly honest in doing so.

Now Mr. Grew calls this "one of the great cleavages between the East and the West." That is not correct. For the Chinese have a strong sense of the binding character of a promise. They will keep their word, they will carry out an undertaking even if it turns out to their disadvantage. Don't fancy that I am cracking up an ally and crying down an enemy just because one is friendly and the other hostile. I have pointed out this difference between Chinese and Japanese very often during the past thirty years, ever since I came to know something of both nationalities. It is a difference caused by their systems of education. The young Chinese are brought up to believe that their ancestors are watching them all the time and that they must not pain them by being dishonest. The young Japanese are taught that they are a master-race, that their Emperor is a kind of god, and that anything is permissible which they

believe will extend his empire and increase his power.

Here is the explanation of those expressions on the faces of the people in my Japanese colour prints. Here is also a revealing light on what we call "national character," which is not inherited, but created by early training. It can be turned this way or that, just as the rulers decide to have this or that taught in their schools. We British used to be taught that we were the greatest nation on the face of the earth. Now we have dropped that nonsense. We are proud of some achievements of our forefathers. We remember some with a frown or a grin. We put on no airs of superiority and we are liked all the better for it.

This change in our "national character" offers hope for the future. Seeing it has been altered in the course of less than three generations, there is no reason to doubt that other national characters can be, if common sense and common honesty prevail over silly pretensions and a morality twisted by self-interest. The Japanese, says Mr. Grew, "love high-sounding formulas and slogans to cover whatever they want and intend to do, with the idea of imparting to their plans the most perfect righteousness, lulling themselves into the belief that their acts are wholly righteous." Now that is just what the mid-Victorians did to justify their actions.

We followed self-interest and pretended—no, we did not pretend, we really believed we were acting on principle, doing the will of God. That is what the Japanese have been led to believe they are doing today. Mr. Grew discovered this and consequently refuses to hope they will soon be overcome. He thinks they will fight on fanatically, even when their hope of winning has disappeared. He has probably had something to do with the forecast or balance-sheet which has been officially published in the United States to counter what it calls the delusion that it will not take long to defeat Japan.

The one chance that this forecast may be falsified lies in a revolt against the rubbish talked about Japanese domination of the entire Pacific area, by the more intelligent among the Japanese themselves and the conversion of the masses to common sense. That there are plenty of such intelligent people Mr. Grew found out, but he does not feel sanguine about their being of any use. When crushing defeat has been inflicted on their army, navy and air force, the masses will be more ready to listen to reason. So far the unreason which has been pumped into them has it all its own way.

CONVERSATION IN TOKYO in 1941—before the treacherous attack on Pearl Harbour—between Mr. Joseph Grew (right), author of the book reviewed in this page, and Vice-Admiral Teijiro Toyoda, who was Japanese Minister of Foreign Affairs, July Oct. 1941. Born in 1880, Mr. Grew was U.S. Ambassador to Japan, 1932 41.

Photo, New York Times Photos

Greek Infantry With the 8th Army in Italy

RIMINI, ON THE ADRIATIC COAST, taken by the 8th Army on September 21, 1944, was finally cleared of the enemy by Greek troops advancing to the River Marecchia : they passed through the City Gate (1) to ruined streets (5) where they " mopped up " in a house-to-house search (3). German prisoners tramped through thick mud (4). Engineers of a British Field Company sweeping for mines at the entrance to the Republican State of San Marino (2). Map shows Allied line on October 3.

Photos, British Official. Map by courtesy of The Times

Going Home in Florence Now That They're Free

PICKING THEIR WAY THROUGH THE DEBRIS of the Ponte Alle Grazie, these Florentines crossed the River Arno to their homes after their city had been occupied and liberated by the Allies on September 12, 1944. Five of the six bridges spanning the Arno in Florence were destroyed by the Germans; the sixth—the fourteenth-century Ponte Vecchio—was left intact, though the enemy mined both banks of the river and mounted machine-guns in adjacent buildings (see also illus. page 227).

Photo, Keystone

Weapons in Brief: The Alphabet Goes to War

Communiqués and newspaper reports refer frequently to Service arms, weapons, secret and otherwise, ships and personnel, by initial letters and names which sometimes can be very puzzling to the reader. This craze for contraction is founded on good reason, for full titles can be cumbersome. These labels—some familiar, some strange—are explained by JOHN FLEETWOOD.

THE first craft to reach Normandy beaches with their spearhead freights were L.C.V.P.s (Landing Craft—Vehicles and Personnel), littlish fellows carried slung from the davits of troopships. The transports lowered their "babies" and, nose to tail, the little craft circled the mother ship, waiting for their crews to board them.

A few thousand yards offshore two patrol ships rode the swell, almost motionless. A mile or so apart, they marked the starting line just beyond the range of effective machine-gun fire. On these ships each wave of landing craft "dressed" like a battalion of infantry, then off they careered for the beaches. As each wave went in a new group of L.C.s advanced to the starting line, and when their turn came they went in too.

Most of the men moved off to find and fight the enemy, destroy his guns, push him back from the beach. A few stayed at the water's edge to signal in the landing craft and regulate the flow of supplies. These

Barge—Kitchen), baking bread and providing hot meals for the men who ferry supplies (see story and illus. in page 251).

It is a queer-looking family, this vast and varied breed of invasion craft. For one class—L.C.F.s (Landing Craft—Flak)—invasion found little work to do, the Allied Air Forces having had from the outset complete mastery of the air. And do you remember L.C.A.s (Landing Craft—Assault), the old originals, from which the men leaped straight over the bows, and whose proper duties were reversed to evacuate our troops from Norway and Dunkirk? When the time came to employ them for the role in which they were cast, the L.C. family had been varied and expanded a hundredfold. Latest in the list is the L.C.T.R. (Landing Craft Tank—Rocket). Everybody knows the M.T.B.s (motor-torpedo-boats), but the P.T.s are less familiar. P.T.s are American M.T.B.s, and America's "plywood navy" is giving a good account of itself.

limbering. The Bofors 40-mm. S.P., long a mainstay of Britain's A.A. defences, is a prime example of the guns of the self-propelled class. It is power-elevated and traversed, and fires 2-lb. shells to a height of 6,000 feet at 120 a minute. The Morris chassis, or modified version of the artillery Quad (tractor), on which it is mounted, gives the Bofors a maximum road speed of 40 m.p.h., rendering it one of our fastest mobile weapons and an invaluable protection for convoys en route.

MOST mobile of all are machine-guns, especially those of the L.M.G. (Light Machine-Gun) class—the Lewis, Bren and the machine carbine, the Sten. But the Heavies run them very close for mobility, since the Vickers and its like are nowadays carried as nearly as possible into action on wheeled transport. To the tank family there has recently been added the A.V.R.E. (Armoured Vehicle, Royal Engineers), the new British mortar tank. (See illus. in opposite page.)

Those responsible for inspecting the ammunition eaten up in such enormous quantities by today's swift-firing guns are persons of vast technical experience, yet the work is being increasingly done by the A.T.S. Ten A.E.s (Ammunition Examiners) of the A.T.S. at one depot alone inspect and supervise the repair, examination and packing of tons of live ammunition every week, working in isolated groups in dispersed sheds.

Girls of one of the manifold branches of work now handled by the A.T.S. are known in the Army, and outside it, as O.W.L.s, though the girls themselves are not smitten with the name. However, the soubriquet was not chosen; it just happened, for the letters mean Operators, Wireless and Line, these Signals girls serving as "linemen" as well as radio operators.

In other spheres there are the P.O.L. units of the R.A.S.C., the men who handle the unshipping and distribution of the life-blood of modern battle—Petrol, Oil and Lubricants; and the F.S.U.s—the Field Surgical Units of the R.A.M.C., whose duties take them close up behind the front line so that they may operate on casualties from one to six hours after injury.

CRUSADER BOFORS A.A. TANK, in operation against the enemy in Europe, is a development of the Bofors 40-mm. S.P. (self-propelled) gun mentioned in this page. Designed primarily for the protection of convoys on the move against low-flying aircraft, it fires 2-lb. shells at the rate of 120 per minute. *Photo, British Official*

were the beach commander and his staff—no kin with the duckmaster of the DUKWS (the factory serial letters for D the boat, U the lorry body, KW the lorry chassis), but a mixed team of soldiers and seamen, whose duties are to see that each specialized section, either of personnel or stores, finds, as it lands, its right place in the beach area.

BACK with the bigger ships were larger landing vessels—L.C.I.s (Landing Craft—Infantry), some of the biggest of landing craft, with two disembarking ramps, one on either side of the bows; and L.S.T.s (Landing Ship—Tanks). Both of these are ocean-going vessels which move under their own power. An L.C.I. is 155 feet long; when she hits the shore, down go the twin ramps, and over 200 soldiers pour out on to the beach.

An L.S.T. is larger still; she is, in fact, a floating garage with vehicles clamped to her lower deck by heavy chains against the formidable roll these ships develop when on the move. Once beached, her mouth opens and trucks and vehicles of every description roll out of her; others are lifted by davits from her hold. By the time these ships go in, the landing is well under way, and their mobile freights quickly build up the power of the assault. In contrast with these large craft are the diminutive L.B.K.s (Landing

Normandy beaches are a glorious page of past history, but it is not too late to pay tribute to the N.B.S.O. (Naval Bomb Safety Officer), who with his Naval and Marine colleagues has immunized hundreds of mines in the sea and on beaches since D-Day. Few serving men were more symbolic of the spirit of Britain during the long dark years of the U-boat and Luftwaffe peril than the M.R.A. At one period in action almost every day and night of the year, more than 7,000 gunners of the Maritime Royal Artillery, spread over the seven seas in ships of the Merchant Navy, were constantly on the alert for aircraft, U-boats and surface raiders. Dubbed "Churchill's Sharpshooters" because they were formed at the instance of the Prime Minister himself, these artillerymen on loan to the Navy can operate 20 different kinds of guns, and other defensive weapons.

Speaking of gunnery, one of the best things that ever came out of our gun laboratories is the Projector, Infantry, Anti-Tank—P.I.A.T., for short—which fires a bomb that will pierce four inches of the sturdiest armour-plate and inflict serious damage on the interior of tanks, often killing the crew.

When is a gun self-propelled? When it is mounted on either a truck or tractor so that it can be fired without dismounting or un-

COMMUNIQUÉS on air activities talk of Emergency Landing Grounds as E.L.G.s. D.E.O.P.S. are supplies dropped from aircraft without a parachute attached. The Special Force referred to in S.E.A.C. (South East Asia Command) communiqués are the Chindits formed by General Wingate. Many of these dispatches allude to Japanese Bunkers. These vary in size from a one-man foxhole with a lid, to a section bunker accommodating from six to 26 men, well provisioned with food and ammunition, and equipped with sleeping bays, cooking quarters and latrines.

Sometimes a cryptic military term must preserve its mystery, unchallenged. The L.C.O.C.U., for instance, is still on the secret list. A weapon lately released from it is the M1-A1, a new type of American "flame-gun," a fearful weapon, as the enemy has learned to his cost. M1-A1 is far superior to anything so far used by the foe, and the intense, all-enveloping liquid fire-power it develops seems largely to have solved the riddle of breaking down the Nazi-developed pillbox defence in depth, without the frequently futile, and far more costly, expenditure of high explosives. An illustrated description of Britain's flame-throwers is given in pages 300 and 301.

A.V.R.E is Added to Allies' Mighty Armoury

BRITISH MORTAR TANK, THE A.V.R.E. (Armoured Vehicle, Royal Engineers) specialises in the assault of powerful fortifications, such as the Siegfried Line, and the "West Wall" defences through which it smashed on D-Day. Resembling a Churchill, it carries a flexible track for carpeting insecure ground or forming a causeway across a hole, ditch or stream—a fascine or bundle of chestnut palings (1), which is unloaded (2) where required. Main armament is a mortar mounted in the turret (3); this hurls a "flying dustbin" (4) containing a great weight of explosive. A.V.R.E.s moving up in France (5).

Photo, British Official

Heroism Beyond Praise: Their Award the V.C.

Sergeant M. W. ROGERS
A battalion of the Wiltshire Regiment was held up by wire and machine-gun fire in Italy. Advancing alone, Sgt. Rogers so confused the enemy defences that his platoon was enabled to attack. He was posthumously awarded the V.C. on Aug. 10, 1944.

Lance-Corporal J. P. HARMAN
Commanding an infantry section in the Queen's Own Royal West Kent Regt., he annihilated an enemy machine-gun post which menaced his company at Kohima, Burma, on April 8, 1944. He was posthumously awarded the V.C. on June 22, 1944.

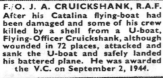

F./O. J. A. CRUICKSHANK, R.A.F.
After his Catalina flying-boat had been damaged and some of his crew killed by a shell from a U-boat, Flying-Officer Cruickshank, although wounded in 72 places, attacked and sank the U-boat and safely landed his battered plane. He was awarded the V.C. on September 2, 1944.

Company Sgt.-Maj. S. E. HOLLIS
On D-Day, C.-S.-M. Hollis, of the Green Howards, dealt with a pillbox threatening disembarking troops. He was the first Normandy V.C.

Private G. A. MITCHELL
A member of the London Scottish, Pte. Mitchell eliminated three enemy posts in single-handed attacks, January 23-24, 1944, at Damiano Ridge, Italy. He fell to the bullet of a German who had surrendered.

Sepoy KAMAL RAM
After the forcing of the River Gari, Italy, on May 12, 1944, the advance was held up by machine-gun fire from four enemy posts. Volunteering to silence them, Sepoy Kamal Ram of the 8th Punjab Regt., Indian Army (here receiving the V.C. from H.M. the King), overpowered the crew of the first post, then attacked the second which he also eliminated. He proceeded to clear up the remaining two, and by his action secured ground vital for the Allied bridge-heads.

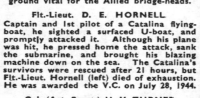

Flt.-Lieut. D. E. HORNELL
Captain and 1st pilot of a Catalina flying-boat, he sighted a surfaced U-boat, and promptly attacked it. Although his plane was hit, he pressed home the attack, sank the submarine, and brought his blazing machine down on the sea. The Catalina's survivors were rescued after 21 hours, but Flt.-Lieut. Hornell (left) died of exhaustion. He was awarded the V.C. on July 28, 1944.

Cpl. (Act. Sergt.) H. V. TURNER
His dwindling platoon seriously harassed by Japanese near Ninhtoukong, Burma, Cpl. Turner (right) counter-attacked single-handed. Taking all grenades he could carry, he threw them " with devastating effect," and five times returned for more. He was killed on his sixth journey. The V.C. was awarded on August 17, 1944.

Photos, British Official; G.P.U., News Chronicle

I WAS THERE! Eye Witness Stories of the War

It Was a 'Tough Do' at the Bridge of Arnhem

A handful of British parachute troops who fought on for three days and nights when surrounded at the end of the Arnhem bridge were taken prisoner, removed to Germany, then escaped to our lines. One of them, Lieut. D. Simpson, told the following story to B.U.P. war correspondent Richard McMillan, at Nijmegen, on Sept. 24, 1944. See also pages 366–370.

ONE OF THE ARNHEM WARRIORS, this member of the British 1st Airborne Division stood guard at Divisional H.Q. there during a desperate phase of the fighting.
Photo, British Official

WE made a perfect drop on the outskirts of Arnhem. Within an hour my section had moved off towards their objective, the bridge over the lower Rhine in the heart of the town. In the darkness we passed through Osterbeek and reached Arnhem without any real opposition. Crouching through the streets, we reached the houses on the northern end of the bridge; our mission was to occupy them.

We got into a school building underneath the approach to the bridge, with the first storey above bridge level. The other section occupied other buildings there. That first night we made a charge against the pillbox guarding the bridge and set fire to an ammunition dump inside the pillbox, which blew up. Twenty Germans ran out with their hands up.

We then pulled back and began fortifying the schoolhouse. By this time the Germans had gathered a force and were attacking the next house with tanks which came along the river embankment and fired from a range of thirty yards. Some of the men driven out of this house crept over to the school under cover of darkness and joined us. Others got through from another battalion to add to our force. We then mustered about fifty.

The next enemy move was to machine-gun the school from the rooftops of adjoining buildings. When this failed, they set several houses on fire, hoping that the wind would carry the flames to the school. That move failed too. About midday a convoy of German half-track vehicles came over the bridge. We opened up with our Brens and Sten guns and killed the men riding in them. The lorries caught fire. That night there were blazing houses and blazing lorries, and the enemy started mortaring.

Then, in the darkness, from the side farthest from the flames, the enemy began stalking towards the school. We spied them in time, and dropped hand grenades on them. After five minutes they withdrew, leaving behind a mortar, two machine-guns and several Bazookas. On Tuesday a Mark III tank appeared with fifteen infantrymen, and began a furious firing. This scrap went on most of the day. One of our men crept across the road and dropped a bomb from a housetop on to the tank and disabled it.

That evening the Germans again tried to burn us out, but our men got out on the rooftop when the flames spread to the school and managed to put the fire out. All night long Tiger tanks roamed round shelling the school until it was riddled like a sieve. The adjoining house burned to a shell. It was a hectic night, mortars adding to the din and havoc. The next day—D-plus 3— was so quiet that we thought the Germans had pulled out, but at 10 in the morning two Tigers starting battering away once more. By this time we had rigged up a radio and were talking from one house to another, comparing notes.

From our second floor we could see Germans working on the bridge and realized that they were putting in demolition charges. It was time for us to take action! We rushed out with fixed bayonets through the enemy fire, cleared the Germans from the bridge, and removed the charges. Then the Germans counter-attacked, and we withdrew to our houses. They set fire to the school, and the building began to fall in.

We had 21 wounded and decided to try to get out with them. There were now 45 altogether in our party. We got as far as the next house when the Germans raked us and pinned us down. Under this very heavy fire we suffered further casualties. The wounded now totalled 35, and it was decided to leave four men with them and give the rest a chance to escape. But as we got clear of the houses, the Germans closed in and forced the last six to surrender.

The rest of the glowing story was told by Corporal Charles Weir, of Richmond Terrace, Aberdeen, and Corporal John Humphreys, of Wormsley, Herefordshire. He and Weir, munching food at an open-air kitchen, paid tribute to the gallantry of their officers. It was just another adventure for Humphreys. He had already been captured in the Italian campaign, and escaped from prison at Ancona.

"It was a tough do on the bridge at Arnhem," Humphreys admitted between hungry bites into a huge meat sandwich. "A tough do!"

STEPPING ASHORE AT NIJMEGEN these survivors from the battle of the bridge at Arnhem, whose adventures are related in this page, reached the British 2nd Army after the small boat in which they made their escape from German captivity had carried them down the Rhine and the Waal. Left to right, Cpl. J. Humphreys, Cpl. C. Weir, and Lieut. D. Simpson, narrator of the story; the fourth man, unnamed, for security reasons. In the background is the Nijmegen bridge.
Photo, British Newspaper Pool

A SINGLE PARACHUTE MINE DID THIS in London's East End. The scene of destruction is at the junction of Arcadia Street and Latham Street, Poplar ; the date, during 1941. London's ordeal in the blitz period 1940-1941 was intensified by the enemy's use of this weapon, which contained between one and two tons of H.E. A comparatively small crater was made when the parachute mine struck, but great devastation was caused over a large area by the terrific blast, as is shown in the photograph above. *Photo, Keystone*

I Watched a German Parachute Mine Explode

A B.B.C. engineer, Mr. L. D. Macgregor, recently broadcast a remarkable story of the 1940 raids on London. Leaving Broadcasting House on a Sunday evening—Dec. 8 of that year—he suddenly saw what seemed to be a "very large tarpaulin" falling. What happened then is related below.

I CROUCHED down in what is known as "Prone Falling Position No. 1." Even at that moment I thought the danger was coming farther up Portland Place. My head was up watching, and before I could reach Position No. 2 and lie down flat the thing exploded.

I had a momentary glimpse of a large ball of blinding white light with two concentric rings of colour, the inner ones lavender and the outer ones violet. The ball seemed to be ten to twenty feet high and was near the lamp-post. The explosion made a noise something like a colossal growl and was accompanied by a veritable tornado of air blast. I felt an excruciating pain in my ears, and all sounds were replaced by a loud singing noise—which was when I lost my hearing.

I felt that consciousness was slipping from me, and at that moment I seemed to hear a loud clear voice shouting, "Don't let yourself go ! Face up to it and hold on ! " It rallied me, and summoning all my will power and energy I succeeded in forcing myself down into a crouching position with my knees on the ground, my feet against the kerb behind me and my hands covering my face.

Just as I felt that I could not hold out much longer I realized that the blast pressure was decreasing, and a shower of dust, dirt and rubble swept across me. Pieces penetrated my face and something pierced my knuckles, causing me involuntarily to let go my hold

on the kerb. Instantly, although the blast was dying down, I felt myself blown slowly across the pavement towards the wall of the building.

THEY HEARD A THUD in the night, but no explosion ; the coming of daylight revealed the presence in this back garden of a house at Finsbury Park, North London, of an enemy mine which had failed to "go off." Yet another which did not explode (left) was discovered hanging by its parachute against a wall of the Royal Free Hospital, London. *Photos, Planet News, Keystone*

I tried to hold on, but there was nothing to hold on to. Twice I tried to rise but seemed held down. Eventually I staggered to my feet, and I looked around. The front of the building was lit by reddish yellow light. A saloon car was on fire to the left of me, and flames from it were stretching out

towards the building horizontally. Pieces of brick, masonry and glass seemed to appear suddenly on the pavement, making—to me—no sound. Right in front of me were two soldiers, one near a breach in the wall of the building where a fire seemed to be raging. He was propped up against the wall with his arms dangling like a rag doll.

I made for the entrance of the building to get help. It was obscured by dust and smoke, and I nearly fell over a large steel plate which was blocking the entrance. Fearing that the car's tank would explode and envelop the injured soldier in flames, I hurried back to him and with him clinging to me we were able to reach the entrance. Soon after that we got help.

It's Like Heaven Now in War-Free Malta

Our Mediterranean strongpoint against complete Axis domination of the inland sea from Gibraltar to Egypt, Malta suffered almost to the limit of endurance. Back in the George Cross island again, George Harrison, News of the World war correspondent, tells what life there is like today, with the people rebuilding their homes as fast as they can.

TWO years ago we were trying to blast history's most famous convoy through to this island in the face of every known horror the Nazis could raise to prevent us. For two and a half days 14 merchant ships ploughed through the Mediterranean under the wings of the Royal Navy escorts from Gibraltar, while Axis bombers, torpedo-bombers, submarines, and E-boats flailed them minute by minute.

Five of the merchant ships, with cargoes of mercy for the besieged islanders got

through, and as the crews came ashore in Valetta the Maltese people—weeping and praying—tossed flowers at their feet and kissed them, openly unashamed at their display of heart-bursting joy.

There was only a week's food in the island then. Luxuries like meat were unknown. The peasants were reduced to snatching grains of corn out of the derelict, bomb-splashed fields to take home and jealously pound into portions of stone-mixed flour—when sufficient had been collected. The legs and arms of the people were scarred with the marks of scabies, which, through malnutrition, had struck viciously at them.

Today, 24 months later, I am here in Malta again, revelling, like its people, in the contrast between then and now. The war has now passed by this island. Even the black-out has gone. Coming from the battle fronts of Italy, it is strange to walk down Kingsway, the main shopping street in Valetta—still showing at every few yards its tumbledown ruins—and see the shop windows gaily illuminated and the street lights blazing brilliantly under the stars, with courting couples, arm-in-arm, pausing to shop-gaze.

Once before when I was here you might buy two small pork chops in the black market for about 30 shillings. Today in the restaurant where I had lunch the menu included : Fillets of fish and chips—two shillings ; mixed grill and veg.—three shillings ; two pork chops and veg.—two shillings. Then there was a whole mass of cold meats with salad for half-a-crown. I ordered steak and chips for the first time for many months. Garnished with onions and tomatoes it was delicious. Afterwards I took Philip Mifsud, the manager of the restaurant, aside and asked him about Malta's food position.

" We serve around 500 meals daily," he said. "Living in Malta today is like Heaven compared with the days of the siege. Take potatoes, which are the mainstay of the Maltese peasant's life. Thanks to the Government aid to our island growers we now receive unlimited supplies at 2d. per lb. In the old days when the whole crop had been eaten, we traded gold rings and bracelets worth pounds for a small sack from some careful farmer who had kept a few by him.

"Then we used to have a soup kitchen issue—twice a week soup, twice macaroni, and twice tinned fish, with a family ration once every two weeks of 2½ ozs. of corned

IN MALTA'S PALACE SQUARE, VALETTA, two bronze tablets, one of which is here shown, were unveiled on September 8, 1944. These commemorated the King's Message bestowing the George Cross on Malta on April 15, 1942, and President Roosevelt's citation commemorating his visit to the Island on December 7, 1943.
Photo, Sport and General

beef. Now, thank God (and he crossed himself devoutly) every man, woman and child in Malta can eat well."

Even "night life" has returned to the island. The bars have whisky, gin and beer. True they are expensive, but that is a minor consideration to those of us who have not tasted them for so many months. Clothing is plentiful in the shops but strictly couponed, and luxuries like chocolates are still under the counter. Lipsticks and cosmetics, which were rarer than diamonds two years ago, are now on show. Malta, one way and another, certainly buzzes with life.

OUR DIARY OF THE WAR

Russian Front.—Soviet troops captured island of Moon, off Estonia.

OCTOBER 2, Monday *1,857th day*
 Western Front.—U.S. 1st Army began new attack on Siegfried Line north of Aachen.
 Air.—Allied bombers and fighters attacked Kassel, Hamm, and the area of Cologne. R.A.F. again bombed Brunswick at night.
 General.—Inhabitants of Dutch islands in Scheldt estuary warned of coming Allied bombardment and flooding.

OCTOBER 3, Tuesday *1,858th day*
 Western Front.—Truce began at Dunkirk for evacuation of civilians. U.S. 3rd Army began attack on Fort Driant, one of Metz defences.
 Air.—R.A.F. Lancasters breached dyke on Walcheren Island. Announced that on night of September 23 Lancasters had bombed and drained Dortmund-Ems Canal. U.S. bombers attacked tank works and airfields in S. Germany.
 Poland.—End of Polish resistance in Warsaw after 63 days' fighting ; Gen. Komorowski (Bor) taken prisoner.
 Russian Front.—Island of Dago, off Estonia, captured by Soviet troops.

OCTOBER 4, Wednesday *1,859th day*
 Western Front.—Perimeter forts north of Antwerp being cleared of enemy.
 Air.—R.A.F. bombers attacked U-boat pens at Bergen. Announced that attack on battleship Tirpitz on September 15 was launched from Russian base.
 Russian Front.—Soviet troops linked up with units of Yugoslav Liberation Army.
 Mediterranean.—Allied bombers attacked Munich and points on Brenner line.
 Balkans.—Units of Land Forces, Adriatic, operating on Greek mainland, entered Patras in the Peloponnesus.

OCTOBER 5, Thursday *1,860th day*
 Western Front.—Allied troops crossed Dutch frontier north of Antwerp.
 Air.—Allied bombers attacked railways and airfields in Cologne and Munster areas. R.A.F. Lancasters bombed Wilhelmshaven, and at night dropped 350,000 incendiaries on Saarbruecken. Mosquitoes bombed Berlin.
 Russian Front.—Soviet troops began attack on Estonian island of Oesel.
 Pacific.—Liberators again bombed Balikpapan oil centre, Borneo.

Germany.—Call-up for military service of all boys born in 1928.

OCTOBER 6, Friday *1,861st day*
 Western Front.—Canadian troops crossed Leopold Canal between Bruges and Eecloo.
 Air.—Hamburg, Harburg and Berlin attacked by U.S. bombers and fighters. R.A.F. bombed oil plants in the Ruhr by day, and Dortmund, Bremen and Berlin at night.
 Russian Front.—Soviet troops crossed Rumanian-Hungarian frontier N. of Arad.
 Balkans.—British and Greek troops captured Aegean island of Samos.

OCTOBER 7, Saturday *1,862nd day*
 Western Front.—U.S. 1st Army broke through German line N. of Aachen. Heavy fighting in Leopold Canal bridge-head.
 Air.—More than 5,000 aircraft from Britain and Italy, in biggest daylight assault of the war, attacked German war plants. Kembs dam on Rhine in Alsace breached by R.A.F. Lancasters.
 Russian Front.—Soviet troops began new Lithuanian offensive towards East Prussia.

OCTOBER 8, Sunday *1,863rd day*
 Western Front.—U.S. 1st Army began new offensive east of Aachen. 3rd Army attacked between Metz and Nancy.
 Russian Front.—Soviet troops broke German defence line in Central Lithuania.
 Pacific.—Marcus Island shelled for first time by U.S. warships.

OCTOBER 9, Monday *1,864th day*
 Western Front.—Canadians and British landed in mouth of Sheldt to relieve pressure on Leopold Canal bridge-head.
 Air.—U.S. bombers attacked areas of Schweinfurt, Cologne and Mainz. At night R.A.F. bombed Bochum in the Ruhr.
 Balkans.—Allied troops entered Corinth.
 Far East.—U.S. carrier-aircraft attacked Ryuku Islands, between Formosa and Japan.
 General.—Mr. Churchill and Mr. Eden arrived in Moscow.

OCTOBER 10, Tuesday *1,865th day*
 Western Front.—Twenty-four hour ultimatum sent to Aachen by Allies after city had been almost surrounded.
 Russian Front.—Soviet troops reached Baltic coast north of Memel.

SEPTEMBER 27 Wednesday *1,852nd day*
 Western Front.—British 2nd Army launched limited attack S. of Arnhem.
 Air.—Railway yards and oil plants at Cologne, Ludwigshafen, Mainz and Kassel again attacked by Allied bombers. R.A.F. bombed Calais.
 Balkans.—Announced that Allied seaborne and airborne troops were operating in Albania and Dalmatian Is.

SEPTEMBER 28, Thursday *1,853rd day*
 Western Front.—Canadians captured citadel of Calais. German swimmers attempted to blow up Nijmegen bridge.
 Air.—Allied bombers again attacked war industries in Central Germany, at Merseburg, Kassel and Magdeburg.
 Russian Front.—Announced that agreement made between Russian Command and Marshal Tito for entry of Red Army troops into Yugoslavia.
 Pacific.—Announced that Allied aircraft from Australia raided Batavia on September 24 in record flight of nearly 3,000 miles.

SEPTEMBER 29, Friday *1,854th day*
 Western Front.—Armistice at Calais for evacuation of civilians. Cape Gris Nez captured by Canadians.
 Air.—Allied bombing, attacks continued on area of Siegfried Line.
 Russian Front.—All Estonia freed of Germans. except islands of Moon, Dago and Oesel.
 Pacific.—Allied aircraft destroyed shipping in Darvel Harbour, Borneo.

SEPTEMBER 30, Saturday *1,855th day*
 Air.—Allied heavy bombers pounded railway yards at Hamm, Munster and Bielefeld and oil plants in Ruhr.
 Russian Front.—Announced that Red Army troops had crossed Yugoslav frontier from Rumania.
 Pacific.—Liberators made attack on Balikpapan, oil centre of Borneo.
 Home Front.—Dover celebrated capture of all German cross-Channel guns.
 General.—Gen. Komorowski (Bor) to replace Gen. Sosnkowski as C.-in-C Polish Army.

OCTOBER 1, Sunday *1,856th day*
 Western Front.—Resistance ended at Calais. German counter-attack south of Arnhem beaten off.
 Air.—At night R.A.F. bombers attacked Brunswick.

★ ═══════ *Flash-backs* ═══════ ★

1939
September 27. *Surrender of Warsaw, capital of Poland.*

1940
September 27. *Tripartite Pact between Germany, Italy and Japan signed in Berlin.*
October 7. *German troops entered Rumania and occupied oilfields.*

1941
September 28. *Lord Beaverbrook and Mr. Harriman in Moscow for Three Power Conference.*
October 6.—*Two-pronged assault*

against Moscow launched by Germans under Von Bock.
October 8. *Russian Command announced evacuation of Orel.*

1942
October 3. *U.S. troops occupied Andreanos group of Aleutians.*
October 4. *Combined Operations raid on Sark, Channel Islands.*

1943
October 1. *Fifth Army captured city of Naples.*
October 5. *Strong U.S. naval and air forces attacked Wake Island.*

THE WAR IN THE AIR

by Capt. Norman Macmillan, M.C., A.F.C.

THE Luftwaffe has attempted to maintain attacks against Greater London with flying-bombs launched from Heinkel bombers over the North Sea. Dark nights, or the periods before moonrise, have been used for launching, but several times the starting of the jet-engine of the flying-bomb, with its tell-tale flame, has revealed the position of the parent aircraft to the watchful eyes of R.A.F. night fighter pilots, and a good percentage of the small number of Heinkels employed on this nocturnal venture have paid for their temerity in encroaching within the patrol area of defending fighters of A.D.G.B. This effort of the Luftwaffe was forecast in page 316, but, as expected, the attacks have been small scale intermittent launchings, sometimes with intervals of several days between them.

current airborne forces are not armed powerfully enough to enable them to hold out against surface forces heavily armed with guns and armour. Against these the 10-ton tanks and 6- and 17-pounder anti-tank guns used by the Airborne Army of today are too light to prevent Units from being compressed into pockets so small that the accurate dropping of supplies of food and war stores by parachute may become impossible. To prevent this they must be relieved rapidly by their own surface heavy armour and guns.

TRANSPORTATION of Heavy Guns and Large Tanks by Air

The notable lesson learned from this greatest-ever airborne operation was that full-scale airborne operations against first-class military Powers will have to include the

It must take about 1,300 h.p. to lift one ton over the divide, and the petrol expended per month on the climbing of the mountain range alone would weigh some 6,000 tons, apart from that used in the flight onward to the destination airfield in China. But this lift of about a quarter of a million tons a year is doubtless but a fraction of what is required by the Chinese to meet the continued onslaught of the Japanese army within China, fed, as it is, by rail from Korea and Manchuria, and by sea from Japan and Korea, with military stores of all kinds. And no doubt in the occupied area of China there are Chinese enslaved by the Japanese war machine to make whatever the Japanese war lords decree.

By comparison with China's needs the air transport lift, great feat though it is, is puny, and the advances through the islands from Australia towards the Chinese coast must seem snail-like, great efforts of organization by white men in tropical conditions though these be. As a result the Japanese have encircled another great slice of China, and have cut off the airfields from which Japan proper was being bombed by Super-Fortresses.

THE work of these giant bombers was valuable, but we know from experience of bombing Germany how vast a total weight of bombs is needed to put a highly organized war industrial machine out of action. It is probable that the bomb load of the Super-Fortresses operating at the range they have had to fly may not exceed some 6,000 lb. of bombs per aircraft per trip. There cannot yet be many of these aircraft in operation ; the production output in the United States was recently disclosed as now scheduled for the rate of about 1,000 a year. So far the bombing cannot have been much more than a token of what is later to come, much as was the British bombing of Germany in 1940-41. At its present stage of development the war in the air in the Far East is necessarily tied by the limitations of the surface forces, and the only way in which the bombing of Japan, and Japanese communications with their armies in China, could be stepped up rapidly would be by carrier-borne aircraft, a hazardous operation with the disposition of forces as they are at present.

Great bombing blows in Western Europe, however, indicate what Japan must eventually face. One was the destruction of a vital length of the Dortmund-Ems canal by a force of 96 Lancasters led by Wing-Commander G. W. Curry, D.F.C., on September 23, 1944, when 14 bombers were lost. This canal was attacked by five Hampdens under Flt.-Lieut. R. A. B. Learoyd in the early morning of August 13, 1940, when Learoyd won the V.C. for his part in the action (see page 222, Vol. 3). It connects the Ruhr with north-western Germany and joins the sea at Emden—another recent target for our bombers. The force of Lancasters used 12,000-lb. bombs and broke the canal banks, leaving it dry for a length of about 18 miles ; this compares with a small section of one of the twin branches of the canal at the aqueducts north of Munster which Learoyd's attack drained, but which was soon blanked off for repair by the enemy. The Lancaster attack on the canal was followed by a heavy bomber attack on Dortmund (important rail centre) in the night following October 5.

ON October 3, 1944, in daylight at high tide, Bomber Command smashed the sea dyke near Westkapelle, Walcheren island, to flood the German gun sites that covered Antwerp. For this operation 12,000-lb. bombs were used. Like the breaching of the Möhne and Eder dams, this was a novel air attack, unlike anything ever executed before. It is noteworthy that only British heavy bombers can make these devastating attacks ; the U.S. heavy bombers cannot transport such huge bombs.

WALCHEREN SEA WALL on the German-occupied island at the Scheldt entrance, was breached by R.A.F. Lancasters carrying 12,000-lb. bombs in a daylight attack on October 3, 1944. Here the waters of the North Sea are rapidly submerging the village of Westkapelle and enemy gun positions covering the approaches to Antwerp. By October 10 flooding had extended to Middelburg in the centre of the island.
Photo, British Official

It has now been stated officially that jet-propelled fighters were used in the defence of London and Southern England against the flying-bomb attack when the Pas de Calais launching sites were in use by the enemy (see page 354). These fast planes are extremely clean in design, and the absence of air-screw means that a shorter undercarriage can be used. Length of undercarriage leg is usually determined by the need to provide safe clearance between the tip of the revolving airscrew and the ground. The jet-plane's shorter undercarriage saves both weight and stowage space ; the saving in space means that there is more room inside the structure for other items, such as fuel, and this is of great importance in a small aircraft like a fighter. People on the ground within the flying-bomb lanes of approach to London nicknamed the jet-propelled fighters "jettys."

The withdrawal of the remaining 2,000 men of the British 1st Airborne Division from Arnhem (see p. 366) disclosed that

landing of heavy calibre guns and heavy tanks from the air. The time will come when 30-ton and even heavier tanks will be transported to their operational zone by air. This will introduce specially designed tank transport aircraft. Incidentally, I observe that it has been announced that it was realized in June 1940 that tank-carrying aircraft would be needed. There must be some mistake here, for on April 18, 1940, I took out a provisional patent for a novel design of tank-carrying aircraft, of which the Air Ministry was promptly advised.

President Roosevelt indicated what is being done already in military air transportation when, on October 5, he said that 20,000 tons of military supplies were being flown into China monthly. From India to China, after the Lashio road was cut, aircraft flew over the southern slopes of the Himalaya Mountains, carrying their load up to 20,000 feet (see pages 716, 717, Vol. 7).

Our Pacific Forces Move Still Nearer to Japan

ADMIRAL NIMITZ'S MEN landed on the Palau Islands, an enemy bastion 550 miles E. of the Philippines, on September 15, 1944, and quickly established themselves in palm-strewn trenches abandoned by the Japanese (2). At the same time, General MacArthur's forces invaded Morotai in the Halmahera group, 300 miles S. of the Philippines; infantry waded ashore from landing craft (1). Columns of smoke (3) marked the destruction of four enemy ships bombed at Haha Jima in the Bonin Islands, only 600 miles S. of Tokyo.   PAGE 381   *Photos, Planet News, Keystone*

Last Shots Fired in Four-Year Channel Duel

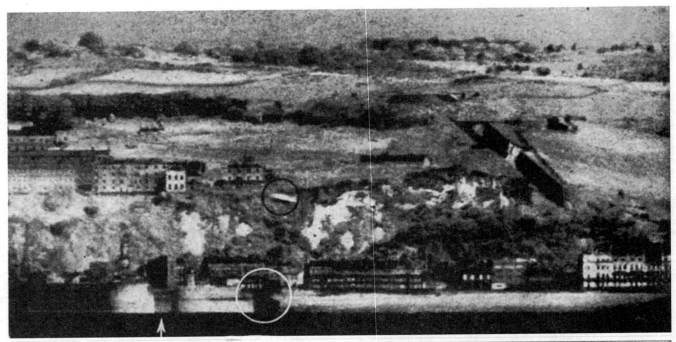

CROSS-CHANNEL SHELLING of the Dover area by the Germans began on August 12, 1940 (see pages 534-535, Vol. 7) and, with our capture of the French ports, ceased in September 1944. A German long-range photograph of Dover (1) taken from a gun emplacement at Calais, shows the harbour entrance (white arrow), a patrol craft (white circle) and its anti-aircraft balloon (black circle).

Scene of a most valiant stand by British troops in 1940, Calais Citadel fell to the 1st Canadian Army on September 28, 1944. During the Canadians' advance, guns of a heavy coastal battery at Dover (4) bombarded German positions.

The garrison of the last fort to hold out at Boulogne surrendered on September 22 : one of the 14-inch guns (2) that were silenced for ever, and its shells in a captured gun-pit (3).

Photos, Canadian Official, Associated Press, Keystone

AUTUMN, the poets have tried to make us believe, should be a "season of mists and mellow fruitfulness," as Keats addressed it in his exquisite Ode. It should have the pensive quality of approaching old age, the quiet serene atmosphere of windless days and clear starry nights. When Collins saw "sallow Autumn" filling its lap with leaves, he did not see those leaves torn off by furious gales or sodden with cold rain: he imagined them floating down through the blue air gently, restfully, to the ground. This year, when weather of that sort would have been immensely helpful to our soldiers and airmen, they have had very little of it. In our island we have been better off than the Continent. After still sunny days we have heard of storms raging in Italy, continuous rain in Holland, roads made scarcely usable by mud in occupied Germany. One exasperated war reporter spoke of the climate in some sector of the front having turned Quisling! Our task has certainly been made more difficult by bad weather and the war in consequence prolonged. A cynical acquaintance of mine says it became markedly worse just after the last Day of National Prayer.

THE announcement the other day that in order to clear off arrears of work the House of Commons would sit till eight o'clock in the evening sounded strange in the ears of one who all his life has been accustomed to the House sitting till eleven or so, and sometimes very much later. It is strange also to hear in the one o'clock News Bulletin that some statement or other was "made in the House of Commons this morning." Not for a very long time, before this war caused its habits to be altered, had Parliament met until the afternoon. This was mainly for the convenience of business men and barristers, but also in order to let Ministers spend the morning in their offices. But for the past forty years at least the business of the House has increased so much that it has suffered from this sacrifice of the best part of the day, the part when minds are at their freshest and energies unimpaired. I hope the new hours will remain. I should like to be able to hope, too, that something will be done to make M.P.s attend to their duties. It seemed to me disgraceful that the House should be obliged to adjourn on a day when important work waited to be done because only a handful of members were on the benches. Very few can have been in the place at all, for when the signal was given that a "count" was to be taken hardly any entered the Chamber. It is unfair to canvass our votes for a job that is so poorly performed.

OF all the contributions now being made to the World-after-the-War discussion, that of J. B. Priestley in his play They Came to a City must rank high. It has now been made into a film, and this is even more effective than the story was on the stage. Or should I say the conversation rather than the story, for there really is no plot and all the characters do is to talk. But it is stimulating, lively talk, and the screen by shifting their background constantly takes off the effect of monotony and makes it seem as if things were happening. The acting is all good, though not much is required of the cast beyond portraying types, a baronet of the Blimp family, a dyed-in-the-wool business man, a bank clerk afraid to "follow his star," a faded aristocratic dowager, and so on. But there is one vivid and pathetic human study—that of an old charwoman with aches all over from her life of toil, but a heart as young as a girl's. I wondered who could be playing that part, and when

the names were screened at the end I was both interested and delighted to see that of Miss Ada Reeve, whom I remember so well as a musical comedy star long ago. She sang wittily, danced like a feather in the wind, and turned somersaults so deftly that the gallery boys used to shout "Over, Ada!" She gives in this film a lovely performance.

IN a previous Postscript I spoke of the number of places in war news which are familiar to British holiday-makers in France. The Italian front reminds us of many towns and rivers known to us in literature. Rimini brings recollection not only of the ill-fated Francesca, who with Paolo was found by Dante in his Inferno, but of W. S. Gilbert, too, for into Patience he introduced the lines:

Francesca da Rimini
Niminy-piminy
Foot-in-the-grave young man

to ridicule the aesthetic type of 60 years ago. The Rubicon everyone seems to have some knowledge of, because it has passed into a phrase frequently used—"crossing the Rubicon," meaning to start irrevocably on some adventure, as Julius Caesar did when he took his army across it to attack Pompey and made his bid for the mastership of the Roman world. The river Po comes into both literature and history with equal prominence. Bologna figures largely in Vasari's Lives of the Italian early painters because so many of them took part in founding the school of painting called after that city. Ravenna calls up memories of Byron as well as Dante, who was buried there. As for Venice, not much farther on, it simply teems with associations.

LIEUT.-GEN. WILLIAM H. SIMPSON commands the U.S. Ninth Army in France. He served with the American Expeditionary Force in 1918 as chief of staff of the 33rd Division. PAGE 383 *Photo, U.S. Official*

NOT long ago there was a "problem" connected with worn-out safety razor blades—blades that were no good any more. How could they be disposed of? Where could they be thrown away without creating danger for anybody? A man who has been fighting in the jungles of Burma tells me there was a keen demand for them there. One of the worst misfortunes that can befall a soldier in the tropical or semi-tropical forest is snake-bite. The snakes are deadly, and though there are remedies that can be carried in your pack, the best thing to do is cut away immediately the flesh which has been poisoned by the bite. For this purpose safety razor blades are the very thing. "Every man who could get one wore it in his hat," the man from Burma told me. "They were precious out there, I can tell you." Surely a most unexpected solution of the razor-blade problem!

SEVERAL parents I know who sent their small children to the United States while the bombing of Britain was at its worst are worried about their probable return with an American accent. One child I am acquainted with who went to Canada, and is back already, was heard the other day calling out, "Motherr, wherre arre my sneakerrs?" His mother had to be told that "sneaker" is American for the rubber-soled shoes which we used to call sand-shoes. But an accent quickly picked up is dropped with equal quickness. An American lady belonging to the English-speaking Union says the children "lost their English accent in six months" and will no doubt recover it in about the same space of time. Even if they retained a little of their Transatlantic pronunciation it would do them no harm and might make their speech more racy and flavoursome than that of persons who have never been out of this island. Half the fun of American humour lies in the tone of voice in which it is made. Many a good story I have heard spoiled by the narrator's flat English (not Scottish or Irish, mark you!) mode of speech.

I SEE Dean Inge, who has ceased to be officially a pillar of the Church, but is still (as a bishop once described him) "two columns in the London Evening Standard," decries the use of certain American and Canadian words such as elevator for lift, suspenders for braces, back of for behind, and so on. This is simply antiquated prejudice. It might be argued that elevator and suspenders are words of Latin descent, while braces and lift are Anglo-Saxon in their origin. That is doubtful anyway in the case of lift, which seems to have come from the same root as elevator. But, whether it did or not, it is absurd to speak of the latter term as "an Americanism to be avoided like the plague." This is the kind of "piking," as Americans call it, which creates ill-will. It is insular in an irritating degree. Such an attitude of mind reminds me of the schoolboy who remarked that the French instead of saying Yes said Oui and the Germans Ja and the Italians Si and the Russians Da. "We alone get it right," he ended complacently. Was that schoolboy Dean Inge in his youth?

THE military mind has long been a puzzle to students of psychology. The ecclesiastical mind often bewilders those who pay attention to the utterances of bishops. For example, the Bishop of Rochester (Dr. Chavasse) has been saying in his diocesan journal that the German leaders and all who have been guilty of criminal acts must be punished, but he prays we may be delivered from the dreadful and hurtful role of being their executioners. His hope is that the German people will themselves play that role. Surely it is sufficiently obvious that from all points of view it would be better if Hitler and the rest were eventually killed by their own countrymen.

Rest from Battle in Nijmegen on the Waal

BRITISH 2nd ARMY INFANTRYMEN rested awhile in this ancient Dutch town from which the surprised German garrison had been routed in prolonged and bitter fighting. Airborne troops and tanks co-operated in chasing the enemy from house to house and street to street, the operation ending in its capture and the securing of the vital Nijmegen bridge—the biggest single objective of the airborne invasion. **The town's pre-war** population was close on 100,000. See pages 325 and 368-369.

Photo, British Official

Printed in England and published every alternate Friday by the Proprietors, THE AMALGAMATED PRESS, LTD., The Fleetway House, Farringdon Street, London. E.C.4. Registered for transmission by Canadian Magazine Post.   Sole Agents for Australia and New Zealand: Messrs. Gordon & Gotch, Ltd.; and for South Africa: Central News Agency, Ltd.—October 27, 1944.   S.   *Editorial Address:* JOHN CARPENTER HOUSE, WHITEFRIARS, LONDON. E.C.4.

Vol 8 # The War Illustrated Nº 193

Edited by Sir John Hammerton

SIXPENCE

NOVEMBER 10, 1944

DOVER'S SYMBOL OF THANKSGIVING—the Town Flag—was hoisted for the first time since the early days of the war by the Mayor, Alderman J. R. Cairns, J.P., on September 30, 1944. He led the rejoicings of Britain's "front-line town," crowds dancing and singing in the flag-hung streets after loudspeakers had announced that after four years' ordeal of cross-Channel shelling all enemy long-range guns mounted in French ports opposite had been silenced or captured.

Photo, Planet News

NO. 194 WILL BE PUBLISHED FRIDAY, NOVEMBER 24

Our Roving Camera Tours the European Scene

FINLAND'S PEACE DELEGATES journeying to Moscow were interrogated by Russian frontier guards. "Cease Fire" was ordered in the Russo-Finnish struggle on Sept. 4, 1944, after nearly 3½ years of bitter warfare.

POLAND'S TRAGIC HOMELESS included citizens of shell-racked Warsaw, who dragged themselves to safety in a refugee-camp after an abortive 63-days revolt which ended on October 3, 1944.

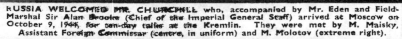

RUSSIA WELCOMED MR. CHURCHILL who, accompanied by Mr. Eden and Field-Marshal Sir Alan Brooke (Chief of the Imperial General Staff) arrived at Moscow on October 9, 1944, for ten-day talks at the Kremlin. They were met by M. Maisky, Assistant Foreign Commissar (centre, in uniform) and M. Molotov (extreme right).

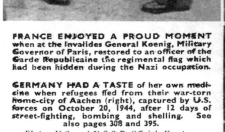

FRANCE ENJOYED A PROUD MOMENT when at the Invalides General Koenig, Military Governor of Paris, restored to an officer of the Garde Republicaine the regimental flag which had been hidden during the Nazi occupation.

GERMANY HAD A TASTE of her own medicine when refugees fled from their war-torn home-city of Aachen (right), captured by U.S. forces on October 20, 1944, after 12 days of street-fighting, bombing and shelling. See also pages 308 and 395.

Photos, U.S. and U.S.S.R. Official, Keystone, Pictorial Press

THE BATTLE FRONTS

by Maj.-Gen. Sir Charles Gwynn, K.C.B., D.S.O.

INFORMATION that has now been released concerning all the measures that the Navy had to take to ensure the build-up of the Armies and their supplies in Normandy should finally convince everyone that there was no avoidable delay in launching major offensive operations. It should also go far to explain the nature of the operations on the whole Allied front since determined enemy resistance was encountered. The ports available, whether improvised or under restoration, have still only a limited capacity which may further be greatly reduced by bad weather. Lines of communication have been immensely lengthened and the number of troops engaged greatly increased, not only in the fighting line but on rearward service of all kinds.

French railways at best are working far below their normal capacity, so that practically all movement of stores, not only those required for day-to-day expenditure, but also those needed to build up adequate reserves in forward areas before embarking on continuous offensive operations, must be moved by road. In Normandy the fighting line and all depots were within short distances of ports of disembarkation, and probably the main difficulty there was to avoid congestion of roads ; but now length of haulage has become the main factor in causing delay. It is not therefore surprising that the chief immediate object is to open access to the great Port of Antwerp which so astonishingly fell into our hands intact.

THE partial lull which has occurred has, of course, given the Germans opportunity to reorganize and restore morale after their shattering defeat, but the respite they have gained has been far from complete. Witness the number of costly, and generally ineffective, counter-attacks they have been compelled to deliver to maintain their defensive positions, and the sacrifice of suicide detachments they have had to make in order to deny us the use of some ports for a time. When General Eisenhower decides that he is ready to renew the offensive on a maximum scale we can, I think, count with some confidence that he will find that the newly-formed crust of German resistance will in places have been worn thin, even if we leave out of account the effects of the intensified air offensive which has been in progress.

How soon General Eisenhower will be ready to strike we have no means of judging, but if he considers the opening of Antwerp an essential factor we must reconcile ourselves to further delays, for it is certain that the Germans will fight to the last to deny us the use of this port.

RUSSIA During the lull on the western front the Russians have made great progress in preparing the way for the great offensive which at the time of writing seems actually to have started. With the loyal co-operation of the Finns they have left Rendulic's depleted army no alternative but a long and difficult retreat to Norway. The capture of Petsamo, moreover, has deprived the Germans of their main source of nickel supplies, while with the closing of the Gulf of Bothnia they will obtain little iron ore from Sweden.

The German armies in the Baltic States, after costly attempts to break south to East Prussia through Bagramyan's encircling force, and failure to carry out an evacuation through Riga, have been driven into the western corner of Latvia, where they are no longer a menace to Cherniakovsky's army

attacking East Prussia. Some part may escape through the ports of Libau and Windau, but they will have to run the gauntlet of Red Air Force attacks, and it is unlikely that they will contribute a substantial reinforcement to German reserves.

South of the Carpathians the German situation is even worse. Malinovsky's offensive through Rumania has penetrated far into the Hungarian plain and is approaching Budapest. His right wing threatens the retreat of substantial German and Hungarian forces belatedly withdrawing from northern Transylvania. General Petrov's Army, advancing through the northern Carpathian passes on a wide front is almost in contact with Malinovsky's right, and a new German disaster seems to be in the making. Horthy's attempt to surrender has apparently been frustrated, but its effects on the Hungarian Army will not so easily be eliminated. Even if they continue to fight, troops that have once been ordered to lay down their arms can no longer be reliable, and Petrov's rapid advance across the Carpathians has almost certainly been assisted by Hungarian defections.

BALKANS Malinovsky's left wing co-operating with Marshal Tito's forces and receiving some assistance from Bulgarian troops has also had remarkable successes which place the Germans, now in full retreat from Greece and southern Yugoslavia, in a desperate situation. The capture of Nish closed their main line of retreat, and the alternative route through Skoplje is long and difficult, passing through country swarming with Tito's partisans. To make matters worse the Germans in northern Yugoslavia, who might have kept retreat routes open, have been roughly handled. Several considerable groups have been surrounded and annihilated, and those that attempted to hold Belgrade, after a suicidal struggle, shared the same fate. Here again the chances that German reserves will be reinforced by the armies retreating from the Balkans are almost negligible, and Kesselring's chances of withdrawing successfully from Italy at his chosen moment are also steadily diminishing.

The whole German south-eastern front covering Austria and southern Germany is therefore desperately exposed, and should there be any considerable defection of Hungarian troops Malinovsky may achieve decisive results, provided always that his communications are good enough to maintain the momentum of his advance. If Rumanian

THRUST TOWARDS THE MAAS at Venlo (indicated by arrow) by troops of the British 2nd Army developed on the fall of Venray and Overbroek on Oct. 18, 1944. Map shows the Allied line on Oct. 20.
By courtesy of News Chronicle

railways are in reasonable working order and an adequate supply of rolling stock is available they may greatly ease supply problems, for there will be no break of gauge to complicate matters. It is obvious that the Germans, with the main Russian offensive in East Prussia and Poland in progress cannot afford to transfer troops from the north in any number to buttress their southern front ; even less can they afford to denude their western front, already dangerously weak.

TIMING of the Russian successive offensives has again been admirable, and there has again been a notable display of patience in Russian strategy, especially so in their northern Carpathian operations. It may be remembered that when Zhukov's offensive in the early spring this year almost reached the crest of the passes there was something approaching general expectation that an invasion of the Hungarian plain was imminent. At the time I can remember expressing the opposite view, that Zhukov for the time being would do no more than establish a footing in the passes and use the mountains as a defensive flank for his westward operations ; for it seemed clear that to enter Hungary without a co-operative attack in the south would be to invite a crushing counter-attack on emergence into the plain.

Malinovsky's offensive has supplied the co-operative factor, providing the opportunity for Petrov's advance at the time when it was likely to be most effective ; but it meant months of patient waiting. An army that holds the initiative can afford to wait to ensure the timing of its blows ; but for an army that is on the defensive, as the Reichswehr is, waiting leads often, as we have seen, to belated decisions.

H.M. THE KING returned to London on Oct. 16, 1944, after a five-day tour in Holland and Belgium. He is here seen in a caravan close to the enemy lines, discussing the campaign with Field-Marshal Montgomery.
Photo, Newspaper Pool PAGE 387

British and U.S. Armies on Germany's Border—

BRITISH 2nd ARMY troops in the Venray and Overloon fighting included the 3rd Division—comprising Scotsmen and men from the Midlands, East Anglia, Yorkshire, Lancashire and Shropshire. Overloon, south of Nijmegen, fell on October 12, 1944 ; Churchills pass the shattered church (left). Occupation of Venray, Dutch road and rail centre, was completed six days later, after house-to-house fighting (right), this successful action reducing the enemy salient west of the River Maas. See map in page 387. *Photos, British Official*

U.S. 1st ARMY AT AACHEN battled in the suburbs towards the centre of the smashed city against fanatical resistance until its capture on October 20, 1944, when it was stated that over 10,000 prisoners had been taken. More than 15,000 civilians also fell into American hands. An American sniper used a tank as protection against enemy fire (left). A 57-mm. anti-tank gun in action during the prolonged street-fighting (right). Thanks to the U.S. gunners' accuracy little damage was done to the city's famous cathedral. See also pages 386 and 395. PAGE 388 *Photos, Keystone*

—And Driving Towards the Po Valley in Italy

5th ARMY FORCES were reported to be on the main Florence-Bologna road within eight miles of Bologna itself on October 26, 1944, and engaged in heavy fighting. Inside the much-vaunted Gothic Line the Germans had constructed strong underground defences on the hillsides, from which they were forced to withdraw. An abandoned Spandau machine-gun nest (left) covered Route 65 to Longhidoro. Brazilian soldiers, going into action for the first time, hauled a captured German anti-tank gun across the River Serchio, assisted by a mule (right).

8th ARMY HAD CROSSED the River Pisciatello and taken Cesena by October 20, 1944, despite heavy rains, swollen rivers and waterlogged roads. A week later they were reported well beyond the River Savio on each side of the Via Emilia, five miles east of Forli. A bogged-down 25-pounder had to be extricated from a flooded emplacement (left) north-east of Scorticana, just across the famous River Rubicon, which at this point (right) is spanned by two newly-erected Bailey bridges (see page 169); in the foreground a bulldozer is in difficulties. The crossing of the Rubicon by Julius Caesar in B.C. 49 began the Roman Civil War.

Photos, British Official

H.M.S. APOLLO, A NEW FAST MINELAYER, of which this is the first picture to be released. In appearance she bears a distinct resemblance to H.M.S. Manxman, survivor of a class of four such ships laid down in 1939. She is a vessel of 2,650 tons with the exceptional speed of 40 knots. Apart from her cargo of mines, she carries an armament of six 4·7-in. guns and sundry smaller weapons. It will be recalled that ships of the Manxman type played an important part in keeping Malta supplied in 1941-42.
Photo, British Official

THE WAR AT SEA

by Francis E. McMurtrie

IN the Far East the pace of the war is increasing. The First Lord of the Admiralty has stated that "a fleet capable in itself of fighting a general action with the Japanese Navy" is being transferred to the Pacific. It will include an immense train of auxiliaries of every kind, from escort aircraft carriers down to landing craft, the need for which will be great owing to the immense distance from Allied bases at which actions are likely to be fought.

With the American landing in the island of Leyte, October 20, 1944, the campaign for the reconquest of the Philippines has opened.

In attempting to expel the attackers by a naval offensive, the Japanese have made their situation infinitely worse. While their fleet still existed as an intact unit it was bound to exercise a certain constraint on Allied movements at sea ; but now it has suffered a severe defeat in the Philippines battle, with the loss of certain of its more important units and the crippling of many others, there is little to prevent the Allied Navies from ranging far and wide, interrupting the vital communications on which depend not only the maintenance of Japanese armies abroad but the sustenance of the population at home.

A fatal mistake was made when the authorities in Tokyo assumed the truth of the claims made by their aircraft to have sunk or damaged a dozen Allied aircraft carriers and various other ships. Relying on this information, they took the risk of sending all their available fighting ships into the waters of the Philippines. No better opportunity could have been wished for by the Allied naval commanders. At the cost of one aircraft carrier of moderate size, the U.S.S. Princeton, two escort carriers, two destroyers and a destroyer escort, losses of a much more serious character were inflicted on the enemy. At the time of writing, these are understood to comprise four aircraft carriers, two battleships, six heavy and three light cruisers and six destroyers. Nearly all the more important Japanese ships were badly mauled, and their repair will take time in the present congested state of enemy shipyards.

H M.A.S. AUSTRALIA, wearing the pennant of Commodore J. A. Collins, R.A.N., in command of the Australian squadron operating with the U.S. Pacific Fleet, received a bomb hit on or near the bridge, killing 19 officers and men and wounding 54, including the Commodore himself. Otherwise, no extensive damage is reported by Admiral Halsey, who commands the Allied naval

forces in the Philippines and is entitled to the chief credit for this important victory.

In the early days of the war it was possible to ascribe the erratic strategy of the Japanese Navy to the fact that it was dominated by the Army under General Tojo. Now that Admiral Yonai has been given a freer hand under the present regime, it might have been expected that such a miscalculation as that which precipitated the Battle of the Philippines would have been avoided. It would seem, indeed, that as the war progresses our Eastern foes are showing increasing signs of being "rattled."

SUPERIOR Strategy Caught the Japanese Napping

It is probable that the enemy were by no means certain where the blow was going to fall, and were thus taken entirely by surprise at Leyte. It is said that preparations had been made to resist an invasion of Mindanao, the great island immediately to the south. Possibly also an attack on Formosa or the Ryukyus was feared. In Far Eastern countries enormous importance is always attached to "saving face," or in other words, avoiding the loss of prestige. To the people of Japan, the loss of the Philippines would not mean much in this way ; and to lose Formosa even would be regarded as a minor blow. Thus it seems likely that what is left of the Japanese fleet will now be husbanded as much as possible, so that it may

FOOD AND AMMUNITION FOR GREECE were aboard this British landing craft in the Mediterranean, and Lt. Greag (above), from Tasmania who repeatedly helped to transport badly-needed supplies was no stranger to the task. PAGE 390 *Photo, British Official*

ultimately fight under the most advantageous conditions, close to its home shores when those are threatened.

There is still a very limited amount of information about the Japanese Navy and its present strength. After its latest losses it may include eight battleships, three of which are new units of 45,000 tons, armed with 16-in. guns. Aircraft carriers may number nine or ten, few of which are first-class vessels. Cruisers have been variously estimated, according to the assessment of losses, but a maximum figure would be about 30. Destroyers, in spite of heavy casualties, may be as many as 80, and submarines are quite as numerous.

The United States Navy should be able to dispose of twice as many ships in each of the foregoing categories without exhausting its reserves. This superiority continues steadily to increase, as American shipyards have an infinitely greater capacity than those of Japan, and also build more rapidly. This does not take into account the very substantial force comprised in the British Eastern Fleet.

THERE is no doubt the Japanese Navy has been heavily handicapped owing to its strategy having been controlled by military men. The Naval Staff in Tokyo would probably have accomplished much more with the material at its disposal had it not thus been fettered. Audacious as the initial attack on Pearl Harbour may have been, it was deprived of any lasting effect by the enemy's failure to follow it up at once with a large-scale invasion of the Hawaiian group. Ultimately this seems to have been grasped, for the Battle of Midway nipped in the bud an enterprise which appears to have had Hawaii as its objective. Incidentally, this action, owing to the heavy loss in aircraft carriers sustained by the enemy, proved the turning point of the whole war in the Pacific.

In the Solomons campaign the same halting strategy can be seen. Instead of overwhelming the Allies at the start by a concentration of the utmost force, the Japanese poured in reinforcements, with sea and air support, in small packets, which always just failed to turn the scale. In the end everything was lost as a result. Much the same process may be expected to follow elsewhere ; Burma is an instance. There, sea communication between Rangoon and Singapore is practically non-existent as the outcome of British submarine operations.

British sea and air attacks on Sabang, Surabaya, the Andamans and the Nicobars, have given the enemy warning that his hold on Malaya and the Netherlands East Indies is growing more precarious. In the near future the Japanese garrison in Singapore may find itself in much the same unenviable position as the Russians in Port Arthur in 1904.

British Commandos Turn Up in Stormy Albania

TAKING SORELY-NEEDED AID to Marshal Tito's Yugoslav partisans and Albanian patriots harassing the German withdrawal from the Balkans, Allied seaborne and airborne forces—mainly British—landed in Albania, it was announced on September 27, 1944. The landings were covered by powerful units of the Balkan Air Force, a composite group of the Mediterranean Allied Air Forces, the formation of which was disclosed on August 5, 1944. Here British Commandos are making their way along the shore after disembarkation.

Photo, British Official

Lifeline to Russia: Tasks Without Parallel

Aid from the Empire and America to Soviet forces has not only resulted in tremendous victories in the field. It has provided one of the greatest stories of supply achievement in the history of war, of feats of engineering, individual effort and courage and ingenuity, of triumph over climatic extremes and vast distances, as told by JOHN FLEETWOOD. See also facing page.

WHEN the last bomb falls on Europe and the last resisting Nazi bites the dust, it will be found that one of the sure foundations on which the United Nations built victory was provided by the legions who opened a back door into Russia and through it poured over 3,750,000 tons of vital war supplies.

As each great Russian drive bites deeper into the fortress of Hitler's tyranny, as each day brings some new story of brilliant Red Army leadership and courage, men far from the battle front yet fighting blinding sunshine, grilling heat, dust-storms, thirst, insect pests, boredom and exhaustion pause for a moment to ponder: " I, too, had a share in that."

These are men of the Persia and Iraq Command (Paiforce), Britons, Americans, Indians, Russians, Poles, men at office desks, in lorry cabins, in river craft, perched on telephone poles in blazing sun or huddled for warmth in dugouts high in mountain passes. And their task ? Aid to Russia—three words that combine great victories in the field with one of the greatest supply achievements in the history of war.

It started when the Allies faced a grim prospect, when the United States were still neutral, in the summer of 1941. Russia had taken so many body-blows in the German advance on Moscow and the Caucasus that observers began to fear she was beaten. British troops had been driven back from Benghazi. Greece and Crete were lost. In Syria, Vichy was ready to co-operate with the Axis. Iraq's Raschid Ali, brave with Nazi gold and promises, had thrown off the mask ; the Persian Shah's attitude was doubtful. To crown the despair of the civilized world, Japan became increasingly hostile.

TRUE to her treaty obligations and in protection of the guaranteed independence of Iraq, Britain rushed reinforcements into Iraq and quelled the Raschid rising, only to be faced with the threat of a German advance from the north. Thus was Paiforce born. Gradually the menace from the north receded, but the armies of the Soviet were in desperate need of tanks, mechanical transport, petrol, oil. And so, from Britain, by the Arctic route, ships of the Merchant Navy battled their way through the icy seas of U-boat alley to north Russian ports.

It was not enough, and soon hard-pressed British armies in North Africa were being denied their urgent needs. British and Indian troops were striking hard from the west and north-west, from the east and south-east, to open the warm-water and overland route to the Soviets, and to keep it open. Ports, railways and roads inadequate to deal with the situation were replanned and rebuilt to form a vast supply route between the Persian Gulf and the Russo-Persian frontier.

Since the British Army Arrived

Tanks, ammunition, trucks, food, steel and rubber from the British Empire and America began to pour into Persian Gulf ports. While these were being unloaded, engineers worked feverishly to enlarge and improve port, road and rail facilities. It is officially estimated that nearly 50 per cent of the total Aid to Russia provided by Britain, Canada and the U.S. has travelled via the Persia-Iraq Command route, playing a vital part in the sweeping Soviet successes.

In his better days the late Shah was an ambitious, energetic, if ruthless autocrat. He set his heart on a railway across Persia from Bandarshahpur to Bandarshah to link the Persian Gulf with the Caspian Sea—868 miles. British engineers surveyed the projected line through the towering mountains. By 1937 the system was working, but it handled no more than a daily average of 200 tons. Since the British Army arrived the capacity of the trans-Persia road-rail route has been geared to tackle up to 300,000 tons a month.

Consider a few more obstacles. The highest point on the line is 7,205 feet above sea level, the lowest is 85 feet below. Duty has to be done in the Euphrates Valley where summer shade temperatures often rise well above 100 degrees, and in scorched deserts of Persian uplands. There, in the heat of mid-day, when work is halted by the sun, long hours have been lived laboriously through, with worries about the delays of mail or desperate guessing as to when the war would end. Even when the mail comes through, when an order of the day records recognition of the value of their work, it is still the dogged courage of these men that saves them from degenerating into the most browned-off troops in the world.

Between the two climatic extremes this great track to Russia soars and falls on gradients which make fantastic demands on engines, brakes and couplings. During the first summer the sun heated the feed-water in the engine tenders until the injectors were unable to deal with it, immobilizing the trains till special hot-water injectors could be flown in from Britain and India. In the high mountains in winter the other extreme prevailed, and trains were ice-bound.

Since the forming of the American Persian Gulf Command, Aid to Russia has been a responsibility divided between Britain and the U.S., and now figures of astronomical proportions appear in the lists of war supplies sent to Soviet forces. Aviation fuel alone amounted to over 53 million gallons ; M.T. petrol used in convoying this and other materials to Russia exceeded 80 million gallons. In the more desperate months the Russians made calls for double and then treble the totals originally promised.

Always there has been the menace of thieves and saboteurs—not of one nation but of many, out for immediate personal gain or in the pay of the Nazis. Here in these huge wastes, where all manner of men can wander at will, thieving is a fine art. The Germans pay well for sabotage ; and black marketeering is a racket more despicable than anything we know at home. More than £400 has been paid for an urgently needed tire, £40 for a car battery.

TO list all the units and services which have thrown their weight into this task would be impossible ; it has been so vast, this aid to Russia, so complex in its many ramifications. So many tiny wheels, interlocking, make the whole mighty machine. Royal Engineers planned and achieved, the Pioneer Corps with their Indian battalions and locally enrolled labour have toiled and sweated, as have the R.A.S.C. and the R.I.A.S.C.

Always the telephones and telegraphs have been kept open for this vital line of communication. Often linesmen of the Royal Signals have had to wear special padding to protect hands from scorching metal or from frost-bite. Famous infantry regiments have patrolled the vast highway, guarded the pipe-line that carries much of the oil. Army Post Offices have fought a long, hard battle to bring mails as often as possible to thousands of soldier nomads.

SUPPLY ROUTE ACROSS PERSIA, stretching from the ports on the Persian Gulf to the Russian frontier, saw an ever-increasing flow of British and American convoys laden with war materials for the U.S.S.R. during the critical years 1942-43. As explained in this page, the long line of communication was kept open often in the face of extremely hazardous conditions. Here an Allied convoy has left the snow-covered mountains in the distance, the laden lorries driving on across lonely countryside towards Russia.

Photo. New York Times Photos

Through Persia to Marshal Stalin's Armoury

AVIATION AND OTHER SPIRIT reaches Russia from Abadan—" City of Oil "—an island in the Persian Gulf where much of the crude oil of Persia and Iraq is converted into its many by-products, including aviation spirit, at the rate of millions of gallons a day. The plant makes its own 4-gallon tins ; thus the petrol is delivered ready-canned (1). Persian mountain passes are patrolled by British military police (2). The forbidding Pa' Yi' Taq Pass in N. Persia, over which the bulk of the Allies' supplies are taken (3). See also facing page.

Photos, British Official

Joyfully the Greeks Greet British Freedom Army

LIBERATION OF GREECE, which culminated in the Allied occupation of Athens (see map above) on October 14, 1944, began when Land Forces Adriatic, under Gen. R. M. Scobie (see illus. p. 415), occupied Patras on October 4. Youngsters quickly made friends with our men (4). British forces landed from Dakota planes (1). Greek E.L.A.S. (Partisans) headed columns that entered Corinth (2) on Oct. 9. Greek collaborators were rounded up by men of the R.A.F. Regiment (3).

Photos, British Official. Map by courtesy of The Daily Telegraph

Germans Sealed the Utter Doom of Aachen City

REICH BORDER CITY 25 MILES S.W. OF COLOGNE, Aachen (Aix-la-Chapelle), scene of the crowning of medieval German monarchs, refused on October 10, 1944, an Allied ultimatum to surrender within 24 hours or be totally destroyed. Bombardment by 200 U.S. heavy guns followed concentrated air attacks, and by Oct. 20 the city was in Allied hands. The ultimatum was delivered by two lieutenants, with a private displaying a bedsheet on a pole (1). Debris in the suburb of Forst (2). Aachen from the air (3). (See also p. 388.)

Commandos With a Hose: Our Soldier-Firemen

Hitler's "scorched earth" policy provides tough work for British fire-fighters. From guarding highly inflammable stores at the docks to extinguishing a blaze in a French or Dutch or Belgian farmhouse their daily routine ranges. There is much of interest about the Army Fire Service and specialist columns of the N.F.S., told here by JOHN ALLEN GRAYDON.

MEN of the Army Fire Service, although little is ever said about their work, are playing an important part in the liberation of Europe. They were among the first troops to land on the Continent, and since D-Day have without respite been in action. The Germans have left in the wake of their retreating armies large numbers of arsonists with instructions to destroy by fire everything possible. The "scorched earth" policy has been perfected by the enemy over a period of nearly five years; but because of their splendid training and knowledge of modern methods, the Army Fire Service has already saved millions of pounds' worth of property in Europe.

During the early days of the invasion, while they were extinguishing the flames that gripped French hamlets, villages, and small towns, they were specially singled out by German snipers. On one occasion, when a party of firemen were guarding an important installation on the beaches, they were subjected to heavy shell-fire. Part of the area was set ablaze—but with sniper's bullets flying around them the firemen went to work and conquered the flames. Then a party of them went looking for the snipers!

The Army Fire Service is under the command of Lieutenant-Colonel S. N. Beattie, whose designation is Inspector of Fire Services. The personnel wear on their shoulder a round 2½-inch diameter badge, with a red background, a blue ring, and a yellow star, with the words: "Army Fire Service." The backbone of this Service are men who have been firemen in civilian life. Many former members of the old Auxiliary Fire Service have found their fire-fighting knowledge, secured perhaps during the 1940 blitz, of great use in Italy and France. Every big Army Depot has its own fire-fighting unit; the six largest have a station organized on the lines of the N.F.S.

ARMY Firemen are trained at a big centre in the North of England, and hundreds every month, under the instruction of experienced firemen, are passed out as qualified fire-fighters. Every man belonging to the Army Fire Service is a trained fighter; tough, quick, alert, and skilled in the use of small arms. Many times they have been thankful for this training. Near Rome a unit found themselves faced by several hundred Germans when they were fighting a fire in a small town; first they turned their hoses upon the enemy—and while the Germans were recovering from their surprise the firemen secured their rifles, took cover in the ruins of what had once been houses, and held off the Germans until a British armoured column arrived on the scene. Then they resumed their fight against the flames!

A GREAT spirit of co-operation sprang up over the war years between the National Fire Service and their counterparts in the British Army. Each calls upon the other where needed, and often the soldier-firemen are of infinite use when a fire breaks out nearer to their camp than the local fire brigade. River fire-fighting plays a big part in the preparation of the army fireman, and N.F.S. men of the River Thames Formation have often assisted in training soldiers for this very specialized form of fighting fires.

Highly trained, the Army Fire Service soldiers, before D-Day, were equipped to tackle burning docks, supply ships, transport vessels, and areas fired as the result of enemy action. Specially-constructed fire-tenders were built for carrying a water supply for immediate first-aid while the water barrage was being brought into action with heavy appliances.

In France the Army Fire Service, with their heavy equipment, cumbersome, and demanding great strength to handle over a long period, have won the praise of more than one battalion, and the gratitude of French farmers and townsfolk because of their promptitude and knowledge of how to deal with a situation that might puzzle less experienced fire-fighters. A case in point was a small farmhouse that was fired by the enemy.

The soldier-firemen found the roof ablaze when they arrived on the scene, and within a matter of seconds they were at work. The enemy were lobbing mortar shells over at the time, but the firemen completed their task and the farmhouse was saved. In their spare moments the firemen, together with men from another unit, helped repair the damaged roof. Within a week the old farmer and his wife were again living in their little home—while the men who had made this possible were still fighting fires, but many miles away. Some time ago Hitler hinted that he would scorch all Europe before the end of the war. His Huns have many times tried to do this. But neither shells, bullets nor bombs will halt these "Commandos With a Hose."

THE Overseas Columns of the National Fire Service and the Fire Float Flotillas were ready in June 1944 to send contingents to the Continent, but owing to the eclipse of the Luftwaffe, it was announced by Mr. Herbert Morrison in October 1944 that only one column and one flotilla need be held for emergencies. The men, distinguished by their blue berets, have perfected themselves in the art of fighting fires in petrol stores, aboard ammunition ships, in military buildings, and storage dumps. In addition to their blue berets they wear khaki webbing, and have a special pack for carrying their kit. The columns had been made available equally to the British and American armies. They were formed of picked men, all volunteers, from all parts of England, Scotland and Wales; a company of skilled Canadian fire-fighters was also included.

FIGHTING A PETROL BLAZE behind the lines in France was only one of the tasks for which men of the Army Fire Service were specially trained. Wherever the Armies of Liberation go, the Army Fire Service are prepared to save not only Service stores and supplies, but civilian property threatened by flames. See also facing page. PAGE 396 *Photo, British Newspaper Pool*

How the Army Fire Service Prepared for France

SOLDIER FIRE-FIGHTING UNITS accompanied the British 2nd Army to France. Specialists in fire prevention and extinction, they are also trained warriors (3). Foam equipment is carried on camouflaged tenders (1) for use against oil and petrol conflagrations. Suction hose for a light pump is brought up (2). A heavy pump is manhandled into position at a stream edge (5) ; it takes water from the stream to "play" on a fire on the opposite bank (4), while a light pump is taken across. At the double, equipment goes forward (6). *Photos, L.N.A.*

Now the Arab States Move Towards Federation

The establishment of a league of independent Arab States was decided on at a preliminary conference held in Alexandria from September 25 to October 7, 1944. The implications of this move by countries whose geographical position makes them of world importance, and the historical background of Arab unity, are discussed here by SYED EDRIS ALI SHAH.

THE long-expected Arab Union is at last to become fact. On October 7, 1944, it was announced from Alexandria that the representatives of five Arab states —Egypt, Iraq, Syria, Lebanon and Transjordan—had signed a protocol to establish a league of the Arab nations. Two other delegates, those of Saudi Arabia and Yemen, not being empowered by their governments to commit themselves to anything, have submitted their reports to King Abdul Aziz Ibn Saud and the Imam of Yemen, who are expected to give their full approval.

The other Middle Eastern Arab state, Palestine, though unable to participate on equal terms in the conference—owing to its status as a British mandate—sent an observer in an unofficial capacity, who will keep the Palestinean Arab leaders posted as to the progress of the project. Article Five of the protocol mentions Palestine thus: "The conference holds that engagements made by Britain, which comprise the cessation of Jewish immigration, the safeguarding of lands belonging to the Arabs, and the advance of Palestine towards independence, constitute rights acquired by the Arabs, and that their execution will be a step forward towards the desired goal, and towards the return of peace and stability."

The clause of the agreement dealing with the Arab League speaks of a council, in which all the member states shall be on an equal footing; its mission would be to co-ordinate their political programmes, so as to safeguard their sovereignty against any aggression, and to concern itself with the general interests of the Arab countries.

This step towards greater unity and stability may be called a Middle Eastern League of Nations, very much on the lines of its Geneva predecessor, with the important difference that it concerns itself mainly with economic and political co-operation between several nations of one common language, area, and cultural and historical heritage. In this respect it is a more solid foundation for practical work than that of the two geographically nearest leagues that were established before the war: the Balkan Entente, inaugurated by Turkey, and the Saadabad Pact, between Iraq, Iran, Turkey and Afghanistan.

To understand the implications of this move, by countries which lie athwart British communications with the East, and owing to the Suez Canal and the Iraqian and other oilfields are a vital factor in world affairs, we must get a good grasp of the meaning and extent of the Arab world. When the conquering Arabs swept out of their deserts they carried with them their language, culture and religion into many countries that were not of true Arab stock or feeling. Naturally, as these Middle Eastern countries came under the sway of the Arabs, a wholesale interchange of ideas took place; with the result that the so-called Arab civilization emerged. Under this, the arts and sciences, poetry, literature, architecture and many other phases of human endeavour became a kind of synthesis; dominating and guiding this were the Arabic language and the Islamic religion.

So this mass of widely differing peoples was welded into one cultural and linguistically homogeneous mass, with preponderant Moslem religious unity. Although the Moslem world contains a population of over four hundred millions, the Arab unit with which we are concerned has about forty-four millions. These Arab lands can be divided geographically into three groups: North Africa without Egypt, having a population

of about sixteen million; Egypt, with another sixteen million; and Arabia proper. This third division, comprising Saudi Arabia, Yemen, Oman, Aden and Transjordan, with the "fertile crescent" countries Iraq, Syria and Lebanon, conforms roughly to the shape of the federation, with the addition of Egypt. Aden and Oman, like Palestine, being British controlled, naturally have to be left out of the calculations.

THE project aims at making these countries into one unit. Main problems that have worried the Arabs so far have been those of differences in currency and economic disparities. Unification of the monetary systems

ARAB STATES, delegates from which signed a protocol at Alexandria for the formation of an Arab League, are shown in black in this map. Saudi Arabia and Yemen were also represented at the conference; Palestine, being under British mandate, was not.

would be a comparatively simple matter under a single government; while the same applies in a far greater degree to questions of trade and industry. It should be remembered that the present divisions of the several States are of comparatively recent origin, following the break-up of the Turkish Empire, and bear no relation to the true economic and strategical demands of their positions. With the rapidly expanding industries that have grown up in the various States owing to the war, and the even greater expansion of industry and commerce that must follow it, lack of planning and the ability to co-operate in these matters might well result in economic disaster in the Middle East, with the inevitable recurrence of disorder.

Naturally a plan of such magnitude as this is no innovation: resistance to alien domination and the desire for unity have been

perhaps the most clearly marked feelings of the Arabs for centuries. But of this long movement, the fruits of which have ripened at this significant phase of the war, it is the more recent history that concerns us now for a fuller understanding of the situation.

After the last war, the secret plans and activities of the various Arab Unity organizations were more free to come into the open. In August 1923, a Congress of the Arabian Peninsula was held on the occasion of the Mecca pilgrimage. Mecca became the headquarters of the movement, and the King of the Hejaz was playing the leading part. A delegation consisting of members from Syria and Palestine met King Hussein in January 1924, and made a declaration of their support of unity under the kings of the peninsula. The work went on until Hussein's kingdom fell, and King Ibn Saud took over the reins.

In the nineteen-thirties Arab feelings were very much stirred by events in Palestine. Significantly, after the 1929 disturbances, the Baghdad Arab Congress executive voted in Jerusalem a programme embodying the two points that all efforts should be made to gain sovereignty for the Arab states, and that the Arab nation constituted one indivisible unity: any division that might have occurred was not recognized by the nation. An Arab Congress took place in Jerusalem in 1936; then followed a treaty between Saudi Arabia and Iraq, while Egypt gained her independence in the same year. The conferences have continued to the present day, receiving impetus from the attainment of independence during this war of Syria and Lebanon.

WHO are the personalities behind all this and to what extent has the idea entered the soul of the Arab peoples? These are the questions that spring at once to mind. In the present political field there are a large number of new faces, together with an impressive array of the "old guard" of Arab national aspirations. Among the old champions of the cause are King Farouk, King Ibn Saud, and the Emir Abdullah of Transjordan. Other outstanding personalities are the Emir Shakib Arslan, General Nuries-Syed, the Prime Minister of Iraq, and H.R.H. the Emir Abd-ul-Illah, Regent of Iraq. Emir Shakib Arslan is a Druse from Syria, who has played no small part in Arab revival in North Africa. He organized the Bludan Arab Congress in 1937, and his periodical, Le Monde Arabe, published in Geneva, has long been the standard-bearer of the Arab renaissance. The Regent of Iraq was prominent at the time of Lawrence of Arabia's campaign, and he is the author of a plan for Arab Federation.

These leaders are all extremely shrewd men, and their planning is not merely selfish and insular; they realize that the world will be a safe place after the war only if nations abandon the policy of an introspective view of world affairs. In short, that the tendency of nations to hold aloof from each other amounts almost to a direct invitation to stronger and less scrupulous States to make them their prey.

As to the attitude of the British Government, and its satisfaction that the federation plan is good and trustworthy, one need only quote Mr. Eden, who said in a speech at the Mansion House on May 29, 1941: "It seems to me that it is both natural and right that the cultural and economic ties between the Arab countries, and the political ties too, should be strengthened. His Majesty's Government will give their full support to any scheme that commands general approval."

Photos, British and
U.S. Official

How the Jeeps Outwit the Japs in Northern Burma

In a country where a 4-mile march may occupy 12 hours and communications are but sketchy, Allied enterprise has tremendous scope. Maintaining flow of vital supplies between Myitkyina and Mogaung, former Japanese bases, jeeps are ferried across the Mogaung River whilst reconstruction of a crazy temporary bridge is in progress (top). The journey continues by railway : rolling stock abandoned by the enemy is hauled by jeeps specially fitted with flanged wheels (bottom).

Through Flooded Jungle and Noisome Swamp—

Violent transition from dust-laden, sweltering heat to continual rain and wind-storms of the monsoon season failed to halt the routing of the Japanese invaders in Northern Burma. Twenty-five miles south of Mogaung lies Pinbaw : moving forward to this objective men of the East Lancs Regiment crossed the Samsan Chaung by rubber assault-boat (1). At this point (2) the river presented a tricky ford ; every available means of porterage was adopted, from mule to jeep.

— *To Battle at Pinbaw on the Road to Mandalay*

Snipers cunningly concealed in the flimsy ruins of Pinbaw were winkled out by these Royal Scots Fusiliers (3) after the first fierce resistance had been overcome. Elephant grass towering in pathless swamps made approach to the village extremely difficult, but this section of Royal Welch Fusiliers made skilful use of the cover afforded by extensive rice fields as they neared the outlying defences (4). Capture of this strongpoint by the 14th Army was effected on August 28, 1944.

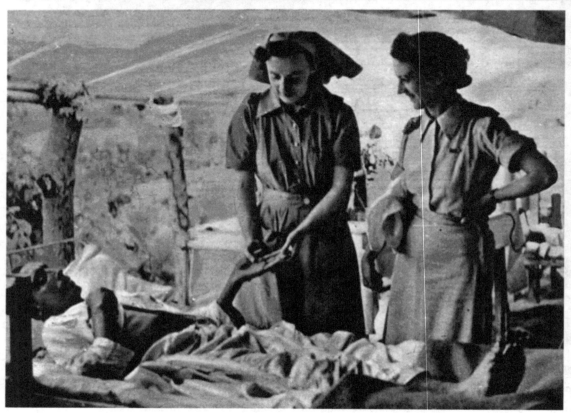

Front Line Women Aid Burma Army

Here the going is not too difficult: Corporal J. Balaam leads his patrol through a rice field (top left). But wading through a stream, in full kit (top right), Sergeant A. Beard and Private W. Pybis appreciate to the full the rigours of the Burma climate and scenery as they go forward to relieve men in an outpost. Sickness cases and casualties are tended by British and Indian girls of the nursing services: Miss I. J. Caldwell, Sister-in-charge of a casualty clearing station, and Sister A. Slade talk to a sepoy of the 13th Frontier Force Rifles (bottom). "In the first six months of the present year," said Mr. Churchill, "the British 14th Imperial Army sustained no fewer than 237,000 cases of sickness." In the same period, "We have suffered over 40,000 battle casualties."

Photos, British and Indian Official

VIEWS & REVIEWS Of Vital War Books

by Hamilton Fyfe

Here is an idea for one of our British universities. Not Oxford or Cambridge. I don't think either of them would give it welcome. Their faces are still turned too rigidly towards the past. I mean one of our newer and more enterprising universities. I wish one of them would start a Public Opinion Research Department, such as exists and flourishes at Princeton University in the United States, and would commission some deserving young man to go through Britain, into every corner of England, Wales and Scotland, with the object of finding out and telling the world what people are doing and saying and thinking at this present time.

A deserving young American named Selden Menefee was sent on a job of that nature all over America last year. In his book, Assignment U.S.A. (Gollancz, 10s. 6d.), he gives his report on what he saw and heard —and guessed. The book is not easy reading. He is not one of those journalists who can make the driest subjects attractive. Mr. Menefee leaves them dry. One has to swallow hard occasionally to get his facts down. But those who persevere are rewarded. They receive a series of impressions which are a great help towards understanding the American people and the reasons for many things they do and say which to most Britons seem incomprehensible.

Why, for instance, do they chaff us about being slow-coaches, unwilling to whip up and get a move on when rapidity is called for? Here is the answer to that. Large movements of population to war industry centres created urgent need for housing schemes, as happened here, too. We coped with it somehow, in rather a hand-to-mouth fashion. Over there, Mr. Henry Kaiser, the shipbuilder, has shown the same imaginative enterprise in building houses that he shows in constructing ships. He has created a town for 35,000 people with everything they can want in the way of conveniences, comforts and recreations, a town guaranteed to last for twenty-five years. A smaller "dormitory development," as Mr. Menefee calls it, has room for 5,000 workers, a restaurant that can feed 1,500 at a time, a library, a theatre, a gymnasium, game-rooms and fields.

Definition of an Employee

That sort of imagination has to be exercised in America. The demand for good living conditions is too insistent to be disregarded. It is true that Mr. Kaiser is a kindly man. To him "an employee is a human being, not an automaton to be used eight hours a day and left to shift for himself in a strange and overcrowded town the other sixteen hours." He has "rediscovered the old principle that men and women will work more efficiently if they live under conditions that do not violate all concepts of human dignity and decency." He has " the social vision to see the need for housing his workers adequately."

But even if Mr. Kaiser were the opposite of all that, he would still have to meet the need. If he failed in this, he would not secure the labour he requires. Labour in the U.S. puts its demands high. It is encouraged to do so by employers like Mr. William Jack and his partner (name of Heintz), who are making aircraft starters and automatic pilots for the Government, near Cleveland, Ohio. They came into public notice for the first time when a Committee of Congress severely criticized the high wages they paid. A semi-skilled mechanic can make £1,500 a year. Many of the women employed take home £25 a week. They work hard for it—twelve hours a day and seven days a week, and "the workers see to it that no one lags."

And it isn't only that Mr. Jack pays high wages to those whom he calls his "associates." He gives them free life insurance policies, free hot lunches, free wrist-watches so that they shan't be late, and at Christmas free turkeys. There is hot coffee on tap all the time in the workshops, and doughnuts are handed round—also free. Cottages in Florida are rented by the company for the

Let's Understand Americans!

workers to spend their fortnight's holiday, with pay, in them. When some had trouble with their feet, Mr. Jack gave an order to a shoe factory for a vast number of shoes such as he wears himself. They cost in the shops £3. He lets his "associates" have them at the wholesale price, thirty shillings. When all this appeared in the papers as a result of the Congress Committee's probing, lots of other employers all over the country "tore their hair," says Mr. Menefee. No wonder. They knew they would be expected more or less to do likewise. That is why Socialism does not appeal very much to the American working-man.

Of the Boeing Aircraft Corporation factories in Seattle, Mr. Menefee has a different story. Last year these were short of 9,000 workers needed to produce the Flying Fortresses urgently required. What caused the disinclination to produce them in the Boeing factories would be too long a story, but there was no doubt it existed. There was dissatisfaction among coal-miners too, and for a time the output dropped heavily. The men had many complaints against the colliery owners and against the Government as well. Their rations did not keep up their strength. Their houses were "unpainted shanties with muddy yards and streets and practically no sanitary facilities," and the rents were high. They followed John L. Lewis because he told them his union could obtain better conditions for them. But Mr. Menefee thinks that, if the Government had taken over the mines, the miners would have "put Uncle Sam above John L. Lewis," and there would have been no more serious difficulty.

Here is another example of the forthright manner in which Americans clear away nuisances which we endure with far too much patient resignation. The city of St. Louis

suffered from a plague of smoke, caused by the burning of soft coal. It was in perpetual twilight. "Motorists had to use their headlights in the daytime. Curtains rotted from the dirt, lawns had to be replanted each year, trees died from gas poisoning."

It was worse than Pittsburg—which is saying a good deal! The curse became so deadly that the population of the city fell. People would not stay in it. They went to live outside. So a campaign of protest was started. The Press went at it with rousing effect. The local authorities were compelled to take the worst offenders into court. Lookouts were employed to spot offenders on a large scale. Householders were induced to spend a little more on smokeless fuel. "The result is a city amazingly free from smoke," except when the wind blows direct from the quarter where most of the factories are, and then it is blown over the city—it does not hang like a pall. Perhaps some day the slums of St. Louis, which are disgraceful, may be cleaned up by a similar effort. But there is no sign of this yet.

Here we come upon one of the bewildering contradictions in the character of Americans generally. They will tackle a problem with immense energy and brilliant imagination when it is forced on their notice or when its immediate solution is necessary to the success of, say, the war effort. But other problems they tolerate, maybe with a wisecrack, maybe with a prayer that God will solve it. The racial problem is one of these. Not only does this affect Negroes. There exists also a strong anti-Jewish prejudice, and in Texas the Mexicans have had a good deal to suffer.

Our Country Right or Wrong

Anecdotes have a way of travelling from one end of the country to the other in very quick time. I was once told a story in New York and heard it everywhere I went until I reached California, where it was waiting for me. One joke that was told everywhere during Mr. Menefee's tour was about the first American soldier landing on foreign soil having an Irish name, and the first American business man to secure a contract for munitions being a Mr. Finkelstein. There is something sinister behind jokes like that if they are repeated frequently. And they are.

Sinister, too, is the veiled isolationism which the report describes in very useful detail. Its prophets are trying to harness it to a revival of nationalism. They want the American people to say, "Our country right or wrong, first, last, and all the time, and let the others rip." They might say it if the attitude Mr. Menefee found in so many parts is not altered by the men who return from fighting. That attitude he calls "lack of enthusiasm for the war," and among the Forces there is said to be a desire "to go back to the same kind of world they knew in 1939." Not a promising frame of mind when they are asked to help in building a new world!

PLANNING FOR PEACE AT DUMBARTON OAKS, Washington, Aug. 21-Oct. 7, 1944, British, U.S., Russian and Chinese representatives included (l. to r.) Sir A. Cadogan, head of the British delegation, Lord Halifax, Mr. Cordell Hull, Mr. A. Gromyko, head of the Soviet delegation, and Mr. E. Stettinius, leader of the U.S. delegation. Facts of great help towards a better understanding of the American people are given in the book reviewed above. *Photo, Topical Press*

The How and Why of Jet-Propelled Aircraft

Brought to the practical stage during this war, jet propulsion is one of the most important aeronautical developments of recent years. The uses in action of aircraft of this revolutionary type by Great Britain, the U.S.A. and Germany, the development of the various classes and their working principles, are dealt with here by Capt. NORMAN MACMILLAN, M.C., A.F.C.

THERE are at present three classes of jet-propelled aeroplanes : (1) those wholly propelled by jet-reaction and controlled by a human pilot ; (2) those wholly propelled by jet-reaction and controlled by robot mechanism ; and (3) those employing jet-reaction during part of their flight only. Germany has employed all three, Britain and the United States the first and third. Italy produced an elementary form of the first class, the Campini two-seater monoplane, which used a normal aero piston engine to drive the blower. There are no reports of jet-propelled aeroplanes in the Russian or Japanese air forces.

Great Britain, the United States, and Germany are thus ahead of all other nations in this aeronautical development, which, coming to a practical stage during this war, has been applied first to military aircraft. It has been stated by leading aircraft designers that jet-propelled transport aircraft are not likely to appear on world air routes for another decade.

At the moment jet-propulsion in the first class has been concentrated into fighter air-

into a combustion chamber into which fuel is injected and fired, initially by electric spark, but when the engine warms up (this takes about 30 seconds) by spontaneous combustion. The gas, under tremendous pressure, then passes through conduits to a turbine which it drives before passing on through the exit tube to the open air.

The driven turbine drives the compressor unit. To start the engine the compressor is speeded-up by an electric starter, much as a motor-car engine is started. High grade aviation fuels are unnecessary ; paraffin can be used—and it does not freeze at high altitudes. Gas turbine, jet-propelled aeroplanes develop their maximum speed at high altitudes where, in the rarefied atmosphere, the gas outflow reaction drives them forward at faster speeds for a fraction of the fuel consumed than when flying at lower heights.

THE prototype plane to test the Whittle gas turbine in flight was designed by Mr. W. G. Carter, of the Gloster Aircraft Co., Ltd., and first flew in May 1941 with the late Flight-Lieut. P. E. G. Sayer as pilot. This aeroplane was an extremely clean-shaped

that two Me 163s were shot down in combat over Germany with U.S. bombers and escorting fighters during the last week in July 1944:

The Me 262, called the Schwalbe (Swallow), and the Heinkel 280 are both fitted with two Junkers Jumo 004 gas turbine, jet-propelling engines, and are single-seater fighters. In the Me 262 the engines are mounted underneath the wings, fairly close to the fuselage. This aircraft carries four 30-millimetre Mark 108 cannon-guns, and can be used as a fighter-bomber. Its speed is in excess of 500 m.p.h. It has a fast rate of climb, but it is reported to be less manoeuvrable in combat than current airscrew fighters of the British and American air forces.

The first enemy jet-plane to fall in Allied lines was shot down over Nijmegen on October 5 by six R.A.F. Spitfires ; it was a Me 262. A single Tempest destroyed another on October 13.

The Bell P59 A Airacomet single-seater fighter is powered with two General Electric Whittle-type gas-turbine engines and carries four 5-in. machine-guns. The engines lie alongside the fuselage below the wings ; this makes the rather low tricycle undercarriage of wider track than usual. The closeness of pilot, controls and engines may make these aircraft vulnerable in combat with other aircraft. The Airacomet weighs more than five tons, has a wing span of 49 feet, and is said to leave no vapour trails in flight. The American gas-turbine was built on reverse lend-lease from British designs. The Bell prototype jet-propelled aeroplane first flew in October 1942.

THE second class of jet-propelled aircraft—robots—is so far confined to the V1 weapon, the flying bombs, fitted with a simplified propulsion unit which is merely a combustion chamber with air intake valves which close when the gas pressure rises, thus forcing the gas through the rear orifice tube and so driving the bomb forward by a series of reactionary discharges. Fuel is fed into the combustion chamber by compressed air carried in bottles within the fuselage, and is fired by the heat within the combustion chamber when the engine is warmed up. (See facing page).

U.S. JET PLANE, the Bell P59 A Airacomet, passed its experimental tests at the beginning of 1944. The improved jet propulsion engines eliminated airscrews on the new aircraft. These power units were developed from Air Commodore Frank Whittle's designs. Top, front view of the Airacomet showing the twin air intake vents. Bottom, the Airacomet in flight. *Photos, Associated Press*

craft. For two reasons : (1) jet-propulsion is specially suitable for high-speed aircraft because its efficiency increases with the maximum speed of the aeroplane using it ; (2) German aircraft priority is for fighters, and the British and American air forces cannot afford to be outclassed in these aircraft.

SIX jet-propelled fighters are nameable today. Three are German—the Messerschmitt 163 and 262, and the Heinkel 280. Two are British—the Gloster prototype and the development aeroplane produced therefrom. One is American—the Bell P59 A Airacomet ; it has not yet been used in operations. Both the Messerschmitts have been in action on the Western Front. The British jet-propelled aeroplane went into action against the V1 flying-bombs during the second Battle of London, June 13 to September 5, 1944.

The engine of the British jet-propelled aeroplane is a gas turbine, based on the pioneer work of Air Commodore Frank Whittle, who built his first engine in April 1937. The principle of the gas turbine is that air is led through a duct to a compressor which forces the air under pressure

single-seater with the single engine mounted within the fuselage. It had the characteristic jet-plane aperture for air entry in the fuselage nose ; a smaller aperture under and behind the tailplane discharged the high velocity gasflow. The tricycle undercarriage had exceptionally short struts, because it was unnecessary to provide the ground clearance that is demanded by the conventional rotating airscrew. This feature of jet-propelled aeroplanes saves both weight and stowage space, both important in an aeroplane, especially a fighter. Tricycle undercarriages are therefore likely to become standard in jet-propelled aircraft. (See illus. p. 354.)

The current British jet-propelled fighter is an improved aircraft. Its performance is secret, but it is very fast and manoeuvrable, and is believed to be better than anything the Germans have. The Messerschmitt 163 is a single-seater, single propulsion unit aeroplane, but it is not fitted with a gas turbine ; a jet reaction unit working on the rocket principle supplies its thrust. It has been described as a flying firework. In appearance it is of the pterodactyl, or bat-like, aircraft. A German radio commentator said

The flying bombs stall, i.e. lose flying speed, at 150 m.p.h. The air valve ceases to function at 170 m.p.h. They must be launched, either from ramps or aircraft, at 185 m.p.h. They carry 130 gallons of fuel, 1,870 lb. explosive, and weigh fully laden 4,700 lb. The engine develops 600 h.p. at a reaction frequency of 40 cycles per second, giving a normal flying speed of 360 m.p.h. Their normal range is 150 miles at 2,000 ft., and their service ceiling is 10,000 ft. Length of fuselage is 21 ft. 10 in. ; propulsion unit is 11 ft. 3 in. long with an overhang of 3 ft. 6½ in. The wing span varies with different types of wings from 16 ft. to 17½ ft. Their flight is controlled by a repeater compass and an automatic pilot. Range is determined by a small airscrew-driven log which can be pre-set to the mileage desired.

The third class of jet-propelled aircraft is fitted with rocket units to assist take-off or increase rate of climb. The rocket units are mounted beneath the wings near the fuselage or on the fuselage near the tail. Junkers Aircraft Works has experimented with rocket devices for over 15 years. American Mitchell bombers have used rocket-propulsion units for take-off. So have Swordfish and other British Fleet Air Arm aircraft. Their discharge lasts for about four seconds.

Nazi Flying Bombs Are Launched This Way Now

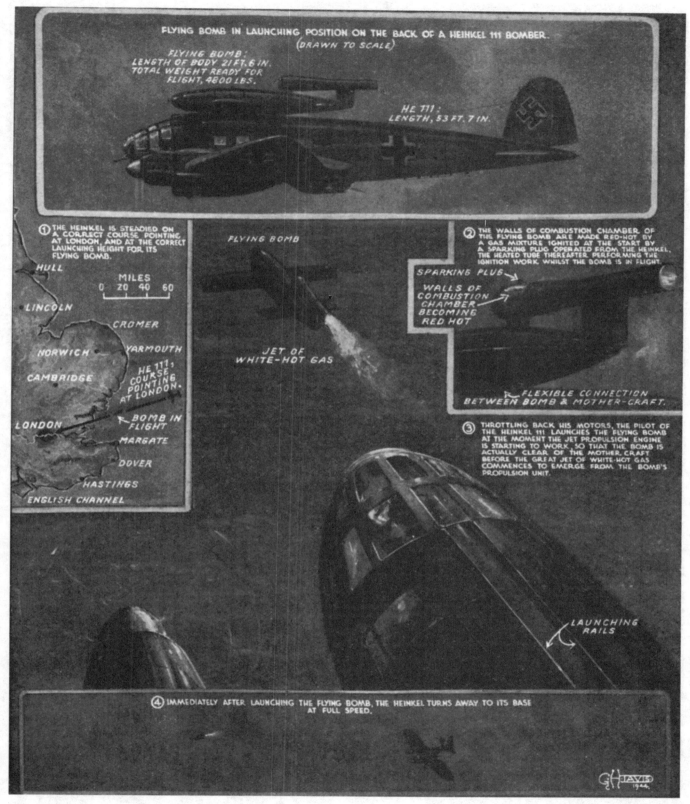

FLYING BOMB IN LAUNCHING POSITION ON THE BACK OF A HEINKEL 111 BOMBER.
(DRAWN TO SCALE)

FLYING BOMB:
LENGTH OF BODY 21 FT. 6 IN.
TOTAL WEIGHT READY FOR
FLIGHT, 4800 LBS.

HE 111:
LENGTH, 53 FT. 7 IN.

① THE HEINKEL IS STEADIED ON A CORRECT COURSE, POINTING AT LONDON, AND AT THE CORRECT LAUNCHING HEIGHT FOR ITS FLYING BOMB.

HULL

MILES
0 20 40 60

LINCOLN

CROMER

NORWICH   YARMOUTH

CAMBRIDGE   HE 111: COURSE POINTING AT LONDON.

LONDON   BOMB IN FLIGHT

MARGATE

DOVER

HASTINGS

ENGLISH CHANNEL

FLYING BOMB

JET OF
WHITE-HOT GAS

② THE WALLS OF COMBUSTION CHAMBER OF THE FLYING BOMB ARE MADE RED-HOT BY A GAS MIXTURE IGNITED AT THE START BY A SPARKING PLUG OPERATED FROM THE HEINKEL, THE HEATED TUBE THEREAFTER PERFORMING THE IGNITION WORK WHILST THE BOMB IS IN FLIGHT.

SPARKING PLUG
WALLS OF COMBUSTION CHAMBER BECOMING RED HOT

FLEXIBLE CONNECTION BETWEEN BOMB & MOTHER-CRAFT.

③ THROTTLING BACK HIS MOTORS, THE PILOT OF THE HEINKEL 111 LAUNCHES THE FLYING BOMB AT THE MOMENT THE JET PROPULSION ENGINE IS STARTING TO WORK, SO THAT THE BOMB IS ACTUALLY CLEAR OF THE MOTHER-CRAFT BEFORE THE GREAT JET OF WHITE-HOT GAS COMMENCES TO EMERGE FROM THE BOMB'S PROPULSION UNIT.

LAUNCHING RAILS

④ IMMEDIATELY AFTER LAUNCHING THE FLYING BOMB, THE HEINKEL TURNS AWAY TO ITS BASE AT FULL SPEED.

GH DAVIS 1944.

DRIVEN FROM THEIR COASTAL LAUNCHING SITES in France and Belgium, the Germans resorted to the "pick-a-back" method of sending their flying-bombs against England—a method founded on the British-built Mayo composite aircraft of 1938. The flying-bomb is perched on launching rails on the top of the fuselage of a semi-obsolete Heinkel 111, flown over the North Sea, pointed at London and then released.

The operation has its dangers, the main problem being to launch the bomb clear of the parent aircraft before the flaming jet of gas begins to stream from the bomb's power-unit. It is conjectured that, to avoid setting the parent aircraft ablaze, the combustion chamber in the bomb is heated, the Heinkel engines sharply throttled back and the bomb launched almost simultaneously. The computed range

of the flying-bomb is not above 150 miles, so that the parent aircraft must fly to within range of the East Coast, aim its bomb, launch it, and return to base, all the time trying to elude our patrols on the watch for the tell-tale flash from the flying bomb's tail. Numbers of these carrier Heinkels have already been shot down, before or after launching their deadly missiles.

As regards the actual launching, the walls of the bomb's combustion chamber are rendered red-hot by a gas mixture ignited by a sparking-plug operated from the parent aircraft. While the bomb is in flight ignition is effected by the heated tail-tube. The gas emerges in a series of jerky impulses at a frequency of 45 per second.

Drawn by G. H. Davis, by courtesy of the Illustrated London News

With British-Trained Fijians in the Pacific Battle

BEATING THE JAPANESE wherever they meet, the Fiji Military Forces were sent by the British authorities to assist in the Pacific war at the special request of the U.S. On Bougainville Island, in the Solomons (invaded on Nov. 1, 1943, by the Japanese and recaptured by April 4, 1944) platoon officers were briefed before battle (1). From a fox-hole a Fijian takes careful aim (2) ; others occupy dug-in night positions (3). A dockyard company unload supplies (4). One of the Fijian troops' trophies was this Japanese motor-cycle truck (5).   PAGE 406   *Photos, New Zealand Official*

Red Army Avalanches Sweep on to the Reich

TROOPS OF THE U.S.S.R., according to an order of the day issued by Marshal Stalin on October 18, 1944, entered Czechoslovakia on a front of 170 miles; a Russian command post is seen in action (1). A Soviet raiding party riding on self-propelled guns pass through a north Transylvanian village (2). In the far north the Red Army, on the shores of the Arctic, freed Kirkenes in Norway on Oct. 25. Heavy artillery (3) pounded enemy positions south-west of Shavli in Lithuania, half-way between Riga and the East Prussian border.

Photos, U.S.S.R. Official, Pictorial Press, Planet News. Map, The Daily Telegraph

Danes Stirred to Resistance by Nazi Decree

THE GERMANS DECREED on Sept. 19, 1944, that all Danish policemen should be disarmed. A fierce clash occurred outside King Christian's residence, Amalienborg Castle, when German Marines tried to carry out the order. Aided by civilians, police erected barricades (I) from behind which they effectively resisted (3). A salt-vendor helped A.R.P. workers to build another barricade from the contents of his barrow (2). Many cycled through the streets to demonstrate against the German declaration of a state of emergency (4). Photos, Keystone

I WAS THERE!

Eye Witness Stories of the War

10,000 Cried for the Blood of Greek Traitors

With the British invasion force that landed on the Greek mainland early in October 1944 went war reporter Walter Lucas. His story of the great welcome that was given and his behind-the-scenes glimpse of life in Greece today appears by arrangement with The Daily Express. See also page 394.

I SHOULD call this landing of Allied troops on the Greek mainland, the first since 1941, a mixture of Aston Villa returning home after winning the Cup and the Battle of Flowers at Nice. From the word go it was welcome. From miles out at sea we could see through the glasses a dark mass of people on the quayside at the little port of Katakolon, on the north-western coast of Peloponnese, and faintly over the water came a peal of church bells. Up to that moment we did not know what we could expect. Omens had been bad,

Within sight of this land of ancient mythology we were struck by a tempest. Two whirlwinds descended upon our convoy like two furies. They thrashed their way hither and thither, travelling before the wind at 30 to 40 miles an hour. As we zigzagged madly one of them lashed our stern so that we spun toplike. We nearly had to jump for it. But that was all our troubles.

When we rounded the little breakwater that shelters the tiny harbour of Katakolon we were met by bouquets and not bullets. Massed along the beach—a sticky mass of gluey mud after the torrential rains—were thousands of people from all over the surrounding country. As we grated the shore the sounds of thousands of clapping hands sent echoes around the bare encircling hills.

Four little girls stepped forward and garlanded Squadron-Leader John Wynne, from

Edinburgh, in command of the R.A.F. Regiment who are supplying an important part of the land forces for this invasion. But the highlight of this story is not military ; it is human. What I found in Greece, the first British correspondent to land on the Greek mainland for three and a half years, is of great importance. I feel that here we have the good will of people who have suffered more than most in this war and who still have deep faith in the British.

My own remarkable experiences will show how the Greeks feel towards us. Shortly after we landed three of us were to go to Pirgos, a large city of 20,000 inhabitants about 12 miles away. With me were Milton Bracker, of the New York Times, the only American correspondent on the expedition, and Flight Officer Bob Williams, of Canadian R.A.F. Public Relations. We were piled into an ancient truck, the only one in the whole district which the Jerries had not stolen, with 30 or more excited Greeks.

We groaned and wheezed along over the muddy, bumpy road, passing through little villages where the cobbled streets were strewn with flowers and branches of trees, beneath flowered arches of welcome and between masses of wildly clapping peasants. In course of time, as was to be expected, the ancient truck gasped to a standstill and nothing would make it budge. We got out and walked the last mile into Pirgos.

It was dark by now. By the time we arrived in the town we were the head of a long procession of cheering and clapping people. We marched through the main street between masses of them, with church bells clanging, and flowers showering on our heads. The main square was packed. We were taken to the town hall, where we were publicly welcomed by the chief priest and the city fathers. Addresses were presented to us in Greek and translated into French, and we replied on behalf of the Allies in French, which was then translated back into Greek

WE were then taken to a balcony and greeted with wildest enthusiasm. Again we had to make speeches. That night we were taken to the Archbishop's Palace and fed and given beds. The archbishop himself was in the mountains where he has been for more than a year the leader of the partisans. We were asked to stay for Solemn Mass for the Liberation in the Greek Orthodox Cathedral the next morning.

As we walked to the service the streets were lined with members of the armed E.A.M., partisan troops, keeping back the masses of excited clapping people. Inside the cathedral there were 2,000 to 3,000 people. We were solemnly led to seats near the High Altar and presented to rows of black-bearded and magnificently robed priests.

Near us were many sad, pathetic, lined and tear-stained faces of widows whose husbands had been killed by the Germans or Greek quisling troops. Some were old and bowed, others were young, but all were miserably poor, and dressed in shabby, torn, stained black clothes. After the cathedral service we were marched back to the town hall with a bodyguard of partisans armed with every type of firearm.

Some were stolen from the Germans, Italians or Bulgars, others were given to them by the Allies. Their uniforms were

TUMULTUOUS RECEPTION awaited our troops when they landed at Piraeus, the port of Athens and 28 miles from the capital, on October 14, 1944. Photographed from an R.A.F. plane, this scene shows crowds assembled at the quayside—a foretaste of the overwhelming welcome that was to be given our men in the capital itself, where thousands of people had surged excitedly through the streets since dawn. An account of Greek reactions to the Allied invasion is given above.

Photo, British Official

equally haphazard, many of them were without boots and all wore rags. Once again we had to appear on the balcony and make speeches while the partisans paraded below and 10,000 people cried for the blood of the Greek traitors.

For the rest of the day we were taken in the same ancient truck, now restored to life, along 60 miles of terrible, muddy tracks to Araxo. We were escorted by the chief priest in his robes, with flowing beard and black cap, and by four of the leading citizens of Pirgos. At every village and town we were again called upon to speak from the town hall while the church bells clanged. We were presented with wine, strong, heady stuff.

Behind all this welcome and misery there is a vicious political quandary facing the Allies in Greece. There is a civil war raging in this country. At Pirgos two weeks ago there was a bitter battle between partisans and Greek quisling forces. Hundreds were killed and many houses burned down with their occupants burned to death inside.

Feeling has run at flood. For the partisan the quisling Greek is almost a greater enemy than the German. Unhappily the issue is not clear-cut as between the partisans and the quislings. It looks as if our military operations against the Germans are likely to be complicated and hindered in many respects by this internecine war.

the bamboo—you can't beat it with any rare Oriental perfume or any bouquet of jasmine. We "come and get it" and bring the good breakfast home, with one eye on the plates and the other on our foothold in the mud. Our food is more than good, it is near a miracle—a miracle about which all cannot yet be told. And the cheerful cooks can work the tin-opener with as much imagination as efficiency. What more can be expected in the jungle?

A few "Penguins" and "Guild Books" add another touch to declare the tarpaulin the abode of men who cling to culture. The books themselves have a struggle with the damp-rot, and it always seems to be the last few vital pages of the detective story that disintegrate first. Still, life is an unsolved mystery, they say. The tent in the jungle isn't home. Home is the place we can't dream about any more. After a couple of years away—and more "away" than the little word can ever mean in other theatres of war—it is difficult even to lie awake and try to picture the suburban villa and the faces of our loved ones. More than time and distance separate us from all that is dear; there is a veil that gets thicker, as the jungle gets thicker beyond the paddy-fields.

Out of one of the swift jungle twilights, when the night-orchestra was tuning-up, came "Bomb-happy," the cat. He looked like a small piece of grey flannel stuck in the mud. Then he picked his delicate way towards the tent. "My God! A——cat!" It was our tent-mate corporal, jumping up as though he had seen a ghost or a hundred Japs. He loves cats, tough as he is, whether they slink along Civvy Street or burst out of the bamboo. "Hell, he's thin, the poor little devil," he said; with the cat in his arms, "Open a tin of sardines, quick!"

His fur is a dusty blue-grey, of a fine texture, making a thick coat. We reckon that without his fur he would cast a shadow like a pencil. But he's had a rough time all his little life, obviously, with his six months or so of bomb-dodging and getting out of the way of retreating Japs. His eyes are stuck wide-open and all over his face like an owl's, as though on the look-out for a Jap boot.

We don't kick him, and he's getting to like it that way. We got him to purr one evening. With all the stroking and the gentle massage of his sardine-lined tummy, while he luxuriated on a dry sack, we thought it was about time he showed a little appreciative acknowledgment. But he must have suddenly become aware of the unusual noise and been startled by it, for he looked sharply at himself and stopped the purr.

And no more caressing or sibilant endearment could get him going again. Cats are like that for independence, from Burma to Brighton. So "Bomb-happy" is on the tent-strength—if we can grab him the morning we move off again. Anyway, we hope to incorporate him with our other scraps of domesticity, our other bits of "home," in the next jungle village.

"HOPING THIS FINDS YOU——." These smiling, perspiring Lancashire Fusiliers write home from the Burmese jungle. How our troops endeavour to " domesticate " themselves in their swampy surroundings is described in this page. The monsoon season ended, the Burma front flared up with the capture of Tiddim by Indian troops of the 14th Army, announced on October 19, 1944. See also illus. pages 399-402.
Photo, Indian Official

Our Home-from-Home in the Burmese Jungle

Back-stage in the vast theatre of war are the fighting men of Burma— with their thoughts like the rest of us. How do they visualize Civvy Street after a long absence? " Home is the place we can't dream about any more," says Sergeant G. C. Smith, in this revealing and intensely human story which we reproduce from the News Chronicle.

Into the Burma jungle village—or what the Japs have left of it—we introduce the elements of domesticity. With a sharp "dah," the wicked-looking jungle-machet, you can go and cut yourself a bed-sitting room from the living bamboo on the doorstep. It's a simple job, and so is the furniture ; and, up to a point, we are simple soldiers.

Under the tarpaulin a temporary home for three takes rapid shape. Maybe a faint spiritual likeness of the far-away upstairs-and-down glows within. But faint is the word, for it's hard to kid yourself here ; things beyond our control or adaptability are too real, too nosey as neighbours.

The monsoon rain is too wet and the sun too hot—yes, and our British sense of humour too all-embracing, enduring, and case-hardened—to allow us to kid ourselves we can set up home on a bamboo basis. The medical category of the mosquito in this semi-liquid area is A1+ and a bit to spare ; it bites straight through green battledress, underclothes, and socks. It is particularly anxious to share our home life in the evening.

Nature is bountiful here and nothing can stop it—but give me Epsom Downs and a

thick overcoat. One of our table-legs, set in the mud floor of the tent, has burst into light-green leaf. It was a small branch sliced off a fig tree ; but we don't anticipate staying long enough to pick figs from the leg of our dining-table. It shows what can happen in a home like ours.

But if Nature is bountiful so is the cook-house. It adds a lot to the atmosphere of homeliness to smell bacon frying every 7 a.m. ; the smell of bacon drifting through

We Do Our Soldiering at the Bottom of the Sea

Doing the lion's share in the work of clearing French and Belgian Channel ports are British sappers of Port Construction and Repair Companies. In these companies are soldiers trained to grope about in the pitch darkness of the sea-bed. Warrant Officer O. Davies, who has been diving in principal ports occupied by the Allies since Algiers, here relates his experiences.

The first thing we do on entering a newly captured port is to make a reconnaissance of the damage done. The main difficulty is the pitch darkness. We find our way about under water by using a line with a weight on the end which is dropped from the tug on the surface. From this vertical line another rope is attached about three feet from the weight,

which you hold on to as you grope about. The attendant on the tug can see where you are by the air bubbles coming to the surface, and by jerking on a rope attached to the diver he guides him to the left or right.

The great thing is never to get panicky. A series of signals, the same used by the Royal Navy and also in civilian operations, is used between the attendant and the diver. These are supplemented by additional signals for local work. One tug on the breast rope means : " Are you O.K. ? "; two tugs mean " I am sending you a slate " (the diver has a pencil and slate for messages), three tugs mean " I am sending you a rope," and four tugs mean " Come up." Four long tugs followed by two short mean " Come up ; I'm pulling you up."

Signals on the air pipe run thus : One means the diver wants less air, two that he wants more air, three " You are holding me too tightly," and four is the emergency signal. This latter is never used except in cases of extreme distress. There is also a telephone in the diver's helmet for exchange of messages, but owing to the difficulty of recharging batteries we rely chiefly on signals.

Our company began the work of underwater salvage and repair during the First Army's landings in North Africa. One of the pleasantest jobs we ever had to do was to repair the ship we'd sailed in from England. She had been damaged ; we dived, repaired the damage with a timber patch, pumped out the water, the ship was refloated and later towed to Gibraltar.

Another interesting job at Algiers occurred when a party of Intelligence Corps officers ran their car into a dock. They came to us and told us there were some valuable documents inside the car, and could we salvage them ? It took us two hours to locate the car, but we found it, hoisted it to the surface with a small mobile crane which is part of the company's equipment, and were then able to hand over the leather case containing the documents. They were still readable.

Also at Algiers a ship blew up which was being loaded with German ammunition for dispatch to England. The explosion blasted a considerable part of the quayside. The wall was constructed of cement cubes weighing a hundred and sixty tons each, and our job was to sling the blocks by crane and drop them into position below water. The

SALVAGING AT NAPLES, the crew of a U.S. Navy tug found this wrecked Italian ship sunk by the enemy in an attempt to block the harbour before the capture of the port by the 5th Army on Oct. 1, 1943. *Photo, U.S. Official*

clear water made this job fairly easy. At Bône we patched up a destroyer and several merchant ships. At La Gaulette, the port for Tunis, we patched the quayside which had been damaged by bombing ; and also widened the canal so that coastal craft, supplying our troops finishing off the Germans in Cap Bon, might pass through. This widening we did by exploding charges of German ammunition under the canal banks.

We had a few minor jobs in Sousse and Sfax, but our next big job was at Naples. The Italians had had, lying about for some time, huge cement tanks which had sprung a leak and sunk in the harbour. We repaired the leaks with tarred rope and pumped them clear of water, when they floated to the surface. We also salvaged a floating crane by patching up its pontoon, pumping out the water, fitting air valves to the pontoon, attaching tubes, and blowing in compressed air.

And then to Anzio. We arrived there three days after the initial landings and

were below water, working on a sunken landing-craft, when Jerry came over and bombed the port. The bombs fell in the sea a mile away from us, but owing to the concussion being twelve times magnified under water it was like getting a crack on the head with a hammer. The main problem at Anzio was the mud. You sank in it up to your chest. By pressing the air valve you made yourself more buoyant, but you had to take care you didn't float straight to the surface. On a hard bottom, of course, you travel heavy.

Our first diving job was to salvage two tugs. We did this at low tide, using two converted Thames barges either side of the tugs. From the barges we passed slings under the keels of the tugs, burrowing in the sand and thrusting the slings through with a pole. At high tide the tugs rose on their slings, and a bulldozer, working from the land, lugged the barges and the tugs ashore.

We had a rush job there when we were called out to unravel a steel cable which had fouled a merchantman's propeller. The ship had to sail that night. It was dark, and we had to do everything by touch. Halfway through the work a smoke-screen was put down, and although we were only two yards from the ship we couldn't see it. Jerry came over and bombed the port. The captain of the ship gave orders for us to abandon the work, and we set off to try to reach the quay.

For two hours, surrounded by fog and dark and shrapnel, we tossed backwards and forwards in the harbour trying to get home. Our little vessel was a Frenchman manned by a French crew and we were going here and there shouting out in English for assistance. After an hour and a half without any response to our English, we thought we'd try yelling in French. We did, and at last we got a response. An angry voice yelled back : " Is there nobody here who can bloody well speak English ? "

OUR DIARY OF THE WAR

OCTOBER 11, Wednesday *1,866th day*
Western Front.—Allied attack on Aachen resumed after rejection of ultimatum.
Air.—R.A.F. Lancasters breached dyke on Walcheren Island. U.S. bombers attacked areas of Cologne and Coblenz.
Russian Front.—Cluj, Transylvania, and Szeged, Hungary, captured by Red Army.
Far East.—U.S. carrier-aircraft attacked Formosa, destroying 221 enemy aircraft.

OCTOBER 12, Thursday *1,867th day*
Western Front.—British troops in Holland retook Overloon, near the Maas.
Air.—Ruhr oil plants, aircraft factories at Bremen and marshalling yards at Osnabruck, attacked by Allied bombers.
Russian Front.—Oradea-Mare, Transylvania, captured by Red Army.
Balkans.—Athens freed by Greek patriots ; Allied glider-borne troops landed at airfield.
Far East.—Formosa again attacked by U.S. Task Force ; 175 more aircraft destroyed.
General.—M. Mikolajczyk, Polish Prime Minister, arrived in Moscow.

OCTOBER 13, Friday *1,868th day*
Western Front.—German armour outside Aachen smashed by Allied aircraft and artillery.
Russian Front.—Riga, capital of Latvia, captured by Red Army.
Far East.—U.S. carrier-aircraft again attacked Formosa. Luzon, Philippines, also bombed.

OCTOBER 14, Saturday *1,869th day*
Western Front.—Allied troops made fresh crossing of Leopold Canal.
Air.—Duisburg hit by more than 1,000 R.A.F. bombers by day, in greatest raid of war on German city. Cologne bombed by more than 1,000 U.S. aircraft. R.A.F. again bombed Duisburg at night.
Balkans.—Athens and the Piraeus occupied by British airborne and naval units.
Russian Front.—Soviet long-range aircraft attacked Tilsit, E. Prussia, and ports of Memel and Libau.
Far East.—Formosa bombed by Super-Fortresses from China.

Sea.—Carrier-aircraft of Home Fleet attacked shipping off Norway.

OCTOBER 15, Sunday *1,870th day*
Air.—R.A.F. Lancasters hit Sorpe Dam on the Ruhr with " earthquake " bombs.
Russian Front.—Petsamo, Finland, captured by Soviet land and naval units.
Hungary.—Adm. Horthy broadcast that Hungary had asked for armistice.
Far East.—U.S. carrier-aircraft attacked airfields at Manila Bay, Philippines.
General.—Death from wounds of Field-Marshal Rommel announced by Germans.

OCTOBER 16, Monday *1,871st day*
Western Front.—German escape gap from Aachen closed. U.S. troops withdrew from Fort Driant, Metz.
Balkans.—British troops landed on Greek island of Lemnos.
Russian Front.—Soviet long-range bombers attacked railway junctions of Insterburg, Gumbinnen and Stalupenen in E. Prussia.
Hungary.—Adm. Horthy deposed by Major Szalasi, head of pro-Nazi Arrow Cross party.

OCTOBER 17, Tuesday *1,872nd day*
Air.—U.S. bombers again attacked Cologne. R.A.F. Lancasters bombed dyke on Walcheren.
Russian Front.—Soviet bombers attacked railway junction of Goldap, E. Prussia.
Pacific.—U.S. carrier-aircraft bombed Luzon, Philippines.
Indian Ocean.—Nicobar Is., Bay of Bengal, bombarded by Eastern Fleet.

OCTOBER 18, Wednesday *1,873rd day*
Western Front.—Venray, road junction near Maas, captured by 2nd Army.
Russian Front. — Announced that Soviet troops had captured five Carpathian passes and advanced into Czechoslovakia.
Germany.—Hitler and Himmler decreed conscription of all able-bodied men from 16 to 60 in Volkssturm (Home Guard).

Far East.—Super Fortresses from China again attacked Formosa.
General.—King George VI returned to England after five-day tour of battle areas in Holland and Belgium.

OCTOBER 19, Thursday *1,874th day*
Air.—U.S. bombers attacked Mainz and Ludwigshafen-Mannheim. At night R.A.F. bombed Stuttgart and Nuremberg.
Burma.—Indian troops of 14th Army captured Tiddim.

OCTOBER 20, Friday *1,875th day*
Western Front.—City of Aachen cleared of German troops.
Russian Front.—Belgrade, capital of Yugoslavia, freed by Russian and Yugoslav troops. Debreczen, Hungary, captured by Soviet forces.
Pacific.—U.S. troops under General MacArthur landed on island of Leyte, Central Philippines.
Italy.—8th Army Forces in Adriatic sector entered Cesena.

OCTOBER 21, Saturday *1,876th day*
Western Front.—Commander of Aachen garrison surrendered.
Pacific.—U.S. troops captured Tacloban, capital of Leyte, and its airfield.

OCTOBER 22, Sunday *1,877th day*
Western Front.—Breskens, port in Scheldt pocket, captured by Allied troops.
Air.—Hamm, Munster, Hanover and Brunswick attacked by U.S. bombers. R.A.F. bombed Neuss, near Dusseldorf, by day, and Hamburg at night.
Russian Front.—Announced that Soviet troops had reached Norwegian frontier west of Petsamo.
General.—Mr. Churchill arrived back from talks in Moscow.

OCTOBER 23, Monday *1,878th day*
Air.—More than 1,000 R.A.F. bombers made night attack on Essen.
Russian Front.—Announced that Soviet forces had broken into East Prussia on 85-mile front.
Pacific.—Naval battles between U.S. and Japanese forces began off Philippines.
General.—Great Britain, U.S.A. and Russia recognized Gen. de Gaulle's administration as Provisional Government of France.

OCTOBER 24, Tuesday *1,879th day*
Western Front.—British 2nd Army troops entered Hertogenbosch.
Russian Front.—Polish town of Augustovo, near S.E. border of E. Prussia, captured by Red Army.

★ ━━━━━━━━ *Flash-backs* ━━━━━━━━━ ★

1939
October 14. *H.M.S. Royal Oak sunk by torpedo in Scapa Flow.*
October 16. *Cruisers Southampton and Edinburgh and destroyer Mohawk damaged in bombing raids on Firth of Forth.*

1940
October 26. *Liner Empress of Britain bombed and sunk.*

1941
October 12. *Briansk evacuated by Red Army forces.*
October 16. *Rumanian troops entered Odessa, on Black Sea.*

October 19. *State of siege proclaimed by Stalin in Moscow.*

1942
October 17. *Schneider works at Le Creusot wrecked in daylight raid by 94 Lancasters.*
October 23. *8th Army launched offensive at El Alamein.*

1943
October 13. *Italian Government declared war on Germany.*
October 18. *Mr. Cordell Hull and Mr. Eden arrived in Moscow for Three Power Conference.*

THE WAR IN THE AIR

by Capt. Norman Macmillan, M.C., A.F.C.

AMERICAN naval aircraft flying from carriers, with Super-Fortress bombers based on China operating in strategic collaboration, carried the war in the Pacific into the Philippine Is., where United States forces landed on Leyte island on October 20, 1944. The Japanese, evidently expecting the first landing to be on Luzon or Mindanao—the two largest islands in the group—were taken by surprise.

The cause of their surprise was the heavy pre-invasion air assault against targets in Mindanao, Luzon, Formosa, and the Ryukyu islands, which concentrated on gun positions, vehicle convoys and shipping at Leyte island only in the final 48 hours. At Leyte island 80 aircraft were destroyed on the ground and four in combat.

air it has already had the effect of inflicting unparalleled losses on the Japanese through the dual air assault from the sea and the Asiatic mainland. From airfields in the Philippines the American and Australian air forces will be able to deal devastating blows at Japan's communications lifeline to the Netherlands East Indies, Malaya and Burma. The Japanese can be expected to fight desperately to hold on to the Philippines, but the seizure of airfields in Leyte will give the Allies the opportunity to use their air power with smashing effect against any of the islands in the group in support of surface forces ; and by October 21 the airfield at Tacloban was captured.

Meanwhile, an interesting air command change was the appointment on October 15,

Bomber Command uses a new armour-piercing delayed-action 12,000-lb. bomb for special targets. One scored a direct hit on the battleship Tirpitz during the Lancaster attack from the Archangel base. The wrecking of the Brest submarine pens' 12-ft. reinforced concrete roof (see illus. page 327) was due to this missile. It was used to burst dykes on Walcheren (see illus. page 380). It was used against the Kembs dam across the Rhine near Mulhouse on October 7 with success. On October 15 a Lancaster squadron escorted by Mustang fighters of A.D.G.B. (now reverted to its former title of Fighter Command) attacked shortly before 10 a.m. the Sorpe dam, the third Ruhr dam not breached by Wing Commander Gibson's special force on May 16, 1943. (See pp. 24 and 25, Vol. 7.)

Direct hits with the A.P. 12,000-lb. bomb were reported during the attack, but so far there has been no report of reconnaissance aircraft confirming the breaching of this dam : which is of unusual construction, having an immense thickness of concrete. It will be interesting to learn whether the new bombs have breached it, or if this attack, like Gibson's, failed to do so. The Sorpe dam appears to be a model for structural engineers to study if it should withstand the bludgeon of the new R.A.F. "earthquake" bomb, as Air Chief Marshal Sir Arthur Harris is said to have christened it.

TWENTY-FIVE Thousand Casualties Saved by 1st Airborne Army

General Dempsey, commanding the forces fighting in the Nijmegen salient, conveying his thanks to the American airborne troops of the 1st Airborne Army, said that the action of that Army saved him a minimum of 25,000 casualties. The composition of the 1st Airborne Army was revealed as the 1st British Airborne Division, the 82nd and 101st U.S. Divisions and one Polish Brigade, equipped with both British and U.S. tanks. The Duke of Cornwall's Light Infantry formed the spearhead of the surface force that tried to relieve the British Division at Arnhem.

Aachen was captured on October 20, 1944, after an American infantry assault lasting eight days from the expiration of the demand to surrender (see illus. page 395). The city had been already so heavily bombed by Bomber Command that further area bombing would have been a wasteful expenditure of the man-power employed in preparations for "drenching" bombing, and tactical air forces were used in support of the final assault. These aircraft were able to pick out individual targets, such as fortified houses, that were holding up the advance, and enemy forces attempting to relieve the garrison. On October 13, German relieving tank assemblies near Wurselen were attacked by aircraft and artillery ; 64 were destroyed.

RECORD BOMBING ATTACK ON DUISBURG, largest inland port in Europe, about 150 miles from the mouth of the Rhine, was carried out on October 15, 1944. This, the R.A.F.'s biggest single night operation, followed a similar attack the previous day, when over 1,000 Lancasters and Halifaxes dropped nearly 5,000 tons of bombs for the loss of 14 bombers. From one of the Lancasters (above) a 4,000-lb. bomb and a shower of incendiaries fall. *Photo, British Official*

The attacks against Formosa began on October 11. The Japanese reported that 1,100 U.S. aircraft, including the Super-Fortresses, were engaged. By October 16 the island had had five raids, in which the bombers smashed harbours, dockyards, industrial buildings, oil stores and shore defences. The Super-Fortresses were flying at shorter ranges than when they attacked targets in Kyushu, southernmost island of Japan proper, and so carried heavier bomb loads, the heaviest they have yet transported. In the first five days Admiral Nimitz reported over 700 enemy aircraft destroyed in the air and on the ground and 43 ships sunk. The success of the Super-Fortresses is reflected in the allocation to them of first priority in man-power and materials in the U.S.A., where five factories now make the complete aircraft, with hundreds of sub-contractors to feed them with parts.

The assault on the Philippines is the natural strategic consequence of the Japanese defeats in New Guinea, the Moluccas, and Palau islands. It conforms to a recognized tactical approach to China and Japan proper. In the

1944, of Air Chief Marshal Sir Trafford Leigh-Mallory to be Air Officer C.-in-C. South East Asia, vice Air Chief Marshal Sir Richard Peirse. The new Air C.-in-C., under Admiral Lord Louis Mountbatten, is primed with the latest battle experience from the invasion of France. His appointment may be the prelude to greater air and surface activity from the west against the Japanese in Burma, Malaya, the Nicobar and Andaman islands, and Sumatra.

IN Europe strategical and tactical air blows have increased in violence. On October 14 and 15, within eighteen hours, more than 10,000 tons of bombs, including 500,000 incendiaries, fell on Duisburg, greatest inland port in Europe. This blow by Bomber Command was a combined daylight and night assault programme. The first attack, made in daylight by a powerful force, dropped 4,500 tons of bombs in 25 minutes : 14 Lancasters, about one per cent of the force, were lost. At night more than 1,500 Lancaster and Halifax bombers dropped the remainder of the 10,000 tons ; eight bombers were lost.

Elsewhere, tactical aircraft have been engaged in disrupting enemy communications to the battlefronts. Take one example. On Sunday, October 15, the weather shut down about midday, yet R.A.F. aircraft supporting Field-Marshal Montgomery's Army Group flew 834 sorties, a relatively small offensive, which nevertheless destroyed 27 railway trucks and damaged 79, cut 15 railway tracks, and destroyed five locomotives and damaged six. Work of this kind proceeds continually, sapping the enemy's strength faster than he can rebuild it. It goes on despite the 500 m.p.h. German jet-planes that make fleeting dashes over the Allied zones. Aircraft may have to operate from strip airfields laid out on the wet ground ; tents and caravans provide sleeping, eating and office accommodation.

On October 12, despite unsuitable weather, British airborne troops landed in gliders on the aerodrome west of Athens. They cleared landmines and made a landing strip for transport and combatant aircraft. Then by air, and from the sea through Piraeus, Allied forces came to the aid of the Greeks who had already liberated their own ancient capital.

Parachute-Borne Fragmentation Bombs in Action

TERRIFIC DAMAGE WAS WROUGHT on Japanese airfields by U.S. Army Air Forces during a raid on Buru Island, near Celebes, in the battle for New Guinea in July 1944. A few seconds after this photograph was taken a direct hit completely shattered the grounded and camouflaged Japanese plane in the foreground. Describing these new " parafrag " bombs, General Henry H. Arnold, head of the U.S. Army Air Force, declared : " They break into 1,000-1,500 pieces, each weighing about ·3 oz. and having velocities up to 4,000 ft. per second." Their design enables low-flying bombing to be carried out with extraordinary accuracy.

Photo, New York Times Photos

This is the Tempest—Bomb-Killer Number One

TEMPESTS OF THE R.A.F. scored outstanding successes against flying bombs, earning the title of "Bomb-Killer Number 1." A wing that had destroyed some 650 doodlebugs during the summer of 1944 was transferred to an airfield in Belgium, whence it operated against German fighters : above, pilots of a New Zealand Tempest squadron at this airfield, their planes in the background. The Tempest is a single-engined fighter in the tradition of the Hurricane and Typhoon, designed by Sydney Camm, C.B.E., of Hawker Aircraft Ltd. (see p. 543, Vol. 3). One of the fastest fighters in service today, it is powered with a supercharged Napier Sabre engine of 2,200 h.p. Armament consists of four 22-mm. cannon guns. The span is 41 ft. ; length, 33 ft. 8 in. ; height (tail down), 16 ft. 1 in. Below, a Tempest in flight ; left, the nose, showing four-bladed airscrew. *Photos, British Official*

LET the end of the War come soon or late, if one may judge from certain straws in the wind we shall have quite a number of those lightheaded busybodies who get a self-righteous thrill from urging the victorious Allies to deal kindly with the vanquished Hun. All of us who remember what followed the last War will have little sympathy with such futile critics who, in the years between the temporary settlement of Versailles and the Germanic revival of war-lust, continued to play the game of the Junkers—those Junkers who we were warned would "cheat us yet," and did cheat us, and will cheat us again, if official opinion should now waver in disposing of them effectively. I have just had a recent reminder of the sort of criticism to which an editor is subjected who tries to be realistic concerning the inborn beastliness of the German race to all outside its pale. The occasion was my coming across a long and friendly letter from a Yorkshire reader, who wrote to me in September 1936, to say that he had many works edited by me on his bookshelves, and these he had treasured for years, but he had just come into possession of some volumes of the first series of THE WAR ILLUSTRATED which he edited throughout the last War, in which he was shocked to discover " such a lurid collection of hymns of hate against Germany, the like of which I never dreamed possible, and it is a sad blow indeed to me to find it coming from one who has produced such wonderful works for our people." As my readers of the present WAR ILLUS-TRATED may be interested to know what I said to this correspondent, I am reprinting here a few extracts from my reply to him, and will only remark that if any readers of the present WAR ILLUSTRATED find it too " anti-German," I should be inclined to reply to them even more strongly than I did to my friendly critic of its predecessor.

MY letter from which these extracts are made was dated September 24, 1936 : "Although even now I am by no means pre-pared to accept your opinion that the Germans are a kindly and peaceable people desiring nothing better than to live in peace and amity with the English, might I ask you if, in common with myself, throughout the duration of the War you were in weekly touch with the Ger-man press and read the articles of your kind-hearted German friends about the English and the French and the Belgians ? You tell me that you are a frequent visitor to Germany (which I cannot pretend to be, having only once since the War made a fairly careful first-hand study of conditions there), and I would suggest that you should, in order to get a proper perspective, look over some of their wartime publications which are still to be found on the files, I have no doubt, of the Illustrierte Zeitung and the Berliner Tageblatt, etc. If you can discover in any of these publications *one* paragraph of sympathy and friendliness towards the British people written by Germans, I should be prepared to bow before the severest criticism you can launch against the contents of THE WAR ILLUSTRATED. As a matter of cold fact the anti-German tone of THE WAR ILLUSTRATED was mild and diffident by comparison with the anti-British tone of every piece of printed matter issued in Germany throughout the War . . . in any other war in which Germany should unhappily find herself fighting against Britain, the same measures of hate would be meted out . . . On re-consideration, I am not prepared to blush for anything that appeared in THE WAR ILLUSTRATED even during the abnormal days of the War. I admire the German people in many ways, having known many of them, but I am not prepared to believe that as a nation they are so kindly disposed towards the British people as, for the time being, it suits Hitler in Mein Kampf to make them appear."

I WAS greatly interested to receive from a correspondent in Italy, Corporal T. M. Burgess, a copy of THE WAR ILLUSTRATED, dated February 16, 1918, which had been handed to him by an Italian civilian when he was passing through a town " somewhere in Italy." This particular issue of THE WAR ILLUSTRATED has been very carefully preserved for no less than twenty-six years, a fact which, Corporal Burgess remarks, " shook me ! " Accord-ing to my correspondent, it went the rounds of all his companions in arms, who were amazed at its age " and the slightly different goings-on it recorded compared with what we are experiencing here today." But what most interested me, as its editor, was the fact that my correspondent had just received, in the midst of all the confusion of the War in Italy, a recent number of its present-day successor ! I could write a whole page about the contents of that copy of February 16, 1918 (it was No. 183, by the way), but can find space here to quote only a few lines from a page-article which I had personally written on a book by General von Freytag-Loringhoven, entitled " Deductions from the World War," wherein that now-forgotten military critic had written, " In the future, as in the past, the German people will have to seek firm cohesion in its glorious Army and in its belaurelled young Fleet."

MY own concluding remarks upon this menacing book, which all Germany was reading at a time when its present Fuehrer was himself an unknown corporal in that " glorious Army " which was, eight months later, to be forced to surrender, are worth reprinting today :

" If anyone tells you that German militar-ism is showing signs of exhaustion, you will

do that person a service by asking him to read this frank study of the World War by Ger-many's foremost military writer who, liar though he be when it suits him to lie, does not hesitate to tell the military truths in which he has been trained, and which he is bent on teaching Germany of today for its wars of the future."

Surely the Allies will see to it this time that when we have disposed of this " glorious Army " for a second time in twenty-six years it will be rendered impotent to renew its evil powers within another quarter of a century. I say " surely," but at the moment I am not too sure ! And that letter from a friendly critic in 1936 is far from reassuring.

HOW wasteful war can be is illustrated by the final reckoning of the number of shells fired by the Germans from their long-range Channel guns on the French coast from the time when they began in 1940 to Septem-ber 1944 when they were captured. The total weight of shells dropped into Dover and Folkestone and other places nearby was 3,700 tons. Of course, they did a lot of damage, but they did not increase the Huns' chance of winning by one ounce. They did not keep convoys out of the Narrows. Our merchant ships went up and down all the time. So far as the result of the war is concerned they had no effect whatever. Those 3,700 tons of shells were utterly wasted.

WHILE the problem of tips to waiters is under discussion, some people holding that you could not obtain good service with-out them and others advocating the addition of a percentage for service to every bill, another difficulty of the same nature is worry-ing many shopkeepers. Numbers of cus-tomers, it seems, are so anxious to get a little bit extra of this or the other that they offer tips to shop assistants. It is a low-down trick in every way. It is an attempt to get the better of other customers by underhand means and it is putting temptation in the way of the shop assistant which, if he yields to it, makes him liable to be dismissed on the spot. For in the event of a tip being taken and the fact coming to the knowledge of the police, the assistant and the customer would both be liable to prosecution under the Prevention of Corruption Act. That many shopkeepers do themselves favour certain customers cannot be doubted. Their method of keeping goods under the counter and producing them only when certain favoured persons enter the shop is sufficient proof. If a shopkeeper is bound to sell what customers ask for, sup-posing he has it, then it must be an offence against the law to refuse. Yet there is much to be said for the shopkeeper who reserves goods for regular customers rather than those who drift about picking up what they can.

I WONDER how many listeners to the B.B.C. "war report" like the confused noise of the direct broadcasts from the Front ? When you hear the distinct but lively tones of Major Lewis Hastings giving his informative com-mentary on the latest events, do you not find it a relief from the untrained voices of the war reporters and all the whistlings, growlings and rumblings that come across with them ? I feel grateful every time the announcer says " We are reading this report." But I suppose there are people who like to feel they are hearing what comes straight from the battlefield. With the matter that we have been given there is no fault whatever to be found. The men who collect it are all good at their job. It is not their business to culti-vate smooth radio voices, and they cannot prevent the hubbub that accompanies their stories. To hear the actual words spoken by General Eisenhower or Field-Marshal Montgomery is something none of us would like to miss. They come over quite well, too. But there has been too much " actuality " for me in the war reports generally. It too frequently defeats its own object.

Lieut.-General R. M. SCOBIE, M.C., whose appointment as Commander of the Land Task Force in Greece was announced on October 15, 1944, was formerly G.O.C. Malta. He was an instructor at the Royal Military College, Australia, 1932-35, and in 1939 became Deputy-Director for Mobilization. He commanded Tobruk fortress in 1941. *Photo, British Official*

Climbing a Mountain Pass to Victory in Italy

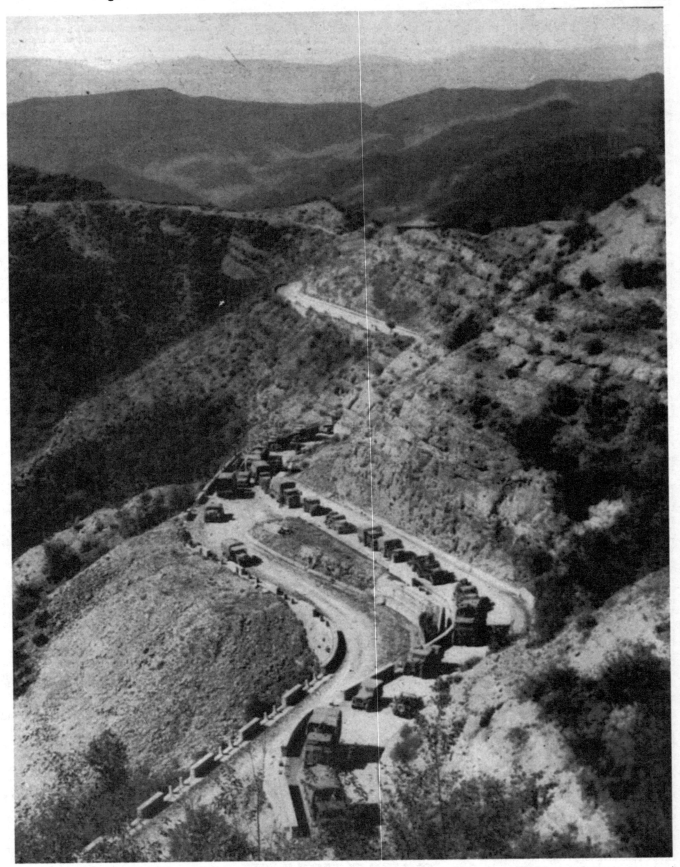

THE MURAGLIONE PASS, 24 miles north-east of Florence and on the highway to Bologna, within eight miles of which city the 5th Army was reported to be engaged in bitter fighting on October 24, 1944, proved hard going for our transport. Stretches of this road running alongside the mountains had been demolished by the enemy, and British engineers have had a tough task putting the zigzag thoroughfare in order for the close-packed streams of traffic moving up to the front.

Photo, British Official

Printed in England and published every alternate Friday by the Proprietors, THE AMALGAMATED PRESS, LTD., The Fleetway House, Farringdon Street, London, E.C.4. Registered for transmission by Canadian Magazine Post. Sole Agents for Australia and New Zealand : Messrs. Gordon & Gotch, Ltd. ; and for South Africa : Central News Agency, Ltd.—November 10, 1944. S.S. *Editorial Address:* JOHN CARPENTER HOUSE, WHITEFRIARS, LONDON, E.C.4.

Vol 8 · *The War Illustrated* · N° 194

SIXPENCE

Edited by Sir John Hammerton

NOVEMBER 24, 1944

MARSHAL JOSIP BROZ TITO, President of the National Liberation Committee of Yugoslavia, and bodyguard, arrived at Nish in liberated territory for talks with Dr. Subasitch, Premier of King Peter's Government. Agreement between the partisans and the Government was announced on June 16, 1944. On October 20, Belgrade, Yugoslav capital, fell to Marshal Tito's forces collaborating with Russian troops under Marshal Tolbukhin. On November 8, Tito was reported in Moscow for talks with Stalin. *Photo, U.S. Official*

NO. 195 WILL BE PUBLISHED FRIDAY, DECEMBER 8

Our Roving Camera Sees Peace Preparations

WAR TO PEACE switch-over in production was to be noted increasingly all over Britain as early as October 1944. An aircraft assembly factory partially turned over to the manufacture of utility furniture (left), with aircraft parts still under construction on the right.

FIELD-MARSHAL'S BATON, the personal gift of H.M. the King to Sir Bernard Montgomery, delivered at the War Office on October 26, 1944, has its base inscribed as seen below. Sir Bernard's promotion from General dates from September 1, 1944.

FROM
His Majesty
GEORGE VI
King
OF
GREAT BRITAIN
IRELAND AND THE BRITISH DOMINIONS
BEYOND THE SEAS
EMPEROR OF INDIA
TO
FIELD-MARSHAL
SIR BERNARD LAW
MONTGOMERY.
K.C.B. D.S.O.
1944.

GERMAN PRISONERS in the autumn of 1944 found themselves faced with the unexpected —and ironical—task of helping to clear British coastal areas of barbed-wire entanglements which had been hurriedly erected during the invasion threat of 1940-41.

WAY OUT ONLY
OPPOSITE SIDE FOR YOUR
SHIRT, TIE, HAT, SOCKS & SHOES

CIVILIAN CLOTHES being drawn under the War Office scheme for ex-soldiers, in operation from October 16, 1944, which was initiated by Private Salter, of the Pioneer Corps, who is seen (above) leaving "Civvy Shop" fully equipped. He received a suit, shirt, collar, tie, shoes, raincoat and a felt hat.

MOBILE LAUNDRY, surrounded by London suburban housewives fly-bombed in the summer of 1944 (left). These women faced up to the new air-terror as cheerfully as they did in the old blitz days.

Photos, Daily Mirror, Planet News, Keystone, Associated Press

THE BATTLE FRONTS

by Maj.-Gen. Sir Charles Gwynn, K.C.B., D.S.O.

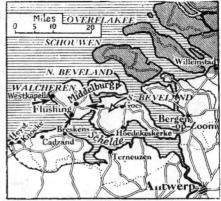

BRITISH COMMANDO units of the 1st Canadian Army made two landings on Walcheren on November 1, 1944—at Flushing and at Westkapelle. In the east the Canadians finally cleared the Beveland causeway. See story in page 441.
By courtesy of News Chronicle

FOR strategic reasons it is often necessary to attack in regions highly unfavourable for tactical offensive operations. That was the case in Italy and now in Holland and East Prussia. In Holland our troops have had to fight under conditions which appear to have been as daunting as those at Passchendaele in the last war, and, moreover, with little prospect of securing tactical success on a spectacular scale. The spirit and determination with which they have fought are therefore all the more admirable, and the results achieved should not be judged by losses inflicted on the enemy, though they have been substantial, but by their strategic importance.

The great dash of Montgomery's Army Group northwards from the Seine was essentially a strategic manoeuvre which entailed comparatively little tactical action; and the capture of the Port of Antwerp intact, the chief prize it secured, resulted from the speed of the thrust. The airborne operation which followed, by making it possible to secure the crossings of the Maas

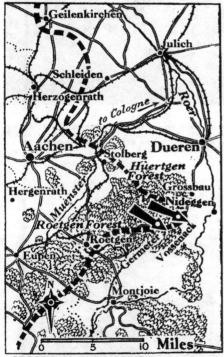

RE-OPENING THEIR DRIVE into the Reich on November 2, 1944, the U.S. 1st Army cleared the thickly-wooded area south-west of Huertgen and west of Vossenack, about 15 miles south-east of Aachen.
By courtesy of News Chronicle

and the Waal, represented a further strategic success gained without inflicting a major tactical defeat on the enemy. The strategic results would, of course, have been greater if a bridge-head over the Lek at Arnhem had also been secured, but even then, before the strategic advantages that had so far been gained could have been exploited, the tactical operations for the clearance of the approaches to Antwerp and the security of the Eindhoven Corridor would still have been necessary, and under conditions no more favourable than those which have actually been encountered.

IN the past, wars were generally decided by one or more tactical victories, and strategic manoeuvres were chiefly designed to bring about decisive battles. But with the growth of armies and the increased com-

plexities of modern warfare, absolutely decisive tactical victories tend to become rarer. Tactical action, therefore, though it has lost none of its importance, must be subordinated to the vastly increased scope of strategy which embraces the employment of practically every form of human activity. The operations in the Scheldt Estuary show, however, what a great part the infantry soldier still plays and how much depends on the physical and moral qualities he develops under well-conceived training.

I have seen it suggested that it might have been better if the full weight of the Allied Armies had been directed northwards, in order to ensure an immediate break-through into north Holland, and that General Patton's drive eastwards from Paris had little chance of achieving further success when it came up against the obstacle of the Vosges and the German frontier defences. I see little reason, however, to support that suggestion. In the first place, it was obviously advisable to apply pressure to the whole of the long front the Germans had inadequate forces to hold and to leave them guessing as to the points of most danger. Secondly, it was obvious from the first that the initial Allied thrusts could not be maintained without a pause after their communications had reached a certain length—and, obviously, the smaller the force the farther it could go without a pause, provided no serious resistance was encountered.

CLEARANCE of Scheldt Approaches Dependent on Supply Services

Montgomery's 21st Army Group has never been held up through lack of numerical strength, but it had practically outrun its supply services by the time it had achieved the amazing feat of capturing Antwerp intact. It was for that reason that it was unable to clear the Scheldt approaches or to continue its advance across the triple obstacles of the Maas, Waal and Lek without a pause. That could not have been done without heavy fighting, for the enemy had fresh troops in Holland, and the supply services were as yet in no condition to meet the expenditure entailed in overcoming serious resistance. A greater concentration of force for the northern thrust would clearly have added immensely to road congestion and would probably have necessitated a pause before Antwerp or even Brussels was reached by the main force. The supply problem and not numerical strength was the dominating factor, and the astonishing thing is that Dempsey's great thrust was able to accomplish so much, not that it was unable to accomplish more.

It should, I think, be realized that if General Eisenhower had concentrated on a northern drive it is possible that the enemy might have been able to mount a counter-offensive in considerable strength from the Lorraine or Belfort gaps, either against his flank or against the head of the army advancing from the south. Judging from the opposition General Patton has encountered that possibility cannot be ruled out, and it might have produced disturbing effects. Furthermore, the enemy's communications, in spite of air attacks on them, are in the main much better than those of the invading armies which had, in the first instance, no usable railways and have had to traverse country in which the retreating enemy could add his own demolitions to those previously effected by air attack. Dispersion of force obviously tended to minimize these disadvantages, reducing congestion on damaged roads and facilitating their restoration.

With the opening of the approaches to Antwerp and the restoration of the railways from Cherbourg and other of the original disembarkation ports to the front, the Allies have now a reasonably good communication system, and the strategic merits of General Eisenhower's disposition I think become apparent. They leave him with a wide choice of points at which to make his main effort, and they have compelled the enemy to disperse his strength in his uncertainty where the blows will fall. The clearance of the approaches to Antwerp manifestly solves all Montgomery's supply difficulties, and it should also meet much of the American 1st Army's requirements; for Antwerp has far greater capacity than any of the ports we depended on in the last war.

Bologne and Calais, when cleared, will also provide useful subsidiary ports for the 1st Army, and General Patton's Army will probably now have exclusive use of Cherbourg and Le Havre except so far as they may be used by the 6th Army Group, which is still, presumably, based on Marseilles. The fact that it has not been thought necessary to proceed with the liquidation of the German garrisons of Lorient and St. Nazaire is a clear indication that General Eisenhower is satisfied that he will have sufficient ports.

RUSSIA

While the build-up for the major offensive in the west has been in progress the course of events in the east has been completely satisfactory. I do not think that it was expected that Chernyakovsky's offensive in East Prussia would achieve rapid sweeping success. It is a frontal attack against a defensive position of great strength and depth with little opportunity for wide manoeuvres. It has, however, probably achieved its main object in compelling the Germans to concentrate a high proportion of their available strength on this part of their immense front, and to make extravagant use of reserves in costly counter-attacks which have achieved little. If, as seems probable, the main Russian offensive, of which Chernyakovsky's and Malinovsky's offensives may be only the forerunners, develops in Poland the Germans in East Prussia would be in a critical position.

MEANWHILE, Malinovsky's campaign in Hungary is proceeding at an amazing pace, and has gained power since his troops, who have been clearing northern Transylvania, have closed up and since Petrov's Army has joined hands with him south of the Carpathians. With the Hungarians showing little disposition to fight with determination the fall of Budapest must be imminent, and without substantial Hungarian assistance it is difficult to see how the Germans can check Malinovsky's further advance. The German armies in Lapland, Latvia and Yugoslavia are in an increasingly hopeless position.

Fiercely Kesselring Clings to Northern Italy

FIFTH ARMY TROOPS continued to make slow but methodical progress against unrelenting German resistance in Italy, south of Bologna, during the first weeks of November 1944. An Allied observation-post on the rugged slopes of Mt. Vigese (left). Pack-mules and jeeps encounter a stiff climb and a slippery descent on this picturesque hump-backed bridge (right) on their way to supply forward units in the hills beyond Castel del Rio in their drive towards the important industrial and communications centre of Bologna.

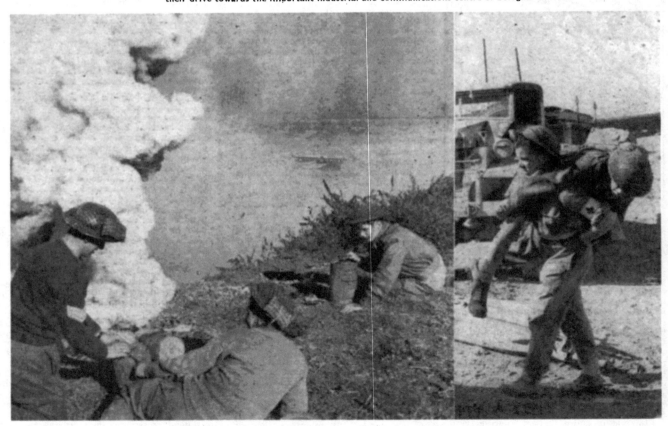

EIGHTH ARMY GUNNERS ignited smoke-canisters (left) to cover our troops on the River Savio near Cesena, which fell on October 19, 1944. On November 10, they were reported to have entered Forli after bitter fighting. Blowing up all the Savio bridges, the enemy day and night shelled the river area to prevent attempted crossings, eventually retiring when threatened with encirclement by New Zealand forces. A British infantryman brings in a wounded comrade from the Savio fighting (right).

　　　　　　Photos British Official

Hun Hordes are Hammered in the Netherlands

AFTER THEIR DEFEAT AT HERTOGENBOSCH on October 26, 1944, the German 15th Army pulled out from south of the River Maas against the onrush of General Dempsey's British 2nd Army and Polish forces of the 1st Canadian Army. Breda, captured on October 29, celebrated its freedom with dancing in the streets (1). After sharp house-to-house fighting, Flushing fell to British troops (2) on November 3. A German 88-mm. shell exploding near Arnhem (3), photographed from a foxhole; the troops in the foreground had a miraculous escape. Swiftly-assembled Bailey bridges made possible communications across flooded Beveland (4).

Photos. British and U.S. Official, Associated Press

THE WAR AT SEA

by Francis E. McMurtrie

ALTHOUGH U-boats are far from being extinct, there being still some hundreds in service, their area of operations has been greatly reduced. There appear to be none left in the Mediterranean, and they have been driven out of the Channel and Bay of Biscay. Their principal ocean bases are now on the coast of Norway. It was from one or other of these Norwegian harbours that the " wolf-pack " issued to make the abortive attack on an Arctic convoy described in the Admiralty communiqué of November 4, 1944. At least three of the enemy submarines were destroyed, and others damaged, some of which may possibly have failed to get back to port. Not a single merchant vessel sustained any damage, our only loss being H.M.S. Kite, a sloop of the war-built "Wren" class.

Operations were conducted by Vice-Admiral F. H. G. Dalrymple-Hamilton, who was captain of H.M.S. Rodney during the action which culminated in the sinking of the Bismarck in May 1941. Complete co-operation between naval aircraft from H.M.S. Vindex and Striker, escort carriers, and a number of escort vessels, which included two destroyers, three sloops and a frigate, proved highly effective in countering enemy efforts to approach the convoy. If the Germans can do no better than this within a limited distance of the bases in which the majority of their U-boats are now concentrated, it does not say much for their chances of renewing the Battle of the Atlantic on terms likely to yield them any advantage.

FULLER reports on the Battle of the Philippines make it plain the Japanese Navy has been dealt a staggering blow. It would seem unlikely that another sea action of importance will be fought until Allied fleets are in a position to advance into Japanese home waters, as the damage inflicted on the ships that regained port may keep them under refit for some time to come.

It is not clear what induced the enemy to give battle in such unfavourable circumstances. Some while back it was announced in a broadcast from Tokyo that the Japanese fleet would fight only when it had the cover of land-based aircraft ; and it may have been the plan to use the airfields in Formosa and Luzon for this purpose. Yet both these islands, as well as Mindanao farther to the south, had been very thoroughly bombed by Allied air forces for more than a week before the action, and a large number of Japanese planes destroyed. So far from this giving pause to the enemy, it seems to have precipitated matters, the concentration of his squadrons being arranged in such a way that the U.S. Third and Seventh Fleets obtained every advantage from their central position in the area of operations.

Probably the Japanese were misled by exaggerated reports of damage inflicted on the U.S. fleets by air attack over a week earlier ; in fact, only a couple of ships were damaged, neither to an extent sufficient to prevent her proceeding to a repairing base. On the other hand, the toll taken of Japanese land-based aircraft was so heavy that their force proved quite inadequate to provide complete cover for the three squadrons into which the enemy had divided his forces, and were themselves outfought by U.S. carrier-borne aircraft.

ANNIHILATION of Japanese Squadron coming from Direction of Singapore

It may have been hoped that the approach of the largest of these squadrons, coming from the direction of Japan, would divert the attention of the U.S. Third Fleet under Admiral Halsey, and the Seventh Fleet, under Vice-Admiral Kincaid, to an extent that would enable the other two enemy detachments to effect a surprise attack. So far from this being the case, the squadron coming from the south-westward (the direction of Singapore) seems to have been the first to be sighted, with the result that it suffered annihilation. Two battleships (the Huso and Yamasiro, of 29,330 tons), four cruisers and seven destroyers were sunk, either in the course of the action or during their subsequent retreat through waters commanded by Allied aircraft. Earlier, this force had been attacked by U.S. submarines during its passage from Singapore, and had thus lost a couple of cruisers before entering Philippine waters.

Air attacks on the enemy force approaching from the north, which seems to have comprised two battleships, four aircraft carriers, five cruisers and six destroyers, were very successful. All four carriers were sunk, as well as a cruiser and two destroyers, before the Third Fleet aircraft engaged were recalled

JAPANESE BATTLESHIP YAMATO, ablaze from stem to stern, with bombs blasting her forward turret, during the furious 3-day engagement in the Philippines toward the end of October 1944. *Photo, Associated Press*

to proceed to the aid of the carriers of the Seventh Fleet, which were being attacked by the remaining Japanese squadron.

This squadron, approaching from the westward, had made its way right through San Bernardino Strait and out into the Pacific, off Samar, early on October 24. It included the new 45,000-ton battleships Musasi and Yamato, with three capital ships of older date, eight cruisers and over a dozen destroyers. One of the cruisers was torpedoed, and capsized before close contact was made, and other ships received damage. In action with ships of the Seventh Fleet a second cruiser was sunk and the enemy force was so severely handled that it retreated through the San Bernardino Strait as darkness fell. A third cruiser was sunk by gunfire.

ALTOGETHER the total Japanese losses in these engagements were summed up by Admiral Nimitz as two battleships, four carriers, nine cruisers and nine destroyers. Severe damage was inflicted on a third battleship, as well as on five cruisers and seven destroyers ; some of these ships may have failed to get home. Almost all the other enemy ships also received injuries, though of a less serious character. Ships of the Third and Seventh fleets lost were the light fleet aircraft carrier Princeton, of 10,000 tons ; two escort carriers; two destroyers; one destroyer-escort, of a type rated as frigates in this country ; and a few craft of less importance. U.S. submarines and aircraft had an important share in the victory.

It is now known that the casualties in H.M.A.S. Australia, mentioned in page 390, were caused by a Japanese bomber crashing on her bridge after its pilot had been killed.

What strength can the Japanese Navy still muster ? It is improbable that there remain in service more than six or possibly seven battleships, seven or eight aircraft carriers, between 20 and 30 cruisers, 70 destroyers and under 100 submarines. This is not a force with which any great enterprise can be attempted. The U.S. Navy alone is capable of putting into the line about three times as many ships in each of these categories.

HEROES OF THE PHILIPPINES—Vice-Admiral Marc A. Mitscher, commander of the famous Task Force 58 of the U.S. Navy (left), and Vice-Admiral William F. Halsey, Commander of the U.S. 3rd Fleet (right). Both were engaged in the momentous three-day sea action in the Philippines in the last week of October 1944, which Admiral Nimitz described as an " overwhelming victory." See illus. page 429. *Photo, Associated Press*

Refuel As You Go is the Navy's Slogan Now

ROUGH WEATHER NO LONGER HAMPERS refuelling at sea, thanks to modern methods. Nowadays the operation often takes place as the supplying ship and the vessel to be fuelled proceed on their courses. The 30-year-old battleship Valiant, 31,100 tons, oiling a destroyer in the Mediterranean (top). A cruiser being refuelled by tanker (bottom); the rating in the foreground grips a marked line which helps the navigator on the bridge to maintain the cruiser's position relative to the tanker. See also page 712. Vol. 7.

Photos, British Official

Looking for Death on the Beaches of Britain

Mines were strewn freely in 1940, when possibility of invasion was very real. Now use of the beaches is required again by the public—and the mines are being searched for and removed. Those engaged in the task know that life and death are separated by the breadth of a hair. The methods of these unsung heroes are explained by MARK PRIESTLEY.

THE official plan clearly showed the position of every mine as planted, but the tides had swept in tons of pebbles in the intervening years and buried the mines in swirling shingle and drifting sand. Some had risen to the surface. Others had sunk to unknown depths. Others, again, had been forced out of position and lay across the safety paths defined on the maps. All the mines, as the official records nicely put it, were "in an uncertain condition." This was the peril that Sergeant

R.A.F. "BEACHCOMBERS" search for shoe-mines after the Normandy landings in June 1944. The article in this page describes the perils of such work on the beaches at home.
Photo, British Official

Arthur Bond-Roose, of the R.E.s, faced for more than two desperate months on an English beach that was in his care.

He saw his commanding officer blown up by a mine, and he made a hazardous crawl across the death-strewn sands to recover the body and rescue the field chart. After that, whenever any of his men recovered a mine, the sergeant personally laid the demolition charges, never knowing but that the mines might explode of their own accord. Ultimately he destroyed over 600. He gained the B.E.M. for his "sense of duty and cool leadership"—and his story is typical of heroism displayed and risks endured today on Britain's least-known field of valour.

IT was a minefield explosion on the Scottish coast, involving the death of two of his friends, that led Lieut. Joseph Kos to invent his "carpet sweeper" detector, which was used with such success in the desert and is now employed in Britain's own minefields. Risks nevertheless remain. In six months, in the South-Eastern Command alone, in the course of minefield clearance operations 19 officers and men have lost their lives. Such is the tragic toll in what a minefield veteran has called the "Battle of the Beaches."

Sometimes an accidental explosion has not been recorded in official registers, and the field parties search with taut nerves for mines that no longer exist. At other times they strike tide-swept mines that have not been charted for that particular spot. One unit

of R.E.s was ordered to remove 450 mines originally laid in 1940. They were about to begin operations when headquarters forwarded an amended chart showing that 50 more mines had been subsequently installed to improve the field, and the position of five was regarded as doubtful!

EVENTUALLY the unit recovered over 650 mines. Some were as mapped, others had been carried by the sea from positions ten and twelve miles away; one was an airborne mine of German type, and there were three magnetic marine mines which must have buried themselves in the sand without touching-off. Thousands of mines were, of course, laid at vulnerable points, inland as well as on the coast, under the imminent threat of invasion. Records were kept as carefully as possible at the time, and have since been amended to keep track of additional mines, or of mines blown up, but the charts are necessarily imperfect.

In one instance, a corporal was killed in a charted minefield and an officer and a sergeant of the Coldstream Guards attempted to recover the body. The sergeant was confident that he knew where the mines had been laid, yet within a few minutes he was killed and the young officer behind him was lying seriously wounded. Cliff falls, the action of tidal currents, and the human element itself have all introduced the unknown factor.

There is the vivid story of an R.A.F. Beach Squadron that took over a seaside villa. Sappers searched the front garden beforehand and disinterred six box mines, each containing 7 lb. of T.N.T. Three days later, the sappers resumed operations in the back garden, where the R.A.F. boys had been feeding the chickens—and dug up another 67, much to the airmen's horror.

Heinz Hounds Nose Them Out

Of late, risks in minefield clearance have been considerably lessened and detection processes speeded up by the use of trained dogs. Lighter than men, dogs have the advantage of being able to move about amongst mines with rather less danger of setting them off. All kinds of medium sized dogs—even Heinz Hounds, as the mongrels are called—are being employed.

Training starts as a game between dog and man, causing the dog to associate the smell of mines—both metal and plastic types—with a reward of food. Twenty dogs can sweep a 200-yard lane, 16 yards wide, in 30 minutes. It is an amazing sight to see several dogs at once "freezing" on finding a mine, as pointers do when they mark a bird. The health of the dogs is so well maintained that their reaction becomes extremely rapid and accurate. The experts of the Veterinary and Remount Service, who are responsible for this aspect of the work and who secure the dogs on loan from private owners, have indeed rendered good service (see illus. p. 180).

THOUSANDS of men have now passed through mine-clearance courses at military-engineering schools. Beginning by gaining knowledge of the principles of explosives, and confidence in handling them, students soon lay and take up their own minefields. The main charge is removed from the mines, but igniter sets are left alive, and they contain sufficient explosive to blow off the hand or foot of anyone foolish enough to disregard all due precautions. "The most famous last words in this industry," the instructors emphasize, "are 'I'll try anything once!'"

It goes without saying that accidents amount to less than 1 per cent.

A dislodged pebble can explode a buried mine. Booby traps with elaborate systems of trip wires have also been thickly sown on home shores. There was an occasion when a disastrous minefield explosion involved a number of N.C.O.s and men and, amid the fatal casualties, four men who had survived with injuries were left marooned, surrounded by unexploded mines. The task of extricating them was made harder by further mines buried beneath the surrounding barbed wire.

MAJOR GERRARD MATTHEWS, the officer who faced the risks and for his bravery received the George Medal, placed planks over the wire and entered the minefield. He missed treading on a mine by only six inches. Against the dangers that are constantly undergone, the number of minefield casualties is remarkably small. Many troops have been decorated for gallantry in Britain's minefields. They include Bombardier James Newby, G.M., who made a rescue crawl of 75 feet through a thickly-sown field on the Tyne when two officers had been killed by an anti-tank mine; and Sergeant Ernest Martin, B.E.M., who recently headed stretcher-bearers into an East Anglian field after a party of R.E.s had met with disaster. Then there are Sergeant W. H. Chick, G.M., and Lance-Corporal Gordon Cowell, B.E.M., who went to the aid of a Spitfire pilot who had crash-landed on a mined beach. The

ENTERING FALAISE on August 17, 1944, Canadian sappers fine-combed even the grass-verged footpaths for mines left by the retreating Germans. *Photo, Associated Press*

impact set off a mine, and the explosion set light to the aircraft's wings, but the two soldiers dragged the airman to safety.

After the last war it took over a year to sweep clear the sea lanes. That is why, this time, the authorities have given warning that risk of explosions on our shores may have to be faced for some years to come. Only a restricted number of sappers can at present serve on home beaches, but thousands will participate in the final clean sweep.

How Our Sappers Tackle German Booby Traps

GERMANS RETREATING through Northern Italy, late in 1944, made increasingly desperate attempts to delay the Allied advance with mines and elaborately-disguised booby traps. Trickiest of all were the "Pappmine" and the "S" mine.

The first is made entirely of glass and cardboard, and having no metal in its composition is not revealed by the normal mine detector. The "S" mine, known familiarly as "Bouncing Betty," leaps into the air to explode at a height of three feet.

A British sapper neutralizes a booby trap made from a child's doll (1). A bottle of wine being disconnected from its deadly charge (2). A cunningly-concealed egg-grenade (friction-fuse type) is removed from the branch of a pear tree (3). Neutralizing an anti-personnel mine intended to be detonated by a trip-wire (4).

Photos, British Official

Buffaloes at Beveland Aid Scheldt Invasion

AMPHIBIOUS TROOP-CARRIERS spear-headed the assault by British and Canadian forces of the British 2nd Army when, heading for Walcheren, they landed on the Beveland peninsula on the north side of the River Scheldt on October 26, 1944. Nicknamed Buffaloes, these armed transport vehicles are propelled through the water by the same rubberized track which enables them to travel ashore. A column advances (1), others return with prisoners (2). Loading the Buffaloes (3). Landing craft go in (4).

Photos, Associated Press, British Newspaper Pool

Dempsey's Men Hurl Enemy Back to the Maas

ON A MOPPING-UP FORAY on Sherman tanks, these smiling troops of General Dempsey's British 2nd Army are seen on the thickly-wooded outskirts of Hertogenbosch which had been finally cleared by October 27, 1944. The capture of this keypoint in the German defence system in Holland was an essential preliminary to opening-up access to the port of Antwerp (see story in page 441), taken intact by the British on September 4. The whole Allied line thereafter moved to the River Maas, leaving behind only isolated enemy rearguards.

Photo, British Official

New Guinea Landing Cuts Off 15,000 Japanese

RECONQUERING THE S.W. PACIFIC, U.S. troops, covered by U.S. and Australian cruisers and R.A.A.F. Kittyhawks, landed in force at Cape Sansapor, near the western tip of Dutch New Guinea, on July 30, 1944, without encountering resistance. This completed the reoccupation of strategic points along the northern coast and cut off a Japanese garrison of 15,000 at Manokwari. Troop-packed L.C.I.s, manned by U.S. Coast Guardsmen, moved inshore (top). Ramps to facilitate landing were constructed on the beach (bottom).

Leyte: General MacArthur Keeps His Promise

THE RECAPTURE of the Philippines began, it was announced on October 20, 1944, with the invasion by combined U.S. and Australian forces, under General MacArthur, of Leyte Island (see map). The Allied invasion fleet assembled at a Netherlands New Guinea base (1). General MacArthur (2, with cane), waded ashore from a landing craft, accompanied by members of his staff. The U.S. flag, "Old Glory" (3), was again raised on Philippine soil.

Photos, News Chronicle, Associated Press. Map by courtesy of the Daily Express

"IN A MAJOR AMPHIBIOUS OPERATION we have seized the eastern coast of Leyte Island, in the Philippines, 600 miles north of Morotai, and 2,500 miles from Milne Bay, whence our offensive began nearly 16 months ago." In these words General MacArthur announced the beginning of the reconquest of the Philippines, thus keeping his promise to return.

The combined skill of the American Army and Navy in the Pacific, assisted by units of the Royal Australian Navy and the R.A.A.F., took the enemy by surprise. Japanese expectation of an attack on Mindanao had caused the enemy to be caught unawares in Leyte, with the result that beach-heads were secured in the important Tacloban area by Gen. MacArthur's forces with "unbelievably low" casualties.

The troops comprised units of the U.S. 6th Army, to which were attached units from the Central Pacific with supporting elements. The naval forces were the U.S. 7th Fleet (Vice-Adml. Kincaid), an Australian squadron and supporting craft of the U.S. 3rd Fleet (Vice-Adml. Halsey). Air support was given by navy carrier forces of the Far East Air Force and the Royal Australian Air Force. General MacArthur, as Commander-in-Chief South-West Pacific, was in personal command. The enemy forces were estimated at 225,000, and included troops of the 14th Army under Field-Marshal Count Terauchi.

Harbours Made in Britain Sailed to France

To enable our forces landed on the Normandy coast on D-Day to be reinforced and kept supplied with utmost speed it was necessary that two invasion ports, each roughly the size of Dover Harbour, should be constructed in this country, then be transported across 100 miles of sea and placed in position off the enemy-occupied coast. The story of this staggering achievement can now be told.

LONG before the invasion was launched it was obvious that vast quantities of stores and equipment would have to be landed on open beaches. It was estimated that about 12,000 tons, plus 2,500 vehicles of all kinds, would have to be handled in this manner each day for 90 days at least. There was only one possible plan: to have ready prefabricated sections which could be assembled at the spot where two vast invasion ports would be most useful.

A harbour for British use was to be located at Arromanches; another, for American use, at Port en Bassin. And each approximately the size of Dover Harbour—which took seven years to complete! These two were to be set up in days, to give full shelter and all usual port facilities to vessels whilst unloading. This entailed the construction of 150 caissons—enormous hollow blocks—for the harbour walls.

The largest of these caissons had a displacement of over 6,000 tons. Each contained crews' quarters for use during the passage, the crew being partly naval, and partly from the Royal Engineers (or American Seabees) for carrying out the operation of sinking. At a later stage, Bofors guns, 20 tons of ammunition, and rough shelters for a gun's crew, were placed on the top of most caissons as additional A.A. protection for the harbour. Caissons were towed across the Channel, each by a tug of about 1,500 h.p.

On arrival they were manoeuvred into position with the help of small tugs, then special valves were opened in each, allowing water to fill it and sink it where it was to remain. It took roughly 22 minutes to sink the largest. These had all been built during the winter months, a few in graving docks, the rest in emergency basins constructed behind river-banks; the banks were then dredged away so that the partly completed caissons could float out and be towed to wet docks for completion of the concrete work. Towing of these to the Normandy coast commenced on D-Day plus one.

ON D-Day blockships sailed to where this work was to be completed, to provide breakwaters for the immediate shelter of hosts of small craft. Sixty ships of various types and sizes were earmarked for this purpose, including old warships. These made the crossing close behind the assault forces and all arrived safely. They were sunk by explosive charges, and their crews were then brought back to this country.

To complete each port, internal equipment such as piers was essential. It is no easy matter to construct a pier hundreds of feet long on a flat beach, with a rise and fall of tide of over 20 feet, and which sometimes may be floating and at other times be resting on sand or, worse still, rock. This problem had been under examination for many months, and in 1942 the Prime Minister took a personal interest in the matter. In typical Churchillian style he wrote, " Piers for use on beaches. They must float up and down with the tide. The anchor problem must be mastered. Let me have the best solution worked out. Don't argue the matter. The difficulties will argue for themselves."

Pier-Heads Built as Ships

The result was eminently satisfactory. After severe sea tests the equipment went into production—amounting to 7 miles of pier and all necessary appurtenances. Pier-heads were built, as ships, in various ports on the coast, from Leith round to Glasgow, four by the R.E.s at military ports in Scotland. Most of the remaining equipment was prefabricated all over the country, and then assembled at the Army depots at Southampton and Richborough. About 240 contractors were employed on this particular task, and 50,000 tons of steel were used.

The work of assembly-on-the-spot went on whilst the sinking of caissons was being completed. By D-Day plus 12 more than half of these were in position, and the harbours were already an impressive sight. Up to this time the operation was going according to plan. Very few accidents had occurred, and our air superiority was such that enemy interference had caused little trouble. Floating breakwaters, consisting of steel floats, had previously been moored end-to-end in a long line, the object of these being to have a damping effect on the sea in strong winds; 15,000 tons of steel were used in their construction. The Army Fire Service helped in sinking the pier-heads to the correct level, as well as manning and floating land-based fire stations.

And then, on D-Day plus 13, there occurred the biggest June gale for 40 years. It blew from the worst possible direction—the harbours were exposed to its full force, and these were only at the half-way stage. The American harbour suffered very severely and the breakwaters were largely broken up, so much so that the work on this harbour was discontinued. All the pier equipment which was on the voyage across when the gale started was sunk, but only one caisson failed to weather the journey.

After the gale subsided the work of construction continued on the British harbour

MR. JACK W. GIBSON, 57-year-old Yorkshireman and Director of Civil Engineering (Special) at the Ministry of Supply, one of the chief figures on the construction side of the prefabricated ports described in this page.
Photo, Sport & General

at Arromanches, though a long spell of rough weather prevented pier equipment from being towed over, so that the remaining harbour was not unloading to maximum capacity until well into July. But even on the worst day 800 tons of petrol and ammunition, as well as many troops, were landed over the piers. Eventually it was completed, and a port bigger than many with famous names had been built in a few weeks against a lonely French beach.

DAY after day, in all weathers, scores of ships of all sizes have moored within its shelter or berthed in unbroken lines along its quays. Never, even at the height of a peacetime trade boom, has so much shipping used such limited accommodation at one time. As a result of the craftsmanship of vast numbers of British workmen hundreds of thousands of tons of vital supplies, scores of thousands of men and many thousands of vehicles have been put ashore in the most rapid military build-up ever undertaken.

The prefabricated port made possible the liberation of Western Europe. Furthermore, when the concrete sections were assembled, for trial, in shoal water off Dungeness shortly before D-Day, they were seen by German air reconnaissance—and led the German High Command to the erroneous conclusion that the Pas de Calais, with its flying-bomb launching sites, was our objective. This inaccuracy caused the retention of large enemy forces in the wrong parts of Northern France, enabling our landings to go ahead before German troops could be switched to the real zone of operations.

GIGANTIC PREFABRICATED PIER for one of our home-made invasion harbours being towed across the Channel. Average speed for this operation was 4 knots, the towing distance for each unit averaging a hundred miles. The total tug fleet available for the assembly of the harbour-parts off the Normandy coast was 85, varying from vessels of 1,500 h.p. to those of 600 h.p.—the latter not generally used in the open sea. Each round trip took about three days, and the transport of well over 1,000,000 tons was involved.

Photo, Planet News

Photos, British Official

Secret of the European Invasion Revealed

Without this crowning example of the British genius for invention it is doubtful if Hitler's West Wall would so readily have been pierced: towed in sections from Britain to Arromanches in Normandy, a prefabricated harbour provided vital accommodation for our shipping. One of the enormous concrete caissons (top) about to be towed across the Channel. The caissons in position (bottom), forming part of the main deep-water breakwater; A.A. guns on platforms guard the harbour.

Tank Landing Ship
Pierhead

Caissons & Blocks

Entrance

Advance to German Frontier Made Possible by—

Steel roadways carried on steel girders run out from the beach at Arromanches to distant pier-heads at which our invasion craft, including 7,000-ton vessels, discharged their urgent cargoes (top). A pier-head, with a displacement of 1,000 tons, complete with crew's quarters, generating sets, and storage accommodation, at the end of the cross-Channel tow (centre left). Ambulances formed part of the traffic using the piers : a convoy (bottom left) proceeds from shore to hospital ship.

—This Masterpiece of British Skill and Daring

Looking towards the invasion coast, long lines of pier roadways straddle calm sea inside the two-miles-long harbour (bottom right) formed by sinking the concrete caissons, in whose making vast quantities of rubble from blitzed sites of London and other cities were used. This sheltered water played a tremendous part in enabling us to achieve so successfully and swiftly "what Philip of Spain failed to do, what Napoleon tried and failed to do, what Hitler never had the courage to do."

Two-Way Traffic on the Prefabricated Piers

Photos, British Official and U.S. Signal Corps

Final erection of the second harbour, for American use, was discontinued, but not before many vehicles and much equipment had been landed (top). At the British harbour (bottom), in the construction of which our " soldiers were sailors and sailors were soldiers and Royal Marines were both," casualties are being evacuated whilst Army vehicles are being discharged at the end of one of the floating piers, so devised as to rise and fall with the 20-foot tide.

VIEWS & REVIEWS
Of Vital War Books

by Hamilton Fyfe

WHETHER you agree with it or not, this remark of a professor at Birmingham University is calculated to make you think. "Never forget the common man," he said. "He is the most important person in the world because there are so many of him."

I don't myself agree with that. It seems to me the professor might just as well have said, "Pebbles on the beach are more valuable than diamonds because there are so many of them." Or even, "Weeds are better than flowers because flowers are few and weeds innumerable." There were a great many million of the common man in this country when the problems of invading the Continent had to be solved. Were they more important than the one man who had the idea of constructing that marvellous prefabricated harbour on the Normandy coast (see pages 430-434), or more important than the man who, when the plan was ready, said, "Now get it done quickly"?

However, that remark by the Birmingham professor was useful because it set a woman thinking. That woman was Miss Verena Holmes, now Technical Adviser to the Ministry of Labour. Some little while before this war began she gave that remark a twist and produced this reflection :

Considering women's engineering work in wartime, the most important person is going to be the common woman—the ordinary munition girl drilling holes or turning shells or making screws, or doing innumerable other operations on millions of different parts. To give her the leadership she requires, to teach her and look after her, to control and encourage her, is in my opinion a work of the very greatest usefulness.

So Miss Holmes started classes for training women to do supervisory and technical work. This enabled many of them to show they really were important, for "a large number who attended those classes are now occupying key positions." The women engineers are naturally best at delicate, precise work, such as instrument making and tending. There are things they cannot do, either because they are not strong enough or because they have not had the necessary experience. But, "although there is a prejudice to be overcome against women doing many jobs," says Miss Holmes in Peggy Scott's new book, They Made Invasion Possible (Hutchinson, 15s.), "yet, when they are given training and encouragement, everyone is astonished at what they can accomplish." Miss Scott thinks men have been more astonished than women.

It does not surprise women to know that women of the Air Transport Auxiliary are piloting our heaviest four-engine bombers ; that women can drive great tractors and what are commonly known as fire-engines ; can work in gas-masks ; can run an aircraft engineering business ; or that a shipyard can be worked with 95 per cent women . . . The men never stop being surprised.

Even women, however, Miss Scott admits, hardly supposed that women could "work as labourers ; dig trenches and lay drain-pipes for an aerodrome site ; shovel soda, after first standing in troughs to smash it with electric drills ; that they can quarry stone." There is still a good deal of doubt among both sexes as to whether women should be given any of the higher appointments in industry. In the factories at present very few indeed have risen above the position of forewoman. But there is no doubt whatever that some of them can make good as directors and managers. Take the case, for example, of the one already mentioned as running an aircraft engineering business.

Miss Rosalind Norman, sister to the founder of Heston Airfield near London,

began by flying herself, then became a maker of scale models of planes. These were bought readily ; she prospered so well that she was able to start making aircraft. No woman had established a business of the kind before. She continued to manage it after she married and became Mrs. Burke ; at one time she had to take with her wherever she went a baby she was nursing—took it even into city offices when she went to keep appointments. "You would have thought it was a bomb if you had seen the faces of some people," she told Miss Scott. But she made her factory

They Made Invasion Possible

flourish, helped the war effort, and brought up a fine healthy child at the same time.

Her energies were not confined to her own plant. She organized in the counties of Surrey, Sussex and Bucks, village part-time teams to work in aircraft workshops near their homes. She created an enthusiasm which was of immense value. There was no effort the teams would not make when she appealed to them in an emergency. Once on a Friday she was asked if she could assemble by Monday morning a million nuts on threads. "Within a few hours every worker in the southern workshops was spinning a nut on a thread. Whole families worked together all night and called in their friends ; hospitals, fire-watchers, mobile Red Cross and many other organizations lent a hand," and at eight o'clock on Monday morning Mrs. Burke delivered the million complete.

ABOUT the future of women such as Mrs. Burke and Miss Holmes there can be no uncertainty. But what about the numbers of ordinaries who will have to find some other employment when war work stops ? Many will not want to go back to indoor jobs after having become accustomed to outdoor life and having liked it as much as did a balloon operator, formerly a clerk, who told Miss Scott, "It's lovely ! I thought I would be frozen stiff in the winter, but if we're moving we don't feel the cold. I wouldn't change

my job for anything." She was not an exception. On that balloon site all the girls who had been indoor workers loved the outdoor life, and it made one realize how many round pegs there have been in square holes. Having found the kind of life they really like, these girls will probably never be content to be always indoors again—although they cannot remain on a balloon site.

A farmer in Sussex, member of the Agricultural Committee, says that any girl in the Land Army who wants to stay on a farm after the war will have the chance to do so. "I admire their pluck," he told Miss Scott. "They don't object to anything. They spread the manure and clean out the pigs, and they do the threshing, which is a dirty job." They can't milk as well as men who have been at it all their lives ; they can't thatch ricks—though perhaps there are girls who could do it. They can't lift weights for feeding the cattle in winter. Their labour is expensive, but they work well together—and how their tongues go !" Whether women carpenters and plumbers will be able to keep on with the work they are doing now is more doubtful ; that they are good at these jobs is beyond question.

Women, it seems, need more entertainment to be provided for them than men usually do. "They want something special for the evenings." They are not content to sit for hours in a pub, or lean against the bar, and chat interminably over pots of ale. Not that they have any objection to drinking at a bar if they want a drink. The old idea that no respectable woman would be seen inside a licensed house has been killed both by the young women of the aristocracy and by those of the women's war services. Will that tarnish their womanhood or harden their natures ?

THE Director of the Wrens, Mrs. Laughton Mathews, shakes her head. She sees no sign of either. "A great deal of what is called masculine and feminine is artificial," she says. "What is artificial will go, what is natural will remain. There is nothing wrong in women drinking at a bar with a man. The great thing is to teach them self-control which will follow them in all walks of life. I think knowledge and experience make for understanding, and for that reason I think Service women will be better people on account of their Service life."

Certainly, if we may judge from the trouble most of the Service women take with their hairdressing, they are anything but masculine in their outlook. They are evidently as anxious to look their best and attract the attention of possible husbands as any girls in "civvies." And why not ?

ONE OF THE MANY thousands of British women in the fighting services, 3rd Officer Audrey Canhan, of Kensington, London, uses this unconventional method of boarding an L.S.T. in Normandy, to check stores. The stirring story of British women's part in the war is told in the book reviewed in this page. PAGE 435 *Photo, British Newspaper Pool*

This is How the Enemy Sniper Gets His Man

Sharpshooters by the thousand have been intensively trained by the Germans to hinder our progress through the woods and lanes and shattered habitations of Europe—fanatically courageous types, masters of camouflage, self-supporting, and above all deadly shots. DONALD COWIE reveals what our troops are up against in their task of disposing of these lone wolves of the battle front.

ONE thing would spoil the thrill if you were allowed as a civilian to visit the Western Front, and that would be the sick feeling at the pit of your stomach every time a vicious crack sounded in the distance and your guide said casually: " Sniper. Better duck your head." Probably there has never been such a widespread outbreak of this military nuisance as at present ; and right across Europe to Berlin it will be encountered increasingly.

The reason why every battlefront report tells of sniping is that—we are winning. The enemy would never use the method in the way that has been described if he were not desperate. Throughout military history the sniper has chiefly been employed by the losing side. When you cannot dominate the battlefield you seek a hiding-place and try to pick off your opponent as he passes.

Thus our men in this war mainly suffer from the sniper *after* a successful battle. They enter towns in Holland and France and presently they will enter towns right across Germany. All seems quiet in the shattered streets, then a shot rings out and a leading soldier falls ; another shot, and our victorious troops must systematically set about rooting out perhaps a score of snipers. These have been ensconced in houses, towers, trees, on rooftops, under derelict tanks and cars, and have been given instructions to do as much damage for as long as possible.

IT is not just nuisance value that these lone-hands have from the enemy point of view. There have been authenticated cases of individual snipers on both sides in this and the last war who have accounted for as many as 200 victims before being caught themselves. On the average in these wars it has taken a ton of lead to kill a man. " Good " snipers get their kill at the average rate of an ounce per time. Therefore the Germans, knowing that they must be forced to retreat and retreat, and studying carefully the experiences of the past campaigns (especially in the Far East), have trained thousands of sharpshooters for our inconvenience.

First the sniper must be an individualist, and second, he must be a good shot. It might be thought that the Germans today would be running short of both. But thousands of German soldiers, in reaction from regimentation, are probably glad of a chance to work on their own ; and modern rifles make it very easy to shoot straight. The sniper is trained to be spiritually and physically self-sufficient, able to endure days of " isolation " and preserve his morale even when he occupies a little island amid a raging sea of the enemy, and when he knows that inevitably he must be discovered by those whom he has so viciously and disturbingly dealt with.

So the man is trained to hate as well as to kill, to take pride in the notches on his rifle butt, to be capable of existing on a minimum of food and drink which he must carry with him, and not to fire unless he is certain of his target—in order to conserve the ammunition which it may be impossible to replenish. After which, he studies the arts of personal concealment.

Sharpshooter in Heap of Hay

He must be a chameleon among a heap of rocks, or a mound of clay in a muddy field ; he must be a clump of waving grass, or little branches beside some bush—a tree, a fallen log, a depression in the ground, a chimney cowl, a church clock, a thick curtain in a window ; he has even been known to be a dignified statue in a market-place.

The sniper's principal concern is to perfect the technique of his shooting. Absolute stillness and steadiness are necessary. He must not fire, even when using ammunition that is quite smokeless, if someone is gazing directly towards his hiding-place. But rigidity can be helped by various devices. There was a sniper in Normandy, caught by our men, who had been firing with uncanny accuracy on to an exposed piece of road at night. They found him by thrusting bayonets into a heap of hay, where he had a carefully-sighted rifle set in a vice.

Telescopic sights are used, but generally the sharpshooter relies on field-glasses. If he lacks a good pair he will take the first opportunity of picking off an officer of artillery and securing his. The Germans have always possessed excellent glasses. Then he will, if possible, choose close targets, anything from 300 to 500 yards away. Good artillery glasses enable him, with trained eyes, to see the hairs of a man's eyebrows before he shoots him.

A SPECIALLY important device is the loop-hole, which is so constructed in the camouflage, wall, tree or parapet, that the sniper has a wide field of vision. It is always a lesson to an ordinary infantryman to take a sight through a sniper's loophole, and compare what he sees with the narrow outlook from one constructed by himself in a trench or earthwork. No wonder the sniper gains such a moral ascendancy. As somebody in France has written : " You have never seen that hidden man. Probably never will. But suddenly you picture him vividly ; not so much his face as his eyes, his mouth. You ' feel ' his cool movement after that last close shot ; he is gently, more steadily aiming and levelling that rifle as he sights along it to make doubly sure he gets you *this* time. Such a feeling can sicken a man."

Yet it is in some ways a foolish feeling, especially under conditions such as those on the Western Front. In static trench warfare, or in those early jungle retreats before the Japanese, snipers are a very great menace because they cannot easily be caught. But when they have been left behind by Germans in occupied Dutch villages and towns it is just a matter of taking careful precautions and sooner or later routing them out. Special squads are detailed for this task. They may draw the sniper's fire deliberately, perhaps using decoys, and once he is located he must submit to encirclement and capture. Note that most of the German snipers are captured—not shot—in their posts. There are no ding-dong battles because today enemy snipers are operating on the whole in unfriendly territory and have no support.

" SNIPER—DUCK YOUR HEAD!" This warning, as the Allies forced their way eastwards through Belgium and Holland, was common enough. Enemy marksmen abounded in many unsuspected places. This German (left), cunningly camouflaged, takes careful aim, whilst his own portrait is " shot." And here (right) is the answer to this deadly threat : Pte. Francis Miller of Leeds, with 17 dead Nazis to his credit, demonstrates how our own sharpshooters " pick them off." He is firing behind cover not shown in the photograph.

Photos, British Official, Keystone

Chinese Regain Ancient City on Burma Border

FIRST CHINESE CITY east of the Burmese border to be freed—ancient Tengchung, 20 miles west of the Burma Road—fell to Chinese troops, it was announced on August 4, 1944. Two thousand Japanese who had dug in for a 6-months' siege became casualties in the 3-weeks' battle, which led to the establishing of contact between British and Chinese forces then under the command of General Stilwell, and Chinese under Marshal Wei Li-huang. Chinese wounded (above) being carried past the battered city walls.

Photo, Planet News

Hungary: Last of Hitler's Allies in Europe

Chaos followed the attempt in October 1944 of Admiral Horthy, Regent of Hungary—last of Germany's European Allies—to escape from the toils of Hitler's war. Dr. E. STERN-RUBARTH writes here of some of the strange contradictions that characterize this country with an almost medieval social structure and which holds a key position in south-eastern Europe.

HUNGARY is once more in the news and with her such names as Horthy, Szalasy, Goemboes, Bethlen, Karolyi and others. It is the country least understandable, and least understood, by the rest of the world ; a country of contradictions and, because of them, of a tragic fate. These contradictions, in some instances, go so far as to appear like Fate's bad jokes.

Hungary is a monarchy, yet without a king, and with a law forbidding the return of the only dynasty laying claim to that vacant throne. As her Regent for nearly 25 years she has had an admiral, yet is without a fleet, or even a port, or an outlet of her own to the open seas. She has a parliament, yet of all Fascist or pseudo-Fascist regimes in Europe, hers is the oldest and most deep-rooted.

Nor are her natural conditions less singular. The Magyar language, in which masterpieces

Hungary has had regents, deputising for a non-existent king, before : Janos (John) Hunyadi, five centuries ago, during the first wars against the advancing Turks, and Lajos (Lewis) Kossuth, in 1848, when Hungary's revolt against the Habsburgs had proved a temporary success. And she had magnates —proud, princely, often virtually independent noblemen owning larger or smaller parts of her territory, with laws, armies, institutions of their own, practically throughout her history—the real masters of her population, her wealth, and her fate.

NOT all were stubborn, narrow-minded and egoistic, as is said of the Prussian Junkers, or the Polish Szlachcics ; there were Liberals, such as Count Stephen Szechenyi, Francis de Deak, Count Gyula Andrassy, Koloman de Tisza and his son Count Stephen (assassinated at the end of the last war) and even fervent practical Socialists like

By no means stupid, the Hungarian politicians indeed considered the Nazis as a last resource, and a most undesirable one. For while they were gratified by securing a considerable area of Slovakia when Hitler dismembered Czechoslovakia, and the better part of Transylvania at Rumania's expense under the Vienna Award of 1940, they were fully aware that this meant giving up their natural ambition to dominate the Danube basin. And, reminiscent of 1918, some of them at least should have gone in fear of another German defeat such as now knocks at Budapest's door.

As for the justification of Hungary's territorial claims, nobody was allowed to doubt, or even to discuss the subject, any more than the mystic virtues of St. Stephen's crown, with its own vault, its own noblemen's guard. Hungary's pre-1918 territory, ruled under the complicated system of the dual monarchy as the Transleithan half of the Empire, embraced 125,000 square miles, with 21 million inhabitants ; her post-1918 area was confined to 37,000 square miles, with 7·6 million souls. True, even their own statistics had to confess that but half the pre-1918 citizens were Magyars, so that, in view of the heavy loss of life incurred by their soldiers, who are world-famous for their daring and bravery, no really large proportion of thoroughbred Hungarians can have been left out of the seemingly so drastically constricted Trianon frontiers.

Ancient Rights of Conquest

But it is an ambitious race, and the magnates possessed large properties, with castles, shooting lodges, studs, and forests outside these new, uncomfortable borders. They had fought for that soil, against the "infidels," for centuries, and wrested it from Turks, and the Venetian Republic, and what-not ; and they were firmly entrenched in their medieval belief that their ancient rights of conquest should prevail over the new-fangled rights of "self-determination."

The little people, smallholders, craftsmen, labourers, care no more about these lofty political principles than do their fellows in other countries. They are poor—most Hungarians, not excluding even many of the proud noblemen, are poor measured by British standards in money—but they enjoy good food, a rich soil, and a most pleasant climate. They are musicians, artists, of a lively temperament, and easily roused to enthusiasm, following their leaders en masse into victory or disaster with a remarkable loyalty. That is the only possible explanation for the frenzy with which, after the last war, they supported first a short-lived Socialist rule, then an even shorter-lived Bolshevik one, and from then onward a series of varied feudal regimes, interspersed with such excesses as those of the early "Awakening Hungarians," or the later "Arrow Cross" (Szalasy) and other varieties of Nazidom. Meanwhile in the castle—the "Kir Palota" above the Danube—the Admiral without a fleet, Nicolas de Horthy, cleverly played upon these emotions.

HUNGARIAN FASCIST LEADER, Ferencz Szalasy (in front), reviewing troops in Budapest after dramatically ousting the Regent Horthy on October 16, 1944. Budapest radio announced on October 15 that Hungary had requested an armistice, but later—seized, apparently, by the Fascists—it broadcast a repudiation. Within 24 hours Szalasy had assumed power. Soviet forces were reported on November 8 to be outflanking the capital.
Photo, Associated Press

of European literature have been written, bears no relation to any other, except very vague and distant ones with Finnish and Turkish. The "racial" problem is complicated by the fact that of the seven tribes which immigrated from southern Russia into Hungary's vast, fertile plains when the Huns had vanished in the 10th century, six were heathen, while the seventh, under the rule of a progressive Chasar khan, had been converted to the Jewish faith a century or so before, and refused to follow their king Saint Stephen when he converted his nation to Christianity.

HUNGARY's kings were, in turn, Slavonic, French, Austro-German, Polish, and of the German-Spanish Habsburg dynasty ; only for short intervals, or as anti-kings, had she occasionally rulers of her own race. For about two centuries she was occupied and ruled by Turkish Sultans through their governors. Small wonder, then, that a semi-oriental mysticism finally endowed the crown itself—St. Stephen's bejewelled golden helmet with the bent cross, gift in part of Pope Sylvester II, in part of the Byzantine Emperor Michael Dukas—with the magic power of rulership, and developed a cult around that symbol preserved to this day.

Count Michael Karolyi, first Hungarian President after 1918, and now in this country. But even so, Hungary's social structure is pervaded by a streak of medievalism such as hardly any other European country has preserved in our day.

This is the basis of a two-fold political trend which (practically to the exclusion of all the other problems, social, economic, and intellectual, which occupied the world since 1918) engaged all the energies of the Hungarian people : the fight for the recovery of lost territory, and the suppression of all movements, communities, or schools of thought whose Liberalism or cosmopolitanism might deflect the nation from that task. A huge, permanently illuminated map of pre- and post-1918 Hungary displayed in Budapest was symbolic of this single purpose ; unceasing propaganda all over the world, far beyond the very modest financial means of the country, kept in evidence the alleged wrongs done to "poor" Hungary by the Treaty of Trianon. That, and that alone, was the keynote of all Hungarian politics. For that, Budapest turned first to the League of Nations, then to Britain, then to Fascist Italy, and finally to Hitler.

HE may have looked down thence upon the Trianon Flag permanently hoisted at half-mast and floodlighted at night, or have heard the people sing the Magyar Hiszekegy (the Hungarian Credo) and the Szozat (the Cry of Warning) often enough with mixed feelings. He may have dreamed of a coming dynasty of his own, but saw this dream shattered by the death of his son on the Russian front and the advance of the Red Army into the green pastures of the Puszta.

Nazis Fall Back on Their 'Last Ditch' Reserves

CONSCRIPTION of every able-bodied German from 16 to 60 was ordered by Hitler on October 18, 1944. Himmler, placed in control, announced that though armed they would wear no uniform, only an armlet (in accordance with international law) ; were to be used against the final Allied assault on the Reich ; and, based on the British Home Guard, would be known as the "Deutscher Volkssturm." Himmler at once proceeded to East Prussia to organize the first battalions—almost within sound of the Russian guns. "Every house, every ditch, every bush will be defended by our men, our boys and our aged people; and, if necessary, by our women," he told conscripts. A Nazi youth being trained to aim a rifle (1). German military police dig anti-tank defences (2). Conscripts listen to Himmler's call to arms near the East Prussian front (3) ; on October 26 they were reported in action for the first time. Wilhelm Scheppman, Volkssturm Training Chief, showing a middle-aged German the bolt action of a rifle (4) ; shortly afterwards, Scheppman was reported ill with a " nervous breakdown."

Photos, Keystone, Associated Press, News Chronicle   PAGE 439

Russians Well Over the East Prussian Border

HEADING FOR the Insterburg Gap, Soviet forces of the 3rd White Russian Front, commanded by General Chernyakhovsky, were reported on October 23, 1944, to have broken through into East Prussia on a front of 85 miles. Massed blows by heavy artillery and aircraft crushed powerful and deeply staggered defences which the Germans had been preparing for years. Soviet heavy guns passing through devastated Schirwindt (1). The shell-shattered town of Eydtkau (2), 35 miles from Insterburg.

GREAT FACTOR in the break-through was the Red Air Force, directed by Marshal Novikov (3) who, as Marshal of Aviation, occupies a position similar to that of Air Chief-Marshal Sir Charles Portal in the R.A.F. Hitler was forced to depopulate a vast area of Reich territory, preparing for the battle which he knew would open the road to Berlin. German tanks were flung into the struggle in suicidal attempts to stem the Russians, who are seen (4) streaming from one of their armoured trains.

Photos, Planet News, Pictorial Press

I WAS THERE! Eye Witness Stories of the War

I Saw the Royal Marines Go In at Walcheren

Westkapelle, keypoint in the Dutch island of Walcheren blocking the entrance to the Scheldt and Antwerp, was in our hands by November 2, 1944. Arthur Oakeshott, Reuters' special correspondent, saw it fall to the combined assault of the Royal Navy, the Royal Marine Commandos, and rocket planes and bombers of the R.A.F. Here he tells of this most hazardous and daring operation as he witnessed it from the H.Q. ship.

As we approached the island, stretching away on either side and astern of us was a vast convoy of landing craft, and we could see the lighthouse tower and the famous 400-yard-wide gap torn in the dyke wall by R.A.F. bombers at Zuidhoofd, just to the right of Westkapelle.

We approached to within some thousands of yards, to the accompaniment of the roar of the 15-in. guns of the battleship Warspite and the monitors Erebus and Lord Roberts. I thought it all seemed very unreal—until a couple of German shells fell among us. Guns blazed away from almost every craft and shells of every calibre went screaming to land on the shore and among the German batteries and beach fortifications. But more and more shells dropped among us and one or two ships were hit.

On an eminence to the left of the town were four large German guns in concrete emplacements, and these were shooting pretty accurately. By this time several landing craft were afire and burning fiercely. Then I saw an unforgettable sight—dozens of landing craft bearing hundreds of men wearing green berets—the men of the famous Royal Marines. They were all singing—yes, singing as they went into that hell of fire and shell and flying metal. "They've got guts," said a sailor.

Still more and more craft swept past us, and all the time the German shells were falling among us, claiming a craft here, a man there. More were in flames. Then above the din of battle we heard the roar of aircraft, and looking up I saw scores of Typhoons screaming down—a puff of smoke, and their rockets flashed in at the German positions.

Deafening Roar of 15-in. Guns

Great spouts of black smoke streamed up into the sky from the bomb bursts, and the smaller fire from the Germans abruptly ceased. But those big batteries continued to take toll of the assault force. By this time the L.C.G.s (landing-craft, guns) were near enough to add their quota, and the noise and crash and banging became almost deafening, while, all the time, wave after wave of Typhoons roared in.

Above the din we heard the steady boom-boom of the "15-inchers" from the two monitors and Warspite, and suddenly I saw a great burst of flame and black smoke come from one of these mighty German gun emplacements. It spoke no more—thanks to the R.N. The other three continued.

Then the rocket-firing landing craft came in. There was a zigzagged flash and a black pall of smoke, and hundreds of rockets sailed high into the air until they looked like a flock of migrating birds, and then dropped to explode with deafening detonations on the luckless German defenders of the island of Walcheren. Another roar of aircraft above us, and once more Typhoons, carrying bombs, sped in on the three remaining batteries and, simultaneously, shells from the monitors and the battleship scored direct hits, and put No. 2 out of action.

Still the other two continued to fire, causing the invading ships considerable difficulty. Again and again I saw landing craft run a gauntlet of shell bursts as they nosed their way shorewards. Some did not get there. Still more shells poured in on the force that crept nearer and nearer the island, and then somebody said : "There goes the third one," and I could see flames belching out of the third of the German gun batteries. Warspite got that one, and a few minutes later the fourth battery was silenced again by the guns of the Royal Navy.

As we steamed away from Walcheren I could see fires here and there on the island and, dotted about the sea, several blazing craft—one burned all night. A wounded Marine Commando officer said to me: "Don't tell them at home that it was easy—it was damned difficult, but we did it—please tell them that !"

I Took a No. 10 Tram to the Front Line

Antwerp itself was taken in their stride by Allied troops on September 4, 1944. The Germans, however, still held the Scheldt estuary below the city in October. George Edinger here describes the fantastic atmosphere of the city and the rapturous welcome given to the Allies on their entry.

NAPOLEON used to call Antwerp a pistol pointed at England's heart, for that superb harbour is only six hours' sail from our shores. But pistols can face two ways. We happen to hold the butt now—and the place is also two hours by road from Germany.

And, thanks to the energy and dash of the Belgian underground and the speed of our autumn advance, we hold Antwerp's 28 miles of docks (they cleared 25 million tons there before the war) virtually undamaged. But the enemy knows that, so he holds fast to the river-mouth below the city ; he is still ensconced away in the remoter mazes of its docks and its canals (he frightened me away with mortar fire when I was trying to help with the minesweeping the other day). A few days ago he was still in the north-east suburbs of the city.

At the fantastic period that I entered into Antwerp, I came in a Canadian jeep through streets lined by delirious burghers. They pressed forward to shake our hands. They strung dahlias over the bonnet of the car ; heaped apples and grapes upon us ; and thrust into our hands bottles of champagne saved for four years for the great occasion. I looked. I marvelled. Surely in all the world there was no city so proud, so seemingly unaltered, so electric in expectancy as Antwerp at that moment. The shop-fronts on the boulevards were gay with things I had long forgotten. There were unlimited caramels, fountain pens, peaches, ice creams, with walnuts and maple syrup, wrist watches, perfumes and silk shirts. The Antwerp women, arrayed in the extravagant steeple-hatted fashion of Liberated France, brought their children in to eat cream cakes in the carpeted tea-rooms.

Young officers of our naval party, installed in the city a few days before (the Germans most unexpectedly opened upon them with machine-guns at 200 yards' range just when they were settling down to tea at headquarters) promised to show me where the best ices were to be got. Well, we ate a strawberry ice, and then a chocolate one before I asked how far the enemy might be at that moment.

"It'll take you about forty minutes to walk," reckoned a sub-lieutenant. "But it's rather a dull walk. I should take a No. 10 tram. Ask the conductor to put you down

ROYAL MARINE Commandos in amphibious fighting craft established a beach-head at Westkapelle on Walcheren, Holland, on November 1, 1944, under smoke from burning shore installations (right). Their gateway was the breach in the sea-wall caused by the R.A.F. Losses among close-support bombardment craft, all manned by British naval and Marine personnel, were heavy—20 out of every 25, many enemy guns believed silenced coming to life again as soon as the landings were launched.
Photo, British Official

at the Town Hall, D——, and walk straight ahead.''

"And you won't have long in the line," added the lieutenant of Marines, "if you want to hear Solomon tonight—his Chopin recital starts at 6.45.''

The sub-lieutenant was generous with his 40 minutes. I got there quicker. I came back quicker still. I was dazed at the unreality of it. But there were greater unrealities. I have mentioned peaches, ice creams, and champagne. That was not all. At lunch on one occasion we had Greek Muscat wine, Burgundy, Bordeaux, and Cognac. But we did not have any meat.

Antwerp, it dawned on me, abounds in all the luxuries, but lacks all the necessities of life. Later I was to hear an explanation. I heard it from a Princess of the royal blood. Her khaki tailor-made, just out of the foremost of fashion houses, symbolized the fantastic world that is Antwerp in 1944. "Of course, we went on making luxuries. It kept our people employed. Then the Germans could not deport them, and they produced things that were not the slightest use to the Germans.''

An Evil Tyrant Built a Castle

"Is it true," I asked the veteran Burgomaster, Camille Huysmans (he is also president of the Second Internationale), "that your shipbuilders managed to work full strength for the Germans for two years without building them a single ship ?''

"And most understandable," he said. "In five centuries we Belgians have only been independent for 120 years. For eight of those we have been occupied. That teaches you a lot about an underground.''

It did. It taught them to raise a secret army, to keep it armed and drilled against the day when it could deliver roads, ports, stores, and bridges undamaged into our hands. Beyond the zoo lies the harbour—long prospects of deserted quay, lines of idle cranes, and grass sprouting through the warehouse floors. It was serenely peaceful.

And there I remembered how the place came to be called Antwerp.

There was an evil tyrant once who built a castle there and raised such fabulous tolls on all the corn and wool that came up the river that all the people were hungry to death. But there came a liberator. His name was Brabo, and he battled with the tyrant and cut his hand off and threw it into the river, whence the place was called Handwerpen (in Flemish, " throwing of the hand"). I told the port minesweeping officer that. "O.K.," he said, "we've got to cut that tyrant's hand off all right. It is gripping the edges of this port ! ''

ANTWERP, GLITTERING PRIZE OF THE SCHELDT clearance operations (October-November 1944), is one of the world's greatest ports (see story commencing in page 441). With its 26 miles of quays, providing 237 berths for ocean-going ships, its 28 square miles of docks and 500 miles of railways sidings, it fell to us without a fight on September 4. *Photo, British Newspaper Pool*

We Sent a U-Boat Down in Five Minutes

Flying-Officer R. W. G. Vaughan, 22-year-old captain of a Catalina of R.A.F. Coastal Command, received the immediate award of a D.F.C. and congratulations from the Admiralty for one of the quickest kills on record. Although his flying-boat was peppered with over 400 holes, one engine had stopped and petrol was leaking from the other, he brought it hundreds of miles back to base. He tells his story here.

Two *members of the crew were wounded— one seriously—but both are recovering. The Catalina was on patrol in Northern waters in daylight when a message was flashed from a Coastal Command Liberator that a U-boat had been sighted. On searching the area, the captain sighted the submarine. To carry out an attack, the captain had to fly through a box barrage sent up by the U-boat's guns. Flying-Officer Vaughan tells what followed.*

As soon as I saw this barrage I took violent evasive action, throwing the aircraft all over the place. The other members of the crew were holding on for grim death. I knew the aircraft was being hit—I could see the flak whistling past my window—but we dropped our depth charges and the gunners banged off several hundred rounds at the conning tower.

By the time I had turned and could see out of my window the stern, or the bow, of the U-boat—I could not make out which—was disappearing beneath the water. At first we were not quite sure if the submarine had crash-dived, but our hearts leapt with joy when we saw 35 to 40 survivors swimming in the sea, and a number of little yellow one-man dinghies. Some of the Germans were trying to swim in a large oil patch left by the U-boat.

F/O K. S. Freeman, of Chester, wireless operator air gunner, was badly wounded in the leg and hand, and F/Sgt. S. M. Audifferen, an air gunner, who comes from Nigeria, was also hurt by shrapnel.

The journey back to base on one leaking engine took six and a quarter hours flying through patches of fog. Two hours from home the engineer reported that he could give no more readings on the fuel gauges and that we should have to go on until our engine gave out. Realizing that the Catalina was badly holed and would sink if I stayed on the water, I "landed" her and raced through the water at speed until she ran up the beach. I found out later we had petrol left for only one more circuit of the base.

Radio Spy in the Jungle of Leyte Island

On October 20, 1944, U.S. troops landed on Leyte, Central Philippines —where for 2½ years Lieut. St. John has lived, leading Filipino guerillas and acting as a " coast watcher " to keep American H.Q. informed by radio of Japanese movements. He told his story, given here by permission of International News Service, to Howard Handleman. See also page 429.

In his jungle headquarters, talking by the dim light of a wick floating in coconut oil, and surrounded by sleeping guerillas, St. John sat up all night to tell me of his adventures. His H.Q. is 18 miles in front of the American lines. To reach him, I

a photographer, and a six-man army patrol had had to cross five miles of open sea in a native dug-out canoe.

As we neared the shore, St. John, another American, and a crowd of Filipinos—guerillas, their families, and the girls who cook

F/O R. W. G. VAUGHAN, D.F.C., of Coastal Command, after sinking a U-boat brought his badly holed Catalina home hundreds of miles on one leaking engine. See story in this page.
Photo, G.P.U.

and sew for the guerillas—were waiting for us. The second American was Ensign James Beattie, a carrier pilot. He had parachuted over the islands and had been taken by the guerillas to St. John.

As we neared the beach three Jap fighters roared out of the clouds overhead. We jumped overboard and waded, chest deep in water, to the shore. Said St. John: "Did you bring bread?"—it was nearly three years since he had tasted bread—and then, to the soldiers: "I've waited a long time to see your uniform—Beattie had to be a navy guy!"

Then he asked for a cigarette. He explained that in three years he had had only ten packets. He led us to his headquarters. A radio operator of the Philippine Army sat at the portable radio set; the guerillas crowded in and sat staring at the "Americanos." "You get used to that," said St. John. And then began the story that lasted all night.

He told how once his headquarters were attacked by 200 Japs, whose shots cut a tuft of hair from his head. He told of meals of monkey-meat and fried locust, of going two years without shoes, of his terrible longing for cigarettes. He told of Filipino friendliness towards him and of Filipino hatred for the Japs.

St. John is an airman, and his story began on Mindanao early in 1942. After the collapse in the Philippines he and 11 others tried to reach Australia in an Army launch. They got to—Leyte. From there they set off for Australia once more, in an outrigger canoe.

Their canoe capsized off Mindanao; they lost their clothing and a treasured bottle of whisky. Filipinos took care of them, the Americans "pairing off" so that one family should not have too many to look after. They almost died from malaria and dysentery. Native medicine slowly restored their health.

SIDELIGHT ON THE PHILIPPINES INVASION announced on October 20, 1944—a U.S. landing craft packed with troops eager to go into action against the Japanese, heading for the beaches at Leyte Island. The invasion was preceded by a devastating naval and air bombardment. See story commencing in facing page, and illus. page 429.
Photo, U.S. Official

But, said St. John, the Americans became so thin that "we had to sit on pillows to prevent our bones paining us." The first Mindanao guerillas were bandits who had fled from the Japs, but with American aid they were properly organized.

It was after recovering from malaria that St. John got in touch with the American leaders of the guerillas. He was offered the choice of going back to his old squadron, then in Australia, or of going to Leyte to watch the Japs. He chose Leyte, because "I began the war in the Philippines and

thought I might as well end it here." So an outrigger canoe took St. John and his radio set to Leyte in August 1943.

"The Filipinos were marvellous," said St. John. "They did my washing and cooking because, they said, I was an 'Americano' helping them, so they would help me. I had to move on every month or so. The Japs knew I was on the island— and there were spies around." As St. John talked, Filipino girls served a meal of rice, bananas, coconut salad and chicken. But St. John did not eat; he was too excited.

OUR DIARY OF THE WAR

OCTOBER 25, Wednesday *1,880th day*
Western Front.—Boxtel, east of Tilburg, captured by British; Fort Frederik Hendrik, Breskens, by Canadians.
Air.—R.A.F. bombers made heavy daylight attack on Essen. U.S. bombers attacked rail yards at Hamm, and oil plants in N.W. Germany.
Russian Front.—Soviet troops captured Kirkenes, North Norway.

OCTOBER 26, Thursday *1,881st day*
Western Front. — British troops crossed Scheldt and landed on Beveland; Canadians advanced on Beveland from mainland.
Air.—Allied bombers heavily attacked industrial and communications targets in Bielefeld, Munster, Hanover and Leverkusen.
Russian Front.—Soviet troops captured Mukacevo in Ruthenia (Czechoslovakia).

OCTOBER 27, Friday *1,882nd day*
Western Front.—British troops entered Tilburg. Bergen-op-Zoom captured by Canadians.
Russian Front.—Soviet troops captured Uzhorod in Ruthenia and Novi Sad in Yugoslavia.

OCTOBER 28, Saturday *1,883rd day*
Air.—R.A.F. bombers gave Cologne its heaviest assault of the war, and bombed U-boat pens at Bergen. U.S. bombers attacked Hamm and Munster.
General.—Announced that Gen. Stilwell had been relieved of his command in S.E. Asia.

OCTOBER 29, Sunday *1,884th day*
Western Front.—Breda captured by Polish troops of Canadian 1st Army.
Air.—R.A.F. Lancasters bombed battleship Tirpitz off Tromso, Norway.
Russian Front.—Railway junction of Csop in Czechoslovakia captured by Soviet troops.
Pacific.—Announced that in sea battles off Philippines, 24 Japanese warships were sunk and 34 damaged, for loss of six American ships; 171 enemy aircraft also destroyed.

OCTOBER 30, Monday *1,885th day*
Western Front.—South Beveland in Allied hands. U.S. 3rd Army troops captured Maizières-les-Metz.

Air.—Cologne had another heavy night attack from R.A.F.
Burma.—New British and Chinese drive south from Myitkyina.

OCTOBER 31, Tuesday *1,886th day*
Western Front.—2nd Army troops reached the Maas N. of Capelle. Polish units established bridge-head on River Mark.
Air.—R.A.F. bombers attacked oil plant at Bottrop in the Ruhr by day and bombed Cologne again at night. Mosquitoes bombed Gestapo H.Q. in Aarhus, Denmark.

NOVEMBER 1, Wednesday *1,887th day*
Western Front.—British troops landed on Walcheren, at Flushing and Westkapelle. Canadians attacked causeway from South Beveland.
Air.—U.S. bombers attacked oil plants at Gelsenkirchen and railways at Hamm and Coblenz. R.A.F. bombed Oberhausen in the Ruhr.
Russian Front.—Kecskemet, 45 miles S.E. of Budapest, captured by Red Army troops.
Mediterranean.—Allied heavy bombers attacked targets in Vienna area.
Balkans.—British patrols in Greece reached Salonika.

NOVEMBER 2, Thursday *1,888th day*
Western Front.—Whole of Belgium freed with German surrender in Zeebrugge, Knocke and Heyst.
Air.—U.S. bombers and fighters attacking oil plants and railways in Western Germany destroyed 208 enemy aircraft. At night more than 1,000 R.A.F. bombers attacked Düsseldorf.
Balkans.—Announced that Marshal Tito's troops had entered port of Zara, on Dalmatian coast.

NOVEMBER 3, Friday *1,889th day*
Western Front.—Domburg, Walcheren, cleared of the enemy. Allied units from Beveland landed in Walcheren. U.S. 1st Army troops captured Schmidt, in Aachen sector.
Burma.—Super-Fortresses from India bombed railway yards at Rangoon.
General.—Announced that Lt.-Gen. Sir Oliver Leese to command 11th Army Group in S.E. Asia, and Lt.-Gen. Sir Richard McCreery to command the 8th Army.

NOVEMBER 4, Saturday *1,890th day*
Western Front.—Flushing cleared of the enemy. Germans retook Schmidt.
Air.—U.S. bombers attacked oil plants at Hamburg-Harburg and Gelsenkirchen and railway yards at Saarbruecken. R.A.F.

bombed Solingen steel works by day and Bochum at night and again drained the Dortmund-Ems canal.
Mediterranean.—Allied bombers from Italy attacked Munich, Regensburg and Linz.
Pacific.—Allied carrier-borne aircraft attacked harbour and airfields at Manila, Philippines, destroying nearly 200 enemy aircraft.
Burma.—Super-Fortresses from India again bombed Rangoon.
General.—Field-Marshal Sir John Dill died in Washington.

NOVEMBER 5, Sunday *1,891st day*
Western Front. — Geertruidenburg, bridge-town on the Maas, captured by Polish troops.
Air.—Railways at Frankfurt and Karlsruhe and chemical works at Ludwigshafen attacked by U.S. bombers. R.A.F. again attacked Solingen.
Russian Front.—Heavy German counter-attacks in East Prussia repulsed.
Far East.—Singapore bombed for first time since Japanese occupation, by Super-Fortresses.
Pacific.—U.S. aircraft again bombed Manila and destroyed 249 Japanese planes.

NOVEMBER 6, Monday *1,892nd day*
Western Front.—British troops entered Middelburg, capital of Walcheren.
Air.—R.A.F. bombers made heavy daylight attack on Gelsenkirchen, and at night bombed Coblenz. U.S. bombers attacked oil refineries and railway yards in western Germany.
Balkans.—Yugoslav forces freed Bitolj (Monastir) and controlled all Yugoslav-Greek border.
Burma.—Kennedy Peak, near Tiddim, captured by 14th Army.

NOVEMBER 7, Tuesday *1,893rd day*
Western Front.—British troops captured Willemstad on Maas estuary, thus clearing south shore except for area around Moerdijk.
Pacific.—In Leyte, Allied troops captured Pinampoan.
General.—Roosevelt re-elected President of U.S.A. for fourth term.
Sea.—Admiralty announced that in passage of convoy from United Kingdom to Russia and back, without damage to any merchant ship, three U-boats were sunk and several damaged.

★ ══════ *Flash-backs* ══════ ★

1940
October 28. *Italians launched attack on Greece from Albania.*
November 5. *Roosevelt re-elected President of United States for third term.*

1941
October 29. *Russians admitted evacuation of Kharkov.*
November 3. *Germans captured Kursk, south of Orel.*

1942
October 26. *Announced that the*

Mosquito fighter-bomber was in service with the R.A.F.
November 2. *Kokoda (New Guinea) recaptured from Japanese.*

1943
October 25. *Red Army troops recaptured Dnepropetrovsk.*
November 1. *U.S. forces landed on Bougainville Isl., Solomons.*
November 2. *German counter-attack in Krivoi Rog sector repelled by Russians.*
November 6. *Kiev recaptured by troops of the Red Army.*

THE WAR IN THE AIR

by Capt. Norman Macmillan, M.C., A.F.C.

IN war it is extraordinarily difficult for the ordinary reader or listener to the radio to attain to a balanced judgement of the course of events. Each opponent uses the art of propaganda to the full ; indeed, as a weapon of war. To me one of the most distasteful of propaganda methods is the innuendo that enemy communiqués must always be tinged with falsehood, or at least with inaccuracies or suppressions. No doubt they sometimes are. But how often does one hear it suggested in a B.B.C. news bulletin after a quotation from a German source intimates that there is a Russian or German attack on a given sector that this should be treated with caution because so far there is no confirmation from our Ally ? Generally the confirmation comes within a few days, but the B.B.C. does not then say that this is confirmation of the previously doubtful news item, and I find that the usual listener is so dulled with propaganda that he or she fails to connect the items in relation one to the other.

THE difficulty about day-to-day accounts of events is that the first impression is not always correct, yet it often secures the largest audience. That is why histories of wars continue to be written long after they have ended. It takes endless patience to sift the facts from the evidence. It is a more difficult task than that of a judge in a complicated murder trial. After this war it is going to be more difficult than ever before.

One of the actions which cannot yet be fully assessed is the great sea/air battle in the waters around the Philippines following the American landing on Leyte Island on October 20, 1944. Before U.S. land-based aircraft could operate from Leyte or Samar islands the Japanese sent a large fleet divided into three forces into action against the Americans. One force of enemy ships was sighted on October 23, 1944, by the 3rd U.S. Fleet commanded by Admiral William F. Halsey, the very strong protagonist of air power in sea war, who ten years ago, at the age of 52, learned to fly. Halsey kept in contact with the enemy ships during the night (presumably by radar), sent up his aircraft at dawn on October 24, and wrought great havoc among the Japanese ships ; this action, in the waters north-east of the Philippines, was assisted by China-based U.S. land aircraft intervention against Japanese land air bases.

PHILIPPINES a Strategic Core in the South-West Pacific

The sea/air action continued for ten days, in a series of sorties. The Americans lost the Princeton, a 10,000-ton cruiser converted into an aircraft carrier, two escort carriers, two destroyers, and an escort ship ; these losses appear to have been suffered while escorting a convoy of 600 ships moving towards Leyte in support of General MacArthur, and were caused by Japanese land-based aircraft, operating presumably from Philippines island bases.

Two Japanese forces approached from the west ; one from Camranh Bay steamed towards the Sibuyan Sea between Mindoro and Panay islands, the other towards the Surigao Strait north of Mindanao. I said in my previous article (page 412), that the Japanese could be expected to fight desperately to hold the Philippines, which form a strategic core in the South-west Pacific. The attacks by 60 Japanese warships, including aircraft carriers, prove how they value the Philippines base.

The forces approaching from the west were attacked by U.S. and Australian warships

and aircraft carriers of the 7th U.S. Fleet under Admiral Kincaid, who divided his fleet, strongly supported by aircraft from carriers, to engage them. The enemy force in the Sulu Sea and Surigao Strait was completely destroyed. Its sortie was accompanied by Japanese air attacks against American shipping in Leyte Gulf, where U.S. carrier aircraft destroyed 53 Jap planes, and A.A. guns another three. Total enemy ship losses were 24 claimed sunk (including two battleships, four aircraft carriers and nine cruisers). Only two of the remaining 36 ships were believed to be undamaged.

THIS appeared a sweeping victory for the U.S. fleet and its sea/air power. So it struck me as curious that Admiral Nimitz should subsequently say that he expected

GESTAPO HEADQUARTERS in Aarhus, Denmark, was demolished by R.A.F. Mosquitoes executing on October 31, 1944, one of the most finely pin-pointed exploits of the war. Over 200 Gestapo officials were killed, and records destroyed, but surrounding buildings were purposely left intact. Our planes returned without loss. *Photo, British Official*

THE FAIREY FIREFLY, shown with wings folded, is a new Royal Navy reconnaissance fighter, with one of the most powerful engines in the world, the Rolls-Royce Griffon. This two-seater aircraft has a performance equal to that of many land-based fighters. Span is 44½ ft., height 13 ft. 7 in., length 37 ft. It is armed with four 20-mm. cannon.
Photo, British Official

the Japanese would again attack in strength, but that the time would eventually come when the U.S. Navy would seek out the Japanese Navy wherever it was and utterly destroy it. If this was a complete victory for the U.S. Fleet (as the first reports indicated) why should not the U.S. Fleet have gone to destroy the remainder of the enemy-fleet at once ?

Was the reason conveyed in the detached news item that came in on November 4 stating that U.S. ships had been attacked by Japanese aircraft in the neighbourhood of the Carolines and suffered losses and damage ? Were these American ships which had been damaged in the Philippines action (about which the communiqués said nothing) limping home to Pearl Harbour for repairs ? If so, the whole story of the battle has not yet been told. Meanwhile it is clear that the Japanese achieved some part of their object, for another communiqué on November 4 stated that Japanese convoys of tanks and transport trucks were seen moving inland in the Philippines towards the battlefield by aircraft which destroyed 36 of the convoy.

HEAVY Accident Loss Rate in Aircraft Carrier Actions

The inference is that the U.S. Fleet must defer its destruction of the Japanese Navy due to damage it suffered. The apparently successful attacks by Jap aircraft in the Carolines indicates that the U.S. ships may then have been insufficiently protected by fighter aircraft, possibly due to heavy losses in combat *and accident* during the Philippines engagement. This is the greatest drawback of carrier actions—the inevitably heavy accident loss rate in aircraft due to the extremely hazardous conditions under which combat aircraft have to operate when in action from aircraft carriers.

This battle will be studied carefully by students of naval air warfare for years to come. The Philippines fight will continue to be a tough one. And the war against Japan will need the help of great air fleets from the R.A.F. before it is won, despite the report that between January 29 and October 27 the carrier group of the U.S. naval task force in the Pacific destroyed 4,425 Jap aircraft and sank or damaged 795 war and merchant ships.

IN Europe the pounding of enemy towns behind the front goes on. The U.S. heavy day bombers continue their assault on oil. On November 2 a force of 1,100 bombers with 900 fighters attacked synthetic oil plants near Leipzig. On October 31, the 2nd T.A.F. sent 24 Mosquitoes, with 12 Mustang fighters, to destroy the Gestapo Headquarters in Denmark in Aarhus University ; all returned, with the job well done.

Assembling Super-Fortresses for the Pacific

CONTROL CABIN   CONNECTING TUNNEL   GUNNERS COMPARTMENT   TAIL GUNNER

NOSE WHEEL WELL   BOMB BAYS   EQUIPMENT AND STORAGE

ATMOSPHERE-PRESSURIZED SECTIONS of the control cabin and gunners' compartments (shown in black in diagram) are built as separate units, fuselage and bulkhead being designed to withstand the artificial internal air-pressure maintained for safety and comfort of the crew (1). On the assembly lines (2). Main wing-section with landing wheels and two of the four 2,200 h.p. engines already in place is lowered to the fuselage (3). Super-Fortresses repeatedly bombed Formosa in mid-October 1944. See also illus. page 189.   PAGE 445   *Photos, Central Press, Planet News*

British Forces Returned in Triumph to Greece

GREECE WAS FREED in 34 days, it was announced on November 9, 1944, when Greek-based R.A.F. reconnaissance aircraft north and north-west of Salonika (taken on November 1), reported that they could no longer find traces of the retreating enemy columns making their way into Albania, and Yugoslavia. The liberation campaign had begun on September 28.

Before evacuating the Peloponnese, to the south, the Germans, leaving devastation behind them everywhere, mined and blocked the famous four-mile-long Corinth Canal with a semi-submerged merchant ship of 3,000 tons (1). Citizens of Athens, freed on October 14, shouted tumultuous welcome to our forces and paraded the streets waving Allied flags (2). British soldiers looked down on the ancient capital from the heights of the Acropolis (3). Our parachute troops formed a guard of honour when the Greek Premier, M. Papandreou, hoisted the National flag in front of the Parthenon (4) on Oct. 18. See map on p. 394.

Photos, British Official

ONE point has been overlooked by those who have protested angrily against American soldiers feeding German children with their rations and fraternizing with their fathers and mothers. This point is that so many American soldiers are of German origin, talk German quite as well as they talk English, have German names, and are more accustomed to German ways of life than they are to those of their fellow-countrymen. There are very large numbers of such people in the United States, and it is next to impossible to prevent their making friends to some extent with Germans in occupied territory. In some ways it might be useful that they should do so. Without any suggestion of propaganda they would show Germans why it is the rest of the world detests them. That is something which it is very necessary for Hitler's dupes to learn. They have not learnt it yet. They never will learn it from official sources. But if it slips out now and then in conversation with men who talk their language and still have relations in Germany, it is likely to have lasting effect. The late Wendell Willkie, whom I could not bring myself to admire, once boasted of his German blood. But how any decent-minded white man could contemplate the history of Germany in the last seventy years and the spectacle of Europe today and be proud, instead of ashamed, of his German blood, just beats me. But it's a human failing to be "proud" of things we couldn't help.

WAR and worry go together with a great many people. They were worrying not long ago about juvenile delinquency. It was shown that children were about as good and as naughty as usual. Now they are disturbed because children are not forced by their parents to eat things they dislike. Wartime diet has no bad effect on them whatever, medical officers of health say. Why not accept that and keep quiet? But no, busybodies are urging mothers (did ever you hear of a father making his children eat anything they didn't want to?) to insist on their little boys and girls polishing off green vegetables, for instance, even if they do not fancy them. Well, I know of a child who was forced to eat Irish stew in the nursery, although he loathed it. The effects on that child were, I should say, almost entirely bad. The best way to persuade children to devour heartily any food that you know will do them good is to tell them they really ought not to have it till they are grown-up and they must only have a very little. Then they will clamour for full plates. But I don't recommend George Meredith's example when the son by his first marriage so persistently screamed to have some of the red wine they were drinking at table that the novelist took up the bottle and poured most of it down the gullet of the irritating child.

A FARMER I've been told about chuckles with satisfaction over the killing of vast numbers of starlings by the beams of searchlights. The searchlight crews have been picking out fly-bombs. The starlings were making their annual migration from the continent to Britain. The beam appears to disturb and puzzle them. They rise from the trees where they roost and circle round and round in the dazzling light until they drop. Have you ever watched starlings at dusk gather and form immense squadrons and fly off to their quarters for the night? Have you ever stood near the trees which form those quarters and listened to the noise the birds make? The farmer has, and he would like to find some means of keeping them away. He says they do a lot of damage to crops. When I told him I liked to see them on my lawn, strutting about in shiny, iridescent suits in the sun, he snorted with indignation. "Ought to be exterminated," he says. Well, if they would only keep to lawns and avoid farms we should both be pleased.

As one contemplates the enormous amount of clearing-up and restoring there is to be done before life can become normal again, it seems sometimes as if it were a task that could never be finished. It will be, of course, but it will take time, and a serious question is, Who shall do it? I am thinking especially just now of the barbed wire entanglements and concrete road blocks that keep people in South Coast holiday resorts away from the front and the sea. These were placed in position by the military. It is hard to see how soldiers at this critical phase of the war can be spared for the job of taking them away. It is equally difficult to imagine local authorities finding enough civilian labour for the purpose, even if they were ready to pay for its being done. At Hove it has been suggested that the Home Guard might undertake this duty, but very naturally their commanding officer demurred. In some places a start has been made by setting German prisoners to the task (see illus. p. 418) and this would seem a most appropriate example of "poetic justice"!

I FOUND myself the other day wondering what treasures the dark unfathomed caves of ocean bear one half so precious as the lowly sponge. The reason for this great thought was that a small sponge in my toilet set had suddenly begun to dissolve and a new one was desirable. So I proceeded to a West End chemist's and asked for the desired item, expecting that it would be

SIR C. BRUCE-GARDNER, M.I.Mech.E., as Chief Executive for Industrial Reconversion at the Board of Trade, will control the change-over from war to peace of British industrial production. He was formerly Controller of Labour Allocation and Supply at the Ministry of Aircraft Production. [Photo, Planet News

much more expensive than the one that I had thrown away; but I was scarcely prepared to read on the price ticket attached to a specimen five inches long by three inches wide, of the commonest sort of sponge, 37s. 6d. Before the war 7s. 6d. would have been an adequate price for the article, and I refused point-blank to pay this monstrous increase, even if I went without a face sponge for the rest of my life. The girl in the shop assured me that it was the cheapest sponge she had in stock and, evidently, she but spoke the truth; for a friend to whom I mentioned the incident said that she had asked to see some sponges in a well-known store, and the cheapest available of the size and type I had required was £2. At another and less exigent store she was lucky enough to find two which bore their old tickets, 9s. 3d. And in purchasing these she was told that they were old stock, but the cheapest price of the next lot on sale would be 17s. 6d., other prices soaring to 175s. Anybody looking for an opening for a promising young son might set him up in the sponge business!

MOSCOW is proud of its tube railway, but the new Kiev which is arising out of the ruins of the ancient city in South Russia will probably be prouder still of its street escalators. Like Rome, it is built on hills and some of these are steep. To get about was tiring. Now all you have to do when you want to go up or down is to step on to a moving staircase, like those in the London Underground railway stations, and there you are! This is the first time such a convenience has been installed in a city, and it shows how go-ahead the local authorities must be. It will be instructive to watch and see whether the example is followed elsewhere. Not many of our big towns are hilly enough to need escalators, though Newcastle and Dundee have several pretty steep streets. In many of our smaller towns such assistance to walkers would be useful if the ratepayers could afford it. In Lewes, for instance, there is one of the most precipitous streets I know anywhere, and Sevenoaks has a long steady rise from the station to its business centre. We shall not get escalators for either of these, I suppose; yet we must not set limits to what the future will do in facilitating movement through crowded streets. The Paris Exhibition of 1900 with its three moving platforms was an object lesson. The noise of these things, however, detracts from their usefulness.

A NEW terror is caused among people who take art seriously, by the proposal made at Hastings that a statue of Mr. Churchill should be put up there as a war memorial. That our Prime Minister is a man who has "done the State," not only "some service," as Othello said, but a very great service indeed, bracing us for a struggle which called for every ounce of determination and dogged courage, no one could or would question. But that he is a suitable subject for the art of the sculptor cannot be included among his characteristics even by his warmest admirers. Indeed, no man in the dress of today—trousers and short jacket or "morning coat" with tails, and collar and tie round the neck—gives the sculptor any chance to produce a thing of beauty; and if a work of art is not a thing of beauty, what good is it? We have enough atrociously bad statues already. That there are among the hundreds in London only three that are tolerable is the opinion of a famous art critic whom I met the other day. These three are the Charles I on horseback at the top of Whitehall, the Carlyle seated figure in the Chelsea Embankment Gardens, and the Arthur Sullivan bust with a woman's figure leaning against it in uncontrollable grief near Charing Cross Underground Station. To have the country flooded with statues of war heroes some of which must inevitably not be of the first rank would remind us of them in a disagreeable way, my art critic friend suggests.

Swastika Ripped From the Old Church Tower

ON THE WAY TO HERTOGENBOSCH, in the advance through Holland, a Royal Engineer climbed the shell-shattered tower of the church at Wijbosch and removed the Nazi flag. Hertogenbosch, important communications centre (peacetime population 45,000), fell to the British 2nd Army on October 25, 1944. Two days later, pushing north from Eindhoven, British troops entered Tilburg. The British salient, from being a somewhat hazardous corridor, was thus completely transformed, the whole left flank pivoting northwards to the sea.

Photo, British Newspaper Pool

Printed in England and published every alternate Friday by the Proprietors, THE AMALGAMATED PRESS, LTD., The Fleetway House, Farringdon Street, London, E.C.4.
Registered for transmission by Canadian Magazine Post. Sole Agents for Australia and New Zealand : Messrs. Gordon & Gotch, Ltd. ; and for South Africa : Central
News Agency, Ltd.—November 24, 1944. S.S. *Editorial Address :* JOHN CARPENTER HOUSE, WHITEFRIARS, LONDON, E.C.4.

Vol 8

The War Illustrated

Nº 195

Edited by Sir John Hammerton

SIXPENCE

DECEMBER 8, 1944

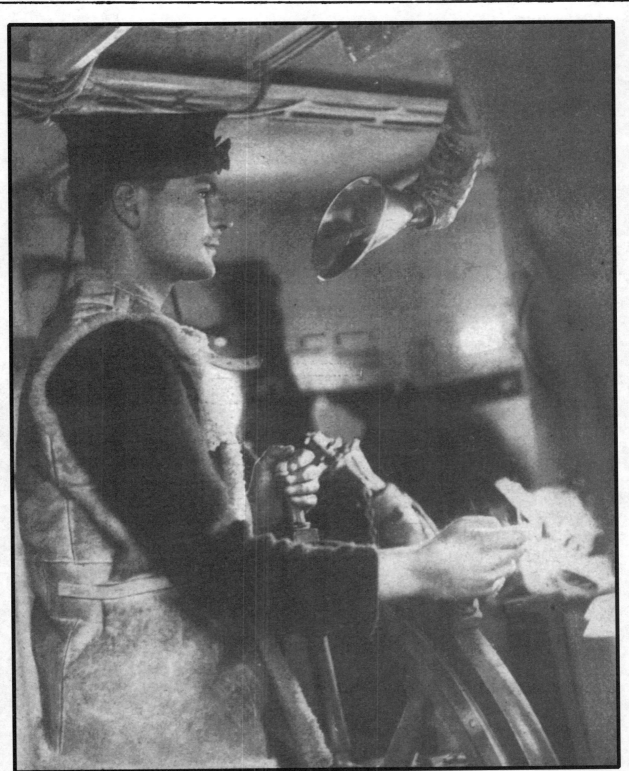

IN THE WHEELHOUSE of one of the landing-craft that braved the crippling fire from enemy shore batteries at Westkapelle on the island of Walcheren on November 1, 1944, the coxswain, Leading-Seaman Tony Cole, of Walthamstow, London, stands unflinchingly by the tiller. The final phase of the battle to free the sea approaches to Antwerp was thus begun, when at dawn Royal Marine Commandos battled their way landwards against German guns thought to have been silenced. See pages 463-466. *Photo, British Official*

NO. 196 WILL BE PUBLISHED FRIDAY, DECEMBER 22

Our Roving Camera Records the London Scene

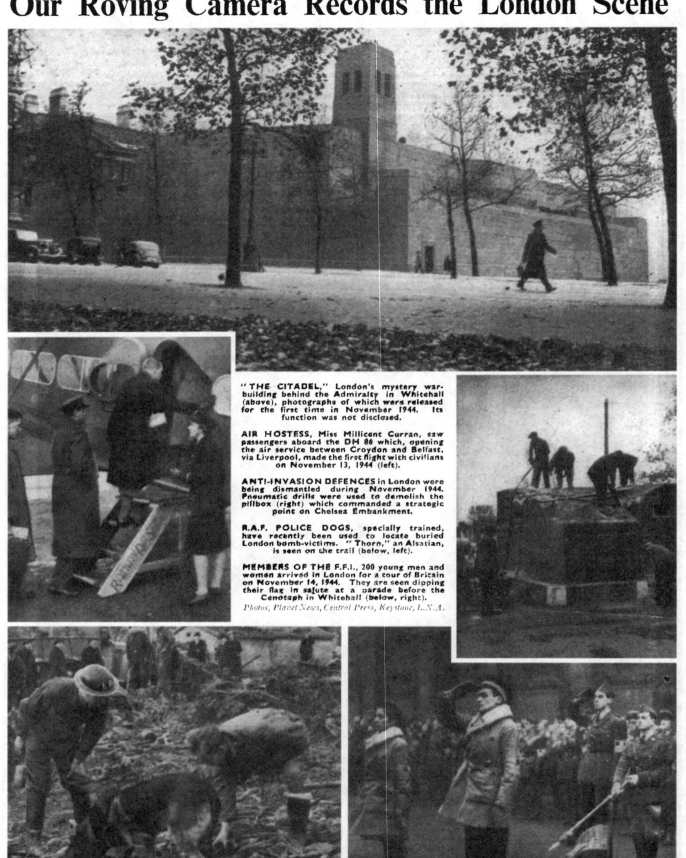

"THE CITADEL," London's mystery war-building behind the Admiralty in Whitehall (above), photographs of which were released for the first time in November 1944. Its function was not disclosed.

AIR HOSTESS, Miss Millicent Curran, saw passengers aboard the DH 86 which, opening the air service between Croydon and Belfast, via Liverpool, made the first flight with civilians on November 13, 1944 (left).

ANTI-INVASION DEFENCES in London were being dismantled during November 1944. Pneumatic drills were used to demolish the pillbox (right) which commanded a strategic point on Chelsea Embankment.

R.A.F. POLICE DOGS, specially trained, have recently been used to locate buried London bomb-victims. "Thorn," an Alsatian, is seen on the trail (below, left).

MEMBERS OF THE F.F.I., 200 young men and women arrived in London for a tour of Britain on November 14, 1944. They are seen dipping their flag in salute at a parade before the Cenotaph in Whitehall (below, right).

Photos, Planet News, Central Press, Keystone, L.N.A.

THE BATTLE FRONTS

by Maj.-Gen. Sir Charles Gwynn, K.C.B., D.S.O.

THE freeing of the approaches to Antwerp (see illus. pages 463-466) marks the end of major operations preparatory to the great final offensive in the west. The enemy's outer defences have been disrupted and the Allied Armies fully deployed, and with secure and adequate bases behind are now within striking distance of his inner positions.

With the attack of the U.S. 9th Army, and the intensification of the preliminary attacks of the five other Allied armies which face east, the great final offensive has clearly actually begun, and there is no longer any question of its being postponed till after the winter, though we may have to wait till the spring or summer of next year for its conclusion. The attacks that have so far been delivered have evidently not aimed at a decisive break-through, but rather to drive in the German covering positions—as in Alsace and Lorraine—and in general to test and weaken the crust of German resistance.

Where General Eisenhower will eventually deliver his decisive blow is not yet apparent, and his final decision may depend on the strategy the Germans adopt. In Lorraine they may fall back fighting to the Siegfried position, and north of the Moselle they may withdraw behind the Rhine in order to avoid fighting a decisive battle with the river close behind them. General Eisenhower, by a premature attempt to gain decisive victory, might run the risk of committing his armies to a blow in the air, particularly since winter conditions militate against rapid pursuit.

WE may take justifiable pride in that the preparatory operations which have been so brilliantly successful were initiated and in the main carried out under the executive orders of a British general, and that troops of the Empire played an outstanding part in them.

Since the original landing and subsequent destruction of Rommel's Army there has been no success of strategic importance equal to the capture of Antwerp and the opening of the approaches to it. Moreover, it involved desperately hard and continuous fighting during a period in which the rest of the front was relatively quiet. I do not mean that the rest of the front was inactive, for pressure was vigorously maintained, but the enterprises undertaken, such as the capture of Aachen and the operations on the Moselle and Vosges fronts, had none of the urgency of those in Holland which had such an important effect on the "maintenance" situation on the whole front. The versatility displayed by the troops of the 21st Army Group and their capacity to adapt themselves to all sorts of conditions has been remarkable.

They have fought with equal determination and skill in the mud and cold of Holland as in summer heat and dust of Normandy. They have displayed immense energy in pursuit and in driving every advantage home, as well as dogged pertinacity in inching their way forward over terrible country in the face of fierce opposition. The number of amphibious operations they have staged testifies still further to their resourcefulness.

HUNGARY

On the eastern front, Malinovsky's great offensive in Hungary continues to make remarkable progress in spite of the slowing down effect of autumn rains. But there is little doubt that the opening of the Russian main offensive is waiting for the winter conditions in which the superiority of Russian troops

and equipment over their opponents' becomes most marked. The partial pause which has continued so long must, however, have allowed the Russians time to consolidate their system of communications and to complete their preparations, whereas such operations as have been undertaken have compelled the Germans to make drastic redisposition of their armies while still uncertain where they will have to meet the main blows. I have noted before now the patience the Russians display in developing their plans, which is as remarkable as the energy with which they strike when the chosen moment arrives.

ALONG A 400-MILE FRONT, from near Arnhem to the Swiss border, six Allied armies —more than General Eisenhower had ever before sent into action at one time—were reported to have opened a mass-offensive against the Germans on November 16, 1944.
By courtesy of The Daily Mirror

PACIFIC

While we are waiting for the curtain to rise for the last act in the European theatre, we have an opportunity to take an interest in the reports that reach us from the Far Eastern theatre, where the first act is over and the second is in progress. Reports cannot, of course, give us as clear a picture of the setting of the stage in that theatre as we have of the western stage, but they do give us an idea of how the drama is unfolding and of the performance of the actors and their parts.

It has, perhaps, surprised us to learn that the actors supplied by the Empire have played such prominent roles. Australian troops conducted the greater part of the land fighting in New Guinea which not only, at Milne Bay, administered the first check to the aggressor's progress, but subsequently won the series of bases which made operations against the Philippines practicable. New Zealand troops took a distinguished part in the Solomons fighting. Ships of both the Royal Australian and New Zealand Navies

have been actively engaged throughout; as has also been the R.A.A.F., which accomplished some wonderful work in New Guinea even when its equipment was wholly inadequate in quantity and obsolete in design.

New Zealand Divisions, as we know, are still, or were till recently, fighting in Italy, and though Australian Divisions were sent home from Egypt one at least remained to take part in Alamein. Twenty thousand Australian airmen and a proportionate number of New Zealanders are still in this country, as the Germans have good reason to know. Apart from that the Dominions have provided an essential base for the American war effort in the Western Pacific. They have been an invaluable source of food supply and, in addition (Australia especially) have developed war industries from scarcely nothing to an almost incredible standard of output and efficiency.

The great recovery and development of American naval and air power in the Pacific has tended to over-shadow the war efforts of the Dominions which, particularly in the earlier stages of the war, have been of such vital importance. Recently, Australian troops have been withdrawn for reorganization and re-equipment in readiness to take part in more exclusively Empire operations pending. Yet even in the recent Philippines operations the Royal Australian Navy and R.A.A.F. have rendered valuable service.

BURMA

In Burma certainly the Empire's share in the Japanese war has been insufficiently recognized. I believe that the general impression is that the situation there has been rather unsatisfactory, relieved only by the spectacular and surprising success of the Chindit operations. Anything in the nature of an irregular enterprise always makes a special appeal to the British public, but it should be realized that amazing and admirable as the Chindits' exploits are they would have little military value except so far as they contribute to the success of the main army—just as Lawrence's exploits would have had little military significance if they had not been confirmed by Allenby's more decisive victories.

Actually the achievements of the 14th Army have been outstanding. It not only repelled a formidable and ambitious Japanese attempt to invade India and to cut the communications of General Stilwell's Chinese force, and of the airfields from which supplies to China are flown, but, by a counter-offensive, it inflicted on the Japanese Army the heaviest defeat it has ever sustained. The counter-offensive was delivered and pressed home in the monsoon season, during which it had previously been held that large-scale military operations must of necessity be suspended.

FURTHERMORE, operations took place in a terrain which it was widely believed would present an impassable barrier to large forces. Not only were the operations continued successfully throughout the monsoon season, but now at the beginning of the dry weather the 14th Army stands at the southern exits of the barrier. It is still true that with long and difficult lines of communication behind it the 14th Army cannot hope by its own exertions to effect the reconquest of Burma ; but it has not only destroyed large Japanese forces but still exercises a threat which will compel the Japanese to weaken their hold on southern Burma, the security of which is essential to them.

In these operations Indian troops have played a glorious and conspicuous part, but it should be remembered that in every Indian Division at least 25 per cent of the combat units are British, and that exclusively British formations, as well as West and East African troops have endured the same hardships and have fought with equal distinction.

Moving Eastward on a 300-Mile Front in Burma

ALLIED FORCES in North Burma, it was announced on November 17, 1944, held an almost unbroken front of 300 miles. Outside Tiddim, pushing on to Kennedy Peak and Fort White, a British tank moves along a mineswept road to the town (1) ; while a British scout watches Japanese draw out (5). Seeing for himself, Maj.-Gen. F. W. Festing, D.S.O., commanding the 36th Division, inspected a north-Burma outpost (3). In November his division achieved the most rapid advance ever made by Allied forces in Burma, moving down the railway corridor south from Myitkyina to Pinwe. Because these mules (4) were liable to panic on seeing the fast-running Manipur River, a camouflaged ferry was built for them. On the withdrawal of Gen. Joseph W. Stilwell from the command of U.S. forces in the China-Burma-India theatre (announced on October 28), Lieut.-Gen. Daniel I. Sultan (2) succeeded him in the Burma-India theatre. U.S. forces in China were placed under Maj.-Gen. Albert C. Wedemeyer.

(See map p. 473.)

Photos, British and Indian Official

From Holland to the Reich the Big Push Goes On

BRITISH TROOPS of the 21st Army Group inspected a German A.A. gun used as an anti-tank weapon at Willemstad (above), on the Maas Estuary, after they had taken it on November 7, 1944. The town was seized in a blinding gale after the enemy had refused to surrender.

DRIVING TOWARDS THE SAAR, General Patton's U.S. 3rd Army—part of the great Allied six-army thrust—had completely, surrounded Metz on November 19, 1944. Guns ploughed through thick mud (above), while convoys splashed along flooded roads (bottom right).

TOMMY'S ODD JOBS in Holland during the winter of 1944 included the removal to safety of many a homeless elderly Netherlander (above). Thousands were helped to transit centres by British Army authorities. (See also illus. p. 461.)

THE WAR AT SEA

by Francis E. McMurtrie

WITH the elimination of the Tirpitz, Germany has lost her last battleship. It is true that the Gneisenau still exists, but only as a dismantled hulk without armament, in dock at Gdynia. Two so-called "pocket battleships," the Admiral Scheer and Lützow, are in fact merely heavy cruisers, inferior in speed to the Prinz Eugen and Admiral Hipper, officially so classed. Two smaller cruisers, the Nürnberg and Leipzig, have not been heard of for some time past, but are believed, like the four ships previously mentioned, to be somewhere in the Baltic. There also are the two old coast-defence ships Schlesien and Schleswig-Holstein, long overdue for scrapping, but capable of being used for bombardment purposes. Two small cruisers, the Köln and Emden, are reported to be in Oslo, where they have been employed as guardships and for training anti-aircraft guns' crews.

None of these ships is of sufficient force to detain in European waters any first-class ships of the Royal Navy which may have been held in readiness to deal with the Tirpitz so long as she remained afloat. Thus it should now be possible to release for service in the Eastern Fleet the majority of the more modern units of the Home Fleet. In fact, it may be assumed that, with a few exceptions, all the principal ships completed for the Navy during the present war will in due course be employed in the Pacific, operating against the Japanese.

THIS fact was tacitly admitted by Admiral Saalwaechter when, in disclosing that the Tirpitz had been "put out of action," he observed frankly but with little tact that the German Navy was "sorry" for the Japanese. It certainly would seem that the tremendous Allied naval force which it will now be possible to concentrate against our Eastern enemies should be sufficient to annihilate the Japanese fleet, already reduced to about half its original strength.

The Tirpitz can hardly be considered a lucky ship, in spite of the numerous attacks which she survived in the course of her brief but inglorious career. There were eight of

these attacks prior to the final one which destroyed her:

(1) By Fleet Air Arm planes at Narvik in March 1942.
(2) By Halifaxes and Lancasters of the R.A.F. in Fotten Fjord, April 27, 1942.
(3) By a Soviet submarine in the Barents Sea, July 8, 1942.
(4) By H.M. midget submarines X6 and X7 in Altenfjord, September 22, 1943.
(5) By Fleet Air Arm planes (Barracudas) at Altenfjord, April 3, 1944.
(6) By Fleet Air Arm planes at Altenfjord between August 23, and 29, 1944.
(7) By Lancasters of the R.A.F. at Altenfjord, September 15, 1944.
(8) By Lancasters of the R.A.F. in Tromsö Fjord, October 29, 1944.

The amount of damage inflicted by attacks numbered 1, 2, 3, 6, and 8 is doubtful, owing to weather and smoke conditions preventing observation of results, but it is certain that in 4, 5 and 7 definite hits were made, resulting in more or less extensive damage. After the attack by midget submarines repairs were going on for some months, the underwater damage being patched up by the use of cement in large quantities. It seems probable that the cumulative effect of this and other damage must have gone far to weaken the structure of the ship below water.

VARYING Effects of Underwater Explosions on a Ship's Structure

In the attack by Lancasters on November 12, 1944, it is recorded that three 12,000-lb. bombs were seen to hit the battleship, while two others exploded near her in the water. It is quite likely that it was the latter which caused the ship to capsize, through a number of compartments being laid open to the sea, so upsetting the reserve of stability.

In a lecture delivered before the North East Coast Institution of Engineers recently, Sir Stanley Goodall, Assistant Controller (Warship Production) at the Admiralty, and formerly Director of Naval Construction, gave some interesting details of the effects on a ship's structure of underwater explosions.

In view of the success with which depth charges had been used in anti-submarine

H.M. THE KING (left), on his visit to Portsmouth on November 16, 1944, inspected the underground plotting-room from which invasion operations on D-Day were controlled.

operations in the last war, full-scale experiments were carried out in post-war years with the battleship Monarch, the monitor Gorgon, and other ships before they were sold for scrap. As a result of these experiments, it was demonstrated that the explosion of a non-contact charge in the neighbourhood of a ship's side would effect damage of less intensity than a contact charge, but the area of destruction would be greater. If, however, the charge was moved from the side round to the bottom, the intensity of the damage was increased, until right beneath the ship the effect was far more devastating than that of a similar weight of explosive in contact with the ship's side.

This may be summed up by saying that a charge exploding beneath a ship is more damaging than a torpedo which strikes her side ; and as a 12,000-lb. bomb contains a much heavier charge of explosive than a 21-in. torpedo, this damage would be further magnified should the former be detonated in such a position. Photographs which have been released of the sunken Tirpitz, lying half-submerged on her side, show two significant breaks in the keel line which may well have been due to bombs exploding beneath her in the way suggested. (See p. 477).

LAUNCHED at Wilhelmshaven on April 1, 1939, the Tirpitz was stated to be of 35,000 tons displacement, but in fact she is now known to have displaced about 45,000 tons, excluding fuel and reserve feed water. She mounted eight 15-in., twelve 5·9-in. and sixteen 4·1-in. guns, besides smaller anti-aircraft weapons. Four aircraft and a couple of catapults were included in the original design, but it seems improbable that these were actually carried, though the sister ship Bismarck is said to have had them when completed. That ship was manned by about 2,000 officers and men when she was sunk, but some of these are reported to have been supernumeraries, not forming part of the normal complement. Over 800 lives are believed to have been lost in the Tirpitz, according to Swedish accounts.

When the Bismarck was lost in May 1941, the Tirpitz had been finished, and had just proceeded from Wilhelmshaven to Kiel to carry out trials in the Baltic. After these had been completed, late in 1941 or early 1942, she seems to have been sent to Trondheim with a view to operating against Allied convoys proceeding to North Russia. In this service she accomplished very little, even when based on Altenfjord, far to the north. Her chief feat was to make a "tip and run" raid in company with other German warships upon the Arctic island group usually known as Spitsbergen, though its official Norwegian name is Svalbard ("Coldland"). (See illus. p. 315, Vol. 7.) The small Norwegian garrison was shelled and some of them taken prisoner, but otherwise nothing effective was accomplished in this sortie, which seems to have been undertaken for propaganda purposes rather than for any sound military reason.

SMALL PROTECTION-CRAFT of the U.S. Navy is lowered to the water from the deck of a transport (above) during the initial stages of General MacArthur's long-promised invasion of the Philippines on October 20, 1944 (see page 429). Well-armoured, and heavily-equipped with A.A. guns, these craft helped to protect the great transport vessels and landing barges seen heading for the shore in the background.

PAGE 454   *Photo, Planet News*

They Help to Keep Our Merchant Fleet at Sea

FOR EVERY BRITISH SHIP'S COMPANY AFLOAT in 1944 as many men again were busy in the docks at home. Despite blackout, raids and other hindrances, 4,415,669 tons of merchant shipping were launched in the first four years of this war, compared with 3,770,170 tons in the four years of the last war, although fewer men and yards were available. Mr. J. F. Cunningham (top left), welder for 27 years, wields the oxy-acetylene torch in a Liverpool yard. Another bustling Liverpool scene (top right), and fitting a new stern to a vessel (bottom). PAGE 455 *Photos, British Official*

With a Red Coastal Battery in the Far North

Russian artillery has gathered great fame : the guns have been a chief factor in securing for Soviet forces resounding victories over the Germans on all parts of the long front. How renown came to one of the coastal batteries that hammered enemy shipping in the bleak and bitter Arctic is narrated here by Captain of the Coastal Service P. NIKOLAYEV. (See also facing page.)

It was a light Arctic night in April 1943, and we were seated in a small dug-out for Marine scouts. Suddenly the window-panes rattled, a light breeze swept through and the distant booming of guns reached our ears. The Marines glanced at each other, and one of them, a short, stocky tommy-gunner, said : " It's Ponochevny ! "

I had heard that word "Ponochevny" mentioned many times. It was the name of one of the naval artillery officers, but I never realized that here in the Far North, on Sredni Peninsula, it stood for the coastal battery of the artillery battalion under the command of youthful Captain Fyodor Ponochevny.

We jumped from the dug-out. On the horizon, at a point closest to the sea, we saw bright flashes of fire. A deep glow fluttered over the place. Suddenly we heard an even more powerful roar of artillery, and the Marines stationed near the dug-out remarked: " That's him firing now."

Soon after I had occasion to visit the famous battery. Deserted, snow-covered hills sloped down towards the sea. Near the shore there was a sparse growth of midget birch trees typical of the Arctic. From there we had a view of the coast of Finland, enveloped in blue haze ; stretching along it were extinct volcanoes and snow-covered cliffs. The battery was stationed at the extreme edge of the right flank of the Soviet-German front covering sea and land. A stairway cut in the ice led towards the gun-post.

Actually, there was no sign of a battery. There was nothing in sight but narrow passages in the rocky ground and black embrasures among the rocks to indicate its presence. An officer in Marine uniform, with the frank, good-natured face of a Ukrainian, came to meet us. Two Orders of the Red Banner decorated his breast. This was Fyodor Ponochevny, commander of the battery.

Born in a whitewashed cottage of a Ukrainian village near Kiev, on the steep bank of the Dnieper, he had entered the Sebastopol naval artillery school at the age of 18 and after graduation had come to the north, where he had been serving for more than four years. Simple and cheerful, exceptionally exacting towards himself and his subordinates, he was liked by all the men of his battery. War is the best test of a man's character : such is Ponochevny's unwritten law, his basis of rating his people.

The Test of a Good Artilleryman

The struggle of a coastal battery against the enemy's surface craft in conditions of the present war demands special precision and speed of action on the part of its personnel, ability to divine the enemy's tactics in good time and counter them by one's own tactics. Any number of enemy shells and bombs may burst all around, showering down thousands of red-hot fragments, but a real artilleryman must hear nothing, except the orders of his commander, must see nothing, except the sights of his gun. If he lives up to this, says Ponochevny, he is a good artilleryman and deserves every respect.

To prove his contention he named from among his crew, Gun Commander Gregory Khomyakov, a robust Marine ; Junior Sergeant Benjamin Koshelev, likewise a gun commander, a restless and lively lad ; the small, red-headed gun-layer Subbotin, a Sebastopolite by birth and a Kronstadter by service ; Sergeant Kovalkovsky, the best " joke-cracker " of the battery ; Leonid Kuznetsov, the cook, and others.

A dense fog obscured the bay. From time to time it merged with falling snow. Suddenly, a barely perceptible hooting was heard from the direction of the sea. The Marines stood tense listening. The sound was repeated. " Ready ! " The order was flashed

to all the crew. Powerful searchlight beams were incapable of penetrating the dense fog. The men were at their posts, peering into the stereoscopes. They were waiting for orders.

The first salvos roared out. A solid wall of fire arose before the German ships.

Fire continued. Abruptly the wind tore apart and lifted the fog, and the searchlight illuminated a big enemy transport. In a moment the transport became a flaming torch. A shell or two hit its centre, another hit was scored to starboard, and a bright glow rose over the bay. Artillerymen switched their fire to the second and third transports, which had not yet managed to vanish behind the bend.

This was a long and hard battle, but it ended in success. The infuriated enemy directed the full might of his coastal artillery against the battery and a heavy duel ensued. More than 300 shells were discharged at this battery, on this bright Arctic night. A tremendous figure ! But this was nothing new. On one occasion 872 shells were hurled against Ponochevny's battery. Eight long-range batteries opened up against it. Nevertheless, Ponochevny's battery survived and continued to sink enemy ships.

Shrapnel hissed overhead. Explosions broke communications, but signalmen rapidly repaired the damage and the artillerymen again and again responded to the orders of their commander. " Faster ! Train all the guns on the second transport ! " The second transport sank. The third went down in flames a few minutes later.

During this war Ponochevny's battery has sunk a total of 16 enemy transports and other ships, among them a big tanker, three trawlers, two patrol ships, and a big motorized barge. In addition, five enemy planes were shot down and an equal number damaged.

LIKE A BEDOUIN OF THE SNOWS, this strangely-garbed Soviet Marine, N. Lebedev, stands on sentry duty in the frozen wastes of the far-north Russian frontier. He was one of the heroic coastal battery under the command of youthful Captain Fyodor Ponochevny, of the U.S.S.R. Karelian Command, whose exploits in destroying enemy transport and aircraft during a highly critical period of the war—a task demanding the utmost speed and precision—are related in this page.

Photo exclusive to The War Illustrated

Amidst Eternal Snows the Great Guns Roar

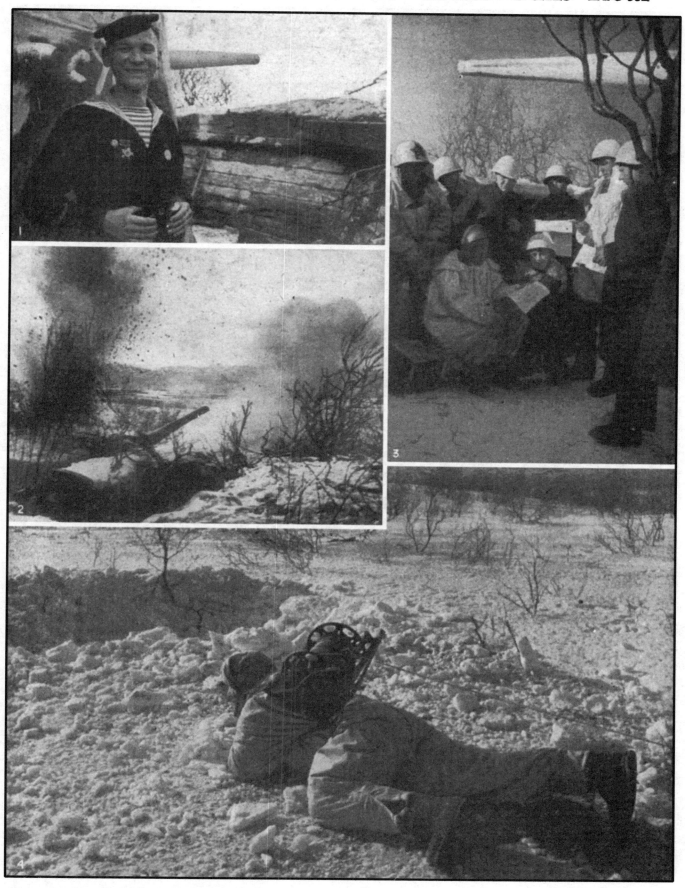

IN THE ARCTIC WASTES of the Sredni Peninsula, on the former Russo-Finnish frontier, a lonely outpost of Soviet Marines—the " Red Banner Battery," commanded by Captain Ponochevny—carried out an epic task harassing enemy transport during the critical winter of 1943 (see facing page). The smiling, bemedalled gun-commander, Sergeant Koshelev (1). Ponochevny's guns crash out (2). The battery read the newspapers (3). Crawling across the snow under fire, Signalman Pankov repairs communications (4).

PAGE 457 *Photos, Exclusive to* The War Illustrated

'Vive Churchill!' Cried 100,000 Parisians

ON ARMISTICE DAY, 1944, the Prime Minister paid a surprise visit to the French capital. He laid a wreath on the Unknown Warrior's tomb and took the salute with General de Gaulle at a gigantic military parade in the Champs Elysées. Ratings from the Chatham Naval Gunnery School headed the British contingent (top). Mr. Churchill, in the uniform of an Air Commodore, waved to the cheering crowds (bottom). This was the Premier's first visit to Paris since the Battle of France in 1940. He returned to England on Nov. 14. PAGE 458 *Photos, British Newspaper Pool*

New Glory for the Guards in the Battle of Italy

GRENADIER GUARDS WITH THE 5th ARMY in Italy took full share of the arduous fighting in the Apennines in November 1944. Earlier in the Italian campaign, from Cassino to the Gothic Line, they won new laurels by covering 315 miles in 108 days of bitter battle and great hardship. A patrol of the Grenadiers is here seen making a steep climb along a rock-strewn mountain track to forward positions in the Central Apennines. Late in November snow had fallen all along the front. See also illus. pages 688-689. Vol. 7. *Photo, British Official*

The Story Behind a Polish Armoured Brigade

From all over the world, and in spite of immense difficulties, Poles have rallied, first in France and later in Britain, to fight for the liberation of their country. In this article HENRY BAERLEIN tells of the history and the adventures of the personnel of a Polish Armoured Brigade he recently visited and which is now in the fighting line

THERE was a time during the last war when Poles, wearing German, Austrian and Russian uniforms, were fighting against one another. But although they had been forced to participate in various theatres of war their leaders saw to it that none of them entered into binding agreements with any one of the warring Powers who tried their utmost to win the Poles' allegiance for their own imperialistic aims. The attitude of the Polish Legion, formed and led by Marshal Pilsudski, is proof not only of the strong nationalistic sentiment of the Poles, which 150 years of slavery could not extinguish, but also of their refusal to co-operate in any policy which was directed against the interest of Poland.

The Marshal had been successfully fighting the Russians when he realized that the promises which the German and Austrian Governments had made regarding the independence of Poland were unreliable. He immediately refused to obey all further orders, and as a result both he and the whole Polish Legion were imprisoned by the Germans.

In the 16th and 17th centuries, before the partition of Poland, one of the most notable features of her army was the cavalry. The horsemen wore breastplates, and fixed to their shoulders they carried lofty contraptions made of eagles' feathers. As the horsemen charged, the wind rushed through these plumes and caused a terrifying noise which was intended to break the morale of the enemy. (It will be recalled that military bands have their origin in the music played by the Arabs when going into battle ; the idea was not so much to encourage their own side as to terrify the foe.)

THIS eagle-feathered cavalry is the ancestor of the tank, and a visit I have just been privileged to pay to one Polish Armoured Brigade has been highly instructive. Officers and men were delighted with their new, fast-moving cruiser-type tanks made in Britain or America. These tanks are much more heavily armed than the Crusaders which they had a year or so ago, and are more easily controlled ; though the Crusader is simple enough to handle, as I discovered when,

after riding in one up and down a mountain-side, our driver showed us that he had done all the driving with his left hand, as his right was bandaged because of a recent injury.

The cavalry regiment—the predecessor of this particular armoured unit was entirely motorized in 1939. From the first day of the war it faced the overwhelming strength of the German Panzer Divisions on the southern front. Heavy clashes occurred at many places, and near Lvov the German 1st Highland Division was encircled and wiped out. When Poland was overrun by the enemy the regiment, reaching France by various routes, gave a splendid account of itself. Later, though somewhat depleted in numbers, it proceeded south, determined to reach Britain. Here, from 1940 to 1942, it formed an integral part of the coastal defence of Scotland, and has since received the singular honour of being presented with a marching flag by the Ancient Royal Burgh of Haddington. Units stationed in Lanarkshire wear on their sleeve the Duke of Hamilton's tartan. These are emblems profoundly treasured by the Poles.

Gamekeepers Turned Snipers

There is something else that is treasured by these men—a rifle fitted with telescopic sights, with the help of which a good shot can scarcely miss his target. An officer told me how his gunsmith in the south of Poland had informed him of a Mauser made in Germany and suitable for Polish army ammunition, but which could be bought only in Danzig. He managed to obtain one five or six days before the outbreak of the war ; and now he has been training snipers whose rifles are furnished with these sights. His men are sportsmen like himself, and hail mostly from the Carpathians, where some had been gamekeepers and others poachers.

It is sometimes asserted that the Poles are not a democratically-minded people. But while on my visit I came across two men who were engaged in conversation : one a sergeant, the other a private. The sergeant had been head of a great petroleum company, while the private, a young man whose mother had been a Habsburg, belonged to one of the most ancient of Poland's noble

GENERAL MACZEK, G.O.C. 1st Polish Armoured Division, paid a front-line visit to Field-Marshal Sir Bernard Montgomery during the Netherlands campaign in November 1944. The General (facing camera) is seen presenting one of his staff to the Field-Marshal
Photo, British Official

families. He seemed to be quite happy, and I was told that he was never excused any of the toil that ordinarily falls to a private's lot.

The Poles have flocked to their standards from all over the world. One man whom I met, for instance, had been smuggled, together with four friends, into a Latvian ship and concealed under the boilers. The Germans took the ship to Stettin, where it remained for three weeks, during which time a sailor brought the fugitives food and water. But the suspicious Germans used tear-gas, which caused one of the Poles to go mad, and the others had to restrain him lest he should "give the show away." Occasionally, at night, the Poles would venture on deck. They escaped from the vessel when she docked at Antwerp.

A NON-COMMISSIONED Pole, a lawyer in civil life, whom I also met in this brigade, had reached Hungary when his own country fell into German hands. He then went to France, where he served as a private in the artillery and, after the collapse of that country, he was interned for a considerable time in Switzerland. Escapes need not always be romantic, and his took place in broad daylight when he strolled across the frontier. He contacted some fellow-countrymen at Marseilles and ascertained that ships were being sent to Beyrout to evacuate those Frenchmen who preferred to come home rather than join De Gaulle. Ten thousand francs quickly changed hands—one of the recipients was a seaman on board such a ship —and on a dark night the Poles were rowed to the far side of the vessel and embarked in secrecy.

"Sir, I Can Tell You Nothing!"

For seven days and nights they lived in the dark, subsisting entirely on scraps that the seaman could save from his own rations. Divided among five men it did not go far and my informant lost a good deal in weight. At Beyrout an Australian officer put no difficulties in the way of the travellers, and the captain of the ship, which, as it happened, had taken the Polish brigade, or part of it, to Narvik some eighteen months previously, said that he would permit them to land on condition that they disclosed how they had arrived on board and who had assisted them.

"Sir," said my informant, "this is the worst moment of my life—for I can tell you nothing !" Thereupon the captain saluted and let them go ashore. The Poles infected the captain's crew. Fourteen of them also went ashore and joined the Fighting French forces of General de Gaulle !

POLISH MILITARY POLICEMAN directs British troops aboard a jeep at Barle Nassau on the Breda-Tilburg front in the Netherlands, where the Poles fought side by side with men of the 1st Canadian Army. This photograph was taken after the Poles, in a hard-pressed struggle, had captured Alphen and Gilza on October 27, 1944, and were moving towards Breda. Later they broke the enemy resistance at Moerdijk.
Photo, Keystone

How We Heartened the Homeless in Holland

AFTERMATH of the great Allied airborne landings at Nijmegen and elsewhere in the Rhine delta of Holland on Sept. 17, 1944, was the succouring of thousands of refugees. Within four days of the landings, Nijmegen, on the River Waal, southern arm of the Rhine and about four miles from the German frontier, was in Allied hands. Its 2,000-yards bridge, taken intact, secured to our troops one of the main objectives of the airborne invasion. See also pages 366-370.

A BRITISH army lorry was one of many boarded by Nijmegen refugees on the way to safety (1). The language of signs came in handy when boy (Canadian trooper) met girl (Dutch, in national costume) outside the town (2). Hot soup was distributed from milk-churns to sabot-shod homeless (3). Against the background of Nijmegen's medieval church, two aged refugees sought information from an Allied soldier in charge of transport (4). Enjoying a much-needed rest, these old Dutch women were housed and tended by nuns in a converted stocking factory (5).

Photos exclusive to THE WAR ILLUSTRATED

Catafighters of the Atlantic Suicide Squad

One of the least-known of the many duties the Hurricane was called on to perform is described by Sgt. A. J. WILSON, R.A.F. Production of this famous aircraft has now ceased. But in the ranks of the Merchant Navy and among the crews of many Naval escort vessels the Hurricane Catafighters will long be remembered for "services rendered." See also page 214.

THE idea came from the Prime Minister, Mr. Churchill. Like most good plans it was simple and direct. In 1941, out in the Atlantic, far beyond the reach of shore-based aircraft of Fighter Command, German long-range bombers were preying on our convoys. We could not spare aircraft carriers to give them protection, and only the guns of the escort ships of the Royal Navy guarded the merchantmen which brought us vital supplies.

The big four-engined Focke-Wulf Condors and Kuriers operated without fear of fighter interference over our convoy routes, sometimes hundreds of miles from their bases in western France. Then came Mr. Churchill's plan. Briefly it was this : Fit out some of our merchant ships with catapult launching apparatus and place aboard them the most suitable fighter which can be rocketed from their decks. When attack threatens, launch the fighter and even if the pilot does not destroy the enemy he will probably save the convoy from attack. The pilot can then take to his parachute and be picked up by the naval escort.

Practical experiments followed. It was not difficult to decide on which aircraft to use. The Hurricane, Britain's most versatile fighter, which has been employed in a dozen different types of operations, was the obvious choice. And one day in May 1941 a small party of pioneers arrived at an airfield on the west coast of England to form what later became known as the Merchant Ship Fighter Unit.

A WING Commander from Coastal Command and a few other officers and airmen, including a Signals Officer from Fighter Command, comprised the party. One room in a hut was their headquarters, and they raided equipment from the airfield's station headquarters to fit it out. They partitioned their room into two ; on one side was the Commanding Officer's office and signals office, and on the other side was the orderly-room, stores, accounts and everything else rolled into one.

When the first two Hurricanes arrived a few days later the Signals Officer took off his tunic and personally fitted the radio equipment. After several days of hard work the big moment came—a trial launching from a ship in port. The pioneers watched anxiously as the pilot gave the signal for the launching rockets to be fired. A few moments later they were cheering as the Hurricane circled above them.

The ships selected as the first M.S.F.U. vessels were equipped with a 30-yards steel runway, along which a trolly, carrying the aircraft, was forced at high speed by exploding rockets. At the end of the runway were hydraulic buffers, and when the trolly struck these the Hurricane was thrown forward into the air. With the Hurricane's engine roaring at open throttle, the explosions of the rockets, and the whole aircraft enveloped in smoke and flame, it looked like death for the pilot. But the din would only last a few seconds and there would be the Hurricane soaring gracefully and only the smell of cordite left to linger about the ship and the bos'n hosing the decks to extinguish the flames.

The first batch of pilots were all volunteers. Most of them were Battle of Britain "veterans" and knew all the tricks of operational flying. They knew, too, that at the end of each combat there was the prospect of an extremely cold ducking in a choppy sea. Jokingly they called themselves the

"Atlantic Suicide Squad." They knew that at any time the fate of the convoy might be thrust into their hands, just as the fate of Britain had been their responsibility some months earlier. They accepted the perils, and off they sailed to meet the enemy.

WITH each went a small R.A.F. maintenance crew—a fitter, rigger, armourer and radio operator. The Navy provided the Fighter Directing Officer, whose job corresponded with that of a controller in a land-based operations room. From the moment the aircraft was launched, he would be in radio-telephone touch with the pilot and direct him to his target ; he would advise him when and where to bale out and arrange for his speedy rescue. The big experiment was on. The heads of three Services waited hopefully for results.

FLIGHT-LIEUT. A. H. BURR, D.F.C., of London, who flew 240 miles over Arctic seas in a determined effort to save his Hurricane, after one of the fiercest air-battles ever fought over a Russia-bound convoy, as narrated in this page. *Photo, British Official*

Twelve months later, when the M.S.F.U. celebrated its first birthday, it was reported that not one merchant ship had been lost through long-range bombing on normal ocean routes when a catafighter had been in the convoy. Cover had been extended from the Atlantic to the Arctic, and the small band of pioneers who had launched the scheme had grown into a strong independent fighting unit with pilots in Canada and Russia.

THIS did not mean that all Condors and Kuriers had been shot out of the sky. The deterrent effect on the enemy was perhaps more significant than the combat results. When a raider knew that if he attempted to attack he would have a Hurricane on his tail, he generally left the ships alone and sought easier prey. But for all that the catafighters saw plenty of action.

One November morning, an enemy aircraft was seen flying astern of a convoy homeward-bound from Gibraltar. It was only a matter of seconds before Flying Officer Norman Taylor, 22-year-old Battle of Britain pilot, of Kenilworth, Warwickshire, was signalling to the ship's chief officer to rocket him into the air.

Brilliant sunshine threw up a dazzling glare from the sea, and at first Taylor could see no

sign of the enemy. Then he spotted the raider—a four-engined Condor, flying so low that to Taylor it almost seemed to be following the contours of the swell. The German pilot pulled on his control column as the Hurricane approached, intending to climb for cloud cover. He was too late. There was a quick exchange of bullets and the huge enemy aircraft dived straight into the sea, leaving only its tail sticking upright out of the water.

Taylor patrolled for another twenty minutes in case the Condor had friends. Then his Fighter Directing Officer heard his voice come crackling over the radio-telephone : "Good God ! I've been hit in the port wing, right through the bull's-eye of the roundel ! "

HE baled out soon after that, and after hitting the water on his back had trouble in releasing his dinghy. The sea buffeted him so much that after ten minutes he gave up trying. When later he wrote his combat report he told in detail of his struggle in the water, explaining blandly that he was in rather a fix as he was a non-swimmer ! Taylor won the D.F.C. for that action, and from the captain of his ship came the comment : "He saved the convoy a bad time and possible disaster to some of its ships."

A few months later, on the same route, two F.W. Kuriers, aircraft as big as our heaviest bombers, were shot down in one evening by two catafighter pilots. Flying Officer J. A. Stewart, of Glasgow, faced the enemy's heavy fire-power at point-blank range as he closed to pour a burst into the cockpit of the first Kurier. The flash which followed was seen by a warship ten miles away. Fierce return fire from the second Kurier was also met by Flying Officer P. J. R. Flynn, a London pilot, who was catapulted from another ship. It was not before his Hurricane's port wing had been badly holed and the panel smashed behind his head that he fired the burst which destroyed the enemy.

NOT all the catafighters lost their Hurricanes. After shooting down two German bombers in one of the fiercest air battles ever fought over a Russia-bound convoy, Flight-Lieut. A. H. Burr, of London, flew 240 miles over Arctic seas in a determined effort to save his aircraft. The convoy had already been attacked by two waves of enemy aircraft before he was catapulted from his ship, and in one of these attacks the launching crew had to repair the electrical installation and they went calmly about their task with bombs falling all around them.

The torpedo-carrying Heinkels swept in to attack, and Burr was shot off to intercept. He sent one down in flames, another swerved and crashed into the sea ; the remainder released their torpedoes too soon, with the result that not one of the ships was hit. Burr checked his petrol and radioed his ship. He had enough for about an hour's flying ; the nearest Russian airfield was 240 miles away. He decided to try to reach it. When he landed there were five gallons of petrol in his tanks—for about seven minutes flying.

Last spring, after two and a half years' service, the ships of the M.S.F.U. made their last voyage. The big steel runways were dismantled, the Hurricanes unloaded and the pilots and maintenance crews sent to other units. In their place came the "Woolworth" carriers (see illus. page 104, Vol. 7), miniature aircraft carriers whose pilots have since done good work with our convoys.

At Westkapelle the Royal Marines Went in at Dawn

Enemy batteries on Walcheren, at the mouth of the West Scheldt, had contrived to survive heavy bombardment when British Marine Commandos invaded the westernmost point of the island on November 1, 1944. Most gloriously achieved, but attended with grievous loss, our object was to clear the approach to the Belgian port of Antwerp. From L.C.T.s (bottom) Marines plunged inland through withering fire. Survivors swam ashore from craft that had capsized (top).

Triumphant Commandos Fought to Link up with—

Subduing enemy batteries in furious battles as they advanced, one body of British troops moved southwards to Flushing, whose liberation was completed two days after the landing at Westkapelle. Snipers concealed in the docks were picked off one by one by our men from behind scanty cover (1). Dutch Commandos took part in this attack; they are seen (2) marching along the waterfront. From the south of Flushing, Allied wounded were evacuated in amphibious Buffaloes (3).

—Comrades Who Meantime had Landed at Flushing

Manhandling their gun to a landing craft at Breskens, on the mainland south of the Scheldt, other British Commandos (4) prepared for the short crossing to the Flushing beach-head. Two hundred ships of all sizes took part in the bloody landings on Walcheren, directed by Admiral Sir Bertram Ramsay, Allied Naval C.-in-C., who is seen (5) talking to Marines who manned the landing craft (6). With the successful link-up of invading forces the mouth of the Scheldt was finally cleared.

Through the Bomb-Blasted Sea Wall of Walcheren

The great gap torn by the R.A.F. in the dike which had prevented the sea from submerging the island formed a perilous gateway for invasion. The bombers' work is being inspected (top, left to right) by Lieut. K. G. Wright, of Sussex, L/Cpl. H. Lindley, of Yorkshire, and an unidentified commando. Landing from an L.C.T., a flail tank (bottom) will beat the earth with its chains to detonate enemy mines as it splashes through the flood-water that now covers four-fifths of Walcheren.

*Photos, British Official
Associated Press*

VIEWS & REVIEWS
Of Vital War Books

by Hamilton Fyfe

I WONDER if other people find, as I do, that books about naval warfare seem so much less attractive than accounts of land fighting, or even fighting in the air—though there is little variety about these latter, all sky warfare being largely the same. What can the reason be ?

Partly it is, I think, because ships when they are engaged in battle are such a long way apart from one another. Effort has to be made by the reader to follow a writer's description of their complicated manoeuvres. So often nothing seems to happen. When vessels are firing at unseen targets miles away, it is hard for anyone who has not taken part in a naval engagement to visualize the ups and downs of the fight. Added to this is the unfortunate fact that naval authors, though they may be thoroughly well acquainted with their subject, are too often not very interesting writers.

I have just finished reading a book called Under Cunningham's Command (Allen and Unwin, 8s. 6d.). It is about the operations in the Mediterranean up to fifteen months ago. These operations were not only of the greatest importance to the cause of the United Nations ; they were of the most varied and often most exciting character. Yet Commander George Stitt's story of them reads like an official report to be laid only before persons whose business it is to learn what occurred. No doubt they would absorb this accurately from Commander Stitt's pages, but the interest of the occurrences for the general public has to be excavated with some pains.

He describes, of course, all the actions already famous—the Battle of Matapan, the attack on Taranto, the Battle of Crete, the supplying of Tobruk, and so on. There is nothing much new in these, except perhaps the light thrown on the dislike of Italian crews for fighting. When the Italian cruiser Pola was captured after putting up no resistance to speak of, one of the prisoners was asked why that was. He said, "Well, you see, we thought that if we opened fire on you, you would sink us." On the upper deck many of the seamen were half drunk ; the whole place was littered with bottles, clothing and rubbish.

A NOTHER episode showing the lax state of discipline in the Italian Navy was the action of a Yeoman of Signals in a vessel that was attacked suddenly without warning. "On seeing and hearing explosions all round him, he made the Sign of the Cross, invoked all the saints he knew, and jumped overboard." There were many stories similar to his. One of them concerned the admiral whose flagship it was. "He is believed to have jumped overboard without a lifebelt."

We do not often hear of submarines attacking one another. They don't often have the chance. And when they do they are more frequently than not prevented from taking advantage of it by the state of the sea. But not always. One day the officer of the watch in our submarine Parthian sighted through her periscope, which was all she had above water, a long, low object on the surface, about three or four miles away. It was coming towards them. It was an Italian submarine. There was a heavy swell and a choppy sea, so the commander of Parthian waited till the enemy came close. At 400 yards' range he fired four torpedoes and blew her up.

Just after she sank, his own vessel was shaken by a violent explosion. This had been caused, it was thought, by something deto-

nating in the wreck under water. Next day, offshore from Tobruk again, another long, low object was spotted through the periscope. Another enemy submarine ? Must be. Very carefully Parthian was manoeuvred back and forth until at last she was in an ideal position to fire. All was ready for the discharge. Then, with a gesture of disgust, the commander turned away from the periscope. What he had thought was an enemy submarine had revealed itself as a long, low building on a spit of sand.

A Diversity of Naval Occasions

The work the Royal Navy did during the disastrous attempts to occupy Greece and later to establish ourselves on Crete would have been immensely valuable if these operations had had any chance of success. As it was, that work mitigated the disasters. The soldiers knew the Fleet would do everything possible. When the brigadier in command at Kalamata, where evacuation was going on, decided that he had better surrender instead of letting his troops be annihilated, many of them made off down the coast, sure that the Navy would not let them down. It did not. At night destroyers patrolled all the time, picking up men who had left the shore in Greek caiques and taking others off lonely beaches where they waited "in blind faith that they would be rescued." Their faith was not misplaced.

H ISTORIANS will discuss in the future whether those Greek and Cretan forlorn hope adventures were justified. Those who defend them say with Commander Stitt that political and moral considerations must sometimes in war outweigh the purely military. I do not myself agree with that view. I hold that those are right who say we should have told the Greeks it was impossible to help them at

H.M.S. PARTHIAN, a British submarine which figured in one of the strangest exploits of the war when, off Tobruk, she attacked and sank an Italian submarine. The incident is fully described in a book dealing with naval operations in the Mediterranean and reviewed here. See also page 406, Vol. 4.

Photo, Wright & Logan

the moment. We should have concentrated on hitting the enemy where we could hurt him, not where he was in a position to hurt us.

Well that, I say, will be debated for a very long time to come. But here is an opinion that is new to me from an admiral, expressed in a speech he made to the ship's company of a battleship after our defeat in the Battle of Crete. He told them he believed this marked the certainty of Germany's final overthrow as nothing had marked it before. First, it had shown the Nazis they could not invade England with any hope of success unless they put into the air at least twenty times more aircraft than they used over Crete. Secondly, it had stopped their eastward advance in the Mediterranean and upset their programme, "which would have a most important effect on the whole course of the war." That is certainly a view which historians will have to take into account.

I F you want a lightly-written, cheerful and not too resolutely comic account of the training an Able Seaman goes through when he is taken from shop counter or clerks' desk or author's writing-table and put into the Navy, I can recommend Godfrey Winn's book, Home from Sea (Hutchinson, 10s. 6d.). Whether it is the war, of which he has seen a good deal as a reporter, or whether it is merely that he has grown older, the plain fact is that Mr. Winn has grown out of his rather miss-ish tricks of sentimentality which once made him a laughing stock and in his writing has become a man. There is still a Victorian lady novelist's touch about his style occasionally—a Ouida-esque flavour, shall we say ? As in such a passage as this, describing his sensations when he saw the lights of a small Icelandic port after being in the Arctic darkness for some time :

> For a moment I was too overwhelmed to call the attention of my companions to what in my quickened imagination had become the lights of Monte Carlo, that coronet upon the brow of a face, raddled, painted, mercifully hidden by the night and still surpassingly beautiful when appraised from someone's yacht anchored in the bay.

But he seldom relapses into that sort of hokum. His book is a straightforward narrative of his entering the Navy, his experiences while he was being taught what it was necessary for him to know (how to tie knots, for example, at which he wasn't very good), of friends he made, of the difference he found between the way he was treated by such people as hotel receptionists when he wore bluejacket's uniform and when he was a smart young man in expensive clothes.

N AVAL uniform he praises warmly. Material first class. "If one went to one's own tailor, he could not, I'm sure, produce better serge." He became accustomed to it quickly. The food, too, he found no fault with. The chief thing wanting was a regular bath. That was almost as hard to obtain on shore as it was on board. How little real comradeship there is between different ranks came out painfully when he applied for the use of a bathroom at a hotel. He had to stand aside while officers were attended to, and then he received a curt refusal. Not everywhere, though. The smaller ones were more kindly. "We always do what we can for anyone in uniform," was their motto.

Anyone interested in Service slang will find here many terms to add to the naval vocabulary. A "sprog" is a recruit, equivalent of "rookie" in the Army. "Tiddley" means looking all right. "Pussar" stands for genuine or "pukka." Ordinary seamen are O.D.s, chocolate is "nutty," in the "rattle" is the same as in clink. No doubt Mr. Winn will go on using many of these expressions for the rest of his life. He thought he had done with writing when he joined up, but he was invalided out and so began again. This book makes one glad to think he will go on.

Germany's V 2 Terror-Weapon Hits at England

A LONG-DISTANCE ROCKET-BOMB falling in southern England in November 1944, caused this damage (above) to property; houses were devastated beyond repair, but only three people were killed. The effects of a rocket that gouged a deep crater (below) in a suburban roadway; the blast radius was noticeably less than that of the flying bomb. *Photos, Associated Press, Keystone*

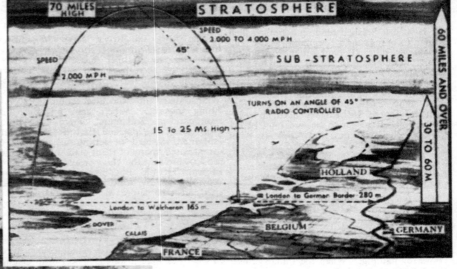

HOW IT WORKS. This trajectory chart shows how, after a vertical take-off to a height of 15-25 miles, the rocket, under radio control, is re-adjusted to an angle of 45 degrees till, outstripping sound, it reaches a maximum height of 70 miles. *By courtesy of The Daily Express*

"ANOTHER ATTEMPT BY THE ENEMY to attack the morale of our civil population in the vain hope that he may somehow stave off the defeat which faces him in the field." In these words, spoken in the House of Commons on November 10, 1944, the Prime Minister made the first official announcement that long-range rockets, Germany's secret V 2 weapon, had been falling on this country. Casualties and damage, he said, had so far not been heavy. Mr. Churchill had already warned Parliament of the possibility of such attacks as long ago as the previous February and again in July.

Reports from neutral sources confirmed British experts in their theories that the V 2 weighed some 15 tons, of which as much as 14 tons represented fuel for consumption during flight, the remaining ton being the content of the explosive warhead. An electrically worked turbine-mixer converted liquid oxygen and alcohol into a gas which, when it exceeded the weight of the rocket, shot the missile vertically into the air.

It is possible that the first V 2 attacks were made from bases on the Dutch coast, including Walcheren (cleared of the enemy by November 9). On three successive days in early September the Germans were seen launching their rockets in the direction of England from a small Walcheren village. Eye witnesses said that the Nazis had to do "some sort of stoking" for almost six hours before they could get the rockets to rise. According to neutral sources, the rockets at Walcheren and elsewhere were shot off from a concrete base the size of a tennis-court, or even from a roadway provided this could be served by the heavy transport required. The rockets were said to be about 45 ft. long, six ft. in diameter, with four fins at the rear on which they were perched for launching. The speed was estimated at between 2,000 and 3,000 m.p.h. Experts were of the opinion that rocket-landings could not be regulated to within many miles of the target. The range was thought to be between 200 and 250 miles. As to cost, they believed that each rocket represented as much in man-hours and materials as the construction of a German fighter-bomber.

Secrets of the New-Style Doodle-Bug Revealed

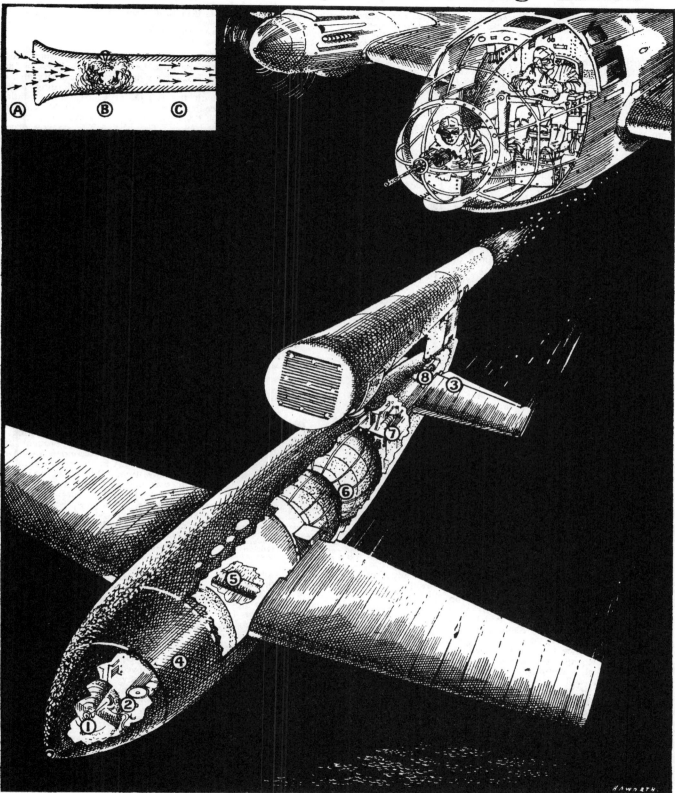

PLANE-LAUNCHED FLYING BOMBS used by the enemy in renewed attacks against this country were described by Mr. Duncan Sandys, Parliamentary Secretary to the Ministry of Supply and Chairman of the Flying Bomb Counter-Measures Committee, on October 31, 1944, as being *under* the launching planes (semi-obsolete Heinkel 111s), contrary to previous principles governing composite aircraft and as shown in page 405. They were probably released in the same way as torpedoes or rockets carried by R.A.F. Typhoons, though the risk to the air crews, as well as the take-off difficulties, were considerable. Carrier-planes were said to fly only a few feet above the sea, rarely venturing nearer than 50 miles to our coast.

In this sectional drawing, pilot and observer in the Perspex "nose" of the Heinkel are seen as the bomb is launched. Points of interest are (1) small propeller driven by the bomb's flight, and (2) the electric

revolution-counter. When the propeller has registered a set number of revolutions, the elevators (3) are automatically moved into "diving" position, thus urging the bomb to earth. Other bomb-parts are (4) warhead, containing 2,000 lb. of explosives; (5) tubular main span passing through the fuel tank, which has a capacity of 130 gallons; (6) wire-bound compressed-air bottles which inject petrol into the engine; (7) automatic pilot, which keeps the bomb on a set course; and (8) rudder- and elevator-operating mechanism.

The inset shows the working of the large impulse-duct engine. (A) Air stream through the grille to be compressed (B) simultaneously with the injection of petrol. The mixture is then fired by a spark, thus closing the valves. The white-hot gases are then emitted (C), propelling the bomb on its flight.

Specially drawn for THE WAR ILLUSTRATED *by Haworth*

British Women's Services are Busy Overseas

In the wake of our victorious armies, serving with the R.A.F., doing more than 30 different kinds of tasks with the Royal Navy, working as clerks, drivers, cooks, orderlies, military police-women: members of the W.R.N.S., the A.T.S. and the W.A.A.F. have an astonishing record of achievements, as told here by PEGGY SCOTT. See also facing page.

WITH the approach of the Japanese to Singapore in January 1942, W.R.N.S. (Women's Royal Naval Service) wireless telegraphists were taken aboard the last ship which got away, without attack by sea or air . . . When the Germans reached Alamein in June 1942, the Wrens were evacuated from Alexandria. How did these young girls take the close proximity of the enemy? Miss Jessie Frith, for 2½ years Superintendent W.R.N.S. Mediterranean, said of the evacuation from Alexandria:

"It never occurred to anyone to be afraid. They all had confidence in the Navy. They just waited to see what they had to do. Their one fear in life was that they might be sent home! There was never a grumble at the discomfort of living in tents in the desert, with sand getting into everything. The girls were very keen and full of the spirit of adventure. As soon as Italy fell I was inundated with offers from Wrens who wanted to serve there. I never had a case of home sickness. The majority of Wrens serving in the Levant area volunteered for further service. They did some very interesting work. They were attached to Admiral Ramsay's planning staff when he was in Cairo, and had a great deal to do with the routeing of convoys in the Mediterranean. They were also responsible for the mail for the Fleet."

Superintendent Frith had the care of Wrens in the whole of the Levant; Alexandria, Cairo, Suez, Ismailia, Port Said, Haifa, Beirut, and later of those in Malta, Naples, Algiers and Gibraltar. When a girl was seriously ill she flew to her so that her parents could be kept advised as to her progress. When a Wren wanted to get married, Superintendent Frith interviewed the prospective bridegroom and wrote to his commanding officer—and she did this an enormous number of times. When leave was due to a Wren her plans had to be approved by the superintendent. The Wrens have plenty to do when their work is finished, swimming, dancing and attending lectures. Some of them are very keen on music and often hear the famous Palestine Orchestra. There are also excellent Service clubs.

WRENS are serving in Italy. Officers who had been working on the Mediterranean coast of Africa and whose work had helped with the Allied invasion of Sicily and Italy first went with the Navy to an Italian port. Wrens are in France too. They sailed on D-plus 69 Day, not expecting easy times. Each Wren had a camp-bed and bedding in a valise, as well as a folding chair, a canvas bucket, washbag and stand. They have quarters, however, in a building that was used by the Germans to house Todt workers.

The most envied, perhaps, of all the Wrens are those at sea. They work on board troop-ships, dealing with communications. There are two cypher officers and three coders to each ship, and they form part of the ship's company. They are allowed four trips, then they have to return to their shore stations to give way to other Wren volunteers. The signals office is close to the bridge. Ratings collect the signals from the Wireless Operator's cabin to be either decoded or decyphered, after which the Wren Officer takes them to the captain on the bridge. The Wrens are aware of the location of U-boats and enemy shipping, or of unidentified aircraft, through these signals, but they also know of the watch over their ship that is being kept by the Naval Operations

staff ashore and they are not afraid. The same spirit is shown by all the Wrens serving Overseas in more than thirty jobs with the Navy, whether in France or Italy, in North, South, or East Africa, in Gibraltar, Malta, India, Ceylon, or in the U.S.A.

When A.T.S. Arrived in Normandy

The A.T.S. (Auxiliary Territorial Service) has been very near the enemy. Twenty-four girls were bilingual switchboard operators in Paris from March 17, 1940, until the fall of France the following June. They stayed at their posts until zero hour, 1.30 p.m. on June 13. Then a message was sent through to London that the Exchange would be closing down—the nearness of the enemy made further service impossible. At 7 p.m. Paris was surrounded by the Germans.

When the A.T.S. arrived at the Normandy

Miss JESSIE FRITH, for 2½ years Superintendent W.R.N.S., Mediterranean, typical of Britain's "front-line" women overseas, examples of whose courage and devotion to duty are given in this page. *Photo, Fayer*

beach-head in 1944 they had expected to "rough it," but the soldiers prepared what they called a "luxury camp" for the girls. Two large marquees had been put up as sleeping quarters. Drinking water was laid on, and electric light. The clerks among the A.T.S. had come by special request of their branches. The A.T.S. moved forward with the Army and most of the girls are now in Brussels. They live in a block of flats which the Gestapo headquarters staff evacuated in a hurry and on the walls of the cellars are scratched names of Belgian prisoners.

THE A.T.S. work as clerks, drivers, cooks' orderlies and military policewomen. For recreation they have N.A.A.F.I., which has come to Brussels. They can hardly deal with the invitations that are showered upon them by the Belgian people—700 in the first three weeks. The girls go everywhere in pairs. They have their own All-Army concert parties, which include A.T.S. artistes. The reception given to the first three "A.T.S. Stars in Battledress" who were allowed to go over and entertain men in the front line was tremendous. Hundreds of A.T.S. are with the British Liberation Army in France and Belgium, and hundreds more are going to the Continent.

A.T.S. have been working in the Middle East for 3 years. Some of their individual jobs are interesting. Junior Commander

R. M. Cotton-Kennedy is Messing Officer for the huge Leave Camp in Palestine, and A.T.S. drivers meet the battle-weary men on arrival. Subaltern Dorothy Harding worked with the R.T.O. at Cairo railway station, centre of military traffic in the Middle East. A.T.S. drivers take convoys of lorries to Palestine. The first A.T.S. convoy drivers to go from Cairo to Palestine had to spend a night in the Sinai Desert.

A.T.S. went to Washington with the British Army in 1941 to help prepare for the Second Front. Sergeant Elsie Chapman and Corporal Louise Allingham, Signallers, were among the first to go. "We were the first British women to appear in uniform in Washington," said Sergeant Elsie Chapman, "and people used to come round us in the street and ask questions. The W.A.C. girls were very good to us and asked us to their homes." Sergeant Chapman was 22 months in Washington.

First W.A.A.F. to Reach Italy

When the first W.A.A.F. (Women's Auxiliary Air Force) Air Ambulance Orderlies arrived in Normandy to bring back the wounded, people were surprised that the R.A.F. had let women go so near to the front. They were not aware that all through the war W.A.A.F. had been going overseas with their units. They went to Canada and the United States, to the West Indies and Bermuda, to Ceylon, Gibraltar, and to the Middle East.

Twelve photographic interpretation officers who were in North Africa interpreting the pictures of Sicily and Italy brought back by the Photographic Reconnaissance Unit, were the first W.A.A.F. to move on with their unit to Italy itself. When they arrived the fighting was only forty miles away. Yet they were glad to be where there was a "nice smell of grass, fresh green fields and cool rain" after the hot sand of North Africa. These twelve W.A.A.F. officers already knew Italy, and the details of bomb damage by Allied aircraft, from examining photographs.

SINCE Air Ambulance Orderlies started to fly to Normandy in the week after the Allied landings they have taken their share of the regular trips to fetch the wounded from France. In the ambulance pool are 150 W.A.A.F., but 800 girls trained for the work are eager to have a share in it. The girl in the blue battledress and a red-cross armlet may be in sole charge of the 24 stretcher cases for which the plane is fitted. The airwomen who have moved forward with their units from Normandy to Belgium have lived sometimes under canvas, sometimes in the local Curé's home, or in an evacuated girls' school. Now they are in luxury flats in Brussels. The sergeant, however, insists on the girls sleeping on their camp beds in case they should become "soft."

The French and Belgian people cannot do enough for "the demoiselles of the R.A.F." They are constantly asking them to their homes and sharing the best they have with them. They admire the Service girls because they are "so feminine"—perhaps they have heard of the hairdresser who accompanied one contingent! Four hairdressers have also gone with five hundred airwomen who have recently sailed for India. Among them are clerks and plotters, wireless, teleprinter and R/T operators, nursing orderlies and equipment assistants. Some will be stationed at a landing ground or flying-boat station, and others at headquarters units in Bombay, Delhi, Kandy or Colombo.

These War-Workers in Uniform See the World

ON AND OFF DUTY, W.R.N.S., A.T.S., and W.A.A.F. have managed to see a good deal of the war zones. Stationed in Syria, these Wrens (1) are hiking in the mountains above Beirut, while W.A.A.F. maintenance-drivers (2) study their new home-base on a map of Paris. Dispatch-riders of the A.T.S., operating between Paris and the fighting-zones, "gas-up" (3). The first A.T.S., nearly 200 all-told, to arrive at the station at Nairobi, Kenya, were welcomed by the King's African Rifles band (4).

Photos, British Official; British Newspaper Pool, Fox

'Aussies' at Home in Netherlands New Guinea

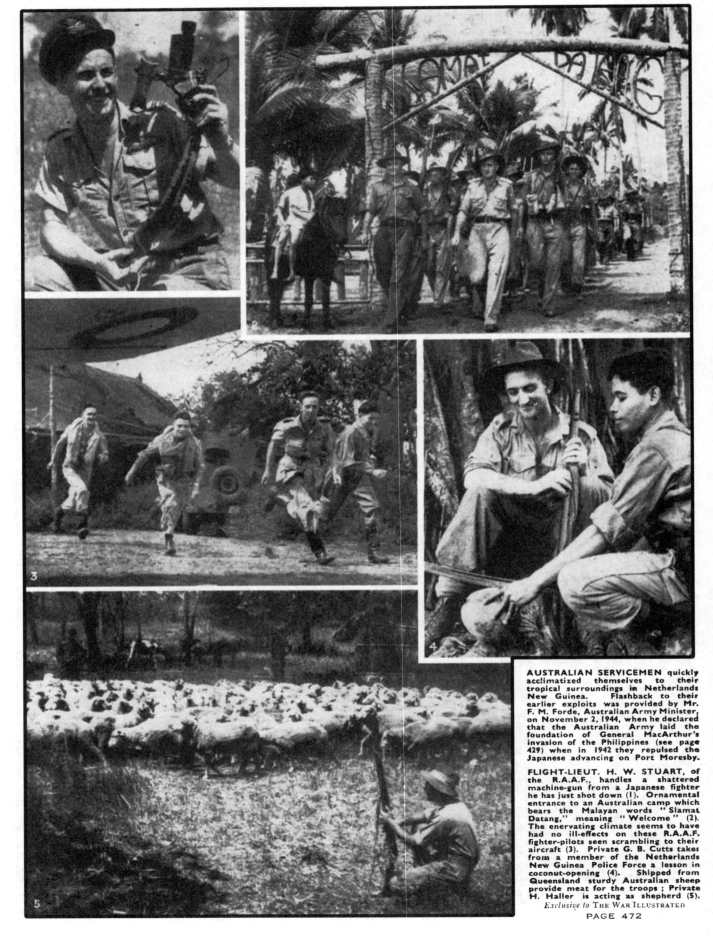

AUSTRALIAN SERVICEMEN quickly acclimatized themselves to their tropical surroundings in Netherlands New Guinea. Flashback to their earlier exploits was provided by Mr. F. M. Forde, Australian Army Minister, on November 2, 1944, when he declared that the Australian Army laid the foundation of General MacArthur's invasion of the Philippines (see page 429) when in 1942 they repulsed the Japanese advancing on Port Moresby.

FLIGHT-LIEUT. H. W. STUART, of the R.A.A.F., handles a shattered machine-gun from a Japanese fighter he has just shot down (1). Ornamental entrance to an Australian camp which bears the Malayan words "Slamat Datang," meaning "Welcome" (2). The enervating climate seems to have had no ill-effects on these R.A.A.F. fighter-pilots seen scrambling to their aircraft (3). Private G. B. Cutts takes from a member of the Netherlands New Guinea Police Force a lesson in coconut-opening (4). Shipped from Queensland sturdy Australian sheep provide meat for the troops ; Private H. Haller is acting as shepherd (5).

Exclusive to THE WAR ILLUSTRATED

I WAS THERE!

Between Battles in the Land of Awful Silence

The Forgotten Army is an unofficial title which has become attached to our 14th Army now fighting the Japanese. Here, in extracts from letters home by a young London officer (published by arrangement with The Star), is a vivid picture of grim conditions our men encounter in the Burma jungles.

TIDDIM ROAD FRONTIER STONE, where India meets Burma, marked yet another mile in the victory-journey of this soldier of the 5th Indian Division in the autumn of 1944. See story in this page. *Photo, Indian Official*

ON the way to Tamu there were abandoned guns and old positions along the roadside, and recaptured machinery with Jap lettering painted over the British and American makers' names. In Tamu itself I went into some of the temples and pagodas, and there were brass and marble Buddhas, gilded, still sitting four and five feet high on their thrones, some incredibly ornate with gilding and coloured mirror inlay.

In one of them, three of the six Buddhas had lost their heads, which lay on the filthy floor beside Jap steel helmets, equipment and clothing. At the end, there was a mangled pile of bones, relics of the act of hara-kiri. They were bare and white, eaten by vultures and rats and disinfected by fire. It looked as though the fellow had pressed a grenade to his stomach from the way the bones were broken. (See illus. page 343.)

The country around Imphal is some of the loveliest I've seen in India, especially when the paddy fields are flooded. You get glorious sunsets, and the mountains take on the most lovely colours. When it rains, it rains like hell, and nothing is dry. But when it is fine, it is invigorating.

At Tiddim you meet a most implacable type of jungle. It takes ages to cut your way through it and troops, when they have to make a detour, are doing well if they cover

Men who have been here some time seem to be used to it, and when I remarked on it they said they hadn't noticed it. But it has affected them. They feel it in lack of friendship and a palling of constant companionship. They admit to a shyness and a fear of meeting a woman again. They say they would not know how to talk to her.

The Japs are fighting a tenacious rearguard action along the road. When they dig in it takes quite a bit to move them, and there is little room to manoeuvre on a road which runs like a thin ribbon through unlimited hills. When they clear out they often leave quite a bit of equipment lying about, but very few prisoners. If they cannot get their dead away they leave them, and if they have been dead for very long, they stink to high heaven.

In one place a landslide had carried away two sections of the road up which our transport must pass to get forward. When the move took place after the capture of the position it was impossible to get even a jeep through, but within an hour or two a diversion had been cleared, and heavy transport was passing up the road, being winched up a hillside at an angle of more than 45 degrees to pick up the road five or six hundred feet higher up.

The feats of sheer endurance and determination to get through and carry out the

job in hand are really amazing. I am afraid that people at home will never fully understand what it means to fight on this front. Though it may lack the catastrophic nature of European battlefields, the job is just as hard in many ways. There are absolutely no amenities, and there is weather and climate of an extremely changeable character to be borne the whole time.

You can never compare it with other war fronts as far as the number of men employed, the enemy casualties, prisoners, and distances covered are concerned. What the men do need, however, is some more concrete assurances than they have so far had that people at home realize what they are doing. Their morale is fine, but they still feel that they are forgotten by people at home. If you saw the conditions under which they have to live their daily lives, you would agree that they deserve more recognition than they have had.

We have reached Manipur River; 40 miles from Tiddim, the township from which this road takes its name. It took us about three hours to cover under thirty miles, and even then we had to leave the jeep about six miles short of our destination as the road was blocked. Last night the conditions were even worse. At one point on the road we

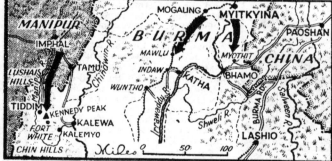

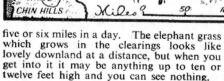

STRIPPED to the waist for the cookhouse parade, this crew (below) of a British 25-pounder reflected the courage of our troops whose lonely life is described here. The advance of the 5th Indian Division along the Tiddim-Fort White-Kalemyo Road in November 1944 rolled up a vital front of more than 60 miles (map left). The capture of Kalemyo, Japanese strongpoint, was announced on November 16.

Photo, British Official. Map, The Daily Herald

five or six miles in a day. The elephant grass which grows in the clearings looks like lovely downland at a distance, but when you get into it it may be anything up to ten or twelve feet high and you can see nothing.

The road itself is shocking to drive over, and even in a jeep you are flying through the air from pothole to pothole most of the time. When it rains everything is turned to mud, and you slither as you try to walk. The most remarkable thing is the feeling of absolute loneliness and isolation.

There are scarcely any villages in this part, and as night falls—there's no lighting except a torch after dark—you feel as though you are being enveloped in a shroud of nothingness. The awful silence may be broken by a flash in the valley below, and a few seconds later you hear the bark of some of our guns. The crickets rattle in a most irritating way, and a jeep may grind its gears rounding a steep corner.

The loneliness is not the bewitching loneliness of an evening at home, miles from the nearest road; it is something much more austere and penetrating. It is the loneliness of country which has never known the habitation of man. It is as though the hills resented the intrusion of the newcomer, with his explosive machinery and weapons.

got through 20 minutes before three landslides completely blocked it. As we passed the spots the stones and earth were already shifting.

The road, which is cut for most of its way out of the hillside, with a drop of anything up to fifteen hundred or two thousand feet on one side, is nothing more than a mud track until the engineers can resurface it. When there is a landslide bulldozers just cut away a bit more of the hill to make a passable track for jeeps.

It is all right when it is dry, but the moment you get rain driving becomes a nightmare, and there is no wall between you and the valley bottom. It had been raining fairly steadily all day yesterday, and so the road was at its worst. By the time we were ready to start back it was getting dusk. After the first few miles it was completely dark, and headlights are of little use on hairpin bends.

Added to this was a new and sudden fall of rain, and the jeep was firing on only two cylinders. We had to struggle the whole way up in bottom gear. The jeep was skidding the whole time like a drunken duchess, and at more than one place she went over in ruts to an angle of about 45 degrees. I was damn glad to get back to our headquarters, and after a double rum in coffee, and some food, slipped out of my soaking clothes into bed and read until I dropped off to sleep.

General Slept While We Took 2,000 of His Men

The last act of the long-drawn out battle for Antwerp ended in farce. The background of it was the canals, the narrow cobbled streets and prim houses of Middelburg in Walcheren Island (see pages 463-466). This dispatch by Alexander Clifford of The Daily Mail was dated Nov. 7, 1944.

THE curtain went up yesterday evening, but even this afternoon the scene was still touched with the Alice in Wonderland atmosphere of a situation for which no one has ever invented any rules. By yesterday afternoon most of the remaining Germans in Walcheren had been washed up like so much flotsam and jetsam into Middelburg. There was no more dry land for them to fight on. A British column was coming in from the Flushing direction and another was threatening to cross the great canal from the west.

Lieut.-General Daser, Commander of the 70th, or Stomach Trouble, Division, decided that he could do no more to keep our ships out of Antwerp. From his narrow little white-panelled room in the Wilhelmina Palace he gave orders to cease fire. Somehow he communicated the fact to the British column coming from Flushing.

But the other column from the west appeared first to clean the situation up. They paddled across the canal in assault boats. Then the comedy began. It was 300 British against 2,000 Germans. It was getting dark and our men did not even know their way around. In a dazed sort of way they began to persuade the Germans to deposit their arms in the fire station.

Night Vigil in the Square

General Daser retired to bed with a raging headache and a bag of aspirin. He said he could not formally surrender till daybreak, and he could not deal with anyone below the rank of brigadier. He pulled his yellow satin eiderdown over him on his blue velvet couch, and they locked him in and spared one man to guard him.

As darkness fell the 300 British began to try to herd the 2,000 Germans into the main square. They scoured the byways and corralled the prisoners as you might corral cattle. When they had filled the square they posted themselves across all the roads leading into it and prayed that no one would start any trouble.

The Germans were not happy sitting in the cold, damp square all night, but it was the only way to deal with them. They had no intention at all of making trouble.

By the morning General Daser had eaten his way half-through the bag of aspirin, but he had not touched the 11 bottles of champagne at the head of his bed. He gave them to the British officer who came to call him. I tried a bottle this afternoon—Veuve Clicquot of an excellent year. By morning the fire station was like a cross between a salvage dump and a war museum. There was a vast mound of German steel helmets that looked like a mammoth caviare.

There was an extraordinary quantity of hand grenades. Quite inexplicably, there were at least 2,000 green tin lampshades. Still the British were enormously outnumbered and they decided to make the Germans help themselves. So you got the 24 rowers, 12 sanitary inspectors, and nine bakers.

ANGRY WITH THE PHOTOGRAPHER, General Daser, German Commander at Middelburg, captured on November 6, 1944, turned his back as he was being escorted to captivity in a British assault-craft, as told in this page. *Photo, British Newspapers Pool*

The rowers were volunteers. But when they found that their job was to paddle boatloads of prisoners across 50 yards of canal the sculling champions and professional oarsmen among them withdrew their offer in disgust. Eventually the prisoners had to haul their boats across by ropes stretched from bank to bank.

The sanitary inspectors were a job lot left over when all the other prisoners had been sorted. Their task was to deal with the electricity and water situation, and they were anxious to be helpful. But it turned out there was nothing for them to do—too much water and no electricity—and they were put back with the others.

The bakers were set to work to produce rations for all the others. This Stomach Trouble Division is on special diet, and its bread is a little whiter than that of the rest of the Army.

I saw General Daser across the canal after lunch. He was a burly figure in a blue-grey leather overcoat, and he turned his back angrily when some photographers pointed their cameras at him. But the boatman spun the boat round so that he was facing the cameras again, and the comedy was repeated. The waiting Germans began to smile. The general sat down stiffly in the stern and went across with his hands on his hips and a scowl on his face.

That End-of-a-Campaign Feeling

By this afternoon the Dutch had hung out their flags and put on all their Christmas gala finery and were parading the streets seeing the sights. They viewed the German equipment dump, and then they examined the British troops' clothes and arms and the amphibious landing-craft. Then they went down to the canal to see the vast queue of German prisoners waiting to cross.

In the crowd of civilians I met a gay little Italian sailor with a rosette in his buttonhole saying "Welcome." He fitted admirably into the crazy scene. He said he had been captured in Toulon last year and made to work for the Germans. Ten days ago he had hidden himself, to avoid being transported to Germany. Now he couldn't get the British to take him seriously. He insinuated that his Ambassador in London would take a grave view of it if he were not properly treated !

Middelburg was cheerful and fantastic today, and you got that end-of-a-campaign feeling—the knowledge that no more guns would be fired and no one else killed here. Middelburg has hardly suffered from this final attack. But its centre is still a weed-grown wilderness as a result of the German Stukas in 1940.

For miles along the road home I passed squads of Germans on the march. It was a day of winter sunshine, with great mounds of white clouds standing around the horizon and a terrific wind. It swept across the marshes, blowing the rushes flat and whipping the floods into waves. The screaming seabirds could barely fly against it. And the Germans marched east, bowed against the wind, and muffled against the cold, through the desolate land they had failed to defend.

The Havoc and Destruction I Saw in Italy

There have been many stories about the conditions under which the Army has to fight its battles. Squadron-Leader Derek Adkins, R.A.F., here describes for "The War Illustrated" the havoc of war on hotly-contested sectors of the 8th Army front in Italy as he saw it.

WHENEVER I visited front-line troops of the 8th Army there was always ample proof of the way in which our light bombers, fighters and fighter-bombers had blasted the enemy from positions in the path of our advancing infantry and armour. Craters and burnt-out wrecks along the roads told of ill-fated attempts made by the Germans to bring up badly needed supplies, while derelict tanks and abandoned 88-mm. guns were evidence of the enemy's failure to withstand the continuous air onslaught that had been maintained against his lines of communication.

I remember one particular occasion when the Army had asked us to attack a road junction just south of Vasto, where the coastal road meets the lateral one running up from the Apennines. Fighter-bombers went out and bombed and strafed the position, and when I motored by the spot a few days later there were craters everywhere. It was some of the best bombing I've seen, and whatever had been holding up our columns must have been either wiped out or quickly withdrawn.

Although most of the villages in the hills escaped destruction from the air, the Germans did turn many of them into strongpoints.

But wherever there were troop concentrations, or concealed gun positions or machine-gun nests, our pilots sought them out and bombed and strafed each one in turn. Isernia was a case in point. It is only a small town in the central Apennines, but after our air attacks there was hardly a building which hadn't been razed to the ground.

At Foggia, too, there were all the familiar signs of accurate bombing. The marshalling yards, for example, were a scrap-heap of twisted metal, with engines up-ended, their boilers burst open by the force of high explosives. Burnt-out railway trucks were still there, loaded with charred remains of German aircraft and engines and other war material. Coaches lay on their side, or were grotesquely balanced half up in the air, with splintered glass windows or no windows at all, their doors and sides smashed by blast.

The most fantastic sight of all I saw was just after the Germans had been finally cleared out of Ortona, a small coastal port on the Adriatic about twenty-five miles south of Pescara. I was living at Vasto at the time, in a villa that had belonged to an Italian painter. It had a superb view right across a sweeping lagoon of the Adriatic, and from the windows of my room I could see all the tiny fishing smacks like wooden toys on a set piece, and down by the beach, 300 feet below, the wide white sweep of the waves as they rippled in.

The weather had been pretty changeable. One day there was a clear sky and wisps of cloud, and the next teeming rain that turned all roads and tracks into quagmires. But one morning the sun must have been shining somewhere, for the complete arc of a rainbow suddenly appeared in the sky like a huge halo over the Apennines. I set off in a jeep with my driver, "Blondie" Wilkinson. Apart from the specific job of work I had to do, I wanted to see what was left of Ortona after the fighting that preceded its capture.

As we entered by the coast road, sappers

WINKLING OUT SNIPERS in shell-shattered Ortona, Italy, which fell to the 8th Army after heavy fighting in December 1943, this Canadian infantryman is "all eyes." Devastation left by the Nazis is vividly described in the accompanying story. *Photo, British Official*

were still picking out mines and clearing a way through, down to the remains of the harbour. From the car I could clearly see the massive curved mole systematically breached along its entire length, with the hulks and twisted debris of a few ships just visible above the surging water.

In the main street leading to the Town Hall

square a bulldozer was carving a passage through piles of rubble from houses blown up to hinder the advance of our tanks. Whichever way I looked the gaunt outline of wrecked and shattered buildings stood bleak and gaping, their sides torn by shellfire and explosions. In one of them a fire was raging on the ground floor. The flames licked upwards and across the narrow street, while the sharp crackle of burning timber mingled with the noise of distant guns and nearby mortars. In some the bare remains of splintered furniture hung in mid-air from twisted girders, the floors drooping pathetically into space. In others the devastation had been more complete.

A Canadian sergeant took me from house to house and showed me how each storey, how each room, had had to be fought for. As soon as one house had been taken a hole was blown into the adjoining one so that the Germans could be methodically cleared out from top to bottom. As we climbed the stairs of a block of flats grim evidence of the recent struggle for this tiny coastal town littered each side. Dead Germans from the picked Paratroop Division lay like wax models prone and stiff, testimony to the stubborn resistance the Canadians had to overcome before the battle was won.

As we stumbled over the heaps of rubble and brick and mortar, threading our way carefully to avoid the mines and booby traps still sown under the white dust and debris, four Spitfires of the Desert Air Force wheeled in the sky overhead. I left Ortona that day with the conviction that nothing more than the reconstruction of a new city was possible from the shambles and carnage the Germans left behind there. But the havoc and destruction I saw in Italy can be nothing compared with the absolute holocaust now taking place in Germany today. And I suppose that will provide many people with some sense of satisfaction, if only as being a measure of retribution.

OUR DIARY OF THE WAR

NOVEMBER 8, Wednesday 1,894th day
Western Front.—U.S. 3rd Army launched attack from south of Metz to east of Nancy.
Air.—Synthetic oil plants at Homberg and Merseburg attacked by R.A.F. and U.S. bombers.
Mediterranean.—Italian-based Allied bombers struck at German troop concentrations and communications in the Balkans.
General.—Germans announced that long-range rocket bomb (V2) had been in action against London.

NOVEMBER 9, Thursday 1,895th day
Western Front.—Resistance of German rearguard at Moerdijk broken by Polish troops. All resistance ceased in Walcheren.
Air.—Allied bombers attacked targets in Metz area and marshalling yards at Saarbrucken.
Burma.—Fort White, south of Tiddim, captured by 14th Army troops.
General.—Germans stated building of U-boats had been stopped to increase production of tanks and guns.

NOVEMBER 10, Friday 1,896th day
Western Front.—Chateau-Salins, N.E. of Nancy, captured by 3rd Army.
Air.—Airfields, industrial plants and communications in Cologne and Frankfurt areas attacked by U.S. aircraft. Mosquitoes bombed Hanover.
Italy.—8th Army troops captured Forli, on Via Emilia.
Home Front.—Mr. Churchill stated that long-range rocket bomb (V2) was in operation against this country.
General.—Mr. Churchill and Mr. Eden arrived in Paris for Armistice Day celebrations.

NOVEMBER 11, Saturday 1,897th day
Air.—Oil plants in the Ruhr attacked by Allied bombers. Harburg-Hamburg and Dortmund bombed at night.
Baltic.—Germans declared East Baltic a war zone in which all ships were liable to be sunk at sight.
Sea.—Announced that H.M. submarines had sunk 45 ships in Far Eastern waters.
Far East.—Super-Fortresses bombed Omura aircraft works in Kyushu, and docks at Nanking and Shanghai.
General.—France invited to be member

of European Advisory Commission, with Britain, U.S.A. and Soviet Union.

NOVEMBER 12, Sunday 1,898th day
Air.—Battleship Tirpitz sunk by R.A.F. Lancasters in Tromso fjord.
Sea.—British naval forces attacking enemy convoy off Norway sank 9 out of 11 ships.
Mediterranean.—Italian-based Allied bombers made third attack in week against Brenner Pass railway route.
China.—Loss of Kweilin, capital of Kwangsi, admitted by Chinese.

NOVEMBER 13, Monday 1,899th day
Western Front.—Verny, fortress near Metz, evacuated by Germans. U.S. 3rd Army captured fort at Thionville.
China.—Announced that U.S. air base at Liuchow, the last in East China, had been evacuated.
General.—Mr. Churchill reviewed French 1st Army on the Jura front.

NOVEMBER 14, Tuesday 1,900th day
Western Front.—2nd Army launched new attack against German pocket west of the Maas.

★ ═════ *Flash-backs* ═════ ★

1939
November 8. *Bomb explosion in Munich beer-cellar shortly after Hitler's departure.*
November 13. *First bombs fell on British soil, in the Shetlands.*

1940
November 11-12. *Fleet Air Arm attacked Italian navy at Taranto.*
November 14-15. *Heavy air raid on Coventry from dusk to dawn.*

1941
November 14. *H.M.S. Ark Royal sank after torpedo attack*

November 18. *8th Army, under General Cunningham, launched offensive in Libya.*

1942
November 8. *Allied forces landed in French North Africa.*
November 13. *8th Army captured Tobruk, Sollum and Bardia.*
November 19. *Russian offensive around Stalingrad began.*

1943
November 20. *U.S. troops landed on Makin and Tarawa in the Gilbert Islands, Central Pacific.*

Pacific.—Announced that Japanese had regained small island in the Palau group.
Balkans.—Allied commando raid on island of Melos.
General.—Announced that Norwegian military mission was attached to Russian command on Arctic front.

NOVEMBER 15, Wednesday 1,901st day
Western Front.—French 1st Army launched attack on Jura front. U.S. 3rd Army took two more Metz forts.
Air.—R.A.F. Lancasters bombed oil plant at Dortmund in the Ruhr.
Balkans.—Yugoslav and Bulgarian troops occupied Skoplje, Yugoslavia.
Germany.—New decree valid from October 1 called for "Nazi activity" by members of the Wehrmacht.
Pacific.—New U.S landing, supported by Royal Navy, in Mapia Islands, between Philippines and New Guinea.
Sea.—Announced that H.M. submarines had sunk 24 more ships in Far East.

NOVEMBER 16, Thursday 1,902nd day
Western Front.—U.S. 1st Army attacked east of Aachen, and 9th Army came into action N.E. of Aachen.

Air.—Allied heavy bombers struck at Dueren, Julich, Heinsberg and Eschweiler, ahead of ground troops on Aachen front.
Burma.—Kalemyo, on Chindwin front, captured by East African troops.

NOVEMBER 17, Friday 1,903rd day
Western Front.—Gressenich, 10 miles east of Aachen, captured by 1st Army.
General.—Air Chief Marshal Sir Trafford Leigh-Mallory missing on flight to take up command in S.E. Asia.

NOVEMBER 18, Saturday 1,904th day
Western Front.—2nd Army launched new attack against Geilenkirchen, north of Aachen. U.S. 3rd Army patrols entered Metz.
Pacific.—Allied aircraft destroyed at least 110 Japanese planes in raids on Manila harbour area.

NOVEMBER 19, Sunday 1,905th day
Western Front.—Geilenkirchen captured by British and U.S. troops.
Mediterranean.—Allied bombers from Italy hit oil targets at Vienna and Linz.
Balkans.—Tirana, capital of Albania, liberated by Albanian patriots.
Pacific.—Escorted heavy bombers attacked Japanese naval base at Brunei Bay, North Borneo.

NOVEMBER 20, Monday 1,906th day
Western Front.—Armour of 1st French Army drove through Belfort Gap and reached the Upper Rhine.
Air.—R.A.F. and U.S. bombers attacked oil plants at Gelsenkirchen and railway yards at Munster.
Pacific.—Allied ground forces completed occupation of Mapia Islands.

NOVEMBER 21, Tuesday 1,907th day
Air.—V2 site in Holland bombed by R.A.F. fighter-bombers. German oil plants at Hamburg, Merseburg and Homberg attacked by Allied heavy bombers and fighters. At night R.A.F. bombed oil plants at Sterkrade and Castrop Rauxel and railway centre of Aschaffenburg, S.E. of Frankfort.
Russian Front.—Soviet troops launched final attack on Germans in Oesel Island, off Estonia.
Far East.—Super-Fortresses attacked Omura aircraft works on Kyushu, and dock installations at Nanking and Shanghai.

THE WAR IN THE AIR

by Capt. Norman Macmillan, M.C., A.F.C.

THE Allied armies in the west opened a, full-scale offensive along the front from Holland to Switzerland in the morning of November 16, 1944. The attack was preceded, accompanied and followed by air action on an unprecedented scale, with British and American bombers co-operating wherever the High Command required.

The U.S. 1st Army attacked first, east of Aachen. Its blow was succeeded by those of the U.S. 9th Army farther north and of the British 2nd Army in Holland. The U.S. 3rd and 7th Armies and the French 1st Army were in action to the south and east. It remains to be seen if winter offensives in Western Europe by modern armies can be more effective than were those of the last war ; if so, it is probable that air power will be largely responsible for the difference. The main pressure of the opening blows was

5,000 aircraft, from which forces less than one-third of one per cent were lost.

It has now been revealed that the battleship Prince of Wales was in Cammell Laird's shipyard in Birkenhead during an attack on the port by German bombers in August 1940. Six H.E bombs fell in the yard, one exploding between the quayside and the battleship. The ship began to list, for blast had burst hull plates and the port tanks were quickly filling. Divers and firemen saved her after nearly three days' work. The following year, as the flagship of Admiral Sir Tom Phillips, the Prince of Wales was sunk by Japanese aircraft off Malaya.

WHEN They Rolled Missiles Down a Precipice at the Tirpitz

In the night of April 27, 1942, Halifax and Lancaster bombers, the former led by Wing Commander D. C. T. Bennett (the

November 12, 1944. Wing Commander J. B. Tait, D.S.O., D.F.C., and Squadron Leader A. G. Williams led the force of 29 Lancaster bombers, each aircraft carrying one 12,000-lb. A.P. bomb. Three more Lancasters accompanied the force for photographic duties. The crew of the 45,000-ton battleship saw the aircraft approaching in clear weather, and opened fire at ten miles range with 15-in. guns. As the aircraft closed in at about 13,000 feet flak also came up from other ships. But one of the first four bombs scored a direct hit amidships on the Tirpitz and all the battleship's guns stopped firing. More direct hits were made and the ship was seen to be burning. The bomber crews were in the air for 13 hours.

One of the photographic Lancasters was piloted by Flight-Lieut. B. A. Buckham, of New South Wales (who was awarded the D.F.C. on the same day for having made a solo attack on Berlin when his bomber was 35 minutes late and he went on alone across the defences). Buckham saw four or five direct hits on the Tirpitz. He had set course for home, after taking 700 feet of film, thinking the ship would not sink, when his rear gunner came up and said, "I think she is heeling over !" Buckham swung round and saw the ship listing at 70 or 80 degrees, with her red-painted keel glistening in the sunshine. So he went round again and got "a grand picture" from 5,000 feet. When the photographic reconnaissance aircraft went out later the Tirpitz had turned turtle. (See illus. in opposite page.)

THE Chief of Bomber Command Sent a Significant Message

The designer of the 12,000-lb. bomb is Mr. B. M. Wallis, of Vickers-Armstrong. He also designed the special mines which breached the Mohne and Eder dams, and was the originator of the geodetic structure used in the Wellesley and Wellington bombers.

In the first attack with 12,000-lb. bombs from Archangel, the Tirpitz was saved by prompt use of a smoke screen, although one bomb hit her. In the second 12,000-lb. bomb attack, after she was moved to Tromsö, the ship was obscured by cloud. After the third attack which sank her, Air Chief Marshal Sir Arthur Harris sent a message to Air Vice-Marshal R. H. Cochrane, commanding the Group from which the Lancasters came, containing this significant phrase : " . . . these operations put precisely that end to this ship which was inevitable as soon as the squadrons got a clear bead on her." Which indicates clearly enough what the Chief of Bomber Command thinks about 12,000-lb. bombs versus battleships.

LAUNCHED BY ROCKET, A SEAFIRE takes off in a blaze of no uncertain glory (above). These fighter-planes of the Fleet Air Arm, it was revealed in November 1944, were being "shot" from the decks of aircraft-carriers in this manner. Each plane, it was stated, was fitted with four rockets—two on each wing. The rockets exploded with a terrific roar, launching the plane almost straight from the deck; thus, only the smallest runway was needed.   *Photo, Associated Press*

directed towards the Düsseldorf-Cologne-Bonn stretch of the Rhine, and the greatest bomber blows were made against targets lying between the fighting front and the river.

TWELVE hundred Fortresses and Liberators with 450 Lightnings and Thunderbolts attacked German strongpoints and military formations in the Dueren-Eschweiler area before and during the opening of the attack. In the afternoon, R.A.F. Bomber Command attacked the Dueren-Julich-Heinsberg area with 1,150 bombers escorted by 250 Mustangs and Spitfires of Fighter Command using Master bomber target location technique to concentrate the bombing. Thousands of 260-lb. fragmentation bombs were used ; these bombs do not crater the surface and so do not make the going difficult for the troops following up ; instead, their blast throws destructive pieces of " shrapnel " at high velocity over a considerable area around the bursting-point. The first day's air co-operation by more than 3,000 aircraft was surpassed on the second day of the ground offensive by the intervention of more than

Australian pilot who flew for Imperial Airways and British Overseas Airways before the war, making several spectacular flights in the float-scaplane Mercury launched pick-a-back from the mother flying-boat Maia), attacked the German battleship Tirpitz in Fotten Fjord off Trondheim Fjord, using relatively small A.P. bombs, mines, and depth charges. They dropped their missiles on the cliff so that they might roll down the precipice and damage the ship below the waterline where she lay safe from direct air attack under the shelter of the rock It was impossible to assess the result of the attack, but the Tirpitz survived, to be subsequently attacked in other fjords of Norway. Bennett had to get out by parachute. He landed in Norway, escaped to Britain, and is now an Air Vice-Marshal and the Officer in Command of the Pathfinder Force.

This tall, slightly built, good-looking Australian must have been particularly interested in the operation that sank the Tirpitz in Tromsö Fjord in daylight on

AROUND Leyte, American air power is reducing reinforcements to the Japanese. On November 9, 1944, when four 5,000-ton ships and 15 destroyers landed Jap troops at Ormoc, U.S. dive-bombers sank three transports and seven destroyers ; fighters shot down 16 Jap planes ; U.S. losses were four bombers and four fighters. Next day another convoy of four transports and six destroyers was wiped out and 19 enemy planes shot down. Estimates gave Japanese landings as 5,000-10,000 troops.

The Japanese Army, witnessing the sea/air threat to their maritime communications in the south-west Pacific, have thrust hard on the Chinese mainland to gain a through overland route to Indo-China, thus forcing American air forces to evacuate airfields at Hengyang, Lungling, Tanchuk, and Paiching. On November 7 at Liuchow the Americans set fire to the buildings of their last airfield, blew up the runways, and burned their petrol stores. The enemy broke into the streets of Liuchow on November 11, and the Americans had lost the last Chinese mainland air base from which their aircraft could effectively cut the Japanese supply lines.

Inglorious Tirpitz Takes the Final Knock-Out

45,000-TON GERMAN BATTLESHIP TIRPITZ was sunk by the R.A.F. as she lay at her moorings in Tromsö Fjord, Norway, on November 12, 1944. The attack was made by 29 Lancasters with 12,000-lb. bombs. Several direct-hits were registered and within a few minutes the last great battleship of the German Navy capsized. Though this was the third attack with 12,000-lb. bombs, it was the first time in which the attackers enjoyed good visibility.

Shortly before 10.30 a.m., the force of Lancasters, led by Wing-Commander J. B. Tait, D.S.O., D.F.C. (5) and Squadron-Leader A. G. Williams, spotted the Tirpitz surrounded by an anti-torpedo boom (1). At 10.30 the ship was hit by at least three bombs and capsized (2). At 10.45 she was on fire (3). Reconnaissance showed that the battleship had overturned with about 700 feet of her keel sticking out of the water (4). The sinking was expected to have far-reaching effects on Allied strategy on the Scandinavian war-fronts. See facing page, and page 454.

Photos, British Official; Planet News

Centre & Starboard Shafts

Bilge Keel

Ship's Side

STERN

Flat Portion of Ship's Bottom

Centre Line of Keel

PAGE 477

V.C. Awards Gained on Five Battle Fronts

Major ROBERT CAIN

During the battle of Arnhem, Holland, in September 1944. Major Cain's company of the South Staffordshire Regiment was cut off and for six days was mercilessly harassed by the enemy. Although wounded, he helped to save " the whole situation of the airborne troops."

Lieut. GERARD NORTON, M.M.

On August 31, 1944, during the breaching of the Gothic Line in Northern Italy, alone and armed with a tommy-gun, Lieut. Norton, of the South African forces, took two enemy machine-gun posts, killing or taking prisoner the entire crews.

Capt. DAVID JAMIESON

In command of a company of the Royal Norfolk Regiment which established a bridge-head over the Orne in Normandy during August 1944, Capt. Jamieson showed " superb qualities of leadership and great personal bravery " in repelling seven enemy counter-attacks, during 36 hours of hard fighting.

C.S.M. PETER WRIGHT

On September 25, 1943, near Salerno, Southern Italy, finding that there were no officers left, C.S.M. Wright took charge of his battalion of Coldstream Guards. Later, single-handed, he silenced three Spandau posts, and reorganized the troops.

Major FRANK BLAKER, M.C.

Posthumously awarded the V.C. for gallantry while leading his company in Burma in July 1944, Major Blaker, 9th Royal Gurkha Rifles, charged a Japanese machine-gun post, and although mortally wounded continued to encourage his men.

Subadar NETRABAHADUR THAPA

Commanding a platoon of the 5th Royal Gurkha Rifles in Burma, which —owing to his inspiration—defied heavy shelling and continuous attacks by vastly superior forces, in June 1944, Subadar Thapa held the position for eight hours and was eventually killed. He was found with his kukri in his hand and a dead Japanese by his side.

Rifleman GENJU LAMA

During fierce hand-to-hand fighting in Burma, in June 1944, Rifleman Lama, 7th Royal Gurkha Rifles, on his own initiative, with great coolness and complete disregard for his own safety, crawled forward and engaged three enemy tanks single-handed, killing or wounding the crews. He is seen (right) in hospital, receiving the congratulations and homage of his father and brothers.

Photos, British and Indian Official, Lenare, G.P.U., Daily Mirror

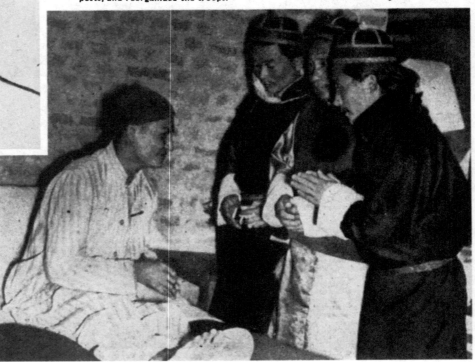

THERE is an interesting difference between the respect in which the German army commanders were held by us at the end of the war in 1918 and the general contempt that is felt for them now. When I say "us" I mean our leading soldiers and politicians and war correspondents. We knew how cleverly the Kaiser's generals had made their plans and how those plans had been beaten, not by better plans—at least not until Foch was appointed to the supreme command—but by sheer weight of numbers, when the Americans arrived in force in France, and by Allied superiority in the air. There was a feeling of almost sympathy with Ludendorff and the other prominent German leaders in the field. Now Hitler's yes-men, who are forced to do whatever this lunatic tells them, and who in consequence have had the most terrific defeats inflicted on their armies, are thought of as third-raters, men who have risen by flattering their crazy Fuehrer and who have during the last 18 months failed to hold the Allied forces in check. It is an instructive contrast, but we must not carry it too far. There is a lot of kick left in the enemy yet.

WHEN Sir John Anderson thanked God that some Home Guards whom he was reviewing had never been called upon to face the foe, he achieved a classic remark of the kind that "would have been better expressed differently." It must have reminded many people of the great Duke of Wellington's reflection, uttered aloud, when he saw the London volunteers who were raised in 1848—year of revolutions in Europe—for the defence of our shores. He took a look at them and walked away, saying "I don't know what impression they would make on an enemy but, by God, they terrify me!" Our present Chancellor of the Exchequer did not mean what he said about the Home Guard to be taken in that way. Nevertheless, we ought to be profoundly thankful that this force of local volunteers, so admirable in many ways, was not called on to offer organized resistance to an invader. I don't mean only because invasion would have been a terrible experience for us all, but because the slightly-trained and inadequately-armed part-time soldiers of 1940 could have put up only a temporary resistance (which was all they were meant to do) and would have been bound to suffer badly before the regulars could take over. So we must be thankful with Sir John Anderson that in those early days they did not have to stand up against professional battalions.

THE extension of murder tactics by Jewish terrorists beyond the borders of Palestine, where they have been carried on for a long time past, will have the unfortunate effect of still further lessening sympathy with the experiment of a "Jewish Home" in the Holy Land. To kill Lord Moyne was not only a cowardly crime: it was a gigantic stupidity. It may have very far-reaching results. Many have thought it was a mistake for us to entangle ourselves in the Palestine business at all. Why Lord Balfour suddenly decided in favour of it has never been fully explained. I have heard told that he asked in his innocent way, "Would all the Jews go there?" and was informed that this was the idea. Upon which he is said to have remarked with satisfaction "Then of course Lord Blank would go!" and to have agreed forthwith. It is also reported, I do not know how truly, that he asked shrewdly why, if the Jews wanted a National Home, they should not buy it in the ordinary way. That undoubtedly would have made their relations with the Arabs very much more satisfactory. The Arabs would not have the feeling that the immigrants have been foisted on them and that their country is no longer their own.

DOES Goebbels really know the first thing about mass psychology? It has always seemed doubtful, and now it appears to me to be proved that he does not, by the song he is trying to persuade young Germans to sing. Instead of giving them a martial air and stimulating sentiment, he sets to a dreary tune such words as:

We are marching in the footsteps
Of the dead heroes of youthful Germany.

and

The Lord God in his lovely heaven
Loves young soldiers who do not run away.

Germans are supposed by people who do not know them at home to be the most musical of nations, just because they happen to have had born among them in the past some of the world's greatest composers. Their failure to produce anything like a good marching song to compare with Pack Up Your Troubles, for example, or Roll Out the Barrel, not to mention Tipperary, shows that they either have no real heart in the war or lack musical ability to translate their emotions into song. Possibly both these explanations hold good.

WHILE the Princess Tsahai of Abyssinia was in this country during her father's exile, she occupied herself by doing good

Surgeon-Captain DOUGLAS MILLER, D.S.C., R.N.V.R., a former Harley Street specialist, who organized the medical operations in the heroic landings of Royal Marine Commandos at Westkapelle, Walcheren Island, Holland, on November 1, 1944. (See illus. pages 463-466.) An eye witness described his work on the beaches, in face of withering enemy fire, as "beyond all praise." *Photo, Associated Press*

work in British hospitals and became imbued with the longing to establish one in her own country when it was freed from the hated Italians. Unhappily, soon after that occurred and the Emperor was able to go back with his family, the Princess died. Her great desire was unfulfilled. Now, however, it is to be carried out. I have had a letter from Lord Horder about the fund that is being raised for the purpose and of which he is the honorary treasurer. The aim is to collect £100,000, rather a substantial sum in these times. Already over £20,000 has been subscribed here, and £10,000 in Abyssinia. In addition, there is a sum of £13,000 with which the Emperor of Abyssinia started the fund. So nearly half the amount required is in hand. Anyone who would like to assist can do so at any branch of Barclay's Bank by paying into the account of Lord Horder, care of H. Reynolds and Co.

WHEN I met in the street a Civil Defence worker with "Warden" on his sleeve, I noticed on his face a melancholy look. I asked him what was the matter. He said "Nothing!" But I gathered in the course of a few minutes' talk that he was gloomy about the war soon coming to an end. He was thinking of the loss of his neat uniform; the consideration paid him by neighbours, the sense of exercising authority, the feeling that he was of some use to his country. After five years it will be hard to let all that drop off and to become once more just an ordinary citizen. I know of others who look forward to the end of the war with something like dismay. One is an oldish dug-out major who has had a cushy job since 1940 and thoroughly enjoyed himself. Another is a young signaller in South Africa, where he has revelled in sunshine for three years and does not at all look forward to the cold and damp and dullness of British weather. A third is an aged newspaper man who has returned to Fleet Street because of the absence of so many young men, and dreads the day when he will not be wanted any longer—not so much for the loss of salary but for the loss of occupation.

I WANTED a few flowers the other day to take to a little girl who is ill and loves gardens. I was asked six shillings each for chrysanthemum blooms. They were beauties, I grant you, but a small bunch would have cost one pound sixteen shillings. I asked if the shop had no cheaper flowers. I was told haughtily, "It does not pay us to sell anything cheap." Well, I could understand that. I was reminded of the man who went into a swagger fruit shop and asked for a basket of peaches. They were three and sixpence each (this was before the war, you understand) and there were five of them. He took the basket, put down a pound note, and turned to go. "Half-a-crown change, sir," said the shop-lady. "No, that's all right," he answered. "I trod on a grape." Are the buyers of chrysanthemums at six shillings apiece the same people who pay five or six pounds for bottles of champagne? Those who pay such prices must keep out of their minds the fact that numbers of their fellow-countrymen are going short of proper food and drink.

EVER since I can remember I have thought the private soldier's tunic very ugly about the neck. The stand-up collar of it spoiled the look of the old scarlet coats, and the khaki ones had just as slovenly an appearance. It is a good thing that an open neck is to be substituted and a collar and tie worn, as officers wear them. It will make a lot of difference in smartness and therefore in self-respect. I hear it was Field-Marshal Montgomery who decided that the change ought to be made and that his view prevailed over the stuffy War Office opinion that "it would make the privates look too much like officers." Very characteristic of both "Monty" and Whitehall!

TAKING ENEMY DEMOLITIONS IN THEIR STRIDE, Royal Engineers with the 5th Army in Italy built this Bailey Bridge near Valsava during heavy fighting below Bologna in the autumn of 1944. Nearly 80 feet high and spanning 530 feet, it was in use within a few minutes of completion, columns of heavy transport hurrying across it on their way up to the front line. Note the curious effect of the bridge's shadow in this photograph which emphasizes its height. See also illus. page 169.

Photo, British Official

Printed in England and published every alternate Friday by the Proprietors, THE AMALGAMATED PRESS LTD., The Fleetway House, Farringdon Street, London, E.C.4. Registered for transmission by Canadian Magazine Post. Sole Agents for Australia and New Zealand : Messrs. Gordon & Gotch, Ltd. ; and for South Africa : Central News Agency, Ltd.—December 8, 1944. S.S. *Editorial Address :* JOHN CARPENTER HOUSE, WHITEFRIARS, LONDON, E.C.4.

Vol 8 *The War Illustrated* N° 196

Edited by Sir John Hammerton

SIXPENCE

DECEMBER 22, 1944

CHINESE GUERILLA, one of thousands fully prepared to pit weapons and skill against the Japanese invader. During their seven years' active resistance to the enemy, such fighters have rendered valuable assistance to the Allied cause. On November 23, 1944, Major-General Albert C. Wedemeyer, who succeeded General Stilwell as military adviser to Chiang Kai-shek, announced that the Generalissimo had accepted in principle a plan which he had submitted for the disposition of Chinese forces. *Photo, U.S. Official*

NO. 197 WILL BE PUBLISHED FRIDAY, JANUARY 5, 1945

Our Roving Camera Sees Latest British Weapons

MARK 10 SELF-PROPELLED 3-in. ANTI-TANK GUN, details of which were released in November 1944, is built on the lines of the Sherman, and designed for use by British and Canadian units. It is manned (above) by Royal Canadian Artillery.

GLIDER-BORNE BOFORS A.A. GUNS played an important part in operations following D-Day. Here one is seen on its runway in the fuselage of a giant British glider ready for action on touching-down. See also illus. p. 504.

THE STAGHOUND ARMOURED CAR—here seen in Italy—has been a closely guarded Allied military secret since 1942. Capable of high speed, it combines the features of tank and reconnaissance car ; is about 17½ ft. long, weighs 14 tons, and carries a crew of five. It is powerfully armoured on all four sides, and mounts a cannon as well as two machine-guns.

MOSQUITO MARK 18, showing the four ·303 mach-ine-guns and the six-pounder cannon (hitherto secret armament) carried in the nose of this R.A.F. Coastal Command aircraft. Its use forced the Germans to change their U-boat tactics. This photograph was re-leased in November 1944. The N.C.O. is displaying one of the six-pounder's shells, which are over 2 ft. in length.

ALLIGATORS are used for transporting ammunition. An amphibious craft (left), it is propelled through the water by its caterpillar tracks and can be launched from a ship at sea and thence direct its course to land.

Photos, British Official, New York Times Photos

THE BATTLE FRONTS

by Maj.-Gen. Sir Charles Gwynn, K.C.B., D.S.O.

SOME time ago (see page 259) I suggested that the Reichswehr generals, realizing that the war is lost, would not lend themselves to Hitler's plan for prolonging the struggle into the heart of Germany; and rather than expose the country to the devastation which that would mean, they would accept decisive battle in the frontier regions. Even if that entailed the quick and final destruction of the regular army it would at least maintain its honour and traditions. The long pause which occurred after the Allied dash through France and Belgium reached its limits, may have raised hopes that General Eisenhower would postpone his final offensive till after the winter and that the Allies, war-weary, might then be induced to agree to terms short of unconditional surrender in order to avoid embarking on another major effort.

If that was their hope, General Eisenhower's announcement that there would be no postponement faced them with the alternative of adopting Hitler's (or Himmler's) policy or of accepting decisive battle in the frontier defences from which there could be little hope of withdrawal and still less of victory. General Eisenhower has made it plain that in his opinion the German General Staff has adopted the latter course, and that they will fight the decisive battle west of the Rhine: that is, in the zone of their frontier defences. Up to the time of writing, all the indications are that his judgement is correct. Wherever the Allies have crossed the frontier the Germans are fighting for every yard of ground, and are flinging their scanty reserves into the struggle in desperate counter-attacks. Only in Holland and in Alsace and Lorraine where the fight has not been on German soil have there been withdrawals under pressure, either as a deliberate policy or by force of circumstances; and there is no sign that the withdrawal will be continued beyond the frontier region.

COUNTER-ATTACKS Delivered by Enemy at Terrific Cost

The decisive battle has undoubtedly been joined on the Aix-la-Chapelle (Aachen) front, and it will, I think, soon be extended to the Saar front. How long it may continue in defences of such great strength and depth it is impossible to predict. Much probably depends on the weather, which up to date has been all in favour of the defence, reducing air co-operation to a minimum and clogging the movements of the attacking troops. Yet the rate of attrition has evidently been very high—much higher than if the Germans could afford to give ground and were not compelled to carry counter-attacking tactics to desperate extremes. Counter-attacks undoubtedly may check the rate of the Allied advance, but delivered in face of an immense weight of artillery fire and met by stubborn resistance their cost is terrific. Ludendorff, it may be remembered, intervened in the Somme battle, in the last war, to prohibit excessive expenditure of troops in counter-attacks delivered simply with the object of recovering worthless trenches. He in that case could afford to give ground, but Von Rundstedt, because he cannot, seems compelled to adopt a practice Ludendorff condemned.

How far the amazing success of the French 1st Army in breaking through the Belfort Gap, and the equally wonderful thrust of the U.S. 7th Army, led by General Leclerc's 2nd Armoured Division, through the Saverne gap to Strasbourg (see illus. page 490) will dislocate German plans for a deliberate withdrawal to the Siegfried Line, remains to be seen. They have certainly added greatly to the rate of attrition and have caused a gap which the Germans may have difficulty in filling, even though a high percentage of second quality troops might be used with reasonable safety since there can be no question of an attempt to cross the Rhine in the reaches exposed. The moral effect of these two remarkable feats may be as important as their strategical results.

THEY must have brought home to the Nazis the fact that the French Army, whose strength and fighting qualities they had probably underestimated, is actually a powerful force of great offensive capacity. They must also have revealed the danger of placing much reliance on their own second or third quality troops. Strategically it is less important that the Rhine has been (or soon will be) reached on a broad front, than that the long active front in the Vosges has been replaced by a strong defensive flank, thereby releasing a considerable part of the U.S. 7th Army and French 1st Army for fresh undertakings.

FIELD-MARSHAL SIR H. ALEXANDER was promoted from General, it was announced on Nov. 27, 1944, with effect from June 4, the date of the capture of Rome. On the first-named date his appointment was also announced as Supreme Allied Commander Mediterranean theatre. *Photo, British Official*

So far, as I have said, it is only on the Aix-la-Chapelle (Aachen) front that the decisive battle has definitely opened. There, despite desperate German resistance and unfavourable conditions, Allied progress has been continuous if slow. It is obvious that the Germans are determined at all costs to cover approaches to the Ruhr. They have concentrated picked troops and have staged counter-attacks on a scale never reached in Normandy, except in the ill-fated attempt to cut General Patton's communications at Avranches. Yet even the heaviest counter-attacks have failed conspicuously to recover ground to any important extent, although naturally in a swaying battle tactical features may change hands several times before the issue is finally decided. There can, I think, be little doubt that General Eisenhower did not count on an early break-through.

He probably hoped to compel the Germans to stand and fight a decisive battle under conditions in which the processes of attrition would be inescapable and opportunities for evasion absent. Under modern conditions of mobility it is very hard by manoeuvre to bring the enemy to decisive battle; he is apt to escape from the most promising pincer movements. Where, however, a vital objective which the enemy must defend can be threatened he may be brought to bay, although that may often entail attacking him frontally in a position of his own selection. With defensive positions organized in depth, coupled with the defensive power of modern weapons, the crisis of such a battle is likely to be long delayed before the enemy is weakened or so thrown off his balance as to give an opening for a conclusive thrust.

GERMAN Armoured Reserve Held for a Desperate Death-Ride

The battle of the Aix-la-Chapelle (Aachen) front is far from over, and there is likely to be much bitter fighting before the line of the Roer is passed and its strong points, such as Julich and Düren, captured. Beyond that line, however, the Rhine plain may afford better opportunities of bringing about a really decisive encounter. The Germans are reported still to have a strong armoured force in reserve, and I believe they would not shrink from using it in a desperate death-ride.

On the Lorraine front the Germans are now back behind the Saar almost everywhere, and in places General Patton's troops are in contact with the outpost zone of the Siegfried Line. He has had much hard fighting, but it is evident that the Germans have not stood with the same stubbornness as on the Aix-la-Chapelle (Aachen) front. They have avoided making heavy sacrifices at Metz, at St. Avold, or in attempts to hold the works of the Maginot Line. They have, however, counter-attacked frequently when Patton's thrust threatened to disturb the orderly conduct of their withdrawal. Their object has evidently been to exhaust his troops and to increase the strain on his long lines of communication before he is in a position from which he can mount a decisive attack on their main defences. If they can delay or repel his attack they might then accept the risk of transferring some of their reserves to the Aix-la-Chapelle front.

The success of the 7th Army will, however, go far to upset any such plan, for obviously it will now be able to advance along the west bank of the Rhine in co-operation with Patton's right, and in ever-increasing strength as the Germans are driven out of the Vosges across the Rhine. There can be no question of either the French or 7th Army attempting to cross the Rhine in its Basle-Strasbourg reaches, but the clearing of the Vosges will open new lines of communication, well protected on their right by the Rhine, for an army operating northwards along the west bank of the river. A powerful attack in this direction will, of course, mean a great increase of the length of front on which the Germans must stand fast.

British Thrust at Venlo on the Ruhr Highway

PRODDING THE VENLO-GEILENKIRCHEN SECTOR of the Western Front (see map in page 451), spearheads of the British 2nd and the U.S. 9th Armies were engaged in some of the stiffest fighting of the war in early December 1944. A heavily camouflaged British M.10 anti-tank gun (see illus. page 482) rumbles through a Dutch border village to the line (1). Armed against cold and rain, this British tank crew wear their new head-to-foot one-piece suits (2).

British sappers clearing enemy minefields near Geilenkirchen (captured on November 19) left warning notices (4). A U.S. soldier fancied pork for dinner (3), though fighting was going on round the corner at Metz, cleared by November 22. Refugees pass British 2nd Army troops (5), during their full-scale attack towards Venlo, on the east bank of the Maas, launched on Nov. 14 (see illus. page 491).

Photos, British and U.S. Official, British Newspaper Pool, Keystone

Marshal Tolbukhin Breaks Through in Hungary

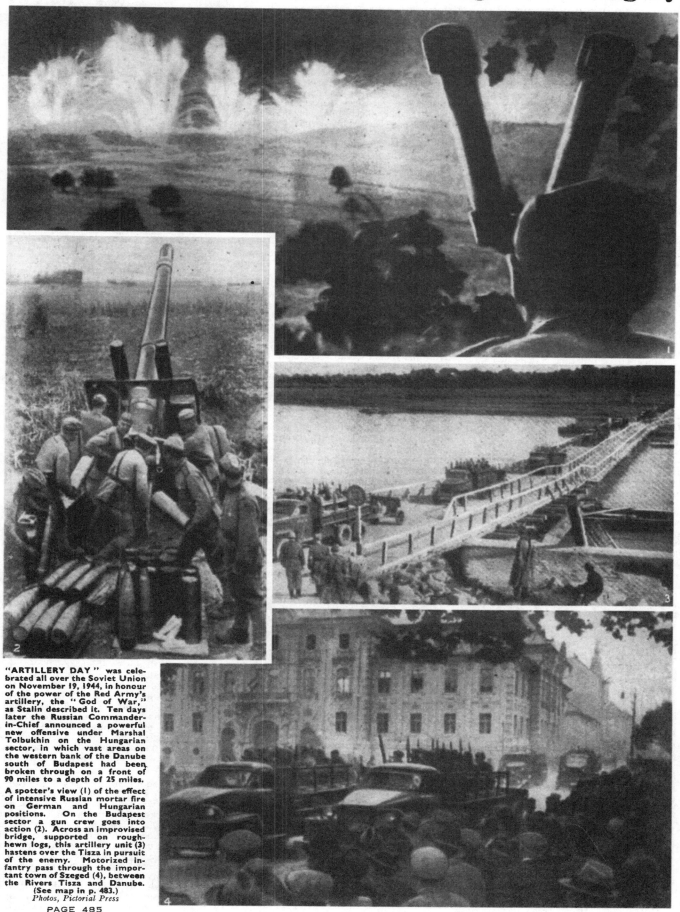

"ARTILLERY DAY" was celebrated all over the Soviet Union on November 19, 1944, in honour of the power of the Red Army's artillery, the "God of War," as Stalin described it. Ten days later the Russian Commander-in-Chief announced a powerful new offensive under Marshal Tolbukhin on the Hungarian sector, in which vast areas on the western bank of the Danube south of Budapest had been broken through on a front of 90 miles to a depth of 25 miles.

A spotter's view (1) of the effect of intensive Russian mortar fire on German and Hungarian positions. On the Budapest sector a gun crew goes into action (2). Across an improvised bridge, supported on rough-hewn logs, this artillery unit (3) hastens over the Tisza in pursuit of the enemy. Motorized infantry pass through the important town of Szeged (4), between the Rivers Tisza and Danube.

(See map in p. 483.)

Photos, Pictorial Press

THE WAR AT SEA

by Francis E. McMurtrie

WITH the clearance of the channel of the Scheldt (see illus. pages 463-466), leading up to Antwerp, one of the finest ports in the world will be at the disposal of the Allies as the main base through which supplies will flow. This will inevitably accelerate the speed of the advance into Germany, for up to now Allied armies have been dependent on the French Channel ports, none of which approaches Antwerp in its capacity or the extent of its equipment. Moreover, the distance overland has been reduced by some 200 miles, a very important matter in view of the damage done to French and Belgian railway communications.

In clearing the Scheldt so quickly the minesweeping service has once more shown that it can always be depended upon to rise to the occasion. After the landings in Normandy on D-Day it was responsible for the removal of 1,600 mines in the areas immediately east and west of Seine Bay.

A belated announcement last month of the award of a D.S.O. to Sub-Lieutenant Causer, R.N.R., and of the Conspicuous Gallantry Medal to A.B. Harry Smith, revealed that the Italian cruiser Bolzano was sunk at Spezia on the night of June 21-22, 1944. Sitting astride a so-called "human torpedo," which was launched from a depot ship under cover of darkness, these two brave men, with their heads just above water, succeeded in approaching the Bolzano undetected and attaching the explosive warhead of the torpedo to her hull.

FROM the parent ship, outside the port, gunfire and searchlights were observed, suggesting that an alarm had been raised. Neither member of the party returned, but Sub.-Lieut. Causer is known to have been made prisoner. Air reconnaissance showed that the cruiser had capsized and sunk, so there could be no doubt of the result of the expedition. Its success was the more remarkable, as the Germans must have been well aware of the danger of such an attempt being made, in view of the previous exploit at Palermo in January 1943 when the cruiser Ulpio Traiano and a transport were sunk by British "human torpedoes" (see illus. page 775, Vol. 7).

Moreover, the Germans themselves have employed "human torpedoes," of a slightly different type, against Allied ships covering landings on the Italian coast and later in the Channel after D-Day, though without much success. The Italians also have used a contrivance of a somewhat similar nature, evolved from an invention by means of which the Austrian battleship Viribus Unitis was sunk at Pola on October 31, 1918. Though they failed to accomplish anything by this means at Gibraltar and Malta in the present war, they did manage to disable the battleships Queen Elizabeth and Valiant in the port of Alexandria towards the end of 1941, a fact which was not disclosed until some two years afterwards.

ROYAL Australian Navy's Great Record Officially Revealed

Particulars of the good work done by the Royal Australian Navy were revealed by its Minister, Mr. N. J. O. Makin, last month. All through the hazardous days of 1941-42 there were never less than one Australian cruiser and five destroyers serving with the Mediterranean Fleet at any one time, while other units of the R.A.N. were in action against the Italians in the Red Sea; they were also engaged in the operations in the Persian Gulf and in the escort of convoys across the Indian Ocean. There are now no fewer than 347 ships in the R.A.N., including four cruisers, 11 destroyers, two sloops, at least four frigates, 55 fleet minesweepers, one repair ship, two auxiliary minelayers, 35 motor launches, three boom working vessels, three infantry landing ships, one fleet oiler, and more than 200 miscellaneous auxiliaries and small craft (see illus. page 264, Vol. 7).

Allied forces engaged in the Battle of the Philippines included the Australian cruisers Australia and Shropshire and the destroyers Arunta and Warramunga, which were attached to Vice-Admiral Kincaid's Seventh Fleet. As already related (page 422, and illus. page 429), H.M.A.S. Australia sustained damage and nearly 100 casualties in this action. The Shropshire engaged a Japanese battleship, possibly either the Fuso or Yamasiro, which later sank; and the Arunta formed one of the units of a destroyer

CREW OF A 4·5 GUN at action stations in one of H.M. ships. This is a dual-purpose gun, capable of high- or low-angle fire. Among the ships equipped with it are the Queen Elizabeth, the Valiant and Renown. *Photo, British Official*

flotilla which closed with the enemy battle squadron and fired torpedoes at short range.

The infantry landing ships Kanimbla, Manoora and Westralia participated in the invasion of Leyte, under cover of bombardment from the Australian squadron. For six hours prior to the landing the Shropshire had been carrying in her paravane (mine defence apparatus), only 15 feet from the ship's side, a Japanese mine which she had picked up at midnight, as the fleet was approaching the island. In order to preserve the element of surprise, no attempt was made to destroy the mine until the assault was launched. Up to November ships of the Royal Australian Navy had been officially credited with the sinking or probable destruction of 27 enemy submarines. Australian ships lost in action number nine, viz., the cruisers Canberra, Perth and Sydney; the destroyers Nestor, Vampire and Waterhen; the sloops Parramatta and Yarra; and the fleet minesweeper Armidale. Casualties to personnel total 269 officers and 2,346 ratings. Awards to personnel number 568.

FURTHER details of utmost interest have been disclosed as the result of a careful expert examination of all the photographic evidence concerning the attack by Lancasters of the R.A.F. Bomber Command on the German battleship Tirpitz at Tromso on November 12 (see illus. page 477). Although only the after part of the ship can be seen clearly in the views taken after she capsized, it is obvious that she sustained two direct hits and one near miss, all on the port side. The first hit is believed to have been in the region of the athwartships catapult, and the second close to the after rangefinder, while the near miss occurred off the port quarter, in the neighbourhood of "Y" turret. It is believed that at least one other direct hit was made, but this cannot be ascertained with certainty from those photographs. As the bombs were dropped, each of the attacking aircraft took photographs of the operation, and in one case films were taken with cine-cameras.

The first bomb dropped (by Wing-Commander Tait) scored the direct hit near the catapult. It was followed by a cone-shaped mass of smoke. The fourth bomb dropped caused a brilliant flash and explosion by the after rangefinder. The ninth bomb burst 30 feet from the port quarter, its explosion being followed by a high column of heavy black smoke, succeeded by a thin and concentrated light-coloured jet from amidships, such as might have been produced by a boiler explosion. Bomb No. 14 was also a near miss, close behind the ship's stern.

80,000-TON LINER QUEEN MARY, completed in 1936, has carried several thousands of troops since the outbreak of war—always unescorted, because she is too fast to sail in convoy. In 1940, when the Nazis learned that she was being used as a troopship, U-boats were ordered to sink her at all costs. They've been trying ever since. *Photo, British Official*

Japanese Navy Routed in Big Philippines Action

FIVE DAYS AFTER the Leyte landings (see illus. page 429) the U.S. Pacific Fleet, on October 24, 1944, routed a large Japanese force, including battleships and carriers, sinking or damaging 30 of the warships and destroying 150 aircraft. Though U.S. losses were slight they included the light fleet carrier Princeton, set ablaze by enemy planes, and here seen (1) being hosed by a cruiser. Outlined against the burning Princeton, a cruiser stands by for survivors (2). Smoke - screened, this stricken Japanese carrier (3) unsuccessfully attempted to escape. An enemy dive-bomber misses the target—an aircraft-carrier (4)—during the U.S. attack on Formosa on October 11-12.

Photos, Keystone, Associated Press

Canada's Mighty Wartime Seafaring Expansion

No navy of modern times has equalled the rate of expansion of the Royal Canadian Navy, and the Dominion's merchant ship output is a feat without parallel ; achievements in building and in action in this war are narrated by HAROLD A. ALBERT who, in close touch with the Wartime Information Board of Canada, is in a position to give these little-known facts.

SOMEWHERE in Canada today a ship was launched. In Canada yesterday a ship went down the slips. Six ships a week for fifty and more weeks a year, and $1,000,000,000 orders piling up for future cargo ships alone ! Is it any wonder if, as Munitions Minister C. D. Howe recently pointed out, Canada's shipyard workers are turning out twice the number of ships produced by an equal number of American workers? This feat is all too little known.

The avenging success of the destroyer H.M.C.S. Haida (*see page 25*), is fresh in our minds. Canadian destroyers have also been Hun-busting and ramming U-boats in mid-Atlantic, and the frigate-Fairmile-M.T.B. dragnet against enemy submarines in the gulf of St. Lawrence has gained innumerable victories.

In the Mediterranean recently Canadian corvettes sank two U-boats within a day or two. Across the North Atlantic—scene of a hundred grim Nazi-Canuck battles—upwards of 100 million tons of food, munitions and essential materials had been convoyed by the Canadians in four years of war. One corvette, H.M.C.S. Matapedia, completed 100,000 miles in 2½ years without having a single ship torpedoed or lost. And for the most part these triumphs have been achieved with Canadian-built ships, Canadian-manned. No navy of modern times has equalled the rate of expansion of the "R.C.N." ; and Britain's own merchant ship output has been surpassed by our Dominion brothers.

EVEN the statistics can be deceptive. Canada's yards in 1943, for instance, turned out only 100 naval and escort vessels against 117 in 1942, but last year's programme was of a more difficult and costly nature. Canada's production of cargo vessels will show a slight drop this year. What wonder when the 1943 figure of 150 ships totalling 1,478,000 dead-weight tons nearly doubled 1942 production ? Of a total of 4,300 orders for small craft, too, 3,600 have been delivered. And there are to be more naval craft this year.

Yet in 1940 there were only 14 yards in all Canada that had ever taken a 130-footer. In the Toronto area only two ferry-boats had been built on the lake-sides in twenty years, and all Canada boasted only 3,000 shipyard workers, the majority engaged on repair work. Most of these yards had been considered pretty busy in the years 1918-1921. In the last two years one cargo shipyard alone built and delivered 30 per cent more tonnage than all 14 yards in those three years.

Deckhand and Ship's Waiter

The boom in shipbuilding, and the swelling strength of the Canadian Navy, are all part of the same big story. It is illustrated in the example of the Simard Brothers, of Sorel, Quebec, one formerly a deckhand, another a ship's waiter. They built up in the course of years a dredging business. While Hitler was flinging his fiery threats at Europe, they dredged out and cemented a launching basin. It has only six large berths, but now the Simards lay 10 or 12 keels at a time, shifting the hulls as they progress on to a marine railway which lowers them to water bow-first.

At the outbreak of war, too, the Royal Canadian Navy mustered a mere token force of six destroyers, five minesweepers, a training ship, a ketch and a couple of tugs, but their reply to the British Admiralty question of when they could start convoy duty was a laconic, "At once !" From a force of 1,800 men, the R.C.N. has expanded to 90,000 —as many as were in the Royal Navy in September 1939—and they are further supplemented ashore by the 5,500 volunteers of the Woman's Royal Canadian Naval Service. One remembers the 25 Canadian midshipmen who arrived at a British port some time ago to serve in battleships and cruisers of the Royal Navy. They were from the first class to graduate from the new Royal Canadian Naval College at Royal Roads, British Columbia.

FOR manpower must keep pace with ships and the latest official figure of *delivered* ships stands at 330 fighting vessels and 100 special service vessels, as well as smaller craft. They range from the powerful destroyer Micmac to the Island class escort trawlers now in service around the British coast.

Glance for a moment at their fighting records, ranging from the valour of the St. Laurent and Restigouche during the time of Dunkirk to the Atlantic battles that have cost us the Valleyfield and the gallant St. Croix. The first of 424 frigates to be built in Canadian yards, H.M.C.S. Waskesiu, was appropriately the first Canadian frigate to sink a U-boat. "We opened up with everything we had," her skipper, Lieut.-Com. William Fraser, told me. "Our No. 1 Oerlikon never wasted a cartridge : they were all dead on the conning-tower. When the submarine came into position, No. 2 Oerlikon picked it up and blasted it."

There was the time when the corvette Ville de Quebec depth-charged a submarine, riddled it with 150 shells from quick-firers, rammed it and sank it, all within nine minutes of a January afternoon in the Western Med. There was the unforgettable duel of the Chambly and Moose-Jaw with a U-boat, whose captain ingloriously jumped on to the attacking corvette and abandoned his ship and crew. Such spectacular incidents typify the team-work of the whole. It can now be revealed, for instance, that enemy submarines mined the approaches to Halifax harbour last summer in an arc intended to close the port to all shipping. R.C.N. minesweepers cleared a channel 1,200 yards wide within one day to permit a convoy to sail, and the channel was maintained till the entire mine-infested area was cleared.

INDIVIDUALLY, one recalls the heroism of ratings of the corvette Oakville, who jumped aboard a U-boat during ramming operations and chased the whole crew into the sea. The crew of the minesweeper H.M.C.S. Georgian were similarly commended recently when, on convoy escort duty amid heavy seas, icebergs and fog, they rescued ten U.S. Army flyers from almost certain death in the North Atlantic. Nearly 2,000 have given their lives in the cause. More than 100 have been decorated for bravery in action and hundreds more have been mentioned in dispatches.

Such is the Royal Canadian Navy, tried, tested and proved in over five years of conflict at sea—a full partner with the navies of Great Britain and the United States. "A most formidable striking force," said the Canadian Naval Minister, Angus Macdonald. "A force which is making its weight felt on many sea fronts." An understatement.

CAPTURE OF THIS U-BOAT in the North Atlantic in a dashing combined action by ships of an escort group under Commander P. W. Burnett, D.S.C., was a typically brilliant exploit of the Royal Canadian Navy, whose remarkable war record is outlined in this page. Forced below for many hours the U-boat, seen between the corvettes Chilliwack and the St. Catharine's, was finally depth-charged to the surface and disabled. The crew surrendered, and the U-boat was then sent to the bottom.

Photo. Canadian Official

The Dominion Takes Over Royal Navy Ships

FIRST OF TWO NEW CRUISERS transferred from the R.N. to the Royal Canadian Navy, late in 1944, was the 8,000-ton Uganda (1), famed " veteran " of Salerno. Among the fastest destroyers afloat, H.M.C.S. Sioux was originally designed for the Royal Navy, but was transferred to the R.C.N. while still being built (2). Minesweepers of the R.C.N. head for port after a prolonged sweep off the French coast (3). An account of the phenomenal expansion of the Dominion's naval and merchant services is given in the facing page.   *PAGE 489*   *Photos, Royal Canadian Navy*

The Tricolour Flies Again Over Alsace-Lorraine

SPEARHEADING FROM SAVERNE, General Leclerc's 2nd French Armoured Division, operating with the U.S. 7th Army, penetrated the city of Strasbourg, capital of Alsace, on November 23, 1944, following their split-up of the German 15th Army. Strasbourg, 2 miles west of the Rhine famous fortress-town since Roman times and French for centuries, was in German hands from 1870-1918. Placarding a portrait of Hitler on their radiator, these French poilus (right) entered the city ; while the retreating enemy continued shelling, setting Allied transport ablaze (left). (See pages 308-9, Vol. I).

STRIKING TOWARDS THE SAAR BASIN, troops of the U.S. 3rd Army took the ancient Lorraine fortress-city of Metz in their stride Reichwards on November 20, 1944. For the first time in 2,000 years this great French bastion was captured by frontal assault. Prisoners waiting for transport to captivity (left). U.S. infantrymen break into a house to clear it of enemy stragglers (right). PAGE 490 *Photos, U.S. Official, Planet News*

2nd Army Infantrymen Dig In Along the Maas

AGAINST A TIDE OF MUD AND MINES, General Dempsey's British 2nd Army on November 14, 1944, launched a new attack south-east of Eindhoven in Holland, to secure the area within the bend of the River Maas, west of Venlo. By December 4 the last enemy pocket had been eliminated at Blerick, and the British forces were solidly established along the west bank of the river: dug-outs and temporary shacks afforded some little shelter from the bleak wintry weather of the Lowlands.

Photo. British Official

Boredom is Banished in Time Off From Battle

In a series of energetic drives against that " fed-up " feeling which threatens to envelop the fighting man in even the briefest intervals of leisure, very real service is being rendered on the various fronts by organizations and teams of entertainers whose one object is to abolish tedium. Some of their outstanding achievements are instanced here by MARK PRIESTLEY.

PROLONGED combat can wreck men's nerves and minds, and boredom can produce an equally real decline in fighting efficiency ; but spare time behind the battle lines today has star attractions. Hardly had we won Poperinghe, in September 1944, when Talbot House, birthplace in the last war of the Toc H movement, was put in order again and flung open to a second generation of soldiers in Belgium as a homely port of call.

Scarcely was the first R.A.F. airstrip laid on European soil, when a 10th century castle, a former German headquarters, was fitted up with showers, baths, billiard-tables, canteens

Marigny Theatre, and seemingly limitless supplies of ice-cream and white wine.

IN the same way, when General Patton's Army gained a brief respite along the Moselle, rest- amps were swiftly established behind the front line, and troops were drafted back, often for several days at a time, for a spell of uninterrupted sleep at night, hot baths, clean clothes and entertainment. The experiment perhaps originated in a rest-cure scheme that is being practised in the Pacific and has proved no less successful. Flyers from such forward bases as Tarawa and Kwajalein have been returned at the

in India, Ceylon and on the Burma frontier. " Nowhere too far ! " would seem to be the motto of most entertainers. One group of ENSA girls recently went 7,000 feet up into the Waziristan mountains to a frontier outpost where no woman had ever set foot, in order to give a show to the largest permanent " men only " military station in the world. Another group, the ENSA Follies, travelled by plane and flat-bottomed river boat through the jungle in order to " cheer 'em up " at Manza Bay, in Tanganyika. " I've heard of these theatres of war," said a Tommy, " but I never thought they'd get quite this far ! " Men of Paiforce gave a hearty reception to concerts given by Miriam Licette, Nancy Evans, Walter Widdop, Dennis Noble, Alfred Cave and Ivor Newton in the deserts of Persia and Iraq.

GERMAN pockets of resistance were still being cleaned up in Antwerp when ENSA took over the largest theatre, and Richard Hearne stood on the roof to watch the progress of the fighting in the suburbs. Forsythe, Seaman and Farrell's sleeping coach stood one night so close to the lines that a German sentry guarded it all night, imagining it to be a Nazi lorry. He realized his mistake with the dawn, but the car driver was quicker. And Gertrude Lawrence nearly wandered into a seaport which was still in German hands, during one of her tours up and down the lines in France.

Yet individual efforts fade in the full panorama of entertainment offered the troops in their time off from battle. ENSA alone has given 30,000 cinema shows and over 12,000 stage shows overseas this year, to attendances totalling nearly 20 million Nor does this include the magnificent range of entertainment provided by ORBS (Overseas Recorded Broadcasting Service). Few people on the home front are aware of the programmes, ranging from dance-bands and musicals to plays like The Ringer and The Amazing Dr. Clitterhouse, and others contributed by the Services themselves.

Rediffusion vans, equipped with libraries of 500 records, have given programmes to troops while actually on the move across Flanders, and natives in a recently liberated village have sometimes stared in wonder to see troops sitting down to listen to a play. As Basil Dean, ENSA chieftain, says, the rediffusion van, with its radio and gramophone, is a secret weapon in the war against that insidious enemy, boredom.

STAINLESS STEPHEN, well-known radio and variety star, mounted on an army vehicle, draws laughs from sunbaked troops of the British 36th Division enjoying respite from fighting on the Arakan sector of the Burma front (above). He did his act within firing distance of the line, and Chindits with machine-guns kept enemy snipers at bay.

and a theatre, and launched with a " Gang Show" as a Malcolm Club attraction. It was the seventh of these clubs—for R.A.F. personnel, founded in memory of Wing-Commander H. G. Malcolm, V.C.—in a hospitality chain stretching from Algiers through Tunis, Bari, San Severo and Naples to Rabat ; others have since opened in Brussels and elsewhere in the wake of advancing troops.

ENSA (Entertainments National Service Association) opened its eighteenth static cinema at Eindhoven, in Holland, when the little town still had a prime place in the war news. NAAFI (Navy, Army and Air Force Institutes) and kindred activities established no less than 160 canteens within three months from D-Day (June 6, 1944).

Never before have armies been backed so well by mobile columns of entertainment. Paris was no sooner open to Allied soldiers when battle-weary boys straight from the line found themselves on leave in the palatial hotel that is now the A.E.F. Club, enjoying free sight-seeing trips, free seats for a Bobby Howes and Frances Day show at the famous

rate of hundreds a week to cattle ranches in the Hawaiian group, and it is found that a few days as cowboys and ranch hands enables them to overcome flying and hospital fatigue alike. " This isn't coddling," say their hosts. " We keep them fit to fight." One ace pilot had a bad crash and even requested to be removed from flying duty. After a spell on a ranch he was ready to go back, and soon he chalked up another success on his score sheet.

There is concern for the lads of the valiant 14th Army in Burma, faced as they are with boredom and communication difficulties of a half-mountainous, half-flooded, sniper-infested terrain. Stars of the magnitude of Vera Lynn, Elsie and Doris Waters and Stainless Stephen have pushed through to Kohima and Arakan. The latter has told how the Chindits posted machine-gunners to prevent snipers picking him off. And concert parties have given performances to forward troops less than twenty miles from Japanese positions. Today, ten concert parties, five play companies, and a pool of artistes are operating

THEN there is the staunch work of the Army Kinema Service, with 150 mobile cinemas in North-West Europe alone, and which have given shows as close as 3,000 yards behind the fronts. In Italy, films were shown in dug-outs in the Anzio beach-head, where an audience of twelve was a full house and the sound of firing mingled with the music and dialogue of the film. On one occasion a mobile unit arrived in a cinema in time to help round-up German prisoners. Today the films which are being seen by the Army and the R.A.F. in Europe and elsewhere overseas run parallel with the programmes of Broadway and London's West End. Even the latest newsreels are delivered twice a week by air, and are shown within three days of their first screening in London.

Grouped behind the mobile cinemas are the mobile cinema workshops and film libraries ready to make immediate repairs, and constantly at work collecting new films and organizing distribution. The men who provide the shows are, of course, trained soldiers as well as technicians.

'Let the Forces Sing' Helps to Win the War

ENTERTAINMENT for the troops behind the battle-fronts is no scratch affair (see facing page). Famous stars, besides artistes among the troops themselves, have given thousands of performances to thousands of serving men and women—sometimes to the accompaniment of enemy guns. "Concert Party," the entertainment unit of the 50th (Northumbrian) Division, gave a show (1) in a Normandy farmyard in the summer of 1944. Formed in 1940, this unit travelled with the Division in the Middle East.

While Tilburg was under fire in November 1944, Ensa artiste Estelle Murison (2) entered it with the British 2nd Army, to display a poster announcing the arrival of the " Five Smart Girls " concert party. Beatrice Lillie entertained officers and ratings in one of our battle-ships (3). Treat for three Londoners on Paris leave was putting out their boots to be cleaned, in a hotel given over to the Forces (4). British artillerymen browsing in a mobile front-line library (5).

Photos, British Official, British Newspaper Pool, Planet News

Where Hitler's Own Last Battle Will Be Fought?

Fantastic as has been the career of "that man," the circumstances of his death may be even more so. The sordid climax approaches, and from information gathered from various sources Dr. EDGAR STERN-RUBARTH pieces together details of the possible manner and place of the passing of the ignoble Fuehrer, after a final outburst of terror and destruction.

IT is safe to say that Hitler was never at any time quite sane, and excesses and privations during his early life have not improved an unbalanced brain. It appears now that he has a fantastic scheme to end his career in an "adequate" way. A mosaic of detailed information makes it possible to visualize this; allusions to a sort of neo-Teutonic "Twilight of the Gods" tally perfectly with the material facts.

The story starts, appropriately, with a cave. Caves have always played a great part in German legends. The Emperor Frederick Barbarossa—drowned, in fact, during a crusade in 1190, in the river Kalykadnos in Asia Minor—sits, according to German saga and poetry, forever in a cave under the Kyffhaeuser Mountain, his beard grown through the table, until a day when, as guardian of the German people, he will be

"ENTER HITLER, HEAVILY CLOAKED," and (right) Himmler, after the attempt on the Fuehrer's life at his H.Q. on July 20, 1944 (see illus. in page 211). The incident, in which it was stated that Hitler was wounded, was followed by many rumours as to his whereabouts. Sinister world-wide plans for the continuance of Nazidom after Allied victory are disclosed in this page.
Photo from a captured German news-reel

called by a raven to mount his horse and lead the Germans to their final victory. Tannhaeuser, the Wagnerian hero, woos Venus in the "underworld" beneath Mount Hoersel, in Thuringia. The treasure of the Nibelungs is made and hoarded in their subterranean kingdom, and so forth. Germany possesses many mysterious or interesting caves, some natural, others remnants of forgotten mining operations. The caves where Hitler's own "last battle" is to be fought—with all the means of modern warfare—belong to the latter category.

AT and around Hallein, a town some five miles from Hitler's mountain haunt at Berchtesgaden and about the same distance from the Austrian town of Salzburg, are enormous caves where, from prehistoric days until two or three centuries ago, rock salt was mined. Inter-connected by new tunnels, and linked with fortifications built all around that area between mountains ranging from 6,000 to 10,000 feet in height, these former salt-mines constitute a bombproof stronghold. There, Hitler intends to assemble his most important lieutenants, his best strategists and technicians, and an army of, say, 100,000 men. From there, by short-wave transmitter, he intends to direct the huge network of underground and guerilla fighters which Himmler commenced to organize many months ago.

This army is a most elaborate and sinister creation. As far as details are available,

it may ultimately consist of three different elements: (1) Nazi, especially Gestapo and S.S. leaders, whose faces, voices and mannerisms are not generally known; (2) selected Hitler Youth trainees, now between 14 and 18 years of age; (3) fervent and proved Nazis of foreign nationality or descent; plus as many minor handymen, cut-throats, spies and liaison-men as possible.

THE No. 1 men, many of whom have "died" of late, according to obituary notices in the Voelkischer Beobachter and other newspapers, in the prime of life, are going to be camouflaged. They may have "died" in order to be provided with authentic identity papers of an inconspicuous—possibly a previously penalized anti-Nazi—citizen of similar size, age, eye and hair-colour, his photograph exchanged, if neces-

sary, for that of the new holder, and duly stamped. The real owner of such papers and passports, killed in an air raid, is meanwhile buried as an "unidentified body." Or they may obtain cleverly forged passports from satellite, even neutral, authorities, duly visa-ed. The tasks of the holders may be manifold: acting as deputies or successors to the present set of Nazi leaders; permeating the future administration of a democratic Germany with subversive and destructive conspirators; directing, in secret, acts of terror and violence, and so on.

Such acts will be the main job of the second category of Himmler's disciples, the cream of the "Ordensburgen"—the dozen or so special training schools for future Nazi leaders. To get into one of them and, finally, after another severe test as to complete fanaticism, discipline, unreasoning obedience, and physical fitness (in short, dehumanization), into one of the secret training camps created earlier this year by the Gestapo boss, a boy must hail from indubitable Germanic peasant or minor civil servant stock, must be strong and healthy, possibly blue-eyed and fair-haired, and brought up to sneer at Christianity, democracy, and other established beliefs.

With awe-inspiring midnight ceremonies, he is eventually sworn in and learns how to use all sorts of weapons, explosives, and other paraphernalia of underground warfare.

He learns how to forge documents and identity papers; how to use invisible inks, Morse and light signals, word and cipher keys; how to preserve, by mnemonic tricks, messages and other confidential, unwritten information; how to apply psychological dodges in dealing with enemies, victims—and friends—in order to gain their help, their knowledge, or their silence. First aid and emergency surgery, chemistry and a number of crafts complete that unique curriculum, based upon a highly developed experience gleaned by the Nazis in fighting the underground movements in France, Poland, Greece and other countries.

Together with the third group, these boys, goaded, misguided, perverted from early youth, are destined to be Nazi "survivors" and tools for continuing, or reviving, the Swastika gospel. This third group has a similar training and task. As non-Germans, non-Nazis, possibly even well-prepared former victims of the Gestapo with authentic scars and forged release-papers from a concentration camp—some even, like a number of high Nazi officials, having voluntarily suffered the torture of such a camp, as a proof of their fanatical loyalty to Hitler—they have to go abroad. Mixing with fugitive foreign workers, or travelling officially by way of neutral countries, theirs is the "holy mission" of spreading discontent and rebellion, of rebuilding, or bringing underground, existing Nazi cells in many countries.

SOME of the most trusted among them, as well as the future leaders among the Hitler Youth special trainees, are provided with secret watchwords, with lists of liaison officers in German and foreign government departments, and with access to the millions in foreign currency salted away abroad in the name of faithful citizens of the respective nationality. They have to finance, to direct, to assemble their subordinates; to pass on the orders, maybe for the assassination of this or that future member of government or parliament, this or that "collaborator" with the Allies; or for acts of terrorism, sabotage and, where possible, guerilla warfare against the victorious powers.

The system, which can be given here only in outline and which is still in development, is meant to be directed from Hitler's or—should he be eclipsed by disease or death—from Himmler's headquarters in the "Alpine Fortress," that network of impregnable caves and fortifications in sight of the Fuehrer's eyrie. The gang outside this citadel, in Germany as well as abroad, should by now be well camouflaged.

AS for a Nazi "Maquis," whatever Himmler's cunning preparations, he cannot produce by magic that enthusiastic support of the population, that outside help and ultimate assault, which all through the bitter years of oppression kept the patriotic guerillas fighting, and sacrificing themselves. Yet for anti-Nazi and democratic Germans themselves, when trying to rehabilitate their country under Allied occupation, such fanatical thugs may constitute a danger.

But, unable to hold his fantastic underground fortress forever, even though it possesses food, water, medical supplies and all comforts in sufficiency for years, Adolf Hitler himself and a number of his most frenetic apostles plan an ultimate sacrifice by blowing up caves and mountains and fortifications with a bang, compared with which the Wagnerian "Twilight of the Gods" would appear as no more than a mere Guy Fawkes display.

kotos, British News-
—per Pool, Keystone

Side by Side the Allies Smash into Germany

Fighting on a big scale for the first time on German soil, British forces attacked Geilenkirchen, important Siegfried Line strongpoint north of Aachen, in conjunction with the U.S. 9th Army. Close-packed armour on the road between Gangelt and Geilenkirchen (bottom) took part in the terrific preliminary barrage. According to enemy report 20,000 shells fell in the town, which was captured by General Dempsey's 2nd Army tanks and U.S. infantry (top) on November 19, 1944.

Royal Navy Shows Its Might in Algiers Harbour

After the Allies secured control in the Mediterranean there took place in Algiers harbour in April 1943 an impressive gathering of H.M. ships (top). Among vessels shown are: (1) Rodney, (2) Nelson, (3) aircraft-carrier Formidable, (4) cruiser Dido, (5) submarine depot ship Maidstone, (6) boom defence ship Leonian, (7) M.L. parent ship Vienna, (8) Tribal class destroyer Ashanti—bows only, (9) Hunt class destroyers, (10) cruiser Carlisle, (11) Hunt class destroyer Oakley.

This U-Boat Now Sails Under the White Ensign

Surrendering to a Hudson aircraft of Coastal Command patrolling from Iceland in August 1941, the German submarine U 570 was taken in hand by the Royal Navy and, as can now be told, renamed H.M. submarine Graph and used to hunt down U-boats! Inside the Graph (centre), and flying the White Ensign as she passes other British submarines (right). H.M.S. Warspite (left), heading for Holland to obliterate with her 15-in. guns enemy batteries on Walcheren, on November 1, 1944.

First Snow Follows the Rain in Italy

Photos, British Off

During the six months' summer campaign in Italy, which carried the Allied armies from Cassino through Rome to just south of Bologna, half of the original German forces—or the equivalent of 15 full-strength divisions—had been destroyed, it was revealed in November 1944.   Then came the snow.   Heavy storms raged over the 5th Army front : a patrol of British riflemen are seen (top) returning to their positions.   Clearing a 25-pounder gun of its white burden (bottom).

498

VIEWS & REVIEWS Of Vital War Books

by Hamilton Fyfe

WHAT makes privates in the Army want to be officers? That is an interesting field for inquiry. But a much more interesting one, it seems to me, is—Why do so many privates prefer not to be made officers, even when they have the chance offered to them?

It is not, I think, that they are afraid of responsibility, for often they come out strong in that line when they are in tight places. It is not that they are doubtful about bridging a social gulf, for many of the young men I know who stay in the ranks from choice are well up in the social scale. I don't know how to explain it.

When Anthony Cotterell, author of An Apple for the Sergeant (Hutchinson, 10s. 6d.), was asked why he had applied for a commission, he replied that " he thought it would be more interesting, because as an officer you had a better idea of what was going on.'' Another man who, at the same interview, was examined as to his motives said they were "to have an easier time, get better food, not have so much to do, and have a batman to clean your buttons.'' No candidate for the O.C.T.U. is ever known to have given as his reason for wanting to join an officers' mess that he would enjoy more intellectual conversation there than in the barrack-room. Major Cotterell found the average of general intelligence among officers, especially regulars, disconcertingly low, though that does not seem to have affected their capability as soldiers.

OF the exceptions the most remarkable was a major-general under whom Cotterell, formerly of The Daily Express staff, brought out "a sort of bulletin" intended to "increase the ordinary soldier's interest in the war, to raise his enthusiasm to go in and win." At the War Office, Cotterell was told, "We want to get rid of this pernicious idea of 'we can take it.' Stop being passive and turn aggressive!'' Whose bright notion this was does not appear. It must have escaped his notice that, while anything issued officially is distrusted and given very little attention, the daily and weekly newspapers are eagerly read by the troops and on the whole regarded as trustworthy. It would have been far better to do what was wanted through them.

However, Cotterell was put on to plan the bulletin, and when the major-general found that he and his assistant were chary of saying just what they wanted, he turned on them and said it would be absolutely fatal if they kept their opinions from him. " What the devil do you think I have you here for?'' he asked, banging his desk. " It isn't for your appearance. It's because you're experts and I want to know what you think. I don't care twopennyworth of cold gin what you say, whether I agree with it or not ; but for God's sake say it !''

THE assistant remarked that in civilian life he was never afraid to speak up, but since he had been in the army his training had been not to do so. To which the major-general replied, "Well, forget it, man. What's the good of fooling about like toy soldiers? Forget I'm a major-general or anything else. What we're here for is to beat Hitler, and we're not going to do that by place-saving and crawling!'' There was in that attitude a refreshing common sense which is not always found in senior regular staff officers.

That particular bulletin doesn't seem to have come to anything. Changes were made so often in its character that its editors "expected to wake up any day and find ourselves a children's annual.'' But Cotterell

was given plenty of work for the Army Bureau of Current Affairs, describing experiences with American units and with R.A.F. raiders over Germany, and as a parachutist being put through training. In an American officers' mess, what struck him most was that "everyone seems to know everybody else and furthermore seems pleased to.'' Otherwise "the funny thing about going from one army to another is the way you find exactly the same characters and behaviour in each.''

There were not, however, among the Americans the same number of soft jobs he noticed in the British forces. For example,

A Newspaper Man In Service Harness

he tells of a Physical Training Instructor who had nothing to do except take a half-hour morning parade. "The rest of the time he spent mainly asleep, in bed with the window shut and the blankets drawn firmly over his head.'" Another man in charge of certain stores "was a regular soldier, otherwise his inactivity would have driven him mad long since . . . He assured me he had never been happier in his life.'' Then there was a young business man being trained for a commission, "an absolutely champion lead-swinger. He was a plausible talker and he fixed things for himself to a quite extraordinary degree, sent himself telegrams asking for himself to be sent on leave for business reasons, wrote himself letters on his firm's notepaper—and got away with everything.''

NOT many men would have wished as keenly as Cotterell did to accompany a bombing raid or to practise parachute jumping. He admits he was scared during both adventures, but that proves he didn't really feel any fear. The first time he dropped from a balloon with a parachute he had a moment of terror, his emotions seemed for that instant out of control, a sort of mental chaos overcame him. Then he felt his hands clutching his trousers and he remem-

bered he had been told to do this, and his mental composure returned.

The jerk when the parachute opened was not so much of a shock as he had been led to anticipate. Of course, when your fall is suddenly brought up short you do feel it, "but you are so keyed up for radical physical experiences that it doesn't mean a thing.'' That first drop was timed to take 35 seconds, not long enough to do more than recover from the sensation of falling and to concentrate on the business of landing. No opportunity to look about and see how things appeared as you fell. As for the landing, that also is not really difficult if you have been well trained, and all our parachute troops receive the very best of training.

NOW and then a man who has been picked for the work shies off jumping at the last moment and has to be sent away at once, "because of the possibly disconcerting effect on the others. When you are jumping, the last thing of which you want to be reminded is the case against it.'' Before the first jump from a plane "people were more jittery'' than they had been before they tried it from a balloon. But they quickly became accustomed to the real thing.

The bombing raid which Cotterell accompanied was over Frankfort. He gives a very sensitive account of the state of mind of the crews before it started. There was "an air of quietly mounting excitement.'' One man put a German dictionary into his pocket. "Come in handy in the Stalag,'' he said, meaning the prisoner-of-war camp if he should have to bale out and be captured. Another said he " hoped those s.o.b.s were not sitting waiting for us,'' and another told him, "Yes, that's what they were doing, just sitting and having cups of tea brought them !''

The "briefing'' is described in some detail. The Weather Officer comes first, then the Intelligence Officer with facts about the nature of the target, then the Wing-Commander who leads the night's force, then the Group Captain. After all instructions had been given, there was a move to the airfield, and the "dull tiredness into which my excitement had faded cleared and was replaced by a sense of high, nay lunatic, adventure.'' He noticed that one of the rules for pilots stuck up in the plane was " steady consistent driving is of far more use than brilliant erratic driving.'' He hoped his pilot had taken that to heart. As they did their work thoroughly and reached home safely, he evidently had taken it to heart !

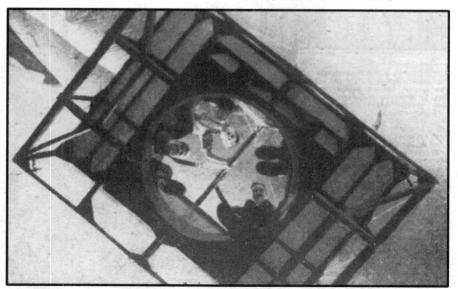

PREPARING FOR A FIRST JUMP, through the hole in a special platform slung beneath a captive balloon, these British parachute troops are more or less enjoying their preliminary training. Use of a balloon makes jumping possible in most weathers. Later they will drop from aircraft. What it feels like to descend by parachute is told in the book reviewed in this page. See also first-hand story in page 92, Vol. 7.

Photo, British Official.

How Petrol is Piped to Our Airfields in Italy

A PIPELINE 222 miles long, for the servicing of Allied aircraft, has been constructed in Italy. The system pumps petrol at the rate of a million gallons a day, thus tremendously speeding-up delivery, lessening road-traffic, and freeing for other duties hundreds of lorries and nearly 1,000 troops formerly needed for fuel transport. The petrol is delivered at terminal points from overseas in giant tankers. (See also illus. p. 652, Vol. 7.)

Overhauling one of the powerful pumps (1): meters (in foreground) keep accurate register of the pressure. Testing the valves of a large terminal storage tank (2), to which petrol is conveyed by way of a buoyed pipeline (3) stretching from shore to ocean-going tanker ; connexion between tanker and pipeline can be distinguished, in background. Marauder pilots, aided by bustling ground-staff (4), prepare to take off on a bombing foray from an east-Italy airfield. Planes from these bases have played a big part in operations in the Balkans.

Photos, British and U.S. Official, Planet News

MacArthur's Men Tighten Their Grip on Leyte

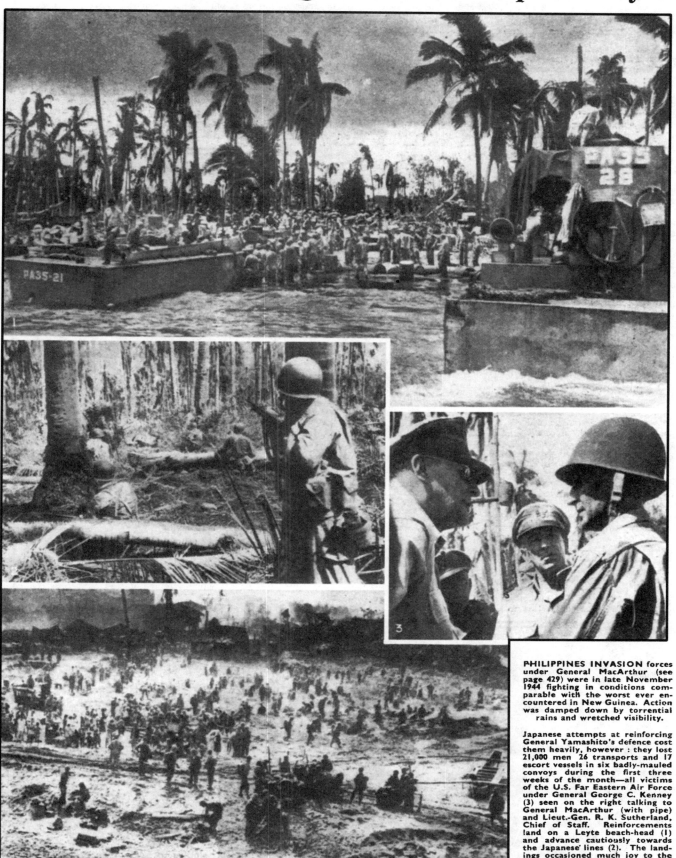

PHILIPPINES INVASION forces under General MacArthur (see page 429) were in late November 1944 fighting in conditions comparable with the worst ever encountered in New Guinea. Action was damped down by torrential rains and wretched visibility.

Japanese attempts at reinforcing General Yamashito's defence cost them heavily, however : they lost 21,000 men 26 transports and 17 escort vessels in six badly-mauled convoys during the first three weeks of the month—all victims of the U.S. Far Eastern Air Force under General George C. Kenney (3) seen on the right talking to General MacArthur (with pipe) and Lieut.-Gen. R. K. Sutherland, Chief of Staff. Reinforcements land on a Leyte beach-head (1) and advance cautiously towards the Japanese lines (2). The landings occasioned much joy to the half-starved, war-weary islanders : down from the hills and up from the cellars they swarmed to greet their liberators (4) with cheers and yells. See also illus. page 487.

Photos, New York Times Photos, Keystone, Planet News PAGE 501

How Mosquitoes Released Doomed Men from Gaol

An amazing feat of low-level precision-bombing, the attack on Amiens Prison is one of the most memorable achievements of the R.A.F. For security reasons eight months had to pass before a full account could be given of this great exploit, which took place on February 18, 1944, and resulted in the liberation of Frenchmen whose death at Nazi hands was imminent.

ONE hundred patriots were awaiting execution in Amiens Prison. Their crime was that of assisting the Allied cause : some had helped our airmen to escape after being shot down in France. Time was shortening. Death sentences might be carried out at any moment.

A Mosquito wing of the R.A.F. Second Tactical Air Force received urgent orders. The walls of the prison courtyard were to be smashed in two places and, simultaneously, both ends of the main building were to be "opened." Way of escape thus provided, the prisoners would dash out to neighbouring woodland, where further assistance would be waiting—at the hands of Free Frenchmen in our confidence as to time and method of the gaol-breaking.

That Mosquito wing had not only to effect the release with least possible injury to the prisoners, but to inflict utmost possible casualties on the German guards. On the day appointed, the selected team of airmen lined up beside their planes on a snow-covered airfield in England. The wing comprised British, Australian and New Zealand squadrons, including R.C.A.F. airmen, commanded by Group Captain P. C. Pickard, D.S.O. and two bars, D.F.C., one of the most outstanding and experienced bomber pilots in the R.A.F. and, incidentally, hero of the film "Target for Tonight." He told his crews, "It's a death or glory job, boys. You have to break that prison wide open !"

SIX aircraft, constituting the first wave, were to breach the wall on its northeast and north-west perimeter. The second wave of six was to divide and open up both ends of the gaol and destroy the German guards' quarters. A third wave was to be in readiness in case any part of the daring plan miscarried. The honour of being the first wave gave rise to heated discussion. The toss of a coin decided the matter. The New Zealanders won, then the Australians beat the British squadron for second place.

A model of the prison had been carefully constructed, and after studying this the crews felt confident that, with just a little luck, they would achieve perfect timing in the attack and, bombing from "deck level," would be able to do unto Amiens Prison all that was required to ensure full success of the plan. So small was the target that almost super-human effort and skill would be called for to avoid collisions. It was perhaps small consolation to the nerve-strung pilots that one Mosquito was detailed to make film and photographic records of the attack !

An hour before midday, with cloud lying low and heavy snow under foot, the squadrons left to rendezvous with their fighter escort on the south coast of England. Flying at sea level across the Channel, they swept around the north of Amiens and approached the target—a gaunt building on the straight Amiens-Albert road. Precisely according to schedule, the New Zealanders went in first.

Mosquitoes 'Lifted' Over 20-ft. Wall

"I saw their bombs explode," an officer of the Australian squadron later reported. "Then it was the turn of my squadron. There were two annexes to the prison, and these housed the German guards. By attacking these we would not only open up the prison, but kill a lot of Germans as well. And that is what we did. We flew so low to drop our delayed-action bombs that we had to lift our aircraft over the high wall and then skid our bombs into the annexe. As we passed over the prison we flew through the smoke and dirt caused by the New Zealanders' bombs."

So accurate were the attacks that the third wave found itself with nothing to do but go home again, whilst the photographic Mosquito, making three runs over the objective, saw the breaches in the 20-ft. high and three-ft. thick courtyard wall, the ends of the building broken, prisoners running out through the breaches, Germans lying on the ground and, on the last run, some patriots disappearing across the snow on the field outside the prison. An R.A.F. officer who was flying this Mosquito which took the "recce" pictures reported :

"We went flat-out through the snow on this side of the Channel and caught up with the bombing aircraft over the Continent . . . We circled to the north of the target . . . When we came in on our first run we saw how accurate and successful the bombers had been. The ends were blown off the building and the outer walls were breached. In the yard we saw a large group of prisoners making good their escape. The fixed cameras in the aircraft were doing their job, and the photographer crouched in the nose was using his hand-held camera. It was his enthusiasm which made us stay longer than I considered healthy. After each run I tentatively suggested going home, but his reply was, 'Oh, no—come on, just one more !' Finally even he was satisfied and we made back for base. His photographs were good. They showed clearly the flattened building and walls, black on the snow-covered ground, and the released prisoners running in all directions across the yard."

Although, as was unavoidable, some of the patriots were killed by German machine-guns as well as by bombs, it is known that the Germans themselves suffered severe casualties. And the operation was not completed

Group Capt. PICKARD Flt.-Lt. BROADLEY
D.S.O. (2 bars), D.F.C.   D.S.O., D.F.C., D.F.M.
The death of these heroes of the raid on Amiens-prison ended one of the greatest partnerships of the R.A.F. They had been flying together for almost four years. Both were born in Yorkshire   *Photos, Topical Press*

without loss on our side, for two Mosquitoes, one of which carried Group Captain Pickard and his navigator, Flight-Lieut. J. A. Broadley, D.S.O., D.F.C., D.F.M., were shot down, as also were two of the fighter escort.

Since the successful invasion of France and subsequent relief of Amiens, it has been possible to collect certain details which had hitherto been unobtainable. All that was originally known of Group Captain Pickard's fate was that his aircraft was last seen circling over the prison, slightly above the height at which the Mosquitoes were attacking. He had detached himself from the main formations in order to take up a position from which, though it was dangerous, he could best see and direct the operations.

IT now seems certain that when he had ordered the third—last—wave to withdraw without dropping its bombs, he saw one of the Mosquitoes brought down by the fierce flak put up by the German defences. About to go down to investigate the crash and discover the fate of the crew, he was pounced upon by two F.W.190s sent up to intercept the raiders—and to them he fell victim.

He was shot down a few miles from Amiens, and his body, with that of his navigator, was removed by friendly villagers who had seen the entire action. The Germans forced them to give up the two bodies, but were unable to prevent the villagers from attending the burial in the cemetery alongside the prison which Group Captain Pickard had helped to "crack" open. After the invasion, when his comrades reached Amiens and sought news of the aircrews' fate, the villagers handed over to them photographs of the graves and personal belongings which they had hidden from the Germans for months.

Whilst Group Captain Pickard's comrades survive not one of them is likely to forget the tragically significant words he uttered after the briefing of the crews at an Allied Expeditionary Air Force intelligence room in England : "It's a death or glory job, boys !"

PAYING A LAST TRIBUTE at the grave, in Amiens Cemetery, of Group Captain P. C. Pickard, D.S.O. (two bars), D.F.C., heroic leader of the R.A.F. raid on Amiens Prison—disclosed on October 28, 1944 and related in this page—are Leading Aircraftman Albert Sullivan, of Newark, Notts., and Marie Yvonne, a grateful Frenchwoman. Buried beside the Group Captain was his navigator, Flight-Lieut. J. A. Broadley, D.S.O., D.F.C., D.F.M.   PAGE 502   *Photo. British Official*

R.A.F. Bombs Cracked Open the Prison at Amiens

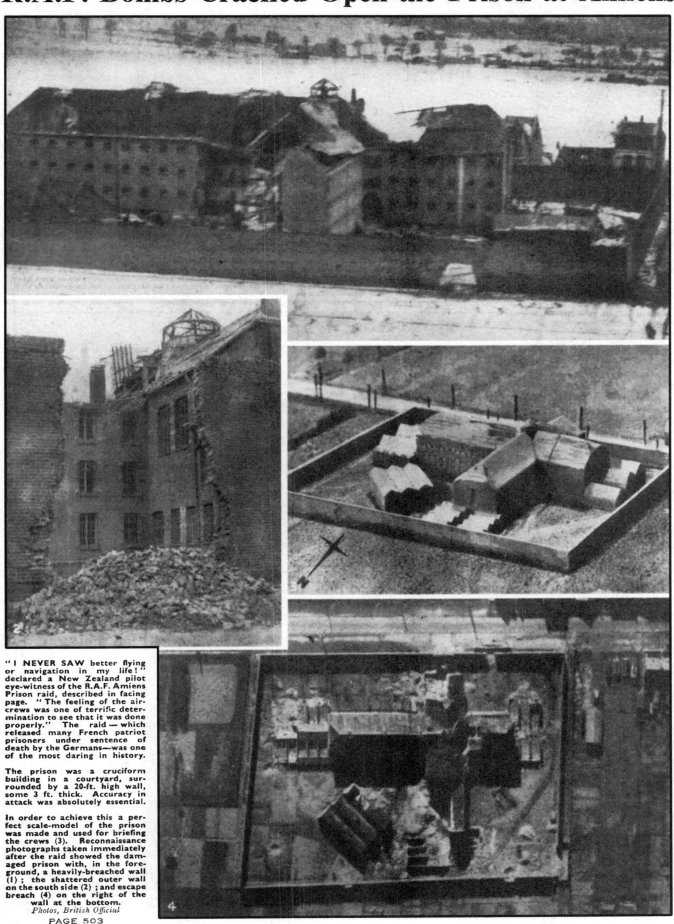

"I NEVER SAW better flying or navigation in my life!" declared a New Zealand pilot eye-witness of the R.A.F. Amiens Prison raid, described in facing page. "The feeling of the aircrews was one of terrific determination to see that it was done properly." The raid — which released many French patriot prisoners under sentence of death by the Germans—was one of the most daring in history.

The prison was a cruciform building in a courtyard, surrounded by a 20-ft. high wall, some 3 ft. thick. Accuracy in attack was absolutely essential.

In order to achieve this a perfect scale-model of the prison was made and used for briefing the crews (3). Reconnaissance photographs taken immediately after the raid showed the damaged prison with, in the foreground, a heavily-breached wall (1); the shattered outer wall on the south side (2); and escape breach (4) on the right of the wall at the bottom.

Photos, British Official

Tank-Carrying Hamilcar: World's Largest Glider

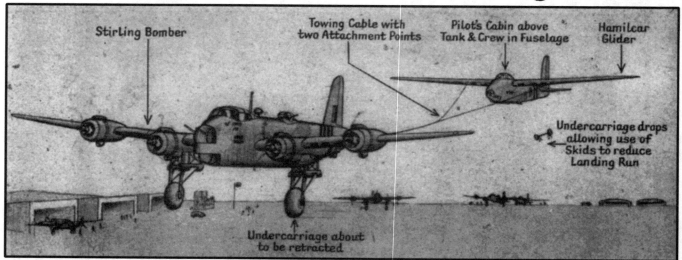

Stirling Bomber — Towing Cable with two Attachment Points — Pilot's Cabin above Tank & Crew in Fuselage — Hamilcar Glider

Undercarriage drops allowing use of Skids to reduce Landing Run

Undercarriage about to be retracted

TAKING OFF, TOWED BY A STIRLING BOMBER, the laden Hamilcar glider rises into a higher position than that of the towing aircraft to avoid the violent slipstream from the airscrews. Besides tanks and howitzers, Hamilcars have carried engineering equipment—the latter enabling our airborne troops in Holland in October 1944 to establish vital bridge-heads and so take the enemy by surprise.

ON BRITAIN'S huge motorless aircraft—the Hamilcar, which the Germans believed to be a troop-carrier—depended much of the success of the Allied airborne landings on the Continent from D-Day onwards. Tremendous punch was given to ground operations by the use of these gliders which, towed by heavy bombers of the R.A.F., carried a Tetrarch tank and other heavy equipment.

In London on November 11, 1944, Major-General Lentaigne —successor to Wingate of the Chindits—disclosed that during the Burma fighting earlier in the year, gliders were used on a large scale for the first time for landings behind the enemy lines. These methods were reported to England, greatly influencing D-Day planning.

On board the Hamilcar the tank, carrying a gun, is started up while still airborne, and is thus ready to go into immediate action. At the moment of landing the nose of the glider swings back and the fuselage sinks to the ground to allow the tank to roll out into operation.

A TETRARCH TANK BACKS INTO A HAMILCAR GLIDER under its own power. This light tank, around which the glider was originally " tailored " to fit, weighs over 7 tons. Its overall length is approximately 14 ft. (including the gun, with remarkable fire power) ; width 8 ft. 5 ins. ; height 7 ft. Its speed is 25 m.p.h., and it is capable of climbing a slope of 35 degrees and negotiating almost any kind of terrain.

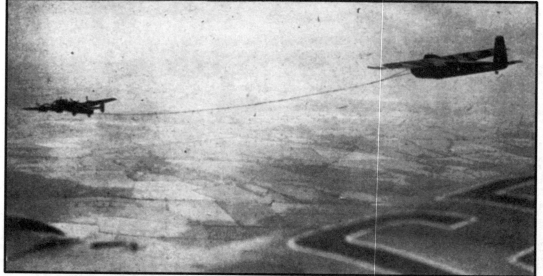

THE GLIDER IN FLIGHT, and its heavy-bomber towing plane, made a familiar sight in Holland during the great airborne invasion of September 17, 1944 (see page 349). Squadron-leader James Stewart, tow-plane pilot at Arnhem, was awarded the D.F.C. for flying his plane deliberately into flak to distract the enemy gunners from gliders on their way down.

Photos, British Official. Drawing by D. C. Burge.

LEADING HAMILCAR PILOT, Major Alec Dale, R.A.F., a Shropshire man, was awarded the D.F.C. for his work with gliders in Sicily in the summer of 1943. " The Hamilcars are beautifully easy to handle, in spite of their weight," he declares, " and the organization of the landings in France was so good compared with the Sicilian show that there was really nothing to it."

Besides airborne troops and tanks these huge gliders have carried 75-mm. howitzers, 3-in. mortars, bridging material and assault boats. At Arnhem in October the assault boats proved invaluable in helping our men to recross the River Lek. The Hamilcar's wing-span is 110 ft., 8 ft. more than that of a Lancaster.

It possesses, however, such manoeuvrability that it can be landed in a small meadow. By daylight and by dark it can touch down with almost mathematical precision from a release point miles away.

I WAS THERE!
Eye Witness Stories of the War

They Told Me 'The Tea Always Gets Stewed!'

Said the captain to Laurence Wilkinson, Daily Express correspondent in Germany: "Now's your chance. No one has ever written about British Army cooks." The result is this pen-picture of the woes of the cooks at the front, and of the transport drivers who have appalling battles of their own to fight as they take the rations up to forward troops.

You drive east, through the happier part of Holland to get to the "dead end" front, near Geilenkirchen, where although shells fall at the rate of about one a second during most of the day, the official communiqué says regularly: "There was little action worthy of note." There is a smile and sometimes a wave for the troops instead of the tragic stare they encounter in the rubble-filled streets of Eindhoven and other Dutch towns to the north.

In the fine city of Maastricht, for example, the war is still a novelty. The great Maastricht bridge was dynamited in spectacular fashion by the retreating Germans, but otherwise there is little damage. The shops, fully lit in the afternoon, are packed with goods unobtainable for years in England. A few miles farther on one is in Germany. The silence is noticeable. The roads are empty; nothing moves. Notice boards on shell-torn trees warn you that there may be mines at the edge of the road.

The guns open up and blast rocks the car. Even the sidelights have to be switched off farther along the road. There is a block; a tank has skidded. A captain says: "It might be dangerous to try to carry on farther." He offers shelter with his cooks in an underground cellar. "Now's your chance," says he. "No one has ever written about British Army cooks."

It is 6.30 and the cooks are preparing tomorrow's lunch for the front-line troops—four slices of bread, thinly spread with melted margarine, and one bully beef sandwich. Then there will be tea. The colour-sergeant explains that the tea is made specially weak because by the time it gets only two miles up the line it will not only be stewed almost black, but will probably be cold as well, so

difficult is the journey. No ordinary transport can make it. Everything has to be taken up on a wide-tracked vehicle, including water for drinking and, if possible, for washing.

The day before yesterday "Unlucky" Cooper, the driver, came back with the tea after 13¼ hours. He could not get through, though the journey was only six miles there and back. Everybody agrees that fighting troops should be supplied with those little cookers which are small enough to slip into the breast pocket, and use solidified methylated spirit fuel. It is smokeless and can be used right up forward where even if the food cannot get through, the men can keep themselves going with a hot drink. Apparently, however, there is a shortage of these cookers. The question is to be referred to the corps commander.

There is a continuous din of shelling, but only occasionally is it close enough to shake the building and make the chief cook look up from the petrol stove. He throws a match

in front of the jet, and leaps back as the flame spurts higher than his head. There is a knack in lighting these No. 1 Hydro burners, which, he said, he learned after he was once burned. But he wonders somebody has not invented a gadget to make it easier.

The driver who left at 4.15 with the afternoon food van comes in. It is now 10.40, and he is dirty and tired. He has to make his journey on a road under German observation, since the other route is knee deep in mud. The forward troops were stopped by heavy mortaring and machine-gunning, and had to dig in where they dropped on the mud. The driver must stop at each mud-hole and call the occupants to collect the food, which is probably stone cold, and hardly worth eating by then.

The men are soaked by days of non-stop rain. They complain of the quality of the food, though, says the driver, it might be some consolation to them to know that the Germans only get their supplies up about once every two days. The shelling goes on all night; so does the cooking and the loading and unloading of food wagons, the clatter of billy cans and containers, and the roar of the petrol stove.

After four hours' sleep, broken only by the blast of the guns on both sides, the cooks are up again. The cannonading outside is terrific. "The gunners usually give them a final pasting before they knock off for breakfast," said the chief cook. "It's just to keep them quiet." Yes, this is a "Dead End" front all right.

For Four Years the Nazis Tried to Catch Me

Emile Declercq, 23-year-old son of a Belgian grain merchant, was known to the Germans as a hard-bitten veteran who fought them from under cover with all the means at his disposal. He told his story, in Nov. 1944, to a News Chronicle reporter, in a hospital near London, whilst recovering from wounds before going back to resume the fight.

The Germans could not catch me, so they took my father away as a hostage.

I learned that he was being taken by car towards Bruges. I got together a few of my men and, mounted on motor-cycles, we overtook the car, forced the driver to stop, and freed my father after a terrific battle.

With wounds in the shoulder and chest and eight ribs broken, I was of no more use

for immediate active service. I lay hidden until the Canadians arrived. Then I was brought to England. All I want to do is to get back to Belgium, to rejoin either the Maquis or the regular Belgian Army.

I was a private in the Belgian Army when the Germans invaded my country. I was taken prisoner, but escaped, took to the woods, and joined the Maquis. After a

MESS TINS IN HAND, men of the British 2nd Army queue for breakfast from an improvised cookhouse in a trench (left) at Breskens, Holland, after its capture by the Canadians on October 22, 1944. Watched by the farmer's wife, a private of the Army Catering Corps makes apple-dumplings in an open-air oven (right) during the advance on Hertogenbosch towards the end of the same month. Preparing meals for front-line men is no "cushy" job, and transporting them is even less enjoyable, as told above.

Photos, British Newspaper Pool, New York Times Photos

EMILE DECLERCQ, Belgian patriot now in England, was the hero of an extraordinary exploit in which he rescued his own father, who was held as hostage for himself, as related here. *Photo, News Chronicle*

while I was made a commandant, with 120 to 130 men. We operated—always by night —in conjunction with other companies in the triangle bounded by Ypres, Bruges and Dixmude. Our orders, from an unknown

leader at headquarters, were always signed by a number. Even now I do not know who he was, but he was a great leader.

The life was full of excitement. We were in deadly peril most of the time—and quislings were almost as great a menace as the Germans. We specialized in night attacks and in sabotage. We destroyed bridges to hold up supply trains; hid Allied airmen who were forced down and in many cases effected their return to England; and, most important of all, we sent messages to England about the fortifications.

The Germans little knew that many of the men they had forced to work for them in building defence lines were in close touch with us. Every alteration, every modification, was notified to us. Our news was relayed to England once a fortnight, at first by a secret radio. When this became too dangerous, we handed written reports to the pilots of Allied planes sent over for the purpose.

We were fed by farmers and villagers, and supplied with arms by parachute. At night we took heavy toll of the Germans and their supply routes. Once we saw some Canadian pilots captured. That night we crept into the camp where they were held prisoner, killed some of the guards and got the Canadians safely away. We kept them hidden until the Allied armies arrived.

SWEEPING FOR MINES IN VORONEZH after its relief by the Red Army in 1943 was a ticklish business in heavy snow. A remarkable story of the evacuation of precious industrial equipment from the town is told in this page. *Photo, U.S.S.R. Official*

Red Army retook the sector. A bunch of sappers helped me to de-mine the factory grounds and to transfer the equipment to the railway. It was loaded on to the trucks during a heavy air raid, and some of it was damaged. In Moscow, when we checked up, we found that the main part of the automatic machine was missing. We had to be patient. There was no question of going back to Voronezh at once to collect it—some of the biggest battles of the war were raging there. I had to wait until the Germans had been kicked out for good.

Then I went back to Voronezh for the third time, and found the missing part. The Germans had used it to shield a trench. We had to put the machine together without the aid of blueprints, and new parts had to be made to replace those damaged in the air raid. And now we are beating our target for chocolate animal production!

How We Saved the Precious Chocolate Machine

Now again in full production, doing the work of 250 people, an elaborate piece of machinery, 150 yards long and nearly ceiling-high, for making chocolates, was in peril of falling into German hands. How he helped to save it is told by Vassili Davydov, by courtesy of Soviet War News.

WHEN the Germans were pushing towards Moscow we had to evacuate our most precious equipment, including a machine which made what we call figure chocolate—teddy bears and golliwogs and that kind of thing. There are only six machines like it in the whole world. We were rather upset at having to let it go, because although we were at that time fully occupied with priority orders for the Red Army—mainly with making concentrates for paratroops—we did hope it wouldn't be long before we could start making sweets for children again.

Now when the Germans overran the Ukraine the Kiev confectionery factory evacuated its equipment to Voronezh, and among this equipment was a new imported machine for making chocolate animals, an improved model, made by a foreign firm to our specification. It had arrived in Kiev just before the outbreak of war. Well, in due course the fighting reached Voronezh. The confectionery factory was badly blitzed, and the Germans sowed mines thickly around. The People's Commissariat knew that the Kiev equipment was somewhere on the premises, and sent me to get it.

I arrived on the Voronezh sector one frosty day in the depth of winter. I had to leave the train some distance from the city, because the battle was raging. In fact, the ground was quaking. I headed in the direction of the gunfire, and soon reached the factory. To my joy, I came across some battered crates and machine-parts, nearly buried in the snow, but just as I was beginning to investigate I heard a yell: "It's dangerous to walk about here, man! Haven't you got eyes in your head?" Then, of course, I noticed the mine warnings.

The chap who yelled at me was a sapper, and he got very suspicious. He didn't like the look of my civilian clothes, and he thought my accent was peculiar. To be on the safe side, he hauled me along to see his commander—which was exactly what I wanted. Clearly I would need expert help if I was to get that machine out of the minefield.

They were very decent about it, cleared a passage through the minefield, and told me to go ahead. I located 85 huge crates containing parts of the new machine, and scores of other boxes containing valuable stuff, well worth saving. But I didn't have a chance to remove a single box. The area was again captured by the Germans, and I had to go back to Moscow empty handed.

I returned to Voronezh as soon as the

From Saipan Our Forts Flew to Bomb Tokyo

Flying with Super-Fortresses to take the war to the Japanese homeland on November 24, 1944, Denis Warner of the Daily Mail certainly did not expect to complete the round trip of 3,000 miles, for reasons made clear in this vivid account written aboard the aircraft in which he was a passenger.

WE bombed Tokyo an hour ago. It was easy, almost over-easy, but now we are fighting a bitter battle to get back to Saipan. The tail-gunner is unconscious with a head wound. We have lost altitude. Our petrol supply is more than dangerously low. It hardly seems worth while writing this story. If we make a night landing on the sea, there is not much of a chance for any of us. We have left Japan's coast behind, and are heading south-east over the Pacific.

It was full daylight when we took off from Saipan this morning. I was immediately behind the pilot and co-pilot. Captain Hamilton, the pilot and veteran of 43 missions in Europe, the only member of the crew with previous combat experience, said: "Ten million guys would give anything to change places with us—and in about seven hours we'll be only too glad to make the change."

Hamilton, 26 years old and grey-haired, did not know then how right he was. The take-off was an awful moment. Hamilton was "begging" the plane to get into the air. Rivulets of sweat were running off his face and neck, and his jacket was soaked.

"Come on, we've got to have 90, we've got to have 90!" he entreated the plane.

Gradually we got speed and swung away northward, then north-westward for Tokyo. Things were moving towards what we hoped would be the climax. Now the bombardier was removing the cover of the bomb-sight. The navigator was making a final check of our position.

We still had a good many miles to go, but there was every chance of fighter opposition. Just now the radio operator has picked up a message from the first Fortress over Tokyo. Brig.-Gen. "Rosy" O'Donnell's plane, with "Rosy" himself at the controls, had hit the primary target—the Nakajima Aircraft Works, nine miles from the centre of Tokyo.

This was good news. The general said the target was visible. That was even better news for us who were to follow him about an hour later, although we knew his planes would have stirred up a hornet's nest of fighters. Suddenly Japan came through the mists—just a glimpse of shadowy outline. I was so excited I couldn't write my notes. As we crossed the coastline the first thing we saw was an immense apparently concreted airfield.

Then, for the first time since leaving Saipan, I began to feel really afraid. My throat was dry, and I could feel beads of sweat forming between my fingers. It was a job to make formation with the rest of the group. It burned up lots of our precious petrol, but it had to be done. There were houses, villages and what looked like another aerodrome. We passed innumerable airfields, and so we came to Fujiyama. Snow-capped, its peak sparkled in the early afternoon. I had always wanted to see Fujiyama. It looks not so good now, but it was our landmark.

Our beam turned to Tokyo. We turned slightly for 60 miles to run up to the target. Clouds still obscured most of the land, but through the long windrift in the clouds above which we flew we could occasionally see the countryside. It could not have taken us long to reach Tokyo, but it seemed an eternity. I was straining my eyes to see it and I was looking for fighters too. I saw fighters first. There was one ahead of us, 2,000 ft. below, but climbing steadily. There was another on our left, also below.

I watched his approach. He came slowly, but always upwards. As I watched, one jumped on our tail and made a pass at our tail-gunner. Our gun and the Jap's rattled at the same moment. Some of us saw the Jap fighter pull out, and all of us wondered why our gun stopped so suddenly. But for 30 seconds there were other things to think about. Lots of light ack-ack was bursting a few thousand feet below us, and now the heavies were right on the mark.

Ten heavy bursts exploded with a shattering roar between us and the plane to our left. Nakajima aircraft factory was obscured, but the main part of the city of Tokyo was visible beneath. On our left, miles below, were waterfront wharves. For maybe 20 seconds we flew with bomb doors open, then I saw Lieut. Ferand squeeze our release. A cascade of bombs fell from other planes.

Bombs fell along the waterfront, and it is certain that the Emperor behind his moat

and hundreds of thousands of other little yellow men heard the concussions and knew that war had come to their homeland. As we swung out seaward we could see more fighters coming up. Off the coast Hamilton checked his crew. There was no reply over the interphone from the tail-gunner.

We depressurized, and sent the co-pilot back to investigate. Five minutes later another member of the crew found the co-pilot had succumbed from lack of oxygen while trying to remove the tail-gunner from his compartment. The gunner was bleeding freely from a wound in the head—possibly from a Jap fighter—and was almost dead from lack of oxygen.

We had no alternative but to descend to where rescue work was possible without oxygen. That almost settled our chances of getting home.

Night is closing in and we have hundreds of miles to go. Now there seems so little chance of getting back I am giving up writing this story, and anyway you can't write when you are as tired and scared as I am.

SAIPAN—*Same Evening :* We got back an hour ago with the tail-gunner dead in the rear compartment and every tank showing "empty." We hit the runway and taxied on two engines draining the last drop. The raid on Tokyo is considered to be more than successful.

TWO PAIRS OF BOMB DOORS are a unique feature of the great U.S. Boeing B-29 Super-Fortresses now carrying the war into the heart of Japan. In the week beginning Nov. 26, 1944, Tokyo was heavily bombed three times, and again on December 3. (See story commencing in facing page.)
Photo, Central Press

OUR DIARY OF THE WAR

NOVEMBER 22, Wednesday *1,908th day*
Western Front.—City of Metz entirely cleared of enemy. Eschweiler captured by 1st and 9th Armies.
Air.—R.A.F. heavy bombers again drained portion of Mittelland and Dortmund-Ems canals on night of November 21-22.

NOVEMBER 23, Thursday *1,909th day*
Western Front.—French and U.S. troops entered Strasbourg.
Air.—Nordstern oil plant at Gelsenkirchen attacked by U.S. and also by R.A.F. bombers.
Russian Front.—Tokay, north-east Hungary, occupied by Red Army troops. Cop (Czechoslovakia) again captured by Russians, after changing hands.
Pacific.—Announced that U.S. task force bombarded Matsura, Kurile Is., on November 21.

NOVEMBER 24, Friday *1,910th day*
Russian Front.—Island of Oesel completely cleared of Germans.
Far East.—Tokyo bombed in daylight by Super-Fortresses based on Saipan in the Marianas.

NOVEMBER 25, Saturday *1,911th day*
Western Front.—9th Army advancing on Julich captured Bourheim and penetrated into Koslar.
Air.—1,000 U.S. bombers and 1,000 fighters attacked Leuna oil plants and marshalling yards at Bingen. At night Mosquitoes bombed Nuremberg.

NOVEMBER 26, Sunday *1,912th day*
Western Front.—Weisweiler, on motor road from Aix-la-Chapelle (Aachen) to Cologne, captured by 1st Army.
Air.—More than 1,000 U.S. bombers attacked oil refinery at Misburg, near Hanover, railway viaduct at Bielefeld and marshalling yards at Hamm ; 138 enemy fighters destroyed. Two V2 sites in Holland bombed by Spitfire bombers.
General.—Gen. Sir Harold Alexander promoted Field-Marshal and appointed Supreme Allied Commander, Mediterranean.

NOVEMBER 27, Monday *1,913th day*
Western Front.—Infantry of 3rd Army entered St. Avold, S.W. of Saarbruecken.
Air.—R.A.F. Lancasters dropped 12,000-lb. blast bombs on Munich. Allied bombers attacked railway yards at

Offenburg, Bingen and Cologne. U.S. fighters destroyed another 102 German aircraft. At night, R.A.F. bombers in great strength attacked railway centres behind Western Front.
Far East.—Super-Fortresses from Saipan again bombed Tokyo.
Pacific.—Japanese fighter aircraft, with heavy loss to themselves, attacked Super-Fortress base at Saipan.
Home Front.—Underground explosion at R.A.F. depot near Burton-on-Trent caused many casualties.
General.—Announced that Lieut.-Gen. F. A. M. Browning had been appointed Chief of Staff, S.E. Asia Command.

NOVEMBER 28, Tuesday *1,914th day*
Western Front.—3rd Army after making progress in Saar region held a front of 26 miles in Germany. 9th Army patrols reached the Roer.
Air.—Very strong force of Mosquitoes bombed Nuremberg. At night, Essen and Neuss were heavily attacked by Lancasters and Halifaxes.
Russian Front.—In Hungary, Soviet troops forced river Tisza north of Nyiregyhaza.
Balkans.—Halifaxes of Balkan Air Force dropped food and supplies over Tirana, Albanian capital.
Sea.—Announced that on night of June 21, British "human torpedo" sank cruiser Bolzano in Spezia harbour.

NOVEMBER 29, Wednesday *1,915th day*
Western Front.—U.S. 1st Army cleared towns of Huertgen, Langerwehe and Jungersdorf.
Air.—More than 1,000 Fortresses and Liberators with 1,000 fighters bombed oil plant at Misburg and railway yards at Hamm. Mosquitoes made daylight attack on Duisburg, and R.A.F. heavies bombed Dortmund. Spitfire bombers made another attack on V2 sites in Holland.
Russian Front.—Announced that Soviet and Yugoslav troops had crossed the Danube south of Budapest, capturing Pecs and Mohacs.
Far East.—Super-Fortresses again raided Tokyo, for first time at night.

NOVEMBER 30, Thursday *1,916th day*
Western Front.—Announced that first Allied convoy had entered Antwerp.
Air.—R.A.F. and U.S. bombers attacked oil plants in Leipzig and Ruhr areas and marshalling yards near Saarbruecken. V2 sites in Holland again bombed. At night, R.A.F. dropped over 2,000 tons of bombs on Duisburg.
Russian Front.—Eger and Sziksző, Hungarian communications centres, captured by Soviet troops.
Pacific.—Japanese convoy bound for Leyte destroyed by U.S. aircraft, the seventh lost in this area.

DECEMBER 1, Friday *1,917th day*
Western Front.—3rd Army reached Saar river above and below Merzig.
Burma.—Scots troops of 36th Division occupied Pinwe.
Home Front.—Announced that Princess Elizabeth had launched new battleship, greatest yet built in British Isles.

DECEMBER 2, Saturday *1,918th day*
Western Front.—Saarlouis (Saarlautern) entered by U.S. troops.
Air.—R.A.F. Lancasters bombed Hansa benzol plant at Dortmund.
Burma.—East African troops entered Kalewa on the Chindwin.
General.—General de Gaulle arrived in Moscow.

DECEMBER 3, Sunday *1,919th day*
Western Front.—3rd Army troops at Saarlouis captured main bridge across the Saar. Saar Union cleared of the enemy.
Russian Front.—Hungarian communications centres of Miskolcz and Satoralja-Ujhely, north-east of Budapest, captured by Red Army.
Far East.—Super-Fortresses from Marianas again bombed Tokyo.
Home Front.—King George VI took salute at " stand-down " parade of Home Guard.

DECEMBER 4, Monday *1,920th day*
Western Front.—2nd Army troops cleared last enemy bridge-head west of Maas. Saarbruecken under fire from 3rd Army.
Air.—U.S. bombers and fighters attacked marshalling yards, etc., at Kassel, Mainz and Giessen. R.A.F. Lancasters attacked Oberhausen, Karlsruhe and Heilbronn.
Mediterranean.—Enemy shipping at Rhodes bombarded by units of Royal Navy.

DECEMBER 5, Tuesday *1,921st day*
Western Front.—3rd Army troops completed clearing of Saarlouis, and crossed Saar at fresh point.
Air.—In battles over Berlin 91 enemy fighters shot down by Allied aircraft. Marshalling yards at Munster, Hamm and Soest also bombed.
Italy.—Canadian and British troops of 8th Army entered Ravenna.
Russian Front.—Soviet troops in Hungary reached Lake Balaton.
Balkans.—In Athens British troops intervened in fighting between rival Greek factions.

★ ═══════ *Flash-backs* ═══════ ★

1939
November 23. *Rawalpindi sunk by pocket battleship Deutschland.*
November 30. *Russians launched attack on Finland.*

1941
December 6. *Russians began big counter-offensive at Moscow.*
December 7. *Japan declared war on Great Britain and U.S.A. Pearl Harbour bombed.*
December 7-8. *Japanese troops landed in Northern Malaya.*

1942
November 24. *Russians advancing from north joined with defenders of Stalingrad, relieving the city.*
November 27. *German troops occupied Toulon. French warships in harbour scuttled by crews.*

1943
November 28. *First meeting at Teheran (Persia) between Roosevelt, Stalin and Churchill.*
December 1. *8th Army broke German "winter line" on Sangro.*

THE WAR IN THE AIR

by Capt. Norman Macmillan, M.C., A.F.C.

ANOTHER American Bomber Command, the 21st, sprang into the news by making the first air attack on Tokyo since the Mitchell bombers, led by (then) Brigadier " Jimmy " Doolittle on April 18, 1942, made the original attack by taking off from the aircraft carrier Hornet, nicknamed " Shangri-La " by President Roosevelt, 800 miles from Japan, and, after bombing, flying on towards land airfields in China (see pages 154–155, Vol. 7).

The 21st Bomber Command, grouped with the 20th Bomber Command, forms the U.S. Army 20th Air Force, whose operations are strategically controlled from Washington by General Henry H. Arnold, Chief of Staff of the United States Army Air Force. The 20th Bomber Command operated from bases in China (until forced to withdraw to India when the Japanese swept over Kwangsi Province), bombing Yawata steel works in Kyushu three times and delivering an equal number of attacks against the Manchurian steel centre of Anshan. In Nagasaki's industrial belt an aircraft plant and other factories were bombed. Oil plants at Palembang and near Medan, docks at Taku, Dairen, Singapore base, Rangoon and Bangkok railheads were among the strategic target operations of this Command.

No doubt the Japanese hoped, by forcing the Fortresses out of China, to save their own islands from air bombardment, at least for a time. Now that 20th Bomber Command operates from India the striking power of the Allies against the Japanese invaders of Malaya, Siam, Sumatra, Java and all the western zone of the South-East Asia Command will be strengthened, while any hope that the Japanese may have entertained of saving Japan proper from air bombing has been falsified by the commencement of the operations of Brig.-General Heywood S. Hansell's 21st Command from bases in the Mariana Islands of Saipan and Tinian. Although the centre of Saipan lies 1,460 miles south-south-east of Tokyo, the long range of the Super Fortress bombers enables them to attack targets within the enemy's capital area.

PHOTOGRAPHIC Flights Over Target Areas of Japan

The first attack on Tokyo from the Marianas bases was made on Friday, November 24, 1944, five months after the surface fighting had wrested them from the enemy. (See first-hand description in p. 506.) The second raid was made on the following Monday, also in daylight. The third raid was made in the night of Wednesday, November 29. Before the attacks were begun, reconnaissance Super-Fortresses had flown over Japan photographing the target areas, so that Intelligence could locate targets accurately and the operational programme be detailed. Among the targets photographed were factories, airfields, docks, hydro-electric power plants vital to Japanese war industry, and dams. The Japanese reported the two daylight raids to have been made each by 40 bombers, flying in formations of ten. The aircraft flew high, using compressor equipment to pressurize the crew quarters while they flew through the sub-stratosphere.

It should be remembered that the term stratosphere is variable in terms of height. The lower level of the stratosphere changes with atmospheric temperature, being highest at the Equator and lowest at the Poles in winter. A bomber might be flying in the stratosphere at 6,000 feet above the North Pole. yet have to fly at over 30,000 feet to

travel within the stratosphere above the Equator. The strain on pilots who have to get huge, heavily laden Super-Fortresses off the runways at nearly 100 m.p.h. in the sticky, damp heat of Saipan's climate must be terrific. With sweat oozing from every pore the pilot has then to climb upward into the cold of the near-equatorial sub-stratosphere, where the temperature of the air falls to 40 or more degrees below zero. No one who has not flown in the tropics can quite understand what this means. We should respect the mental courage and superb physical condition of these aircrews. Among the Tokyo targets attacked was a factory of the Nakajima Aircraft Co., Ltd., which makes Army and Navy fighters, torpedo-bombers, transport aircraft (including the Douglas DC-2), and aircraft engines.

Japan is a mountainous country, with a generally damp climate, and a sky much obscured by clouds. Consequently, at the great range of attack from Saipan, the aircraft crews cannot know when they leave base if it will be possible to bomb visually. Fortunately this is not now a vital factor in bombing—as it once was. For, as the result of much scientific research in Britain, a form of radar " X-ray " or " television " sighting has been devised, which enables the bombardier to see targets through miles of cloud or darkness. Electrical impulses emitted from the aircraft are " echoed " from objects on the ground and, working like a fluoroscope, the " gen-box," as the R.A.F. calls it, produces the invisible rays upon a glass screen as visible rays which form a picture of the groundscape.

IDENTIFICATION Now Possible Even in Zero Visibility

The picture can be reduced in scale to cover a greater area of the ground and so permit the navigator to see where he is going ; or it can be increased in scale to enlarge details of targets. Ships, particular parts

R.A.F. THUNDERBOLTS IN BURMA, on an advanced airstrip, are here being serviced by ground crews. Two planes are coming in to land after a raid on Japanese military targets.
PAGE 508   *Photo, British Official*

TAIL OF A V2 ROCKET ends its faster-than-sound journey as salvage loaded on to a lorry in England. Dimensions of this devilish contrivance can be gauged by contrast with the men.   *Photo, Daily Mirror*

of towns, and industrial targets can be identified even in zero visibility. The phrase used in official communiqués : " Bombing by instruments " means use of this instrument. After the R.A.F. had used the method the Americans adopted it, and this British invention enabled their bombers to operate over Europe on days when they would otherwise have been grounded, owing to weather conditions obscuring targets. The device has already been used against Japan, and will be invaluable in prosecuting the air war against the Japanese war industrial machine.

Hitherto the R.A.F.'s big 12,000-lb. bombs, both the block-buster blast type and the streamlined armour-piercing variety, have been used only against special targets such as isolated factories and warships. For the first time the block-buster 12,000-lb. bomb was used against a German city during a 15 minutes attack on Munich, begun at the moonless hour of 5 a.m. on November 27, 1944. The 270 Lancaster bombers employed all got back, only one landing away from base, after a flight of over ten hours. The destructive effect of these bombs is claimed to be nine times more powerful than that of 4,000-lb. bombs. Many incendiaries were also dropped, and Munich was left in flames. Note the high concentration of this attack, which was controlled by master-bomber tactics, in which a Pathfinder bomber flown by a super-expert aircrew identifies the target from a very low altitude, and directs the bombing by radio code.

WING COMMANDER G. P. GIBSON, V.C., D.S.O., D.F.C., was operating as master-bomber during an attack on Rheydt on September 19, 1944. He was last heard giving radio instructions while his aircraft was flying at a low altitude. He did not return, and is now posted missing. This must have been his fifth period of operations, counting his leadership of the attack on the Mohne and Eder dams as the fourth. I have always wondered why men like Gibson (whose value is immense) cannot be given a sufficiently important staff appointment to keep them available to impart to others their valuable knowledge, instead of risking losing them for the remainder of the war and perhaps altogether. (See page 33, Vol. 7.)

From the outbreak of war to June 1944 Britain built 102,609 aircraft, including 10,018 heavy bombers, 17,702 medium and light bombers, 38,029 fighters, and 6,208 naval aircraft ; rise of output was from 110 fighters per month in 1939 to 940 per month in the first half of 1944 ; heavy bomber output rose from zero in 1939, 41 in 1940 (a staggering under-production) to 2,889 in the first six months of 1944 ; monthly output of all types rose from 730 in late 1939 to 2,435 in first half of 1944. The aircraft industry (20,000 in 1935) employed 1,750,000 workers in 1944.

Civil Defence in Action After a V-Bomb Raid

A CASUALTY IS LOWERED from an upper storey of a bomb-shattered building in Southern England. Many magnificent feats of rescue stand to the credit of National Fire Service and Civil Defence workers collaborating in circumstances of great danger. On October 7, 1944, Mr. Herbert Morrison, Minister of Home Security, announced that C.D. casualties by enemy action (excluding police and N.F.S.) totalled about 2,300 killed and 8,300 seriously wounded. The man in the white helmet (top right) is an officer of a public utility company.　PAGE 509　*Photo, Sport & General*

V2 Rocket-Bombs' Home Obliterated by R.A.F.

FIRST PHOTOGRAPH OF A V2 in flight (above) was taken by a U.S. photo-reconnaissance pilot in a Lightning aircraft 20,000 ft. over Germany in November 1944 as the missile flashed by overhead. He said it was approximately 5 ft. in diameter and 50 ft. long, with a 30-ft. "tail" of flame, but that it was in sight for only 4 seconds. Another Lightning is shown in the circle.

SOARING VERTICALLY into the skies in November 1944, rocket-bombs were seen by R.A.F. patrols who were flying at great heights over enemy-occupied Holland. "You get no warning of their approach," said a pilot who, on one mission, saw no fewer than three. "At one moment there is nothing there, and then, apparently from nowhere, the rocket swishes past, climbing at terrific speed and leaving an extraordinary and distinctive trail behind it."

Spitfire fighter-bombers of an Australian squadron bombed a V2 storage, erection and launching site in Holland on November 21. Diving from 8,000 ft., in cloudy weather, the leader placed his bombs dead on the target, and the others followed with equal accuracy. (See also page 468.)

V2 EXPERIMENTAL STATION AT PEENEMUNDE on the German Baltic coast was again attacked by the R.A.F. on August 4, 1944. The station, hidden in woods (top), before the raid, showing light flak positions (A); and cradles for carrying rockets (B), two of which are on the ground (C). After the raid (bottom) the site, in ruins.

Photos, British Official and U.S.S.T.A.F.

Have you heard of the B.O.A.S.? I never had until a week or two ago, when I received from Sydney, Australia, the fourth annual report of the British Orphans' Adoption Society. This was started in 1939, within a few weeks of the commencement of the war. A young man in New South Wales foresaw that thousands of children would be orphaned in Great Britain and he believed that Australian homes would be opened to them, if the right appeal were made. There were many childless couples who might be glad to bring them up as their own. There were many families which could easily add one to their number. So that young man called some of his friends together and they founded the B.O.A.S. When the sending of children out of Britain to Australia had to be stopped, owing to the dangers which threatened shipping, the Society decided to hold up its adoption plans for the time being and to take up other wartime work for children—chiefly, of course, the children of Australian Servicemen. These have been helped in many ways, and a lot of clothes for air-raid victims have been sent to this country. I expect to hear more of the B.O.A.S. when travel to the Southern Hemisphere becomes normal again.

The Crystal Palace, as most readers know, was put up originally in Hyde Park for the first International Exhibition 93 years ago. When the idea of a great glass structure was suggested by a gardener named Joseph Paxton, who had much experience of conservatories, all the architects cried it down. However, they could not produce any better plan, and Paxton was a man of great energy. He had his Crystal Palace built, and it was considered at the time one of the wonders of the world. Then it was transported to the pleasant suburb of Sydenham and for many years attracted large numbers of people to attend its famous concerts, watch its celebrated firework displays, wander in its large grounds, crowd into its theatre, buy all sorts of knick-knacks at the stalls which occupied the indoor space along with enormous groups of statuary. Gradually it became shabby and its attractions diminished. Between thirty and forty years ago a fund was raised to preserve it. Lord Northcliffe gave the support of The Times newspaper. Someone on his staff asked, "What on earth do you want to save the Palace for? It's a dreadful place!" And Northcliffe replied in his schoolboy way, "I know. I'd just as soon support a fund to blow it up!" Some repairs were done and then, just over 8 years ago, it caught fire and was destroyed. Now it is proposed to build again on the site—as a sort of war memorial—not a glass structure, though it would still be called the Crystal Palace. The idea seems thoroughly bad to me.

Here is a sidelight on what I have said about jobs for ex-Servicemen after the war. A newspaper advertised for an office boy. Two of those who answered were a man discharged from the Army at the age of 23 and one, aged twenty, who had been in the R.A.F. There was nothing against them ; they had left the Services on health grounds. They could not, apparently, find work. Unless we are ready to deal with cases of this kind, which will be very numerous as soon as demobilization gets going, we shall have the same wretched procession of ex-Servicemen from door to door, trying to sell paper and envelopes, cutlery, brushes and combs, vacuum cleaners, and so on. In this connexion the demand of the Trades Union Congress that the "direction" of people to jobs should cease at once when the European War ceases is not helpful. If men and women who need work cannot find it for themselves, it must be found for them. The

T.U.C. agree with that, but they don't agree that the workless should be obliged to take the work that is found for them. In short, the Trade Unionists seem to want it both ways.

I hear that there is strong possibility of the Royal Observer Corps continuing to do its work in peacetime. Its members—there are women among them—identify and plot every aircraft that flies over Britain. That will be desirable, if not absolutely necessary, after the war. These observer stations have done most valuable work, of which very little has been heard. That is as it should be. Theirs is eminently a hush-hush job. Few people would be able to say what their uniform is. Usually they wear it only when they are at work. All through the twenty-four hours they are on the watch, and made it possible to give warnings which sent us into shelters and so saved many lives. To show the nation's appreciation of their services they were given the title Royal Observer Corps. They are paid, but not too well, for they must bring to their task both a high degree of intelligence and the closest concentration. A fuller description of their duties was given on p. 758, Vol. 7, of The War Illustrated.

I do not suppose many persons outside the "surveying" profession know what a heavy burden of work the destruction of buildings by German V-bombs has thrown on to those who have to estimate the amount of damage done. I had a conversation in the train with one of them, a surveyor belonging to an old and highly respected firm. He told me that, although it was Saturday, he had gone to London early and, though he would not get home till seven, he would go up again on the Sunday to put

GENERAL DE LATTRE DE TASSIGNY, commanding the French 1st Army which, on November 19, 1944, drove through the Belfort Gap to the Rhine. The Vichy regime sentenced him to 10 years' imprisonment in 1943, but 8 months later he escaped and came to London.   *Photo, French Official*

in a full day's work. He often stayed out of bed till one o'clock, he said, dealing with masses of figures, and he rose between five and six to tackle them again. He was a man of over sixty, I should guess, and did not look as if he could stand such a strain much longer. The claims for compensation under the Government insurance scheme had to be presented, he told me, in the most meticulous detail. Sheets and sheets of figures had to be prepared and carefully checked. The officials went over them with the utmost vigilance, in the public interest. I could not help saying I was glad to hear that. He smiled wearily and nodded. But when it is a matter of millions and you have to reckon up certain kinds of damage in shillings and pence, no wonder the poor man looked tired.

Someone at the War Office wants to know what soldiers feel about soldiering. A request has been issued to a number of them to draw up "a profit and loss account" of their Army service. I have seen a good many of their balance-sheets, and almost every one insists on the value of the friendships made and the prevalence of the spirit of comradeship. This seems curious, at first. Men thrown together compulsorily, or even voluntarily, almost always hate one another. Explorers do, schoolmasters do, crews on small ships do. Why should there be this difference in Army life? It is because there is so wide a choice of friends. If a man gets into a set he does not care about, he can switch over into another. Disappointed in one friendship, he can form another. Those who have ideas and feelings in common come together. There is, as a rule, no need to consort with anyone you dislike. When that rule does not hold good, when a small number of soldiers are forced to be with each other for any length of time in a confined space—see what happens then !

I met a Dutch naval officer. He was in high spirits. "It is good," he said to me, "that after all you have done and are doing for us we can give you a little help." I asked in what way. "Well," he said, "we have for long past built our naval vessels that were intended for service in Eastern waters, to guard our colonies Java and Sumatra, in a manner that suits the hot weather of that part of the world. A warship is not a very pleasant place to live in at the best of times. In the Tropics it needs a great deal of ventilation, and it has other differences from the ships that go about in colder climates. Your ships are being prepared for the Japanese campaign and you have taken some hints from us, which is a very wise thing to do ! " British sailors, too, are to dress differently when they go East. They will wear much lighter clothing ; in fact, very little clothing at all.

My old friend Kennedy Jones, whom I knew long before he joined Lord Northcliffe and helped to found The Daily Mail, once told me how he brought a gardener to his London home from Scotland and how the man asked him when he arrived, "Whose funeral was it the day?" Jones replied "Nobody's. Why?" The gardener explained that he had seen on his ride from the railway station "so many lum hats." Now a lum hat is Scots for a chimney-pot hat, and in Scotland at the end of last century these were worn only at funerals. They were in London worn with tail coats by all men who wished to be considered respectable. For a long time now they have been seen only on the heads of undertakers and bank messengers. The Duke of Windsor, when he was Prince of Wales, discouraged the wearing of them at weddings. More gradually they went out of fashion for mourners at burial services. But they are still worn by undertakers, and their scarcity has sent the price of secondhand ones soaring. If you have an old one among your junk in a box-room or under-the-stairs cupboard, fish it out. You might get four or five pounds for it.

Shattering Man-Traps on the Road to Berlin

Photo, Keystone

UP GOES A GERMAN MINE and down, for safety, go these U.S. infantrymen during the Allied six-army advance on a 400-mile front in the West, which opened on November 16, 1944. Four U.S. armies—as well as the British 2nd Army, under Gen. Dempsey, and the French 1st Army, under Gen. Tassigny—took part. They were : the 1st (Gen. Hodges) ; 3rd (Gen. Patton) ; 7th (Gen. Patch) ; 9th (Gen. Simpson). Gen. Patton entered Metz on November 22. All organized enemy resistance west of the Roer, between Altdorf and Barmen, had ceased by November 29.

Printed in England and published every alternate Friday by the Proprietors, THE AMALGAMATED PRESS, LTD., The Fleetway House, Farringdon Street, London. E.C.4.
Registered for transmission by Canadian Magazine Post. Sole Agents for Australia and New Zealand : Messrs. Gordon & Gotch, Ltd. ; and for South Africa : Central
News Agency, Ltd.—December 22, 1944.   S.S.   *Editorial Address* : JOHN CARPENTER HOUSE. WHITEFRIARS. LONDON. E.C.4.

Vol 8   The War Illustrated   Nº 197

Edited by Sir John Hammerton

SIXPENCE

JANUARY 5, 1945

MEN OF ARNHEM—400 "Red Devils" of deathless fame—marched proudly away from Buckingham Palace after a special investiture by H.M. the King on December 6, 1944. The numbers were so unprecedented that, for the first time in history, the ceremony had to be held in the spacious entrance hall of the King's London home. Sixty-one of the noble band (see pages 366-70) received decorations. They included a V.C. (Major R. H. Cain), two C.B.s, seven D.S.O.s, 19 M.C.s, seven D.C.M.s and 25 M.M.s.   *Photo, Daily Mirror*

NO. 198 WILL BE PUBLISHED FRIDAY JANUARY 19

Our Roving Camera Visits the Airborne Troops

"RED DEVILS" of Arnhem (3), on their way to and from Buckingham Palace on December 6, 1944 (see page 513), brought to spectators' minds recollection of exploits of the famous Allied Airborne force. The Airborne army—glider-borne, as distinct from parachute-troops—was originally formed in Nov. 1941. The consolidation of Allied airborne forces in one command, approximating to an army in size and importance, was announced on August 11, 1944, when it came under Lieut.-Gen. Lewis H. Brereton, formerly commanding the U.S. 9th Air Force (see page 287), with Lieut.-Gen. F. A. M. Browning C.B., D.S.O. (see page 543), Deputy Commander. Airborne troops must be under 32 years of age, not more than 13 stone in weight or over 6 ft. 2 ins. in height. Equipment includes a No. 22 wireless set in container (1), and a folding motor-cycle (2).

British parachute-trooper in full kit (4) wearing a camouflaged jumping jacket and carrying mortar bombs and mortar leg case; back view is seen in (5).

Photos, British Official; Keystone

THE BATTLE FRONTS

by Maj.-Gen. Sir Charles Gwynn, K.C.B., D.S.O.

JUST when it seemed that their offensive in Hungary and Slovakia (see map in page 483) had lost its impetus, the Russians produced another of those extensions of their front which have so often been a feature of their strategy. As usual, the new blow had been well timed and well designed to set the previous offensive again in motion. When German reports admitted that the Russians had established a bridge-head a short distance above the junction of the Drava with the Danube, it was not clear whether this was only a tentative effort by the left wing of Malinovsky's army, for he had already made several attempts to establish a foothold across the Danube south of Budapest, and had suspended his direct attacks towards the city.

Confident claims by the Germans that they had sealed off the bridge-head suggested that only a part of Malinovsky's army was engaged, but when it was announced that Tolbukhin had broken out of the bridge-head and widened its frontage it was evident that the Germans were confronted with a new and serious danger. I had originally expected that Tolbukhin's army would be used in support of Malinovsky's great drive into Hungary, but when it was reported that he had been diverted to bring an end to Bulgarian hesitations and had later been reported to be acting in support of Marshal Tito's forces against German pockets in the Morava valley, it seemed he might not be able to co-operate directly with Malinovksy.

BOLD and Rapid Exploitation of Success with Red Armour

There was obviously a possibility that he might be employed against the Germans retreating from Greece and Yugoslavia and those still fighting in the Sava valley west of Belgrade. That would have implied the dispersion of his army on a number of secondary missions and not, as is now evidently the case, its mass employment in a major operation. I have followed Tolbukhin's career with special interest, for he has a number of remarkable achievements to his credit, both in breaking through strong German defences and in particularly bold and rapid exploitation of success with his armour. He came into prominence when he broke the German Mius position in the Donbas, captured Taganrog (August 1943) and swept along the shores of the Sea of Azov.

THEN came his victory on the Melitopol line, and his steady pursuit which drove the Germans across the lower Dnieper and isolated the Crimea. During the last winter campaign little more was heard of him until in the spring, when his liquidation of the Crimea was rapidly carried through with astonishing skill and determination; his use of armour in the initial drive which threw the Germans back to Sebastopol being particularly remarkable. After that, nothing was heard of him for some time, and when his 4th Ukrainian army appeared in the Northern Carpathians it was under Petrov's command. Not till the Rumnian offensive started was it learnt that he had taken over the 3rd Ukrainian army from Malinovsky in the general shift of commanders that occurred when Zhukov's temporary command of the 1st Ukrainian army (after Vatutin's death) was terminated. In all these achievements Tolbukhin had largely an independent role and in all he showed exceptional drive and vigour. It is not surprising that his latest achievement has shown the same characteristics.

Again he has forced a strongly held German position and has exploited success with amazing speed. This time, however, his operations are evidently closely co-ordinated with those of Malinovsky, and it would be interesting to know if Zhukov has returned to his former post of chief strategical co-ordinator under Marshal Stalin. Tolbukhin's drive we know has been two pronged, northwards and westwards. The northward thrust in addition to securing a passage at the north end of Lake Balaton was evidently designed to clear the west bank of the Danube and thus enable Malinovsky's left wing to force a crossing and encircle Budapest from the south.

IT is not yet certain if the main weight of Tolbukhin's army will be employed north of Lake Balaton after Malinovsky is well established across the river. It is, I think, more probable that his main thrust will develop westwards round the southern end of the lake. For the Austrian frontier is only 40 miles ahead and there are no intervening natural obstacles. In that case Tolbukhin would have the somewhat independent role of dealing with the German forces in Southern Austria and Slovenia, which presumably hope to cover the retreat of the German army from Yugoslavia and from which they might receive reinforcements. Probably, however, part of his army would continue to co-operate directly with Malinovsky and provide a link with the southern force.

Meantime, Malinovsky took every advantage of the assistance Tolbukhin had given him. He crossed the Danube south of Budapest and is attacking the city from the south-west as well as renewing his assault from the east. Furthermore, in a drive north-west he broke through the German front between Miskolcz and Budapest and has reached the frontier of Slovakia, 100 miles to the west of the strong German group which was fighting stubbornly north of Miskolcz. This group has, therefore, lost all direct contact with the Danube valley and will be forced to retire through Slovakia. In his drive north-west Malinovsky also reached the elbow of the Danube where it turns westwards, and by capturing Vacs opened the door to the corridor leading to

Bratislava and Vienna between the mountains of Slovakia and the Danube. Having secured these positions, Malinovsky turned part of his force southwards from Vacs to attack Budapest from the north and clear the east bank of the Danube between the two cities.

It is clear that the capture of Budapest—and it is closely threatened on three sides as I write—will enable Malinovsky's army to drive westwards towards Vienna on both sides of the Danube, with the co-operation of Tolbukhin on one flank and the protection of Petrov's army on the other against any counterstroke that might be attempted by the Germans from Slovakia. It is, no doubt, in order to delay such a development and to gain time for the organization of the defence of Austria that the Germans are fighting so obstinately to hold Budapest, even at the risk of withdrawal becoming desperately difficult. They may have the additional motive of realizing that once Budapest falls the Hungarians will have few inducements to continue the struggle, and be less sensitive to the pressure that can be exercised on them while the city remains as a hostage in German hands.

ACCURATE Timing of Thrusts a Source of Soviet Triumphs

There seems every prospect that the climax of the Hungarian campaign will be reached, and the threat to Austria will mature, just at the time that the Russian winter offensive in Poland and East Prussia, evidently brewing, is due to start. Whether that has resulted from long-term calculations or not may be doubtful, but in the event it will not be surprising if we see another example of that accurate timing which has so often been a feature of Russian strategy.

For the time being, the threat of the coming winter offensive obviously immensely increases the difficulty the Germans have of finding reserves to intervene in the constantly deteriorating situation in Hungary. They cannot afford to withdraw troops from East Prussia or Poland, for their only hope of escaping a decisive disaster is to prevent the main Russian offensive, when it comes, acquiring momentum. They are reported to have transferred two divisions from Italy to Hungary, but obviously having clung so long to the Italian front they cannot afford to weaken it without risking a disastrous and almost certainly a belated retreat. The timing of German strategical moves, possibly from Hitler's influence, has all along been as faulty as the Russian has been accurate.

EXPERT BRIDGE BUILDERS, these South African engineers with the 8th Army in Italy upheld their great reputation when they restored enemy-shattered communications across the river Unito. This was the first obstacle encountered outside the historic city of Ravenna, which fell to Canadian troops of Princess Louise's Dragoon Guards on December 4, 1944, after a brilliant encircling movement.

Photo, British Official

German Escape Routes Hammered in Yugoslavia

BRITISH LAND FORCES IN THE ADRIATIC co-operated with Marshal Tito's army in the battle of the German escape routes in Yugoslavia (see map), it was disclosed on November 10, 1944. Yugoslav troops guard prisoners at Ledenice (1); while at Risan (taken on December 3), on the Gulf of Kotor, two R.A.F. planes attacked this German stronghold (2), from a height of only 100 feet, firing rockets and pumping machine-gun bullets into it. Tito's snipers harass the enemy retreating along the Niksic Road (3). A mountain howitzer (75 mm.), manned by the Royal Artillery, in action at Risan (4).

Photos, British Official

In Holland Where the Nazi Floods Swirled

BLOWING UP THE LOWER RHINE DAM south-east of Arnhem on Dec. 3, 1944, the enemy succeeded in hindering our progress. Taking advantage of the lull, British troops wrote home for Christmas from their trenches and dug-outs (1). Thinking of Xmas presents, maybe, our men were warned against a profiteering shopkeeper (2). Organizing a children's party, near Nijmegen, on the eve of St. Nicholas's Day (Dec. 6), the Yuletide festival in Holland, Canadians disguised as St. Nicholas and his "black boy" took a jaunt in a Bren carrier (3). Across the waste of waters, chilly vigil was kept by an outpost at Elst (4).

Photos, British Official; British Newspaper Pool. Associated Press

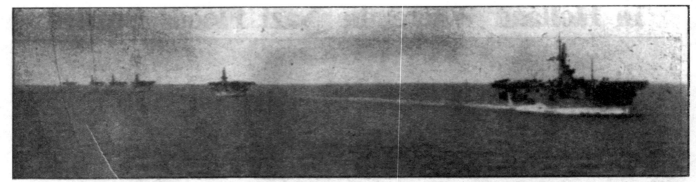

BRITAIN'S MIGHT IN THE AEGEAN is suggested by this photograph taken from the escort carrier Attacker, showing the carriers Khedive, Stalker, Emperor, Hunter, Searcher and Pursuer, which in the winter of 1944 harassed the remnants of German forces still in that area. From Sept. 9 to Oct. 27, Royal Navy and Allied warships, by sinking 101,000 tons of enemy shipping and making daring raids on several islands, had established complete naval and air superiority throughout the whole of the Aegean.
Photo, British Official

THE WAR AT SEA

by Francis E. McMurtrie

IN assessing the results of the second Battle of the Philippines, fought on October 23-24, 1944, it was pointed out that the severity of the Japanese defeat must ultimately entail the interruption of the vital communications upon which the maintenance of enemy armies overseas depends (see page 390).

With the latest American thrust, from Leyte into the island of Mindoro, the threat to these communications is enhanced. Its strategical position, 70 miles to the southward of Manila Bay, gives Mindoro an importance out of all proportion to its dimensions, 100 miles long by 60 miles broad. By occupying this island the United States forces under General MacArthur have cut the Philippines in half, isolating Japanese garrisons in the southern islands from those in Luzon. Already new airfields are being prepared in Mindoro from which planes will be able to operate in either direction. Ships and aircraft are also well placed to strike at the main shipping route through the South China Sea, the width of which between Mindoro and the nearest point of French Indo-China is little over 750 miles. Enemy forces in the latter territory, as well as in Siam, Burma, Malaya, Sumatra, Java, Borneo and Celebes, must obtain the bulk of their munitions and reinforcements from Japan by this sea route.

SHORTAGE of shipping has for some time affected the regularity of such supplies. In China the Japanese had advanced far into the province of Kweichow, threatening to cut the Burma-India road and even to drive the Chiang Kai-shek Government from Chungking (see p. 536). This threat has been averted by a retreat of over a hundred miles, brought about, it is believed, by the collapse of the enemy's supply arrangements. Thus Allied sea power, by destroying Japanese shipping, is already exerting its influence over the campaign in China. Moreover, the recent withdrawals in Burma are due to similar causes, for traffic by sea between Singapore, Sumatra and Rangoon has been brought to a standstill by the operations of British submarines, leaving all supplies to come by the slow and difficult land route from Siam.

With the transfer of the principal British fleet in the East from the Indian Ocean to the Pacific, the process of severing the tentacles of the Japanese octopus is likely to be accelerated. After reaching his new base at Sydney, Admiral Sir Bruce Fraser proceeded to the U.S. base at Pearl Harbour for a conference with Admiral of the Fleet Chester Nimitz and General MacArthur. Measures will there be concerted for the destruction of Japan's still substantial resources of naval and military strength.

In the conquest of Leyte and Samar the United States forces are now known to have killed 82,554 Japanese soldiers. Many of these were lost in transports sunk by American sea and air attacks. Some further information has also been released concerning the fate of enemy aircraft carriers in the Pacific. When war began, the Japanese Navy is known to have included eight fleet aircraft carriers. Two of these, the Ryuzyo and Hosyo, were quite small ships of between 7,000 and 8,000 tons displacement, useful mainly for training. The remaining six were all employed in the surprise attack on Pearl Harbour on December 7, 1941.

FATEFUL Days for Aircraft Carriers of the Japanese Navy

Four of these carriers were sunk in the Battle of Midway in June 1942. These were the Akagi and Kaga, each of 26,900 tons, and the Hiryu and Soryu, each of 10,050 tons. This left the two newest, the Syokaku and Zuikaku, still in service as the backbone of the enemy carrier force. Their exact dimensions are unknown, but they were certainly over 20,000 tons in displacement. In the first Battle of the Philippines, fought between U.S. naval aircraft and a Japanese squadron last June, the Syokaku was destroyed, together with a smaller carrier of escort type. Thus the Zuikaku was left as the sole survivor of the original six that were in operation against the U.S. Navy at Pearl Harbour. Her end came in October, when she was overwhelmed by the attacks of carrier-borne aircraft of the Third Fleet under Admiral Halsey, during the second Battle of the Philippines. Three smaller carriers were also sunk.

THERE have been many speculations about the identity of the carrier the enemy lost in the Battle of the Coral Sea in May 1942. At the time her name was reported as Ryukaku, and she was supposed to be a third ship of the Syokaku type. It is now understood that her name was Shoho, and the Japanese official statement that she had been converted from an oil-tanker is quite possibly true. Other enemy carriers that have been sunk are believed to have been similar conversions, either from tankers or from large passenger liners. Exactly how many ships were so transformed it is difficult to ascertain, but the number may have reached a dozen. If so, it is improbable that more than half of them are still afloat.

Photographs of sinking Japanese destroyers that have been published recently support the belief that a great many of small size have been built. They appear to be somewhat smaller than our "Hunt" types, or the American "destroyer-escorts," and are possibly no larger than the average corvette, though in appearance they come closer to the destroyer form. This explains to some extent the fact that, in spite of very heavy losses, the Japanese supply of destroyers does not yet seem to be exhausted.

THERE have been expressions of surprise in uninformed quarters at the news that in the Pacific the chief command of the Allied fleets will be exercised by the American Admiral Nimitz. There is, in fact, nothing remarkable in this, when it is considered that the United States Navy will be contributing by far the largest proportion of the Allied sea forces operating in that ocean. It is only logical that the nation with the biggest contingent should have the senior command, and in the past this principle has been well understood. In the last war the chief command in the Mediterranean was exercised by a French admiral, subordinate commands being held by British and Italian flag officers. For three years past an Australian squadron has formed part of the United States fleet in the Pacific, so with the transfer of Admiral Fraser's fleet this arrangement is perpetuated on a larger scale.

In the invasion of North Africa, the landings at Salerno and Anzio, and the invasion of Normandy, American flag officers served under the chief command either of Admiral of the Fleet Sir Andrew Cunningham or Admiral Sir Bertram Ramsay. So smoothly did everything work that it has been emphasized in official reports that for all practical purposes the naval forces concerned operated as one fleet. It may be assumed that in the Pacific results will be equally satisfactory.

The situation has been further simplified by the promotion of Admiral Nimitz to the newly created rank (in the U.S. Navy) of Admiral of the Fleet.

VICE-ADML. SIR ARTHUR POWER, whose appointment as Commander-in-Chief, East Indies Station, was announced on December 11, 1944. PAGE 518 *Photo, Elliott & Fry*

Our Mightiest Home-Built Battleship Launched

" MAY GOD BLESS ALL WHO SAIL IN HER ! " said Princess Elizabeth when (as announced on December 1, 1944) she launched at a northern port the greatest battleship yet built in the British Isles. Though the ship's name, type, and class were not disclosed for security reasons, it was stated that her ultra-modern equipment would include " electric eyes," a British invention capable of piercing the thickest fog and darkness and detecting the enemy's position, speed, and course.

Photo, P.N.A.

When the Bombed and Blazing Apapa Went Down

IN A U-BOAT INFESTED SEA survivors were taken off a blazing British liner bombed by enemy aircraft—thanks to the skill of the rescue ship's captain. That, briefly, is the story behind these remarkable photographs released for publication on December 1, 1944, though the incident occurred in 1941. The liner was the Elder Dempster 9,000-tons Apapa. The rescuer was the much smaller Highland Star ; the captain brought the stern of the vessel (extreme right) so close to the Apapa that a large part of the latter's complement was able to jump across to safety. The Apapa's officers, having braved danger in their search for survivors, cleared the sinking liner in a whaler (top). The ship goes down (bottom) while U-boats lurk close by. *Photos, Central Press*

Royal Navy Swept Clear the Scheldt to Antwerp

CLEARING THE SEA APPROACHES to Antwerp, Europe's third greatest port, presented the Royal Navy with one of the biggest minesweeping tasks ever attempted, declared Sir Bertram Ramsay, Naval C.-in-C. Allied Invasion Forces, on November 21, 1944. Though the Germans used "every type of devilry" to blockade the Scheldt Estuary before and after the Belgian city's capture on September 4 (see illus. page 442), a fleet of 70 R.N. minesweepers began operations under fire even before enemy guns had been silenced. By the end of November, Antwerp was receiving large convoys.

The first Liberty cargo ship sails up the Scheldt (1) and unloads supplies on a quayside hung with Allied flags (3). Against the background of a half-sunk ship (2) a mine explodes close inshore. Netherlanders cheer the first minesweeper to reach Terneuzen (4).

Photos, British Official ; Associated Press

How They Built Up R.A.F. Transport Command

Not so long ago all military aircraft crossing the Atlantic made the trip lashed to the decks or in the holds of cargo ships. Now bombers fly the North and South runs every day of the year despite ice or scorching heat or raging tempest. How this triumph has been made possible is told here by R. H. MEEK. See also page 362, Vol. 7

THE organization responsible for today's efficient functioning is known as the Atlantic Group of the Royal Air Force Transport Command ; on its duty rosters are listed the names of Fighting Frenchmen, Cubans, Norwegians, Poles, South Americans, Netherlanders, as well as men from the U.S.A. and Canada.

Three months before the outbreak of war a conference in London of international postal authorities decided that a North Atlantic route was not feasible for any regular airmail run, especially during winter. Also falling into line, wartime aviation authorities agreed on surface crossings for aircraft in spite of the time lag involved in taking aircraft apart, crating, loading, unloading, reassembling and retesting before any machine finally reached European battle stations.

Then the fall of France in June 1940, precipitated a revolution in methods of air-craft delivery, and a group of Canadian

During the next year President Roosevelt offered to form in the U.S.A.A.F. a ferry command, part of whose duties would be to fly bombers from the U.S. to Canada. The President wanted these men to hand over on the Canadian side to a military organiza-tion, so the R.A.F. Ferry Command was born. The business of landing the aircraft at the border to have them towed across an imaginary line by a team of horses was elimin-ated. The United States turned over to the British for the period of the war all American personnel employed on the Atlantic bomber ferry. In April 1943 the organization became known as the R.A.F. Transport Command.

It all sounds simple, but its effects were far reaching. In 1941 the bomber ferry business was outgrowing its stove-pipe pants ; more space and facilities were needed. The Canadian Government went to work on a marshy stretch of land 12 miles out of Montreal, at Dorval, and four months later

past one and a half years around Goose Bay. This is probably why Transport Com-mand people enthuse over the post-war possibilities of their pioneer work. It is true they have literally altered the centre of gravity of the world's communication routes. It is now obvious, say the experts, that express air traffic of the future will fly the northern routes from North America through Canada to Europe and Asia. The northern hemisphere contains nine-tenths of the world's population and the majority of the large cities ; the shortest route from San Francisco to Moscow goes through Edmon-ton, Alberta. When Montgomery faced Rommel at El Alamein, and the whole of North Africa was in danger, Transport Command flew bombers from America through Dorval to Cairo, just behind the fighting front.

Flying School for Ferry Pilots

A civil pilot of Transport Command, Capt. Maurice Gill, accomplished the fastest flight yet made across the Atlantic, on Nov: 29, 1944. He was flying a Canadian-built Mos-quito, and the flight of 2,230 miles from Goose Bay, Labrador, to a north British base took six hours and eight minutes. The fastest trip recorded thus far on the bomber ferry from Montreal to Britain was 11 hours and 35 minutes ; this was done by a fully loaded bomber on the 3,200 mile run. Flying time from the coast of New-foundland to the coast of Britain has been as low as six hours and 10 minutes. How-ever, the average bomber flight to Britain is 14 hours and the return trip against the prevailing winds takes 16½ hours.

To provide an adequate supply of com-petent pilots, British Overseas Airways per-sonnel got together with Canadian Pacific Airlines officials, and a flying school for ferry pilots was instituted in Canada in 1940. Requirements for a pilot's job with Trans-port Command are so tough that R.A.F.T.C. is virtually breeding a new race of airmen. A man must first be supremely physically fit. He must have not less than 750 hours flying time on two-engined craft, have a commer-cial licence, and be "top-drawer stuff" on blind flying. If a man fulfils these con-ditions he then attends T.C. schools at Dorval or North Bay, Ontario. Pilots and co-pilots coming from the R.A.F. and R.C.A.F. must have completed a tour of 30 bombing operations over enemy territory before they become eligible for Transport Command. Some pilots on the bomber ferry have done 80 sorties over Europe and most of these men have won decorations for gallantry.

Capt. R. ALLEN   **Capt. C. W. A. SCOTT**   **Capt. G. R. BUXTON**
PIONEERS OF TRANSATLANTIC WINTER FLYING, these pilots are employed on the all-the-year-round England-America return service of the British Overseas Airways Corporation—the only civil air line to have operated in both directions throughout three winters. Up to the end of November 1944, Captain Scott had made 97 Atlantic crossings, Capt. Buxton 96, and Capt. Allen 95.
Photos, Planet News

business-men, flyers, and engineers decided to take a crack at flying bombers to Britain. Airminded officials of the Canadian Pacific Railway Company begged for a chance to back the scheme. They received it.

But there were many obstacles to be over-come before that first bomber could land on British soil. A route had to be chosen. Landing fields had to be torn out of the wilderness. There was a law about flying aircraft across the Canadian-U.S. border. Competent crews had to be found. Finally 50 Lockheed Hudson bombers were flown to the Canadian-U.S. border. The U.S. was not yet at war, so to avoid legal entangle-ments the planes were towed across the line by horses and tractors. Then the pilots climbed back behind the controls and the planes were flown to St. Hubert Airport, Montreal.

AWAITING the intrepid airmen and their precious charges at the end of the next leg of the trip were runways which had been flattened out of the snow in the wilds of Newfoundland ; and on November 10, 1940, 10½ hours after a handful of people had stood and watched while seven Hudson bombers roared down the makeshift runway and spread their determined wings above the Newfoundland evergreens, the R.A.F. in Britain was richer by seven aircraft and the trans-Atlantic ferrying of bombers had become a reality.

one of the safest airports in the world was ready for use. Today Dorval is the nerve centre of the north and south Atlantic bomber express. British W.A.A.F.s send and receive one high priority secret code message every minute.

AT the same time the Canadian govern-ment sent engineers and workmen to build an airport in Labrador. Men, food and equipment were flown to Goose Bay, and working 24 hours a day they completed the biggest airport in the world within six months from the time of discovery of the site. Goose Bay airport cost about 15 million dollars and is still growing. Since the first plane landed there in December 1941 thousands of bombers—the exact figures would be a breach of security—have landed on its 6,000-ft.-long runways. Suffice it to mention that this huge airport in the icy north has handled—received, serviced and dispatched—as many as one hundred big bombers in a single day. (See page 88, Vol. 7).

Another great airport had been completed previously at Gander, Newfoundland. (See pages 98-99, Vol. 4.) Subsidiary bases for the north Atlantic run were also laid out in Maine, U.S.A., Nova Scotia, New Brunswick, Greenland and Iceland. Flyers using the Labrador base were delighted to find that the weather there was in their favour. There has not been a single non-flying day in the

DAILY flights both ways across the Atlantic are handled by the British Overseas Airways Corporation for the R.A.F.T.C. These flights carry urgent war freight, diplo-matic mail pouches, as well as diplomats and officials of the United Nations on urgent war business. They carry mail and bring back to Dorval the air crews which have delivered bombers overseas. The Montreal airport is the home base of the Commando, the four-motor Liberator used to fly Prime Minister Churchill on many of his long trips.

Transport Command is continually develop-ing new equipment and methods for long-range big plane flights. When the order is given to cease fire the organization will be in a position to switch over from carrying war supplies to the fast transport of medicine, food, machinery and other necessities for rehabilitation of the nations ravaged by years of war.

British Troops in Conflict with Greek Rebels

CIVIL STRIFE IN ATHENS broke out on December 3, 1944, when police fired on an EAM (Left Wing) demonstration against the Government of M. Papandreou. Troops were detailed by General Scobie, commanding British land forces in Greece, to keep order among the newly liberated populace, but without success. By December 12, General Scobie's demand that the guerillas should hand in their arms having been ignored and after casualties had been suffered by our troops as well as by the opposing Greek factions, the situation had grown so serious that Field-Marshal Sir Harold Alexander, Supreme Allied Commander in the Mediterranean, and Mr. Harold Macmillan, British Resident Minister, Mediterranean, were dispatched to Athens.

EAM is the political, and ELAS, whose guerillas are said to number 60,000, is the military organization of the Left Wing. EDES, the army of Gen. Zervas, represents the Right Wing partisans.

A BRITISH-MANNED SHERMAN gate-crashed the heavy door (1) barring the entrance to the EAM headquarters in Athens, on December 3, 1944, and men of the Royal Armoured Corps rushed in ; one N.C.O. was killed. General Scobie, commanding British land forces in Greece, confers (2) with General Stephanos Seraphis, leader of ELAS (left), and General Zervas, commander of the EDES (right); while British parachute troops (3) manned a Bren gun post at street corner. See eye-witness story in page 537.

See eye-witness story in page 537.

Photos, British and U.S. Official

Scientists Battle for Precious Lives in the Far East

Mosquitoes can be as deadly as Japanese. By both pests—insect and human—are the lives of our fighting-men in Burma and the Pacific imperilled. How Allied scientists and the medical services are conducting a vigorous war-within-a-war is explained here by T. S. DOUGLAS. On the outcome of these battles against jungle diseases a great deal depends.

THE Allied armies in the Far East are fighting two wars—one against the Japanese and another against diseases that flourish in the jungle. Malaria, dengue fever and other afflictions are quite as dangerous as the bullets of the Japs, and only constant war on them makes fighting possible at all. Conditions for medical units are far more difficult in the East than anywhere else, but with new methods and new drugs have been performed what only a few years ago would have been considered "miracles" in keeping down casualties.

Just how serious a menace malaria can be was shown when Dr. H. V. Evatt, Australian Minister for External Affairs, revealed that more than 80 per cent of the Allied forces in New Guinea were attacked by malaria. In the first Burma campaigns up to 85 per cent of the men suffered from malaria. To-day the position is very different. Malaria remains the great menace, but our armies have got to grips with it and a great degree of control has been achieved.

MALARIA is spread by the blood-sucking female mosquito. The basis of prevention, then, is destruction of the mosquito, draining or otherwise dealing with its breeding grounds, and the wearing of protective clothing that prevents the little flying pest from biting. Destruction of the insect itself is not easy, for Anopheles—the malaria-carrying mosquito—thrives everywhere in the East. The new insecticides, and especially the insecticide "bomb" which sprays the air with a deadly and very effective poison, enable huts, tents, and so on, to be cleared simply and effectively. A "bomb," about twice the size of a grenade, contains some hundreds of charges. One is enough to kill every mosquito in a small tent; a dozen will clear the fuselage of a bomber.

But unless the tent is mosquito-tight, others will eventually get in; and Anopheles will enter a hut every time the door is opened. Destruction of mosquitoes will, of course, reduce the chances of being bitten. But for thousands of men in the front line who have to sleep in the open insecticides can help little, although an anti-mosquito cream rubbed on the exposed skin has been helpful. One of the difficulties is that the great heat leads men to discard clothing, thus increasing the area available for a mosquito bite. Now they realize that profuse sweating in clothes is generally better than getting bitten.

Aeroplanes Versus Aquatic Larvae

Clearing the breeding grounds of the mosquitoes near all camps is one of the most effective measures. The mosquito lays its eggs on the surface of stagnant water—ditches, ponds, swamps, fresh water of any kind. If the water is sprayed with oil, the aquatic larvae which hatch out of the eggs are suffocated. Great quantities of oil are used for this purpose, and the spraying has to be repeated at weekly intervals. Paris green is also used on marshes, and aeroplanes with special spraying devices have been used for this "dusting," covering in an hour areas that would take a week or more to treat from the ground.

But, obviously, such measures cannot be taken by troops when they are fighting and moving into new areas. Protective clothing, and especially mosquito netting, is helpful. But it is not easy to rig mosquito nets under active service conditions, and a hand or foot has only to protrude from the net for a minute during the night for Anopheles to do her deadly work. In some of the U.S.

MULES TAKE SURGEONS TO THE BURMA WOUNDED

A MOBILE surgical unit, carrying its equipment on mules, has crossed the Chindwin and is pushing steadily forward with British and Indian troops of the 14th Army, ready to carry out the most delicate operations within 20 minutes of arrival in any battle area. A medical staff officer said:

"Battle experience has proved that we must try to bring the surgeon to the patient. The specially blacked-out operating tent can be erected in five minutes. Most of the operations will be carried out by the light of a specially constructed headlamp. The patient will receive two to three days' post-operation treatment and will then be evacuated.

"Our mobile surgical unit has performed almost every type of operation. During the siege of Imphal 5,000 cases were dealt with in one month. Penicillin will be air-dropped with other medical requirements."

Major K. van Someren, of Park Road, Edinburgh, is in command, and Major J. D. Laycock, of Rockland Road, Grange-over-Sands, Lancs, is the unit anaesthetist.

camps one man does a mosquito-net patrol all night, pushing back under the net the feet and arms of sleepers.

The most effective weapon against malaria, where front-line troops are concerned, has been a drug—mepacrine, or atabrine as it is called in the U.S. It is a little yellow pill and taken regularly it will ward off malaria. Mepacrine has proved virtually one hundred per cent effective in preventing malaria, as long as it is taken regularly. When the drug is stopped a certain number of takers may develop malaria, for it does not give immunity—but it certainly enables the men to have their malaria in comfort, so to speak. That is, the malaria is warded off until the soldiers have returned to base, where they can be given hospital treatment. One U.S. correspondent reported that when beds were short, doctors were naming the date when soldiers could have their malaria!

Recently it was announced that 33 million doses of mepacrine were being prepared, and it is now a routine matter for men in the fighting lines to take their pills. It has proved so effective that the Japanese have been putting out special propaganda designed to discourage men from taking mepacrine.

ANALYSING SWAMP-WATER on the Moluccas island of Morotai, in the S.W. Pacific, a U.S. Navy malaria control team is grateful for the protection of a gunner, for there are snipers about as well as disease. *Photo, U.S. Official*

But long and detailed experiment has shown that it cannot in any way harm the taker. It is worth noting that the Japanese are no more immune from malaria than our men—the mosquito bites without prejudice as to race or colour. Japanese anti-malarial measures are less effective than those of the Allies, despite the fact that in the East Indies they captured almost the whole of the world's sources of quinine, great specific for malaria.

One of the big problems in Burma has been the removal of men when they are sick or wounded, for many units are cut off from motor transport. Now, moving casualties by air has been brought to perfection. Small landing strips are continually being cut behind the advanced units. From these, light planes (see illus. p. 343) carry the casualties to larger strips, whence they are transferred to specially equipped Dakotas. These fly them to base hospitals, thirty at a time. Whatever the conditions, sick and wounded have never been left behind. By mule, or on an improvised stretcher borne by comrades, the casualty may be carried over difficult trails to the nearest airstrip.

Clouds of Insects Everywhere

On arrival at an advanced hospital a casualty is at once classified. If he needs special treatment or is unlikely to be fit again within a couple of months, he is flown, or taken by boat or hospital train, to India. Incidentally, every division in Burma has a front-line psychiatrist, for jungle warfare is particularly liable to produce shock and nervous strain. Statistics show that 90 per cent of the men they have treated return fit and well.

Just how far the Allies have gone in the prevention and treatment of malaria, dengue fever and other insect-carried diseases was revealed by Brigadier-General R. W. Bliss, assistant surgeon of the U.S. Army, after he returned from a tour of the Far East front recently. "When we first took over the Pacific Islands," he said, "there were clouds of insects everywhere, actually making it difficult to see. Today, if we locate one mosquito we consider it comparable to finding a four-leafed clover!"

He described how, on Saipan, medical sanitary squads divided the island into squares, like a chess board, and proceeded to kill every mosquito and drain or spray every potential breeding ground. D.D.T., the wonderful insecticide which ended the typhus epidemic in Naples, was sprayed from tree-top height by daring pilots. Dengue fever, also passed on by mosquitoes, was rife but has now practically disappeared. And Saipan island has a "quarantine" so that no new mosquitoes can get in or out: every plane arriving or leaving has an insecticide bomb fired off in it before it lands or takes off.

ON Saipan, Japanese medical stores were captured intact. They showed the poverty of their equipment compared with our own. The standard Japanese outfit consists of eight items. The standard U.S. equipment consists of 600 items. There seems no doubt the Japs have suffered much more heavily from sickness, and their surgeons have had orders to kill sick and wounded who showed little hope of rapid recovery.

There was recently tested a new "insect-proof" uniform. A number of men, who volunteered, sat for an hour in a mosquito infested spot, half of them wearing the new uniform, half the old. The men in the new uniform averaged less than one bite apiece, those in the old uniform averaged 19 each.

Annihilating the Deadly Malaria Mosquitoes

BATTLING AGAINST MALARIA, experts in 1944 reduced the incidence of the disease to 80 cases per 1,000 men, as told in the facing page.   Method of draining a mosquito-breeding swamp in New Guinea (1). Where drainage is impracticable, oil—or the highly effective new chemical Aerosol—is spread on the water : in North Burma a Chinese soldier is taught to spray oil on water-filled shell-holes (2). Adjusting an oil drip-can over a New Guinea stream (3), and testing a jungle pool for the presence of larvae of the virulent Anopheles (4).   PAGE 525   *Photos, U.S. Official*

A Simplified Guide to the Burma Campaigns

Our readers may not find it easy to follow the course of events in Burma, with fighting raging in widely separated areas whose geography is unfamiliar and with few outstanding names to serve as guide-posts. Maj.-Gen. Sir CHARLES GWYNN, K.C.B., D.S.O., in this broad outline of past and present operations makes clear the nature and purpose of the war in this arduous country.

AFTER the retreat of General Alexander's troops and General Stilwell's Chinese forces from Burma in the spring of 1942, the primary object was to prevent a Japanese invasion of India. For that the C.-in-C., India, General Sir Archibald Wavell, was responsible, and with that object the counter offensive into the Coastal Arakan district of Burma was undertaken in 1942. General Wingate's experimental Chindit operations were also authorized. (See p. 46, Vol. 7.)

But at the Quebec Conference (August 1943) plans were approved envisaging a counter-offensive against Japan which would have overburdened the C.-in-C. in India, and the South-East Asia Command (SEAC) was therefore established (August 1943) with Admiral Lord Louis Mountbatten in Supreme Command. His headquarters were moved to Kandy, in Ceylon, in April 1944. One of the chief tasks envisaged for SEAC was the reconquest of Burma and the reopening of land communication with China.

OWING to shortage of shipping and demands in the European theatre, amphibious operations for the time being were out of the question ; but it was decided that land operations might be undertaken in support of General Stilwell's project of opening a road between Ledo and that part of the Burma road still in Chinese hands. The task of covering the construction of the road was left to General Stilwell, with his Chinese troops, trained and re-equipped in India after their withdrawal from Burma, assisted by American specialized troops and native levies. In order to interrupt the communications of the Japanese opposing his advance, the 3rd Indian Division, trained under General Wingate as an airborne force, was to be landed near the Mandalay railway and from there operate, on Chindit principles, under his general directions.

In order to maintain pressure on the Japanese, the operations in Arakan were to be resumed, and the troops from Manipur were to improve communications to the Chindwin valley and operate across the river. Both these operations were to be carried out by the 14th Army under General W. J. Slim, composed of the 15th Corps in Arakan, the 3rd Corps in Manipur, with the 33rd Corps in reserve.

Japanese Caught Between Two Fires

With the opening of the dry season, in January 1944, the 7th and 5th Indian Divisions advanced in Arakan. After some progress had been made the Japanese counter-attacked strongly by sending a powerful force round the flank of the leading 7th Division, cutting its communications and isolating it. The Division formed a defensive " box " and beat off all attacks ; while the 5th Division, which was following, undertook operations to clear the road. Eventually, with the help of the 26th Indian Division attacking from the north, the Japanese encircling move was caught between two fires and was heavily defeated by the end of February 1944.

Early in March interest was transferred to the Manipur front. Patrols operating in the Chindwin valley discovered that the Japanese were advancing in strength, and it soon became apparent that though the 4th Corps, with heavier armament than the Japanese could bring up, could confidently withstand attack in the open country round Imphal, the capital, its communication with the Assam railway at Dimapur might be cut, and the railway which provided General Stilwell's only line of communication endangered.

It was therefore essential that the 4th Corps should have sufficient offensive power to contain the main Japanese force, and the 5th Division was flown from Arakan to reinforce it—a remarkable feat of the air transport service, which also was able to relieve all anxiety about maintenance of supplies. The most immediate danger was that the 17th Indian Division, covering the improvement of the road to the Chindwin at Tiddim 100 miles to the south, might be cut off and overwhelmed. The Division was heavily attacked, but most skilfully and gallantly fought its way back to Imphal, which by the beginning of April was completely isolated.

THE danger to the railway at Dimapur matured when the Japanese sent a lightly armed column through very rough country to strike the main road, beyond reach of the Imphal force. But it found

NORTH BURMA FRONT, where by mid-December 1944 the 14th Army had taken Kalewa and bridged the Chindwin ; and the 36th British Division with the Northern Combat Area Command had reached Katha.
By courtesy of The News Chronicle

the road blocked, 40 miles short of Dimapur, by a small mixed force holding Kohima, which included men of the Royal West Kent Regiment. Violently attacked by greatly superior numbers, the force stood a memorable siege and saved the railway.

Meantime, the 33rd Corps, with the 7th Indian Division flown from Arakan, and the 2nd British Division, recalled from training areas, concentrated at Dimapur in order to undertake the reopening of communications with Imphal. By the end of April the garrison of Kohima was relieved ; but the Japanese held stubbornly to their grip on the road, and it was only after fierce fighting that contact with Imphal was again established, in the middle of June. The monsoon

by then was in full blast, but General Slim was determined in spite of the weather to continue the offensive.

Actually it was the enemy that wilted under climatic conditions. Three Japanese Divisions that had risked the thrust towards Dimapur without adequate communications were thrown back to Ukhrul as a disorganized rabble and practically annihilated. Other forces, fighting hard, were driven back along the two better roads leading to the Chindwin by Tamu and Tiddim respectively, by which the enemy's original main advance was made.

With the opening of the dry season in October, General Slim's offensive gained strength, and the enemy was thrown successively out of his strong positions at Tiddim, Kennedy Peak, and Fort White. And by the end of November his advanced bases in the Chindwin valley at Kalemyo and Kalewa had been captured. By the beginning of December, bridge-heads were established across the Chindwin ; and the 14th Army has now good prospects of co-operating with the Northern force in an advance on Mandalay.

Chindit Column's Daring Thrust

We now turn to the Northern operations. By the beginning of March 1944 General Stilwell had extended the road from Ledo 50 miles across the frontier covered by his Chinese troops, and had begun to encounter stiff resistance by the 18th Japanese Division in the difficult Hukaung valley. Undeterred by the threat to his communications at Dimapur, he continued to press on.

About the middle of March, as had been planned, General Wingate's 3rd Division was landed in the Katha region and set about the disruption of the enemy's communications, though it lost its Commander in an air accident. With the threat in their rear, the resistance of the 18th Japanese Division weakened, and General Stilwell, having cleared the Hukaung valley, organized a two-pronged drive—his main force advancing on towards Mogaung, while an American Commando force made a brilliant surprise thrust through jungle tracks to Myitkyina, capturing the airfield there on May 17. The Japanese, however, left a suicide force in the town, and to avoid unnecessary casualties our attack was not pressed home till much later (August 3).

The main column, meantime, encountered strong resistance at Kamaing, short of Mogaung, but a Chindit column (South Staffordshires, Lancashire Fusiliers and Gurkhas) by a daring thrust gained a footing in the latter town and with the co-operation of a Chinese force that had by-passed Kamaing, captured it on June 26. General Stilwell had now gained, by early July, a firm footing in the dry region of Northern Burma, including valuable airfields. And at Mogaung he had captured the main Japanese Northern supply depot. His main body, reinforced by the 36th British Division, began to advance steadily along the Mandalay Railway, while his Chinese troops thrust towards Bhamo, the head of navigation on the Irrawaddy and the starting-point of a road which links with the Burma-China highway near the frontier. Now, in December, a footing in Bhamo has been won, and another Chinese column has crossed the Irrawaddy between Bhamo and Katha, which the 36th Division captured on December 10. Ahead lies open country in which tanks can operate freely and air strips are plentiful, so that with the co-operation of the 14th Army, it is reasonable to hope that Mandalay may be reached and the Burma Road reopened.

Royal Welch Fusiliers are Bound for Mandalay

Here crossing the Nankye Chaung, troops of this famous Welsh regiment in General Festing's 36th Division began on Oct. 30, 1944, a fresh drive down the Myitkyina-Mandalay "railway corridor," through Hopin and Mawlu, which they captured on Nov. 2. From Hopin to Mawlu, which is north of the junction leading to Katha, key town on the Irrawaddy, is 75 miles—a 14-days' journey, with many road blocks to surmount, with jagged rocks or clammy clay of river-beds to hinder weary feet.

Japanese Fortresses Set in Mud and Scrub—

Through steamy little villages, all strongpoints of enemy resistance, the 36th Division of the British 14th Army in Burma, consisting of Royal Welch Fusiliers, Royal Scots Fusiliers and the East Lancs Regiment, advanced from Hopin to Mawlu against obstacles or resistance almost step by step. A patrol (1) edges its way through razor-sharp grasses in the jungle on the way to Mohnyin (2). Bomb-wrecked rolling-stock (3) was strewn over Mawlu station. (See map page 526.)

—Wiped Out by British 36th Division's Drive

A 25-pounder gun captured by the Japanese and turned on to our lines was later abandoned in the mud of a deep crater, whence it was retrieved by our gunners and used (4) to hurry the retreating enemy. Beyond the captured fortress-village of Mawhan supplies had to be carried forward by mule (5) to Mawlu. Stretches of open trail were few and far between ; mostly the advance down the " railway corridor " was through jungle so tangled as to be impenetrable even to the versatile jeep.

529

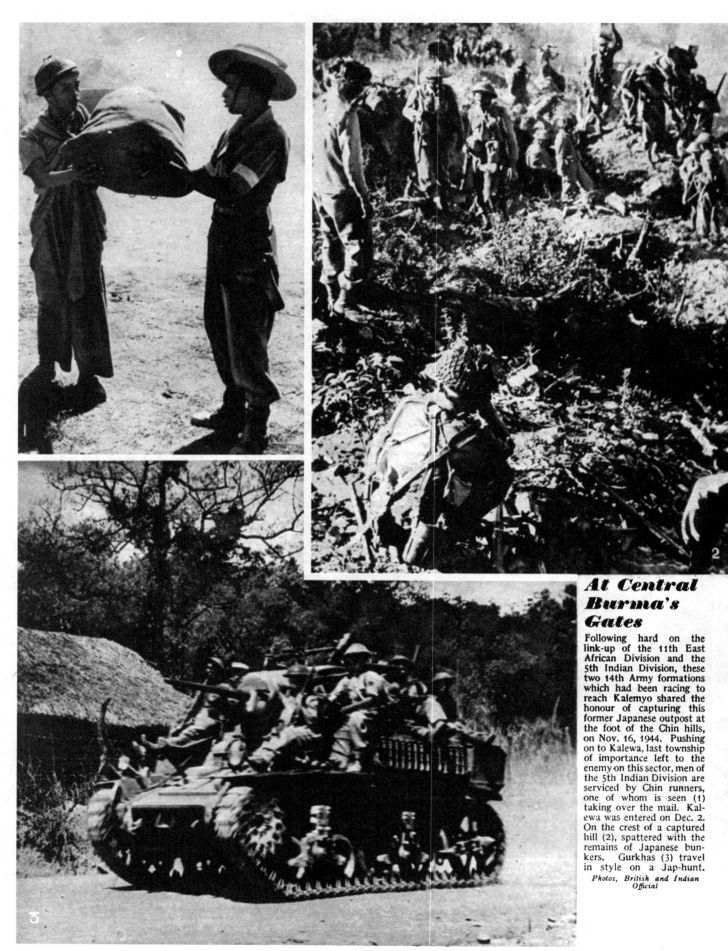

At Central Burma's Gates

Following hard on the link-up of the 11th East African Division and the 5th Indian Division, these two 14th Army formations which had been racing to reach Kalemyo shared the honour of capturing this former Japanese outpost at the foot of the Chin hills, on Nov. 16, 1944. Pushing on to Kalewa, last township of importance left to the enemy on this sector, men of the 5th Indian Division are serviced by Chin runners, one of whom is seen (1) taking over the mail. Kalewa was entered on Dec. 2. On the crest of a captured hill (2), spattered with the remains of Japanese bunkers. Gurkhas (3) travel in style on a Jap-hunt.

Photos, British and Indian Official

VIEWS & REVIEWS Of Vital War Books

by Hamilton Fyfe

It is amusing to remember that not long after James Thomson wrote Rule Britannia and started the legend that the English were a race of seafaring heroes, ruling the waves, Dr. Johnson was making the remark that in his opinion "no man would be a sailor who could get himself into gaol. For," he went on, "being in a ship is being in gaol—with a chance of being drowned. A man in a gaol has more room, better food, and commonly better company."

We cannot attribute that to the Doctor's ill-humour or whimsicality. It was a view generally held and there was justification for it, not only in his day but long after. Indeed, we are told by Mr. Stanton Hope in his Ocean Odyssey, a "record of the Fighting Merchant Navy" (Eyre and Spottiswoode, 12s. 6d.), that even twenty years ago there were "famous liners in which saloon passengers made their voyage in super-luxury, while the sailor, fireman and steward, to whom the ship was workshop and home, pigged it in cramped quarters, snugged down sleeping and eating their meals in an ill-ventilated fo'c'sle, damp from drying clothes and reeking with tobacco smoke."

Post-War Period Expectations

Some ships had wooden bunks, but more often than not hammocks were used which swung about with the motion of the vessel, banged their occupants against iron stanchions and made them prefer resting and "easing their bruised ribs" on the hard floor. Now, says Mr. Hope, there have been drastic changes which "will set the standard of accommodation expected in the post-war period." The crews' living quarters are being placed amidships in the newest types of tanker and cold storage freighter. There are two- and four-berth cabins. There is running water, hot and cold, with proper arrangements for washing clothes and drying them, and warm shower-baths instead of tubs filled with cold sea-water from the pump.

The food in merchant ships has also been greatly improved. Instead of salt pork and ship's biscuit forming the staple diet, there is variety—"fresh meat, fresh fish, eggs, smoked ham, bacon, green peas, butter beans, rolled oats, marmalade, jam, syrup, and butter of a quality and quantity to satisfy even the incorrigible 'sea-lawyer.'" The result of treating seamen as human beings has been that the traditional type of sailor has almost disappeared. They are no longer regarded as being outside the pale of common decency and common sense when they come ashore after a voyage. They are not the "easy meat" they used to be "for crimps in the noisome doss-houses to which they had to resort owing to their poor pay and the lack of better arrangements for their stay on land." They are not liable to be "robbed, drugged and shanghai'ed to awaken eventually in some hell-ship bound half-way across the world." Entertainment for them when they are in port is not left to missions managed by "well-meaning volunteers with elementary ideas of how to interest them." Tracts and cups of tea altogether failed to do so.

Mr. Hope tells of a concert he once attended in China when he was a seaman himself. It was arranged by British residents, who evidently enjoyed their own performances a great deal better than their audience did. The sailors would have liked to dance and could have obtained their tunes from a gramophone, but this "was not considered quite proper in the mission hall." Now recreations and amusements of many kinds are provided. The problem is not "What

shall we do with the drunken sailor?" but "How can we make the men on whom our very existence has depended comfortable and contented?" Better educated than their forerunners, their "prestige was never higher" —never, indeed, so high. This is due to the change in their environment. Treat men like pigs and they will behave piggishly. Treat them as intelligent, responsible, decent-living people and they will respond immediately.

Mr. Hope has no difficulty in proving what magnificent work the Merchant Navy has

A Seaman Looks at the Merchant Navy

done during this war. He takes a number of episodes, describes them in picturesque detail, and shows how resourceful as well as courageous, how adaptable as well as dogged, our seamen are. Here is one example. The captain of a collier was ordered to take aboard a cargo, not of coals but refugees from the Riviera. He found himself suddenly and for the first time entrusted with the care of several hundred passengers. Not in safe seas, but in the Mediterranean infested by Nazi submarines. It was "the most alarming crisis in his long sea-going career." He faced it as if it were just part of his normal everyday duty. At the other end of the scale we have the story of a young stewardess whose cool handling of her very grave responsibilities when her ship was sunk helped to save many lives and counteract any inclination to panic.

Quisling Ship That Lost Herself

The stories Mr. Hope has picked are full of many-sided interest. There is one of a "quisling" ship in a British convoy, which made an attempt to slip away. The attempt was foiled by a British boy who had shipped in the "foreign-built vessel, flying a different flag, captained by a foreigner and manned by assorted foreigners." The lad's suspicions was aroused by several odd happenings. The ship was "lost" and it seemed pretty clear that the captain did not want her to be found. At last the boy discovered that she was being headed for German-occupied Norway instead of taking the course prescribed for the convoy. He went up to the bridge and told the captain what he thought of him. This might easily have cost him his liberty, perhaps his life. But luckily just at that moment a British destroyer hove the quisling ship to, gave the foreign skipper his course, and added "If you don't get on it inside two minutes, I'll sink you." The fellow gave no more trouble. When the convoy reached its destination, a Court of Inquiry was held. Some day we shall know the result of it.

Some of the seamen taken prisoner reported that German naval officers used stereotyped arguments which had evidently been supplied to them for use in conversation with Britons. One asked "Why do you come to help the Russians? You are not Bolsheviks." Another inquired "Why don't you British give up the war, causing all this suffering?" and added references to "pig-headed Churchill" and "the Jewish plutocrats" who were the "over-lords" of Britain. All this sort of talk was completely wasted, of course; but it is interesting to see how Nazi propaganda on the home front has

twisted German mentality and made even their naval officers, who were once considered unusually sensible for Germans, talk such rubbish and ignore facts.

On the whole, they seem to have behaved more humanely than army officers. One told a batch of captives that they had behaved well and he hoped they would be well treated in return when they reached Germany. "In the last war," he said, "I was a prisoner in Australia and I have not forgotten the very good treatment I had there." Men who were in a Vichy-French prison camp gave a disgusting description of it, though it was admitted that some of the guards were kindly in their attitude and tried to diminish the discomfort of the "noisome" place. The food was very bad and all they had to sleep on was a straw palliasse with two thin blankets.

The average Briton's amazing, and occasionally tantalising, capacity for understatement comes out very vividly in these lively yet harrowing pages of Mr. Hope's. Here, at random, is a choice example:

One merchant seaman of my acquaintance spent three days alone on a raft, tossed continuously in the long Atlantic rollers until taken off by a seaplane. When I commented sympathetically on his ordeal he responded, "Ay, I was damn glad to get out of that plane—it didn't 'alf make me sick !"

None of their experiences at sea or on land had the effect of making the cheery souls who figure in Mr. Hope's book want to give up their occupation or seek secure, cushy jobs at home. They did not speak about it, but they knew how their fellow-countrymen depended on them. The question which Admiral Lord Cork and Orrery puts in his Foreword to the book is, "Do their fellow-countrymen mean to see them let down again after this war, as they so shamefully were after the last ?" They were allowed, he says truly, "to go through a terrible time and there was no national cry for justice to them." Lord Cork evidently thinks that a British Government might play the same low trick again. It rests, he tells us, "with our people as a whole to decide whether it does or not."

MAIL DAY FOR THE MERCHANT NAVY may mean the delivery of 6,000 letters to vessels in a single port, and a launch like the one shown here can take six hours on its rounds of ships at anchor. The incomparable M.N. is the subject of the book here reviewed.
Photo, British Newspaper Pool

Why Britain's Achievements Astound the World

In the sixth year of hostilities, Britain's War Cabinet has made possible the world-wide assessment of our stupendous effort—an almost incredible total of self-sacrifice and labour which has brought us to the threshold of victory. Facts and figures hitherto secret, presented dryly in White Papers, have stirred the imagination of mankind and evoked wonder even from our Allies.

GREATER than that of any other belligerent : thus can be summed up the war effort per head of the population (45 million) of Great Britain. Mobilized for every sacrifice, living and working under complete black-out for five years, "family life has been broken up, not only by the withdrawal of men and women to the Services, but by evacuation and billeting," says the White Paper (Statistics Relating to the War Effort of the United Kingdom, published by H.M. Stationery Office, 1s.).

"Production has been made more difficult by the dispersal of factories to frustrate the air attacks of the enemy and by the need for training new labour to unaccustomed tasks. There have been two long periods when work was carried on under constant and severe air attacks. Since 1940, 1,750,000 men have given their limited spare time, after long hours of work, for duty

JERRICANS—NEW-STYLE PETROL TINS—are here seen in great numbers being refilled from petrol lorries at an advanced air base on the Continent. Millions of them, produced at top speed by British factories during the first half of 1944, helped in the winning of the Battle of France, as told in this page.
Photo, U.S. Official

in the Home Guard. Most other adult male civilians and many women have performed part-time Civil Defence and Fire Guard duties out of working hours."

Such is the background of toil and "leisure" in the Britain which, in long agony of blood and sweat and tears, has been converted to a miraculously efficient war machine. Hinging upon this, the White Paper brings generous comment from America (New York Times), as reminder to those in the U.S. of short memory, that " the British were fighting Hitler, part of the time almost alone, for two years before the Japanese bombed us into the war."

OF the 13 million houses in the United Kingdom when war broke out, 4,500,000 have been damaged by enemy action. Of these, 202,000 have been totally destroyed or smashed beyond possibility of repair. Bombed out, blacked out, taxed to the extreme limit, " the people who performed these prodigies of labour," comments Mr. Brendan Bracken, Minister of Information, "were fed on a monotonous ration and a dull diet, and have had a constant worry about coupons for this and that."

The terror by night, and oft-times by day, the privations, and the miseries of separation, have fallen heavily upon our children : 7,250 have been killed by the enemy on our home soil : the total of wounded and maimed has yet to be revealed. This grim toll of

flesh and blood totalled, to the end of August 1944, 57,298 civilians killed (including 23,757 women) and 78,818 injured and detained in hospital. In the Armed Forces of the U.K., from the outbreak of war to September 3, the killed numbered 176,081, the missing 38,275, the wounded 193,788, and prisoners amounted to 154,968. Our Merchant Seamen list on their roll of honour the names of 29,629 killed.

BY mid-1944 there were in our Armed Forces 4,500,000 men. In the auxiliary services, wholetime Civil Defence, or industry, there were over seven million women and girls. The aircraft industry alone absorbed two million workers—and up to June we had built 102,609 aeroplanes. In these five years we have produced more than 35,000 guns : heavy and light artillery for field and A.A. purposes. And, in addition, 3,729,921 machine- and sub-machine-guns, and 2,001,949 rifles. Tanks amounted to 25,116, and wheeled vehicles of all kinds 919,111. Our shipyards have turned out 5,744 naval vessels.

The severe drain on our man and woman power for war work and services dislocated home and other living conditions to an abnormal degree. The building trade, textile, clothing and other industries suffered a loss in workers equal to almost one-half of the pre-war total ; in 1944 the number was 2,900,000 as against 5,798,000. Imports, because of the acute pressure on Allied shipping, sank to an all-time low level.

Even firewood became so rare as to be unobtainable : except in districts devastated by enemy action. Expenditure on boots and shoes was cut by a quarter, clothing by one-half, hardware (pots and pans generally) by two-thirds, furniture by three-quarters, bicycles and cars by nine-tenths. And the fighting and the working went on, increasing in volume. Our war expenditure has mounted to nearly £25,000,000,000. In direct taxation we paid in 1943 the sum of £1,781,000,000, in indirect taxation £1,249,000,000. In the same period government spending amounted to £5,782,000,000.

Equally surprising revelations, affording both friend and enemy more food for serious

thought, are given in another White Paper (Mutual Aid, Second Report, from H.M. Stationery Office, 2d.), concerning Britain's reverse Lend-Lease to America and other Allies. " The total of Mutual Aid furnished by His Majesty's Government in the United Kingdom to their Allies," the Report says, " exceeds £1,000,000,000. All this has been given, without payment, in furtherance of the principle that the resources of the United Nations should be pooled for the common war effort."

Success of the Allied landing in France depended largely on the prefabricated harbours—one for British the other for U.S. use—which were designed and constructed in this country (see pages 430-434). Among other items handed over to the U.S. forces were two complete floating docks ; pontoon units numbering 2,110 ; 200 cranes ; 12 coasters and 30 lighters ; 3 hospital carriers.

TRAINING requirements for U.S. forces in Britain gave rise to serious problems, but these were all surmounted—regardless of cost. " In one agricultural area about 3,000 civilians were removed, and eight villages evacuated in order to give space for training with live ammunition." Movement about this country of American troops in the six months ending June 30, 1944, involved 9,225 special trains and 650,000 wagons ; hundreds of thousands of tons, in addition, were transported by road and canal. British ships carried 865,000 U.S. troops across the Atlantic; the Queen Mary (see page 486) and the Queen Elizabeth brought over 320,500.

In many cases our factories met the entire requirements of the U.S. forces, including sparking plugs for certain types of aircraft : 558,500 up to June 30, 1944, and a further 600,000 plugs had been shipped to the U.S. Other supplies comprised 2,104 aircraft (500 were gliders), with an additional 570 aircraft engines ; 137,000 jettison fuel tanks to increase the range of fighter planes ; 50,000 pieces of armour plate for aircraft ; 29,000 aero tires and 22,000 aero tubes ; and 7,087,802 jerricans (petrol containers) were delivered in the first 6 months of 1944.

Those jerricans, turned out by the million in British factories, played an immense part in winning the Battle of France. " Without them," declared President Roosevelt, "it would have been impossible for our armies to cut their way across France at that lightning pace, which exceeded the German blitz of 1940." The special point about these petrol tins is that they are oblong, enabling them to be packed in great numbers on a lorry or other vehicle, and they are known as "jerricans," because "Jerry" invented them. British production followed the capture of one of Rommel's petrol convoys by the 8th Army.

We supplied to U.S. forces food grown in the United Kingdom to the value of close on £8,000,000. To Russia we shipped material for the Soviet fighting forces, numerous items, in one year, including 1,042 tanks, 6,135 miles of cable, and two million metres of camouflage netting ; naval supplies were represented by 195 guns of all calibres with 4,644,930 rounds of ammunition. To China, to European Allies, to Portugal and Turkey vast streams of arms, munitions, equipment or other aid flowed from our shores. As fitting conclusion to a severely condensed account of part of the Homeland's effort comes President Roosevelt's declaration that all this has made a "life and death difference in the fighting this year."

Colossal War-Efforts of the Homeland Revealed

 Men of the United Kingdom under Arms

(In June of each year)

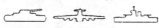

EACH SYMBOL REPRESENTS **250,000** MEN

1939

1941

1942

1943

1944

Total number of men who have served or are serving

Including the number killed, missing, taken prisoner or released on medical and other grounds, the total during this war is over **5,500,000**

The striking development of Britain's warplane industry

 ONE EXAMPLE **HEAVY BOMBER OUTPUT**

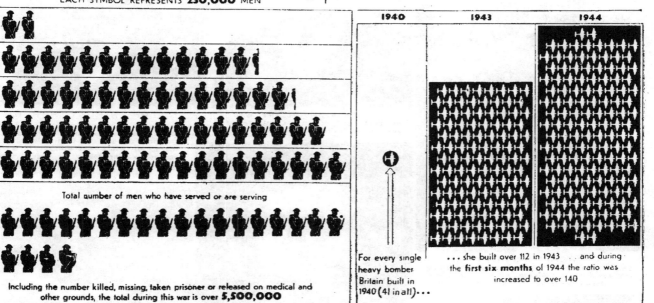

| 1940 | 1943 | 1944 |

For every single heavy bomber Britain built in 1940 (41 in all) . . .

. . . she built over 112 in 1943 . . . and during the **first six months** of 1944 the ratio was increased to over **140**

Britain mobilized with all her might

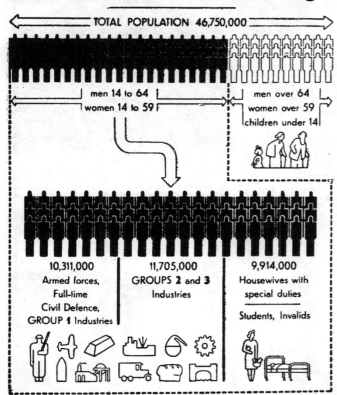

TOTAL POPULATION 46,750,000

men 14 to 64
women 14 to 59

men over 64
women over 59
children under 14

10,311,000
Armed forces,
Full-time
Civil Defence,
GROUP **1** Industries

11,705,000
GROUPS **2** and **3**
Industries

9,914,000
Housewives with
special duties

Students, Invalids

JUNE 1939 — JUNE 1944

DISCLOSED FOR THE FIRST TIME, in a White Paper issued on November 28, 1944, are details of Britain's prodigious war achievements (see facing page). Here part of the story is told in pictorial form. In the diagram at bottom left, Group I industries include munitions and all warlike stores—engineering, aircraft, motors, shipbuilding and repairing, metal goods manufacture, chemicals, explosives, oils, etc. Group 2 industries embrace all basic industries and services, including agriculture, mining, government service, gas, water, transport, food, etc.; and Group 3 building, civil engineering, clothing, distributive trades, commerce and professional services.

British Official Diagrams

The part played by women in Britain's war effort

<u>REPLACING MEN</u>

4 examples from Group 2 Industries

Each BLACK symbol represents **10,000** women added
Each WHITE symbol represents **10,000** men withdrawn

AGRICULTURE ETC.
 IN
OUT

LOCAL GOVERNMENT SERVICE
 IN
OUT

PUBLIC UTILITY SERVICES
 IN
 OUT

TRANSPORT. SHIPPING AND FISHING
 IN
 OUT

The total number of men in all branches of Group 2 industries fell by 600,000 and the number of women rose by 800,000

Home Front Civilians Honoured for Bravery

Mr. THOMAS KNIGHT, B.E.M.
This 37-year-old Ramsgate diver groped along the sea-bed to salvage a torpedo which threatened to explode at the slightest touch.

Mr. BENJAMIN GILBERT, G.C.
Engine-driver hero of the Cambridgeshire ammunition train explosion on June 2, 1944.

Mr. ANTHONY SMITH, G.C.
A Chelsea chimney-sweep, this C.D. Rescue Service worker was honoured for "outstanding gallantry and devotion to duty in conditions of the utmost danger and difficulty." Burrowing beneath blazing debris, he rescued a trapped casualty in the basement of a bomb-wrecked house which was about to collapse.

Dr. E. BOYTON, M.B.E.
This 61-year-old doctor (above), of Battersea, performed an amazing deed of heroism in a V-bomb raid when the staircases were demolished in a block of flats. Though fearful of heights she tended a casualty trapped on the 5th floor, by climbing up a swaying N.F.S. turntable ladder (as at left) and entering the crumbling premises over a broken window frame. She remained with the man until he was removed.

Sergeant B. E. WOODS, B.E.M.
An officer of the Metropolitan Police, he saved three buried raid victims by raising the roof of a bombed house on his shoulders, enabling rescue work to proceed. Bricks were falling at the time, and the roof later collapsed.

Dr. J. BEESTON, G.M.
This Willesden doctor gave a blood transfusion while gas escape threatened to overcome workers in a tunnel where a woman lay trapped, and thus saved her life.

Dr. H. SPARLING, M.B.E.
C.D. Casualty Officer of Croydon he was held by the heels while giving injections and binding fractures in a large house which had collapsed on top of people.

Photos, L.N.A., G.P.U., Topical, News Chronicle

Stand-Down Parade of Britain's Home Guard

IN LONDON ON SUNDAY, DECEMBER 3, 1944, over 7,000 Home Guards, drawn from all over Britain, marched past H.M. the King, who took the farewell salute (above), the Queen and the Princesses, at Stanhope Gate, Hyde Park. Three men from each unit in the Kingdom attended, together with some 3,500 from the London district, most of whom had enrolled when the Home Guard was formed, as the L.D.V. (Local Defence Volunteers), in May 1940. See eye-witness story in page 538.

Photo Planet News

Chinese are Called on to Summon All Resources

"CHINA IS FACING the most critical situation of the war," disclosed a Chungking dispatch dated December 1, 1944. The Japanese were advancing rapidly and in very considerable strength towards the vital Burma Road base of Kweiyang, junction town of the highways leading to Kunming, terminal for air supplies, and heading towards Chungking (see map). Four days later Generalissimo Chiang Kaishek called on the Chinese people to summon all their resources.

The developing threat to China's lifeline precipitated the flight of countless refugees all along her eastern front. Every available inch on this train (1) about to steam westwards from Liuchow was crammed. A forlorn Chinese mother and her two children (3) rested on the track, hoping for a lift. Suspected civilians were rounded up: a Chinese Army colonel is seen (2) interrogating one (with back to camera) accused of espionage. See also illus. p. 544.

Photos, Planet News, Paul Popper.
Map by courtesy of News Chronicle

I WAS THERE! *Eye Witness Stories of the War*

Behind ELAS Lines in Dissension-Torn Athens

Political differences in Greece, partly submerged during the fight against the common enemy, flared into open fighting after Athens had been freed of the German yoke. On December 8, 1944, B.U.P. correspondent James Earl-Roper sent this dispatch from the Greek capital, where the insurgent ELAS (Greek partisans) were being dealt with by Greek Government and British troops. (See also illus. page 523).

WITH a group of American war correspondents (our armbands served as safe-conduct passes) we moved through ELAS "territory" for three hours. I saw well-armed men, well supplied with ammunition, manning German-built pillboxes and putting the finishing touches to air-raid shelter trenches and firing points. The ELAS soldiers were carrying a variety of rifles, all had bandoliers and seemed to have plenty of ammunition, including German "potato masher" hand grenades.

I saw one woman guerilla. She was about 23, and was proudly carrying a red-snapper concussion grenade of the Italian type. The rattle of small arms fire sounded almost

IN AN ATHENS STREET, in December 1944, a British soldier stands rock-like, alone, while the tide of civil war, typified by banner-carrying political demonstrators, swirls around him.
Photo, British Official

Suspicion thawed when the Greeks made out the armbands of the war correspondents.

Most of the ordinary civilians I saw looked very tired. Many of them seemed hungry and some seemed nervous. It was easy getting into the ELAS lines. I walked out towards the ELAS strongholds, shook off a British soldier who warned me not to go farther, and then ran into an ELAS guerilla, who passed me back to another trooper, and so on.

Getting out again was not so easy. As we started to infiltrate back to the British lines, a volley of rifle bullets slammed suddenly down the boulevard. I made a dash for it, racing across the open street with the rifle bullets speeding my progress. I ran on until I reached the middle of the next street, when a pretty Greek girl flagged me down with a wave of the hand and a laugh.

Bullets were still flying around, and the position looked none too happy until a British armoured car rolled up to the scene with British soldiers on the look-out for trouble. Then a jeep came along and we got a lift back to central Athens.

My Amazing Escape from an Exploding Bomb Dump

From dark hells of falling rocks and choking gas and violent explosions men miraculously escaped; others perished where they were working deep underground, when the great bomb dump near Burton-on-Trent blew up on November 27, 1944. Jack Gorton tells his extraordinary story, given here by arrangement with The Daily Herald.

M. GEORGE PAPANDREOU, the Greek Prime Minister, against whose Government the ELAS (Left Wing) troops broke into insurrection on December 3, 1944. A glimpse of the Athens scene five days later is given in this page. *Photo, British Official*

continuously, except when we reached points deep in the ELAS positions in the rebel-held part of Athens. Sitting at a street corner on a camp stool with stretchers near him was a Greek doctor, waiting for casualties.

House windows were shuttered, but there were people living in those houses. Sometimes the shutters flew back suddenly and suspicious faces peered out and down at us.

WE work—my pals and I—separated by a solid door of cement seven feet deep from those thousands of tons of stored bombs. On Monday morning with my mate George Shepherd I walked into the galleries. A hole in the hillside is our way in. We go with wicker food baskets slung over our shoulder on pieces of string and it's a walk of five-and-twenty minutes to our job 160 ft. down.

There are miles of galleries. It's like an underground maze. George and I got on the job. We talked about the week-end football results and joked a bit. Then, round about eleven, it happened. We heard a thump, a terrible thump. It sent me flying into the rock face.

I got up and said to my mate, "What the hell is this?" But we were still alive, we could slap our thighs and feel that our bones were still unbroken. We decided to go into the main roadway to see if we could get to the boys—there were 21 of them—to see if we could get into the daylight and fresh air.

Charlie Gibbs, a loader, took a light in his hand and walked off. Soon he came back and said: "Boys, there's gas on the main roadway!" Charlie Gibbs faced us squarely and asked for volunteers to go into the main roadway to see if we could find our friends. We heard Charlie saying, "We must have some more help!"

We walked on and I found Willy Watson, a loco driver, lying in the main roadway. He was unconscious. They took him back. I walked on another 200 yards and smelt gas, like sniffing burnt sugar. We took Willy Watson through a relief door, a wooden door, because we knew that on the other side of it there was fresh air, and laid him down. We twisted his ears and worked his left arm around like a pump. We saw his eyes flicker and then we knew that Willy was still alive.

We went on for two other men who were on the same roadway, through two pockets of gas before we got to them. I saw George Smith crouched down, unconscious. And this is where I started to go under. A piece of rock fell on one of my hands. I suddenly realized that that piece of rock had never caused me any pain. Then I went under. I don't remember anything more, but I

A DERBYSHIRE VILLAGE "JUST VANISHED" when a R.A.F. bomb-dump blew up near Burton-on-Trent on November 27, 1944, and 68 people were killed or missing. Huge cracks and craters appeared in the earth as seen here; houses, cottages and farm buildings in a village a few miles away collapsed like packs of cards, and people more than 50 miles away, in Northampton and Daventry, heard the explosion and felt the blast. A miraculous escape-story by a near-victim is related above.
Photo, The Daily Herald

know now that my mates dragged me back to safety. Up on the surface a farmer, who is a C.D. worker, had refused to leave the mouth of the tunnel because he thought that some of us might get a message up to him. Somebody did shout. It is 90 feet deep there, but the farmer heard the cry.

They got a rope lowered down and, the boys tied it round me and I was hauled up.

And they hauled up my wicker food basket with me. There it was, perched on my chest on the stretcher when I came round. I must be the luckiest man alive. I've heard people say that before, but now I know. I managed to get out of an explosion that has churned up our bit of countryside into a mudheap. Five of my mates down there are dead. Many more of them on the surface are dead.

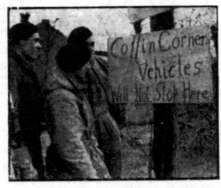

COFFIN CORNER was the apt nickname for a dangerous position near Geilenkirchen (captured on November 19, 1944). Members of a British tank crew inspect the warning notice. There are other warnings our men must most carefully observe, as related below.
Photo, British Official

The British Soldier's Lot is Tough in Germany

Until quite recently the British soldier has been the liberator wherever he went, always greeted as a friend. Now that he has crossed the frontier of the Reich he has become an avenger—a role that doesn't suit him at all, for reasons given here by a military observer on the spot.

I'VE watched Thomas Atkins—the friendliest creature on God's earth—moving into billets in French farms, Belgian side-streets, Dutch villages. He's a stranger in those places for about twenty seconds ; then suddenly he's at home, a friend of the family, of the street, of the village. He's chatting away in the accents of London, Wessex or the North Country, always with the grin that seems magically to make it all comprehensible to his new-found friends.

Out come the sweets and chocolate for the children and the cigarettes for the old man, and perhaps a tablet of soap for Ma—the first real soap she's seen for years. And though he represents an army which has stood up to the toughest fighting of the war, made spectacular advances and won great victories, he will never play the conquering hero. He never boasts and he never informs the French, Belgians or Dutch how much better everything is in England. Though he's popular with the girls, as with everybody else, you'll never see him rounding up the local glamour girls for joy rides. He's a family man. He misses his own home more than he could ever say and he loves to "get his feet under the table," to share the family life of whatever spot on the map he's sent to.

That's why invading Germany makes things tough for him. He knows the German

soldier, and though he respects some of his enemy's soldierly qualities he has implacable hatred for the methods of the Nazi. He knows his job is to make the Nazi pay for the ruined streets of London, Plymouth and Hull, for the separation from loved ones he has suffered, and the far worse sufferings of the Gestapo's victims in occupied countries. But when he enters his first German village he finds only children who look much the same as English children, hard-working housewives and quiet old people. It's against all his warm-hearted, easy-going instincts to hold himself aloof, to discard the friendly grin and act the stern, relentless conqueror.

Is It Loot from Holland ?

Yet those are his orders. All fraternization is absolutely forbidden. Forbidden because he's naturally unable to discriminate between the few Germans who all along have been Hitler's enemies and the many who cheered his victories, condoned the vile methods of the Gestapo, and now protest that they were always anti-Nazi. That quiet, respectable woman who looks rather like his own mother —why should he be forbidden to pass the time of day with her ? She seems to bear no ill-will. Yes, but if he only knew she probably has a son in the S.S., maybe one of those who booby-trapped British wounded or shot Russian civilians for acts of peaceful resistance.

That big radiogram in her parlour is probably loot from Holland, and even her Sunday coat may well have been looted from the shop of a Frenchman who paid the penalty for refusing to collaborate. If the average British soldier were allowed to fraternize in a "harmless" way—give sweets to pale children and return the greetings of humble old folk— his genius for friendship would almost certainly betray him and play into the hands of his bitterest enemies.

So it's grim, this entry into Germany, for our men. When they're out of the line and the day's duty is done, they can no longer look forward to evenings at a homely fireside, nursing the old cat, playing games with the children, tracing their travels since D-Day on an old map, while Ma darns their socks and the pretty daughter's smiles help just a little to ease the ever-present ache of absence from loved ones.

When I asked the Commanding Officer of a battalion of a famous infantry regiment how his men were taking it, he said : "I have given my orders and they are being obeyed. The men have been told that we can't afford to be friendly with any of the Germans here. Except for the bitter few, they seem to be ill at ease living here among people they must ignore. It will be better when they evacuate these villages."

A dispatch rider, plastered with German mud from head to foot, gave me his view. "Seems funny not to be able to answer the kids when they speak. Still, I s'pose it wouldn't do to treat many of the Jerries decently. They'd only think we were soft." And he parked the bike that had carried him all the way from the Normandy beaches and walked off down the village street—alone. He'd never been alone in France or Belgium or Holland. Always there'd been at least a couple of children hanging on his arms, a dog round his feet, and greetings from every doorway. But now he was alone—one of the newly arrived army of friendly souls in a friendless country.

We Cheered the Home Guards' Last Parade

Great crowds lined London's bomb-scarred streets on the grey Sunday afternoon of December 3, 1944, to honour the farewell parade of Britain's Home Guard, who for over four years had held themselves ready to repel any invader. Grace Herbert of The Daily Express here gives her impression of marchers and spectators on this moving occasion. See illus. page 535.

THEY marched through Hyde Park, sere and leafless in the typical December weather, saluted the King, their Colonel-in-Chief, went off down Piccadilly to the Circus, up Regent Street, turned left along Oxford Street to Marble Arch, went by Tyburn Gate, then down through the Park again to the Ring Road to disperse, officially for ever . . . unless called on for some fateful emergency.

A spectator can stand only at one place along a route, see one aspect of a marching man's face, one set of expressions. I felt a strange, unusual wish to cry. Why ? These were ordinary men, our grocers, bank managers, husbands, sons. Men we see every day.

But for this day they were uplifted into something different. They wore great coats and tin hats, some carried new rifles, others

had last-war rifles. Some wore new boots which were hurting them ; some were young —very young ; some were old—though not too old. Men of 70 walked beside boys of 17. And they were comrades. It was the comradeship, not the militancy, of this procession which made me want to cry.

I stood near the dais where the King, the Queen and the two Princesses were to take the salute. The Royal Standard curled in a soft breeze. People crowded the roof tops of the Dorchester Hotel and the houses of Stanhope Gate just behind. Park Lane was still.

In the middle distance we heard a low cheering. Five grey horses of the Metropolitan Police came into view. Behind them bobbed the khaki tin hats of our voluntary army. Several of us stood on park seats so that we could see both them and the King and Queen, and the Princesses. The King

MONTY IN GERMANY : Field-Marshal Sir Bernard Montgomery (left) paid his first visit to German territory in December 1944, and met men of the British 2nd Army who had occupied it just a short while before.
Photo, British Official

HOME GUARDS SWINGING DOWN PICCADILLY on December 3, 1944, had taken part in the special stand-down parade in London, described in the story commencing in facing page. H.M. the King broadcast an appreciation of their services, in which he described them as "mighty in courage and determination." See also illus. page 535.   *Photo, New York Times Photos*

wore Field-Marshal's uniform ; the Queen, a black fur coat, a black hat, and fox fur.

With them on the saluting dais were Sir James Grigg, War Secretary, in a plain black coat, and General Sir Harold Franklyn, Commander-in-Chief of the Home Forces. The Irish Guards band, stationed opposite the dais, played "Colonel Bogey." Princess Margaret whispered to Elizabeth. They strained forward past their mother and father to see the men advancing.

The King raised his hand to the salute as men of the London district marched past. Then came the anti-aircraft gunners ; then

the Eastern Command contingent. For 45 minutes they marched by, 29 contingents, 11 Home Guard bands. The crowd cheered and clapped. Nearly every person in that crowd was looking out for somebody they knew in the parade.

It was an amazingly large, good-natured crowd. But it did not cheer loud and long. One woman said : "We are still at war !" Which seemed to sum up the general feeling. There were many Home Guards in the crowd,

both in and out of uniform. And they made remarks like these :

"Well, it shows the war's nearing its end." "Our job's done." "We won't forget the friends we've made in a hurry." "Fancy every one of those 7,000 men wearing his own socks." "Now I remember when we only had sticks." "Now mum'll have me back on her hands." "Old Home Guards never die. . . ." The last line passed. The police closed in. It was over.

OUR DIARY OF THE WAR

DECEMBER 6, Wednesday   *1,922nd day*
Western Front.—3rd Army troops entered outskirts of Sarreguemines. Floods caused by German breaching of dykes S.W. of Arnhem held up movement on 2nd Army front.
Air.—Leuna oil plant at Merseburg again attacked by U.S. bombers by day and R.A.F. at night. Railway yards at Bielefeld and Osnabruck also bombed.
Pacific.—U.S. warships repulsed Japanese air attack on Super-Fortress base in Marianas.

DECEMBER 7, Thursday   *1,923rd day*
Western Front.—3rd Army troops penetrated Siegfried defences northwest of Saarlouis.
Russian Front.—Soviet troops cleared southern shore of Lake Balaton, Hungary, of the enemy.
Philippines.—Announced that U.S. troops had landed on west coast of Leyte, three miles from Ormoc.
Far East.—Super-Fortresses attacked aircraft plant at Mukden and other targets in Manchuria.
Pacific.—U.S. warships and bombers attacked Japanese base at Iwojima, Volcano Islands.

DECEMBER 8, Friday   *1,924th day*
Western Front.—Fort Driant, west of Metz, fell to U.S. troops.
Air.—Marshalling yard and oil plant in Duisburg area attacked in daylight by R.A.F. Lancasters.
China.—Tushan, south-east of Kweiyang, recaptured by Chinese troops.

DECEMBER 9, Saturday   *1,925th day*
Western Front.—3rd Army troops made two more crossings of the Saar and threw back counter-attack at Saarlouis.
Air.—Railway yards and airfield at Stuttgart bombed by U.S. 8th Air Force.
Russian Front.—Red Army troops reached Danube north of Budapest and orced new crossing to the south.

DECEMBER 10, Sunday   *1,926th day*
Air.—Railway centres at Coblenz and Bingen attacked by U.S. bombers. Spitfire bombers again attacked V2 sites.
Sea.—Announced that new British fleet would operate in Pacific theatre, under command of Admiral Sir Bruce Fraser.

Burma.—Troops of British 36th Division entered Naba, Indaw and Katha.
Philippines.—Japanese base of Ormoc, on west coast of Leyte, captured.
General.—Soviet-French Treaty of Alliance signed by Gen. de Gaulle in Moscow.

DECEMBER 11, Monday   *1,927th day*
Western Front.—U.S. 7th Army troops entered communications centre of Haguenau, on road to Palatinate.
Air.—More than 2,000 U.S. heavy bombers from Britain and Italy attacked railway yards at Frankfurt, Giessen and Hanau and oil plant and ordnance depots in Vienna region.
Russian Front.—Soviet troops closed in on Budapest from north, east and south.
Greece.—Fighting continued in Athens between British supporting Papandreou Govt. and reinforced ELAS. troops.

DECEMBER 12, Tuesday   *1,928th day*
Air.—More than 1,250 U.S. bombers and 900 fighters attacked Leuna oil plant and railway yards at Hanau, Darmstadt and Aschaffenburg. R.A.F. bombed Witten in the Ruhr by day, and at night made a heavy attack on Essen.

Mediterranean.—Allied bombers from Italy attacked Blechhammer oil plant in Silesia.
Greece.—Field-Marshal Alexander and Mr. Harold Macmillan visited Athens.

DECEMBER 13, Wednesday   *1,929th day*
Western Front.—Last Metz fort, Jeanne d'Arc, fell to Allied troops.
Burma.—Announced that 14th Army had built Bailey Bridge across the Chindwin near Kalewa.
Far East.—War production centre of Nagoya, Japan, bombed by Super-Fortresses.

DECEMBER 14, Thursday   *1,930th day*
Western Front.—Germans launched counter-attack at southern end of front, around Colmar.
Greece.—Announced that reinforcements and supplies had been flown from Italy to British troops in Athens.
Burma.—Super-Fortresses from India attacked Bangkok and Rangoon.

DECEMBER 15, Friday   *1,931st day*
Western Front.—Troops of 7th Army crossed German border from Alsace.
Air.—R.A.F. bombed E-boat and R-boat

pens at Dutch port of Ijmuiden, and at night attacked chemical works at Ludwigshafen. U.S. bombers attacked railway targets at Hanover and Kassel.
Burma.—Bhamo, last big Japanese stronghold in northern Burma, captured by Chinese forces.
Philippines.—Announced that U.S. troops had landed on island of Mindoro, south of Manila.
General.—Mr. Churchill stated that Britain supported Russian plan of Curzon Line as Poland's eastern frontier, with East Prussia as compensation in the west.

DECEMBER 16, Saturday   *1,932nd day*
Western Front.—Germans launched series of large-scale counter-attacks against 1st Army front in the Ardennes.
Air.—R.A.F. Lancasters bombed railway centre of Siegen, east of Cologne. U.S. bombers attacked Stuttgart.
Italy.—Troops of 8th Army captured Faenza, on road to Bologna.
Mediterranean.—Allied bombers from Italy attacked oil plant at Brux, in Czechoslovakia.
Burma.—Chinese and U.S. troops of Mars Task Force entered Tonkwa, 120 air miles from Mandalay.

DECEMBER 17, Sunday   *1,933rd day*
Western Front.—Germans forced four penetrations of U.S. lines.
Mediterranean.—Allied bombers from Italy attacked oil targets at Blechhammer and Odertal and railway yards at Salzburg.

DECEMBER 18, Monday   *1,934th day*
Air.—Cologne, Coblenz and Mainz attacked by U.S. bombers. R.A.F. bombed German warships at Gdynia.
Russian Front.—Soviet troops from Hungary crossed Czechoslovak border.
Far East.—Super-Fortresses bombed Nagoya and Hankow.

DECEMBER 19, Tuesday   *1,935th day*
Air.—Allied heavy bombers attacked road and rail communications behind German counter-attack in the West.
Balkans.—Montenegrin town of Podgorica captured by Yugoslavs.
Far East.—China-based Super Fortresses attacked Omura, Japan and Shanghai and Nanking.

★ ══════════ *Flash-backs* ══════════ ★

1939
December 13. *Battle of River Plate between Graf Spee and Exeter, Ajax and Achilles.*

1940
December 9. *Wavell's offensive opened against Italians in Western Desert of Egypt.*
December 17. *Sollum on Egyptian frontier captured by Wavell.*

1941
December 8. *Imperial forces raised 8-months' siege of Tobruk.*

December 9. *Japanese landed on island of Luzon, Philippines.*
December 10. *Prince of Wales and Repulse sunk off Malaya.*
December 11. *Germany and Italy declared war on U.S.A.*

1942
December 16. *Red Army opened offensive in Middle Don area.*

1943
December 12. *Rommel appointed C.-in-C. of "European Fortress."*
December 15. *U.S. troops landed on coast of New Britain.*

THE WAR IN THE AIR

by Capt. Norman Macmillan, M.C., A.F.C.

THE V2 rocket-bomb which has been used by the Germans to "shell" southern England can be launched from a simpler site than is needed for the flying bomb. The latter requires a launching ramp or a mother-aircraft (see illus. p. 469). To fire V1s in rapid succession from the surface demands the advance preparation of ferro-concrete engineering works of considerable size ; it was the large V1 launching sites that Bomber Command concentrated on during their 1944 attacks against the Pas de Calais area of France, often using 12,000-lb. armour-piercing bombs to shock-damage the massive concrete works of the enemy. Remembering that these large bombs were frequently employed in those counter-attacks

erection and launching sites in Holland, firing cannon shells into buildings attached to the sites and setting alight surrounding woods with bombs and incendiary cannon shells.

ALTHOUGH these counter-measures must reduce the frequency of V2 discharges, as must Bomber Command's attacks against factories believed to be engaged on the manufacture of the weapon, and the 2nd Tactical Air Force attacks on railway rolling stock used to transport the V2s from factories or main stores to launching zones, it is improbable that air action can eliminate the V2 weapon. The only way to do that is to drive the enemy back from all surrounding territory within an area whence his flying-

the Allies can prevent Germany and Japan from prosecuting such research in secret, and also succeed in arranging reciprocity in research among themselves, the future world will be an uneasy place for all mankind to live in. Apart from any other factor, imagine the problems attached to the provision of practice firing ranges in peacetime in most countries for testing weapons with a range of upwards of 200 miles !

Meanwhile, passing over all Germany, Allied bombers in great and growing fleets continue to attack enemy supply lines by railway, canal, road and sea. On December 1, 1944, the enemy admitted that he had been forced to move his anti-aircraft batteries back from the Western fighting zone (where they were employed against both aircraft and tanks) to guard against air attacks on his vital supply points within his defensive belt. The railway system of the Ruhr, the canal system linking the Ruhr with Berlin and the North Sea and Baltic, the oil plants near Leipzig and in Austria have all been heavily bombed, as have towns situated in the zone ahead of the Allied armies through which enemy supplies for his fighting lines must pass.

HEAVY Bombers' Normandy Tasks are Repeated Inside Germany

Among recent town targets have been Osnabruck, Munster, Dortmund, Essen, Bochum, Holde, Hagen, Mulheim—Ruhr, Oberhausen, Hamborn, Barmen, Düsseldorf, Mulheim-Cologne, Bonn, Coblenz ; within this area the heavy bombers are repeating the task which they carried out so effectively over and behind the Normandy battlefield, but here, within Germany, it may take longer to gain results, because the surface conditions are so different, and the enemy is defending his own land and buildings.

In China the position remains critical following the Japanese drive on Kweiyang in Kweichow province, thereby threatening to cut the Burma Road at Kweiyang at the moment that the United Nations troops had cleared it far to the west in the Tengueh-Lungling-Bhamo area. General Chennault's U.S. Army 14th Air Force continued to attack the Japanese columns, and a China-based Liberator was reported to have sunk an enemy ship about 20 miles off Hong Kong. But American aircraft have been forced out of Kwangsi province ; tactical aircraft were withdrawn into Yunnan province, while the Super-Fortresses of the 20th Bomber Command were recalled to India (see map in p. 536).

SHIPFINDER FORCE WELLINGTON is loaded up with drip flares by a R.A.F. ground crew of Coastal Command. Of immense candle-power, these flares, dropped by Wellington bombers, silhouette the night targets for Wellington or Beaufighter striking forces which in powerful formations attack what survives of enemy shipping in the North Sea.   *Photo, Planet News*

makes it easier to realize how it came about that Bomber Command expended over 100,000 tons of bombs against the V1 sites within a few months.

BUT the V2 is a different proposition (see facing page). The quality of the target it offers is not so suited to the shock assault of heavy bombers. Indeed, it has been officially stated that the V2 can be fired from an ordinary level road with a good surface and stout ballast. The rocket weighs about 12 tons, and the starting thrust is about 26 tons, which enables it to take off from a standing start ; any level platform capable of supporting a standing weight of 12 tons and the momentary thrust of 26 tons will do for the discharge of the weapon. Around the launching site, however, must be arranged quarters for the V2 handling crews, stores and workshops, but these small buildings do not offer a target of importance to Bomber Command. Hence Fighter Command has been the mainspring of the V2 counter-offensive Spitfire fighter-bombers, well able to make the accurate pin-point attacks necessitated by the dispersed and small units of the target, have been employed to attack V2

bombs and rocket-bombs cannot reach a target outside the Reich. But by the time that is done Germany will have been militarily defeated, for the Allies will have met from the east and the west, simply because Germany is approximately 400 miles across, and 200 miles is the present range of the V2. Thus Germany can continue to fire V2 rockets of the present pattern right up to the moment of her capitulation, knowing that they will explode in the territory or cities of other nations.

The problems which have been introduced into this war by the introduction of new weapons, such as these, the 12,000-lb. A.P. bomb, radar, teleradar, the aircraft cannon-gun up to 75 millimetres, and the aircraft rocket shell with a 55 to 60-lb. explosive head, are bad enough, but their subsequent application in the post-war epoch will be even worse. Following the lines which this war has opened up, scientific research during the post-war period might place in the hands of some one nation the power to win a war against all other nations with a speed equal to the rapidity with which Germany knocked out Holland, Belgium and France in 1940. Unless

LATEST news from the zone is that Chinese troops, counter-attacking, have driven back northward-pushing enemy columns in Kweichow province almost to the Kwangsi border. The outcome of this most critical of all the battles of China will go far to determine the duration of the war against Japan. If the Burma Road is cut in China by the Japanese, the carriage of supplies by air over the Himalayan hump to bypass the area held by the enemy in the west will be useless, and the fate of the pipeline now under construction to carry oil into China (see illus. p. 544) will become problematical.

Meanwhile, Super-Fortresses have again bombed the enemy home base zone from the Marianas islands. Targets in Korea and Manchuria (important iron and steel areas) were attacked. On December 13, 100 Super-Fortresses bombed Nagoya, a centre of silk and cotton, textile and pottery manufacture. Japanese attempts to land reinforcements on Leyte were defeated eight times by air attack, sometimes aided by surface, sea or land artillery action, and U.S. forces captured the port of Ormoc before mid-December.

R.A.F. leading night fighter aircrew in defence of Britain—Wing Commander John G. Topham, of London, and his observer, Flight. Lieut. H. W. Berridge, of Sutton—have destroyed 14 night raiders while flying on operational tours during four years.

V2 Holds No Secrets from Our Experts Now

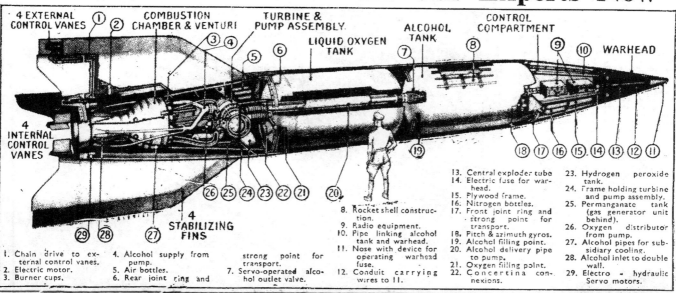

4 EXTERNAL CONTROL VANES ① ②
COMBUSTION CHAMBER & VENTURI ③ ④
TURBINE & PUMP ASSEMBLY. ⑤ ⑥
LIQUID OXYGEN TANK
ALCOHOL TANK ⑦
CONTROL COMPARTMENT ⑧ ⑨ ⑩
WARHEAD

4 INTERNAL CONTROL VANES

⑲

⑱ ⑰ ⑯ ⑮ ⑭ ⑬ ⑫ ⑪

㉖ ㉕ ㉔ ㉓ ㉒ ㉑

⑳

㉙ ㉘ ㉗

4 STABILIZING FINS

13. Central exploder tube.
14. Electric fuse for warhead.
15. Plywood frame.
16. Nitrogen bottles.
17. Front joint ring and strong point for transport.
18. Pitch & azimuth gyros.
19. Alcohol filling point.
20. Alcohol delivery pipe to pump.
21. Oxygen filling point.
22. Concertina connexions.

23. Hydrogen peroxide tank.
24. Frame holding turbine and pump assembly.
25. Permanganate tank (gas generator unit behind).
26. Oxygen distributor from pump.
27. Alcohol pipes for subsidiary cooling.
28. Alcohol inlet to double wall.
29. Electro - hydraulic Servo motors.

1. Chain drive to external control vanes.
2. Electric motor.
3. Burner cups.
4. Alcohol supply from pump.
5. Air bottles.
6. Rear joint ring and strong point for transport.
7. Servo-operated alcohol outlet valve.
8. Rocket shell construction.
9. Radio equipment.
10. Pipe linking alcohol tank and warhead.
11. Nose with device for operating warhead fuse.
12. Conduit carrying wires to 11.

ROCKET AND TRANSPORTERS

ROCKET TRANSPORTER

GROUND RECLAIMED FROM THE SEA

ROCKET SURROUNDED BY SERVICING VEHICLES

ROCKET IN VERTICAL POSITION READY FOR FIRING

ROCKET TRANSPORTERS

ROCKET VERTICAL

CONCRETE BASE

FROM A R.A.F. RECONNAISSANCE PHOTOGRAPH taken when experimental work with V2 rocket bombs at the German research station of Peenemunde (see illus. page 510) was in progress, the artist secured data for the reconstruction drawing above. Three rockets are seen in their vertical launching positions, one surrounded by special servicing vehicles. Dotted about are the transporters which carry the rockets from concealed storage galleries to the firing site, and there hoist them into a vertical position by means of rams. The V2, now known to be 46 ft. long and 5½ ft. in diameter, stands on its fins on a camouflaged concrete platform, ready for the launching from a well-protected firing-house situated at a safe distance. See also facing page, and illus. pages 458 and 508. (It should be noted that the word "Perspex" used in connexion with V1 in page 469 is the proprietary trade mark for the particular material made by I.C.I. Ltd., and the enemy therefore has no access to supplies.)

British Official and G. H. Davis (by courtesy of The Illustrated London News)

Britain's 7·2 Howitzer is Now in Action Overseas

FIRING 200-lb. SHELLS up to 16,000 yards, this New British howitzer (photographs of which were released late in 1944) weighs ten tons, and is mounted on a twin-wheel carriage with pneumatic tires 5 ft. 6 in. in diameter (2). It is fitted with hand-controlled brakes; but often when the howitzer is fired the recoil is so powerful that the weapon runs up on the steel ramps placed behind the firing position, in spite of the fact that the brakes are " on " (1). Note the height the wheels have risen from the ground during the vigorous recoil.

The 7·2 is quite mobile in relation to its weight, constituting a compromise between the gun that is too heavy to move, and the gun whose power has to be sacrificed for the sake of mobility. It was put to severe test on narrow, hairpin bends of roads on the Italian front (4), and later during the great Allied sweep across France and Belgium. Cleaning some of the 7.2's 200-lb. shells (3) at the side of a roadway in France as the guns take up their firing positions.

Photos, British Official

Editor's Postscript

BY the time these lines are read I hope the deplorable events which are taking place in Athens while this is being written will have become a thing of the past. But I think we must be prepared for many more clashes such as have happened already in Greece, in Italy, in Belgium, among the Poles and the Yugoslavs. What puzzles me is that no one so far as I know has publicly pointed out the inner meaning of these happenings. It is a long time now since a friend of mine, with wide experience as a newspaper correspondent and an almost uncanny knowledge of what other people are thinking, told me he thought the Resistance Movements in the occupied countries would have little use for the official Governments which had been set up in London (though the Greek was in Cairo), and that few of the ruling men of pre-war days would be likely to get back into their old jobs. Those who had borne the burden and heat of the day, my friend predicted, would resent having thrust on them persons who had been living in comfort and comparative safety. None the less, I am sure that without these recognized "national" governments which London has sheltered, the task of the guerillas in some of the captured countries would have been vastly more difficult if not entirely hopeless.

SINCE I wrote in this page about the necessity of inducing large numbers of tourists to visit Britain other papers have been full of the subject. All sorts of suggestions are being made for the improvement of our hotels and guest-houses ; all manner of criticisms are being passed on their shortcomings. Especially in the food line. But the idea that we ought to try to give visitors the kind of food they are accustomed to at home strikes me as being wrong altogether. In the first place, we could not do it. We try imitating French dishes, and the result is almost always deplorable. In the second place, people from other countries like a change of meals as well as changes of air and scenery. Often have I heard foreigners praise warmly the merits of real British cooking. I remember once in a train from Marseilles to Paris talking to a Frenchman who had paid us a visit not long before. He spoke with tender recollection of "your English steak pie," "your English roast shoulder of mutton," "your English apple tart with cream," "your Scottish soups—how do you call them ?—yes, I have it, barley broth and cockieleekie—very strange name !" Half the pleasure of his holiday, he assured me, had been due to the meals he had at hotels where they had the sense to serve genuine British dishes prepared with appreciative taste, instead of serving tinned soup, and bad copies of foreign dishes, with tinned pineapple and watery milk pudding to follow. There are not many such hotels, but they can be multiplied, and must be if we want people from overseas to come and spend money here.

IT is not wise to complain every time an American film is produced which seems to claim too much credit for our Allies. Such little annoyances are better passed over. But I must say I am in hearty agreement with critics who have condemned March of Time's picture of D-Day, called Strategy of Liberation. It seems that it gives the impression of an operation in which only Americans took part ; and the climax comes when the manufacture and placing in position of the prefabricated harbour which enabled the invasion of the Continent to be carried out are represented as being the work of American engineers. Now that is really too much to bear without protest. I do not suppose the March of Time films, which are as a rule so good, last long ; perhaps this one has already ceased to be shown. But in any future case of the kind the exhibitors ought to stand together and decline to show it. The story of these British prefabricated harbours was told in pages 430-434.

I AM afraid that variations on the Enoch Arden theme are very numerous just now, as they were at the end of the First Great War. Tennyson made the story of the sailor who came back after long absence to find his wife living with another man and decided to go away and not disturb them, familiar to all who read poetry. It is not very good poetry. The last line is a ludicrous example of bathos. After paying tribute to "the strong heroic soul" who passed away without revealing himself, the Laureate announced that the little port where he died

Had seldom seen a costlier funeral.

But the appeal of the story is strong enough to triumph over the mediocre verse. It is one of those situations which stir the feelings even of the unimaginative. When they are encountered in real life, they do so all the more deeply. Here is one example. I went into an estate agent's office, and a small-sized soldier looking terribly disconsolate, passed me on his way out. The young woman at the counter had tears in her eyes. She had been receiving the rent for a little house from the soldier's wife. A few weeks before it had stopped. The soldier had come home on leave from Italy and found the place shut up. Where his wife was he had no idea, though he had been told by neighbours about another man. He could not even get into the house. What a home-coming !

A YOUNG friend of mine, a recently qualified engineer, who passed with honours, has gone into one of the great aircraft-making

LIEUT.-GEN. FREDERICK BROWNING, C.B., D.S.O., who led the ever-memorable Arnhem-Nijmegen airborne operations in September 1944, received the Order of the Bath at a special investiture in London on December 6 (see page 513). He was appointed to succeed General Sir Henry Pownall as Chief of Staff to Lord Louis Mountbatten at S.E.A.C. Headquarters on November 28.
PAGE 543   *Photo, Associated Press*

firms. I was surprised when I heard he was getting six pounds a week to start with. He is nineteen. It is easy to understand why firms pay high wages. The argument is that they may just as well hand out money to their promising young men and so secure their loyalty (if that is the right word !) as pay it over to the Treasury in the shape of Excess Profits Tax. But I wonder if it is quite fair to the young men ? Starting them on that scale will make them not only expect to keep it, but to soar far above it. This boy has been told to look forward to a rise in a few months' time. Can he and his like reasonably count on being paid as highly under normal peace conditions ? If not, they are likely to complain of having been led up the garden, I fancy. Another thing the boy says is that he finds there is very little to do. That seems more surprising still.

IN a little suburban house the other day I saw a bowl of magnificent chrysanthemums. I knew they must have cost at least three or four shillings a bloom. I knew the occupants of the house could not afford to pay that price for flowers. When I said how beautiful they looked, I was told proudly that they were a present from one of the sons of the house who is with his regiment in Italy. "They just came one morning, with a card to say who they were from, and we *have* enjoyed them !" The way this is made possible has been worked out by Naafi in the various fighting areas and by the Women's Voluntary Service at home. The men at the front give their orders, and their friends receive the flowers with very little delay. I hear that the number of orders placed is approaching ten thousand and that more men are taking advantage of the scheme every month. Their gifts range from ten shillings-worth of any flowers the florists have in stock to special bunches of a named flower, which cost between two and three pounds. This is a happy development of the American "Say it with Flowers" idea.

HERE is a case in which a war-worker lives resolutely in the present. An A.T.S. sergeant, who is sixty-nine, is in charge of 28 young women privates in a hostel. She enjoys it thoroughly and keeps them in excellent order, winning their affection as well as their respect. She believes she will not be able to secure another job of the kind when she has to give up this one. Of course, there is really no reason why, if she remains fit and energetic as she is now she should not be given employment such as she would like. But so many of us are still inclined to be hide-bound in this matter of age. Not so very long ago men and women in the sixties did feel their years. After seventy they acquiesced in being laid on the shelf. Today we have changed all that. People do not grow old anything like as soon as they used to in the 19th century. Was Shaw's Back to Methuselah a sound prediction ? It does seem in some ways to be coming true.

WHEN it was announced that women's shoes were to be made with wooden soles, most people imagined that this would make them cheaper than shoes with leather soles. But a friend of mine tells me she bought for fifty-five shillings a pair supposed to have leather ones and found they began to wear out before she had had them on more than once. The leather was so unresistant that small stones in the roadway made marks on it. So she thought she would try wooden soles and perhaps give rather less for them. To her astonishment they cost her seventy-seven shillings. It is difficult to see the justification for that. I have more than once bought *sabots* in France to wear in the garden and they were very cheap indeed. I found them most useful, quite comfortable to the feet, and a protection against wet grass or damp soil. I have often wondered why we never adopted them here.

Oil from India to be Pipelined to China

CLOSELY GUARDED SECRET OF THE BURMA CAMPAIGN was disclosed on November 19, 1944, with the news that a gigantic oil pipeline, conveying thousands of tons monthly, runs from India to Burma and will eventually take precious fuel to China.   An amazing triumph for Allied engineers, the pipeline rises from sea level near Calcutta, 4,000 feet up through Assam and North Burma, and is now crossing high ranges separating Burma from China.   Above, valve installations are being checked as the task of pipe-laying proceeds.   *Photo, New York Times Photos*

Printed in England and published every alternate Friday by the Proprietors, THE AMALGAMATED PRESS, LTD., The Fleetway House, Farringdon Street, London, E.C.4. Registered for transmission by Canadian Magazine Post.   Sole Agents for Australia and New Zealand : Messrs. Gordon & Gotch, Ltd. ; and for South Africa : Central News Agency, Ltd.— January 5, 1945.   S.S.   *Editorial Address:* JOHN CARPENTER HOUSE, WHITEFRIARS, LONDON, E.C.4.

Vol 8   *The War Illustrated*   Nº 198

SIXPENCE

Edited by Sir John Hammerton

JANUARY 19, 1945

WHENCE THE CHINDITS TOOK THEIR NAME: Major-General F. W. Festing, D.S.O., commanding the 36th British Division (left), and Lieut.-General Dan I. Sultan, the U.S. Commander in Burma (centre), stroll thoughtfully past one of the great Chin Taes at Mawlu in North Burma. These startling guardians of Burmese temples were originally erected to keep away evil spirits. From them the late General Wingate's force (see page 46, Vol. 7) took its undying name.   *Photo, British Official*

Home Scenes Recorded by Our Roving Camera

GERMAN PRISONERS in Norfolk helping to lift the sugar-beet crop under the watchful eyes of a British soldier (left), while a German corporal stands by to pass on the orders. It was announced on December 14, 1944, that small parties of German prisoners were being employed on agricultural and forestry work, without supervision. Their uniform is chocolate-dyed battle-dress, and the maximum pay for this work ranges from 3s. to 6s. a week.

MR. LEWIS J. STURGE 70-years-old barrister (above), appointed Chief Enforcement Officer for the Ministry of Food to wage war against black marketeers.

44,000 L.M.S. WORKERS (two-thirds of the railway system's vast energies) have been building tanks, guns, planes, assault craft, bridges, and armoured trains for the past five years. Troops (above) test a unit construction bridge outside a L.M.S. workshop.

CHRISTMAS COMPETITION was organized by London Transport for the most attractively decorated Tube-station canteens for shelterers. The prizes consisted of War Savings Certificates. The canteen at Gloucester Road, London, S.W. (above) reflects the air of Christmas cheer achieved under tremendous difficulties.

MEN OF THE SERVICES, as well as hundreds of Italian prisoners of war, helped the railway companies to sort out the mails and luggage at the great London termini during the holiday rush at Christmastide. British troops (left) amid the welter of mailbags at Waterloo. *Photos, Daily Express, Topical Press, Fox Photos*

THE BATTLE FRONTS

by Maj.-Gen. Sir Charles Gwynn, K.C.B., D.S.O.

WHEN I last wrote it was well known that the Germans had during the autumn been able to form a powerful reserve with a large armoured component, and that it was located in the Cologne region.

The Allied High Command apparently considered that it was intended for use in a defensive counter-stroke in case the west wall was breached. They presumably thought that Von Rundstedt, in view of Allied air superiority, would not dare to undertake a counter-offensive operation which, if it achieved any success, must involve a lengthening of his lines of communication and an advance out of the area in which he possessed well fortified defensive pivots.

The prospects of such a counter-offensive achieving anything of decisive importance would be small and the risks of ultimate disastrous defeat very great. It is not, therefore, astonishing that Von Rundstedt secured surprise as good generals have often done, by accepting apparently prohibitive risks. Surprise gave him the initiative and initial success, but it remains to be seen whether he has not followed a will o' the wisp. The situation while I write is still too fluid to justify any attempt to forecast the outcome, although personally I have never wavered in the belief that Von Rundstedt's success, such as it has been, would be short lived. I considered that the utmost he would achieve would be to disorganize and delay General Eisenhower's offensive preparations and thus gain a breathing time on the western front before the main Russian offensive started.

RESERVES Thrown Piecemeal Into Battle in a Defensive Role

The risks he ran of being caught on the rebound were, however, obviously very great if he attempted too much, especially in view of Allied air superiority which would test German skill in disengaging to a dangerous degree. I cannot believe that Von Rundstedt seriously hoped that he would succeed in disrupting the Allied front and reach Paris or Antwerp; although to stimulate his troops he may have announced that these were his objectives. It should, I think, be noted that the battle has been mainly between the reserves on both sides.

The greater part of both armies face each other on a long stabilized front (see map), and there are not, in the faster moving operations of today, the same opportunities of applying the "roulement" system used extensively in the last war to maintain a long drawn out struggle such as the Somme and Passchendaele. By taking the initiative Von Rundstedt was able to complete the concentration of his reserves before striking his blow, while, on the other hand, the numerically superior Allied reserves were widely dispersed and had to carry out much regrouping before they could deliver an effective counter-blow. Some had of necessity to be thrown into the battle piecemeal in a defensive role.

VON RUNDSTEDT's plans were skilfully laid and executed, but were adapted to gain initial and temporary rather than major success; for with the bulk of the German Army tied to Russia he has not the force behind him—as he had in 1940—required to achieve anything of a decisive character. It is, in fact, surprising that, with the Allied air arm grounded by fog, his thrust so quickly lost its momentum, and for that we have to thank the very gallant resistance offered by the American troops, even when isolated and fighting under most trying conditions. The climax of the battle has not yet been reached

at the time I write, for Von Rundstedt still has fresh reserves uncommitted and may be able to regroup those partly expended for an attempt to recover the momentum of his drive before the Allied reserves can be brought fully into action. There can be no doubt, however, that he put his best troops and greatest strength into his opening effort, and that the Allies were then at their weakest. The chances that a second blow might succeed when the first has failed must therefore on all accounts be small. It would be a gambler's bid which, if it failed, might well shorten the war, but that consideration would not, I think, as I have before suggested, deter Von Rundstedt. (See map, p. 549.)

HUNGARY

Meanwhile, in Hungary the German situation has rapidly deteriorated and Tolbukhin has added another great achievement to his remarkable record. When the Germans decided to hold Budapest at all costs they must have been confident that they would be able to keep communications with the city open. They had established and strongly entrenched a position stretching from the north end of Lake Balaton to the Danube, which could not be outflanked. Good lateral communications also facilitated the movement of reserves to meet any danger of penetration by frontal attack, and the large town of Szekesfehervar provided a strong defensive

WESTERN FRONT after the Allied armies had stemmed Rundstedt's violent counter-offensive launched on December 16, 1944, and U.S. troops of the 1st Army encircled at Bastogne had been relieved on December 27 by U.S. 3rd Army forces. *By courtesy of The Times*

pivot in its centre. Provided the position held, communications with Budapest were amply assured; and the fact that Tolbukhin's Army was split in two by Lake Balaton and that its communications not only were of great length but had to pass through a bottle-neck at the Danube crossing, seemed to make it improbable that he could achieve a break-through.

IT is true Malinovsky had secured a crossing of the Danube south of Budapest, but with his army engaged in widespread operations to the east and north of the river it was unlikely that he could give Tolbukhin much direct support. By maintaining pressure on Pest he had immobilized a number of enemy divisions in defence of the city; but decisive and rapid success depended on Tolbukhin's ability to break through the strong flank position, and it is clear that he displayed generalship of a very high order in accomplishing the feat. By vigorous feint attacks and concealment of his main striking force he succeeded in misleading the enemy and achieving surprise. Under cover of a sudden concentrated bombardment his infantry broke through and his armour followed, fanning out and widening the gap.

Thrown into confusion, part of the German force appears to have retired into Budapest, and Szekesfehervar was taken with astonishing rapidity. As on former occasions it was, however, the speed and boldness with which Tolbukhin employed his armour to exploit success that made the whole operation decisively complete. Driving north it not only cut the roads and railways leading into the capital, but it reached the Danube, making contact with Malinovsky's troops on the north bank of the river. The city was thus completely encircled and no time was lost in widening and strengthening the ring against any attempt of the garrison to break out to the west, or attempts by a relief force to re-establish communication with it. The garrison had no alternative but to stand a siege. Tolbukhin may attempt to carry Buda, on the west bank of the river, by storm, for he has already occupied the suburbs and defences are probably not well organized to stand an unexpected attack from the rear.

OUTMANOEUVRED and Outfought by Malinovsky and Tolbukhin

Pest, on the other bank, is, however, still strongly held and the garrison should be able to put up a stubborn defence. In that case, although the communications leading through the city would be invaluable to them, the Russians may be content to invest the place and concentrate their efforts on a drive westwards towards Bratislava and Vienna, Malinovsky on the north and Tolbukhin on the south bank of the Danube. The Russians have shown before now that they are not easily diverted from their main object by a tempting bait. Much may, however, depend on the attitude of the Hungarian troops who probably furnish a considerable part of the force in Pest. They might not offer much resistance to an attempt to storm the city which would have devastating effects.

In any case the mere isolation of so large a force in the capital is bound to have a far-reaching effect on the whole situation in Hungary. The troops which failed to hold Szekesfehervar must need much reorganization before they become again an effective force. They are, moreover, in danger of being cut off from all communication with those opposing Malinovsky on the north side of the Danube, and they are not likely to receive much reinforcement from those facing Tolbukhin's left wing south of Lake Balaton.

Seldom have the Germans been so completely outmanoeuvred as well as outfought, and on this occasion I do not think that the disaster can be attributed to Hitler's obstinate determination to hold on to untenable positions at all costs. (See map, p. 553.)

All Wet and Quiet on British 2nd Army Front—

VOYAGE BY ASSAULT-CRAFT was the only means of transport available to these infantrymen of the British 2nd Army holding the "Island"—the flooded tract of land north of Nijmegen on the road to Arnhem.

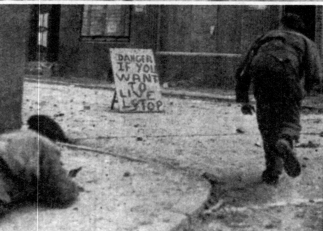

GRIM WARNING ON XMAS DAY faced these men at a street crossing swept by enemy fire. Luck of the draw decided which of these troops (left), should go on leave, beginning January 1, 1945.

ACROSS THE FLOODS a British Bren-gunner of Field-Marshal Montgomery's forces keeps a steady look-out from an old Dutch farmhouse stacked high with sandbags. Towards the end of December 1944 enemy patrols were reported to be operating along the banks of the Maas by night, trying to edge silently along the canal into our positions—only to be dispersed. The U.S. 1st and 9th Armies were placed under Montgomery shortly after the Rundstedt offensive began (see facing page)

PAGE 548

Photos, British Official, British Newspaper Pool

—As Rundstedt Struck Savagely Farther South

CLOSING DAYS OF 1944 witnessed a full-scale German counter-offensive, deeply penetrating the frontiers of Luxembourg and Belgium, notably in the Ardennes (see page 569). This map shows the front on December 28, when General Patton's 3rd Army, mightily counter-attacking, had narrowed the "bulge" north of Bastogne. The enemy was also held at Celles and Ciney, four miles from the Meuse.

U.S. FIELD ARTILLERYMEN hurriedly manhandle their guns into fresh-positions in the early stages of Von Rundstedt's powerful counter-offensive launched on December 16, 1944. Fourteen days later Gen. Patton's U.S. 3rd Army went over to the offensive on a 35-miles front. American machine-gunners (below) cover a front-line bridge.

"GIVE YOUR ALL IN ONE LAST EFFORT!" was Field-Marshal von Rundstedt's order to his troops assaulting the U.S. 1st Army in the west. Among his heavy supporting armament were the new Royal Tiger tanks, one of which is seen here knocked out during the U.S. 1st Army's recapture of the Belgian town of La Glieze. The Royal (or "King") Tiger is reputed to mount a 105-mm. gun, to have front armour a foot thick and to weigh over 70 tons. Note the exceptionally wide tracks.

Photos. U.S. Official, Planet News, Keystone. Map, News Chronicle

THE WAR AT SEA

by Francis E. McMurtrie

IN a speech at Sydney, Admiral Sir Bruce Fraser, Commander-in-Chief of the British fleet in the Pacific, has hinted that there will be some surprises for the Japanese at sea as the year advances. A leading part was promised for the Fleet Air Arm, which would be called upon to meet the attacks of Japanese shore-based aircraft, thus neutralizing the enemy's airfields and covering troop landings.

How successfully this can be done is illustrated by the progress of the American invasion of the Philippines. By the end of last year practically all resistance had ended in the island of Leyte, where a total of 117,997 Japanese troops had been disposed of, equivalent to a complete army. Mastery

would necessarily imply the postponement of any fleet action until the mainland of Japan is threatened by invasion or blockade.

American estimates of the strength remaining to the Japanese Navy vary. According to one commentator, there may still be from eight to ten capital ships in fighting condition. This probably is slightly exaggerated, and has been arrived at by taking into account either new 45,000-ton battleships which have still to be completed, or the nebulous and probably mythical ships of a glorified "pocket battleship" design, supposed to be under construction when war began.

There is no evidence that any new battleships have been completed other than the Musasi and Yamato, which took part in the

SHIP-CARRYING SHIP might be the description of this fast new military cargo vessel (above), built in Britain. Equipment includes three 120-ton derricks. Note the smaller craft rising above her holds, fore and amidships.

Assembled and launched within 4½ days are Britain's new "Tid" tugs (right), "Tid" being short for "Tiddler." Prefabricated, the components are assembled in shipyards. The engines develop 1,000 h.p.

Photos, British Official

of the air has been an essential feature of the reconquest of Leyte and Mindoro. It has been achieved by means of an overwhelming force of aircraft carriers. The total number of these in service in the United States Navy at the end of 1944 was 124, comprising 15 of the 27,000-ton Essex class; eight of the 11,000-ton Independence class; the Saratoga, Enterprise and Ranger, all built before the war, and no fewer than 98 escort carriers. Since it may be assumed that the bulk of this formidable fleet of carriers is employed in the Pacific, it follows that the U.S. fleet there is able to put into the air when desired some thousands of aircraft. It is not surprising, therefore, that Japanese air losses have been extremely heavy.

ADMIRAL FRASER observed that he did not rule out the possibility of an ultimate clash between Allied capital ships and the enemy's, though it might be assumed that Japanese tactics would be to hold back their fleet until the fullest possible air cover could be provided by shore-based planes. This

Battle of the Philippines last October. A third of the class may be nearing completion, in which case she may have to be reckoned with some time in 1945. The only other battleships are the Nagato. Hyuga, Ise, Haruna and Kongo, and there is a possibility that one of these may have foundered as a result of severe damage received in the Battle of the Philippines. The Hyuga and Ise have both been fitted with flight decks aft, so are probably no longer in a position to use the whole of their armaments. What has become of the Mutu, sister ship of the Nagato, is doubtful. She did not figure in the Philippines action, when every other known Japanese capital ship was thrown in, and it is suspected that she no longer exists.

It would be more accurate, therefore, to estimate the enemy's capital ship strength at six or seven units. Such a force has little hope of making headway against the weight which the Allied fleets in the Pacific are capable of bringing to bear:

Excluding the obsolescent New York, Texas and Arkansas, the U.S. Navy now possesses 20 efficient battleships, ten of which have been completed since 1940. This calculation does not include the Arizona and Oklahoma, neither of which was found worth rebuilding after the shattering damage received when they were sunk at Pearl Harbour three years ago.

No information has been released concerning the composition of the British fleet in the Pacific, beyond the fact that the battleship Howe is Sir Bruce Fraser's flagship. (See illus. pp. 560 and 561). It has, however, been intimated that the new ship launched by Princess Elizabeth on November 30 last— which according to a German broadcast is the 45,000-ton battleship Vanguard—will be ready in time for the war against Japan.

These two facts apart, it seems reasonable to conclude that all the modern capital ships in the Royal Navy will ultimately proceed to the Pacific. In addition to the possible use of the Vanguard, these would include the Howe, Anson, King George V, and Duke of York, and presumably the Nelson and Rodney. It is also gathered from what has been published in the Press that the modern French battleship Richelieu has been assigned to the Pacific theatre, making the British fleet's potential battleship strength up to eight.

BATTLESHIP Superiority Over Japanese will be Approximately Four to One

Thus it would appear that the Allies will be in a position to muster a possible total of 28 battleships against the Japanese, giving them a superiority of about four to one. How different from the bright prospect that seemed to be opening for Japan at the end of 1941 ! United States battleship strength was then temporarily reduced to half-a-dozen modern and undamaged units, one of which was under refit, against ten Japanese battleships in full commission and two more nearing delivery. At that date, too, this country had no modern capital ships available for service outside European waters.

It may be argued that Japanese strategy was faulty, in that the spectacular success at Pearl Harbour was not followed up quickly by a landing in the Hawaiian group. If the efforts directed against Burma and the Netherlands Indies had been postponed while Hawaii was overrun, the task of the United States in recovering from the Pearl Harbour disaster would have been immeasurably more difficult. The battleships Nevada, California, Tennessee and West Virginia could not have been salved and repaired, as they were during 1942-43, and American strength would have been reduced by four important units; while the loss of Pearl Harbour would have been a tremendous handicap.

IT would seem as though, too late, the Japanese began to appreciate these facts. At any rate, it is generally believed that the large force of transports and warships which was intercepted and broken up by American air attack in the Battle of Midway, before it had got as far as that island, was intended to operate against Hawaii. By that time six months had elapsed, and the chances of the enemy succeeding in such a distant enterprise were considerably reduced ; but it still represented a serious menace, and its defeat is rightly regarded as the turning point of the Pacific war.

Today the prospects for Japan are distinctly gloomy. Her ally in Europe is losing strength daily, and at sea has been reduced to a feeble defensive. Of late the only naval activity by the Germans has been in the shape of night raids by small craft, in which their losses have been heavy, and the use of "secret weapons" such as midget submarines and human torpedoes (see page 551). Though these may be useful as propaganda to bolster up the morale of the home front, they have achieved nothing of practical value.

Fantastic Nazi Frog-Men and Human Torpedoes

SPECIALLY TRAINED NAZI SABOTEUR-SWIMMERS in rubber tights, with frog-like webbed feet and oxygen masks, swam six miles down the River Waal on September 29, 1944, only to be captured by British troops after an attempt to blow up the Nijmegen Bridge. A net (1) camouflages the swimmer's face. Returning from action (2) he is hauled aboard an escape-craft. Fully-equipped (5), he poses for the camera. Other new enemy naval weapons are the one-man torpedo (3), and light craft with explosive charges (4). *Photos, Associated Press, Keystone*

Troopships That Never Fail the Battle-Lines

Behind official totals of Allied troops successfully carried over the seas are many half-divulged stories of brilliant achievements of troopships by the hundred. All types and sizes of vessels are these, from the 80,000-ton peacetime luxury liner turned war-worker to the humdrum little steamer of the trippers' holiday. Something of the superb romance of these adventurous ships is outlined below by MARK PRIESTLEY.

UP to the end of September 1944, 10,600,000 British Army personnel had been moved by sea—with the loss of 2,978 lives, or only 0028 per cent of the total. In just over three months from D-Day (June 6) more than 2,200,000 men were landed in France and the Low Countries; and even the loss of stores due to enemy action totalled a mere three-fifths of one per cent of all stores landed !

Anyone who saw the Canadian assault troops streaming from the Canterbury into the landing craft off the Normandy beaches will never forget the spectacle. Since then, under the command of Capt. G. D. Walker,

PEACETIME LUXURY VESSEL, the S.S. Canterbury, known to thousands on the Dover-Calais route and here seen in " battle-dress," has won new fame as a troop transport. Built in 1924 and with a tonnage of 2,900, her speed is 22 knots. *Photo, Southern Railway*

D.S.O., this famous peacetime steamship of the Dover-Calais luxury run has been foremost in the shuttle service between Britain and the forward European ports. Down in the engine-room, the Chief Engineer, Mr. Stanley Belchamber, has an amazing record. He was with the first ship to land troops in France in 1914, and with the first ship to land troops in 1939. "I had hoped to repeat it in 1944," he said, "but we lost by four seconds."

That is typical of the magnificent seamanship that has conducted the transport of our men with such safety and success. The first Allied landing on European soil, the operation against Sicily, was headed by Captain M. H. Williams, a ship's master with a record of 44 years at sea. He had trained for weeks beforehand, off a remote stretch of British coastline, to make sure that the high-spot of his voyage would be perfect.

One famous troopship, the Royal Ulsterman, has scarcely paused for four years in her specialized work of carrying troops to and from Iceland, to the Gold Coast and South Africa, to Madagascar, Italy and France. Her sister ship, the Royal Scotsman, which has steamed 50,000 miles since the evacuation of Narvik in 1940, once sailed from Malta to Bombay and back, a remark-

able operation for a vessel primarily intended for a peacetime coastal run.

Then there is the Ben-My-Chree (Girl o' My Heart), once on the Liverpool-Douglas "tripper line," and now with a record of 100,000 miles safely behind her. Her skipper, Capt. Radcliffe Duggan, has been 53 years at sea, and was the Dunkirk hero who deliberately steamed four miles through a minefield as the lesser risk to his passengers than sailing past a line of enemy batteries which had plastered his ship on the way in. Since then he has undertaken round trips of 2,700 miles through Atlantic winter gales to serve the Iceland garrison, and he finds the present-day routine service to Europe "almost monotonous."

Her best voyage was undoubtedly the recent occasion when she re-entered Cherbourg harbour, for she had been the first ship to enter that port, carrying 1,400 French reservists, on September 4, 1939. Her worst voyage was, strangely enough, one she made without a soldier on board. It occurred en route to her refitting as a first-wave assault ship, when during a storm she was caught in the millrace off the Pentland Firth, off the north tip of Scotland. Waves twenty feet high crashed over her stern, and hundreds of tons of water swept through the lower decks, sweeping away everything movable in their path. None on board thought she could survive, but she came through.

THE Royal Scotsman once ran into a sand-storm at sea ; it whipped the paint off the weather-side of the ship, and in 48 hours worked its way so thoroughly into the guns that they had to be completely stripped and cleaned. The Prins Albert, formerly a passenger ship on the Ostend run, has had many narrow escapes, but has never been hit and has never missed a landing. At Salerno she was singled out for attack by seven E-boats, and a torpedo missed her by two feet. "Aircraft were overhead, we were firing, our destroyer escort was firing, the Erebus was smacking 15-in salvos into the shore batteries which were firing as well—it was some party !" one of her officers said.

A troopship, with the reputation of being Britain's luckiest, was actually landing troops

in Italy when the enemy reported her as sunk in the South Atlantic ; and when she recently put into Gibraltar it was with a trail of four doomed U-boats bagged by the destroyers in her wake. She once reached Gibraltar without a rudder, and the officers decided to run her without passengers and with a volunteer crew back to England. She hugged the occupied coast safely across the Bay of Biscay, but was sighted by a U-boat when 30 miles from Brest. The fog that suddenly swept down and saved her was typical of her luck. Twice raided when in port, every bomb fell wide and the rudder was repaired. When she sailed again, a 12-in. shell amidships damaged her only slightly. Subsequently involved in a collision, she was sailing again within a few weeks, and now carries troops to within 60 miles of Germany.

Four Invasions in Five Months

The Manxmaid, brought back into active service a couple of years ago after running thousands of aliens to the Isle of Man, for some months acted as the German battleship Tirpitz while our planes were training for the real attack !

No record of the "troopers" would be complete without mention of the Canadian landing ship Prince David, which possesses the proud distinction of having been in four invasions in five months. She lost every assault craft sent to the beaches of Normandy. She was in time, however, to land the French Commandos seven hours before the main assault on Southern France. For nearly two miles on the way in they travelled on a parallel course to some light German craft, but the Prince David was not seen. Then, on the way out, she found herself the centre of a mêlée between Allied warships and a batch of Nazi corvettes ; once again she escaped. Three weeks later came her support to the landings on Kithera, an island off the tip of Greece. That was followed by her arrival at Piraeus, the port of Athens. The Greeks came out to meet the David's flotilla, in everything that would float—from schooners to tin bath-tubs.

THE goliaths of the British troopships are the Queen Elizabeth and Queen Mary, luxury liners converted to war-work. The 80,000-ton Queen Mary (see illus. page 486), with a good turn of speed on two occasions ploughed unharmed through a pack of 20 U-boats. In the first three years of this war she made six voyages to Australia, and took thousands of Australian troops to the Middle East and Singapore—and, by way of a change, she has carried large numbers of Italian and German prisoners to captivity.

OUTSTANDING AMONG THE HIGH ENDEAVOURS of the Empire's war effort have been the achievements of our troop-transports. Characteristic example is the fine record of the Royal Canadian armed merchant cruiser Prince David, built at Birkenhead in 1930. With a displacement of 7,000 tons, she carries a complement of 241. Sister ship of H.M.C.S. Prince Henry, her speed is 24 knots. *Photo, Royal Canadian Navy*

Two Irresistible Soviet Armies Encircle Budapest

SWEEPING WESTWARDS, the 2nd and 3rd Ukrainian fronts of the Red Army had completely encircled Budapest (see map) by December 26, 1941. Four days later the enemy rejected a Soviet ultimatum, and fierce house-to-house fighting immediately ensued in the suburbs. Soviet tanks close in (1) on the Hungarian capital. Russian gunners open fire (2) at point-blank range. A Red Army tank is replenished with water from the Danube (3); while horsed artillery units (4) dash into action.

Photos, U.S.S.R. Official, Pictorial Press.   Map by courtesy of The Times

McCreery's Die-Hards Take Faenza in Italy

FAENZA—ITALIAN KEY-TOWN—was captured on December 16, 1944, by British, Canadian, New Zealand, Indian and Polish troops of the 8th Army fighting in close co-operation (see map). Before the final push, Lt.-Gen. Sir Richard McCreery, 8th Army Commander, visited British sappers (1, centre) on a demolition job. New Zealanders in a jeep (2) were bogged down in the seas of mud, while their fellow countrymen (3) entered the town. Sexton self-propelled guns (4) harassed the enemy north of Ravenna

Photos, British Official. Map, The Times

Political Prisoners Dash From Alsace Gaol

DELIRIOUS WITH JOY at their unexpected liberation, these French women political prisoners rushed from Haguenau prison in Alsace where 300 of them had been incarcerated by the Nazis. When Haguenau, last important town before the German border, was taken by the U.S. 7th Army on December 11, 1944, the Germans were so eager to quit that they forgot the prisoners. Some of the latter had been held for two years, their "crimes" ranging from making insulting remarks about Hitler to listening to the B.B.C.

Photo, Keystone

Miracle of South-East Asia Air Command

Lack of planes, airfields, constructional and repair organizations and personnel, plus enormous distances from supply ports, grievously handicapped us in the early days of the war against Japan. Now, air backing for Allied operations in South-East Asia has reached mighty proportions. Its development in the past two years is traced by Squadron-Leader DEREK ADKINS.

WHEN war was declared in September 1939 urgent operational requirements in other theatres made it impossible to reinforce or modernize the pre-war air force in India, although the need did not really arise until Japan entered the war in 1941. Up to that time the Royal Navy had protected India's 3,000-mile coastline from seaborne attack, and her armies had defended her land frontiers and maintained internal peace.

When Air Chief Marshal Sir Richard Peirse arrived in India at the beginning of March 1942 he found no more than four Royal Air Force squadrons, whose most modern aircraft were a handful of Mohawks, and three Indian Air Force squadrons of out-of-date Harts and Lysanders.

IN Burma the situation was little better. There were four fighter, three bomber and two Army Co-operation squadrons, but they lacked proper repair or maintenance-organization and their warning system consisted of inadequate observer posts. The result was that, in spite of their own gallant efforts and those of the American Volunteer Group, the Japanese advance could not be halted. These squadrons, sadly depleted in equipment and personnel, were forced to retreat with the Army into Indian territory.

In Ceylon there was little reason for confidence, but capable improvisation enabled fighters to operate in the nick of time and beat off enemy naval bombers dispatched from the Japanese battle fleet on Easter Sunday (April 5) 1942. No further attacks were launched against either Ceylon or India before the 1942 monsoon, which gave time for the position to be consolidated.

The chief problem was the lack of airfields suitable for modern operational aircraft. A huge priority programme was planned which aimed at multiplying the number of airfields more than fifteenfold at a cost of over £15,000,000. In spite of the shortage of suitable constructional equipment and supervisory staff (the bulk of the labour being carried out manually by coolies), well over 200 airfields in India and Ceylon were available to the British and American air forces before the end of 1943.

A second difficulty was to build up an adequate maintenance system in a country where heavy industries are practically non-existent and the number of highly trained Indian workmen consequently small. The enormous distances from the ports at which supplies arrived to the scene of operations in Assam and Bengal imposed additional burdens on a railway system already strained to the limit by existing war commitments. Nevertheless, by the end of 1943 a civilian repair organization had been started, and several civilian maintenance units had begun operating under the supervision and guidance of a small nucleus of Service personnel. Storage space expanded 33 times, and the rapidity and efficiency of the expansion can be judged by the fact that compared with the average output of the first six months of 1943 nearly four times as many aircraft were in fact erected during the whole of that year.

THE third problem was that of personnel. The small drafts that became available from the United Kingdom and other theatres were insufficient to meet the growing man-power needs in South-East Asia. The Indian Air Force was therefore increased to ten times its previous strength, and training organized in every trade and flying category. Many thousands of young Indians came

forward to join India's youngest fighting service, and are today playing their part beside the Royal Air Force and the U.S. Army Air Force in the war against Japan.

The need for the safe conduct of the convoys bringing men and supplies and equipment to India resulted in the development of an organization designed to fulfil over the Indian Ocean the responsibilities of Coastal Command over the sea approaches to Great Britain. From a small beginning there are now numerous medium and long-range general reconnaissance squadrons regularly patrolling the sea lanes from the coasts of Africa, the Persian Gulf and the Sea of Oman, to the shores of India and Ceylon and as far east as the Japanese occupied islands of Andaman, Nicobar and the Netherlands East Indies.

AIR CHIEF MARSHAL Sir Richard Peirse, K.C.B., D.S.O., A.F.C., Allied Air Commander-in-Chief, South-East Asia Command, the exploits of which, since 1942, are related in this page. *After the portrait by Simon Elwes*

The main theatre of operations, however, has been India and Burma, the bulk of the squadrons being located in Bengal and Assam. After night fighters had dealt sternly with random raiders attacking Calcutta in January 1943, offensive operations began in the spring. Although the Army had failed in its objective of securing forward positions in the Arakan and holding them during the 1943 monsoon, air supremacy was maintained throughout the fighting and direct support given to the troops. In addition, bombers and long-range fighters had vigorously attacked enemy airfields and dislocated his rail, road and river lines of communication.

WITH the advent of the monsoon in June 1943 the Japanese almost entirely stopped air operations and withdrew their units for training, rest and re-equipment. Despite the weather, however, Allied air operations were continued against the enemy in order that his communications and reinforcement activities should be disrupted as much as possible. These hazardous operations met with such success that the Japanese were forced to move the bulk of their supplies and troops by night. The intensification of operations that took place after the 1943 monsoon was made doubly effective by the

reorganization of the air forces, resulting in the formation, in December 1943, of Air Command, South-East Asia, with Air Chief Marshal Sir Richard Peirse as the Allied Air Commander-in-Chief under the direction of the Supreme Commander, Admiral Lord Louis Mountbatten.

RESPONSIBILITY for the prosecution of the air war against Japan from Eastern India was vested in the new Eastern Air Command, of which the American Major-Gen. George E. Stratemeyer became Air Commander. This Command is staffed jointly by British and American officers and controls all R.A.F. and U.S.A.A.F. squadrons based in Assam and Bengal (see facing page).

Under Eastern Air Command there are four integrated forces—the Strategic Air Force, the Third Tactical Air Force, Troop Carrier Command and the Photographic Reconnaissance Force. The general reorganization was implemented by modern aircraft, notably Spitfires, Beaufighters, Vengeance dive-bombers, Mosquitoes, Liberators and Thunderbolts (see illus. page 508).

It may be said that the introduction of the Spitfire to the Third Tactical Air Force proved a turning-point in the air war against Japan, for previously Hurricanes had struggled against enemy aircraft that usually possessed the advantages of height and manoeuvrability.

The medium and heavy bombers, however, have been the main offensive weapon. Throughout a campaign that was for so long fought largely on a strategic defensive by all three Services, these aircraft have been the arm that has reached forward to strike. The tenuous communications that exist throughout Assam and Burma have laid so many duties on the R.A.F. Dakotas of Troop Carrier Command that they have now become as indispensable as the fighters and bombers to the success of ground operations.

AIR supply, too, has been one of the deciding factors in the work of the 14th Army. The 7th Indian Division, for example, was wholly dependent for food, ammunition and fuel on supplies dropped from the air, when isolated in Arakan in February 1944. The West African Brigade, fighting in the Kaladan valley and cut off by rivers and mountain ranges, was supplied almost entirely by air, and the 5th Indian Division, including thousands of men, hundreds of animals and jeeps and all the Divisional artillery, was transferred by air from the Arakan to the Imphal front in March 1944.

In Imphal itself British and U.S. Dakota squadrons, flying unarmed, successfully accomplished the biggest air supply feat of the war. For three months they maintained and reinforced over four divisions of our troops who were in full action against a completely surrounding enemy. Such was our air supremacy that we lost under 20 planes. The fly-in of the late General Wingate's forces (the Chindits) behind the Japanese lines was another outstanding feat of 1944.

The Mosquitoes and Spitfires of the Photographic Reconnaissance Force are carrying out regular missions over Burma, Siam and also the Andamans, bringing back vital information for intelligence purposes.

The course of the war in the East will depend to a large extent on India's capacity and stability as a base. Today the Supreme Allied Commander in South-East Asia can plan future operations in the sure knowledge that his Allied Air C.-in-C. can provide whatever backing is required.

Assam and Bengal Squadrons Smite Japanese

BLASTING enemy-held roads, railways and bridges in Burma, the Eastern Air Command, with H.Q. at Calcutta, set up a new bombing record in December 1944. Air-Marshal W. A. Coryton, C.B., D.F.C. (1), commanding the 3rd Tactical Air Force, greets Maj.-Gen. H. C. Davidson (right), commanding the U.S.A. 10th Air Force on a Burma airfield. Hurricanes wreak havoc (2) near Paletwa in Arakan. Bound for Rangoon, a R.A.F. Liberator of the Strategic Air Force (3) is loaded with bombs. Maj.-Gen. G. E. Stratemeyer (4), Air Commander of the Eastern Air Command. Air-Commodore F. J. W. Mellersh, A.F.C., commanding the Strategic Air Force (5) holds a conference at his Bengal H.Q.

Photos, British, Indian, and U.S. Official

Armour Again Saves Our Fighting Men's Lives

Resourceful minds have been concentrated tirelessly on the modernization of ancient devices for securing protection for vital parts of the body, with the result that today our soldiers and airmen can be equipped with safeguards against injury in battle. How the cumbersome armour of the knight of old has been transformed to meet present needs is told by HARRIMAN DICKSON.

SOME of the most highly specialized types of armour used by British and American forces are produced by a London company which has been making chain mail and swords since the middle of the eighteenth century. Here one may meet men who have been at the business all their lives, and their fathers and grandfathers before them.

Take Mr. Lennard Barrat, for instance. A great deal of thought and research went into the production of the bullet-proof vest which has since saved hundreds of Allied airmen from death or serious injury. Each vest consisted of over 200 overlapping steel plates which would stop a revolver bullet at point-blank range. But there was one drawback. If the airman wanted to bale out, the 23 lb. of armour might cause disaster. It was imperative to find some way whereby the elaborate straps of the vest could be released rapidly and the whole thing jettisoned. That was were Mr. Barrat came in. He was responsible for devising the release mechanism which brings the whole process down to one simple pull on a red tab. Today an airman can free himself of the vest, and bale out, at high speed.

OTHER problems have been faced by skilled workmen in that factory for months before a solution has been discovered. At the very beginning of their investigations it was obvious to the experts that a suit of

amongst the factory workers is 83-year-old Tom Beasley, whose family has been in the trade for over two hundred years. Tom Beasley was the man who forged the beautiful Stalingrad sword (see illus. pages 495 and 499, Vol. 7).

The Germans have reported that some of our shock troops wear a light belt of armour which gives them good protection against machine-gun fire, and the German radio has talked about "bullet-proof uniforms." The astonishing thing about the latest types of armour used by British and U.S. troops is that they derive from that worn by Henry VIII.

THIS dip into history began when a Mr. Stephen Grancsay, U.S. historian and curator of the New York Museum of Art, heard that a group of experts were testing various armours at the ballistic testing ground, Aberdeen, Maryland. Mr. Grancsay knew a lot about the armour worn by the knights of old, and he began to consider ways of effecting improvements to meet modern war conditions. He set to work and in a very short time submitted a new type of armour which surprised the military experts. He then confessed that this armour was modelled on the lines of that once worn by no less a person than King Henry VIII. It was true, of course, that Mr. Grancsay used very different materials, but both the armour suit and helmet were certainly inspired by designs

TOM BEASLEY forging the famous Stalingrad sword at a London factory where "armour" is made for our troops, as told in this page.
Photo, Topical Press

belonging to XVI century British history. The final product was composed of innumerable small steel plates, each connected to the other by minute springs and shock-cords.

Meanwhile, in Britain, Mr. Kenneth Walker, the surgeon, had carried out a number of similar experiments with new types of material, in the hope of finding something which was not only much lighter than steel but which had the same tensile strength. One such material is coir fibre. Then others were discovered and now several new plastic materials which have superseded steel in industrial production, are said to be very suitable for armour.

During the last war, Mr. Kenneth Walker served with the R.A.M.C., and was selected by Mr. Churchill to become " expert in armour to the Forces." In those days the steel helmet was still something of a novelty. Now every aspect of the armour problem has been thoroughly explored, and some of the results appear to be highly satisfactory.

BULLET-PROOF BODY ARMOUR is worn by certain branches of the U.S. armed forces. In France, a front-line bulldozer detail is so equipped (above). Pilots of the U.S.A.A.F. are also protected in this way (right).
Photos, Keystone, G.P.U.

armour which would give complete protection against the high velocity modern missile was out of the question. They therefore concentrated on partial protection. It was found that in the last war no less than sixty per cent of casualties were due to chest or trunk wounds. Many armoured devices were then tried out to protect those parts of the human body, including a steel plate fitted to the back of the respirator box, and the steel vest now in extensive use today.

There also you may see some of the latest armour devices in production, in which women play a big part. Since many of the women came from the dress trade before the war, they handle the intricate strips of cotton canvas and magnesium steel with an adroitness born of long practice. Prominent

In Flooded Holland Our Men Stand By

The British 2nd Army's front in Holland, between Nijmegen and Arnhem, was plunged under water early in December 1944, when the enemy breached the dykes. Meanwhile, on our right flank, Von Rundstedt—on December 16—launched his massive counter-offensive against the U.S. 1st Army threatening the Ruhr. A British light A.A. gun team (top) goes about its task in the downpour; (bottom) a cheerful party of Royal Engineers plug a sodden Dutch road with logs.

New British Pacific Fleet is Formed—

Among the most powerful battleships afloat, the 35,000 tons H.M.S. Howe, of the George V class (here seen closing an Egyptian felucca in the Suez Canal), will act as the flagship of Admiral Sir Bruce Fraser, G.C.B., K.B.E., Commander-in-Chief of the British Pacific Fleet, it was announced on December 12, 1944. Thus a strong new British fleet, based on Australia, has been established to operate in the Pacific, as well as an East Indies fleet under Vice-Admiral Sir Arthur Power, K.C.B.

—To Sweep Nippon Navy From the Seas

"We must get nearer to Japan," declared Admiral Fraser on arriving in Australia on December 12. He hoped that the first ship to enter the new Sydney graving dock—biggest in the southern hemisphere, and capable of taking the largest ships in the world—might be one of Britain's mightiest battleships. " The country with the greatest sea power must win the war—and we have it," he added, pointing out that Japan had still to supply her army in Burma by sea.

The 'Jocks' Return to St. Valery

Celebrating its three-months' freedom from the Nazi oppressor, the Normandy seaport of St. Valéry-en-Caux, on December 12, 1944, gave a lusty welcome to the famous 51st Highland Division—the men who had come back. In June 1940 after fighting a valiant rearguard action around the town (see pages 86-87, Vol. 3), the 51st were finally forced to surrender. Just over four years later men of the same division retook St. Valéry. Its liberation was marked by a day of ceremonies when officers and men of the Scottish Division were toasted at a banquet held in their honour. Followed a parade and a church service of thanksgiving to which the whole town gathered. Later, an impressive service was held in the cemetery and wreaths were laid on the graves of the men of the Division who fell in 1940. Headed by their pipes and drums, the "Jocks" (top) march to the church; (left) sounding the Last Post for the fallen. *Photos, British Official*

VIEWS & REVIEWS
Of Vital War Books

by Hamilton Fyfe

THE mass of books about the Second Great War will be as dead in ten years' time as those about the First have been for a couple of decades. A few, a very few, will be still treasured because they are pervaded by personality—not for what the writer has to tell us, but for his way of telling it. I think one such book will be The Golden Carpet (Faber, 15/-) by Capt. Somerset de Chair, M.P. It tells the story of the rapid advance across the desert from Palestine to Iraq, which in 1941 stopped the Nazi-planned insurrection in Baghdad by capturing that city almost without a shot being fired. All this seems to be already ancient history. It may have been, as Captain de Chair claims, " one of the greatest marches" in the annals of war. " Never since the days of Alexander the Great had an army succeeded in crossing the desert from the shores of the Mediterranean to the banks of the Euphrates." That may be true enough, but probably it only makes the majority of folks yawn. Many people may not want to know how it was done any more than they yearn for meticulous details of the Syrian campaign—interesting as these may be—which the book covers also.

But if you pick up The Golden Carpet and open it anywhere and start reading, you will very soon find yourself tremendously interested, not in the campaign, but in a whole lot of people from generals to car-drivers, Arab interpreters, cipher clerks (who had to code and decode messages), and Bedouins who flicker in and out of the picture, looting as a rule, not amenable to any kind of discipline, but very useful at times. Capt. de Chair makes you see and hear all these people. They impressed themselves on his imagination so sharply that he is able to pass them on to us with vivid effect.

A Battle Won by Telephone

Perhaps at first you may wonder why he describes things in such close detail. It may even annoy you to read that a handkerchief lent to him had thin blue lines on it, or that he had sardines and biscuits for breakfast. But you will quickly discover that it is this photographic quality of the narrative which makes it grip, and gives every figure, every landscape, every scene a quality which you feel you are not going to forget.

One of the most dramatic incidents is the intercepting of the enemy's telephone in a building from which the Iraqis had been ejected so hastily that they had no time to destroy their installations. Capt. de Chair, who was Intelligence Officer to the expedition, did not speak Arabic (which seems to the non-military mind exceeding strange, seeing that his duties were entirely among Arabs), but he had a very useful native interpreter with him, whom he put on at once to converse with the Iraqis as if he were one of them. He received a warm welcome. " I've been trying to get you for two hours ; what has been the matter ? " asked a voice from the other end.

He quickly repeated this with his hand over the mouthpiece, and I said " Tell them that we are surrounded by the British, that the British have got tanks, and that the tanks are already across the floods. Reading (the interpreter) spoke to the distant operator in an admirably excited voice, laying horrified stress on the word Bababa—tanks. Consternation followed at the other end.

Before long word came that an Iraqi patrol had been sent out to locate the British tanks and had reported fifty of them ! There were actually none at all in the whole area. But rumour once started soon created alarm. Later on, after Baghdad had been surrendered, an Iraqi officer, who had been

through a course at the R.M.A., Woolwich, spoke perfect English, and knew the situation, political and military, from inside, told a war correspondent that the Iraqi army had to give in " because you British had fifty tanks there, and we had only two old anti-tank guns on that front." But whether Capt. de Chair's ingenious invention of a tank force was recognized as having contributed more than anything else to our victory does not appear.

WHEN it had at last been arranged for the British troops to march into Baghdad, it seemed to Capt. de Chair " of the first importance to capitalize the propaganda

Backstage Story of Iraqi Revolt

value of this romantic and in many ways spectacular achievement." He hoped the ceremonial entry would be filmed, so as to let the world know what this little British force had accomplished. General Kingstone—Commander of the British troops—said firmly "No." His refusal is attributed to " the inherent aversion to publicity of the professional British soldier." Another defect in far too many British officers is disinclination to follow a course that seems to them necessary, when the civil authority does not agree. The Foreign Office, for some reason never made clear, did not wish the British troops to enter the city at once, although everyone who knew anything about the Iraqis said there would be looting if they did not. There was no immediate occupation, and the looters had their way for a whole night.

All who dared to defend their belongings were killed, while eight miles to the west waited the eager British force which could have prevented this. . . . Genius is a grasp of the essential

BRIGADIER GLUBB PASHA, commandant of the Arab Legion, is here seen with Field-Marshal Sir Harold Alexander (extreme left) during an inspection of this famous corps in the Middle East. Its exploits are vividly described in the book reviewed above.
PAGE 563 *Photo, British Official*

CAPT. SOMERSET DE CHAIR, M.P., whose outspoken book describing in detail the campaign in Syria and the Iraqi revolt is reviewed in this page. *Photo, Elliott and Fry*

and after victory the essential is to keep control of the situation.

Genius was deplorably lacking at this juncture. There was a lack even of ordinary common sense. Worse than that revealed itself when the campaign against the French in Syria started. The advance on Palmyra, in which the author took part and was badly wounded, was expected to be a walk-over. Little air support was given to our men, and the enemy, in this case the French, had plenty of planes and used them murderously. After being wounded by a low-flying aircraft, Capt. de Chair was hit again while in the ambulance, although it had a huge Red Cross on it. The arrangement for disposing of casualties had completely broken down : Those who drew up the time-table of the advance (" silly time-table," Capt. de Chair calls it with complete justification) assumed that Palmyra would be taken at once and that all casualties could be sent there.

'A Worse Hell Than That of Crete'

" No one had stopped to wonder what would happen to the wounded if Palmyra did not fall on Day One." It held out till Day Thirteen, and while our troops were suffering a worse hell than that of Crete, " senior staff officers were saying behind the stout defences of their mahogany desks, ' We may have to send some aircraft up to Palmyra after all. Our chaps seem to be having a rough time of it.' And as they sipped their drinks in the bar they added, ' It is worrying about those casualties up there—not being able to get them back. We should have thought of Palmyra not falling. It is most annoying.' " (See page 55, Vol. 5).

But don't think the general tone of the book is bitter—or even critical. It is light-hearted, full of boyish humour, entertaining in a hundred different ways. The solemn account of the dinner at the British Embassy in Baghdad just after that night of horror I have mentioned, could not be bettered. From the drawing-room with its oil paintings, gilt furniture and soft carpets, to the dining room, " where the dinner-table was of polished shining mahogany in which the brightly silver and shaded candles were rosily reflected "—thence to the library for after-dinner bridge, all followed the routine of pre-war English upper-class existence. One can't help wondering if devotion to that routine has not perhaps something to do with—well, the sort of stupidity that led to the massacre in Baghdad.

How the Army's Amazing Bailey Bridge is Built

A revolution in military engineering has earned high praise from Field-Marshal Montgomery —a permanent way which can be assembled on the spot to span a river or gap and carry the weight of the heaviest tanks. Speed and simplicity are its keynotes. How a Bailey bridge can be erected in three hours by 40 men is explained below by T. S. DOUGLAS. See also p. 169.

A RETREATING enemy endeavours to burn his bridges behind him, and almost since the beginning of warfare the construction of emergency bridges has been a matter of prime consideration. In modern war a bridge has no longer simply to support the weight of marching infantrymen and of artillery. It has to carry the enormous lorries and massive tanks of a mechanized army.

It was the increasing weight of British tanks that early in this war led to the invention of the Bailey bridge, which has enabled us to pursue the German panzers during the last two years. The Germans have nothing like it.

FIRST of all, it is easily transportable. No special transport vehicles are required. Every part fits into a three-ton lorry, and a small group of these vehicles can move everything required for a complete bridge. The exact number of vehicles varies with the length and strength of the bridge that is to be erected. The way that length and strength can be varied is another advantage. Without supports or pontoons, the Bailey can span a gap of up to 240 ft. Using the supports of a bridge that has been destroyed, or pontoons, the bridge can cover almost any distance. The longest Bailey bridge so far constructed is believed to be the 1,200 ft. bridge over the Sangro River in Italy, a triumph of military engineering. The longest floating Bailey bridge (1,096 ft.) was thrown

over the Chindwin in Burma in December 1944. The bridge can be constructed with single panels and single tiers so as to take moderately heavy traffic immediately. Additional panels and tiers, greatly increasing the load it will carry, can be added while it is actually being used. There is nothing to undo—you simply add.

There are other advantages. Two footways for infantry are carried outside the roadway, so that there is no confusion between foot and wheeled traffic. If the bridge is damaged by shells or bombs, the damaged section is easily removed and a new one inserted. Most of the bridge is built on the near shore where there is a certain amount of cover, and it can be built between banks of different levels. It is not surprising that Field-Marshal Montgomery said not long ago, " There is never enough Bailey bridging. This bridge is quite the best thing in that line we have ever had ; it does everything we want ! "

The principle of the bridge is simple. Standard parts are fitted together, largely by means of strong pins each weighing six pounds which in turn are held by split pins. The vital part is the lattice-work panel which is carried ready assembled, and in fact strongly welded. Six men can carry this part by special handles. These panels, locked together, support the roadway which is of wood and is assembled as the bridge is built. Road guides not only keep the traffic central but also hold down the standard wood pieces

which form the roadway. The wooden footways are supported outside the panels.

It is the method of "launching" that makes the Bailey bridge so novel. Each 10-ft. section is built up on shore, complete with roadway, then pushed forward on special rollers, which are part of the equipment, almost to the point of balance. The next section is then added and the bridge pushed forward again. A false "nose" is fixed, and when this has crossed the gap it gives support while the final panels are completed ; after which "nose" and rollers are removed so that the bridge can be locked in position.

Forty Men Can Construct a Bridge

There are only 17 parts used in making the bridge itself, and another nine in constructing the supports on which it rests. The tools required are of the simplest, but very ingenious. All these parts, with the necessary tools, are packed into standard lorries. The number of men used on construction varies, of course, with the size and speed required. But forty men can construct a complete bridge. In ideal conditions a short and single-tier bridge can be assembled in three to four hours, a little longer at night. But conditions are rarely ideal in war. One of the finest feats was the construction of a 300-ft. bridge over the Trigno in Italy within 36 hours of the bridge-head being cleared of enemy infantry. A remarkable feat was also performed on D-Day in Normandy, when engineers bridged the Caen Canal (see illus. p. 169) and the Orne River while under fire of every kind from the enemy. They had the advantage of having rehearsed the bridging again and again in Scotland.

One of the secrets of the bridge is precision in the manufacture of its parts, and the greatest credit is due to the firms and their employees who have turned out miles of Bailey bridging. When the bridge was approved, none of the factories normally undertaking this kind of work was available. All kinds of factories were enlisted to the task of production—some had been making greenhouses, window frames, bedsteads and even canoe paddles ! The parts have to be exactly the right size, those vital holes that take the pins in exactly the right place, and all parts interchangeable. Just to make sure, every piece is tested by being built into a bridge before it leaves the factory. The test consists in constructing a continuous bridge, but in the factory as soon as it reaches "the other side" it is taken to pieces section by section.

MR. DONALD C. BAILEY, O.B.E., the designer of this bridge, is a civil engineer in the Ministry of Supply (see illus. p. 169). He was not a specialist in bridge construction when the call came for an improved military bridge, and is said to have sketched out the first designs on the back of an envelope while returning with other officials from an unsuccessful trial of a bridge in 1940. Every military invention has its "growing pains," but those of the Bailey bridge seem to have disappeared very quickly, and for once everyone was satisfied from their own special angle. By the end of 1943 engineers were actually averaging two Bailey bridges a day, and all the time the vast store of them required for D-Day was being built up.

The Bailey bridge will cross any kind of gap, and although it goes up so quickly it is permanent. All the bridges, long and short, "easy" and difficult, have averaged 24 hours in construction. Some of the first are still in use, having carried hundreds of thousands of tons of traffic.

IN ITALY, during the winter campaign of 1944, as well as in France following the D-Day operations, the Bailey bridge literally paved the way to Allied victory.

Stacks of Bailey bridges in sections (above) lined the road to Ferrara after the fall of Ravenna to the 8th Army on December 5, where the enemy had systematically destroyed all river and canal crossings. British sappers—six men to each lattice-work panel—build up one of the last spans of a Bailey bridge (right) across the Caen canal in Normandy.

Photos, British Official

Our Engineers Triumph Over Sheer Destruction

TWELVE HUNDRED FEET ACROSS, and spanning the Sangro River in Italy (crossed in November 1943), is the largest Bailey bridge in the world, seen (top) while still under construction. Another noteworthy Bailey bridge strides the Arno (above) at Florence; it was erected on the piers of the former Ponte San Trinita (see illus. p. 227). Before the enemy quitted Florence on August 11, 1944, they systematically destroyed all the city's bridges except the world-famous Ponte Vecchio.

Photos. British Official

London's Battle for Homes Reaches Its Peak

"HOUSING IS THE MOST THREATENED SECTOR on the home front," declared the Prime Minister on November 29, 1944. Eight days earlier the appointment had been announced of Mr. Duncan Sandys, M.P., as Minister of Works, in succession to Lord Portal. In a subsequent debate Mr. Sandys disclosed that the bomb-damaged houses in London alone totalled over 800,000 and that the cost of repairs undertaken up to December 7 amounted to well over £35,000,000. Over 200,000 men and women, he said, were engaged on London repairs, which had been granted a priority second only to urgent work of operational importance.

The new Minister further revealed that General Eisenhower had placed 3,000 U.S. sappers at the Government's disposal for the clearing of London bomb-sites and the building of temporary dwellings. While the pressed-steel bungalows—known as "Portals"—would not be produced till after the war he was considering calling for the manufacture of prefabricated houses from contractors who had built the invasion harbours (see pages 430-434.)

RE-HOUSING of London's bomb-victims proceeds apace. The Phoenix house (1), which is to replace the original Portal dwelling (see page 2), is still on the "secret list"; it contains a living-room, 2 bedrooms and a kitchen with a refrigerator. Steel-framed, this type is built largely of concrete and asbestos. The all-electric kitchen (2) is a feature of the new B.I.S.F. houses built on rolled-steel frames.

U.S. sappers took only 7 days to clear a bomb site and erect the first of many temporary dwellings (3) they are constructing in Lambeth; it is of the curved asbestos type. Just over a fortnight was taken to complete the first prefabricated semi-detached homes at Burnt Oak, Middlesex (4) which have both framework and window-frames of steel. In the badly-blitzed district of Poplar, in London's East End, single-storied houses built in the Midlands and brought south by lorry are being put up on bombed sites (5).

Photos, Sport & General, Planet News, Associated Press, Fox Photos

People of Britain Square Up To V-Bomb Terror

V-BOMBS HAVE FALLEN, and Britain's courageous and efficient Civil Defence organization goes swiftly into action. The beams of Army searchlights aid rescue-workers amid tottering masonry (1), besides helping the work of house-repairers (2) fitting temporary windows to bombed-blasted dwellings. When a large wall collapsed after a raid, burying rescue-workers and killing a N.F.S. boy-messenger, onlookers and would-be rescuers scrambled for safety as the wall crashed in a cloud of dust behind them (3). A bomb-victim, badly injured about the head and with his feet still pinned (4) was tended by a Light Rescue worker when flats in a working-class district were hit. Silence is called for on a bomb-site (5) while a R.A.F. police dog (see page 450) tracks down buried casualties among the rubble and wreckage. Under a new system of observer posts, Civil Defence services usually reach an "incident" in less than three minutes.

Photos, Daily Mirror, Keystone, Associated Press

Master of Most Jobs is the Wonderful Tractor

CATERPILLAR TRACTORS are capable of a greater variety of war-front tasks than any other single piece of mechanism. In the foreground (above) a bulldozer is seen cutting a road. Its huge scraper (A) can shift several hundred cubic yards of soil in an hour, break off or uproot massive trees, rip the undergrowth from tangled jungle or forest. The scraper is carried on stout metal arms (B), and can be raised by powerful rams (C) worked by small levers (D).

Power is supplied from a diesel engine (E) capable of 100 h.p. and more. There is no normal gearbox, the drive being through two separate clutches, one for each track, which can be engaged or slipped by means of the two track levers (F). The driving sprocket is at (G), and at the other end is the idler wheel. Between these is the track-tensioning spring (H) for keeping the track in adjustment.

In the left background is a small bulldozer ready for transport by air. On the right a tractor hauls a heavy gun and limber. A 45 h.p. tractor can haul up to 100 tons. Farther back a tractor fitted up as a crane is moving heavy stones.

Inset (bottom left) an armoured tractor is engaged in shallow water nosing out grounded barges and smoothing down sandbanks.

One of the most serviceable of all tracked vehicles is the "alligator," which won fame in the Walcheren landings in November 1944 (see pages 441 and 463-466). It resembles in appearance a last-war tank, but it floats. Cup-like treads move it through the water. Its official title is "Landing vehicle, tracked."

Specially drawn for THE WAR ILLUSTRATED *by Haworth*

I WAS THERE! Eye Witness Stories of the War

Tanks Ran Right Over the American Foxholes

When the Germans launched their counter-offensive in the Ardennes in the foggy weather of December 16,–1944, penetrations were made in the U.S. 1st Army front. Wes Gallagher, of the Associated Press, sent this dispatch from Belgium on December 20, telling of American heroism in the confused fighting that was then still in progress.

DOUGHBOYS slugging it out with Nazi tanks until they are ground to death in their foxholes—rescue in Western thriller fashion of nurses and wounded from a field hospital captured by the Germans—infantrymen trapped behind German lines picking their way back to their outfits—these are only a few of the tales of heroism in the First Army's bitter struggle to smash the West Front German counter-offensive, as I have seen it.

But it is not all a story of acts of cool bravery, as there are others of American formations cracking under the Nazi onslaught. It is a front of wild confusion as officers and men, trapped for several days behind German lines, smash through into the First Army side with titanic tales, only to be greeted with calm disapproval by tough doughboy veterans who now have succeeded in plugging the holes and stabilizing the front in this sector.

Sergeant Ronald Johnson of Creekside, Pennsylvania, stood beside me in a crowded casualty clearing station. He had just helped two wounded G.I.s over the mountain from behind German lines.

"When the attack started, artillery hit our company command post, killing everyone but myself and another fellow," he told me wearily, while at his feet a blood-stained G.I. with a bullet in his neck was slowly dying on a stretcher.

"The Germans came in and took us prisoner, but some of our boys attacked and we escaped in the woods. We made our way back to our units, or what's left of them. And the boys dug in again when we were attacked by those big German tanks. Some of those boys stood right in there fighting until the tanks ran right over their foxholes and smashed them. I got away again with two wounded boys, and by keeping to the

woods was able to bring them over to the American lines. That's all I guess."

An American field hospital of which I was told was overrun by Nazi tanks and

parachutists. The parachutists started loading nurses and wounded on trucks to be taken to Germany, when Lieutenant-Colonel Charles Horner of Doylestown, Pennsylvania, dashed into town in a jeep, followed by two half tracks, and started shooting from the hip and recaptured the base. The doughboys took over the town just in time to shoot up two jeep loads of Germans who raced into town in captured American cars, thinking their forces held it. Tanks appeared next and Yankees and tank destroyers slugged it out with the Nazis, who were on the receiving end for the first time in four days, until the town was firmly held again.

But this section of the front has been stabilized now, and the Germans are finding the going harder hour by hour.

AT PISTOL POINT, a German prisoner, survivor of a tank left burning by the roadside somewhere in the Ardennes, is marched to captivity by a U.S. sergeant. Accurate anti-tank fire from the U.S. 1st Army severely mauled Rundstedt's panzer drive into Belgium, which began on December 16, 1944. An account of American heroism is given in this page. *Photo, U.S. Official*

How We Captured a Member of the Gestapo

A surprise capture was made in Italy when a member of Himmler's Gestapo was brought in to our lines for interrogation. How this happened is told in the following narrative by Squadron-Leader Derek Adkins, who was serving with the Desert Air Force at the time.

IN all our successive moves from El Alamein across the arid wastes of the western desert, the more fertile country of Tripolitania, the olive and orange groves of Tunisia and Sicily, no more pleasant camp site had been found than the one we had at Lucera. It was in the heart of the Italian

countryside, in the midst of a rich oak-tree plantation, with the Apennines looming in the distance, and from which you could occasionally hear the rumbling of gunfire. I must say that the sight of long-forgotten English trees, after the monotony of olive groves and vineyards and cactus plants, was just like a breath of Richmond Park!

The weather had been appalling, with a strong nor'-wester blowing up and down the straggling mountain passes so that one almost expected to see the miniature villages perched on the top of each summit blown away. For a week or more a fine rain had hung from the clouds like a thin transparent curtain, dancing through the valleys and across our aerodromes, slanting now this way, now that.

Cocksure—but Cornered!

I had been visiting the Wing Headquarters of some fighters of the South African Air Force when I was told that a German prisoner was being brought in for interrogation. The trailer that served as an office was cleared, and within a few minutes the prisoner arrived under escort. He was a typical Nazi, sullen and arrogant, broad-shouldered, with square-cut features and closely cropped hair. He answered every question at first in a cock-sure manner that seemed to say, "You can't catch me!" But we knew rather more about his case than he thought.

It all began a year or two ago when a Croatian patriot, who was serving in a unit well behind the front line, had his name put down by the Germans as a "volunteer" for the Russian front. He soon realized that he was being watched by the Gestapo, but twice he contrived to make the German authorities believe that he was medically unfit. The first time he took large quantities

GERMAN SHOCK TROOPS push forward past blazing U.S. vehicles, including a jeep and a heavy half-tracked lorry, on the Western Front during the full-scale enemy drive into the American lines in December 1944. An eye witness story of the initial stages of this menacing German offensive is narrated above. PAGE 569 *Photo, U.S. Official: from a captured German film*

of salt immediately before his medical examination, and another time feigned illness so successfully that his transfer was postponed.

Meanwhile, the Croat had been making plans to escape, but just before they were complete a member of the Gestapo arrived and placed him under arrest. Accompanied by some of his fellow countrymen he was going to be escorted to a German headquarters and placed in "protective custody."

The Tables Were Turned

The climax was reached after the party had set forth on the first stage of the journey. The Gestapo man was sitting happily with a bottle of wine to his lips, innocently thinking he was taking his victims to captivity. The Croat, however, had other ideas and by a carefully prepared ruse, which I can't disclose here, the tables were turned. The Gestapo gangster found himself on the way to Italy!

Of course he had a very plausible tale to tell. But his bewilderment at finding himself a prisoner was soon betrayed by a display of complete panic. After a short time in the office trailer this was replaced by a clumsy appearance of willingness to serve the Allied cause, coupled with the belated statement that he was really of Austrian origin.

But his bluff was called, and we were soon able to disprove his story by producing evidence that he had in fact assisted in some

SUNBAKED AND SMILING, these troops of the Royal Scottish Fusiliers contemplate a useful array of rubber boats taken from the Japanese north of Mawlu in Burma. A curious story of a captured enemy supply dump is told in this page. *Photo, British Official*

of the worst atrocities for which the Gestapo are renowned. The last I saw of him he was muttering "Ach! du lieber Gott!"

Our Submarine's Fight with Nine Japanese Ships

Lieutenant-Commander E. P. Young, first R.N.V.R. officer to command a submarine, in a remarkable exploit off southern Burma took on seven Japanese supply ships and two escorts at once. In 36 minutes two escorts and one coastal vessel were sunk, two other vessels were damaged, and one M.T.B. was hit. Lieutenant-Commander Young tells his story here.

WE surfaced and opened fire at the rear ship at a range of 2,000 yards, obtaining eight fairly destructive hits. She turned away and limped towards the shore. We then attacked and stopped the ship ahead of her, but both the escorts were now racing towards us, firing their machine-guns. I turned to port to bring them both on to the starboard bow, and directed the fire of all our guns on to them. In turn they were both hit and stopped by direct hits from the 3-in. gun.

This part of the action was most exciting, the range eventually closing to 400 yards. Both of these escorts were carrying Japanese, presumably troops. One of them released a depth charge when it was 500 yards away, which rocked the submarine. Then one of the escorts got out of control, and eventually drove itself under.

Meanwhile, an M.T.B. was sighted coming for us at great speed, so this was the next target to be engaged. She fired two stern torpedoes, the tracks passing about 100 yards astern of us. We scored a direct hit on the M.T.B. as she was retiring, and she took little further interest in the proceedings. And now some vessel had

opened up with a pom-pom. We had not previously noticed this vessel, which was probably a motor gun boat. She got one direct hit, which struck our bridge casing but caused no casualties. There was a perpetual

whine of machine-gun bullets, but it was difficult to see exactly which ships were firing.

It was now decided to finish off the coaster which had been stopped earlier—the second target engaged, and also the other escort. They both sank after a few short range water-line shots. Then fire was directed at another ship. Two direct hits were obtained and his bridge demolished.

By this time the barrel of our 3-in. gun was so heated that the next round jammed. Moreover the remainder of the convoy was getting out of range and we had exhausted all our Oerlikon and Vickers ammunition, and I was getting anxious about the navigation. I decided to call it a day, to avoid the risk of running the submarine aground.

Hot Burma Jungle Race for a £1,500,000 Store

When the victorious 14th Army was following up the Japanese retreat across the Chindwin it became known that the enemy had a vast supply dump east of the river. How an Allied fighting patrol raced through the jungle to capture this £1,500,000 store is told by Capt. R. F. Hearn.

AN exhausting three-day trek took us over the last mountain range before the Chindwin, and we reached a village on the west bank opposite Settaw. The natives had no knowledge of the dump, but told us that there were some Japanese skulking around near Settaw.

There was no time to be lost, so I crossed the river with a fighting patrol to investigate. We went on for about three miles through the thick jungle, and found the dump. Piles of equipment were scattered around. There were brand-new assault and outboard motor boats, heaps of radio stores, seven 105-mm. guns still in their grease-proof wrappings, approximately one million rounds of all types of ammunition, mines and grenades. I got back across the river, and that night we heard that about 50 Japanese and many coolies were encamped near Settaw.

Early next morning we went over again. This time our fighting patrol had been swelled

by a platoon of infantrymen. It was tricky country, and we moved cautiously. We had gone about a mile when our defensive screen bumped some Japanese, who made off into the jungle. It looked suspicious. Anticipating an ambush, we halted a while before going on. Behind us Lieut. Ensminver had rounded up a whole village to help move whatever stores we decided to take. He also brought along a small Royal Engineers party for demolishing the rest.

When we finished what we had to do, the sappers put explosive charges with five-minute fuses in each of the seven guns. Going back through the dump to the river, we set fire to the basha huts where the ammunition was stacked. Fourteen hours afterwards we could still hear them exploding. That night we recrossed the Chindwin, and were told that a large enemy force, transport and porters, were nearing their dump. They were welcome to what they found!

Stone Age Terrors I Saw in Devastated Russia

On a 600-mile journey through what was "guerilla" country when the Germans were in Byelorussia, Soviet war correspondent Boris Yampolsky was appalled by unforgettable sights. Now freed by the Red Army, industries are reviving, and guerillas are back at their old jobs. Yampolsky's story appears here by courtesy of Soviet War News.

FOR many years the Byelorussian people dug canals, built dams and bridges and drained the swamps. In place of whispering reeds, a sea of golden grain rippled in the wind. Then German airmen

dropped incendiaries on the reclaimed boglands so that they burned day and night. Smoke rolled over the swamps, and from the sky ashes fell like rain. Ashes covered the ground, our faces, the horses.

LT.-COMMANDER E. P. YOUNG, D.S.O., a 29-year-old London publisher, and the first R.N.V.R. officer to be given command of a submarine, tells his story above.

We rode into a vast wilderness. The roads were overgrown with high grass and the fields with rank weeds. Black, burned villages, felled orchards—and in them, like tombstones, overturned beehives. Tall black crosses at the roadsides. While the Germans were still in Byelorussia I went on a journey through what had been the most thickly populated district of the Polessye region. For three days and nights I rode and saw not a single village, not a solitary house. I met only a boy tending a cow in a misty field, and a half-blind old woman who emerged from a hole in the ground at the sound of my horse's hoof-beats.

The hillocks bore graves with huge crosses adorned with wreaths of maple in autumnal yellow and red. You could see them from a long way off. I rode from hillock to hillock, from cross to cross. It was from the half-blind old woman that I first heard the fearful words : "round-up." The Germans had ringed the area and closed in from all sides. In one of the biggest villages of the Pinsk region all the people were burned in the church. In another all the children were burned in the school. In a third the people were burned on bonfires. In the fourth they were burned in their homes. S.S. men stood by and saw to it that nobody escaped through the windows.

I made these notes in a dugout tunnelled deep into a hill in the forest and camouflaged to tone with the face of the earth. It was only by sparks from the chimney that I found it. It was just as though I had found my way into a cave of the Stone Age. The tunnel ran deep beneath the roots of the trees. It was hard to tell how many people were there. Three tiers of bunks lined the walls at the entrance. In the depths people lay on the floor. When I entered, tommy-gun in hand, a woman screamed. The people's eyes were dim with the darkness, their senses mazed with the silence.

BYELORUSSIAN GIRLS, natives of Bialy-stok, welcomed their Red Army liberators with flowers in July 1944. See story in this and the preceding page. *Photo, Pictorial Press*

Sometimes a wolf crept up and glared into the den with green eyes. In swinging cradles were babies with wax-like faces. The sick peered out from bundles of rags and grimy sheepskins. I sat in the den until morning. There was no place to stretch my limbs. A girl at a spinning-wheel sat all night spinning a thread, unending as the people's woe.

Someone else was weaving bast shoes. An old man with a frostbitten face was sitting on the ground and slowly turning a handmill with wooden millstones. He ground hour after hour, all night long, day after day, to get flour for his bread. When I spoke to him of a windmill his eyes shone as he remembered the spreading sails that threw shadows across the field. To him it was like some fairy tale heard in childhood.

While the old man ground, an old woman pounded in a mortar. Thump, thump,

thump. By midnight she had a few handfuls of millet. She poured it into water and put it on the fire. The fire here, just as in prehistoric times, burned always in the home. If it died, it was a great calamity. Fire must then be sought again.

Next morning I rode on through fields hazy in the autumn mist. Two peasant women were harnessed to a wooden harrow. Behind them followed a boy, barefoot, with a tray swinging on his chest, scattering seed. Thinking of that life in the hole in the earth, and gazing at the sower, I thought : That's what will happen to all the world, to all humanity, if the Nazi is not exterminated.

There was not a bed, not a chair, not a frying-pan or a bucket anywhere. For a hundred miles around you could have found neither needle nor knife. All had burned in the German fire. In Polessye they ate potato bread seasoned with potash—the fertilizer of the peat bog. They smoked birch leaves. I saw wooden knives, wooden needles, stone axes, just as if they had dropped from a book on ancient history.

The Germans thought : "All is burnt. The ashes will be scattered by the winds, and that's the end." Never were they more mistaken. The tenacious memory of the people cannot be burned by fire, slain by the knife, or strangled by the rope.

Not far from the River Sluch there was a burial mound raised by the people during the German occupation. A wooden cross bore the inscription : " The people's curse on the German murderers to all eternity. May the memory of those who died in agony be unfading." The Germans broke the cross and scattered the grave. The very next day, as though it had grown out of the earth, a new cross appeared, bearing the same epitaph. Towns will crumble to dust, rivers change their course, old roads will vanish, new ones appear, but never will those burial mounds entirely vanish.

OUR DIARY OF THE WAR

DECEMBER 20, Wednesday *1,936th day*
Western Front.—German penetration of 35 miles reached Laroche. Monschau, northern limit of German advance, recaptured by 1st Army troops.
Far East.—Tokyo bombed by small force of Super-Fortresses.
Pacific.—Royal Navy carrier-aircraft attacked harbour and oil installations on Sumatra.

DECEMBER 21, Thursday *1,937th day*
Western Front.—Stavelot and Malmedy recaptured from enemy.
Air.—R.A.F. Lancasters attacked Trier by day, and marshalling yards at Cologne and Bonn and oil plant near Stettin at night.
Far East.—China-based Super-Fortresses bombed aircraft works at Mukden.

DECEMBER 22, Friday *1,938th day*
Western Front.—German force which had encircled Bastogne reached St. Hubert, 35 miles from Sedan gap.
Sea.—E-boats attacking Allied convoy route off the Scheldt routed by British warships.
Far East.—Nagoya, Japan, again bombed by Super-Fortresses.
Hungary.—National Provisional Government set up by Hungarian National Assembly at Debreczen.
General.—British Government announced new army call-up to provide 250,000 more fighting men.

DECEMBER 23, Saturday *1,939th day*
Air.—Allied aircraft attacked Trier and marshalling yards at Ehrang and Kaiserslautern.
Burma.—British 36th Division, making deepest penetration yet, occupied Tigyiang, on Irrawaddy island.
Greece.—Fighting broke out between ELAS (Left-wing) and EDES (Right-wing) troops in north-west Greece.
Home Front.—V-bomb attacks on Northern England reported for first-time.

DECEMBER 24, Sunday *1,940th day*
Western Front.—Enemy armour penetrated to Ciney and Celles, four miles from Dinant on the Meuse. With abandonment of American pocket round St. Vith, German salient was 40 miles wide at base.
Air.—More than 2,000 U.S. bombers and over 900 fighters attacked supply lines

and airfields behind enemy front. Allied Tactical aircraft flew more than 6,000 sorties in attacks on enemy transport.

DECEMBER 25, Monday *1,941st day*
Air.—Roads, railways and bridges in Ardennes battle area attacked by Allied aircraft ; 864 motor vehicles destroyed and 332 damaged.
Greece.—Mr. Churchill and Mr. Eden arrived in Athens by air.
India.—Japanese bombers shot down in small-scale attack on East Bengal.

DECEMBER 26, Tuesday *1,942nd day*
Western Front.—German columns driving on Meuse from Rochefort halted at Celles and Ciney.
Air.—Major force of R.A.F. bombers attacked German troops and supplies at advanced railhead of St. Vith.
Russian Front.—Red Army troops completed encirclement of Budapest.
Italy.—German attack on 5th Army front caused withdrawal from Barga in Serchio valley sector.
Greece.—Conference attended by delegates from all Greek parties opened in Athens under chairmanship of Archbishop Damaskinos.
Philippines.—Japanese warships driven off by air assault after shelling Allied positions on Mindoro.

DECEMBER 27, Wednesday *1,943rd day*
Western Front.—3rd Army troops broke through from south and relieved garrison of Bastogne after eight days' stand supplied by air.
Far East.—Tokyo again bombed by Super-Fortresses from Saipan.
Greece.—Conference in Athens adjourned after unanimous agreement in favour of Regency.

DECEMBER 28, Thursday *1,944th day*
Western Front.—Allied troops recaptured Echternach at south of German salient.
Air.—R.A.F. bombers attacked railway workshops and marshalling yards in Cologne area by day and Bonn and Munchen-Gladbach at night.
Pacific.—U.S. Liberators again attacked Iwojima, Volcano Islands.

DECEMBER 29, Friday *1,945th day*
Western Front.—U.S. troops began attack on Rochefort at westerly point of German bulge.
Air.—Allied bombers attacked marshalling yards at Bingen, Frankfurt and Aschaffenburg. R.A.F. bombed Coblenz and E-boat pens at Rotterdam.

Pacific.—U.S. warships and aircraft bombarded Iwojima in Volcano Islands.

Italy.—5th Army troops reoccupied Barga.
General.—Mr. Churchill and Mr. Eden returned to London from Athens.

DECEMBER 30, Saturday *1,946th day*
Air.—U.S. heavy bombers in great strength attacked marshalling yards at Kassel, Mannheim and Kaiserslautern.
Russian Front.—Germans rejected Russian surrender ultimatum at Budapest.
Pacific.—U.S. aircraft attacked targets in Palaus, Carolines and Wake Island.
Greece.—King George of Hellenes agreed to appointment of Archbishop Damaskinos as Regent.
General.—Hungarian Provisional Government declared war on Germany.

DECEMBER 31, Sunday *1,947th day*
Western Front.—Rochefort captured by Allied troops. Germans counterattacked 3rd Army on Saar front.
Air.—Strong force of U.S. bombers attacked oil refineries, jet-plane factories, U-boat yards and railway bridges in N.W. Germany. Mosquitoes bombed Gestapo headquarters in Oslo by day and Berlin at night.
General.—Polish Committee of National Liberation at Lublin proclaimed itself Provisional Government of Poland.

JANUARY 1, 1945. Monday *1,948th day*
Western Front.—3rd Army attacked between Bastogne and St. Hubert.
Air.—Luftwaffe made many attacks on Allied airfields in Belgium and Holland ; 364 German aircraft estimated destroyed by aircraft and guns. R.A.F. Lancasters breached Dortmund-Ems canal for fourth time. Day and night attacks by Allied bombers on oil plants and railway targets behind German front.
Burma.—Indian troops in Arakan occupied Rathedaung.
General.—France officially joined the United Nations.

JANUARY 2, Tuesday *1,949th day*
Air.—Daylight attacks by over 1,000 U.S. bombers on railways, bridges and troop concentrations. Night attacks by over 1,000 R.A.F. bombers on Nuremberg and Ludwigshafen.
Russian Front.—Fierce house-to-house fighting continued in Budapest.
General.—Admiral Sir Bertram Ramsay killed in air accident.

★———— *Flash-backs* ————★

1940

December 29. *Night fire raid on City of London ; Guildhall and other famous buildings burned.*

1941

December 22. *Japanese launched major attack on Philippines.*
December 24. *Japanese captured Wake Island in the Pacific.*
December 25. *Hong Kong garrison surrendered to Japanese.*
December 30. *Kaluga, on Moscow front, recaptured by Russians.*

1942

January 2. *Manila and Cavite in Philippines taken by Japanese.*
December 24. *Admiral Darlan assassinated in Algiers.*
December 29. *Kotelnikovo S.W. of Stalingrad, captured by Russians.*

1943

January 1. *Veliki Luki, Nazi defence bastion, taken by Red Army.*
December 24. *General Eisenhower appointed Supreme Commander of Allied Expeditionary Force.*

THE WAR IN THE AIR

by Capt. Norman Macmillan, M.C., A.F.C.

WITH the island of Leyte securely in American hands, General Mac-Arthur turned his attack upon Mindoro island, south of Luzon on which the Philippines capital, Manila, stands. The convoy conveying the American 6th Army troops from Leyte was attacked during each of the two days it steamed through the Mindanao Strait and the Sulu Sea, and 24 Japanese aircraft were shot down. The convoy was protected by cruisers, destroyers, aircraft-carriers, and night fighters based on Leyte.

On December 14 the carriers of Admiral Halsey's U.S. Third Fleet attacked Japanese defence airfields. On the 15th 400 carrier-based planes swept over Luzon, 100 attacking latest Tempest fighters were in action, shooting down eight F.W. 190s and one Messerschmitt 262 "jet-job" without loss.

The purpose of the Luftwaffe was to assist the ground forces by laying strips of anti-personal fragmentation bombs in front of the German attack forces. The Germans employed V-weapons in the offensive, using flying bombs and rockets against rear areas behind the Allied lines, and "silver balls" in the forward areas. The shock of the attack forced the U.S. 1st Army into the first Allied retreat since the invasion of Normandy. On Sunday 17th, the enemy were reported to have put 1,000 single-engined fighters and fighter-bombers into the air over the Aix la Chapelle sector. By the following day two

first five targets, using more than 1,300 bombers and losing 17 ; 500 attacked Duisburg. The Americans lost three of their 500 bombers and five of the 600 fighters, shooting down three enemy fighters ; they used a new type of fragmentation bomb weighing 265 lb., and dropped over 4,000 tons in one day.

WHILE the U.K. heavy bombers were diverted to tactical assaults, the U.S.A. 15th A.F. from Italy continued the strategic offensive against Germany's oil supplies. On December 17 and 18 they attacked Silesian oil refineries at Blechhammer, Odertal and Oswiecim. On the first day the enemy sent up from 120 to 155 interceptors to meet the force and in an air battle north of Brno, Czechoslovakia, 48 were shot down ; the Americans that day lost 29 aircraft. On the second day enemy resistance was light.

On December 19 and 21 Bomber Command Lancasters, escorted by U.S.A. 9th A.F. attacked the communications centre of Trier, and 300 Fortresses attacked the railway and road junction from Trier north to Gemund, opposite the U.S. First Army front, on the first of those days.

APPALLING Weather Conditions Surmounted by U.K. Heavy Bombers

Still the German advance rolled on, and the U.S. 101st Airborne Division, equipped as ground forces, were encircled in Bastogne on December 20. This division dropped from the air on D-Day in Normandy and again dropped into action at Nijmegen. Now they were called upon to fight another isolated action from a different cause. Dakota transport aircraft began to drop supplies to them on December 23, and in four days 842 transports and more than 50 gliders flew in supplies in the largest-scale effort of its kind throughout the war ; only one supply—of food—fell outside the held area, fortunately of larger extent than Arnhem, which probably accounts for the difference between the relative success of the two supply dropping operations. The 101st Division in Bastogne also possessed heavy tanks, which the Arnhem men did not. Their success, for they held out for seven days until relieved by forces of General Patton's 3rd Army, proves (as I suggested in a previous article, page 380) that means must be found to transport heavier equipment by air for future "Arnhems" if they are to succeed.

During most of the first week of the German offensive fog grounded the Allied tactical air forces, but the heavy bomber forces in the U.K. continued to operate whenever they could in the worst weather they had ever taken off in. Bomber Command and the 8th Air Force bombed enemy communications at Ehrang, Kaiserslautern, Coblenz, Bonn, Fulda, Gerelstein, Cologne, Saarbruecken, Aschaffenburg, Frankfort and Bingen. In addition, Bomber Command attacked Politz oil plant, near Stettin, (Dec. 21) ; troop concentrations and enemy armour at St. Vith (Dec. 26) ; and E- and R-boat pens at Ijmuiden (Dec. 15) and Rotterdam (Dec. 29) with 12,000 lb. bombs as counter to enemy opposition to Allied convoys sailing to Antwerp.

ON December 24 and 25 Allied sorties exceeded 10,000 for less than 1,000 by the Luftwaffe. On December 24 over 2,000 Fortresses and Liberators attacked escorted by over 900 Mustangs and Thunderbolts. No doubt Allied air power played an important part in blunting Rundstedt's attack—for by then nearly 3,000 enemy vehicles were destroyed and 1,250 damaged from the air—and before the end of December the German troops were forced back several miles, there to dig in, while the Allies took the initiative on the southern flank of the new salient.

V-bombs fell in Northern England for the first time at the Christmas week-end ; the Germans said London, Manchester and Antwerp were so attacked.

PARACHUTES CARRYING AMMUNITION AND FOOD drift down near Bastogne in the Ardennes from a U.S. Dakota transport, while a sky train with further supplies (top left) circles over the area. This photograph was taken just before the U.S. 3rd Army had broken through to the rescue of their comrades of the 101st Airborne Division in Bastogne (relieved on Dec. 28, 1944) who had been isolated by Rundstedt's counter-offensive of mid-December. *Photo, U.S. Official*

Clark Field aerodrome, near Manila, as the Americans landed on Mindoro to capture the town of St. José and its adjacent airfield five miles inland. Their penetration took them seven to nine miles inland from a coastal beach-head nine miles across. With them was an airfield construction unit of the R.A.A.F., the first Australian ground forces to enter the Philippines campaign. Clark Field and Manila were again attacked by air over the Christmas week-end.

AT dawn on Saturday, December 16, Von Rundstedt attacked the U.S. front in Western Europe from north of Monschau to west of Trier, employing 20 divisions with two Panzer armies. The Luftwaffe appeared in its biggest concentration for many months. From dusk on Saturday until Sunday afternoon it was estimated that 500 enemy aircraft were in action, including jet-propelled fighters. The British 2nd Tactical Air Force assisted the American 9th Air Force, and Britain's

Groups of the British 2nd T.A.F. were flying wing to wing with the U.S.A. 9th A.F. But the fast Me. 262s frequently slipped silently down from the clouds to drop A.P. bombs, and then speed off. The enemy dropped parachute troops behind the American lines to spread confusion and effect demolitions.

While the American troops fought and retreated, the Allied heavy bombers were switched on to strategico-tactical bombing behind the enemy attack zone. The first group of targets included the vital railway centres in the great network of tracks that interlink this important German industrial area. More than 2,400 Allied aircraft (including a fighter escort of 600 Mustangs of the U.S.A. 8th A.F.) between early night of December 17 and dusk on December 18 bombed Ulm, Munich, Hanau, Munster, Duisburg, Cologne, Coblenz and Mainz in that order. All the aircraft operated from U.K. bases. Bomber Command attacked the

Premier Flies to Athens to Call Peace Parley

IN A DRAMATIC BID FOR PEACE, Mr. Churchill, accompanied by Mr. Eden, flew to Athens on Christmas Day 1944, and at once called a conference of the conflicting parties presided over by Archbishop Damaskinos, who was appointed Regent five days later. The Premier is assisted from his armoured car (1). Sappers remove explosives (2) found outside the British H.Q. The conference at work (3), before arrival of ELAS delegates. L. to r. Mr. Eden, Mr. Churchill, Archbishop Damaskinos, Field-Marshal Alexander. Mr. H. Macmillan, Gen. Scobie.

News from the Airways of the World at War

AIRCRAFT have fought their own battles in the skies, carried constant war to the back areas and the deep seas, and taken part in almost every battle at sea, on land, and in combined operations. They have carried troops and supplies, equipped underground armies in enemy-occupied countries, and as ambulances have saved thousands of lives by transporting wounded swiftly from the battlefields. Without aircraft the assaults on the Pacific islands, on Sicily, Italy, Normandy and the French Riviera would have been far more costly, and in some cases perhaps impossible.

As the war has continued, the number and variety of aircraft used by the Fighting Powers have so increased as to make it impossible for anyone not specializing in the subject to keep really well-informed. The series of books entitled Aircraft of the Fighting Powers, of which the fifth annual volume (1944 Aircraft), edited by D. A. Russell, M.I.Mech.E., has just been issued (The Harborough Publishing Co. Ltd., one-and-a-half guineas) solves the problem for all who have been otherwise engaged, and at the same time provides a valuable work of reference for those who have been in close touch with aviation throughout the war.

PRODUCED on art paper, with photos and scale drawings, Vol. V. covers 24 American, 22 British, 10 German, eight Japanese, five Russian, and one Australian aircraft. These include heavy, medium and torpedo-dive-bombers, flying-boats, fighters, transports, tugs, gliders, photo-

VICKERS-WARWICK, R.A.F. dual-purpose aircraft, has two 2,000 h.p. Double Wasp engines ; carries a motor lifeboat for rescue purposes ; and is armed with three multiple gun-turrets. See also illus. page 62.

HEAVIEST ARMED AIRCRAFT is the B-25 Mitchell bomber, which carries 18 guns in all. Eight ·5-in. machine-guns jut from its nose.

graphic reconnaissance aircraft, prototypes, auto-giros, a helicopter, and the V1 flying bomb. Technical details of engines, weights, armament, size, and performance (except when still secret) and a brief but fascinating history of each aircraft are given in the text.

When describing the Russian IL-3 two-seater Army attack aircraft the writers say, "The IL-3 is the two-seat version of the IL-2, the original Stormovik (not a type name but the Russian name for ground-attack and assault aircraft)." References like that give this book something of the touch of Dobson and Young (those incomparable popularizers by radio of good music).

A COMPENDIUM of aircraft designation systems, international aircraft markings and colour schemes, D-Day invasion markings, a colour plate reproducing the colour standards of the British Ministry of Aircraft Production—and, of course, the front, profile and plan drawings of aircraft are of particular interest to modellers and artists. The standard scale is 1/72, but, to fit the page size, 1/144 is used for exceptionally large aircraft, such as the Russian TB-7, the heavy bomber in which M. Molotov flew to Britain and the United States, and the German Me 323 which flew supplies to Tunisia in 1943.

One trifling thing I noticed. In page 50 : Staraya Russa was spelt Staraya Russia. Wartime materials may be the reason, but I would like a heavier binding-case to stand up to the handling that this interesting volume is sure to receive.

NORMAN MACMILLAN.

VICKERS-ARMSTRONG SEA-OTTER MARK I, seen in flight, is a single-engined amphibian biplane designed for naval reconnaissance and air-sea rescue purposes. It has catapult equipment and is powered with a Bristol Mercury 30 engine of 870 h.p.; is armed with three Vickers " K " guns and carries a crew of three or four.

NORDEN BOMBSIGHT, here being uncovered by a U.S. bombardier, ensures pin-point bombing from any altitude and in most weathers.

Photos, British Official, Charles E. Brown, Keystone, Planet News

Editor's Postscript

Few persons who have studied public opinion, as all journalists must do, have much use for the "polls," or widely-collected cross-sections of popular notions, which profess to show what the masses are thinking about public affairs. To begin with, only a very small proportion of the masses think at all, consecutively or logically, about matters beyond their own personal interest. They do not take the trouble to collect the facts and assemble the historical background which alone can provide a basis for rational judgement. Therefore their answers to questions put by the gatherers of opinions depend very largely on the manner in which those questions are phrased. We heard a great deal about the League of Nations Union Ballot in 1935, which showed a large majority in favour of stopping Mussolini's attack on Abyssinia. But nothing was done to stop it. People signed the ballot paper, but didn't really care. Indeed, many of them did not understand what they were signing. This was proved by a London daily paper which canvassed a district where the vote had been overwhelmingly against letting the Italians break the peace, and received an equally heavy poll in favour of doing nothing to restrain them! Not much value need be attached therefore to the result of the same journal's well-intentioned endeavour to find out how long we want control and direction of labour to continue. "Not until Japan has been beaten" was the prevailing view, but I doubt if many of the "polled" could give reasons for it.

Many useful changes that were turned down in peacetime have been adopted during war. It looked as if there might be a chance to run a short Bill through the House, giving Ministers who are members of the House of Lords the right to speak on the affairs of their Department in the Commons. That has often been mooted, and it is difficult to see any practical objection to it. But Mr. Churchill is a staunch believer in tradition—as he showed by his insistence that the House of Commons should be rebuilt on the lines of the one destroyed, inconvenient as it was in many ways. He cannot see any reason for not keeping peers who hold important offices in their own place and letting under-secretaries explain the views of their chiefs in the Lower House. In many Legislatures Ministers can speak in both Houses, and there are obvious advantages in the practice. One of them is that there would not be the same feeling in the Commons as there is now when Cabinet office is given to men who sit in the Upper House and cannot be questioned or argued with face-to-face by the representatives of the people.

Those who think of a National Park as merely a much bigger open space of the kind we are familiar with in towns, with their asphalt paths and trim hedges and well-kept grass, are entirely in error. National Parks are described in a paper circulated by the Committee which is busy even in war-time spreading the idea of them as "regions of our finest landscape brought into full public service—preserved in their natural beauty, continued in their farming use, and kept or made accessible (in so far as they are not cultivated) for open-air recreation and public enjoyment, and particularly for cross-country walking." In our small island such preservation is essential if we want the men who are fighting our battles all over the world, and their children, to be as proud of Beautiful Britain as their fathers were. We have allowed far too much of it to be smirched and uglified by ribbons of hideous little bungalows and tin shacks; by scattered buildings of a squalid type such as deface the lovely South Coast and much of the Downland scenery; by cheap and nasty additions to old farmhouses or labourers' cottages. To stop that in future everywhere, and not only in National Parks, is our plain duty to those who will come after us. National Parks would be at any rate a good start.

When even the chairman of the Kennel Club calls the prices now being asked (and paid) for dogs "iniquitous," it is obvious that there is something like a ramp in the dog market. For puppies that used to cost two or three pounds, people are giving twenty or thirty. For a St. Bernard—if you should happen to fancy one, which I never did as a house companion, suitable enough though they are on a snowbound Swiss mountain—you would probably have to give £50. A dachshund will cost you £20, a Sealyham £15, and so on. This is not due to the number of dogs in Britain having diminished. There are just about as many as there were at the outbreak of war, although a great many were destroyed when rationing made it hard to feed dogs. The cause of the great rise in prices is apparently the increased demand for dogs of any and every kind. Even mongrels which used to be given away now fetch several pounds apiece.

If it is true that letters from Marshal Pétain to Hitler and Hitler's answers to them have been discovered in a house where Pétain lived for a time, they will probably throw light on both men's characters. I can imagine, for instance, Pétain writing, "Dear Adolf, as you told me to call you, can you not let me have Laval liquidated? He is such a nasty piece of work. He puts me off my food. And really he is not much use to you. I will not take his orders, yours respectfully, Marshal of France." To which the following reply is sent, "Marshal, Laval, I agree, is simply dirt. But dirt is useful in its place. Therefore, he will stay where he is—at your right hand, and you will do what he tells you, because I communicate my wishes to you through him.

By the way, you should put Heil Hitler! at the beginning and end of your letters to me. Heil! to you from your affectionate Adolf."

A Metropolitan magistrate referred recently to "the epidemic of stealing" which broke out during the last war, continued more or less through the uneasy peace, and has become worse since 1939. At first it was heard of mainly among soldiers, but it has spread now to many other sections of the community. Here is one example. From the lavatory attached to the restaurant of one of London's big department stores some dozens of soap tablets and hundreds of towels have been stolen, with the result that the management has had put up a notice to say it cannot supply either. In another big shop everything purchased is tied with a special kind of tape. One customer who bought some small article and said "Never mind about tying it up; it will go in my pocket" was told that it was the rule to put the tape round everything that had been paid for. If anyone was found in possession of something without the tape, that something had clearly been stolen.

My friends among the publishers have long had a stout champion in Stanley Unwin, himself a past President of the Publishers' Association and controlling more than one of our best-known London houses. Unwin has just sent me his newest outburst against the powers that be. It is a sixpenny pamphlet entitled "Publishing in Peace and War," in which he prances once again into the arena on his favourite hobby-horse—the meagreness of the paper ration for book-publishing which, despite the recent 2½ per cent increase, is still less than 22,000 tons a year. This may seem a lot—if you don't happen to know anything about publishing and until you reflect that the present ration for H.M. Stationery Office alone is 100,000 tons, while the newspapers have a quota of some 250,000 tons. It came as no surprise to learn that at least two-thirds of the total tonnage used for books in Britain goes in reprints of educational text-books and the classic writings of all ages, and that what we generally term fiction is merely the froth on the surface of the stream. Which is, of course, as it should be. An aggravating feature of the present situation is the fact that books are now selling in Britain to the lively tune of £18,000,000 a year, as compared with £10,000,000 pre-war, and yet the demand vastly outstrips the supply. Unwin contends that another 8,000 tons of paper a year on the publishers' ration would make all the difference. I wonder if, for once, he isn't being a bit too modest in his demands.

None of my friends has ever numbered among his desert island reading the "Agony" column of The Times. Yet a well-known social historian I know not only makes it his breakfast-time reading but card-indexes it for reference—as an invaluable and (he swears) infallible guide to the foibles and peculiarities of the strange age we live in. I wonder under what section of his card-index he classified the following advertisement:

Artist-Scientist (Oxford). 33 languages, comparative philology, paints portraits from sitters or from photographs, undertakes all branches engineering, architectural design; designs, executes wall, ceiling frescoes, furniture, sculpture; undertakes all branches literary, scientific research (any language), physical chemical analysis, mathematical calculations, abstractions.

How many readers, I wonder, could name 33 languages without turning up a book of reference—let alone read and (presumably) write them? Offhand, I can think of only 23, including Basque, the mystery language they speak in the Pyrenees which is said to have no affiliation with any other tongue in the world.

Lieut.-Gen. COURTNEY H. HODGES, Commander of the U.S. 1st. Army, against which Von Rundstedt opened his violent counter-offensive on December 16, 1944.

Photo, Associated Press

They Also Serve Who Guard the Arctic Seas

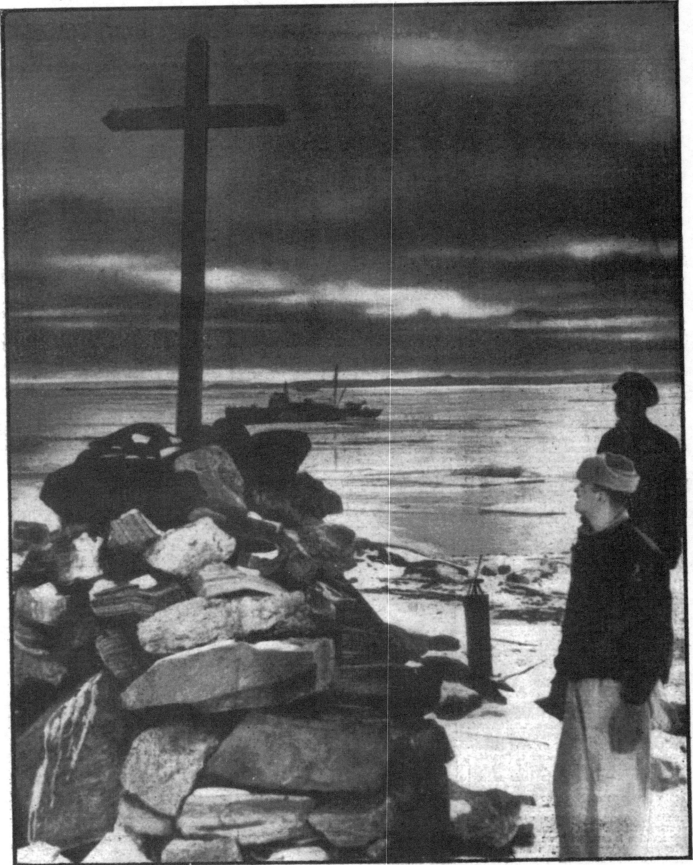

U.S. COAST GUARDSMEN IN GREENLAND keep lonely vigil among the grey Arctic wastes. The American protection of this vast island, some 850,000 sq. miles in area, dates back to April 11, 1941—eight months before the U.S. was at war with Germany—when President Roosevelt signed an agreement with the Danish Minister in Washington providing for the establishment of U.S. naval, military and air bases on Denmark's only colonial possession. A coastguard cutter is seen in the bay.

Photo, Paul Popper

Printed in England and published every alternate Friday by the Proprietors, THE AMALGAMATED PRESS, LTD., The Fleetway House, Farringdon Street, London, E C.4. Registered for transmission by Canadian Magazine Post. Sole Agents for Australia and New Zealand: Messrs. Gordon & Gotch, Ltd.; and for South Africa: Central News Agency, Ltd.—January 19, 1945. S.S. *Editorial Address:* JOHN CARPENTER HOUSE, WHITEFRIARS, LONDON, E.C.4.

Vol 8   *The War Illustrated*   Nº 199

SIXPENCE   *Edited by Sir John Hammerton*   FEBRUARY 2, 1945

ON BOARD THE "BLIGHTY EXPRESS," London-bound from a southern port, men of the British Army of Liberation, aided by the ever-ready Naafi, celebrated in the buffet-car the beginning of their 7-days home leave (the first since D-Day), which began on January 1, 1945. Leave was balloted for among units serving in France, Belgium and Holland. To be eligible a soldier must have served abroad for six months. Special trains equipped with canteens were run from the landing ports.   *Photo, New York Times Photos*

NO. 200 WILL BE PUBLISHED FRIDAY FEBRUARY 16

Our Roving Camera Greets the Home-Leave Men

FIRST BATCH OF D-DAY MEN ON 7-DAYS' HOME LEAVE raised a mighty cheer as the transport docked at a southern port (1) on the night of January 1, 1945. Off the ship, a Welsh N.C.O. was one of several who telephoned home (2). Some travelled north in a luxury train drawn by a specially-labelled streamlined engine (3). At a London terminus a Tommy on leave from Burma proudly displayed a Japanese sword (4). The 4½-year-old daughter of Lance-Corporal F. Burford, of Balham, tried on the shoes her father had brought from Holland (5). Congleton, Lancs, welcomed its local V.C.—Sergeant G. H. Eardley. —with cheers, flags, bunting and banners (6). See also page 577.

Photos, Topical Press, G.P.U., Central Press, Daily Mirror, Fox

THE BATTLE FRONTS

by Maj.-Gen. Sir Charles Gwynn, K.C.B., D.S.O.

LUZON ISLAND, in the Philippines, where General MacArthur made a successful surprise landing on Jan. 9, 1945 (see heavy black line above), in what was described as " one of the biggest amphibious operations of the war." *By courtesy of the News Chronicle*

VON RUNDSTEDT's offensive has been a severe shock to our complacency, but I think I can claim that I was not unduly optimistic when a fortnight ago I wrote that I expected that his success would be short-lived. In the first week of the New Year it became evident that he had definitely failed to achieve any of the more ambitious objects it may have had. He struck us a shrewd blow and sent us reeling back in some confusion, as Field-Marshal Montgomery has admitted, but our recovery has been rapid. There can be no doubt that Rundstedt had pinned his hopes on the success of his initial blow, for which he had used his best troops and practically the whole of his strategic reserve, made as strong as possible. But presumably he had always intended to make subsidiary attacks to exploit success when the Allies were compelled to suspend their previous offensive operations and to use their reserves in counter-measures against his main thrust.

For such subsidiary attacks his troops that had been on the defensive could then turn to the offensive, utilizing their local reserves which it would not have been safe to withdraw to take part in the major operation. The counter-offensive he has delivered against the U.S. 7th Army in the Palatinate is clearly a subsidiary operation of this nature, although owing to the failure of his main offensive it is probably designed rather to limit the Allied counter-measures than to exploit the initial success in the Ardennes.

AT the time I write Rundstedt, aided by the weather, which has reduced air co-operation to a minimum, is withdrawing under pressure in the Ardennes salient, but his subsidiary offensive in the Palatinate, though it has been checked, has not definitely been brought to a standstill. The question which naturally invites speculation is, what will he do now ? Will he revert to the defensive, withdrawing altogether from the Ardennes salient which clearly has no value as a permanent defensive position, for it would always be a source of danger and entail a considerable lengthening of the line to be held ? A cautious general would almost certainly withdraw, especially as an improvement in the weather would release the Allied Air Force for a devastating attack on his forces in the salient, unprotected by permanent fortifications, and with restricted lines of communication. But there are as yet no signs that his withdrawal will be complete, and since he had openly announced to his troops when he launched his attack that they were to make a final effort to win the war, it is safer to assume he may still make a desperate attempt to recover the initiative.

That he has any chance of doing so successfully I cannot believe, but that he will make the attempt seems probable if only because of the shattering reactions on German morale a definite reversion to the defensive would cause. There is ample evidence that the counter-offensive and its initial success restored a shaken morale to a notable degree, but admission of the failure of a proclaimed final effort could hardly fail to damp the spirits of even the most fanatical troops. Rundstedt has his back to the wall, and however hopeless he may realize the struggle to be I am convinced he will go down fighting with all the offensive spirit that is traditional in the German army, even if it should accelerate final disaster. What form his final effort may take it is impossible to predict ; the Ardennes salient clearly no longer provides a springboard for a renewal of his original plan, but he may cling to what remains of it as a bait to draw in the bulk of the Allied forces.

LOOKING for Opportunity to Catch Montgomery on the Wrong Foot

The terrain is highly defensible, and the defence is being increasingly confided to infantry formations. He may therefore be withdrawing his armoured formations secretly for employment elsewhere, or be massing them for a major tactical counter-stroke. In the one case they may reappear on another sector of the front, possibly to strengthen his offensive in Alsace. In the other, he may be looking for an opportunity to catch Montgomery on the wrong foot—though that I do not think will be easy, for the way in which Montgomery tidied up a confused situation and brought about the recovery which has placed the Allies again on the offensive should give us every confidence in his leadership.

We who for so many days had had to depend on the scraps of belated and often confusing information which was allowed to come through the screen of security silence should be very grateful to the Field-Marshal for the very clear picture he gave to correspondents of the stages by which the recovery was effected, and of the factors on which it depended. We had, I think, realized that the defence organized and conducted by the U.S. 1st Army on the Monschau-Stavelot front, and the gallant resistance offered by isolated American detachments, had made a great contribution to recovery by slowing down Rundstedt's thrust and forcing it to change direction. We had admired, too, the characteristic speed and vigour of General Patton's counter-offensive against Rundstedt's left flank, but I think only professional soldiers can have appreciated the more complicated situation on the north side of the salient which made the organization of a well co-ordinated counter-stroke difficult.

I IMAGINE many people wondered why a counter-offensive on this flank was not synchronized with General Patton's drive immediately. But it must now be recognized that not only had the situation to be stabilized on General Hodges' 1st Army front which had borne the weight of Rundstedt's attack, but that in the development of counter-measures four armies were concerned, and that the assembly of formations to provide a striking force involved difficult movements across congested lines of communication al under separate commands. The obvious necessity of placing the whole operation under the control of a single commander was at once realized by General Eisenhower, and that it was carried through as speedily as it was, and without confusion, gives proof of clear planning and admirable staff work. In General Patton's case the problem was simpler, because he was employing his own reserves. Nevertheless, his change of front and delivery of attack in a new direction so promptly was an outstanding feat.

Rundstedt has, of course, succeeded in so far as he has disturbed General Eisenhower's original plans and compelled him to suspend his previous offensives on the Roer and Saar fronts. But the Allies are now engaged in a new offensive. A large part of Rundstedt's strategic reserve has already been expended, and what remains is still committed to a fight from which he may find it difficult to disengage. His losses, already heavy, may therefore continue to mount rapidly. That might be compensated to some extent by a reduction in the rate of attrition on the Roer and Saar fronts, but replacement of the high-class personnel and special armaments of picked divisions must become increasingly difficult. The truth is the Germans, both in west and in east, are making a somewhat reckless use of their reserves.

IN Hungary they used them prodigally in a belated attempt to rescue the remains of the Budapest garrison, apparently mainly with the object of avoiding the loss of prestige its surrender would involve ; for they have clearly no intention of re-occupying the city or of establishing a defensive front again on the Danube if they succeed. Failure in either case may leave gaps which will be difficult to fill. This readiness to expend their reserves is characteristic of the extreme offensive doctrines on which the German army is taught to rely, and it has on many occasions in Russia got them into trouble. There they were generally able to escape the worst consequences by skilful evasive manoeuvre, but neither in the west nor east is there now room for retreat without exposing German territory. The extreme offensive doctrine therefore fits badly with Hitler's plan of contesting every yard of ground in an effort to prolong the death struggle, and Rundstedt's failure, if it can be made complete, may lead to a collapse which would materially shorten the war.

IN ATHENS, before the truce between General Scobie and the E.L.A.S. forces came into operation on January 14, 1945, a British sniper was interested in insurgent troops as they hurriedly left a burning building.
Photo, British Official

Winter Camouflage for Monty's Men and Armour

SNOW SUITS WERE A GENERAL ISSUE for U.S. troops serving under Field-Marshal Montgomery during the rolling back of the enemy's Ardennes "bulge," the western extremity of which was sealed off by the occupation of Houffalize by the U.S. 1st and 3rd Armies on January 16, 1945. A section of the 30th Division Field Artillery (above) in their snow camouflage near Stavelot (retaken December 21, 1944). Hoping that it will be harder for the wily Hun to spot against the wintry background, a tank man whitewashes his M-4 Sherman (below). PAGE 580 *Photos, Fox*

Snow and Rain Saved the Hun in the Lowlands

FOUL WEATHER IN ALL ITS FORMS, ranging from torrential rains to blinding blizzards, held up Allied operations in Holland and Belgium from early December 1944 until the capture of Laroche, Rundstedt's defensive swivel-point in the Ardennes salient, on January 11, 1945. In flooded Holland, three of our "Water Weasels," amphibious tracked half-ton cargo-carriers (above), demonstrate their adaptability. R.A.F. ground staff (below) sweep the snow from Mitchell medium bombers on a chilly airfield in Belgium.

Photos, British Official

AUSTRALIA'S MAMMOTH NEW GRAVING DOCK, AT SYDNEY.—the largest in the southern hemisphere and capable of taking the mightiest ships afloat—was begun in 1941, and will doubtless play an important role in the war against Japan (see pages 560-561, 584-585). One of the towering dock-walls is here seen under construction. The enormous overhead gantries are employed in pouring concrete used in building the walls, and to haul the concrete supplies around the site requires a fleet of miniature locomotives. Bulldozers, mechanical scoops and steam shovels have excavated almost 500,000 tons, including the gouging out of over 130,000 tons of solid rock. When completed, the dock will cost about £7,000,000 and will make Sydney one of the foremost centres of world trade after the war.
Photo, Royal Australian Navy

THE WAR AT SEA

by Francis E. McMurtrie

GOLDEN HIND is the name that has been given to the depot that has been established for the Royal Navy at Sydney, the main base of the Pacific Fleet under Admiral Sir Bruce Fraser. Seldom has a happier choice been made by the Admiralty. It was in the Golden Hind, first English ship to sail from the Atlantic into the Pacific, that Drake circumnavigated the world in 1577-1580. At the start of the voyage she was the Pelican, but the name was changed to Golden Hind—the crest of Sir Christopher Hatton, principal patron of the expedition—when Drake entered the Straits of Magellan on August 20, 1578.

It was in the Golden Hind at Deptford that Queen Elizabeth knighted Drake on April 4, 1581. There the old ship was ordered to be laid up for preservation, but in the following century her timbers had decayed and she had to be taken to pieces. Charles II presented a chair made out of the remaining sound wood to Oxford University. Now, after a lapse of 366 years, the name Golden Hind has returned to the Pacific.

DEFINITE confirmation of the loss of the Japanese battleship Musasi is further evidence of the fact that the Battle of the Philippines was a decisive victory. With a displacement of about 45,000 tons and a main armament of nine 16-in. guns in three triple turrets, the Musasi was in the same category as the new United States battleships of the Iowa class, the German Bismarck and Tirpitz, and the British battleship that was launched by Princess Elizabeth on November 30, and which, according to statements from abroad, is named Vanguard.

It appears that the Musasi's magazines blew up after she had been torpedoed from the air. So far as is known, she has only one sister ship in service, the Yamato, which received damage on the same occasion. A third ship of the class may be completing. Otherwise, the Japanese are believed to have only five old battleships left. Thus they cannot muster sufficient strength to intervene effectively in the American invasion of Luzon, which is striking a heavy blow at Japanese prestige.

SUBMARINE-Launched Flying-Bombs With New York as the Target?

Further evidence of enemy weakness at sea is the fact that a convoy of 200 transports intercepted by U.S. aircraft off Camranh Bay, Indo-China, was protected by a slender escort of destroyers and smaller craft, headed by one of the seagoing training ships of the Katori class, which was bombed and sunk. These are ships of 5,800 tons, with a speed of 18 knots and an armament of four 5·5-in. guns and two 5-in. anti-aircraft weapons. The Singapore naval base has been heavily raided by Allied bombers, which also attacked Penang, second city of the Straits Settlements.

Some apprehension has been aroused on the Atlantic seaboard of the United States as the result of a statement made by Admiral Jonas Ingram, to the effect that New York might be attacked by flying bombs from the sea within the next month or two. Though the probability of this was rather discounted by the Navy Department, there has since been a good deal of speculation on the subject. It would not be impossible for flying bombs to be launched from a submarine, though from the point of view of waging effective war it would seem to be a somewhat futile proceeding. Bombs could be carried in some form of hangar on deck, as has been done with aircraft in British and Japanese submarines. It is improbable that more than one, or possibly two, would be accommodated in a single submarine.

Certainly the Germans have been showing greater under-water activity of late, more U-boats having been encountered in the Atlantic during December than for some time past. It is probable that they can still dispose of at least 300 submarines, though all may not be of the latest ocean-going type. A certain percentage have been fitted with the special arrangement of air-intake and exhaust pipes known as the "schnorkel," of which the enemy have boasted so often lately. According to some accounts, these not only enable the batteries of a submarine to be recharged without coming to the surface but have given her the ability to move under water at higher speed.

THOUGH this device may assist U-boats to evade observation it is improbable that it will afford them any permanent advantage, for it is more in the nature of a defensive measure than an offensive one. For the time being it is possible that the hunting of U-boats may become a somewhat longer and more difficult job ; but even if the enemy boasts that U-boats can now remain submerged for as long as a month be true, it is not going to help the Germans much in the long run. Submarine crews that are always striving to keep below water in case they may be spotted are scarcely likely to become enthusiasts for attack. Those with the most enterprising captains will take greater risks and thus will have a shorter life, leaving the cautious still more inclined to evasive tactics.

That the Japanese Navy is not the only enemy with which Allied naval forces have to contend in the Pacific is shown by the announcement earlier this month that three U.S. destroyers had been lost in a typhoon in the Western Pacific. One of these, the Spence, of 2,100 tons, was launched as recently as 1942. She was one of over 150 vessels of the Fletcher type, armed with five 5-in. and several smaller guns, besides depth charges and ten torpedo tubes. Her complement numbered about 250 officers and men. The other two destroyers, the

ICE-COVERED DESTROYER on convoy duty in Northern waters. The crew are seen applying a touch of " ship-shape and Bristol-fashion " to their frost-bound vessel.
Photo, British Official

Hull and Monaghan, were sister ships of 1,395 tons, launched during 1934-35. They had four 5-in. guns and eight torpedo tubes, and a complement of over 200 each.

THESE are not the first United States warships lost in heavy weather during the present war. In the Atlantic coast hurricane of September 14 last the destroyer Warrington, of 1,850 tons, two Coast Guard vessels and a small minesweeper, the YMS 409, foundered. In February 1942, an older destroyer, the Truxtun, of 1,190 tons, was wrecked in a gale on the coast of Newfoundland, together with the supply ship Pollux. Early in 1943 a converted minesweeper, the Nightingale, was lost in a gale off the coast of Oregon ; and in the same region another minesweeper, the YMS 133, capsized a few weeks afterwards. Two motor torpedo-boats, PT 31 and PT 33, were sunk through running on to reefs in the Philippines during January and February 1942 ; and a submarine rescue vessel, the Macaw, met her end through striking a coral reef in the Pacific in February 1944. In June 1942, the storeship Capella was lost in unreported circumstances off Narragansett. A small Coast Guard cutter, the Wilcox, foundered in a gale off the Atlantic seaboard in September 1943. With a fleet (including landing craft) of some 6,000 units, it is inevitable that a certain number of such casualties should occur.

AFTER A DARING RAID IN THE AEGEAN, these officers of one of H.M motor-launches display their trophies, including the ensigns of a German schooner and its escort vessel. On offensive night patrol they boarded and captured two ships of an enemy convoy nearing its destination. On the extreme left is the motor-launch's 23-year-old commanding officer, Sub-Lieut. Robin A. Barr, R.N.V.R.
Photo, British Official

Proud Record of the Royal Australian Navy

Ever since the outbreak of war in 1939, vessels of the R.A.N. have been vigorously assaulting the enemy. Great renown has come to many of her ships, especially by way of Mediterranean exploits ; but, as ADRIAN BALL here writes—specially for " The War Illustrated "—much remains to be told of great doings in the Pacific, where today the R.A.N. is fighting—stronger than ever.

WHEN war broke out in the Pacific on December 7, 1941, the strength of the R.A.N. was deployed throughout the Mediterranean, the Indian and Pacific Oceans. The "N" class destroyers were in the Mediterranean, destroyers and corvettes were on patrol duties around the Australian coast, and larger units were searching for enemy raiders in the Indian Ocean. Because of the shortage of British escort vessels in the Far East at that time, the destroyer Vampire and the fleet minesweepers Burnie, Bendigo, Goulburn and Maryborough were engaged in patrol and escort duties in Malayan waters when Japan struck at Pearl Harbour. These minesweepers are often referred to in Australia as corvettes, but actually their design corresponds closely with that of the "Bangor" class sweepers of the R.N. and R.C.N.

On December 10 the Vampire, fighting with a group of R.N. destroyers escorting H.M.S. Prince of Wales and Repulse, rescued 22 survivors from those two ships. Her next encounter with the enemy came on the night of January 26–27. In company with H.M.S. Thanet, the Vampire attacked a Japanese force of one cruiser and three destroyers off Endau in the Malay Peninsula. In the fight which followed one large Japanese destroyer was sunk, and the Thanet was lost.

Famous Battle of the Java Sea

During January 1942 the cruisers Perth and Hobart, the sloop Yarra and the minesweepers Ballarat, Toowoomba and Woollongong reinforced this little squadron. These minesweepers took part in the evacuation of Sumatra, rendering sterling service at Oosthaven, Merula and Palembang.

H.M.A.S. Perth formed part of an Allied force which was thrown into action against a superior Japanese fleet on February 27. In this great fight, destined to go down in history as the Battle of the Java Sea, the Allied fleet was all but annihilated. The R.N. lost the cruiser Exeter and the destroyers Electra, Encounter and Jupiter ; the U.S.N. lost the cruiser Houston and destroyer Pope ; and the R. Netherlands Navy the cruisers De Ruyter and Java and the destroyers Evertsen and Kortenaer. After surviving the battle itself, the Perth (in company with the Houston and Evertsen) attempted to slip through Sunda Strait in darkness, but went down fighting an overwhelmingly strong force.

WHEN it was seen that resistance in Java could not be prolonged, the minesweepers were ordered to evacuate personnel from Tjilatjap. Braving the enemy bombers and surface craft, they accomplished their task and carried out efficient demolition. While escorting a convoy back to Australia, the Yarra was attacked by a force of three heavy cruisers and four destroyers. Lieut.-Cmdr. Rankin laid down a smoke screen to give the merchant ships a chance, and the Yarra met a glorious death, her three 4-in. guns barking defiance at the heavy cruisers and destroyers. Although put out of action quickly, the sloop did not sink for over two hours ; thirteen of her gallant crew were picked up by a Dutch submarine and taken to Colombo. A similar fate befell H.M. destroyer Stronghold and the U.S.S. Edsall, Peary and Asheville. After continuous attacks by bombers the minesweepers eventually reached Australia.

Between May 4 and May 8, 1942, Australian warships fought for the first time in home waters in the series of actions known as the Battle of the Coral Sea, which saved Port Moresby and, incidentally, Australia from invasion. This series of engagements began when U.S. planes struck at Japanese warships and transports at Tulagi. On May 7 a second raid was made on Jap forces in the Louisiade Archipelago ; the following day the Japs made a furious counter-attack, sinking the U.S. aircraft carrier Lexington. Meanwhile, the Australian squadron, which included the Australia and the Hobart, was withstanding a terrific attack by bombers and torpedo bombers. The attack failed, the squadron suffering neither casualties nor damage. Japanese losses for the action included the aircraft carrier Shoho, a cruiser, and several other vessels, mostly transports, in addition to vessels seriously damaged. On the night of August 8, 1942, a force of Allied cruisers was caught in a surprise attack by Japanese destroyers and cruisers. In this action, known as the Battle of Savo Island, the R.A.N. lost the Canberra, the U.S.N. the cruisers Vincennes, Quincy and Astoria, all torpedoed—a severe blow for the Allies at a critical period in the war in the Pacific.

Commodore H. B. FARNCOMB, D.S.O., R.A.N., took command of the Australian squadron when Commodore J. A. Collins, R.A.N., was wounded in H.M.A.S. Australia off Leyte in October 1944. *Photo, R.A.N.*

During 1942 the Japanese began to harass lines of communication between Australia and the U.S., and Australian and American warships accounted for at least 8 submarines. On May 31 four midget submarines entered Sydney Harbour. They were detected by vessels of the auxiliary patrol and destroyed by Australian motor launches of the " Fairmile " type. Then came the turning-point in the Allied fortunes, with Australian victories in the Owen Stanley Range and at Milne Bay, and U.S. successes in Guadalcanal. The submarine menace was nullified by the convoy system, H.M. Australian ships escorting 6,000 vessels of 25 million tons with the loss of only 10 ships in one year of war. Numbers of Japanese warships and transports were destroyed in battles in the Solomons area, and the Allies swept into the offensive.

IN this offensive the R.A.N. has taken a leading part. Its policy for the last 18 months has been, broadly, to keep the sealanes open, while sending the larger units into battle. These " larger units " have been the heavy cruisers Shropshire (presented by the R.N. to replace the lost Canberra) and Australia, and the Australian-built "Tribal" type destroyers, Arunta and Warramunga. On November 29–30 the two last-named ships took part in the attack on Gasmata. The heavy cruisers and the two "Tribals" figured prominently in the attack on Arawe, New Britain. The assault transport (infantry landing ship) Westralia also played a great part.

When U.S. troops invaded the Admiralty Islands at Seeadler and Hauwei the Shropshire and Warramunga were in the van. Meanwhile the "N" class destroyers were serving with the Eastern fleet and took part in attacks on Sabang, Sumatra. The destroyer Quiberon then returned to join the R.A.N. in the Pacific, after a highly successful record in the Mediterranean. Approximately 12½ per cent of the total personnel of the R.A.N. were engaged in the landings at Tanamera, Hollandia, Aitape, and Humboldt Bay, when U.S. and Australian troops "leap-frogged" over hundreds of miles of Jap-occupied territory to Dutch New Guinea. Australian vessels engaged included the cruisers Shropshire and Australia, the destroyers Arunta and Warramunga, the assault transports Manoora, Westralia and Kanimbla, the armed surveying vessel Moresby, the rescue tug Reserve, the minesweepers Benalla and Shepperton, and two auxiliary vessels, Cape Leeuwin and Polaris. With H.M.A.S. Moresby, the two corvettes and the two last-named vessels formed a survey group which carefully mapped out the coastline prior to the Allied landings.

Bataan Has Joined Her Sisters

During the last few months most of the R.A.N. has returned for service in Pacific waters—Norman, Napier, and Nizam from the Eastern fleet, and minesweepers such as the Cairns, Ipswich, Tamworth, and Launceston, which did useful work in the Mediterranean. One of the latter, H.M.A.S. Bundaberg, played a lone hand in the occupation of Sek Island on April 26 of last year. The following day the same vessel in the company of the destroyer Vendetta and escorted by Fairmiles carried Australian troops to Madang and Alexishaven, which they occupied within a few hours. The first of the Australian-built frigates to arrive in New Guinea waters, the Barcoo, took part in the bombardment before the Australian occupation of Karkar Islands and Bunabun alongside minesweepers Stawell and Kapunda.

Today the R.A.N., fighting in the Pacific, is stronger than ever. All the "N" and "Q" class destroyers are there, and another Tribal, the Bataan, has joined her sisters, the forerunner of others. The minesweeper programme of 60 vessels has been completed, and frigates are coming off the stocks in ever-increasing numbers. More " Fairmiles " are being built to sweep what is left of the Japanese landing craft from the seas. At least 230 vessels have been built in Australian yards since the outbreak of war. A £6,750,000 graving dock, to accommodate the largest vessels in the British and U.S. fleets, has been built in Sydney (see illus. page 582), and a £1,000,000 dock at Brisbane. In the year from November 1942 to November 1943, 13,815,099 tons of Allied shipping were repaired in Australian docks. In December 1944 Admiral Sir Bruce Fraser's newly formed British Pacific Fleet based on Australia found a tough, strong, experienced R.A.N. ready — and proud and superbly equipped—to fight alongside it !

The next development in the progress of the R.A.N. will be the construction of a cruiser in a Commonwealth shipyard. As the guns and armour are to be made in Australia, this ship is likely to take five years to build.

Aussies Prepare to Erase Japs from the Pacific

ALREADY FAMED IN ACHIEVEMENT the Royal Australian Navy (see facing page), is preparing for the final show-down with the Japanese. Taking stores to the "gate" ships on boom-defence duty (1) at a Commonwealth port. An Australian Wren petty officer (2) checks Verey cartridges at a naval base. In action off New Guinea the gunner of a Fairmile motor launch takes a crack at the enemy with his ·50 Browning machine-gun (3). H.M.A.S. Bataan destroyer of the Tribal class (4), slides down the slipway. Guns of an Australian naval squadron supported Gen. MacArthur's landings on Luzon, Jan. 9, 1945.

Photos, Royal Australian Navy

New Line-Up of Armies to Crack Belgian Bulge

ACROSS THE ARDENNES SNOWS, U.S. troops, not yet issued with winter camouflage (see page 580), approach the front-line (1). British infantry—who, with armoured units, it was announced on January 4, 1945, had joined in to halt Von Rundstedt's drive—wait for the order to attack near Marche (2). Field-Marshal Montgomery (3), after taking over the U.S. 1st and 9th Armies in the salient in December 1944, with his generals. Left to right, Lieut.-Gen. Sir Miles Dempsey, G.O.C. British 2nd Army; Maj.-Gen. Hodges, U.S. 1st Army; "Monty"; Maj.-Gen. Simpson, U.S. 9th Army; General Crerar, Canadian 1st Army. A 155-mm. gun (4) of the U.S. 3rd Army being cleaned. Forces of the U.S. 1st and 3rd Armies, approaching from the north and west respectively, entered Houffalize, pivotal point of the bulge, on January 16. (See map p. 601.)

Photos, British Official; British Newspaper Pool, Fox

Gay Setting for Our Troops on Paris Leave

PALATIAL DINING-ROOM OF THE GRAND HOTEL, PARIS, provides a dazzling change for our fighting men on leave. They have been using it since the building was transformed into the Allied Expeditionary Forces Club. During the German occupation the French waiters refused to serve meals here, declaring that they did not wish to be killed by falling chandeliers in the event of R.A.F. raids. The real reason, of course, was their implacable hatred of the invaders.

Photo, Associated Press

The Price Norway is Paying for Her Liberation

After nearly five years of Nazi oppression and exploitation a piece of Norway almost as big as Scotland is being freed. But the cost of this newly-won liberty is high indeed, and how Norwegians are struggling to restore some semblance of normal life to their ruthlessly devastated country is told by R. B. NYQUIST in this article specially written for "The War Illustrated."

Do not imagine that that liberated territory is in any way comparable with other liberated parts of Europe. It is not, for Finmark, as the area is called, is the northernmost county in Norway, lies well within the Arctic Circle, and its civilization—the most northerly in the world—has been built up only at great cost and over a period of hundreds of years. The pre-war population of this vast tract of Arctic country was only about 60,000 people, mainly fishermen operating from the scores of little hamlets along the rugged coastline, and small farmers.

The liberation of Finmark has caused the deportation of nearly 40,000 of those people, and the almost complete destruction of their formerly prosperous little towns, fishing villages and farmsteads—even mountain holiday huts. Places like Berlevaag, Gamvik, Honningsvag, Hammerfest, Lakselv, and Alta no longer exist. This Arctic front—it may almost be called the forgotten front—is far away and the distances to it and on it are tremendous. Communications are few and the German destruction there has been thorough. Thus it is only now—over three months since Red Army troops stormed across the frontier in chase of Rendulic's Finnish Army, and put them and other German forces totalling altogether about 120,000 men to flight in North Norway—that a fairly complete picture of the situation in this Arctic country can be painted.

It is a grim picture, but one, nevertheless, which means the liberation of Norway has begun. If, however, the Germans are allowed to carry out their scorched earth policy down the whole length of Norway, the country will be ruined. As it is, it will be a great many years before economic life in Finmark can be resumed. Norwegian troops now in Finmark, working shoulder to shoulder with their Russian comrades-in-arms, are doing everything in their power to open up the communications which will allow them to get to grips with the Germans, who are now believed to be holding the Lyngenfjord line, north of Tromsö—about 600 miles from the starting point of the retreat. But Finmark is in the grip of Arctic winter, with deep snow and cold reaching as much as 30 degrees below zero. The only road has to be cleared of German-made devastation, bridges have to be rebuilt and ferries across the fjords devised. Every piece of material necessary to carry out these repairs has to be shipped great distances and then transported by road.

When Allied troops do catch up with the Germans, the latter may continue their withdrawal in a blaze of destruction, and this may well be carried right down the thousand-mile length of the country. Norwegians, therefore, believe that the only way to prevent complete devastation of Norway is by an Allied operation from the west—an operation which will sever the slim German communications, put a stop to premeditated destruction, and at the same time keep eight or ten divisions from the western front whither German soldiers in Norway are now making their way—and at their own pace. When the time comes for this operation, orders will be given to the Norwegian Forces of the Interior to cut the enemy lines of communication on land in order to drive the enemy out on to the sea. Crown Prince Olav, the Norwegian C.-in-C., has already told this to his countrymen at home.

The liberation of Norway began with the capture by the Red Army of Kirkenes, the Germans' biggest Arctic military base—it was a naval depot, army headquarters in the north, and Luftwaffe base from which attacks were made against the Russia-bound convoys. When this port fell after a brilliant Russian outflanking move, Rendulic, the German general who brought his Lapland army of about eight divisions out of Finland, knew that his position in Finmark had now become untenable. The Red Army was advancing right across Finland, which has an almost 600-mile-long frontier with Norway, and unless the Germans could pull right out of Finmark and North Tromsö they would be in danger of being cut off. Complete evacuation and a ruthless scorched earth policy was ordered. No shelter was to be left anywhere

Hr. TERJE WOLD, Minister of Justice and first member of the Norwegian Government to return to Eastern Finmark, Norway's northernmost province, until recently under the Nazi heel. *Photo, Royal Norwegian Govt.*

which could be used by the Russians—or the Norwegian civilians ; all food stocks, all boats, all cattle which could not be carried away as loot were to be destroyed.

The Germans were in such a hurry to get out of Eastern Finmark, however, that they did not have time to do all these things thoroughly. They fired Kirkenes before they fled—only 26 houses were left standing—and they destroyed the ironworks there (the damage to these works alone has since been estimated at over three million pounds). But the majority of the Norwegian civilians there escaped deportation. When the battle had approached, these people hid in the iron mines at Björnevatn, some miles outside Kirkenes, or in the countryside. Only those who could be rounded up immediately—such as prisoner of war slave workers—were driven westwards with the retreating army.

Between 18,000 and 20,000 Norwegian civilians in Eastern Finmark escaped, and hoisted their flags among the ruins, greeted the Russian soldiers as liberators, and then helped them in every possible way to continue their advance. The Germans pushed on westwards, and as they put some distance between themselves and the Russians their pace slowed and with devilish precision they began to destroy, loot, and round-up civilians. At every fishing port they reached they commandeered all seaworthy craft. Into these they packed as much war equip-

ment as they could ; if there was any remaining room civilians were crammed aboard to be taken hundreds of miles round the North Cape and down the stormy coast under unbearable conditions. Short of food, and suffering from exposure, a great army of men, women and children did not survive the nightmare journeys.

Those who were not deported by boat were ordered to march in columns. Nazi sadism was at its height during this evacuation. Norwegians were forced, just for the delight of the Germans, to watch their homes and their possessions go up in flames. People who refused to leave their homes were shot, and many who had managed to escape to the mountains were later hounded down and taken away. During the forced marches, sandwiched between Nazi troops in wagons and trucks, many Norwegians died. Hardy though they are, they could not face the rigours of days of forced marching over an Arctic road swept by a searing wind and fierce snowstorms. That, briefly, is what happened all the way from Vardö down to Tromsö. It was in Tromsö Fjord that the Tirpitz met her fate (see page 477).

Tromsö was the first assembly point, but the evacuation and deportation has by no means ceased here. Thousands of Norwegians are being funnelled farther south, and 200,000 are threatened. Meanwhile, all those German soldiers not required to hold the Lyngenfjord line are believed to be passing south by road and fishing boats to Mosjoen, the most northerly railhead in Norway. Then in comparative comfort those who are not needed are being taken back to Germany to defend the Fatherland.

Meanwhile, Norwegians in Finmark are struggling hard to restore some semblance of normal life. Norwegian troops were dispatched from this country as soon as the Russian advance became known, and at 10 a.m. on November 10, 1944, the first of them crossed the frontier from Russia into Norway. After nearly five years' impatient waiting and training in Britain they were on Norwegian soil again. Norwegian inhabitants had already begun to do everything they could to restore something approaching reasonable conditions, and public officials who had been removed by the Germans during occupation were reinstated. Since then the first urgently needed supplies of food, clothing, and medical requirements have arrived, but life is still far from easy.

Although it is believed that most of Norway north of the Lyngen Line is now clear of Germans—except perhaps for a few bands of S.S. rearguards left to complete their destruction—the coastline is by no means immune from further German terror actions. Of those Norwegians in liberated territory a large number are volunteering for the armed forces. They have something to avenge, and Hr. Terje Wold, Norwegian Minister of Justice, summed up their attitude when he said on his return from Finmark :

"The inhuman conduct of the Germans will undoubtedly have an influence on the fight of the Norwegians both at home and abroad. Anything is better than to let them burn our country unhindered, step by step. We will do everything we can to make our contribution towards preventing this from happening, and our view coincides completely with that of the Russians. Every possible effort from abroad, every reasonable counter-measure from within, must be made in Norway's continued fight."

Retreating Nazis in Finmark Burn and Destroy

IN NORWAY'S northernmost province of Finmark (see map) grim were the scenes as the Germans retreated before the Red Army advancing through Finland after the capture of Kirkenes on October 25, 1944. Driving the peasantry before them, the Germans burnt and destroyed savagely (see facing page).

For 4½ years the Germans' biggest Arctic base, Kirkenes, ice-free all the year round, was invaluable to them. In peacetime it supplied 70 per cent of Norway's iron ore. Not a house was left standing in Berlevaag (1) where of a population of 1,600 only 70 remained. At Gamvik this rough wood-and-earth structure (2), with an upturned boat for roof, housed eight people, two cows and a goat. King Haakon's proclamation announcing Soviet-Norwegian collaboration was read (3) at Havningberg. First Norwegian troops (4) marching into Kirkenes. Operating independently of direct Russian support, Norwegian forces were reported on Jan. 17, 1945, to have advanced 125 miles west of Kirkenes and to have captured the airfield at Banak.

Photos, Norwegian Official, Keystone

VIEWS & REVIEWS
Of Vital War Books

by Hamilton Fyfe

THERE is a fine phrase in the British official report on the Battle of El Alamein—a phrase with a touch of poetry in it which you don't expect to find in documents of this kind.

"The 9th Australian Division," it says, "put up a magnificent effort. They fought themselves and the enemy to a standstill, till flesh and blood could stand no more."

Well, what do you expect after that ? To be told that the Division had to be withdrawn or that the survivors were compelled by sheer physical exhaustion to surrender ? Not a bit of it. The report goes on—and here the touch of poetry comes in— "Then they went on fighting." Flesh and blood could stand no more, but "they went on fighting." Their persistence, their dogged refusal to allow Nature to call a halt to their efforts, contributed to the victory of El Alamein.

THAT illustrates one of the characteristics of the Australian soldier. Another is his astonishing adaptability. In a booklet recently published for the Australian Army Staff by H.M. Stationery Office, entitled The Australian Army at War (9d.), there is a brief, matter-of-fact reference to the adventures of a battalion cut off during the fighting in Greece, in April 1941, that ghastly blunder undertaken for mistaken reasons of political "honour." This battalion "withdrew to mountainous country and in small parties made its way to the coast. Some were captured, but a surprisingly large number reached safety. A substantial party, disciplined and under command of its own officers, arrived in Palestine months afterwards."

AUSTRALIAN COMMANDOS IN TIMOR —an illustration from the booklet reviewed in this page. The Commonwealth Government dispatched troops to help the Dutch hold this East Indian island in the Sundra group four days after the Japanese had struck at Pearl Harbour. *Photo, Australian Official*

I happen to know something about that journey lasting for months. I doubt if any other unit in any army could have done it. Not that the Australians were hardier, or braver, than other troops. It was their resourcefulness that stuck out, their quick acceptance of new conditions, their ingenious surmounting of obstacles, the mood half-playful, half-grim, in which they tackled the most tremendous difficulties. I wish the booklet could have gone into that adventure a little more fully.

I first came to understand the qualities of Australian soldiers when I stayed with them on the Somme in 1918. The earliest impression

The Australian Army at War

made on me then, before I had been with them twelve hours, was caused by the enormous amount of tea they drank. Tea first thing in the morning, tea last thing at night, tea at every meal and between meals. I had never seen anything like it—not even in Yorkshire. The old type of British Tommy, the Mulvaneys and Learoyds and Ortherises of Kipling's great book, Soldiers Three, would have sneered at this. But if they had gone into action with the Aussies, if they had been on patrol with them in No Man's Land on pitch-black nights, if they had gone with them to carry out the order, "Get some German prisoners !" and seen how they burst into the enemy trenches and secured their prey, from whom information was wanted—they wouldn't have sneered then : they would have admitted with enthusiasm that, like Alan Breck, in Stevenson's Kidnapped, every one was a "bonny fighter."

THEY seemed to know by instinct what to do. That was largely the explanation of what appeared to some observers of the old school to be lax discipline. Partly this was due to the absence among them of those stiff and stupid class distinctions which in so many armies keep officers and men apart. The Australian officer is like one of those people who in civil life are given authority in business or industry, in a steel-making plant or a shipbuilding yard. While they are on the job they exact instant obedience to orders, but off duty they put on no side ; they do not assume airs of social superiority—they are just men. This works so well in the Australian Army, as I have seen it work well also in the Russian army, that I should like to see it followed everywhere.

But, as I have suggested, it is partly the Australian soldier's instinct for knowing what to do which accounts for the less oppressive insistence on spit and polish, saluting, mechanical precision, which prevails among them. Once I had an amusing experience of the Aussie's ability to deal with any situation. Some British soldiers had secured a sheep's carcase, they were hungry, the meat would be in good condition—but they had no idea what to do with the sheep in order to get their teeth into that meat ! A few Australians happened along. Instantly they set to work, and within an hour or two a savoury stew was ready.

It is not altogether a result of wider experience. It owes a good deal to the sublime self-confidence of the Australian. He believes he

can do anything and if you believe that strongly enough you can. The Aussies don't sit down before obstacles. Sometimes they don't take enough time considering how best the impediment can be cleared away. They just go in and clear it away. In the jungle fighting on New Guinea this "dash-and-be-damned-to-you" spirit was vastly effective. No matter how toughly the Japanese tried to defend themselves, they had to give way time after time until the threat of an invasion of Australia had been finally removed.

HERE is one example of the swift and fierce actions in the New Guinea campaign. It was the Battle of Gorari, which gave to "an evil-smelling and unhygienic jungle the name of Death Valley." Five hundred Japanese fresh troops just brought into the line died there. Their lines of communication were systematically cut in several places and then "the Australians closed in, killing off the enemy in scores in almost continual close fighting. The bayonet was used and 150 Japanese protected by earthworks were killed in the first charge. Then followed the mopping-up and encirclement and destruction of pockets, trapping and annihilating an enemy who was still vicious when cornered."

The struggle across the Owen Stanley Range will be for ever famous in Australian history—and in the history of the British Commonwealth of Nations. As at Alamein, the Australian troops accomplished the impossible. They had Nature against them as well as the enemy. Whether in the mountains or on the coast when they had surmounted the ridge, everything in the way of weather and other natural conditions hampered and attacked them. Do you recollect how day after day at one period, which now seems far back, we used to hear of Buna and Gona, beach strongholds which were hard to get past ? No wonder they resisted a long time. The Japanese method of defending them was to build " a maze of earthworks and pill-boxes in the construction of which they used coconut palms. Trunks up to a foot in diameter formed cover for strongposts which were able to stand hits from even 25-pounders."

In these posts Japanese soldiers for weeks, ate, drank and slept in filthy pits only a few feet square. They obeyed the order to " stay there," and rarely showed any initiative or attempted to gain ground. " Reliefs, ammunition and stores were taken through a maze of communicating trenches four feet deep. They were living underground and fighting from almost impenetrable strongposts."

BUT the Aussies penetrated them one by one until they had cleared almost the whole island of the enemy. Their plan has been the same throughout and everywhere. " Attack, always attack.'' It was a dire necessity as well as a sure key to success. "It was completely beyond the capacity of a country with a population of only seven millions to defend even its most vulnerable areas, particularly as it had been committed to the maintenance of a substantial contribution to the Empire air programme and to the maintenance of its divisions abroad, while the small Australian Navy was largely on service in European waters."

There were twelve thousand miles of coastline and almost the entire population was settled in the east, south and south-west regions. The part of the country where the invader would have made his landing was sparsely inhabited and distances were enormous. "It was because of this that Australian strategy contemplated meeting the Japanese wherever he would make the fight outside the Australian mainland."

That strategy was sound and has been brilliantly put into operation. When the Japanese are at last disposed of, the credit for at all events the earlier part of their discomfiture will certainly go to the Australian Army and Air Force.

Battle Trails in Icy Skies

In support of Allied ground operations against Von Rundstedt, R.A.F. Bomber Command—despite widespread fog and bad weather —dropped nearly 10,000 tons during the first week of the breakthrough, from Dec. 17, 1944, and 14,000 tons from Dec. 24 to 31.

Homing from targets deep in Germany, a flight of Lancasters, unable to land on their own airfield, came down on this U.S.A. 8th Air Force heavy bomber base (above) guided by flares arching into the bitter sky and by ground-lights and welcome signals from the control tower. Fortresses are ready to take the air.

Our attacking fighters and bombers frequently return these winter days with airframes ice-encrusted, ground-crews chipping away the frozen burden as machines touch down. Silhouetted against the German sky (right) streaked with vapour trails from Allied and enemy planes engaged in a dog-fight on Christmas Day, this American A.A. battery waited to pick off an oncoming target.

Photos, P.N.A., U.S. Official

German Breakthrough in the Belgian Ardennes—

Pho

Field-Marshal Montgomery declared on Jan. 7, 1945, that Von Rundstedt's invading forces were " now being written off."
U.S. tank-destroyers (1) covered the Bastogne area as American troops forged slowly into the German salient. Dashing
tank commander of the U.S. 3rd Army, Lieut.-Col. Creighton Abrams, standing in the turret of his tank (2) gives orders
through the " mike " during the drive into Bastogne, whose defenders were provided with food and munitions by air (3).

— Stemmed on South Flank by Gen. Patton's Men

Covering the lower arc of the ominous bulge driven into the American lines in Belgium on Dec. 16, 1944, the 4th Armoured Division of Gen. Patton's U.S. 3rd Army smashed through from the south and on Dec. 27 relieved the elements of three divisions trapped in Bastogne for eight days. Parachutes were used to supply them: containers are seen (4) still attached. Vehicles of the relieving division lined up in the town square (5). An American corporal repairs a puncture in a tire of his jeep (6).

Burma's Chindwin Crossed

Closing weeks of 1944 saw substantial advances by Allied troops on all sectors of the Burma front. An important link-up was effected by the crossing of the Upper Chindwin River, near Sittaung, on Nov. 17 by British and Indian troops of the 4th Corps. Pushing east, these joined forces with the 36th British Division during the week ending Dec. 15. Between those dates the 4th Corps captured vital townships on the Mandalay railway. Preparing for the crossing (left) that won the Chindwin bridge-head, with mules, horses and jeeps lined up on the bank. Troops of a Welsh regiment safely over (below).

Photos, British Official

I Helped the 14th Army in Burma to Laugh

Write to them as frequently as possible. Send them newspapers and magazines, razor blades and shaving soap and toothpaste. This urgent suggestion is offered to relatives and friends of the gallant 14th Army by that great-hearted comedian STAINLESS STEPHEN, who has been among the men and has written this light-hearted chronicle specially for "The War Illustrated."

ON March 2, 1944, under the light of a full moon, a bowler-hatted comedian, using two tank transporters as a stage, was giving a show to 5,000 assorted fighting men near a certain Milestone on the Imphal-Kohima road. Fifteen weeks later, to the very day, at that self-same spot, the 4th Corps, driving north from Imphal, met the 33rd Corps, working south from Kohima. The Japanese dream of a speedy conquest of India had been shattered—General "Bill" Slim's 14th Army had won a great victory. Something else had died during those four months besides 50,000 Japanese, namely, the idea that the foe was invincible in his own chosen terrain of the jungle.

What sort of men are these who so decisively smashed the enemy? It has been my privilege, as that bowler-hatted comedian, to do a hundred shows before a hundred thousand of the "Forgotten 14th." From Calcutta I flew direct to Imphal, using a basha as headquarters for several weeks. Here I met the B.O.R. (British Other Rank), which initials distinguish him from the I.O.R. (Indian Other Rank).

In the Jungle for Thirty Months

Exposure to sun and air has turned them the colour of teak, and they are as tough. It's an individual war out there: personal initiative counts more than anything. No overwhelming artillery barrage precedes the attack. The enemy must be winkled out of his bunkers by hand-to-hand fighting of the cloak-and-dagger variety. The Jap is a fanatical warrior whose ambition is to die for his Emperor; and with the co-operation of the 14th Army many thousands of them have realized that ambition. And rather than surrender, the "Nip" commits hari-kiri by blowing himself up with one of his own grenades.

"Smile Awhile," the first E.N.S.A. outfit to play to the 14th, gave a series of shows on the Imphal sector. We appeared, often, in the open; at other times in wigwams made of bamboo poles interlaced with rushes. Capacity was infinity; sometimes there were as many behind the stage as in front. As the shows were free, no seats were reserved. Armed with rifles, Bren guns and knives, the audience squatted on the mud floor of the basha. At a well-known spot near Palel we entertained a famous Highland regiment, the majority of whom had been in the jungle for thirty months. Little wonder they listened to us open-mouthed, for we recalled memories of a dim, pre-war existence.

IN the River Chindwin area, I left Imphal at daybreak and sped in the Corps General's car via Palel to Tamu. By the way, this road is one of the outstanding engineering achievements of all times. Whoever designed it must have been a snakes-and-ladders specialist. There were hairpin bends every hundred yards, and in fifty miles we climbed 4,000 feet. Dust was three feet deep most of the way; talk about "sand in your shoes," I had grit in my gizzard, and the continual swaying of the car round innumerable bends made me feel more dizzy than any blonde. However, we reached Tamu, eighty miles in five and a half hours.

The only building left there was a derelict Buddhist temple. Not a soul was to be seen, and I almost trod on the General's aide-de-camp, the fox-hole being used as Divisional Headquarters was so well camouflaged. After the inevitable mug of char, I was shown the stage—an ammunition box, and

the rest was up to me. The audience had appeared as though by magic from the dense tropical undergrowth. You may have read in books about the silence of the jungle; it's a myth. Myriads of cigalas, a species of grasshopper, combine to make a shrill ear-piercing screech. Add to this the raucous squawks of gaily plumaged birds, and you have some idea of this eerie jungle atmosphere. Two more shows to some Chindits and anti-tank gunners, and I left by jeep for my deepest penetration into Burma.

THIRTY miles down the Sittaung road brought me to my fourth audience, a West-Country infantry regiment who were awaiting my arrival in Devon Wood, overlooking the banks of the Chindwin. Here hundreds of chattering monkeys swung in

SOUTH WALES BORDERER after nearly a week of constant patrol in Burma—typical of the grand men whom the inimitable Stainless Stephen has entertained "on the spot." See also page 492. *Photo, British Official*

the trees above us, one of the noisiest galleries I have experienced. Incidentally, during all these performances, sentry groups were posted round about in case we were disturbed by roving Japanese patrols. And that particular matinee audience had to withdraw many miles towards Tamu that same night to escape infiltration. I used to tell the troops that the initials E.N.S.A. meant "Every night something 'appens," and there it almost did. I was so near the Japs they could hear my teeth chattering.

And so back to the airstrip with me less Stainless than ever, in my coating of Burmese dust. Here, standing on the bonnet of a jeep, which was so burning hot I had to mark time all through my 40 minutes show, I staggered through my fifth performance to these fellows behind the back-of-beyond, just as the sun was setting. Remember, there is no twilight in Burma; darkness and stand-to were close at hand, and the jungle was no place for a solitary civilian. Overhead sounded a familiar drone, and silhouetted against the sun was a welcome sight—the Harvard that was to fly me back to Imphal.

Tired? Yes, I'd had it! No wonder, 150 miles massage by road, 70 miles by plane,

five shows, not one of them less than forty minutes, and all in a temperature of over a hundred degrees. But it was worth it; my memories will never fade of those jungle warriors, second to none, in their lonely outposts of Empire. En passant, I had no trouble whatever with piano or microphone, for the reason that they didn't exist.

What did I say to these men? What did they laugh at? I usually began with a gentle leg-pull describing the delights of India in general and the Burma front in particular; how I'd have to change my name from Stainless to Spineless if I did any more jeeping. I told them I'd eaten so many soya links (sausages made from soya beans) that I'd had to report sick with square tonsils. Incidentally, many of these men have never tasted spam—bully-beef is their stand-by. Scotsmen were more than interested to hear that Scotch whisky was so scarce in Britain that when a "wee hauf" was poured on the haggis at the Burns' supper, the haggis stood up and sang "Mother Machree." Or so 'twas said!

Bend Down to Let the Moon Pass

Gags on the personalities of the unit were sure-fire. To wind up, I crooned an original ditty, "News from the Homeland," which included couplets about the principal cities and towns at home, a rapid comic survey of the British Isles. I promised the boys that I would contact their relatives at home whenever possible (so far I've met over 3,000), and concluded by inviting them to join me in a pint as soon as possible. Recently in Plymouth five gunners from Imphal turned up, which is the reason my wife's housekeeping allowance was cut somewhat.

My farewell performance on this part of the front was at Kohima, 7,000 feet up in the Chin Hills. At nights here it was almost necessary to bend down to let the moon pass! Half of our audiences were convalescents from the rest camp, who, with the Royal West Kents and the Assam Rifles, held out against vastly superior enemy forces for thirteen days in the fiercest hand-to-hand fighting on the whole front.

I next worked my way north via Dibrugarh as far as Ledo, about 200 miles from the borders of China. Here we had very cosmopolitan audiences, British, Americans, Indians, West Africans, Chinese and a platoon of sun-worshippers from Manchester! American military police, complete with tommy-guns, acted as ushers. I should like to mention that American audiences were always most appreciative.

AFTER flying back to Calcutta I took the air again, for the Arakan front, in south Burma. Here I did 22 shows in seven days. My total kit comprised a bowler-hat, shaving outfit, toothbrush and mosquito net. At Bawli Bazaar the audience numbered 4,000: the Corps Commander sat on the ground amongst his troops. This was a cine-variety show. A three-tonner vehicle was my stage, and I stood in the light of the projector of the portable cinema. And did the insects buzz round! The high spot of my appearances hereabouts was on one of the peaks of the Mayu mountains, to some Scottish troops. To reach them I had to motor up the "jeep-track" gradient of one in two. On Easter Sunday I did five shows, visited two casualty clearing stations, and attended two church services. On this part of the front I lived in fox-holes for five nights, with plenty of rifle fire at night to remind me that there was a war on!

George Medals for These Factory Heroes

ALMOST INCREDIBLE BRAVERY amid flames 2,000 feet high, bursting bombs and red-hot metal, in an explosion at the Royal Ordnance Factory, Hereford, on the night of May 30, 1944, was reported in The London Gazette of January 9, 1945, which announced the award of two O.B.E.s, five George Medals, and nine British Empire Medals to gallant members of the staff ; fifteen others were Commended for brave conduct. The fire started inside a large filled bomb and spread to other bombs, mines, and a container of explosive. The bomb split and exploded, sending up a sheet of flame 2,000 feet high. White hot girders and concrete blocks were flung over a wide area. Other explosions followed, and the filling house was completely demolished.

"The spirit of the factory was magnificent," stated the Gazette. "The staff and workers who were off duty hurried to help. Women ambulance drivers and stretcher-bearers ignored the risks of blast, debris, and further explosions. The men of the Factory Fire Brigade faced the risk of death and fought heroically to give the mass of workers time to get to the shelters."

REALIZING that the danger was focussed in an area within which a thousand tons of powerful explosives were housed, and that any spot therein upon which burning debris fell would be a source of extreme peril, the factory Superintendent, Mr. R. E. D. Ovens (awarded the O.B.E.) at once set up his headquarters in the open, and conducted operations throughout the night. His " courage, coolness and resource, his complete disregard of his own safety in his concern for the lives of the workers and his selfless devotion to duty," stated the official account, " were beyond praise." Meanwhile, inside the blazing building astonishing feats were being performed by members of the staff.

THE Director-General of Filling Factories, Mr. C. S. Robinson, in presenting the ribbons of the awards in the factory canteen on January 9, revealed that some of the men, including Fireman Davies, Mr. F. J. Tyler and Mr. J. W. Little (whose heroic deeds are described in greater detail below) poured sand or water into the open mouth of the blazing bomb for 20 minutes, knowing that at any moment they might be blown to pieces.

It was also disclosed that thirty-one 2,000-lb. bombs, or their equivalent in mines, exploded. Yet, despite this and thanks to the incomparable heroism of the firemen and the workers, only two people were killed. Between 700 and 800 operatives were evacuated from the factory to safety during the holocaust.

H. E. DAVIES

This fireman (right) tried to deflect with his hands fire-blanketing " foam " into the bomb where the blaze had originated. When no more foam was available he seized a hose and played water on the bomb casing until this was red-hot and the contents were shooting out. He then rushed for the emergency doors, stopped, and returned, intending to get the hose right into the bomb. Before he could do so it exploded, and he was blown out of the building and covered with debris. Rescued by F. J. Tyler (below), he was being taken to an ambulance when another explosion occurred. He at once returned to the scene, to rescue another fireman trapped in the wreckage. In spite of yet another explosion he saved his comrade.

F. A. LEWIS

Assistant Fire Brigade Officer at the factory, whose " energy, grit and determination seemed inexhaustible. Under his leadership his men returned again and again to face almost incredible risks." When the building collapsed about him he got out, assisting other injured firemen and leading them into an explosive store which was on fire ; ordering his men to spray him, he forced open the red-hot steel doors, which had become jammed, and got the fire under control. After the explosion, in which he was flung 30 yards out of the building, he fought one fire after another, inspiring his men.

FREDERICK J. TYLER

A process-worker, this fire-fighter was directing a hose on the blazing bomb when it exploded. He was blown through the emergency door and pinned under debris. Recovering consciousness, and despite severe injuries, he dragged hot debris, metal girders, and a part of the collapsed roof off Fireman Davies (above), saving his life. Tyler himself was then taken away in an ambulance.

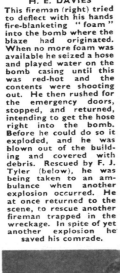

JAMES WINTER LITTLE

This Senior Overlooker was assisting in efforts to extinguish the contents of the red-hot bomb when it exploded. He was tossed into the air, over the bomb rack, hit a girder and was flung against the wall before dropping to earth. He was severely injured. Said the citation, " He displayed outstanding courage, tenacity and devotion to duty."

Photos, British Official

ST. VINCENT DE LISLE CAREY

He led a party of stretcher-bearers straight to the inferno as flames and white-hot explosives were shooting through the roof. A number of bombs exploded, the building collapsed, men were blown in every direction. Though badly injured he had set to work rescuing them when another explosion blew him out of the corridor. He displayed " courage and cool judgement in the highest degree."

Where Kesselring's Fierce Attack Was Held

Lieut.-Gen. L. K. TRUSCOTT, Jr., who succeeded Gen. Mark Clark as Commander of the 5th Army on the latter's promotion to C.-in-C. Allied Forces in Italy, announced on Nov. 26, 1944.

IN THE SAN CLERMONTE SECTOR in Italy, this 5th Army gunner (1) built his own winter quarters from stones, sandbags and tarpaulins. Snow-canopied transport line a roadside in the Serchio Valley (2) where the 5th Army held Kesselring's strong counter-blows in late December 1944. Of stout assistance in the campaign were snow-clearing men of the African Pioneer Corps (3). Mortar platoon (4) with the 8th Army advancing north of Faenza.

Photos, British Official; Associated Press. Map by courtesy of The Times

The Story of the Little Bronze Cross for Valour—

The most famous decoration in the world—the highest of its kind—the Victoria Cross is but an ounce of bronze. But the award itself is without price. This story of its record up to the present day—told by J. M. MICHAELSON—is of particular interest in connexion with the series of portraits of V.C.s which have appeared in "The War Illustrated" since its commencement

ANOTHER stirring chapter in the history of the Victoria Cross was written recently, when a D.C.M. awarded for a very courageous act in battle was later replaced by the higher award of a V.C. (C.S.M. Peter Wright—see illus. p. 478). It is believed that this was at least partly on the suggestion of H.M. the King, who had personally decorated the soldier concerned.

All honours come from the King, but the V.C. is peculiarly a royal honour. The idea of a new cross as a decoration for the highest courage in the face of the enemy was Queen Victoria's, and each sovereign subsequently has contributed something to the V.C. and the manner in which it is awarded. Apart from the original idea, Queen Victoria personally suggested the nobly simple words "For Valour" on the cross. The first suggestion was that the wording should be "For the Brave." Queen Victoria objected that this might lead to the inference that only those who received the Cross were brave. After some thought she suggested "For Valour," and no one had any doubt it was a happy inspiration.

King Edward VII secured a change in the warrant governing the conditions, by which the V.C. could be awarded posthumously. Previously, the rule had been that if a man died during the performance of an act that might entitle him to a V.C., or at any time before the Cross was presented, the Cross was withheld although the record remained. Many V.C.s since have been awarded posthumously, the presentation as a rule being made to the next-of-kin.

KING GEORGE V, who presented 633 V.C.s for supreme acts of courage in the war of 1914-1918, changed the warrant so that it was not restricted to men in the fighting services but could be given to anyone performing an act of great courage "in the face of the enemy," with the proviso that the individual was acting under someone in the regular services. This made women and even civilians eligible in certain circumstances. The actual words of the supplementary warrant speak of "every grade and rank of all grades of all branches of H.M. Forces, British and Colonial." Eligibility, originally confined to men in the home forces, had already been extended to Indian soldiers by a change in the rules in 1911. In the present war, at the time of writing, there have been 17 V.C.s awarded to members of the Indian Army, 22 to members of the Dominion Forces and one to a member of a Colonial Force—that of Fiji.

It is not easy to visualize conditions in which a civilian could receive the Cross, and it was for this reason that the King instituted the George Cross in 1940, for gallantry in air raids in this country and not in face of the enemy as with the V.C. In spite of the great number of women in the military nursing services, the W.R.N.S., the A.T.S. and the W.A.A.F., conditions under which a heroic act might be performed within the scope of the V.C. do not often occur and no award has so far been made to a woman.

The V.C. was officially announced on January 29, 1856, and the first awards were made in the following year when a considerable number of the Crosses were presented simultaneously. Altogether in the "minor wars" of the 19th century and the Boer War, 525 V.C.s were presented; and the fact that only some 120 have been awarded in the present war reflects the very high standard of courage required and, perhaps, the changing conditions of war in which individual heroism counts less than "team work."

Crosses Made from Crimean Cannon

The first V.C.s were struck from the metal of Russian cannon captured at Sebastopol during the Crimean war and the custom remained until early in the present war, the supply of this metal ran out. It is now supplied by private contract. Unlike all other medals, the V.C. is not struck at the Mint, but made by a private firm of London jewellers. They made the first V.C. and have continued to make the Crosses ever since. In a special ledger is recorded the name of every man for whom a Cross has been made, the number now totalling well over 1,200. The first entry is Charles David Lucas, a midshipman who in 1854 handled a burning shell to save his ship and comrades.

VALUE of the metal is about threepence, and the weight is one ounce. The award itself is, of course, without price. It is recognized not only in Britain but all over the world as the hardest honour to win. It has never been made "cheap" by numerous awards and is harder to win now, perhaps, than ever it was. Courage is always hard to grade, and the special committee who have the task of deciding finally about recommendations, even when they have ensured that only recommendations complying with the warrant are considered, can have no easy task. It must not be forgotten, also, that many acts of great courage in modern warfare are performed when there are no witnesses who survive. The exact words of the warrant are " some

signal act of valour or devotion to the Country" performed in the face of the enemy. "Signal" means, presumably, outstanding, and it is therefore not enough to perform an act of great heroism. It must be outstanding. For a short period during the last century the warrant was amended so that acts of gallantry not in the face of the enemy could be rewarded; one such award was made—to a soldier after a Fenian raid in Canada.

ORIGINALLY the ribbon of the V.C. was dark red if the wearer was in the Army, blue if he was in the Navy. The institution of the R.A.F. would have called for a third colour. Instead, a single colour for all the Forces was decided upon. Today, the V.C. ribbon is always dark red. When the ribbon is worn without the medal, a miniature V.C. is in the centre. If a bar to the V.C. has been awarded, a second miniature Cross is added to the ribbon. A bar to the V.C. has been awarded only twice in the history of the decoration: to Captain Chevasse (second award was posthumous), and Lieut.-Col. A. Martin-Leake, both of the R.A.M.C.

Crosses are not made individually for each recipient. A very small number are kept in stock and sent as required to the Service Ministries. The V.C., is, of course, the most treasured of decorations, but occasionally one has come into the saleroom. The prices paid have varied from £50 to £170. A Cross is not permitted to be sold until after the death of the recipient. Every winner of the Victoria Cross not an officer receives automatically ten pounds a year, and a bar to the decoration brings another five pounds a year. Where there is need, up to £50 a year can be given by the terms of the warrant.

FOR those who have never seen a V.C., technical details will be of interest. Name, rank and unit of the recipient are engraved on the reverse of the clasp. The date of the act which won the Cross is on the reverse of the Cross itself. The clasp is decorated with a "laureated spray," and when there is a bar to the V.C. it is of similar design to the clasp fixed half-way up the riband. The V.C. is worn before all decorations or insignia of any kind.

There have been a number of pleas in the Press for more V.C.s to be awarded. During the first years of this war, the number of V.C.s averaged only one a month, compared with twelve a month in the war of 1914-18. The number of Crosses awarded has increased recently, and a short time ago five awards were announced on a single day.

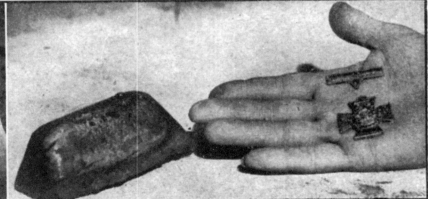

MAN WHO MAKES THE CROSSES is Alec Forbes, 60-year-old London craftsman, seen (left) moulding his 751st. He has cast all the crosses for the past 40 years. Fifty can be moulded from this one bronze ingot (right). The metal originally used was from cannon captured during the Crimean war; now the bronze is supplied by private contract. This highest possible award for heroism was instituted in 1856, and first awards were made a year later. Since 1920 it has been extended to include nurses and civilians.

Photos, G.P.U.

—And Seven Brave Men Who Have Lately Won It

Cpl. SIDNEY BATES
When troops of the Royal Norfolk Regiment were sorely pressed in Normandy in August 1944, Corporal Bates, armed with a Bren gun, charged the enemy single-handed, firing from the hip until mortally wounded.

Wing-Cmdr. G. L. CHESHIRE, D.S.O. (2 bars), D.F.C.
Described as "probably the greatest bomber pilot of any Air Force in the world." Wing-Commander Cheshire accomplished daring low-flying exploits. Awarded the V.C. on Sept. 9, 1944.

Naik YESHWANT GHADGE
This N.C.O. of the 5th Mahratta Light Infantry captured an enemy machine-gun post single-handed, in Italy in July 1944, killing its crew before himself being killed by snipers. His was the first Mahratta V.C.

Captain MICHAEL ALLMAND
Hero of two magnificent exploits in Burma, in June 1944, in which, though in great pain, he inspired his men to capture two important bridges, this officer of the 6th Gurkha Rifles later died from wounds.

Cpl. SEFANAIA SUKANAIVALU
The first Fijian V.C. of the war, this N.C.O. of the Fiji Infantry Regiment fell badly wounded while rescuing casualties under fire in the Solomon Islands, in June 1944. To dissuade his comrades from endangering their lives by attempting to rescue him, he raised himself before the enemy—and was riddled with bullets.

Coy. Havildar-Major CHHELU RAM
Though mortally wounded in Tunisia in April 1943, this N.C.O. of the 6th Rajputana Rifles rallied his company to hold a vital outpost with only bayonets and stones. This is the only known portrait of Chhelu Ram.

Major DAVID VIVIAN CURRIE
Of the Canadian Armoured Corps, Major D. V. Currie (right) is seen being congratulated on his V.C. award, by the Commander of the 1st Canadian Army. In three days and nights of fierce fighting in August 1944, near Falaise, Major Currie and his small force cost the Germans seven tanks, 12 88-mm. guns, 40 vehicles, 300 dead, 500 wounded and 2,100 prisoners.

Photos, British, Indian and Canadian Official, Daily Mirror, Planet News

Nazis Failed to Establish Greenland Radio Base

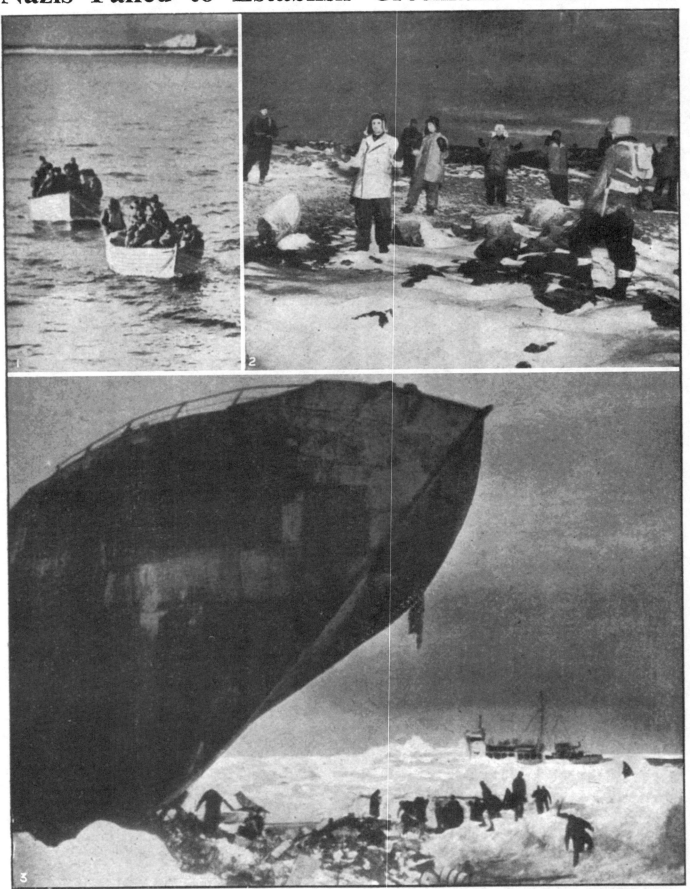

THREE DETERMINED ATTEMPTS by the Germans, between July and October 1944, to establish radio and meteorological bases on Greenland were foiled by U.S. Coast Guards, the enemy losing three armed trawlers, their equipment and over 60 officers and men. After scuttling their ship, the Nazis approached the U.S. combat cutter which had trapped their trawler in the ice (1) ; while others (2) surrendered their gear. The cutter Northland (3, in background) hemmed in the ice this German trawler after a 70-mile chase.   PAGE 600   *Photos, Planet News, Associated Press*

I WAS THERE!

Eye Witness Stories of the War

British Fought Like Tigers at the Ardennes Tip

Operating under Field-Marshal Montgomery's new command, troops - mostly of the British 6th Airborne Division—in early January 1945 battled magnificently for the fortress-village of Bure, at the extreme tip of the northern section of Von Rundstedt's salient in Belgium, which Hitler's crack 2nd Panzer Grenadiers fought like madmen to hold. The action is described by Richard McMillan, B.U.P. war correspondent.

I WATCHED them go into action in a wilderness of snow and ice resembling the Russian front at its worst. The Germans hung on at the cost of great bloodshed until they were forced back yard by yard by the superior fighting power and superhuman valour of the British. For a whole day and a whole night the British hurled themselves in waves against the fiercely defended fortress into which Bure had been converted.

The fighting was grim, but it was hardly grimmer than the weather. The whole battlefield was like a cake of ice, with snow several inches deep and a frost which turned the normally gentle landscape of the Ardennes into a scene of iron. Against this background, fierce for human beings but fairy-like as the snowclad trees and frosted hedges sparkled in the light of the gun flashes, the town of Bure stained the white night with a thunderous flame. The British attacked just before dawn, and were thrown back. They went in again, held a few houses, attacked again, and got to the other end of the village.

Tribute to 'Those British Boys!'

There they were cut off. Then their comrades smashed through the snow and ice and the hail of death from the German self-propelled guns, tanks and spandaus to start the battle all over again. So it went on throughout the day. At one time it looked as if those deadly self-propelled guns, shoehorned into the ruins of the once-pleasant wooded village, would win the day. We took a heavy toll of the enemy, but our dead lay there, too, many of them, sprawled across the roads or huddled gruesomely in ditches. Our tanks, too, had gone to ground. Flames from their idle hulks added to the fury of the inferno which blotched the silvery hills and valleys of a Christmas-card scene. Fresh troops are now forging forward to consolidate the ground gained and drive the enemy back towards Grupont.

Two platoons which had been cut off at the eastern end of the village were relieved, but they, too, had casualties. The Germans had turned tanks at the closest range against the houses in which they sheltered. Their gallant resistance alone is described as an epic. But they knew the quality of their comrades, and knew that they were never forsaken. It was the spirit of Arnhem all over again, only this time with the certainty of victory for us. A U.S. officer who came up from the scene of that bloody shambles exclaimed : "You couldn't believe it unless you had seen it, that human beings could fight like these British boys. They are tigers ! "

As I went up towards the line the crags of the Ardennes peaks showed as patches of grim grey through the white. Then we came on scenes of war. German tanks and tracked troop carriers were smouldering, making black smudges in the quiet glades. Next we came on a team of London gunners, struggling and slipping uphill with their huge lorries dragging medium guns to the tops of the peaks to add to the bedlam which reached our ears more clearly every minute from the other side of the hills. "I think we'd manage better with skis or sledges !" remarked a man from Balham. Theirs looked like an impossible task—this struggle to haul those steel monsters from the valleys up these icy passes. But they won through.

Then I met a group of three solitary British soldiers. They came down from the snows where they had been on patrol, seeking out any stray German skulking in the higher woodlands. They too could crack a joke in the glacial grip of this Arctic battle scene. One of them, Corporal George Oakes, told me, "I come from Old Trafford, Manchester. I'd sooner be having a game there than playing these winter sports !" "As for me," grinned Lance-Corporal Harold Leader, from Street, Somerset, "I just wish I could get some real Somerset cider !" And a lad from Birmingham said, "We've seen Monty on the job. He looked in grand fettle as he tramped through the snow, chatting as usual with the men." That was the spirit I found everywhere among the troops—not only in the British but also in the American sector—tremendous élan because of the knowledge that Field-Marshal Montgomery had taken over.

Frozen and Terrified Prisoners

Americans with whom I talked all told me, "We know how highly you British rate Monty, but we know his value, too. He led you to victory in the desert, but don't forget he led both us Americans and the British in Normandy. Of course we're bucked, and already he is producing the goods." And so I went on over the pass and down to the battlefield. A group of German prisoners came past, shivering and looking hungry and terrified. The guards told me they had found them wandering in the snow. "It was too much for them," they said. "They'd had a night out and were freezing to death, so they came in with their hands up." But that did not mean those still in the line were not tough. "They are fighting more savagely than ever !" a British major told me. From the snow and dirt-blackened shell of the still smouldering village, sparks and eddies of smoke drifted up towards a sky of Alpine blue.

In the Front-Line Foxholes North of Bastogne

The way Allied troops were living and fighting and dying in snowbound foxholes on the southern flank of the German bulge into Belgium makes this Western Front battle a grim narrative indeed. Vividly the "atmosphere" is translated into words by Walter Farr, war correspondent of the Daily Mail, in this dispatch dated January 8, 1945. See also illus. pages 592-593.

I THINK I've found the war's worst job. It is worse than dodging flying bombs, worse than being fired on by rockets, worse than making a landing on a hostile beach, worse than fighting in submarines or bombing a well-defended target in a plane or attacking Japs in the jungle.

The war's worst job is fighting this winter battle in a frozen front-line foxhole out among the snow-covered hills north of

FIELD-MARSHAL MONTGOMERY'S EMERGENCY COMMAND is shown (left) facing General Bradley's 12th Army Group across Rundstedt's narrowing Ardennes salient on January 10, 1945. British troops, as narrated above, fought with magnificent gallantry at Bure, which was finally freed by the same date. Hooded crews mounted their Churchills (right) for a successful thrust in the Marche area : the attack began on January 4 from the line Marche-Hotton, in support of the U.S. 1st Army assault from Hotton. PAGE 601 *Photo, British Official. Map, Evening News*

NEAR BASTOGNE, IN THE ARDENNES SALIENT, these men of an armoured division were moving up on the U.S. 3rd Army front to dig for themselves foxholes in the snow-covered ground. Writing from the front on January 10, 1945, war correspondent Alan Moorehead declared that had Americans lost Bastogne " there was a reasonable chance of the Germans sweeping through to the coast and taking Antwerp, which would have meant the encirclement of the British armies." See also illus. pages 592-593.
Photo, U.S. Official

Bastogne. When you try to size up what this Western Front fighting is all about I advise you to consider the way our men out here in the foxholes are living and fighting in their first real winter war.

I came up to snowbound "Foxhole Row" today to get its story. For whether Rundstedt keeps on coming or is smashed depends very little on the high strategic talk back in the rear areas and very much indeed on "Foxhole Row."

"Foxhole Row," of course, runs—apart from a few gaps—for five or six hundred miles from the North Sea to the Mediterranean. At the moment this part in front of Bastogne is the worst of it and the job here is about the toughest. To get to "Foxhole Row," Bastogne, you park your jeep two or three miles behind it and walk down a road swept by the enemy guns. You take a narrow, slippery path between the wrecks of Jerry tanks, step over a dog that got its head blown off, turn left past a shell-shattered wayside crucifix, and cross the brow of a hill.

"Foxhole Row," Bastogne, is the extreme tip of the Patton pincer and a very sharp tip it is, too. The occupants took up residence 19 days ago, and for 19 days and, most unpleasant of all, 19 nights they have stuck it out. These "undesirable residences" have no heating at all, no running water laid on, no modern conveniences, but plenty of modern inconveniences.

Back at Division and Army Headquarters they told me that some foxhole occupants get little heaters and can keep quite warm with them and even make tea or coffee. "Foxhole Row," in fact, has got no little heaters or anything like that. You keep warm by taking a brisk walk out on patrol in no man's land or by half-burying yourself in the straw and twigs in the bottom of your foxhole.

Science of Foxhole ' Comfort '

Each hole is approximately 6 ft. long, 3 ft. wide, and 3 ft. deep. It takes just over an hour to dig, though men have been known to dig holes in 20 minutes or even less when under fire. Having dug deep enough you put in a three- or four-inch layer of small twigs. Then, if you can get it, you put in a four- or five-inch layer of clean straw over the twigs.

You drive in a wooden stake, cut from the nearest bush, at each corner and rest a piece of board on top of the stakes, filling in the spaces round about with earth. Over all that you put a piece of white cloth, to make your foxhole look part of the snow-covered hill.

The temperature has been around zero for weeks, and standing guard is hard going.

You stare out across the snow. By day, after you've stared at the great, white, unbroken landscape for hours, you begin to see "Germans" all over the place. A flurry of snow blown up on the crest of a hill by the wind looks like a German raiding party. You can look at a snow-covered bush or a shrub 400 yards away and slowly convince yourself it is a crouching German. The wind, the whiteness, and the cold strain your eyes.

Often it is difficult to move about enough to keep warm or keep awake, yet you cannot relax, for a swarm of German tanks and infantry can, and occasionally does, take you completely by surprise. "Foxhole Row" thinks the winter nights much worse than the days. Out on patrol, every crunch your feet make in the snow sounds so loud you are sure the waiting enemy can't fail to hear you. And when you are listening for enemy patrols every noise sounds like a footstep.

The Germans have devised some little tricks intended to annoy our men in "Foxhole Row." Sometimes, in the middle of the blackest night, a huge German police dog comes bounding at you. The Germans facing us have a lot of such well-trained dogs.

Astonishingly enough, not a man up here in "Foxhole Row" has a cold or cough, thanks, I believe, to their tremendous stamina and the fact that, as good soldiers, they have quickly learnt how to look after themselves.

Most of the people in "Foxhole Row" haven't had such a thing as a whisky, a cognac, a drop of gin, or even of beer, since they came here. Five of them went down the hill to a house in the valley this morning because they thought they saw a face flash past one of its broken windows. They surprised 20 Germans, brought them back, and eagerly seized two pleasant-looking bottles they were carrying.

The bottles had no labels, but they gave promise of whisky. "Foxhole Row" was excited—but they turned out to be full of vinegar! " Foxhole Row's" opinion of the fighting ability of the Germans—and it is worth noting carefully—is that they don't fight as well as they used to, but that they can still put up a remarkably good show. The bitter cold here not only freezes the soldiers' feet. Unless they're careful it freezes the oil in their guns. It even freezes the water in their water bottles.

Mud-Slogging with the 5th Army in the Apennines

No swift, spectacular advances are being made in the British part of the 5th Army sector in Italy. It would be miraculous if things were otherwise, for weather and ground conditions are almost incredibly bad. In this story, dated December 30, 1944, a Military Observer writes of seas of mud, rocky gorges and appalling hills, cantankerous mules, and ordeals of the wounded on their way to the dressing-stations.

BRITISH troops for three months now have been pushing forward, hill by hill (some of them higher than Snowdon), under filthy weather conditions, through the barren fastness of this Apennine range. The prize of the rich Lombardy plain is now within sight, tantalizingly close, but there are still more hills and a tenacious enemy to overcome before our men plant their feet finally on flat ground.

The other day I went forward almost as far as one can get. To reach there one has to climb through a range of mountains some 3,000 feet high, over a narrow, twisting road spread with a coffee-coloured soufflé of treacherous mud which conceals a multitude of potholes. This road is the supply route for two divisions. One grinds up through the clouds, wearing chains on one's wheels, past what was once a pine forest. Woodcutters have finished what American artillery began, and now all that is left of the tall trees is an expanse of splintered stumps, not un-

like the masts of a vast, derelict shipyard. One then loops down into a valley, passes through a long, rocky gorge down the sides of which waterfalls tumble, like skeins of white wool, and climbs again up a road even more atrocious, until one can go no farther—because the enemy are just down the road. The Germans, unfortunately, are not only down the road, they are in the hills themselves between this road and the next one, and as there are only a few roads through the Apennines there are devilishly long stretches of hills in between each.

From where one turns off the main road one can get up in a jeep for about a mile, along a track of pine logs, laid by the engineers, like a venetian blind unrolled up the side of the hill. These hills have been turned, by the passage of guns, mules, and human feet into a brown sea of mud, and here and there, floating on the mud, is a little encampment of bivouacs dug into the side of the hill and strengthened with sandbags, for the enemy throws over an odd shell. A few unkempt little houses, straw stuffed into holes made by shellfire, give a little better protection from the almost incessant rain, but they are mostly taken by headquarters, and those who live there, braving a legion of rats, can count themselves lucky indeed.

Where the track ends one stands on the shore of this sea of mud ; if one wants to go forward now one does so on foot. This spot, known as the Mule Base, is the meeting place for a million mules, tough, scruffy little animals that will not march for more than a couple of miles with a full load without demanding a rest, and if someone should dare to put one box of ammunition too many on their shoulders they contrive to throw it off in the first hundred yards. They eat vast quantities of hay, and as this all has to be brought up in the few available jeeps it means a corresponding reduction in other supplies. But it would be hard to carry on the war here for a day without them, for they carry everything—ammunition, water, food, clothing, and a hundred and one other things—needed by the men in the forward positions.

From Mule Base to the forward companies takes about three hours of slogging through the worst mud in the world. Even the mules sink up to their hocks. Wellington boots are useless ; one either dislocates a joint trying to free them from a vice of mud or leaves the boots behind and goes on barefooted. Most people wear hobnail boots with sacking wound round their legs, and carry a stout staff. Even so, in the darkness, when one cannot pick one's way, one falls continually, and if it wasn't for the telephone wires one would easily get lost altogether.

I went forward with one mule train as far as it goes in daylight—the last part of the journey, which is under enemy observation, is made at night—and I can tell you that when I got back I was pretty exhausted, so you can imagine what it is like for the infantry carry-

AT A MULE BASE IN THE APENNINES men of the 5th Army load their wiry beasts with supplies for forward troops. Some 3,000 feet above sea-level, the use of vehicles of any kind on the steep mountain tracks is impracticable—as explained in this and the facing page. *Photo, British Official*

ing their arms and equipment. On this particular day there was a thick mountain mist, a not infrequent occurrence, which lent a rather macabre effect to the scene : the long line of mules, grunting and sweating, those in the rear shrouded by the mist ; the persuasive cries of the Italian muleteers in their feathered Alpine hats ; little, broken farms, with doleful children standing with wide, incurious eyes ; abandoned German trenches strewn with rusting machine-gun belts—ground that our men had fought over not long before.

An almost eerie stillness hung over the rolling hills, over the ploughland and the vineyards and the sudden steep ravines, broken only by an occasional burst of

machine-gun fire or the muffled thump of a gun. In the trenches and the farmhouses that are the front line the strain on such days must be intense, for one cannot see what is moving out there in the mist, and the nearest Bosche positions are only eight hundred yards away.

The worst problem is the evacuation of wounded. Not long ago an officer wounded in a night attack lay for eight hours in an area that was being heavily shelled before he was found. He had been conscious all that time with a compound fracture of the leg. It took a further eight hours to get him back on a stretcher to the nearest dressing-station, where he could receive comprehensive treatment. Somehow he survived the journey.

OUR DIARY OF THE WAR

January 3, Wednesday   *1,950th day*
Western Front.—U.S. 1st Army launched attack in Grandmenil area of Ardennes salient.
Air.—Over 1,100 U.S. bombers attacked road and rail centres in Ruhr and Rhineland. R.A.F. Lancasters bombed oil plants near Dortmund.
Greece.—Gen. Plastiras formed new Greek government.
Burma.—Allied forced landed in Akyab, abandoned by Japanese.
Philippines.—U.S. troops landed on Marinduque Island.
Far East.—U.S. carrier-aircraft attacked Formosa and Ryukyu Islands for second day running. Super-Fortresses again bombed Nagoya, Japan.

January 4, Thursday   *1,951st day*
Western Front.—U.S. 7th Army troops withdrawn from German soil between Sarreguemines and the Rhine.
Mediterranean.—Allied heavy bombers attacked rail yards on Brenner route.
Philippines.—35 Japanese ships sunk or damaged off Luzon. U.S. bombers attacked Clark airfield near Manila.

January 5, Friday   *1,952nd day*
Western Front.—Announced that from Dec. 17 Field-Marshal Montgomery had assumed command of Allied armies (including U.S. 1st and 9th) north of German salient.
Air.—R.A.F. attacked German pocket near Bordeaux, and at night made heavy attack on Hanover. More than 1,500 U.S. bombers and fighters attacked rail centres from Cologne to Karlsruhe and from Siegfried Line to Frankfurt.
Philippines.—U.S. carrier force bombed Luzon ; warships bombarded Kurile Is.
Poland.—Moscow announced that Soviet Govt. recognized Polish Provisional Govt in Lublin.

January 6, Saturday   *1,953rd day*
Western Front.—German bridgeheads over Rhine near Strasbourg were counter-attacked.
Air.—U.S. bombers attacked road and rail bridges at Cologne and Bonn. R.A.F. attacked German troops near Houffalize by day, and rail centres of Hanau and Neuss at night.
Far East.—Super-Fortresses attacked Kyushu, southernmost Japanese island.

January 7, Sunday   *1,954th day*
Air.—Over 1,650 U.S. bombers and fighters attacked railway yards and bridges in W. Germany. R.A.F. Spitfires bombed V 2 sites in Holland, and at night Lancasters attacked Munich, Hanover, Hanau and Nuremberg.
Russian Front.—N. W. of Budapest Russians evacuated Esztergom.
Burma.—Indian troops of 14th Army entered Shwebo.
Philippines.—U.S. aircraft bombed harbours and airfields on Luzon.

January 8, Monday   *1,955th day*
Western Front.—German position on west bank of Maas eliminated by Allied troops.
Far East.—U.S. carrier-aircraft again bombed Formosa and Ryukyu Is., sinking or damaging 137 ships and 98 aircraft.
Pacific.—Announced that Australian troops had relieved Americans in Solomons, New Guinea and New Britain.

January 9, Tuesday   *1,956th day*
Philippines.—Large U.S. forces landed on Luzon Island, in Lingayen Gulf.
Far East.—Super-Fortresses bombed industrial area of Tokyo and again attacked Formosa.
Sea.—Announced that in December,

1944, renewal of U-boat activity led to increased losses in Allied merchant shipping.

January 10, Wednesday   *1,957th day*
Western Front.—In Ardennes salient Bure and Samree were taken by Allies after heavy fighting.
Air.—U.S. bombers attacked airfields, road and rail bridges in areas of Cologne, Bonn and Karlsruhe.

January 11, Thursday   *1,958th day*
Western Front.—On north of Ardennes salient Allies captured Laroche, and on south St. Hubert was entered.
Far East.—Super-Fortresses from India made daylight attacks on docks and shipping in Singapore and Georgetown, Penang. U.S. carrier-aircraft sank 25 enemy ships and damaged 12 off Indo-China.
Greece.—Truce signed in Athens between Gen. Scobie, British G.O.C., and E.L.A.S. Central Committee.

January 12, Friday   *1,959th day*
Western Front.—British patrols from north of salient joined up, in St. Hubert with U.S. troops from south.
Air.—Lancasters with 12,000 lb. bombs attacked U-boat shelters at Bergen.

Russian Front.—Red Army troops under Marshal Koniev opened offensive on Sandomierz front, south of Warsaw.
Sea.—Ships of Home Fleet wrecked German convoy off Norway.

January 13, Saturday   *1,960th day*
Western Front.—U.S. 1st Army launched new attack south of Stavelot and Malmedy.
Air.—More than 1,300 U.S. aircraft attacked seven rail bridges across the Rhine. At night R.A.F. bombed oil plant as Politz, north of Stettin.

January 14, Sunday   *1,961st day*
Western Front.—Allied troops cut Houffalize–St. Vith road near Cherain.
Air.—Over 1,750 U.S. bombers and fighters attacked oil plants and storage depots in Germany ; 189 Luftwaffe aircraft destroyed. R.A.F. attacked by day V 2 sites in Holland, and at night bombed Leuna oil plant near Merseburg and fuel depot near Munster.
Russian Front.—Soviet troops of 1st White Russian Front under Marshal Zhukov launched offensive in central Poland.
Far East.—Super-Fortresses from Saipan attacked Japanese island of Honshu, and from China again bombed Formosa.

January 15, Monday   *1,962nd day*
Western Front.—Allied patrols entered Houffalize.
Air.—Lancasters bombed benzol plants in Ruhr. U.S. bombers attacked railway yards in southern Germany.
Russian Front.—In southern Poland Koniev's troops captured Kielce.
Burma.—First China-bound convoy from Ledo reached Myitkyina, present terminus of Ledo Road.

January 16, Tuesday   *1,963rd day*
Western Front.—British launched attack at Sittard against German salient east of the Maas. Troops of U.S. 1st and 3rd Armies met in Houffalize.
Air.—U.S. bombers attacked oil and tank plants at Dresden and Magdeburg.
Russian Front.—In central Poland Zhukov's forces captured Radom.
Far East.—U.S. carrier-aircraft made third consecutive attack on enemy shipping in China ports of Canton, Swatow and Hongkong.

★══════════ *Flash-backs* ══════════★

1940
January 8. Food rationing (of sugar, butter and bacon only) started in Britain.

1941
January 5. Bardia surrendered ; over 30,000 Italian prisoners.

1942
January 10. Japanese invaded Celebes, Netherlands E. Indies.
January 12. In Libya South African troops captured Sollum.

1943
January 4. Caucasian centre of Nalchik recaptured by Russians.
January 14. Churchill and Roosevelt met at Casablanca, French Morocco, to plan enemy's " unconditional surrender."

1944
January 4. Russian offensive opened on Ukraine front.
January 11. Red Army opened offensive in White Russia.
January 15. Russian offensives on Leningrad and Novgorod fronts.

THE WAR IN THE AIR

by Capt. Norman Macmillan, M.C., A.F.C.

THIS war has been responsible for the introduction of new methods to solve old problems in aviation. Often these new ideas have been put into practical use long before security restrictions have allowed the public to be let into the secret. Three of these innovations have just been made "officially" known, and at least one has been "secretly" employed for at least two years. They are (1) the anti-blackout suit; (2) an aircraft equivalent of the dictaphone; and (3) a new flak curtain to protect aircrews.

The anti-blackout suit has been called in some reports a flying pressure suit. This is an erroneous term, because it might be confused with the pressure suits worn by Squadron Leader F. R. D. Swain and Flight-Lieut. M. J. Adam, of the R.A.F., who successively broke the world altitude record for aeroplanes in September 1936 and June 1937. Those were real pressure suits, worn with a circlip around the waist so that the pressure of the oxygen fed into the upper part would induce respiration in the high atmosphere where atmospheric pressure falls too low to "feed" normal breathing.

THE purpose of the anti-blackout suit is to maintain equilibrium in the bloodstream when an aircraft is manoeuvring, irrespective of height. When an aeroplane changes direction, loads are imposed on its structure and, naturally, on the persons flying in the aeroplane. The greatest loads occur when the aeroplane makes a fast turn or pulls out of a steep dive. The effect is to force the occupants down into their seats. The blood feels the pressure of this force, and the heart becomes unequal to the task of pumping the blood upward to the head against it. The result is brain anaemia, with loss of sight, until the force causing it is removed, when the vision returns to normal.

In war, fast manoeuvring with full competence of faculties is vital, and one anti-blackout suit was invented by Wing Commander W. R. Franks, of Toronto University. It is a rubber suit, filled with fluid in columns, and worn close to the body from feet to chest. The force exerted on the fluid drives it downward so that external pressure is automatically created around the lower limbs, and relieved around the torso, thus restoring an even balance of forces so that the heart functions normally. Pilots say it is quite comfortable and that they can make terrific pull-outs without noticing them. The American Berger suit, waist-high, is operated by air pressure fed to five airbags from the exhaust side of the vacuum pump. On January 11 a Mosquito shot a Me. 109 into the sea off Norway after making a terrifically fast turn inside the circle described by the Messerschmitt. A second Me. pilot who saw the phenomenal turn sped off to safety. It is possible that the Mosquito's aircrew were wearing anti-blackout suits.

OBSERVATIONS Dictated by Air-Crews Over Enemy Territory

All reconnaissance pilots and observers used to have to write notes. A midget recording apparatus has been invented so that they can "dictaphone" their information. A four-in. spool carries 11,500 feet of ·004 inch diameter wire. This wire records the voice from a microphone in the same way as on a gramophone record. Aircrews over enemy territory are able to dictate their observations, a much faster and therefore more accurate method than recording them by pencil on paper with a constant struggle to catch up with the trains, road transport, tanks, gun flashes and other items of military information that pass underwing.

The third device is an anti-flak curtain made of overlapping squares of manganese steel and able to stop a 20 millimetre cannon shell bursting two feet away. The curtains are placed in sheets and strips around crew stations in aircraft. They enable the heavy armour plates to be taken out of Fortresses, Liberators, Havocs and Marauders, and so enable them to carry bigger bomb loads. They were designed by Brig.-General Grow, chief surgeon to U.S. Strategic Air Forces in Europe, whose headquarters has recently moved to France to correlate the activities of the 8th and 15th Air Forces based in the U.K. and Italy.

Britain's Bomber Command has been returning to old targets. Gestapo headquarters in Oslo was again bombed by Mosquitoes on New Year's Eve. (First attack was on Sept. 25, 1942.) The Dort-

HOT AIR FROM A PRE-HEATING VAN being pumped to the air intake and radiator of a R.A.F. Typhoon fighter-bomber during a bitter spell on a Dutch airfield in January 1945. *Photo, British Official*

mund-Ems canal received its fourth breaching attack on Jan. 1, 1945; this was the first attack to be made in daylight against this target. Bomber Command "Mossies" have been lobbing 4,000-lb. bombs into railway tunnel entrances with good results as part of the anti-Rundstedt air plan.

For a long time convoy escort carriers have been Jekyll and Hyde ships, carrying 7,000 tons of grain in addition to aircraft. These converted merchant ships have done good work. News of them has just been released. Swordfish were their aircraft.

ON January 1, waves of German fighter bombers attacked Allied airfields on the Western Front. They effected a surprise and caught many aircraft on the ground or about to take off. German claims were 579 Allied aircraft destroyed, 400 on the ground. Allied counter-attack claims were 364 German planes destroyed out of about 500. The enemy were probably lucky in having the fog clear from their airfields first. They flew in low and down strip runways with blazing guns.

In Western Europe the Allied air forces have continued to attack enemy communications behind the front where fighting continued. U.S. bombers had dropped 13,250 U.S. tons on Cologne by January 10, more than they have unloaded on Berlin or any other city.

In Burma, Rathedaung was captured on Jan. 1, and Akyab on Jan. 3. Akyab should greatly aid the air offensive against the Japanese in lower Burma, as it provides a supply port and airfields. The Japanese air base of Iwojima in Bonin Islands was bombed for 24 consecutive days up to December 30, 1944, to neutralize counter air attacks against Super-Fortress bombers attacking Japan targets from the Marianas Islands; Guam is now the H.Q. of U.S. XXI Bomber Command. U.S. air attacks against tactical targets in Luzon island, Philippines, were followed by four assault landings on January 9. Enemy air attacks against this biggest Pacific convoy began three days out from the landing beaches of Lingayen, but few Japanese planes penetrated the defence screen round the ships. They lost 79 aircraft. Counter air attack was made against Formosa, Ryukyu islands, and French Indo-China Jap-occupied bases by carrier planes of the U.S. 3rd Fleet. Singapore naval base, and Georgetown (Penang) submarine base, were bombed on Jan. 11 by Super-Fortresses flying from India.

TOKYO-BOUND, AN 8,800-h.p. SUPER-FORTRESS takes off on its 2,600-mile ocean flight from Saipan in the Mariana Islands of the Pacific. Raids on the Japanese capital by Saipan-based aircraft began in late Nov. 1944. Flying more than 3,500 miles, from a base in India, Fortresses bombed Singapore Island in daylight on Jan. 11, 1945. *Photo, Planet News*

With the 2nd Tactical Air Force of the R.A.F.

AIRFIELD OBSTACLES—wooden tripods mounted on wheels—were designed by the Germans to prevent the landing of Allied glider forces as we advanced in Holland and Belgium: workers, under the supervision of a R.A.F. officer, assisted in their removal (1). The enemy left these anti-tank weapons (3) behind them on an abandoned Dutch airfield; resembling the bazooka, they are fitted with fins which open on being fired.

Surprising factor in the German offensive in the Ardennes was the come-back staged by the Luftwaffe. It did not last long, however. On January 1, 1945, Allied fighters and A.A. guns shot down 364 enemy aircraft during violent attacks on our airfields. With another 81 probably destroyed, the Luftwaffe thus sustained its greatest one-day loss of the war. The 2nd Tactical Air Force of the R.A.F. magnificently helped to stem the enemy advance: loading up Typhoons with 1,000-pound bombs (2 and 4) on a captured airfield.

Photos, Fox Photos

Blazing Hellcat Roars Home—to Fight Again

HIS 400 M.P.H. SINGLE-SEAT FIGHTER spouting flames and the odds of survival piled heavily against him, a U.S. pilot landed the 2,000 horse-power aircraft successfully on the carrier Cowpens, during operations in the Pacific late in 1944, saving both his own life and the Hellcat.

With superb skill he jockeyed for position (1), made a level approach (2) and a perfect touch-down. As the carrier's fire-fighters played on the blaze he struggled from the red-hot cockpit and, scorched and near blinded with smoke and still burdened with his parachute-pack, ran along a wing (3), then leapt to the safety of the flight-deck (4). So efficient were the firemen that only one minute and thirty seconds elapsed between the time the Hellcat touched down and the flames were extinguished. Astonishingly, the plane was soon refurbished to fight again. *Photos, Keystone*

THAT oil has been worked in England for some time past and that we are now obtaining 375 tons a day from our own wells for the use of the Forces, is good news. It surprised most people—indeed almost everybody, for the secret of the little Nottinghamshire village where the oil-field is centred has been a well-kept one up till now. Eakring the village is called, and it used to be mainly agricultural, with mining taking second place. Now about a thousand men are employed on the 238 oil-wells in the vicinity. Since the outbreak of war about 78 million gallons have been produced there. The first oil-field I saw—it was in South Russia—made me think that a town must have been wiped out by fire. The whole landscape was filled with tall poles, forming the derricks, which are necessary for the boring of a well; and all the oil-fields I have seen since in various parts of the world have had the same desolate, sinister appearance. Fortunately, this area of our countryside is not thus disfigured; all that can be observed are the leisurely-moving arms of electrically-operated pumps (dotted occasionally about the fields) bringing the crude petroleum to the surface, with cows grazing contentedly on the surrounding pasturage.

I CANNOT pretend to feel much commiseration for Germans whose cities and towns are bombed. They gloated when we were the victims of their raids on this country, and the only way to cure that sort of savagery is to give them a dose themselves, and a good stiff one. But I must admit to being sorry when I hear of beautiful places I have known being devastated and smashed. Bonn, for instance, was in the news the other day as having been heavily bombed, and I found it hard to imagine the serenity of that university town being shattered by four-thousand-pounders. Built on the banks of the Rhine, with all its streets lined with trees, and with graceful modern blocks among the old ones that were lovingly preserved, it has always remained in my mind as a home of ancient peace. About Budapest, of which there cannot be much left, I do not feel the same at all. The old city of Buda, with its palaces and wooded heights overlooking the Danube, had a charm of past greatness, but the modern Pest on the other side of the river was garish, artificial, over-sophisticated. It was the creation of a ruling caste without ideas of their own and without the taste to imitate the best in architecture. For it I feel no regret.

I HAVE received already a mass of propaganda from a London Committee representing the rival Polish Government which has been set up at Lublin since its liberation by the Russians and which has the backing of the Soviet authorities. Its aim is, of course, to persuade those who wade through it that Codlin is the friend not Short. The Polish nation is said to be behind the Lublin Cabinet and to have no use whatever for the one that has had its headquarters in London for the past five years. Equally, of course, this latter body claims to have the support of the Polish people. What would be the result of a plebiscite, no one can say.

I LISTENED to an animated discussion between two acquaintances of mine on the question, started by letters in The Times, whether it would be a good or a bad thing to keep on Identity Cards after the war. One argued that this would be a monstrous interference with the liberty of the subject, and also that no useful purpose would be served. The other maintained it would be most useful to make everyone carry about a history of his or her life: he wanted, you see, to expand the present card, which does not even state the age of the holder, into a record that would include honours and convictions, successes and failures, offices held and countries travelled through or lived in. To this it was replied that no self-respecting person would consent willingly to have his career thus laid bare. The retort was that if there were nothing to be ashamed of in it, no loss of respect need be felt. I did not take part in the controversy. I do not think there is any likelihood of the life-history idea developing. On the other hand I should be surprised if the present Identity Cards were to be given up, though I cannot find confirmation of the statement by one of The Times letter-writers that they are marked as being available till 1960.

ONE is accustomed to shortages of so many kinds that I suppose I ought not to have been astonished when I was told in a big men's outfitting shop, "We have no pocket-handkerchiefs, sir, I am sorry to say." Yet somehow one does not think it possible that the manufacture of such absolute necessaries, which are so small and require so little raw material, could be interrupted. One explanation offered was that "it's just after Christmas, you see, and so many handkerchiefs were bought as presents." Like all other articles that have to be "sent to the wash," they have nowadays much shorter lives than they had formerly. The way laundry machines tear clothes to pieces used to be a joke; now it is a tragedy. Fortunately we are just at the beginning of a new coupon period, so it is possible to replace some of the shirts that are returned in tatters; but even so the difficulty of keeping a shirt on one's back is formidable. In those countries where washing of clothes is done by washerwomen who come in for a couple of days a month and clear it all up, clothes last three times as long. No machinery for them!

POST-WAR visitors to Paris may well bless General de Gaulle for the request he has just made to the local authorities. While, as he says, he is "very appreciative of these expressions of recognition," he does not favour the use of his name to designate public thoroughfares. Immediately after the last war, the French—especially in the small towns of the *Midi* and the south—had a passion for renaming their streets and squares after some local nine-days' war hero, to the bewilderment of visitors accustomed to the age-old nomenclature and the detriment of shopkeepers. I, for one, hope that the General's hint will be taken through the length and breadth of France and not merely in Paris alone. While South America, as can be imagined, tops the list when it comes to a quick-change in street names, nearer home in neutral Eire they have made confusion even worse confounded by renaming streets after I.R.A. "heroes" whose names—in their Gaelic spelling—are not only meaningless to the bulk of the population but unpronounceable. And yet a few years ago when it was proposed to rename a back street in Dublin—actually it was his birthplace—after John Field, the Irish composer who invented the Nocturne and inspired Chopin, the Corporation turned it down—because someone discovered that the composer's grandfather on his mother's side had been English. In other words, as Goebbels would have it, he wasn't pure Eireann!

IT surprised me that until recently no one thought of Hitler's later speeches as being refabricated from old gramophone records —which is what some of the papers have been saying. The notion that there is something new in the piecing together and editing of a speech from bits and pieces of previous records of the same speaker—or that it is of German origin—will amuse those who know anything of the film business or the recording work of the B.B.C. The most remarkable piece of editing of this kind may now be told. It occurred during the Proclamation of the then Prince of Wales as King Edward VIII. During the reading of the proclamation outside one of the royal palaces, where the B.B.C. recording van was in attendance, a cannon went off unexpectedly. The elderly Court official "fluffed" his "script," as the actors say, and apart from nearly falling off the tasselled dais, made such a mess of his words that when the record was played over at Broadcasting House not a single sentence was in its proper order. But the Recorded Programmes Department weren't to be beaten. Within a few hours they had made something like sixty copies of that unintelligible jumble record, and from them (with the aid of a copy of the Proclamation) had placed together one complete record with the words in the correct order—all in time for the six o'clock news!

IN its sixth year the war still brings us odd surprises—on the home no less than on the battle fronts. A friend has been telling me of a strange and wonderful sight he saw recently in his Thames-side garden—the bomb-torn and bark-stripped branch of an ancient chestnut tree which, though wrenched from its parent-trunk and in mid-winter, had put forth its pink-and-white "candles." In the heart of London too, Nature, I notice, has been up to strange tricks. Shortly after a flying-bomb had beheaded the plane trees that make almost a boulevard of our Kingsway and Aldwych, their mutilated trunks were vigorously sprouting leaves once more. Though the plane tree came here from the Lebanon only two-and-a-half centuries ago it has already taken on the resilient character the true Cockney. When its bark becomes encrusted with soot and grime it sheds it and goes on growing as if nothing had happened —just like your Londoner in wartime!

Lieut.-Gen. SIR MONTAGUE STOPFORD, commanding the 33rd Indian Corps, knighted by Lord Wavell, the Viceroy of India, in the name of the King, watched the decoration ceremony at Imphal on December 15, 1944.

Photo, British Official

Shattered Relic of Rundstedt's Offensive

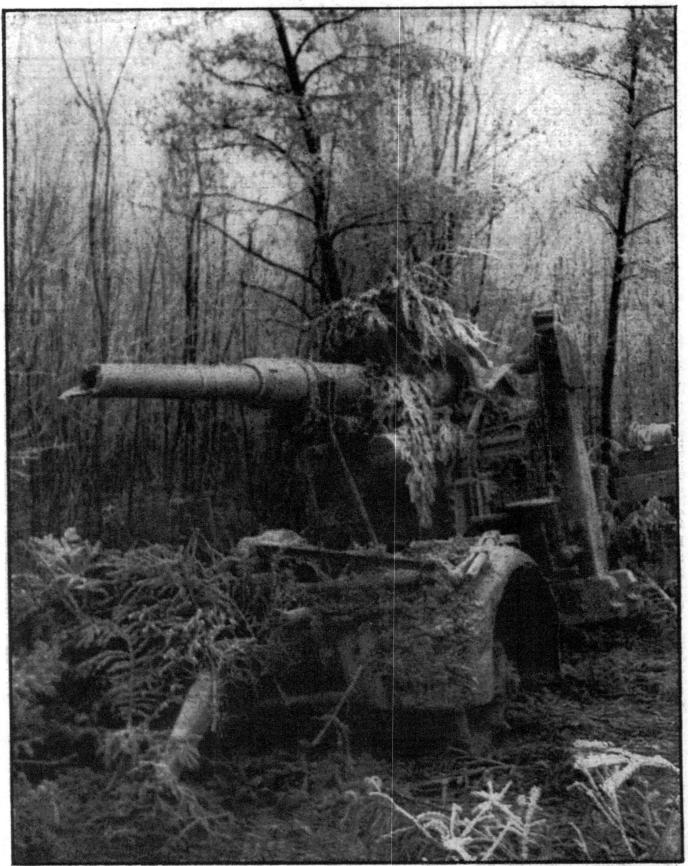

Photo, British Official

GERMAN MOBILE GUN, camouflaged with fir branches, spangled with frost and wrecked, was found abandoned in the Ardennes after Field-Marshal Montgomery, temporarily commanding the U.S. 1st and 9th Armies in addition to British and Canadian Armies, had halted the northern flank of the German thrust towards the Meuse, in early January 1945. Before leaving the weapon the enemy blew out the muzzle. It is of the 88-mm. type, as employed extensively by the Afrika Korps in Libya ; originally intended for A.A. purposes it was later adapted to fire at any angle.

Printed in England and published every alternate Friday by the Proprietors, THE AMALGAMATED PRESS, LTD., The Fleetway House, Farringdon Street, London, E.C.4. Registered for transmission by Canadian Magazine Post. Sole Agents for Australia and New Zealand : Messrs. Gordon & Gotch, Ltd ; and for South Africa : Central News Agency, Ltd.—February 2, 1945.   S.S.   *Editorial Address :* JOHN CARPENTER HOUSE, WHITEFRIARS LONDON, E.C.4.

Vol 8

The War Illustrated

Nº 200

SIXPENCE

Edited by Sir John Hammerton

FEBRUARY 16, 1945

ASKARI WARRIOR OF THE SUDAN DEFENCE FORCE, he patrols the Abyssinian border country. These native troops—100 per cent equatorial Africans—are under the command of 22-year-old Bimbashi (Captain) J. T. Weekes, of Sussex, whose nearest white neighbour is 250 miles distant by road. S.D.F. units collaborated with General Platt's forces in the liberation of Abyssinia (see page 675, Vol. 7). At Debra Marcos, in 1941, a unit of only 300 successfully held at bay a force of 12,000 Italians. *Photo, British Official*

NO. 201 WILL BE PUBLISHED FRIDAY, MARCH 2

Soviet Hosts March on Main Roads to Berlin

SIX MIGHTY RUSSIAN ARMIES made stupendous advances on a 600-mile front in January 1945. The map shows the area covered from January 12 to 19 (in dark grey), and from January 19 to 26 (in white). By February 5 Marshal Zhukov was within 40 miles of Berlin, on the main roads.

GERMAN PRISONERS TAKEN BY THE RED ARMY in Czechoslovakia (1). In their headlong retreat the enemy destroyed whatever they could lay their hands on: they blew up this bridge (2) near Tilsit, and set Pultusk (3), near Warsaw, ablaze. A rooftop view of Tilsit (4) after its fall on January 20, 1945: smoke in the background is from a large petrol dump. Supplementing the Soviet advance, over 1,000 Allied heavy bombers on February 3 gave the Reich capital its heaviest raid.

PAGE 610

Photos, U.S.S.R. Official, Planet News, Pictorial Press.   Map, Evening News

THE BATTLE FRONTS

by Maj.-Gen. Sir Charles Gwynn, K.C.B., D.S.O.

THE success of the Russian offensive has evidently been the result of brilliant strategical planning and wonderfully efficient administrative organization. The timing of the blow appears on the whole to have been as skilful as we have learnt to expect in Russian operations. It may have seemed to many of us that by launching the offensive so late there was a risk that the period of frozen ground might prove to be too short to allow of full exploitation of success. But the speed with which the offensive has developed goes far to prove that the date was well chosen.

I think we may safely assume that the date was deliberately fixed to provide the greatest opportunity of developing speed, and the whole execution of the plan has shown how speed has been used to dislocate the German defensive arrangements. The timing of the main blow has also evidently been skilfully co-ordinated with the progress of operations in Hungary which had attracted important elements of the German reserve, and with those of Cherniakhovsky on the other flank which had already pinned down a strong German force in East Prussia. The speed with which the offensive has developed and the comparatively small number of prisoners claimed in its earlier stages has given rise to a belief that the Germans were not holding the Vistula line in strength and that they carried out a deliberately planned withdrawal. No doubt the Germans, if only as a matter of Staff routine, would have prepared plans for retreat in case their front on the river line was broken, but I find it hard to believe that they voluntarily weakened the Vistula defences in anticipation of the Russian onslaught; for it would obviously be dangerous to fight the decisive battle, in less strong positions, in close proximity to a region as important as Silesia.

REFUGEES Streaming Westward Hinder the Regrouping of German Forces

Furthermore, it is obvious that, if the main defence position was close to the Silesian frontier, East Prussia, where there was no possibility of carrying out elastic defence without abandoning German territory, would become a dangerously exposed salient. The only arguments in favour of such a course would be, on the one hand, that German communications would be shortened and improved and that the network of Silesian railways would facilitate the movements of reserves to threatened points or for counter-attack; and, on the other, that the Russians by the time they reached the frontier might have exhausted some of their strength in overcoming delaying resistance and would be operating at the end of long and indifferent communications.

WHATEVER the German plans may have been, they have manifestly broken down under the speed and power of the Russian steamroller. The Vistula line, whether held weakly or in strength, has been broken, and if the withdrawal from it was deliberate it is admitted by the Germans that many detachments did not make good their escape. Moreover, it is clear that neither Koniev's nor Zhukov's Armies have encountered well-organized and properly manned defences as they approached the German frontier. In places resistance has been determined, but apparently it has generally been offered by troops, sometimes of second-class quality, hurriedly rushed into position; and reserves do not appear to have been suitably located to intervene quickly and effectively. German commentators suggest that reserves are being regrouped for a major counterstroke, but

even assuming that they exist in adequate numbers their regrouping before the front is stabilized will be a difficult matter, probably made more difficult by the streams of refugees flowing westward.

Up to the time of writing there are few signs of the front becoming stabilized, but of course there is the possibility that the Russians may outrun their supplies and that the offensive will lose its momentum. The Germans evidently hoped that this would occur before the frontier was crossed, relying on the resistance of detachments which the Russians had overshot to block the main avenues of communication. So far there are no indications that this has happened, and the Germans are complaining that with the ground frozen the Russians have been able to by-pass such centres of resistance as still exist (many of them have probably been mopped up, judging from the rise in Russian claims at the end of the first fortnight).

THERE remains, however, the question of the lengthening distance of the front from the Russian bases. That, undoubtedly, may compel the Russians to pause, especially if and when they encounter solid resistance. But I think that any pause that may occur will be of short duration. It is safe to assume that the Russian commanders have taken every possible step to enable them to sustain the impetus of their advance. They have the advantage of a wide base on the Vistula with each Army Group operating from its own sector; and, in hard weather, there must be numerous routes leading forward.

It is interesting to compare the situation with that on the Western Front after the break-out from Normandy. In that case the Allies, up to the reopening of Antwerp, were operating from a single restricted base and by few roads. Moreover, before they were brought to a halt by increasing German resistance and by supply difficulties, they had traversed at least twice the distance the Russians have had to go before reaching the German frontier—in East Prussia and in the attack on Southern Silesia the distances were actually much shorter.

I have seen it argued that the loss of East Prussia, since it is a non-industrialized Province, would not materially weaken Germany; and that although Silesia con-

tains vital war industries its loss would have long-term rather than immediate effects. Both these contentions are, I think, unduly cautious. Admittedly, East Prussia as a territorial objective is not of much importance except that it might provide a base for a counter-offensive against the flank of the main Russian offensive. But obviously the target there is the strong German Army, largely composed of first-line troops committed to the defence of the Province, and probably maintained at strength with a view to counter-offensive action although sentimental considerations may also have dictated the size of the force committed. Whether that army is ultimately annihilated or not it is quite clear that it has now been securely bottled up.

OUT-MANOEUVRED Wehrmacht's Expenditure of Slim Reserves

As regards Silesia, it may be true that the loss of its products will not immediately affect German power of resistance, but its loss must convince many Germans that the war cannot be indefinitely prolonged, more especially as the output of the Ruhr and Saar has been greatly reduced by the air offensive. Furthermore, the losses of men and material suffered in defence of Silesia are bound to have a crippling effect.

On the whole I see no reason for underestimating the achievements of the Russian offensive or for believing that it will be brought to a halt before it can achieve even greater—possibly decisive—results. Undoubtedly the Germans still possess a strong and on the whole a well-equipped army which might still for a time offer stubborn resistance if it was considered that anything would be gained to compensate for the loss of life and destruction involved. The dispositions of the army have, however, been so completely dislocated that there seems no possibility that it could stage a counter-stroke that, at best, could achieve more than limited success.

The persistent counter-attacks delivered against Tolbukhin's Army in Hungary have at last been abandoned after a wasteful expenditure of reserves, which proves how completely the Wehrmacht has been out-manoeuvred. The relief of Buda, their chief object, has not been achieved and their limited success can in no way affect the main issue. Von Rundstedt's counter-offensive similarly has proved to have been little more than a waste of reserve power—possibly to a disastrous extent. I can well believe the rumours that the German Army commanders, as far as they dare, are advising Hitler that it is time to throw up the sponge.

Army-Gen. CHERNIAKHOVSKY
3rd White Russian Front

Marshal K. K. ROKOSSOVSKY
2nd White Russian Front

Marshal I. S. KONIEV
1st Ukrainian Front

Marshal Gregory ZHUKOV
1st White Russian Front

Army-Gen. I. F. PETROV
4th Ukrainian Front

Marshal R. Y. MALINOVSKY
2nd Ukrainian Front

Photos, U.S.S.R. Official. Pictorial Press

Flame-Throwers Support Our Advance in Belgium

HEAVILY ENGAGED IN THE SITTARD SECTOR, in Belgium, British infantry, in open order, crossed the snow-blanketed fields (1) near Heinsberg (captured January 24, 1945). A Crocodile flame-thrower is seen (2) supporting our troops approaching the village of St. Joost, which they entered on January 23 after the Crocodiles had done their red-hot and terrifying work (3). Hands-on-head, half-frozen enemy troops surrendered (4) in the Bocket area. See pages 300-301 for full description of British flame-throwers. *Photos, British Official: British Newspaper Pool*

Now Rundstedt's Western Drive is Written Off

THROUGH ARDENNES SNOWS British infantry march cheerfully to the battle front. All that was left of Von Rundstedt's "bulge"—against which British troops were flung to stem the tide—was eliminated on January 22-23, 1945, when Wiltz, Nazi "anchor" town in Luxembourg, fell to Gen. Patton's U.S. 3rd Army, and St. Vith, Belgian key outpost, was taken by Gen. Hodges' U.S. 1st Army. Only the atrocious conditious—deep snow and ice-bound roads—saved the enemy from an annihilating pursuit; as it was, on the few days favourable to flying, his retreating transport was harried and battered by Allied aircraft. See also illus. pages 624-625.

Photo, British Official

THE WAR AT SEA

by Francis E. McMurtrie

RUSSIAN progress along the shores of the Baltic threatens very soon to involve the ports of East Prussia, Poland and Pomerania. These, from east to west, include Königsberg, Pillau, Elbing, Danzig, Gdynia, Kolberg, Stettin and Stralsund. While the three first are already invested at the time of writing, and the next two are being approached by the advance guards of the Soviet armies, it is unlikely that the remaining three will be affected until Berlin has been occupied. In these circumstances the Germans are doubtless hastening to remove to harbours farther westward all shipping, including vessels of the Reichsmarine that may be capable of proceeding under their own power. Efforts may also be made to tow away ships incapable of propulsion ; though this would be a hazardous proceeding in view of the tempting target offered to aircraft, submarines and torpedo craft by a vessel moving slowly in tow.

So far as is known, the only important ship left in Königsberg is the 10,000 ton cruiser Seydlitz. This ship was launched at Bremen as long ago as January 1939, but for unknown reasons she has never been completed, and it is even doubtful whether her engines are fully installed. Presumably, the concentration of all available shipbuilding resources upon the construction of U-boats and of light surface craft, from destroyers down to motor torpedo boats, has prevented work proceeding on the Seydlitz. She may also have suffered structural damage of a serious nature as the result of the bombing of such harbours as Bremen, Hamburg and Kiel.

AT Elbing are the shipbuilding yards and engine works of the Schichau concern, which has specialized in the construction of destroyers, though merchant vessels have also been built there. It is estimated that there are probably half-a-dozen new destroyers in various stages of construction here.

In default of their being launched and able to escape, they will doubtless be destroyed by the enemy.

At Gdynia there were until recently quite a number of German warships, including the two 10,000-ton cruisers Prinz Eugen and Admiral Hipper and the so-called "pocket battleships" Lützow and Admiral Scheer, as well as the smaller cruiser Leipzig, which had been disabled through collision with the Prinz Eugen. Also, in a complete state of dismantlement, there was the only remaining German battleship, the 26,000-ton Gneisenau. All these ships had been stationed at the former Polish naval base, a spot too remote to be frequently bombed.

SOVIET Baltic Fleet Watching Coastal Waters of N. Germany

Now it may be assumed that the harbour will speedily be emptied, except for the hulk of the Gneisenau and possibly the Leipzig, if she is still in dry dock. Where will all these ships go ? It has been reported that preparations were being made for the reception of some of them in the Royal dockyard at Copenhagen, Danish vessels having been transferred elsewhere to free berths for this purpose. Possibly Stettin will be utilized as an intermediate harbour of refuge, but owing to its situation at the head of a long and narrow channel, which could easily be blocked, the port is not altogether desirable for use as a haven in wartime.

In anticipation of such movements of warships and merchant vessels from east to west, submarines, motor torpedo boats and aircraft of the Soviet Baltic Fleet are reported to be keeping the coastal waters of North Germany under close observation. There has been no sign of any activity from the heavier ships of the Russian Navy, however ; this is probably owing to the existence of German minefields.

A forgotten fleet of which the fate was in doubt has just come into the news again. In 1939 there was a substantial French naval force in the Far East under Admiral Découx, consisting of the 7,249-ton cruiser Lamotte-Picquet, the large sloops Amiral Charner and Dumont d'Urville, the patrol vessels Marne and Tahure, and six or seven gunboats, with various subsidiary craft. In January 1941 the first five of these ships were in action with the Siamese Navy in connexion with a boundary dispute, exacerbated by Japan. In this engagement the French ships appear to have suffered little or no damage, but two Siamese torpedo boats were sunk, and two coast defence ships, the Ayuthia and Dhonburi, were put out of action. One if not both had to be beached, and afterwards refitted by the Japanese, who had originally built them.

LITTLE was heard of the French fleet for some time after this, but with the virtual occupation of Indo-China by a Japanese army in the summer of 1941 it was assumed to have passed under enemy control. Admiral Decoux, appointed Governor-General of Indo-China by Vichy, appears to have been ordered to comply with Japanese demands. Apparently the sloop Dumont d'Urville was detached from the station, or else her captain took the initiative and proceeded elsewhere, for according to the latest information she is now operating with the Allied fleets. A gunboat, the Francis-Garnier of 639 tons, also contrived to escape the Japanese net by ascending the Yangtse into the heart of China. She has been presented by France to the Chinese Navy, who have renamed her Fa Ku. Of the remaining ships, the patrol vessel Tahure, of 644 tons, was bombed and sunk off the island of Hainan by United States Army aircraft operating from a Chinese base on April 29, 1944.

INTENSIVE Japanese Air Attacks on Lingayen Gulf Ships

Now comes news that in January 1945, in the course of attacks by United States naval aircraft, on enemy shipping off the coast of Indo-China, the cruiser Lamotte-Picquet was set on fire and sunk. Apparently she was being employed by the Japanese to escort a convoy. One of the Japanese so-called training cruisers of the Katori type, of 5,800 tons, was also destroyed in the course of these operations.

It is disclosed that while covering the landing of American troops in Lingayen Gulf, early in January, a number of casualties were incurred in H.M.A.S. Australia, a 10,000-ton cruiser, and H.M.A.S. Arunta, a destroyer of 1,900 tons. Japanese aircraft appear to have made intensive attacks on these two ships and on H.M.A.S. Shropshire, which escaped without injury. Three officers and 41 ratings of the Australia were reported killed or missing, and one officer and 68 ratings were wounded. In the Arunta seven ratings were wounded, two of whom died from their injuries.

COMMANDER H. B. FARNCOMB, R.A.N., was flying his broad pendant in the Australia. It will be recalled that he relieved Commodore J. A. Collins, R.A.N., when the latter was disabled during an enemy air attack on the ship off Leyte in October 1944. (See illus. p. 584). Neither the Australia nor the Arunta was put out of action, despite bomb damage.

Several fires broke out in the Australia, but damage control parties were successful in mastering the flames, while fresh gun-crews took the places of those who became casualties. It must not be imagined, therefore, that the Japanese are no longer to be taken seriously in the air ; even though they are outnumbered and outclassed in the quality of their pilots, their naval airmen are desperate opponents who may be expected to fight to the death whenever encountered.

" PUDDLE JUMPER." they call it in U.S. Army slang ; its official title is " powerful landing ship, medium," and it is seen disgorging its cargo somewhere in the Philippines. The U.S. 8th Army—in action for the first time—added to the Luzon landings on January 29, 1945, by a successful invasion just north of Bataan.

Photo, Associated Press

Grain Ships That Also Carry Aircraft

DUAL-PURPOSE SHIPS in the service of the Allies kill two birds with one stone. With great ingenuity merchantmen have been provided with flight-decks so that they act as escort carriers while continuing to function as grain-vessels ; here one is being loaded up at a Canadian port with 7,000 tons of grain, through orifices in the flight-deck. The latter is only 380 feet long, but Swordfish torpedo-bombers of the Fleet Air Arm can take-off and touch-down on it with ease.

Photo, Keystone

Home Fleet Action Destroys Nazi Norway Convoy

DAZZLING FLASH FROM H.M.S. NORFOLK'S 8-in. GUNS stabbed the darkness (1) off the Norwegian coast, south of Stavanger, on January 11, 1945, when an enemy convoy was almost completely wiped out by ships of the Home Fleet, including the cruisers Norfolk and Bellona. After the action, in which our ships were engaged by shore batteries and aircraft, gunners of the Norfolk piped down among empty shell-cases on deck (2). H.M.S. Bellona (3) homeward bound.

Photos, British Official

How Master-Bombers Control the Aerial Fleets

Directing our bombing by radio code, the fighting "master of ceremonies" has perhaps the toughest task of all. He stays over the target the longest, endures to the full the worst of which the enemy is capable and, to complete his mission, must remain unflurried and coldly calculating to the very end. What manner of men these are is revealed by MARK PRIESTLEY.

I HAVE just visited a R.A.F. school in England where ace officers of Bomber Command—men of the stamp of Squadron-Leader Maurice Pettit, D.F.C., and Flight-Lieutenant John Hewitt, D.F.C.—are being trained in the new technique of master-bombing. Over lonely moors and wasteland I have seen complete raids held in rehearsal —raids that Germany will experience in reality—from the arrival of the pathfinders and the dropping of target indicators to the final run-in of the bombers.

Over the range in their Lancasters and Halifaxes go the master-bombers, learning their technique. They check whether the markers have fallen on the bull's-eye, they make dummy runs, weaving through imagined flak and other defences, and give repeated instructions over the radio-telephone, telling their main force how to attack.

Who are these master-bombers? They are the men who now actually direct and control every air raid on enemy territory. They control the great attacking fleets of bombers while over the target in much the same way as a naval flagship controls its warships during an engagement.

A MASTER-BOMBER'S responsibility is much like that of a commander in the field. In an attack on a German industrial city, he ensures that the incendiaries are evenly distributed over the whole area and thus cause maximum destruction. When bombs demolish a factory, he makes sure that bombs to be delivered a few seconds later do not waste themselves on the same building. Over the battle lines, in attacks made in close support of the Army, it is the master-bomber's job to see that all missiles fall ahead of the bombing line.

The dense concentration of attack that obliterates targets such as the strongly fortified towns of Duren and Julich is directly due to the supervision of a master-bomber. Thanks to this fighting master of ceremonies, raiding forces of two or three hundred

Group-Captain J. SEARBY, D.S.O., D.F.C. personally directed many important R.A.F. raids on enemy targets by means of the "Master-Bomber" technique described in this page. *Photo, New York Times Photos*

planes are achieving as much as a thousand bombers were doing not long ago.

It was Group-Captain Jack Searby, D.S.O., D.F.C., who decisively proved the value of master-bombing tactics in the first big raid on Turin in 1943. He was on the scene that night ahead of the pathfinders. As they arrived to drop their sky markers, he double-checked them. Some markers fell in the wrong place. Then in simple code words he told the following pathfinder crews to overshoot or undershoot with the next marker. When the bombers arrived, dead on time, it was to hear Group-Captain Searby's confident 'tones adding encouragement to their final instructions.

SCARCELY a week later he was there again, directing the main force to distribute its bombs equally between three aiming points, almost counting the bombs. In all, he made eight runs over the target in the course of the fifty-minute attack. Results were so satisfactory that when three aiming points had to be attacked at Peenemunde, Hitler's secret weapon centre, it was decided that the main force would again have to be controlled by one mind.

That is how Wing-Commander Geoffrey Cheshire, V.C., D.S.O. (two bars), came back into operations. He had already scored nearly a century of attacks over Germany, Italy and occupied Europe. He was already accustomed to "target hovering," for he had been picked for the first observer-reporter tactics over Mainz, when the first bomber crews in dropped their loads and then circled the target for the remaining forty-five minutes of the raid. One of the few men to have the distinction of a second bar to his D.S.O., courageous and always cheerful, he became a natural master-bomber, and adapted this technique to the tactical bombing which speeded the way of the D-Day invasion (see illus. p. 599).

The majority of master-bombers are drawn from the most experienced pilots in the Pathfinder Force, men who have proved themselves by bringing back numerous

photographs of the aiming point in dozens of German cities. But they have to face still sterner tests before they are allowed to control an attack over an enemy target.

A fleet of bombers set out one rainy day not long ago to deliver their loads on an industrial target in eastern Holland. The weather rapidly deteriorated while they were crossing the North Sea and the master-bomber called off the attack and wheeled his boys for home rather than endanger civilian lives by inaccurate bombing. Such decisions are entirely his to take. At one time, unless precise instructions were given at briefing, it was left to each individual pilot to determine the height of his bombing run. Now it is the master-bomber's duty to observe weather and cloud conditions and decide from what level the main attack shall be made.

SOMETIMES the master-bomber has failed to return. Wing-Commander G. P. Gibson, V.C., D.S.O., D.F.C., was leading a main force in Sep., 1944, and flying far below the bombers, giving instructions to the massing Lancasters, when his calm, easy voice suddenly ceased. The deputy master-bomber immediately took over. There is even a deputy to a deputy, although, fortunately, his services are seldom needed (see page 508).

One night when Lancasters and Halifaxes were attacking a marshalling yard, every bomber heard a quiet voice over the radio saying, "Close bomb doors and return home." Nobody paid any attention, and the attack proceeded to its successful end. The slightly foreign voice did not pass muster. It was an attempt by the enemy to interfere with our tactical method. Even if the master that night had not been a Canadian, other factors would have prevented the German fake "master" from getting away with it.

With practice, master-bombing has reached an amazing pitch of efficiency reflected in our diminishing bomber losses. Wing-Commander Jimmy Tait, master-bomber on the Tirpitz attack (see illus. page 477), has been called " the man who never makes a mistake." As a 14-year-old schoolboy, he made up his mind to be an airman—and 14 years later he was a master-bomber with the coveted D.S.O. (three bars) and D.F.C. Veteran of attacks on the Dortmund-Ems Canal, he led a task force on October 17, 1944, against the Kembs barrage. It was a completely successful raid despite the flak that was tearing the sky. Another flyer on the raid told me that with Tait so calm he didn't give a thought to the shell-bursts. When they reached base the pilots found the master-bomber's plane had been hit early in the action and had been wobbling all over the sky.

THEN there is Wing-Commander George Curry, D.S.O., D.F.C., the boy who was at his North-country enlisting station in 1939 and has come unscathed through scores of raids. He has had his plane shot up many times, never with any effect on his ice-cold judgement. There is Wing-Commander Tom Bingham-Hall, D.S.O., D.F.C., who a few weeks back headed one of the toughest attacks ever made on the Ruhr in broad daylight. As he zoomed again and again to check the target indicators his plane was holed like the proverbial colander. A few days later he was detailed to control the attack on another vital target in North-West Germany. This time his plane had an engine knocked right out, and the aircraft was cut almost in two. "Get ready to take over, just in case!" Wing-Commander Bingham-Hall told his deputy. He carried on with his task—and successfully completed it.

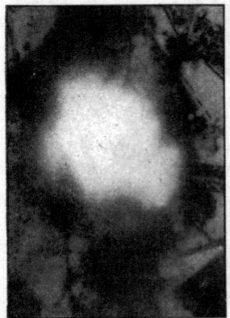

THE TARGET INDICATOR makes a vast patch of light during a raid by R.A.F. Lancasters, on January 1, 1945, on the oft-drained Dortmund-Ems canal, thus marking the position for the following attacking aircraft
Photo, British Official

Strange Truce Outside Beleaguered St. Nazaire

EVACUATING 13,000 civilians from the closely invested St. Nazaire area on January 17, 1945, Allied and German officers standing side by side watched the torn-up railway track outside the great French Atlantic port being repaired (1) in readiness for the first "mercy train."

A German soldier, waving a white flag, halted the train for inspection (2); it was thoroughly searched before being permitted to steam into St. Nazaire, drawn by a locomotive name-plated "Laval." The German delegation negotiating the seven-days' truce, which began the following day, was headed by medical officer Captain D. Mueller (3 centre), surrounded by American and French officers and an official of the International Red Cross. Only passengers carried on the train's inward journey were two French Red Cross nurses, one of whom (4) received final instructions from a U.S. officer, German soldiers looking on. St. Nazaire had been besieged since August 6, 1944; the German garrison was said to number over 35,000.

Photos, Keystone

Business as Usual in Threatened Strasbourg

CAPITAL OF ALSACE was menaced when the enemy, ferrying forces across the Rhine, approached Gen. Patch's U.S. 7th Army and Gen. de Lattre de Tassigny's French 1st Army (reported on January 7, 1945). Many of the city's 200,000 population were evacuated; otherwise life went on much as usual.

In the Place Kléber—named after Napoleon's Strasbourg-born general—news-thirsty citizens surrounded a newspaper kiosk (1). Favoured by the women (2) were " slacks " tucked in at the ankle. Outside the Bank of France (3) a girl cyclist read French posters ("We shall get 'em. Long live France!") pasted over anti-Soviet slogans stencilled on the walls by the Germans.

When the enemy forces occupied the city in 1941 they renamed the Place Broglie " Adolf Hitler Platz." Now it is as before (4)—called after the Marshal de Broglie, a famous 18th-century governor; here, in 1792, the " Marseillaise " was first sung. (See also illus. pages 308 and 309, Vol. 1, and 490, Vol. 8).

Photos, Planet News

PAGE 619

'Josef Stalin' is Russia's New Monster Weapon

THE SOVIETS' MAMMOTH TANK, named after the Premier of the U.S.S.R., made a dramatic debut on General Cherniakhovsky's Polish front in mid-January 1945. The Nazis reported it as completely outclassing their own Royal Tiger (see illus. p. 549), mounting "the biggest tank gun in the world"—a 4·8-in. weapon, as compared with the Royal Tiger's 3·4-in. and the Sherman's 3-in. guns—and weighing nearly 100 tons. Five Stalin tanks in action (above) in Poland. Self-propelled guns (top) in East Prussia.

PAGE 640   *Photos, Pictorial Press, Planet News*

Polish Capital Resounds to the Victory March

AFTER THE RECOVERY OF WARSAW on January 17, 1945, Marshal Zhukov chose soldiers of the 1st Polish Army who, with troops of his 1st White Russian Front, had taken part in the city's liberation, to lead a procession through their capital: they are here seen passing the Church of the Holy Redeemer. Next day the Lublin Provisional Government took up residence. By January 29, Marshal Zhukov had left Warsaw over 200 miles behind and had crossed the frontier of Pomerania, 95 miles from Berlin. See story in page 633.

Photo, Pictorial Press

Channel Islanders Look Daily for Deliverance

To avoid slaughter and destruction, the British Government evacuated the armed forces and thousands of civilians from the Channel Islands in June 1940. The following month the Germans landed and commenced their occupation of territory which has belonged to Great Britain since 1066. The life that friend and foe alike are leading there is revealed by HAROLD A. ALBERT.

NEVER was any ship more eagerly awaited than the S.S. Vega as, towards the close of 1944, she ploughed through wintry gales and fog with her first cargo of food and medical supplies for the German-occupied Channel Islands. A Swedish vessel chartered in Lisbon by the British Red Cross, she carried 1,000 tons of Canadian-packed food parcels and some 5,000 invalid diet supplement parcels, as well as salt, soap, drugs and medicines, and bags of mail from prisoners of war in Germany. And her sponsors can perhaps claim that her truly international errand of mercy was organized in record time.

On December 12, 1944, the Home Secretary announced in the House of Commons, "H.M. Government have decided that it would be right to supplement the rations of the civil population of the islands by sending supplies of medicines, soap and food parcels on the basis of those supplied to prisoners of war. The German Government have now agreed to this procedure, and have granted a safe conduct to the ship." Although held up by bad weather, barely a fortnight later the Vega dropped anchor in the harbour of St. Peter Port, the capital of Guernsey, and Colonel Iselin, the Swiss Red Cross delegate, stepped down the gangway.

IT was the first link the Islanders had with the friendly outside world since the fall of France. Since July 1940 they have lived under the yoke of the swastika, enduring German rule, starving, suffering; and the arrival of a relief ship must have seemed the first ray of hope in their long ordeal.

Not long ago the General Hospital in St. Helier, the capital of Jersey, had torn up the last of its sheets for bandages, and was reported to have no remaining drugs or anaesthetics of any kind. Patients on the operating table had to suffer. Heating difficulties have been so great that doctors have sometimes been unable even to sterilize their instruments, and some patients when gravely ill have counted themselves fortunate in being allowed an extra blanket, or a handful of rice as extra food.

Children are still allowed supplies of watery milk, though this is diminishing, for the Germans are said to be killing off the cows. Rations have shrunk to almost microscopic proportions: 4 lb. of bread per week, 2 oz. of fats, a few potatoes, and less than 1 oz. of meat, if and when obtainable. But meat is seldom seen, and bread has become largely bran, sawdust, and potato. There is no sugar ration, and tea and coffee are unknown. Horses have vanished—slaughtered to make sausages. Cabbages form the staple diet, and seed potatoes, eked out with syrup made from sugar-beet.

The shortage of soap—reduced to a tiny tablet of fats, sand and bone-meal, issued every three months—has led to an outbreak of skin diseases. Diphtheria and influenza have ravaged the Islands. To compensate for the lack of salt, filtered sea-water is peddled round the streets in little carts and sold at 2d. a gallon, for cooking vegetables and making bread. There are, of course, no tinned foods, few matches or candles, no jam, and no cheese.

In both Jersey and Guernsey the electric current is cut off for six hours a day, there is no gas, and only the Germans have coal or coke. A weekly ration of 10 lb. of wood is allowed to householders, but the merest twigs count as weight; and a boy who picks up a piece of wood can be heavily fined for stealing fuel. With paper and writing materials at a premium and bicycles laid up for lack of tires, with no new clothes and scanty repairing materials, one wonders how any semblance of normal life can be carried on. Even the coinage has practically disappeared as a result of pennies and shillings being greedily pocketed by German troops and sent home by them as souvenirs.

THIRTY thousand women and children, and men of military age, were evacuated from the Islands by the British Government in June 1940, but 60,000 civilians remained, and the armed forces were withdrawn to England. Then, on June 28, in spite of the demilitarization, the Nazis bombed and machine-gunned Jersey and Guernsey, and on July 1 enemy troops were landed by air. The local States, as the parliaments are known, immediately put into action a scheme of compulsory labour to produce every possible ounce of foodstuffs from the rich island earth, and the Germans at first made little attempt to interfere with local government. Occasional extra supplies—cigarettes and cheese, shirts at 35s. apiece and shoddy frocks

at £20—filtered in, together with saccharin and coffee, from the French mainland.

The towns were placarded with posters showing German soldiers smiling at children. The local newspapers had immediately become Nazi-controlled and gave their own distorted views and news. Until the paper shortage grew too severe, William Joyce (Lord Haw-Haw) ran columns of his own in the Guernsey Star and Evening Press. When the Gestapo arrived, all non-native-born British subjects were deported to Germany. Nearly all the Guernsey police force, in addition, was deported on a charge of stealing German supplies.

Thus to the "lovely gardens of the sea" came the horrors of occupation. Thousands of extra troops were drafted in to supplement the garrison of occupation and maintain sterner watch on civilians. With them came regiments of labour slaves entitled to draw extra rations from the already slender island stocks. The remaining children were compelled to go to school to learn German and study the "glories" of German history. Radio sets were confiscated, save the concealed sets the Gestapo never found, but nightly showers of leaflets dropped from aeroplanes soon renewed longed-for news from London.

EVEN in the worst days the Islanders never lost hope. They stripped themselves to ensure that deportees to Germany went provided with clothing and food. They organized classes and concerts to help pass the waiting years; Guernsey amateurs even produced Rio Rita and The Desert Song with the aid of a moth-eaten store of carnival costumes. But when Feldkommandant Knackfuss ordered a command performance, the performers forgot their words and the musicians played the wrong notes. "Our hands were cold," they said.

On the Islands, as I write, there remains a German garrison estimated to number about 35,000; they were cut off from the mainland when the Americans stormed St. Malo last August. And, ironically, they share now with the civilians the hardships and misery which the Nazi occupation helped to bring about. The clothing of officers and men, like that of the civilians, is tattered and worn thin. But the Islands are not besieged. They are of no military importance; they have been by-passed in the war. In early Feb. 1945 it was Jersey's turn to welcome the Vega—with salt, medical supplies, boot-repairing materials, and oil for harbour cranes.

There is a typical British "bobby" in St. Helier who used to be much pestered by German newsreel men anxious to impress Berlin cinema audiences with the fact that the Germans were indeed on British soil. Now there are no German cameramen. There is no more German traffic to direct. That same policeman patrols past empty shops and shuttered boarding houses, and into his belt he has tucked a pair of natty white gloves. And you and I and Feldkommandant Knackfuss know that it will not be long before he wears them!

NAZI TROOPS IN ONE OF THE CHANNEL ISLANDS, at a lecture outside the school taken over as a billet. Life was easier for them when this photograph was taken. Much less spick-and-span and soldierly in appearance are they now, for the garrisons have been isolated since August 1944, and occupying troops and civilians are all in "the same boat."
Photo, Keystone

Above the Bhamo Wreckage a Burmese Idol Looms

On the line of advance down Burma from the north the Japanese stronghold of Bhamo was stormed on Dec. 16, 1944, after a month's siege, by troops of Maj.-Gen. Li Hung's 38th Division, part of the 1st Chinese Army in Lieut.-Gen. Dan Sultan's northern combat area command. On its way to take part in this reopening of the Burma Road, a light tank manned by Chinese (top) rumbles past peasant ox-carts. Through the remnants of the conquered town the storm-troops file (bottom).

Holding the Line in Holland and Alsace

Conditions under which men of the British 2nd Army holding the Maas line in Holland were living are typified by this slit-trench (1) in a pine wood, occupied by Cpl. Hall of Newcastle and Cpl. Alder of Kelso. Snow-camouflaged infantrymen (2) dive for cover as a mortar bomb bursts near. On the Strasbourg front (3) a patrol of the U.S. 7th Army, similarly camouflaged against the tell-tale snow, file cautiously through Domaniale Forest near Bitche, then dominated by German guns.

Photos
B

Nature's White Mantle a Tricky Foe to Outwit

Men, weapons and equipment all wrapped in concealing white, a British " Recce " patrol crawls through the snow on German territory (4) ; from 100 yards away they are invisible.   Past a blazing vehicle filled with exploding ammunition at Laroche, in Belgium, a tank grinds its way, driven by Sgt. J. Brown, of Wigan (5), to clear a passage for an ambulance convoy of wounded.   From a crude dugout (6) a member of the U.S. 10th Armoured Division emerges for a breath of fresh air.

Photos, Associated Press,
Sport & General

Mars Men Beat the Jungle in Southward Drive

A new American battle-group known as the Mars Task Force includes former members of " Merrill's Marauders," famed for exploits in earlier campaigns.   Men of this Force, reported on Jan. 24, 1945, to be engaging the Japanese 75 miles north of Lashio on the old Burma Road, are seen (top) crossing a footbridge on their way to Myitkyina, Allied base in Central Burma.   Before advancing towards Mandalay, Chinese troops (see page 623) mopped-up in Bhamo (bottom).

VIEWS & REVIEWS

Of Vital War Books

by Hamilton Fyfe

A LONG time ago a king of Bohemia who had brought vines from Burgundy and hoped to produce from them vintages as rich and mellow as those he had drunk in France, was disappointed at first with his experiment. Later he was better pleased. He compared the wine to the soul of the Czechs. "It tastes somewhat bitter to begin with," he said. "You have to get used to it. But in the end you rather like it."

The Czechs don't mind that story. Two of them who have written a book entitled Czechoslovakia, Land of Dream and Enterprise (Lindsay Drummond, for the Czechoslovak Ministry of Foreign Affairs Department of Information, 15s.) actually tell it—without comment. Czechs are like a certain sort of Scot ; they don't object to being described as having a rough rind covering sound and rich fruit.

T HAT certainly is true of the Czechs. Everyone who has been in their country for more than a passing tourist visit will admit it. "They take some knowing," will be the unanimous verdict. But when they do know you, and you have learned to know them, you have to agree that they are a nation worthy of respect and liking, even if they do not inspire immediate affection. As for their energy, it compels admiration.

I have called them a nation. That is not accurate. The Republic of Czechoslovakia includes Slovaks, Moravians and Ruthenes as well. But in the twenty years of its existence as an independent State the Czechs took the lead in everything, and in consequence were not too well liked by the rest. Energetic and competent people are inclined to disregard the protests and prejudices of those who are easy-going and disinclined for changes. The Slovaks are far apart from the Czechs in temperament. They are very largely a shepherd people. They cling to the old ways. They were long under Hungarian domination, and their masters deliberately kept them ignorant and poor. The only way by which a clever boy who wanted to be something other than a small farmer, a tender of sheep, a craftsman or a small trader, could satisfy his ambition was to become Hungarianized.

The discontent of the Slovaks after they had been freed was due mainly to their dislike of anything new—education, for example, though they soon began to understand its value. But they had certain genuine grievances, as had the German part of the population. The latter lived in that Sudetenland we heard so much about during the year or so before this present war broke out. Strangely enough, there is no mention of the Sudeten inhabitants in the book ; they do not figure in the index. The authors, Jan Cech and J. E. Mellon, evidently decided it would be better to ignore them. It is pretty safe to foretell that there will not be any Germans in Czechoslovakia when the war is over.

S OME people who know both are thinking that trouble might have been avoided if the Czechs had not been so masterful and had allowed their fellow-citizens of German origin more participation in the work of government. Hitler would not then have had a pretext for interfering and stirring up the Sudetenland folk to revolt. But, on the other hand, the Czechs knew that the Germans, who had been top-dogs when Bohemia was under Austrian rule, resented the liberation of the country and were not really loyal to the new State. It would have been prudent to hold out the hand of friend-ship to them, but such generosity is rare and not quite in the character of the general run of Czechs.

If they had a less "rough rind," they would not be so vigorous and so successful in their undertakings. They were by far the most go-ahead and enterprising of all the populations in the Austrian Empire, which they helped so much to bring down in 1918. "Czechoslovakia's industrial importance can be seen from the fact that no less than 75 per cent of the former Austro-Hungarian Empire's industries was concentrated on her territory." Coal and iron ore abound, so the heavy industries flourished. Among lighter products most of us remember

---

Land of Dream and Enterprise

Bohemian glass and Pilsner beer, and more recently Bata shoes. Paper, china, leather goods, gloves, furniture, chemicals, and textiles on a vast scale were other products of Bohemia, while in late years the Moravian capital Brno (formerly Brunn) became known as "the Manchester of Czechoslovakia" because of its manufactures, especially woollen cloth.

B UT you must not think of the Czechs allowing their industry to turn towns and countrysides into hideous factory areas and wildernesses. They will not tolerate any ugliness that is avoidable. There is an illustration in this book of a cement works in Bohemia. In a clear atmosphere the buildings stand out white and gracious ; they might pass almost for Greek temples. No more damning contrast between them and the huddle of dirty sheds and iron-roofed erections which mark so many British cement factories, could be imagined.

In this and most other ways the Czechs are among the most "modern" nations. They went ahead of the Russians in proving that the Slav nature is anything but backward and lethargic once it is aroused. They were set a hard task when they came into possession of their country after the First Great War and had to reorganize almost everything. Presidents Masaryk and Benes receive a great deal of the credit for this, and they deserve a great deal ; but the rapid recovery in all fields of the national life was due in the main to the qualities of leadership displayed by large numbers of Czechs and to the steady work and communal effort of the mass of the population.

One of the earliest changes concerned the ownership of land. The large estates in the possession of German, Austrian or Hungarian landlords were broken up and divided among small farmers. Nobody was permitted to own more than 625 acres. All who had land above that amount were obliged to sell it at a 1914 valuation. The State bought it, sometimes paying more than the owners could have obtained in the open market, and then sold or leased it to cultivators who farmed in a modest way. Thus one-eighth of the soil of the Republic changed hands in a very short time and agriculture was greatly improved.

I N Slovakia especially there was rejoicing over the freeing of the soil from the Hungarian overlords. They had so long tyrannized over those who worked it with small advantage to themselves. Magyar rule had been particularly oppressive and corrupt. There was no attempt to govern for the benefit of the people. The "magnates" were utterly selfish, for the most part, though exceptions did exist here and there. In Ruthenia there were under Hungarian rule only eighteen elementary schools. Within two years the Republic had more than 500 going, and these were not enough. By the end of fifteen years the Ruthenians had over 1,000 schools of various kinds. They are taking full advantage of them.

I hope education and the opening-up of larger prospects will not too much alter the habits and the outlook of the Ruthenian, Slovak and Moravian populations. I have found travelling among them made a continual delight, not only by the varied and frequently magnificent mountain scenery, but by the kindliness of the people.

I hope, too, the picturesque and sometimes really beautiful costumes the country people wear on Sundays and holidays will not give place, as they have done elsewhere—in Serbia, for instance—to trousers and felt hats and the year-before-last's Paris or Vienna fashions. Efficiency coupled with a preference for having things done decently and in order, and not letting Nature be spoiled, has been the aim of the Republic so far, and will no doubt remain so.

PETROL-DRIVEN PUMPS FOR FIRE-FIGHTING, mounted on trailers, produced by a firm which came to Britain from Czechoslovakia just before the war. In addition to satisfying a considerable proportion of our own requirements, the concern supplied pumps to Malta, the Near East and elsewhere. Photograph reproduced from the book reviewed in this page.

By courtesy of the Czechoslovak Ministry of Foreign Affairs

Little-Known Regions to be Wrested from Japan

For lasting peace to be secured in the Pacific, three remote regions—Formosa, the Pescadores and Korea—must be removed from Japanese control. Even after the defeat of their Nippon "protectors" the problems will not easily be surmounted. Meanwhile, as DONALD COWIE points out, their strategic importance in the impending campaigns of the South-East Asia and South-West Pacific Commands is paramount. See also pages 342, Vol. 8, and 590, Vol. 7.

FORMOSA, the Pescadores and Korea are to be taken from Japan. That is a declared war-aim of the United States and Britain. Already the naval and air fighting has begun to swirl round Formosa, at least. But what do we know of these remote places ? Are they really important, and what will be their strategic significance tomorrow ? Korea, for example. Probably there are few who realize that Korea is a land as big as Portugal, with thrice the population, and that it is as wide as Scotland and twice the length, that it was a famous independent kingdom for centuries, and still has an underground freedom movement like any occupied country of Europe.

Consult the map, and look for a rugged peninsula which descends from Manchuria and points like a dagger in the direction of southern Japan. Korea also looks like a potential causeway leading from Japan to Northern China, and thus the unfortunate country was regarded by the expansionist Japanese who extended their "protection" to it in 1910. That was after China and Russia had been thoroughly beaten by the Japanese hereabouts, so that poor Korea, without any local friends, and backward in the kind of civilization that makes for success in modern war, had no option but to accept the inevitable.

Hemmed in and Handicapped

"The Hermit Kingdom" was the ancient name given to Korea, and it explains a great deal. Geography has always kept the country diffident and peace-loving. Hemmed in completely, it has suffered repeated invasions from Chinese, Tartars, and Japanese. Then the configuration of the land—"as plentifully sprinkled with mountains as a ploughed field with ridges," says one old writer—has divided the inhabitants into mutually-exclusive clans, and has hampered the development of material civilization on the modern scale.

Yet the native Koreans, superficially resembling the Chinese in appearance and customs but definitely *not* Chinese, have contrived to retain a spirit of independence. Even the Japanese have never been able to crush this spirit. They had to speak of extending their suzerainty over Korea, not of making the country an integral part of Japan. Outwardly the people are what we would call soft and easy-going, like the Burmans, but underneath they do not yield.

Ports and Harbours Modernized

All this is said because it leads to the future, when we do at last liberate Korea, perhaps using the peninsula as a dagger indeed. The task looks formidable on the map, but will certainly be aided by the disposition of the Koreans themselves. The Japanese have modernized the ports of Gensan on the east, Masanpo on the south, and Mokpo, Chemulpo and Chinampo on the west coast—good harbours—and have built railways linking these towns with the capital, Seoul. They have intensively developed the chief industries of cotton and silk growing, agriculture and salt, and they have exploited mineral deposits about which we know little. But—the Japanese have never conquered the real Korea, which, when suitably aided, may separate them fatally from their armies in Manchuria and China, while giving their liberators an excellent vantage-point from which to take the Japanese homeland in flank. (See map in opposite page.)

So we come—or hope we will come—to Formosa. This is an island as big as ten Trinidads, with a population of aboriginals twice that of New Zealand. It is situated a long way from Korea, right down the Chinese coast south of Shanghai but east of Hong Kong. The map shows how it controls the entrance to the East China Sea, which is, in turn, the road to the Yellow Sea and—Korea.

Therefore, Formosa (otherwise Taiwan) is an obvious war-aim, both for immediate strategic purposes and for helping to secure the Pacific peace afterwards. The intention is that the island shall be restored to China, from whom it was taken by the Japanese as a trophy of the Sino-Japanese War in 1895. It has always belonged to China. But the very primitive inhabitants represent a peculiar stock, and the Chinese never bothered to develop Formosa.

Targets for Invading Forces

Today the island has thriving industries —mining, salt, tobacco, tea, rice, sugar— and a railway from the northern port Keelung via the considerable town Taihoku, the capital, to Tainan and the port of Takow in the south-west ; and there are nearly 5,000 miles of roads and several large airports. But all this has been the work of the Japanese, who have really made Formosa an integral part of their country, so that it may not prove an easy conquest for us. Already raided by U.S. and Chinese bombers in 1943, Formosa was heavily attacked by carrier-borne aircraft and Super-Fortresses from China in October 1944, just before the American landing on Leyte in the Philippines, and again in January 1945 during Gen. MacArthur's invasion of Luzon.

The island is mountainous and afforested, with a rough coast on the Pacific side, but contains alluvial plains on the China side and in the south which might be the obvious target for invading forces, provided they first secured the Pescadores. The latter are scarcely visible on the map, a group of 48 small islands between Formosa and the China coast. But possibly it can be seen already why they were singled out by Roosevelt, Chiang Kai-shek and Churchill in conference at Cairo, as a main Pacific war aim, along with Korea, Formosa, Manchuria and the Pacific mandated islands. He who holds Formosa can control the entrance to the East China Sea and the paths to Japan and Korea. But the Pescadores (bombed by Liberators in August 1943) provide a series of stepping-stones across the Formosa Strait, between the big island and China. They bear the same strategic relation to Formosa and China as Malta did to Sicily and Tunisia.

APART from that, the islands are primitive, undeveloped, with a population of no more than 60,000 backward peasants and fishermen. They are to be restored to China after the war, as is right, but China never did much for them in the past. (Concerning which it must be remembered that China had more than enough to look after elsewhere, and did not believe in colonial development, anyway.) But the pattern may be plain. There is an amphibious link between China and Formosa—the Pescadores. Formosa itself bestows control of the East China Sea which leads to Shanghai and Korea. Korea is disaffected, vital to the Japanese as a link with Manchuria.

Apart from which, it may be pointed out that all these places could carry bombers to pound Japan at short range : and that another series of islands, the Ryukyu (attacked by a U.S. naval task force in October 1944 and again in January 1945), jump away from Formosa in a north-easterly direction and do not stop till they reach Japan again. Thus it can be imagined with what interest Admiral Mountbatten and Gen. MacArthur and Admiral Nimitz study the charts of these parts.

OFF FORMOSA a smoke-cloud 5,000 feet high obscures a Japanese ship struck by a U.S. warplane of Admiral Halsey's 3rd Pacific Fleet when, on October 11, 1944, over 200 enemy vessels were sunk. Formosa was heavily raided in Jan. 1945 by carrier- and China-based U.S. aircraft, including Super-Fortresses, both before and during General MacArthur's landings at Luzon (Jan. 9), thus severing the enemy's Philippines supply-lines.

Photo, Keystone

Our Zones of Advance in the Western Pacific

Legend:
- ■ Allied-held areas
- □ Japanese-held areas
- ⊛ Allied-held Islands
- ○ Japanese-held Islands

SOVIET UNION
SINKIANG
OUTER MONGOLIA
MANCHURIA
Harbin
PARAMUSHIRU
SAKHALIN
KARAFUTO
KURILE IS.
Peiping
Vladivostok
HOKKAIDO
TIBET
CHINA
Chinampo
Gensan
Seoul
KOREA
Chemulpo
Masanpo
Mokpo
YELLOW SEA
HONSHU
JAPAN
1500 M.
TOKYO
Yellow
INDIA
Ledo
CHUNGKING
Yangtze R.
Hankow
SHIKOKU
KYUSHU
1500 M.
LEDO RD.
Shanghai
EAST CHINA SEA
Wenchow
1000 M.
RYUKYU IS.
BONIN IS.
BURMA ROAD
Lashio
Kweiyang
Kunming
Weilin
Foochow
Amoy
Keelung
Taihoku
Tainan
Takow
FORMOSA
Formosa Str.
PESCADORES IS.
1000 M.
VOLCANO IS.
500 M.
BUR o MA
Mandalay
Akyab
HANOI
Canton
Hong Kong
Swatow
PACIFIC
MARIANAS
RANGOON
HAINAN
SIAM
FRENCH INDO-CHINA
PHILIPPINES
500 M.
SAIPAN
GUAM
BANGKOK
SOUTH CHINA SEA
LUZON
MANILA
MINDORO
OCEAN
Saigon
PALAWAN
SAMAR
LEYTE
YAP
MALAYA
MINDANAO
PALAU IS.
CAROLINE IS.
SINGAPORE
BRUNEI
SARAWAK
SUMATRA
BORNEO
MOROTAI
HALMAHERA
BIAK
WAKDE
CELEBES
Hollandia
Aitape
NETHERLANDS INDIES
NEW GUINEA
JAVA
BALI
TIMOR

500   1000
MILES

FROM THE "BACK DOOR" OF AUSTRALIA—New Guinea—which the Japanese reached in 1942 in the limit of their southward thrusts in the Pacific, the Allies had by mid-January 1945 driven them back to Luzon, northernmost of the Philippines. From bases in China and the Marianas, U.S. Super-Fortresses flew vast distances across the Pacific to bomb war factories at Tokyo, as well as Formosa, Japan's island stronghold off South China. On January 11, 1945, U.S. carrier-borne aircraft of the 3rd Fleet sank 23 enemy ships in an attack on four convoys off Saigon, Indo-China. Most spectacular Allied advances to date have been the Philippine landings at Leyte (October 22, 1944, see page 429); and at Luzon (January 9, 1945,

see page 579) by U.S. forces under General MacArthur, C.-in-C. South-West Pacific, assisted by units of the Royal Australian Navy. The formation of a powerful British fleet to operate in the Pacific, under Admiral Sir Bruce Fraser, was announced on December 10, 1944.

Admiral Halsey, Commander of the U.S. 3rd Fleet, declared on January 29, 1945, that Japanese control of the South China Sea had been smashed and that Allied warships could operate there at will. The Philippines campaign had virtually isolated Japan proper from areas which she had seized in 1942 and from which she derived much of her war material. See facing page.

By courtesy of The New York Times

Premier Ranges War Fronts in Confident Review

Speaking for one hour and fifty minutes in the House of Commons on Jan. 18, 1945, Mr. Churchill threw light on matters in connexion with the securing and maintenance of a just peace in liberated countries, indicated the trend of the war and gave the world a sober reckoning of sacrifices the United Nations have made. Excerpts from Mr. Churchill's speech are given here.

STATING bluntly that "we have one principle about the liberated countries or the repentant satellite countries," Mr. Churchill described it as:

Government of the people by the people, for the people, set up on the basis of free and universal suffrage, and elections with secrecy of ballot and no intimidation . . . It is not only our aim, it is our interest and it is our only care.

The thorny subject of Greece in her transition throes was given considerable attention, the Premier declaring that of the correctness of our policy there he was sure wise obtained, with a plan to seize the power of the Greek State in Athens once the Germans cleared out and went away.

Whilst food was being distributed and efforts made to restore order, the E.A.M. and Communist Ministers

threw sand in the wheels of the Cabinet at every stage. They did their best to hamper the landing and distribution of food by promoting strikes on some occasions. I am against private armies. We are not going to have private armies . . . However, the "Cease fire" has sounded. The rejoicing people of Athens have once again proclaimed the British troops. At any

Omar Bradley. Many other consequential movements were made, and rightly made. Judging from the results, both these highly skilled commanders handled the very large forces at their disposal in a manner which, I think I may say without exaggeration, may become a model for military students in the future. Field-Marshal Montgomery at the earliest moment, acting with extraordinary promptitude, concentrated powerful British reserves on the decisive strategic points, and, having been placed in command, as he was, by General Eisenhower of American forces larger than those he holds from H.M. Government or from the Canadians, larger than those he holds in the 21st Army Group, he fell unceasingly on the enemy on the north and has fought the battle all the time from that part of the assailed front.

Superb and Titanic Events

Reminder of the part being played by the British Commonwealth and Empire in battles on the Continent and in the general war was given in terse facts and figures.

We are maintaining at the present time in the field, and in our garrisons the equivalent of upwards of 100 divisions, apart from the vast Navy and the Air Force and all the rest . . . We are fighting incessantly on three separate fronts—in North-West Europe, in Italy, and in Burma. Of all the troops landed in France the losses sustained in the fighting by the British Empire and United States troops have been very low in proportion to the numbers engaged. Of course, there are over twice as many American troops on the Western Front as there are troops of the British Commonwealth, and we have in fact lost half as many as our American Allies. If you take killed only, the British and Canadians lost a larger proportion than the United States, heavy though the United States losses are.

More likely to shorten this war than to lengthen it was Mr. Churchill's opinion of the Rundstedt attack—apparently designed to throw the Anglo-American Armies out of gear before the onslaught of the Russian Armies from the east.

Marshal Stalin is very punctual. He would rather be before his time than late in the combinations of the Allies. I can't attempt to set limits to the superb and titanic events we are now witnessing or on their reactions in every theatre.

IN the Philippines fighting "we must marvel at the triumphant military strength of the United States." And of that campaign on which we and India have expended such great effort he said:

The advance of the Fourteenth Army in harmony with the Chinese on their north flank has carried the fighting front against the Japanese at some points almost 200 miles forward from Imphal. Now is the time when the fearful fighting of last year is reaping its reward. The stuffing was beaten out of the Japanese troops in the terrible conflicts in which we had very heavy losses—14,000 men at least, British, Indian, and others—and in which far higher toll was taken by disease.

No negotiated peace with "the terrible foe" was emphatically reiterated.

I am quite clear that nothing should induce us to abandon the principle of unconditional surrender or to enter into any form of negotiation with Germany or Japan under whatever guise. Both the President of the United States and I in your name have repeatedly declared that the enforcement of unconditional surrender on the enemy in no wise relieves the victorious Powers of the obligations of humanity and of their duties as civilized and Christian nations.

A word of warning, followed by a hearty profession of supreme confidence, reminded us that

We must keep our eye on the jet-propelled fighter aircraft, on the "V" rockets, and, above all, on the renewed U-boat menace. No doubt there are other dangers, too. But, taking the position as a whole, I have never, at any time, been able to present a more confident statement to the House of the ever-growing might and ascendancy of the United Nations or of the military solidarity of the three great Allies.

FOOTNOTE TO THE PREMIER'S SPEECH is this map showing how the Allies, massing from east, west and south, had closed in on Germany between D-Day (June 6, 1944) and January 25, 1945, when British, U.S. and French armies stood poised near the Rhine and six Russian armies had cut across Poland to isolate East Prussia and threaten the very heart of the Reich.
Map by courtesy of The Daily Herald

in mind and conscience. It was with the approval of the U.S. and Russia and with the invitation of the Greek Government that we had gone there to allay the confusion left by the departure of the Germans.

We came with a small force of troops and took up our positions from no military point of view. We scattered our troops at a number of places—on the coast and at a number of points inland—where we hoped to be able to bring in a large number of supplies to a very hungry people . . . We had made Greece safe for U.N.R.R.A. before the outbreak took place. Meanwhile, over a period of six weeks or so the Greek Government, representative of all parties, was distracted by internal divisions and street demonstrations, and all the time the Communist-directed forces were drawing down from the north and infiltrating into the city of Athens, in which they had also a strong local organization. We had furnished these men over several years with arms in considerable quantities in the hope that they would fight against the Germans. They accepted the arms and kept them and other arms which they had captured or bought from the Germans in their retreat or other-

rate, something in the region of 1,500,000 people—men and women—can earn their daily living without fear of being killed in street fighting.

As a result of these events, and also of the complete clearance of the city, which was preceded for several weeks by heavy fighting night and day, the various alphabetical groups have, I have been informed, submitted themselves to the best available leaders, and have subtracted themselves from E.A.M., leaving now only the K.K.E., the Communists, in complete isolation.

GENEROUS praise was accorded our American Allies for their tackling of the Rundstedt incursion into the lines on the Ardennes front, "the greatest American battle of the war." The taking-over by Field-Marshal Montgomery of American Armies at the crucial moment was resolute, wise and militarily correct.

General Eisenhower at once gave the command to the north of the gap to Field-Marshal Montgomery and to the south of the gap to General

From Athens at Last Fades Grievous Turmoil

AFTER FIVE WEEKS of fighting (see pages 523, 537), the signing of a truce (1) between General Scobie, British C.-in-C. in Greece, and delegates of ELAS (left) was announced on Jan. 12, 1945. It came into operation at one minute past midnight on Jan. 14.

During the conflict R.A.F. heavy bombers ferried hundreds of tons of food from Italy to feed the Athenians while General Scobie established an Army unit, run by operational troops, for the issue of 34,000 rations a day. A British military policeman (2) shepherded children to one of the kitchens.

Archbishop Damaskinos, appointed Regent on Dec. 30, 1944, walked to the gates of the Foreign Office to acknowledge the cheers of the crowds after his proclamation, a guard of Evzones presenting arms (3). Men of the newly-formed Greek National Guard (4) marched in single file through the streets. On Jan. 29 it was announced that ELAS had agreed to free all civilian hostages, numbering several thousand. Eight days later 1,025 British prisoners, including 525 R.A.F. personnel, and 700 Greek hostages, after weeks of bitter hardships in the snowbound Greek mountains arrived in Athens. See also facing page.

Photos, British Official　　PAGE 631

Triumphant Return to the Arakan Port of Akyab

BITTER LOSS TO THE JAPS was the recapture, on January 3, 1945, of the important Arakan coastal town of Akyab, which only a year ago figured as their base from which India was to be conquered. Wing-Commander Bradley R.N.Z.A.F., the town's pre-war Civil Administrator, was garlanded and welcomed back by the inhabitants (1). With its great all-weather airfield, and port capable of berthing 10-000-ton cruisers, Akyab was Burma's most-bombed target; first British bombs fell on it in July 1942, two months after the Japanese occupation. The airfield, serviceable for all types of aircraft, has become "the Croydon of the Arakan."

The ill-supplied Japanese had been withdrawing for some time by sampans, launches and rafts, and the island fell to troops of the 15th Indian Corps, assisted by British Commandos, the Royal Navy and the R.A.F., without a shot being fired. The invasion in progress (2); landing craft are moving inshore, while troops wade to the beach. The town and port (3) seen from a R.A.F. plane of Eastern Air Command during the operation. *Photos, British Official*

I WAS THERE! Eye Witness Stories of the War

I Talked to the People of Stricken Warsaw

Every town and village in liberated Poland hung out flags when troops of the Red Army and the 1st Polish Army freed the city of Warsaw, Jan. 17. 1945. Crowds cheered, churches held thanksgiving services. But behind the joy in the Polish capital was grief and desolation, as told by a correspondent with Marshal Zhukov's men. His dispatch is published here by courtesy of Soviet War News. See illus. page 621.

WHEN our soldiers entered Warsaw they found not a single civilian. The wind roared through the empty streets. Then a few hungry families, with nowhere to go, straggled from the debris. Since then thousands of people have returned. Today the city echoes to the westward tramping of Soviet and Polish soldiers, avenging armies. Tanks, guns, lorries and troops are pouring through Warsaw.

And from the west the civilians keep coming back. Their hearts are heavy with anger. Most of their city is gone. They stand dumb with sorrow in the streets. Those who have lost their homes drag oddments from cellars—tattered mattresses, pillows, blankets. They finger them in a desultory kind of way, then go wandering on.

I began talking to a Polish worker, Stanislav Wjechowski. He showed me round the part where he had lived. "There used to be a school here," he said, pointing to an anonymous chaos of stone. "And this was the museum." A marble memorial tablet still hung precariously to a ruined wall. Wjechowski read out the inscription, "Here lived and worked Frédéric Chopin." The Germans pulled down the Chopin monument as long ago as 1942. The people of Warsaw commented, "They are afraid in case Chopin plays them a funeral march !"

We walked through Nowy Swiat, Warecha Street, Napoleon Square—everywhere the same gruesome spectacle. The sixteen-storey general post office, the tallest building in Warsaw, was in ruins. The main railway station, the Sejm building, the Polish Theatre, were wrecked, the university was burned, the cathedral blasted, everything that was dear to the people of Poland, everything they had taken pride in and preserved through the centuries—everything defiled and ruined.

Tragic Note in a Bottle

I have seen heartbreaking things in the streets of Warsaw. A girl standing in front of what had been a house in Szpitalna Street. Her name was Eva Gutkowska. On the eve of the uprising, they told me, she had gone to stay with relatives in a village outside Warsaw, leaving behind her father, mother, two sisters and a brother. When she wanted to return home, the Germans would not allow her. Now she had returned to her home. What did she find ?

WARSAW'S PRESIDENTIAL PALACE, formerly Belvedere Castle, destroyed by the Nazis. The city's most beautiful monuments, including the Unknown Soldier's tomb and the Chopin memorial, were razed to the ground.

She found a heap of rubble, and in the midst of it a rough cross made from a packing case, with the inscription, "Five people are buried here." She began to tear at the rubble with her hands, until some Polish soldiers gently stopped her. They found a bottle hidden near the cross with this note inside, "The Gutkowski family died here in a bomb explosion." Then followed their names.

On the wall of a burned house someone had chalked, in Polish : "We will restore you, our native Warsaw." Under this is the inscription, "Stalin will help us."

THIS WAS MARKET SQUARE, blown up by the Germans. During the abortive Warsaw rising in August 1944 they wrought destruction with sadistic brutality, methodically reducing street after street to rubble and ashes.

On this Tiny Island of Peleliu 17,000 Died

The weird story of Peleliu got lost in the excitement of our landing in the Philippines, but the island saw the toughest fighting of the Pacific war. The Americans, who landed on Sept. 14, 1944, so far have killed 16,000 Japanese there and lost 1,600 dead themselves. Henry Keys, The Sunday Express war reporter in the Pacific, tells what he saw there.

I HAVE just visited an island of death—Peleliu, in the Palaus. Its age hangs over it like the brooding evil of senile corruption. It is a little island only five miles long by two miles wide. From the air it looks as if it had been hung on the blue sea like a discarded jockey's cap, the ledge on which the Marines landed representing the visor and the remainder the crumpled crown.

The landing was savage enough, made over a narrow reef ringing the shoreline like a necklace, a verdant coconut palm estate spewing death and impaling flaming tanks on the reef. Now the dazzlingly white coral shelf is pounded and beaten into a mass of airstrips. But it is back in the crumpled crown of the jockey's cap that the grim fighting took place.

This section is a mass of jagged ridges and escarpments 200 or 300 feet high. It took the Americans a month to inch their way far enough into them to be reasonably sure they would not be flung back into the sea, and another six weeks to break all organized resistance. The fighting is not over yet.

Twelve miles away is Babelthuap, with 25,000 Japanese. Every night some 300 walk across the reefs connecting it, except for two narrow channels which they swim. Each man is a walking arsenal. His object : a swim to an anchored Allied ship or a dump, and destruction by high explosive. Every night some 300 Japanese who ventured to take that walk died.

The island's commander, Marine Brigadier-General Harold Campbell, who was for a year the American adviser to Lord Louis Mountbatten in England, drove me over Peleliu. He headed for Bloody Nose Ridge,

IN THE DESOLATE POLISH CAPITAL the Nazis "planted" squads of incendiarists to burn everything left standing after the evacuation. Soviet officers here question a group of these whom they had dragged from hiding. Before quitting, the Germans blew up the power station and destroyed the water supply and the drainage system.

Photos; Pictorial Press, Planet News

which sticks out towards the airfields. Our jeep bounced and twisted over the crazy, inadequate coral trail which the ant-like Japanese had made by hand.

We climbed almost vertically up to the hogsback of the ridge. Then we plunged down the side. The coral kept crumbling and breaking, and the jeep slid crazily down. I shivered as we fell from sunlight to gloom and the silence of the gulch.

We were at the mouth of a big cave, one of Peleliu's thousands, in which the Japanese fought to the death. We went in. There was the dank, heavy smell of a dead Japanese. We were soon able to see the outline of his broken body. Then other things became clearer; this was an old enemy dump. A broken caisson leaned drunkenly, one axle amid the filth of the floor of the vast cavern. There were burst ration cans, shells, shell-cases and a small field piece.

The Silence Was Tomb-like

Everything was wet and rotting. Water dripped from the roof of the cavern, echoing like the tapping of a hammer. "Don't go too far," warned General Campbell: "we haven't had a chance to clean this out yet. There are plenty of booby traps." We drove on into the heart of the ridges. Everywhere there were caves, some high in the faces of the ridges. The entrances to most were jagged little orifices, big enough only for a man to crawl through on his belly. Many were hidden behind rubble and the blackish brown mounds of coral. Whenever the jeep stopped the silence was tomb-like.

"We killed and buried 12,000 Japs in these ridges alone," said Campbell. "It was a terrible job. There was nothing in books to help us, in a country like this. Look at that cave up there." He pointed to a hole 100 feet above us. "We put a 155-mm. rifle back 500 yards and just blasted at that for six days and nights. At the end of that time two Japs came out and crawled round the face of the cliff. But we had men round the shoulder of the ridge who picked them off.

"We kept shooting for another four days and nights, and six more came out cocky as the devil. We got them the same way. The main entrance of that cave was down at the bottom of the ridge, and we sealed it up with a bulldozer."

The general drove on. "I am going to show you the cave where we finished them off." We slid down the other side into ugliness and desolation. The general was cryptic. "Death Valley," he said. Death Valley was not 50 yards wide. The ridges went up sheer on either side, blackened and brown with the dead trunks of trees, amputated by shells and burned by flame-throwers, pointing ruefully to the sky.

Skulls Showed How They Died

In the middle of the valley's floor was a muddy hole. The rest of the floor was a forest of stalagmitic coral needles closely grouped like a vast cluster of pine trees. You could look down between them, as I did, and peer into inky nothingness. There were big bomb craters among them, for the Japs braced themselves against these columns for cover and fought from there. The skulls and skeletons wedged in the crevices showed how they died.

"The Japs were without water," said Campbell, "and they just had to come over our side, 15 or 30 a night. We killed most who reached that filthy pool. There are still a few Japs hiding in the caves. We kill some now and then."

We took a last look at the ridges. "You wouldn't believe that the whole island and all the ridges were just one green carpet when we came," the general said. "Every foot has been scorched and seared by battle."

I Kicked My Captor Crashing Down a Hillside

Leaving the rest of his troop just as dusk was falling, to look at a tank which had been in difficulties during a battle the previous day, Capt. Law, a Tank Officer from Canada serving with a famous British cavalry regiment on the Burma front, relates how presence of mind and a ready boot transformed him from a prisoner to a free man.

As I made my way back darkness came on quickly, and before long I realized that the short-cut track I was following was taking me too far from the road. Suddenly, as I crossed a ridge on the way back to the road, I felt something pressed into my back and was aware of a small, aggressive figure behind me. Knowing that some Indian patrols were active in the area that night, I thought the man might be an Indian Sepoy, so I shouted in Urdu, "It's all right, Johnny. I'm a tank man!"

I was certainly surprised when I heard the guy behind me babble in some unknown tongue, and found his weapon—which turned out to be a knife—stuck closer into my back. Then, of course, I knew he was a Japanese. My captor was then joined by another Japanese—a huge fellow who had a rifle and an altogether unpleasant manner. As the pair marched me up the road I realized that they might shoot me as soon as they were clear of our patrolling area. Just as I was formulating some plans for escape, the big man suddenly hissed in a startled way to draw attention to some slight noises coming from the jungle. From that moment both the Japanese were definitely scared, for they seemed to know that our patrols were out in strength.

Reaching some cover, my captors indicated that I must lie low with them on the side of the hill. As one of them left the track, he slipped. I gave him a cracking kick and he went toppling down the hill, but not before he had stabbed me in the hand with his knife. With one Japanese doing involuntary ju-jitsu down the hillside and the other out of view for the moment, I ran for some undergrowth and, avoiding the road where our own patrol might have shot me at sight, made my way through the jungle to a safe hiding-place where I tried to plan how to get back. Taking a bearing on the sound of the British guns shelling a village, and guided by the North Star, I marched through the jungle all night until I met a British patrol making their morning brew of tea.

LAST-DITCH STAND BY THE JAPANESE was being made in a cave on shell-shattered Peleliu (story in this page) when the above photograph was taken. U.S. Marine sharpshooters stand by for the kill as the enemy is assaulted in his lair by the far-reaching, scorching jet of the flame-throwing amphibious tractor on the right. *Photo, New York Times Photos*

When the Earth Was Burning at Mandalay

The most concentrated air attack of the Burma war, in which the load of bombs dropped in ten minutes was as heavy as the biggest London blitz, was made, on Jan. 14, 1945, on Japanese troop concentrations in Mandalay and Sagaing. The bombers were R.A.F. and American Liberators, and with them went News Chronicle special correspondent Stuart Gelder, whose narrative, dispatched from Bengal, is given here.

We were without fighter cover, but derived some comfort from the fact that American Thunderbolts were going in five minutes before our arrival to shoot up flak positions.

We took off from bases in Bengal in brilliant mid-morning weather and flew straight to the Irrawaddy. From 50 miles away thick columns of smoke were rising where the American heavies are attacking Sagaing and R.A.F. Mosquitoes are going in to finish the job. By the time we pass by we have ample evidence that there is not much of the town which is not burning.

Five minutes more and an enormous column of black and white smoke stands out from the flat lands beyond. It hangs stationary. Round its base sudden gusts of flame appear. This is, or was, Mandalay.

Over the outskirts. Hundreds of huge high-explosives are falling in straight lines from the flights ahead. I leave the flight deck and sit on the edge of the bomb-way to watch our load away. Below, through the gaping bay, as I hang on with my hands against the screaming wind, the earth is burning.

We are right over the centre now. My feet are jolted from the steel floor. There is a loud cracking cough in my right ear and a gush of smoke past my head. There is at least one Jap gunner left alive in the flaming city below.

Down They Go In Hundreds

Seven more bursts of flak near our nose. There will be a nice high tea of bacon and eggs and whisky waiting for us at home— or a long, long walk through the hills.

Another jolt and another, but now the cough of flak and roar of engines are lost in a shout through the intercom. Our little lot is away, and from where I am it looks as though the entire bottom of the aircraft has fallen out.

Bombs are raining down in hundreds. They illuminate the smoke with the fierce light of magnesium flares. A piece of cake for us! As we leave, the target is almost completely obscured by smoke and fire, but we can still see the gaol house. We had to miss that one. We hope our men who are prisoners there enjoyed the show.

And this was not only a perfect example of precision bombing. It was an example of the perfect comradeship and co-operation which has grown up between British, Dominion and American flying men.

BOMBING OF TAUNGUP, chief Japanese supply base for the Arakan, 130 miles below Akyab, on December 24, 1944, as seen from a Liberator. R.A.F. and U.S.A.A.F. struck by daylight, dropping 250 tons of high explosives and incendiaries in 25 minutes. This was the most concentrated raid on a single target in Burma up to that date.
Photo, British Official

OUR DIARY OF THE WAR

JANUARY 17, Wednesday 1,964th day
Western Front.—U.S. troops occupied Vielsalm, west of St. Vith. At night Allied Commando troops attacked Dutch island of Schouwen.
Russian Front.—Warsaw occupied by Zhukov's troops. Czestochowa, in southern Poland, captured by Koniev.
Air.—After night attack by R.A.F. on oil plant at Brux, Czechoslovakia, and Magdeburg, U.S. bombers attacked oil refineries and U-boat yards at Hamburg.

JANUARY 18, Thursday 1,965th day
Western Front.—First train left with civilians evacuated from German-held St. Nazaire.
Russian Front.—Rokossovsky's troops captured Modlin, N.W. of Warsaw.
General.—Vice-Adm. Sir Harold M. Burrough appointed Allied Naval Commander, Expeditionary Force.

JANUARY 19, Friday 1,966th day
Western Front.—Germans launched heavier attacks in Northern Alsace, threatening Strasbourg.
Russian Front.—Lodz captured by Zhukov's army, Cracow by Koniev's. New attack launched by Petrov in northern Carpathians.
Far East.—Super-Fortresses from Saipan bombed aircraft works at Akashi, near Kobe, Japan.

JANUARY 20, Saturday 1,967th day
Western Front.—French 1st Army opened attack against Colmar pocket of 35,000 Germans.
Russian Front.—Tilsit in East Prussia captured by Cherniakhovsky.
Far East.—U.S. carrier-aircraft bombed Japanese shipping off Formosa.
General.—Hungarian Provisional Government signed armistice with Allies.

JANUARY 21, Sunday 1,968th day
Russian Front.—Koniev's army invaded Silesia on 60-mile front in Breslau direction. Cherniakhovsky captured Gumbinnen in East Prussia. Rokossovsky's troops crossed southern frontier of East Prussia and captured Tannenberg.
Air.—Heavy force of U.S. bombers attacked marshalling yards at Aschaffenburg, Heilbronn and Mannheim. At night R.A.F. bombed Kassel.
Burma.—Allied troops made new landing on Ramree Island, south of Akyab.

Far East.—U.S. carrier-aircraft bombed Ryukyu Islands in strength.

JANUARY 22, Monday 1,969th day
Western Front.—U.S. 3rd Army occupied Wiltz, east of Bastogne.
Air.—Allied air forces caused great destruction to 3,000 enemy vehicles retreating from Ardennes salient.
Russian Front.—In double advance in East Prussia, Russians captured Allenstein and Insterburg.
Burma.—British and Indian troops entered Monywa, west of Mandalay, without Japanese opposition.

JANUARY 23, Tuesday 1,970th day
Western Front.—St. Vith, road junction in east of Ardennes salient, captured by Allies. British 2nd Army advancing from Sittard occupied Waldenrath and St. Joost.
Russian Front.—Bromberg (Bydgoszcz) captured by Zhukov's troops. Koniev's army reached the Oder on 37-mile front in Breslau area.
Air.—U.S. bombers attacked railway yards at Neuss. Allied aircraft renewed attacks on bridges and railways leading to V2 sites round Leiden and The Hague.
Far East.—Super-Fortresses bombed Nagoya, Japan.

JANUARY 24, Wednesday 1,971st day
Western Front.—British troops entered Heinsberg, west of the Roer.
Russian Front.—In Upper Silesia, Koniev's troops captured Oppeln on the Oder. Zhukov captured Kalisz, between Cracow and Poznan. New Russian offensive in Slovakia.
Far East.—U.S. aircraft bombed Japanese air base on Iwo Jima, Babelthuap in the Palau Islands, and Yap in the Carolines.

JANUARY 25, Thursday 1,972nd day
Western Front.—Germans launched offensive in Alsace, crossing River Moder west of Haguenau and cutting road to Sarreguemines.
Russian Front.—Gleiwitz, in heart of Upper Silesia industrial region, and railway junctions of Oels and Ostrow captured by Red Army.
Philippines.—U.S. troops captured Clark Field, main air base on Luzon.

JANUARY 26, Friday 1,973rd day
Western Front.—Ardennes bulge cleared of the enemy. German attacks in Alsace held on river Moder.
Russian Front.—Soviet troops reached

General.—Commons agreed to compulsory posting of A.T.S. overseas.

Gulf of Danzig, cutting off East Prussia. In Silesia, town of Hindenburg was captured.
Burma.—Royal Marines of East Indies Fleet landed on Cheduba, off Arakan.
Far East.—U.S. aircraft bombed airfield and bridges at Nanking.

JANUARY 27, Saturday 1,974th day
Russian Front.—In East Prussia, Russian armies broke through Masurian Lakes defence system.
Air.—Allied air forces continued to attack enemy trains and road transport moving east in the Ardennes.
Far East.—Super-Fortresses bombed Tokyo against stiff opposition and also attacked Saigon, Indo-China.

JANUARY 28, Sunday 1,975th day
Western Front.—U.S. 1st Army launched new attack east of St. Vith. Germans lost bridge head over Moder.
Air.—U.S. 8th Air Force marked third anniversary with 1,000-bomber attack on oil plants in the Ruhr and road and rail bridges over the Rhine. R.A.F. bombed marshalling yards near Cologne and Stuttgart by day and night.
Russian Front.—Capture of Memel by Red Army completed liberation of Lithuania. Katowice and Beuthen in Silesia also captured.
Burma.—First convoy crossed into China by Ledo-Burma Road.

JANUARY 29, Monday 1,976th day
Western Front.—U.S. 3rd Army troops crossed German frontier north of Luxembourg.
Russian Front.—Zhukov's forces crossed German frontier W. and N.W. of Poznan and invaded Pomerania. In the Carpathians, Petrov's troops captured Nowy Targ.
Air.—Railway marshalling yards and junctions at Hamm, Munster, Coblenz, Kassel and Krefeld heavily attacked by U.S. and R.A.F. bombers. Berlin again bombed by Mosquitoes at night.
Philippines.—U.S. troops made new landing in Luzon, north of Bataan.

JANUARY 30, Tuesday 1,977th day
Western Front.—Gambsheim, German bridge-head over Rhine north of Strasbourg, re-occupied by Allies.
Sea.—Carrier-aircraft of Royal Navy struck at enemy shipping off Norway.

★══════ *Flash-backs* ══════★

1941
January 18. *Dive-bombing attacks on Malta shipping began.*
January 22. *Australians under General Wavell entered Tobruk.*

1942
January 19. *Russians recaptured Mojaisk, on Moscow front.*
January 22. *Japanese landed at Rabaul, New Britain.*
January 25. *Japanese made landing at Lae, New Guinea.*
January 26. *American troops arrived in Northern Ireland.*

1943
January 20. *Lewisham school bombed in day raid on London.*
January 23. *Tripoli entered by General Montgomery's 8th Army.*
January 30. *Russians cleared Maikop oilfields of the enemy.*

1944
January 20. *Novgorod recaptured by Red Army troops.*
January 22. *5th Army troops landed near Nettuno and Anzio.*
January 30. *5th Army troops pierced Gustav Line N. of Cassino.*

THE WAR IN THE AIR

by Capt. Norman Macmillan, M.C., A.F.C.

ALL the news is dominated by the Russian offensive which began in Poland on January 12 and spread all along the Eastern front from the Lithuanian Baltic coast to Budapest, swiftly engulfing within the battle area East Prussia, Poland, parts of German Silesia, and the Carpatho-Ukraine area of Czechoslovakia. The initial assault by the Red Army was made in weather so bad that the Red Air Force was grounded, and the advance preparation for the surface forces was made by artillery without aircraft support. From this it is possible to draw several inferences ; but they are no more than inferences at the moment, and must remain so until the full facts are historically and without any doubt established.

First is the importance of artillery in the modern surface land action. (The part played by artillery in the opening stages of the battle of El Alamein under Montgomery

It should be remembered that before Rundstedt's counter-offensive on the Western Front there was a call (particularly to the U.S.A.) from General Eisenhower for more shells. There was, apparently, an artillery fire-power shortage. That may explain the comparatively slow and infinitely laborious advance that the Army of Liberation made on the Western Front before Von Rundstedt counter-attacked. (Weather was no doubt another factor ; the Red Army remained static until the ground froze in Poland, whereas on the Western Front, as in 1917, the Allies tried to push on despite most adverse ground conditions.)

ENEMY Communications Congested by Heavy Western Front Bombing

No doubt much of the Red Army artillery success is due to the employment of mobile heavy guns, able to move forward as units on their own tracks as the German defences are

of the Allies there. Meanwhile, heavy bombers from the West were devastating the heart of the Reich. On January 19 the German radio stated that Munich, Freiburg and Nuremberg had been completely destroyed. Munich was the first city to receive the R.A.F.'s 12,000-lb. bombs. Oil plants in Silesia and Pomerania were bombed, prior to the opening of the Soviet offensive, by British and American bombers operating from bases in the U.K. and Italy in strategic preparation for the Soviet assault. (The advance air attrition of Rommel's oil was an integral part of the Alexander-Montgomery-Tedder plan of attack in Egypt.)

NO part of Europe now in German occupation lies outside the range of heavy bombers based in Britain and Italy. It would not be possible to drop the concentrations of bombs that fell in Normandy or on the railway system behind Rundstedt's salient, but it is possible for the Western-based Allied heavy bombers to attack whatever German defended urban strongpoint the Red Army Marshals may indicate for reduction from the air. That is important, for the Red Air Force is equipped mainly with light bombers and fighters, the Soviet strategic heavy bomber force being comparatively small.

It is not surprising that there are reports (emanating from enemy and neutral sources) that both Germany and Japan are building ramming aeroplanes. The Japanese rammer is to be used against Super-Fortress bombers attacking Japan. The German version is said to be a jet-plane with an armoured nose.

SORELY Depleted Luftwaffe in Action on the Eastern Front

When the weather cleared on the Eastern Front the Red Air Force tactical aircraft swarmed over the battlefields. The enemy reported them to be operating in several thousands. Two thousand were reported operating in aid of the Red Army in one sector alone. The Soviet capture of East Prussian airfields and abandoned German aircraft is important for the continued air offensive.

Meanwhile, British and American air attacks against Germany's oil were made on plants and storage depots in the Ruhr, Merseburg, Munster, Heide, Magdeburg, Derben, Brunswick, Bochum, Recklinghausen, Dresden, Harburg, Brux, Leipzig, Wanne, Eikel, Vienna, Duisburg, and elsewhere. When not engaged against oil targets, the heavy bombers, and at all times the tactical aircraft on the Western Front, have been engaged in congesting enemy communications behind the most active parts of the Western Front. Road and rail vehicles, marshalling yards and railway junctions have been attacked. Berlin has been repeatedly bombed by Mosquitoes at night.

FAR to the north, Norwegian parachute troops have been dropped to sabotage railway bridges carrying the lines running through the valleys between Trondheim and Oslo, thus obstructing reinforcements withdrawing from Norway to the main fighting fronts. One troop train crashed into a ravine, killing, it is believed, about 180 Germans and injuring about 300. Another use of air power was the attack by South African rocket-firing Beaufighters on a hotel (at Cigale Cove, Lussin Island, northern Adriatic, on January 25) which was the living quarters of the crews of German human torpedoes. It was destroyed.

In Luzon the advancing American forces have captured the important Clark Field aircraft runway. Seizure of this airfield should give them full tactical air control over Manila, the Philippines capital. Tokyo and other Japanese targets and Jap-occupied bases in Indo-China have been strategically bombed by Super-Fortresses and carrier-aircraft.

R.A.A.F. OFFICERS AT TACLOBAN, capital of Leyte Island, in the Philippines, which was officially pronounced " mopped-up " on December 26, 1944. During the campaign the R.A.A.F. played an important part in airfield construction. They landed at Mindoro, one of the larger islands, with the U.S. 6th Army and built an airfield while the site was still under fire. *Photo, Australian Official*

will be remembered.) Artillery did not have this significance during the German assault in 1940 ; then tanks and aircraft were in the spearhead of the attack. Why has the situation changed ? Probably the explanation is that after five years' experience of modern war, defensive preparations are much more developed than they were when the first B.E.F. was in Belgium in May 1940. Indeed, the B.E.F. can have had the scantiest of cover on the Dyle. Belgium relied on a series of fixed forts, France on a fixed Maginot Line. Today, defences of earthworks, concrete, metal, wire, bunkers and mines are arranged in depth, often to considerable extent, with the object of slowing up an advance.

IT has been demonstrated that there are two ways of smashing these obstructions. One is by massed artillery. The other is by the use of massed heavy bombers. Army co-operation air attacks in which fragmentation bombs are dropped, rocket projectiles, cannon-gun shells, and machine-gun bullets fired, is ideal when the front is on the move, but it does not provide the sheer weight and penetrative power required to effect the first break-through.

reduced and stormed by the infantry. Man-power favours the Red Army. Faced with this mobile form of assault it is probable that the German commanders could have countered the continuous weight of the surface attack only if they had had means to attack and disrupt the Soviet rear area communications and organization. This they could do by one means only—air power, and that means they did not possess. The continuous air offensive waged against the Luftwaffe in the air by British and American fighters and American heavy bombers, the unremitting attacks upon German aircraft factories by British and American bombers, and their attacks against German aircraft grounded on their own aerodromes had so reduced the Luftwaffe that it was a depleted air force that Guderian and Manstein had to deploy against the Russian rear. It has been reported that there were but some 1,000 German aircraft of all types in action upon the Eastern front.

Germany could not withdraw her air force from the West without facing catastrophe because of the overwhelming air superiority

Escort-Carrier H.M.S. Fencer in Convoy to Russia

NORTHWARD - BOUND in convoy, continual sweeping of snow from H.M.S. Fencer's flight-deck (1) is needed to keep it serviceable. At a Russian port Soviet naval officers (2) watch operations. Below-decks, in the hangar, sailors of the Red Navy (3) entertain their hosts with a vigorous display of dancing.

The convoy sails at sundown—a striking study in silhouettes (4) as seen from H.M.S. Fencer, which has added to her laurels by attacking enemy shipping off the Norwegian coast and on the fringe of the Arctic Circle.

For three years British convoys have been running supplies to Russia, and more than 88 per cent of the cargoes have got through. As long ago as May 1944, Mr. Churchill told Parliament that, besides more than £80,000,000-worth of raw materials, foodstuffs, machinery, medical supplies and comforts, well over 5,000 tanks and 6,000 aircraft had reached the U.S.S.R.

Photos, British Official

By Sea, Land and Air with Our Roving Camera

DR. JAMES HALL, of Deal, sailors' emergency surgeon famed far and wide, has turned out many times in blizzard and storm, in response to S O S signals from ships carrying someone in urgent need of medical attention. His log of time spent at sea exceeds 400 hours, his journeyings totalling 1,500 miles. The lifeboat (left) in which on Jan. 18, 1945, he spent four hours in a raging gale.

CROSS-CHANNEL SERVICE TO FRANCE reopened on Jan. 16, 1945, after 4½ years. Passengers on the first day—here seen arriving—numbered 80, all on urgent business. Note British and French soldiers either side of the gangway.

COALMAN IN KHAKI is Pte. C. Eggleston, of Bristol, one of hundreds of soldiers who helped London merchants to "deliver the goods" to fuelless houses during Jan. 1945. PAGE 638

THE LANCASTRIAN, civil version of the Lancaster bomber, is a fast long-range luxury air-liner to be used when the England-Australia service, via India, is resumed. It carries nine passengers besides freight or mail; range, 4,150 miles, cruising speed, 265 m.p.h. The passengers' cabin (centre right).

Photos, Daily Sketch, Fox, British Newspaper Pool, News Chronicle, Barratt's

HAVE you ever noticed that people who are loud in their professions of patriotism, genuine professions too, refuse to alter their habits and methods of business to meet a national need ? Here is a case that has come under my notice. A brewery sends out to customers who order beer, first, an invoice to acknowledge the order and say it will be carried out. With the beer is sent a large sheet in duplicate to record the delivery. Then arrives a bill which, like the other documents, is far larger than it need be. Sheer waste of large quantities of paper that are urgently required for munitions ! The head of the brewery is a man who loves his country and would make sacrifices for it; but he cannot bring himself to alter the ways of his office in order to save paper. The same shrinking from change even in such small matters makes some people continue to write their letters on double sheets of note-paper when one sheet would be quite enough. And I know at least one man who will not use envelopes that have been through the post. "Never done such a thing," he mutters. "Not going to begin now."

ANOTHER matter in which change is dis-liked and even bitterly resented is that of dress. Men who have stuck to the bowler hat are furious because this style of head-gear has almost disappeared from the hatters' shops. They look at the soft felts, which are offered to them, with disgust almost as great as that which used to be felt for these when they first came in. I re-member wearing one in the early nineties, when they were a novelty, and being chaffed or abused by all my friends for having taken to what they called a "photographer's hat." But before long King Edward VII was wearing one during his trips to Marienbad and even in the country at home—though not, of course, in London. Soon they became the usual wear for the majority, in Town as well as out of it. By this time the top-hat, essential at one time as a mark of respectability, was disappearing. Neither it nor the bowler could compare in comfort with the Homburg or Trilby, and in my opinion that has a far better appearance as well.

WILL the Riviera ever be again what it was in its most prosperous days, when all its huge luxury hotels were built and vast sums of money were taken and left there by visitors from all lands, especially Britain ? I am prompted to ask the question because I see it announced that the Promenade des Anglais at Nice is to be rebuilt after being destroyed by the Germans. That was one of the most famous esplanades in the world, four miles long and planted with palms and other semi-tropical trees and shrubs. I have many pleasant recollections of walking along it in hot sunshine at a time of year when London was miserably cold and foggy. But for some years the attractions of the Riviera had been diminishing. It cultivated a summer season for a time, which helped it along. But it is doubtful whether it can again be-come the playground of the rich—for there may not be any !

WHILE I was having my hair cut, I had my attention called by the barber to a naval officer a few chairs away who had a bushy black beard. The barber shook his head disapprovingly. He recalled the trimness and smartness of naval beards in his young days—he called them "torpedo beards." Half as many wore them, he said, as went clean shaven. I can recollect the time when most admirals were bearded and they certainly did not look as wild and woolly as the naval officers of today who have cheeks and chin covered by hair. "Makes 'em look older, too," the barber

said. I'm not so sure about that; Bernard Shaw with a beard in his twenties was the youngest-looking thing ever, I have heard. But it is a natural view for hairdressers to take. Why should they encourage what a wit of my acquaintance, named Frank Richardson, a generation ago used to call "face fungus" ? He gained quite a reputation by making fun of beards and whiskers and there was, some said, a movement among barbers to put up a statue of him in Air Street. He certainly did them a good turn.

WHEN the scholarly young man in the club library asked me "How many ounces in an hour ? " I must confess I thought he was conundrumming and felt tempted to reply with the old teaser : " Why is a mouse when it spins ? " There was something in the question after all, however, for he pointed to a footnote in a new edition of the anonymous 14th-century English classic, The Cloud of Unknowing, which he was studying. Here it is—an unbeatable example of the tortuous and fantastical methods of calculation employed (though not often, I hope) by our medieval forebears :

> A point is the fourth part of an hour ; a moment is the tenth part of a point ; an ounce is the twelfth part of a moment ; and an atom is the forty-seventh part of an ounce. So that in one hour there are four points, forty moments, 480 ounces, and 22,560 atoms.

As the Scot might put it—Whaur's your Albert Einstein noo ?

FEW men who had held various important Cabinet offices can have had the truth told about them when they died, so frankly and pitilessly as it was told about Gerald Balfour the other day. Brother to the more famous Arthur, who finished up as an earl, he was put at the head of several departments of State and failed in all of them. He belonged to the clique known as the Hotel Cecil,

Mr. HAROLD C. EMMERSON appointed Director-General of Man-Power at the Minis-try of Labour to implement the Government's call-up of 250,000 more men for the Services (announced on December 23, 1944). He suc-ceeded Sir Godfrey Ince.
PAGE 639   *Photo, Barratts*

headed by Lord Salisbury, whose nephew he was, so his failures were not chalked up against him. Had he died thirty years ago, they would have been glossed over by the newspapers. But he seemed to be so com-pletely a figure of the past that for once the incompetence of a once-prominent "states-man" was laid bare. It is a good thing that this should be done every now and then. It would cure the masses of the delusion that Cabinet Ministers are of necessity supermen.

ALTHOUGH I make a point of closely following the deliberations of the House, it was a paragraph in an evening paper which drew my attention to the fact that the Requisitioned Land and Works Bill, of which I had not heard, was soon to have its second reading. I have not seen the text of the Bill, but it deals, my paper tells me, with common land taken over early in the war for camps, hutments, balloon sites, and so forth. The land (most of it used in peacetime for recreation purposes) would, in the ordinary course of events, have been restored after the war, but the Bill plans to give the Govern-ment the " choice of restoring it or disposing of it if restoration proves expensive." Chief opponent of the measure is that sturdy champion of hikers and campers, Sir Law-rence Chubb, who, besides being a successful London business man, is Secretary to the awkwardly named Commons, Open Spaces and Footpaths Preservation Society. He is now rounding up M.P.s. to denounce the Bill, which he himself has described as "a scandal." I am told that it would take less than £1,500,000 to make the requisitioned sites suitable for their peacetime purposes and thus save them from the speculative builder—by modern standards of Govern-ment spending a miserly sum which would barely cover the cost of a single all-out artil-lery barrage on the Western Front. It is obvious that some cheese-paring official in Whitehall feels that by means of the Bill he may enhance his reputation as an "econo-mist," and that that's all there is to it. That it should have survived its first reading, how-ever, is just a little disturbing in these days when the rights of the Little Man are being trumpeted from every political platform.

FEW recent items of war news have given me such pleasure as this which comes from David Woodward, Manchester Guardian correspondent with the 21st Army Group, and, as far as I know, has not appeared elsewhere :

> Vast stocks of maps for the invasion of Germany have been printed by the Royal Engineers' survey companies on the backs of maps origin-ally prepared by the Germans for the invasion of England.

It will be recalled that when Brussels was liberated depots containing millions of these maps fell into our hands. If ever there was a case of Time's whirligig bringing its revenges—here, surely, it is. Historians, please copy !

TWICE in the past few days social observers have given me accounts—and conflict-ing ones at that—of what is going on in the queueing world. According to one informant, housewives are getting even more fun out of queueing than they did in far away 1940 before rasher-and-egg had joined the aloof company of truffles and peacock-pie in the gastronome's Calendar of Succulent Rarities. Informant No. 2, boldly contradictory, declares that another twelve months of queue-ing and the housewives of Britain will be in danger of nervous collapse, suggesting in semi-seriousness that any woman who has queued consistently for four years and up-wards should be awarded a Government decoration. (The Q. Cross ?) From my own somewhat restricted observations on the matter I am inclined to deprecate both these theories. Like poets, bridge-players and cross-word puzzlers, queuers, I suggest, are born and not made.

Rocket-Showers Shatter Mindoro Defences

INTENSE BOMBARDMENT BY ROCKET-FIRING CRAFT preceded the successful storming by U.S. troops under Gen. Walter Kreuger of Japanese-held Mindoro, one of the larger Philippine islands (see map, page 629) on December 15, 1944. Of this operation General MacArthur said, " It will enable us to dominate sea and air routes which reach to the China coast." Mindoro is 75 miles south of Manila, capital of Luzon, on which landings were made three weeks later. See also illus. in page 358.

Photo, New York Times Photos

Printed in England and published every alternate Friday by the Proprietors, THE AMALGAMATED PRESS, LTD., The Fleetway House, Farringdon Street, London, E.C.4. Registered for transmission by Canadian Magazine Post. Sole Agents for Australia and New Zealand : Messrs. Gordon & Gotch, Ltd. ; and for South Africa : Central News Agency, Ltd.—February 16th, 1945. S.S. *Editorial Address* : JOHN CARPENTER HOUSE WHITEFRIARS. LONDON. E.C.4.

Vol 8 *The War Illustrated* Nº 201

SIXPENCE

Edited by Sir John Hammerton

MARCH 2, 1945

THE NATIONAL FIRE SERVICE has sent a unit, with their own vehicles, to the Western Front as the First Overseas Column for fire-fighting duties with the U.S. Army, it was announced in January 1945. They wear N.F.S. uniform with Army webbing equipment and a beret, but carry no arms. Trailer pumps are here seen being hauled across a disused English gravel-pit by way of training, while N.F.S. girl motor-cyclists essay battlefield conditions on the stony track below. (See also illus. p. 34).

Photo, Daily Mirror

NO. 202 WILL BE PUBLISHED FRIDAY, MARCH 16

Stalin's Berlin Thrusts Approach Journey's End

RED ARMY TRAFFIC GIRL FLAGGED THE TANKS AND INFANTRY speeding through Poland towards Germany: the signpost (1) reads "Moscow-Berlin." In E. Prussia, Soviet tanks rumbled through Neidenburg (2) towards Elbing (captured Feb. 10, 1945). Southwards, troops of Marshal Koniev's 1st Ukrainian Front took Gleiwitz (Jan. 25) in street and house-to-house fighting (3). On Feb. 12 it was announced that Marshal Koniev had eliminated the Oder as Germany's great defence line, leaving Breslau surrounded in the rear, and was within 60 miles of the Frankfurt fortress. Map shows lines reached by Soviet forces on Jan. 26, Feb. 2 and Feb. 9.

Photos Pictorial Press   Map, News Chronicle

THE BATTLE FRONTS

by Maj.-Gen. Sir Charles Gwynn, K.C.B., D.S.O.

GEN. DWIGHT D. EISENHOWER, General of the Army and Supreme Commander Allied Expeditionary Force—a new portrait. Note the SHAEF flash and the five-star cluster, which together with the Great Seal of the U.S. is the insignia of "General of the Army."
Photo, U.S. Official

WHEN the Russians were once again confronted by a great river line strongly held—the Oder—it was interesting to see if they would pass it as successfully as on former occasions. If the frost had held, it is possible that the momentum of Zhukov's great drive would have carried him across the river on a narrow front at some point where the ice would bear tanks. Koniev a year ago, after routing the Germans at Uman, took the Dniester in his stride without that assistance, but then there was little resistance to be overcome and little fear of meeting a counter-stroke on the other side.

Zhukov was bound to be more cautious, for it is certain that much of his supporting infantry had been left far behind and that his communications had been stretched to the limit of their capacity; moreover, the Germans had had sufficient time to muster a defence force, numerically powerful, though probably composed largely of partly trained and inadequately equipped Volkssturm troops, while in addition it was almost certain they were making strenuous efforts to assemble a reserve army capable of delivering a formidable counter-attack. I cannot believe, therefore, that even if hard going had enabled Zhukov to force a crossing he would have pressed straight on towards Berlin without making a considerable pause and waiting to extend his front; though no doubt he would have established strong bridge-heads on the west bank.

WHY Zhukov's Spearhead Force Paused on the Oder's Bank

It was certainly fascinating to read of the ever-shortening distance to Berlin, but I imagine it produced a misleading impression of what remained to be accomplished and, in turn, an exaggerated feeling of frustration when an untimely thaw came. It is certainly probable that thaw checked the speed of Zhukov's movements and may have caused him to modify his original intentions. It must have added greatly to the difficulties on his lines of communication, but it is unlikely that it was the real reason why a pause on the Oder was necessary.

The true reason, I am sure, was that his spearhead force was entirely unsuitable to carry by assault a large city prepared for defence, and any attempt to do so would have involved it in desperate street fights, probably with disastrous results. It was a force which maintained the speed of its advance by by-passing centres of serious resistance, leaving them to be dealt with by supporting forces. It was capable of dealing with resistance in the open and could play havoc with the enemy's communications; but the farther it went the narrower the front on which it could operate was bound to become, both to facilitate supply and to ensure sufficient concentration to enable it to deal with such minor centres of resistance as had to be overcome in order to keep lines of supply open.

THERE is no doubt that it was able to cover such immense distances without a pause only because transport was available to motorize a large infantry component. Yet it obviously made no attempt to capture such strong centres of resistance as Poznan and Thorn (Torun) and minor places of which we heard nothing until they were finally mopped up by slower-moving supporting troops. Much less could it have hoped to rush a great city like Berlin, and there could have been no question of by-passing or investing it till adequate forces were available. It is true that in the earlier stages of the break-through, large towns like Lodz and Radom

may have been rushed by the spearhead armour because the defence had no time to organize resistance, but in any case the supporting main body had not yet been out-distanced and may actually have been responsible for the capture.

WHATEVER his original intentions were, when the thaw came Zhukov was wise to slow down his advance into a partial pause and to confine his operations to widening his front and clearing the east bank of the river while his supporting troops closed up. Although Moscow makes no such claim, from German reports it appears probable that he also secured small footholds on the west bank which might be expanded later, and which would also leave the enemy in doubt as to where the main crossings would eventually be attempted.

On Zhukov's front, Kuestrin and the eastern suburbs of Frankfort are bastions which called for elimination. At the time of writing, Zhukov is still engaged in these preliminary operations and has apparently not yet attempted a major crossing. Koniev, on whose progress Moscow had maintained a security silence, appears to have adopted a similar course to Zhukov, but has carried it a stage further by securing bridge-heads sufficiently large to admit the deployment of strong forces on the western bank. Having had a much shorter distance to go, he not only reached the Oder first but required less time to close up his army. The speed with which he captured Oppeln and the industrial towns of southern Silesia which would otherwise have left the enemy with a strong base for counter-attack east of the river, evidently laid the foundation for his success.

But we have now also heard the astonishing story of how small footholds were established on the west bank. The main bridge-head Koniev has now secured must go far to reduce the value of the Oder as a defensive position.

WESTERN FRONT on Feb. 8, 1945, when British and Canadian troops of the Canadian 1st Army opened Field-Marshal Montgomery's new offensive into Germany, penetrating outer defences of the Siegfried Line.
By courtesy of News Chronicle

It may not of itself provide a starting point at present for far-reaching operations, but it is certain to engage a considerable part of the German reserve and open the way for exploiting the strategy of alternating blows which the Russians have so often skilfully employed.

WEHRMACHT Split to Fragments for Elimination Separately

All the indications are that the Oder will be added to the long list of great rivers that the Russians, by brilliant strategy and admirable tactical determination and initiative, have successfully passed with exceptionally short pauses for elaborate preparation. Berlin ahead provides, of course, a wonderful incentive and it is undoubtedly an objective of great military as well as of political importance. Yet if and when Zhukov crosses the Oder I should be surprised if attempts to attack it directly are made before, possibly in collaboration with Koniev, he is in a position to encircle the city and to trap its garrison. As I have suggested, a premature attempt to carry the city by storm might involve entanglement and exposure to a counter-stroke which the Germans may still be able to deliver. It is possible that even before he attempts major operations west of the Oder he will develop his thrusts north-westwards towards Stettin, in order to achieve the encirclement of the German forces in Pomerania and the Danzig area—which can hardly be dealt with by Rokossovsky.

The Wehrmacht is still too huge a force to be crushed by a single blow, and Russian strategy has consistently adopted the policy of splitting it into fragments which can be eliminated separately. The escape of any group which could be isolated, particularly if it is composed of first-line troops, would tend to prolong the war; for although the Germans evidently intend to fight in Berlin, its capture might not be immediately decisive if a powerful army still remained in being.

The great part that has been played since D-Day by the Allied Armies in the west is perhaps hardly sufficiently appreciated, especially since they ceased to recover territory at a sensational pace. They may make further great contributions in the near future, but the mere fact that Hitler was induced to commit his main strategic reserve to Rundstedt's abortive offensive at the critical time may have accelerated German collapse more than previous victories or liberation of territory.

At Colmar the Nazi 19th Army Was Destroyed

ARMOURED COLUMNS OF THE FRENCH 1st ARMY entered Colmar, third largest city in Alsace, on Feb. 2, 1945, to write off the German 19th Army : they and their U.S. comrades were welcomed (1) by this little girl in national costume seen with the Mayor, as well as by vast crowds (2). A giant Nazi pill-box, containing 30,000 lb. of explosives, was blown up by U.S. sappers near Kesternich in Germany (3). Civilians in Sarralbe, Alsace, boated about their business when, after blizzards, a sudden thaw set in (4).

Photos, U.S. Official, Planet News, Keystone

From War to Peace in a Central Burma Village

VILLAGERS OF CHANTHA, near Yeu (see map in page 650), were led by rumour to believe Allied troops would arrive on Dec. 18, 1944, and a thanksgiving service was held. But the Japanese came instead, and carried off the priest, the Mother Superior and several nuns. Then, when 14th Army troops appeared, in Jan. 1945, villagers and soldiers worshipped together. Leaving the church (1); happy women and children gathered outside (2). At the approach to Chantha troops manhandled girders (3) to build this Bailey bridge (4) across the River Mu. PAGE 645 *Photos, British Official*

H.M.S. INDEFATIGABLE, BRITAIN'S NEWEST AIRCRAFT CARRIER, was first reported in action off Sumatra on January 24 and 29, 1945, when battleships and aircraft-carriers of the British East Indies Fleet totally destroyed the Palembang refineries, source of 75 per cent of Japanese aviation fuel. The force was commanded by Rear-Admiral Sir Philip Vian, K.C.B., D.S.O. (inset), in the battleship King George V. An improved type of the Illustrious class, the Indefatigable was built at John Brown's, Clydebank. With a length of over 800 feet, she is believed to carry at least 100 aircraft, besides about 2,000 officers and men. Her defensive armament is said to include sixteen 4·5-in. dual-purpose guns. Our first quadruple-screw carrier, 30,000 tons, her speed is computed at 32 knots. See also facing page.

Photo, British Official

THE WAR AT SEA

by Francis E. McMurtrie

IT is a truism to say that modern warfare depends entirely upon supplies of oil being plentiful. Ships, aircraft, tanks and transport all rely for propulsion upon petroleum in a more or less refined form. Nowhere is this fact better exemplified than in the Far East. One of the reasons which deterred the Japanese from risking war with the United States at a much earlier date was the lack of mineral oil deposits in the chain of islands which constitute Nippon. Similarly, it was the abundance of petroleum in the East Indian archipelago which made that area such an attractive target for Japanese invasion.

Now that the tide has turned and the enemy is slowly but surely being expelled from island after island, the oil problem is bound to be a main factor in hastening Japan's downfall. In the millions of tons of shipping destroyed by Allied submarines and aircraft, oil tankers have figured prominently. As a consequence, there are no longer enough of these valuable vessels to transport to Japan in adequate quantities the petroleum that is needed to keep the war going. For the time being, no doubt, the stocks previously accumulated in Japan may suffice, but a future shortage seems inevitable.

To conserve home supplies as far as possible, oil has been refined near the places where it is produced, so that ships and aircraft might take in their fuel at bases in the East Indies. It will be remembered that the bulk of the Japanese fleet which took part in the Battle of the Philippines last October came not from Japan, but from Indo-China and Borneo. Undoubtedly it had been based on those regions with a view to the conservation of oil supplies, despite the obvious objections to dividing forces in this way. As a result, the fleet arrived on the scene of battle in three detachments; it could not therefore concentrate its full strength in one blow, and so was defeated.

SAFETY of Vital Oil Refineries A Very Real Worry to Japan

It is clear that one of the weakest features in the enemy's oil situation is the fact that most of the crude oil has to be refined before it can be utilized. This work has to be carried out at a number of refineries in Sumatra, Java and Borneo; it may be assumed that every effort has been made by the Japanese to extend the capacity of these installations. By far the biggest of them are at Soengei Gerong and Pladjoe, close to Palembang, in Sumatra, which had a combined capacity of over 60,000 barrels daily before the war. Another important refinery is at Pangkalan Brandan, in the north-east of the same island, with a pre-war output of 12,000 barrels a day.

On December 20, 1944, British naval aircraft of the East Indies Fleet were ordered to attack the Pangkalan Brandan refinery, but low cloud over the target prevented this from being done. Bombs were dropped instead on the harbour and shipping at Belawan Deli, where oil and petrol tanks were ignited. A second attempt on January 4, 1945, was more successful, bombs and rockets being showered on the refinery, most of the buildings of which were set on fire.

THREE weeks later, on January 24, a heavy attack was launched on the Pladjoe plant. It was found to be defended by large numbers of Japanese fighters, an inner and outer ring of anti-aircraft batteries and an extensive balloon barrage. Fighters were first encountered by our carrier-borne aircraft some miles short of the target. At least 13 and probably 19 of the enemy planes were shot down, while 34 more were destroyed and about 25 damaged on the airfields around the refinery.

ON January 29, Soengei Gerong, the bigger of the two plants, was dealt a heavy blow, the attack being pressed home in spite of the balloon barrage and heavy anti-aircraft fire. Many of the principal buildings received direct hits, and were afterwards set on fire through the adjacent oil reservoirs igniting. One particularly violent explosion shook our aircraft at a height of 3,000 feet. There was less fighter opposition than on Jan. 24, the enemy evidently having been unable to replace the losses then suffered. At least 12 and probably 15 Jap aircraft were accounted for in the air or on the ground.

SURVIVORS FROM H.M.C.S. CLAYOQUOT—a minesweeper torpedoed and sunk in the North Atlantic in January 1945—climbed aboard the Canadian corvette Fennel, from rubber dinghies. Eight of her complement of 81 were missing. The Clayoquot was the third Canadian minesweeper and the 20th Canadian warship to be lost in this war. *Photo, Canadian Official*

Attacks on the fleet by enemy aircraft were repelled, six being brought down in flames by British fighters or the guns of the ships. The fleet included four fleet aircraft carriers, the Indefatigable, of 30,000 tons (see illus. facing page) and the Indomitable, Illustrious and Victorious, of 23,000 tons; the battleship King George V, of 35,000 tons; the cruisers Argonaut, Black Prince and Euryalus; and the destroyers Grenville, Kempenfelt and Ursa, all under the command of Rear-Admiral Sir Philip Vian.

IT may be assumed other refineries in the East Indies will be attacked in due course. There are at least three in Java: at Theope, Kalantoeng, and Kapoean, with a combined capacity of between 15,000 and 20,000 barrels; an important one at Miri, in Sarawak; and a very big one at Balikpapan, in South-East Borneo, which has been bombed at least twice by U.S. naval aircraft in recent months. Its pre-war capacity was 35,000 barrels daily; it may be greater today.

Unless the Japanese can repair these refineries very quickly, or re-establish them underground, their ability to provide enough refined oil fuel for the navy and mercantile marine—to say nothing of high octane spirit for aircraft—will soon be at an end. From the reconquered bases in the Philippines the United States Navy is already ranging far to the southward. Air attacks will inevitably be followed by naval bombardments where necessary, and in due course Allied troops will be landed to occupy strategic positions for use as bases for further advances. It has been estimated that Japan may have an army of 250,000 in the Netherlands East Indies, but this force has had to be scattered over various islands to hold the conquered peoples in subjection, and is thus liable to be overcome in detail.

DESTRUCTION of Japanese Fleet May Now be Regarded as Certain

What part the British Pacific and East Indies Fleets will play in this programme remains to be seen; but undoubtedly it will be an important one, as the attacks on the oil refineries in Sumatra have already illustrated. Singapore and Hong Kong must eventually be cut off from all communication with Japan, and their fall cannot be averted. The former fortress has been heavily bombed on several occasions by United States aircraft, coming presumably from bases in India or Ceylon; and the great floating dock, salved with such difficulty by the Japanese in 1943, has again been sunk in the channel between Singapore Island and the mainland of Johore, where the naval base is situated. (See illus. p. 666.) Loss of this dock to the Allies will be offset to some extent by the building of the mammoth new graving dock at Sydney (see illus. p. 582).

THERE is nothing the Japanese can do to arrest the steady crumbling away of their conquests. If their depleted fleet should again sally out to meet the Allies in battle, its destruction may be regarded as certain, dissipating the main defence which the enemy can still muster to guard the homeland of Nippon, so long inviolate. It is scarcely surprising, therefore, that the Government, headed by General Koiso, should already be showing signs of decay, which are not likely to be arrested by the replacement of two or three of its less prominent members.

These Men and Ships Aid Burma's Liberation

THE ROYAL INDIAN NAVY spares two motor launches to undergo a refit at a rear Indian base (1) where they put in for periodical overhaul. The Arakan Coastal Forces have taken part in the Burma campaign by patrolling enemy waters in search of Japanese shipping, bombarding coastal positions and supporting Allied seaborne raids. Ratings strip and clean Lewis guns (2).

As towns along the Kaladan River in the Arakan are freed, villagers row out to greet our men and ships, waving the Burmese flag (3). The fleet minesweeper Punjab (4, in background), of the Bathurst class, passes the sloop Jumna which, since she was completed in 1941, has steamed over 50,000 miles. Her principal task—as with the rest of such craft attached to the R.I.N.—is escorting warships and merchantmen bound for the S.E. Asia theatre of war.

Outstanding among engagements in which the R.I.N. was concerned was the landing on Ramree Island, bastion protecting Taungua, one of the main supply harbours on the Arakan mainland, Jan. 21, 1945.

Photos, Indian Official

How India's Proud New Navy Came Into Being

Continuing our series on the Empire Navies (Canadian in page 488, Australian in page 584), this authoritative account of the building-up of the Royal Indian Navy from practically nothing to the magnificent Service which it is today has been specially written for "The War Illustrated" by Vice-Admiral Sir HERBERT FITZHERBERT, from 1937-1943 Flag Officer Commanding R.I.N.

ALTHOUGH the Royal Indian Navy has a record and a tradition dating back to 1615, its history during recent years has not been a happy one. It has suffered from neglect and disappointment ever since it was rechristened the Royal Indian Navy, and unless there had been a splendid spirit animating those officers and men who constituted the Service before the present war it would have died a natural death.

In this short article I must confine myself to setting out the principal incidents connected

Vice-Adml. SIR HERBERT FITZHERBERT, K.C.I.E., C.B., C.M.G., Flag Officer Commanding the Royal Indian Navy from 1937 to 1943, and the author of this article.

with the growth and expansion of a Service that started from practically nothing and finished up as a Navy complete in its training and organization with a large number of modern men-of-war and many thousands of fully trained and efficient officers and men.

THE story is one of striving against difficulties, most of which, fortunately, were successfully overcome. In order to allow the reader to visualize the conditions under which the work had to be done I would refer to the fact that in those pre-war years the sea was given no thought by any authority in India. Such plans for expansion as were envisaged had, therefore, to take into account a mental attitude that had to be completely altered if any success were to be achieved in the building-up of an efficient Naval Fighting Service. Lack of understanding, lack of funds and a tradition that gave the Army first and only place in India's defences all had to be eliminated if any success was to be hoped for. I hitched my wagon to a star which gave me and those who helped me so splendidly an ideal which, even if it was not completely achieved, spurred us on to continued effort.

The Chatfield Commission which visited India in 1938 did a great deal to help the progress of the Royal Indian Navy. The crisis of September 1938 was another event that enabled plans for the expansion of the Service to be pressed forward. The outbreak of war found India unprepared, but the Naval plans, having already been thought out, were ready for immediate implementation and no delay was encountered in the commencement of a very large and rapid development.

With an expansion such as was envisaged, the provision of adequate training staff and facilities became one of the most serious bottle-necks. This difficulty, like most of the others, was overcome and it was found possible to provide fully trained officers and men for the rapidly increasing fleet. The technical schools of the Royal Indian Navy today are all of a very high standard, and it is considered that the training given is comparable to that received by the personnel of the Royal Navy.

MANY major factors had to be considered in this large-scale development. Shipbuilding was one of these and it presented a number of problems. Where were the ships to come from ? By 1942 Hong Kong and Singapore had gone, and India had no shipbuilding industry worthy of the name. Eventually ships were built in England and Australia, and Indian shipbuilding capabilities were examined and organized so that in time every available slipway in India was utilized. It was indeed heartening to visit Calcutta when the Naval programme was well under way and to see lines of hulls in various stages of completion where no activity was to be seen before the war.

Naval bases were non-existent in India, so these too had to be provided. But before long there were well equipped and efficiently run Naval bases on both sides of the peninsula capable of dealing with the care and maintenance of all vessels that were likely to use the ports. The question of personnel was, without doubt, the crux of the problem ; provision of adequate numbers of the right type of officers and men was far from easy and their training presented another major difficulty. But I am happy to say that even these obstacles were successfully overcome and the Royal Indian Navy produced not only the requisite number of ships but a full complement of officers and men.

The R.I.N. Fought in Many Seas

Ships of the Royal Indian Navy were employed in many seas. The Battle of the Atlantic claimed some of India's men-of-war while the Red Sea, Persian Gulf, Arabian Sea, Bay of Bengal and Indian Ocean were also the scenes of much of their activity. Royal Indian Navy craft also operated in waters around Singapore and as far South as Australia. In the Arakan campaigns of 1944 and 1945 full scope was offered for the employment of the smaller ships and on many occasions they played an important part in these operations. Wherever they were used they gave an excellent account of themselves and a very fair proportion of awards for war service fell to their lot.

THE ROYAL INDIAN NAVY suffered its full quota of casualties. Ships were sunk by torpedo, mine and gunfire ; aerial attack became a matter of routine for many of them. Perhaps the most outstanding performance was the action fought by H.M.I.S. Bengal (Lieut.-Commander W. J. Wilson) on her way from Australia to India in Nov. 1942. This fleet minesweeper was escorting an oiler to India. One fine morning smoke was sighted on the horizon, and the Bengal closed to investigate. She found two Japanese armed merchant cruisers, one of 10,000 and the other of 6,863 tons, each armed with a broadside of five 5·5-in. guns. Without hesitation the Bengal closed the nearer enemy ship at full speed and opened a rapid fire which was not long in taking effect. The Japanese vessel returned the fire and the situation became critical.

Undeterred, the Bengal pressed on and maintained her fire, gallantly supported by the oiler, the Dutch Ondina, which received such severe damage that at one stage of the action she had temporarily to be abandoned. Soon the result of the Bengal's good shooting began to show and in a short time the larger of the two enemy ships, Kikoku Maru, was ablaze from stem to stern, finally sinking as the outcome of a heavy explosion. Her consort, seeing how the battle was going, made off at full speed and was not seen again. Armed with nothing heavier than a single 4-in. gun and handled with the greatest determination and courage, the Bengal had achieved a notable victory.

Looking back upon the record of the Royal Indian Navy, I have nothing but praise to offer to the Indian sailor. He has done his work unremittingly in extremely difficult and hazardous conditions. At all times and in all places he has shown himself courageous, determined and excellently disciplined. When well led he is capable of anything. To the officers also must be accorded their meed of credit. Starting from the very beginning, as so many of them had to do, they took their work seriously and learned all there was to learn in a remarkably short space of time. Their keenness and enthusiasm were of the highest order.

NO account of the creation of India's new Navy would be complete without reference to India's Press. I found them extremely helpful at all times ; indeed all the Royal Indian Navy owe them a great debt of gratitude for their unstinted help and assistance offered freely at all times.

The building up of a navy is a work that is not given to many people, and I count myself proud and fortunate that it should have fallen to my lot to create the Royal Indian Navy as it is today. The battle was a long one and at times difficult, but I think that I can say that most of our problems were overcome and that, in the end, we did produce something of which India could be proud.

Security prevents me from giving numbers of ships and personnel, but it may be taken as correct that the increase registered would need a large figure by which to multiply the numbers that existed before the expansion was commenced.

[*According to Jane's Fighting Ships, the ships include 10 sloops, one corvette, 16 fleet minesweepers, 40 trawlers, a surveying vessel, and numerous light craft and auxiliaries. Personnel in Nov. 1943 numbered 27,000.*]

Commander J. W. JEFFORD, R.I.N., and his Navigating Officer, Lieut. P. S. Mahindroo Singh, R.I.N.R., on board H.M. Indian sloop Godavari, typical personnel of India's new navy.
Photo, British Official

Bound for Mandalay Across the Shwebo Plain

SHERMAN TANKS AND ARMOURED VEHICLES of Lieut.-Gen. Slim's 14th Army in Burma (1) waited for the signal to advance again after a brilliant 30-mile dash between Kalewa and Shwebo, rail town (finally cleared of the enemy on January 11, 1945) and last important centre before Mandalay, 50 miles away. Near Pyingaing, British armour was assembled in strength for the first time in the Burma campaign on Christmas Day and Boxing Day 1944: three days later, against stiff Japanese resistance, it had advanced 30 miles, linking up with other Allied forces. British troops (2) display a Japanese flag captured in the village of Payan, an enemy stronghold holding up our progress from Zigon to Shwebo. Vitally important in our advance across the Shwebo plain to Mandalay was the Kabo weir on the River Mu, and General Slim's men approached it with such speed that the enemy abandoned it intact. This is Burma's dry belt and each division of troops needs 20,000 gallons of water per day. Anticipating a Japanese counter-attack, British troops, well dug in, guarded the approaches to the weir (3).

Photos, British Official.   Map by courtesy of The Times

On Myebon Peninsula in Jap-Infested Arakan

RECONQUERING THE ARAKAN, whose ancient capital, Myohaung, was occupied on January 25, 1945, Indian troops were ferried along a tributary of the Kaladan in landing craft of the Royal Indian Navy (1). British commandos (3) en route to the Myebon Peninsula, 60 miles south-east of Akyab (see page 632, and map opposite), where they landed on January 13—the fourth Burma landing in three weeks. A Sherman tank of the 25th Indian Division (2) pursuing the enemy beyond Myebon.

Photos, British and Indian Official

Can Hitler Wage War Without Front Lines?

Elaborating the fascinating and widely discussed subject as to how Nazi Germany might fight on when the last of her organized forces has been smashed, Dr. EDGAR STERN-RUBARTH outlines the probable plan of Nazi strategy after her inevitable collapse. His statements are based on special information and searching study. See also page 494.

A first sight it would seem an inevitable consequence of the complete breakdown of Hitler's coherent and organized front lines that Germany would have to acknowledge defeat. That means, of course, " unconditional surrender," since the Allies have announced that there will be no negotiation.

But because they realize what that means for them, Hitler and his gang long ago decided otherwise. And, if without a hope of turning the tables, they have an eye to protecting their forfeited lives, possibly by making us weary, negligent, and more tractable after a number of months.

This, then, is their scheme : all that is left of the German forces, seasoned, reliable—and that means " Nazified "—is prepared to follow the leaders and therefore must be salvaged. In larger or smaller units—armies, corps and so on—they must be kept together and positioned in a new variety of Hitler's once successful defence areas, the famous " hedgehogs," each under a faithful and reliable commander, provided with huge stocks of food and ammunition, surrounded by impregnable fortifications and with indestructible shelters for the whole garrison. These hedgehogs would be connected with each other and with their central command by short-wave transmitters—centres of resistance intended to become thorns in the flesh of any army of occupation.

" WE cannot hold lines any more ? Well, we shall hold fortresses ! We cannot defend cities ? Then let us hold mountains, caves and tunnels ! We cannot enforce a favourable decision ? Then let us go on harassing the enemy until he compromises ! We cannot rule the country any longer ? Then let us intimidate it ! " That, approximately, is the Nazi logic which dovetails with Hitler's mania, which for the last six months or so has occupied his attention to the exclusion of other military interests : the survival of National Socialism as a doctrine, a religion, for a thousand years, irrespective of losing this war, the latter to be dismissed as a " mere episode."

It is crazy and blasphemous in its intended parallel with Christianity forced underground, into the catacombs when proscribed and outlawed by Roman Caesars. There exist a number of these hedgehog-citadels of the Nazi forces, and four of them have stood siege for over half a year. One comprises the three Atlantic strongholds of Lorient, St. Nazaire, and the larger one embracing La Rochelle and the whole coastal area of western France down to and including the mouth of the Garonne, one of France's main doors to the sea.

Another is Col.-Gen. Schoerner's domain in Latvia where, with the encircled 16th and 18th Armies, he holds the country from Riga to Libau. The one around Budapest has just been liquidated by the Russians. In East Prussia, the C.-in-C., though less successful than Schoerner, had orders not to evacuate his forces, the 3rd Tank Army and the 4th Army, even had there been a fair chance of doing so ; but while the armies in the Baltic prove able to prevent the huge Russian forces from compressing them in a narrow corridor, General von Tippelskirch's defence lines were overrun when the fortification chain of Lötzen, and the natural protection of the Masurian Lakes, fell to Cherniakhovsky's and Rokossovsky's astutely planned onslaughts.

There are at least five more hedgehogs, mostly of much greater importance and size,

HEDGEHOG DEFENCES

EXISTING ● PREPARED ▨ POTENTIAL ⬚
Ⓐ Underground Citadel
Ⓑ Alpine Fortress

Statute Miles
0   200   400

" HEDGEHOG" MAP OF HITLER'S UNDERGROUND EUROPE from which he may continue to wage war after the inevitable defeat of the Wehrmacht in the field—as suggested in this page. Defences of this nature already in existence or being hastily prepared range from La Rochelle and Venice in the south to Bergen and Königsberg in the north. Some have already fallen to the Allies.

under preparation, and they are likely to be well stocked when the time comes for investing them. The first is the southern Norwegian bulge, including the country's two main outlets Oslo and Bergen, and controlling the entrance, through Skagerrak and Kattegat, of the Baltic Sea, possibly with some subsidiary stronghold across the straits, in north-western Jutland. The second, and the only other territory outside the Reich itself that the Nazis deem it essential for their purpose to hold, is behind the Adige-Brenner Line, in the province of Venice and including that city and port.

FOR both, fortifications have been under construction at least since last summer, when the Allied landings in Normandy sounded the death-knell of Hitler's regime. Two more have since been started : one for the protection of both Germany's main seaports, Hamburg and Bremen, and the Frisian islands along their coast-line, and another in the Black Forest, behind Germany's strongest fortress north of the Swiss frontier, Istein, and in exploitation of the huge, wooded mountain ranges and deep ravines and rushing streams of that sub-alpine landscape.

The fifth, and main giant hedgehog, Hitler's own perfect fortress (see page 494), is of incomparably larger size and elaborate design. Its outer lines cover, and exploit, practically the whole Austrian chain of Alps, from the Swiss border to the neighbourhood of Vienna, in the south, and the Bavarian outskirts of the Alps, probably meant to include Munich, in the north. Within that outer fortress, covering an area of about 10,000 square miles, there is an inner citadel of much smaller size, with Hitler's own eyrie at Berchtesgaden, the town of Salzburg, and the natural range of caves—ancient salt mines adapted to this new purpose—interconnected and equipped with all the latest gadgets, in the middle of it. Here will be the nerve centre and headquarters of a Nazi army spread and dissolved into fragments, waging war without front lines.

THERE are at least four more potential hedgehogs—if the Nazi organization and German forces can stem the Allied assault long enough to prepare and equip them. The first is Berlin itself, or at least part of her huge wooded area intersected with many river-arms and lakes. The second, in the Iron Mountains, 3,000 to 4,000-foot ridges along the Czech border (round Annaberg), where remnants of the former formidable Czechoslovak " Maginot Line " could be combined with the natural defences of the thickly wooded heights.

The third (round Detmold), in the Teutoburg mountains west of the river Weser, a minor yet difficult chain of hills which might be preferred to the higher Harz. The fourth, the Danish island of Bornholm south of the tip of Sweden, 112 square miles in area, was long ago selected as an experimental station for new weapons, ultimately to become a well-garrisoned stronghold. This has its historical associations, for from there, the old " Burgundarholm," more than seventeen centuries ago the Germanic tribe of the Burgundians, later the heroes of the Nibelungen Saga, started their fighting and conquering trek which ultimately led them to the wine lands of France.

It may seem ludicrous to connect up-to-date military planning with considerations of national mysticism. But since the scheme of this future war—possibly preceded by a giving-up of the North-German plains and a strategic move for protecting southern Germany as a whole—originated in a maniacal mind, and was backed and elaborated by its henchmen, it is no more incredible than Hitler's other dreams and blunders. Averting his eyes for the last six or seven months from military realities, he seems totally unaware of the fact that the sweeping Russian armies have made light of his hedgehogs as originally planned. It remains now for the Nazi leaders to realize that their new, perfected, gigantic variety is similarly doomed.

With Sinews of War Through the Persian Gulf

FOUR-AND-A-HALF MILLION TONS OF SUPPLIES TO RUSSIA were delivered through the Anglo-U.S. Persian Gulf route by the end of 1944. A heavily burdened convoy (top) alongside the new Allied-built docks at Khorramshahr on the Persian Gulf, from which by rail and lorry, across some of the most difficult terrain in the world, supplies are carried to Caspian seaports of the U.S.S.R. Lorries climb the zig-zag route (bottom) to Persia's central plateau. (See also pages 392-393.)

Photos, New York Times Photos

Enemy Forces Lured to their Doom by Bluff

Hand-in-hand with the tricky art of large-scale camouflage goes wholesale deception of the enemy with dummy tanks and guns, fake towns and wharves and railways. Even non-existent fighter-pilots have done their bit. Efforts of the "deception officer"—specialist in make-believe—can have rich and sometimes spectacular results, as instanced by ALEXANDER DILKE.

ONE of the most ingenious tricks of the war, resulting in two fighter planes being shot down by a "ghost" pilot, has been revealed in the official story of the air battles of Malta. It was in April 1942, when the Luftwaffe in strength was making its most determined efforts to finish off that "unsinkable aircraft-carrier." Ammunition and planes were short. Sometimes the handful of planes went up without ammunition and bluffed the Messerschmitts, which showed great respect for the few Spitfires and never knew whether these were armed or not.

One day German bombers came over with a fighter escort when no British planes could be sent up. Group Captain A. B. Woodhall, in charge of the Operations Room, had a happy inspiration. He created an imaginary "Pilot Officer Humgufery" and started giving

strongpoints and refused to reveal themselves. It was therefore decided to mount a fake attack to stir them up.

In darkness the four dummy guns and about twenty dummy men were placed in position. Then the party's one real field gun was concealed about 400 yards from the Italians' position. The attack was made at dawn, with a maximum of noise and much bomb throwing, which the Italians apparently mistook for shelling. They decided to retire into the fortress in the face of such a strong attack, and were followed up by the one real gun firing shells as fast as it could.

WHEN they reached the fortress, the Hussars began to prepare to follow up the unexpected success of their attack. But before they could do so the defenders, convinced they were surrounded by a

Sudan was full of enemy spies and the deception officer had to back his bluff with some real stuff. He persuaded the Royal Navy to start lengthening a wharf at a Red Sea port. He had hundreds of men extending a railway. He erected a field hospital and even sent doctors and nurses there. The wharf was never used, and it was not until long after that the Navy discovered its leg had been pulled. No troops ever travelled along the railway extension, and doctors and nurses waited at the field hospital in vain for casualties. But the bluff was completely successful. Spies sent back plenty of information which was correct, and for that very reason the Italians were completely deceived. The attack on Kassala was successful, and although hundreds of men had laboured at installations never intended for use they had not laboured in vain.

DUMMY tanks were probably the invention of the Germans, and when the full truth is known it may be found they carried out one of the biggest bluffs in history in the years immediately before the war. We used them effectively in North Africa at different times. On one occasion 7,000 Axis soldiers surrendered to 25 wooden tanks and eight wooden guns. Success at El Alamein was at least partly due to the way the enemy was bluffed over the 10th Corps. This Corps was engaged in very convincing training some fifty miles from the front just before the battle. It was moved up at night at the critical moment and the enemy thoroughly deceived.

One of the quiet pieces of bluff carried out by deception officers was discovered when we captured Tobruk in January 1942. Documents complete with many details were found in the Italian headquarters, describing a newly-arrived Australian division in Egypt. The Italians even had the exact date of disembarkation, figures for the equipment and names of the ships from which it had landed. This would have been splendid for the Italians if the Australian division had existed. But it was entirely imaginary. Someone had "planted" it on the enemy, who probably paid quite a lot of money for the "information."

THE air war has given rise to camouflaging of vital targets, and the Germans have spent millions on building dummy towns, concealing landmarks and so on. It is all a very delicate business, calling for keen appreciation of the enemy's psychology. On one occasion the Germans bluffed the R.A.F. They put a few landing lights on a dummy airfield, and turned all the lights full on at the real aerodrome. They guessed our bombers would go for the dummy, thinking that the excessive lighting at the other aerodrome was intended to catch the eye. This trick, of course, does not work twice. We have been equally successful, and have attracted bombs to dummy targets by camouflaging them just badly enough to enable them to be detected.

The simplest bluffs are often the most effective. Three men ordered to delay advancing Germans in a village took six beer bottles and placed them across the road at even intervals, then retired to a house to watch. A German appeared, eyed the bottles cautiously, and went back, evidently to report. Others appeared, but another half-hour was wasted before the Germans picked off the bottles one by one from a safe distance, then, finding nothing happened, they became even more cautious, thus lengthening the delay we desired.

NO WOODEN HORSE OF TROY but a dummy found on an abandoned airfield in Holland taken by our troops in their advance late in 1944. The retreating Nazis "stocked" many of their airfields with these "lath-and-plaster" horses and cattle, hoping to delude the R.A.F. into the belief that they were quiet farmsteads.
Photo, British Newspaper Pool

him orders over the radio. The orders were "received" by a Canadian pilot with an unmistakable voice who happened to be in the Operations Room at the time. He replied in the name of Humgufery as if he were in the air.

THE Germans intercepted the messages, and soon came the cry "Achtung! Spitfeuer!" The enemy had picked up the "ghost plane," which presumably they imagined was above them and coming out of the sun. Just what they thought we shall probably never know, but their confusion was such that they proceeded to shoot down two of their Messerschmitts. Those two planes were credited to the imaginary "Pilot Officer Humgufery."

One of the most spectacular bluffs was carried out in Libya by a small party of the South Nottinghamshire Hussars. It was necessary to keep the Italians in Maktila, which they held very strongly, while an attack was mounted in another direction. The instruction to the Hussars was, "Keep them on the hop!" They were given a fairly free hand—and four wooden guns with a number of dummy men. For some days they patrolled round the Italians' outer defences but the Italians stayed in their

powerful force, put up the white flag and surrendered. Over 5,200 men laid down their arms to a handful of live men, twenty dummies and four wooden guns!

Armies now have officers who are specialists in the art of bluffing. An officer appointed to carry out a big deception has to go to work like a stage manager—in fact, one of the experts was formerly a famous stage manager. He must be prepared to use his ingenuity in producing "props" to convince the audience of enemy reconnaissance pilots that his "show" is genuine, and may have to carry realism a long way, hoodwinking friends as well as enemies.

General Platt, when he was G.O.C. for East Africa, revealed after the Abyssinia campaign that on one occasion a "deception officer" he selected for a vital task was so good that he deceived everyone, including General Platt. The occasion was the attack from the Sudan, when it was planned to go for Kassala. But the Sudan is not an easy country in which to conceal large numbers of troops, and it was important to deceive the Italians about the direction of the attack, because if they had had time to reinforce the attack would have been fruitless.

Marshal Gregory Zhukov: His Target Berlin

Once a private in the army of the Tsar, now First Deputy of Marshal Stalin (Supreme C.-in-C. of the Soviet Armies), 50-years-old Marshal Gregory Konstantinovitch Zhukov on Jan. 14, 1945—in command of the 1st White Russian Front— launched in Central Poland the mighty offensive which liberated Warsaw and within three weeks was closely threatening the Reich capital.   Saviour of Moscow in 1941, he organized the defence of Stalingrad in 1942, and relieved Leningrad in 1943.

Italy's Worst Winter in Living Memory—

The snows came, and biting wind and bitter frost gave skating-rink surfaces to the roads. On-the-spot ingenuity and improvisation became the order of the day: gunners of an anti-tank regiment of Royal Artillery used home-made ploughs drawn by oxen to clear a mountain path (1). Moving up to relieve forward troops of the 5th Army a section nears the end of an arduous climb (2). Fighting alongside British on the 8th Army front, Italians man a 17-pounder anti-tank gun (3).

— *Froze Contending Forces to Immobility*

Only skis and ski-sticks enabled Lieut. W. Cheney, of Kent, in charge of an 8th Army report post in the Apennines, to attempt his daily rounds (4). Gargantuan icicles failed to impair the appetite of Sapper R. Vass, of Surrey, resting by the Santerno's bank (5). After a thaw on the 5th Army front, the Santerno promptly rose three feet, became a raging torrent and ripped this pontoon bridge (6) to pieces, whilst Royal Engineers made desperate efforts to save what they could of it.

No German Remains in Warsaw or Memel

Through the stricken streets of Warsaw, reconquered Jan. 17, 1945, marched troops of Marshal Zhukov's 1st White Russian Front (top) with men of the Polish 1st Army who shared in the battle for the capital. Completing the liberation of Lithuania with the capture of Memel, German stronghold-port, with its naval base and shipyards, on Jan. 28, these warriors (bottom) of the 1st Baltic Front, commanded by Army-General Bagramyan, were among the first to reach the Baltic coast in that area.

Photos, U.S.S.R. Official, Pictorial Press

In the Wake of Our Armies Marches U.N.R.R.A.

Mighty labours of the United Nations Relief and Rehabilitation Administration (U.N.R.R.A.) are under way. Of its various Liaison Missions to Allied Governments in Europe, those to France and Luxembourg are already in operation, and there is an U.N.R.R.A. Yugoslav camp in the Sinai Desert. Work to be accomplished is explained by JOHN ALLEN GRAYDON. See also page 46.

THE freeing of the countries in Europe occupied by the Germans is being accomplished in two ways : from the military aspect, and with relief measures necessary for the life and health of the community. The Allied Armies have already gone far on the military side. Now experts are studying more closely than ever the full meaning of the word "Relief," and in this sphere of operations U.N.R.R.A. is playing a leading role.

In Europe today the people are in their lowest state of health for many years. That is why Dr. Wilbur Augustus Sawyer, World Director of Health for U.N.R.R.A., has prepared vast plans for the speedy relief of those who have for so long suffered at the hands of the Germans. Dr. Sawyer, who fought as a

IN ATHENS during the recent disturbances, this American U.N.R.R.A. relief-worker frequently distributed food and medical supplies under fire. *Photo, British Official*

United States Army infantryman in the last war, is 61 years of age, and for the past nine years has been Director of the International Health Division of the Rockefeller Foundation. Best-known for his vaccine against yellow fever, he has an international reputation as an organizer. Without doubt his present post makes colossal demands upon his skill. A native of Wisconsin, he has twice visited Britain since the outbreak of war : the first occasion was during the blitz of 1940, the second in September 1944.

The department of U.N.R.R.A. which Doctor Sawyer heads has called upon medical science for all latest developments ; as an example, the new D.D.T. insecticide, so efficient against malaria, will play a prominent part in keeping down epidemics. During their occupation of France and Belgium the Germans sent to the Reich most of the medical drugs they could lay hands upon. Hospitals were destroyed, and trained medical staff were put to work in war factories. The result is that many health services will have to be built up all over again.

EMERGENCY medical units, each with enough drugs and other requirements to meet the demands of 100,000 people for one month, have been constructed, and every unit has a hospital with beds for 200 patients, an operating theatre and X-ray equipment. Five small hospitals, with forty beds, for use in small towns and villages are included. There is also a standard unit which has supplies for one million people for three months.

Eighty crates of medical supplies provided by U.N.R.R.A. were in January 1944 being flown from Britain to Moscow on the first stage of their journey to liberated Czechoslovak territory. This consignment, consisting of

drugs, dressings and instruments, is only the first instalment. A much larger consignment, from the U.S., will shortly go by sea, including drugs and dressings packed as units to supply 100,000 people for one month, hospital units with equipment for 40-bed and 200-bed hospitals, laboratories and X-ray units with mobile diagnostic sets, for the use of a team of Czechoslovak doctors. The shipment of these supplies to Czechoslovakia and also of U.N.R.R.A. relief to Poland was facilitated by the Soviet Union agreeing to the use of Black Sea ports.

ONE of the most urgent and important of the Health Department's problems is the return in the quickest possible time of millions of displaced persons to their homes without increasing the health hazards of Europe by the spread of epidemics. In so far as Military and Allied Governments do not undertake this responsibility themselves, the Displaced Persons Division of U.N.R.R.A. will be in charge, advised on health matters by the Health Division.

The object is to ensure that uniform and co-ordinating measures of medical inspection, delousing, immunization, and so on, are carried out in the countries of departure, transit, and arrival ; so that, on the one hand, the danger of epidemics is reduced as far as possible, and on the other that displaced persons are not unnecessarily detained in quarantine on frontiers and their return delayed.

150 Million Distressed Europeans

Another high U.N.R.R.A. official to whom Europe looks for assistance is Toronto-born Miss Mary Craig McGeachy, 39 years old Welfare Director. Her duty is to supervise essential relief for distressed people in liberated areas, and it is thought she may have about 150 million Europeans relying upon her for help before the end of the present year. As Britain's first woman diplomat, in 1942, she became First Secretary of the British Embassy in Washington, and it was while filling that post that she showed such skill that the Welfare Directorship of U.N.R.R.A. was given to her. A complex organization such as U.N.R.R.A. has always to be preparing for new tasks, and one of the latest developments has been the establishment of a residential Staff College at Reading under the charge of Mr. W. E. Arnold-Forster. At this College members are prepared for the work of assisting the Army in the repatriating of 10 million Allied Nationals now in Germany and Austria. Forty-five members took part in the first course. They spent two weeks in an

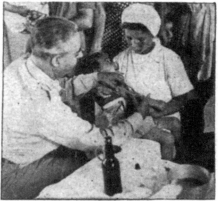

INOCULATING A SMALL CHILD against diphtheria, at an U.N.R.R.A camp set up in Palestine for refugees of Greek origin. *Photo, British Official*

intensive study of the purpose and organization of U.N.R.R.A. ; the relations of the organization with the Governments and citizens of the United Nations, as well as the Military. The repatriation of Displaced Persons also received a careful examination.

NO attempt is made to train experts in a particular field, for the members on the course are already specialists when U.N.R.R.A. engages them. Many are Welfare Workers, Doctors, Nurses or Administrators. The men and women who study at the Reading Staff College are of different nationalities. Several are ex-soldiers with experience in transport, feeding services and camp administration ; others are experts at civilian relief ; many have lived in Europe under the Germans ; still more gained their experience during the blitz on Britain. All, in their respective roles, have an important niche to fill in Europe. The Staff College helps them to understand in full their responsibilities.

When the students have finished their two-weeks course they give way to another class, returning to London for a further fortnight of hard training. When the first batch of students returned to London they met U.N.R.R.A. officers newly-arrived from the liberated countries and who gave them accounts of conditions there. Also the students talked with officials of interested Governments, who explained special problems and backgrounds of their own nationals who await liberation when the Allies march into Germany in strength.

U.N.R.R.A. OFFICERS AT SCHOOL AT READING, ENGLAND. In this residential Staff College members are intensively trained to undertake the highly responsible work described in this page. They include soldiers, airmen, policemen, tea-planters, chemists, engineers, nurses, solicitors and journalists, all specialists in some particular field. PAGE 659 *Photo, Sport & General*

VIEWS & REVIEWS Of Vital War Books

by Hamilton Fyfe

IF we did not know that Governments are frequently deceived—or deceive themselves—about the intentions of other Powers and their own readiness to meet any sudden attack, it would be matter for astonishment that both the British and American Governments were caught unprepared by the Japanese onslaught in the Pacific at the end of 1941.

That onslaught is often described with indignation, both here and in the United States, as "treacherous" and "dastardly." Why use these epithets? Why affect surprise that a nation taught by the others to play Power Politics should take the trouble to play that game as skilfully as possible? Morals and Power Politics have nothing whatever to do with one another. That is why we must get rid of Power Politics if we want decency and honour in international dealings. We must use power for the benefit of all, and not allow it to be used for selfish national ends.

Obviously, so long as power is used for those ends, we must regard such sudden opening moves as the Japanese made without warning, not as infractions of a rule (because in war there are no rules) but as part of the game. If I were apportioning blame for the events in the Pacific between December 1941 and the summer of the following year, I should be inclined to find less guilt in Japanese action than in the failure of the British and American Governments to make full preparations to meet that action. Yes, and I would include the Netherlands Government in that condemnation, for it had taken few precautions to safeguard its colonies Sumatra

and Java against blows long foreseen by everyone who watched the course of Japanese policy and knew what the military and naval cliques in Tokyo were aiming at.

THIS view may shock some, but it is the rational view. Nothing can be more futile than to mix up sentiment with war. How foolish to describe our soldiers as fighting magnificently like lions, while we say the enemy fought fanatically like rats in a trap! There is a little too much of this in the very fine tribute to our troops in Burma which South-East Asia Command issues at the low price of threepence and under the title SEAC Souvenir. (Original issue printed by A. D. Bose in the office of The Statesman, Calcutta, who provided facilities as a war gift). Everyone defends himself fanatically when his life depends on it. Everyone attacks ferociously when properly worked up—and it is the business of those who train troops to work them up. Over and over again in this stirring record

we are given proof that in ferocity the men of the Fourteenth Army could give the Japanese points every time.

The enemy could not, of course, have entered Burma so quickly if the French in Indo-China and the Siamese in what is now called Thailand had not given them a great deal of assistance. Thanks to this, the Japanese were able to strike at India—with very fair chances of success. An Order of the Day to the invaders issued by the general in command of this operation said it would "engage the attention of the whole world and was eagerly awaited by a hundred millions of people in Japan." Its success would have a profound effect on the course of the war and might even lead to its conclusion. "We must therefore," he ended, "expend every ounce of energy and talent to achieve our purpose."

Tribute to Our Troops in Burma

WELL, they did all they could. That general could not blame his armies for the failure which probably led to his suicide. They were thoroughly well equipped, they were well trained, they were clever in jungle warfare, they were almost incredibly tough. But his effort collapsed because he brought them up against men who, though not so hardy by nature and not so plentifully supplied with the machines that war today requires, fought better than they did and threw them back. There were times when it seemed as if only miracles could prevent the Japanese from invading India. Every one of those times the necessary miracle happened—or rather, it didn't "happen"; it was worked by the courage and doggedness and skill in fighting under terribly difficult conditions of the men of the Fourteenth Army, that army which has earned a place in history that will never die away.

When Imphal Was Besieged

There was, however, something in the nature of a miracle on conventional lines which helped a great deal. This was born in the quick, inventive mind of General Wingate. When he proposed to lead a force that would operate far behind the Japanese lines and play havoc with their communications, he was asked, "What about your own supplies?" He said, "We'll get them by air." And that was how they did receive them. Regularly the aircraft loaded with all the expedition needed found out where it was and dropped parachute cargoes, scarcely any of which missed their mark. This method more than once warded off disaster.

For instance, when Imphal, that place we used to hear of every day at one time, was besieged last spring, the enemy counted on forcing our surrender by starving out the garrison. They relied on this so confidently that they announced the town's capture in Tokyo. But they had not reckoned with the method of supply from the air. "Day after day the hungry Japs on the surrounding hills saw the stream of troop-carriers bearing in food, fuel, ordnance, ammunition, stores, men and even water. They brought out the wounded over the very gun-sights of the enemy. Behind them supply units, transport

Lieut.-Gen. SUN LI JEN, Commander of the 1st Chinese Army (left), and Lieut.-Gen. Dan I. Sultan, commanding Allied Forces in the Northern Combat Area of Burma, entering Bhamo after its capture on December 15, 1944.
Photo, L.N.A.

men and L. of C. troops slogged to keep the dixies and the magazines filled for the men in the line. Unbelievable reports flamed round the world of impending grief. The men of the 4th Corps on duty at Imphal serenely stuck it out."

THE use of that word "serenely" is an example of the fault I have mentioned. It is silly to suggest that any troops in such a position as those at Imphal are "serene." It was a lie to suggest, as Japanese radio did, that "confusion and alarm" prevailed. It was a stupid lie to be put about by a commander whose forces were being destroyed daily by the "confused and alarmed" garrison. But though those 4th Corps men were neither rattled nor bewildered they would grin grimly at the idea that they felt "serene."

Except for the Australians in New Guinea, no troops have ever had to fight a prolonged series of battles in such frightfully difficult country against an enemy who had managed to occupy the best positions before we were able to turn and rend him. Of the Mayu range of mountains in the Arakan area the Japanese command wrote, in an order to its forces, "It is a fortress given to us by heaven, to furnish us with defences, obstructions, concealment, with water, with quarters, with supplies of building material unlimited. Its heights and rivers will shortly become an unforgettable new battleground."

ALL that was true. The prediction in the final sentence was fulfilled. But the battleground proved fatal to the invaders, not to the British defenders. The events of that campaign will never be forgotten by us, but the enemy will try not to think about them, for with all those catalogued advantages on their side the Japanese were soundly defeated.

Full tribute is paid to those who were not actually fighting, but whose brave and untiring toil made victory possible. Everything depends on the regular arrival of all that an army needs. Without that the most daring courage, the most carefully laid plans, can accomplish nothing. Throughout the Burma campaigns "Admin," as they call it (short for Administration), never failed. "So the vast spaces, the dark, dense, treacherous jungle, were overcome; the evil beasts and insects and snakes, the leeches, lice and ticks, the sun's high blaze, the night's dew and lonely terror; rain, mist, mud, and the foulest of all, the Japanese enemy"

This is How South-East Asia Command Works

FORMATION of South-East Asia Command, with Headquarters at New Delhi, India, was announced at Quebec on Aug. 25, 1943. In April 1944 its Headquarters were moved to Kandy, Ceylon. On Nov. 28, 1944, Lt.-Gen. F. A. M. Browning succeeded General Sir Henry Pownall as Chief of Staff.

AIR COMMAND S.E.A. was set up in Dec. 1943 under Air Chief Marshal Sir Richard Peirse; on Oct. 15, 1944, this appointment was transferred to Air Chief Marshal Sir Trafford Leigh-Mallory, who was reported missing while flying to the East on Nov. 17. Air Marshal Sir Keith Park is now Allied Air C.-in-C. S.E.A.

Adm. Sir A. J. Power's appointment as C.-in-C. East Indies Fleet was announced on Dec. 11, 1944.

SUPREME ALLIED COMMANDER SOUTH-EAST ASIA

Adm. Lord Louis Mountbatten

DEPUTY SUPREME COMMANDER

Lt.-Gen. R. A. Wheeler (U.S. Army)

CHIEF OF STAFF

Lt.-Gen. F. A. M. Browning

EAST INDIES FLEET

Adm. Sir A. J. Power

ALLIED LAND FORCES S.E.A.

Lt.-Gen. Sir Oliver Leese

ALLIED AIR C.-in-C. S.E.A.

Air Marshal Sir Keith Park

EASTERN AIR COMMAND

Maj.-Gen. G. E. Stratemeyer

14th ARMY

Lt.-Gen. Sir William Slim

N. COMBAT AREA COMMAND

Lt.-Gen. Dan I. Sultan (U.S. Army)

1st CHINESE ARMY
Gen. Sun Li Jen

XV CORPS

Lt.-Gen. Sir P. Christison

XXXIII CORPS

Lt.-Gen. Sir M. Stopford

IV CORPS
(Commander not announced)

3rd TACTICAL AIR FORCE

Air Marshal W. A. Coryton

10th U.S.A.A.F

Maj.-Gen. H. Davidson
U.S.A.A.F.

STRATEGIC AIR FORCE

Air Commodore E. W. Mellersh

TROOP CARRIER COMMAND

Brig.-Gen. W. D. Old
U.S.A.A.F.

When the G.I. Joes Swarmed Ashore at Luzon

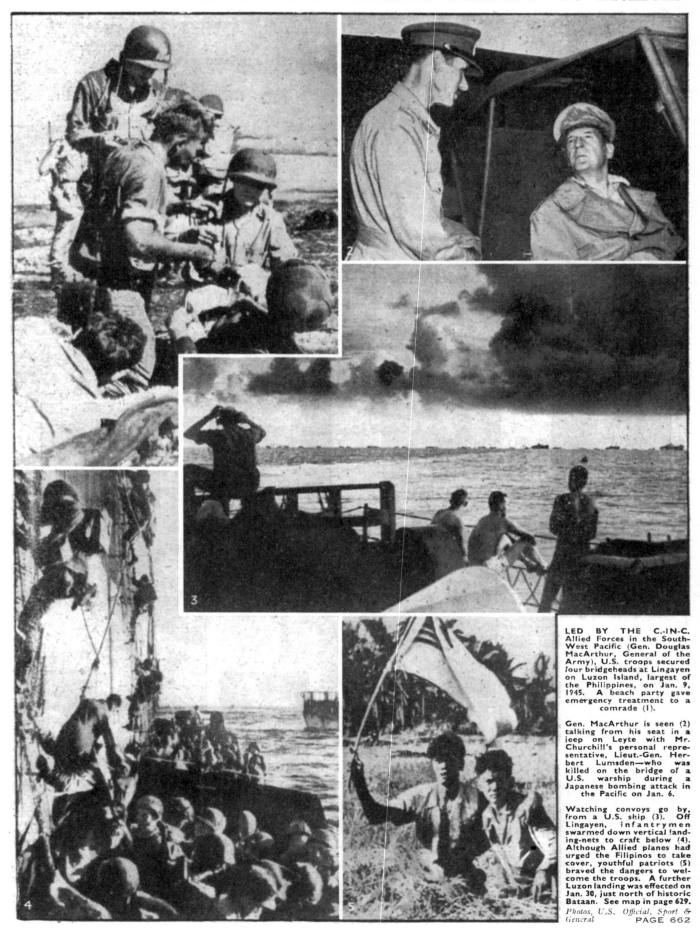

LED BY THE C.-IN-C. Allied Forces in the South-West Pacific (Gen. Douglas MacArthur, General of the Army), U.S. troops secured four bridgeheads at Lingayen on Luzon Island, largest of the Philippines, on Jan. 9, 1945. A beach party gave emergency treatment to a comrade (1).

Gen. MacArthur is seen (2) talking from his seat in a jeep on Leyte with Mr. Churchill's personal representative, Lieut.-Gen. Herbert Lumsden—who was killed on the bridge of a U.S. warship during a Japanese bombing attack in the Pacific on Jan. 6.

Watching convoys go by, from a U.S. ship (3). Off Lingayen, infantrymen swarmed down vertical landing-nets to craft below (4). Although Allied planes had urged the Filipinos to take cover, youthful patriots (5) braved the dangers to welcome the troops. A further Luzon landing was effected on Jan. 30, just north of historic Bataan. See map in page 629.

Photos, U.S. Official, Sport & General

Australian Forces to Clean-up the 'Island Front'

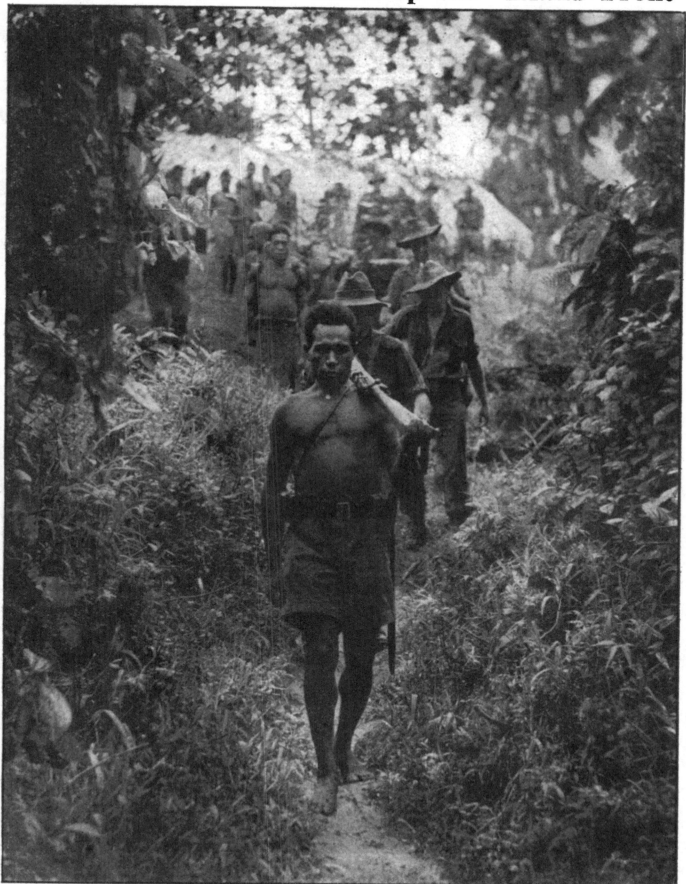

MIXED PATROL OF AUSTRALIANS and native Melanesian troops sets out from Awit in New Britain in search of Japanese rearguards. Australian forces, it was announced on January 10, 1945, have largely taken over from U.S. troops the "Island Front" in the South-West Pacific, to deal with by-passed units of crack Japanese divisions strongly sited at strategic points in the Solomons, New Britain and New Guinea. A further Australian amphibious landing on New Britain—on the eastern end of the island—was reported on February 6. *Photo, Australian Official*

V.C.s of Burma, Italy and the Western Front

Naik AGANSING RAI
On June 26, 1944, a company of the 5th Royal Gurkha Rifles was ordered to recapture from greatly superior enemy forces two outposts seriously menacing our lines in Burma. Under devastating machine-gun fire and showers of grenades, Naik Rai (left), armed with a tommy-gun, advanced alone, killing ten Japanese and so inspiring his men that they routed the enemy and captured the positions. In the words of the citation, his "magnificent display of initiative, outstanding bravery and gallant leadership" saved the situation.

Rifleman T. PUN
During an attack on the railway bridge at Mogaung, Burma, on June 23, 1944, a section under Rifleman Pun (right) was eliminated—all but himself. In the face of "the most shattering concentration of automatic fire," he continued to advance alone, ankle-deep in mud, through shell-holes and over fallen trees, then killing three occupants of a Japanese machine-gun post. His action enabled the remainder of his platoon to reach and secure their objective.

Sgt. GEORGE H. EARDLEY
Near Overloon, Holland, on October 16, 1944, Sergeant Eardley, of the King's Shropshire Light Infantry, armed with grenades and a Sten gun, destroyed three German machine-gun posts single-handed "under fire so heavy that it daunted those with him."

Private R. H. BURTON
Attacking an enemy-held height, through mud and continuous rain, in Italy on October 8, 1944, this private of the Duke of Wellington's Regiment, displaying "magnificent gallantry," dashed forward and put out of action the crews of three Spandau posts.

Private E. ALVIA SMITH
While protecting a wounded comrade, during a fierce action on the Savio River in Italy on October 21, 1944, Private Smith, of the Seaforth Highlanders of Canada, beat off attacks by two German tanks besides enemy infantry.

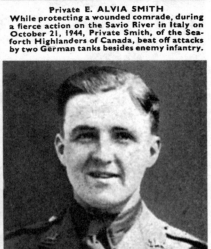

Capt. J. N. RANDLE
This officer of the Royal Norfolk Regiment, at Kohima, in Assam, on May 6, 1944, charged a Japanese machine-gun post alone, and although mortally wounded silenced it with a grenade hurled through a bunker slit. He then flung himself across the slit so that the aperture should be completely sealed. His battalion gained its objective.

L/Sgt. J. D. BASKEYFIELD
Hero of Arnhem, Holland, this N.C.O. of the South Staffordshire Regiment, on September 20, 1944, held enemy tanks at bay till his gun was silenced. Then he crawled to another 6-pounder, the crew of which were dead, and fired it till he was killed. Stories of his valour were a constant inspiration to all ranks.

Lieut. TASKER-WATKINS
Superb gallantry which saved the lives of his men during an action against numerically superior forces at Balfour, Northern France, on August 16, 1944, secured the supreme award for this lieutenant of the Welch Regiment, the only officer left of his company.

Photos. Indian Official, G.P.U., Keystone, Daily Mirror

I WAS THERE!  Eye Witness Stories of the War

Back in Manila, the Philippines Capital

Entered by U.S. troops on Feb. 4, 1945, Manila (see map in p. 629) was wrenched from the Japanese after being in their hands for more than three years, as told here by B.U.P. correspondent Frank Hewlett. Gen. MacArthur's campaign in these islands had started 26 days before this success, with landings over 100 miles to the north, in the Lingayen Gulf.

THREE years ago I said "Goodbye" to my wife Virginia. I went to Bataan with General MacArthur's forces, but she insisted on staying behind as a nurse at the Santa Catalina Hospital in Manila. Today we were reunited. It might give the world some idea of the ordeal of this town under Japanese occupation if I say, simply, that my wife's weight today is only 5 stone 10 pounds!

No wonder that the half-starved people in the concentration camp in the Santo Tomas University in Manila managed to summon up enough strength to hoist me on their shoulders when I broke into the main building there during the fighting last night. It was an honour that should have been reserved for the troops, but they were busy killing the Japanese outside.

Inside, it was pandemonium. Women wept, children screamed with joy, men broke down as they shook hands with us and could

while it pushed aside some determined Japanese opposition, but all along the road brushes with the enemy were frequent.

As we broke into the city the column split in two, one half heading for Santo Tomas. The citizens of Manila went crazy with joy as we tore through the city. They stood by the sides of the road cheering until it seemed their lungs would crack. They offered us some of their own tiny rations and found some beer for us, too.

There was fighting at some points when we reached the University buildings. At others, Japanese troops were holding out on the second and third floors of some of the buildings. Below them the windows were filled with internees, wildly cheering the relieving troops. To have started a battle would have meant death to scores of them, so, finally, a truce was reached. The Japanese were allowed to leave the building in return for the safe release of the internees.

GENERAL MACARTHUR, C.-in-C. South-West Pacific, inspected—no doubt with grim satisfaction—this Japanese monument to their dead on Luzon, after his invasion of that Philippine island on Jan. 9, 1945. See also illus. page 662. *Photo, Keystone*

soldiers who were guarding the American internees, 221 of them, in one of the University buildings where they were holding them as hostages. It was then that the truce was reached, but it was an uneasy one.

Led by their commanding officer, Colonel Hayashi, the Japanese soldiers filed out of the building one by one. The American commanding officer shouted to his troops, "The Japanese gave us the alternative of freeing them all or having all the American hostages killed. We will march down the road with them between us, and at a given point we will halt and they will go on. I don't want any of you fellows to get trigger-happy but, if they shoot, give them hell!"

Japs Would Have Died in 10 Seconds

The Japanese, carrying guns and sabres, marched off silently, covered on both sides by grimy American soldiers fingering their tommy-guns. Not a man spoke, but everyone knew that if one Jap had touched a trigger of his gun every one of them would have died within ten seconds. After a few hundred yards the U.S. soldiers halted and the Japs kept marching on. "Down with MacArthur. Down with America!" we heard one Jap soldier screech as they moved out of sight. The Americans fondled their guns for a moment. Then all was quiet . . , nobody had been taunted into shooting.

To a British missionary, Ernest Stanley, goes much of the credit for saving the hostages. Mr. Stanley handled the negotiations between the American commander and Col. Hayashi, and agreed to walk unarmed across no man's land to meet Hayashi and get the matter settled.

NOTORIOUS CONCENTRATION CAMP AT SANTO TOMAS, MANILA, was the scene of great poignancy when U.S. troops rescued thousands of prisoners, including many British and Americans, who had been starved by the Japanese and ill-treated there. The photograph was taken as the rescuers made their way inside. *Photo, Fox*

not utter a word, but just stood, their lips moving silently. Then they asked for food. They looked as if they had not eaten for weeks. Last June the Japanese had banned all outside purchases of food, and for the past two months conditions had been terribly bad, each person getting less than 700 calories a day. And it takes 2,400 calories daily to sustain a normal person!

IT was a nightmare last few hours before 3,700 internees in the camp had been released. I came in with a flying column under General Chase, which consisted of a small force of tanks, lorries filled with troops, and jeeps. At one o'clock in the morning we started off on a reckless dash towards the city, over a rough and seldom-used road. At Novaliches, 10 miles from Manila, the column had to stand and fight

The most critical moment of all—it could easily have led to the murder of more than two hundred men, women, and children—came at dawn. For six hours U.S. troops had been exchanging shots with 65 Japanese

Down a Mine for a Night's Work with a Bevin Boy

Serving the nation equally with those of their age who join the Armed Forces, the boys who are called up for work in the pits have no aura of glamour. But they have the satisfaction of knowing we could not get on without them. This contribution by a Bevin boy, Mr. T. Buckland, written specially for "The War Illustrated," will interest parents—and others.

I WORK at a pit called Glapwell Colliery, at Glapwell in Nottinghamshire. To get there I have to travel five miles by bus. I then go into the locker rooms—the pithead baths. We walk in at one side, take off our clean clothes, walk leisurely

through the showers to the dirty side, then change into working clothes. We each have a tin water-bottle—which we call a "Dudley" —and a snap tin which holds lunch and keeps out the dust and the rats down the pit.

We fill our "Dudley" with fresh water (it holds four pints) and along we go to the pithead. We each have a numbered pay check, and as we pass through a kind of barrier we shout out our numbers and a man clocks us in. Then to the lamp cabin, where we leave lamp check and locker key and receive a hand-lamp, which is quite weighty to carry about. We walk to the pit-top where the cage (lift) is. It is roughly a thousand yards from pit-top to pit-bottom, and when you are in the cage water is dripping all over you. There are holes in the bottom of the cage, and when we reach the middle of the shafting we are travelling at about 60 m.p.h., with the draught through the holes blowing right up our legs, and it's cold !

When we get out of the cage at the bottom we report to the cabin where all the deputies are, and they tell us where to go ; every coal face is numbered. The nearest one to me is number 25, and it is quite a distance. For part of the way it is cold, but gradually it becomes warmer and you have to deposit your coat somewhere. It is roughly four miles from the pit-bottom to the point where I work, which makes it about nine miles from where I live.

Even Standing Still We Sweat

It is a steep, downhill walk, and parts of the way we have to bend very low. I leave you to imagine what it is like when one is returning, tired out ! When we get to our working-place we undress, keeping on only short pants, hat and boots. My present job is making a new roadway, which they call a heading, in a temperature of about 70 degrees, and believe me, even when standing still you sweat. First, we see if there are any empty tubs handy. If there are not, we have to walk 500 yards for them. We get four each time, and we lower them down the slope by a cable running off a small haulage motor.

I am working with two other miners, and when we start shovelling up the rock the sweat really begins to roll. It gets into your eyes, and it stings. Soon we are sweating from head to foot. Shovelling and picking at the rock all the time we fill eight tubs right off, and begin to feel there is no more sweat left to come out. Half-way through a shift I have generally drunk my four pints of water, and then have to go thirsty. It makes you value water !

THE eight tubs filled, we have our " snap," which takes twenty minutes to half an hour. Then we lower another four tubs, and by the time we have filled them and hauled them to the top of the slope it is just about time to start walking back to the cage that will take us to the surface again. We fill between 12 and 16 tubs a night, each tub holding about one ton of rock. Twelve to 16 tubs a night isn't bad, is it ?

BOY TRAINEES for the pits, at Markham Colliery, near Chesterfield, listen to an old hand's advice. Conscription of boys of 18 to work in the mines was announced by Mr. Ernest Bevin, Minister of Labour, on Dec. 3, 1943. *Photo, Topical.* PAGE 686

THIS WAS THE £1,200,000 DOCK TARGET at Singapore, sent to the bottom, as told below. To operate the 855-ft. dock, water was let into its hollow walls ; this caused it to settle down and fill up sufficiently to admit a big ship due for repairs. Then water would be pumped from the walls, the dock rising and carrying the ship propped up and high and dry, as above. *Photo, Associated Press*

Singapore's Giant Floating Dock Was Our Target

In the great bombing raid on Singapore on Feb., 1, 1945, the 50,000-tons dry dock was sunk—for the second time. Built in Britain and towed in sections 8,000 miles to Singapore, it was sunk by us when the fall of Singapore seemed imminent, and raised by the Japanese. The raid is described by Reuter's correspondent Alan Humphreys, who was in one of the Super-Fortresses.

I AM taking part in this raid on the Singapore naval base, the biggest installation of its kind in the South Seas, of which the King George V Dock, towed out from Britain before the war, is the main target. The raid is being made by the 20th Air Force. The first wave of giant aircraft has already made its attack through cloud and A.A. fire. My plane is in the second wave and is just making its run over the target.

It is 9 a.m., and this hour for the attack involved departure from a 20th Air Force Bomber Command base in India after midnight. We flew towards Singapore throughout the night. About 7 a.m. I learned that we were about opposite Penang, but little could be seen in the early dawn of the outline of that northern Malayan island. I also learned that Singapore radio was still on the air—500 miles to go and no apparent suspicion by the Japanese.

The Malayan coast was followed roughly all the way down the Straits of Malacca.

At Port Swettenham a number of ships could be seen hastily leaving port, and the pilot, Capt. John Siler, said, "I bet the radio is getting busy now ! " He began to whistle, "On the road to Mandalay ! " In a short talk to the crew before leaving, Captain Siler had stated, "Petrol will be the problem—we shan't wait long at the rendezvous, and go in and get it over ! " This, however, was not necessary and we approached Singapore island in formation.

In seven years since I left Singapore, I had often wondered about going back there. But never did I think to see the city again as a passenger in an American aircraft going to bomb it. Certain features were easy to

spot—the first was the aerodrome, a red-brown smear among the green of the western part of the island. The King George V dock was empty, and Keppel Harbour, where the Far Eastern liners used to dock, also seemed empty. There were, however, many small craft lying in the roads of Singapore Harbour. The Pandang Singapore Cricket Club sports ground and recreation ground showed as a green oblong along the seashore, but the hardest peering could not make out either Singapore Cathedral or the Raffles Hotel. The civil airport at Kallag was easy, but it was difficult to see if there was anything on it, and the same with the R.A.F. aerodrome at Seletar.

BY now we had put on all our trappings, and the door by which we should drop if necessary was also cleared for quick use. Now we are over the target—I see one Japanese fighter coming in head-on to attack. The guns of the leading aircraft are quiet while our guns thump briefly. Smoke clouds from bursting A.A. shells float by. Twice more our guns fire, and then the bombs are away.

Later the bombardier told me, "We had hit our target—buildings at the Naval base ! " The journey back was very much like the approach in reverse. Though we follow the Malayan coast all the way up nobody comes up to challenge us. This is a new Super-Fortress on its first operational mission, but for most of the crew it is the thirteenth and the pilot's fourteenth mission. The final comment on the opposition was this from the nose gunners, " Those Jap fighters at Singapore are amateurs ! "

They Wear as Badge the Burma Peacock

These stalwarts of the Burma Rifles are the eyes and ears of every Chindit column, though they have been given little publicity up to now. This account of them is condensed from a broadcast talk (Jan. 25, 1945) given by Brigadier Bernard Fergusson, D.S.O., who commanded a column in the first Wingate expedition and a brigade in the second.

I STOPPED for a night just outside a Kachin village a few miles north of Indaw, and a hundred odd miles behind the enemy lines. I had some Kachins of the Burma Rifles with me, and I told them they could go and have a " jolly " down in the village, so long as they were ready to join me as I marched through next morning.

When I arrived, just after dawn, I saw Rifleman Pawai La putting on his pack and kissing all the girls. I said to old Agu Di, the Kachin officer, " Pawai La hasn't lost much time, has he ? " And Agu said,

" Well, sir, this is his own village ; he hasn't been home for five years. That's his mother he's kissing now."

Pawai La hadn't even asked me for leave ; he was all ready to move on with the rest of us. When I asked him if he'd like three months leave there and then, he said he certainly would ! I remember, as we moved off, seeing him digging a hole to hide his kit and uniform in, in case the Japs should come into the village on our track behind us.

I could give you fifty instances of how all the people of that country have shown their sympathy for us at the risk of their lives. I remember especially an old Burmese in a town which was known to be a nest of Japanese spies; he stood on his balcony in full view of half the town, and shouted out, "God Save the King! Long Live the King!" at the top of his voice. That was in April 1943, in Tigyaing, which has just been liberated by the 36th Division.

These fellows wear as their regimental badge the peacock of Burma. They are all natives of Burma—Karens from the Irrawaddy Delta, Kachins and a few Chins. Once inside Burma, there's nothing to stop them putting on plain clothes and disappearing to their homes. But they haven't. They came out with General Alexander in 1942, leaving homes and families behind them. They went in again and shared our hardships in 1943 with the first Wingate expedition—and came out again, those who weren't killed or taken prisoner. And they went in with the Chindit show of 1944 and out a third time.

They're not very big. I suppose they average round about five feet six, and when you see them marching along with a pack on their back they look as if they were all pack. They're very cheerful: they smile and laugh a lot, and they sing most beautifully—European music chiefly, not like a lot of snake-charmers.

They're the most marvellous chaps in the water, both as boatmen and swimmers, and they can make anything out of bamboo—chairs, tables, boats, drinking vessels and cooking pots. They'll eat anything, too. I've eaten bits of monkey and snake and all sorts of other tit-bits with them: and they get on frightfully well with the British soldier. It's a waste to use them as shock-troops, we've found, but you'll never get better guerilla fighters. They've got all the guts you could wish for, and more.

Here's another case rather like Pawai La's. In 1943, one fellow passed within two miles of his own village; and when he asked for news of his family he was told that his wife and daughter had died, and that his two sons, just in their teens, were living alone. He sent a message to them to meet him at the next halting place, spent an hour with them, and carried on back to India. He hadn't seen them for three years.

Another time two of them who were acting as scouts for me got caught by the Japs in a village. We didn't know what happened to them; we only knew they were overdue. But all the other Riflemen volunteered to go and find out what had happened to them; and I chose a couple who went boldly into the village in plain clothes, even though their accent gave them away as strangers to that part of Burma. On their way back with the

KAREN OFFICER of the famous Burma Rifles, subject of the story in this page. Note the peacock badges on his collar.
Photo by courtesy of the India Office

news that their comrades had been caught, they found fifty Japs trying to find the place where I was lying-up.

These two men each had a couple of grenades: they chucked the lot at the Japs to attract their attention, and then led them away on a false trail through the jungle, away from my bivouac. No wonder Wingate himself said that he never asked to command better troops. You didn't often get praise from Wingate, and when you did get a pat on the back you'd certainly earned it.

The Burma Rifle officers are mostly young Scotsmen from the big rice and timber firms of Burma, and are immensely fond of their Riflemen as their Riflemen are of them. But a growing number of officers are Karen or Kachin. One of them, Captain Chit Khin—we all call him "Chicken"—is a young Karen who got a fine M.C. on the first show, and I picked him out of lots of others to come with me on the second.

He's got a large grin which is one of the best known landmarks in the force. This last show, Chicken marched his complete platoon into a fortress which was entirely surrounded and closely watched by the best part of a brigade of Japs. Once inside, he discovered that the order which sent him there had been a mistake, so he marched his whole platoon out again, both ways without so much as a casualty.

In their temporary wartime depot in India there's a long and growing list of decorations which they've won with the Chindits. We who know them, who have marched and fought and slept beside them for many months in hard conditions, don't need that list to remind us what sort of stuff they're made of. I see great hope for the future of Burma **if** there are many more such men as these, and the part they have played in restoring freedom to Asia must never be forgotten either by their country or by ours.

OUR DIARY OF THE WAR

JANUARY 31, Wednesday *1,978th day*
Western Front.—Vanguards of U.S. 1st Army crossed German frontier east of St. Vith.
Russian Front.—Zhukov's forces, invading Brandenburg on a broad front, captured Landsberg.

FEBRUARY 1, Thursday *1,979th day*
Western Front.—In N. Alsace, U.S. 7th Army crossed river Moder and entered Oberhofen.
Air.—Day attacks by R.A.F. and U.S. bombers on railways at Munchen-Gladbach, Mannheim Ludwigshafen and Wesel; heavy night attack by R.A.F. on Mainz, Ludwigshafen and Siegen. Mosquitoes again bombed Berlin.
Russian Front.—Rokossovsky's troops captured railway centre of Torun on the Vistula, previously by-passed by advancing Russians.
Philippines.—U.S. troops made new landing in Luzon, S.W. of Manila.
Far East.—Floating dry dock at Singapore sunk by Super-Fortresses.

FEBRUARY 2, Friday *1,980th day*
Western Front.—Troops of 1st French Army and U.S. forces entered Colmar.
Air.—R.A.F. bombers made night attack on Wiesbaden, Karlsruhe, oil plant at Wanne-Eickel, Mannheim and Magdeburg.
Russian Front.—In new advance towards Stettin, Russians captured Soldin and Drossen, N.E. of Frankfurt-on-Oder.

FEBRUARY 3, Saturday *1,981st day*
Western Front.—U.S. 1st Army captured two more towns in Siegfried zone, Schoneseiffen and Harperscheid.
Air.—In heaviest attack on centre of Berlin, 1,000 Flying Fortresses, with 900 fighters, dropped 2,500 tons of bombs.

FEBRUARY 4, Sunday *1,982nd day*
Western Front.—Advances by U.S. troops finally cleared Belgium of Germans.
Air.—Liberators of Coastal Command bombed enemy naval vessels, including U-boats, in the Baltic. R.A.F. bombers attacked Bonn, and benzol plants in the Ruhr.
Russian Front.—Marshal Koniev's troops began to force the Oder S.E. of Breslau. In East Prussia, Russians captured Landsberg and Bartenstein.
Far East.—Super-Fortresses from the Marianas bombed Kobe area of Japan.
Philippines.—American troops broke into Manila.

FEBRUARY 5, Monday *1,983rd day*
Russian Front.—Zhukov's troops reached the Oder N. and S. of Kustrin.
Pacific.—Announced that on January 24 and 29 East Indies Fleet, including four aircraft-carriers, attacked Japanese oil supplies at Palembang, Sumatra.

FEBRUARY 6, Tuesday *1,984th day*
Western Front.—U.S. troops occupied Neuf Brisach, at west end of bridge over Rhine east of Colmar.
Air.—More than 1,300 U.S. bombers and 850 fighters attacked communications targets in Magdeburg, Leipzig and Chemnitz areas. Spitfire bombers attacked V 2 sites in Holland.
Russian Front.—Koniev's troops in bridge-head over the Oder S.E. of Breslau advanced up to 12 miles on a 50-mile front.

FEBRUARY 7, Wednesday *1,985th day*
Western Front.—U.S. 3rd Army troops made new crossings into Germany over River Our.
Air.—R.A.F. bombers made night attack on enemy troops at Cleve and Goch, between the Maas and the Rhine.
Russian Front.—N. and S. of Kustrin, Red Army troops cleared eastern bank of Oder and occupied Kunersdorf.

FEBRUARY 8, Thursday *1,986th day*
Western Front.—Canadian 1st Army launched attack south-east of Nijmegen, between the Maas and the Rhine.
Air.—R.A.F. Lancasters attacked with 12,000-lb. bombs E-boat shelters at Ijmuiden. At night Lancasters made two attacks on synthetic oil plant at Politz, near Stettin.
Russian Front.—Koniev's army began to force the Oder north-west of Breslau. In East Prussia, Kreuzberg fell to Russians.
Pacific.—Rocket-firing Venturas attacked radio and lighthouse installations in Kurile Is. Australian Liberators made second attack on power-station in Java.

FEBRUARY 9, Friday *1,987th day*
Western Front.—U.S. 3rd Army crossed River Prum and captured Olzheim.
Air.—In the early hours Halifaxes bombed Wanne-Eickel synthetic oil plant. Later, 1,300 U.S. bombers attacked Lutzkendorf synthetic oil plant near Halle and armament works at Weimar.
Russian Front.—In East Prussia, Soviet troops captured Frauenberg and surrounded Elbing.
Pacific.—Liberators bombed Japanese base on Iwo, Volcano Is.

FEBRUARY 10, Saturday *1,988th day*
Western Front.—Germans opened flood gates of Schwammenauel dam on the Roer before U.S. troops reached it.
Air.—Allied bombers attacked motor fuel depot at Dulmen, east of Cleve, and submarine pens at Ijmuiden.
Russian Front.—Elbing, Vistula port on Berlin-Königsberg railway, and Preussisch-Eylau, S.E. of Königsberg, captured by Rokossovsky's troops.
Far East.—Super-Fortresses bombed Nakajima aircraft works at Ota, N.E. of Tokyo. Mustangs attacked Chinese seaport of Tsingtao.

FEBRUARY 11, Sunday *1,989th day*
Western Front.—Scottish troops entered Cleve; Canadians captured Millingen on the Rhine.
Russian Front.—Koniev's troops in Oder bridge-head N.W. of Breslau, advanced up to 37 miles on 100-mile front, capturing Liegnitz, Luben and Steinau. In Pomerania, Zhukov captured Deutsch Krone and Maerkisch Friedland.
Burma.—Super-Fortresses and R.A.F. Liberators made attack on Rangoon.

FEBRUARY 12, Monday *1,990th day*
Western Front.—Cleve wholly in British hands; Gennep, near the Maas, also captured. U.S. troops in Prum.
Russian Front.—On Carpathian front Petrov's troops captured Bielsko. Koniev's forces west of the Oder captured Bunzlau on River Bober.
Greece.—Agreement signed in Athens between Plastiras Government and representatives of E.L.A.S.
General.—Crimea Conference of Roosevelt, Stalin, and Churchill issued statement on joint plans for defeat of Germany and settlement of Europe.

FEBRUARY 13, Tuesday *1,991st day*
Western Front.—U.S. 3rd Army completed clearing of Prum. British troops cleared the Reichswald.
Air.—Two heavy night attacks on Dresden by R.A.F. bombers.
Russian Front.—Budapest completely occupied by Red Army after six weeks' siege. In Silesia, Russians captured Beuthen, on west bank of Oder, and Neuhammer, and surrounded Glogau.
Mediterranean.—Italy-based bombers attacked goods-yards in Vienna and Graz.
Philippines.—MacArthur's troops cleared Nichols Airfield, Manila, and occupied Cavite naval base.

★ ━━━━━━━ *Flash-backs* ━━━━━━━ ★

1940
February 10. H.M.S. Cossack rescued British from Nazi prison-ship Altmark in Norwegian fjord.

1941
February 6. Benghazi surrendered (first time) to Australians and British under General Wavell.

1942
February 8-9. Japanese landed on N.W. coast of Singapore Island.
February 12. Scharnhorst, Gneisenau and Prinz Eugen dashed from Brest through Straits of Dover to German harbours.

1943
January 31. Field-Marshal Paulus and 15 German generals surrendered at Stalingrad.
February 2. At Stalingrad remaining Germans capitulated.
February 8. Red Army captured Kursk in drive to Ukraine.

1944
January 31. U.S. forces launched attack on Marshall Islands.
February 3. First German major offensive on Anzio beach-head.
February 8. Russians recaptured Nikopol in the Dnieper bend.

1,700 h.p. **CARRIER-BORNE AVENGER TORPEDO BOMBERS** of the East Indies Fleet formed up for their successful high-precision swoop on the Japanese-held Sumatra oil refinery at Pangkalan Brandan on Jan. 4, 1945—the second in a fortnight. These and the attacks on the Palembang refinery unmistakably demonstrated the strategical mobility of carrier-borne aircraft. Rocket and cannon-carrying Fireflies were used in these operations for the first time east of Suez.
Photo, British Official

THE WAR IN THE AIR

by Capt. Norman Macmillan, M.C., A.F.C.

IN their advances into East Prussia and Brandenburg the Red Armies moved over frozen ground and water which offered a continuous unbroken surface for the passage of armour and transport. (I have seen the ice on the Vistula more than a metre thick at Warsaw.) In these conditions, and provided there is not excessive snow—or, worse, a sudden thaw—conditions are almost better for an army on the move than in summer, when dust can do considerable harm to mechanism, both of engines and tracks. In an attempt to interfere with Red Army communications, the Luftwaffe bombed the ice on the Masurian Lakes of East Prussia and on the River Oder.

It is not known how effective this operation was, but the enormous surface of ice would probably take a lot of bombing to destroy it as a usable method of getting across. It is probable that Bomber Command of the R.A.F. would make the best air ice-breaker, because it is the only force in Europe which specializes in 12,000-lb. armour-piercing bombs ; it would be interesting to know whether the armour-piercing or the block-buster type of bomb would give the best results. Perhaps, if the Wehrmacht has to retreat over frozen lakes before a continued Soviet advance, Bomber Command may demonstrate what it can do to hamper the German withdrawal.

ONE classic example of air action against the use of a frozen lake for military purposes was the Luftwaffe counter-attack against the Gladiators of No. 223 Squadron of the R.A.F. on Lake Lesja, near Aandalsnes in Central Norway, in 1940. The R.A.F. squadron was put out of action within 24 hours by comparatively light bombs. But it was defeated by the damage its aircraft sustained, not by the smashing up of its ice airbase. There the bombs went plop through the ice, leaving a small hole, but not breaking up the surface catastrophically. Probably in future bombing operations against ice the answer will be found by using special bombs timed to explode just below the ice surface by means of a hydrostatic fuse.

Bomber Command has co-operated strategically with the Red Army during its rapid advance (Marshal Koniev's force averaged 14 miles a day for 18 days from January 12) by bombing German rail communications to hamper the movement of troops

across Germany from west to east. On the afternoon of February 1, and during the succeeding night, Bomber Command dropped 4,750 tons of bombs on four main railway centres at Munchen-Gladbach, Mainz, Ludwigshafen, and Siegen. (Previously Frankfort-on-Main, Mannheim and Karlsruhe had been bombed.) Bomber Command used 1,450 bombers to make the rail attacks on February 1 and 2 ; twelve were lost from this force.

STRATEGIC Function of Bomber Forces in Surface Land War

After ordinary bombing it is possible to restore railway communications fairly quickly. Repair gangs can get the track straightened out and levelled and new rails laid with astonishing speed in war when all labour is mobilized. But difficulties are greatly increased by the individual weight of the large bombs used by Bomber Command, which do proportionately more damage than an equivalent weight of smaller bombs. The linkage of the German railway system in western Germany, which was strategically designed for war, lays itself open to renewed blows at a succession of important junctions, so that as one is repaired another is damaged.

In these two entirely different examples—one of the Luftwaffe attacking the ice communications of the Red Army and the other of Bomber Command attacking the railway communications of the Wehrmacht—is exemplified the strategic function of bomber forces in surface land war ; the tactical aircraft employed for close work with the armies in the field are not able to concentrate the weight of bombs upon specialized targets, and the Army commanders must turn to the strategic air forces for this aid.

An important aspect of the work of Bomber Command and the United States Army 8th Air Force is the capacity of both air forces to continue to operate from the United Kingdom as a base, despite the advance of the Army of Liberation to the German frontier. If they were unable to do so, and it were necessary to move them to the Continent, it would be difficult to find bases, and every strategic unit sited in France, Belgium or Holland would displace a tactical unit.

Not only that, but every bomb they dropped in Germany would have to be transported to the Continent by ship and taken forward to the airfields by rail or road truck, thus adding

tremendously to the strain on the traffic lines. But these two strategic air forces are their own transport organization to the Continental battlefields for both fuel and armaments. The 8th Air Force is the only U.S. air force now operating from the United Kingdom. In three years of war the 8th Air Force, the first U.S. air force to go into action against Germany, has lost more than 5,000 bombers, 2,500 fighters, 40,000 men killed; it has destroyed 12,500 enemy aircraft.

WHILE the heavy bombers have continued attacks against communications and oil-producing plants, the Light Striking Force of Bomber Command, equipped with Mosquitoes, has punched steadily at Berlin. The Mosquitoes can make the trip to Berlin and back to their bases in the Midlands in from four to four-and-a-half hours, carrying either one 4,000-lb. bomb or 2,000 to 3,000 lb. of smaller bombs. For this journey they have an additional 100 gallons of fuel, in outboard tanks, one under each wing.

Sometimes these Mosquitoes make one attack a night against Berlin, sometimes two. In the night of February 1-2, two forces of about 75 to 100 Mosquitoes dropped between them some 300 tons of bombs on the Reich capital, adding to the demolitions that the Wehrmacht were themselves making by blowing up bomb-damaged buildings to obtain materials for the construction of defence works within and around the city. These night bombing Mosquitoes rely mainly on their speed for safety. Their operational speed of nearly 300 miles an hour is obtained by flying at about 30,000 feet, with the crew of two seated in a slightly pressurized cabin.

FROM Berlin a Swedish correspondent reported to his newspaper that the demolitions being made by the Wehrmacht in the capital did not matter much, as the city was already so badly damaged ! Possibly this is a factor which the Nazis took into account when they decided to defend Berlin and turn it into a fortress. Time and time again during this war a great city has been shown to be the most powerful obstacle to an advancing army. Berlin is far the largest city to be prepared to resist imminent attack by modern surface forces.

But it will be informative to see what part can be played in the assault by the strategic bomber forces of the R.A.F. and U.S. Army. No surface army assaulting a fortified city has ever had the prospect of such powerful air support as has the army that has fought its way forward to within 60 miles of the German capital. Perhaps we may see a United Nations strategic air H.Q. working with the Red Army before Berlin.

Snow was the R.A.F.'s Bitter Enemy in Holland

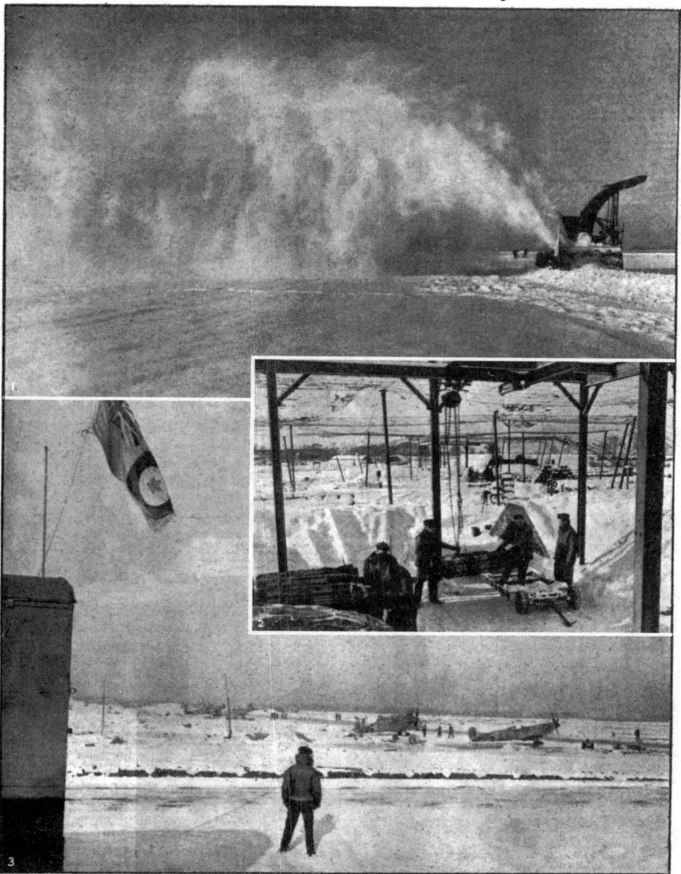

CLEARING THE RUNWAYS on a deeply covered bomber station in Holland (1) was a task for a snowplough during the Arctic spell in January 1945 so that the battle against V2 might go on. One airfield used its entire year's ration of salt—15 tons—in one day in an attempt to make the runway usuable : squads of snow-shovellers included almost the entire personnel—bar the cooks. The ground crew load a bomb-trolly with incendiary clusters (2). Spitfires in the snow : general view of a R.C.A.F. fighter station (3). PAGE 669 *Photos, British Official*

Our Roving Camera Salutes Balloon Command

DISBANDED on Feb. 5, 1945, Balloon Command had been in operation for 5½ years : the Air Minister, Sir Archibald Sinclair, said farewell at a massed parade (right) at Stanmore, Middlesex. Air Vice-Marshal W. C. C. Gell, D.S.O.,M.C.(below), its A.O.C., was the first Auxiliary Air Force Officer to reach the rank of Air Vice-Marshal and be given a command. Balloons will still be flown, but under other R.A.F. commands : the original personnel will be employed in other ways. One thousand balloon crews from over 40 barrages were concentrated in S.E. England to operate a curtain of nearly 2,000 balloons between the V-bomb sites and London (see illus. pp. 334 and 337). They stopped 278 flying bombs.

MECHANICAL STEERING TRAINER aids a Merchant Navy recruit on board the Toureg, one-time French passenger ship now used by the National Training School at Gravesend. Three other schools are also conducted by the Shipping Federation.

WORLD TRADES UNION Conference opened at the County Hall, Westminster, London, on Feb. 4, 1945, when Mr. George Isaacs, M.P. for Southwark N., and chairman for the day (left), welcomed 240 delegates representing 50,000,000 workers. Largest delegation was the Russian (35), said to represent 27,000,000 workers. Representatives came from as far afield as China, Poland (the Lublin Government), Nigeria, Arabia and Latin-America ; no ex-enemy countries were invited. Sir Walter Citrine (above), just returned from Greece, addressed the conference.

Photos, British Official, Sport & General, Keystone

OPINIONS about the film based on the life of Woodrow Wilson differ widely. Many think these biographical pictures are a mistake altogether. They certainly present, as a rule, very misleading views of public characters, and often they deliberately falsify history. One aspect of President Wilson which seems to be completely absent from the film is his humour. He had a strong sense of fun and he could laugh at himself, which not many of the great ones of the earth can do. He was once in company with a number of people who were talking about beauty and ugliness, and whether these are decided by cast of features as settled by nature, or by expression which is under our own control. He contributed to the discussion this limerick :

As a beauty I am not a star,
There are others more handsome by far ;
But my face, I don't mind it,
For I am behind it ;
It's the people in front get the jar.

Wilson used to go regularly once a week to a variety theatre in Washington and always laughed at the knockabouts and back-chat comedians. It seems to me that schoolboyish enjoyment of slapstick when it is cleverly put across goes a long way towards making one feel that Presidents, Prime Ministers, and such are likeable human beings.

THAT the employment of prisoners of war in various ways, chiefly on farms, is necessary few would deny. That it has a good many unpleasant consequences all who know anything about its working would readily allow. One result of putting Italians on the land is that in some districts they are exterminating the small birds, especially the song-birds—thrushes, blackbirds, and larks in particular. In their own country they kill everything that flies, and they have practically destroyed bird life in many parts of Italy. Partly this is because they are so miserably poor (because they are so wretchedly ignorant) that they want the birds for food. That cannot be so in this country. As prisoners of war they are well fed. They ought to be warned that we have a law against the slaughter of song-birds, and punished severely if they transgress it. Trying to persuade them that birds and their music add enormously to the pleasures of life would be useless. Appealing to their "better nature" would be futile for, so far as animals are concerned, they have none. They are brought up to consider all animals created for their benefit, to be treated by them as harshly as they please.

WHILE books on the last war were mainly about maps—and the great events worked out on them—this time, to adapt E. C. Bentley's famous clerihew, they're mainly about chaps. I am forcibly reminded of this by an anonymous little masterpiece, called Arnhem Lift, published by the Pilot Press at five shillings and running to fewer than a hundred pages. No one ignorant of what the penny papers have for once very properly described as the "Arnhem Epic" would gather from it that here was an episode in the annals of British arms as deathless as the Charge of the Light Brigade ; but they would learn something in its way quite as important—the psychology of the ordinary soldier when faced with what seemed inevitable, slow-creeping destruction. Looking back on his ghastly seven-days' dilemma, the author records that in their conversation neither officers nor men mentioned those hardy staples of soldiers' talk—sex, home, and family. "I really don't think any of us thought at all," he says with telling naïveté. "We were too busy living and we seemed to act almost entirely by instinct. None of us will

probably ever be so natural again as we were there. We were completely without inhibitions, there wasn't time for them." All of which may make the so-called psychoanalysts furiously to think. Or will it ?

AMID all the talk of the different "freedoms" which we want all the peoples of the world to enjoy, I cannot help feeling grateful to the Town Council of Sudbury, in Suffolk, who have refused a request from a Sunday School Union that children should be refused admission to Sunday picture shows. "A matter for parents to decide," the Councillors say. Very good sense in that reply ! If Sunday schools find they cannot compete with cinemas, they should alter their methods. They could give picture shows themselves. To demand a monopoly, to suggest that children shall be forced to attend schools against their will, is both a confession of failure and an attempt to smother freedom. I have known of one or two Sunday schools managed so well that children preferred them to any other form of entertainment.

HERE is a note of a conversation, not one in which I took part but which I could not help overhearing, while I was in a bus, which was at the starting place with some minutes to spare before its next journey began. The inspector had boarded the bus and was talking to the conductress. They talked loudly so all of us in our seats received the benefit of it. "No, I don't hold with it," said the inspector. What he did not hold with was putting soldiers under the command of A.T.S. officers. A file of them had passed him with a woman in charge. Three of them ran across the road to a tobacconist's shop. She called out sharply, "Come back, two

Maj.-Gen. R. N. GALE, successor to Lieut.-Gen. F. A. M. Browning as deputy commander to the U.S. Lieut.-Gen. L. H. Brereton of the 1st Allied Airborne Army. The appointment was announced on January 18, 1945.

Photo. Topical Press

of you. I said only one could go and buy cigarettes ! " She was obeyed, but the inspector did not think it was right. I listened with interest to hear what the conductress would say. Well, she cordially agreed. She did not think men ought to be ordered about by women, though she looked rather the sort that would order her husband about, if she had one !

THE election of Mr. Churchill and President Roosevelt to be members of the Académie Française makes me smile when I recall what famous Frenchmen of letters have said about that Institution. Anatole France described how he was instructed to set about getting a seat among the Immortal Forty. He must go and see So-and-so, and pay extravagant compliments. He must call on this and that countess and speak of certain authors of the past whom these ladies condescended to favour. He came to the conclusion that the whole business was one of intrigue, not of literary value at all. In fact, as Lord Melbourne said about the Order of the Garter, "there's no damned merit about it." From time to time the Academy is forced to elect authors who have won their reputation with the reading public, which in France is a much larger proportion of the population than it is here. But its choice, when free, falls usually on writers who are forgotten as soon as they are dead. Long ago an epitaph on a feeble poet proclaimed :

Ci-gît Piron, qui fut rien
Pas même académicien.
(Here lies Piron, who was nothing, not even
an academician.)

I doubt if the Académie has raised itself in public estimation since that rhyme set all Paris laughing at its expense.

THE other morning I passed through a district that had been stricken over-night by the V-blight. In one long avenue hardly a house mounted its tiles in their proper place. Thick as Milton's autumnal leaves in Vallombrosa they strewed the pavements and the gardens of trim red-brick villadom. No one was about ; no one, that's to say, except one indomitable little man who, with his shattered slates piled up neatly along the garden path, was proceeding to refurbish his patch of faded greensward with a lawn-mower ! I was instantly reminded of something I'd seen many years ago, during a fire in Santiago—a native woman hurrying from her still-burning house, clasping for dear life, not her jewels, as you might suppose, but a geranium in a flower-pot ! In moments of stress we clutch at strange straws. How many English aspidistras, I wonder, have thus been salvaged from the unkindly incendiary ? Recent news of German civilians streaming west before the Red Army provides further instances. Roadsides were littered with discarded objects such as vases and oil paintings which had been snatched up by the refugees in the moment of their flight.

ONE splendid effort made during this war, with a great deal of success, is the finding of jobs for ex-Servicemen who in the past would have been considered too badly hurt for anything but the shelf. The things such men can be taught to do, and which they do well, are really astonishing. Who would suppose that a soldier who was blinded and lost both hands in battle could work a lift ? Yet that is what Mr. Frederick Higgs of the Hampshire Regiment will be doing. He will have artificial hands and the lift will be fitted with an instrument for telling him which floor is calling. St. Dunstan's has provided Mr. Higgs with this occupation and the ability to cope with it. This grand Institution takes in many who are not only sightless but mutilated in some way as well, and it manages to place them nearly all somewhere or another. The days when a man whom war left helpless had to eat his heart out in idleness and penury are, happily, gone.

Pay Day Aboard One of India's Little Ships

IN TRADITIONAL NAVAL MANNER, a native rating aboard a motor launch of the Arakan Coastal Forces receives his pay on top of his cap. These small craft of the R.I.N. steam long distances with supplies for Allied troops in Burma, often through minefields and waters infested with Japanese submarines. They played a proud part in the Arakan invasion of January 1945, when four Allied landings were achieved in three weeks. See also pages 648-649.

Photo, Indian Official

Printed in England and published every alternate Friday by the Proprietors, THE AMALGAMATED PRESS, LTD., The Fleetway House, Farringdon Street, London, E.C.4. Registered for transmission by Canadian Magazine Post. Sole Agents for Australia and New Zealand: Messrs. Gordon & Gotch, Ltd. ; and for South Africa: Central News Agency, Ltd.—March 2, 1945. S.S. *Editorial Address:* JOHN CARPENTER HOUSE, WHITEFRIARS, LONDON, E.C.4.

Vol 8   *The War Illustrated*   Nº 202

SIXPENCE

Edited by Sir John Hammerton

MARCH 16, 1945

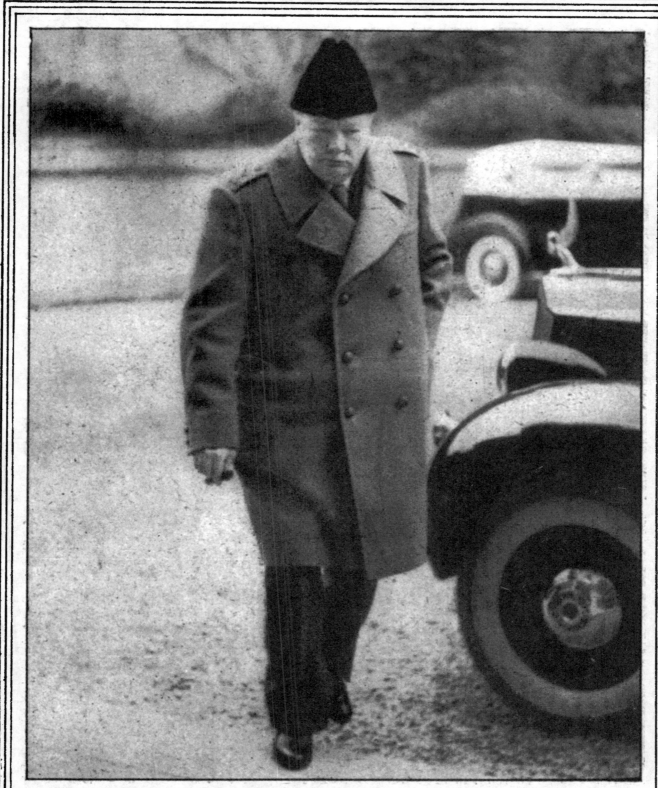

MR. CHURCHILL ARRIVING AT YALTA FOR THE CRIMEA CONFERENCE (see pages 682-83) early in February 1945. Returning to England on Feb. 19 by way of Athens, where he was given a tumultuous welcome, he discussed the war against Japan with President Roosevelt at Alexandria, and at Cairo met the Emperor of Ethiopia, the King of Saudi-Arabia, the King of Egypt, and the President of the Syrian Republic in '' the most important conversations ever held on the future of the Middle East.''   *Photo, British Officia'*

NO. 203 WILL BE PUBLISHED THURSDAY, MARCH 29

Red Army Keeps a Birthday as it Nears Berlin

FOUNDING OF THE RED ARMY 27 YEARS AGO was celebrated by the Soviet people on Feb. 23, 1945. Five days before that great anniversary one of its foremost leaders, Army-Gen. Cherniakhovsky, was killed in action : he is seen (1, centre) on the E. Prussian front. Street fighting in the E. Prussian town of Muhausen (2). Marshal Koniev (3, right)—30 miles south of Frankfurt-on-Oder on Feb. 21—and Marshal Rotmistrov. Marshal Malinovsky (4, extreme left) congratulates his staff officers in Budapest, completely occupied by Feb. 13. *Photos, Pictorial Press*

THE BATTLE FRONTS

by Maj.-Gen. Sir Charles Gwynn, K.C.B., D.S.O.

KONIEV'S great drive westwards towards Dresden and northwards to link up with Zhukov's armies, which when I last wrote had started, made astonishingly rapid progress. It has been suggested that the Germans believed that with the Oder in flood and laden with ice blocks it would be impracticable to maintain bridges across it capable of meeting the requirements of a major offensive, and that in consequence they had used their best troops to deal with any attempt Zhukov might make to drive towards Berlin or Stettin. It is perhaps more probable that they were satisfied that the Russians would be compelled to make a fairly prolonged pause in order to improve their communication and to build up their resources, which would afford time for the assembly of a strong counter-offensive army.

IF that was their interpretation of the situation it is reasonable to suppose they confided the defence of the Oder line and the centres supporting it to second-class troops while they withdrew the best of their divisions and armour to their main strategic reserve. Whatever their policy may have been, the power and speed of Koniev's offensive clearly took the Germans by surprise, and many of their troops offered feeble resistance, though perhaps rather through lack of training and competent leadership than lack of will to fight. Having established himself in depth west of the Oder, encircled Breslau and joined hands with Zhukov on his right, it seems probable that Koniev may now pause to close up preparatory to making a fresh bound, for he has begun to encounter German counter-attacks in considerable strength. Such success as these have had was short-lived and was probably gained only against mobile troops sent far in advance to seize points of tactical importance.

GERMANS Draw on Main Reserve to Meet Immediate Danger

There are, however, no indications that they represent the opening of a major counter-offensive, but rather that the Germans have been compelled to draw on their main strategic reserve to meet immediate danger. Meanwhile, Zhukov is evidently almost ready to attempt the forcing of the Oder on his front. The Germans report that he has already secured footholds on the west bank and Koniev is now in a position to protect his left flank in any further operation. During the pause on the Oder, Zhukov brought up his right in a thrust towards Stettin, which increases the danger the German forces in Pomerania and Danzig are in. Furthermore, Rokossovsky is now advancing up the Polish corridor west of the Vistula and has cut the Danzig-Stettin railway. This extension of his front has enabled Zhukov to draw in and concentrate his right wing.

In East Prussia the Germans are being driven steadily into a smaller space with their backs to the sea and Königsberg is under close attack. Here the Russians have suffered a great loss by the death of Cherniakhovsky ; but the Red Army has produced such a brilliant group of generals—who may rank even higher than Napoleon's marshals—that it should not be difficult to find a successor to him. Bagramyan very probably will assume command on this front.

DOWN on the Hungarian front Tolbukhin and Malinovsky's well co-ordinated operations made, as was expected, a clean job of Budapest, and the Germans suffered a disaster which must have cost them over 200,000 men, apart from the heavy losses in their abortive rescue attempts. Once again

it has been shown that a commander can commit no greater strategical error than to allow his field army to become involved in the direct defence of a fortress, sacrificing its power of manoeuvre and thereby imposing on his remaining mobile troops tasks not in keeping with the main strategic object.

THE dispatch of Panzer Divisions from reserve in Poland to take part in rescue operations in Hungary almost certainly contributed largely to the collapse of the Vistula front. Moreover, these divisions have apparently been retained in Hungary and been used to counter-attack Malinovsky's spearhead on the north bank of the Danube with little prospect of achieving any result of importance. German strategy is indeed difficult to understand, and one can only suppose that it is still subject to Hitler's malign influence. With the storm brewing

in Pomerania and Danzig, which would then have been a real menace to Zhukov's flank as he drove to the Oder. Moreover, the lower Vistula would have provided a strong defence line on which to check Cherniakhovsky's and Rokossovsky's advance, and at the worst a further retreat to the lower Oder would still have been possible. In the event the East Prussian force is encircled and has lost strategic significance even should it maintain the struggle for a considerable time. The forces in Pomerania and Danzig seem liable to share the same fate if they make no attempt to retreat behind the Oder. They are not a serious menace to Zhukov's flank.

HAMMERING at Back Door of the Southern Stronghold

Thus on the whole there has been an amazing and unnecessary dispersion of German military strength. The situation has grown so desperate that it has been suggested in many quarters that the Germans have abandoned all intention of using their remaining strategic reserve for the defence of Berlin and northern Germany and that they intend to retreat into the more defensible regions in the south and there prolong the struggle.

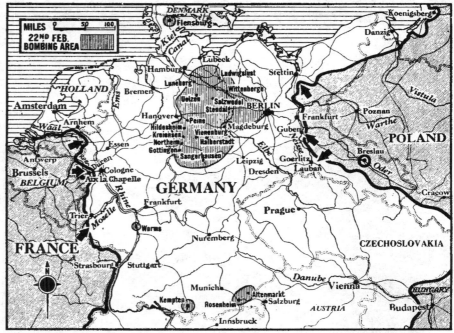

NON-STOP BOMBING OF THE REICH : shaded zones in centre show general targets most heavily attacked during the vast operation of February 22, 1945. This involved more than 8,000 Allied aircraft—25,000 men in all were airborne—and it was the heaviest blow to date against Nazi communications. Four days later Berlin had its biggest daylight raid, from over 1,200 Fortresses and Liberators covered by 800 fighters.
By courtesy of News Chronicle

on the Vistula Rundstedt's offensive in the west has proved, as it seemed to be from the first, a desperate gamble in which the best of the German reserves were staked.

The defence of Budapest, justifiable in the first instance, was maintained with characteristic Hitler obstinacy till it became a fatal commitment which led to further dispersal of the main strategic reserve. Then when the blow on the Vistula came the Germans clung to East Prussia, and no attempt to withdraw was made until Rokossovsky had closed the ring round it. Before that it must have been evident that under Cherniakhovsky's pressure the East Prussian Army was incapable of counter-offensive action against the flanks of Rokossovsky's and Zhukov's armies. There can seldom, therefore, have been a clearer case for the abandonment of territory which was neither defensible nor afforded a springboard for a counter-stroke.

A rapid withdrawal would have secured greater concentration and would have substantially reinforced the already strong forces

That, it is argued, would account for the obstinate stand at Budapest and the transfer of reserves to the south in an attempt to halt Malinovsky and Tolbukhin who were already hammering at the back door of the southern stronghold. It is I suppose possible, though I find it hard to believe, that some such plan may exist based on the hope that if the struggle can only be prolonged for a sufficient period the Allies will fall apart or from sheer war weariness concede terms.

There is certainly little justification for that hope, and my own opinion is that the intention had been to assemble as strong a force as possible, probably between Dresden and Berlin, which might have delivered an effective counterstroke if Zhukov had attempted to press on to Berlin without adequate support. Zhukov has not fallen into that trap and all the indications are that the difficulties of forming a substantial counter-offensive reserve proved insuperable. I believe, therefore, that the Wehrmacht will go down fighting fanatically with such forces as it is able to muster in final defensive battles, and with little if any thought of retreat.

All Clear Again in Philippine Islands Capital

THREE WEEKS AFTER the Americans entered Manila city, supported by tanks (1), the battle for the Philippines capital ended, on Feb. 24, 1945, when troops completely occupied the Spanish walled city of Intramuros, Manila's central fortress. Infantrymen gazed around the gutted and burning buildings which lined Ascaraya Street (2), on the watch for snipers. Brigadier-Gen. William C. Chase (3), Commander of the 1st Cavalry Division which freed more than 3,000 prisoners—among them several Britons—from the notorious Santo Tomas internment camp (see story in page 665). Threading their way through the blackened and shattered streets, a Filipino family (4) inspect the destruction wrought by the Japanese garrison during their last stand. Not all the enemy were true to the suicide code; on the night before the fortress fell many tried to escape in native canoes to join the Japanese remnants in the rugged Sierra mountains, but were intercepted.

Photos, Associated Press

'Nothing's So Bad that It Couldn't be Worse!'

THIS CHEERFUL REJOINDER—typical of the British soldier—was made by the injured man, here seen receiving expert first-aid from a stretcher party, in response to reassuring words from the cameraman. The scene is Montgomery's British-Canadian assault south-east of Nijmegen in Holland towards the Rhine, which commenced on Feb. 8, 1945. Sten gun still in nerveless hands, the wounded infantryman's comrade lies crumpled in the shellhole. Beyond, empty hands raised in token of surrender, Germans stumble to captivity.　　PAGE 677　　*Photo. Keystone*

H.M.S. KING GEORGE V docked at Alexandria on her way to Far Eastern waters. This 35,000-ton battleship was among H.M. ships which on Jan. 24 and 29, 1945, took part in the devastating air-sea assault on Japanese-controlled oil refineries at Palembang in S. Sumatra. The attack was made by a powerful East Indies Force, commanded by Rear-Admiral Sir Philip Vian, K.C.B., D.S.O., including the aircraft-carriers Illustrious, Victorious, Indomitable and Indefatigable. None of our ships sustained damage. See illus. page 646.
Photo, British Official

THE WAR AT SEA

by Francis E. McMurtrie

In the Pacific events continue to demonstrate the immense advantage which command of the sea confers upon the Allies. In the latter part of February it enabled a strong force of aircraft carriers under Vice-Admiral Mark A. Mitscher, U.S.N., to approach the eastern shores of Japan while flying off planes to the total estimated number of 1,500. These aircraft attacked various military objectives in the main industrial area, notably around Tokyo and Yokohama, but their prime object seems to have been to prevent the use of airfields by the Japanese and to destroy hangars and grounded planes. An escort carrier in Yokosuka Dockyard was so badly damaged that she capsized.

This operation was mainly intended as a diversion to prevent any interference from the mainland of Japan with the attack which was simultaneously being made by the main body of the U.S. Fifth Fleet, under Admiral R. A. Spruance, against Iwojima.

Iwojima is actually two words, the second of which, " jima " (often written " sima " or " shima "), means "island." For this reason American communiques invariably speak of this place as Iwo, without the termination. Though few people had heard of it before the war, Iwo had been made into an extremely strong fortress by the Japanese. It is the only one of three islands composing the Volcano group which was suitable for the purpose. It is about eight square miles in extent, with a volcanic cone 644 feet high at the western end. There is only one satisfactory anchorage, protected by a reef running out to seaward for a distance of 2½ miles, and most of the island's surface is bare rock, with occasional bushes.

To protect the two small airfields laid out on the island's flattest spots, the Japanese mounted numerous guns around the circumference of the island. Their calibre has not been reported, but they may well have been 9·4-in. coast defence pieces on disappearing mountings, of which Japan bought a large number from the Schneider armament concern at Le Creusot many years ago. It was never explained for what purpose the Japanese could require so many

weapons of this type, but the present war has solved the puzzle.

For four days the island's defences were bombarded by Admiral Spruance's forces, the principal units in which were the battleships Nevada, Tennessee and Idaho, armed with 14-in. guns, and the New York, Texas and Arkansas, mounting 12-in. Two of these ships, the Nevada and Tennessee, received a considerable amount of damage from Japanese bombing at Pearl Harbour on December 7, 1941, and have since been modernized. The New York, Texas and Arkansas are the oldest capital ships in the U.S. Navy, and in the normal course would have been scrapped before now. All three formed part of the Allied covering force during the invasion of Normandy last June, an example of the mobility of naval forces.

FIERCEST Fighting in Pacific
Cost 5,372 U.S. Casualties

Occasional attempts at interference came from Japanese aircraft, but though some damage was inflicted on the American ships their fire did not slacken, and the enemy planes were shot down or driven off by U.S. fighters and anti-aircraft weapons. These enemy aircraft seem to have come from bases in the Ogasawara (or Bonin) Islands, lying a hundred or more miles to the northward. These are larger and more numerous than the Volcano Is., though it is doubtful if they are so strongly fortified as Iwo.

It is remarkable how the three obscure and almost unknown islands which compose the Volcano group have suddenly sprung into fame. They were first discovered in 1543 by the Spanish navigator, Bernard de Torres, who called the smallest of them, 28 miles to the southward of Iwo, San Agustino (now Minami Iwo). Similarly, Kita Iwo, which lies at a somewhat greater distance to the north-westward of Iwo, was originally named San Alessandro. Forgotten for over two centuries, the islands were rediscovered in 1779 by Captain King, who succeeded to the command of Captain Cook's third expedition after the latter's death at Hawaii. King gave the name Sulphur Island to Iwo, sulphur being its only exportable product.

Though the islands were, by virtue of King's survey of them, long regarded as British, they were formally annexed by Japan in 1877 ; and in view of their important strategic position, 600 miles from Japan's biggest naval dockyard at Yokosuka, their fortification was later undertaken. Following the intensive bombardment already mentioned, U.S. Marines succeeded in effecting a landing on Iwo, and after over three days strenuous combat, gained the summit of Suribachi, an extinct volcano on the southern side of the island, which the Japanese had converted into a fortress. This success, which included the fiercest fighting yet known in the Pacific, cost 5,372 casualties, including 644 killed.

In their desperate resistance the Japanese garrison, thought to have numbered 30,000, used rifles, machine-guns, hand grenades, demolition charges, and a species of mortar, firing rockets. Heavy rain did much to hamper the progress of the assailants, whose numbers, according to the latest reports, have been increased by reinforcement to about 45,000. Tanks and heavy artillery have also been landed, but the nature of the ground—soft ash alternating with volcanic rock—does not lend itself to the use of these weapons. Wherever it is possible to get at the Japanese, whose strongpoints are said to consist of caves dug deep into the rock, fierce bayonet fighting is proceeding. In due course the island's resistance will be subdued, enabling its airfield to be used to extend the range of U.S. bombing. No doubt the next step will be to occupy the adjacent Ogasawara group, whose airfields have already been under attack.

In the Philippines, Vice-Admiral Kinkaid's Seventh Fleet has been instrumental in effecting the occupation of Biri and Capul, two small islands in the San Bernardino Strait, between Luzon and Samar. This strait is on the direct route connecting Manila with American bases at Guam, Saipan and Hawaii. Only small forces of Japanese were on these islands, and their occupation was rapidly completed. In Manila Bay itself the island fortress of Corregidor was stormed by American troops after a heavy bombardment. Its possession gives full control of the entrance to the bay, the peninsula of Bataan opposite having already been secured. Thus with the extermination of the remnant of the Manila garrison, the port and naval base are again firmly in U.S. hands.

Loud Sounds the Knell of Fate for Nippon

ASSAULT ON THE HEART OF JAPAN began on Feb. 16, 1945, when 1,500 U.S. carrier-borne planes struck at Tokyo (map inset). Three days later U.S. marines landed at Iwojima, to make possible fighter-escorted attacks on the enemy capital. Mighty battleships of the U.S. 7th Fleet (1) entered Lingayen Gulf in the Philippines on Jan. 9 (see page 662). An Iowa-class battleship and an Essex class carrier make heavy weather in the Pacific (3). Vice-Admiral Marc Mitscher (2) commanded the Tokyo task force. Rear-Admiral R. K. Turner (4), commander of amphibious forces in the Pacific Fleet, directed operations at Iwojima. PAGE 679 *Photos, U.S. Official, Central Press, New York Times. Map, The Daily Telegraph*

U-Boats With Funnels Are Prowling the Seas

The menace of German submarines, abated for a while, has broken out again. Now the threat is greater than ever, and our shipping losses have risen. R.A.F. Coastal Command has had a large hand in forcing the U-boats to adopt new devices, of the kind shown in the facing page and commented on here by Capt. JOSEPH HAWKINS, who has spent 40 years at sea.

"YOU keep your schnorkel out of this!" is a remark that may be heard in any sailors' tavern alongshore any night of the week. Thus Hitler's latest secret weapon, the Schnorkel, has become a salt joke—of sorts. These men who jest with Death, as is the way of all seafarers, know that the Schnorkel device may bring a U-boat within harbour, or enable it to approach unseen up to the side of their ship at sea.

The Schnorkel is a tube or funnel device fitted aboard a U-boat, enabling the latter to draw down fresh air from the surface and to discharge exhaust gases from the engines and used air from the crew's quarters. By this means the vessel can remain submerged almost indefinitely—invisible from the air and from the decks of ships; it can approach convoys unseen, and perhaps penetrate harbours when the booms are opened for our ships.

THIS latest weapon would also enable German designers to plan a craft sea-worthy enough to ride winds and waves on the surface as well as glide fish-like in the depths; completely new designs of sub-marines able to travel fast underwater and to go deeper will certainly be evolved. Submarines up to now have had to surface for an hour or more in every twenty-four, to renew air aboard and recharge the electric batteries used for underwater travel, batteries being necessary because the fumes of Diesel engines could not be tolerated below the surface. But electric motors give only a poor underwater speed—usually 4 or 5 knots. On the surface, Diesels give a speed of over 20 knots. Underwater Diesels, if they could be used, would give, perhaps, half that speed or more, thus doubling the effective underwater speed of a U-boat and enabling it to keep pace with a convoy without ever surfacing and showing itself.

Though the Schnorkel may be an Allied seaman's joke, it is likely to be the death of a good many of them; for it was very largely due to aircraft of Coastal Command and the Fleet Air Arm that the U-boat was beaten earlier in this war, after grievous losses. If aircraft lose their effectiveness almost completely against U-boats that can remain submerged all the time, and yet keep pace underwater with the convoys they are shadowing, the Hun will have a fruitful innings. Hitherto, aircraft forced them under water, and under water meant a speed of no more than 4 or 5 knots, and that was too slow to keep near a convoy.

Extreme Discomforts for Crews

But that innings, however short it may prove to be, will be packed with discomforts to an extreme degree. For the new Schnorkel U-boats are a nightmare to the most hardened Nazi crews; for one thing, the submarine with this new breathing device cannot, whilst on a mission, surface at all. U-boat Command spokesman Heinrich Schwich has said on the German radio, "Not a single man, throughout the cruise, ever has a dry piece of clothing on his body; the crews are subject to a physical and psychological strain for which the term gigantic is not an over-statement."

AGAIN, a Nazi radio commentator has said: "We sometimes live under the water, 'breathing' through the funnel, for as long as ten weeks. The hardships and strain are incomparably greater than ever before. There is hardly a quiet moment, and no chance to come up for fresh air or to smoke. There is no distraction. Lights can be used only for essentials, to save current. The men cannot even listen to the radio. As the days pass, and then weeks, the atmosphere gets more and more humid" . . . And, on top of it all, hunted and depth-charged and bombed in this frail underwater vessel that at any moment of day or night may prove the entire crew's grave—what a prospect for Hitler's mariners! They plumb the depths of misery.

Another secret weapon boasted of by German prisoners and German radio is the "electric eye" torpedo, a development of the acoustic mine. The torpedo is fitted with magnetic-electric apparatus which, attracted by the vibration of a ship's engines, turns the torpedo towards the ship out of whatever course it may have been running on, as soon as it comes within a few hundred yards of the hull. Other new devices are the "water-donkey" (decoy craft) and the gyroplane (see facing page).

Further, the German propagandists claim to have an "anti-Asdic" apparatus aboard the

PERISCOPE MINE is another example of Nazi ingenuity. Purpose of the "periscope" may be to deceive planes or surface craft into belief that the mine is a U-boat.

new U-boats. This seems unlikely, but we have to consider its possibility. The Hun should never have known anything about our Asdic device—that was one of the things that fell into his hands when France collapsed in 1940. From the merchant seaman's point of view France has a long row to hoe before she wipes out the harm which that loss did to our shipping.

Royal Navy's 'Surprise Packets'

I can speak of the bitterness on this point of some of the Masters who are my acquaintances. There have been times when we have not stepped out of our clothes for two months at a time, and hardly slept—just a cat-nap now and then with the First Officer's elbow in your ribs as soon as you shut your eyes, to fetch you back to the bridge again for some emergency. Some skippers I know have been torpedoed ten times. One ship, the Dan-y-Bryn, once had six "tin fishes" running parallel with her after she had made a sharp turn to port to avoid taking them broadside-on. As many as 30 U-boats have been sighted from the air in a single convoy battle with assembled wolf-packs.

What of the coming days when the 30 raiders will still be there, but invisible beneath the waves, and able to keep pace with us unseen? Well, we still have our 4-in. guns, our 12-pounders and our half-dozen Oerlikons. Aboard the escort vessels they still have the Asdic, and the depth charges, and one or two other surprise packets I am not at liberty to mention. If the enemy have developed a target-seeking torpedo, we shall have to perfect a torpedo-diverting device, or a U-boat-seeking bomb!

OUR shipping has been decimated, and our losses of seamen have been very heavy. More than 4,000 of them still languish as prisoners on German soil today. But every sun that rises sees more than 2,000 vessels flying the old Red Duster actually out on the sea-roads of the world, and British seamen alone equal about eight Army divisions, bringing us more than a third of our food, as well as most of the fertilizers that enable British farmers to produce the rest. Not a ship, not a man of them all will be missing from his job, and as for the new U-boats —well, they had better keep their damned Schnorkels out of this!

BALL - LIKE FLARES, dropped by a Sunderland of Coastal Command during a successful attack on a U-boat lurking in wait for our invasion fleets in 1944. The stricken submarine can be seen (bottom left) in the swirl of the sea.
Photo, British Official

Nazi Navy Throws Up Fantastic New Devices

WATER-DONKEY is the Germans' name for their new decoy craft (top). This dummy U-boat is hauled by a real submarine by means of a lengthy tow-rope (1). The hull (2) rides just beneath the surface. Water-donkey and U-boat are connected by electric cable, and on spotting the enemy (plane or ship) the U-boat commander starts a sound-machine (3) ; when the chasing plane or ship—picking up the sounds—attacks the water-donkey under the impression that it is a genuine U-boat, air is released from (4) and oil from containers at (5). Air bubbles and oil patches are then formed at (6). After the bombs or depth-charges begin to fall, the water-donkey releases fragments of wreckage from (7), and is sunk by flooded tanks (8).

R.A.F. COASTAL COMMAND'S SUCCESSES have forced the Wilhelmstrasse to equip its still-considerable U-boat fleet with new weapons to reduce their under-surface vessels' vulnerability. Among these is the man-lifting gyro-plane (above, left) in which an observer ascends several hundred feet for reconnaissance purposes and from which he is in constant touch with his " base " by telephone. Aboard the U-boats, the gyro-plane is carried in a special container (above centre). Most serious of the new threats to the Allies is the Schnorkel, which enables the U-boat so equipped (right) to extend its under-water endurance very considerably, and obviates the need to surface every night to recharge the electric batteries which supply the motive power when sub-merged; also, the vessel can cruise submerged on its Diesel power. The Schnorkel device is an extendable air-shaft divided into two sections and projecting well above the surface, one section acting as air intake and the other expelling the exhaust gases. From German sources come reports that hardship and strain in these new-style U-boats are " incomparably greater than ever before."
See also facing page.

From the German paper "Signal." Schnorkel diagram by News Chronicle

Crimea Conference: The Big Three Determine—

THE Big Three—Mr. Churchill, President Roosevelt and Marshal Stalin—held at Yalta, in the Crimea, one of the most momentous conferences of the war, it was announced on February 7, 1945. Five days later they issued an epoch-making communiqué—extracts from which appear in this and the facing page—covering plans for the final defeat, occupation and treatment of Germany; the establishment of an international organization to maintain peace; and recommendations for solving the urgent problems of Poland, Yugoslavia and other countries released from Nazism. At Marshal Stalin's suggestion, the 8-day talks are to go down in history as the Crimea Conference. Yalta—30 miles from historic Sebastopol and 850 air miles from Moscow—is set against hillsides, snow-capped in winter, covered with vineyards and cypress woods. In Tsarist Russia it was a rich man's playground; since the Soviet regime it has become a health resort for workers.

MARSHAL STALIN enjoys a joke with Mr. Churchill. The Premier wore the uniform of a colonel of the British Army; the Marshal's only decoration was the star of the Hero of Socialist Labour.

ARRIVING AT YALTA, Prime Minister and President inspected the Moscow Guards' guard of honour. Behind Mr. Roosevelt (driven in a jeep by a civilian tractor-driver) are detectives who, according to U.S. law, must accompany the President on all public appearances. On the extreme left is M. Molotov, People's Commissar for Foreign Affairs.

FOREIGN SECRETARIES WITH THEIR STAFFS AND INTERPRETERS met each day at the Vorontso Palace, the British H.Q. Mr. Eden and General Sir Hastings Ismay, Chief of Staff, are seen (centre); Mr. E. R. Stettinius, Jr., U.S. Secretary of State (extreme right), and M. Molotov (fourth from left). In future they will meet in rotation in the three capitals.

Defeat of Germany

WE have considered and determined the military plans of the three Allied Powers for the final defeat of the common enemy.

The fullest information has been interchanged. The timing, scope and co-ordination of new and even more powerful blows to be launched by our armies and air forces into the heart of Germany from East, West, North and South, have been fully agreed and planned in detail.

We believe that the very close working partnership among the three Staffs attained at this Conference will result in shortening the war. Nazi Germany is doomed.

Occupation and Control

WE have agreed on common policies and plans for enforcing the unconditional surrender terms which we shall impose together on Nazi Germany after German armed resistance has been crushed. These terms will not be made known until the final defeat of Germany is accomplished.

Under the agreed plans the forces of the three Powers will each occupy a separate zone of Germany. Co-ordinated administration and control has been provided for under the plan through a Central Control Commission consisting of the Supreme Commanders of the three Powers with headquarters in Berlin.

It has been agreed that France should be invited by the three Powers if she should so desire, to take a zone of occupation, and to participate as fourth member of the Control Commission.

It is our inflexible purpose to destroy German militarism and Nazism and to ensure that Germany will never again be able to disturb the peace of the world.

We are determined to disarm and disband all German armed forces: break up for all time the German General Staff that has repeatedly contrived the resurgence of German militarism; remove or destroy all German military equipment; eliminate or control all German industry that could be used for military production; bring all war criminals to justice and swift punishment and exact reparations in kind for the destruction wrought by Germans; wipe out the Nazi Party, Nazi laws, organizations and institutions; remove all Nazi and militarist influences from public offices, and from the cultural and economic life of the German people.

It is not our purpose to destroy the people of Germany, but only when Nazism and militarism have been extirpated will there be hope for a decent life for Germans and a place for them in the comity of nations.

Reparations

WE have considered the question of the damage caused by Germany to Allied Nations in this war and recognize it as just that Germany be obliged to make compensation for the damage in kind to the greatest extent possible. A Commission for the Compensation of Damage will be established, to work in Moscow.

—Germany's Fate and Reshaping of the World

THE Crimea Conference took place in an atmosphere of the utmost informality. Much of the business was done over or immediately after meals, at which the food was exclusively Russian, prepared by the staff of a leading Moscow hotel brought for the occasion. The three leaders each had their own quarters. Mr. Churchill lived at the Palace of Prince Vorontsov, son of a former ambassador to Britain ; it had been used by a German general during the Occupation. President Roosevelt stayed in the Livadia Palace, whose large banqueting hall was used for the main conferences ; while Marshal Stalin's headquarters were at the Palace of Prince Yousoupov. These three palaces were almost the only buildings left standing by the Nazis ; at the Livadia Palace they had removed even the door-knobs. The general procedure followed at the talks was for the three Foreign Ministers to meet first, followed by the Big Three. Meetings took place every day and some lasted into the small hours.

IN SERIOUS MOOD. President Roosevelt and Mr. Churchill go into conference on their own. Each was accompanied by a daughter—the President by Mrs. John Boettiger, and the Premier by Section Officer Oliver, W.A.A.F.

Forthcoming Conference

WE are resolved upon the earliest possible establishment with our Allies of a general international organization to maintain peace and security. We have agreed that a Conference of United Nations should be called to meet at San Francisco, in U.S.A., on April 25, 1945.

Liberated Europe

THE establishment of order in Europe and the rebuilding of national economic life must be achieved by processes which will enable the liberated peoples to destroy the last vestiges of Nazism and Fascism and to create democratic institutions of their own choice.

This is a principle of the Atlantic Charter—the right of all peoples to choose the form of Government under which they will live—the restoration of sovereign rights and self-government to those peoples who have been forcibly deprived of them by the aggressor nations.

To foster the conditions in which the liberated peoples may exercise these rights, the three Governments will jointly assist the people in any European Liberated State or former Axis Satellite State in Europe to establish conditions of peace ; to carry out emergency measures for the relief of distressed people ; to form interim Governmental authorities pledged to the earliest possible establishment through free elections of Governments responsive to the will of the people.

Poland

THE Provisional Government which is now functioning in Poland should, therefore, be reorganized on a broader democratic basis.

The three heads of Government consider that the Eastern frontier of Poland should follow the Curzon Line. Poland must receive substantial accessions of territory in the North and West.

Yugoslavia

WE have agreed to recommend to Marshal Tito and Dr. Subasic that the agreement between them should be put into effect immediately, and a new Government formed on that basis.

Unity for Peace

OUR meeting here in the Crimea has reaffirmed our common determination to maintain and strengthen in the peace to come that unity of purpose and of action which has made victory certain. We believe that this is a sacred obligation to the people of the world.

Only with continuing and growing co-operation and understanding among our three countries and among all the peace-loving nations can the highest aspiration of humanity be realized—a secure and lasting peace which will, in the words of the Atlantic Charter, "afford assurance that all men in all the lands may live out their lives in freedom from fear and want."

WINSTON S. CHURCHILL,
FRANKLIN D. ROOSEVELT,
J. V. STALIN.

LEADERS OF THE THREE GREAT POWERS pose for the camera man in the Italian courtyard of the Livadia Palace. Mr. Churchill's headgear is a Canadian sealskin cap with which he was presented by journalists at Teheran in 1943. Marshal Stalin, in cavalry boots, appears to be a keen listener. Meeting in Malta on Feb. 2, the Premier and President travelled to Yalta by air.

LIONS GUARD THE ENTRANCE to Livadia Palace, which was hastily restored by Russian workmen to make it habitable for the Three-Power Conference. It is about 2½ miles from Yalta, and was once the property of the Tsar, to whom it was presented almost a century ago by Count Leo Potocki. It has a magnificent estate covering over 700 acres.   *Photos, British Official*

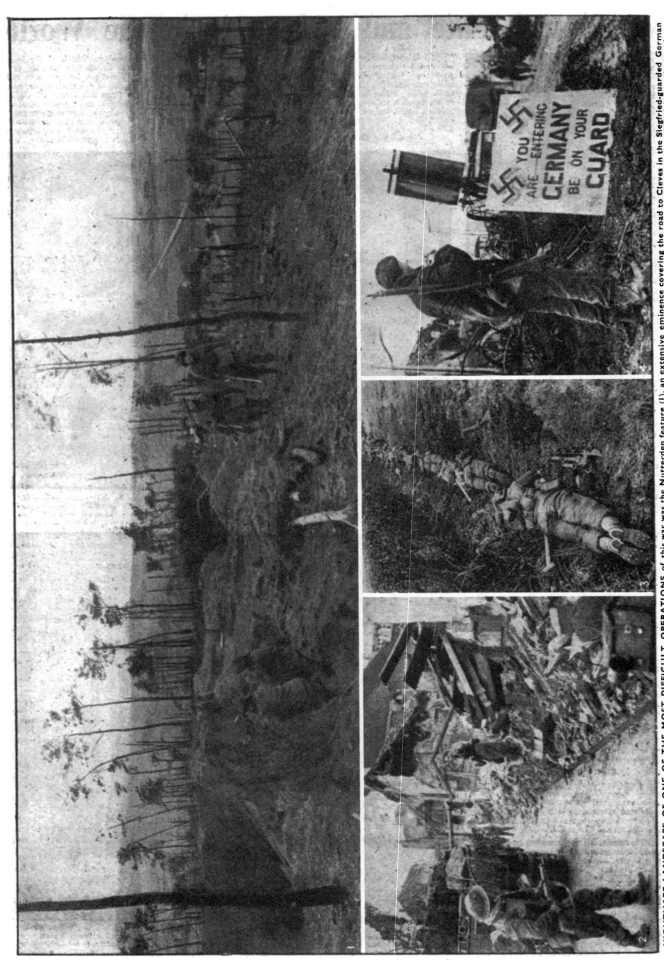

NIGHTMARE LANDSCAPE OF ONE OF THE MOST DIFFICULT OPERATIONS of this war was the Nutterden feature (1), an extensive eminence covering the road to Cleves in the Siegfried-guarded German Rhineland: British troops are seen taking up new positions after an advance. This offensive by General Crerar's Canadian 1st Army—three-fourths of whose troops were English, Scottish and Welsh—at the northern end of the Western Front was launched on February 8, 1945. In Cleves, snipers held out in isolated buildings; a tank and an infantryman were needed to draw this one (2) from his lair. British troops took hasty cover (3) as shells burst over them. A youthful Canadian corporal studied a warning notice posted on the Reich frontier. See also illus. pages 688-689. *Photos, British and Canadian Official, British Newspaper Pool, Keystone*

YOU ARE ENTERING GERMANY BE ON YOUR GUARD

Has Tito the Key to the Macedonian Problem?

Deeply rooted in the Yugoslav political conflict is the centuries-old Macedonian question which Marshal Tito proposes to settle by incorporating Macedonia in a federated Yugoslavia. Here HENRY BAERLEIN presents the problem in its intriguing historical perspective, offering a glimpse of a people for years the victims of terrorists, politicians—and propagandists.

THERE are Yugoslavs who look askance upon Marshal Tito because, although he was born in Croatia, his parents were Czech and Hungarian. But if he succeeds in only one of his ambitions—the settlement of the age-long Macedonian question—the Yugoslavs will owe him eternal gratitude. He now proposes that this province should form a link between Serbia and Bulgaria, and should take its place in a federated Yugoslavia that would, of course, include Bulgaria.

The Macedonians were for centuries at such a distance from the other Slavs that they lost their national consciousness—which many thousands of them, in the days of the vast, loose empires of Dushan and Simeon, never possessed. Sir Charles Eliot, author of Turkey in Europe, and a well-known authority on the Balkans, was of the opinion that it is not easy to distinguish Serb and Bulgar beyond the boundaries of their respective countries, that it is wiser to note that those who became Exarchists were commonly called Bulgars, while the Patriarchists were called Serbs. ("Exarchists" and "Patriarchists" are the names of two politico-religious parties in the Near East; the former repudiate, while the latter support, the jurisdiction of the Greek patriarch of Constantinople). But even here we are up against difficulties; for instance, at Tetovo I found that the priest Missa Martinov was an Exarchist and president of the Bulgarian community, while his brother Momir Martinovitch was a Patriarchist and president of the Serbian community.

THERE have been learned dissertations on the Macedonian dialects, as to whether they are more Serbian or Bulgarian. Investigators have travelled through the province measuring heads, but thousands of Macedonians have themselves not the least idea whether they are more Bulgarian or Serbian. A French observer said some years ago that Macedonia was a school of brigandage and ethnology. He said it was the prey of

Albanians, who were a scourge in the old Turkish days, and the professors—that is, of unconscionable savages and of laborious agents of foreign propaganda.

Devoid of an innate national sense, the Macedonian Slavs have Bulgar or Serb sentiments, for the most part thrust upon them or created by these foreign propagandists. Very rapidly they transform themselves into Serbs or Bulgars; and in their wavering they have thousands of precedents—about the year 1400, for example, a Slav chieftain called Bogoja attacked the town of Arta and, in order to gain an easier victory, announced, the chroniclers tells us, that he was of Serb, Albanian, Bulgar and Greek descent. One must therefore be a little dubious of maps which ascribe the Macedonian Slavs to any particular nationality. Kiepert's famous ethnographical map was adopted by all the statesmen of the Berlin Congress, but, alas, not one of the travellers whose observations Kiepert used was acquainted with the Serb or Bulgar language !

Wanted—Another Solomon !

Serbia having gained her independence a good many decades before Bulgaria, rendered the name of Serb more disagreeable to the Ottoman Turk, so that the Bulgar name was more popular. The Serbs were looked upon by Turkey as a revolutionary element, while the Bulgars were then apparently aiming at nothing more than an independent Slav Church, the Exarchate, within the limits of the Turkish boundaries. Of course, after Bulgaria's deliverance and her annexation of Eastern Roumelia, there was less eagerness on the part of the Slavs to let their Turkish masters think they were Bulgars.

The Macedonian question was being discussed by a Bulgarian professor and a British military attaché. The latter suggested a division between Serbia and Bulgaria. "No," said the professor, "let the country remain whole, like the child before Solomon." "Would you be satisfied," asked the attaché, "if this question were now decided once and

DEBATABLE LAND OF MACEDONIA, lying part in Greece, part in Yugoslavia and part in Bulgaria, has been the most disturbing factor in the Balkans since they were freed from Turkish rule in the nineteenth century.

for all ?" "Yes," said the professor, "if the judge be another Solomon !"

Those who were most active in trying to settle the question were the terrorists whose field of operations extended from the parts contiguous to the Bulgarian frontier and as far as possible into the interior of Macedonia. It was their object to play a predominant role in a greater Bulgaria, and they were not going to be reconciled to the Macedonian problem being peacefully solved without their co-operation. They vetoed the idea of it being included in a Serb-Bulgarian federation.

FOR many years they compelled the peasants of Macedonia to give them shelter, to feed them, and to subscribe to their funds. No guerilla chief presented a balance-sheet, and it was generally known that the celebrated Boris Sarafov allowed himself, each year, after his exertions, a few months in Paris. Their activities were often turned against each other; the pavement of Sofia's main square was frequently darkened by the blood of a dying member of one of the bands.

"I used to be a Bulgar and now I am a Serb," said a man with whom I was walking one day in Monastir, "and so long as I have work I shall be perfectly contented." The Macedonians might have done worse than to echo his words. At Resan I stayed at the house of an old gentleman called Lapchevitch, whose brother was my friend Liapchev, the Bulgarian Prime Minister. At Resan the Serbian authorities were certainly trying to smooth away these wretched divisions. They retained not only the priests who were in office during the Bulgarian occupation, but the male and female Bulgarian teachers. "What is required of the Balkan Christians," said Ljuben Karavelov in 1869, years before his country achieved its liberation and he the premiership, "what is required is union and union and union."

TITO has had some predecessors in his admirable ambition to put an end to Serb-Bulgar rivalry, the deplorable rivalry of cousins. Prince Michael of Serbia, who flourished in the middle of the nineteenth century, displayed such qualities that the Bulgars were eager to associate themselves with him, and if he had not been assassinated (apparently by an Austrian emissary, for the union of the two Balkan countries was not desired in Vienna) the Balkans would have been spared a good deal of bloodshed.

Between the two European wars the Bulgarian peasant leader Stambulisky worked for the same object, and he was foully murdered. Let us hope that the efforts of Tito will be crowned with success.

IN THE RUGGED BALKAN PENINSULA are a medley of races and conflicting ambitions. The village of Bansko (above) is in southern Bulgaria, whose relations with Yugoslavia were strained for years after the last war owing to the activities of the Internal Macedonian Revolutionary Organization which, with headquarters in Bulgaria, carried on agitation to unite Macedonia into an autonomous state.

Photo, Paul Popper

The Fruits of Allied Control of Burma Skies

The virtual air monopoly which we have established in the South-East Asia Command largely accounts for the fact that the Japanese in Burma are now on the high-road to defeat. On the air forces the Army depends for almost everything, and the close support which they give to the troops has been brought to a fine art. Here, Sqdn.-Ldr. C. GARDNER, R.A.F. reviews the situation.

AIR power is indeed the key to defeating the Japanese in Burma, and I think it is true to say that on no other front in this world war is air supremacy such a prerequisite to victory. On the Western Front, Von Rundstedt's salient was reduced and held by ground forces alone at a time when all the massive air strength of the Allies was grounded. In Burma, in the some-ways-similar instance of the Japanese offensive at Imphal, the opposite was true ; the grounding of our air forces would have spelt certain defeat and may well have let the Japanese invaders through the gateway into India.

The Japanese, who knew the value of air power and used it so efficiently when they set out on their vast scheme of conquest, now appear to have forgotten the lesson which put them on the high-road to success. The result is they are now on the high-road to defeat.

On the Burma front in 1944 they made two major attempts to invade India. On both occasions their land plans met with some measure of success. In Arakan they surrounded our defending 7th Indian Division and cut all its land lines of communication. They stopped up every escape hole and every reinforcement hole. Our troops were veritably "in the bag"—except for a third hole : the hole in the top of the bag. Through that hole our air power poured in the supplies which were necessary to defeat the Japanese plans, and which ultimately resulted—on January 3, 1945—in the recapture by our forces of the port of Akyab, our objective for two and a half years in the Arakan campaign (see illus. page 632).

Jap Invasion Tide Smashed

Later in 1944 the Japanese land plan successfully surrounded a major part of the British Army on the plain at Imphal, and again we were without lines of supply. Again our air power won the day. For three months supply carrying Dakotas poured in reinforcements, petrol, bullets, guns and food, and on their return journeys evacuated the wounded. The British and Indian Divisions fought on, and against their heroic air-supplied defence of Kohima and the Imphal plain the Japanese invasion tide smashed. Our troops then turned and followed them and, fighting through the drench of the monsoon, they forced them back and back. And now, fine weather having returned, we have the enemy with his back to Mandalay. The foiling of the Japanese plans and the placing of our feet on the road to victory was due, in the main, to air supply. The troops fought with unequalled heroism, but it was the air which brought them the means to fight.

Had the Japanese been able to interfere, in even a medium way, with our unarmed Dakotas flying to Imphal, we might have lost that vital battle. As it was, these lumbering troop-carriers, unarmed and unescorted, flew hundreds of sorties each day in skies which were well within range of Japanese fighters, but into which the Japanese fighters never dared come.

AFTER the battle of Imphal and after the heroic decision had been taken to chase the Japanese retreat through the monsoon, General Slim again based his plans on the Dakotas. The Japanese in their dispositions once again, for the third time in one year, reckoned without our air power. The result was that the 5th Indian Division was able, during the so-called "close season" of the rains, to chase the Japs 160 miles down the Imphal-Tiddim road to Tiddim itself. Down

on the ground the weather was unbelievable. "Impossible to fight in," said many. The road was in many places washed away ; large slabs of rain-soaked mountain collapsed on it regularly ; everywhere there was mud. Every stream was a river and every river a flood. But broken bridges and blocked roads meant nothing to the Dakotas. Every day they came through with supplies to the 5th Indian Division, while that Division achieved the impossible and pressed on through the rains.

Hundreds of miles away, to the north-east, another British column was forcing its way towards Mandalay—the 36th Division under Major-General Festing. These men were reaping the benefit of the Wingate expedition of 1944—an expedition which was almost entirely airborne, both in its original spearhead and in its maintenance. Wingate had

AUXILIARY FUEL TANKS go as cargo into an aircraft of R.AF. Transport Command in Burma—where lines of communication are sketchy ; most of the roads are impassable during the monsoon and almost everything is carried by air. *Photo, British Official*

used the air to plant his Chindits into what he called "the very guts of the enemy." At the time of writing we threaten Mandalay from the north and the west, but if it were not for the Allied control of the Burma skies it is doubtful if one British soldier would be standing within 200 miles of that city.

All of this is history, even if not widely known history. The question is, "What is our air power doing now ?" In the immediate future the Allied air forces in South-East Asia Command have two main functions to perform. These are (a) to continue to relieve the tortuous and over-long land lines of communication to our troops by carrying as much of their supplies as possible to them by air ; and (b) to prevent the Japanese from reinforcing and disposing of the remainder of his troops in Burma.

THE first main function continues to be fulfilled, and in the air war against Japanese communications we are having singular success. I think it is true to say that the Japanese can now hardly move a man or a vehicle along the Burma railways, roads and rivers during the hours of daylight. Their all-important supply railway, built with the sweat and agony of the prisoners of war, from Bangkok

to Rangoon is a shambles. Our heavy bombers have ranged along every one of its 365 miles of single track, and any Japs that do go into Burma by this route walk far more miles than they ride.

Inside Burma itself things are even worse. Enemy traffic moving north from Rangoon towards the battlefields is bombed and shot at and attacked 24 hours a day. Night technique has been involved, and the bridge-busting technique too. When the Japanese were retreating eastward along the road from Kalewa to Yeu, every one of the 22 bridges behind them was broken by the special "bridge-busting" squadron.

Almost Resigned from the Fray

On the ground, the men of the 14th Army and of the Northern Combat Area Command have a comradeship and understanding with the flyers which transcends even the high degree of co-operation achieved on the Western Front. The air forces know that the Army depends on them for almost everything—even for the regular delivery of the SEAC daily newspaper. When the 3rd Tactical Air Force goes out to give close support to our fighting men, as often as not the ground troops know the names of the pilots who are doing the dive-bombing for them.

It is doubtful whether close support has elsewhere been brought to the fine art which has been achieved on the Burma front—bomb lines 30 yards ahead of our own troops have been given and accepted—and the job done with no mistakes.

"And what," you may well ask, "has the Japanese Air Force tried to do about this virtual air monopoly which we have established in the South-East Asia Command ?" The answer, as far as we can see it up to the present, is that the Japanese Air Force has almost resigned from the fray. It has never recovered from the blow given it in the spring of 1944, when, in two months, the equivalent of the whole front line Jap air strength in Burma was wiped out either in the air or on its own aerodromes.

LET us be quick to say this is not because the Japanese are inferior pilots or have inferior aircraft. Their pilots are good and their aircraft are certainly more manoeuvrable than our own, though not so fast nor yet so heavily armed. What has cost the Japanese Air Force dear and has brought it to its present low strength of aircraft and of initiative is its High Command. We have, however, for the time being, established our air monopoly by virtue of better organization, better tactics and careful planning.

They may yet, of course, attempt to stage some sort of air come-back in Burma ;. because, unless they do, their final defeat on that front must appear to be as inevitable to them as it is to us. Today we have air bases at Akyab, at Shwebo and Tiddim ; from these Mountbatten is free to strike. If the Japanese are to attempt to forestall our offensives they must make a serious attempt to regain some control of the air. On all the other Eastern fronts their air power is hotly engaged. In Tokyo urgent appeals are being broadcast to speed up aircraft production. "Have the Japanese enough resources to stage this come-back ? " The answer is, "We shall see ! "

"Have they enough resources to check the air supremacy of Eastern Air Command ?" The reply is, "No !" Bomb-blasted Mandalay is sufficient answer.

With Thunderbolts of Eastern Air Command

In the brisk rubbing-out of the Japanese blight in Burma, the R.A.F. is as ready to work closely with the infantry as it is to fly far afield on errands of its own. Thunderbolt fighters (top) help to clear the ground as well as the air. Members of another Thunderbolt squadron (bottom) are F/O L. A. Dennahy of Essex, indicating a target to (left to right) Flt.-Lieut. I. L. J. Lowen of Winnipeg, F/O P. C. Walker of Ottawa, and Flt.-Lieut. J. E. Franks of New South Wales.

First German City to Fall to British Arms

Road and rail junction and enemy troop concentration area, S.E. of Nijmegen and beyond the Reichswald Forest, Cleves was captured by Montgomery's infantry and armour on Feb. 11, 1945. Bombardment flattened it, so that even Bren-carriers had difficulty in surmounting the rubble: here (top left) one is towed by an A.V.R.E. Churchill, with its powerful mortar. From this strongpoint at Cleves (bottom) our infantry extracted 90 prisoners, then checked up on captured equipment.

Ph

Massed to Enter Blasted Reichswald Forest

British and Canadians under General H. D. G. Crerar smashed through the horror that was the Reichswald Forest—barrage-blasted, thick with German defence posts, its roads incredibly muddy and potholed. Deep in its heart advance units were fighting when fresh British infantry rolled up to support them : crowded on tanks and anti-tank guns they jammed the approach road. The forest, along whose northern side runs the Siegfried Line, was cleared of the enemy by Feb. 13, 1945.

Burma Airstrips Bulldozed from the Jungle

Photos, British Official

Keeping pace with the advancing Allied battleline, R.A.F. airfields have a way of appearing from " nowhere." At a forward airstrip, local Manipur natives paused to stare at a Thunderbolt fighter with Flight-Sergeant F. W. Richard of North Harrow, Middlesex, in the cockpit (top left). Men of the R.A.F. Regiment (top right) go on guard. At the open-air " Ops " room of this airstrip (bottom) pilots of a R.A.F. Hurribomber squadron study their target maps.

VIEWS & REVIEWS
Of Vital War Books

by Hamilton Fyfe

As hopes of the war in Europe ending rise higher so we are shown more and more clearly what discussions and controversies will follow as soon as that happens. It has been suggested that an effort may be made to modify the Atlantic Charter and the plans for a new League of Nations, that "Power Politics" may return again, that we may even see traditional British effort to maintain the "Balance of Power" renewed.

Let us first of all get into our heads what these terms really mean. Power Politics means that each nation arms itself as stoutly as it can for its own protection in the event of its being attacked. The Balance of Power, which Britain tried to maintain during the 19th century among the large Continental States, was an equilibrium between groups of Governments united for their own special purposes, so that Britain, standing as it were in the middle of the see-saw and putting her weight now on this side, now on that, as circumstances required, might be able to maintain a well-poised position.

Well, that is generally regarded as having failed. And the failure to organize nations as the States of the American Union, or more loosely the component parts of the British Empire and Commonwealth, are organized must in some measure go to explain the undercurrents of the two world wars, though in both of these catastrophes the aggressor power was clearly Germany.

In order to prevent these catastrophes being followed by others, the rulers of the Allied nations have decided that a new and more energetic effort must be made to set up an international organization. This has met with little open opposition so far, but now there are plainly visible the beginnings of the campaign that is going to be carried on against it. The League of Nations which came into being after the war of 1914-18, and largely on the initiative of the U.S. President, was handicapped from the start by the abstention of the U.S.A., and unless whatever new international organization for peace that is erected has the fullest co-operation of the United States and the Soviets its ultimate power for world peace will be illusory.

I have just read a pamphlet containing articles from Blackwood's Magazine strongly denouncing the "delusion" that any world Council or Assembly could be of any value; and on top of that I have read also a book by Dorothy Crisp, Why We Lost Singapore (Dorothy Crisp & Co., Ltd., 12s. 6d.). Miss Crisp is a regular contributor to certain widely circulated newspapers in Britain and Australia, so what she has to say reaches a large number of readers. Her book might be described as a rather violent attack on those statesmen who have managed our affairs generally, not only for what they did in the past, which she believes led to the loss of Singapore, among other misfortunes, but for what she assumes they intend to do in the future.

I THINK myself she would have been better advised if she had stated her case more moderately. To abuse our Foreign Secretaries between the wars as "idiots whose heads should all be on chargers"; to say that "for the last generation the main aim of the Foreign Office has been to lessen and belittle the power of Britain and promote the humiliation of her subjects"; and to declare that "a child of three" could have improved on our Foreign Office dealings with Siam (Thailand), suggests weakness of case rather than strength of conviction. In another connexion she remarks scornfully that "any child of

two" could have told General MacArthur what the consequences of making Manila an open city would be. She accuses the British War Cabinet in 1940 of not understanding "things which were apparent to the meanest political intelligence."

Such language will make readers who want facts rather than invective throw the book aside. But it should be read, and read through to the end. For it shows the line, as does the Blackwood pamphlet, which a good many people not without political influence may be expected to take.

Stated briefly, this line is that the British Empire should keep clear of all "entanglements" and lead the world towards "ordered life and stability." Miss Crisp quotes

Was This Why We Lost Singapore?

approvingly a speech by an unnamed public man who believed that, "in the English character there is more of real religion, more probity, more knowledge and more genuine worth than exists in the whole world besides." She also endorses, "Cecil Rhodes's ringing proclamation: 'We are the first race in the world and the more of the world we inherit, the better it is for the human race.'"

HOLDING those views, it is natural that Miss Crisp should think Mr. Churchill made mistakes when he sent tanks and other equipment to Russia instead of sending them to the Far East for the defence of Singapore. "We lost Singapore," she writes, "because we supplied Russia." She accuses the Prime Minister and his Government of "steadily preferring to supply foreigners with arms instead of our own men." She blames them also for being more anxious in 1941 to make certain we should not have to fight Japan without the aid of the United States than "to ensure our being well-placed strategically in the East and our troops and supplies there being used to greatest advantage."

Whether we should have been better off if Japan had attacked us without attacking the United States and so bringing them into the war is, fortunately, not now a practical question. Miss Crisp has a low opinion of Americans in general. Their Presidents "think in terms of vote-catching" and the voters are half of them "foreigners." They believe they won the last war and "have a right to criticize us on any and every occasion."

JUST how far such sentiments towards America and Russia would animate the British Empire in giving a lead to the world cannot be foretold. Nor can we tell whether Miss Crisp's attitude towards the Chinese would be adopted. She tells us that to think of them as simple, gentle, honest, faithful, kindly folk is "rubbish—dangerous rubbish." They have not really been fighting the Japanese, Miss Crisp suggests, and the Japs are not doing much either, for they are as much in effective control of the country as any Chinese central Government has ever been. Between Chinese and Japanese she makes no distinction, as those who have lived in both countries invariably do. Both the British and American Governments were "completely fooled" about the war in China, and "they are keeping their people fooled now."

SOME who have read so far may ask how Miss Crisp can expect Britain to lead the world if British Governments are so gullible, so blind to our national interests. Evidently she looks forward to a drastic change of rulers among us. There must be, for example, "a regular holocaust at the Foreign Office," and in all departments of State some single person should be given power to purge them ruthlessly. It was, in her view, the fault of all of them that we lost Singapore. Diplomats and highly placed soldiers contributed equally to the disaster. The Colonial Office rebuked "the Governor of an important colony who communicated facts concerning the movements of U-boats" by telling him to "remember he was not Governor of the entire British Empire." The Ministry of Economic Warfare, with "between one and two thousand officials," has done nothing but "announce enemy 'shortages' that have been invariably disproved by events."

It is a long and fierce indictment, and no doubt some part of it is justified. How far such arguments will convince the electors we shall not know, of course, till the General Election is over.

AT DUMBARTON OAKS, U.S.A., where from August to October 1944 preliminary steps were taken in the formation of an international organization to maintain peace and security, discussions took place between (left to right) Sir Alexander Cadogan, head of the British delegation; Mr. Edward Stettinius, Jnr., chairman of the American group; and M. Andrei Gromyko, leader of the Russian delegates.

Photo, Associated Press

Australia's Task in the South-West Pacific—

Now that Australian forces have taken over from the Americans in New Britain—turbulent-historied island, largest of the Bismarck Archipelago—the occupying Japanese are facing a bleakly final prospect. This article, specially written for "The War Illustrated" by ROY MACARTNEY, has the authority of the Australian Army Staff. See facing page and illus. page 663.

RABAUL, once Japan's most forward major base for the invasion of Australia, is again in the news. Australians have landed on New Britain in force and are closing in on the former capital of British mandated territory where 40,000 Japanese have lain skulking since by-passed by General MacArthur's northern drive more than a year ago.

The whole of New Britain, west of a line traversing the Gazelle peninsula between Open Bay and Wide Bay, is in Australian hands. Patrols pushing along the northern coast have encountered first enemy resistance in the area of Mavlo River. Other patrols in the Wide Bay area on the southern coast have closed within fifty miles of Rabaul without encountering first enemy outposts.

It is a bizarre war being waged between the aggressive Australians and the trapped Japanese in this South-West Pacific backwater, nearly three thousand miles behind the fighting on Luzon. Since the Allied landings on Arawe and Cape Gloucester, at the western tip of New Britain, late in 1943 and in January of last year, the enemy garrison have displayed remarkable resignation to playing little further part in the Pacific war.

Loss of Arawe and Cape Gloucester with their airfields also meant to the Japanese the loss of control of Dampier and Vitiaz Straits. Thereafter, New Britain with its large garrison was doomed to virtual isolation. A surprise Allied landing in the Admiralty Islands to the north-west in February 1944 completed the isolation of these enemy troops. Shortly after over-running the thousand enemy who offered mild resistance to the Arawe and Cape Gloucester landings, American troops moved east along the northern coast and occupied Talasea (March 10, 1944). With other forward outposts established on the south coast to protect their western foothold, the Americans were not disposed to worry further about the Japanese garrison. What was strangest of all, the Japanese garrison showed no inclination to worry about the Americans either!

Daily Air Drubbing for Rabaul

Instead there ensued a steady withdrawal of all their forces to the east. Gasmata, once a strongly held base on the southern coast, was voluntarily evacuated. By March of last year the bulk of the 40,000 enemy had withdrawn to the north of the Gazelle peninsula and were busy building up a string of fortifications across the narrow neck.

Although Allied ground policy in New Britain last year was passive, air policy was to the contrary. From January to March the full fury of the 5th Air Force based on New Guinea and the 13th operating from the Solomons, was unleashed against Rabaul and its four airfields which once harboured hundreds of Japanese bombers and fighters. American and Australian planes were over the town daily to give it its usual drubbing. Simpson harbour, which had once sheltered powerful units of the Japanese fleet, was cleared of shipping, only a few rusting hulks

being left to rear their heads out of its troubled waters. Lakunai, Tobera, Vunakanau and Kopopo airfields, clustered around the harbour, suffered a terrible battering.

From the early days of January 1944, when sixty to seventy Japanese fighters opposed each raid, to the end of February when the enemy was unable to put a single fighter in the air to tackle the American and Australian bombers, his air force underwent an incessant ordeal. By March, Allied bombers were able to carry out their daily missions without fighter escort, such was the once-proud enemy's state of impotence.

TOKYO Official Radio, on March 11 of last year, broadcast in its home service an amazing dispatch from one of its Army correspondents in the beleaguered fortress which shows something of the real hysterical Japanese temperament. "Rabaul has become a ghastly terrific scene," he declared, "with insufficient planes to ward off the constant rain of bombs day and night. Even though we stay in shelters we are forced to cover our ears and eyes. When we climb out of the shelters we can see incendiaries floating down and painting the area a flaming red. One hero told me, 'I often think perhaps there are no more planes left in Japan and I worry greatly.'"

While 40,000 "heroes" prepared to repel an assault on Rabaul, Allied forces quickly furthered their drive towards the heart of Japan. From April to September 1944 swift landings at Aitape, Hollandia, Wakde, Biak, Noemfoor, Sansapor and Morotai carried the Allies clear of New Guinea and on to the doorstep of the Philippines. Quiet continued on New Britain, with the Americans content to cover their vital western bases and the Japanese to enjoy the seclusion of bomb-shattered Rabaul.

Effectively blockaded by air and sea, the only contact the garrison had with Japan, other than by wireless, was an occasional visit by a submarine. Key personnel and senior officers were evacuated in these underwater craft. The garrison was well supplied with arms, ammunition and stores from the tremendous reserves which had been built up when preparations for further southward invasion were in full swing. Food stocks were not unlimited, however, and the Japanese began intensive cultivation of native gardens throughout the north-eastern tip of the island still in their hands.

Right through this period, Australian reconnaissance patrols had been active.

Led by former residents of the mandated territory who knew the island thoroughly, they had been constantly probing right up to the defences which the enemy was constructing across the Gazelle peninsula. There was little enemy activity which was not soon known to Australian intelligence.

Early in October 1944 Australian troops, rested after earlier strenuous operations on the New Guinea mainland, took over from American troops at Talasea on the north coast, and the following month established a major base at Jacquinot Bay in the south. News that Australians had taken over full responsibility in New Britain was not released until January 1945. By early February Australian headquarters was able to report that what had previously been a thin vein of men stretching out from Jacquinot Bay towards the Gazelle peninsula, was now a "thick, healthy artery."

Garrison Was Stormed by 17,000

When the Japanese swept southward in January 1942, the port which promised to make such a fine naval base was pitifully, inadequately defended. It was garrisoned by only 1,400 Australians and in its defence had only two 6-in. guns (destroyed in the first enemy air raid), protected by five obsolete Wirraways—Australian-built army co-operation machines. Displaying tragic heroism, the Wirraway pilots opposed the first intensive attack on Rabaul on January 20 by eighty Jap planes. They accounted for two enemy machines before every one of their planes was shot out of the sky.

Seventeen thousand Japanese stormed the garrison the following day and overran their rich prize without a great deal of trouble. Only a few of the officers of the Australian garrison have been since listed as prisoners of war. Nothing has been heard of most of the rank and file who defended the ill-fated base. A handful escaped to the west through some of the wildest jungle in the world. Many of the Australians who did get back to their own forces are among those today fighting in New Guinea!

Headquarters of the Japanese South Seas Expeditionary Force were established at Rabaul. No other base in the Pacific has been more expensive to the enemy. It proved a suppurating sore which helped greatly to drain away the early Japanese aerial and naval superiority. It was the base from which the convoy, repelled in the Battle of the Coral Sea (May 1942) set out on its apparent attempt to invade north-eastern Australia. It dispatched the ill-fated Milne Bay expedition in August, and fed the skies over Guadalcanal in the autumn of 1942 with constant reinforcement of planes quickly eaten up by superior American aircraft.

THE crushing defeat of the Bismarck Sea battle was inflicted in March 1943 on a large convoy which the enemy tried to slip forward from Rabaul to reinforce Lae and Salamaua (see page 747, Vol. 6). Enemy shipping lost in Simpson harbour, together with the number of planes destroyed over Rabaul, would present staggering figures.

Forty thousand Japanese today ring Rabaul, left with only the mangled remains of hundreds of fighters and bombers and the shattered dreams of the Greater East Asia Co-Prosperity Sphere they once planned to establish. Now they, like millions of decent people before this war, desire only to be left in peace. But Australians on New Britain are determined to see to it that their last days on the island will not be memorable for their tranquillity.

ADVANCES BY AUSTRALIAN TROOPS in this South-West Pacific area are being maintained. New ground has been broken by them with unvaried success in New Britain and northern New Guinea after bloody, gruelling struggles. The Royal Australian Air Force has combined with ground forces to smash Japanese resistance.

—Includes Round-up of Japs in New Britain

MAIN RESPONSIBILITY NOW OF AUSTRALIAN TROOPS in Pacific islands is the clearing of by-passed areas, fanatically held by large and well-organized enemy forces. Elimination of these—an extraordinarily difficult task, because of the nature of the country—calls for skill and superb fighting quality. Australian infantry (top) in a march-past ceremony after formally taking over from U.S. comrades-in-arms. At Jacquinot Bay, New Britain, an Aussie advance party (bottom) heads into the jungle. See also facing page.

Photos, Military History Section: Australian Army

Over to Belgium With the A.T.S.

FIRST MIXED A.A. BATTERY FOR OVERSEAS SERVICE was one which helped to defend Britain in the blitz. Some of its girl members chat with Belgian children by a wayside shrine (1) near their new gun-site (in the centre, Junior Commander Mary Churchill). Private Marie Smith, of Barnet, on look-out (2). En route through snowclad Ghent (3) to their site where they help to build their own quarters (4). The Smith twins, of Didsbury, Manchester, with their pin-up gallery (5). This particular battery numbers 250 A.T.S. girls and 70 men.

Photos, British Official

War-Stricken Dutch Children Happy in Coventry

FIVE HUNDRED HOMELESS youngsters from battlefront towns of the Netherlands, adopted by Coventry, arrived in England on Feb. 11, 1945. After two months in a country hostel as guests of the citizens of that city all the children will be billeted-out in private homes. Awaiting transport in a Dutch village (1). At Coventry they were welcomed by English schoolgirls with smiles and handshakes (2). Their first breakfast (3) was served against the background of a Netherlands fresco and simple instructions in their own tongue. Sabot-shod comrades (4) triumphantly bore off their issue of new clothes, as did the grinning little girl (5) whose quaint garb had been made from a blanket.

Photos, Pictorial Press, Topical Press, Keystone, New York Times Photos

Brave Birds and Animals Have Their Own V.C.

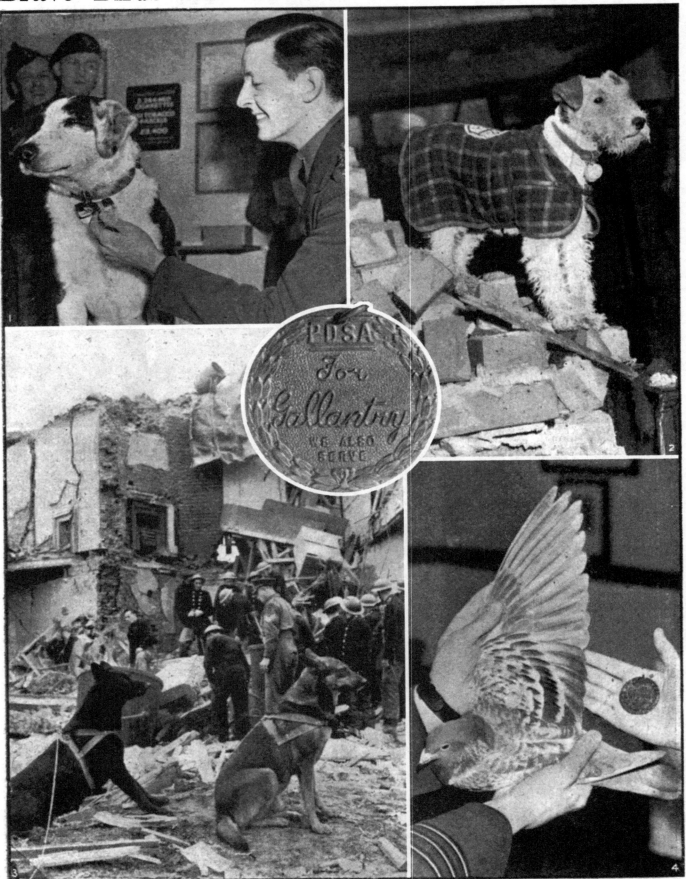

CAPTAIN PHILIP SIDNEY, V.C., PRESENTS "BOB," cross-bred collie (1)—saver of many 8th Army men's lives—with the Dickin Medal for Gallantry (inset), known as the animals' and birds' V.C., and awarded by the People's Dispensary for Sick Animals. Other medallists include six-year-old terrier "Beauty" (2), rescuer of 63 people buried in London raids; "Jet," an Alsatian seen (3-left) on a bomb-site, also searches for victims; "Winkie," R.A.F. messenger pigeon (4), saved the crew of a bomber down in the sea. PAGE 696   *Photos, Topical, Associated Press, Fox*

I WAS THERE!

Eye Witness
Stories of the War

It's a Watery War on Our Part of the Front

The first seven days spent in Germany by General Crerar's British and Canadians, following the grand assault south-east of Nijmegen on Feb. 8, 1945, are summed up here by The Daily Express war reporter Paul Holt. His story from the Western Front is dated Feb. 16. See also illus. pages 688-689.

GEN. H. D. G. CRERAR, C.B., D.S.O., whose Canadian 1st Army mounted a full-scale offensive in the Nijmegen sector of the Western Front on Feb. 8, 1945, drives his jeep—when floods permit. See col. one. *Photo, Planet News*

WE have turned the original Siegfried Line and its supporting Kriemhild Line from the north and now, seven days after the attack, the British and Canadian forces have a sure foot in Hitler's dying Third Reich. There is devastation here worse than any I saw in Normandy, Belgium or Holland, save maybe for the town of St. Lo. This is the death we are bringing to the Germans. The longer they resist us the wider still the devastation must spread.

Back in Holland a week ago I saw the graves of German soldiers. They were neat. They had the cross at the head, the helmet on the breast, and round the graves white tape, fluttering a warning lest tanks coming on should disturb the soldiers whose battle is done. But here in Germany the German dead lie in the rain, for nobody has had time to bury them. There is more work to be done by the living.

Now we have that dreary Reichswald Forest behind us. In it, behind the fighting, the Gordons, the East Lancs, the Welshmen, the Somerset men, the Seaforths sit round pine fires and brew up their tea, waiting for the next battle to begin. The shattered trees cry and crack over their heads and the mud of the tracks on which their lives depend bubbles greasily.

The first tank into Cleves, first city of the Reich to fall to British arms, veered its great gun warningly from window to window. The turret top was down. But round the muzzle of the gun was spiked a four-by-four picture of Hitler, and perched on the "fender" of the tank there rode a happy little man with a blazing petrol tin, brewing up the tea.

So wet is this battle that the troops now call their commander Admiral Crerar. The men mostly sing the Bing Crosby ditty, " Or would you rather be a fish ? " The wounded come back from the battle front riding high

in ducks across the floods. The general directing the battle wears fisherman's waders, a paratrooper's camouflage smock and fisherman's jersey.

At any hour you are likely to meet Field-Marshal Montgomery among the floods. Then this happens : A patient column has been waiting on the road for many hours. The flood laps slowly at the wheels of the lorries, rising higher. The troops jump from fender to fender, singing out, " Aye, aye, sir ! " and less printable nautical remarks.

Suddenly, along the sodden road marked " Cleared of mines only to verges," there comes a busy little jeep with a great red light flashing on and off by the radiator. Two grim-looking M.P.s with red caps ride the bumps with stiff backs. Behind them comes the biggest car I ever saw, shining black and shining silver with an outsize Union Jack fluttering at the bonnet. And inside alone sits Monty, who never misses a salute.

In the upland, where our gliders landed at Arnhem time, there are search-parties out, for although the Germans have been here now for four months, they did not bury our dead. In the rich and gloomy suburban houses of Cleves there is no sign of war shortage. The linen is good and ample. The black-out material is neat and good. The kitchenware is perfect.

Talk of the week here has been the fight of the Seaforths against the paratroops to the south around Gennep. The Jocks had their pipers playing at full blast in the forest to pin the attention of the enemy while they sent a company round to take them in the rear. The Jocks went in with bayonets and took heavy losses, but won the day.

It has been fighting like the American Civil War in the forest, with both sides

AT THE CORNER OF HERMANN GOERING STREET in the Rhineland town of Cleves (centre) a keen-eyed British infantryman watched for snipers. Before retreating across the Rhine in the face of our offensive early in February (story in this page), the enemy breached the swollen river-banks, flooding large areas, including the main roads. Here—as seen from the air—is the highway from Nijmegen to Cleves, along which splash DUKW amphibious trucks (" ducks ") carrying supplies.

PAGE 697

Photos, British Official, Associated Press

FIELD-MARSHAL MONTGOMERY, jeep-riding to forward positions on the Western Front in Feb. 1945, was caught in a mud-cluttered traffic jam. The fall of Goch in this area on Feb. 20 and of Calcar on Feb. 27 laid open a vast stretch of Reich territory where 50 German battalions were reported to be facing the British forces.
Photo, British Official

coming out into clearings, seeing the enemy, and charging resolutely. The infantry have been predominant. The Nazis are fighting well, almost as well as we do. They have boys of 18 in their paratroop units against our boys of 18 who have taken the place in the " cutting edge " of the British infantry of the men lost since D-Day.

The German boys are fighting well because they do not know any other way to live. They lack any picture in their minds of a world at peace, and do not want the quiet way. It is an asset to be added to the tally of this offensive that we have brought elements of seven German divisions to the battle to be beaten west of the Rhine.

How the Parachutists Came Down on Corregidor

Island fortress at the mouth of Manila Bay in the Philippines (see map in page 629), Corregidor was the Allies' last stronghold in the Western Pacific when it fell to the Japanese on May 6, 1942. On Feb. 16, 1945, U.S. troops under Corregidor's old commander, General MacArthur, made a successful come-back, as told by News Chronicle war correspondent Dickson Brown.

AFTER three days of almost continuous daylight bombardment from the air and sea, American paratroops and ground forces stormed this island fortress early today. In the past days Corregidor has taken a terrific pounding, during which more than 2,000 tons of bombs and shells have rained down on the island.

Zero hour was at 8.30 a.m. Just before the landing was due, Liberators and Bostons went over the fortified areas, dropping heavy bombs, incendiaries and anti-personnel bombs, while a protective screen of fighters circled overhead and a swift-moving fleet of P.T.s went close inshore. Shortly after 8.35 the first C47 Douglas transport planes, carrying troops, were sighted.

As far as the eye could see from the flagship were transport planes, stretching for miles in a line. The last-minute bombing was like one prolonged explosion, with smoke, flames and dust rising high into the air. When this cleared, against a background of clouds, the first 47s sailed in low and parachutists were soon seen floating down where only a few minutes ago the bombs had rained. White, green, red and yellow parachutes opened every second as each Douglas loosed its human cargo.

Our flagship lay only 4,000 yards from Corregidor's shore. Surrounding us were invasion landing-craft of all descriptions, while, forming a protective screen farther out, were the cruisers, destroyers and minesweepers. As the parachutists descended the fleet of 47s circled overhead, together with plenty of P 38s.

Slightly to the east, in apparently never-ending formations, Bostons were diving low, strafing areas in an effort to cut the island in two and prevent the Japs from rushing up troops to the high ground on the western extremity, where the paratroops were just then descending.

Aboard the flagship the crew and the commanding admiral, Rear-Admiral Arthur Dewey Struble, remained on the alert as from the loudspeakers came the warning : " Be on the look-out for floating mines ! "

1,000 Descended in 40 Minutes

Bostons still kept coming over, and I was near enough to see their guns open up as they dived low and then turned and swooped up. More smoke came up from the strafed and bombed area, while the paratroops kept coming down, some appearing perilously near to falling into the sea. Some actually hit the steep barren cliffs and were seen to scurry or slide down to the beach, where the watchful P.T.s were on the look-out for them.

In 40 minutes 1,000 paratroops descended with supplies and equipment on the high fortified ground where before the war the Americans had most of their defences. So far as can be ascertained at the moment not a single shot has been fired by the Japs.

But the paratroops are not the only invasion forces. The flagship, at the head of the task force, has taken up its position and is leading hundreds of invasion craft to a selected spot near San Jose, on the southern side of the island, where the boats will disgorge the ground forces.

At this point there is a fairly good landing beach and a small jetty which the bombardment has fortunately spared for our own use. It is now 10.30 and the first craft have made for the shore in a calm sea where no Jap warship sails and under a blue sky where no Jap plane flies.

Now the first signal from the shore has come, giving the pleasant news that the landing on the fortress of Corregidor has been accomplished without opposition.

Rear-Adm. ARTHUR DEWEY STRUBLE, U.S. Navy, in charge of operations off Corregidor—see story above. He also commanded the great U.S. convoy during the Mindoro landing on Dec. 15, 1944.
Photo, Associated Press

I Watched Koniev's Tankmen Cross the Oder

First bridge-heads over the River Oder were gained by Marshal Koniev's troops south-east of Breslau on February 4, 1945. How infantry scrambled across to a foothold on the western bank and armour and guns were ferried over the ice-covered river to support them is told by Lieut.-Col. K. Bukovsky, of the Red Army, by courtesy of Soviet War News.

IT was a frosty day. The tank crews took off their furlined " cover-alls," rolled up the oily sleeves of their tunics, and started to fell trees in the woods. They lopped off the branches and hauled the logs down to the bank. German shells crashed into the woods from time to time. The tankmen flopped down, then grabbed their axes and got busy again.

I confess that at first I could not guess what they were intending to do. Surely they could not be building a bridge—there were no piles in the river. And it seemed absurd to build rafts in winter. The ice was thick enough to impede a raft, though too thin to bear a man's weight. Anyway, what raft could carry a heavy tank ?

Meanwhile, the infantrymen were busy on their own account, building something that was neither bridge nor raft—something they called a siege bridge, a flimsy affair, but it served to get them across the bending, cracking ice. Beyond the river, they at once engaged the enemy. Fresh German divisions were rushed to the Oder. Tanks and infantry poured along the highways and railways from the heart of Germany, even from Holland. The panzers tumbled off the train at the nearest railway stations and careered towards the river.

It was clear that our infantry, no matter how high their courage, could not hope to do more than hold the small bridge-head they had established on the enemy bank. If they were to advance and widen their foothold, the punching strength of armour would have to be added to human daring and skill. And now the feverish work of the tankmen in the woods bore fruit, and my curiosity was satisfied. The crews dragged two large barges down to the river and launched them, smashing the ice by the bank. A log platform connected the two. This contrivance, neither raft nor ferry, answered the purpose best under the circumstances. It was a little over one hundred yards to the opposite bank. The tankmen reckoned to manage without a cable by breaking up the ice in front, and pushing along the edges of the ice corridor they had made.

At last everything was ready. It only remained to roll the first tank on to the log platform linking the barges. The tankmen, to keep their spirits up, called this clumsy, shaky affair "the battleship," but I could see that they were keeping their fingers crossed. Would the thing tip over ? Or would it simply settle on the river bottom, together with the tank ?

We all held our breath. The barges slumped heavily under the weight of the tank, and rocked violently. Pieces of broken ice tumbled inside. Then the rocking stopped, and we breathed again. The barges stayed on the surface. They were going to get the armour across all right.

Meanwhile, the infantrymen, dug in on the far bank, resisted all attempts to press them back into the water. Next morning a gun turned up—it had been ferried across on logs. Half-an-hour later, men with armour-piercing rifles crawled up and lay down beside the tired infantrymen. The mortar crews dragged their cast-iron mounts across the ice on the end of ropes. Self-propelled guns made the trip on the stout little contraption that had brought the tanks across—by this time everyone had dropped the nickname "battleship" and was calling it affectionately and not inappropriately "Noah's Ark."

The sight of all this material was a real tonic for the infantrymen. They went into the attack in high spirits, widened their hold

MASSIVE TANK OBSTACLES forming an apparently impregnable defence line confronted troops of the late Army-General Cherniakhovsky's 3rd White Russian front approaching Neidenburg in East Prussia, in Jan. 1945. But the city fell. Even a broad river may prove as ineffective when determined tankmen confront it, as told in the story commencing opposite. *Photo, Pictorial Press*

along the river, and joined up with a series of similar footholds to left and right, forming a place d'armes of respectable size.

About this time a big tank clash occurred. More than a hundred enemy tanks rushed the Soviet infantry positions in an attempt to break through to the crossings and reach a town where a large German garrison was surrounded. The danger that the bridgehead would be sliced in two was averted by the Soviet tankmen, whose intervention turned what the Germans had fondly thought to be a wedge into a sack. After several hours eighteen enemy tanks were burning in the fields, while the rest raced up and down the sack, looking for a hole !

OUR DIARY OF THE WAR

FEBRUARY 14, Wednesday *1,992nd day*
Western Front.— Gen. Crerar's troops repelled four enemy counter-attacks east and south of Reichswald.
Air.—Daylight attacks by U.S. bombers on Dresden, Chemnitz and Magdeburg. Chemnitz bombed at night by R.A.F.
Russian Front.—Koniev's troops captured more Silesian towns west of the Oder, including Neusalz. Zhukov's forces completed capture of encircled city of Schneidemuhl.
Burma.—14th Army troops began most southerly crossing of Irrawaddy, near Pagan.

FEBRUARY 15, Thursday *1,993rd day*
Western Front.—Canadian 1st Army on 10-mile front on west bank of Rhine. Kessel captured, S. of Reichswald.
Air.—1,100 Fortresses and Liberators bombed Dresden, Cottbus and Magdeburg.
Russian Front.—In the Oder loop, Marshal Koniev's troops captured Grunberg in Silesia and Somerfeld and Sorau in Brandenburg.
Philippines.—Allied forces made amphibious landing on Bataan peninsula.
Far East.—Nagoya, Japan, bombed by Super-Fortresses from Marianas.

FEBRUARY 16, Friday *1,994th day*
Air.—More than 1,000 U.S. bombers attacked benzol plants and oil refineries in the Ruhr, and railway yards at Hamm, Osnabruck and Rheine. R.A.F. bombed Wesel, on east bank of Rhine.
Russian Front.—Koniev's troops reached River Bober west of Grunberg and completed encirclement of Breslau.
Philippines.—U.S. parachute and ground troops landed on Corregidor.
Japan.—More than 1,500 U.S. carrier-borne aircraft bombed airfields and other targets round Tokyo.
Sea.—Announced that at least two U-boats were sunk during recent passage of convoy to Russia ; no ship attacked.

FEBRUARY 17, Saturday *1,995th day*
Air.—Railway yards at Frankfurt-on-Main and Giessen bombed by U.S. aircraft.
Russian Front.—In East Prussia Red Army captured Wormditt and Mehlsack, south-west of Königsberg.
Burma.—British and Indian troops of 15th Indian Corps made another landing on Arakan, at Ruywa.

Japan.—Tokyo area again bombed by U.S. carrier-borne aircraft.

FEBRUARY 18, Sunday *1,996th day*
Western Front.—3rd Army troops broke through belt of Siegfried Line northwest of Echternach.
Russian Front.—Sagan on River Bober captured by Koniev's troops. Germans counter-attacked between Stargard and Landsberg in Pomerania, and on Danube near Komarno.
General.—Army-Gen. Cherniakhovsky died of wounds on East Prussian front.

FEBRUARY 19, Monday *1,997th day*
Western Front.—Scottish infantry broke into Goch, S.E. of Reichswald.
Air.—U.S. bombers attacked railway yards at Munster, Osnabruck, Rheine and Siegen. At night R.A.F. bombed synthetic oil plant at Bohlen and communications centre of Erfurt in Saxony.
Russian Front.—German garrison at Königsberg counter-attacked in attempt to clear road to Pillau.
Pacific.—U.S. Marines landed on Iwojima in Volcano Islands.
Japan.—Tokyo bombed by Super-Fortresses from Marianas.

FEBRUARY 20, Tuesday *1,998th day*
Air.—Heavy daylight attack on Nuremberg marshalling yards by U.S. bombers. At night R.A.F. bombed Dortmund, and oil refineries near Düsseldorf.
Mediterranean. — Thunderbolts of M.A.A.F. attacked railway yards at Berchtesgaden.
Russian Front.—In Brandenburg, Red Army captured Crossen, 30 miles south of Frankfurt-on-Oder.
Sea.—Aircraft of Coastal Command struck at E-boats attempting to attack Allied shipping on way to Antwerp.

FEBRUARY 21, Wednesday *1,999th day*
Western Front.—U.S. 3rd Army made surprise thrust into Moselle-Saar triangle and entered Saarburg.
Air.—Another heavy attack on Nuremberg by U.S. bombers. At night R.A.F. bombed railway centre of Worms.
Russian Front.—Czersk, 45 miles from Danzig, captured by Red Army.

FEBRUARY 22, Thursday *2,000th day*
Western Front.—U.S. 3rd Army crossed Saar at several points below Saarburg ; Vianden and Dasburg taken.
Air.—Allied air forces from Britain and Mediterranean made biggest bid to wreck German rail system to West and Italian Fronts.
Russian Front.—South of Guben, in Brandenburg, Red Army troops reached River Neisse.

FEBRUARY 23, Friday *2,001st day*
Western Front.—U.S. 1st and 9th Armies launched offensive across the Roer east of Aachen.
Air.—U.S. bombers attacked railway junctions between Kassel, Leipzig, Regensburg and Stuttgart. R.A.F. bombed Essen and Gelsenkirchen by day, Pforzheim at night.
Russian Front.—Poznan captured by Red Army after month's siege. Encircled town of Arnswalde, Pomerania, also taken.
General.—Turkey declared war on Axis.

FEBRUARY 24, Saturday *2,002nd day*
Air.—U.S. bombers attacked oil refineries at Hamburg, Harburg and Misburg, and U-boat yards at Hamburg and Bremen.
Philippines.—U.S. troops completed occupation of Manila.

FEBRUARY 25, Sunday *2,003rd day*
Western Front.—1st and 9th Armies broke into Cologne Plain ; Duren and Julich captured.
Russian Front.—In Pomerania, Red Army captured Preussische-Friedland.
Japan.—Tokyo again attacked by U.S. carrier aircraft and Super-Fortresses.

FEBRUARY 26, Monday *2,004th day*
Western Front.—Canadian 1st Army resumed offensive round Calcar, U.S. 1st Army reached Blatzheim, and 9th Army pushed into Erkelenz.
Air.—In biggest daylight attack of the war on Berlin, U.S. bombers dropped 3,000 tons of high explosive and incendiaries. R.A.F. bombed Dortmund.
Burma.—Capture of Pagan, S.W. of Mandalay, announced.

FEBRUARY 27, Tuesday *2,005th day*
Western Front.—3rd Army troops entered Bitburg, N. of Trier. Canadian 1st Army captured Udem and Calcar.
Air.—Forts and Liberators bombed Leipzig and Halle, while R.A.F. bombers made daylight attack on Mainz.
Russian Front.—Rokossovsky's troops drove into Pomerania.

★ ══════════ *Flash-backs* ══════════ ★

1941
February 25. *Mogadishu, capital of Italian Somaliland, captured by East and West African troops.*

1942
February 15. *Singapore surrendered to Japanese. Large-scale Japanese landing in Sumatra, Netherlands East Indies.*
February 19. *First Jap raids on Port Darwin, Northern Australia.*
February 27. *Battle of Java Sea began ; Allies lost cruisers Exeter, Perth, Houston, Java and De Ruyter and six destroyers.*

1943
February 14. *Capture of Rostov and Voroshilovgrad by Red Army.*
February 15. *Germans attacked the Faid Pass (Tunisia) and penetrated American positions.*
February 16. *Kharkov, gateway to the Ukraine, taken by Red Army.*

1944
February 15. *Cassino Abbey was bombed and bombarded.*
February 16. *Russians recaptured Staraya Russa, S. of Lake Ilmen.*
February 22. *Krivoi Rog, in Dnieper Bend, recaptured by Russians.*

THE WAR IN THE AIR

by Capt. Norman Macmillan, M.C., A.F.C.

BOTH strategic and tactical air warfare increased in scale during February 1945 in all theatres of war. The failure of the Luftwaffe to defend Germany against the increasing blows of the Allied air forces was a certain pointer to the inevitable, and accelerating, disintegration of German air power. At this stage of the war it is difficult to say which of the contributory factors has been most potent in bringing about the wane of German air-to-air defence.

There have been (1) the continuous blows of Bomber Command against German industry ; (2) the destruction of German aircraft in the air and on the ground by the U.S. Army 8th, 9th and 15th Air Forces, and their determined attacks upon the German aircraft assembly plants ; (3) the combined R.A.F. and U.S. attacks upon German fuel plants and storage tanks ; (4) the assault by strategic and tactical aircraft against the German rail, road, canal and sea communications ; (5) the deterioration of German aircrew training resulting in less efficient tactical handling of the defence ; (6) the earlier German switch from day to night fighter defence, resulting in poverty in day fighter aircraft and aircrews ; (7) the overrunning of German training airfields in Silesia and Pomerania by the Red Army ; (8) the concentration of German industry upon V1 and V2 weapons and A.A. guns.

It is now the exception to find German aircraft over the zone of Western Europe from which the Wehrmacht has been driven. When a Nazi aircraft or small formation does come over there is terrific competition among Allied pilots to score a kill.

HANDLING of Air Forces Not an Art with Nazi Commanders

Yet, if a small air force is well handled it can achieve much. That was demonstrated in the battles of Britain, Malta and North Africa: The German commanders do not appear to have learned how to handle air forces. In the past they literally threw them away. Recently they have reversed their policy, conserving their small forces to the point of hesitant folly ; for aircraft destroyed on the ground are a dead loss, but aircraft destroyed in combat have at least had a chance to inflict damage on the enemy.

Both the strategic and tactical handling of the Luftwaffe have been often inexplicably faulty. It almost appears that the German air force leaders never really learned the art of using air power—fortunately for the United Kingdom and its people. How differently has Allied air power been wielded ! And yet there is no mystery about the employment of air power. Its processes are coldly logical, more logical than the unfolding of either land or sea power.

Recently Air Chief Marshal Sir Arthur Tedder, the chief British exponent of strategic air-army integration, visited a Russian headquarters to give his counsel on the merging of air action over all Germany to produce the most favourable conditions for the surface forces on the West and East Fronts to defeat decisively the last concentrations of the Wehrmacht armies. No doubt his conclusions will affect the overall strategy of Allied air action, particularly from the U.K., Western Europe and Italy ; for in his capacity as deputy to General Eisenhower, the overall commander in the west, Tedder's views will carry weight with the Chiefs of Staff Committee, the War Cabinet, and the United States supreme executive.

The initiation of a combined east/west air attack plan became news on February 13, 1945, when, after nightfall, Bomber Command Lancasters made two heavy attacks on Dresden. Subsidiary attacks were made on a synthetic oil plant at Bohlen and railway targets at Nuremberg, Dortmund and Bonn. These attacks were covered by Bomber Command night fighter and intruder attacks against airfields whence air-to-air opposition to the main bomber force might have been expected to come. The force totalled 1,100 aircraft. Six bombers were lost.

NEXT day, 1,350 Liberators and Fortresses of the U.S. 8th Air Force based in the U.K., escorted by more than 900 Mustangs and Thunderbolts, again bombed Dresden—and Chemnitz, Magdeburg and Wesel. Losses were eight bombers and five fighters ; 19 German fighters were destroyed. In the following night Bomber Command aircraft attacked Chemnitz twice. On February 15 the U.S. bombers attacked Dresden, Kottbus, and an oil refinery near Magdeburg.

In these attacks, levelled mainly against towns behind the German armies opposing the Russian forces, there is evidence of a co-ordination of effort among the Allies. The Red Air Force is not equipped with many strategic heavy bombers, and the application of British and American heavies to focal points feeding German resistance to the Eastern Front must be of great value to Marshal Zhukov and his associated commanders, and should save life among the forward troops of the Red Army.

LIBERATOR'S CREW, on patrol over the Indian Ocean, keeping a look-out for Japanese submarines. R.A.F. Liberators and Catalinas maintain constant patrol in these waters, flying 12-20 hours at a stretch.
Photo, British Official

On February 22, after a five days' lull in the air on the Western Front (due to the grounding of the tactical air forces by bad weather) between 8,000 and 9,000 aircraft attacked communications throughout the Reich under almost cloudless skies but through a ground haze. The purpose of this assault, which was delivered against 158 targets in Germany, Denmark, Austria and Yugoslavia, was to impose a temporary paralyzation upon the Wehrmacht's communications by road, railway and canal. The big American bombers from the U.K., 1,400 strong, each dropped ten 500-lb. high explosive bombs (see map in page 675).

MOST Widespread Demonstration of Air Fire-Power Ever Seen

Italy-based aircraft bombed the southern zone of German-held Europe. The tactical air forces from France and the Mediterranean added their quota of bombs, rockets, shells and bullets. The skies were filled with almost every type of British and American aircraft—Fortresses, Liberators, Mitchells, Bostons, Invaders, Tempests, Typhoons, Spitfires, Thunderbolts, Lightnings. It was the most widespread demonstration of air fire-power ever seen in war, and it followed night bombing of Worms and Duisburg communication centres by 1,100 Halifaxes and Lancasters.

Before dawn on February 23 the forward elements of the American 1st and 9th Armies attacked across the flooded river Roer, crossing the four-knot current in various forms of boats and amphibious craft, to seize bridgeheads on the eastern bank from enemy forces who should have been cut off from substantial reinforcement by the strategic bombing of German communications.

IN the Orient the air war has reached new proportions. On Feb. 16 a force of 1,600 aircraft raided Tokyo, Yokohama, and their environs for nine hours, attacking air bases and other military objectives. Fifteen hundred of the aircraft flew from a carrier task force protected by warships. One hundred Super-Fortress bombers flew from their Marianas island bases. The task force sailed under the flag of Vice-Admiral Mark Mitscher, and among the ships were some of America's newest and largest battleships. Here is proof, were proof needed, that the United States is now the leading sea-air Power. The two-ocean navy policy has produced the world's greatest marine-air fleet, which has not yet reached its full expansion.

This attack on Tokyo covered an assault on Iwojima, the island base in the Volcano group from which the Japanese have sent interceptor fighters to attack the Super-Fortress bombers operating from the Marianas. Capture of Iwojima will give the U.S. air forces an advanced island "aircraft carrier" whence fighters will be able to escort the Super-Fortresses to the Japanese mainland, and so bring about the preliminary air conditions there which in Europe preceded the collapse of Germany's military power.

BURMA'S FIRST BALLOON BARRAGE guards the famous floating Bailey bridge over the Chindwin at Kalewa, longest in any theatre of war (see page 564). Above, one of the balloons is being inflated.
Photo, British Official

At Balikpapan in Borneo Jap Oil 'Goes Up'

"RIGHT ON THE BUTTON" was the pilots' description of how bombs from Liberators of the U.S. 5th Air Force rained down on Japanese oil installations at Balikpapan in Borneo, sending up dense smoke clouds to a height of 10,000 feet. Making a record 2,600-mile round flight from their Australian bases, Liberators, in September and October 1944, delivered four powerful attacks in which they unloaded 390 tons of bombs destroyed 146 enemy aircraft for the loss of 16 bombers and 6 fighters, and completely wiped out the refinery area.

Photo, Fox

From Ypres to Lambeth with Our Roving Camera

AT THE MENIN GATE, YPRES, in Feb. 1945, British troops of the present war—tankmen of the Hussars and Lancers—paid tribute to their comrades-in-arms who fell in 1914-18. A band of the Hussars paraded in the Place Vandenpeerefoom and were inspected by a brigadier; from there they marched to the Menin Gate (right) where a solemn service of remembrance was held.

DRAWING THE LUCKY LEAVE NUMBERS from the drum at a ballot in the Middle East, an A.T.S. lance-corporal (below) breaks the good news. On Feb. 22, 1945, an official statement was issued declaring that the ballot system for leave ensured no favouritism.

ONE OF BRITAIN'S NEWEST SUBMARINES enters the fitting-out basin after being launched. According to the novel rota-scheme in operation at the shipbuilding yard concerned, the ceremony was performed by Mr. Thomas Beacham, an assistant foreman-driller, one of the many "hands" who had helped to build her.

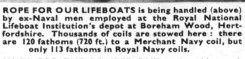

ROPE FOR OUR LIFEBOATS is being handled (above) by ex-Naval men employed at the Royal National Lifeboat Institution's depot at Boreham Wood, Hertfordshire. Thousands of coils are stowed here: there are 120 fathoms (720 ft.) to a Merchant Navy coil, but only 113 fathoms in Royal Navy coils.

HUTS FOR THE BOMBED-OUT at Loughborough Gardens, Lambeth, South London, were erected by U.S. troops. Of curved asbestos each has two bedrooms, 9 ft. by 10; a living-room 10 ft. by 12; and a kitchen 9 ft. by 12. Gas and water are laid on. Fourteen homeless families moved in during Feb. 1945. More than 330 similar huts are being built there (right).

PAGE 702   *Photos, British Official, Fox*

A SIGN of the times is the growing tendency of people to exchange views on how to celebrate the coming of peace. Is it to be public whoopee or private meditation, a binge in a fashionable restaurant or a simple family jubilation at home? Such discussion is harmless enough amusement, but it pre-supposes an end to the war as clear-cut as in 1918; whereas the exact manner in which the present war will end is still as unpredictable as the exact hour. In 1918 people were taken unawares. There was no precedent for the occasion, and the reaction was spontaneous, unpremeditated—and therefore impossible to repeat. The most remarkable thing I recall about that great November morning was the first irresistible instinct of everyone to get out into the open. All the undignified yelping and mafficking came later. Incidentally, if the end is as sudden this time, there is one class of worker who will be too busy for much celebration. This is the harassed journalist, who will be working overtime to change his next day's or next week's issue into one that will more accurately reflect (he hopes) the prevailing mood.

DONALD WOLFIT and his company recently returned from a short season at the back of the Western Front, where their Shakespeare shows aroused more enthusiasm among the troops, so Wolfit was told, than " anything since the Hallé orchestra." I have no doubt that they will meet with equal success on their next venture, which is a trip to the Middle East. The standard of public taste has improved enormously since the last war, and people are broadly if not invariably right when they say that a man's taste does not change because he gets into uniform. Compare a 1945 list of London's entertainments with one of, say, 1917. Think of the crowded Promenade concerts, or the popularity of Gielgud's current productions at the Haymarket Theatre, or the patient queues on the opposite side of the street waiting to book for the film version of Henry V. Nevertheless, I hesitate to deduce too much from these facts. While Beethoven and Shakespeare draw their thousands, the crooners and cross-talk comedians still draw their tens of thousands, both in and out of uniform. What is important is that the men and women of the Forces shall have the very best entertainment, for they deserve nothing less.

A GOOD many people lately have been telling me sad tales about eye-strain, and usually they blame the small print of wartime newspapers and other journals. I doubt if type-size is nearly as much the cause of their trouble as the present quality of paper and printers' ink. The one is less white, the other less black than in happier times, and the words do not therefore leap to the eye as readily, especially if you are straining to read in the black-out by the dimmed lights of a train, bus, or tram, as the foolish habit is with so many of us. Most newspapers reverted to a smaller type when the cuts in newsprint came, and more columns were squeezed into a page. The width of the column governs the size of type to a great extent, because the eye is accustomed to read in groups of words at a time and a large type in a narrow column upsets the grouping and makes for slow reading. Anyway, so far as THE WAR ILLUSTRATED is concerned, we have managed to maintain a fair measure of legibility in such typographical and paper changes as circumstances have forced upon us.

THE manager of a big transport company—who ought to know—writes to the papers to protest against the " haphazard way street names are placed—some on the ground level

and others anything up to 20 feet high, and often only on one side of the street. Could not something be done by the municipal authorities to standardize the position and height of all street names?" he asks. In London, the only district which seems to have tackled this problem at all seriously is the Royal Borough of Kensington, which has set itself as a model—especially as regards its distinctive lettering—though just before the war Westminster ran it close. As for the inner and outer suburbs, one has only to journey to them by taxi after dark to realize how inconspicuous street names can become—and how good-tempered our taxi-drivers are, for the most part, in the face of wholly unnecessary mystification. While on this subject might I express the faint hope that in the New World of the Planned Age on which we are about to enter, suburban house-owners abandon once for all their fancy nomenclature—" The Pines," " The Firs " " Mon Repos," " Balmoral," and so forth—and resort to honest-to-God numbers easy to be identified by postman, taximan and stranger-to-the-neighbourhood alike. There was talk, some fifteen years ago of the G.P.O. inflicting a small charge on house owners wishing to name their houses instead of numbering them. But nothing—unfortunately—ever came of it. I wonder why?

ON my desk is a ninepenny pamphlet, titled Atlantic Bridge, which re-tells in seventy pages one of the most significant stories of this or any other war. It is a story—"The Official Account of R.A.F. Transport Command's Ocean Ferry" is its somewhat drab

Rear-Admiral R. H. PORTAL, D.S.C., appointed Flag Officer Naval Air Stations (Australia) on Dec. 15, 1944, is a younger brother of Air Chief Marshal Sir Charles Portal. He served in the R.N. 1914–18, as pilot in the Fleet Air Arm 1925, commanded H.M.S. York 1939–41, H.M.S. Royal Sovereign 1941–42, and was Assistant Chief of Naval Staff (Air) 1943–44.
Photo, Topical Press

sub-title—which would have delighted old Hakluyt and his sturdy navigators as few things else in this neo-Elizabethan age of ours. There's plenty of excitement in it, but that's not its chief quality, for me at any rate. What attracts me, oddly, is its detachment. Not that it isn't highly personal and, I might add, thrillingly personal at that. For the anonymous author (why should he be anonymous?) has seized on the not sufficiently realized fact that the formation of Transport Command in November 1940 was, like the Battle of Britain, a turning point in the history of the war. In the dark fall of that year Britain, to appearances, was all but out for the count. Even Mr. Kennedy, the U.S. Ambassador, thought so when he left St. James's for Washington. And then, on the morning of November 11, and without the flicker of a single fanfare, seven Hudson bombers, crossing the Atlantic from Newfoundland, touched down on the runway of a British airport. History had been made overnight; bombers were no longer being shipped but *flown* from the U.S. As Atlantic Bridge has it, "As fundamental and far-reaching as the introduction of railway supplies into the pattern of infantry warfare in the 19th century, the trans-oceanic delivery of the Hudsons opened a supply bridge of incalculable value." To have lived through History is not enough. We must have its significance pointed out to us as well. That is what this pamphlet—prepared for the Air Ministry by the Ministry of Information—does so unmistakably and yet so unobtrusively.

WARTIME bread, I am assured by more than one doctor of my acquaintance, has been largely the cause of the wonderfully good health of the British people during the past five and a half years. It is almost wholemeal bread. Instead of the most nourishing parts of the wheat being separated from the white flour and sold for cattle food, flour that has in it the best of the wheat must now be supplied. Up to the seventies of last century wholemeal bread was eaten by pretty well everybody. Teeth were better then, folks were haler and heartier, constipation was far less common. Then a Hungarian made white bread, with the germ and other valuable properties of the wheat removed; and "Vienna bread" became fashionable. Many people still hanker after it because they have a feeling that it is more "genteel." We shall be very foolish, my medical acquaintances tell me, if we go back to it. Our present bread has in several ways improved our national wartime vigour and fitness, they say.

AN M.P. asked some time ago in the House of Commons whether gipsies had been called up for service in the Forces. Mr. Bevin said some had been, but he did not know how many. I should like to ask if they were any use when they were put into uniform. I myself should doubt it. Many people sympathize with gipsies, always on the move in their caravans, sitting round their fires of brushwood and waiting for the pot to boil, making their way through the streets of little towns with baskets of white heather, which are really no more than an excuse for begging. But those who know them best say they are incorrigible thieves who from their earliest childhood have been brought up to steal and never do a stroke of honest work. George Borrow managed to sentimentalize them in The Romany Rye and Lavengro, two of the most readable books in our language, and there may have been gipsies such as he drew in his time, the first half of the 19th century. But today they are regarded by the country-people as vagabonds in the bad sense. Few of the old gipsy families are represented among them. They gather recruits from the dregs of the population. Lately the police pounced on a Romany camp and found as many as 22 deserters from the Army there.

Roll Out the Barrel : Philippines Style

DRUMS OF PRECIOUS PETROL come to a Luzon beach-head from U.S. landing craft to keep General MacArthur's planes, armour and vehicles going, after the whirlwind invasion of this Philippine island on Jan. 9, 1945 (see illus. page 662). Highlight of the campaign came a week later, with the storming by U.S. parachute troops and ground forces, after a three-days' blasting by air and sea, of the historic island-fortress of Corregidor at the entrance to Manila Bay. Story in page 698.

Photo, Planet News

Printed in England and published every alternate Friday by the Proprietors, THE AMALGAMATED PRESS, LTD., The Fleetway House, Farringdon Street, London, E.C.4. Registered for transmission by Canadian Magazine Post. Sole Agents for Australia and New Zealand : Messrs. Gordon & Gotch, Ltd. ; and for South Africa : Central News Agency, Ltd.—March 16, 1945.   S.S.   *Editorial Address :* JOHN CARPENTER HOUSE, WHITEFRIARS, LONDON, E.C.4.

Vol 8 **The War Illustrated** Nº 203

SIXPENCE

Edited by Sir John Hammerton

MARCH 29, 1945

BOMB-LINE PROVIDED A BRIDGE across the flooded airfield for this L.A.C. of the Mediterranean Allied Air Force on the 8th Army's front in Eastern Italy where, in February 1945, heavy rain and snowfalls transformed many of our forward fields into lakes. The M.A.A.F., it was reported on Feb. 13, were concentrating on one of Kesselring's few remaining oil-sources—the sugar-beet refineries in the Po Valley, known to have been converted to the production of industrial alcohol. *Photo, British Official*

NO. 204 WILL BE PUBLISHED FRIDAY, **APRIL 13**

Tokens of Defeat Once the Rhineland's Pride

IN COLOGNE'S DEAD CITY smoke-blackened spires of the Cathedral (top) rise starkly above acres of desolation ; the great spans of the Hohenzollern Bridge sprawl broken in the Rhine. Below is all that devastating Allied air attacks left of the main railway station, situated immediately behind the Cathedral. Less than twenty-four hours after the city's fall, on March 6, 1945, the U.S. 1st Army crossed the Rhine at Remagen, 10 miles south-east of Bonn (map in page 717). See also illus. page 713, and story in page 729. *Photos, British Official*

SEEING THE WAR AT FIRST HAND

"The War Illustrated" Sends its Own Representative to the Front
CAPT. NORMAN MACMILLAN'S FIRST IMPRESSIONS

*I*N *response to an official invitation received by the Editor of " The War Illustrated " some time ago to make a personal visit to the British Armies now advancing into the very heart of Germany, we nominated Capt. Norman Macmillan, M.C., A.F.C., our well-known Air Correspondent, for this important task, and brilliantly has he discharged it. Although Capt. Macmillan, from his long and varied flying experience, is one of the foremost authorities on the War in the Air, he is also a devoted student of the War in all its aspects, and our readers will not merely be deeply interested in what he has to tell about his experiences in the forward zones, during a visit of considerable duration, but will derive much new knowledge about the course of the war which will help them to a better understanding of the struggle, so far as the British and Canadian armies are particularly concerned, and generally to comprehend the nature of the Allies' effort in the West as seen by a privileged and unusually well-equipped observer. Subjoined is the first of the series of articles which Our Own Representative will contribute to our pages.*

I**F** I were asked to say what was my basic impression of the war after visiting the British 21st Army Group and the Royal Air Force 2nd Tactical Air Force fighting in or from Holland, Belgium, France and Germany, I would answer without hesitation in the following words : *The changed character of war.*

No one who has not seen the present war in the field can fully appreciate how it is conducted. Those who visualize it through middle-aged eyes that in youth gazed on the scarred battlefields of the First Great War cannot comprehend how different war has become. The young men, aye, and women, too, who are immersed in this great conflict as the first grand-scale experience of their lives, take it in their stride and scarcely question that war can ever have been different since the days of the long-bow portrayed in the colour film of Henry V which many of them are flocking to see while on leave in London or Brussels.

I**N** that film there is a scene of the English archers erecting a palisade of sharpened wooden stakes, driving them into the ground to stop the charge of the French horse ; except for the materials there is not so great a difference between that scene and the concrete teeth of the Siegfried Line, and the purpose of both is the same. Yet at Agincourt there was fought a pitched battle in the space of Hyde Park. Today the battle line runs from the North Sea eastwards along the course of the river Waal (Rhine) as far as Emmerich, where it turns south to follow a long line, curving in salients and re-entrants, to the Swiss frontier. In places there are Allied bridge-heads across the Waal/Rhine, at other parts of the broad river the Germans are on one side and ourselves on the other.

It may be asked why we do not attack towards the north to drive the enemy out of the Netherlands altogether and free the great Dutch cities of R o t t e r d a m, Amsterdam, The H a g u e and Utrecht. From the area around The Hague, A m s t e r d a m and Rotterdam, and from farther east, between the D u t c h - G e r m a n frontier and the Zuider Zee, come the V-bombs that fall in Southern England. Could we not end altogether the ordeal of England by capturing all Holland ? Perhaps we could. But it would almost certainly be at a greater

sacrifice of life and property among our own forces and among the Dutch civilian population.

T**WICE** we have nearly captured that part of Holland without firing a shot. On the first occasion, when the Allied advance after the break-through at the Falaise gap carried the columns in one fast surge to Antwerp, the Germans began to pull out of Holland. They evacuated Breda and many other places. When they found that our swift advance had outrun our supplies, so that the spearheads had to halt, they returned and looted Breda.

Again, during the airborne battle around

CAPT. NORMAN MACMILLAN, M.C., A.F.C., Air Correspondent of " The War Illustrated," the first of whose special articles describing his recent visit to the Western Front appears here. He is seen (centre) with the British crew of a captured German tank which, repainted with Allied markings, was moving up into action with the Canadian 1st Army on the left flank of the Reichswald Forest on February 9, 1945.

PAGE 707

Arnhem, they prepared to evacuate Holland west of that Gelderland town. For the second time they returned. If they clear out for the third time, as they may be forced to do by the present penetration into Germany, they should not be able to return, and Holland will have been liberated without adding the total destruction of the principal Netherlands cities to the other miseries suffered by that unfortunate people. (I will tell you later of my impressions of the Dutch people I met, and what their rations were while I was among them.)

I**T** was therefore a drive to the east that was set in motion by the Allied High Command after the counter-thrust by Von Rundstedt had been stopped and driven back. There was no second attempt to get across the Lek (the upper arm of the Rhine) at Arnhem. Instead, on February 8, 1945, the Canadian 1st Army (part of which is formed of United Kingdom troops) attacked from the Nijmegen zone, eastward and south-eastward across the Dutch frontier into Germany, to clear the area westward of that part of the Rhine where it bends to the west from Wesel to enter Holland on its last course to the sea.

This opening move by Field-Marshal Montgomery's 21st Army Group (containing the C a n a d i a n 1st Army, the British 2nd Army, and the U.S. 9th Army disposed in that order from north to south) was succeeded by the all-American attack across the Roer river, farther south, in the direction of Cologne and Düsseldorf.

A**HEAD** of the Canadian 1st Army lay the Reichswald, a German State forest, whose trees grow not on flat ground but on low rolling hills, ideal country for defence, where the new types of dugout defence posts with entrances camouflaged by trees and branches are difficult to spot. The Germans used this forest for storage dumps ; they concentrated a heavy flak defence within it, so that R.A.F. pilots on sorties had a healthy respect for it on their outward and homeward routes ; and the aircrews were glad when the Canadian 1st Army winkled the enemy out of it.

But I was writing of the changed character of warfare. It was well illustrated in the zone over which was made the initial attack that led to the capture of the R e i c h s w a l d Forest. All a r o u n d the eastern side of Nijmegen, wherever there was an open field, lay the skeletons of Waco gliders. Only when there were woods or farmsteads—this is farming country—or roads bordered with elm trees, there were no gliders. But on sloping hillsides, on grass fields, on rough ploughlands I saw them in great numbers, certainly running into some hundreds, with their wings torn, their fabric-covered fuselages ripped by the storm of bullets and shells and by the winds and snows of Nature. German artillery had shelled them to put them out of action. It was not hard to visualize the struggle for Nijmegen—the billowing canopies of the parachutists the twisting, turning gliders making for the ground and bucking to a standstill in every direction as their pilots put them down in the quickest possible way ; the men out-pouring quickly, clad in their airborne equipment, wearing small, close-fitting hel-mets, scattering, and perhaps digging-in in shallow slit trenches. Behind them the valuable Grave Bridge over the River Maas was taken intact, although one span was later slightly damaged by a Jerry dive-bomber.

Hastily Scratched-up Earthworks

The most advanced of the gliders landed on a flat area below a dip down into the Rhine valley ; there the drive halted, and the field of action became No Man's Land ; on February 9, 1945, the corpses of both American and German soldiers still lay unburied on the battleground, in the open or behind hastily scratched-up earthworks.

Over that field the advance thrust its way in the attack that began at 10.30 a.m. on February 8 to the north flank of the Reichs-wald Forest. And the set grin on the up-turned face of an American paratrooper's corpse somehow seemed to lose its horror, and to accord with the sense of triumph that the airborne battlefields of Nijmegen were at last all cleared of the invading Boche.

On the rising ground behind, batteries of 25-pounders barked, their muzzles recoiling into their armoured mobile carriages as a tortoise retracts its head within its shell. These mobile guns are part of the changed technique of war. Their shells whined away across the Rhine valley, broadly watered by floods which the Germans had purposely created, to burst among buildings only dimly visible in the winter haze enshrouding the farther side of the river.

PROJECTORS BEING LOADED WITH ROCKETS in the Reichswald Forest area in Feb. 1945. A group of 12 projectors or " guns " each with 32 barrels can lay down a barrage whose fire-power is comparable with that of two hundred and eighty 5·5-in. guns firing 100-lb. shells. A battery of rocket projectors can be handled by fewer than 200 men, whereas the equivalent fire-power from 5·5-in. guns would require nearly 3,000 men. *Photo, British Official*

OVER the whole battle zone in front there was a stillness like the hush that por-tends a thunderstorm. There was no sound of small arms fire. As I went forward over the No Man's Land that had existed since the airborne action of September 1944, there was evidence of the great change in tactical warfare. There was no trench line. There was no elaborate wiring system—just a thin solitary line of coiled wire pegged crudely down to the ground.

How different from the First Great War, with its fantastic barricades of wire and wood, its continuous trenchlines in depth one behind another, its communication trenches leading from the firing line ! Here there was no communication trench, no front line trench. Merely a few slit trenches each a few yards in length ; and on the side of the narrow road that ran across the farmlands, little circular hideouts were cut out of the steep but shallow bank of sandy soil. Little notices were stuck into the ground by the roadside, like the *Keep Off the Grass* tablets in a public park. But these read *Road and Verges Only Cleared of Mines*. Mines have taken the place of trenches and wire.

WHAT has brought about this difference in the waging of war ? It is the inter-nal combustion engine, whose power carries men and weapons up to the fighting zone and into action, that enables them to ride into war in armoured vehicles. Extensive earthworks are no longer valuable against this mobile fire power. The continuous line has given place to the screen of outposts, with perhaps a thousand yards separating the opposing armies' most advanced troops. In an attack these outposts are quickly driven in or overrun, and the mobile units cannot be stopped until they come up against the main defences of guns, armoured vehicles, pillboxes, anti-tank obstructions, and built-up areas situated, perhaps, several miles behind the men who manned the slit trenches and camouflaged hideouts. So it is the modern mobility of fire-power that has altered war. And Allied outbuilding of the Wehrmacht's surface and airborne mobile fire-power is now surely driving the German Armies in-wards to defeat upon their own territory.

WITH THE CREW OF " Y " FOR YORK Capt. Norman Macmillan, M.C., A.F.C., is seen during his visit to a medium bomber station of R.A.F. 2nd Tactical Air Force on his tour of the Western Front. The crew of the Mitchell bomber were about to take part in the great raid of Feb. 22, 1945, when between 8,000 and 9,000 Allied aircraft attacked German rail communications from the Baltic to the Italian Alps. PAGE 708 *Photo, British Official*

THE BATTLE FRONTS

by Maj.-Gen. Sir Charles Gwynn, K.C.B., D.S.O.

So far the great—I am tempted to write final—offensive has gone far better and faster than could have been expected when at the end of last year Germany appeared to have made a remarkable recovery. In the east she was strongly entrenched on the Vistula and in East Prussia, while in the west, where the Siegfried line had been breached at Aix la Chapelle (Aachen), she had formed a stronger line on the Roer. It is true that she had lost the line of the Danube and had been tempted into committing a large force to hold Budapest in order to maintain a block on the main communications across the river.

Her chief weakness lay in the lack of a really adequate strategic reserve, owing very largely to her having clung to the Baltic States till her armies there became isolated in Latvia, and to her having refused to withdraw in Italy to a shorter front. Her determination to hold the dangerous East Prussian salient with a strong contingent of her best troops also tended to reduce her reserve strength. Nevertheless, Germany was in a strong defensive position, and if her High Command had not committed a series of strategical mistakes the task of the Allies would certainly have been much more difficult. Without in any way underrating the power of the Allied offensives or the skill with which they have been conducted both in the east and west, I feel convinced that by these mistakes Germany threw away her prospects of prolonging the war.

MISTAKES Generally Attributed to Hitler's Own Influence

That she would have succumbed eventually under the processes of attrition and the ever-increasing weight of air attack cannot be doubted, but it is improbable that we should have seen the rapid collapse of her defensive position that has occurred. Most of the mistakes were of the same type—the type generally attributed to Hitler's influence—obstinate determination to hold on to untenable positions, followed by belated decisions to carry out rescue operations that made heavy demands on the main strategic reserve. The decision to hold on to Budapest when it was threatened with encirclement by Malinovsky's and Tolbukhin's armies was the first of this particular series of mistakes, and it was true to type.

Once the city was surrounded the chances that the garrison could cut its way out rapidly diminished, and its ultimate fall was inevitable unless rescued from outside. The loss of the large force committed to its defence would naturally greatly weaken the Austrian front, and rescue attempts which a timely withdrawal might have made unnecessary had to be undertaken. But the rescue operations would have had no chance of success without reinforcements from the central reserve. In the event, the reinforcements were insufficient to make the rescue successful, and, what was equally serious, they could not be returned to reserve without fatally weakening the Austrian front.

This dissipation of reserves was all the more important in its results since so large a part had already been assigned to Rundstedt's counter-offensive. One can only believe that in the first instance the Germans underrated the danger that Tolbukhin's encircling thrust implied and were unwilling to face the loss of prestige a timely withdrawal from Budapest would have entailed.

HISTORIANS will, I suppose, dispute whether Rundstedt's offensive was a justifiable gamble or a far-reaching strategic mistake which should not have been made.

Alarming and brilliantly executed as it was, I agreed from the first with those who believed that the utmost it would achieve would be to disturb temporarily General Eisenhower's dispositions, and that its eventual effect would be to accelerate Germany's final defeat. Rundstedt's plan, which made such heavy demands on reserves, seemed to ignore the danger in the East, even more formidable than that in the West. Some day we may learn whether Rundstedt himself fathered the plan or whether it was made in compliance with Hitler's directions. I am disposed to think that it was Rundstedt's own idea, though presumably it had to receive Hitler's sanction.

FOR one thing, we can be fairly certain that Rundstedt had originally advocated meeting invasion by a powerful counter-offensive, and although Rommel's opposing views at the time carried the day, we may be reasonably certain that when Rundstedt was in charge again he would be on the look-out for an opportunity to carry his original ideas into effect. Furthermore, he probably felt that the situation was such that a gamble that held out any possibility of a major success was justifiable in view of the inevitable final defeat by attrition. I suspect, too, that obsessed with the danger on his own front and his own ideas for meeting it he was less concerned about the threat in the East. It would not be the first time that a general has displayed parochial tendencies in pressing the Higher Command for support of his own plans to the detriment of others.

WHEN the Russian storm broke on the Vistula, the German reserve had been disastrously weakened by the reinforcements sent to Hungary and by those given to Rundstedt for his offensive. It was a gift to Zhukov and Koniev. The East front immediately called for reinforcements, with the reconstruction of a central reserve a primary necessity. Rundstedt had consequently to give back the Panzer Army on which all his hopes of continuing offensive operations depended. Furthermore, the heavy losses he had sustained in the Ardennes

left him weaker than he originally was. On all counts, therefore, we can now see that his offensive was a strategic failure of a major order. How far it actually delayed the development of General Eisenhower's plans we do not know.

WE do know it caused the postponement of the Canadian 1st Army's offensive, but the delay may in the long run have been advantageous, for it is questionable whether the operation could have been closely co-ordinated with the Roer offensive so long as Rundstedt retained control over the reservoir dams. I suggest that without reinforcements from central reserve Rundstedt might well have been able to maintain the menace of the dams, and if the Roer offensive had been attempted while the possibility of flooding the river existed the chances of its rapid immediate success would have been small. It is true that eventually the Canadian offensive had perforce to be launched under desperately unfavourable conditions of weather and inundations. But Rundstedt was not strong enough to retain his hold on the dams and was forced to blow the sluice gates prematurely.

SEVENTY-FIVE-mm. SELF-PROPELLED GUNS, such as these positioned in an Italian farmyard, took part in many operations against enemy forces on the River Senio, Northern Italy, early in 1945 when bad weather—including both fog and snow—rendered air attacks and infantry operations by the 8th Army impossible. See also page 374. *Photo, British Official*

On the whole, therefore, it is evident that his gambling offensive not only led to the weakening of the Eastern Front, but in the long run left him in a more dangerous position than if he had never embarked on it. The employment of the reserves he still retained to check the Canadian advance has no doubt facilitated his retreat to the Rhine, but it left him disastrously weak to meet the U.S. 9th and 1st Armies' offensive.

RUNDSTEDT's offensive was an effort to exploit advantages of interior lines, but only with the result that at the critical time reserves, rushing from one front to the other, were available on neither. To make the situation still worse the force in East Prussia which by a timely withdrawal and sacrifice of territory might have supplied a potential reserve, allowed itself to be isolated by Rokossovsky's drive to the Baltic, and now the forces in Danzig and eastern Pomerania have been in turn isolated by Rokossovsky's and Zhukov's further drives to the Baltic.

Surely these were two great strategical mistakes once it became apparent that the Oder was the final defence line available in the East, and that it required to be buttressed with all the reserves that could by sacrifice of territory be made available.

SECTION OF A "MULBERRY" PORT in the making in England: 6,000-ton concrete caissons, two of 150 which went to the construction of the famous prefabricated D-Day harbours (code word Mulberry) towed over to Normandy, as seen—while nearing completion in a British dockyard—by the official Admiralty artist, Sir Muirhead Bone. His drawing shows workmen engaged on the huge structures mounted on their floating bases and

+++++++

lying in a shallow dock where bulldozers (centre foreground) and a "grab" (right) are dredging the river-bed so that the caissons may float out in preparation for the astonishing Channel crossing. Some of the units of the harbour had to be moved to the South Coast from as far away as Scotland. Workmen in their hundreds swarm over the steel-tubing scaffolding; while from the quayside gigantic cranes unload material into the

+++++++

caissons' decks and under-decks. These caissons, towed across the Channel and then sunk in position off the enemy-held shore of Arromanches, helped to form a great harbour, later known as "Port Winston," whereby a preliminary force of 250,000 men was landed on Hitler's French seaboard, effecting a complete strategic and tactical surprise on the Germans. The whole vast organization of preparing, towing and placing in position was

+++++++

handled, under the direction of Admiral Sir Bertram Ramsay (killed in an air accident in France on January 2, 1945), by Rear-Admiral W. G. Tennant. On December 6, 1944, Mr. A. V. Alexander, First Lord of the Admiralty, disclosed that the first person to suggest the use of prefabricated harbours for a European landing was Commodore Hughes-Hallett in the summer of 1943. See also pages 430-434.

Crown Copyright Reserved.

A DESTROYER OF THE BRITISH EAST INDIES FLEET, helping to cover the successful landing by Royal Marines on Cheduba Island, south-west of Ramree, in the Arakan, on January 26, 1945 (see page 724), delivers a broadside while an assault-craft (left) pushes shorewards. The fleet of the East Indies Station, as it was called—a command which passed into abeyance when the Japanese took Singapore—was reformed as the British East Indies Fleet, it was announced on December 11, 1944, under the command of Sir Arthur Power, K.C.B., C.V.O.   *Photo, British Official*

THE WAR AT SEA

by Francis E. McMurtrie

MANY inquiries have reached me as the result of certain statements made in Australia by an American correspondent whose surname happens to be the same as my own. These statements were contained in an article written from Pearl Harbour for Australian consumption. As briefly summarized by cable, the main contention appears to be that joint offensive operations by British and American fleets in the Pacific are impracticable, "because British warships are slower than American, and cannot put enough aircraft into the air." It is suggested that the British fleet was designed for " close-range defence of the British Isles," and for "engagements such as the Battle of Jutland."

Unless these assertions are deliberate distortions of the truth, it is evident that the correspondent responsible for them is wofully ignorant of naval matters in general and of British warship design in particular. If there is one thing beyond question concerning the British Navy it is that the majority of its fighting ships are designed to be able to fight in any of the Seven Seas, a necessity enforced by the world-wide extent of the British Empire. Moreover, " close-range defence of the British Isles " is an idea utterly opposed to the offensive spirit which has always animated British naval strategy and which has been particularly prominent during the present conflict, as the Italian and German navies know to their cost.

EVEN in peacetime a considerable part of the British fleet is always to be found at great distances from the United Kingdom, on foreign stations where there are important interests needing protection. In 1939 it was the cruisers already stationed in South American waters that tackled the German raider Admiral Graf Spee and fought her to a standstill.

If individual ships of the British and United States Navies of similar size and date are compared, it will be found that there is, in fact, no great difference between their main characteristics. Examples of this may be found in comparing details of H.M.S. King George V with those of U.S.S. North Carolina. Both these battleships were laid down in 1937, and have a standard displacement of 35,000 tons. Other details are :

	King George V	N. Carolina
Extreme length	745 ft.	729 ft.
Armament	Ten 14-in.	Nine 16-in.
	Sixteen 5·25-in.	Twenty 5-in.
Maximum speed	30 knots	Over 27 knots

It is evident that so far from the British ship being slower she is the faster by over two knots. To obtain this extra speed, which implies a greater weight of machinery and boilers, a slightly lighter armament has had to be accepted, but the critic does not seem to

have complained of British ships being too lightly armed for operations against Japan.

Comparison of aircraft carriers also shows no exceptional disparity. Our latest aircraft carrier of which particulars have been released is H.M.S. Indefatigable, of nearly 30,000 tons. She is reputed to have a speed of 32 knots. to mount sixteen 4·5-in. guns and to accommodate at least 100 aircraft. The U.S.S. Essex, of contemporary design, is over 27,000 tons ; her speed has been unofficially given as 33 knots. She mounts eight 5-in. guns and can carry 100 aircraft.

IT is true that there are 15 or more of the Essex class in service, and others building or completing, while so far it is not known what sister ships H.M.S. Indefatigable may have, beyond the Implacable, but the same applies to various other categories of warships, in which the vastly superior shipbuilding resources of the United States have enabled a greater quantity of tonnage to be constructed in the past five years. In any case, the relative totals of warships available was not the point under discussion.

In heavy cruisers a comparison may be

H.M.S. ARGONAUT, 5,450-tons British cruiser, was first reported in action with the East Indies Fleet when an attack was made on the Japanese oil refineries at Palembang in S. Sumatra, on Jan. 24 and 29, 1945. See also illus. page 678.   *Photo, British Official*

made between H.M.A.S. Shropshire, of 10,000 tons. and the U.S.S. Chester, of 9,200 tons, which were launched in 1928 and 1929 respectively. The former ship is armed with eight 8-in. and eight 4-in. guns, the latter with nine 8-in. and twelve 5-in. While the Shropshire is designed for a speed of 32·25 knots, the Chester is half-a-knot faster. In radius of action the Australian ship has a distinct advantage over the American, with an oil fuel capacity of 3,200 tons against one of 1,500 tons.

DEFINITE Assurance Given by Admiral Sir Bruce Fraser

It is possible that the correspondent may have been referring only to lighter craft, though this seems improbable from the sweeping character of the remarks cabled. However, assuming that the latest type of U.S. destroyer, the 2,200-ton Barton or Allen M. Sumner class, may have been in his mind as specially designed for long-range work in the Pacific, it has only to be observed that no particulars have been published of contemporary British destroyers of the Carysfort class, and there is nothing to show that they are inferior.

In view also of the definite assurance given by Admiral Sir Bruce Fraser that there are no operational difficulties in the way of our fleet in the Pacific operating against the enemy, it may be assumed that the views emanating from the Pearl Harbour correspondent have no basis in fact. His only other complaint appears to have been that, while the United States fleet " is capable of striking with 2,000 carrier-borne planes," it would be impossible for the British to put " a fraction " of that number into the air.

HOW far this is from the truth may be judged by raids on oil refineries in Sumatra carried out from four British carriers during the latter part of January. Though the number of aircraft engaged on this occasion has not been mentioned, the carriers included the Indefatigable, which as already mentioned is believed to accommodate over 100 planes. It is reasonable to suppose that each of the others, ships of 23,000 tons, may have carried 80 or more each, which gives a total of about 350, a very substantial " fraction " of the estimated American total of 2,000. Nor does it necessarily follow that these are the only aircraft carriers operating with our fleets in the East.

It is too often forgotten that this country has, if anything, a bigger score to settle with the Japanese than has the United States. Though the United States Navy lost two battleships at Pearl Harbour, we were deprived of the Prince of Wales and Repulse in the same week. All the territory lost to America, with the exception of small islands like Guam and Wake, was in the Philippines. British territories still to be wrested from the aggressors include Lower Burma, Malaya, North Borneo, parts of New Guinea and the Solomons, and Hong Kong, to say nothing of many important commercial properties in Chinese cities such as Shanghai and Tientsin.

How We Stormed and Crossed the Roer River

WHEN MANY BRIDGES WERE DESTROYED during the desperate fighting on the Roer in late February 1945, in the Allied drive to Cologne and Düsseldorf, a medical party of the U.S. 9th Army in an assault-boat (1) bent to their paddles to cross the swollen swift-flowing river and evacuate wounded comrades. Under heavy fire, Allied combat engineers in this sector of the Western Front flung temporary bridges across, only to see them smashed by German artillery. Abandoned assault-craft in which the infantry had effected a successful surprise crossing early on the morning of Feb. 23 drifted down-river to a shattered bridge (2). Undaunted, engineers built other bridges while still under fire. The bridge at (3) is of the pontoon type, on inflated rubber floats, and U.S. tanks are crossing it. *Photos, U.S. Official, Central Press*

Precision-Bombing Spared Cologne's Cathedral

MORE REMNANTS OF HITLER'S WEHRMACHT SURRENDERED, outside the world-famous cathedral in shattered Cologne, when Germany's third largest city (peacetime population over 700,000) fell on March 6, 1945, after two days' attack by the 3rd Armoured Spearhead Division and the 104th (Timber Wolf) Infantry Division of Gen. Hodges' 1st U.S. Army. Though Cologne had been laid flat by over 40,000 tons of bombs, the main structure of the Cathedral (founded in 1248) was almost unscathed. See also illus. page 706, and story in page 729. PAGE 713 *Photo, British Official*

Secrets Behind the Names That Sail the Seas

There is far more in the christening of a ship than meets the landsman's eye. Why is it necessary to conceal the names of vessels when these are launched in wartime? How are the names selected, and what special significance have they? Why is a number sometimes substituted for a name? Little known facts in this connexion are revealed by ALEXANDER DILKE.

WE had to wait three months to be told officially that Vanguard was the name which Princess Elizabeth gave to Britain's newest battleship—the greatest yet built in the British Isles—when she launched it on Nov. 30, 1944 (see illus. page 519). The name was kept secret because it was considered it might enable the enemy to guess a good deal about her and any ships of the same class; nevertheless a German broadcast gave the name at the time of launching.

Names of the battleships of the King George V class were announced before the outbreak of war, as international agreements called for the nations exchanging details of all warships under construction or projected. But the names of completed ships in this class have never been announced until they have been some time in commission, with evidence that the enemy knew their identity.

It is the custom in the Royal Navy to christen warships in "classes," the names of all the ships in one class, similar in size, speed, armament, and so on, being consistent. Among our destroyers is the "Hunt" class, so named because each bears the name of a famous British pack, such as the Quorn, Pytchley, Garth and Southdown; one carried the idea further, the wardroom being labelled "The Kennels" and the captain's cabin "Master of the Hounds."

OBVIOUSLY, if the enemy knew the name of a new warship he might thus discover its "class" and judge its speed, armament and other details. Knowing that in the King George V class we had announced the names King George V, Prince of Wales, Duke of York, Anson and Howe and that two battleships in another class—Lion and Temeraire—had been begun, the enemy might have been able, from the name of the new battleship previously mentioned, to make deductions. Those deductions might have been wrong, of course!

In the 1914-18 war the Germans puzzled long over a British destroyer named H.M.S. Zubian. They could not place the name in any of the known destroyer classes, and their encyclopedias did not help them to discover its meaning. Only after the Armistice was it revealed that the name Zubian was made in the same way as the destroyer to which it was given—by joining together Nubian and Zulu. Those sister ships were both damaged and a new destroyer built from the fore part of one and the aft part of the other!

There is a definite rule against using the names of living admirals; and, of course, a sense of proportion is maintained. "County" names have been kept to cruisers. Flower names are more suited to corvettes than to battle-cruisers. A numerous class of sloops bearing flower names, which did brilliant work in the last war, was sometimes known as the "Herbaceous Border."

The U.S. Navy is more consistent in christening its warships, since it has definite rules that certain names are used only for certain types. For instance, a vessel called after one of the States will be a battleship: Montana, Ohio, Maine, New Hampshire, and Louisiana were the names announced for the projected 58,000 ton class. The gigantic building programme of the U.S.A. gives rise to wonder as to what name would be used if there were more than 48 battleships! If you see a ship named after a large city in the U.S., then she is a cruiser. Although U.S. and British naval authorities might be consulted over names, one frequently finds two warships with the same name. Enterprise, Franklin, Birmingham, Rochester, Anthony, Duncan, are just a few examples of the duplications that are recorded.

U. S. DESTROYERS are not so easy for us to identify from their names, for they are christened after famous men associated with the United States Navy, including Secretaries of the Navy, Congressmen, sailors—ratings as well as officers—and inventors. American battles and famous old warships provide names for U.S. aircraft-carriers. The Lexington's name was "handed on" after that aircraft-carrier was sunk in the Battle of the Coral Sea, to a new carrier originally intended to be called Cabot. The name comes from the battle of 1775, but there are at least five towns of various sizes called Lexington in the U.S.A. The Lexington of the battle is in Massachusetts.

U.S. submarines get their names from fish and marine animals, fleet minesweepers from birds, oilers from American rivers. There is a group of names for every type of ship and some of them are very curious. Vol-

H.M.S. WATCHMAN, 27-year-old British destroyer of the "W" and "V" class (see this page), was built on the Clyde during the last war. She has a displacement of 1,100 tons and in January 1945 completed a fine record of 200,000 miles steamed in this war alone.
Photo, British Official

canoes and the ingredients of explosives provide names for ammunition ships, and names of Indian tribes as well as mythological characters are used. The Germans seem to prefer names of men famous (or infamous) in their history—Bismarck, Tirpitz, Spee, Zeppelin, and so on. When the cruiser Lützow was transferred to the Soviet Navy early in 1940, her name was given to the former Deutschland, a "pocket-battleship," apparently as a clumsy attempt to conceal the transaction.

With British submarines the substitution of names for numbers first came into operation in the case of those built soon after the 1914-18 war; by 1939 only a few numbered ones were in existence, and the experiment of again giving numbers instead of names was not a popular one when it was tried, early in the war. Submarine officers and men found it difficult to entertain any feeling of pride, enthusiasm or affection for an impersonal number: which is another way of saying that a name, with its associations, has the morale-supporting effect which a number so completely lacks. It is a matter of esprit de corps; the name is a rallying-point, as it were, comparable to a ship's badge or a regimental Colour. The Germans, however, have always numbered their U-boats, but not consecutively as completed.

THOUSANDS of merchant ships have been launched in recent years, and it must on occasions have been difficult to decide on an appropriate name. At one stage of the war, place-names that came into prominence during the North African campaigns were given to merchant ships. Years hence, when that fighting has been forgotten by most people, it will no doubt be wondered how such curious names for ships were found.

Months ago, when it was feared that the enemy was gaining information from the names of ships stencilled on packages that were to form their cargo, it was decided that henceforth all such packages should carry an identity number, which gave no information to any enemy agent who might have watched them being transported by road or rail to the port of dispatch

H.M. SUBMARINE TALLY HO with her cheering crew on their return to base in Northern England after 12 months in Far Eastern waters. The Jolly Roger records the "kills" the submarine has made, including a Japanese cruiser, submarine, submarine-chaser, 1,000-ton escort vessel and 17 other ships, mostly carrying supplies to Burma. PAGE 714 *Photo, Planet News*

The Howe at Sydney Ready to Smite the Japs

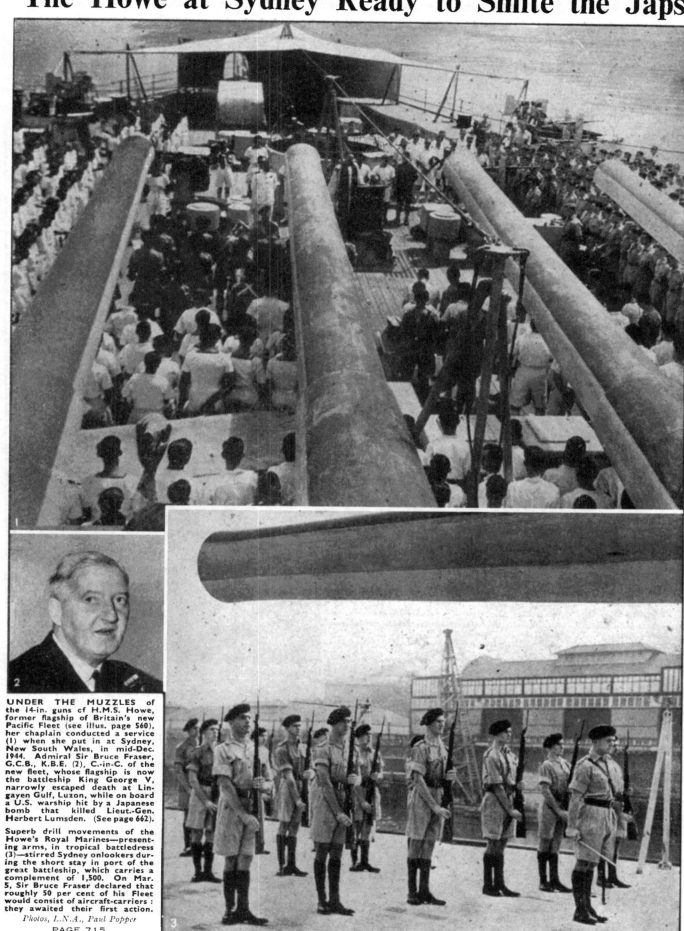

UNDER THE MUZZLES of the 14-in. guns of H.M.S. Howe, former flagship of Britain's new Pacific Fleet (see illus. page 560), her chaplain conducted a service (1) when she put in at Sydney, New South Wales, in mid-Dec. 1944. Admiral Sir Bruce Fraser, G.C.B., K.B.E. (2), C.-in-C. of the new fleet, whose flagship is now the battleship King George V, narrowly escaped death at Lingayen Gulf, Luzon, while on board a U.S. warship hit by a Japanese bomb that killed Lieut.-Gen. Herbert Lumsden. (See page 662).

Superb drill movements of the Howe's Royal Marines—presenting arms, in tropical battledress (3)—stirred Sydney onlookers during the short stay in port of the great battleship, which carries a complement of 1,500. On Mar. 5, Sir Bruce Fraser declared that roughly 50 per cent of his Fleet would consist of aircraft-carriers: they awaited their first action.

Photos, L.N.A., Paul Popper

Red Guns and Cavalry Eat Deep into Germany

THROUGH SNOWY STREETS of Beuthen (1), large industrial centre north-west of Cracow, taken by troops of Marshal Koniev's 1st Ukrainian Front on Jan. 28, 1945, Soviet heavy guns rumbled whilst civilians went about as usual. In the Frankfort sector where Marshal Zhukov's 1st White Russian Front took Kuestrin on March 12, prisoners ranged from youths to grandfathers (2). When Marshal Rokossovsky's 2nd White Russian Front entered the area round Neidenburg, E. Prussia, they found defences utterly deserted (3). Glorious is the war record of the Red Cavalry: Lieut.-Gen. Oslikovsky and his staff greet their " Mounties " as they move across snow-clad plains of E. Prussia (4). Marshal Zhukov, in a thrust of over 60 miles, had reached the Baltic in the Kolberg area (see map), it was announced on March 5, 1945, when Marshal Rokossovsky had taken Koeslin and also reached the sea, cutting off Danzig and the German Northern Army Group.

Photos, Pictorial Press, Planet News.
Map, courtesy of The Daily Telegraph

Line-up of Allies for 'One Good Strong Heave'

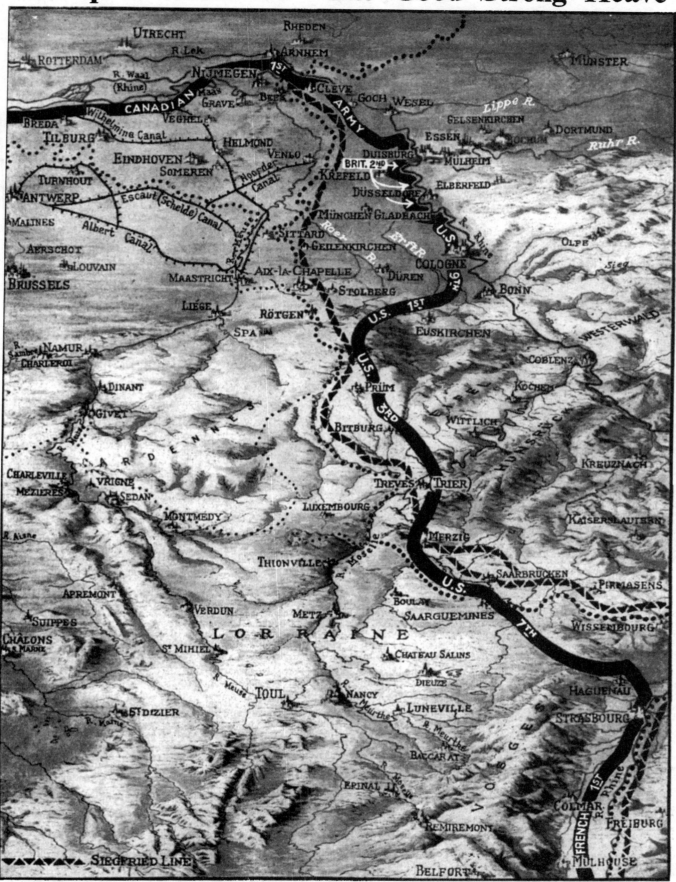

500-MILE WESTERN FRONT BEFORE COLOGNE FELL on March 6, 1945, and the Rhine crossing south of Bonn 24 hours later. North to south: 21st Army Group (Can. 1st, Brit. 2nd, U.S. 9th), Field-Marshal Montgomery; 12th Group (U.S. 1st and 3rd, plus 15th—under Lt.-Gen. L. S. Gerow—it was revealed on March 9), Gen. Omar Bradley; 6th Group (U.S. 7th, French 1st), Gen. Jacob Devers. Relative distances: Brussels-Cologne, 120 miles; Brussels-Belfort, 250 miles. "One good strong heave all together will end the war in Europe," said Mr. Churchill on March 4 in a speech, delivered on German soil, to officers and men of the 51st (Highland) Division.

'Turkey is Our Ally, Turkey is Our Friend'

Those words were uttered by Mr. Churchill on February 11, 1943, in acknowledging the services Turkey had rendered to us by standing firm in the darkest days of the war. Two years later, on February 23, 1945, Turkey declared war on the Axis. An appreciation of the Turks of yesterday and of today is expressed here by HENRY BAERLEIN

IT would have been of great service to the Allies if Turkey had entered the war in the autumn of 1943. The supply line to Russia would have been vastly shortened, not only because we would have enjoyed open passage into the Black Sea but on account of the direct rail connexion between Turkey and Egypt, which was capable of handling far more Allied traffic than the Trans-Iranian route. An Anglo-American invasion of Bulgaria, the Aegean Isles and the Greek mainland would have been facilitated by the use of Turkish sea and air bases, while the Germans would have been deprived of vital materials such as cotton, mohair, wool and chromium.

But if one is critical of the Turks for not throwing themselves heroically into the conflict in 1943, let us not forget the service they rendered us in the spring of 1941 when

all that in a few strenuous years they had succeeded in building up after the scrapping of an evil past, the past which a hated regime had imposed upon them.

LET us, then, with understanding of Turkey's special position, consider what will now be her contribution to the cause of the Allies. It is said that her army is anxious to take the field. Of their military virtue there has never been a doubt ; she had nearly a million men under arms, the majority of whom are professional soldiers, trained in all branches of modern warfare. Turkey has leaders of military genius. In the war which only two decades ago raged over Anatolian soil, her President of today was Commander-in-Chief on the Western front and victor over the Greeks in 1922 at the decisive battle of Inonu, from which Ismet Pasha, as he

miles from Kara Burnu on the Black Sea to the Sea of Marmora. When, in the spring of 1943, Field-Marshal Sir Henry Maitland Wilson inspected the Chataldja Lines, he praised them as the most formidable fortifications in Europe. (It is a fact that nearly all the heavy batteries were not mounted into position until a year after the beginning of this war.)

The use of Turkish sea and air bases will render very unpleasant the sojourn of those Germans who still remain in the Dodecanese and other islands of the eastern Mediterranean. When we landed in the Azores in October 1943 it was necessary to construct aerodromes ; whereas in European Turkey and in Anatolia there are aerodromes fully prepared for all military purposes. Hitherto Izmir (Smyrna), the main harbour of Anatolia, has been threatened by the German occupation of the Dodecanese, which since 1912 were under Italian rule and a constant danger to Turkish security. After the liberation of this island group, Smyrna's obvious strategical value as an invisible bridge between Asia, Africa and Europe will be possible of exploitation.

Peasantry the Country's Backbone

Turkey's strength lies largely in her healthy farming community. Although industries have been established on a considerable scale, the men working in the cotton mills and aeroplane factories of Kayseri (the Roman Caesarea) do not normally stay to become skilled workmen, but return for good to their villages when they have earned enough, say in two years, to set up as farmers. This peasant stock is indeed the backbone of the country, as it is of the army.

Alone and with no help from without, this nation of 16 millions has achieved what others have failed to do. They sought out the old and imperishable treasures of their culture and history, discarding all false romanticism, taking advantage of the latest discoveries of the whole world, though this never degenerated into servile imitation. They had determined to be and to remain Turkish. Thus, in place of the former Agricultural Bank, the only Turkish bank existing in Ottoman times, they established the Sumer Bank and the Eti Bank, whose names evoke the most ancient Turkish States which are known to history, the Sumerian and the Hittite.

AMONG the traits which this vigorous young nation has in common with ours is the love of sport. The Turkey of today is a young nation, but her devotion to sport goes back to other days. A tablet with a Hittite inscription, discovered not long ago at Boghaz-Keuy, shows that before the Greeks or the Persians appeared in Asia Minor sport had reached a high stage of development. Foot races took place regularly among the priests, and wrestling, without which no fête or wedding in Anatolia today is complete, was centuries ago the occasion of great public festivals.

In the margin of a book in the library of St. Sophia is an annotation on wrestling, made by the celebrated champion Mehmed Pehlivan, who died in 1651. His epitaph shows that the Turks share with us an occasional extravagance in the admiration of the heroes of sport. " M.P. Kak ber Kaf " says that epitaph, meaning that his reputation stretched from the one to the other of the mountains which in Asiatic mythology were the limits of the world.

TURKISH TROOPS LOAD LEND-LEASE BOMBS into a railway truck en route for an airfield. The Turkish Parliament, on February 23, 1945, unanimously decided to declare war on Germany and Japan, thereby entitling them to be represented at the United Nations Security Conference due to open at San Francisco on April 25. *Photo, New York Times Photos*

Syria was under the control of Vichy, when in Iraq Raschid Ali had revolted, when in Persia a Nazi organization was ready to assume power and when Rommel had driven the Allied army back to the borders of Egypt. Only the Turkish Army and people with their will to remain free, and the Anatolian mountains, stood between the main body of the Wehrmacht and India, Egypt and the complete isolation of the Soviet Union from the rest of the world.

THEN the Turks stood firm—and with no illusions, for if Germany had attacked no one could have gone to their aid. Britain was at bay, Russia was obviously playing for another winter. And Turkey was very inadequately armed, owing to the undeveloped state of her heavy industries. A defensive war of movement in depth, taking advantage of the natural configuration of Anatolia, would alone have been possible.

In 1941 the Turks were steadfast: chiefly, of course, for the reason that it was for their own independence. Nations do not sacrifice themselves for the sake of other nations, and if we are a little apt to look askance upon those who fly to the rescue of those who are on the point of victory we must have sympathy for a people reluctant to fling away

was then, took his present name. Field Marshal Fevzi Chakmak, head of the Great General Staff, was Ataturk's military adviser and closest collaborator until the latter's death in 1938.

While the Turkish Air Force is as yet somewhat small in numbers it has made a satisfactory start, after Soviet experts came to inaugurate it about twenty years ago. It includes British and American bombers and fighters, as well as Heinkel bombers of the latest type. Such is the enthusiasm that it evokes among the Turks that several women have entered its ranks and qualified as pilots, including Sabiha Goece, formerly Ataturk's protégée, who is regarded as Turkey's best bomber pilot.

Turkey's Navy consists of one old battle cruiser, the reconditioned Goeben, and another large and two smaller cruisers of later design, nine or ten destroyers and torpedo-boats, and seven, possibly eight, submarines. The small State-owned merchant marine could hardly be transferred to active war service. In the very unlikely event of a German attack on Turkey the world would be hearing again of the famous Chataldja Lines, which stretch for forty

First Convoy to Break Land Blockade of China

Of tremendous significance to the United Nations was the brief ceremony on Feb. 1, 1945, marking the opening of the Ledo-Burma (Stilwell) Road and the welcoming at Kunming of the first overland convoy with war supplies : the three-years' land blockade by Japan was ended.   Part of the 100-vehicle convoy is here seen on its way to China.   For over 1,000 miles this road runs from Ledo in Assam, through Burma and on to Kunming, capital of the Chinese province of Yunnan.

Phot
Plan

In Siegfried Defences Approaching the Rhine

Near the northern end of the great Rhine battlefront the Canadian 1st Army (75 per cent British troops) foot-slogged along the road to the German town of Goch (1) south-east of the Reichswald Forest. Scottish infantry broke into this Siegfried bastion on Feb. 19, 1945, and together with Welsh troops within two days accounted for the last Hun sniper. Then on again to further conquests, with a dense smoke-screen, belching oilily from close-massed generators (2), to cover the advance.

Rounding-Up Beaten Huns In Their Own Land

Ready for the prisoners' pen, unperturbed and even smiling because for them the war is over, captured Germans sat at their ease under the guard's watchful eye (3) after heavy fighting near Keppeln, south of Calcar, which fell to the Canadians on Feb. 26, 1945.   Before the Keppeln attack, troops waited for zero hour in the lee of a blasted building (4).   Members of an amphibious assault fleet marooned by heavy floods (5) in the dykelands on the banks of the Rhine east of Nijmegen.

SERGEANT HAMPSHIRE, MIDDLESEX HOME GUARD

CORPORAL SMITH, ARGYLL HOME GUARD

PORTRAYED BY ERIC KENNINGTON, an original L.D.V. and several of whose pictures belong to the Nation, these grand types of Britain's Home Guard are representative of a number painted during the artist's travels all over the country, to form a souvenir of hard times and good times experienced by that unpaid army of nearly 2,000,000 which "stood down" in the autumn of 1944.

COMPANY SERGEANT-MAJOR WATERS, LANCASHIRE HOME GUARD

CORPORAL ROBERTSON, CITY OF EDINBURGH HOME GUARD

VIEWS & REVIEWS
Of Vital War Books

by Hamilton Fyfe

As I have been looking through Eric Kennington's brilliant series of drawings in colour in Britain's Home Guard, by John Brophy (Harrap, 6/-), portraits from life of typical members of the force in all parts of the country, my memory has naturally enough gone back to the early days, the days when I joined and served in it as orderly-room clerk—those warm, cloudless, delicious summer days of 1940. Can it be—I ask myself as I turn these pages—that the scratch lot we were then, without any soldierly qualities except that of determination to stand up and be killed after we'd had a shot or two at the enemy—can it be that we developed into such men as Kennington shows us —soldiers every ounce of them, hard-bitten, wearing their uniforms with a professional air, men whom you feel instinctively form part of the Army proper ?

Yet that is what happened, and happened very quickly, marvellously so when you remember that they were only spare-time soldiers and had to acquire their training after their day's work was done and at weekends. I saw something of the transformation. It did not begin until we were "issued with" uniforms. (I hate the expression, but it has become so general that I have to use it instead of saying grammatically "until uniforms were issued to us.") Even then, in our denim battledress, we looked more like sacks of sugar or cement until the stiffness of the stuff relaxed a bit ; and even then we had to share our small stock of rifles.

Those Molotov Cocktail Drills

John Brophy, who has written the "character study" of the Home Guard which accompanies Kennington's drawings, and is well worthy so to do, knows how bitterly that was resented. He says it is "traditional, a survival from the past, and particularly from 1914 to 1918, that every British soldier is apt to feel that he is not a soldier at all unless he is given a rifle which is his and his alone . . . So it was a shock to many a man in the Home Guard when he discovered that until some unspecified date in the future he was to share his rifle with others."

This tradition of which Brophy speaks goes back a very long way. In Soldiers Three, Kipling showed Private Stanley Ortheris treating his rifle like a favourite child. And a large proportion of the first to enlist in the Local Defence Volunteers, as they were called to begin with, were men who had been in the Army. They had been longing for a chance to contribute to the war effort :

> At long last they were required to act and were given a job they could get their teeth into . . . Most of them calculated that their personal task would be sacrificial ; the utmost they could hope for was to fire a few shots from behind a hedge or a wall—perhaps, if they were lucky, to throw some petrol-bottle grenades and see a German tank or lorry catch fire—before they were blasted out of this life.

How well I remember those Molotov cocktail drills ! Before we had our horrible denim battle-dresses, before we had one rifle among five of us, we learned how to throw these missiles at approaching tanks, waiting until they were level with us, as we crouched by the roadside, and then smashing the bottles just in the right place ! Looking back, it seems funny, but we were dead serious about it. Few of us, Brophy says, "believed it possible that the Germans would not invade. Every night, whether it was their turn to patrol and watch the skies or to sleep at home, they had to face the question, 'Will the Nazis come before morning?' Such awareness is not to be lightly borne in the hours of solitude by men who have outgrown the irresponsibilities of youth."

This uneasy apprehension never overcame me. I was one of the minority who did not believe it possible that there should be an invasion so long as the British Navy remained unbeaten. Long, long before, in my boyhood, I think, I had been told the story of Von Moltke, the famous Prussian general of the war of 1870-71, being asked whether it was true that in the War Office at Berlin there were plans for invading Britain. He answered without a glint of a smile, "There

---

In Praise of the Home Guard

(See portraits in facing page)

are a number of such plans. They fill many pigeon-holes. But no one has ever produced a plan for getting the invasion forces out of Britain again !"

I KNEW in 1940 that this was still true. German forces might land—from the air if not from the sea ; but their communications would be cut instantly. They would be marooned in a hostile land. They might do some damage. They might cause panic here and there for a short while. But a full-scale invasion such as Brophy seems to have considered feasible I never for an instant believed in—so long as the Royal Navy held the seas.

Brophy suggests that the German General Staff were deceived by our appeal for volunteers from fifteen to sixty-five and for shotguns to be used by them. "The German generals must have suspected a colossal

Mr. JOHN BROPHY, novelist and broadcaster and member of the old L.D.V., whose book, in collaboration with artist Eric Kennington, is the subject of the present review. See also facing page.

bluff, a trap baited with too much cheese ; otherwise the invasion of Britain would surely have been undertaken forthwith, by slamming the troops into any and every sort of air- and sea-craft available." But we were not bluffing, we were just letting ourselves indulge in bureaucratic silliness.

NOR were the Germans humbugged by the error which substituted "fifteen" for "eighteen" as the minimum age of enlistment, or by the belief that we really meant to pot at them with sporting firearms as if they were rabbits. They were as well aware as was Von Moltke in the seventies of last century that, although they might succeed in establishing some sort of a force in Britain, they would never get it out of the country again —unless they could first defeat and dispose of the British Navy.

Answer to Friends' Forebodings

The value of the Home Guard was that it prevented nuisance raids by parachute troops, which might have done a great deal of damage. It formed the second line of defence behind a very thin front line. It gave us more confidence, it strengthened our resolve never to give in—and don't forget that in 1940 all the world, not only the French but the Americans, not only the friends of Hitler but our friends everywhere, believed that we should have to give in. The Home Guard was the answer we gave to those gloomy forebodings.

> By its continued existence and increased strength it enabled Britain not only to outlive the threat of German invasion, but to send great forces abroad, to Africa, Burma, the Middle East, Italy, France, and ultimately into Germany. It was an army which was never called upon to fight, yet helped to win one of the decisive battles of world history by being always ready to fight.

It does one good to look at the faces Kennington has drawn and to see what splendid types could be picked out almost haphazard from the ranks of the Home Guard. In their faces, kindly though resolute, intelligent as well as sternly self-disciplined, you can find the qualities that have made us what we are. There are townsmen and countrymen. Brophy says he noticed a good deal of difference between them. Town units had more ceremonial, more spit and polish, more bands playing, more of "the old-time rigidities of parade-ground drill." The officers established messes on "an intermittent dining-club-cum-smoking-concert basis." There was too much of the old Army atmosphere surrounding most of the Home Guard town units. Brophy preferred the country companies on that account.

IN both he says there was far too much of what the French call *paperasserie* (in our Army there is a less decorous name for it). Far too much "instructional paper—printed, cyclostyled or typewritten—was produced and circulated. There seemed to be a paragraph and sub-paragraph to cover every tiniest event which could possibly happen, not only to every man but to every buckle and bootlace. In consequence, the administration of Home Guard units tended to follow the placid, careful, and elaborate course of Civil Service routine, and many a man felt encouraged to take shelter behind an appropriate regulation rather than think and act for himself."

I saw this growing even before my age was detected and I was discharged (not "with ignominy," but without any particular politeness). It became a curse, as it has too long been the curse of all our Government Offices, and to some extent of our local administration also. It sapped some of the first fresh vitality out of the Home Guard, Brophy says. "But only some of it ; on the whole, the Home Guard suffered less from bureaucracy than either the full-time fighting services or Civil Defence." But the disease, he adds, is serious. He is terribly right.

In Burma Lord Louis Keeps Touch With His Men

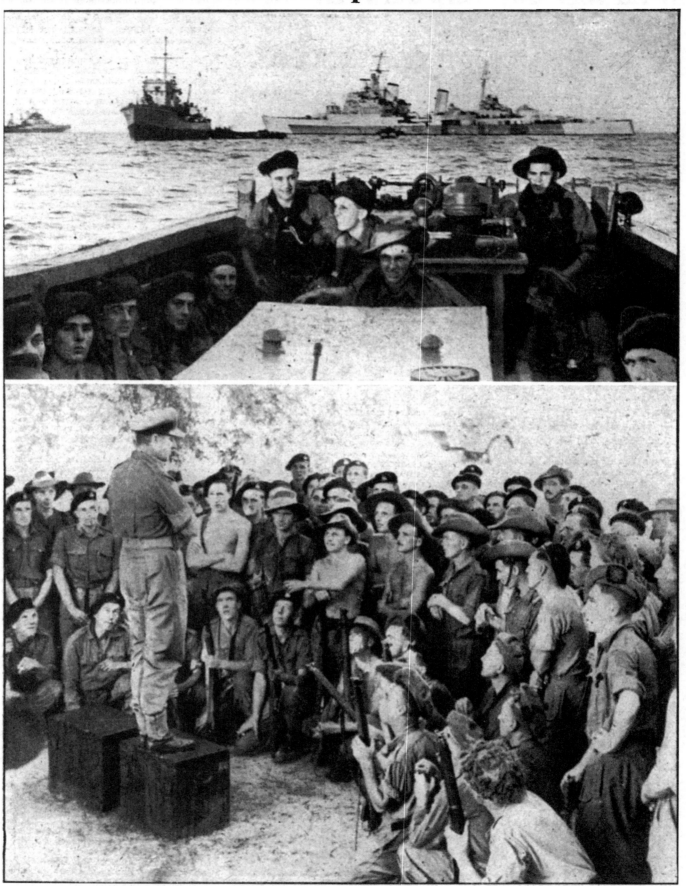

ROYAL MARINES OF THE BRITISH EAST INDIES FLEET (top) headed in landing craft from cruisers for Searle Point in their successful attack on Cheduba Island, south-west of Ramree (cleared by the 26th Indian Division on February 18, 1945) off the Arakan coast, on January 26.   Lord Louis Mountbatten, Supreme Allied Commander, South-East Asia (bottom), gives an informal talk to seasoned warriors in a forward area in Burma, on one of his frequent visits to the battle areas.

Photos, British Official

The Stilwell Road Artery to Hard-Pressed China

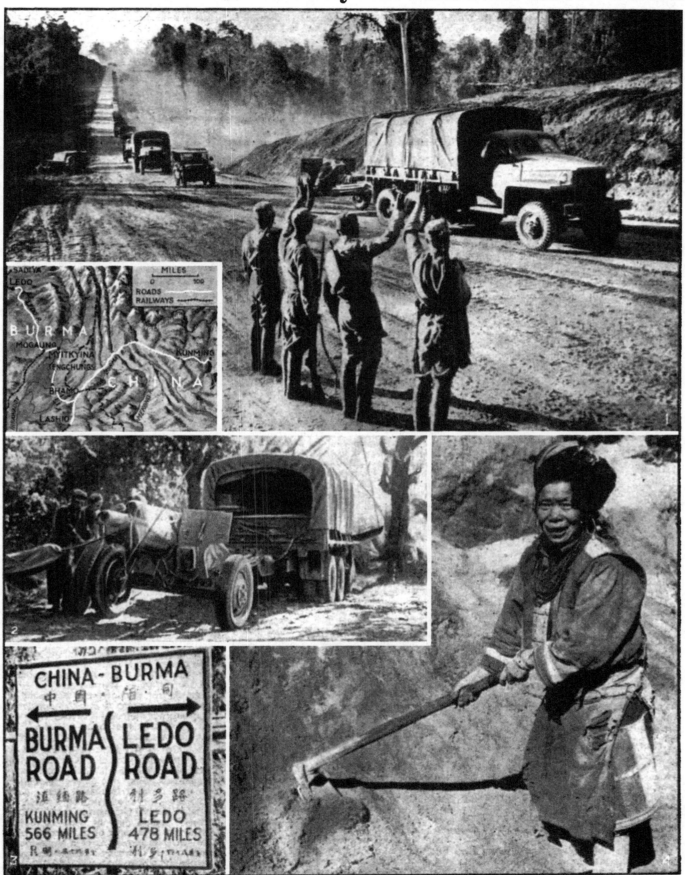

ENTERING MYITKYINA ON THE STILWELL ROAD (the 478-mile highway from Ledo in north-east Assam to Mongyu east of Bhamo on the Burma Road, opened on February 1, 1945, the first overland convoy since the Japanese invaded Burma, was cheered by Chinese troops (1). The road is named after the U.S. General Joseph W. Stilwell. Among precious cargo was the first gun to go through (2). A new signpost points the way (3). One of many Chinese women (4) who helped to build the highway. See also page 719. PAGE 725 *Photos, L.N.A., News Chronicle, New York Times Photos*

Behind Our Lines Hun Hordes Await Their Fate

By-passed on the grand scale months ago by the forward-pushing Allies on the Western Front, and now far in the rear, considerable pockets of resistance are hopelessly isolated from Hitler's main forces. The fantastic position of scores of thousands of Germans bottled-up in fortresses, with their backs to the Allied-controlled sea, is explained by J. V. GUERTER. See also p. 652.

STILL fighting hundreds of miles behind our front lines in France and Belgium are some 100,000 Germans who refused to surrender when we broke through last September. They are besieged in some six major pockets covering hundreds of square miles from Bordeaux to Dunkirk, but the idea that they are just lost units which at any moment may be starved into surrender has been shown to be false. The position is one of the most fantastic ever known in the history of war.

The Allied High Command has refused to be enticed into detaching major formations to carry out the assault of the pockets. It was undoubtedly the hope that it would do this and thus weaken the assault on Germany that led Hitler to order the pockets to " fight to the last man." On the other hand, the Germans in the pockets while strong in defence are well contained, and too weak to break out of them. There is no major fighting, but all along the perimeters of the pockets there is continuous patrolling and

CMDR. J. C. HIBBERD, D.S.C., R.C.N., of the Canadian destroyer Iroquois, greets Col. Gros, leader of the F.F.I. besieging the Nazi garrison in the La Rochelle area. Canadian warships are assisting British and Polish naval units on patrol in the Bay of Biscay.
Photo, Canadian Official

periodical shelling. On the seaward side—and all the pockets have their backs to the Atlantic wall—the Royal Navy takes good care that the E-boats, trawlers and possibly U-boats trapped in the ports are ineffective. Our planes have to avoid flying directly over the pockets as the Germans are well supplied with A.A. guns, but this is no particular handicap to their operations.

APART from Dunkirk, there are five major pockets, each of them round a port. The Morbihan sector includes the port of Lorient and the islands of Groix and Belle Ile, as well as the Quiberon peninsula. There are estimated to be some 25,000 Germans in this sector. As in the other sectors, they are a mixed crowd of submarine crews and other naval personnel, A.A. gunners, pioneers and Luftwaffe ground crews.

Round the Loire estuary is the sector the French call the Loire-Inférieure pocket. This is the largest pocket, containing perhaps 35,000 Germans. It varies in depth up to 15 miles and has a total length of over 50 miles on both sides of the Loire estuary.

The territory includes two islands and has the advantage of being protected in the north by marshes.

Farther south is the La Rochelle sector. The sea approach is protected by two small islands which have been fortified. The town itself in the centre has been fortified, and there is an airfield. The Gironde estuary is closed by the Royan and Pointe de Grave sectors. This makes Le Verdon and Bordeaux useless.

Nazis Prepared for the Worst

In spite of boasts about the impregnability of the Atlantic Wall, it is evident that plans had been prepared by Rundstedt for the defence of these pockets if disaster overtook the armies. The general plan of the defences is the same in each sector. In the centre is a highly fortified redoubt, making use of the concrete pens built for E-boats and U-boats, and the general fortifications of the Atlantic Wall. There are also aerodromes at St. Nazaire, La Rochelle and Lorient. Other aerodromes can be brought under shell-fire by the besieging troops.

ROUND this inner fortress is a " zone of occupation," varying in depth. It serves the purpose of keeping the inner fortress out of range of all but the heaviest artillery, and also of producing a certain amount of fresh food to supplement the rations the Germans stored. At the end of last year (1944) it was estimated that there were up to 175,000 French civilians trapped in these " zones of occupation." Since then there have been a number of truces for evacuating civilians, as they were-suffering badly; 13,000 were got out of St. Nazaire pocket on a single day in January (see illus. page 618). Nevertheless, there still remain many thousands under the German heel. Evacuations of these continue from time to time.

In this zone the Germans have mounted artillery. Some of it is very heavy, and naval guns have thrown shells into French towns 15 miles away. But generally the Germans conserve their ammunition unless there is movement in the no man's land which is separated from the zone of occupation by trenches and similar earthworks forming the perimeter. They are nervous of movement here, and immediately open up.

ON the other side of no man's land the besiegers, largely F.F.I., keep watch. They have not the necessary tanks, heavy guns and other assault weapons necessary to wipe out the pockets. They have to be content with ensuring that the Germans do not make sorties, which they have attempted on a number of occasions, chiefly with the object of looting neighbouring villages for food, and so on. These F.F.I. have suffered considerably during the winter, for they have had to fight with a minimum of weapons, and on occasions there has been a shortage of rations. Earlier, an appeal was made to the French public for clothing for the soldiers. The French are becomingly increasingly bitter about these pockets, especially since they have seen the insolence of the Germans during the truces—one officer was cool enough to ask for new gramophone records to be obtained for him as his were nearly worn out ; and another wanted to have a telephone line kept open permanently to the nearest French town ! The French would like to see the pockets assaulted and wiped out, but they realize this would be a diversion that would lengthen the war ; and so they accept the position. Recently a newspaper urged

FROM LORIENT IN BRITTANY to near Bordeaux, on an almost unbroken 200-miles stretch of France's western seaboard, Hun pockets of resistance hold out, providing one of the strangest situations of the war, as described in this page.

the French workers to make for the F.F.I. the weapons it needed to attack the pockets.

Last October there were signs that the Germans were getting ready to surrender. Then a number of S.S. men were dropped by parachute on the pockets. They dealt with the " weaklings " and greatly improved morale. Hitler has " pampered " these pockets, arranging parachute mail services and so on. Supplies are periodically dropped on the aerodromes by planes which " run the gauntlet," probably coming in from the sea. If any attempt to make a landing, it must be a dangerous business.

Return as Heroes—Perhaps !

The Germans are not uncomfortable, and apparently are well supplied with food. They are reported to distil their own spirits, even. Boredom must be the chief danger to their morale, but apparently the line taken in propaganda now is that if they hold out they will be the last German troops to surrender and will go home heroes ! The line that they only had to wait a few weeks for Rundstedt's tanks to break through and relieve them is now, of course, worked out. In the case of the Dunkirk pocket, there was a carefully arranged plan for breaking out to meet the onrushing German troops. Unfortunately for the Germans the Ardennes salient never became a break-through, and the spearheads never approached the positions where they should have " met " the sortie from Dunkirk.

As far as it was intended to reduce the Allied potential against Germany, the pocket plan has failed. We do not need the German-held ports. No units of importance have been diverted to assault them. For all the effect they are having on the war, the estimated 100,000 Germans in the " Atlantic pockets " might just as well be behind barbed wire in prisoner of war camps. And there—in spite of visions of a " glorious " march back to Germany after the collapse—is probably where they will end the war. The French will be glad to continue to watch them for as long as may be necessary after the " armistice." It is likely to be long enough to deflate the Germans considerably.

Cassino of Bitter Fame to Rise in Part Again

SEVENTY MILES SOUTH-EAST OF ROME, scene of terrific fighting in 1944, Cassino town, finally captured by the 5th Army on May 18, is being partly restored. Public Works officials discuss the plans (1). Against the background of the shattered Monastery atop the hill, Italian women, baskets on head (2), help to rebuild Cassino's lower part : new buildings will arise where are rubble and the stumps of blasted trees (3). The town's upper part will remain in its wrecked condition as a memorial. See pp. 653, 655, Vol. 7.   PAGE 727   *Photos, Planet News*

De Gaulle Attends Opening of French Assembly

FRANCE'S PROVISIONAL PARLIAMENT—THE " ASSEMBLÉE CONSULTATIVE "—meets in the famous Palais du Luxembourg in Paris (1),
until 1940 the home of the French Senate. The President, M. Felix Gouin, welcomed the head of the State, General de Gaulle (2), at the opening
session on February 7, 1945, and later addressed the members from the rostrum (3). From the floor of the House the General, seated beside
M. Pleven, Finance Minister (4) followed the Budget debate.

Photos, French Ministry of Information

I WAS THERE!

How We Surged Into the Outskirts of Cologne

Three divisions of the U.S. 1st Army, striking from north, west and south, on March 5, 1945, pierced the outer defence belt of Cologne, proud city of Prussia. "For me," writes Stanley Baron, News Chronicle war reporter whose story of the entry is given here, "there has never been a more exciting day in my six months in Germany!"

WE are in it! We are there, and what a great and glorious day! The first blocks of houses in this city we have talked of, dreamed of, and debated as a military proposition ever since we crossed the German border six months ago are ours. They fell to the tank men and attached infantry of Gen. Maurice Rose's 3rd Armoured Division.

I followed them in, 20 minutes after the Engineers, racing in a half-track ahead of us, had removed the last steel beam of the tank barrier at the railway bridge at Bickendorf, in the north-west corner of the city. As I begin to write this message the fighting has shifted ahead to within three miles of the cathedral. From three thousand yards or so away to the right comes the crash of mortar and artillery fire as the infantrymen of the 104th (Timber Wolf) Division begin thrusting in from the west at Junkersdorf.

There has been a great race between the two outfits, and the tank men have won by a short head. The first tank crunched past the city boundary sign at 7.10 a.m., two hours and 13 minutes before the infantry flashed back the news that they were there, too. There is a hole in the ground where the sign stood. Gen. Rose himself drove past it, dashing alongside the tank column as the spearhead fought its way to the first house-rows of the built-up city fringe.

A moment later the Engineers began digging it out, and now that yellow sign with the simple plain black name "Köln" is being carried in triumph as a divisional emblem. For me there has never been a more exciting day in my six months in Germany. It began with an attempt to get in with the infantry. An open space 800 yards wide, between Weiden and Junkersdorf,

was swept with 88-mm. gunfire, and mortar shells from a row of houses and the Cologne Sports Palace opposite topped that.

Then began the race to get round to the north-west, through a series of burned and powdered villages, some of them still on fire and sending huge, billowing streamers of smoke across the plain to merge with the dove-grey puffs from our own artillery firing heavily into the city. Events and impressions flit so quickly in this battle that it is difficult to sort them out. I remember passing through an avenue of plane trees, painted orange right down the twig-tips by the brick-dust blasted out of a smouldering factory.

Then we came out to the riverside plain and saw the city full and clear for the first time. The two great towers of the cathedral dominated the skyline. There are rumours that the building is not seriously damaged. So round to the advance command post of the Third Armoured Division.

ONE glance at a 100-yard-long column of shambling prisoners marching north-ward through the village as we humped and bumped over the shell-hillocked road to the south-east was enough to show how well the battle was going. Some of them said the Hohenzollern bridge spanning the Rhine with road and rail tracks 1,395 ft. long was believed to be down in the water.

The report at the Command Post was terse. "Col. Leander Doan's task force got away at 4 a.m. They have advanced 5,000 yards and they are going like hell. Resistance is light. You might catch them up at Bockel-muend." At a corner we asked the question we have waited to speak so long: "Which way to Cologne?" "Straight ahead," the military policeman answered, "straight on."

R.A.F. DISPATCH-RIDER checks up on his map on the outskirts of Cologne. The sign-post in German indicates the boundary of the city, which fell on March 6, 1945.
Photo, British Official

No houses now, but plenty of people—trudging out from the city still heading west. Groups of them hauling all their belongings on handcarts. Ones and twos with babies in arms and young children at their side. Old men and women dragging their feet under the weight of their bundles. Now the first roadside houses and now the hush, the strange, deadly hush between spasms of racking noise that falls on a dying city.

We looked for the bomb damage, but this outskirt has been lucky. The tram-track was beside us now. Broken-up cars lay along it. Others had been pushed down on the railway bridge.

We came up with the cars while the Engineers were still thrusting the last of them out of the way. I talked to Pte. (First Class) Edward Fleming, born at St. John's, Newfoundland. "They jammed the underside of the bridge with them and laid steel beams across between the windows, with cross-beams sticking up from a hole in the road. We cleared them out in 40 minutes," he said.

EIGHTY-FIVE PER CENT OF GERMANY'S THIRD LARGEST CITY, Cologne, was wrecked by Allied bombing and shell-fire : men of a U.S. patrol (above) found the going hard across the rubble in a main suburb. Lancaster and Halifax squadrons of the R.A.A.F. magnificently contributed to the heavy pounding of the city and its approaches in preparation for the final assault. After its fall some 150,000 civilians were found in hiding : they had gone underground during the bombardment. See also illus. pages 706 and 713.

Photo, British Official

MARINE-LADEN AMTRACS RUSH THE BEACHES AT IWOJIMA. These amphibious tracked vehicles of the U.S. Fifth Fleet spearheaded the landing operations (top) 675 miles south of Tokyo, on Feb. 19, 1945, as described in the story below. Men of the invading units, which totalled 30,000, moved up from the beach (bottom) against desperate Japanese resistance. See also pages 678-679.
Photos, New York Times Photos, Associated Press

Assault on Iwojima—Remote Pacific Stronghold

Fearful battles raged for this five-miles-by-two island of the Volcano Group, stiff with Japanese defenders. Writing on Feb. 19, 1945, B.U.P. correspondent William Tyree tells of the landing by U.S. Marines. And Reuters reporter Barbara Finch, flying in the first Allied hospital plane to put down on that now historic ground, records her experiences.

WHEN I flew over it today, Iwojima looked like a pork chop sizzling in a frying pan. The island was smoking from end to end. Battleships, cruisers, destroyers and bombers poured shells and bombs into the defences. From a height of 1,000 feet I could see the Marines advancing inland from the south-eastern beach. Some were far inland, nearing the airstrip which is one of the first objectives. It looked as if they had had a tough fight.

The Japanese are fighting desperately from underground defences. I listened-in as the Marines called for fire support from the fleet. Seconds later; bursts of orange flame sprang from the muzzles of the Navy guns and huge columns of smoke rose from the island. It was systematic destruction, and I could see many formidable pillboxes along the beach which had already been put out of action. The battleships New York, Texas, Nevada, Arkansas, Idaho, and Tennessee joined in the shelling.

The Marines stormed ashore after one of the heaviest naval bombardments of the Pacific war. Iwojima was known for this operation as "hot rock." Twice as our plane swung over the Mount Suribachi crater, at the southern end of the island, the Japanese opened up with anti-aircraft fire.

As our plane approached the island I could see hundreds of small craft moving to the beach, releasing thousands of rockets. A wave of Marines followed in less than forty-five minutes. There was not a single Japanese plane in the sky. By the middle of the afternoon none of our surface forces had been disturbed by any enemy counter-action. The invasion armada was spread over scores of miles and the water seemed to be alive with forces heading for the shore.

I WAS carried over Iwojima by a Navy plane called "The Lemon." It lived up to its name, and three hours after we started it sprang a petrol leak and we had to return to base. We took off again in a bomber and arrived over the target at 10 a.m., just as the fight began to get rough. Already 30,000 U.S. Marines have stormed ashore, from an armada of 800 ships. They have seized a beach-head on the south-east coast.

Flying across hundreds of miles of the Pacific in the first Allied hospital plane to put down on this island, Barbara Finch, Reuters reporter, was the first woman to land on shell-battered Iwojima. In her dispatch she said :

Our plane was strictly a mercy one. It contained doctors and medical supplies, 2,000 lb. of mail to "Leathernecks" who have been fighting the Pacific war's grimmest battle for the past eleven days, tents and shovels for the building of a temporary clearing hospital for the wounded, later to be evacuated by air. As the plane dipped to land, my first glimpse of Iwojima was idealistic—a pastel-coloured Japanese print dominated by the conventional volcano.

But then Japanese guns on high ground beyond Motoyama airfield No. 3 got our range. It was a hot reception, and we were literally shot on to the airstrip. After most of the cargo was dumped on the field, I crawled, tottering slightly under the weight of a helmet, a trench-knife, a canteen, and a web belt, from the plane.

"How in hell did you get there ?" asked the first Marine I saw. He was disguised by a black stubble of beard, as are most of the other men who have been living on Iwojima since the island's D-Day. Wounded were put on a plane and soon we took off again, out over an armada of ships, up through the frosty air, until Iwojima—island of blood, courage, death—was just a memory.

The Lifeboat Came Down from the Skies

A twenty-three-ft.-six-in. lifeboat supported by five parachutes is dropped from an aircraft flying at 1,500 ft. to rescue ditched airmen adrift in a small rubber dinghy—one of the almost daily miracles wrought by the Air-Sea Rescue Service of Coastal Command. Patricia Ward, Evening Standard reporter, tells the story of a typical "drop."

MULTIPLE - PARACHUTE LIFEBOAT has been dropped by a Warwick aircraft of Coastal Command near to airmen adrift in a dinghy. An Air-Sea Rescue launch stands by. Story in this page. *Photo, P.N.A.*

FROM the pilot's cockpit of the aircraft, the R.A.F. rubber dinghy 1,500 ft. below looked at first sight like a black-backed gull bobbing up and down on the waves. The pilot circled, and came down to 700 ft. "Going to take a closer look," he told me over the inter-com. When next we flew over the dinghy I could see the expressions on the faces of its five occupants clearly as they stood up to wave their flying-helmets and cheer and cheer again.

I was sitting beside the pilot of a twin-engined Warwick beneath the long belly of which was slung a 23-ft.-six-in. lifeboat, which in a minute would be launched by parachute to the men below. In this case the dinghy was only five miles from the coast and the airmen drifting in it had not been "ditched" for long, but the pilot and crew of the Warwick, who belong to the Air-Sea Rescue Service of Coastal Command, have more often than not during the last six months launched lifeboats to rescue men who have been drifting for as long as four or five days, storm-tossed and helpless in their rubber dinghy many miles away from the coast of Britain.

We circled again, and this time as we approached the dinghy the pilot, Flying Officer W. Thomson, pressed a button in the instrument panel and released two smoke-floats to point the direction of the wind. The navigator, spread-eagled over the glass panel in the nose of the aircraft, picked up the switch-cord controlling the release of the lifeboat, and as we circled to come in down the narrow lane between the smoke-floats his voice came over the inter-com., "Dead on them now, boss—steady, steady, right"—he pressed the release button—"Boat away!"

I felt the aircraft lift slightly as the boat went away : we banked steeply to watch it going down on its five parachutes, looking from that height like a pencil attached to a bunch of toy balloons. We saw it settle on the water a hundred yards from the dinghy ; next time we flew over them the airmen were already in the lifeboat and hauling their rubber dinghy over the side.

I asked the pilot how they had managed to transfer themselves so quickly. " There are two rockets, carrying life-lines, in the bow of the lifeboat which fire automatically as soon as it hits the water : they catch hold of the lines to haul themselves alongside," he explained. " If this were a real 'show' we would keep on circling over them until we were relieved by another aircraft, or saw them picked up by a fast motor-launch, sent out by us or by the Navy."

Ten minutes later our Warwick landed at the East Coast air-sea rescue base, from which we had started on this demonstration flight, and with Flying Officer Thomson and his crew I went to the maintenance sheds on the airfield, where the spare lifeboats are kept, to get a closer view of the type we had launched, known as the Mark IA. Pilot Officer B. Plumbridge, of Dulwich, the navigator who had launched it, showed me the ingenious gadgets.

"As the boat leaves the aircraft an automatic fitting inflates two buoyancy chambers fore and aft. Here and here and here"—he pointed to a number of wooden chests fitted down the sides—"are stowed special exposure suits, medical supplies, ever-hot water bags, food, cigarettes, and water-purifying units. There's enough of everything to look after seven men.

"The boat is fitted with two outboard engines, and it carries a wireless ; its range and cruising speed is 100 miles at 6 knots. It's a grand job, and a great improvement on the smaller type of boat we used to use. And, of course, it's the difference between life and death from exposure to the boys it goes down to."

OUR DIARY OF THE WAR

FEBRUARY 28, Wednesday *2,006th day*
Western Front.—U.S. 1st Army crossed River Erth at Modrath, 6½ miles from Cologne.
Air.—Allied heavy bombers attacked rail centres in Ruhr and Rhineland.
Russian Front.—Neu Stettin and Prechlau in Pomerania captured by Russians.
Balkans.—Allied troops landed on island of Piscopi, in Dodecanese.

MARCH 1, Thursday *2,007th day*
Western Front.—München-Gladbach captured by U.S. 9th Army. Advance units of 3rd Army entered Trier.
Air.—U.S. bombers heavily attacked rail centres in southern Germany. R.A.F. bombers attacked Mannheim and oil plant near Dortmund.
Philippines.—American infantry invaded island of Palawan, S.W. of Manila.
Far East.—U.S. carrier-aircraft bombed Ryukyu Islands. At night Okinodaito, island 450 miles S. of Japan, was bombarded by U.S. warships.

MARCH 2, Friday *2,008th day*
Western Front.—U.S. 9th Army troops reached Rhine at Neuss, captured Krefeld and occupied Venlo and Roermond on the Maas. Welsh troops cleared Weeze and Kervenheim.
Air.—R.A.F. twice bombed Cologne by day. U.S. bombers attacked oil plants at Magdeburg and Bohlen and railway yards at Chemnitz and Dresden.
Far East.—Singapore again bombed by Super-Fortresses from India.
Philippines.—U.S. troops seized Lubang Island, between Luzon and Mindoro.

MARCH 3, Saturday *2,009th day*
Western Front.—Units of U.S. 9th Army and Canadian 1st Army linked up between Maas and Rhine. The U.S. 3rd Army crossed River Kyll.
Air.—Big day attack by U.S. bombers on oil plants, arms factories and railway yards in central and eastern Germany. Night attacks by R.A.F. on Dortmund-Ems Canal and oil plant near Dortmund.
Burma.—Meiktila, S. of Mandalay, finally cleared of the enemy.
Japan.—Very large force of Super-Fortresses attacked Tokyo area.
Home Front.—German piloted aircraft attacked England, for first time since June, 1944.

MARCH 4, Sunday *2,010th day*
Western Front.—Armour of U.S. 1st Army reached Rhine, between Cologne and Düsseldorf.
Air.—Allied bombers attacked railway yards and ordnance depots in S.W. Germany and the Ruhr.
Russian Front.—Soviet troops reached Baltic at two places, Zhukov's near Kolberg and Rokossovsky's beyond Köslin.

MARCH 5, Monday *2,011th day*
Western Front.—U.S. 1st Army troops broke into suburbs of Cologne.
Air.—Marshalling yards at Chemnitz and oil plants at Harburg bombed by Fortresses and Liberators. R.A.F. attacked benzol plant at Gelsenkirchen by day and Chemnitz at night.
Russian Front.—Stargard, Naugard and Polzin, in direction of Stettin, captured by Zhukov's troops.

MARCH 6, Tuesday *2,012th day*
Western Front.—Cologne captured by U.S. 1st Army. The 3rd Army made swift advance N.E. of Bitburg towards Rhine.
Air.—At night R.A.F. bombers attacked Wesel on the Rhine and also Sassnitz, on Baltic island of Rügen.
Russian Front.—Zhukov captured Belgard and Cammin, N.E. and N. of

Stettin. Rokossovsky completed capture of encircled garrison of Grudziadz.

MARCH 7, Wednesday *2,013th day*
Western Front.—Troops of U.S. 1st Army crossed the Rhine at Remagen, S. of Bonn. 3rd Army reached Rhine N.W. of Coblenz.
Air.—Oil refineries and railway yards in Ruhr bombed by U.S. aircraft. At night R.A.F. made heavy attack on Dessau.
Russian Front.—Rokossovsky captured Gnied and Starogard on approaches to Danzig. Zhukov took Gollnow, Stepenitz and Massow, near Stettin.
Burma.—Chinese troops captured Lashio, terminus of Burma Road.

MARCH 8, Thursday *2,014th day*
Western Front.—British troops fought their way into Xanten.
Air.—U.S. bombers again attacked oil plants and railway yards in the Ruhr. At night R.A.F. bombed Kassel and U-boat yards at Hamburg.
Russian Front.—Soviet troops captured Bütow and Koscierzyna on approaches to Danzig.
Burma.—Tanks of 19th Indian Division entered Mandalay.

MARCH 9, Friday *2,015th day*
Western Front.—U.S. 1st and 3rd Armies linked up. The 3rd Army captured

Mayen and Andernach. German commandos raided Granville on Normandy coast.
Air.—U.S. bombers made heavy attacks on Kassel and Frankfurt-on-Main.
Russian Front.—Soviet troops captured Stolp, on Danzig-Stettin road.
Japan.—Night attack on Tokyo by Super-Fortresses from Marianas.
Far East.—Japanese went over to offensive against French in Indo-China.

MARCH 10, Saturday *2,016th day*
Western Front.—Organized enemy resistance ended on Canadian Army front opposite Wesel. Allies on Rhine from Nijmegen to Coblenz.
Russian Front.—In Hungary, German counter-attacks made some progress near Lake Balaton.

MARCH 11, Sunday *2,017th day*
Air.—Over 1,000 R.A.F. bombers dropped 4,500 tons of bombs on Essen. Over 1,000 U.S. bombers attacked U-boat yards and oil refineries at Hamburg, Kiel and Bremen.
Philippines.—Announced that U.S. troops had landed on Mindanao.
Far East.—Singapore again bombed by Super-Fortresses from India.
Japan.—Super-Fortresses from the Marianas attacked city of Nagoya.

MARCH 12, Monday *2,018th day*
Western Front.—Remagen bridgehead now 10 miles wide and 4 deep. Hönningen cleared of the enemy.
Air.—Over 4,900 tons of bombs dropped on Dortmund by R.A.F. in heaviest attack of the war. U.S. bombers attacked Swinemunde in the Baltic.
Russian Front.—Küstrin, on E. bank of Oder opposite Berlin, fell to Zhukov's troops. Rokossovsky captured Tczew, Neustadt and Puck, reaching Danzig Bay N. of Gdynia.

MARCH 13, Tuesday *2,019th day*
Air.—R.A.F. bombers attacked Barmen and other communications centres in the Ruhr by day and night.
Russian Front.—Soviet troops closing in on Danzig captured Reimerswalde, Langenau, Bohlschau and Gnesdau.
Burma.—14th Army troops captured Maymyo, N.E. of Mandalay.
Japan.—Industrial city of Osaka bombed by Super-Fortresses.

★━━━━━━ *Flash-backs* ━━━━━━★

1941
March 4. *British naval raid on Lofoten Islands off Norway.*
March 11. *Lease-Lend Bill became law in the United States.*
March 13. *First of two successive night-bombing attacks on Glasgow and Clydebank.*

1942
February 28. *Combined Operations raid on Bruneval, Normandy.*
March 1. *Japanese landed at three points in Java, East Indies.*

March 8. *Large-scale Japanese landings in New Guinea.*

1943
March 3. *Rzhev, W. of Moscow, stormed by Red Army troops.*
March 4. *Battle of Bismarck Sea ended ; Japanese convoy sunk.*

1944
February 29. *U.S. troops landed at Los Negros, Admiralty Islands.*
March 10. *Red Army in Ukraine broke through on 110-mile front.*

THE WAR IN THE AIR

by Capt. Norman Macmillan, M.C., A.F.C.

IN what the Germans call Mitteleuropa, the tactical and strategic pounding of targets has risen to new records in consort with the advance of the armies in the West to the left bank of the Rhine, the sweep of Rokossovsky's army in the Danzig region, and of Zhukov's army to the coast of Pomerania. These Russian moves were to be expected, because the wild country on the frontier of Pomerania and the Polish corridor, with steep hills and lakes and few roads, is bad for military operations; thus we see that the Red Armies have by-passed this difficult country and struck northwards to the east and west of it after having cut it off to the south.

LARGE bodies of the enemy have been forced across the Rhine or pinned against its left bank, and in the east have been cut off and surrounded within areas of considerable size at Koenigsberg, Danzig, and in eastern Pomerania. The supply of their cut-off forces with war materials is an almost insurmountable problem for the enemy, faced as he is with superior air power that cuts his communications by land, sea and air.

In the East, the Red Air Force bombed Koenigsberg and Stettin in the night of March 5, in addition to their usual tactical air support for the armies in the field. In the same night R.A.F. Bomber Command, using Halifaxes and Lancasters, bombed Chemnitz, a key railway centre for German communications with their eastern front. Chemnitz had been bombed a few hours before by the U.S.A. 8th Air Force.

BY March 7 the Red Army under Zhukov was on the eastern shore of the Stettinerhaff, the lagoon-like basin into which the Oder flows, and which forms the connexion between the port of Stettin and the Baltic. With this Russian advance the ports of Sassnitz and Stralsund assumed greater importance for the Germans' sea supply routes linking Germany with the beleaguered forces in Pomerania, the Polish corridor and

East Prussia; and in the night of March 6 Bomber Command Lancasters bombed Rügen, the island on which Sassnitz stands and to which the railway runs through Stralsund (see map in page 716). These air blows by British and American heavy bombers are evidence of the close liaison between the three principal Allied armies in their combined use of strategic bombing.

TACTICAL bombing is generally carried out by air forces working in close contact with the armies in the field, and the tactical air forces usually operate with their national armies. But at any time the heavies of Bomber Command and the U.S.A. 8th A.F. can be switched to provide an increased weight of bombing upon a tactical target. Coblenz and Wesel received special attention from Bomber Command; at Wesel Mosquitoes flying in daylight with fighter escort attacked German troops, armour and transport. Tactical air forces attacked the Rhine bridges to prevent the exodus of the German army from the area west of the Rhine. In the northern sector of the fighting front only two bridges remained, both at Wesel, and both were damaged by air attacks made on March 5.

CONCENTRATED Bomb-Damage a Clue to Future Design of Cities?

Cologne, captured by General Hodges' American 1st Army, was found to be a city shattered from previous bombing. But the bombing was concentrated, and it was the industrial and railway centres of the city that had been blasted and burnt out. The outer residential areas were not severely damaged. Does this give a clue to the design of future cities, when today's ruins will have been rebuilt to house peoples who have known what air warfare means, and who will want to have whatever protection architects can provide against the risk of a recurrence of these frightful sufferings? The ruins of Cologne really date from June 28, 1943, when Bomber Command's first modern-method attack of 1,700 tons was made. So much has been learned about air assaults on cities since —including those by robot weapons—as to suggest that the concentration of great multitudes into enormous urban areas must invite disaster should there be war again.

In the night of March 7, Berlin received its 16th consecutive air attack by Mosquitoes of the Light Night Striking Force of Bomber Command. The strength of these attacks has not been disclosed, but it is usual for the Mosquito force to operate in units of from 60 to 100 or more aircraft, and each aircraft is capable of carrying one 4,000-lb. bomb or a lesser weight composed of smaller H.E. or incendiary bombs.

ONE feature of the air war in the West worth notice is the regularity of operation of the U.S.A. 8th A.F. and Bomber Command bombers during the period in February and early March, when the Tactical Air Forces based on the Continent were frequently grounded by bad weather. Aircraft are usually grounded by inability to land safely, due to reduced visibility on the ground. Apparently the weather in the United Kingdom has been on the whole better, while the use of instruments for bombing has enabled the U.K. based aircraft to operate over Continental targets despite the conditions that have grounded the T.A.F. This is a case where concentration of all aircraft into the battle area—assuming that to have been possible—would not have given the best results.

Some facts were given by Sir Archibald Sinclair, Secretary of State for Air, when

ROCKETS TO ASSIST TAKE-OFF give carrier-borne planes greater speed and weight-carrying capacity; mounted on each side of the fuselage, their action lasts four seconds. Capt. C. L. Keighley-Peach, D.S.O., R.N., is here seen entering a rocket-boosted Seafire fighter of the Fleet Air Arm. *Photo, Keystone*

introducing the Air Estimates in the House of Commons on March 6, 1945. In 1942 Bomber Command lost 4·1 per cent of aircraft dispatched; 3·7 per cent in 1943; 1·7 per cent in 1944, and 1·1 per cent in the first two months of 1945. From April 1 to Sept. 30, 1944, Bomber Command alone suffered more than 10,000 casualties in killed, missing and wounded. During the fifth year of the war, from Sept. 1943 to August 1944, Bomber Command dropped a greater weight of bombs on Germany than the total of the four previous years. In the week ending Feb. 12, 1945, 16,000 tons of bombs were dropped by Allied air forces; 23,000 tons the next week; 41,000 tons the next, and in the following week at least 32,000 tons.

LUFTWAFFE Piloted Attacks Against Britain Resumed

At one time in the war against Japan three divisions were maintained solely by air transport. The greater part of the troops that took Meiktila, Burma, 75 miles south of Mandalay, on March 3 were carried there and all are being nourished there by aircraft of Transport Command.

It has been disclosed that a V2 rocket can be launched from any space of ground which is hard or artificially hardened measuring 23 ft. by 23 ft. On Saturday night, March 3, a force of about 70 German fighter bombers and Heinkel 188s raided Southern and Northern England. This was the first Luftwaffe piloted attack against Britain since June 13, 1944. Six and probably eight of the raiders were shot down. A smaller number of enemy aircraft made a second attack on the following night.

THE name of the current jet-propelled R.A.F. fighter has been disclosed as the Meteor. No details have yet been given, except that it is faster than the flying bomb. This statement was made in the House of Commons. The speed of the flying bomb is about 360 m.p.h. The Mediterranean Allied Tactical Air Force in Italy kept the Brenner Pass railway line into Italy blocked during every day in February.

EIGHT ROCKET PROJECTILES with 60-lb. heads, four ·303 machine-guns in the nose and four 22-mm. cannon just below are the weapons with which R.A.F. Mosquito fighter-bombers of Coastal Command attack enemy shipping. *Photo, Charles E. Brown*

R.A.F. Mosquitoes Range the Rhine with Films

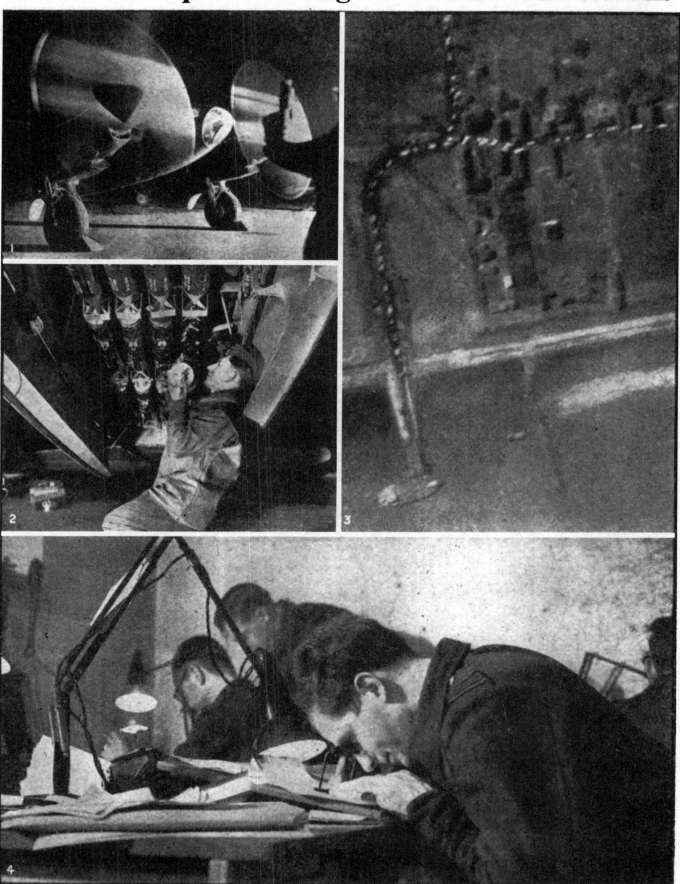

READY FOR A FLASHLIGHT RAID ON GERMANY, a Mosquito's engines are warmed up (1) for a night flight to photograph enemy troop movements. The armourer loads up flash-bombs (2) to illuminate the targets. A snap of the ferry at Hitdorf, near Cologne, showed many vehicles waiting to embark eastwards in retreat across the Rhine (3). As soon as possible after the high-speed films are developed, R.A.F. photographic interpreters examine the results of the reconnaissance (4). See also illus. page 797, Vol. 7.   PAGE 733   *Photos, British Official*

Our Roving Camera Goes to Buckingham Palace

IN THE GRAND HALL at Buckingham Palace, where H.M. the King recently decorated members of the Services, the impressive ceremony was for the first time photographed for the Press. The King is seen (right) decorating Flight-Sergeant Edward Durrans, R.A.F Bomber Command, with the Conspicuous Gallantry Medal.

AT BRIGHTON, concrete anti-invasion defences (below) erected in 1940 are being removed from one of the beach ramps overlooking the Lower Promenade. It was officially announced on March 8, 1945, that the famous undercliff walk and foreshore from Black Rock to Saltdean would be opened to the public almost immediately, but other beaches would remain closed.

ROYAL MARINES, with faces blackened, prepare for jungle warfare in the English countryside where, at the Eastern Warfare School, they learn to negotiate Japanese-style ambushes and booby-traps and become proficient in hand-to-hand fighting.

BRICKS-AND-MORTAR SENTINEL, it stands alone on a blitzed site in London, at the corner of Boswell Street and Theobald's Road, W.C.2. A catering establishment, it miraculously survived widespread devastation by the Luftwaffe during the raids of May 1941. The building suffered only superficial damage and now is spick-and-span.

Photos, British Official, Topical Press, Fox

THE doubts and criticisms in certain quarters, following so soon after the universal enthusiasm with which the first news of the Crimea Conference was acclaimed, reminded me once again of Marshal Foch's dictum to the effect that no news is ever as good, or as bad, as it first appears. I have often found this a fairly useful corrective to premature optimism or undue pessimism, on my own part or that of others, and I remember Mr. Duff Cooper, when he was Minister of Information, quoting the phrase in a broadcast designed to reassure us about the Battle of France in 1940. Nevertheless, its truth has been disproved on at least two occasions during this war—disproved at each end, so to speak. For even as Duff Cooper was speaking, the news from France, bad as it seemed, was in reality far more black than either he or the rest of us dared to imagine at the time. Again, only two months later, when men in Hurricanes and Spitfires high above the yellow fields of Kent were shooting down " bandits " in the ratio of four to one, we knew the news was good, but we did not then know how good. It was only later we began to realize we had been witnesses of an upward turning-point in the world's history.

BEFORE Dr. Arnold revolutionized the English Public schools they were run on the principle, " Always believe the worst of boys, never trust them an inch, give them no credit for decent feelings." Then came the experiment of putting boys on their honour and bringing out their good qualities by showing that these were believed in. I hope we are not going backwards in this matter. One is made to feel uneasy about it by the comment of a Royal Horticultural Society official on the suggestion that we might have our country roads lined with fruit trees, as they are in some parts of the Continent and as they are now being planted in County Wexford, Southern Ireland. The comment was " not practicable in England," because children could not be counted on to leave the fruit alone. This is a return to the old doctrine of original sin and the view that " man is vile." I don't believe this any more than Dr. Arnold did.

NO one in the House of Lords had a good word to say for statues as war memorials when the subject of how best to commemorate local efforts was discussed. The most sensible suggestion thrown out was that we should look well after those who came back and the dependents of those who didn't. Lord Chatfield's idea of a great garden space as a national memorial in London, with a " shrine " in it for memorial services, was a happy one and might be carried out locally also. Anyway, " No statues ! " seemed to be the general feeling. The prevalence of life-size effigies of public men and national heroes in this country, which has a climate singularly unsuited to such display, is one of the many misfortunes planted on us by the classical tradition, harking back to the Greeks and the Romans. While boys at Public Schools and the older universities are condemned to spend most of their time over the authors who were famous in Athens and Rome between two and three thousand years ago, we have to endure the sight of stone or bronze figures, mostly grotesque, just because Romans and Athenians had them scattered about their cities !

YOU remember the old rhyme about God and the soldier being alike adored when danger threatens and war comes and being forgotten as soon as war is over ? Well, the Navy, it seems, used to have a similar jingle some two hundred years ago. That was when Admiral Hawke had been beating French fleets, especially one under Admiral Conflans, and helping in that way to found the British Empire overseas. The jingle ran :

When Hawke did bang Monsieur Conflang,
    You gave us beef and beer—
Now Monsieur's beat, we've naught to eat
    Since you have naught to fear.

Capt. Russell Grenfell, R.N., tells us in a most interesting little book, Service Pay (Eyre & Spottiswoode, 10s. 6d.), that the Navy has always been treated scurvily in the way of pay, food and accommodation on board ship. He does not think we have yet made up for the injustice of the past. I suppose the official answer to this would be that we have always been able to attract enough men into the Navy since we gave up press-gang methods, and they have not complained overmuch. But then they aren't allowed to complain ! Whatever the rights and wrongs of the case, Capt. Grenfell's is a most readable statement of one side of it.

TRAVELLING once from New York to Chicago on the Twentieth Century Limited, which did the journey of a thousand miles in a thousand minutes, I went to the barber's shop on the train for my hair to be trimmed. Then I thought I might as well be shaved too, so as to save me from having to do it myself under difficult conditions in the smoking-room wash-place next morning. Not until I felt the razor running over my throat did I recollect that we were running at more than sixty miles an hour and that any swerve or sudden jerk might end my career. However, I went through with it and I have often been

Col. BALWANT SINGH, of the 300-year-old 1st Rajindra Sikhs (Indian State Forces), who have fought the Japanese in Burma's jungles for the past 2½ years. His battalion alone claims over 1,000 enemy dead and wounded.
Photo, Interservices P. R. Directorate (India)

barbered on trains since then. Now I see that among L.M.S. suggestions for improving this railway's service is the addition of hair-dressing saloons. Shops on trains are also proposed. These I have never seen in America, but the boys who walk through trains there sell all sorts of things, from chewing gum to lead pencils, from whatever fruit is in season to the latest best-selling novel.

AUSTRALIA has been an experiment ever since we began to send settlers there. Most of it is unsuited to white settlement. Its cities contain far too large a proportion of its inhabitants. With so small a population it has done marvellously well, but the war has made it more plain than ever that it cannot go on with so few people. The Australians themselves realize this and they are paying more attention to what visitors to their country say on the subject. To the view, for example, of Sir Clive Baillieu, a leading British industrialist, who has been saying in Melbourne that " if we do not increase the population we may in 15 or 20 years find ourselves in a sorry state." But the question has to be seriously considered : Can settlers of British stock be induced to go to Australia ? That efforts to attract them will be made is, I believe, certain ; but so long as they have been able to exist in this country, even if it was only on the dole, very few have shown any inclination to emigrate anywhere. Those who went to Canada and Australia in earlier days went because they could not exist here. Can the right sort of emigrant be persuaded to go now ? Much depends on the answer.

IT may seem absurd, but I feel sure a good deal of the prejudice felt against the Poles (and there is much of it) is due to the crack-jaw appearance of Polish names. They seem to be all c's and z's and w's, mixed up in what looks like a hopeless muddle. Take the name Wiktor Trojanowski, for example. The way to pronounce it is Victor Troianovski. That sounds all right. Take an even more extreme example —Skrzeszewski. That ought to be written, if we want to get the sound correct, Skrishevski. Spelt as it is in our newspapers, it doesn't make sense. The Polish and the Russian languages are very much alike; indeed, to a great extent almost the same—in sound. But the Poles long ago abandoned the Russian alphabet, which Shaw says is so much more practical and convenient than our own, and they adopted the letters used in France and Britain. But they made a hash of it by disregarding sound altogether. A reform in this direction would be a step towards the better international understanding which is so necessary.

I SUPPOSE I ought not to have been surprised at a youngish chartered accountant being reserved from National Service in virtue of his profession. I ought to have remembered how dependent modern industry is on the work of accountants, who cannot be replaced or done without. I recall what a shrewd City man said to me some few years ago. " I'm going to make both my boys accountants. Whatever happens, even," he added with a smile, " if we went Bolshevik, there would still be accountants wanted." He might have mentioned that it was a very well-paid profession also, and might even lead to a peerage. One member of it who died recently left close on £100,000. In the same newspaper which announced this was the will of Sir George Clausen, one of the finest painters of the past half-century. He left a little less than £5,000. That illustrates the different scales on which artists and accountants are remunerated in our society. It is fair enough, however, when you think what great pleasure Clausen must have obtained from his art compared with the sheer tediousness of spending one's whole life adding up other people's figures !

Smoke-Markers Point Berlin Bomb Targets

H.E.s CASCADED ON BERLIN in its biggest daylight raid on Feb. 26, 1945, when over 1,200 Flying Fortresses and Liberators of the U.S. 8th Air Force, escorted by 700 Mustangs and Thunderbolts, dropped some 3,000 tons on the railway termini. The photograph shows precision bombing in operation as B-17 Fortresses, reaching the smoke-markers—used in daylight attacks—over the targets, released showers of explosives during this fourteenth successive day of the great daylight air offensive on the Western Front.

Photo, U.S. Official

Printed in England and published every alternate Friday by the Proprietors, THE AMALGAMATED PRESS, LTD., The Fleetway House, Farringdon Street, London, E.C.4. Registered for transmission by Canadian Magazine Post. Sole Agents for Australia and New Zealand: Messrs. Gordon & Gotch, Ltd.; and for South Africa: Central News Agency, Ltd.—March 29, 1945. S.S. *Editorial Address:* JOHN CARPENTER HOUSE, WHITEFRIARS, LONDON, E.C.4.

Vol 8

The War Illustrated

Nº 204

SIXPENCE

Edited by Sir John Hammerton

APRIL 13, 1945

THROUGH THE SHATTERED MEDIEVAL GATEWAY OF XANTEN, ancient Rhineland town founded by the Romans, a German prisoner is seen being marched under British guard. The town was entered by a battalion of Somerset Light Infantry on March 8, 1945. Capture of Xanten meant the wiping-out of the Wesel pocket and the line-up of the Allied armies along the west bank of the Rhine on an unbroken front from Arnhem to Coblenz.

Photo, Associated Press

NO. 205 WILL BE PUBLISHED FRIDAY, APRIL 27

On the Eve of Last Big Battles in the West

JETTISONED BY THE WEHRMACHT fleeing across the Rhine, the limber of this wrecked gun (1) provided a firing-point for troops of the Canadian 1st Army street-fighting south-west of Wesel (taken on March 24, 1945). A Nazi medical-aid party surrendered to men of the U.S. 87th Division (2) who entered Coblenz on March 16. When Field-Marshal Montgomery visited British and Canadian troops in the Nijmegen area in February he talked with Lieut.-Gen. B. G. Horrocks, C.B., D.S.O. (3, centre) commanding the 30th Corps, and Maj.-Gen. G. I. Thomas, G.O.C. the 43rd Division. A hefty Canadian in this sector was dwarfed by a German Jag Panther tank (4) knocked out by one of our 17-lb. shells, which had completely stripped its track.

Photos, British Official, L.N.A., Planet News

WHY OUR SOLDIERS ARE FITTEST IN THE WORLD
The Marvel of Britain's Field Medical Services described
by Captain NORMAN MACMILLAN, M.C., A.F.C.

No one who has studied the present war can fail to be struck by the relatively low fatal casualty rate in the British and United States land forces. This is not due solely to the kind of war that is now fought, which offers the protection of armour to a large percentage of the fighting troops. Indeed, the armour has brought in its train the inevitable counter-weapons of long-barrelled high muzzle-velocity guns that can smash through the armour, and flame-thrower tanks with both long-range and short-range flame projectors, and landmines.

And the fact that fatal casualties at sea have risen while their incidence on land has decreased is in itself significant. The reason is to be found in the modern organization for the collection and care of the wounded, which has made a remarkable reduction in the number of men who succumb to wounds.

The first thing I noticed in the battlefields to the east of Nijmegen was their extreme cleanliness. The recollection of the nausea occasioned by the smell of putrefying flesh, that was so common as an experience of those who visited the front areas in the First Great War, was not revived by a visit to the fighting area on the Dutch-German frontier. Mud there was in abundance. The dirt roads were mud canals along which vehicles ploughed their way axle-deep, relying often on their four-wheel drive to pull them through. The men's clothes and faces were mud-bespattered, but when it dried it made an excellent natural camouflage.

But, though there was mud, and water, there was an absence of odour of death. In this modern mobile warfare, conducted in a series of wave-like advances, the Red Cross can conduct its work far more swiftly than it could in the stagnation of the trench warfare of the First Great War. Today, Red Cross trucks can often drive right up to the wounded. I saw Medical Officers driving up through Krannenburg in armoured Red Cross trucks. Each battalion has its own mobile medical section. No longer do the wounded have to lie in the pitiless sun as they did in the soldiering days of which Kipling wrote, or in the merciless rain of the last Flanders war.

Surgical Centres in Forward Areas

They are picked up quickly, given first aid, and sometimes a blood transfusion, loaded into stretcher-carrying trucks (when they are lying cases) and taken swiftly back to the Casualty Clearing Station. I saw light little Recce (reconnaissance) cars moving back fast with a couple of canvas-covered stretcher cots mounted on the roof and projecting over the body both in front and rear, passing through a procession of transport that pressed forward to the fighting front—tanks with 6-pounder and 17-pounder guns, supply trucks, self-propelled 25-pounder guns, half-track White scout cars, close-support and distant flame-thrower tanks, mine-clearing flail tanks, M.10 U.S. mobile guns, 25-pounder mobile guns, Ducks.

Mobility has made it possible to take the surgeon to the wounded, by the establishment of advanced surgical centres in the forward areas. Their curative work is aided by penicillin and sulphonamide drugs for the control of infection ; and by the blood transfusion service which enables a wounded man to be brought up to the strength required to stand an operation. Even after an enormous loss of blood a wounded man can be restored to life by the promptness and adequacy of a transfusion. In the First Great War such cases would probably have been fatal.

The Army Blood Transfusion Service has a base headquarters, advanced blood-bank, and the field transfusion units which work with the forward surgical centres. Blood is supplied in three forms—stored blood which, with refrigeration, can be kept for about a month ; fluid plasma and dried plasma (plasma being the colourless coagulable part of blood wherein the corpuscles float). Plasma, especially dried plasma, remains constant without need for refrigeration ; dried plasma only has to be dissolved in saline or water to make it ready for use. Plasma requires no grouping test for compatibility, as does blood, and it can therefore be administered to anyone without troubling about his blood group.

But, in cases of heavy blood loss, a proportion of blood must be given in addition to plasma, to reintroduce the necessary oxygen-carrying power of blood, and in this case blood compatibility tests must be made. Blood supplies are sent by air from the United Kingdom. When necessary they can be dropped by parachute, with the blood supply packed in airborne round wicker baskets fitted with shock-absorbing inserts. In the war zone one can see the Red Cross refrigerator wagons, marked Blood Bank, on the move distributing their supplies, which are carried in bottles about the size of beer bottles.

Interlinked with these modern services for the care of the wounded are Mobile Field Hospitals and the Air Evacuation Units. I visited a Mobile Field Hospital situated in a French town. This M.F.H. is a R.A.F. establishment under the command of Squadron Leader G. Gray. Sister Long, with rank equivalent to Flight Lieutenant, is the senior sister of the P.M.R.A.F.N.S. nursing side. This mobile hospital handles both R.A.F. and Army casualties, and can move at 24 hours' notice, carrying its own supplies,

KRANNENBURG, GERMAN FRONTIER VILLAGE, SOUTH-EAST OF NIJMEGEN, had been badly damaged by the 2nd Tactical Air Force when Captain Norman Macmillan, M.C., A.F.C. (centre), Air Correspondent of "The War Illustrated," watched tanks and transport of Gen. Crerar's Canadian 1st Army pass through, shortly after its fall on Feb. 8, 1945. This was the opening of the offensive which secured Cleves, the Reichswald Forest, Goch and Xanten. The present article is the second in the series describing Capt. Macmillan's visit to the Western front.

one Scottish—cases for evacuation come to the hospital. (During the severe winter weather the hospital dealt with 250 men of the Pioneer Corps who were sick.) The day's patients arrive at about 11 to 11.30 a.m. The nominal roll is examined and the serious cases are seen first, then the stretcher cases, and finally the walking cases.

The transport aircraft land at an aerodrome nearby, and by 11.55 a.m. aerodrome control can say how many planes are there and if flying will or cannot take place. Stretcher cases may remain in the ambulances unless there is no flying, when they can be taken in. The longest time of hold-up was six days during which bad weather prevented flying. The dangerous abdominal wound cases receive special attention, and are kept for 10 days before flying. Pilots avoid bumpy air, but generally fly low—1,000 to 2,000 feet—so that patients will not suffer from any marked change in atmospheric pressure. All aircrew members of the R.A.F. automatically go back to the United Kingdom when they are involved in an accident that results in injury. Erks go back if likely to be off duty for over three months.

tented accommodation and stores. It has its own transport section with 14 Bedford trucks, six ambulances, two car vans, two water towsers, two 15-cwt. utility vans and one jeep. It has its own sanitary squad. Its normal field establishment is for 100 cases, but it is capable of carrying 150, and in the town where it was when I saw it, it could expand to take 400.

The wards were bright. Each had a solarium at one end. The patients looked as happy as any I have seen. They were obviously well-cared for. Some were reading, some smoking. They looked up with a smile as we passed. In one ward a radio receiver was playing softly. We met one patient who had come out of a ward and was shuffling along a corridor, slowly. "Where are you going?" asked the C.O. The patient smiled but did not seem to know. "You'd better get back to bed," said the C.O. Still smiling, the patient turned and shuffled back. The C.O. told me, "He's just had a shot of penicillin. It often affects them like that."

From R.A.F. Wings and three Army hospitals—one Canadian, one British, and

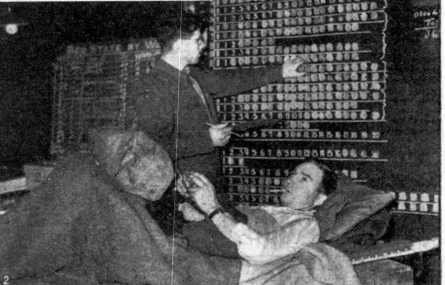

I heard great praise of Archibald McIndoe, civilian consultant in plastic surgery to the R.A.F., for his work on facial maxillary (jawbone) injuries; and of Reginald Watson-Jones, civilian consultant in orthopedic surgery to the R.A.F. There is no doubt that the British medical service is far ahead of the German. British airfields have their own disinfectors. Army and R.A.F. have mobile laundries. But when we overran France and Belgium about 50 per cent of the Jerry mattresses were found lousy. At Tournai about 2,000 German patients were under the care of two doctors, and many were in a terrible state, some even maggoty. German amputations are done by guillotine driving straight through the limb, with no flaps. With abdominals they shoot in serum (the non-coagulable liquid constituent of blood) and leave things at that, without worrying.

I talked with Flight-Lieut. D. H. Drummond (from Bethlehem, Orange Free State) in his mobile dental surgery, in which he spent half the week in one town and the other half in another town, taking the surgery half-way to the patients. The dental laboratory at the M.F.H. makes about 20 to 30 false teeth sets a week. In the mobile surgery Flight-Lieut. Drummond deals with about 300 to 400 dental patients a month. He is responsible for about 1,700 men, serving both the R.A.F. and the Army.

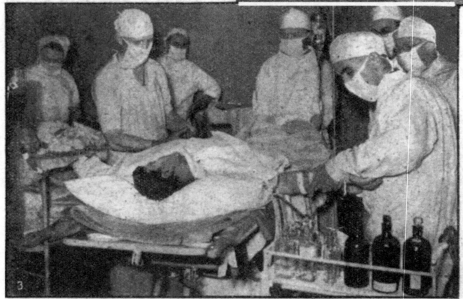

FROM BATTLEFIELD TO OPERATING TABLE. British stretcher-bearers brought in this Canadian 1st Army casualty (1) during the big offensive east of Nijmegen in March 1945, when quagmire roads prevented the use of vehicles. A stretcher case lights a cigarette (2) while waiting at the hospital reception-centre for a bed. Surgeons operating at a British forward hospital (3); the inverted flasks suspended at either side of the table contain blood plasma and penicillin ready for use. *Photos, British Newspaper Pool, Keystone*

THE BATTLE FRONTS

by Maj.-Gen. Sir Charles Gwynn, K.C.B., D.S.O.

WHEN I wrote last the Allies had successfully carried through the first phase of the final Western offensive. Nevertheless, the enemy still possessed very large forces, his picked troops were still fighting fanatically, and those of inferior quality could be coerced into putting up formidable resistance so long as they were under control. In these circumstances it was clear that before the next major phase of the offensive could be launched, with a reasonable prospect that it would prove irresistible and decisive, a considerable amount of "tidying up," to borrow Field-Marshal Montgomery's phrase, required to be done, including the softening processes of the air offensive, the elimination of such enemy force as retained nuisance potentialities and could be dealt with in detail, the establishment of threats which would force the enemy to disperse his available forces, and the build-up of resources on a scale which would enable the final blow to be delivered and "followed through" with maximum power.

We are told from day to day what air power is doing, and it is certain that it must be steadily reducing the enemy's material resources and affecting his power of movement, although apparently not yet to a decisive extent. We have learnt, in his territory that has been occupied, what amazing measures he had taken to reduce the effect of air attacks on civilian morale and interruption of work. Presumably much vital machinery has also been well protected. Nevertheless, at best he can only slow down the cumulative effect of air attacks and cannot give anything approaching complete protection, his transportation system in particular remaining vulnerable. It is easier to assess definitely the progress and importance of preliminary land operations.

ANNIHILATION Threatens German Army Groups in East Prussia

In the east the German Army in East Prussia has been split in two, and with their backs to the sea by which there is little chance of escape. The two groups, crowded into small areas, are approaching complete annihilation. In the Danzig region and in the small part of the Polish corridor still in German hands the position is very similar, although a partial evacuation by sea is probably still feasible since the encircled groups are receiving some support from German warships, and there are very strong rearguard positions available. There have, however, as yet, been no signs of evacuation, although continued resistance would seem to serve no military purpose except so far as it denies the use of the Danzig and Gdynia ports to the Russians, and of course contains part of Rokossovsky's attacking army.

BETWEEN the Gulf of Danzig and the Oder estuary inclusive, the whole of east Pomerania has been cleared. Zhukov's right flank is therefore completely protected, and he is probably in a position to force a crossing of the Oder in the neighbourhood of Stettin should that be part of his plan. By the capture of Kustrin, the only bridge-head the Germans still held on the east bank of the Oder on the direct route to Berlin, he must have almost completed his preliminary operations. On Koniev's front, Breslau and Glogau still remain as serious blocks on his line of communication, but much of Breslau has been captured, and he also is ready for the final phase.

South of the Carpathians, Malinovsky has made important advances in Slovakia, but in the Lake Balaton region the Germans made a fierce and prolonged attempt to drive Tolbukhin back across the Danube. Tolbukhin, as might be expected from his record, evidently fought a skilful defensive battle, yielding little ground and inflicting heavy losses on the enemy. He is now reported to be taking the offensive again against an enemy who must have exhausted the greater part of his reserves.

IN the west, General Eisenhower's operations preliminary to his maximum effort have developed with more far-reaching effect than probably was anticipated, and it is evident that the disastrous consequences of Von Rundstedt's offensive are not yet exhausted. The preliminary operation that, after the Roer victory, had immediately to be carried through was the elimination of the Wesel bridge-head which the Germans still held with fanatical determination. It was an essential task, made difficult by the defensive possibilities of the position and the quality of the defending troops. Its successful accomplishment reflects credit on Montgomery's British, Canadian and American troops out of all proportion to the scale of the operation.

While that battle was in progress General Hodges was advancing southwards from Cologne towards Bonn, and General Patton was continuing to press eastwards through the Eifel and on both sides of the Moselle from Saarburg to Treves (Trier). His advance was characteristically energetic, but difficult passages of a series of tributary rivers involved heavy fighting, and the Rhine lay some 50 miles east of Trier with the intervening country hilly and wooded.

No immediate attempt to reach the Rhine appeared to be likely. Then, suddenly, came the news that Patton's armour had broken through north of the Moselle and was racing eastward audaciously, encountering little resistance from the confused German troops who did not know what had happened. In two days he had reached the Rhine a few miles north of Coblenz, while almost at the same time General Hodges' armour, apparently taking advantage of the confusion into which the Germans had been thrown, broke through from the north and made its unexpected capture of the Remagen bridge.

Junction between the two forces quickly followed and the whole of the seven or eight divisions of the German 7th Army were encircled. Both forces had made large captures of prisoners and material, but the net was still wide-meshed, and though retreat eastwards across the Rhine was barred, no doubt some disorganized groups escaped southwards to the Moselle.

We have still to learn whether this great coup had been deliberately planned and the possibility of the opportunity arising fore-seen, or whether it resulted from a brilliant recognition of an opportunity at once seized and daringly exploited, first by General Patton and then by General Hodges. I believe it must have been the latter, and that neither general was working to a programme. Certainly the seizure of the Remagen bridge was unforeseen and resulted from the initiative of a junior commander on the spot. If I am right, all the more credit is due to those concerned for the enterprise displayed.

Generals Eisenhower and Patton have lost no time in exploiting success still further. Patton, having cleared the north bank of the Moselle, where the enemy were attempting to hold open an escape gap for 7th Army parties, forced a crossing of the lower reaches of the river and sent his armour racing through the dangerous defiles of the Hunsruck mountains, causing confusion and alarm on the enemy's communications with the Saar front. At the same time he intensified pressure from his Saarburg-Trier pocket south of the Moselle.

IN the south, General Patch's 7th Army and the French have launched their offensive, the date for which Eisenhower may have advanced. The Germans in the Saar region are therefore under attack from three directions with their communications in danger, and under intensive air attack. The situation has great possibilities, for unless they withdraw across the Rhine promptly there may be another disastrous encirclement with desperate attempts to escape under devastating air attack. As this situation develops, the Remagen bridge-head now well established and steadily expanding acquires greater value, and these southern operations may merge into and become part of the still awaited main offensive.

WESTERN FRONT ON MARCH 20, 1945, before the U.S. 3rd and 7th Armies had linked up along the Rhine from Mainz to Karlsruhe and mass crossings of the river had been made by all the Allied armies on this front.
By courtesy of The Evening News

Italians Join Us in Cracking Their Late Ally

ON THE 8th ARMY FRONT IN ITALY so hard was the going in the early spring of 1945 that ammunition for the Royal Artillery mountain regiments had to be brought up by mule-train (1). Royal Signals linesmen put through a test call after hasty repairs (2). In the Senio Valley, Sherman tanks were on reconnaissance (3) beside the river. There, Italian partisan troops, seen supported by our 4.5-in. guns (4) and riding on British tanks (5), were reported on March 6 in action with British and Polish forces. By March 20, Allied bombers having kept the Brenner Pass closed for 51 days were reported to be " starving out " the 300,000 German troops in N. Italy. See also page 768.

Photos, British Official

THE WAR AT SEA

by Francis E. McMurtrie

WITH the island of Iwo (Iwojima) firmly in American hands, it was to be expected that further operations would soon be undertaken by the United States Navy against objectives in Japan. Nor did the enemy have long to wait. On March 21, first day of what promises to be a dismal spring for the Japanese, it was announced that a task force under Vice-Admiral M. A. Mitscher had approached Japanese territorial waters closely enough to fly off from their carriers a large number of aircraft, estimated by the enemy at fully 1,400. These aircraft, besides attacking shore installations, sought out Japanese warships lying in ports of the Inland Sea and bombed them heavily.

Lying between the three islands of Honshu, Shikoku, and Kyushu, the Inland Sea may be regarded as the centre of Japan's maritime power. It provides some hundreds of miles of sheltered water, with numerous ports, including some of the largest in Japan. Osaka and Kobe, for example, are two of the biggest commercial cities, with extensive shipbuilding yards and a flourishing trade in peace time. Kure is a great naval arsenal, comparable with Portsmouth. Hiroshima, Wakayama, Okayama and Moji are other important places on the Inland Sea, Moji being at its western entrance and Wakayama near its eastern end.

DESPERATE Efforts by Japanese Aircraft to Reach U.S. Carriers

Preliminary reports indicate that in addition to destroying 475 enemy aircraft, the American planes succeeded in inflicting heavy damage on 15 or more ships, including the battleship Yamato, of 45,000 tons, two large fleet aircraft carriers, two smaller carriers, two cruisers, four destroyers and a submarine. Half-a-dozen cargo vessels were sunk. Desperate efforts were made by the Japanese aircraft to reach the United States carriers, and some hits were scored by the enemy, but only one American ship was badly damaged, and she managed to reach port under her own power. In all probability the Japanese warships were lying at Kure, where some of them may have been undergoing repairs after the mauling they received in the Battle of the Philippines last October.

It is believed that the Yamato is the only large modern battleship left in the Japanese fleet ; her sister ship, the Musasi, was sunk in the Philippines battle, and there is no evidence that any more ships of the type have been completed. In size and power they are comparable with the U.S. battleships of the Iowa class, the German Bismarck and Tirpitz (both sunk), or the British Vanguard, launched on November 30, 1944. All these are ships of about 45,000 tons displacement. The Yamato is reported to be 870 feet long, with an armament of nine 16-in., six 6·1-in. and numerous smaller guns.

How many aircraft carriers Japan has left cannot be determined failing more exact information of the number sunk. It is possible there are still three or four large fleet carriers of 30,000 tons or more, besides some of smaller size. One of the latter, it will be recalled, was seen to capsize during a recent American air attack on Yokosuka, the Japanese naval base in Tokyo Bay. There is nothing to prevent the United States Navy from repeating their attacks at frequent intervals, and as time goes on they are bound to be intensified. What are the Japanese to do ? Their own air forces are clearly incapable of repelling such heavy raids, and have already suffered heavily, according to official reports, in their attempts to do so.

One course would be to send the bulk of the Japanese fleet to some distant harbour such as Port Arthur, on the Yellow Sea, but this would merely defer the inevitable, while leaving the country without a fleet to protect its home waters. Another possibility is that the Japanese Navy, now that it is no longer able to lie in harbour free from attack, will take an early opportunity of seeking an action at sea with the United States fleets, despite its discouraging experience last October.

THAT great concern is felt by the Japanese High Command may be judged from the fact that within the last month three flag officers holding senior appointments in command of bases have been called upon to fill seats on the Naval Staff at Tokyo—or wherever the Naval Staff now sits. Evidently the views of as many experienced admirals as possible are being sought to enable a decision to be reached. Probably the immediate cause of these emergency appointments was the loss of Iwo after a desperate struggle that lasted for 26 days. An American official summary of the operations was recently issued, which states that in the conquest of Iwo the U.S. Marine Corps was called upon to fight under conditions which have had no parallel in the present war. With every natural advantage, the enemy had contrived a series of fortifications which approached absolute impregnability.

Had not the concentrated fire of half-a-dozen battleships, supported by vessels of other categories, been successfully used to beat down the island's defences long enough for the troops to gain a foothold, the taking of the island would have presented an almost insuperable obstacle. One of the biggest troubles was volcanic ash, which immobilized even tracked vehicles and turned them into motionless targets. Enemy artillery had been carefully ranged on every possible landing place, so as to interlock and mutually support the strongly defended pillboxes and other fortifications. There were underground labyrinths extending over many miles of passages, the result of years of military planning and construction. In fact, the defences were limited in depth only by the coastline of the island. (See illus. page 747.)

MAGNIFICENT Fighting Spirit of Marines Storming Iwojima

Its garrison was composed of specially trained units, taught to utilize every natural advantage of the island terrain. This is characterized by a tall volcanic cone, cliffs and deep gulleys, several commanding hills and a series of terraces rising from the beaches to plateaus and prominences, every one of which had to be stormed. All these obstacles were overcome by the magnificent fighting spirit of the U.S. Marines, who by March 21 had killed over 21,000 of their enemies. In winning this victory the American forces lost 3,189 officers and men killed, 441 missing, and 15,308 wounded. The escort aircraft carrier Bismarck Sea was sunk by Japanese planes on Feb. 21. Iwo was the toughest nut yet encountered in the course of the war in the Pacific, eclipsing Leyte, Saipan, Kwajalein or Tarawa.

Though in a recent official broadcast it was suggested that naval news was no longer to be expected from the Mediterranean, there seems to have been a smart action, or rather a couple of actions, fought by two of H.M. destroyers off Cape Corse (Corsica) in the early morning of March 18. In the first, which opened shortly after 3 a.m., H.M.S. Lookout (Lieut.-Com. D. H. F. Etherington) was hotly engaged with three German-manned destroyers, one of which she sank. Nearly an hour later the two survivors were encountered 13 miles away by the Meteor (Lieut.-Com. R. D. H. Pankhurst). Enemy torpedoes having missed their mark, the Meteor sank one of her opponents, and the other escaped under cover of smoke. No casualties or damage were suffered by the British ships, which must have been remarkably well handled. Further details would be of interest ; it is not even clear whether the enemy ships were ex-French or ex-Italian destroyers.

SELF-PROPELLED FLOATING DRY DOCK, constructed of concrete, has no grace of design but is a most efficient American production. It goes to a ship needing repairs or other on-the-spot facilities it provides, and operation is on the lines of the great dock recently bombed and sunk at Singapore (see illus. and story in page 666).

Photo, Keystone

Saved From Destruction by 10 Vital Minutes—

LUDENDORFF BRIDGE AT REMAGEN, south of Bonn (1), was saved by only 10 minutes when, on March 7, 1945, U.S. 1st Army men cut the wires to the enemy explosive charges, and crossed the Rhine. The bridge (2), carried a double-track railway which the Germans had converted to a roadway (3). Second-Lieut. Karl Timmermann (4), first U.S. officer to cross it, led the way (5). Later, the Nazis executed four of their officers for leaving the bridge intact.

Photos, British and U.S. Official.   Diagram by courtesy of The Evening News

—For 10 Days It Bore Them O'er the Rhine

GENERAL WEAKENING OF THE STRUCTURE caused the bridge at Remagen to collapse suddenly, on March 17, ten days after its capture, many U.S. Army engineers at work upon it at the time losing their lives. But so rapid had been the extension of the Allied bridge-head beyond, that Maj.-Gen. C. R. Moore, Chief Engineer European Theatre of Operations, considered rebuilding to be unnecessary. Reinforcements continued without interruption across pontoon bridges which had been built within a day or two of the first assault.

Photo, Associated Press

Vanishing Battle-Scars of Valiant Leningrad

IN THE U.S.S.R.'s SECOND CITY women workers are seen (top) repairing the roof of the Maryinsky Palace; in the background is St. Isaac's Cathedral, Leningrad's largest church, built in 1819-1858. Alongside the Griboyedov Canal (bottom) splintered railings are being refurbished. Founded by Peter the Great in 1703, the city—formerly St. Petersburg—was besieged by the Germans for 28 months, including 24 months of continuous shelling. The siege was formally declared raised on January 27, 1944. See also pages 622-626, Vol. 7.

Photos, Pictorial Press

First Slice is Lopped From Mikado's Empire

ON THE VOLCANIC BEACH OF IWOJIMA, Pacific island air-base 650 miles from Nippon's war industries, and the first territory of the Japanese Empire to be captured by the Allies in this war. American Marines as they landed took cover from withering fire (top) and awaited the word to advance. Iwojima was finally cleared on March 16, 1945, after 26 days of combat. Supplies were run ashore (bottom) as bulldozers made a road. Six days after the island fell it was announced that cannon-carrying P.51 Mustang fighters, escorting Super-Fortresses, were operating between Iwojima and the Japanese mainland. See also pages 678-679 and story in 730.

Photos, Sport & General, Keystone

They Help the R.A.F. to Keep Up With the Army

Hard on the heels of the enemy our specialists produce, in almost magical manner, new landing strips or airfields. And where captured aerodromes have been left thoroughly wrecked by the Germans they make these swiftly serviceable again. ALEXANDER DILKE throws some limelight on the work of the R.A.F. Airfield Construction Service and Army Airfield Construction Groups.

"IN spite of unfavourable weather, planes of the Tactical Air Force made 700 sorties yesterday . . ." We have become so used to statements such as this in the communiqués that we hardly notice them, and certainly do not stop to think what 700 sorties means in the way of aerodromes just behind the lines in territory that was only recently in enemy hands.

Construction of these aerodromes and air-strips by the score since we landed in France is the story of R.A.F. and Royal Engineer and Pioneer units whose names have very rarely figured in the news, but who have done vital work in enabling the R.A.F. to keep up with the Army. Units of the Army Airfield Construction Groups and the R.A.F. Airfield Construction Service went ashore on the Normandy beach-heads just as soon as there was room for them to work; the first landing strip was constructed within range of enemy guns and was ready in less than 48 hours from the moment when the first soldiers set foot on the beaches.

As the beach-heads expanded, new landing strips and aerodromes were constructed. At one time there was the astonishing sight of soldiers cutting and carting wheat while specialists laid out the landing ground, and bulldozers went to work levelling, and tractors towed away felled trees. Altogether about twenty landing strips and emergency aerodromes were built in Normandy before the breakout. From these fields flew hundreds of planes that pounded the German army when it broke. And fighters from them made possible the protection of the prefabricated harbour (see pages 430–434, 710) and the beaches against air attack.

WHEN the Germans were routed and the Allies took up the astonishing chase across France and Belgium, the Airfield Construction Units also became mobile and followed hard on the heels of the armour. So hard that once they started work on new airfields before the infantry had caught up. The Airfield Construction Groups have their own reconnaissance units with armoured cars, and on one occasion one of them worked at repairing an airfield for four days with nothing but their own weapons to protect them from attack.

During this period new airfields were reached, repaired after the heavy bombing they had received from Allied planes, and then left behind within a few days. It is on record that in a single week a single unit covered over 200 miles in France and Belgium and made 14 aerodromes fit for use again en route.

When the German retreat ended and lines were once more established, the Airfield Construction Units had harder if less spectacular work to do. The weather broke, and the Germans resorted to flooding. Water became the enemy. Construction Units have fought a four months' battle with water on the low-lying fields of Belgium and Holland, and that the number of days on which Tactical Air Force planes have been unable to operate is so small is the measure of their triumph over the conditions.

Hard Training and Rehearsal

What is the secret of the success of these comparatively new units? The first answer is organization. Experience has shown what was necessary. In North Africa, and again in Italy, the incalculable value of air bases right up with the front line was demonstrated, and some of the problems of keeping them there when the line was advancing rapidly solved. With organization went specialized training and rehearsal. In Britain the units had not only had exact maps and models of the areas in which they would construct the first landing-strips in Normandy, but also rehearsals before D-Day.

With this went specialized equipment. One of the most vital pieces of equipment has been Sommerfeld track, which has been used by the mile. It is special steel netting constructed in standard lengths with long steel spikes to hold it down on the ground. The netting enables a sandy beach or stretch of grass to be turned into a firm track in a matter of hours. For making roads round the aerodrome or landing-strip it can be used alone. For runways and landing-strips it is used with bitumenized hessian or other matting. The track is made in pieces 10–11 feet wide, and about fifteen side by side are required to make a runway. There is a regular "drill" for laying it, and if possible it is stretched tight by bulldozer before being pegged. The beauty of it is its portability and its lightness. A score of trucks can carry a runway. The material for a concrete runway would fill thousands of trucks. Even so,

an immense weight of the steel track and matting has been carried to the Continent—probably close on a hundred thousand tons since our armies landed last June. (See p. 267.)

In addition, the Construction Units carry all the instruments needed by the surveyors, the best available contour maps and photographs, as well as time and labour-saving tools such as a mechanical saw operated by a small engine which fells the thickest tree in a matter of minutes. The bulldozer, of course, is the maid-of-all-work, filling depressions, levelling hedges, removing tree-stumps and then filling the holes. (See illus. p. 568.) Mine detectors are a vital part of the equipment, for unless the enemy has abandoned an aerodrome in a panic he is sure to have distributed mines and booby traps.

The Airfield Construction Units are concerned not only in making new landing-strips but also in improving airfields which have had emergency repairs. In the sodden, low-lying country of Belgium and Holland this has meant a tremendous amount of drainage, and the construction of solid runways to make the aerodromes usable in winter. The Germans naturally destroyed the drainage of their aerodromes before retiring, and in some places placed mines under water for good measure. Miles of drains have had to be dug and hundreds of ditches cleared and mended.

To save transport, local materials are used wherever possible for making permanent runways. Rubble from neighbouring towns which have been bombed has been used, the dual purpose of clearing the streets and securing solid foundations for a new advance being served. In one case the Construction Units got local brick-kilns going again to provide the millions of bricks necessary for the construction of a runway.

Most of the time the work done by the Engineers, Pioneers and men of the R.A.F. Airfield Construction Service is unspectacular. Especially in Holland and Belgium it was not possible to make aerodromes overnight. Weeks of work in cold, rain and snow were required to produce the dry runways and dispersal points of the finished aerodromes.

The uniform of the R.A.F. Airfield Construction Service is khaki battledress and blue cap—similar to that of the R.A.F. Regiment which undertakes the defence of the airfields they construct and repair.

R.A.F. AIRFIELD CONSTRUCTION SQUAD pegs down wire-mesh tracking (left) on the first Normandy airfield to be built for the R.A.F. by the R.A.F. in the summer of 1944; the task occupied about a week. Previously, airfields in the British sectors had been constructed by the Royal Engineers. In Holland, construction specialists (right) "feed" a cement-mixer while making a road around an airfield. A powerful bulldozer (background, left) is being halted at the end of its "furrow." See also illus. page 765

Photos, British Official

Norway's Spirited Resistance to Hun Occupation

ARMED PATRIOTS in one of the war's most daring coups in Norway, on February 8, 1945, seized eleven tugs and a salvage vessel under the noses of the Germans, sailed them across the Skagerrak and berthed them in a Swedish port (left). The tugs had been moored in the German-controlled port of Fredrikstad, on the Oslo Fjord, one of them alongside a Nazi warship, and were boarded in early morning; they sailed out of port past German patrol ships, harbour fortifications and the outer batteries in full daylight, then set course for Sweden. And on March 14, Norwegian patriots cut off every railway line connecting Oslo with German disembarkation ports in Southern Norway. See also story in page 761.

BIGGEST PROBLEM in Finmark—Norway's northernmost province, forcibly evacuated by the Nazis in November 1944 (see pages 588-589)—is that of relief : clothing is distributed (centre left) to those who escaped to the mountains when the enemy burned down their houses. In these primitive shacks (centre right) thousands of Norwegians in Finmark were forced to spend the winter.

Then the Germans sent motor-torpedo-boats and other small craft to take away the remaining population. In March 1945 the food situation in liberated Finmark was reported as being under control, since the Germans, taken by surprise by the Russian offensive, had failed to destroy the stocks, which have since been greatly supplemented by supplies from Britain. In their picturesque traditional costume of padded knee-boots and reindeer-skin tunics, dating back to the 17th century, Laplanders help to distribute newly arrived food supplies (bottom) among the people of freed Finmark.

Photos, Norwegian Official

Mighty Mechanical 'Brain' Helps the War Office

It knows everything about everyone in the Army and the A.T.S. It will help with the problems of demobilization. It works 24 hours a day, is foolproof and cannot lie. How this astonishing record-system, known as the War Office Central Card Index—WOCCI for short—deals with an incredible mass of statistical detail is explained by MARK PRIESTLEY.

IF the Prime Minister calls for the latest casualty figures if a unit in the field needs special technical reinforcements, if a front-line soldier is medically downgraded and needs a new job, WOCCI will provide. And it will fix the demobilization date of millions of men and women in the Army and the A.T.S. "Favouritism or wangling cannot op:rate in this scheme," said Mr. Arthur Henderson, Financial Secretary to the War Office, on March 13, 1945. "It will be impossible to influence the electrically controlled War Office central card index."

At the headquarters of this astonishing index system, I watched an A.T.S. operator sorting numerical cards at the rate of 9,000 an hour. And, as a demonstration, I saw a machine picking out all the fishmongers in the R.A.M.C., R.E.M.E., and Pioneer Corps. It took less than six minutes.

Suppose the Ministry of Labour, or any other Ministry should decide to arrange priority demobilization for fishmongers of over 40. WOCCI can enable the officials to see at a glance the date of birth, present age,

religion, nationality, medical record, marriage and home details of the men who qualify. It can even distinguish, if need be, between wholesale fish splitters and fish graders and show where they are stationed and when they are normally likely to be released.

THOUSANDS of new cards arrive for classification nearly every day ; amendments are never less than 50,000 a week and may rise to as many as 30,000 a day. If a "brass hat" wants to know the record of Private John Smith—just one particular John Smith—the department can unerringly provide the fullest information within six hours.

It is all done by cards and by machines that punch, count and analyse them, shuffling, stacking, discarding. And by a staff of 350 girls—key punch operators, coding clerks, file clerks, form reviewers, sorters, actuaries and other experts—who for three years kept WOCCI a closely guarded secret.

Every Serviceman knows the forms he fills and the questions he answers on joining up—birthplace, number of children, occupation and so on. Operators with lightning fingers transform these facts into the ingenious punch-hole language which the machines can later read and classify. The unit to which he is assigned, transfer from one unit to another, medical disability, prolonged sick leave or wounds can all be translated into

THREE OF THE 350 GIRLS who operate the amazing War Office index-system described in this page are seen at work. In a corner of the coding-room (1) the " punch " operator (2) perforates the appropriate holes in the cards ; the sorting-machine operator (3) can ascertain the numbers available in any trade or calling among Forces personnel. *Photos, Topical Press*

perforation language. Eventually a Serviceman or woman becomes to the mathematical brain of WOCCI no more than a group of 70 to 80 holes punched in a $7\frac{1}{2}$-in. by 3-in. card. Thus are the details "potted."

IN the coding section a key punch first makes a card from each enlistment form, while a gang punch makes wholesale batches covering the same data. These are specialized by the algebraic sleight-of-hand of another machine which produces a master name card. John Smith, in fact, often says that he is a "cog in a machine" without realizing that WOCCI is the machine. Even if he is reported missing or becomes a prisoner of war, there are cards to cover his new condition, transferred to a special section and amended on machines resembling typewriters.

There is no need for a check of discrepancies against the original forms ; mistakes are automatically counteracted. If the operator makes a slip, the machine locks. If a machine goes wrong, the customary clicking and roaring ceases, a green light turns red—and a stand-by mechanic becomes busy.

It is in collating statistics such as the number of press tool setters aged 30 in the Army, or the number of infantry N.C.O.s supporting both wives and mothers, that WOCCI best demonstrates its high-speed accuracy. Scores of tiny, electrically-operated fingers read the holes in the cards infinitely faster than a blind expert reads Braille. As the cards whirr by, at up to 400 a minute, each finger catches in a lightning flash at the hole location for which it is set. In the sorting machines, the fingers open slots which send the cards into their respective compartments. In the tabulating and enumerating machines each finger contact on the card registers another tally for a given punch-hole fact.

The machines can add up to sixty separate columns at a time. As Colonel A. G. Stats.

the officer in charge of the department, says, "The machine cannot lie. We are producing the vast amount of statistical information required with the return of the Army to civil life, and we are doing it by the most modern method." And with startling success.

The Central Card Index is only the "cash register" of the service echelons which, in turn, act as general clearing houses of information about personnel. It is noteworthy that Junior Commander Florence Tiffin, of Liverpool, who is in charge of the P.I.M. (Provision Information Miscellaneous) Branch, is the first A.T.S. officer who has ever replaced an Army officer in any echelon formation in the whole of the British Army.

Every day embarkation rolls, casualty lists and returns of all kinds enter her office. If Private Smith is in Holland, P.I.M. transmits to the Index details of when he was embarked. If he is wounded, P.I.M. tells which hospital he is in, and how he is progressing. And warm, human values are actually asserted behind the systematic and ice-cold efficiency. The A.T.S. assistants

make it their job to see that everyone is spared unnecessary anxiety and to ensure that a soldier's wishes are carried out.

IF Private Jones, for example, names his mother as next-of-kin, but would prefer any bad news to be broken to her by his sister, they see that if he is wounded, missing or killed the telegram goes to the right person. If a man is in hospital in France and notified as on the danger list, and no further news is received after 21 days, the echelon sends an urgent request for a progress report so that his family can be told the latest news—and WOCCI ensures that this is done on time.

Another busy branch governs enemy prisoners of war, and when this branch works overtime it means that another few thousand Germans are out of the fight. The cards can tell how many thousand prisoners we have taken, who they are, and what possessions were found on each man at the time.

Yet WOCCI is more than a mere wartime agglomeration of military facts and figures. Officials agree that it is capable of infinite adaptation, and such departments as the Ministry of Labour are making full use of it. The world's biggest book-keeping job will last into the Peace as a permanent guide to all Government departments—an eventual improvement that may cut red tape, and red tapers, by more than half.

Dawn Breaks on Britain's East Indies Fleet

Returning in early morning through the tumbling waters of the Indian Ocean from a mighty attack against the enemy naval base at Sabang, Sumatra, are some of the ships of our great East Indies Fleet now sharing prominently in the smashing of Japan.   They are (left to right) the cruiser Black Prince, aircraft carrier Victorious, a destroyer, aircraft carrier Illustrious (prominent in the centre), French battleship Richelieu, and the battle cruiser Renown.

751

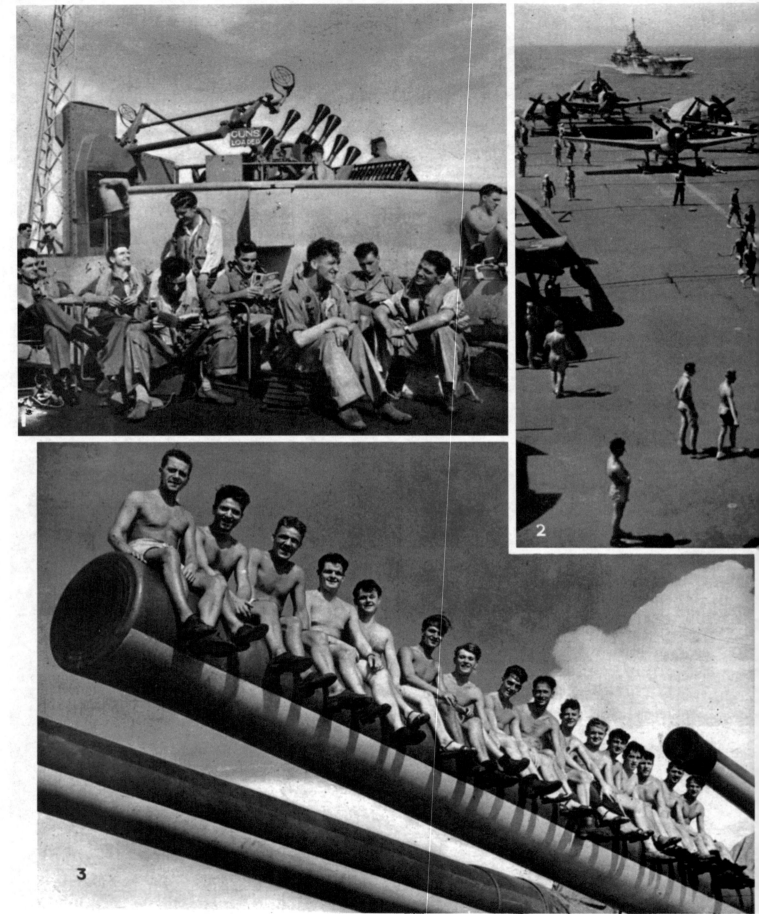

They Thrash the Japs in Far Eastern Seas

"A large share of the task of defeating Japan will fall on the men of the Royal and Merchant Navies," declared the First Lord of the Admiralty on March 7, 1945. Responsibility sits lightly on the capable shoulders of these pilots (1) on board the aircraft carrier Indomitable, waiting to deliver the next blow. Elsewhere on Indomitable deck-hockey is played, in a temperature of 100 degrees (2). Members of H.M.S. Queen Elizabeth's company sun-lounge on one of her 15-in. guns (3).

Phot

'Savage Parent of More Savage Offspring'

Sister ship of the Indefatigable is our newest aircraft carrier H.M.S. Implacable (4), now very much On Active Service. Her motto is " The Savage Parent of More Savage Offspring." A destroyer approaches H.M.S. Queen Elizabeth (5), of the East Indies Fleet, during her return from operations against Sabang : a seaman prepares to fire to the destroyer a line which is held coiled up in a canister by a second seaman ; the line will facilitate the passing of mails, or other small articles.

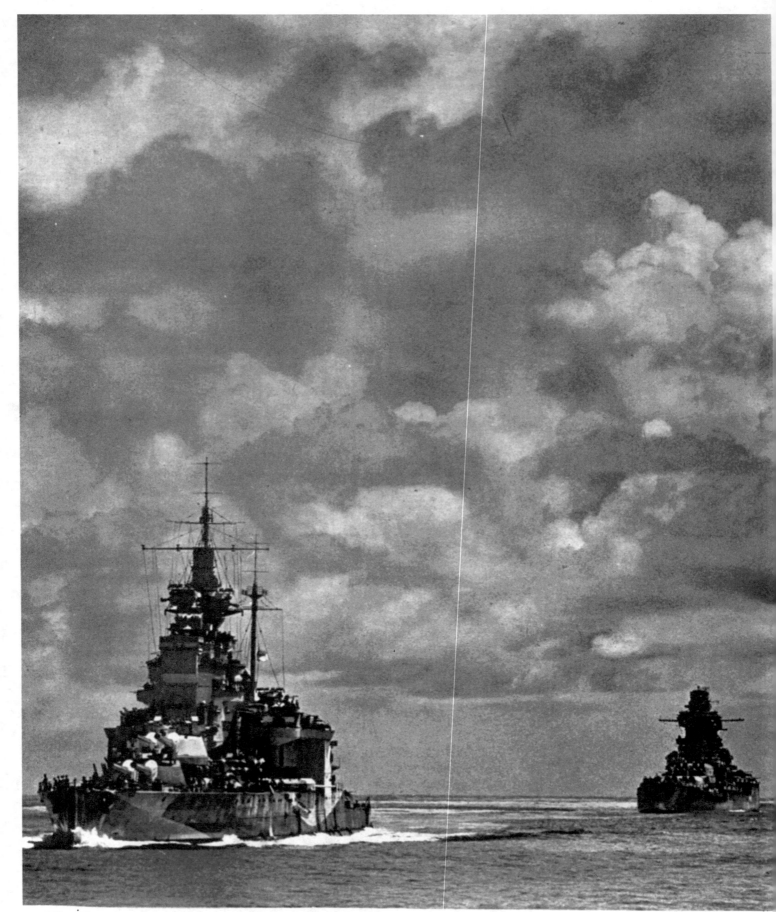

Valiant and Richelieu Fought at Sabang

Photo, British Official

The Japanese naval and air base guarding the entrance to the Malacca Straits was twice attacked in 1944 ; on the second occasion, battleships, cruisers, destroyers and aircraft carriers almost completely destroyed the harbour installations and heavily damaged the wireless station (see story in page 249).   Engaged in the operations were H.M.S. Valiant and F.S. Richelieu (background) of the East Indies Fleet now under the command of Admiral Sir Arthur J. Power, K.C.B., C.V.O.

VIEWS & REVIEWS

Of Vital War Books

by Hamilton Fyfe

INDIA! Most puzzling of all the problems, most disturbing of all the difficulties that will have to be solved and surmounted after the war ends in Europe and the Far East. India, the land where the contrasts are so startling and the variety of points of view so apparently irreconcilable that one can hardly believe it possible to hit on any settlement which would please more than a small minority of a population that before many years are past will number 400 millions or more.

Here is one of the contrasts. The leaders of the Hindu majority are mostly in prison or under strict supervision, yet there are two million Indians who have volunteered for service to fight alongside British troops and who in many campaigns have won the warmest praise. Field-Marshal Alexander said to Major Yeats-Brown, author of Martial India (Eyre and Spottiswoode, 8s. 6d.), "The Indian soldier is a splendid fighting man. You can't praise him too highly and you can say I said so." That was on the Italian Front. Wherever they have fought the Indian troops have merited the same commendation. Yet the impression most people have, I suppose, is that Indians generally are anti-British.

WELL, that certainly can't be true of the two million volunteers, nor are they likely to go home any less friendly to us than they were when they started. For the terms on which they and their British comrades-in-arms live create mutual liking and respect, and everything possible is done to make the Indian troops understand that we value their co-operation. For example, they get special radio programmes in eight different languages, and seven different kinds of music are broadcast to them, so as to satisfy all ears. They have a weekly newspaper, which is printed in five languages, and one which appears twice a week in eight languages. This is the sort of thing they will not forget.

Unfortunately this book of Yeats-Brown's is the last he was to write. He has died since he finished it. Nobody who read Bengal Lancer, which made his name, could doubt that whatever he wrote about Indians would be well worth reading, for he wrote with sympathy as well as knowledge. Some of the best parts of this book are his descriptions of life in the villages from which the soldiers are drawn. Descriptions of city life, too, for many of them are city-bred. Here is an impression of the main street in Delhi, rich and busy, gay and peaceful :

What is it that first strikes a European in an Eastern city? To judge by myself, it is the air of leisurely contentment. In our cities nine out of ten passers-by look hurried, harassed, worried. Not so here. The people seem to be enjoying the congestion of the bazaars and byways. Poverty is not so dreaded and wealth is not so eagerly sought as with us . . . a free-and-easy atmosphere.

Apparently, few places could seem pleasanter. But—as striking contrast to the magnificent Government of India buildings in one part of Delhi —the poor quarters have "no drainage system except the gutter in the street." Village life, as Major Yeats-Brown saw it in a district of the Southern Punjab, from which Sikh soldiers come as well as Hindu and Moslem, seems on the surface almost idyllic.

Women in many-coloured saris—glittering groups of pink and daffodil and sky-blue, with some black saris spangled with silver—sit by the roadside with their plainly dressed menfolk (an off-white loin-cloth and drab shawl) eating barley porridge and drinking buttermilk. Their naked children, adorned with silver earrings and nose-rings, are sharing the meal or playing noughts and crosses in the dust beside them.

The domestic arrangements of the people have changed but little in the last thousand years. They buy ornaments for their

Can India Become a Democracy ?

daughters in the shape of brooches and anklets costing about £10 each (brides wear eight anklets on their wedding day), but they do not think of having "modern living conditions in their homes." Their rooms are scrupulously clean in spite of their mud floors and walls ; they have no glass windows, "only apertures of bricks placed chequerwise provide light and ventilation." In cold weather these apertures are covered with blankets and the room is dark, except for the dim glow of a hurricane lamp ; "however, life is chiefly passed in the sunlight, and soon after sunset the family sleeps."

THE homes from which the Indian soldiers come are mostly those which keep old customs. The women are secluded and wear veils over their faces. The religions, both Hindu (Brahminism) and Moslem, keep the masses ignorant and contented. The caste system is as powerful as ever. Some of the many disadvantages of this are pointed out in another book on India, titled The

W.A.C. ON PARADE IN DELHI, when on Feb. 3, 1945, more than 600 officers and auxiliaries of the Army, Navy and Air Force branches of the Women's Auxiliary Corps of India were inspected by the Countess of Carlisle, Chief Commander. Problems of the great Indian Empire are discussed in books reviewed above. PAGE 755 *Photo, Indian Official*

Future of India (Pilot Press, 5s.), written from another point of view, but also most enlightening. The writer, Mr. Penderel Moon, was high up in the Indian Civil Service ; he retired only a short while ago. His theme is mainly political and economic India. He therefore deals not only with the masses but with the small educated class who have been influenced by Western ideas and habits and who lead, but do not in any sense represent, the mass of their fellow countrymen who form the subject of Yeats-Brown's study.

THOUGH Mr. Moon is convinced that India must be induced to frame, or be supplied with, a system of self-government, he does not consider this class yet satisfactory as leaders. "The forces of evil ranged against them" he describes as enormously strong. "Only the rarest virtue can rise above them. Most young men of the Indian middle classes have no chance of developing the requisite strength of character. Both at home and at school they are inadequately disciplined, and they are brought up in a world in which greed, falsehood, suspicion and communal hatred prevail." Therefore "India's educated few will lead themselves and the uneducated masses to disaster unless the rising generation can establish higher standards of sincerity and integrity and thus promote in society at large greater mutual toleration and trust."

Those are wise words and brave words, and they do not in the least mean that the writer of them advocates waiting until there has been a marked change before we make it plain that we are ready to give India its independence. "A cardinal element in the present situation is Indians' distrust of our good faith ; and this distrust must continue so long as our determination to hand over power remains in doubt. At present our determination is qualified, not absolute. It is still hedged round with some 'ifs' and 'buts' and even seems likely to disappear altogether if Indians cannot themselves settle their own differences." Should they be unable to do this, we ought, Mr. Moon contends, to give up our position as masters and hand over political power to some group or groups of Indians and let them carry on the functions of government.

Here again we come up against one of the contrasts I mentioned which make the democratization of India seem so much more difficult than in any other country. What have the men who manage the Tata steel works, the largest in the world, in common with the peasants who live from hand to mouth in the villages, hungry most of the time, and disliking the idea of going to work in a factory as heartily as Mr. Gandhi hates industry worked by machines? How reconcile the outlook of those who built the big blocks of modern tall offices in Calcutta with the outlook of those who say that the cows which wander in the streets below must not be driven away because they are "sacred" cows ?

"THE cultivator," says Mr. Moon, "is an illiterate peasant, still employing the methods and implements of Homeric times. He ploughs with a wooden plough, reaps with a hand sickle, treads out the grain with oxen and winnows it by tossing it in the air." Living on the very margin of subsistence it might be supposed that peasants in the slack season, when there is little to do on the land, would engage in some industry such as weaving or tanning. But it is not "proper" for them to do that.

Whatever political changes are made, whether the Moslems have their separate regions (Pakistan) or come to some agreement with the Hindus and form a united India, the problem of the peasants must be faced. Perhaps the two million soldiers when they return may introduce new ideas. Without new ideas India will remain as it is now, no matter what government it has.

Burmese Post-War Problems Are Looming Large

As a land-link between India and China, Burma occupies a place of great and growing strategic importance. Economically the people have been badly hit, and political problems revolve around the strong nationalism which has been furthered by the Japanese grant of "independence." The tangled position is discussed here by a special Burmese correspondent.

Now that the war in Burma is about to enter a decisive stage, attention is again focused on that country's post-war status and on the economic problems which face the Burmese people. It is in that connexion that Sir Reginald Dorman-Smith, the Governor of Burma, is at present on a visit to this country. Unlike the position in October 1941, when the then Burmese Prime Minister, U Saw, came to England and sought to obtain from the British Government a promise of full Dominion Status for Burma after the war, the political problem is complicated as a result of the Japanese invasion of the country.

With the construction of the Burma Road in 1937-1938, Burma became the only link between war-torn China and the Western democracies, the remaining life-line, by which the Chinese armies continued to receive, until the invasion of Burma in 1942, supplies and munitions with which to defend themselves against the Japanese. Realizing the new strategic importance of Burma, Japanese interest and activities there increased considerably about that time. Japan began to exploit Burmese nationalism.

Japanese propaganda was particularly successful amongst members of the socialistic Thakin Party, an extreme nationalist organization whose followers are politically sophisticated young Burmese. Some months before war broke out in the Far East, a number of leading Thakins were smuggled out of the country by the Japanese across the Burma-Siam border. They were then taken to Japan, where they were given military training in anticipation of the war in East Asia and the Pacific.

Fifth Column Behind Our Lines

When the Japanese armies, supported by elephant supply columns, invaded Burma in January 1942, through the Kawkareik Pass—an ancient invasion route between Burma and Siam—the Japanese were accompanied by the nucleus of the Burmese Independence Army, composed of members of the Thakin Party. Though some did actively fight by the side of the Japanese invaders, their main task was to obtain recruits chiefly amongst members of their own party and to organize fifth column work behind the British lines.

According to Sir Reginald Dorman-Smith, 4,000 Burmese fought against the British, while Field-Marshal Alexander stated that ten per cent of the Burmese were pro-British, another ten per cent pro-Japanese, and the rest were indifferent. As the British withdrew towards the Indian frontier, Dr. Ba Maw, a former Burmese prime minister and leader of the Sinyetha Party (Poor Men's Party), who represented Burma at the Coronation in London in 1937, was rescued by his followers from the jail at Mogok where he had been interned for his numerous seditious speeches.

After encouraging Burmese nationalists to rebel against the British, the Japanese realized that they were in no position to antagonize the Burmese, especially as Burma occupied a vital strategic position on the South-East Asiatic mainland. Instead, Japan decided to pursue a politically subtle policy in Burma. Soon after the British withdrawal, Dr. Ba Maw's Sinyetha Party and the Thakin Party were amalgamated, and Dr. Ba Maw was entrusted with the task of forming a Central Administration, though the country in fact was being ostensibly run by the "gunsei," the Japanese military administration. In March 1943 Dr. Ba Maw visited Tokyo to confer with the then Japanese

Premier, General Hideki Tojo, and on his return an Independence Preparatory Commission was set up. On August 1, 1943, Burma was declared an independent State, and Ba Maw as Head of State and Prime Minister pledged Burma to work whole-heartedly with Japan for the establishment of Greater East Asian collaboration and prosperity.

This shrewd manoeuvre was clearly part of Japan's political warfare in South-East Asia. It has been the aim of the Japanese to fan flames of Burmese nationalism and thereby gain the support of the Burmese nation in their fight against the Western Allied Powers. Though in some respects Burmese independence is perhaps nominal, it nevertheless must have had a profound psychological effect on the Burmese people. Apart from a few Japanese technical advisers,

SIR REGINALD DORMAN-SMITH (left), Governor of Burma since 1941, discussed the Burmese situation with Mr. L. S. Amery, Secretary of State for India and Burma, during a visit to London. *Photo, Topical Press*

the internal administration of the country is in the hands of the Burmese. Renzo Sawada, a former Japanese envoy to France, was sent as the first Japanese ambassador to the newly created Burmese State, while Burma sent Dr. Thein Maung as the Burmese Special Envoy and Plenipotentiary to Japan.

In the cultural sphere steps were taken by Dr. Ba Maw's Government to eradicate British influence. After the declaration of Burmese independence, English as the official language of the country was abolished, and replaced by Burmese. The Burma Society, a literary organization, launched a movement to standardize the Burmese language, and a new dictionary was being compiled. Buddhism was recognized as the religion of the State. A Burmese National Army was also formed, and a military academy opened in Rangoon.

Economically, the Burmese have been very badly hit. The yearly surplus of three million tons of rice could not be exported, while millions of Indians were dying of starvation across the frontier in Bengal. Various industrial installations had been " scorched " by the British to prevent them from falling into the hands of the Japanese. Communications between Upper and Lower Burma having been paralysed through constant Allied air attacks, there was a shortage of rice in Upper Burma while there was a glut in Lower Burma and there was an abundance of cooking oil and vegetables in Upper Burma and a shortage of those foodstuffs in Lower Burma. Japanese propaganda in

Burma blamed the Allies for the country's economic hardships, while the Japanese themselves were unable to do anything. Steps were, however, taken by Dr. Ba Maw's Government to mitigate the plight of the farmers by arranging for the purchase by the State of part of the rice crop at fixed prices. And special measures were taken by Dr. Ba Maw to enable the Burmese cultivators, whose land had been expropriated by Indian moneylenders, to recover their lost rice holdings. The fact that a Burmese Government had helped them to recover most of twenty-five per cent of the 12,000,000 acres of rice land which had passed into the hands of Indian moneylenders must have created a deep impression amongst the Burmese farmers, who constitute eighty per cent of the population.

In Burma before the war almost all commerce and industry was in the hands of foreigners. This resulted in an acute form of Burmese nationalism, for the Burmese felt that they had no stake in their own country as far as its economic wealth was concerned. Further, the Burmese cultivators were burdened with outstanding loans, amounting to £60,000,000 yearly, to Indian moneylenders, of which £40,000,000 was advanced to finance agriculture. As compared with this enormous sum, the Burma Government advanced only £150,000 yearly under the Agricultural Loans Act of 1884.

Development of Communications

What of the future ? The first and foremost task naturally will have to be the settlement of the land problem, the elimination of Indian moneylenders, and the providing of proper financial facilities to Burmese farmers. Then there is the question of re-establishment of the petroleum, lumber and mining industries, and the part the Burmese as such will be allowed to play in their future development. Though more Burmese may invest in these industrial enterprises than was the case hitherto, there are few Burmese with ready capital. The Burmese will insist, therefore, that a certain percentage of the capital be subscribed by the State. They will also want a substantial number of Burmese to be trained as technicians and employed by the various British industrial undertakings.

A form of independence having been granted by the Japanese, it will not be easy to impose a pre-war administration on the Burmese people. Whatever political arrangements are made between Britain and Burma, it would go a long way towards establishing cordial relations between the two countries if due regard were to be given to the national and cultural sentiments of the Burman nation. It must be remembered that before Burma became part of the British Empire the Burmese Kingdom had never been ruled over by a foreign power, though Burma was wedged between two mighty neighbours, China and India.

With the return of peace in East Asia the strategic importance of Burma will be far from diminishing. On the contrary, the development of communications which the war has brought about between Burma and her neighbours will assure Burma's geographic importance in the Far East. The completion of the railway connecting Burma and China would mean that Burma would become a vital trade link between the outer world and Yunnan, a part of China which has scarcely been developed. It would therefore be to the advantage of the British Commonwealth to have a politically and economically stable Burma.

E.N.S.A. Cheered Our Troops on to Mandalay

GLADDENING THE HEARTS OF THE TROOPS IN BURMA, an E.N.S.A. party calling itself "Coming Your Way" gave an impromptu show on a forward R.A.F. airstrip on the road to Mandalay (captured on March 20, 1945, when Indian troops of the famous 19th "Dagger" Division entered Fort Dufferin), after a previous performance had been interrupted by the Japanese. To the accordion accompaniment of Freddie Everard of Peckham Rye, Carolyn Wright of Woodham Cherrers and Roberta Robertson of Folkestone gave a highly appreciated display of tap-dancing on a dismantled work-bench top.   See also pages 492-493 and 595.

Photo, British Official

War Graves of British Commonwealth of Nations

Years after hostilities cease, constructional work on the British Commonwealth and Empire graves of this war, from Belgium to Burma, from Abyssinia to the Aegean, from Normandy and Norway to Tunis and Timor, will still be in progress. VICTOR HYDE, M.C., here relates the progress made and relieves anxieties of next-of-kin. See also pages 44-45, 748-749, Vol. 7.

"ONE of our aircraft is missing . . ." On Whit Monday, 1943, an aircraft of R.A.F. Fighter Command failed to return from operations over the Atlantic. On Whit Thursday I stood—am I ever likely to forget ?—by an open grave overlooking a bay in a remote island 30 miles from the English mainland while we buried the pilot. He was my elder son.

He is one among 282,162 British Empire slain (the latest available figures, including U.K. losses of 199,497, but excluding 80,580 Empire Missing, covering the period September 3, 1939 to November 30, 1944), most of the parents of whom had said, "No, it couldn't happen to *him* . . . They wouldn't take *our* Derek . . . *We* shan't get that dreaded telegram." Yet it did happen . . . Their Derek—my Derek—was taken . . . Each one of us opened that dreaded telegram. Over 282,000 Empire war graves are to be

and Sicily they are described as the "main" ones in these theatres. In Normandy they include Bayeux. first town captured by the Allies after D-Day, and Tilly, scene of bitter fighting before the break-through. Others are situated at Ranville, Bernay, Sequeville-en-Bessin, Barneville, Cambes, Rauray, Rosée and St. Mauvieu.

GRAVES of officers and men who lost their lives on the landing beaches have been brought together in one cemetery. It will be known as Hermanville Beach-head cemetery. Two of the twenty invasion burial grounds, at Beny-sur-Mer and Bretteville-sur-Laize, contain graves of Canadian troops only. Some of these places, as La Delivrande and Juaye-Mondaye—known also as Jerusalem —are comparatively small villages shown only on a large-scale map. The remaining five of these twenty Normandy cemeteries

triumphant campaign. They include El Alamein, Tobruk, Halfaya-Sollum, Acroma (Knightsbridge), and Benghazi and Tripoli military cemeteries in the Western Desert, Mareth (Guards) cemetery, Sfax, Enfidaville, Medjez-el-Bab, Thibar Seminary, Beja, Massicault, Tabarka (Ras-Rajel) and Oued Zarga cemeteries in Tunisia, and Algiers (El Alia), Bone, Bougie (La Reunion) and Dely Ibrahim cemeteries in Algeria.

EARLY actions in the Italian campaign will be commemorated in the Salerno Beach-head cemetery, and in the Sangro and Morro River cemeteries. At Anzio there will be built two more "silent cities of the slain," to be known as Anzio Military and Anzio Beach-head cemeteries. Of the three principal Sicilian burial grounds, two are British— at hotly-disputed Catania and at Syracuse —and the remaining one Canadian, at Agira.

Architects appointed by the Imperial War Graves Commission and already at work in these areas include Mr. J. H. Worthington, of Alderley Edge, Cheshire, in North Africa ; Mr. Louis de Soissons, of Welwyn Garden City, in Italy ; and Mr. Philip Hepworth, of Chiswick, West London, in Northern France. One of the first decisions of the Commission in 1940 was to erect headstones of the same pattern as that which marks the graves of the First World War. With the exception of North Africa, Eritrea, Abyssinia and similar regions where the tide of battle has long since ebbed serious constructional work must inevitably wait, first upon the regrouping of isolated graves, and secondly upon the end of hostilities.

The Only Money Asked of Us

Then there are such problems as design, shipping of the headstones, and the assembly of skilled labour, including the stonemason and those sterling fellows whom, in the decades between the two wars it was a privilege to know—the ex-Servicemen caretaker-gardeners. These, in the final count, are the backbone of the Commission. Carved on each headstone, in serried rows by the right as the warriors beneath them dressed on earth by the right, are the name, age, rank, unit and Service number of the casualty, together with his corps or regimental badge.

WAYSIDE CEMETERY AT MAY-SUR-ORNE, in Normandy, where lie many brave Canadians fallen in this war, the Union Jack flying above them. The padre requested that the shattered trees on the right should be left standing—cut off in their young lives, as these men were.
Photo, British Newspaper Pool

constructed, cared for, maintained, and perhaps six and seven times that number of relatives, each in different ways anxious for information concerning one particular grave, are rightly full of questions.

"In which cemetery is our boy buried ? When will the headstone be erected ? What will be its wording ? Are we given any say in the choice of words ? Does any part of the cost devolve upon the next-of-kin ? How about post-war maintenance ? Shall we be able to obtain a photograph of his grave ? Will facilities exist for visiting our military cemeteries ? How can we arrange for wreaths to be placed on the grave on the anniversary of his passing or on his birthday?"

THOSE are among the most pressing anxieties. Let us look at the answers together, you and I, who in this moment of common sacrifice feel for each other so deeply.

Fifty-eight military cemeteries of this war have so far been named. Twenty are in Normandy, six in Belgium, nine in Italy, three in Sicily, twenty in North Africa. Work has begun on others in Holland. Few of these totals are final ; they represent only those cemeteries for which names have been approved, while in the case of Africa, Italy

are situated at Ryes, Couville, Hottot-les-Bogues, Lingevres, and Fontenay-le-Mesnil.

FAMOUS names in the headlines of the fighting of last summer in Belgium, where permanent cemeteries are also to be constructed, include Bourg Leopold, Antwerp, Gheel and Louvain. In Holland, up to the present, only a few have been laid out, including one at Nijmegen. Service plots are being formed in certain civil cemeteries in all three countries, to be known, as were similar plots of the First World War, as communal cemetery extensions.

The twenty main North African cemeteries provide a poignant picture of the tide of battle in the critical years of 1941 and 1942, and of Field-Marshal Alexander's final

AT the moment of going to press we learned with deep regret of the sudden death of Mr. Victor Hyde, author of this article. For years he had been accepted as the leading authority on the subject and as special correspondent of our national newspapers he had visited the battlefields many times.—ED.

In every case provision is made for a personal inscription chosen by the next-of-kin and restricted to sixty letters, to appear at the foot of the headstone. For this the nominal sum of 7s. 6d. is asked ; should this impose a hardship, then the Commission will bear the charge itself. That is the only money it asks of us. Each grave in time and in season will be planted with flowers, shrubs and plants indigenous to the country ; none will ever lack its floral quilt. In certain theatres, notably France and Belgium, the Commission will establish new or restock old nurseries, from which millions of plants will be propagated and transplanted. Unto our children's children—unto perpetuity—the Commission is charged in this way with the maintenance of the graves of our boys, and well enough endowed never to want for funds.

You yearn for a picture of his grave ? You long to visit it ? You want to remember him with your own personal tribute on his birthday ? All these affairs are best arranged through a reputable ex-Servicemen's association. For those—the very poor—who want to visit a distant cemetery but lack the funds for the trip, free passages might possibly be provided. More than one organization extended a helping hand in this way after the First Great War.

For Them the Tumult and Discord Has Ceased

ON A DALMATIAN ISLAND OVERLOOKING THE ADRIATIC the Bishop of Lichfield, Dr. E. S. Woods, travelling by Baltimore bomber, recently consecrated a cemetery for Allied war dead (top). Only a few miles of water separate it from German-held territory. On the island is also an advanced R.A.F. airfield used for strikes into Yugoslavia. A U.S. soldier pays silent homage to fallen comrades in a temporary U.S.-British cemetery at El Alia in N. Africa (bottom) over which fly the Union Jack and Old Glory. See facing page. PAGE 759 *Photos, British Official, Keystone*

Hue-and-Cry for Nazis in the Vale of Glamorgan

SEVENTY GERMANS made a daring mass-escape from a prisoner-of-war camp (I) at Bridgend, Glamorganshire, on March II, 1945, tunnelling a narrow 27-ft. passage from their sleeping-quarters to beyond the barbed-wire (2). Though 16 were caught before they could run a hundred yards and another 12 within as many minutes, the remainder for a time eluded capture, the hue-and-cry over the Vale of Glamorgan and beyond developing into one of the biggest man-hunts ever seen in Britain. R.A.F. planes, thousands of armed troops, including U.S. soldiers equipped with tear gas, police, Home Guards, girls of the Women's Land Army and civilians joined in the chase.

A patrol checks up on a motorist's identity card (3). After 40 hours of freedom, these prisoners (5), including S.S. troopers, Luftwaffe pilots and naval men, were escorted back to camp. By March 17 all the fugitives were recaptured. Four Nazi prisoners unsuccessfully tried to seize a Mustang on a North-country U.S. airfield in December 1944; they are seen (4) after recapture.

Photos, U.S. Official, Topical Press, News Chronicle, Keystone

Royal Navy to the Rescue of Hunted Norwegians

Mostly women and children, 525 Norwegians were collected by a small Military Mission of their own countrymen, then brought safely to a British port (announced March 18, 1945) by Royal Navy and Royal Canadian Navy destroyers. How this rescue was effected was told to Evening Standard Naval reporter Gordon Holman by a Norwegian Army officer.

Maj.-Gen. T. W. REES, D.S.O., M.C., Commander of the 19th Indian ("Dagger") Division, broadcast a running commentary of the fierce fight for Fort Dufferin, Mandalay, which we entered on March 20, 1945. Story is told below. *Photo, British Official*

THESE are very simple people. They not only had no desire to work for the Germans, but they also hated leaving their homes. They know little of the outside world and all they wanted was to be left to their fishing. But the Germans showed them no mercy and when we set out we knew that they were living in the most desperate conditions.

We arrived in a bay off the island one morning. The land appeared to be deserted, but then we caught sight of one or two people. They were trying to get away up the steep mountain. We shouted to them, but, like timid and frightened animals, they still wanted to get away.

Then we managed to persuade one of them that we were really Norwegians. The others stopped, and presently the news was being carried all over the island that help had come. We had food with us on this small relief patrol, and we gave it to them and then began to collect the old and sick people. There was very little daylight, and we took some time to get 200 ill and old inhabitants into our boats.

I lived in a small tent. There was nowhere else to live unless you crowded into the caves and peat houses and rock crevices in which

One night my patrol went out in a heavy snowstorm and the Germans were searching along the seaboard aided by a searchlight from one of their vessels. Often men dug themselves deep down into the snow to avoid detection by the Nazis.

Finally more than 500 people were collected ready for the great moment when Allied warships came to evacuate them. One man carried his grandmother on his shoulders 18 miles to be ready at the point of evacuation.

Then there were days of great suspense, but one morning British warships steamed in and men, women and children were taken aboard them, given hot food and treated once again as human beings.

The British sailors gave everything they could to them. Thirty children were in the captain's cabin in one destroyer. It was wonderful to see them no longer afraid.

Mandalay Battle Was Fought with Burning Oil

Second city of Burma, Mandalay had been in Japanese hands for close on three years when troops of the 19th Indian ("Dagger") Division captured it on March 20, 1945. Fort Dufferin was the centre of Jap resistance in fighting that was still in progress on March 11, when this dispatch was written by Daily Herald war reporter Arthur Halliwell.

JAPANESE resistance is stiffening as troops of General "Thruster" Rees's 19th Division push on into Mandalay. Those of us who watched the Japs repulse yesterday's gallant attack on Fort Dufferin got a very good idea of what we can expect in the next few days. They are resisting from pagodas, from deep air-raid shelters built by Burmese, and from immensely strong concrete pillboxes.

And they are fighting with all their old fanatical indifference to death. The Jap in this mood is the most difficult soldier in the world to beat. Some of them have crept back on to the slopes of Monastery Hill and gone to earth like moles in the maze of tunnels connecting the various pagodas with which the mountain is studded. There has been some gallant and spectacular fighting up there during the last 24 hours.

Gurkhas have been sitting on the tops of pagodas, lobbing grenades at the Japs inside in a grim game of pitch and toss. Today they have been employing "Ali Baba and the Forty Thieves" technique by pouring boiling oil and petrol into the tunnels and literally frying the Japanese alive.

Meanwhile, the slow encirclement of Fort

these poor people were existing. For four months they had watched the Germans come day by day and burn dwellings and any form of human shelter. The Nazis did not always trouble to give a warning. In one house two women were burned to death ; one was aged 90, the other 27.

The Germans came in armed trawlers and R-boats, and destroyers were known to be in the region. One day I watched them blow up what I think was the last remaining building in Hammerfest just across the sund where they used to have a U-boat base. We organized the evacuation despite these daily visits from the ruthless German patrols.

I saw Germans come ashore one day and wade up to their armpits through snow just to burn a shed in which there was some hay.

BRITISH NAVAL FORCES STOOD BY in the fjord (above) whilst Nazi-hunted Norwegians tramped through the snow of Soroy Island (left) with all the haste they could muster to the safety of the waiting rescue-ships, which transported them to Scotland, where they were then billeted. See story above, and page 749 ; also pages 588-589. PAGE 761 *Photos, Norwegian Official*

IN MANDALAY, British troops of the 19th Indian Division guarded a pagoda entrance, waiting for the emergence of Japanese who had "gone to earth" in tunnels beneath, before the city fell on March 20, 1945.
Photo, British Official

Dufferin continues. To the east Gurkhas are making a sweep outside the city boundaries, while men of the Royal Berks are working down the western moat against comparatively slight resistance.

At times yesterday the warfare seemed to hark back to the days of the Thin Red Line

and the Crimea. A crew of five ran their gun right up to Fort Dufferin to blast breaches in its 20-ft. walls, over open sights.

I went up to watch the shoot. The red battlements of the fort were only 200 yards away when the gun unlimbered. We were so close that fine dust from the walls smothered us as 100-lb. shells hammered into them. We could see the great walls crumbling. Bricks and mortar flew high. Soon a wide breach has been made. Then the crew shifted the sights and pounded the Japs inside the wall at two other points in preparation for a charge of the Frontier Force Regiment that was to follow.

"It's the best shoot we've ever had," Sergt. Gus Pratt, of Leeds, told me. "We've done some bunker-blasting over open sights, but we've never fired at such close range. It gave all the lads a kick to see our shells knocking hell out of the wall." The gun had fired 50 rounds before Jap snipers managed to work round on the flank.

As the gun withdrew, its work well done, tanks and infantry began moving up. I watched their assault from the shelter of foxholes. The tanks moved up to within 50 yards of the fort, hammering the walls with shell fire, and spraying machine-gunners on the battlements with small arms fire.

The whole of the main gateway was soon ablaze. It burned like a torch, spouting flames 50 feet into the air. Great timbers came crashing down in cascades of sparks, while the sappers crawled forward to cut the Japs' wire and locate the mines. Those sappers were heroes. They went in right under the enemy's guns. I saw one pitch forward on his face and lie still. But his comrades crawled resolutely forward without pause.

FORT DUFFERIN was the last Japanese stronghold in Mandalay, surrounded with a wide moat and high battlemented wall, both of which were heavily attacked by R.A.F. Hurribombers of Eastern Air Command before the final assault *Photo, The Times*

so we drove on, and saw a little girl who could not have been more than about eight, running madly towards the back yard of her home with her hands up in the air. We left this village and clattered into another. Again white flags, again the same scared faces at the windows. There were, however, a few fresh highlights. There was a woman, for example, who put up her hands as we approached, and when the lieutenant signalled her to put them down, began waving frantically with both hands.

Then there was an unforgettable little scene as we passed a large, prosperous-looking house. We caught a brief glimpse of the interior, of the family seated at their Sunday dinner. Suddenly, someone ran out from the back of the house and began waving and blowing kisses at us. She was a middle-aged, rosy woman with high cheek bones, wearing a coloured handkerchief round her head, and high Russian peasant boots. She was calling out greetings in Russian to us.

There was no need to wonder what was behind this scene. She was obviously a Russian domestic slave of this prosperous German family, greeting her liberators. As we rounded the bend of the village street we saw some more people frantically dashing into their houses, and the lieutenant shrewdly guessed they were going to warn German soldiers hiding there that we were coming.

And so we lumbered on towards the small town Patton's men had taken four days ago. Here the atmosphere was entirely different. People had become accustomed to the idea of being "occupied," and were wandering about engaged in a Sunday afternoon stroll. They were dressed in their Sunday best.

First Into White Flag Villages on the Rhine

Driving 52 miles in 58 hours, armour of Gen. Patton's U.S. 3rd Army made a cross-country dash from the region of Trier, to reach the Rhine, near Coblenz, on March 7, 1945. Sam White, with one of the tank columns, describes in this story from The Evening Standard the scenes in Rhineland villages which they were first of the victorious Allies to enter.

WE mounted our tanks, and the lieutenant almost whispered into the mouthpiece, "Let's go!" One after another, heaving slightly like cruisers in a heavy swell, six tanks in our column moved off to see what fire we could draw from the opposite bank of the Rhine, and to round up some of the hundreds of German soldiers waiting patiently to surrender.

I watched the east bank of the river intently. It was like a film travelogue in slow motion. The villages and small towns,

smokeless factory chimneys and deserted fields, slipped by us looking as though some magic had robbed them of all life.

Then we saw our first village approaching and the lieutenant said, "None of our boys have been through here yet. Keep an eye out for snipers . . ." As we neared it we could see white flags fluttering everywhere. Some were as large as tablecloths.

The main street was crowded with civilians busily looting a wrecked German convoy. Immediately they saw and heard us they scattered, and when we entered the village street looked deserted. It was strange to see the first immediate impact on German civilians of American armour clattering down their street. Everywhere faces peered at us from nervously drawn window blinds.

A few of the braver spirits, almost invariably middle-aged men, stood in the doorways of their houses. Some smiled sheepishly; others raised their caps; one or two attempted something like a wave. One man in complete panic gave the Nazi salute. The lieutenant gazed sharply round at him, then grinned, "Say, that guy was scared!" And

WHITE FLAGS AT DURENBACH, in the Rhineland, suggested washing-day when the 11th Armoured Division of the U.S. 3rd Army seized it in March 1945. *Photo, U.S. Official*

I'm Running a Railway in Battered France

Taking a rest from actual war, an American soldier in France—Lieut. S. B. Valentine, Corps of Engineers—has recorded in letters home something of the lighter side of active service and how even in the most unpromising circumstances a good time may be had by all! His stories are reproduced by arrangement with the New York Times Magazine.

I AM now running a railroad. The system in these parts was knocked out by the Air Force; it is our job to get it functioning again. I feel like a kid who has got a new set of tracks for Christmas, and, although I will soon have to turn it over to

the N.C.O.s and go back to saying "yes" and "no," at the moment I am out there all day and most of the night batting cars around, pulling switches, blowing whistles and hopping on and off trains like a dancer.

Theoretically, I am trying to co-ordinate our rail activities with those of the French, but for reasons I will describe this sensible idea seldom becomes a fact. First, there is that little matter of the language barrier. My French has improved, but it's not up to conversations on technical subjects. Usually when I ask for a schedule of their trains I get a detailed drawing of a switchbox. If I tell them I will have a train for them at such and such an hour they turn up at that time expecting dinner.

Then, too, the French seem to be capable of what I can only call enthusiastic inefficiency, especially now that anybody is an "official" of the railroad—if you order two locomotives for Thursday you don't get them on Thursday; instead, the following Saturday you get four. Much of my time is spent in conferences with the Chef de Gare. Before we can begin one, there must be a pause while he takes off his beret and puts on his official hat with the stars on it. This done, we settle down to argue about schedules.

My aim is to find out if anything is coming through at a given time. I am assured a thousand times no—it is impossible—the road is bombed out above or below, nothing could pass. Still dubious, but somewhat reassured, I rise; the Chef removes his official hat and puts his beret back on. We adjourn for a glass of wine next door. At this very moment I hear a familiar sound, and blanketa, blanketa, blanketa, an express comes "balling the jack" down the line. The Chef looks at it, gives an enormous shrug and says to me, "Ce n'est pas possible."

Some day soon, of course, all this will be straightened out. When it is I hope we will have moved on, because things will be damn dull. We work from dawn to 8 p.m. and by the time we have had our chow it is about 9. So, for lack of any other diversion, we get in a jeep and drive around, stopping to talk to groups of French. A few nights ago on one such trip we got ourselves involved in some local happenings.

As we drove through the winding, house-smothered streets we could dimly see people standing in the doorways, or leaning against trees, talking and waving their hands as usual. In one village we came to a complete standstill because we couldn't get through the knot of people standing in the middle of the road. We were promptly surrounded and everybody started spitting French at us like a battery of machine-guns.

By concentrating on one set of speakers that were chattering in front of me I learned that there was a fire at a near-by farm. When I started to translate for T., he said: " Hell, I knew that, because there are two French firemen in our back seat ! "

Arriving, finally, at the fire it proved to be something of an anticlimax, to us anyway. Only a haystack was burning, in the middle of a square of barns. Everything was confusion : there were horse-drawn water-tanks, firemen in full regalia (which is very fancy here), other firemen on bicycles, and villagers snarled up in hose lines that were still dry. Everyone was yelling for "l'eau !" at the top of his or her lungs. T. and I had to leave shortly, but not before we saw a tiny, tired trickle of water come out of one nozzle and land about three yards short of the stack. The whole thing would have disgusted Mayor La Guardia, but a high old time was had by all.

REPAIRING THE RAIL BRIDGE AT CAEN, Normandy, wrecked by Nazis in July 1944, a typical example of the work of the Royal Engineers, Pioneer and Railway Construction Corps. By March 19, 1945, they had restored 80 railway bridges, and repaired 1,020 miles of main-line routes in north-west Europe since D-Day. Experiences of an engineer operating a battered French railway are told in the accompanying story.
Photo, British Official

OUR DIARY OF THE WAR

MARCH 14, Wednesday 2,020th day
Western Front.—U.S. 3rd Army infantry crossed Moselle S.W. of Coblenz.
Air.—R.A.F. ten-ton bombs used for first time in daylight attack on viaduct at Bielefeld. At night, R.A.F. bombed enemy troop concentrations in Zweibrucken and Homburg.
Russian Front.—In the Carpathians Soviet troops captured Zvolen, N. of Budapest.
Mediterranean.—Allied bombers from Italy attacked Hungarian oil plants 35 miles from Russian front.

MARCH 15, Thursday 2,021st day
Western Front.—U.S. 7th Army launched attack on the Saar Basin.
Air.—U.S bombers attacked H.Q. of German General Staff at Zossen. R.A.F. dropped ten-ton bombs on viaduct at Arnsberg, and at night made heavy attack on Hagen, east of Ruhr.

MARCH 16, Friday 2,022nd day
Western Front.—U.S. 1st Army troops cut Ruhr-Frankfurt motor-road. 7th Army captured Bitche.
Air.—At night R.A.F. heavy bombers attacked Nuremberg and Würzburg.
Russian Front.—German counter-attacks N. of Lake Balaton slackened after loss of 600 tanks and 20,000 men in 13 days' battle.
Pacific.—Organized Japanese resistance ended on Iwojima.
Japan.—Super-Fortresses made heavy attack on port of Kobe.

MARCH 17, Saturday 2,023rd day
Western Front.—U.S. 3rd Army troops stormed into Coblenz.
Air.—Strong forces of Allied bombers attacked German oil plants, tank factories and railway yards.
Sea.—Coastal forces of Royal Navy and aircraft of Coastal Command scattered E-boat formations in the North Sea.

MARCH 18, Sunday 2,024th day
Western Front.—U.S. 3rd and 7th Armies converged on Germans west of the Rhine; tanks entered Bad Kreuznach and Bingen.
Air.—Over 1,300 Fortresses and Liberators made greatest daylight attack on Berlin. Typhoons made low-level attacks on headquarters of Gens. Blaskowitz and Christiansen in the Netherlands.

Russian Front.—Baltic port of Kolberg, N.E. of Stettin, captured by Soviet troops.
Japan.—U.S. carrier-aircraft attacked airfields in Kyushu. Super-Fortresses bombed Nagoya.
Pacific.—U.S. warships bombarded Japanese positions in Kurile Is.

MARCH 19, Monday 2,025th day
Western Front.—French troops of U.S. 7th Army crossed German frontier. Coblenz cleared of the enemy.
Air.—U.S. bombers attacked jet-aircraft installations in southern Germany. Lancasters attacked viaduct at Arnsberg with ten-ton bombs.
Burma.—Troops of 2nd Division occupied Ava, south of Mandalay.
Philippines.—U.S. troops landed on island of Panay.
Japan.—U.S carrier-aircraft bombed Kobe and Kure. Carrier task-force also attacked units of Japanese Fleet in the Inland Sea.

MARCH 20, Tuesday 2,026th day
Western Front.—U.S. 3rd and 7th Armies linked up W. of Kaiserslautern. 3rd Army reached Mainz and captured Worms. 7th Army captured Saarbrücken and Zweibrücken.
Air.—Fortresses and Liberators attacked U-boat yards and oil refineries at Hamburg. R.A.F. bombed railway

yards at Hamm and Recklinghausen and at night attacked oil plants near Leipzig and Heide.
Russian Front.—Soviet troops took Braunsberg, E. of Danzig, and by capturing Altdamm wiped out German bridge-head on Oder E. of Stettin.
Burma.—All Mandalay freed with capture of Fort Dufferin.

MARCH 21, Wednesday 2,027th day
Western Front.—Ludwigshafen, opposite Mannheim, entered by U.S. 3rd Army. Kaiserslautern cleared.
Air.—U.S. bombers attacked jet-aircraft bases near Dutch-German border. R.A.F. dropped ten-ton bombs on railway bridge near Bremen. Mosquitoes bombed Gestapo H.Q. in Copenhagen.

MARCH 22, Thursday 2,028th day
Western Front. Troops of U.S. 3rd Army crossed Rhine at Oppenheim, S. of Mainz.
Air.—R.A.F. and U.S. bombers attacked advanced bases and army concentrations east of Wesel and in the Ruhr.
Russian Front.—In Silesia Koniev's troops broke through W. and S. of Oppeln, capturing Neustadt and Steinau.

MARCH 23, Friday 2,029th day
Western Front.—British, Canadian and U.S. forces under Montgomery began

to cross Rhine in Wesel sector. Speyer and Landau captured, Mainz cleared, by U.S. 3rd Army.
Air.—R.A.F. and U.S. bombers again attacked railways with object of isolating the Ruhr.
Russian Front.—Zoppot, between Danzig and Gdynia, captured by Soviet troops.
Far East.—U.S. battleships and carrier-aircraft attacked Ryukyu Islands, between Formosa and Japan.

MARCH 24, Saturday 2,030th day
Western Front.—Allied airborne troops dropped east of Rhine and linked up with Montgomery's land forces. British Commandos captured Wesel.
Air.—Sixteen German airfields bombed by U.S. aircraft. R.A.F. bombed marshalling yards near Sterkrade. Bombers from Italy attacked tank works at Berlin.
Russian Front.—In Hungary, Tolbukhin's troops made sweeping advance, capturing Szekesfehervar. In Silesia, Koniev captured Neisse.
Australia.—New graving dock at Sydney (Captain Cook Dock) opened.

MARCH 25, Sunday 2,031st day
Western Front.—Four landings across Rhine between Rees and Wesel merged into 30-mile bridgehead. U.S. 3rd Army crossed Main and captured Darmstadt.
Air.—R.A.F. attacked railway centres of Munster, Osnabruck and Hanover. U.S. Liberators bombed buried oil depots in Hamburg area.
Russian Front.—Malinovsky's troops broke through W. of Budapest and occupied Esztergom, Neszmely, Felsogalla and Tata. In Baltic, Heiligenbeil was captured.
Far East.—Liberators wrecked hydro-electric plant on Formosa.

MARCH 26, Monday 2,032nd day
Western Front.—Scottish troops of 2nd Army cleared Rees; U.S. 1st Army reached Limburg; 3rd Army tanks entered Bavaria at Aschaffenburg; 7th Army crossed the Rhine N. of Mannheim.
Russian Front.—Malinovsky captured Banska-Bystrica in Slovakia. Tolbukhin took Papa and Devecser on approaches to Austria.
Far East.—U.S. carrier-aircraft and battleships again attacked Okinawa in the Ryukyu Islands.

★ ════════ *Flash-backs* ════════ ★

1941
March 20. *British Somaliland cleared of Italian troops.*
March 24. *El Aghella occupied by Axis forces; first appearance of Afrika Korps in Libya.*

1942
March 17. *Gen. MacArthur arrived in Australia as C.-in-C. of Allied Forces in South-west Pacific.*
March 23. *Japanese occupied Andaman Is., in Bay of Bengal.*

1943
March 15. *Russians evacuated Kharkov (held since Feb. 16).*
March 20. *8th Army began assault on Mareth Line in Tunisia.*

1944
March 15. *Cassino town attacked with 1,400 tons of bombs.*
March 19. *German troops began occupation of Hungary.*
March 24. *Major-Gen. Wingate killed in air crash in Burma.*

THE WAR IN THE AIR

by Capt. Norman Macmillan, M.C., A.F.C.

TECHNICALLY and practically, the most important development in the air war is the introduction of the 22,000-lb. streamlined bomb. Designed by Mr. B. N. Wallis, of Vickers-Armstrongs, its development was the responsibility of the Ministry of Aircraft Production, with the English Steel Corporation of Sheffield, who cast the first bodies, playing a great supervisory part in the technique of metallurgy. Complete bomb bodies are now being supplied from the U.S.A., although the only aeroplane so far modified to carry this huge bomb is the Lancaster. It takes a ground crew of six half-an-hour to load one bomb into a Lancaster with special hoisting tackle.

The development of large bombs has continued progressively throughout the war.

piers supporting seven spans of the southern viaduct had entirely disappeared and only the stumps remained of the piers carrying seven spans of the other. It should be borne in mind that a viaduct is a most difficult target. (See illustration in this page.) On March 15, Bomber Command's 22,000-lb. bombs were again used, this time against the railway viaduct at Arnsberg. On March 19, Lancasters carrying 22,000-lb. and 12,000-lb. bombs again attacked this viaduct, and another in the area of Bielefeld ; they were escorted by Mustangs of Fighter Command.

These attacks were part of a strategic assault from the air upon German communications. On March 10, the U.S.A. 8th A.F. sent 1,350 Fortresses and Liberators with 500 Mustang fighters as escort to bomb the Ruhr

R.A.F.'s NEW 10-TON BOMB, designed by Mr. B. Neville Wallis (left), did this to Bielefeld twin viaducts, first enemy objective to feel the enormous missile's weight. The structure carried one of the two last remaining double-track railways east from the Ruhr before it was thus dealt with by Lancasters in daylight on March 14, 1945.
Photos, British Official, Associated Press

In March 1941 the R.A.F. dropped its first 4,000-lb. bomb. Early in 1943 came the 8,000-lb., and early in 1944 the 12,000-lb. bombs. All these were of the "blockbuster" type, intended to destroy built-up area structures such as factories, largely by blast effect. In June 1944 came the streamlined 12,000-lb. bomb which sank the Tirpitz, but failed to burst the Sorpe dam. Will the latest 22,000-lb. bomb break this massive concrete dam that its forerunners have failed to break ? Up to the moment of writing it has been used only against railway viaducts between the Ruhr and central Germany.

THE first 22,000-lb. bomb attack was made on March 14, 1945, on twin viaducts at Bielefeld. Photographic reconnaissance disclosed that they were wrecked over more than 100 yards, or nearly one-third of the overall length of the structure. The great

railway marshalling yards. On March 11, medium bombers of the M.A.A.F. for the first time flew over German-occupied Austria to bomb the railway bridge near Drauburg, 105 miles south-east of Munich, on the line between Lienz and Klagenfurt.

Next day over 1,000 Lancaster and Halifax bombers with a fighter escort attacked the Ruhr communications centre of Dortmund ; more than 5,000 tons were dropped, and nearly 75 per cent of the force carried a 4,000-lb. bomb in their load, while some had 12,000-lb. bombs ; Dortmund has now received about 22,000 tons of bombs. On the same day about 700 Fortress and Liberator bombers attacked railway yards between Frankfort-on-the-Main and the Ruhr. On March 13, Halifaxes with a fighter escort bombed the repaired town of Barmen, on the last main route then open to the Ruhr.

In addition to its nightly raids by Bomber Command Mosquitoes, Berlin had two big

daylight communications raids by the U.S.A. 8th A.F. heavy bombers. On March 15, 1,350 Fortresses and Liberators, escorted by over 750 fighters, bombed military targets near Berlin, including the railway yards at Oranienburg, 20 miles north of the capital. These yards were hit by 3,500,000 lb. of bombs, many of them 2,000-lb. bombs— the first mention of bombs of this calibre being used by these day bombers.

On March 18 nearly 1,000 Fortresses dropped their loads on Berlin's Schlesischer Station traffic centre two miles east of the German Air Ministry, and the North Station freight yards two miles north of the Ministry, while more than 300 Liberators struck at armament works in Tegel and Hennigsdorf, six and eleven miles north-west of Berlin. From noon a ton of bombs fell every second, until more than 2,700 tons were dropped. Me. 262 jetplanes attacked the bombers, and three Fortresses were lost.

OIL Plants Systematically Paralysed by Bomber Command

The second great strategic bombing plan, that against oil targets, was continued. Bomber Command attacked Scholven-Buer synthetic oil plant in the Ruhr (March 10) ; the synthetic oil plant at Lutzendorf, near Halle, Saxony, on March 14-15 ; benzol plants at Castrop Rauxel and near Essen on March 15 ; one benzol plant near Huls and another north-east of Dortmund (March 17) ; two benzol plants, one 10 miles east of Bochum and one north of Hattineen (March 18) ; an oil refinery at Bremen (March 20). On March 15, U.S.A. 15th A.F. Fortresses flew 1,400 miles to bomb the Ruhland oil refineries between Berlin and Dresden—the greatest effort yet from Italy ; while Liberators of the same force bombed Moosbierbaum, Floridsdorf and Schwechat oil refineries near Vienna. On March 17, the U.S.A. 8th A.F. sent 1,300 Fortresses and Liberators to bomb oil targets at Bohlen, Ruhland, Moblis, Hanover, and Munster.

Other objectives attacked in Germany were Ruhr Valley targets by 1,350 U.S. bombers (March 9) ; over 500,000 incendiaries on Dessau by Bomber Command (March 7-8) ; 4,000-5,000 tons on Essen by Bomber Command (March 11) ; over 1,600 tons on Swinemunde by U.S. bombers (March 12). Fortresses and Liberators bombed the H.Q. of the German General Staff at Zossen, 20 miles south of Berlin, on March 15.

U.S. forces landed on Iwojima island on February 19 following an air and sea bombardment. Resistance ended there on March 16, and Iwojima's southern airfield is now one of the busiest in the Western Pacific. The first Super-Fortress came in early in March, and before the end of that month Super-Fortresses were landing there on their way back to base after almost every mission over Japan. (Their bomb load can be increased because Iwojima cuts the distance from the Marianas bases almost by a half.) Super-Fortress targets in Japan were Tokyo for the twelfth time on March 9-10, when about 15 square miles of factories and buildings were destroyed by fire ; and Nagoya on March 11, when 2,000 tons of incendiaries were dropped ; while Osaka, second largest city in Japan, received 2,000 tons on March 13.

On March 19 about 1,400 U.S. carrier aircraft, operating with a naval force that sailed into the Inland Sea, attacked targets in Kyushu—mainly Kobe, Kure and other bases—while Super-Fortresses attacked farther north ; 475 Jap aircraft were destroyed, mostly on the ground. Much damage by fire was caused in these raids against Jap cities by a new incendiary cluster bomb. At about 5,000 feet this 500-lb. bomb releases a shower of 6-lb. bombs filled with jellied petrol, each of which spreads flaming petrol for about 30 yards.

How Transport Command Serves Us Overseas

ON A BELGIAN AIRF.ELD British Army lorries line up (1) ready to rush supplies from Dakota aircraft of R.A.F. Transport Command to forward positions on the Rhineland front. While Allied armies probe deeper into the Reich, the Support Group of Transport Command fly priority supplies—ammunition, rations, medical requisites, letters from home—to the front lines. They carry troops homeward on leave, and wounded to hospitals in Britain.

Inside a Dakota (2), showing mail and newspapers being unloaded for forward units. Belgian civilians assist Allied wounded on board a homeward-bound plane (3). When Transport Command took over a Belgian airfield, the aircraft using it brought their own 1,200 yards of runway carried in the form of steel netting in large sections (later to be covered with matting when in position), one of which is seen (4) being unloaded by civilian workers. See page 748.

Photos, Brit. Official

Smiles and Ships Snapped by Our Roving Camera

CHEERY GIRLS OF THE LAND ARMY, whose smiles and spades have helped carry us through grimly critical times, about to go ditching. They retain their cheerfulness in spite of Mr. Churchill's announcement that our Women's Land Army would not qualify for post-war gratuities.

BROADSIDE LAUNCH down the slips at a Southern England dockyard. This ship, the heaviest yet launched by this method, with a displacement of 1,000 tons, will be used as a Fleet Air Arm ferry and is expected to go to the Far East for service against the Japs.

"HEART OF OAK," English all-timber ships, famed since King Alfred's day, are still being made and launched at Rockchannel, Rye, Sussex. In this cradle of the Royal Navy, workmen whose craft is a thousand years old are building these ships for duty in the Pacific. With hulls of Sussex oak—100 trees go to each vessel—they are fitted with Diesel engines and have a displacement of 120 tons.

N.F.S. WOMEN proudly marched past Mr. Herbert Morrison, the Home Secretary (left), in Hyde Park, London, on March 18, 1945, when 4,000 part-time members of both sexes of the N.F.S., representing their 30,000 comrades, took part in a farewell parade. Following the official stand-down order on February 1, this was their last appearance in the familiar red-and-blue uniform. Said Mr. Morrison, "I should be doing less than my duty if I did not say that you deserve and are given the thanks of the Government for your public spirit."

Photos, Fox, New York Times Photos, Planet News

ON an overnight journey to The Land o' Cakes recently I was approached in my sleeper by the guard of the train who asked at what time I wished to be called, adding *sotto voce*, " And perhaps you'd like a cup of tea and some biscuits, sir ? " I was so overcome at the thought of morning tea (on a wartime railway journey) that I tipped the man there and then, telling him to call me (with tea) half an hour before we reached Glasgow as I had an important appointment early in the day. Thanks to a tiring afternoon in town I slept like a log, confident in the guard's assurance that I should not oversleep. Judge of my horror when I woke to find the train already in the station at Glasgow, with the passengers streaming past my window and not a sign anywhere of either the guard or the much-needed tea ! And the moral ? Of this, frankly, I'm not sure, though I feel it has something to do with the perils of tipping in advance. And yet how often in peace-time have I secured the maximum of atten-tion from stewards, waiters and railway guards by the judicious application of a not too substantial preliminary tip in antici-pation of favours to come. Perhaps the real moral has something to do with the absurdity of not only expecting to be called on a wartime train but imagining that mere money can buy a cup of tea on it as well.

I CONFESS that until today I hadn't heard that of our many wartime shortages one of the most acute is that of schools. A friend of mine recently went to live in one of the Home Counties within half-a-dozen miles of four fairish-sized towns with populations of 30,000 and upwards. For two months his wife has been trying to find a school for their 12-year-old daughter—any school, anywhere in the neighbourhood. But all report " House Full," with waiting-lists stretching well into 1946. The nearest, and in many respects the most suitable, schools are those evacuated from London since the war. But these are not permitted to take pupils other than from their home-district in London. Even the elementary schools have no vacancies : it is, they explain, purely a matter of desk-room with them and any extra pupils would have to do their lessons standing up. In desperation, my friend thought he would force a con-clusion. Writing to the County Educational Authority, he invited them to prosecute him for not sending his child to school. That was three weeks ago. So far he has had no reply—not even an acknowledgement in the shape of a call from a visitor in blue. If conditions are as bad elsewhere—and I find that in some districts they are—why bother to raise the school-leaving age until the pre-sent fantastic situation has evened itself ?

I HAVE noticed lately that when people— tradespeople, hotel servants and others —wish to be excused from observing some of the commoner courtesies they no longer plead " there's a war on." The newest catch-phrase (usually uttered a little breathily) is, " Oh, we don't do that now." There is a certain stale genteelness about the phrase which the older, blunter one lacked, an implication that whatever one has re-quested is somehow " not done." In a big three-starred hotel in the North recently, for instance, that was the answer I got when I asked the receptionist to telegraph a request for advance reservations for my party at the company's hotel in another town : a highly necessary precaution, as anyone acquainted with wartime travelling well knows, and one with which I am sure even the over-worked postal staffs concerned would have had full sympathy. Litt'e

common courtesies like this neither hamper the war effort nor are hindered by the labour shortage. Though they take up a minimum of time, they certainly help to make life easier for hurried and harried business people on their travels. The disturbing thing is that, neglected as they are today, they may be lost for ever in the world after this war. If they are to be resumed— incidentally, will there be a general signal for a resumption of peacetime " good manners " ?—it will take fully a generation to " re-educate " our young people in their usage. As the melancholic Wordsworth put it almost a century and a half ago :

> Turn wheresoe'er I may,
> By night or day,
> The things which I have seen I now can
>   see no more.

THERE must be plenty of people in Britain who will envy Mr. T. P. Bennett his new job. For Mr. Bennett is an architect who is to be responsible for the design of a large number of Britain's post-war public-houses, and part of his job is to go " pub-crawling " round the country—if he will forgive my putting it that way—watching how men and women drinkers behave themselves, whether they prefer to do their drinking standing up or sitting down, so that he may make his plans and designs accordingly. I have no particular fondness for public-houses, preferring to imbibe my few odd pegs, when I can get them, under my own roof or at my club, where I can choose both my time and my company. But the news of Mr. Bennett's scientific Design for Drinking, as it might be termed, is a sign of the times as welcome as it is revolutionary. To

Maj.-Gen. F. W. MESSERVY, C.B., D.S.O., whose appointment as commander of the 4th Corps in Burma was announced on March 13, 1945. He commanded the 7th Armoured Division in Libya in 1942. **See also page 661.**
PAGE 767   *Photo, British Official*

most people the words " Gin Palace " conjure up the coarser canvases and engravings of Hogarth, with their eighteenth-century scenes of almost indescribable drunken-ness and squalor. Yet such sad scenes have I witnessed in my own youth in Glasgow as well as in the less savoury districts of London, when public-houses in some quarters kept open all day and more than half the night. The new public-house must live up to its old name, while abandoning for ever its tradition of furtiveness and squalor. It must—and will be, I feel—a place for the public of all ages and both sexes, and from which drunken-ness and drinking-for-drinking's sake will be banished as it is from most other modern places of entertainment.

I MUST confess to a certain admiration for the advertiser in The Times newspaper who recently offered for sale a pair of sock-suspenders of " elastic and 14 ct. gold, engine-turned," which had originally cost £20. Diamond studs we all know, and mink coats and other such ostentatious marks of wealth. Sock-suspenders are different. There is a touch of finer breeding about the man who chooses to keep his magnificence secreted so closely to himself or reserved for only the most privileged few. Or did the wearer perhaps practise a studied negligence in crossing his legs so that a glint of the treasure was allowed to peep out to the impressionable world ? That he should be obliged to part with so unique a possession is one of the minor tragedies of the war. And who will buy them ? I never before heard of anyone wearing second-hand sock-suspenders, how-ever golden. In these times most of us would imagine our own suspenders were on their very last legs in more senses than one.

RESPECT for authority is generally considered a good thing. It can be overdone. The Germans overdo it. The Americans and the French, on the other hand, are inclined to treat law and order with some contempt. In this country we seem, to me, to hit the happy mean. When we know that rules and regulations are sensible and necessary, we abide by them cheerfully. If we disregard them, it is because they are mere evidence of officialism. I saw an illustration of this the other day at Brighton. The stretch of Marine Parade which had been closed for four years and a half because there were guns there was to be reopened on a Monday for traffic. On the Saturday the roadway had been cleared. But the notices "Road Closed" still re-mained. I was glad to see that on Sunday, in spite of them, any number of people were getting under the poles set up to keep them out and walking on the promenade that had been shut against them for so long. They saw authority being exercised in a fussy, needless fashion, and they put authority in its place.

A WARTIME example of American lawless-ness is the determination of a number of New Yorkers to evade the order that night clubs must close at twelve o'clock. These inveterate gamblers now frequent unlicensed premises where they can sit up playing cards, or throwing dice or spinning roulette wheels until dawn. These new haunts of folly are run by the sort of persons who used in the days of Prohibition to provide the "speak-easies," where drink could be bought in defiance of the Law. Such pests are always ready in big cities to assist weak and silly men and women to fly in the face of authority. Entrance to their rooms costs 25s. at the lowest, and they take a percentage on the money that passes, besides selling drink at exorbitant prices. No consideration of decency, no wish to help the war effort, no obligation to do their share in meeting the national danger, deters such people as these harpies and the imbeciles they prey on from flouting the Law, if they can. And too often they are able, by bribing the police, to escape the consequences that ought to follow.

Mid Snow and Ice on Europe's Alpine Front

GUARDING THE FRENCH-ITALIAN FRONTIER IN THE MARITIME ALPS a rifle section of the 44th U.S. (Alpine) Brigade is here seen ready for action. Fighting always in snow and ice, this Alpine force has held these strategic heights against the enemy's right flank since the Riviera invasion which began on August 15, 1944. Supplies have had to be transported by mule-train, and a funicular line was constructed between mountain-tops to enable the gunners to get their 75-mm. howitzers to new positions.

Photo, Planet News

Printed in England and published every alternate Friday by the Proprietors, THE AMALGAMATED PRESS, LTD., The Fleetway House, Farringdon Street, London, E.C.4. Registered for transmission by Canadian Magazine Post. Sole Agents for Australia and New Zealand : Messrs. Gordon & Gotch, Ltd. ; and for South Africa : Central News Agency, Ltd.—April 13, 1945. S.S. *Editorial Address :* JOHN CARPENTER HOUSE, WHITEFRIARS, LONDON, E.C.4.

Vol 8 | SIXPENCE

The War Illustrated № 205

Edited by Sir John Hammerton

APRIL 27, 1945

SEEING THE 'BIG HEAVE' FOR HIMSELF, MR. CHURCHILL drove in an armoured car through ruined Xanten to cross the Rhine and watch troops of the British 2nd Army in action in areas still under enemy fire. In the uniform of a Colonel of the Royal Sussex Regiment he visited the 3rd Division, which is composed largely of English county regiments, with battalions from Scotland and Northern Ireland. During his trip (disclosed on March 26, 1945) a shell exploded only 50 yards from him.   *Photo, British Official*

NO. 206 WILL BE PUBLISHED FRIDAY, MAY 11

Desperate Last Stands Routed by Russians

AT DANZIG, where Nazi forces made a desperate stand, big guns (1) in the dockyards are being examined by a Soviet officer, after the great Baltic port had been stormed by Marshal Rokossovsky (2nd White Russian Front) on March 30, 1945. German women cleared away street barricades in the Silesian town of Naumburg (2), entered by Marshal Koniev's troops of the 1st Ukrainian Front.

At Kuestrin, on the Oder 40 miles from Berlin, men of Marshal Zhukov's 1st White Russian Front patrolled the streets of the town (3), which they took on March 12. On his way through a Czech village, a mounted Red Army reconnaissance rider of Marshal Malinovsky's 2nd Ukrainian Front was welcomed by gaily dressed inhabitants (4). Marshal Tolbukhin, commanding the 3rd Ukrainian Front, captured the centre of Vienna on April 9, after bitter fighting, and penetrated the important Semmering Pass, only 150 miles from Hitler's Berchtesgaden eyrie.

Photos, Planet News, Pictorial Press

Seeing the War at First Hand

HOW THE TIDE OF BATTLE SWEPT INTO GERMANY
by Captain NORMAN MACMILLAN, *M.C., A.F.C.*

I VISITED a R.A.F. Casualty Air Evacuation Unit in Belgium that was formed in November 1944. Commanding it is Wing Commander J. Clarke Taylor, graduate of Glasgow University, a R.A.F. regular M.O. The unit has three Flights, with the H.Q. and B Flights at one Belgian aerodrome and A Flight at another. This unit evacuates patients from eight base hospitals. Squadron Leader J. G. M. McMurchy of Manitoba is O.C. B Flight. Each Flight has one Senior Nursing Sister with the equivalent rank of Flight Lieutenant and three Nursing Sisters with the equivalent rank of Flying Officer. There are three doctors per Flight, and each Flight has an operating theatre.

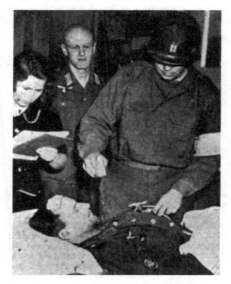

DE-LOUSING WOUNDED PRISONERS is a necessary precaution as the Allies advance into Germany. This military hospital at Linz, on the Rhine, is exclusively operated by German military medical experts who work under U.S. direction.　*Photo, U.S. Official*

From an Advanced Landing Ground type of evacuation centre in Holland severe cases are evacuated direct by air to the U.K. Light cases fly back to Belgium, go into Base Hospital for treatment, and are kept in base hospital if they can recover within 31 days. At the base hospital the Medical Air Liaison Officer makes arrangements for the more serious cases to be evacuated thence by air to the U.K. The Unit made a record in transporting one casualty from the front line to U.K. hospital in 12 hours. But a paratrooper holds the absolute record. He was shot while in the aircraft, went back to the end of the line and in due course flew home in the same plane.

THE forward shuttle between Holland and Belgium began in mid-September 1944, and is carried out by Handley Page Harrows converted to Sparrows. This flying unit, known officially as the Sparrow Flight, has six aircraft, one of which had been damaged by flak, and the first pilot and one of the wounded passengers hit. In command is Squadron Leader I. C. Murison, of Edinburgh. The main evacuation is carried out by Dakota air transports. The aircraft carry 13 lying and seven sitting cases, and on their return journey fly in blood stores, stretchers, and other articles. They do not bear the Red Cross, because they may be used for the carriage of men or stores not within the Convention. There are no

Red Cross aircraft, as such, in Europe, although the R.A.A.F. has Red Cross aircraft in the Far East.

This C.A.E.U. can reach a peak of 500 cases per Flight per day—a total capacity for dealing with 1,500 cases daily. In the main airfield casualty clearing ward men lay in rows on stretchers waiting for the ambulances to take them to the Dakotas. Their stretchers stood high off the floor on the special steel stands (these were made in Belgium) that are now used in the field for stretchers. I spoke to one of the men. He smiled. It was a sad smile. Yes, he was glad to be going home, but he had not expected to be going home like this. " How did you expect to go home ? " I asked. " On my own pins," he said. Poor fellow ! He was an amputation case. But, in an earlier war, he might never have gone home at all.

The ambulances ran up close alongside the aircraft. Orderlies lowered the upper stretchers to the floor of the ambulances with smooth operating winding-gear, lifted the stretchers out carefully and carried them the few yards to the open door in the side of the Dakota. They were lifted in manually and placed in position in tiers of three on either side of the tunnel-like interior of the aluminium alloy fuselage. Sitting cases were helped up the companion that the aircraft carries for ordinary passengers. Each Dakota had a W.A.A.F. Air Ambulance Orderly, quietly going about her work of seeing that all her patients were comfortably settled. During the flight she can provide food or drink, administer morphia or oxygen as required. They seemed to like their work, and take pride in it. One I spoke to had completed 43 trips and flown 200 hours, duly entered in her logbook.

All kinds of patients come to the air ambulances from the C.A.E.U. One of the ladies of the Sadler's Wells Ballet company contracted antrum trouble, and as a member

of E.N.S.A. was treated in the base hospital and then home by air. The big hatch in the fuselage is closed. The engines start. The air ambulance taxies to the end of the runway, rises and climbs away above our heads. An hour later the casualties will be passing over England, soon to be landed on their destination airfield.

WHERE the Allies First Broke Into the Reich

WE entered Holland by crossing the swollen river over a wood and pontoon bridge, for the original bridge lay wrecked in the Maas. The Germans had evacuated Belgium too rapidly for much damage to be done in the towns and villages by fighting, and the first badly damaged place I saw was Sittard, Dutch Limburg town of 15,000 inhabitants.

We were then on our way to the active front, and visiting the sector where the first bitter fighting took place on German soil, the area between the Maas and Roer rivers, from Aachen in the south to Roermond in the north. Here stands Sittard in the coalmining district of Holland. The slag heaps made familiar pyramids. Underground the mine galleries continue across the frontier into Germany, and at that time the farther shafts and galleries were in German hands, so that it was impossible to work the Dutch seams ; this undoubtedly aggravated the coal situation on the Continent, and must have had an adverse reaction on the coal situation in Britain.

IT was past midday and we stopped at a hotel in Sittard, but there was nothing to eat or drink—no tea, no coffee, no beer. Fortunately we carried sandwiches in the car. Continuing along a narrow road we crossed the frontier into Germany. In Hongen, a small agricultural village, there was not a house undamaged ; roofs and floors were fallen in, and thatch lay about the ground ; the air was filled with the horrid odour of

ON THE SOUTHERN FLANK OF THE REICHSWALD FOREST, Captain Norman Macmillan (centre), Special Correspondent for "The War Illustrated" with the British Forces, watches a fine black Labrador search for mines with Sapper Robert Coote. In the background a transport column, including a Bailey bridge in sections, waited to move up. Nearly 3,000 dogs of various breeds, loaned by the people of Britain, have passed through the War Dogs' Training School in Britain. Men who are to handle them in action are trained alongside the mine-searching dogs, and battlefield conditions are realistically reproduced. See also page 180.　　PAGE 791 burnt-out homes. Heinsberg, two miles from the Roer river, was worse. It was smashed up, not just knocked down. (Heinsberg, Düren and Jülich were bombed by Bomber Command in daylight on November 16, 1944, the first support of its kind given to U.S. forces.) Heinsberg had the appearance of having been burgled, an effect created by the evacuation of the place by its former inhabitants, who had fled deeper into Germany, taking what possessions they most

fallen when someone fled. Among a road block of military vehicles held up by mud more than axle deep amid treacherous bomb-and-shell-holes, I saw a solitary German woman civilian walking through the village; it was the short daytime period free from curfew.

WHEN such villages are captured, German civilians, who remain behind, usually in hiding, are sorted out. They are examined,

internees, but when it was safe to allow it some of them were given permission to return to their homes.

It struck me how few birds were to be seen. In the course of a whole day I saw only three magpies and four crows. I saw no song bird anywhere in Holland, and few in Belgium. Whether they had migrated in search of food, or had themselves been killed for food, I cannot say, but only in the desert have I before travelled so far and seen so few birds. The only wild animals I saw over a wide area were two hares.

Just ahead, above the Roer river, little Auster planes were spotting amid clustering flak bursts; higher up a big formation of Thunderbolt fighters came west returning from a mission. United States troops were taking over from British in that sector. In the wide space of a harrowed field an American A.A. battery was setting up its 90-mm. guns. Many of the men came from the north-eastern States and preferred the dry cold of the period of snow and frost to the damp weather that had followed. A tiny white puppy gambolled about one gun platform; they called him Snowflake.

Taking a short cut, we stuck more than axle deep in the mud of a road that had been but a farm road before war swept over it, and had a hard job to reach Sittard again, recognizing our direction from the fighter that had belly-landed in a field where unrecovered mines lay still buried; this is one of the hazards of the modern forced-landing in time of war.

WE passed over the magnificent Juliana Canal to reach Susteren, Dutch town less than two miles from the German frontier and three from Maeseyck in Belgium, at the narrowest part of the Maastricht appendix. Here several houses were newly damaged, and their Dutch owners were removing their belongings and taking them back on horse-drawn vehicles. From Maeseyck we wanted to go to Weert, but the direct road was too badly damaged by frost, flood and traffic, and in the growing dusk our Humber car roared away up the fine road towards Roermond, a Dutch town then in German hands, on the farther side of the confluence of the Roer and Maas. A short distance from the river we turned left for Weert, where the canal was dry and barges and boats were stranded on the canal bed.

ON THEIR WAY TO MÜNSTER, troops of the U.S. 17th Airborne Division clustered on Churchill tanks of the 6th Guards' Armoured Brigade, manned by British crews. The town fell to both divisions, on April 2, 1945, depriving the enemy of the vital group of fighter airfields in the Rheine-Münster-Osnabruck triangle, previously battered by the 2nd T.A.F. *Photo, British Newspaper Pool*

valued with them, and leaving the remainder scattered about by the fury of their search to find what they thought most worth taking.

A cash register stood awry in one shop, still marking the last sale made. Outside one house the pavement was strewn with cheap professional photographs of German soldiers, lying, presumably, where they had

and disinfested with DDT (dichloro-diphenyl-trichlorethane), the disinfestor that saved Naples from disastrous typhus. This white powder, shot inside their garments by a spray gun, kills all lice. Many German civilians from this frontier area were sent back to Holland to live in camps which the Germans had formerly prepared for Dutch

FIELD-MARSHAL MONTGOMERY ADDRESSED HIS MEN OF THE 6th AIRBORNE DIVISION when he visited troops of the 21st Army Group during their swift advance from Coesfeld to Osnabruck, which they entered on April 3, 1945. The capture of Osnabruck opened the way into the Hanover plain; two days later Monty's men reached the river Weser and seized Minden, site of the historic Westphalian battlefield in 1759 when British and Hanoverian troops defeated the French.

Photo, British Official

THE BATTLE FRONTS

by Maj.-Gen. Sir Charles Gwynn, K.C.B., D.S.O.

WITH the Allied armies across the Rhine deep into the heart of Germany, and with prisoners daily coming in by the thousand, it would seem that any day now the enemy must accept the inevitable. I am quite sure that the mass of the German Army and the great majority of its officers realize that it is useless to prolong the struggle, yet until they are prepared, and are in a position, to turn their weapons if necessary against the fanatical minority it would be over-optimistic and dangerous to believe the end is in sight.

Sporadic resistance unless suppressed by the Germans themselves is almost certain to continue, and there is always the possibility that a substantial force composed of diehard troops may be withdrawn into the more inaccessible and defensible parts of the country. It has, however, become evident that the Volkssturm is not likely to make an important contribution towards continued resistance, and I suspect that one of the main aims of Allied strategy is to prevent the retreat of any organized force into mountain strongholds.

Why, for instance have Zhukov's and Koniev's main armies not yet resumed their main offensive ? It is clear that Koniev is in a position of readiness, except so far as Breslau blocks one of his main lines of communication. That, however, can hardly now be the reason for delay. Zhukov has certainly established bridge-heads across the Oder, but we may be sure that he has made no attempt to break out from them or we should have heard of it from German sources even if Moscow as usual made no announcement until substantial success had been achieved. To my mind, though, of course, it is pure surmise, the somewhat intriguing delay in the development of the Russian attack towards Berlin indicates a timing programme arranged between the High Commands of the Eastern and Western Fronts. Zhukov and Koniev, standing poised, contain the bulk of what remains of the German armies, and every day the Allied offensive in the west is closing up behind it, making retreat southwards increasingly difficult.

IN particular, General Eisenhower's s o u t h e r n w i n g operating in the Main and Neckar valleys threatens to break into the valley of the upper Danube, while on the other side Tolbukhin and Malinovsky are pressing up its middle reaches. These encircling arms are still 300 miles apart, but an advance of about 100 miles by the latter to Regensburg and by Tolbukhin of the same distance to Linz would cut the main lines of communication of the German n o r t h e r n a r m i e s with the projected fortress region of the south.

Meanwhile, the advance of Eisenhower's c e n t r a l a n d northern forces makes it increasingly difficult for the enemy in the north to disengage without exposing the rear and communications of the forces facing Zhukov and Koniev. If the Germans, therefore, seriously contemplate withdrawing to the south every day the danger of the manoeuvre becomes greater, and every day a break-through by Zhukov and Koniev on the

flank of a retreating army would promise more decisive results than if effected prematurely. That is why I think they are biding their time, waiting for the moment at which they can strike most effectively. There may also be political motives which render it advisable that Russian armies should not advance beyond the zone of occupation assigned to them, and perhaps it is desirable that Berlin should be entered simultaneously by the combined forces of the Allies. Changes in the machinery of control might thus be avoided.

ENEMY'S Best Available Troops Assembled to Oppose Crossing

Montgomery's crossing of the Rhine was effected after deliberate and meticulous preparation with the knowledge that the enemy had assembled all his best available troops to oppose it. No precautions could be neglected, and in particular it was essential that a bridge-head once secured should rapidly be reinforced in strength. Immediate deep penetration was of less importance. As a consequence when the moment for a breakout from the bridge-head arrived there were ample troops to support the thrusts, and bridges available.

General Patton's crossing, on the other hand, was only made possible by his annihilation of the enemy's forces on the western bank in the Saar-Moselle triangle, which left the line of the Rhine in this sector practically undefended. His crossing was hardly opposed, and his armoured spearheads were able to make deep penetration before encountering serious opposition ; consequently there was no need to establish a secure bridge-

head. But few bridges could be established immediately, and it took time for his main bodies to close up and for his communications to develop. His spearheads made amazing progress of immense importance through country where any delay might have enabled resistance to be organized, but; as was to be expected, when resistance was encountered a pause became necessary. It was, in the circumstances, of surprisingly short duration, but thereafter the rate of progress became less spectacular.

IN General Hodges' snap capture of the bridge at Remagen there was no question of selecting the point of crossing, and although the enemy was completely surprised, his resistance soon materialized. It was necessary, therefore, as in Montgomery's case, to fight for a bridge-head and to fill it with troops before a breakout could be attempted. But since, unlike Montgomery, General Hodges had no adequate bridging equipment immediately available, the build-up of his bridge-head took much longer. By the time he was ready to advance, however, General Patton's operations to the south and Montgomery's in the north had greatly reduced the enemy's power of resistance so that Hodges' armoured thrusts were almost as spectacular as those of Patton.

What is remarkable is that these three crossings, involving operations of very different type should, as they were exploited, have been so admirably co-ordinated. The enemy nowhere was able to make a properly organized stand, and no awkward bulges developed which might have entailed waiting till the front could be to some degree straightened. On the contrary, it was the enemy who suddenly found himself in a dangerous salient in the Ruhr and unable to escape from it before the pincers closed round him. Every credit should, of course, be given to the commanders of individual armies, or groups of armies, for the manner in which they dealt with their special problems, but I cannot believe that under such diverse conditions the front of the offensive would have presented such a well-balanced picture if the highest co-ordinating authority, presumably General Eisenhower, had not retained control and been very loyally supported by his subordinates. A healthy rivalry no doubt existed, but it never appears to have been detrimental to the rapid development of well-conceived plans. Discipline in the highest ranks was clearly well maintained and, especially where Allied armies are working in close co-operation, that is not easy to achieve.

THE same spirit of loyalty and mutual co-operation has been displayed by Marshal Stalin's subordinate commanders. It has been from the enemy's side that rumours of quarrels and dissension have come and the list of higher commanders whom Hitler has removed is long, although we may well believe that their suspension in many cases was due to justifiable protests against the Fuehrer's strategical conceptions. The old saying that " the fish gets rotten from the head " has seldom been more fully exemplified. But the processes of decay and disintegration would probably have been much more rapid but for the fanatical devotion of the German officer class.

WESTERN FRONT ON APRIL 6, 1945, when British armour of Field-Marshal Montgomery's 21st Group had reached the Weser, last natural barrier before the triangle whose corners are Hanover, Bremen and Hamburg—all vital in the Allied plan to engulf Germany. Hanover fell to Gen. Simpson's U.S. 9th Army on April 10.

By courtesy of News Chronicle

Royal Navy's Fast Ferry Service on the Rhine

ENTIRELY NEW AMPHIBIOUS TECHNIQUE was brilliantly executed by British and U.S. Naval Forces to help the Allied crossings of the Rhine : a fast cross-river service to carry tanks, bulldozers and mobile guns had to be established before bridges even of a temporary nature could be thrown across. Royal Navy's craft consisted of L.C.M.s (Landing Craft Mechanized) and L.C.V.P.s (Landing Craft Vehicles Personnel) ; and these huge vessels, to operate 200 miles from the sea, had mostly to be transported over hundreds of miles of damaged roads.

The L.C.M. is a 50-ft. all-steel boat, with a crew of five and speed of 12 knots, weighs 26 tons, can carry any armoured vehicle up to a Sherman tank, or 6,000 81-mm. mortar projectiles, or 750 155-mm. shells, or 7,500 gallons of petrol. The L.C.V.P. is 36 ft. long, with crew of four, speed of ten knots, weighs nine tons, and can carry 50 combat-equipped troops, or one bulldozer, or one 105-mm. infantry cannon and one 57-mm. anti-tank gun, or two 75-mm. howitzers, or 1,000 gallons of petrol in five-gallon cans.

These had to be launched mostly from muddy banks, and manoeuvred against strong currents. Operations were under the overall direction of Admiral Sir Harold M. Burrough, K.C.B., K.B.E., D.S.O., Allied Naval C.-in-C. of the Expeditionary Forces.

BRITISH NAVAL OFFICERS conferred in a Rhineland forest while organizing the momentous crossings. The senior officer of the British Naval Units was Captain P. G. H. James, R.N. (1, centre). This base was administered by Royal Marines, and craft from it were soon operating. Ratings lend a hand in lowering a landing vessel into the Rhine (2) by means of a powerful mobile derrick.

The White Ensign flew as a captain of the Royal Army Service Corps directed the crossings through a microphone (3) ; in the background British engineers were building a Bailey bridge. With a depth charge exploding close astern, U.S. navy men patrolled the river (4) in search of mines and enemy-laid explosives intended to blow up our pontoons.

Photos, British Official, British Newspaper Pool, Associated Press

REAR-ADMIRAL R. R. McGRIGOR ON THE BRIDGE of the carrier Campania (left) during the fiercest air attack on an Arctic convoy in two years, reported on March 31, 1945. Carrying 500 Norwegians rescued from Soroy (see story in page 761), the convoy was attacked by both aircraft and U-boats ; Fleet Air Arm fighters secured many Ju.88s. In the convoy was the carrier Nairana (right), seen in heavy seas.   *Photos, British Official*

THE WAR AT SEA

by Francis E. McMurtrie

A FTER the action in the East China Sea on April 7 it becomes clear that the setting sun is now a more appropriate emblem for the Imperial Japanese Navy than the rising sun, which has hitherto constituted its flag. It is difficult to follow the conception of strategy which induced the Japanese High Command to order to sea on that date a weak and unbalanced naval force, destitute of any form of air cover, when powerful Allied fleets were known to be within striking distance. In the case of H.M.S. Prince of Wales and Repulse, in December 1941, the situation was such that grave risks had to be taken by the British admiral in the hope of intercepting enemy transports ; but no such considerations existed to influence the enemy on April 6.

Late in the afternoon of that day a strong force of Japanese aircraft attacked Allied ships and shore installations in the vicinity of Okinawa. Though attacks were pressed home with desperation, they were successful only to the extent of sinking three U.S. destroyers. Damage was inflicted on other destroyers and smaller vessels. As the result of the energetic counter-measures taken, 55 enemy planes were brought down by American fighters and 61 by the anti-aircraft guns of the fleet. By the evening the attacks had been definitely defeated.

JAPANESE Admiral's Folly Was Exploited by Allied Forces

No sea activity appears to have been detected at this stage ; but early next morning American reconnaissance aircraft observed a Japanese naval force, comprising the battleship Yamato, a cruiser of the Agano class, one other small cruiser and a number of destroyers, passing to the southward of Kyushu, the westernmost island of Japan, on a W. or S.W. course, towards the East China Sea.

Possibly reports from the survivors of the previous day's air attack had persuaded the Japanese admiral that the Allied forces had been rendered incapable of dealing a serious blow at his weak and ill-balanced force. Even so, it was the height of folly to have neglected to provide for contingencies by ordering land-based aircraft to keep in close touch with the force in case of need.

Naturally, such a golden opportunity was seized by the U.S. Commander-in-Chief, who

at once dispatched a fast force of aircraft carriers, under Vice-Admiral Marc Mitscher, in the direction of the enemy. Contact was established about noon, when Admiral Mitscher's aircraft began a series of intensive attacks on the Japanese. Anti-aircraft fire from the Yamato and her consorts was intense, but there was no sign of air opposition. Hit by about eight torpedoes, besides bombs and rockets, the Yamato ultimately sank at a spot some 50 miles south-west of Cape Satanomi, the southernmost point of Kyushu. This would be somewhere to the westward of Yakushima, one of the largest of the group of islands extending in a S.W. direction from Kyushu. Both the enemy cruisers and three of their destroyers were sunk in action with the American aircraft, and three more destroyers were on fire when last seen.

N EWS of this defeat was received by Japan's new premier, 77-year-old Admiral Suzuki, with the gloomy statement that, " The war has come to its most important and crucial stage, and warrants not the least bit of optimism for our nation's survival." Certainly the chances of the fleet being able to do much to help the country out of its troubles seem to be slender. By the loss of the Yamato, the only modern battleship left after the sinking of the Musasi in the battle for Leyte last October, it is calculated that Japan's naval strength is reduced to five old battleships, the Nagato, Hyuga, Ise, Haruna and Kongo ; five or six aircraft carriers ; about ten cruisers ; and a doubtful number of destroyers. Any one of the several main divisions in which the Allied fleets in the Pacific are organized should be capable by itself of dealing with the entire Japanese Navy in its present plight.

Though the enemy defeat was inevitable, it certainly would not have come so swiftly had it not been for the ineptitude with which naval operations have been conducted by our Eastern foes. How far the supremacy of the Army in the conduct of affairs may have contributed to this is not known ; but instances of mismanagement are plentiful. Thus, after the sinking of H.M.S. Hermes, Dorsetshire and Cornwall in April 1942, the Japanese fleet was withdrawn from the Indian Ocean just as it seemed possible that it might succeed in enveloping and destroying

Admiral Sir James Somerville's hastily collected force. The backbone of that force, as the admiral has since stated, was composed of the four slow and somewhat antiquated battleships of the Royal Sovereign class.

In its various engagements with United States forces in the Solomon Islands area the Japanese Navy never concentrated in full strength, with the result that its substance was gradually frittered away in side-shows. When it came to a full-scale engagement, in the Philippines last October, enemy forces arrived on the scene separately from different directions and were each beaten in turn. In short, Japanese naval strategy has been found wanting on nearly every occasion of critical importance.

WARSHIPS Transferred by U.S. and Britain to Soviet Navy

Messages from Moscow recently disclosed the fact, already known to a great many people in this country and the United States, that these two countries last year transferred a number of warships to the Soviet Navy under Lend-Lease arrangements. Originally it had been suggested that some of the ships of the Italian Navy surrendered in September 1943 should be given to the Russians ; but the latter apparently had more confidence in British and American naval design and construction.

Ships which were transferred are understood to have included the battleship Royal Sovereign, of 29,150 tons, launched in 1915 ; she had been earmarked for replacement when war began, but is a powerful and well-protected vessel. The principal American ship presented is the 7,050-ton cruiser Milwaukee, launched in 1921. These two ships have been renamed Arkhangelsk and Murmansk respectively. Eight destroyers of the American flush-deck design, which were given to this country in 1940 in exchange for the lease of a number of Atlantic bases, have also passed into Russian hands. They are believed to include the Lincoln and St. Albans, which until recently operated under the Norwegian flag, and six others of similar type. They are now known as the Derzki —Audacious—class.

S EVERAL British submarines of the Ursula type, of 540 tons, are also said to have been included in the transfer ; they are now known as the Pchelka—Bee—class. Another submarine of a slightly larger design, the Sunfish, is also reported to have gone to Russia. A dozen or more motor torpedo boats, 12 steel submarine chasers, 70 wooden submarine chasers, and a number of wooden minesweepers have been acquired from the United States Navy.

Men Who Planned the Great Airborne Landings

GLIDER TRAIN WAS 500 MILES LONG when the mighty Allied airborne armada descended east of the Rhine on March 24, 1945; Hamilcar gliders and Halifax towing-craft (1) lined up on an R.A.F. airfield in England ready to take off.

Curtiss Commandos (C.46 type), carrying 36 paratroopers instead of the usual 18, were employed for the first time. This 4,000 h.p. super-transport has a range of 1,800 miles, a speed of over 250 m.p.h. and can lift almost 4 tons; it drops parachute troops from both sides simultaneously. (See illus. p. 161, Vol. 6).

Col. G. J. S. Chatterton (2), commanding the Glider Pilot Regiment, evolved the new plan for the glider attack on the Rhine defences. Air Vice-Marshal Scarlett-Streatfeild (3), A.O.C. 38 Group, responsible for the Rhine airborne operations. Gliders down near Hamminkeln (4); parachute troops prepared for action (5) north of Wesel.

Photos, British Official, Newspaper Pool, News Chronicle

From the Skies Into Action Beyond the Rhine

WHEN TROOPS OF THE BRITISH 6TH AIRBORNE DIVISION descended east of the Rhine, north-west of Wesel, on March 24, 1945, in the Allies' greatest airborne operation, men and mechanism were ready for instant action; immediately on touching-down this quick-firing gun (1) left its glider. Airborne troops prepared to dash into blazing Hamminkeln (2), between Rees and Wesel, which they captured within a few hours. Two of our men inspected a sign-post outside the town (3), while civilians quietly submitted to a round-up (4). PAGE 777   *Photos, British Official*

With Our 7th Armoured Division in the West

THE FUEHRER'S FACE AS THEIR TROPHY, doughty warriors of the British 7th Armoured Division relaxed (1) at Gemon, Westphalia, which they entered during a security black-out on Western Front news. Against the background of a village church near Stadtlohn (occupied April 1, 1945), heavy armour took up position (2) as our men picked off stray snipers (3). An upturned kitchen stove (4) served as cover at Bocholt during the final clearance of this north Rhineland town on March 29.

Photos, British Official, British Newspaper Pool

Dortmund-Ems Canal Now a Negligible Ditch

BRITISH 6th AIRBORNE DIVISION crossed the famous 150-miles long Dortmund-Ems canal, ten miles south of Osnabruck, on April 2, 1945, after retreating Nazis had destroyed all the bridges. Thanks to persistent draining of the canal by heavy bombers of the R.A.F., the water was only knee-deep, as this photograph of airborne troops transporting a wounded companion shows. Major-Gen. E. L. Bols (inset), Commander of the 6th Airborne Division, is one of the youngest of our generals.

Photos, British Official, Newspaper Pool

What Speedy Liberation Means to the Dutch

In occupied Holland nothing is normal. . Impoverishment, soul-numbing weariness and dreariness and hunger are afflictions common to all— whilst the people await, with anguished patience, the day of liberation. A Dutch Correspondent in that Nazi-oppressed land writing specially for "The War Illustrated," in early April, indicates how you would spend your day if there.

Y OU rise. Let's hope you have had a good night, that you have at least sufficient blankets to protect you against the cold. But that is by no means certain, because in many places the Germans have requisitioned all textiles.

As it is spring-time you can rise comparatively early. In the winter this was more difficult, because here there is no electricity and your stock of candles is exhausted. Therefore you have spent the long nights of December, January and February in bed. It was not pleasant, because no one can sleep sixteen hours at a stretch, so you have spent a good deal of time worrying. And hunger kept you awake.

But it is spring-time. The sun shines in the room. Fortunately the sun is not

Fortunately, somewhere in the neighbourhood a house has collapsed and you have been able to buy some firewood. This has swallowed up the last of your savings. Or you have felled a tree or taken down a fence. One of my friends did a neat little job : he pulled a couple of heavy wooden posts out of the ground in front of a shelter used by the German military. For weeks these have stood in his living-room to dry. Anyone stealing wood is immediately shot . . ; officially, but one often "gets away with it." But you have no choice— you *must* have fuel to prepare your food. You will probably not go to work, because business and industry are virtually paralysed.

Your water main is clogged. (How long shall we have our water supply ? In many places the water has been cut off for several

In the afternoon you and a friend plan to make a trip to North Holland, about 50 miles. You still have a blue suit, which you may be able to exchange for wheat. You become very angry because you have heard that a certain farmer has *sold* wheat. The scoundrel asked approximately £530 for 4 bushels. Fortunately, one morning the "underground boys" gave him the biggest hiding of his life.

You still have a bicycle, in spite of requisitions made by the Germans and the "Landwacht." But you have no tires. Six months ago you could get pneumatic tires for about £14 each. You thought it too expensive, but you are sorry now. Then you tried it with wooden tires, but that is worse than riding on the rims. Suppose you get the wheat, how are you going to carry it ? The best plan for you and your friend will probably be to hire a barrow and to take turns in sitting on it and pushing it.

Bulbs Fried in Oil for Supper

The relief organization instituted by the churches has distributed bulbs. You have also got a couple of pounds (although you do not belong to any church)., Your wife has fried them in a little oil, the only fat you have received since last November. With three slices of bread it makes a grand supper.

Let us hope that on your way to the farmer's you will find someone who is interested in your suit. Because if you do not get a small stock of food soon you will not be able to carry on, and your parents (if they are still alive) will die of hunger. Those hunger expeditions are no fun. Frequently one sees people collapsing by the wayside.

Six o'clock ! Now comes the highlight of the day. Hasn't the paper come yet ? But you have long since ceased to read the official newspaper. Far better get your news from the underground sources, and you don't need the newspaper for the food announcements. Someone will tell you the numbers of those miserable bread and potato vouchers. Therefore the stencilled paper called Het Parcol, Je Maintiendrai, Nederland zal Herrijzen (The Netherlands shall rise again), Trouw or Het Oranje Bulletin (The Orange Bulletin) is *the* newspaper.

The paper tells you *why* Holland's food situation is desperate. The Huns have blighted the country like a swarm of locusts. Then they used hunger as a means of breaking our morale. They deliberately allowed loads of potatoes to rot, rather than divide them among the population. But the paper says : "Carry on !" It is read out during mealtimes in the family circle . . . The Americans are advancing in the Far East. Berlin bombed again. The resistance movement has blown up a recruiting office which organized deportations to Germany. Monty is going for the Huns hot and strong. "It's going well, boys. Carry on !"

QUEEN WILHELMINA OF THE NETHERLANDS received a rousing welcome when she returned on a visit to liberated Holland, on March 13, 1945, after an absence of nearly five years. In Sluis (above) she was cheered everywhere, children waving flags, as she walked among them chatting informally. Life in the "hunger provinces" is described in this page. *Photo, British Official*

affected by human folly. The sun is, at any rate, "normal." And it would be normal for you if you went to the kitchen to prepare your porridge. But for months you have had no porridge oats, no milk and no gas.

A ND yet you have been lucky ! At the beginning of the week you stood in a queue for an hour and a half for the baker's shop to open, and you got your full ration. You are an old customer and the baker winks at you. Every member of the family has had his full bread ration this week —one loaf, and each gets one thin slice for breakfast. Some people take a slice and a half, but you think it more economical to take another half slice for your "elevenses."

Tea ? There is a tin containing tablets with which you can turn hot water into a brown liquid without affecting the taste. An excellent substitute ! But how will you get hot water ? You have a special cooking stove which in the cold months never raised the temperature of the room above 45 degrees, but on which you can heat four or six pans. At any rate no normal fuel, because there has been no fuel distribution since the middle of 1944.

hours in the day.) The plumber comes only when you offer him a sandwich or a cup of soup. That means he does *not* come. But you will have to see him today : perhaps he will come when you give him a darning needle which your wife can spare.

Then you go with your pan to the communal kitchen. You get a spoonful of soup or mashed greens and potatoes for each member of your family. Soup ? This usually consists of water with a few green pieces floating in it and sometimes a slice of carrot. But soup is a delicacy compared with the mashed greens and potatoes, as the never-failing sugar-beet gives them a sickly sweet taste. Moreover, the family's digestive organs can no longer cope with those indigestible turnips.

T HERE are no potatoes. You have surrendered your ration vouchers to the communal kitchen. Yesterday you had a violent argument with the man in the flat above, who maintained that the municipal food office give you less than you should have. You have denied it, because the communal kitchen is a Dutch institution and not a German one. Moreover, the municipal food office deals extensively in the black market.

B UT the number of those who can no longer believe in liberation is growing. Yes, "it's going well," but *when* are we going to be liberated ? When we are all dead and buried . . . "Buried" . . . There are no more coffins and no funeral carriages. We say, "May God grant that we will be liberated before we die of starvation or before we are so far gone that we are beyond aid." The German has not broken Holland, but hunger is stronger than strength of mind. Four and a half million Dutchmen in the "hunger provinces" remain at their posts. The enemy cannot break us, but tonight hunger will keep us awake again.

Canadians On the Way to the V-Bomb Bases

TORN UP BY THE " TRACK RIPPER," NAZI SABOTAGE WEAPON, the railway lines near Emmerich (1), 20 miles south-east of Arnhem and captured on March 29, 1945, were rendered useless by the enemy retreating before the Canadian 1st Army on the northern shoulder of the lower Rhine sector. British and Canadian armour passing through shattered Emmerich (2). Netherlands children (3) cheered Canadian troops and armour hurrying through the Hummelo area (4) to the V-bomb bases at Zutphen (seized April 8).

Photos, Planet News

Feats of the Royal Regiment of Artillery

The one-word motto of the Royal Artillery—Ubique—means "everywhere." And that is where individual R.A. regiments are expected to be! It has no fixed composition in the field, and under its command may be formations from other Allied artillery groups. Something of the Royal Regiment's great story in this war is told by MARK PRIESTLEY.

WESTERN Front barrages are now synchronized by the Greenwich time signal pips, sent out on certain radio services every hour of the day and night so that gunners may correctly set their battery watches. This has been done ever since D-Day (June 6, 1944), at the special request of Field-Marshal Montgomery—and the precision is worthy of the heroes of the Royal Regiment of Artillery. Whenever the battle mounts to a fresh phase of fury, as in the 1,000-gun barrage that heralded the Allied break across the River Roer (see illus. page 712), the gunners live and sweat through hours of dangerous glory. How comes it, then, that the activities of the Royal Artillery are still largely anonymous?

The numbers by which they are identified have a less personal touch than the historic names and county associations borne by infantry regiments. The 94th, 112th and 179th Field Regiments, all of them West Country units, were among the first to go into action on German soil, and an Anti-Tank Battery had the honour of providing the first units to cross the Rhine. The 181st Field Regiment, too, has collected no less than four Military Crosses, six Military Medals, a D.S.O. and four C.-in-C.'s certificates for gallantry all within three months, a notable record of valour.

IN the channels of the Netherlands, artillery and naval personnel have worked together with land artillery mounted on landing craft. It has been the Navy's job to keep the ships aimed and give the orders to fire; the gunners man the guns and do the rest. The technique has been successfully used in covering landing forces before the establishment of shore artillery posts was practicable, and perhaps results were best exemplified in a recent battle on the Dutch coast when infantry faced a German attack at brigade strength for 15 hours without yielding an inch of ground. The seaward gunners brought fire to bear on minute-by-minute objectives as soon as they were signalled by their observation officers. "And the gunners saved the day," an infantry officer afterwards commented. "Not a doubt of it!"

AGAIN, a Scottish infantry regiment had scarcely taken a certain canal after hard fighting when they found the R.A. units coming forward for further action. The gunners were admittedly surprised to see infantrymen manning their posts in trenches, and an infantry sergeant gazed back in amazement at them. "You guns here already!" he exclaimed. "That's fine! But we didn't think guns could cross that devil's ditch for hours!"

On another occasion, a Gun Position Officer's transport went forward in advance to establish a new position and gave a surprise to the Americans. "We thought you were Recce," they said. "Jerry's only just gone. You don't waste any time, do you?"

Behind such tributes there lies the training that has created efficiency. The 181st Field Regiment, for example, was built around a converted infantry battalion and the men come from every walk of life. Today each man is an expert at his particular job, whether gunnery, signalling, wireless operating, driving, line-laying or acking, but each individual could do another man's job if necessary. All have become cogs in the great machine behind the shells, and their periods of inactivity have been all too few in the chase from Normandy into the Reich itself.

There is a Survey Regiment of the Royal Artillery which landed in Sicily and for nineteen months has been slogging slowly up Italy. Names like Ortona, Cassino, Florence and the Gothic Line recall but a few of the battles in which it has played a part. Theirs is the task of locating and observing enemy batteries. One way to do it is to sit out in forward observation posts, often under enemy fire, and wait for a gun-flash. When it is observed a geometrical bearing is taken and sent back to H.Q. (see illus. pages 205, 210). There the information is collated with "gen" from other posts. In time, when the locations have been checked, the guns receive a position and the enemy point is bombarded out of existence. Alternatively, in bad visibility, sound-ranging is worked out in a complicated system of microphones and wires on the ground.

The courage of the observation officers as they feel out the enemy positions, the skill of the signallers and line-layers, thus all form part of the successful work of the R.A. tanks moving forward, or enemy fire may tear the gun telephone lines to shreds and these have to be laid and relaid. In Italy, survey parties and layers have sometimes been lost in fifteen-foot snowdrifts, microphones have been removed by Nazi patrols, and sometimes it has been impossible to move equipment by truck or carrier. Then the drivers have had to drag four-hundredweight of equipment by blanket!

Just Ahead of the Foot-sloggers

A barrage is often the outcome of weeks of watching and planning directed against enemy defences in depth. One artillery group has expended 5,600 shells in a day to this end. In other units, meeting normal demands for fire in battle, guns may fire more than 3,000 rounds each in three weeks "not somewhere near but on the target."

When a barrage supports an infantry attack, the line for opening fire may be just ahead of the foot-sloggers and shells must land in the right place. Too short, they would fall among the infantry; too far, their effect would be wasted. Plotting the targets by the "acks" and laying the guns by the layers calls for and gets 100 per cent accuracy.

Add to this 100 per cent courage. For the enemy is similarly spotting and range-finding our own guns all the time. When Lance-Bombardier Jimmy McGuire received the M.M. it was because his section of a line had been cut no less than 70 times by enemy shellfire and he had kept the cable route mended. In another instance, a gun crew found the camouflage net of their gun ablaze; the fire spread quickly over the whole gun-pit—and they leapt in and out of the flames to throw the ammunition clear.

ANOTHER group on a 9·2-in. gun were knocked about by fragments of a heavy calibre shell. Still they attempted to continue the action, until another enemy shell scored a direct hit on the emplacement and put the gun completely out of action. With communications severed, a message had to be run to an information point nearly 400 yards away on the other side of no man's land, which was being heavily shelled. The Number One on the gun took the message and brought up aid for the wounded.

Perhaps the gunner's saga can best be underlined by the story of the 90th Middlesex, now in North-West Europe. Veterans of the Battle of Britain, they were once exclusively ack-ack. Then their 3·7-in. guns were tested as field artillery. The experiment was brilliantly successful. Today the 90th is anti everything Nazi, whether in the sky, on the ground or in water, for the men who serve the 3·7s have been trained in the field role and share in fire tasks previously given mainly to 25-pounders. Since the 90th joined the B.L.A. it has fired 100,000 rounds at field targets, tank and troop concentrations

WATCH ON THE RHINE (NEW STYLE) as two medium batteries of the Royal Artillery lined up ready for the momentous crossings of March 23-24; the river embankment can be seen in the background. These 4·5-in. guns were of the type used against Rommel in the Western Desert in 1942-43, counterblast to the German 88-mm. gun. PAGE 782 *Photo, British-Official*

*Photos, British Official,
Planet News*

Over the Rhine With Monty's Men

Opening of the final round of the war with Germany came on the night of March 23-24, 1945, when on a 25-mile front north of the Ruhr the Rhine was forced by Field-Marshal Montgomery's 21st Army Group. Among the first to cross were troops of the 15th and 51st Scottish Divisions. Jocks are seen (top right) leaving their assault craft. By the wrecked bridge at Wesel men of the Cheshire Regiment (bottom) landed from Buffaloes, which also carried supplies (top left) to the far side.

Photos, Brit
Newspaper

Royal Engineers Make Ferries and Bridges—

Twenty-one hours after men of the 15th Scottish Division had crossed Hitler's last great water barrier in the West, the first bridge had been completed and troops and supplies were pouring across. Well over 10,000 Sappers were engaged, and more than 1,000 lorries brought up the 5,300 feet of bridging and rafting. A self-propelled gun of a Highland Division anti-tank regiment embarks on a raft (1), and guns and supplies go over (2). The first Bailey pontoon bridge across the Rhine (3).

— For 21st Army Group's Dramatic Leap

Amphibious craft scurried to and fro as engineers assembled pontoons (4) for the bridging. For this vital work of construction the men were intensively trained on Yorkshire rivers. In the darkness of the night before the assault, bulldozers cut approach roads to the bridge and ferry sites. Then, as assault troops took the plunge in their Buffaloes the Sappers moved forward to the banks with all their weighty gear. Within a few hours two ferries and three bridges were operating.

Our Spearheads Borne by Air and Water

Greatest air-swoop of the war carried glider and parachute troops of the famous British 6th Airborne Division beyond the Rhine in advance of the 2nd Army. Glider crew ready for action immediately after crash landing (top left). In Hamminkeln (top right), an anti-tank gun landed by glider is set up. 1st Commando Brigade crossed by boat at 10 p.m. on Mar. 23. ahead of any others, and by 2 a.m. had taken Wesel, where some of their 350 prisoners (bottom) crouch in a crater.

VIEWS & REVIEWS

Of Vital War Books

by Hamilton Fyfe

EVOLUTION is to me of all subjects the most interesting. It combines the elements of a first-class fairy-tale with the wonders of science. That is true not only of the evolution which is a process of Nature ; it applies equally to the development of machinery invented and constructed by man. Many, perhaps most, of these human inventions have been developed in response to the necessities of war. Sometimes it seems as if mankind exerted its powers to their utmost only in order to destroy and kill.

There is no more fascinating story of ingenuity in the overcoming of difficulties than that of the gradual perfecting of landing craft for the use of troops invading a country from the sea or across a wide river like the Rhine. Such craft are no new thing. Napoleon had a fleet of them at Boulogne when he thought of invading Britain. But if he could now see the difference between his flat-bottomed boats and the Buffaloes, the Alligators, and other types of amphibious warfare vehicle-vessels which are working today, he would gasp with astonishment.

STILL more amazed would he become if he were told that this progress was accomplished in a space of less than five years. Landing craft did not have a chance to develop normally, gradually, bit by bit. Building them was a rush job all the time. When this war began they scarcely could be said to exist. Some had been built in order to land troops and stores on the Gallipoli Peninsula and in Mesopotamia. But, says Mr. Gordon Holman in his book on the subject, called Stand By To Beach ! (Hodder & Stoughton, 7s. 6d.), " if anyone remembered landing craft in the twenty years' gap between 1918 and 1938 it was probably with a smile at the very idea of their freakishness."

Not till 1939, a month before this war started, did the first of a new kind of landing boat have its trials on the Clyde. These were built just in time to be employed for a purpose of which their designers and constructors never dreamed. They were needed, not to land British troops on beaches, but to take them off, in order to save them from the enemy. They did this in Norway in April 1940, and again at Dunkirk in the following month ; they were a very present help to those two melancholy evacuations.

Then came an illustration of the British quality which some call dogged courage and others call conceit—the quality that refuses to acknowledge, when we get into a tight place, just how tight that place is. At the moment when we seemed to be on the verge of disaster, when we had almost no defence for our island, not more than forty tanks, a very poor supply of ack-ack guns, and not nearly enough aircraft, we began to prepare for the day when we should turn the tables and strike at the Nazis on the continent of Europe. It reminds one of the immortal saying attributed to Foch at the time of the Battle of the Marne, but actually, I believe, much older : " My centre is giving ground ; my right retiring ; situation excellent ; I am attacking."

WE were not in a position to attack in 1940, but we did the next best thing— the thing that would have seemed crazy to the Huns if they had known about it : we set about making preparations for the day when we should attack. That we were going to do this some day was in all minds.

The trouble was that the shipyards were full up with what was considered to be—and at the time was—more urgent work. They could not be expected to do the whole

job. So " the Admiralty set about organizing production in branches of British industry which had never before had any association with ships or the sea." The method of prefabrication was adopted. Parts were made by engineering works, furniture factories, carpentering shops, locomotive builders, firms that took orders for bridges and other large constructions, even wayside garage and repair outfits. Boats were built in sections, taken to the coast to be assembled.

All over the country the work went on and " many of the workmen and women who were engaged in this vast programme in its early stages must have wondered when and

Build-up of a Great Invasion Fleet

how the results of their labours would be put to use." Silence was, of course, essential, and they kept silent.

Although our supply of tanks was still lamentably short in spite of the vast effort being put into their construction, some of the new craft were designed to carry tanks. There really is something sublime about the way the British race disregards difficulties and even disasters, and fixes attention on the day when these will be inflicted on the foe.

THE tank landing craft are about 200 feet in length and about 30 wide, with a displacement of about 350 gross tons.

Nearly all the weight is aft, and this helps to trim the vessel for landing purposes. A large ramp set at an angle of around 45 degrees forms the squared-off bows, and where the lower part of the ramp enters the water the craft draws no more than three feet. The whole of the flat bottom of the vessel slopes gently until in the stern she draws seven feet. The ramp in the bows is hinged at the bottom and can be lowered quickly by hand or power-driven winches. When it is down it provides a runway on to the beaches for the vehicles carried.

Two-thirds of the space is available for tanks, which are lashed to the metal decks to prevent them from moving while aboard. The craft is powered by two 500 h.p. Diesel engines. The living quarters of the crew are right aft and can only be described as cramped.

But the crews, consisting of two officers and

Cpl. G. E. TANDY of the Royal Marines (second from left) and three of his comrades display pieces of the damaged assault craft which the young corporal, as coxswain, steered in the remarkable manner related in this page.
PAGE 787

ten petty officers and men, make the best of it. " Although they have to live very much on top of one another, there is the usual standard of naval discipline to be observed." and they turn out smartly when occasion calls for smartness.

As in all small ships, there is a fine comradeship added to, no doubt, in this case by the fact that almost invariably the men are " hostilities only " ratings, and the officers have earned their promotion after serving on the lower deck.

The first time the new types of landing craft were used for attack was at the end of 1941, when the Lofoten Islands, off Norway, were raided. They behaved well, did all that was expected of them. So they did at Dieppe in August of the next year. This was the final testing for the " new branch of the Navy," and " it proved a very hard test indeed," but " they came through with flying colours." All the tanks were put down on the beaches, though in places the fire from the shore batteries was heavy ; and when the time came to take off the troops who had been fighting up the cliffs and on the top, " the naval crews displayed outstanding gallantry."

We learned a lot from that operation at Dieppe, which in itself was such an unhappy failure. It helped greatly towards later operations which were almost complete successes. In Sicily, for instance, the landing craft assisted in putting ashore within forty-eight hours of the first assault 80,000 men, 300 tanks. 7,000 vehicles and 700 guns. Now there appeared a new type " produced with amazing speed in American shipbuilding yards." These were on a far bigger scale and they looked more like ships because they had shaped bows. But these bows were, in fact, two huge doors. When these opened, a ramp came down as it did in the smaller vessels. The interior was like a vast hall or warehouse ; nothing was allowed to interfere with the need for loading space.

Time went on, and at last D-Day arrived. All the craft needed were ready. All the men required had been thoroughly trained. They were about to do, as the late Admiral Sir Bertram Ramsay put it, " what Philip of Spain failed to do, what Napoleon tried and failed to do, and what Hitler never had the courage to try." They were about to take part in " the greatest amphibious operation in history " (another of Admiral Ramsay's stirring phrases). How well, how skilfully, how bravely they did it, everyone knows.

WHERE all behaved so magnificently it may seem invidious to single out any deed of heroism. But I must relate one such deed because it was performed not in the heat of battle, when the blood is summoned up and the sinews stiffened by danger, but in conditions of a totally different colour. Cpl. George Tandy of the Royal Marines was coxswain of an assault landing craft which had to travel seven miles before putting its load of 32 soldiers ashore on the Normandy coast. The sea was running high ; the steering-wheel was smashed. What could be done ?

Tandy knew. He slipped over the stern into the water, " placed one foot on the rudder guard-rail and directly controlled the rudder with his other foot. He had only the shallow rim of wood round the stern of the boat and a little iron cleat to hang on to. In this way he faced a seven-mile journey to the French shore."

Nor was that all. When he had landed his passengers, Tandy decided to take his craft back to its parent ship in the same way. He did that, too, and after being in the water for nearly three hours he was not more than half alive. Yet he declared that any one of his shipmates would have done as he did if they had had the opportunity.

How find words to fit such devotion, such determined, dogged courage ? As usual, Shakespeare supplies them. " What a piece of work is a man ! "

Allied Military Control at Work in Wesel

AT LIPPSTADT, when the U.S. 9th and 1st Armies entered it on April 1, 1945, thus closing a ring of steel round the Ruhr, the local police had fled and the people were engaged in an orgy of looting; women, seen emerging from a big wine store (1) joined in. Villagers at Haltern were huddled outside their sandhill shelter (2) as Allied troops arrived on March 29.

A joint Allied military control took over in ruined Wesel (captured by British Commandos on March 24), appointing German civilians to enforce their instructions to remaining townsfolk. A sergeant of the Middlesex Regiment and a U.S. private stuck up the Allied proclamation (3); such notices must all be posted up in the presence of at least one German civilian. The British officer commanding at Wesel issued his instructions to German civilians (4) chosen by their own towns-people to represent them with the Allied military government.

War Factories Wrenched from the Hun Intact

PREFABRICATED U-BOATS were among the booty taken by the U.S. 1st Army at Rheinbrohl, east of the Rhine and north of Coblenz, during General Hodges' big push in late March, 1945; partly finished submarines are seen on the stocks (1) at the factory from which their predecessors were dispatched to coastal assembly yards. Among the prisoners released were Russian slave-workers, including women and girls, who celebrated their freedom with dancing (2).

Of special interest to these U.S. Army engineers (3) was the prefabricated section of a U-boat. Prefabricated U-boats came in for their mightiest pounding on March 30, 1945, when 1,400 Fortresses and Liberators of the U.S. 8th Air Force struck at Bremen, Hamburg and Wilhelmshaven in the greatest U.S. attack to date on naval installations in the West. On the Eastern front, a Soviet soldier guards another type of German factory, this one underground (4), captured near Berlin.

Photos, Associated Press, Pictorial Press

In Rapid Succession the Nazi 'Plums' Fall

AT FRANKFORT-ON-MAIN, BIRTHPLACE OF GOETHE, Germany's greatest poet, youthful civilians crowded the streets (1) as men of General Patton's U.S. 3rd Army moved in on March 28, 1945. When General Patch's U.S. 7th Army took over in Mannheim the following day, refugees crept from a huge air-raid shelter, raising the white flag (2). At Heidelberg (3), ancient university town taken almost undamaged on March 30, captured Nazi snipers were marched away—out of the war.

A New Use for Germany's Famous Motor-Roads

ON THE BROAD FRANKFORT AUTOBAHN, hordes of Nazi prisoners marched westwards to captivity after the swift seizure of Giessen, important rail-and-road junction in the Lahn valley, by General Hodges' U.S. 1st Army on March 28, 1945. As the captives moved thickly along the grass-covered dividing line of this Frankfort motor-road, tanks and transport of the 6th Armoured Division of General Patton's U.S. 3rd Army rolled in a one-way stream towards Cassel, which they cleared on April 4.

Photo, U.S. Official

Red Army Advance Freed British Prisoners

RESCUED FROM NAZI P.O.W. CAMPS overrun by the Russians in their rapid sweep westwards, and magnificently cared for by the Soviet Government, over 1,000 Allied Servicemen arrived at a northern British port on March 30, 1945 ; travelling by way of the Middle East, a smiling group in fur caps (I) chatted with a Soviet officer before embarking at Odessa. These (2), liberated at Poznan, trudged through the snows to a repatriation centre. Ex-captives cheered themselves hoarse as their ship docked at last (3), ; four of them sported a Nazi flag and armlet as trophies (4). The repatriates included officers and men of the British Army, the Royal Navy, the R.A.F., R.C.A.F., the Canadian Army and the Royal Norwegian Army.

Photos, Pictorial Press, New York Times

I WAS THERE! Eye Witness Stories of the War

From Above the Rhine I Saw the Sky-Men Pounce

Field-Marshal Montgomery in March 1945, in a personal message to his troops included this memorable phrase, " 21st Army Group will now cross the Rhine." Here James Wellard, The Sunday Express Correspondent, tells what he saw from an observation plane manoeuvring over that river on March 24. See also illus. pages 776, 777 and 783-786.

GENERAL SIR MILES DEMPSEY, British 2nd Army commander, opened a 1,420 ft. long British-built Bailey bridge over the Rhine, across which he is seen passing in a jeep, on March 30, 1945. *Photo, British Official*

IT is 11 o'clock, Saturday morning, and as far as the eye can see to the east, from 1,200 feet above the Rhine, Germany is flaming and smoking. What is now going on in the skies around me, on the ground and in water, is like a futurist painting of Armageddon. For the Germans on the east bank of the Rhine it is Armageddon.

This is D-Day concentrated. Filling the sky, transport planes, two-engined American Dakotas, four-engined British Halifaxes, are streaming across the sky in two columns. I saw the first wave of this airborne armada just go in. From each plane there was a series of tiny explosive puffs which blossomed out into parachutes. Suddenly, a thousand men were swinging to the ground. German flak reacted strongly to the first wave. Despite tremendous artillery and fighter-bomber barrage some flak batteries survived. From them, dirty black puffs are blotting the sky. From others, red tracers are coming up.

I see one Dakota plunge suddenly to earth. Two more are smoking. One of them breaks into a snarling blaze. The planes get across the Rhine. The crew bale out. Still the planes come in. Now the second wave is approaching. I look through the glass roof of the observation plane, and see giant tow-planes pulling, on long nylon ropes, two gliders apiece. These are the smaller American Waco gliders, which fly either one behind the other or in line abreast.

NEXT come the big British Horsas, heaving along behind Halifaxes. They come by hundreds, suddenly break loose from the tow-planes and start circling and diving to the earth. Mercifully the German flak seems almost to have stopped now, and we speculate whether the flak gun crews have panicked under the monstrous spectacle of this air armada and abandoned their positions.

As we sail slowly along the Rhine between Xanten and Wesel and cross to the other side to take a close look at the flaming German town of Blisslich, I can see that resistance has collapsed for miles inland. My pilot is looking for enemy flak and artillery positions. We can find none, and during an hour in the air see only one enemy shell land on the west bank. It fell between two Alligators lined up along the white road waiting their turn to go down into the river.

At the river banks the scene is almost as peaceful as a Saturday afternoon on the Thames. The countryside is lush and flat on both sides of the Rhine. Our ferries are scuttling back and forth like water beetles with nothing to hamper them. I can see men standing in boats waving to us.

There are vehicles, British and American, stacked on both banks. Crews stand around leisurely. Some are lying on their backs in the beautiful sunshine, some are eating. Everything, as a field commander said, is "going like a house afire."

I see our pontoon bridges already reaching out across the river. The Alligators need not wait for them, and waddle down through the mud, plunge into the water and start swimming across. Trucks on ferries are starting across. Already hundreds of vehicles with coloured recognition panels atop them are moving eastward across the Rhine.

Every German town and village inland is buried under mushroom-like clouds of smoke. Our artillery has killed them. Rubble is so deep our traffic is going around over fields marked out with white tape. Along one road, walking west, comes a line of men in blue-grey uniforms. They are 200 German prisoners with one Tommy escorting them to the river.

We fly south to Wesel; Wesel flattened and looking from the air like the embers of a bonfire. Our vehicles are already moving in. Last night the R.A.F. gave its most perfect demonstration of night precision bombing. Wesel is small, compact. They say every bomb went plumb into the target. If there are Germans in Wesel they must still be digging their way out of the rubble.

To the north, somewhere, another wave of gliders were going down. Fields for miles were dotted now with white, red and orange parachutes. Gliders with their infantrymen and supplies have to make a steep, dangerous descent into fields, and down they go, wheeling like big birds all over the sky.

I see them grinding to a halt against fences and trees, and men leaping out and running towards ditches. But the fantastic thing about it all is the absence of enemy opposition.

Slaves of the Reich on the Westward Trek

Tragic is the march of the freed peoples who had been pressed into Hitler's hated service ; tragic, too, will be the homecoming for thousands of them. Pathetic is their gratitude to their liberators. Colm Wills, News Chronicle War Correspondent with the British 2nd Army, sent this dispatch on April 2, 1945, depicting scenes on the roads of Western Germany.

WE have burst the walls of the prison land, and through the gaps the slaves are streaming westwards in scores of thousands, amazed by the light of freedom. They line both sides of every road, trudging on through dust or damp, continually stepping aside out of the way of our onrushing columns. Some carry bundles, some push makeshift handcarts laden with the bundles of four or five companions of the road. But very few have any belongings at all beyond their ragged civilian suits or patch-work uniforms.

These uniforms are as diverse as the poor wretches who wear them. Some are the uniforms of Allied armies to which the wearers belonged before they were captured and drafted into German labour gangs. Others are the garb of the Todt organization and other similar slave groups. Inevitably the eye becomes accustomed ; after a while the trudging columns become part of the un-noticed landscape.

And then suddenly one is aware of a face, glimpsed in passing, and the mind photographs the expression of the eye, the cruel sculpture wrought on the grey flesh by years of suffering. Suddenly one realizes what is going on. These are men and women recalled to life.

Slowly, painfully, they are making their way homewards. The home they left years

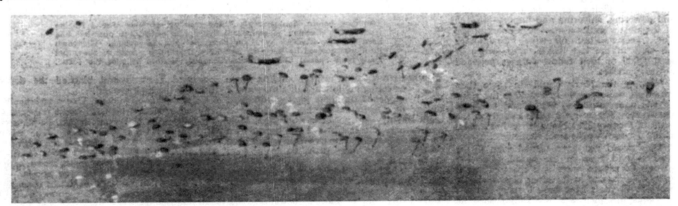

OUT OF FLAK-FILLED SKIES OVER THE DROPPING-ZONE in the Rees-Wesel area parachute troops of the British 6th Airborne Division descended in mass, as narrated in the story above, to aid the British 2nd Army's crossing of the Rhine. The plane from which this remarkable photograph was taken was shot down a few minutes later—the first aircraft victim of the gigantic operation. Parachute troops and glider-borne infantry totalled 40,000. See also illustration page 776. *Photo, U.S. Official*

ago may no longer exist. Their families and friends may be dead. But they have got to go and see. They are weak, weary and ill, some of them crippled.

Only the irresistible call of home can keep them going—that and the unbelievable experience of freedom. For they are free. Free. They walk the roads, and the very dust they shuffle through is blessed to walk upon. Free. They eat their meagre meals in ditches by the road, and the dry crusts taste sweet. They all move westward, though many come from the east and bear on the sleeve or breast a letter P, for Polish, or the word "Ost," to show they come from somewhere in Germany's eastern European reservoir of helots.

Many are Russians, and these raise a proud smile as they point to themselves and shout to you, "We Russki," and if you stop and tell them the latest news of the Red Army the smile becomes a broad grin and they pace with longer strides and squarer shoulders.

They all move westward—easterners along with French, Belgians and Dutch, Czechs and Yugo-Slavs, along with Danes and Norwegians, because westward they will find Allied organizations ready to deal with them and send them home when possible.

Already these organizations are penetrating well into the battle zones, but cannot keep pace with the Allied spearhead. So the freed slaves march west to meet them. In the last few days war prisoners have begun to swell the ranks of the marching men. Several Stalags have been overrun, and many prisoners cannot wait for official transport. They must start homewards instantly.

I have met scores of French and Belgian soldiers walking west, shaken their hands, given them cigarettes, talked with them. It is wonderful to see the joy in their faces, hear their voices rise with excitement.

Some of them somehow have managed to make themselves little cockades in their national colours, wherewith to adorn their shabby Army caps. Others have even been able to muster a little gaiety and wear bright scarves picked up somewhere along the road. One even marched solemnly in the silk top hat of some fleeing German burgher.

There is immense satisfaction in rolling into Germany with the conquering armies. But there is deeper satisfaction in realizing that even in Germany these are still armies of liberation. For, however pathetic these columns of pilgrims are, however tragic their past, however difficult their future, this is an hour of wonder for them—the hour when they can say, as they do say over and over among themselves, in all their diverse tongues: "We are free!"

a final hopeless battle. Their deaths were as useless as the gutted arsenal they defended. The main gates were blown off their hinges by grenades hurled by G.I. Joes as they passed by on to Duisburg. Inside the gates I was met by half a dozen nervous caretakers who had been in the works' fire service. Their eyes were watery and red-rimmed either by weeping or sleeplessness.

They told me that several thousand employees were living down below in the works' shelters, as their homes had all been destroyed. "We were not allowed to go to shelters during raids, as it interfered too much with production," they told me. The works had been repaired six times in the past four years but had never been in full production since the first R.A.F. raids in 1941.

DOWN in the shelters was one of those scenes that are familiar in Germany today—a whole community living deep underground in appalling conditions. There must have been 1,500 in this one shelter. All over this area about 40,000 people are today coming up out of the ground.

Within the past 24 hours nearly 500,000 more German civilians in this corner of the Ninth Army front have been added to the cares of the over-taxed Military Government officials. In the bomb-cratered courtyard of the Thyssen main works I saw only a small group of Russian slave workers, found locked down the works coal mine, obviously left to starve.

Not far from the Thyssen works are canal docks, where the plant's output used to be loaded into barges for their journey up "Happy Valley" (the Ruhr). I saw at least 100 sunk or wrecked barges on the canal banks. You could see there had been no activity here for many weeks.

I Saw Hitler's Great Arsenal Cold and Dead

The 15-square miles of the Thyssen steel works, where Germany's war weapons had been forged, have taken the final knock-out. Writing from Duisburg on March 30, 1945, Daily Mail Special Correspondent Noel Monks, with the U.S. 9th Army, records his visit to this smashed-up "arsenal of hate."

A LARGE white flag droops over the administration building of the once mighty Thyssen steelworks here, a fitting sign that Hitler's game is up.

For the Nazis' plans of world conquest were cradled in the thousand blast furnaces within sight of where I am writing this.

And a thousand German workers today came out of their holes in the ground—timid and cowering, shivering and hungry—in one of the most significant mass surrenders of the war. They had been on strike since January 22—date of the last R.A.F. raid—when at least 5,000 of their fellow-workers perished at their benches.

Nothing the Nazis could do since then could get these people to evacuate the ruins of the once throbbing works and continue elsewhere. The war for them ended on the night of January 22. Not a wheel has turned in the Thyssen works since that night.

They could not have turned even if the workers had been in the mood. For the plant's 15 square miles is a mass of rusty, twisted ruins, and in the giant blast furnaces that for 12 years have been forging Hitler's war weapons there are now only stone-cold ashes. Strangely enough, hundreds of tall chimneys still stand, gaunt and smokeless. Wandering through the ruins of the Thyssen plant today was like walking over the graves of millions of men, for it was the Thyssen brothers who dazzled Hitler with blueprints of tanks, guns and battleships and led him to make war.

I came to the main Thyssen plant past the bodies of a dozen Volkssturmers who died in

Battle of Rheine Town and Its Aftermath

Two days before Montgomery's Rhine crossing, airfields around Rheine from which German jet-propelled and fighter squadrons operated had been heavily attacked by 1,300 Fortresses and Liberators. The town itself was entered by the 11th Armoured Division on April 2, 1945, and Daily Mail Special Correspondent Alexander Clifford tells of the battle.

I WATCHED it from the farm building where I was eating my lunch, half a mile away.

It happened on some high ground just beyond the Dortmund Canal. The Somerset Light Infantry had got across the canal some time before. The last bridge had been blown up in their faces, but the new bridge had been swiftly built. Then they drove on up the road in the usual way.

And suddenly they found themselves faced with a battle. The Germans had cleared out an N.C.O.s training school at Hanover, formed the pupils into a battalion, and marched them on foot to the canal. They were only very lightly armed, but they occupied a wood and blocked the defiles through the high ground.

They were good soldiers. They even launched counter-attacks, which is almost unheard of these days. A real attack had to be planned. It went on from three sides. The Monmouths had gone round behind the ridge and the Herefords had attacked from in front of it. On the canal side tanks stood in the fields and spouted shells into the woods.

In about ten minutes of battle one saw what is happening to this country. Two farmlands and a wood were abolished and the German battalion broken into fragments.

Mortar shells began dropping into the wood, bursting about the treetops and snapping off the trunks this way and that. The tanks on the right swung their turrets slightly and played the hose of their machine-gun fire into a farmhouse. The pink tracers looked like golf balls, with a slight slice because of the wind.

The house began to burn in the roof with a brilliant red flame. One knew that the farmer and his children were almost certainly in the cellar. One knew the cattle were dying in the fields—the mortality among cows in war is astonishing. Quite quickly the battle spluttered to a finish. So much explosive had crashed on to that wood that none could have continued to fight out of it.

As the battle finished, a file of German soldiers marched down the road, turned into Brigade H.Q., saluted the military policeman, and gave themselves up. The astounded policeman accepted their surrender.

One of them simply happened to be in the neighbourhood on leave from the Russian front. Another prisoner was a tough, handsome specimen, Sgt.-Major Haner, from the Italian front. He had fought at Cassino and he was back in Germany for the first time in four years.

He was interrogated, and he answered the questions with stiff correctness. His face was drawn and his eyes were hollow. Suddenly he burst into tears. "Can I ask something?" he said. "Can I write a note for my mother and my wife?"

"No, of course not," answered the British officer. The German pulled himself together and turned to go. "Why do you want to write?" asked the British officer. The German said, "I haven't been home for four years. I will show you where my home is," and he pointed on the map to a place that lay a mile away. It had been captured by the British an hour before.

It's the sort of thing that is bound to keep happening. No one has yet got used to the newness and excitement of being in Germany. For all of us there is an endless fascination in watching the reactions of the civilians and discussing psychological theories about them. You then drive away down a lonely country road and find farms with nothing but a white flag to show they have ever heard of our approach. And you stop to get eggs and you know that you are getting genuine spontaneous reaction from the farm people.

This afternoon a laughing buxom girl brought us the eggs, wished us a happy Easter, and asked, "When are tanks coming?" We refused to discuss military details and she was frankly disappointed.

VOLKSSTURM R.S.M. captured by the 53rd Welsh Division in Bocholt, cleared of the enemy by March 29, 1945, displays his armlet.
Photo, British Official

She liked soldiers and she wanted to see ours. Her little sisters waved to us as we left.

What are you to make of it? One really gets the impression that they want to be friendly. And that is astonishing when you see their towns. Take Rheine, which is the Second Army's biggest to date. It isn't flat entirely, but empty and uninhabitable.

Once again the stout old church seems to have been miraculously spared. It is uncannily quiet save for the spasmodic crack of the sniper's rifle. There is really nothing to say about Rheine. It is the typical wrecked town that is becoming sickeningly familiar.

It was bombed because it was the centre of a ring of airfields. It was shelled because it lies on the Ems and some odd German units attempted to hold the crossings. It was entered, and it went through the harsh purging- that is known as being "cleaned." That is to say, it was made safe to our troops. So you thread its silent streets with glass and woodwork crackling under your wheels and empty windows staring blindly at you from either side.

You find that everything has obviously been left at a moment's notice—half-cooked food on cold stoves, cash still in the cash registers, wine on the café tables. All of it half-wrecked, of course, but all recognizably there. You find a clothing shop burst wide open and you wonder at the astonishing display of garments.

I suppose that none of it was much good, but I saw enough artificial silk stockings lying in the roadway to turn any comparable English town green with envy. Just now and again you become conscious of the mass of personal tragedy that lies around. A half-finished letter on a desk, or an umbrella left to dry before a now cold stove, makes you realize that here some thousands of people have suddenly deserted their homes. If you don't believe the Germans are being punished, you should walk through Rheine's streets.

OUR DIARY OF THE WAR

MARCH 27, Tuesday   2,033rd day
Western Front.—U.S. 1st Army reached Limburg and joined with units of 3rd Army south of Coblenz.
Air.—R.A.F. dropped 10-ton bombs on U-boat pens at Farge, near Bremen.
Russian Front.—Soviet troops broke into Danzig and Gdynia.
Philippines.—Announced that U.S. forces landed on Cebu Island.
Far East.—Units of British Pacific Fleet joined with U.S. Fleet in attacks on Ryukyu Islands.

MARCH 28, Wednesday   2,034th day
Western Front.—9th Army took Hamborn. 3rd Army entered Wiesbaden. Frankfort-on-Main cleared.
Air.—Flying Fortresses bombed tank plants at Berlin and Hanover.
Russian Front.—Gdynia captured by Rokossovsky's troops. Malinovsky captured Gyor and Komarno.

MARCH 29, Thursday   2,035th day
Western Front. — British and Canadians cleared Emmerich and crossed German-Dutch frontier. Montgomery's armour broke out from Rhine bridge-head. Mannheim fell to U.S. 7th Army.

MARCH 30, Friday   2,036th day
Western Front.—Heidelberg captured by U.S. 7th Army. 3rd Army reached Lauterbach.
Air.—U.S. bombers made heaviest assault on Hamburg, Bremen and Wilhelmshaven.
Russian Front.—Town and fortress of Danzig stormed by Rokossovsky. Tolbukhin crossed Austrian frontier from Hungary.
Burma.—Kyaukse occupied by 14th Army troops.

MARCH 31, Saturday   2,037th day
Western Front.—French 1st Army crossed the Rhine between Mannheim and Karlsruhe.
Air.—Halle, Brandenburg and Brunswick attacked by U.S. bombers. R.A.F. bombed U-boat yards at Hamburg.
Russian Front.—Soviet troops captured Ratibor on Upper Oder.
Far East.—Super-Fortresses bombed airfields and aircraft factories at Nagoya.

APRIL 1, Sunday   2,038th day
Western Front.—Link-up of 1st and 9th Armies near Lippstadt sealed off the Ruhr. Paderborn captured.
Russian Front.—Soviet troops captured Sopron, at approaches to Vienna. Koniev captured encircled town of Glogau on the Oder.
Far East.—Okinawa, largest of the Ryukyu Islands, invaded by Allies.

APRIL 2, Monday   2,039th day
Western Front.—British and Canadians occupied Enschede and Rheine. Münster entered by British and U.S. forces.
Russian Front.—Nagy Kanisza, oil centre in Hungary, captured by Soviet troops.
Italy.—8th Army forces landed on spit of land dividing Lake Comacchio from Adriatic, N. of Ravenna.

APRIL 3, Tuesday   2,040th day
Western Front.—Canadian 1st Army captured Nordhorn and crossed Twenthe canal between Zutphen and Hengelo.
Air.—German troop concentrations at Nordhausen, N.E. of Cassel, bombed by Lancasters. U-boat yards at Kiel attacked by Flying Fortresses.
Russian Front.—Tolbukhin's troops captured Wiener Neustadt.
Japan.—Super-Fortresses attacked aircraft works on Honshiu Island.

APRIL 4, Wednesday   2,041st day
Western Front.—Cassel and Gotha cleared by 3rd Army. French entered Karlsruhe. Aschaffenburg cleared by 7th Army.
Air.—U.S. heavy bombers again attacked U-boat yards at Kiel and Hamburg.
Russian Front.—Bratislava, capital of Slovakia, stormed by Malinovsky. Baden and Zwoelfaxing captured, S. and S.E. of Vienna.

APRIL 5, Thursday   2,042nd day
Western Front.—Allied tanks and infantry crossed the Weser. Osnabruck cleared by 1st Commando Brigade, Minden by 6th Airborne Division.
Air.—U.S. bombers attacked ordnance depots and railway yards in southern Germany.
General.—Soviet Govt. denounced Russo-Japanese neutrality pact.

APRIL 6, Friday   2,043rd day
Western Front.—Eisenach and Hamm cleared of the enemy. In Holland, Canadians captured Coevorden, and reached the Ijssel river.

Far East.—Liberators from Luzon bombed Hong Kong harbour.
Philippines.—U.S. troops landed in Sulu Archipelago near British North Borneo.

Air.—Railways at Leipzig and Halle attacked by U.S. bombers.
Russian Front.—Soviet troops broke into defences of Vienna.
Balkans.—Serajevo captured by Yugoslav troops.
Pacific—Japanese air force attacking Allied ships off Okinawa had heavy losses ; 3 U.S. destroyers sunk.

APRIL 7, Saturday   2,044th day
Western Front.—At night Allied parachutists landed in N. Holland east of the Zuider Zee.
Air.—U.S. bombers attacked airfields and railways from Hamburg to Nuremberg ; 63 enemy fighters shot down. Mosquitoes bombed Berlin from Continental bases for first time.
Japan.—Tokyo and Nagoya bombed by 300 Super-Fortresses.
Pacific.—Allied carrier-aircraft attacked Jap fleet in East China Sea, sinking battleship Yamato, two cruisers and three destroyers.

APRIL 8, Sunday   2,045th day
Western Front.—Canadians captured Zutphen. U.S. troops entered Gelsenkirchen and Götingen. French 1st Army captured Pforzheim.
Russian Front.—Soviet troops forced Morava and Danube N.W. of Bratislava.
Baltic.—Danish patriots escaped with 21 ships to Sweden.

APRIL 9, Monday   2,046th day
Western Front.—Krupps works at Essen surrendered to Allies. Canadians in Holland linked up with airborne troops.
Air.—U.S. bombers attacked jet-aircraft bases near Munich. R.A.F. bombed U-boat yards at Hamburg by day and at Kiel by night, sinking pocket-battleship Admiral Scheer.
Russian Front.—Koenigsberg captured by Vassilievsky's troops. Tolbukhin broke into centre of Vienna.
Italy.—8th Army crossed Senio river after heavy air bombardment.

APRIL 10, Tuesday   2,047th day
Western Front.—U.S. 9th Army captured Hanover and cut road to Brunswick. Occupation of Essen completed.
Air.—Jet-aircraft bases in Berlin area attacked by U.S. bombers ; 305 enemy aircraft destroyed. R.A.F. bombed railway yards at Leipzig.

★ ====== *Flash-backs* ====== ★

1940
April 9. *Denmark and Norway invaded by German Armies.*
April 10. *First battle of Narvik ; destroyer Hardy sunk.*

1941
March 28. *Battle of Cape Matapan ; Italian fleet routed.*
April 6. *Yugoslavia and Greece invaded by Germans.*

1942
March 27-28. *Combined Operations raid on port of St. Nazaire.*

April 9. *American resistance ended on Bataan, Philippines.*

1943
March 28. *Mareth, Toujane and Matmata captured by 8th Army.*
April 10. *8th Army occupied Tunisian port of Sfax.*

1944
March 31. *Red Army crossed frontier into Rumania.*
April 10. *Black Sea port of Odessa recaptured by Russians.*

STREAMING TO CAPTIVITY IN THEIR THOUSANDS, relics of the Wehrmacht in the eastern Rhineland passed in procession (1) to the cages, following the U.S. 3rd Army's spectacular surge across the river, launched on March 22, 1945. In a message to his troops on March 30, Lieut.-Gen. Patton declared that in less than two months they had captured 140,112 enemy soldiers and killed or wounded 90,000, "thereby eliminating practically all the German 7th and 1st Armies." These Nazis (2) abandoned their arms before surrendering to a soldier of the British 2nd Army. Among the 8,000 Germans taken by Patton's troops in the Saar triangle were these (3). At Wesel, on March 24, the 1st British Commando Brigade captured the German commander, Lieut.-Col. Ross (4).

Photos, British Official, P.N.A., Associated Press

THE WAR IN THE AIR

by Capt. Norman Macmillan, M.C., A.F.C.

FOR seven days before the 21st Army Group crossing of the Lower Rhine, massed formations of aircraft of the 2nd T.A.F., the U.S.A. 9th A.F., Bomber Command and the U.S.A. 8th A.F. rained bombs, rockets, cannon-shells and bullets upon tactical targets east of the river barrier, attacking guns, troop concentrations, and bridges as far forward as the river Weser (at Bremen, on March 23, with 10-ton bombs). The earlier cloud-covered skies had changed to blue.

The co-ordination of all British and American air forces engaged in the operation (whether based on the Western Continent or the U.K.) was controlled by Air Marshal Sir Arthur Coningham, commander of 2nd T.A.F. Through their combined effort all rail communication to the chosen combat area was smashed on the enemy side, and the battlefield isolated. British heavy bombers attacked the strategic rail centres of Münster, Hanover and Osnabruck; subsequently, on April 3, Lancasters attacked enemy troop concentrations 60 miles northeast of Cassel.

BETWEEN 9 p.m. on March 23 and 3 a.m. on March 24, 21st Army Group forces crossed the Rhine in Buffaloes and naval mechanized and vehicle personnel landing craft. After daylight on the 24th the greatest airborne force ever seen was placed into position ahead of the surface forces in areas east of Rees and Wesel. More than 40,000 troops invaded Germany from the air that day. The glider train was 500 miles long, and between 5,000 and 6,000 aircraft of all types flew in this one operation: tugs, gliders, bombers, fighters. Curtiss C.46 Commandos able to carry 36 paratroopers were used for the first time. One airborne formation carried an anti-tank unit. In one convoy some British gliders carried two jeeps, 6-pdr. guns, other artillery, automatic weapons, blood plasma. Liberators following the gliders dropped from a few hundred feet supplies weighing 600 tons, including 4,400 canisters and bottles containing food, fighting equipment and medical supplies.

LUNCH-TIME Attack on Berlin by Soviet Heavy Bombers

Fifty per cent of the Glider Pilot Regiment pilots who landed the troops east of the Rhine were volunteers from the R.A.F. They went into battle after landing. No. 38 Group, 1st Allied Airborne Army, commanded by Air Vice-Marshal J. R. Scarlett-Streatfeild, was responsible for the British airborne operation. (See illus p. 776.)

From Italy heavy bombers of the U.S.A. 15th A.F. flew to bomb Berlin for the first time on March 24. Lightning fighters escorted them at the Italian end of their double journey; Mustangs met them over the target area and protected them there. Two days later Berlin was attacked at lunch-time by Soviet bombers.

By March 25 the parachute and glider-borne forces and the ground forces east of the Rhine had linked up. Forces from the three main bridge-heads across the Rhine at the Wesel, Remagen and Mainz crossings advanced deeper into Germany, and resistance began to crumble. By March 28 the forward moves were so rapid that pilots of the tactical air forces reported the enemy fleeing eastward, and the Allied bomb-line (demarcation behind which bombs must not be dropped because of the risk of hitting Allied forces) had to be advanced at short intervals throughout the day. Some attack sorties had to be recalled for rebriefing before they could drop their bombs.

As the armies pushed on to capture town after town—Speyer on March 23, Darmstadt on March 25, Frankfort-on-Main on March 26, Cassel on April 3, Osnabruck and Hengelo on April 4 and Almelo on April 5—and swung wide to bypass the Ruhr, the bombers maintained their strategic war; on Good Friday, March 30, the U.S.A. 8th A.F. sent its biggest force of 1,400 bombers escorted by 900 fighters to bomb the U-boat yards and other targets at Bremen, Hamburg and Wilhelmshaven. The cruiser Köln and other ships were sunk.

The day was indeed a good Friday for England. V-weapon bombardment ceased, and up to the time of writing has not been resumed. This is partly due to the bombers' cutting of the railways, but more to the Germans pulling out of Holland through the gap between Arnhem and the Zuider Zee

PREPARING FOR THE WESEL LANDINGS, March 24, 1945. British parachute troops became proficient in rope-climbing as part of the instructional course laid down at a training school in England. Before his first descent a learner goes through a programme in which over 20 mediums of jumping and landing are used. See also story in page 92, Vol. 7.

under the increasing pressure of the Canadian 1st Army and the tactical aircraft working with it. (This confirms the forecast in my first special article [see page 707] written after visiting the Western Front.) That day 2nd T.A.F. was ordered to hold fire because of the swift advance of the bomb-line ahead of Montgomery's now fast-moving "break-out" forces: British tanks entered Münster. But this gave the aircraft the more opportunity to bomb the German columns evacuating Western Holland in the biggest smash attack since Falaise; from the evening of March 31 the escape roads were jammed with German traffic.

ALLIED aircraft moved forward across the Rhine to operate from captured German airfields, and so maintain with greater ease their close air support for the surface forces. Strategic tonnage in March broke all records. Bomber Command dropped 67,500 tons and the U.S.A. 8th A.F. 65,625 (British) tons—all on Germany; the U.S. bombers flew 28,500 sorties, carrying an average bomb

load of 46 cwt. On April 3, 750 Fortresses, with 650 Mustangs in escort, bombed ship-building yards at Kiel, and a smaller force of Liberators bombed Hamburg.

IN the Far East, after a preliminary bombardment by British and American carrier-borne aircraft, U.S. forces landed on Okinawa in the Ryukyu Islands, 370 miles south-west of Japan, on April 1. This American invasion was a continuation of Pacific strategy in which the larger islands—in this case Formosa and Kyushu—are bypassed and a smaller island seized to serve as a fixed aircraft carrier. British support to the American landing was given in opening attacks on March 26 and 27 against the Sakishima Islands by Avenger bombers, rocket-firing Fireflies, and Hellcat and Corsair fighters. The carriers were led by the Illustrious. The objectives were aerodromes, radio and harbour installations, administrative buildings and vessels.

Okinawa island is 50 miles long and averages over 10 miles across. Little opposition was met at first and two airfields were quickly captured. But on April 6, Japanese resistance stiffened, and a great air/sea action followed a Japanese bomber attack on the U.S. fleet; 417 Jap aircraft were shot down, 39 by the British.

JAPANESE sources state that in the Far East are the British aircraft carriers Illustrious, Victorious, Formidable, Implacable, Indefatigable, Furious and Eager: this force should be able to place about 400/450 aircraft into the air, but it is likely that some of these carriers are in the Indian Ocean.

A small force of Super-Fortress bombers attacked Nagoya on March 30. On April 6, Super Fortresses bombing Tokyo and Nagoya (about 300 in the force) were escorted for the first time by fighters of the U.S.A. 7th A.F. On that day Liberators based in the Philippines bombed Hong Kong targets for the third consecutive day. On March 30 F/Lt. H. C. Graham flew a Canadian-built Mosquito 2,184 miles from Newfoundland to Scotland in 5 hrs. 38 mins. at a speed of 6½ miles a minute. On March 31, 1945 the Joint Commonwealth Air Training Plan for training air-crews ended.

From Home to Rome With Our Roving Camera

PREFABRICATED HOUSE (left), one of 30,000 being prepared for shipment from the U.S.A. to ease the plight of bombed-out Londoners, was on exhibition at Washington, D.C. On March 6, 1945, Mr. Duncan Sandys, Minister of Works, declared that London house repairs were nearing the 719,000 target.

ACTING AS POLICEMEN with the Inter-Allied Control Commission in Germany after the cessation of hostilities, British Public Safety Officers will wear a uniform (below) of dark blue with silver buttons, resembling Civil Defence battledress.

IN A ROME NAAFI (above) a British sergeant records a message for home. Thousands of families in Britain are to hear the voices of their men recorded on gramophone records in Italy and the Middle East.

TEN-TON BOMB of the R.A.F. (below) rides to the filling-centre on a specially designed lorry with 90 h.p. Diesel engine. These gigantic missiles softened up the Reich for the big advance. They are flown to their targets in Lancaster bombers, which themselves weigh just over ten tons. See also illus. in page 764.

FOOD FOR LIBERATED HOLLAND stored in an Allied warehouse, including sacks of sugar and flour, ready for distribution. Desperate plight of the inhabitants of the occupied region of the Netherlands is described in page 780.

Photos, British Official, Keystone, Planet News

RECENTLY, within the space of a few days, B.B.C. listeners lost three of their favourite entertainers, among them my brother-Savage—the inimitable Jetsam of the "low notes." Which leads me to the obvious reflection that of all forms of contemporary fame none is so immediate and yet so transient as that of the ether. Who, for instance, remembers the early Savoy Hill artists—John Henry, Uncle Caractacus, the Pianist with the Soft Voice, A. J. Alan and the rest—all of whom had their little half-hours? The news that plans are already under way to re-establish Britain's pre-war lead in television sets me wondering whether this new art-form will also produce perishable stars and satellites. If I were asked my opinion I should say "Yes." The fault, dear Brutus, lies not in our stars but in ourselves—we who nowadays have only to turn a knob or put on a gramophone record or slip round the corner to the cinema to experience the musical and theatrical talents of the world. We flit from one to another, sipping genius as a bee or a butterfly, yawning in our embarrassment of riches. How different from the days of our youth when many of us (myself included) queued-up for the "early doors" for hours at a time! Things come too easily nowadays, and television can only make us more blasé than ever—unless Whitehall rations it. Which mightn't be so daft a decision after all.

WHETHER you personally enjoyed them or not, the "crazy" shows invented by the late George Black for the London Palladium had at least the merit of being "in period." In retrospect they seem to have been an apposite comment on the general craziness of a most regrettable decade. The antics of the so-called Crazy Gang, especially their trick of jumping out of the picture-frame, so to speak, and mocking at the picture with an air of saying, "It's all nonsense anyway," together with their wilful puncturing of all the classical unities and accepted standards, could have been extended with profit to a larger stage. Just as in the country of the blind the one-eyed man is king, so in a world where accepted standards had fallen low, amid the cynicism of political manoeuvre and complacency that conspired to close both eyes to unpleasing reality, a Crazy Gang to tear all pretences to ribbons in a riot of ribaldry might have turned out to be a Sane Gang after all. I am reminded, somewhat sadly, of the words of Greville, Lord Brooke, the Elizabethan poet: "Man is the only creature with the power of laughter; is he not also the only one that deserves to be laughed at?"

A SLIM, six-shilling story of the sea—Northern Escort, by Lieut.-Comm. J. E. Taylor, which Allen and Unwin have published—reminds me of one of the many-and-odd differences between this war and the last: the vast improvement in the literary quality of the books it has produced. The sailor, whether he be William McFee, David Bone or Marryat, invariably writes well about his job; but Lieut.-Comm. Taylor does it exceedingly well, infusing his nautical technicalities (and how seamen love them!) with what I can only describe as a sort of Whitmanesque gusto. I commend the Lieut.-Commander to the notice of the British film industry, should they ever be shamed into producing a really big naval film (pace Mr. Noel Coward) which won't bring the blush of embarrassment to hardened seamen's cheeks. Perhaps John Grierson, when he returns from Canada, might make a documentary of Northern Escort which, as it stands, is the semi-fictionalized account of four terrible days during an actual convoy trip to Murmansk, as seen from a British destroyer in the days when air-cover was simply non-existent. I shall value this fine little book most of all for its lively and moving portrait-gallery of the strangely diverse types that go to make up the Wavy

Maj.-Gen. T. G. RENNIE, C.B., D.S.O., M.B.E., commander of the 51st (Highland) Division since before D-Day, survivor of St. Valery in 1940, and hero of El Alamein, was killed in action during the Rhine crossings, on March 24, 1945. *Photo, British Official*

Navy—not least the resourceful Surgeon-Commander in that grisly scene where he "de-hypnotizes" shell-shocked casualties and gets them staggering back to their action-stations. It is a scene worthy of Victor Hugo, and executed in less than a twentieth of the space Hugo would have taken.

FROM his charming little estate in Herefordshire, my old friend Rafael Sabatini, the novelist, in a recent letter, tells me of an unusual press-cutting he has just received. From the Birkenhead News, it announced that a British soldier in France recently fished up from the bed of a river a book belonging to the Birkenhead Public Library, and which turned out to be a copy of Sabatini's novel The Minion. "I don't know," comments my novelist friend, "whether the implication is the wide diffusion of my stories or that the proper place for them is at the bottom of the river!" Sabatini is himself a keen salmon-fisher and rents about a mile of the Severn, on the banks of which stands his home, Clock Mill. Somehow I feel that his sympathies were all with his fellow-angler who hooked a story and missed a fish, though, books being at a premium and a Sabatini yarn always making good reading, perhaps the soldier felt he hadn't done so badly. Had it been the Sabatini which got away, no one would have believed him—not even a fellow-angler!

THE birthplace of Beethoven at Bonn had the narrowest possible escape during the Allied bombardment which led to the town's capture on March 8, 1945, the next house in the row being completely destroyed by one of our shells. Another split second, and what hypocritical howls would have gone up from the people who befouled, devastated, and finally set fire to the house of Leo Tolstoy at Yasnaya Polyana, crying: "We will burn everything connected with the name of Tolstoy!" The particular pride of the Tolstoy shrine was that it had been sedulously kept just as it looked in the writer's lifetime. The indefatigable Russians have restored it to that condition as nearly as possible. But it can never be the same again: the spell is broken. It is all too reminiscent of the American showman who used to exhibit the axe with which George Washington cut down his father's cherry tree. Since Washington's day the axe had had two new blades and three new handles, but it was still the same axe! In Concord, Massachusetts, you are shown Emerson's study, and this too is claimed to be exactly as it was on the day he died, open books, MSS, and old pipes on the desk, the faded block calendar for 1882 torn off to the actual date, April 27. Most impressive—until you realize you are not in Emerson's house at all, but in the Concord museum! The entire contents of the room were transferred bodily from Emerson's house in the same road.

OUTSIDE St. Paul's Cathedral the other day a friend of mine was stopped by three young Scots-Canadians in uniform, obviously "rubbernecking" among the City ruins. "Pardon me," inquired one, jerking a thumb towards Wren's masterpiece, "but is this the Museum?" Taken aback, my friend quizzed them. Didn't they know the building? Hadn't they seen pictures of it? But they all shook their heads. So he told them, and waited for "Why—of course!" But they just went on shaking their heads; and then, thanking him, moved away. It seems incredible—but there it is.

Reich's Greatest River a Bulwark No Longer

EASTWARD OVER THE RHINE, ACROSS A 400-YARDS PONTOON BRIDGE, after the enemy had destroyed all the permanent bridges—except at Remagen—equipment for General Hodges' U.S. 1st Army streamed into the Reich. When not flooded the Rhine is from 900 to 1,600 ft. wide, the current 3½ to 5½ knots, and the depth normally 20 ft., when flooded 40 ft. It was announced on March 26, 1945, that Royal Marines were guarding the pontoons against Nazi saboteur-swimmers carrying explosives.

Photo, U.S. Official.

Printed in England and published every alternate Friday by the Proprietors, THE AMALGAMATED PRESS, LTD., The Fleetway House, Farringdon Street, London, E.C.4. Registered for transmission by Canadian Magazine Post. Sole Agents for Australia and New Zealand : Messrs. Gordon & Gotch, Ltd. ; and for South Africa : Central News Agency, Ltd.—April 27, 1945. S.S. *Editorial Address :* JOHN CARPENTER HOUSE, WHITEFRIARS, LONDON, E.C.4.